THE CAMBRIDGE HISTORY OF LAW IN AMERICA

VOLUME II

The Long Nineteenth Century (1789–1920)

Law stands at the center of modern American life. Since the 1950s, American historians have produced an extraordinarily rich and diverse literature that has vastly expanded our knowledge of this familiar and vital yet complex and multifaceted phenomenon. But few attempts have been made to take full account of law's American history. *The Cambridge History of Law in America* has been designed for just this purpose. In three volumes we put on display all the intellectual vitality and variety of contemporary American legal history. We present as comprehensive and authoritative an account as possible of the present understanding and range of interpretation of the history of American law. We suggest where future research may lead.

In the long century after 1789 we see the crystallization and, after the Civil War, the reinvention of a distinctively American state system – federal, regional and local; we see the appearance of systematic legal education, the spread of the legal profession, and the growing density of legal institutions. Overall, we learn that in America law becomes a technique of first resort wherever human activity, in all shapes and sizes, meets up with the desire to organize it: the reception and distribution of migrant populations; the expulsion and transfer of indigenous peoples; the structure of social life; the liberation of slaves and the confinement of freed people; and the great churning engines of continental expansion, urban growth, capitalist innovation, industrialization. We see how law intertwines with religion, how it becomes ingrained in popular culture, and how it intersects with the semi-separate world of American militarism and with the "outside" world of other nations.

The Cambridge History of Law in America has been made possible by the generous support of the American Bar Foundation. Volumes I and III cover the history of law in America, respectively, from the first moments of English colonizing through the creation and stabilization of the republic; and from the 1920s until the early twenty-first century.

Michael Grossberg is the Sally M. Reahard Professor of History and a Professor of Law at Indiana University. His research focuses on the relationship between law and social change, particularly the intersection of law and the family.

Christopher Tomlins is Senior Research Fellow at the American Bar Foundation in Chicago. His research encompasses the relationship among labor, colonization, and law in early America; the conceptual history of police in Anglo-American law and politics; and the place of historical materialism in legal theory.

THE CAMBRIDGE HISTORY OF LAW IN AMERICA

VOLUME II

The Long Nineteenth Century (1789–1920)

Edited by

MICHAEL GROSSBERG
Indiana University

CHRISTOPHER TOMLINS
The American Bar Foundation, Chicago

CAMBRIDGE
UNIVERSITY PRESS

CAMBRIDGE UNIVERSITY PRESS
Cambridge, New York, Melbourne, Madrid, Cape Town, Singapore, São Paulo, Delhi

Cambridge University Press
32 Avenue of the Americas, New York, NY 10013-2473, USA

www.cambridge.org
Information on this title: www.cambridge.org/9780521803069

First published 2008

Printed in the United States of America

A catalog record for this publication is available from the British Library.

Library of Congress Cataloging in Publication Data

The Cambridge history of law in America / edited by Michael Grossberg,
Christopher Tomlins.
p. cm.
Includes bibliographical references and index.
ISBN 978-0-521-80306-9 (hardback)
1. Law – United States – History. I. Grossberg, Michael, 1950– II. Tomlins,
Christopher L., 1951– III. Title.
KF352.C36 2007
349.73–dc22 2007017606

ISBN 978-0-521-80306-9 hardback

CONTENTS

EDITORS' PREFACE

In February 1776, declaiming against the oppressive and absolute rule of "the Royal Brute of Britain," the revolutionary pamphleteer Tom Paine announced to the world that "so far as we approve of monarchy . . . in America THE LAW IS KING"! Paine's declaration of Americans' "common sense" of the matter turned out to be an accurate forecast of the authority the legal order would amass in the revolutionary republic. Indeed, Paine's own fiery call to action was one of the stimuli that would help his prediction come true. We know ourselves that what he claimed for law then mostly remains true now. Yet, we should note, Paine's claim was not simply prophecy; it made sense in good part because of foundations already laid. Long before 1776, law and legal institutions had gained a place of some prominence in the British American colonies. The power and position of law, in other words, are apparent throughout American history, from its earliest moments. The three volumes of *The Cambridge History of Law in America* explain why Paine's synoptic insight should be understood as both an eloquent foretelling of what would be and an accurate summation of what already was.

The Cambridge History of Law in America belongs to a long and proud scholarly tradition. In March 1896, at the instigation of Frederick William Maitland, Downing Professor of the Laws of England at Cambridge University, and of Henry Jackson, tutor in Greek at Trinity College, the syndics of Cambridge University Press invited the University's Regius Professor of Modern History, Lord John Dalberg Acton, to undertake "the general direction of a History of the World." Six months later Acton returned with a plan for a (somewhat) more restrained endeavor, an account of Europe and the United States from *The Renaissance* to *The Latest Age*. Thus was born *The Cambridge Modern History*.

Acton's plan described a collaborative, collectively written multivolume history. Under general editorial guidance, each volume would be divided among "specially qualified writers" primed to present extensive and authoritative accounts of their subjects.[1] They were to imagine themselves writing less for other professional historians than for a more general audience of "students of history" – anyone, that is, who sought an authoritative, thoughtful, and sophisticated assessment of a particular historical subject or issue. Acton envisioned a history largely clean of the professional apparatus of reference and citation – texts that would demonstrate the "highest pitch of knowledge without the display," reliant for their authority on the expertise of the authors chosen to write them. And although it was intended that the *History* be the most complete general statement of historical knowledge available, and to that extent definitive, Acton was not interested in simply reproducing (and thus by implication freezing) what was known. He desired that his authors approach the task critically, strive for originality in their research, and take it on themselves to revise and improve the knowledge they encountered.[2]

Acton did not live to see even the first volume in print, but between 1902 and 1911 *The Cambridge Modern History* appeared in twelve substantial volumes under the editorial direction of Adolphus Ward and Stanley Leathes. The *History* quickly found a broad audience – the first volume, *The Renaissance*, sold out in a month. Other Cambridge histories soon followed: *The Cambridge History of English Literature*, which began to appear under Ward's editorship in 1907; *The Cambridge Medieval History* (1911–36); *The Cambridge History of American Literature* (1917–21); *The Cambridge Ancient History* (1923–39); *The Cambridge History of the British Empire* (1929–67); *The Cambridge History of India* (1922–60), and more. All told, close to a hundred Cambridge histories have been published. More than fifty are currently in print. Cambridge histories have justly become famous. They are to be found in the collections of libraries and individuals throughout the world.

Acton's plan for *The Cambridge Modern History* invoked certain essentials – an ideal of collective authorship and a commitment to make expertise accessible to a wider audience than simply other specialists. To these he added grander, programmatic touches. The *History* would be "an epic," a "great argument" conveying "forward progress . . . upward growth." And it would provide "chart and compass for the coming century." Such ambitions are

[1] When, early on, Acton ran into difficulties in recruiting authors for his intimidating project, Maitland gently suggested that "his omniscient lordship" simply write the whole thing himself. Acton (we note with some relief) demurred. There is humor here, but also principle. Collective authorship is a practice ingrained in the Cambridge histories from the beginning.

[2] Our account of Acton's plan and its realization gratefully relies throughout on Josef L. Altholz, "Lord Acton and the Plan of the *Cambridge Modern History*," *The Historical Journal*, 39, no. 3 (September 1996), 723–36.

characteristic of Acton's moment – the later nineteenth century – when in Britain and Continental Europe history still claimed an educative mantle "of practical utility," the means rather than science (or law) to equip both elites and ordinary citizens "to deal with the problems of their time." It was a moment, also, when history's practitioners could still imagine filling historical time with a consistent, standardized account – the product, to be sure, of many minds, but minds that thought enough alike to agree on an essential common purpose: "men acting together for no other object than the increase of accurate knowledge." Here was history (accurate knowledge) as "the teacher and the guide that regulates public life," the means by which "the recent past" would yield up "the key to present time." Here as well, lest we too quickly dismiss the vision as naïve or worse, was the shouldering of a certain responsibility. "We have to describe the ruling currents, to interpret the sovereign forces, that still govern and divide the world. There are, I suppose, at least a score of them, in politics, economics, philosophy and religion. . . . But if we carry history down to the last syllable of recorded time, and leave the reader at the point where study passes into action, we must explain to him the cause, and the growth, and the power of every great intellectual movement, and equip him for many encounters of life."

Acton's model – a standard general history, a guiding light produced by and for an intellectually confident elite – could not survive the shattering effects of two world wars. It could not survive the democratization of higher education, the proliferation of historical scholarship, the constant emergence of new fields and subdisciplines, the eventual decentering of Europe and "the West." When, amid the rubble and rationing of a hastily de-colonizing post–World War II Britain, Cambridge University Press's syndics decided a revised version was required – a *New Cambridge Modern History* for a new day – their decision acknowledged how much the world had changed. The revised version bore them out. Gone was Acton's deep faith in history's authority and grandeur. The general editor, G. N. Clark, wrote, "Historians in our self-critical age are aware that there will not be general agreement with their conclusions, nor even with some of the premises which they regard as self-evident. They must be content to set out their own thought without reserve and to respect the differences which they cannot eradicate" – including, he might have added (but perhaps there was no need) the many fundamental differences that existed among historians themselves. Cambridge histories no longer aspired to create standardized accounts of the way things had been nor to use the past to pick the lock on the future. The differences in perspective and purpose that a less confident, more self-critical age had spawned were now the larger part of the picture.

Yet the genre Acton helped found has now entered its second century. It still bears, in some fashion, his imprint. The reason it has survived, indeed prospered, has less to do with some sense of overall common purpose than the more modest but nevertheless essential precept of continued adherence to certain core principles of design simply because they have worked: individual scholars charged to synthesize the broad sweep of current knowledge of a particular topic, but also free to present an original interpretation aimed at encouraging both reflection and further scholarship, and an overall architecture that encourages new understandings of an entire subject or area of historical scholarship. Neither encyclopedias nor compilations, textbooks nor works of reference, Cambridge histories have become something quite unique – each an avowedly collective endeavor that offers the single best point of entry to the wide range of an historical subject, topic, or field; each in overall conceptual design and substance intent not simply on defining its field's development to date but on pushing it forward with new ideas. Critique and originality, revision and improvement of knowledge – all remain germane.

Readers will find that *The Cambridge History of Law in America* adheres to these core goals. Of course, like other editors we have our own particular ambitions. And so the three volumes of this Cambridge history have been designed to present to full advantage the intellectual vitality and variety of contemporary American legal history. Necessarily then – and inevitably – *The Cambridge History of Law in America* dwells on areas of concern and interpretive debates that preoccupy the current generation of legal historians. We do not ignore our predecessors.[3] Nor, however, do we attempt in the body of the *History* to chart the development of the field over their time and ours in any great detail. Readers will find a more substantial accounting of that development in the bibliographic essays that accompany each chapter, but as editors we have conceived our job to be to facilitate the presentation of as comprehensive and authoritative a rendition of the present understanding of the history of American law as possible and to suggest where future research may lead.

Cambridge histories always define their audiences widely; ours is no exception. One part of our intended audience is scholarly, but hardly confined to other legal historians; they are already the best equipped to know something of what is retailed here. So to an important extent we try to look past legal historians to historians at large. We also look beyond history to scholars across the broad sweep of law, the humanities, and the social sciences – indeed to any scholar who may find a turn to law's history useful (or simply diverting) in answering questions about law and society in America.

[3] See, for example, the graceful retrieval and reexamination of themes from the "imperial school" of American colonial historians undertaken by Mary Sarah Bilder in Volume I, Chapter 3.

A second part of our audience is the legal profession. Lawyers and judges experience in their professional lives something of a practical encounter with the past, although the encounter may not be one they would recognize as "historical." As John Reid has written, "The lawyer and the historian have in common the fact that they go to the past for evidence, but there the sim ilarity largely ends." Here lawyers and judges can discover for themselves what historians do with evidence. In the process, they will also discover that not inconsiderable attention has been paid to their own lives and experiences. Legal historians have always known how important legal thought and legal education are in the formation of the professional world of the law, and both feature prominently in this *History*. Here the profession encounters the history of its activities and of the medium it inhabits from a standpoint outside itself.

The third segment of our intended audience is the general public. Our purposes in this encounter are not Acton's. We do not present this *History* as the means to educate a citizenry to deal with the problems of the moment. (Indeed, it is worth noting that in America law appropriated that role to itself from the earliest days of the republic.) Like G. N. Clark, today's historians live in self-critical times and have lower expectations than Lord Acton of what historical practice might achieve. That said, readers will find that this *History* touches on many past attempts to use law to "deal with" many past problems: in the America where law is king, it has been law's fate to be so employed. And if their accounts leave some of our authors critical in their analysis of outcomes or simply rueful in recounting the hubris (or worse) of the attempts, that in itself can be counted an education of sorts. Moreover, as Volume III's chapters show repeatedly, Americans continue to turn to law as their key medium of private problem solving and public policy formation and implementation, and on an expanding – global – stage. In that light, there is perhaps something for us to learn from Acton's acknowledgment that the scholar-expert should not abandon the reader "at the point where study passes into action." We can at the very least offer some reflection on what an encounter with the past might bring by way of advice to the "many encounters of life" lying ahead.

In reaching all three of our intended audiences, we are greatly assisted by the pronounced tendency to "demystify" and diversify its subject that has characterized American legal history for a half-century. To some, the field's very title – "legal history" – will conjure merely an arcane preoccupation with obscure terminologies and baffling texts, the doctrines and practices of old (hence defunct) law, of no obvious utility to the outsider whether historian or social scientist or practicing lawyer or just plain citizen. No doubt, legal history has at times given grounds to suppose that such a view of the discipline is generally warranted. But what is interesting in American legal history as currently practiced is just how inappropriate that characterization seems.

To read the encomia that have accumulated over the years, one might suppose that the demise of legal history's obscurity was the single-handed achievement of one man, James Willard Hurst, who on his death in 1997 was described in the *New York Times* as "the dean of American legal historians." Indeed, Hurst himself occasionally suggested the same thing; it was he who came up with the aphorism "snakes in Ireland" to describe legal history in America at the time he began working in the field in the 1930s. Though not an immodest man, it seems clear whom he cast as St. Patrick. Yet the *Times*' description was merited. Hurst's lifework – the unpacking of the changing roles of American law, market, and state from the early nineteenth to the early twentieth centuries – set the agenda of American legal historians from the 1950s well into the 1980s. That agenda was a liberation from narrower and more formalistic preoccupations, largely with the remote origins of contemporary legal doctrine or with the foundations of American constitutionalism, that had characterized the field, such as it was, earlier in the century. Most important, Hurst's work displayed some recognition of the multidimensionality of law in society – as instrument, the hallmark with which he is most associated, but also as value and as power. Hurst, in short, brought legal history into a continuing dialogue with modernity, capitalism, and the liberal state, a dialogue whose rich dividends are obvious in this *History*.

Lawyers have sometimes asked aggressively anachronistic questions of history, like – to use an apocryphal example of Robert Gordon's – "Did the framers of the Constitution confer on the federal government the power to construct an interstate highway system?" Hurstian legal history did not indulge such questions. But Hurstians did demonstrate a gentler anachronism in their restriction of the scope of the subject and their interpretation of it. Famously, for Hurst, American legal history did not begin until the nineteenth century. And when it did begin it showed a certain consistency in cause and effect. As Kermit Hall summarized the view in 1989, "Our legal history reflects back to us generations of pragmatic decision making rather than a quest for ideological purity and consistency. Personal and group interests have always ordered the course of legal development; instrumentalism has been the way of the law."[4] The Hurstian determination to demystify law occasionally reduced it to transparency – a dependent variable of society and economy (particularly economy) tied functionally to social and economic change.

[4] Kermit L. Hall, *The Magic Mirror: Law in American History* (New York, 1989), 335.

As a paradigm for the field, Hurstian legal history long since surrendered its dominance. What has replaced it? In two words, astonishing variety. Legal historians are aware that one cannot talk or write about economic or social or political or intellectual history, or indeed much of any kind of history, without immediately entering into realms of definition, prohibition, understanding, practice, and behavior that must imply law to have meaning. Try talking about property in any of those contexts, for example, without implying law. Today's legal historians are deeply engaged across the full range of historical investigation in demonstrating the inextricable salience of law in human affairs. As important, the interests of American historians at large have never been more overtly legal in their implications than now. To take just four popular areas of inquiry in American history – citizenship and civic personality, identity, spatiality, and the etiology of social hierarchy and subordination – it is simply impossible to imagine how one could approach any of these areas historically without engaging with law, legal ideology, legal institutions, legal practices, and legal discourse. Legal historians have been and remain deeply engaged with and influenced by social history, and as that field has drifted closer and closer to cultural history and the historical construction of identity so legal history has moved with it. The interpretive salience of race and ethnicity, of gender and class is as strong in contemporary legal historical practice as in any other realm of history. Add to that the growing influence of legal pluralism in legal history – the migration of the field from a focus on "the law" to a focus on the conditions of existence of "legality" and the competition of many alternative "legalities" – and one finds oneself at work in a field of immense opportunity and few dogmas.

"Astonishing variety" demonstrates vitality, but also suggests the benefits of a judicious collective effort at authoritative summation. The field has developed at an extraordinary rate since the early 1970s, but offers no work that could claim to approach the full range of our understanding of the American legal past.[5] *The Cambridge History of Law in America* addresses both

[5] The field has two valuable single-author surveys: Lawrence M. Friedman's *A History of American Law* (New York, 1973; 3rd ed. 2005) and Kermit Hall's *The Magic Mirror*. Neither approaches the range of what is on display here. The field also boasts volumes of cases and commentary, prepared according to the law teaching "case book" model, such as Stephen B. Presser and Jamil S. Zainaldin, *Law and Jurisprudence in American History: Cases and Materials* (St. Paul, MN, 1980; 6th ed. 2006) and Kermit Hall, et al., *American Legal History, Cases and Materials* (New York, 3rd ed., 2003). There also exist edited volumes of commentary and materials that focus on broad subject areas within the discipline of legal history; a preponderance deal with constitutional law, such as Lawrence M. Friedman and Harry N. Scheiber, eds., *American Law and the Constitutional Order: Historical Perspectives* (Cambridge, MA, 1978; enlarged ed. 1988). Valuable in

the vitality of variety and its organizational challenge. Individually, each chapter in each volume is a comprehensive interrogation of a key issue in a particular period of American legal history. Each is intended to extend the substantive and interpretative boundaries of our knowledge of that issue. The topics they broach range widely – from the design of British colonizing to the design of the successor republic and of its successive nineteenth- and twentieth-century reincarnations; from legal communications within empires to communications among nation-states within international law to a sociology of the "legalization" that enwraps contemporary globalism; from changes in legal doctrine to litigation trend assessments; from clashes over law and religion to the intersection of law and popular culture; from the movement of peoples to the production of subalternship among people (the indigenous, slaves, dependents of all kinds); and from the discourse of law to the discourse of rights. Chapters also deal with developments in specific areas of law and of the legal system – crime and criminal justice, economic and commercial regulation, immigration and citizenship, technology and environment, military law, family law, welfare law, public health and medicine, and antitrust.[6]

Individual chapters illustrate the dynamism and immense breadth of American legal history. Collectively, they neither exhaust its substance nor impose a new interpretive regimen on the field. Quite the contrary, *The Cambridge History of Law in America* intentionally calls forth the broad array of methods and arguments that legal historians have developed. The contents of each volume demonstrate not just that expansion of subject and method is common to every period of American legal history but also that as the long-ascendant socio-legal perspective has given way to an increasing diversity of analytical approaches, new interpretive opportunities are rife everywhere. Note the influence of regionalism in Volume I and of institutionalism in Volume II. Note the attention paid in Volume III not only to race and gender but also to sexuality. The *History* shows how legal history

their own right, such volumes are intended as specific-purpose teaching tools and do not purport to be comprehensive. Finally, there are, of course, particular monographic works that have proven widely influential for their conceptual acuity, or their capacity to set a completely new tone in the way the field at large is interpreted. The most influential have been such studies as James Willard Hurst, *Law and the Conditions of Freedom in the Nineteenth-Century United States* (Madison, WI, 1956), and Morton J. Horwitz, *The Transformation of American Law, 1780–1860* (Cambridge, MA, 1977).

[6] Following the tradition of Cambridge histories, each chapter includes only such footnotes as the author deems necessary to document essential (largely primary) sources. In place of the dense display of citations beloved of scholarly discourse that Acton's aesthetic discouraged, each author has written a bibliographic essay that provides a summary of his or her sources and a guide to scholarly work on the subject.

has entered dialogue with the full array of "histories" pursued within the academy – political, intellectual, social, cultural, economic, business, diplomatic, and military – and with their techniques.

The Cambridge History of Law in America is more than the sum of its parts. The *History*'s conceptual design challenges existing understandings of the field. We divide the American legal past into three distinct eras and devote a complete volume to each one: first *Early America*, then *The Long Nineteenth Century*, and last *The Twentieth Century and After*. The first volume, *Early America*, examines the era from the late sixteenth century through the early nineteenth – from the beginnings of European settlement through the creation and stabilization of the American republic. The second volume, *The Long Nineteenth Century*, begins with the appearance of the United States in the constituted form of a nation-state in 1789; it ends in 1920, in the immediate aftermath of World War I, with the world poised on the edge of the "American Century." The final volume, *The Twentieth Century and After*, concentrates on that American century both at home and abroad and peers into the murk of the twenty-first century. Within each of these broad chronological divisions occurs a much more detailed subdivision that combines an appreciation of chronology with the necessities of topical specialization.

Where appropriate, topics are revisited in successive volumes (crime and criminal justice, domestic relations law, legal thought, and legal education are all examples). Discussion of economic growth and change is ubiquitous, but we accord it no determinative priority. To facilitate comparisons and contrasts within and between eras, sequences of subjects have been arranged in similar order in each volume. Specific topics have been chosen with an eye to their historical significance and their social, institutional, and cultural coherence. They cannot be walled off from each other, so readers will notice substantive overlaps when more than one author fastens on the same issues, often to create distinct interpretations of them. History long since ceased to speak with one voice. In this *History*, readers are invited into a conversation.

Readers will notice that our chronology creates overlaps at the margins of each era. They will also notice that some chapters focus on only particular decades within a specific era[7] or span more than one era.[8] All this is

[7] Chronologically specific topics – the American Revolution and the creation of the republic in Volume I, the Civil War in Volume II, the New Deal era in Volume III – are treated as such. Chapters on the legal profession in Volumes II and III divide its development at the Civil War, as do those, in Volume II, on the state and on industrial organization.

[8] Volume II's chapter on the military deals with both the nineteenth and twentieth centuries, as do Volume III's chapters on agriculture and the state and on law and the environment. The latter chapter, indeed, also gestures toward the colonial period.

intentional. Historians construct history by placing subjects in relation to each other within the continuum of historical time. Historians manipulate time by creating periods to organize the placement of subjects. Thus, when historians say that a subject has been "historicized," they mean it has been located in what they consider its appropriate historical-temporal context or period. Slicing and dicing time in this fashion is crucial to the historian's objective of rendering past action coherent and comprehensible, but necessarily it has a certain arbitrariness. No matter how familiar – the colonial period, the Gilded Age, the Progressive period, and so forth – no historical period is a natural division: all are constructs. Hence we construct three "eras" in the interests of organizational coherence, but our overlaps and the distinct chronologies chosen by certain of our authors allow us to recognize different temporalities at work.

That said, the tripartite division of these volumes is intended to provide a new overall conceptual schema for American legal history, one that is broad and accommodating but that locates legal history in the contours of American history at large. Maitland never forgot that, at bottom, just as religious history is history not theology, legal history is history not law. Notwithstanding law's normative and prescriptive authority in "our" culture, it is a phenomenon for historical inquiry, not the source of an agenda. And so we take our cue, broadly, from American history. If it is anything, American history is the history of the colonization and settlement of the North American mainland, it is the history of the creation and expansion of an American nation-state, and it is the history of that state's place in and influence on the world at large. The contents and the organization of *The Cambridge History of Law in America* speak to how law became king in this America and of the multitudinous empire of people and possibilities over which that king reigned. Thus we address ourselves to the endless ramifications, across more than four centuries, of the meaning of Tom Paine's exclamation in 1776.

The Cambridge History of Law in America could not have been produced without the support and commitment of the American Bar Foundation, Cambridge University Press, and our cadre of authors. We thank them all.

The American Bar Foundation housed the project and, together with the Press, funded it. The Foundation was there at the creation: it helped initiate the project by sponsoring a two-day meeting of an ad hoc editorial consulting group in January 2000. Members of that group (Laura Edwards, Tony Freyer, Robert Gordon, Bruce H. Mann, William Novak, Stephen Siegel, Barbara Young Welke, and Victoria Saker Woeste) patiently debated the editors' initial thoughts on the conceptual and intellectual direction that the *History* should follow and helped identify potential contributors. Since then, the project has benefited from the support of two ABF directors, Bryant Garth and his successor Robert Nelson, and the sustained and enthusiastic interest of the Foundation's Board of Directors during the tenure of four Board presidents: Jacqueline Allee, M. Peter Moser, the late Robert Hetlage, and David Tang. We owe a particular debt of gratitude to Robert MacCrate for his early support and encouragement. As all this suggests, the American Bar Foundation's role in the production of *The Cambridge History of Law in America* has been of decisive importance. The part the Foundation has played underlines its standing as the preeminent research center for the study of law and society in the United States and its long tradition of support for the development of American legal history.

Cambridge University Press has, of course, been central to the project throughout. We are grateful to the syndics for their encouragement and to Frank Smith and his staff in New York for their assistance and support. Frank first suggested the project in 1996. He continued to suggest it for three years until we finally succumbed. During the years the *History* has been in development, Frank has accumulated one responsibility after another at the Press. Once we rubbed shoulders with the Executive Editor for Social Sciences. Now we address our pleas to the Editorial Director for Academic Books. But Frank will always be a history editor at heart, and he has maintained a strong interest in this *History*, always available with sage advice as the project rolled relentlessly onward. He helped the editors understand the intellectual ambitions of a Cambridge history. Those who have had the privilege of working with Frank Smith will know how important his advice and friendship have been to us throughout.

Finally, the editors want to thank the authors of the chapters in these volumes. A project like this is not to every author's taste – some took to it more easily than others. But together the sixty authors who joined us to write the *History* have done a magnificent job, and we are deeply grateful to every one. From the beginning our goal was not only to recruit as participants those whom all would identify as leading figures of our field but also to include those who, we were confident, would be leading figures of its next generation. We are delighted that so many of each were willing. We acknowledge also those who were unable for one reason or another to see an initial commitment through to the end: their efforts, too, helped us define and establish the project. And obviously, we owe a particular debt to those others who came later to take the places of the fallen.

To oversee a project in which so many people have at one time or another been involved has seemed on occasion like being the mayors of a village. People arrive and (much less frequently, thank goodness) depart. Those who settle in for the duration become a community of friends and neighbors. Over time, one learns much from one's friends and neighbors about the joys and vicissitudes of life. One learns who (and whose family) may be ailing, and who is well. One learns of hurts and difficulties; one revels in successes. And one may learn, as we did so sadly in August 2006, of an untimely death. Notwithstanding the demands of his immensely successful career in academic administration, our colleague Kermit Hall never laid down his historian's pen and was an enthusiastic participant in this project. He died suddenly and unexpectedly. His contributions to the field have been great, and he is greatly missed.

Throughout, the many authors in this project have responded courteously to our editorial advice. They have reacted with grace and occasional humor to our endless demands that they meet their deadlines. Sometimes they even sent their manuscripts too. Most important, they have striven to achieve what we asked of them – the general goals of a Cambridge history and the specific goals of *this* history, as we have described them in this preface. Their achievements are evident in the pages of each volume. In an individualistic intellectual culture, the scholarship on display here demonstrates the possibilities inherent in a collective intellectual enterprise. In the end, of course, the editors, not the authors, are responsible for the contents of these volumes. Yet, it is the authors who have given the *History* its meaning and significance.

Michael Grossberg
Christopher Tomlins

I

LAW AND THE AMERICAN STATE, FROM THE REVOLUTION TO THE CIVIL WAR: INSTITUTIONAL GROWTH AND STRUCTURAL CHANGE

MARK R. WILSON

From Tocqueville in the 1830s to scholars in the twenty-first century, most observers have found the state in the antebellum American republic elusive and complex. As any student of American history knows, the new nation that emerged from the Revolutionary War was not ruled by uniformed national officials. In place of a king the United States had popular sovereignty and the law; instead of strong central authorities it had federalism and local autonomy; lacking administrative bureaucracy, it relied on democratic party politics. In the Constitution, the new nation wrote a blueprint for government that called for separation rather than conglomeration of powers. It would prove remarkably successful in endowing the American state with both flexibility and durability, as Madison and other founders had desired.

The state in the early United States did not look like an entity approaching the Weberian ideal-type of the modern state: an organization capable of enforcing a successful monopoly of violence over a given territory, ruled through a legal-administrative order. But for all its apparent distinctiveness, the state in the early United States, no less than its counterparts in Europe and Asia, performed the fundamental tasks of any state: managing its population, economy, and territory. The history of how it did so suggests that the American state in the early nineteenth century was more substantial and energetic, especially at the national level, than many have suggested.

As Tom Paine famously put it, the Revolution created a new America, in which law was king. But we should be wary of overemphasizing the importance of the law in early American governance. We should instead embrace a broad conception of the law, in which the Constitution, statute law, and judge-made law all figure as parts of a larger legal order that also included coercive law enforcement and administration. Certainly, we cannot understand the state in the early United States without considering the Constitution and the courts, as well as federalism and party politics. But these institutions did not alone comprehend the American state between the Revolution and the Civil War. Along with the structural characteristics that made it distinctive from a global perspective, the early American state – like other states – performed major administrative feats that required guns and even bureaucracy. Often overlooked by students of comparative politics, history, and law, these less exceptional dimensions of the early American state were crucial in the formation of the new nation and its survival through the Civil War.

Generalizing about the early American state poses special challenges, but also promises significant rewards. As recent political theorists have emphasized, writing in general terms about any state tends to exaggerate its coherence. In the case of the United States in particular, any general discussion of "the state" must recognize the complexities induced by the occurrence of state action at three levels of governance: not just national, but state and local too. Here I attempt to avoid confusing these different levels of state authority by treating them as distinct subjects whose relationships and relative powers changed over time. Nevertheless, one should not be deterred from considering what broad conclusions one can reach by examining the general character of the work of public authorities (whether national, state, or local) as such. Complexity for its own sake does not get us very far. While necessarily crude, broader claims may be unusually fruitful when it comes to the state in the early United States, precisely because its complexity is already so well understood.

Whereas the conventions of historical and social-scientific writing may have imbued many states with an artificial coherence, in the case of the early United States we face the opposite problem. That is, the early American state is understood to have been so exceptionally weak, decentralized, or otherwise unusual that it defies the conventions of analysis applied to contemporary European states. One finds this "exceptionalist" paradigm of American distinctiveness promoted assiduously after World War II, most obviously by Louis Hartz in *The Liberal Tradition in America* (1955). A more refined version of the argument was advanced by James Willard Hurst in his *Law and the Conditions of Freedom in the Nineteenth-Century United States* (1956). Hurst explained that the early United States was remarkable not for any "jealous limitation of the power of the state," but rather because it was a new kind of state that worked in positive fashion to achieve "the release of individual creative energy."[1] Hurst comprehended Tocqueville's most astute observations about the paradoxical capacity of liberal states to do more with less better than did Hartz, indeed better than many others since. But like Tocqueville, Hurst implied that the American state was abnormal.

[1] James Willard Hurst, *Law and the Conditions of Freedom in the Nineteenth-Century United States* (Madison, 1956), 7.

Decades after Hurst, more recent authorities on the early American state have broken much new ground, but mostly they still accept American distinctiveness. Above all, the decentralization of early U.S. political authority, described (and praised) at such great length by Tocqueville, continues to figure centrally. Before the late nineteenth century, the United States was a state of "courts and parties": those two institutions alone served to coordinate a radically decentralized political and economic system. Some of the best new histories of the early American state have outdone Tocqueville in their assumptions about the hypersignificance of local governance. In the history of American political economy, meanwhile, the several states continue to figure as the central subjects, just as they did in the classic monographs on Pennsylvania and Massachusetts written by Hartz and the Handlins in the mid-twentieth century. The leading legal historian Lawrence Friedman summarized the message of a half-century of scholarship on state institutions and political economy in the antebellum United States as follows: "Nobody expected much out of the national government – or wanted much." The national government "was like the brain of a dinosaur: an insignificant mass of neurons inside a gigantic body."

The impotence of national authority and incoherence of state action in the United States through the Civil War era are part of a well-established story. But that does not make them correct. Here I take a different direction. In doing so, I build on the work of a handful of scholars – among them Richard R. John, Ira Katznelson, and Bartholomew Sparrow – whose research recommends reconsideration. In their effort to chart the dynamics of the complex American political system, I argue, students of the early American state have overlooked the most important single characteristic of the early United States: its astounding growth. In comparison with European states, the early American state was confronted with problems arising from unusually rapid demographic, economic, and territorial expansion. Between 1790 and 1870, the national population increased from 4 million people to 40 million. The economy grew roughly twice as fast: between 1820 and 1870 alone, national product increased by a factor of eight. Perhaps most remarkable of all, the territory over which the early American state presided expanded from 864,000 square miles in 1800 to nearly 3 million square miles in 1850. From a gaggle of colonies hugging the Eastern seaboard in 1776, by the time of the Civil War – less than ninety years later – the United States had become the peer in population, economic output, and territorial reach of France, Britain, and Russia.

The early American state was less top-heavy than those others. In 1860, when all three states had similar numbers of inhabitants, central state expenditures in Britain and France were roughly five times what they were in the United States. Nonetheless, along with its tremendous growth in population, economy, and territory, the early United States saw a remarkable expansion of state institutions. By 1870, twenty-four new states had joined the original thirteen, and hundreds of new towns and counties had been created. National government had undergone significant expansion and specialization. By 1849, the original executive departments of State, War, and Treasury had been joined by three more cabinet-level departments: Navy, Post Office, and Interior. In Congress, a variety of specialized standing committees had appeared in both houses by the 1810s; the number of House members had tripled between the 1790s and the 1870s, from 102 to 292. In 1836, Congress reorganized the patent system by establishing a new Patent Office, which became an important arbiter of technological innovation. Even the federal judiciary, set in its structure for the most part in 1789, saw a newcomer by the end of this era: the Court of Claims, established in 1855 and empowered during the Civil War.

Institutional expansion allowed the early American state to manage its population, economy, and territory – the three fields of greatest concern to all modern states. Here I use these three related fields as the means to organize a multidimensional account of the early American state. My account confirms some long-established notions and extends – or challenges – others. For example, students of American history will not be surprised to learn that early American governmental institutions failed to deliver on the most radical and egalitarian promises of the Revolution. But what happens when we probe beyond the obvious racial and sexual inequalities of early America to consider matters of causation and chronology? In its symbolic and legal construction of the national population, the early American state deliberately segmented its population along a color line. Furthermore, state construction of whiteness and its cognates became more energetic over time.

In the field of political economy, the pattern of chronological change was more complex. Here, a non-linear narrative, which considers the activities of various levels of American government, helps us reconcile a basic dispute among political and legal historians of the early United States. Both sides in this dispute have managed to assemble powerful evidence: on the one hand, of considerable state promotion and regulation; on the other, of impressive growth – not only in America, but around the Atlantic world – in capitalist enterprise. But we rely too heavily on evidence from the 1830s and early 1840s for broad characterizations of the development of the market economy during the whole antebellum era. If we consider more carefully the final years of the antebellum period and if we look beyond the various states to both local and national initiatives, we find that the oft-discussed trend toward private enterprise during the latter part of this era was actually quite weak.

In the governance of population and economy, the national state shared the stage with the various states and localities. In the governance of territory, on the other hand, the national state – which contemporaries frequently called "the General Government," if not "the Union" or simply "the United States" – was the leading player. It was the national state, through treaties and military operations, which claimed vast new territories during this period. And it was the national state that created and administered the laws and policies that transformed much of this territory into land. The country's greatest landowner and realtor, the national state transformed the landscape and the lives of the millions of people who settled beyond the original thirteen states by extending the common law of property over the continent and creating administrative agencies necessary to divide vast spaces into manageable commodities. By the middle of the nineteenth century, territorial governance and consolidation stood as the early American state's central accomplishment and central problem. That this field of governance touched the lives of the entire population, and not only a minority in the far West, became especially evident by the end of this period, when disastrous new territorial policies in the 1850s led directly to the Civil War.

Taking fuller measure of the early American state leads us to an unexpected conclusion: that the early national state, dismissed by many observers then and since as extraordinarily weak and irrelevant, was in fact the most innovative and influential level of governance in the multitiered American political and legal order. Between 1861 and 1865, the national state extended its influence significantly, but this extension was built on an already considerable foundation. The emergence of a powerful national state in America did not occur during or after the Civil War, but before.

I. POPULATION

Historians and legal scholars lead us to consider the early American state's management of its population in terms of two hypotheses. First, a variety of state institutions worked to individualize the populace; over time the state came to recognize and have a more direct relationship with the individual human beings residing in its territory, including those who lacked full citizenship rights. Second, the early American state increasingly sorted the population according to discriminatory racial categories, which simultaneously expanded the boundaries of a favored social class identified as white and increasingly denigrated those persons who fell outside the boundaries of this category.

Any discussion of the early American state's activities in the field of population may logically begin with a consideration of the Constitution and the census. Although the racialization of the population had certainly been proceeding for decades in British North America before the Revolution, the language of the Constitution suggests that the infant American state was not yet devoted to full-blown white supremacy. The Constitution's most direct sorting of the population is found in Article I, in which it describes the rules for determining the apportionment of the House. Here, the Constitution differentiates among three social categories: "free persons," "Indians not taxed," and "all other persons." For apportionment purposes, as is well known, the number of people in the last of these categories – a euphemism for slaves – was multiplied by three-fifths; members of the second category were excluded altogether. The Constitution refers to neither sex nor color. Thus, while it certainly provides tacit recognition and even support for slavery, the basic blueprint for the new national state uses condition of servitude, rather than race, as a social sorting device.

By contrast, the census, which should be understood as one of the institutions of the early American state with the greatest symbolic power, used the term "white" from the beginning. The first U.S. national census, required by the Constitution, was conducted in 1790, a decade before the first national censuses of Britain and France (although after the pioneering efforts of Sweden). It divided the population into "white," "other free," and "slave." The white population was further divided into three categories: females, and males over and under the age of 16. By 1820, the census had dropped the adjective "other" for "colored." In subsequent decades, increasingly complex census schedules would continue to divide the population according to the same handful of basic variables: color, sex, age, condition of servitude, and place of residence. In 1830, it began to enumerate persons described as deaf, dumb, and blind; in 1840, it counted "insane and idiots" as well. In 1850, the census added a new racial subcategory, "mulatto," which was left to field enumerators to interpret. (In 1850, more than 11 percent of the people falling under the larger category of "colored" were placed in this new subcategory.)

As sectional tensions increased, census regional and racial data were paraded for a variety of political purposes. When poorly designed 1840 census forms led enumerators in some Northern states to register hundreds of non-existent "insane and idiot" African Americans, some Southerners seized on the false data as evidence of the salutary effects of slavery. Another wrongheaded interpretive leap, which spoke to the increasing dedication to the idea of white supremacy within the boundaries of the state during this period, came from the census itself. In 1864, as he presented the final official population report from 1860, long-time census chief Joseph Kennedy hailed figures showing that the nation's free white population had grown 38 percent over the preceding decade, in contrast to 22 percent growth among slaves and 12 percent for free blacks. Disregarding the inconvenient fact that the free black population was on a pace to double in size over the next century, Kennedy announced that the data indicated an ongoing "gradual extinction" of "the colored race."

Along with this apparently increasing emphasis on racial hierarchy and difference, the development of the census over time suggested a more general shift in the relationship between state and population in antebellum America, toward individualization. As we shall see, this was evident in the development of family law across the various states. At the census, the key innovation occurred during a massive expansion of data collection in 1850, when enumerators first recorded the names of individuals other than household heads. Pushing toward a new level of social knowledge, the census forged a direct relationship with named individuals, including women and children. Here, as elsewhere, the state's willingness to have its relationship to persons mediated by a patriarchal or corporate head was declining. At the same time, there was necessarily a corresponding increase in bureaucratic capacity. While the 1840 census was processed in Washington by a clerical force of only about 20, the 1850 tally required 170 clerks. According to its leading historian, this made the Census Office, at its peak, "the largest centralized clerical operation of the federal government at the time." There were no comparable operations in the private sector during this era.

More important than its bureaucratic achievements was the symbolic work that the census did. Again, racial sorting had been going on throughout the colonial period (both in popular culture and in law); it was certainly not pioneered by the census or any other post-Revolutionary state institution. But through its administrative and legal institutions, the early American state encouraged the reproduction of a national social order in which racial hierarchies became more important over time, rather than less. Through the census and other legal and administrative institutions, the early American state encouraged its populace to think in terms of whiteness and non-whiteness in a way that the Constitution did not.

While colonial developments made it likely that the new national state would continue to emphasize racial categories in the definition of its population, other available categories were eschewed. Most important among these was religion. Here, in contrast to its operation with regard to race, the symbolic power of early national state institutions was used against the entrenchment of poisonous social divisions. The census that so diligently classified according to sex and race avoided interrogation of religious identity, even in its detailed, individualized schedules of 1850. This need not have been the case. Before the Revolution, seven of the thirteen colonies had state-supported churches; in Europe, of course, established religion was the rule. But the immediate post-Revolutionary period proved one in which disestablishment was especially attractive. Many American leaders were true Enlightenment men whose qualifications as Christians were dubious. Many members of fast-growing non-established churches, such as Baptists and Presbyterians, found the end of established Congregationalist and Anglican churches an attractive prospect. Virginia led the way with a 1786 law "for Establishing Religious Freedom" that banned government assistance to any church and established a policy of tolerance toward non-Christians. Soon after, the Constitution, which made no reference to a deity at all, proscribed religious tests for federal officeholders; the First Amendment, of course, prohibited the federal government from religious establishment. By 1802, when President Jefferson wrote a letter to a Baptist congregation in Danbury, Connecticut, referring to "a wall of separation between Church and State" erected by the Constitution, the national state's refusal to define its population according to religious categories was clear.

Over time, and despite a marked rise in popular Christian enthusiasm during the first decades of the nineteenth century, the early American state moved further away from the religious sphere. To be sure, the Constitution had never banned state-supported churches or religious tests at the state level.[2] Massachusetts did not abandon establishment until 1833. The early national state lent indirect assistance to religious authorities in a number of ways, such as offering tax exemptions for churches and providing military chaplains – two measures opposed by the strictest of disestablishmentarians, including James Madison. And in *People v. Ruggles* (1811), a New York case, leading American jurist James Kent upheld the blasphemy conviction of the defendant, who had reportedly said, "Jesus Christ was a bastard and his mother must be a whore." Such speech, Kent ruled, was "in gross violation of decency and good order."[3]

The generation that followed Kent, however, was less willing to use state power to defend Christianity. By the 1840s, when one Pennsylvania judge mocked the idea of a "Christian state" in America, blasphemy convictions were exceedingly rare. The direction of change was clear: the whole country moved steadily toward the standard established first by pro-toleration colonies like Pennsylvania and then by the new national state and state governments such as Virginia in the immediate post-Revolutionary period. Certainly, churches and their members could have great political influence, and they often lobbied successfully for legal change to support

[2] In a 1947 case involving the use of state funds to transport children to parochial schools, the Supreme Court approved such use in a 5–4 decision, but Justice Hugo Black's majority opinion claimed – erroneously, it seems clear – that the establishment clause applied to the various states, as well as the federal government. *Everson v. Board of Education*, 330 U.S. 1 (1947).

[3] *People v. Ruggles*, 8 Johns. (N.Y) 290 (1811).

temperance or other reform causes. But even when it came to public policy decisions in which Christians might have been expected to prevail easily via democratic politics, the effective secularism of the state – rooted, it is worth noting again, at least as much in anti-establishment and anti-clerical sentiment as in what might be called modern secular thought – proved surprisingly robust. In 1830, Congress failed to satisfy hundreds of petitioners who demanded the end of Sunday mail deliveries, which caused many post offices to remain open on Sundays. In the vigorous debates on this issue, Senator Richard M. Johnson of Kentucky, a post office committee chair and future U.S. vice president, not only defended the Sunday mails as a necessary element of an efficient national communications system, but went so far as to refer to the equal rights of Jews and pagans. He warned that his opponents were flirting with "religious despotism." Although some Sunday mail routes disappeared in the coming years (the last post office open on Sunday was closed in 1912), Johnson's victory over the petitioners in 1830 stands as a notable example of the early national state's unwillingness to protect favored segments of the population according to religion.

When it came to race, the reverse was true. From the beginning, but increasingly over time, statutes, constitutions, and court decisions promoted the formation of a privileged class of white men. In some areas, at least, early actions by the national state encouraged the subsequent extension of white privilege by state lawmakers. Unlike the Constitution, early Congressional statutes encouraged Americans to associate whiteness with full citizenship. In its 1790 Naturalization Act, Congress offered full citizenship to "all free white persons" with two years of residence in the United States. The Militia Act of 1792 required every "free able-bodied white male citizen" to participate in military service. In the coming decades, as new state constitutions denied suffrage and other civil rights to free blacks, some proponents of these measures would justify the racial discrimination by claiming that their absence from the ranks of the militia demonstrated that blacks were never full citizens.

The rising legal inequalities between white and black developed simultaneously with growing egalitarianism among whites. During the first half of the nineteenth century, tax or property requirements for suffrage disappeared in state after state. Decades ahead of England, the United States experienced the rise of a popular politics. The presidential election of 1840 saw a total of 2.4 million votes cast; just sixteen years earlier, John Quincy Adams had managed to become president with fewer than 109,000 votes. Well before the Civil War, then, universal white male suffrage had become the rule. Full citizenship was now a function of race and sex; it did not depend on birth, wealth, religion, or nationality.

Some would have had it otherwise. Throughout the period, there was plenty of popular anti-Catholicism, from the published diatribes of the inventor Samuel Morse to major mob actions in Boston and Philadelphia. From the heyday of the Federalists to the rise of the Know Nothings in the 1850s, political nativism was easy to find and sometimes succeeded in creating new legislation. But all in all, U.S. immigration and citizenship law remained remarkably open to European men. With the Naturalization Act of 1790, Congress provided for citizenship after two years' residence, an inclusive and open system that at least indirectly challenged the sovereignty of European states by encouraging their subjects to depart. Although the residential standard soon became five years, efforts to establish much more restrictive systems were defeated on several occasions. Throughout the period, the national government and the various states both regulated immigration through a variety of laws, including the federal Passenger Acts that limited the numbers of arrivals by setting tonnage requirements and the states' efforts to force shipmasters to accept liability for potential social welfare spending on the newcomers. But these rules did not prevent some 2.5 million people, mostly Irish and German, from coming to the United States during the decade starting in 1845 – one of the largest waves of immigration in all of American history. Overall, the governmental institutions that these people encountered in the United States tended to promote white solidarity, rather than divisions among Europeans. Even as the Know Nothings won short-term victories in New England, for example, many Midwestern and Western states were allowing non-naturalized white aliens to vote.

While the circle of white citizenship expanded, the legal denigration of those outside it also increased. This was true even for slaves, in the sense that the well-established institution of slavery, which seemed in the immediate post-Revolutionary period to be on the defensive, became more legally entrenched over time. Before the 1810s, proponents of emancipation had reason for optimism. In 1782, the Virginia legislature legalized manumission, which had been banned in the colony earlier in the century; other Southern states also allowed masters to free their slaves. Meanwhile, in the North from 1790 to 1804 the states abolished slavery altogether, though often with gradual emancipation plans. In 1807, when Congress banned slave imports, the vote in the House was 113 to 5. During the first quarter-century after the Revolution, then, the early American state did relatively little to promote slavery in an active way, although Southern slave owners were always extraordinarily well represented in all three branches of the national government.

By the antebellum years, by contrast, many Americans became convinced that a variety of governmental organizations, including Congress and the federal courts, were acting positively in favor of slavery. To be sure, there was some evidence to the contrary. For much of the 1840s and 1850s, the U.S.

Navy operated an African Squadron, which cooperated with a more active British naval force in an effort to interdict the slave trade. And many Northern states had enacted personal liberty laws, which challenged the interstate privileges of slave owners ordained in the Constitution and the Fugitive Slave Act of 1793. But even before 1850, when Congress enacted a stronger fugitive slave law, most of the evidence suggested that slavery was gaining legal support. In 1820, South Carolina banned owners from freeing any slave during the owner's lifetime; by the 1850s, most Southern states had blocked manumission completely. To the dismay of the members of the American Anti-Slavery Society, established in 1833, Congress adopted a "gag rule" in 1836 that officially tabled any petitions on the subject of slavery. Six years later, in *Prigg v. Pennsylvania* (1842), the U.S. Supreme Court upheld the 1793 Fugitive Slave Act, ruling the 1826 Pennsylvania personal liberty law unconstitutional. (Undaunted, the state responded by passing a new personal liberty statute.) New developments during the 1850s would give Northerners even more reason to think that a minority in the slave South was using the state to promote slavery against the wishes of a national majority.

Even more than developments in the law and politics of slavery, the changing legal status of free blacks best demonstrated the early American state's growing devotion to organizing its population in a racial hierarchy. By the end of the antebellum period, most Northern states had joined Southern states and the federal government in making whiteness a qualification for full citizenship. This marked a distinct change from the post-Revolutionary years, when the laws of eleven states allowed free black men to vote. Although we should not romanticize race relations in the Early Republic, these early suffrage laws suggest that in the aftermath of the Revolution race was not fully coupled to citizenship. (The relationship between citizenship and suffrage was no less complicated.) This would soon change, as popular discourse and law both became increasingly racist. As Harriet Martineau observed in her 1837 book *Society in America*, the Revolutionary War general, the Marquis de Lafayette, had expressed great "astonishment at the increase of the prejudice against color" when he returned to the United States in 1824.[4] By that time, many states had reversed their previous policies by explicitly denying the vote to free blacks. Even slave states became stricter in this area: it was not until 1834 and 1835, respectively, that Tennessee and North Carolina passed laws ending black suffrage. In the 1820s, as it moved to give the vote to white men regardless of wealth, New York imposed a new $250 property requirement on black men. In

[4] Harriet Martineau, *Society in America* [1837], ed. Seymour Martin Lipset (Gloucester, MA: Peter Smith, 1968), 123.

1838, Pennsylvania – where Tocqueville had noted only a few years earlier that the "tyranny of the majority" created a kind of de facto disfranchisement – made whiteness an official qualification for voting. Ohio's new 1851 constitution did the same; so did Oregon's original constitution in 1857. Meanwhile, the majority of states passed laws prohibiting free blacks from entering them at all. By the eve of the Civil War, only five New England states, in which lived only 4 percent of the free black population, failed to link whiteness and suffrage. We should not exaggerate the novelty of Chief Justice Roger Taney's decision in *Dred Scott v. Sandford* (1857), declaring that those outside the "white race" had no citizenship rights in the United States. In some ways, this was merely the logical extension of the principles that both Northern and Southern states had been adopting over the preceding decades. Three years earlier, Congressman John Dawson of Pennsylvania had already declared that the "word *citizen* means nothing more and nothing less than a white man."[5]

From census methods to suffrage laws, most governmental institutions in the field of population and personal status enforced distinctions of sex as well as race. In part because these two categories overlapped, however, the state's changing relation to women followed a different trajectory than it did with persons designated non-white. While women were never allowed full citizenship rights, they were increasingly provided with legal rights that brought them into a more direct relationship with the state, just as the individualized 1850 census schedules implied. This is not to overlook the considerable inequalities imposed by the state throughout this era, which were thoroughly criticized at Seneca Falls in 1848 and in a wave of subsequent conventions for women's rights. Indeed, when it came to suffrage, there were grounds here too for a narrative of declension: in New Jersey, propertied single women had enjoyed the vote from the Revolution until 1807, when they were disfranchised even as the vote was extended to a wider circle of men.

While the champions of woman suffrage would not begin to triumph until well after the Civil War, in other areas the antebellum state began to treat women more as individual subjects. This was evident in both property law and family law. Under the traditional coverture doctrine, husbands were allowed full legal control over the property brought to the relationship by their wives, who in the eyes of the state had no independent economic status. But starting with Mississippi in 1839, married women's property laws proliferated. By 1865, twenty-nine states had enacted laws allowing wives more control over property. While conservative courts continued to favor husbands in property cases, this was still a significant change. Immediately

[5] *Congressional Globe* 33rd. Cong., 1st Sess., Vol. 28 (28 February 1854), 504.

before the Civil War, Massachusetts and New York went one step further by passing laws allowing married women control over their wages. When it came to divorce and child custody, there was also a clear trend toward liberalization. While fathers continued to be favored by the courts until the end of the era, mothers were increasingly seen by the courts as deserving consideration in child custody cases.

There were many reasons for the changing legal status of women during these years, which surely included the efforts of early feminists, as well as the long-run revolutionary potential of Revolutionary rhetoric. But the rise of whiteness as a social and political marker also contributed to the change. Although the hierarchy with which the early American state came to imagine its population clearly privileged white men above all others, white women enjoyed at least a residual effect of the growing association between race and legal rights. In this sense, race trumped even sex, to say nothing of alternative social categories such as religion, in the politics of population in the early United States.

II. ECONOMY

The role of the early American state in the economic sphere is a subject that has engaged scholars for several generations. It was also, of course, a matter of great concern to the Americans who lived during the years from the Revolution during the Civil War. National politics, as well as those at the state and local levels, often turned on debates over the state's proper economic role. From Jefferson and Hamilton to the Jacksonian Democrats and the Whigs, leading statesmen and major political parties identified themselves by articulating specific programs of political and economic policy; much of the work of courts and legislatures pertained directly or indirectly to this issue. To most observers, it was evident that commerce and industry in the new nation promised unprecedented growth, as well as disorder. But Americans' differing understandings of the proper balance between energy and stability (to use the language of the *Federalist*) and the proper distribution of power in the economic sphere made political economy a contentious subject.

Historians have debated three distinct narratives of the development of early national political economy and law. The first stresses the growing tendency of legislators and courts to abandon traditional regulations and common law doctrines in a way that facilitated the development of private capitalist enterprise. The second, largely in reaction to the first, emphasizes the continuing robustness of government regulation and republican moral economy. A third narrative, less linear than the first two, uses the history of federal and state policy on transport infrastructure to describe a rise and fall of government promotion and administration of enterprise during this period.

Each of these three narratives is valuable. Together they tell us a great deal about the direct and indirect activities of the early national state in the field of economy. Each, however, projects a story that is excessively linear and rather narrow. Histories that stress the continuity of regulation and the traditionalism of courts successfully demonstrate the defects of a narrative in which law increasingly serves entrepreneurial ends, but turn a blind eye to clear evidence of trends in the direction of deregulation. Studies that concentrate on the crucial subject of internal improvements, on the other hand, exaggerate the rise of privatization in the late antebellum era by assuming, mistakenly, that trends in the 1830s and 1840s continued into the last decade of the period. Nor, in any case, was all the world Ohio and Pennsylvania; nor were internal improvements the only important field for state enterprise. Histories that point to a decline of state enterprise and state promotion sit uneasily with the record of state activity in Southern and Western states and with the work of national and local government. While it is indisputable that competitive capitalism and private capital had become more important over the course of this period, government enterprise and state promotion remained an essential part of the early American political economy, all the way into the Civil War.

As several generations of historians have taken great pains to establish, the early United States should not be understood as some kind of libertarian laissez-faire paradise. The state was a major economic actor during the antebellum period, not only as a promoter of internal improvements and other enterprises that might have been left to the private sector but also as a regulator. Municipal regulation enforced by local and state courts was particularly vigorous, much of it lasting through the end of the period. The early American state did not leave the problems of local road building, fire protection, pollution, and public health to private markets. Instead, local officials and judges drew up and enforced elaborate lists of regulations, which they saw as legitimate manifestations of state police power necessary to maintain harmony and order. For every statute or court decision that served to promote capitalist enterprise during this era, evidently there was another that bolstered traditional arrangements or even demanded more public responsibility from private entrepreneurs.

For anyone laboring under the illusion that political economy and law in the early United States were either overwhelmingly laissez faire or unambiguously dedicated to advancing the interests of leading merchants and industrialists, accounts of considerable and continuing regulation serve as an especially important corrective. But they fail to tell the whole story. To be sure, late antebellum cities regulated, just as their colonial predecessors did. Courts often served as a conservative force in early America, just as Tocqueville said they did. But the era was shaped by powerful historical tides that ate away at older arrangements. Even at the municipal level, the regulatory environment changed dramatically. Take, for example, one of the most important everyday manifestations of state power: the regulation of food markets. In the 1790s, many cities and towns confined produce and meat sales to exclusive state-owned markets; they also fixed prices for bread. By the 1830s and 1840s, these measures were dropping away as food marketing became increasingly privatized, first illegally, and then under legal sanction. In New York City, the common council responded in 1821 to years of pressure from bakers by substituting standard loaf weights for fixed prices. By the 1850s, New York mayor Fernando Wood openly rejected any vestiges of "the practice of the old cities of Europe," hailing the privatization of meat marketing as a superior system. This was just one important indicator of the decline of traditional state regulation.

Outside the field of municipal regulation, the direction of state policy ran even more clearly in favor of competition and innovation. Business corporations, for instance, became increasingly common and less bound to public oversight and public purposes. In the 1790s, most corporations were non-profit organizations; they were widely understood as highly regulated public or semi-public entities. But by the middle of the nineteenth century, several states had passed general incorporation laws, which allowed businesses to incorporate legally by applying to state legislatures for special charters. Meanwhile, courts increasingly supported state charters of new corporations that competed with older ones, which had previously enjoyed a monopoly. As it claimed broad federal powers over commerce in *Gibbons v. Ogden* (1824), the Supreme Court had ruled against a steamboat monopoly chartered by New York State. But a more direct blow to the old monopolists came from the Taney court in the case of *Charles River Bridge v. Warren Bridge* (1837), which upheld a Massachusetts court ruling that rejected exclusive franchise in favor of competition.

In property law, state courts moved to favor development over stasis. This was evident in judges' changing attitudes toward the use of streams and rivers, which became increasingly important – especially in the Northeast – as potential sources of industrial power. In colonial New England, farmers and iron makers had struggled over water use, with each side winning significant victories from the legislature. But in the nineteenth century, courts became increasingly sympathetic to the arguments of industrialists, who claimed that the economic benefits of a new mill outweighed the costs to farmers and fishermen downstream. The courts' changing understanding of this field was evident in the Massachusetts case of *Cary v. Daniels* (1844), where the court stressed the public benefits of economic development over traditional usages and rights.

In the fields of contract and labor law, the state moved away from a conservative paternalism and toward a liberal political economy that imagined a market consisting of countless dyads of freely associating individuals. This was not at all the case, clearly, when it came to slavery. But elsewhere, courts came to favor competition, mobility, and efficiency. This doctrine could benefit employees, who by the eve of the Civil War had become the majority of the American labor force. By the 1830s, for example, an employee who wished to leave a job in the middle of the term stipulated in a contract would almost certainly not be compelled by a court to serve out his or her term. Instead, he or she would face a monetary penalty of forfeited wages, which in many cases might be preferable to compelled service or jail. And the courts' growing interest in promoting economic competition could sometimes even work in favor of labor unions. In the Massachusetts case of *Commonwealth v. Hunt* (1842), the state's highest court overruled a lower court's ruling that a union of boot makers was illegal under the common law doctrine of criminal conspiracy. Unions and even the closed shop were permissible, ruled the Massachusetts high court.

But even the most worker-friendly decisions of antebellum courts left plenty of room for anti-union rulings in subsequent cases. By the 1870s certainly, courts were routinely ruling against unions. More broadly, in the context of an ongoing process of industrialization in which economic power was increasingly concentrated, the move away from concerns about equity in contract and labor law served in many cases to favor employers over employees. While customers or passengers were often successful in winning tort cases against businesses, employees – who were understood to have agreed to at least a temporary condition of subordination – fared less well in the courts. In the well-known Massachusetts case of *Farwell v. Boston & Worcester Railroad Co.* (1842), for instance, the court ruled against an employee whose hand was crushed in a workplace accident. Such cases demonstrated that, while the changing legal environment promoted the development of an increasingly flexible labor market, employees' formal privileges and powers in the workplace often failed to extend much beyond their ability to quit.

While state and federal courts tended increasingly to favor mobility, competition, and innovation in many fields of the law, state and federal legislatures also acted deliberately to promote economic growth. Here, there was considerable disagreement about the means by which government – and which level of government – should act. This debate played out most spectacularly in the fields of banking, communications, and internal improvements, which were among the most important political issues of the day at the local, state, and national levels. While the development of the political economy of banking and transport infrastructure did not proceed in a linear fashion, between the Revolution and the Civil War there had been a notable rise and fall of direct government administration in these fields; in communications, the change was less dramatic, but moved in the same direction.

Banking

In banking, of course, one of the most important developments was President Andrew Jackson's campaign against the Bank of the United States, which led to the rise of "free banking" in the states. Chartered by Congress in 1791, the first national bank was a semi-public institution, in which the United States held a 20 percent ownership share. In 1811, this first bank was allowed to die, by a one-vote margin in the Senate. Five years later, after a war in which a national bank was sorely missed, Congress chartered the Bank of the United States anew, again with the federal government owning a one-fifth share. Easily the largest bank and largest business corporation in the country, the Bank had considerable indirect power over the money supply. It also had a large public profile. Protected from state-level taxation by the Supreme Court's decision in *McCulloch v. Maryland* (1819), the Bank was an embodiment of federal and Federalist power, well after the death of Hamilton and the rise of the Jeffersonian majority. Owned largely by private investors – many of them overseas – and often promoting deflation through conservative reserve policies, it was a prime target for attacks by populists and soft money men. Jackson, who issued a surprising challenge to the Bank in his first presidential message to Congress in 1829, went to open war against it in 1832, when he vetoed a bill that would have renewed its charter. Attacking the Bank of the United States as a monster that oppressed the common man, Jackson won a landslide victory in the elections that fall. Then, by moving U.S. Treasury funds into twenty-three state-chartered "pet banks," Jackson ended the national state's support for the nation's most powerful financial institution. In 1836, Congress refused to renew its charter.

The death of the Bank of the United States demonstrated the Jacksonians' ideological commitment to the decentralization of economic power. Decentralization was certainly not the same thing as laissez-faire or anti-developmentalism. In banking, as with corporations more generally, the early American state came to favor a policy of competition via low barriers to entry. Beginning with Michigan in 1837 and New York in 1838, a total of eighteen states passed "free banking" laws in the antebellum era, allowing the formation of banks without special charters from the legislature. These banks were still subject to state regulation, which normally required that any notes they issued be backed by government bonds. By the late antebellum era, then, the national state had little control over money supply. There was no national currency, not even of the limited sort that the Bank of the United States had effectively provided in the 1820s, and Treasury funds were strictly segregated from the banking system. Equally important, the state had little symbolic presence in this field. Awash in a bewildering array of bank notes issued by institutions all over the country, the United States was not yet bound together by the greenback.

Communications

In the field of communications, the early United States provided considerable direct and indirect subsidies through a world-class postal service and liberal press laws. With the Post Office Act of 1792, Congress created what would quickly become a giant state enterprise; for the next eight decades the postal system was rivaled only by the military in its reach and cost. (Unlike the military, the postal system came close to paying for itself: although it absorbed $230 million in U.S. funds before the Civil War, it brought in $171 million.) By 1828, there were about 8,000 post offices in the United States, serving an area of 116,000 square miles and delivering 14 million letters and 16 million newspapers a year. Considerably larger than the postal systems of Britain and France, to say nothing of Russia, this national state enterprise dwarfed any governmental institution at the state or local level. And its influence clearly went well beyond its sheer economic size. To the extent that the early United States came to be bound together culturally during these years, across regional and state boundaries, it was due in large part to the communications network managed by the Post Office Department.

Certainly, the American state was especially active in giving its subjects access to information. Thanks to postal subsidies and low taxes on publishers, by the 1830s, per capita circulation of newspapers in the United States was triple that in Britain. But in communications, as in banking, it was possible to see a retreat of the state during the antebellum period. Telegraphy, originally sponsored by the national government, became a private concern in the 1840s.

Internal Improvements

In the field of internal improvements, historians have charted a similar rise and fall of direct government promotion at both the national and state levels.

Here again, the Jacksonians worked to reduce the national state's presence in the economic field. Before it crystallized as the "American System" identified in the 1820s with Henry Clay and President John Quincy Adams, a policy of major national state assistance to transport infrastructure had been advocated by several leading American statesmen, including Albert Gallatin and John C. Calhoun. In 1817, Calhoun urged Congress, "Let us . . . bind the Republic together with a perfect system of roads and canals. Let us conquer space." The support in Washington for such a policy, always shaky, crested in the 1820s. In 1822, President Monroe signed a bill that provided for the extension into Ohio of the National Road, which had been originally authorized in Congress in 1806 and began in earnest after the War of 1812. Then, with the General Survey Act of 1824, Washington tapped the Army Corps of Engineers – really the only group of formally trained engineers in the country – to work on internal improvements projects. Over the next decade and a half, the military engineers surveyed fifty railroads. Meanwhile, President Adams, who called not only for more federal aid to canals but also for a national university and the adoption of the metric system, went well beyond what Congress was willing to support. His successor, Jackson, signaled his rejection of the American System with an 1830 veto for an extension of the National Road into Kentucky, as well as with his war against the Bank of the United States. Although federal internal improvements spending continued to be high under Jackson's watch, there was a significant shift in resources toward the western part of the country, which received large appropriations for roads and river improvements. Not until 1837, with the economy in recession and President Van Buren in office, was there a sharp drop in federal spending in this field. All in all, from 1790 to 1860, the federal government distributed about $43 million in direct outlays for internal improvements, plus another $77 million in indirect grants, including land grants and a major distribution to the states in 1836 of the Treasury surplus.

State-level outlays on internal improvements during these years were even higher. And here too, historians have found it easy to construct a narrative of early action followed by retreat. While the states did invest in turnpikes, railroads, and other infrastructure projects, they did the most with canals. From 1815 to 1860, of the $188 million spent on canals in the United States, about three-quarters of the money came from governments, mostly at the state level. The Erie Canal, begun in the 1810s and completed in 1825 for about $7 million, was a spectacular success that led other states to emulate New York's example. After Jackson replaced Adams in the White House in 1829, it became clear that the states could not expect much aid for canals from Washington. The states responded with massive borrowing to finance their canal projects, many of which faced more difficult terrain and lower anticipated revenues than the Erie Canal. By 1840, the various states had accumulated $200 million in debts, a thirteen-fold increase on their debt burden of twenty years before. In 1841–43, a total of eight states and one territory defaulted, enraging the British investors who held most of the debt. Over the next decade and a half, eighteen states altered their constitutions to limit state outlays and indebtedness. The canal era was over.

Or so it has seemed. By using a chronological frame running from the 1810s through the 1840s, and by concentrating on the fields of banking and internal improvements, it is easy to describe a narrative of the rise and fall of state enterprise in the early United States. But this story should be questioned. Even in the field of internal improvements, government continued to be quite active. In the 1850s, a Democrat-majority Congress passed a new river and harbor bill, authorized four separate surveys for the transcontinental railroad, and provided large land grants to two railroads in Alabama as well as a 2.5 million-acre grant to the Illinois Central Railroad – to become one of the nation's leading lines. Many of the various states, like the national government, continued to invest in transport infrastructure. In 1859, New York spent more than $1.7 million, or half the state budget, on its canals. True, only about a quarter of the $1 billion invested in U.S. railroads by 1860 came from public sources, whereas close to three-quarters of canal funds came from government; but in total the actual public moneys spent on railroads were about as much as the canal outlays. In the late antebellum era, several Southern states promoted railroads with considerable energy. Whereas Pennsylvania spent about $39 million on canals and only about $1 million on railroads before 1860, Virginia's outlays were $14 million for canals and $21 million for railroads. In Georgia, where the Western & Atlantic line was fully state owned, public funds accounted for half of the $26 million invested in railroads by 1860. Across the antebellum South, more than half of all investment in railroads came from government.

Most public spending on railroads came from local governments, rather than the states. State support for internal improvements did not disappear after 1840, in other words, but shifted away from the state governments toward the local level. In Pennsylvania alone, local governments raised about $18 million for railroads. In 1840, local government debts associated with internal improvements stood at about $25 million; by 1860, they had risen to $200 million – the same amount that the states had owed at the height of the canal finance crisis.

Outside the field of internal improvements, other activities of local government also suggest deficiencies in a narrative of a rise and fall of state enterprise during this era. When it came to police and education, two of the most important areas of practical state activity, there was no trend in the direction of privatization, but rather the opposite: a significant increase in state enterprise. During the 1840s and 1850s, the country's largest cities abandoned informal, voluntary watch systems for large, professional, uniformed police forces. In 1855, Philadelphia counted 650 full-time police officers, organized into sixteen districts. This was a powerful new governmental institution, which embodied a rather sudden shift away from a less formal administration of municipal criminal justice, in which politicians and private citizens had formerly exercised considerable discretion.

Even more impressive was the continuing expansion of state enterprise in the field of education. Federal land policy, which provided the various states with nearly seventy-eight million acres for the support of public schools, helped the United States join Prussia during this era as a world leader in public education. But the most important work was done by state and local governments. At the state level, there was a significant increase over time in school administration and spending. Starting with Massachusetts in 1837, many states created boards of education, which regulated local efforts. In the South as well as the North, education took up an increasing share of state budgets: during at least some years in the 1850s, spending on schools and universities accounted for at least a quarter of all state expenditures in Alabama, Connecticut, Louisiana, Michigan, New Jersey, North Carolina, Pennsylvania, Tennessee, and Wisconsin. Overall, the fraction of state budgets devoted to education rose from an average of 4 percent in the 1830s to 14 percent in the 1850s. Even more governmental activity in the field of education occurred at the local level, where public enterprise became much more important over time, rather than less. In New York City, one key shift occurred in 1842 when the city established an elected Board of Education, taking the business of public schooling away from the voluntary associations that had previously overseen it. By 1850, the public schools were teaching 82 percent of New York City pupils; just two decades earlier, nearly two-thirds of the students had been taught in private institutions. By the eve of the Civil War, when from Massachusetts to Alabama more than half of white children attended school, public schools were quickly growing in number and offering more days of instruction out of the year.

By the eve of the Civil War, local governments had thus embraced public enterprise to a very significant extent. This fact clashes with any narrative of the development of antebellum political economy that attempts to use the history of national and state-level internal improvements policy to suggest that by the late 1840s state enterprise was dead as an idea and a practice. It was not. Nor was it the case, despite some significant innovations in court-made property and contract law, that the early American state became progressively more devoted overall to promoting private enterprise. Local governments' large investments in modern police forces and large new public school systems are among the more important pieces of evidence to the contrary.

Such local activities serve to confirm many traditional accounts of the early American state. But they were not the whole story. Contrary to what many historians of this era have suggested, the various states were overshadowed before the Civil War not only by local governments but also by the national state.

III. TERRITORY

In his 1889 comparative legal treatise on *The State*, Woodrow Wilson declared that "the great bulk of the business of government still rests with the state authorities" (meaning the various states), implying that it had always been so. For later observers, tracing American political development from the nineteenth century though the World Wars, New Deal, and Great Society, it was even easier to describe an earlier political order dominated by state and local government, which gave way only in the twentieth century. There was something to this view: the nineteenth century never saw the emergence of the kind of national state that existed in the United States in the late twentieth century – the kind that absorbs fully 20 percent of total national income in peacetime. Still, the Wilsonian assumption ignores the considerable evidence pointing to the great power and influence of the early national state. Perhaps the most notable change in the United States during this period, it is worth repeating, is the tripling in size of its territory, to a land area of nearly three million square miles. This territory was gained by the diplomatic, military, and legal activities of the national state; it was also managed by the national state for many years thereafter. Even in the early twenty-first century, nearly a third of the land area of the United States is controlled directly by federal agencies. Traditional understandings of the early American state assume, rather than establish, the insignificance of the national government. They simply fail to recognize the importance of territorial acquisition and management to the national state's growth and consolidation.

One basic fact about the early American state, often overlooked, is that the economic footprint of the combined states was considerably smaller than that of the national government, and also less than local government. Even at the height of the canal era, the combined expenditures of all the states amounted to only about two-thirds of federal outlays; more often, they came to only one-third. Combined local government expenditures, which are difficult to measure, appear to have been greater than those of the states, but still slightly below U.S. outlays. In other words, not only in the twentieth century but also in the nineteenth, the federal government outspent its state and local counterparts.

Nearly all U.S. revenues during this era came from customs duties; in a few years, land sales were also significant. Where did the money go? Well over half of it went to the largest of all enterprises, public or private, in early America: the U.S. postal system and the U.S. military. For nearly every year of the first half of the nineteenth century, the military alone absorbed close to three-quarters of federal spending. We must understand that although the economic and military footprint of the early American state was smaller than that of its European counterparts, it, like them, was nonetheless at heart an organization that concentrated coercive power with an eye to territorial domination.

In terms of land area, the infant United States was already an outsized national state relative to those in Europe, even before the Louisiana Purchase and the Mexican War. The territory over which this network operated grew tremendously during these years in two giant leaps and several smaller steps. The Louisiana Purchase of 1803, of course, was the first giant territorial expansion. This event, like the War of 1812, must be understood in the context of the giant conflict then taking place on the European continent among national states then considerably wealthier and more powerful than the United States. At war with most of his neighbors, Napoleon had an immediate need for the $15 million that Jefferson happily paid for lands that stretched from New Orleans up to and beyond the Yellowstone River in the northwestern plains. The Napoleonic Wars were also the most important force behind the War of 1812, in which the United States managed to emerge with its sovereignty and territorial boundaries intact, despite British troops' burning of the new national capital at Washington.

In the years leading up to the War of 1812, events on the Atlantic that were of relatively little concern to the European belligerents took on high importance in the new American nation, which was sensitive about affronts to its sovereignty – even if many of them derived from American merchants' efforts to profit by supplying both sides of the war in Europe. From 1798 to 1800, the United States engaged in an undeclared naval war with France. After a settlement was reached with France, offenses by the British took center stage. From the American perspective, these offenses were considerable: in the decade before 1812, Britain captured more than 900 American ships and impressed as many as 10,000 U.S. citizens into the British navy. In 1807, in one of the incidents that most enraged the American public, the British ship *Leopard* fired on the American ship *Chesapeake*, causing twenty-one U.S. casualties, before British sailors boarded the American vessel to haul off four alleged deserters. This famous violation of U.S. sovereignty was met in Washington with a disastrous new trade policy: the Embargo

Act of 1807, which cut U.S. exports by 80 percent without doing much to affect British behavior. Five years later, a Congress divided along party lines declared war on Britain, which after years of fighting the giant French armies now faced a return to the transatlantic logistical nightmare that it had known a generation before. Even after the French collapse in early 1814, Britain chose not to pursue another extended conflict in North America, in part because of successful American resistance. Two weeks before the most celebrated American military victory of the conflict, Andrew Jackson's defeat of the British at New Orleans in January 1815, a treaty was signed.

Naturally, the War of 1812 stressed the American state and changed its relationship with the people living within its boundaries. During the war itself, the national state struggled to manage the economic mobilization, a task made especially difficult by the recent death of the first Bank of the United States and the refusal of Federalist bankers to assist the war effort. For the tens of thousands of men who moved into the armed forces, as well as for many of their friends and relatives on the home front, the war provided a new connection to the national state that was incarnated in symbols – banners and patriotic songs. But for the development of the American state, the immediate aftermath of the War of 1812 was at least as important as the conflict itself. When the war was over, many U.S. military institutions were expanded and thoroughly reorganized, taking a form that they would hold through the end of the century. As Secretary of War from 1817 to 1825, John C. Calhoun created a new staff system, demanding much higher levels of organization and accountability. The army supply bureaus that would later fuel American troops in the Mexican War and Civil War, including the Quartermaster's Department, Subsistence Department, and Ordnance Department, were rooted most directly in the Calhoun-era reforms. Meanwhile, the U.S. Military Academy at West Point, created in 1802 under President Jefferson, was reformed after the War of 1812 under a new superintendent, Captain Sylvanus Thayer. Now modeling itself after France's L'Ecole Polytechnique, West Point became the nation's first engineering school. As we have noted, several dozen of its graduates would be detailed for work on civilian internal improvements projects under the General Survey Act of 1824. By 1860, West Point graduates comprised more than three-quarters of the army officer corps. The officer corps stood out in early America as an unusually professionalized group with an unusually practical higher education.

The U.S. Navy also saw expansion and reform. The navy's equivalent to West Point, the U.S. Naval Academy at Annapolis, was created in 1845. Meanwhile, the navy was reorganized according to a bureau system that resembled that of the army. No less than the army, the navy extended its reach during this era. By the 1840s, it had separate squadrons operating in the Mediterranean, the Pacific, the West Indies, the East Indies, the South Atlantic, and off the coast of Africa. Still no match for the giant British fleet, the U.S. Navy nevertheless came during these years to have a global reach. One sign of its growing influence came in the early 1850s, when Commodore Matthew C. Perry led a U.S. naval force that compelled Japan to open its ports to the West.

Throughout this era, military institutions and installations were among the most important manifestations of the American state. Largely through its military, the national state served as an extraordinarily important actor in the fields of high-technology manufacturing, exploration, and overseas trade. Innovations in small-arms manufacture, including the development of interchangeable parts, were pushed forward by the army's two national armories, at Harpers Ferry, Virginia, and Springfield, Massachusetts. Like the army, the navy, which ran its own construction yards in ports up and down the Atlantic seaboard, employed a mixed military economy that combined contracting with large-scale state enterprise. One of the most important state institutions of the late antebellum era was the army's Corps of Topographical Engineers, authorized by Congress in 1838 as a full-fledged sister to the Corps of Engineers. Over the years that followed, the Topographical Engineers became a leading source of territorial knowledge. Serving the technical purposes of the state, this knowledge also became popular. The reports of the 1842–45 journeys of the team of one Topographical Engineer, John C. Frémont, became best sellers. After the Mexican War, the Topographical Engineers literally created the boundaries of the United States, with their surveys of the new borders with Mexico and Canada. During the 1850s, the army engineers built thirty-four new roads in the far West. They also conducted four major surveys for a new Pacific railroad.

The military was never far from state-supported scientific efforts during this era; such efforts in turn accounted for a considerable proportion of all scientific knowledge generated in the early United States. By one estimate, close to a third of all scientists in antebellum America worked directly for government. At the state level, support for science came largely in the form of government-sponsored geological surveys, which helped chart the riches of Pennsylvania coal and California gold. More important for early American science was the national government, which funded leading scientific enterprises, such as the U.S. Coast Survey and Naval Observatory. The most important American global exploration effort of the era, the U.S. Exploring Expedition (or "Ex Ex") of 1838–42, used six ships and nearly $1 million in federal funds; among its accomplishments was the co-discovery, with French and British ships, of the continent of Antarctica.

This ongoing institutional expansion and influence on the part of the military echelon of the national state were not matched by the military activities of the various states. Many states effectively reneged on the constitutional and statutory military obligations established just after the Revolution. In theory, the states should have maintained viable public militias through conscription, upholding the non-regular reserve side of the much-hailed American "dual military" tradition. In practice, state militias withered away during the early nineteenth century. During the 1840s, seven states ended compulsory service altogether. While voluntary militia companies sometimes expanded to take their place, this was still an important development away from a federal military system and toward a more fully nationalized military.

One of the central tasks of the U.S. Army, of course, was to serve the early American state's management of Native Americans. It did so not only through active military operations but also routine administration. Significantly, the Bureau of Indian Affairs (also called the Office of Indian Affairs) was established in 1824 as a division of the War Department, by order of Secretary of War Calhoun. This formalized the existing War Department oversight of "Indian agents," the U.S. officers authorized by Congress to oversee trade and other aspects of U.S. policy toward Native Americans in the early nineteenth century. Starting in 1796, Congress demanded that the Indian trade be conducted through official government "factories," or trading posts, which effectively regulated an important part of the American economy. The factory system ran until 1822, when the private fur trade lobby convinced Congress to kill it. But well after this, the War and Treasury Departments continued to oversee a different aspect of economic exchange on the frontier: the payment of annuities, which were a common feature of U.S. treaties with various tribes. By 1826, these annuities amounted to $1 million a year, about 6 percent of all federal outlays. When Congress streamlined the Indian service in 1834, army officers became even more responsible for the distribution of annuities, to which was added regulation of the liquor trade and other basic tasks of administration. Fifteen years later, in 1849, the work of Indian affairs was moved out of the War Department and into the new Interior Department. Only in the last decade of this whole era, in other words, did the U. S. military lose direct oversight of all aspects of Indian affairs.

Along with routine administration, of course, the military enforced the Indian policies of the early American state with naked coercion. This was certainly the case in the aftermath of the Indian Removal Act of 1830. Over time, the United States became less willing to recognize groups of Indians within its territory as independent sovereign states. Supporting the drive of European-American settlers for more land, the early American state turned increasingly to force to meet this end. None of this was new in 1830. For instance, the 1795 Treaty of Greenville, in which the United States formally acquired the southern two-thirds of Ohio in exchange for $20,000 cash and a $9,500 annuity, followed a military victory by Revolutionary War general Anthony Wayne. This victory reversed a crushing defeat suffered in 1791 by a European-American force led by Arthur St. Clair, the territorial governor. During the 1810s, two future U.S. Presidents, William Henry Harrison and Andrew Jackson, won victories over Shawnee and Creek forces in the Indiana and Mississippi territories.

Despite all this early military activity, however, there was still an important shift in state policy between the Revolution and the Civil War away from treating Native Americans as sovereign or even semi-sovereign entities. In the cases of *Johnson v. M'Intosh* (1823) and *Cherokee Nation v. Georgia* (1831), the Supreme Court held that Indian tribes lacked full sovereignty. In *Worcester v. Georgia* (1832), the Supreme Court appeared partially to reconsider. But the state of Georgia and President Jackson, who wanted the vast Cherokee lands for white settlers, simply ignored the ruling. By 1840, some 60,000 members of the southeastern Indian tribes had been forcibly resettled in the new Indian Territory (now Oklahoma). From an earlier policy of treaty-making backed by military force, the American state had moved toward one of direct coercion and control. The vast majority of Native Americans, who were not U.S. citizens, were turned into stateless peoples living under imperial rule.

While the Indian removals of the 1830s and the annexation of Texas and Mexican War of the following decade stand as powerful evidence of the early American state's appetite for territorial domination and expansion, this hunger had limits. This was true especially when it came to dealing with the European powers, with which the United States continued to forge diplomatic rather than military solutions to potential territorial disputes. Many military officers who served along frontier flashpoints, as well as Congress and the State Department, were wary of violating the existing international order of state sovereignty. It was through an 1819 treaty that the United States took over Florida from Spain, and despite many calls for U.S. control of Cuba, the island remained in Spanish hands until the end of the century. The Monroe Doctrine of 1823 warned European powers against additional territorial colonization in the Western hemisphere, but the U.S. quietly acceded to British annexation of the Falkland Islands in 1833. An equally important non-war occurred in the 1840s in the far northwest, where President James Polk, among others, claimed to seek an expanded U.S. territory that would reach above the 54th parallel. But in 1846, Congress agreed to a boundary along the 49th parallel, the line that Britain had proposed more than two decades before. And while American private citizens violated the sovereignty of foreign states by launching filibusters in Central America and elsewhere, they failed to gain U.S. approval. In each of these cases, it appears that many governmental institutions and officers tended to restrain, rather than promote, the territorial expansion through military action demanded by many settlers, newspaper editors, and elected officials.

The one great territorial acquisition of the immediate antebellum era, of course, did come from military conquest. By 1848, Tocqueville's prediction of Anglo-American continental hegemony, made only a decade before, had been realized rather abruptly by the Treaty of Guadalupe Hidalgo, ending the Mexican War. The vast preponderance of land in what would be the continental United States was now under the direct and exclusive authority of the national state. By 1850, the nation counted 1.2 billion acres of public land. With the giant territorial leaps of 1803 and 1848, the management of vast physical spaces became far more important for the early American state than it had been in the day of President Washington. The state's greatest resource, territory was also the state's greatest challenge.

Throughout the period, the national state used property law and land policies, in addition to its postal and military institutions, as a way of managing territory. These policies, which must be understood as among the most important facets of state action in early America, altered the nature of the physical spaces over which the state claimed hegemony. An economical means of territorial consolidation, they suggested the potential power and efficacy of a new, liberal form of statecraft. They also led to the fracturing of the state itself, in a terrible civil war. All of this demonstrated the relative importance of national state policy and administration.

Even before the Louisiana Purchase, the infant American state had struggled with the problem of territorial management. After the Revolution, many of the American states ceded to the Union their claims to lands on their western frontiers. Cession of claims, it was hoped, would bolster the legitimacy and fiscal health of the new national state while reducing interstate conflict. This was a significant enhancement of national state power. The first Congresses then passed critical legislation that would shape the American landscape and the American polity for decades to come. The Northwest Ordinance, enacted in 1787, created a standard mechanism – in advance of the ratification of the Constitution – for the political consolidation of western territories. This measure established a three-stage process for the formation of new states, through which U.S.-appointed territorial governors would serve until replaced by full-fledged state governments. The basic blueprint for the expansion of American federalism, the Northwest Ordinance applied to the territory that between 1803 and 1848 would enter the Union as the states of Ohio, Indiana, Illinois, Michigan, and Wisconsin. (The remainder of the original territory became part of Minnesota, which achieved statehood in 1858.) While the actual paths taken by many of the new territories to statehood departed somewhat from the original plan, in every case the national state had tremendous influence over the early political development of the West. Not especially wild, the West was organized from the beginning by law, from Congressional statutes to the workings of local justices of the peace and county courts, which spread the common law and other old English institutions across the American continent.

No less important than the Northwest Ordinance was the Land Ordinance of 1785, with which the Confederation Congress established procedures for the transformation of territory into land through a national rectilinear surveying system. While it is possible to overstate the extent to which the early American state consolidated its rule by thus enhancing the legibility of the landscape, there can be no doubt that this was a field in which the national state exerted powerful influences over the U.S. spatial and economic order. Under the 1785 law, the basic unit became the township, a square six miles long and six miles wide, which created a total of thirty-six "sections" of one square mile (640 acres) each. Four sections per township were reserved for the use of the United States, and one to provide moneys for public schools. Over time, U.S. land policy was modified in a way that tended to promote faster settlement. At first, the United States sold only whole sections, but the minimum dropped steadily, until in 1832 it was possible to buy as little as a sixteenth of a section (40 acres). Across much of the Midwest, the landscape had been transformed by a proliferation of square-shaped family farms of 80 or 160 acres, as well as much larger estates. In 1820, the minimum per-acre price, which would become a sort of national institution in itself, was set at $1.25, down from the $2.00 level established in 1790. In 1854, a longstanding Jacksonian land policy initiative was instituted by Congress with a Graduation Act, which allowed reduction of price on unsold public lands to as little as $0.125, or one-tenth the normal minimum. Thus well before the Homestead Act and Morrill Act were passed by the Republican-dominated Congress during the Civil War, national state policy favored both rapid settlement and the use of public lands to fund education.

The massive project of converting territory into land was managed in large part by one of the most important of early American state institutions, the General Land Office. Established in 1812 under the Treasury Department, the Land Office was faced immediately with a major jump in land sales, promoted in part by the acquisition of new lands formerly held by Native Americans, by treaty and by force, during the War of 1812. By 1818, the Land Office's Washington headquarters employed twenty-three clerks, one of the largest clerical forces of the day. Overseeing a minor mountain of paperwork, Land Commissioner Josiah Meigs found himself signing his name on roughly 10,000 documents a month. Two decades later, in 1837, there were sixty-two district land offices across the country, along with seven surveying districts. By then, the Land Office's surveyors ranked among the leading government contractors of the day; its district registers and receivers, who earned commissions on land sales, were – no less than territorial judges and justices of the peace – some of the most powerful men in the territories. In 1835–36, one of the great land booms of the century, the national state was selling off between 1 million and 2 million acres a month. Along with the postal and military departments, the Land Office was another national state institution conducting economic enterprise on a scale far larger than any private sector institution.

To some degree, certainly, the land business may be understood as a kind of negative state enterprise, in which immense national resources were quickly privatized. In the half-century from 1787 to 1837 alone, the United States sold 75 million acres. But the notion of privatization takes account of only one side of early American statecraft in this field. As early as the 1790s, Washington and Jefferson understood that, by promoting settlement on its frontiers, the American state might achieve a more thorough consolidation of territory than it could ever hope for through direct military action and at far less expense. After the Louisiana Purchase, the paramilitary dimension of the state's pro-settler land policy became even more important. Occasionally this dimension became explicit, as in the so-called Armed Occupation Act of 1842, which granted 160 acres to any civilian who agreed to settle and fight for five years in Florida, where the Seminoles were continuing to mount the most successful military resistance to Jackson's removal policy.

The military dimension of early land policy was also evident in the association during this era between military service and government land grants. During the Revolutionary War, several states, as well as the federal government, promised land grants to soldiers. For veterans of that conflict, the compensation in land was eventually complemented by cash pensions. In the years following the Pension Act of 1818, pensions for Revolutionary War veterans regularly accounted for more than 10 percent of all federal outlays. Men who served in subsequent antebellum conflicts did not receive federal cash pensions and got land alone. Soldiers in the War of 1812 received more than 29,000 warrants, involving 4.8 million acres. During the Mexican War, in 1847, Congress passed the Ten Regiments Act, which compensated just one year of military service with 160 acres of land located anywhere in the public domain. Soon after the Mexican War, veterans of the War of 1812 convinced Congress to award them more land as a sort of quasi-pension. Together with the Ten Regiments Act, new Congressional statutes in 1850, 1852, and 1855 generated a total of 552,511 land warrants for veterans, involving 61.2 million acres. The explicitly paramilitary dimension of this element of U.S. land policy and settlement can be exaggerated, since many veterans never moved west but simply sold their warrants to brokers; furthermore, plenty of land was available outside the military warrant system. But these land grants can be seen as an important early form of militarily inflected national social policy, as well as a major part of antebellum land policy. Favored initially as a cheap enticement to enlistment, the military warrants took on a new significance over time as they served increasingly as a manifestation of the national state's acceptance of its special obligations to a certain class of citizens.

During the 1850s, even as Congress was granting unprecedented amounts of land to military veterans, the national state's territorial policies became the center of a political crisis that led directly to the Civil War. This well-known chapter in American history was written as a result of the intersection of the fields of population, political economy, and territory that have been discussed above.

While the numbers of Northerners dedicated to the abolition of slavery were not nearly enough to win a national election or back a major war effort, many more Northerners objected to the changes in U.S. territorial policy in the 1850s, in which the American state openly endorsed slavery as a national institution. During the Mexican War the U.S. House had twice passed the so-called Wilmot Proviso, which, taking the Northwest Ordinance as a model, would have prohibited slavery in the vast new territories then being seized from Mexico. Blocked repeatedly in the Senate by John C. Calhoun – once a leading nationalist state-builder following the War of 1812, now the country's leading spokesman for states' rights – the Wilmot Proviso divided the country and the national political parties sharply along regional lines.

Apparently a desert wasteland, with the exception of the Pacific Coast and the California gold fields, the massive new territorial acquisition that came from the Mexican War created great stresses on the American state. In the famous Compromise of 1850, Congress agreed to admit California as a new free state, but allowed the settlers of the large new Utah and New Mexico territories to decide whether to permit slavery. For any Americans familiar with maps of the continent, this evidently challenged a thirty-year-old policy in which it appeared that slavery would be banned in western territories located north of an imaginary line extending westward from Missouri's southern border. In 1854, the Kansas-Nebraska Act more directly cancelled the territorial policy on slavery enacted in the Compromise of 1820, by allowing "popular sovereignty" to decide the issue in the Kansas territory, which lay well above the 36°30′ parallel.

The new policy proved to be a disaster. Pro-slavery and anti-slavery settlers flooded into Kansas, where they prepared rival constitutions and, on more than one occasion, killed one another. In 1857, following the Supreme Court's *Dred Scott* decision, President Buchanan endorsed the pro-slavery Lecompton constitution. At the same time, concerns about Mormon theocracy in Utah territory led Buchanan to order a major U.S. army march westward from Kansas. Military logistics were already the biggest item in the federal budget. Buchanan's Utah campaign only heightened the fiscal strains associated with managing the new territories. When the economy entered a severe recession at the end of 1857 and a new Utah Expedition was mounted in 1858 to reinforce the first one, fiscal difficulties increased markedly. The Utah dispute was settled peaceably, but the expeditions drained the Treasury and bankrupted the nation's leading military contractor. After he conducted a vain and illegal effort to assist the contractor, the Secretary of War was forced out. By the end of the 1850s, disputes over U.S. territorial policy had not only reshaped party politics along sectional lines, they had also undermined many of the early American state's most important institutions.

CONCLUSION

The Civil War tested and transformed the American state. But it did so to a lesser extent than one might have expected, in part because of the antebellum developments described here. In the fields of population, economy, and territory, many of the same state institutions that had been so important between the Revolution and the Civil War continued to be key nodes of state action during the war years of 1861–1865 and beyond. While the war gave rise to many changes in American government, those innovations were shaped and in the long run constrained by the antebellum state order.

The secession of Southern states in 1860–61 challenged the territorial integrity of the nation that had been expanding over the previous eighty years. The North's willingness to fight suggested that territorial integrity was important to many Americans. It was no accident that the war started not over a conflict between two of the various states, but rather with the crisis at Fort Sumter, part of the continental network of military installations maintained by the national state. To fight the war, the North drew on the officer corps and national military bureaucracies that had been schooled and refined during the antebellum expansion of continental empire. The South, which was able to tap part of the same officer corps, created military organizations virtually identical to those of the North. When the Union won the war after four years, a single national state regained territorial mastery. Postbellum territorial consolidation, which concentrated to a remarkable degree not on the South but on the West, followed antebellum precedents.

In the field of political economy, the Civil War mobilization challenged governments in both North and South. While the two sides' economic capacities were far apart, the differences in their mobilization styles should not be exaggerated. Certain aspects of the Confederate mobilization, including state enterprise in ordnance manufacture and regulation of prices and labor markets, appear to resemble the kind of state-managed efforts that would be seen in the World Wars of the twentieth century. But there was also a remarkable lack of central coordination in the South, evident in its chaotic fiscal policy and the resistance of individual states to central authority. In the North, by contrast, the national state quickly took many supply and fiscal concerns out of the hands of the various states. And while the North had the luxury of a large, diverse economic base, filled with thousands of potential private contractors, it – no less than the South – created a mixed war economy. In several of the largest war industries, including those that supplied small arms, ammunition, uniforms, and ships, state-owned and operated facilities manufactured a quarter or more of the goods consumed by the Union armies. The North's supply system was overseen largely by career military officers, rather than businessmen. It was financed by a new national income tax and the unprecedented popular war bond drive. Thus while the Northern state lacked many of the powerful wartime administrative mechanisms that the United States would create during the World Wars – boards to control prices, allocate raw materials, and renegotiate contracts – it nevertheless played a substantial managerial role in the war economy of 1861–65.

One of the most important effects of the Civil War was to remind Americans of the potent authority of government, which from 1861 to 1865 demanded hundreds of thousands of soldiers and hundreds of millions of dollars. Although only about 10 percent of the nearly three million Southern and Northern men who served as soldiers were formally drafted under new conscription laws, many more were pulled into the armies by bonuses paid by national, state, and local governments. (In the North alone, bonuses totaled roughly $500 million, compared with about $1 billion in soldiers' regular pay.) During the war, many county governments, especially, found themselves borrowing unprecedented sums to provide extra compensation to soldiers and their families. In the decades that followed the war, the national state led the way in providing yet another form of additional compensation: military pensions. Anticipated by antebellum precedents, the Civil War pension system reached an entirely new scale. By the early 1890s, the United States was paying pensions to nearly one million Union veterans, absorbing more than 40 percent of the national state's income. The Pension Bureau in Washington, which employed more than 2,000 people, then qualified, according to its chief, as "the largest executive bureau in the world."

Accompanying the wartime expansion of the state that came with the mobilization of men and materiel was the rise of the kind of activist, pro-developmental national state that some Whigs had dreamed of during the antebellum period. During the war years, the U.S. Congress enacted a high tariff, issued large land grants for Pacific railroads and state colleges, and created the Department of Agriculture. Another important wartime innovation, symbolically and substantively, was the greenback – a new national currency that replaced the bewildering array of notes that had been issued by banks across the country during the antebellum period. The new paper money was circulated through a new national banking system, yet another creation of the Republican-dominated Congress. While the national bank network did not have the controlling authority that would be created a half-century later in the Federal Reserve system, and while banks chartered by the various states continued to be important parts of the American economy, the war marked a distinct break away from the radically decentralized Jacksonian financial system. The state's wartime financial requirements, met almost entirely at home rather than in Europe, also fueled the growth of Wall Street, which became increasingly interested in the activities of the Treasury.

While the Civil War partially transformed the American political economy, it was in the field of population that it had – in the short and long run, if not in the medium run – its most revolutionary effects. The Thirteenth, Fourteenth, and Fifteenth Amendments to the Constitution banned slavery, created a new category of national citizenship in which African Americans were included, and appeared to proscribe racial discrimination at the ballot box. Briefly, the United States during the 1860s and 1870s saw an extraordinary political revolution occur, as African Americans became not only voters but also important leaders at all levels of government across the South. By the end of the century, however, African Americans would lose much of what they had appeared to gain just after the Civil War. Due in part to the counterrevolutionary activities of Southern whites, their loss also came about as a result of Northerners' shallow commitment to Reconstruction – surely the consequence of the enduring institutionalized racism that had prevailed across the nation for generations before the war, a racism assiduously encouraged by the state at all levels.

In 1867, Illinois Congressman Lewis Ross harkened back to "the earlier and better days of the country, when the Democratic party was in power," when "we had a Government resting so lightly on the shoulders of the people that they hardly knew they were taxed." For Ross and his party during Reconstruction, and for others in subsequent years who wanted to limit the powers of the national state, it was important to promote an understanding of American political and legal history in which government (especially central government) had always been puny and punchless. But that understanding is simply incorrect. It owes as much to the fantasies of anti-statists – including white supremacists in Ross's day and champions of "free enterprise" in the twentieth century – as it does to the historical record.

Taxes were indeed relatively low in the early United States, but the powers and achievements of the state were considerable. Slavery and white privilege, while antedating the Revolution, were reproduced energetically by new laws. Popular suspicion of concentrated governmental power may have been widespread, as the success of the Jeffersonians and Jacksonians suggested, but all levels of American government raised large sums for public works. Many critical industries and services, including transport, communications, education, scientific research, and security, were managed on a large scale by public, as well as private, authorities. Far from anarchic, the trans-Mississippi West, no less than the East, was explored, surveyed, and maintained by governmental organizations and laws.

Even acknowledging all this evidence of a robust state in the early United States, some may maintain that the state was still insignificant in relative terms. A cursory examination suggests that, even in comparison to the most powerful European states of the era, the state in the early United States was not especially impotent or anomalous. In the realm of political economy, much of the nationalization and heavy regulation undertaken by European states that diverged from American practice began in the second half of the nineteenth century, not in the first. Similarly, it was largely in the second half of the century that the modern British and French empires took shape; before 1850, the consolidation of the U.S. continental empire suggested that American achievements in military conquest and territorial administration were no less considerable than those of other leading powers, even if they cost less. Finally, the early American state was evidently at least as energetic as its European peers in measuring its population and discriminating legally among different classes of persons.

When it comes to government, there was no original age of American innocence. To the extent that the American state can be understood today as exceptional relative to its peers around the world, it owes its distinctiveness more to the developments that would come after 1865 than to its early history.

2

LEGAL EDUCATION AND LEGAL THOUGHT, 1790–1920

HUGH C. MACGILL AND R. KENT NEWMYER

The years from 1790 to 1920 saw the transformation of American society from an agrarian republic of 4 million people huddled on the Atlantic seaboard to a continental nation of some 105 million people, recognized as the dominant financial and industrial power in the world. Legal education (and legal culture generally) responded to and reflected the historical forces behind this radical transformation. In 1790, aspiring lawyers learned law and gained admission to practice by apprenticing themselves to practicing lawyers. Law office law unavoidably tended to be local law. By 1920, 143 law schools (most affiliated with universities) dominated – indeed, all but monopolized – legal education and were close to controlling entry into the profession. Through their trade group, the Association of American Law Schools, and with the support of the American Bar Association, they had by the beginning of the 1920s created the institutional mechanisms for defining, if not fully implementing, national standards for legal education. In legal education as in many other areas of American society, institutionalization and organization were the keys to power, and power increasingly flowed from the top down.

The normative assumptions of this new educational regime emanated from the reforms first introduced by Dean Christopher Columbus Langdell at Harvard Law School in 1870. Langdell's ideas were stoutly resisted, initially even at Harvard. They were never implemented anywhere else in pure form, and they were rooted more deeply in tradition than Langdell acknowledged. Nevertheless, his institutional and pedagogic innovations became the common denominator of modern legal education. Langdell's success owed much to the congruence of his ideas with the version of legal science prevailing in the late nineteenth century. No less important, it responded to the changing nature of legal practice in the new corporate age: a shift from courtroom to board room, from litigating to counseling, from solo and small partnership practice to large law firms. More generally, Langdell's reforms at Harvard were symbiotically connected to the demographic, intellectual, political, and economic forces of modernization at work as the nineteenth century ended. Our goal, hence, is to describe and analyze legal education as it responded to (and influenced) these transformative changes.

I. THE COMMON LAW FOUNDATION: LEGAL EDUCATION BY APPRENTICESHIP

No single factor had greater impact on American legal education than the transplantation of the English common law to America. Sizeable portions of English law had to be modified or jettisoned to fit American circumstances, but what remained as bedrock was the adversary system of dispute resolution. In this common law system, a lawyer was a litigator. It followed that the primary objective of legal education – first in England and then in America – was to teach lawyers the art of arguing cases in court. From the outset, practicing law took precedence over theorizing about it.

What better way of learning the practical skills of lawyering than by studying those who practiced them on a daily basis? Apprenticeship training was essentially learning by doing and by observing, and in both the burden rested mainly on the student. Even after law-office training was supplemented by a few months in a proprietary or university law school, an opportunity increasingly available by the middle decades of the nineteenth century, legal education remained largely autodidactic.

Apprenticeship was the dominant form of legal education in British North America from the outset, although a few sons of the well-to-do, chiefly from the Southern colonies, attended one of the four English Inns of Court. English legal education carried considerable cachet even though by the eighteenth century, when American students began to appear in London, the Inns had deteriorated into little more than exclusive eating clubs. They left no mark on legal education in the United States, except to generate a negative reaction to anything suggesting a national legal aristocracy. Even in England, real instruction in law took place in the chambers of barristers and solicitors.

The rules governing apprenticeship training in America, like those governing admission to practice, were established by the profession itself – by judges in conjunction with local associations of lawyers. In new states and territories, where the profession itself was ill defined, the rules were fewer and less likely to be enforced. In most states, students were required to "read" law in the office of a local lawyer of good standing. Three years of reading appears to have been the norm, though time spent at one of the early law schools counted toward the requirement. Fees paid by apprentices, set informally by the bar, generally ranged between $100 and $200, but in practice the amount and means of payment were up to the lawyer. The level of literacy expected of apprentices probably excluded more aspirants than the schedule of fees, which was flexible and often laxly enforced.

Students were admitted to the bar after completing the required period of reading and passing a perfunctory oral examination, generally administered by a committee of lawyers appointed by the local court. Occasionally an effort might be made to make the examination a real test, as when the famed Virginia legal educator George Wythe opposed, unsuccessfully, the admission of Patrick Henry (who became a leader of the Richmond bar). Since apprentices were sons of people known in the community and known to their mentors, the examining committee was unlikely to offend a colleague by turning down his protégé. Few students who fulfilled the terms of apprenticeship, had a nodding acquaintance with Blackstone's *Commentaries*, and were vouched for by their sponsors failed to pass. Admission to appellate practice as a rule came automatically after a prescribed period of practice in the trial courts.

Immediately prior to the Civil War even these minimal standards were subject to dilution. In Lincoln's Illinois, for example, the price of a license for one lucky candidate was a dinner of oysters and fried pigs' feet. As Joseph Baldwin put it in *The Flush Times of Alabama and Mississippi* (1853), "Practicing law, like shinplaster banking or a fight, was pretty much a free thing. . . . " The popularity of "Everyman His Own Lawyer" books during this period makes the same point. Admission to practice was less a certification of the applicant's knowledge than an opportunity for him to learn on the job.

Compared with legal education in eighteenth-century England or twentieth-century United States, law-office education was strikingly egalitarian. Even at its most democratic, however, the system was not entirely open. To women and black Americans, it was not open at all, exclusions so rooted in the local culture (like apprenticeship itself) that no formal rules were required to enforce them. Though not based on class distinctions, the system operated to favor the sons of well-connected families. Fees were beyond the reach of most working-class young men; for those who could afford them, it was advantageous to read with the best lawyers, in the best offices, with the best libraries. Most of George Wythe's students at William and Mary, for example, were from Virginia's ruling class. Their Northern counterparts who could study at Harvard with Joseph Story and Simon Greenleaf also had a leg up on their competition. Access to the profession, and success within it, depended on being literate, articulate, and disciplined – qualities difficult to develop for those on the margins of American society. Still, judging by the large number of lawyers who achieved eminence without benefit of social advantage, professional status had less to do with pedigree than with success in the rough-and-tumble of circuit-riding and courtroom competition.

Though comparatively open to achievement, apprenticeship was also open to abuse. Often the most able jurists did not have the time to devote to their apprentices: consider for example the complaint of one of James Wilson's students that "as an instructor he was almost useless to those who were under his direction."[1] Many lawyers had neither the knowledge nor the ability required to teach others. At the worst, they simply pocketed student fees and exploited their apprentices as cheap labor for copying contracts, filing writs, and preparing pleas. The learning-by-suffering approach was justified on the grounds that students were actually mastering the rudiments and realities of practice. In fact, even this modest goal was not always reached; witness the confession of John Adams that, after completing his apprenticeship, he had no idea how to file a motion in court.

The chief weakness of law-office education did not lie in the practical matters of lawyering, however, but in its failure to teach law as a coherent system – or, as contemporaries liked to say, as a science. James Kent's description of his apprenticeship in Poughkeepsie, New York, in the 1780s identified the problem and the solution. Kent received no guidance from Egbert Benson, attorney general of New York, to whom he had been apprenticed by his father. Unlike his officemates, however, who spent much of their time drinking, Kent plunged into Blackstone's *Commentaries* on his own. Mastery of Blackstone brought order out of the chaos of case law and, as he later claimed, launched him on the road to success. Kent repaid the debt by writing his own *Commentaries on American Law*, a work designed to do for American lawyers in the nineteenth century what Blackstone had done for him in the eighteenth.

For the great mass of American law students who lacked Kent's discipline and thirst for knowledge, the apprenticeship system did not deliver a comprehensive legal education. Neither, however, did it exclude them from practice. Indeed, apprenticeship education, like the common law itself, fit American circumstances remarkably well. A system that recognized no formal class distinctions and placed a premium on self-help resonated with American egalitarianism. Even the local character of law-office training, a serious weakness by the late nineteenth century, had its uses in the Early Republic because it guaranteed that legal education would respond to the diverse, and essentially local, needs of the new nation. What Daniel Webster learned in the law office of Thomas W. Thompson in Salisbury, New Hampshire, for example, prepared him to serve the needs of farmers and merchants in the local market economy of the hinterland. His later education, in the Boston office of Christopher Gore, with its well-stocked library, was equally suited to practice in the state and federal courts of that major commercial center. Gore's students could also learn by watching

[1] Quoted in Charles Warren, *History of the American Bar* (Cambridge, MA, 1912), 167.

Boston's leading lawyers in action, whether in the Supreme Judicial Court of Massachusetts, the federal district court of Judge John Davis, or Justice Joseph Story's U.S. Circuit Court. A legal education for students in Richmond in the 1790s similarly included the opportunity to observe appellate lawyers like John Marshall and John Wickham argue cases before Judge Edmund Pendleton and Chancellor George Wythe. The law they learned – English common law and equity adjusted to plantation agriculture and chattel slavery, operating in an international market – suited the needs of the Old Dominion.

Whether in Salisbury or Boston, New York or Poughkeepsie, Richmond, Baltimore, or Philadelphia, apprenticeship training adapted itself to American circumstances, even as those circumstances changed. By failing to teach legal principles, the system at least avoided teaching the wrong ones. Circumstance more than deliberate planning assured that American legal education in its formative years, like American law itself, remained open-ended, experimental, and practical.

II. THE AMERICAN TREATISE TRADITION

Apprenticeship education received a bracing infusion of vitality from the spectacular growth of American legal literature. Through the War of 1812, American law students educated themselves by reading mainly English treatises. What they read varied from region to region and indeed from law office to law office, but the one work on every list was Sir William Blackstone's four-volume *Commentaries on the Laws of England*. Published in 1764, the work was quickly pirated in the American colonies. It went through many American editions, beginning with that of St. George Tucker, published in Richmond in 1803, which was tailored to American circumstances and annotated with American cases. A staple of legal education until the 1870s, Blackstone's *Commentaries* did more to shape American legal education and thought than any other single work.

Blackstone's permeating influence was ironic and paradoxical. A Tory jurist, he celebrated Parliamentary sovereignty at the very time Americans were beginning to challenge it. His subject was English law as it stood at mid-eighteenth century, before the modernizing and destabilizing effects of Lord Mansfield's new commercial doctrines had been felt. Even as a statement of English law circa 1750 the *Commentaries* were not entirely reliable. In any case, English law was not controlling in the courts of the new republic.

Despite these limitations Blackstone remained the starting point of legal education and legal thought in America from the Revolution to the Civil War. Law teachers could select the portions of the four volumes that fit their particular needs and ignore the rest, a case in point being Henry Tucker's *Notes on Blackstone's Commentaries* (1826), prepared specifically for the students at his law school in Winchester, Virginia. For book-starved apprentices everywhere, the work was an all-purpose primer, serving as dictionary, casebook, a history of the common law, and guide to professional self-consciousness. Above all, the carefully organized and elegantly written *Commentaries* imparted to students and established lawyers alike a vision of law as a coherent body of rules and principles – what Samuel Sewall, advising his student Joseph Story, called "the theory and General doctrines" of the law. By providing a rational framework, Blackstone helped law students bring "scientific" order out of case law and offered relief from the numbing tasks of scrivening. With English law rendered by a Tory judge as their guide, American students set out to chart the course of American legal science.

To aid them in mapping the terrain, apprentices were advised to keep a commonplace book – a homemade digest of alphabetically arranged legal categories including relevant case citations, definitions, and other practical information. Students often supplemented Blackstone by consulting such works as Matthew Bacon's *A New Abridgement of the Laws* (1736), which went through several American editions before being replaced by Nathan Dane's nine-volume *Abridgement of American Law* (1826–29). Dane was to Bacon what Kent was to Blackstone; both American transmutations appeared at the end of the 1820s. Among other synthetic works consulted by American students during the late eighteenth and early nineteenth centuries were Thomas Wood's *Institutes of the Laws of England* (1722), the forerunner to Blackstone; Rutherford's *Institutes of Natural Law* (1754–56); and John Comyn's *Digest* (1762–67). Until they were replaced by American treatises in the 1820s and 1830s, continental works in English translation also were frequently consulted for specific doctrines and for general ideas about law. Among the most widely used, especially in regions where maritime commerce made the law of nations relevant to practice, were works by Hugo Grotius, Jean Jacques Burlamaqui, Samuel Pufendorf, and Emmerich de Vattel. Under Joseph Story's direction, Harvard built a great collection of civil law treatises on the assumption that the common law could profit by an infusion of rationality and morality from the civil law tradition. As it turned out, the practical-minded law students at Harvard were much less interested in comparative law than was their famous teacher.

In search of practical, workaday principles of law, students could choose from a surprisingly wide range of specialized treatises – again English at first, but with American works soon following. Although their reading was apt to be limited to the books available in the office where they studied, there were some standard subjects and accepted authorities. At the end of the eighteenth century and in the first decades of the nineteenth, serious students were advised to read Hargrave and Butler's edition of the venerable *Coke upon Littleton*, a seventeenth-century work so arcane that it brought the most dedicated scholars to their knees. Fearne's *Essay on Contingent Remainders and Executory Devises* in its various editions was the classic authority on wills and estates in both England and America. For equity, students had to rely on English treatises until the publication in the 1830s of Story's commentaries on equity and equity jurisdiction. Given that the formal writ system of pleading survived well into the nineteenth century, practical guides to pleading and practice were essential. One of the most widely used was Chitty's three-volume *The Practice of Law in All of Its Departments*, published in an American edition in 1836. Justice-of-the-Peace manuals, on the English models set by John Dalton and Giles Jacob, were standard fare in every part of the country.

Case law was central to legal education from the beginning. Prior to the early 1800s, when printed reports of American court decisions first made their appearance, students had to rely on English reports. As a "guide to method and a collection of precedents," Kent particularly recommended those of Sir Edward Coke, Chief Justice Saunders (in the 1799 edition), and Chief Justice Vaughn. For equity, Kent urged students to consult the Vesey and Atkyns edition of the opinions of Lord Hardwicke. The library of the Litchfield Law School included two dozen sets of English reporters. Once they became available, American judicial decisions gradually displaced English case law as sources of authority, but English decisions continued to be studied and cited for the legal principles they contained until late in the nineteenth century, by no less an authority than C. C. Langdell, the founder of the case method. Attention to English and American reports reminds us of the practical-minded, non-theoretical nature of American legal thought and education during the formative period.

Law students were also expected to understand the ethical obligations of the profession, a theme presented in Blackstone's *Commentaries* and echoed in countless law books and lawyers' speeches during the course of the century. What students made of this uplifting professional rhetoric is difficult to say, but clearly the emphasis on the morality of law and the ethics of practice was useful to a profession still in the process of defining and justifying itself. As it turned out, the failure of the apprenticeship system to instill a sense of professional identity was an impetus for the law school movement and the rebirth of bar associations in the 1870s and 1880s.

Much more threatening to the apprenticeship system was the exponential growth of printed American judicial decisions – "the true repositories of the law," as Story called them. Federal Supreme Court reports, available from the beginning, were soon followed by those of the several federal circuit courts.

State reports, beginning with Kirby's Connecticut reports in 1789, became the norm by the first decade of the nineteenth century. By 1821, Story counted more than 150 volumes of state and federal reports that lawyers needed to consult – enough, he feared, to overwhelm the profession. Each new state added to the problem, as did the growing complexity and quantity of litigation in the wake of the commercial and corporate revolution that began before the Civil War. In 1859, speaking at the dedication of the law school at the first University of Chicago, David Dudley Field estimated that American lawyers faced no less than two million common law "rules."[2]

The struggle to organize this burgeoning body of case law helped shape legal education. Before printed reports, the problem for students was the inaccessibility of judicial decisions; as published reports proliferated, the problem became one of extracting sound principles from them. Commonplacing, a primitive approach to the problem, gave way to the use of English treatises footnoted to American decisions, on the model of Tucker's Blackstone. These were gradually superseded by domestic treatises, Dane's *Abridgment* and Kent's *Commentaries* being the most ambitious. Oliver Wendell Holmes, Jr.'s famous twelfth edition of Kent, published in 1873, contained an index of largely American cases that ran to 180 pages of small print. Charles Warren believed that *Angell on Watercourses* (1824), with "96 pages of text and 246 pages of cases," may have been the first American casebook.[3] Joseph Story, who suggested the case emphasis to Angell, also saw to it that Harvard maintained a complete run of all American and English reports. Extracting principles from this ever-expanding body of decisions, which was the function of treatise writers, also was the chief objective of Langdell's case method. Working in this mode reinforced the belief that law was autonomous, with a life of its own beyond the efforts of lawyers and judges to make sense of it.

As authoritative expositions of legal principles, treatises were the primary means of organizing case law in the nineteenth century. The publishing career of Justice Joseph Story, the most prolific treatise writer of the century, is exemplary. Story's *A Selection of Pleadings in Civil Actions* (1805) appeared only one year after Massachusetts began to publish the decisions of its highest court. By his death in 1845, Story had published commentaries on all the chief branches of American law (except for admiralty), each of them focused on principles. By bringing a measure of system and accessibility to his topics, Story pursued the ever-receding goal of a nationally

[2] David Dudley Field, "Magnitude and Importance of Legal Science," reprinted in Steve Sheppard, ed., *The History of Legal Education in the United States: Commentaries and Primary Sources* (Pasadena, CA, 1999), 658.

[3] Warren, *History of the American Bar*, 541.

uniform common law. Updated regularly in new editions, Story's volumes were standard reading for law students and practicing lawyers into the twentieth century. Abraham Lincoln, himself a successful corporate lawyer, said in 1858 that the most expeditious way into the profession "was to read Blackstone's Commentaries, Chitty's Pleading, Greenleaf's Evidence, Story's Equity and Story's Equity Pleading, get a license and go to the practice and still keep reading."[4]

Lincoln's comment highlights two major characteristics of apprenticeship training: first, it was largely a process of self-education that continued after admission to practice; and second, self-education consisted mainly in reading legal treatises. The period from 1830 to 1860 in particular was "one of great activity and of splendid accomplishment by the American law writers."[5] Merely to list some of the most important of their works suggests the variety of material available to law students and lawyers. Angell and Ames's *The Law of Private Corporations* (1832) was the first book on corporate law. Story's treatises – *Bailments* (1832), *Agency* (1839), *Partnership* (1841), *Bills of Exchange* (1843), and *Promissory Notes* (1845) – made new developments in commercial law available to students and lawyers all over the country and remained authoritative for several generations. Greenleaf's *Evidence* (3 vols., 1842–53), recommended by Lincoln, had an equally long life. Parsons's highly regarded book on contracts, published in 1853, went through nine editions and was followed by several treatises on commercial paper. Hilliard's *Real Property* (1838) quickly replaced previous books on that subject. *Angell on Carriers* (1849) was followed by Pierce's even more specialized *American Railway Law* (1857). Treatises on telegraph, insurance, copyright, trademark and patent law, and women's property rights literally traced the mid-nineteenth-century contours of American economic modernization.

And so it went: new books on old subjects, new books on new subjects. Thanks to the steam press, cheap paper, new marketing techniques, and the establishment of subscription law libraries in cities, these books circulated widely. New treatises gave legal apprenticeship a new lease on life. So did university law lectureships and private and university-based law schools, both conceived as supplements to apprenticeship training. The treatise tradition, which did so much to shape law-office education, also greatly influenced the substance and methods of instruction in early law schools.

[4] Terrence C. Halliday, "Legal Education and the Rationalization of Law: A Tale of Two Countries – The United States and Australia," ABF Working Paper #8711. Presented at the 10th World Congress of Sociology, Mexico City, 1982.

[5] Charles Warren, *History of the Harvard Law School* (New York, 1908), I, 260.

III. AMERICAN LAW SCHOOLS BEFORE 1870

Langdell's reforms at Harvard Law School in the 1870s are generally seen as the beginning of modern American legal education, but Harvard under Langdell was built on a foundation laid by Story. As Supreme Court justice and chief judge on the New England circuit, with close personal connections to the leading entrepreneurs of the region, Story was attuned to the economic transformation of the age. As Dane Professor, he was in a position to refashion legal education to fit the needs of the market revolution. Dynamic entrepreneurs operating in the nascent national market needed uniform commercial law if they could get it, consistency among state laws if they could not. At the least, they needed to know the rules in each of the states where they did business. The emergence in the nineteenth century of a national market economy generated many of the same opportunities and challenges presented by globalization in the twenty-first. The question was whether lawyers trained haphazardly in local law offices could deliver. Could they master the new areas of law that grew from technological and economic change? And, even with the help of treatises, could they extract reliable, uniform principles from the ever-growing body of decisional law? Increasingly the answer was no, which explains the remarkable expansion of free-standing and university-based law schools in the antebellum period.

Public law schools connected with established colleges and universities – ultimately the dominant form – traced their origins to university law lectureships. The model was the Vinerian professorship at Oxford, of which Blackstone was the most famous incumbent. The first law lectureship in the United States was established at the College of William and Mary in 1779 by Governor Thomas Jefferson. Others followed at Brown (1790), Pennsylvania (1790), King's College (Columbia) (1794), Transylvania University in Kentucky (1799), Yale (1801), Harvard (1815), Maryland (1816), Virginia (1825), and New York University (1835).

These lectureships addressed the perceived failure of the apprenticeship system to teach law as a system of interrelated principles. Their success defies precise measurement. Aspiration and execution varied widely, and they were all directed principally at college undergraduates. Judging by the number of his students who later distinguished themselves, George Wythe at William and Mary had considerable influence. On the other hand, James Wilson's lectures at Pennsylvania, James Kent's at Columbia, and those of Elizur Goodrich at Yale failed to catch on. Isaac Parker's lectures as Royall Professor at Harvard inspired little interest, but his experience led him to champion the creation of a full-fledged law school there in 1817.

The efforts of David Hoffman, a prominent Baltimore lawyer, to do the same at the University of Maryland were unsuccessful, partly because his vision of a proper legal education was too grandiose and partly because American law was changing more quickly than he could revise his lecture notes. Nonetheless, his *Course of Legal Study* (1817) was the most influential treatise written on the subject of legal education prior to the Civil War, and it bore witness to the deficiencies of apprenticeship education. These early lectureships pioneered the later development of public, university-based law schools.

Private, proprietary law schools also flourished during the years before the Civil War. The prototype of many that followed was the law school founded in 1784 by Judge Tapping Reeve in Litchfield, Connecticut. Reeve, a successful law-office teacher, was joined by a former student, James Gould, who headed the school on Reeve's death in 1823. In contrast to the haphazard and isolated nature of most apprenticeship arrangements, Litchfield was full-time learning and serious business. During their required fourteen months in residence, students took notes on daily lectures organized on Blackstonian lines. Directed treatise reading was supplemented by moot courts and debating societies. Above all, Reeve and Gould taught legal science. Gould believed that the scientific approach demanded that law, especially the common law, be taught "not as a collection of *insulated positive rules*, as from the exhibition of it, in most of our books . . . but as a *system of connected, rational principles*. . . ." At its peak in 1813, the school had 55 students in residence; by the time of its demise in 1833 it had graduated more than 1,000 students, drawn from every state in the union, including many who went on to eminence in law and politics, Aaron Burr and John C. Calhoun among them.

Litchfield was the model for a dozen or more proprietary schools in seven states, and there were other home-grown variations as well. In Virginia, for example, there were several private law schools during the antebellum period. Although none attained the longevity of Litchfield, they attracted a considerable number of students. By 1850 there were more than twenty such schools around the country. Even then, however, they were being outdistanced by the larger and better financed university-based law schools. The last proprietary school on the Litchfield model, in Richmond Hill, North Carolina, closed in 1878.

The concept of a full-time law school affiliated with an established university took on new life at Harvard in 1815, when Isaac Parker, Chief Justice of the Supreme Judicial Court, was appointed the Royall Professor, to lecture on law to Harvard undergraduates. The full-time law school began two years later with the appointment of Asahel Stearns as resident instructor. Stearns was simultaneously teacher, adviser, librarian, and administrator;

in addition to being overworked, he was plodding and narrow. Parker was enthusiastic about the new school, but his superficial lectures failed to attract students. Only in 1828, when Justice Joseph Story was appointed Dane Professor, did Harvard Law School come into its own. Under the leadership of Story, Nathan Dane, and Josiah Quincy, Jr., the newly invigorated school set out to train lawyers who would facilitate the Industrial Revolution then underway in New England. Story also hoped that Harvard law students, trained in his own brand of constitutional nationalism, would rescue the Republic from the leveling forces of Jacksonian democracy.

Several factors account for the success of the school, starting with Dane's generous endowment (from the proceeds of his nine-volume *Abridgement of American Law*). The growing reputation of Harvard in general was advantageous to its law school, as were the cordial relations between Story and Quincy, president of Harvard. As Dane Professor, Justice Story attracted able students from across the nation. A growing student body meant rising income from fees. With fees came a library and a part-time librarian. Under Story's guidance, the law school began to acquire the materials necessary for the scientific study of American law. A complete and up-to-date run of federal and state reports and a comprehensive collection of American, English, and continental treatises laid the foundation for what Harvard advertised as the best law library in the world. Years later, Langdell would celebrate the library as the laboratory for the study of law. Story built the laboratory.

With the appointment of Simon Greenleaf as a full-time resident professor in 1833, the school was up and running. Greenleaf handled the daily administration of the school and much of the teaching. Story focused on the scholarship he was required to produce under the terms of the Dane endowment. In their many editions, his commentaries became standard texts not only for students at Harvard, but for judges and lawyers across the nation, and for the apprentices who studied with them.

Measured by the demand for Story's commentaries in all parts of the country and by the nature of the student body, Harvard Law School was a national law school – the first in the nation. Other antebellum law schools, independent or college based, responded more to the perceived needs of their respective locales. Some, including the Cincinnati Law School, founded in 1833 by Timothy Walker, one of Story's students, were modeled directly on Harvard, but soon assumed a regional tone. Yale, by contrast, followed a different route (one that would be widely replicated elsewhere) by absorbing Judge David Daggett's New Haven law school, but no pretense was made of integrating this new initiative with the college, and it would be many decades before Yale had a full-time instructor in law on its payroll. At Jefferson's insistence, the law department at the newly founded University of

Virginia aimed to reach students from Southern states with law congenial to Southern interests, including states' rights constitutional theory. Whatever the dictates of their markets, all of these new law schools, whether in rural Connecticut, the new West, or the Old South, claimed to offer systematic legal instruction that apprenticeship training could not deliver.

The impact of the early law schools on legal education is hard to assess because formal instruction was auxiliary to law-office training and because most schools retained many of the practices of the apprenticeship system. And, as one might expect, their quality varied widely. Still, it is reasonable to assume that schools offered students better access to the growing body of treatises and case reports than most law offices could furnish. Students learned from each other and sharpened their skills in the moot court competitions that were common features of school life. The fortunate student might encounter a gifted teacher such as Theodore Dwight. His historically oriented lectures, directed treatise reading, and "oral colloquy," developed first at Hamilton College in the 1850s and refined at Columbia over three decades, was the accepted standard for first-rate law school training prior to the Langdellian revolution of the 1870s, and for some time thereafter.

Dwight at Columbia, like Greenleaf at Harvard and St. George Tucker at William and Mary, was a full-time professor. But the profession of law teacher was several decades in the future. Instruction, even at many of the law schools, generally was offered by judges and lawyers working on a part-time basis. Not surprisingly, they continued to teach law-office law. The substance of law school education prior to the 1870s was intensely practical. Scant attention was paid to legislation, legal theory, comparative law, legal history, or any other discipline related to law. Even dedicated scholar-teachers like Story were more interested in the practical applications of law than in investigating its nature and origins. Student opinion forced the University of Virginia's law department, initially committed to a relatively broad-gauged course of study, to narrow its focus in order to maintain enrollment. Story was forced to modify his ambitious Harvard curriculum for the same reason. Not long after his death, his great collection of civil law treatises was gathering dust on the shelves because students found it of little practical use.

In law schools as in law offices legal education was chiefly concerned with preparing students to litigate, and that meant coping with judicial decisions. As early as 1821, Story and Dane had decried the unmanageable bulk of case law. Increased population and the creation of new states and territories helped turn the problem into a crisis that neither law offices nor law schools as then constituted could manage.

IV. THE 1870S: A NEW ORDER STIRS

The appointment of Langdell at Harvard in 1870, the turning point in American legal education, was an incident in the emergence of the modern research university. The academy, however, was hardly the only segment of society to be affected by the broad changes that swept through America in the decades following the Civil War. The reunification of the nation was confirmed by the end of Reconstruction in 1877. The Centennial Exposition of 1876 dramatized the national reach of market economics, bringing the reality of the Industrial Revolution – mass production and consumer culture – to millions for the first time. America celebrated free labor and individualism, but the reality beneath the rhetoric was order at the top imposed on chaos below. Business organizations of increasing scale were among the principal engines of change. The nature and structure of law practice evolved, especially in cities, in response to the changing needs of these lucrative clients. The subordination of courtroom advocacy to the counseling of corporations accelerated, as it became more important to avoid litigation than to win it. Corporate practice called increasingly for legal specialists and larger firms.

Bar associations, which had yielded in the 1830s to Jacksonian egalitarianism, began to re-emerge. The Association of the Bar of the City of New York was formed in 1870 in response to scandalous conduct among lawyers during Boss Tweed's reign and the Erie Railroad Wars. In 1872 the Chicago Bar Association was established in an effort to control the unlicensed practice of law. By 1878 there were local or state bar associations in twelve states. In that year, at the prompting of the American Social Science Association, a small group of prominent lawyers convened in Saratoga Springs to form the American Bar Association (ABA). The ABA would follow the lead of the American Medical Association, founded in 1847 (but attaining effective power only at the end of the century), in attempting to define the profession, requirements for entry, and standards for professional work.

Comparison between the lofty stature ascribed to the legal profession by Tocqueville and the low estate to which it had fallen furnished the more prominent members of the bar with an additional impetus to action. If membership in the profession was open to people with no more (and often less) than a secondary general education, who had completed no prescribed course of professional training, and who had met risible licensing requirements, then professional status itself was fairly open to question. Unsurprisingly, one of the first subgroups formed within the ABA was the Committee on Legal Education and Admissions to the Bar.

The significance of Christopher Columbus Langdell's work at Harvard in the 1870s is best understood in this context. In 1869 Charles W. Eliot, an analytic chemist from MIT, was appointed president of Harvard. Touring Europe earlier in the 1860s, Eliot had been impressed by the scientific rigor of continental universities. To make Harvard their peer, he would "turn the whole University like a flapjack,"[6] and he began with the medical school and the law school. To Eliot, the education offered at both schools was so weak that to call either profession "learned" bordered on sarcasm. He brought both confidence and determination to the task of reform. When the head of the medical school stated that he could see no reason for change, Eliot replied, "I can give you one very good reason: You have a new president."

The law school Eliot inherited, in common with the thirty others in operation at the time, was intended to supplement apprenticeship, not to replace it. It had no standards for admission or, other than a period in residence, for graduation. The library was described as "an open quarry whence any visitor might purloin any volume he chose – provided he could find it."[7] Its degree was acknowledged to be largely honorary.

To dispel the torpor, Eliot appointed Langdell first to the Dane professorship and then to the newly created position of dean. Langdell, an 1854 graduate of the law school, had twelve years' experience in appellate practice in Manhattan, which convinced him that legal reform was urgently needed and that it should begin with legal education. Eliot's offer gave him a chance to implement his ideas.

Langdell saw law as a science whose principles had developed over centuries through judicial decisions. A properly scientific legal education would study those principles through the decisions in which they had evolved. The scholar's attention must be focused on the best decisions of the best judges, for "the vast majority are useless, and worse than useless, for any purpose of systematic study." An amateur botanist, Langdell added a taxonomical dimension: If the doctrines of the common law "could be so classified and arranged that each should be found in its proper place, and nowhere else, they would cease to be formidable from their number."[8]

Because it was a science, all of its ultimate sources contained in printed books, law was a fit subject for study in a modern university, especially one designed by Charles W. Eliot. Indeed, because it was a science, it could only be mastered by study in a university, under the tutelage of instructors who had studied those sources systematically, working in a library "that is

[6] Dr. Oliver Wendell Holmes, Sr., quoted in Warren, *History of the Harvard Law School*, I, 357.

[7] Samuel L. Batchelder, "Christopher C. Langdell," *Green Bag*, 18 (1906), 437.

[8] C. C. Langdell, *A Selection of Cases on the Law of Contracts* (Boston, 1870), viii.

all to us that the laboratories of the university are to the chemists and the physicists, all that the museum of natural history is to the zoologists, all that the botanical garden is to the botanists."

To put Langdell's premises about law and its study into practice, the Harvard Law School had to be reformed institutionally and intellectually. Langdell inaugurated a structured and sequenced curriculum with regular graded examinations, offered over two years of lengthened terms that would increase to three years by 1878. Treatises would be replaced by books of selected cases (to alleviate pressure on the library), and lectures by the classroom give-and-take that became "the Socratic method." Apprenticeship, fit only for vocational training in a "handicraft," had no place at all.

The law to be mastered was common law, judge-made law, and above all private law – contracts, torts, property. The principles to be found in appellate cases were general, not specific to any state or nation. To Langdell, whose generation was the last to study law before the Civil War, the primacy of the common law was unquestionable. Statutes, unprincipled distortions of the common law, had no place in scientific legal study. Since law was entirely contained in the law reports, it was to be studied as an autonomous discipline, unfolding according to the internal logic of its own principles, largely unaffected by the social sciences, unrelated to social policy, unconcerned with social justice. "Soft" subjects such as jurisprudence (law as it might be, not law as it was) that were impossible to study scientifically were beyond the pale. Because close study of cases, many old and English, might tax students with no grounding in the humanities, the prior preparation of law students assumed a new importance. Initially Langdell raised the general education standard for law school admission to roughly the level required for Harvard undergraduates. By the turn of the century, the standard would become a bachelor's degree, and gradual adoption of that standard by leading law schools in the early part of the twentieth century would confirm the study of law as a graduate program.

Adoption of the case method appeared to require the abandonment of established modes of instruction and the acceptance of a new conception of law. In fact, the new method drew heavily on antebellum legal culture: the assumption that the law was found in judicial decisions, and that legal science consisted in ordering cases under appropriate general principles and relating those principles to one another in systematic fashion. This taxonomic approach could be found in Story's treatises or Dwight's lectures at Columbia. The resulting edifice led logically, if not inevitably, to deductive reasoning starting with principles, some as broad as the infinitely disputable concept of justice itself. Langdell stood the old conceptual order on its head, however, by reasoning inductively from the particulars of appellate decisions to general principles – or at least by training students to do so.

To determine which opinions were worth studying, he had to select those – assertedly few in number – that yielded a "true rule." A student who had grasped the applicable principle and could reason it out could say with assurance how a court should resolve any disputed question of common law. The essential element of legal education was the process of teasing the principles from the cases assigned. The instructors, however, had first to discriminate the signals from the static, sorting through the "involved and bulky mass" of case reports to select those whose exegesis would yield the principle, or demonstrate the lines of its growth. To develop a criterion for picking and choosing, they had first to have identified the principle.

In 1871 a student was no more able to make sense of the mass of reported cases without guidance of some kind than anyone in a later century might make of the Internet without a search engine. Langdell's selection of cases was that engine. It determined the scope and result of student labor as effectively as though Langdell had taken the modest additional trouble required to produce a lecture or a treatise rather than a collection of cases without headnotes. To have done so, though, would have deprived students of the opportunity to grapple directly with the opinions, the basic material of law, and to master principles on their own, rather than take them at second hand.

The intellectual challenge presented to students was therefore something of a simulation, neither as empirical nor as scientific as Eliot and Langdell liked to think it. The fundamental premise, that the common law was built from a relatively small number of basic principles whose mastery was the attainable key to professional competence, may have proceeded from Langdell's undergraduate exposure to the natural sciences, from the crisis he encountered as a New York lawyer when the common law forms of action gave way to the Field Code, or to the constrained inductivism of natural theology and popular science prevalent when Langdell himself was a student. The latter resemblance may have been in the back of Holmes's mind when he characterized Langdell as "perhaps the greatest living legal theologian," who was "less concerned with his postulates than to show that the conclusions from them hang together."[9]

The logic of the case method of instruction demanded a different kind of instructor. The judge or lawyer educated under the old methods, no matter how eminent, whether full- or part-time, was not fitted to the "scientific" task of preparing a casebook on a given subject or to leading students through cases to the principles they contained. If law was a science to be studied in the decisions of courts, then experience in practice or on the

[9] Book Notice, *American Law Review* 14 (1880), 233, 234 (reviewing C. Langdell, *A Selection of Cases on the Law of Contracts*, 2d ed., 1879).

bench was far less useful than experience in the kind of study in which students were being trained. Langdell needed teachers trained in his method, unspoiled by practice – scientists, not lawyers.

In 1873, with the appointment of James Barr Ames, a recent graduate with negligible professional experience, Langdell had his first scientist. The academic branch of the legal profession dates from that appointment. As Eliot observed, it was "an absolutely new departure . . . one of the most far-reaching changes in the organization of the profession that has ever been made. . . . " Ames, and Langdell himself, spent much of the 1870s preparing the casebooks needed to fill the added hours of instruction. Ames, warmer and more engaging than Langdell, also became the most effective evangelist for the Harvard model. In 1895 he would succeed Langdell as dean.

Eliot's resolute support of Langdell notwithstanding, he was aware of the hostility of the bar to Langdell's regime and of the competition from Boston University. He saw to it that the next several appointments went to established figures in the profession, preferably men with an intellectual bent. The Ames experiment was not repeated until 1883, with the appointment of William R. Keener to succeed Holmes. It had taken more than a decade before Langdell had a majority of like-minded colleagues.

Only at Harvard did the case method exist in its pure form, and then only before 1886. For in 1886, Harvard introduced elective courses into the curriculum. The principles of the common law proved to be more numerous than Langdell had anticipated or could cover in a three-year curriculum. Since it could no longer be asserted that mastery of the curriculum constituted mastery of the law itself, the case method of study now required a different rationale. The method, with its intellectual discipline, came to be justified – less controversially – as the best way to train the legal mind. Substance had given way to process. "The young practitioner is . . . equipped with a 'trained mind,' as with a trusty axe, and commissioned to spend the rest of his life chopping his way through the tangle."[10]

Even the skeptical Holmes had acknowledged, during his brief stint on the faculty, that the method produced better students. Ames contrasted the "virility" of case method study with the passive role of students under the lecture method. A whiff of social Darwinism spiced the enterprise. The ablest and most ambitious students thrived. Survival, and the degree, became a badge of honor. Students and graduates shared a sense of participating in something wholly new and wholly superior. Ames observed that law students, objects of undergraduate scorn in 1870, were much admired by the end of Langdell's tenure. An alumni association was formed in 1886 to promote the school and to spread the word within the bar that "scientific"

[10] Alfred Z. Reed, *Training for the Public Profession of the Law* (New York, 1921), 380.

study under full-time academics was also intensely practical. The students who, in 1887, founded the *Harvard Law Review* (which quickly became one of the most distinctively Darwinian features of legal education) were moved in part by the desire to create a forum for their faculty's scholarship and a pulpit for propagating the Harvard gospel. In this period Harvard's enrollment, which had dropped sharply when Langdell's reforms were introduced, began to recover and to climb, a sign that the severe regimen was reaching a market. As established lawyers gained positive first-hand exposure to the graduates trained on the new model, some of the bar's initial hostility to Langdell's reforms abated. Eliot's gamble was paying off.

Langdell's new orthodoxy was asserted at Harvard with vigor, not to say rigidity, even as its rationale was changing. In the 1890s, when Eliot forced the appointment of an international lawyer on the school, the faculty retaliated by denying degree credit for successful completion of the course. In 1902, William Rainey Harper, president of the new University of Chicago, requested Harvard's help in establishing a law school. The initial response was positive: Joseph Beale would be given leave from Harvard to become Chicago's Langdell. But when it was learned that Harper also planned to appoint Ernst Freund to the law faculty, the atmosphere cooled. Freund had practiced law in New York, but he held continental degrees in political science, and he expected Chicago's new school to offer courses such as criminology, administrative law, and political theory. Harper was informed that the Harvard faculty was unanimously opposed to the teaching of anything but "pure law." Harvard, wrote Beale, turned out "thoroughly trained men, fit at once to enter upon the practice of a learned and strenuous profession."

"Learned," to be sure; even "trained"; but "fit" and "strenuous" as well? Purged and purified by the ritual of case study, lean and stripped for the race of life? It is as though Beale saw the muscular Christianity of an earlier day revived in the person of the new-model lawyer, trained in "pure law" and ready to do battle with the complexities of the modern business world. Harvard's sense of mission had a quasi-religious pitch. Indeed, the young lawyer coming out of Harvard found a fit in the new-model law firm as it developed in response to the needs of corporate clients. An emerging elite of the bar was forging a link with the emerging elite of the academy; "the collective ego of the Harvard Law School fed the collective ego of the bar."

By the early 1890s Harvard graduates were in demand as missionaries to other law schools, frequently at the behest of university presidents anxious to speed their own institutions along the scientific path – new Eliots in search of their own Langdells. Iowa adopted the case method in 1889; Wigmore and Nathan Abbott took it to Northwestern in 1892; Abbott carried the torch on to Stanford.

The tectonic shift occurred in 1891, when Seth Low, recently appointed president of Columbia, forced a reorganization of the law school curriculum, and William Keener, recruited the previous year from Harvard, became dean. Theodore Dwight, the Columbia Law School personified, had long resisted the case method, one of his reasons being the intellectual demands it placed on students. The case method might be all very well for the brightest and most highly motivated, but what of the "middle sort" of student Dwight had taught so successfully for so long? Such softness had no place at Harvard, which shaped its admissions policy to fit its curriculum, not the other way around. Neither did it at Keener's Columbia after its conversion. The conversion of Columbia, which alternated with Michigan as the largest law school in the country, brought Langdell's revolution to the nation's largest market for legal talent.

In Keener's hands, however, the revolution had moderated considerably. He did not condemn all lecturing as such; he pioneered the production of the modern book of "Cases and Materials," which Langdell would have anathematized; and he acquiesced in Low's insistence on including political science courses in the curriculum. Even so, Columbia's conversion met strong resistance. Adherents to the "Dwight method" formed the New York Law School, which immediately attracted an enormous enrollment. Conversions still were the exception, not the rule, even among university law schools. It would be 1912 before members of the Yale law faculty could assign a casebook without the approval of their colleagues and Virginia held out until the 1920s.

In the early years of the new century, however, as old deans, old judges, and old lawyers retired and died, their places all across the country were filled by academic lawyers trained in the case method. They developed what Ames had called "the vocation of the law professor" and advanced from school to school along career paths that remain recognizable a century later. Casebook publishers kept their backlists of treatises alive, covering their bets, but the case method and the institutional structures associated with it could no longer be dismissed by the legal profession as a local heresy peculiar to Harvard.

Langdell had elaborated and implemented a view of law and legal education that made it a respectable, even desirable, component of the science-based model of American higher education. In a period when all of the social sciences were struggling to define themselves as professional disciplines and to succeed in the scramble for a place at the university table, Langdell accomplished both objectives for law as an academic subject. Further, his conception of the subject effectively defined legal knowledge, and his first steps toward the creation of the law professoriate defined the class of those who were licensed to contribute to it. With the case method, moreover, a university law school could operate a graduate professional program at the highest standard and, at the same time, maintain a student-faculty ratio that would not be tolerated in most other disciplines. The fee-cost ratio made the expenses of operating a modern law school – the purchase of books, for example – an entirely tolerable burden. Eliot numbered the financial success of the Harvard Law School among Langdell's great achievements.

V. THE ACADEMY AND THE PROFESSION

Except for medicine, no other emerging academic discipline was intimately tied to an established and powerful profession. Reform in legal education might build momentum within the upper echelon of American universities, but the extent to which the emerging standards of that echelon could be extended downward depended in part on the organized bar. The post-bellum bar association movement, contemporaneous with the rise of law schools, was shaped by a similar desire for the market leverage conferred by professional identity and status.

In its first twenty years, the American Bar Association failed to reach a consensus on the form or content of legal education. The Committee on Legal Education and Admissions to the Bar presented to the ABA at its 1880 meeting an elaborate plan for legal education, prepared principally by Carleton Hunt of Tulane. The plan called for the creation of a public law school in each state, with a minimum of four "well-paid" full-time instructors, written examinations, and an ambitious three-year curriculum that owed more to Story, Hoffman, and Francis Lieber than to Langdell. After the "well-paid" language was struck, the entire plan was defeated. One eminent member noted that "if we go farther . . . we shall lose some part of the good will of the legal community."

Most members of that community, after all, had attained professional success without the aid of a diploma. They were unlikely to see why a degree should be required of their successors. Another delegate, mindful of the problems that gave rise to the bar association movement but acquiescing in the result, observed that "we must do something to exterminate the 'rats.'"[11]

Chastened, the Committee waited a decade before submitting another resolution. In the interim, the Association turned its attention to a matter of more immediate concern: the wide variations in standards and procedures for bar admission. The movement to replace ad hoc oral examinations with uniform written tests administered by a permanent board of state bar examiners, which began in New Hampshire in 1878, enjoyed the ABA's

[11] *Record of the American Bar Association* 2 (1880), 31, 41.

support. It may incidentally have increased the demand for a law school education, but was intended to raise standards for entry into the profession.

The founders of the ABA appear to have grasped, if intuitively, the profound changes at work in the profession. However, it was more difficult to agree on the role of law schools. Sporadic discussions of the potential role of law schools in raising the tone of the bar were punctuated by skeptical comments about Langdell's innovations. The mythic figure of Abraham Lincoln loomed behind all discussion of the relative value of formal schooling. How would the Lincolns of the future find their way to greatness if schooling were required for all? It was conceded that schooling could be substituted for some time in a law office and might be a satisfactory alternative, but little real energy was expended on the problems of formal education.

A standardized model for education, if it could have been implemented nationally, would have facilitated the admission in every state of lawyers licensed in any one of them. In the long term, it would also have improved the administration of justice. Judges and lawyers, all trained to a similar standard instead of being educated poorly or not at all, would develop a shared language and culture. The mischief of litigation, appeals, reversals and, worst of all, the endless proliferation of decisions, many of them ill considered and inconsistent, would be ameliorated. Law school education might, therefore, have been a large part of the answer to some of the principal concerns of the ABA at its founding. Langdell's hard-nosed new model for legal education might have furnished the standard. His insistence on the worthlessness of most case law, and the importance of selecting only decisions that reflected the basic principles of the common law, might have been welcomed as a bulwark against the unending flood of decisions, aggravated in the 1880s by the West Publishing Company's promiscuous National Reporter System. Up to the turn of the century, however, most leaders of the bar had been apprentices. The minority who had been educated in law schools looked to the revered Dwight at Columbia or the eminent Cooley at Michigan, both of them practical men, not to the obscure and idiosyncratic Langdell, aided by "scientists" like Ames. The gap between the profession at large and the academy widened as the teachers grew in number and in professional definition. It would take a generation before market pressures would drive the bar and the new professoriate into each other's arms.

VI. ENTER THE AALS

In 1900, appalled by the "rats" in their own business and frustrated by the low priority the ABA attached to the problems of legal education, a group of 35 schools organized the Association of American Law Schools (AALS). The membership criteria of the AALS reflected "best practices" and the higher hopes of the founding schools. Members required completion of high school before admission, a hurdle that would be raised first to one, then to two years of college. Members had to have an "adequate" faculty and a library of at least 5,000 volumes. Part-time programs were strongly disfavored, and as a general matter, the cost of compliance excluded the very schools the Association sought to marginalize, if not to drive out of business altogether. But that was just the problem: the marginal schools could not be eliminated, for reasons that were uncomfortable to acknowledge. Law schools organized on Langdell's principles offered superior students a superior education that was well adapted to the needs of big-city practice. There might be a close fit between Harvard, for example, and the Cravath system, which became as influential in the emergence of the corporate law firm as the case method had become in legal education. But many could not afford that kind of education, and a great deal of legal work did not require it.

Most schools paid lip service to the standards of the AALS, and some extended themselves mightily to qualify for membership. A few, however, made a virtue of condemning the elitism of the AALS. Suffolk Law School in Boston, for example, secured a state charter despite the unanimous opposition of the existing Massachusetts law schools. If that lesson in political reality were not sufficiently sobering, Suffolk's founding dean drove it home with repeated blasts at the educational cartels of the rich, epitomized by Harvard. Edward T. Lee, of the John Marshall Law School in Chicago, contended with considerable persuasiveness that the requisites for teaching law – books and teachers – were readily to be found outside of university law schools, and even in night schools, often at higher levels of quality than that obtained in some of the more rustic colleges. The movement to require two years of college prior to law study would inevitably – and not coincidentally – exclude many of the poor and recently arrived from the profession. Opposing that change, Lee emphasized the religious, ethnic, and national diversity of night school students, declaring that "each of them from his legal training becomes a factor for law and order in his immediate neighborhood.... If the evening law schools did nothing more than to help leaven the undigested classes of our population, their right to existence, encouragement, and respect would be vindicated."[12] The scientists and the mandarins were unmoved.

These were the principal themes in the educational debate at the turn of the century. Ultimately, every university-affiliated law school in the United States came to adopt some form of Langdell's model of legal education, but

[12] Edward T. Lee, "The Evening Law School," *American Law School Review* 4 (1915), 290, 293.

they traveled by routes that varied enormously according to local institutional circumstances, politics, and professional culture. Although no single account can stand for all, the evolution of the law schools at the University of Wisconsin in Madison and Marquette University in Milwaukee, and the strained relations between them, furnishes the best illustration of the practical playing-out of the dynamics at work in legal education at the beginning of the twentieth century.

Wisconsin: A Case Study

The University of Wisconsin's 1854 charter provided for a law school, but it was only after the Civil War that one was established – not on the university's campus, but near the state capitol so that students could use the state library for free. The law school did not come into being at the initiative of the Wisconsin bar. Rather, the university found it prudent to add a practical course of study in order to deflect criticism of its undergraduate emphasis on the humanities, which some legislators thought irrelevant to the needs of the state. Care was taken to cultivate leading members of the bench and bar, and it was Dean Bryant's boast that Wisconsin offered the education a student might receive in "the ideal law office." In a professional world where apprenticeship opportunities were inadequate to meet the demand (and where the invention of the typewriter and the emergence of professional secretaries reduced the value of apprentices), this was not a trivial claim.

In 1892, however, Wisconsin installed a new president, Charles Kendall Adams. Adams had taught history at Michigan for more than twenty years before succeeding Andrew Dixon White as president of Cornell. Like Eliot, he had toured European universities in the 1860s and was similarly influenced by the experience. At Michigan, he introduced research seminars, which he called "historical laboratories," where young historians could work with original documents.

Aware of Langdell's case method and predisposed in favor of the idea of the library as laboratory, Adams set out to bring Wisconsin's law school up to date. It would have been impolitic to bring in a missionary from Harvard, so Adams hired Charles N. Gregory, a well-connected local lawyer, as Associate Dean. Gregory was charged with remaking the law school, distressing Dean Bryant as little as possible in the process. Gregory spent part of his second summer at the country house of James Barr Ames, now dean at Harvard, where Ames and Keener, now dean at Columbia, drilled him in the case method and the culture that came with it. Gregory did what he could to convert Wisconsin, holding off the faculty's old guard and hiring new people trained in the case method when he had the opportunity, before leaving in 1901 to become dean at Iowa. In 1902, Dean Bryant finally retired, and his successor, Harry Richards, a recent Harvard graduate, completed the make-over Gregory had begun. "The ideal law office" was heard of no more. Something resembling Harvard emerged in Madison, and Wisconsin was a founding member of the AALS, which Gregory had helped organize.

In the mid-1890s, while Gregory labored in Madison, a study group of law students in Milwaukee preparing for the Wisconsin bar examination evolved into the Milwaukee Law School. The school offered evening classes taught by practicing lawyers, held in rented rooms – the classic form of urban proprietary school. In 1908, this start-up venture was absorbed by Marquette University, an urban Jesuit institution that hoped to confirm its new status as a university by adding professional schools in law and medicine.

The reaction in Madison to a competitor in the state's largest city was not graceful. In 1911 Dean Richards attempted to block Marquette's application for membership in the AALS. He did not do so openly, lest he appear interested solely in stifling competition. In fact the two schools appealed to rather different constituencies. Marquette's urban, relatively poor, often immigrant, and Catholic students were not Richards's ideal law students, nor were they his idea of suitable material for the bar. To his distress, Marquette was elected to the AALS in 1912, with adept politicking, compliance with many of the membership standards, and every indication of a disarming desire to meet them all. Richards was skeptical, perhaps with cause, but he lost the round.

The following year a bill was introduced in the Wisconsin legislature that would have raised Wisconsin's educational requirement for admission to the bar and would also have provided a paid secretary for the board of bar examiners. These were reforms that Richards normally would have supported. But the bill, thought to be backed by Marquette graduates, also would have abolished the diploma privilege (admission to the bar on graduation) that Wisconsin graduates had enjoyed since 1870. The privilege was inconsistent with the standards advanced by both the ABA and the AALS, and Wisconsin could hardly defend it on principle. To lose it to a sneak attack from an upstart competitor, however, was a different matter. After an exchange of blistering attacks between partisans of both schools, the bill was defeated.

Another conflict erupted in 1914, when the Wisconsin Bar Association became concerned over low ethical standards, "ambulance-chasing," and comparable delicts. Some of the offending conduct might have been merely the work disdained by the established practitioner, for the benefit of an equally disdained class of clients, but it was not so characterized. Richards proposed to solve the problem by requiring all prospective lawyers to have two years of college preparation, three years of law school, and a year of apprenticeship. The schooling requirements happened to be those of his own institution, but it was unlikely that Marquette could meet them – nor would it necessarily have wished to. Had his proposal succeeded and Marquette failed, Richards would not have been downcast.

Richards was upset over the large enrollment in night law schools (Marquette would offer classes at night until 1924) of people with "foreign names," "shrewd young men, imperfectly educated . . . impressed with the philosophy of getting on, but viewing the Code of Ethics with uncomprehending eyes." But the Wisconsin bar, its still largely rural membership unaffected by immigration, did not adopt Richards's proposal. Indeed, it did not accept his premise that increased educational requirements would lead to improved ethical standards. His effort to elevate educational standards, to the disadvantage of Marquette and its ethnically diverse constituents, was dismissed by many as retaliation for the diploma privilege fracas.

Richards's fears and prejudices notwithstanding, this feud was not Armageddon. It was, however, a museum-grade exhibit of the characteristics and developmental stages of two different but representative types of law school: Wisconsin exemplified the twentieth-century shift to technocratic elitism, whereas Marquette represented the nineteenth-century ideal of open, democratic opportunity. Wisconsin, so recently accepted into the Establishment, was especially severe in seeking to impose the Establishment's standards on a deviant institution. Richards could not see Marquette for what it was. A school open to the urban alien poor, it seemed to him the very nursery of corruption. In reality, Marquette started on a different track altogether, one not marked by Langdell. Had Marquette been thrust into the outer darkness in 1912, its graduates would still have found their way into the profession. If bringing Marquette into the AALS came at some initial cost to the nominal standards of that association, it had the long-term effect of improving, by those standards, the education its graduates received.

VII. "STANDARDS" MEET THE MARKET

As the "better" schools ratcheted up their entrance requirements (completion of high school, one year of college, two years), increased the length of the course of study (three years was the norm by 1900), and raised their fees along with their standards, a large percentage of a population increasingly eager for a legal education was left behind.

Would-be law students excluded from the most prominent schools for want of money, time, or intellectual ability constituted a ready market for schools that were not exclusive at all. In the absence of restrictive licensing standards for the bar or accreditation standards for law schools, that market was sure to be met. The number of law schools doubled every twenty years from 1850 to 1910; by 1900, the total had grown to 96. From the beginning of the twentieth century to the end of World War I, law schools continued to multiply rapidly as demand increased and as unprecedented waves of immigration produced a more heterogeneous population than American society and American educators knew what to do with.

The schools that sprang up to meet this market had little in common with the leading schools, and did not care. The "better" schools, though, were troubled indeed. Although enrollment at the established schools grew at a healthy rate, their percentage of the total law student population actually declined. Schools were indeed winning out over apprenticeship, but which schools? Wisconsin's Richards, president of the AALS in 1915, reported that the number of law schools had increased by 53 percent since the Association was organized in 1900, and the number of students, excluding correspondence schools, had risen by 70 percent. The number of students enrolled in member schools had increased by 25 percent, to 8,652, but enrollment in non-member schools had risen by 133 percent, to 13,233. Member schools accounted for 55 percent of all students in 1900, but for only 39 percent in 1915. Law schools had won the battle with apprenticeship as the path to practice, but the "wrong" schools were in the lead.

The universe of academic legal education was divided into a few broad categories. The handful of "national" institutions at the top implemented Harvard's reforms of a generation earlier and adopted some form of the case method. Sustained by their wealth and prestige, they were not dependent on trade-group support. The next tier, close on their heels, superficially similar but less secure, constituted the bulk of AALS membership. Below them, more modest schools offered a sound legal education to more regional or local markets, on thinner budgets, with uncertain library resources. These schools relied heavily on part-time instruction, and many offered classes at night for part-time law students who kept their day jobs. Many aspired to membership in the AALS and worked so far as their resources permitted to qualify for membership. Then there were the night schools, conscientious in their efforts to train the newly arrived and less educated. And there were proprietary and commercial night schools who simply crammed their customers for the bar examination. The lower tiers would remain as long as they could offer a shorter and cheaper path to practice, and a living for those who ran them, regardless of the standards of their betters. The AALS, acting alone, could not be an effective cartel.

Parallel developments in medical education and the medical profession are instructive, and they had a powerful influence on the legal academy and the bar. Through the offices of the Carnegie Foundation (whose president, Henry S. Pritchett, had been, not coincidentally, head of the Bureau of

Standards), Abraham Flexner was commissioned to prepare a study of medical education in the United States. Flexner was a respected scholar, but not a doctor. His independence permitted him to use terms more blunt than the AMA itself dared employ. He grouped medical schools into those who had the resources and will to provide a scientifically sound – i.e., expensive – medical education, those that would like to but lacked the means, and the rest, denounced as frauds. He urged that the middle tier be helped to move up and that the bottom tier be eliminated. Following publication of his report in 1910, this is exactly what happened. Philanthropists and research foundations followed Flexner's criteria in their funding decisions, putting the leaders still further ahead. State licensing standards were tightened, and the applicant pool for the bottom tier dried up. By 1915 the number of medical schools and the number of medical students had declined sharply.

The Carnegie Foundation had already sponsored one study of legal education, a relatively brief report on the case method prepared by Josef Redlich of the University of Vienna after visits to ten prominent law schools. Redlich blessed the method but noted its narrowness, giving some comfort to proponents and detractors alike.[13] In 1913, a year before publication of the Redlich Report, the ABA Committee on Legal Education turned again to Carnegie, hoping for a Flexner of its own. Alfred Z. Reed, not a lawyer, was commissioned to study legal education in the United States. He visited every law school in existence at the time, plowed through all available statistical compilations, and analyzed structures, politics, and curricula.

Reed admired the achievement of Harvard and the other leading law schools, and acknowledged that the case method succeeded splendidly in the hands of instructors of great ability, teaching well-prepared and able students in first-year courses. It was not clear to him, however, that the method was equally effective in advanced courses or in institutions with thin financial and intellectual resources, whose students might be of Dwight's "middle sort." Instead of following Flexner in recommending a one-size-fits-all approach, Reed concluded that the bar, in terms of work done and clients served, was in fact segmented rather than unitary and that legal education should be so as well. He recommended that the role of night schools in preparing those who could not take their professional education on a full-time basis be acknowledged and supported. Expected to condemn the schools that produced the bulk of the dubious applicants to practice, he instead declared that there was both room and need in the United States for lawyers who would not be Tocqueville's aristocrats and for the schools

[13] Josef Redlich, *The Common Law and the Case Method in American University Law Schools* (New York, 1914).

that trained them. The Reed Report remains the most comprehensive study of legal education ever conducted. Reed's research was prodigious and his prose was marvelous, but his recommendations were not wanted and they were rejected immediately.

VIII. THE BAR MILITANT

Leaders of the bar had become increasingly alarmed at the condition of legal education as it related to professional standards. The magnates of a profession that, at its top, was distinctly homogeneous shared a genuine concern about standards for admission to practice and were dismayed at the impact on the status of the profession of the recent infusion of large numbers of imperfectly schooled recent immigrants. "Character" loomed large in their discussions, and in the Canons of Ethics, published in 1908 to establish the ABA's position as arbiter of the profession. While xenophobia and, more specifically, anti-Semitism were rarely overt in the public statements of the leaders of the bar, neither were these elements perfectly concealed. Plainly there was a question whether the character required for a grasp of American legal institutions and the ethical dimension of the practice of law might not be an Anglo-Saxon monopoly.

The bar was nearly as white and male at the turn of the century as it had been before the Civil War. Several schools were established to overcome the obstacles African Americans encountered in attempting to enter the profession, the Howard University Law School being the best known and most successful, but the path to practice remained a very stony one for black Americans. Women fared hardly better. Michigan, and a few other schools in the mid and far West, could boast of their openness to women, but it was only in 1919 that a woman was hired as a full-time law teacher (at Berkeley), and it took Harvard until 1949 to admit women at all. To these familiar patterns of prejudice, nativism was now added.

In his 1916 presidential address to the ABA, Elihu Root stressed the role of the lawyer as public servant, neatly subordinating the democratic notion of open opportunity to the paramount consideration of fitness for practice. Apprenticeship had given way to schooling. Therefore the standards of law schools had to be raised in order to screen out the unfit: the "half-trained practitioners [who] have had little or no opportunity to become imbued with the true spirit of the profession," which is not "the spirit of mere controversy, of mere gain, of mere individual success."[14] Harlan F. Stone, dean at Columbia and, in 1919, president of the AALS, agreed with Root. John Henry Wigmore, clearly envious of the AMA's success, made the same

[14] Elihu Root, "The Training of Lawyers," *American Law School Review* 4 (1916), 188, 189.

point with brutal directness. "The bar," he declared, "is overcrowded with incompetent, shiftless, ill-fitting lawyers who degrade the methods of the law and cheapen the quality of service by unlimited competition." To meet this problem, "the number of lawyers should be reduced by half," and he concluded, stricter pre-law educational requirements would be a sensible "method of elimination."[15]

Finally the explicit connection was made between higher academic standards and the exclusion of "undesirables" from the profession. Both legal education and the practice of law at their least elevated levels remained "pretty much a free thing," as Joseph Baldwin had put it before the Civil War. Unregulated markets for education and for lawyers perpetuated the democratic openness of the Jacksonian era. That very openness, however, was an obstacle to the attainment of the dignity sought by the bar and of the stature sought by the academy. Wigmore's candor identified competition as an additional and crucial element: entry of the unwashed into the profession was not merely damaging to its pretensions, but to its pocketbooks as well. If the lower depths of the bar had taken over criminal defense, personal injury, and divorce work – all beneath the dignity of the corporate lawyer – what would prevent them from moving into real estate, wills, trusts, and other respectable work as well? Once the bar grasped that threat, the need for regulation became clear.

Increasing state licensing requirements to include two years of college prior to admission to law school could cut out many "undesirables" and socialize the remainder in ways that could repair the deficiencies of their birth and upbringing. There was no risk of creating the "caste system in its worst form" that the president of Yale feared,[16] because a college education was within the reach of anyone with character, grit, and stamina, regardless of family wealth. Doubtless Root, Stone, William Howard Taft, and their peers were sincere in this belief. In 1915, however, only 3.1 percent of the college-aged population was enrolled in degree-granting institutions of any kind. Something more tangible than grit was required, and most people knew it.

Root and his associates, armed with a pre-publication copy of Reed's work, prepared their own report for presentation to the ABA in 1921. They realized that, if the bar was to be mobilized, they would have to do the mobilizing themselves. The Root Report sought at long last to commit

[15] John H. Wigmore, "Should the Standard of Admission to the Bar Be Based on Two Years or More of College-Grade Education? It Should," *American Law School Review* 4 (1915), 30–31.

[16] Arthur T. Hadley, "Is the B.A. Degree Essential for Professional Study?" *American Law School Review* 1(1906), 379, 380.

the organized bar unequivocally to the standards long urged by the AALS, specifically to a three-year course of study and a minimum of two years of college preparation. Academics showed up in force at the 1921 meeting of the ABA to help secure the report's adoption.

At this conjunction of the bar and the academy, long-ignored political realities forced themselves on the attention of all. The leading law schools, through the AALS, had set a standard for education, but they had no means of enforcing it on non-members. They had a carrot but no stick. The ABA was equally powerless to enforce educational standards against non-conforming schools. The ABA represented a minuscule fraction of the profession (1.3 percent in 1900, 3 percent in 1910, 12 percent in 1920) and had no authority over the 623 state and local bar associations, some of which had the effective connections with state governments that the ABA lacked.

The ultimate form of professional recognition is the sanction of the state. The American Medical Association, with the Flexner Report, had indeed exterminated its "rats." But it had done so because it stood at the apex of a pyramid of state and county medical societies, whose local influence, aided by Flexner's findings, secured higher local licensing standards. Medical schools that could not train their graduates to the requisite level lost their market and folded.

The ABA, with many generals but few troops, did not have that local political influence. At its 1921 meeting, therefore, the ABA leadership decided to convene a conference the following year of representatives from all state bar associations, in order to sell the Root Report to people who might be able to put teeth into it. All the powers of the legal establishment were brought to bear on this National Conference of Bar Associations, held in Washington in 1922. The influence of William Howard Taft, the encouragement of the dean of the Johns Hopkins Medical School, and the dread of socialism were all deployed successfully on behalf of the Root Report. For the moment the academy and the profession were united. From that moment of unity much would flow, but not quickly. In 1920, no state conditioned admission to the bar on a law degree, still less a college degree beforehand. In 1920, there was no nationwide system for accreditation and licensing of law schools. The contours of practice would continue to change, affected by the Depression and the New Deal. The hard edge of Langdell's model for law schools would become progressively softer, as increasing numbers of academics – some later to be called "realists" – looked to empirical work and the social sciences for a thicker description of law and the lawyer's social role. The last vestige of "scientific" justification for the case method would be discredited, but the method and its accompanying structures survived. Lest they be thought too impractical, some schools would create clinical programs, a distant echo of apprenticeship first sounded in 1892. But the road that would lead to higher licensing standards for lawyers and a national system of law school accreditation was clearly marked, and the elements that would lead to legal education in its modern, apparently monolithic form were all in place.

3

THE LEGAL PROFESSION: FROM THE REVOLUTION TO THE CIVIL WAR

ALFRED S. KONEFSKY

The American legal profession matured and came to prominence during the century prior to the Civil War. The profession had entered the Revolutionary era in a somewhat ambiguous state, enjoying increasing social power and political leadership, but subject to withering criticism and suspicion. Its political influence was clear: twenty-five of the fifty-six signers of the Declaration of Independence were trained in law; so were thirty-one of the fifty-five members of the Constitutional Convention in Philadelphia; so were ten of the First Congress's twenty-five senators and seventeen of its sixty-five representatives. And yet, just three weeks after the signing of the Declaration of Independence, Timothy Dwight – Calvinist, grandson of Jonathan Edwards, soon to be staunch Federalist, tutor at Yale College and, within several decades, its president – delivered a commencement address in New Haven full of foreboding, particularly for those among the graduates who would choose the legal profession. What would await them? Little but "[t]hat meanness, that infernal knavery, which multiplies needless litigations, which retards the operation of justice, which, from court to court, upon the most trifling pretences, postpones trial to glean the last emptyings of a client's pocket, for unjust fees of everlasting attendance, which artfully twists the meaning of law to the side we espouse, which seizes unwarrantable advantages from the prepossessions, ignorance, interests and prejudices of a jury, you will shun rather than death or infamy." Dwight prayed that, notwithstanding, "[y]our reasonings will be ever fair and open; your constructions of law candid, your endeavors to procure equitable decisions unremitted." And he added an historical observation:

> The practice of law in this, and the other American States, within the last twenty years has been greatly amended; but those eminent characters to whom we are indebted for this amendment, have met with almost insurmountable obstructions to the generous design. They have been obliged to combat interest and prejudice, powerfully exerted to retard the reformation: especially that immoveable bias, a

fondness for the customs of our fathers. Much therefore remains to be done, before the system can be completed.[1]

In one short valedictory diagnosis Dwight captured the essence of the dilemma that would stalk the profession throughout the succeeding century. Was law a public profession or a private profession? Did lawyers owe a special obligation through their learning, education, role, and place in society to the greater good of that society, or was their primary loyalty to their clients (and by extension to themselves)? Could lawyers credibly argue the intermediate position, that by simply representing the private interests of their clients they also best served society?

Dwight's address, first published contemporaneously in pamphlet form, was later reprinted in 1788 in *The American Magazine*. Alongside Dwight's lofty sentiments there also appeared a far less elevated essay, "The Art of Pushing into Business," satirical advice from an anonymous author, Peter Pickpenny (reportedly a pseudonym for Noah Webster). This essay has been largely ignored. Nevertheless Pickpenny's observations deserve attention, for he too picked up on the old refrain. "Are you destined for the *Law*?" he wrote. "Collect from Coke, Hale, Blackstone, &c. a catalogue of hard words, which you may get by heart, and whether you may understand them or not, repeat them on all occasions, and be very profuse to an *ignorant* client, as he will not be able to detect a misapplication of terms." And again: "As the success (or profit, which is the same thing) of the *profession*, depends much on a free use of words, and a man's sense is measured by the number of unintelligible terms he employs, never fail to rake together all the synonymous words in the English, French and Latin languages, and arrange them in Indian file, to express the most common idea." And finally, "As to your fees – but no *true lawyer* needs any advice on this article."[2]

Peter Pickpenny in his own way reinforced Dwight's disquisition on the danger and temptation of the pursuit of purely private gain. Lawyers chased their own private, selfish interest. Contrary to professional lore, they would dupe their own clients while professing to represent them. At the very moment that the Republic was relying on lawyers to reconstitute the form of government, the repository of the ultimate public virtue, their capacity for public virtue was – at least for some – in doubt. Legal ideas were about the nature of the state and the theory of republican civic virtue,

[1] Timothy Dwight, "A Valedictory Address: To the Young Gentlemen, who commenced Bachelors of Arts, at Yale College, July 25th, 1776," *American Magazine* (Jan. 1788), 99, 101.

[2] "Peter Pickpenny," "The Art of Pushing into Business, and Making Way in the World," *American Magazine* (Jan. 1788), 103, 103, 105.

but lawyers lived in the marketplace constituted by private interests. That crucial intersection between public and private was where lawyers' roles and reputations would be determined, rising or falling depending on the perception and reality of whether the twain could ever properly meet.

It is tempting to invoke for the legal profession in the century after the Revolution the iconic category (or cliché) of a "formative" or, perhaps, a "transformative" era. But it is not exactly clear that any such label is satisfactory. What we know is that the legal profession evolved in some ways and not in others. The century was clearly of critical importance in the growth of the profession. In 1750 the bar was in many respects an intensely local, perhaps even provincial or parochial profession, more like a guild than anything else. By 1860 it was poised on the verge of exercising truly national political and economic power. During the intervening years, lawyers began to exhibit the classic signs of modern professionalism. They began to cement control over admission to what they defined as their community, through education (knowledge, language, technical complexity) and social standards. They began to regulate their own behavior after admission to practice, to shape the market for their services, and generally to enhance their status in society. Lawyers encountered values, ideas, and self-images embedded in a world of developing and expanding markets, increasingly at a remove from the rhetoric of republican virtue. This new world provided both opportunity and temptation.

Though they never missed a chance to lament their changing world, lawyers displayed a remarkable ability to adapt to opportunity and temptation. Their educational methods slowly altered, the numbers admitted to the profession expanded, the organization of practice gradually shifted, lawyers adapted their practices to legal change, and they occasionally forged that change themselves. The profession helped reshape professional rules of conduct to meet the demand of new marketplaces. Lawyers simultaneously complained about change and embraced it. The public did not really understand what they did, they said, so attacks on their behavior were misplaced. Yet they also tried to convince the public it was wrong, or – subtly – changed their conduct to address the criticism. The public's skepticism always haunted the profession, particularly as lawyers began to exercise political power. In a society that moved in theory from trust that elites would exercise their judgment in the best interests of all to suspicion of the legitimacy of elites to retain or exercise power at all, lawyers believed they had no choice but to open up their profession. Still, in a culture outwardly unwilling to tolerate signs of special status, lawyers kept struggling to maintain control of their own professional identity.

I. LAW AS A PROFESSION IN THE NEW REPUBLIC

The legal profession prior to the Revolutionary era is not amenable to easy summary. Across some 150 years, lawyers in different colonies underwent different experiences at different times. Before 1700, colonies occasionally regulated various aspects of lawyers' lives, from bar admission to fees. The bar's internal gradations and hierarchies in England (between barristers and solicitors) did not entirely survive transplantation in America, where the paucity of lawyers seemed to undermine the necessity of creating ranks. Suspicion of attorneys, often as a carryover from religious life, existed in some places. The Massachusetts Bay Colony's system of courts and judges flourished at times without lawyers at all – no doubt viewed by the Puritan elders (perhaps contrary to their sensibilities) as some evidence of heaven on earth.

By the beginning of the eighteenth century, more lawyers were entering professional life. Lawyers followed markets for their services; they were to be found primarily in seaboard areas where the colonial populations tended to cluster. Accurate figures for the number of lawyers in colonial America have not been compiled, but estimates suggest about a half-dozen in the Pennsylvania colony around 1700 rising to at least seventy-six admitted between 1742 and 1776; about thirty to forty in Virginia in 1680, many more a hundred years later, and prominent and prosperous as well; about twenty in South Carolina (primarily Charleston) in 1761, thirty-four or so in 1771, and fifty-eight in 1776. Figures vary for New York, from about 175 from 1709 to 1776, to about 400 for the longer period from 1664 to 1788 (about 50 in New York City alone from 1695 to 1769). In Massachusetts, there were only fifteen trained lawyers in 1740 (one lawyer per slightly over ten thousand people); in 1765, there were fifty lawyers for a population of about 245,000; in 1775, a total of seventy-one trained lawyers. With an estimated population of one-and-a-half million people in the British colonies in 1754, the numbers of lawyers were trifling, if not insignificant.

The social power and influence of colonial lawyers far exceeded their numbers. As the colonial economy expanded, trade increased, and populations grew, the number of lawyers followed suit. Some prospered (though others struggled financially). More important, as the Revolution approached, arguments both for and against independence were forged by lawyers, drawing on their education, training, and experience. Attorneys familiar with arcane land transactions and property rights or routine debt collections came to represent the public face of a political class seeking revolution and independence. Some were cemented to Revolutionary elites through marriage and kinship networks, but other than personal ties and a familiarity with political and historical ideas related to law, it is unclear why law practice should have become associated with the Revolution: revolution might just as easily be construed as a threat to law. Aware, perhaps, of the anomaly, lawyers recast the Revolution as a purely political act that changed the form of government, but maintained and institutionalized reverence for law. The outcome was somewhat paradoxical. On one hand, it became accepted in the new United States that the sanctity of law lay at the very core of civic virtue; on the other, that the actual business of representing clients involved in legal disputes was potentially corrupting. In public roles, lawyers might be admired. As attorneys in private practice, they were condemned all too often.

II. IDEOLOGY AND THE PROFESSION

In the aftermath of the Revolution the legal profession appeared in disarray. Tory lawyers – by some estimates, 25 percent of all lawyers – fled. The remainder struggled to adapt to a new legal environment, untethered from the English common law and its authority. But the profession's disarray has been exaggerated. Though there is no question that there were Tory defections (particularly in Philadelphia, Boston, and New York), their numbers were rather fewer than reported, particularly in some of the new states. As for the remainder, they quickly burnished their images in the glow of republican ideals while grasping new market opportunities.

Lawyers' Republicanism

To understand the social function of the nineteenth-century American bar, it is necessary to crack the code of republicanism. Republican ideals focused on the identification and pursuit of a public good or interest that, in theory, was located in a shared belief in civic virtue. Private interest was to be subordinated, and responsibility for administering the public welfare delegated to a natural elite that would place the commonwealth's interest above all else. Republican governors would derive their authority from general recognition of their character, merit, and demonstrated ability, not from their inherited role or hierarchical position in society.

The republican ideal presented both opportunity and challenge for the legal profession. The American version of revolution was primarily driven by ideas. One might consider lawyers an unlikely repository of revolutionary fervor, but patriot practitioners certainly had preached ideas – notably separation from the crown – and were responsible, therefore, for developing a replacement. The public good was thus deposited substantially into the hands of lawyers; their responsibility was to frame forms of government that would guarantee the civic virtue on which the future of the Republic depended.

For lawyers turned politicians/statesmen, the keys were twofold, constitutions and the common law, both envisaged as foundations for institutions that would restrain or limit the power of the state and ensure liberty. Rules were the purview of lawyers. Pay attention to the carefully crafted and drafted rules distilled from the voices of experience drawn from the ages. You will get social order and control, and avoid the threat of licentious freedom. Or so the lawyers believed.

But the lawyers were reluctant to leave anything to chance. Here opportunity met its challenge. The lawyers who drafted the Republic's constitution were afraid that the document itself, placing sovereignty in the people and deriving its authority from the consent of the governed, might in fact be more democratic than republican. Lacking faith in the capacity of the people to abide by the limits of the Constitution and behave within its restraints, the founders hence sought to create additional means to mediate between the Constitution and its core values and popular rule; to protect the people from their own excesses. Fifty years after the Revolution, lawyers were still delivering anxious jeremiads that reflected on their fears for the republican legacy with which they had been entrusted. In 1827, Lemuel Shaw, then practicing law in Boston a few years before being appointed Chief Justice of the Massachusetts Supreme Judicial Court, enjoined his colleagues of the Suffolk County bar to "[guard] with equal vigilance against the violence and encroachments of a wild and licentious democracy, by a well balanced constitution." Well balanced meant "a constitution as at once restrains the violent and irregular action of mere popular will, and calls to the aid, and secures in the service of government, the enlightened wisdom, the pure morals, the cultivated reason, and matured experience of its ablest and best members" – people like themselves.[3] It was not enough to write the documents and then get out of the way. Lawyers should be the checks and balances too.

The danger was that the public would accuse lawyers of being undemocratic for intervening in the political process, for trusting neither the constitutional institutions they had created nor the citizens they had placed in positions of responsibility to undertake their own wise self-government. Ironically, however, the public documents of revolution were rule-bound. Lawyers were positioned to interpret and apply them in two distinct capacities, first as participants in the public process of creating rules of self-government (laws), and second as interpreters and practitioners of law – as

[3] Lemuel Shaw, An Address Delivered before the Suffolk Bar, May 1827, extracted in *American Jurist and Law Magazine* 7 (1832), 56, 61–62.

providers, that is, of services to fellow citizens who were, in their own interests, navigating the system the lawyers had themselves developed.

Here we meet the second hallmark of the post-Revolutionary profession: its new, enhanced role in the process of dispute resolution. As the meaning of republican virtue changed and became increasingly contested, what emerged was a new kind of constitutional faith that interests and factions would ultimately balance each other out and that no one interest would ultimately dominate the polity. Given that a lawyer's job was to represent interests, the new republicanism dovetailed neatly with a professional norm that insisted on pursuing the best interests of clients in an adversarial environment. If the Constitution and the common law created a framework within which private interest had to be recognized, who better than lawyers to mediate between these interests by getting everyone to play by the rules, by laws, and by procedures so that social order and not chaos would ensue? The problem, of course, was that lawyers could be accused of fomenting private disputes for their own personal gain and of tearing at the fiber of society, rather than preserving it. The lawyers' response was that they were only representing the interests that the country's constitutions recognized and that they would be shirking their republican responsibilities if they did not participate in the system of resolving disputes that helped preserve the rule of law. There was public virtue in representing the interests of others.

But lawyers still wanted to be the "best men," the dedicated, dispassionate elite that would guide the Republic. Lawyers by training and education, familiar with classical antiquity and its lessons, would form a learned profession, a natural calling, that would replace the ministry as society's preferred leaders. Particularly well situated by preparation to participate in a government of laws, attorneys could as a profession shepherd post-Revolutionary America through daily life, or through the most trying times, just as they had through the Revolution itself.

To accomplish all these tasks, lawyers had to maintain some control over who was admitted to the practice of law. From an early date they emphasized moral character as a determining factor in bar admission almost as much as acquired knowledge. Lawyers acted as gatekeepers to the profession: only those judged safe in the wake of the Revolution were deemed worthy of admission and its consequent public and social responsibilities. A half-century after the Revolution, Tocqueville captured part of this idea when he referred to lawyers as an "American aristocracy." Tocqueville's observation had many meanings, but as part of his characterization of this aristocracy he noted "[t]hat the lawyers, as a body, form the most powerful, if not the only, counterpoise to the democratic element."[4] Elites, independent and

[4] 1 Alexis DeTocqueville, *Democracy in America* (Phillips Bradley ed., 1945), 278.

not dependent members of society, could be trusted to identify the true public interest in a society reduced to competing, potentially ungovernable, and exuberant private interests. Or at least, so the rhetoric of the bar proclaimed. The risk was that elites could be corrupted by their own private interests (always just around the corner in a market society) or that the bar could be viewed through its admission control mechanisms as a monopoly restricting opportunity or, in a related sense, could be accused of a lack of commitment to democracy and, even worse, of resisting change or the will of the people by asserting a preference for order. Republicanism, then, appeared to grant post-Revolutionary lawyers three major vocational opportunities – mediating between government and the sovereignty of the people by fostering the public good, providing the services of dispute resolution in a society of competing interests, and maintaining a disinterested bar trained to exercise enlightened leadership. All, however, would turn out to be unresolvable tensions in the life of the bar between the Revolution and the Civil War. The difficulties they posed were played out over and over again – in legal education; in bar admission, composition, and structure; in the organization of practice; in law reform; in ethics; and elsewhere. The bar never could quite escape the ambiguity of its role in American society.

Anti-Lawyer Critiques in the Republic: Defining the Public Good and the Nature of Community Under Law

Not everyone thought American lawyers were living up to the republican creed. There has long been an anti-lawyer tradition in America, although it is not exactly clear whether the Revolution exacerbated or eased it. But some post-Revolutionary critics, for political and other reasons, clearly believed that lawyers were far from paragons of civic virtue, and their attacks tried systematically to stymie the attempts of attorneys to align themselves with the constituent elements of republicanism. There was a certain irony to this criticism, for it showed that lawyers' dual capacities rendered them vulnerable as well as powerful. Through their active participation in the founding of the nation, lawyers had worked hard to institutionalize the insights of republican theory as well as to situate themselves as public representatives of it. As private lawyers, however, they could be found wanting in a wide variety of interrelated ways that served to undermine their carefully constructed public role.

First, there was the perpetual, vexing problem of the complexity of law. Law in a republic ought to be accessible to all, not the special province of experts. The more technical and complex the law – with only lawyers qualified to administer, superintend, or interpret it – the more costly and the less accessible it became. The call came to simplify the words and cut the costs. One radical program, suggested in Massachusetts by Benjamin Austin in 1786 (and republished in 1819), was simply to abolish the "order" of lawyers altogether. Similarly, the citizens of Braintree asked for laws that would "crush or at least put a proper check or restraint on that order of Gentlemen denominated Lawyers" whose conduct "appears to us to tend rather to the destruction than the preservation of this Commonwealth."[5]

If the state found it impractical to control lawyers, then perhaps communities could reduce reliance on the artifice of law as practiced by lawyers. Lawyers' "science," some critics charged, cut law off from its natural roots in justice. In the immediate post-Revolutionary generation, they proposed ways of restoring the quasi-utopian, pristine quality of law. Massachusetts, Pennsylvania, and Maryland all considered legislative proposals to embrace arbitration procedures that would wrest control of the administration of justice from lawyers and simplify the legal process. Arbitration was also occasionally linked to court reform. As one Maryland observer noted, "The great mass of the people have found business to proceed much faster by mixing a little *common sense* with *legal knowledge*. . . . I know many private gentlemen, who possess more accurate legal erudition than the majority of attorneys, although, perhaps, not so well acquainted with *trick* and *finesse*."[6]

Second, as practicing attorneys, lawyers appeared merely self-interested, rather than interested in the public good. As the citizens of Braintree hinted, self-interest threatened the fabric of the community by pitting citizens against each other. At the very least, lawyers exacerbated conflicts by representing opposed parties. Worse, as Jesse Higgins observed in 1805 in *Sampson Against the Philistines*, lawyers might actually foment conflict for their own purposes, rather than prevent or resolve disputes. In 1830, in *Vice Unmasked*, P. W. Grayson stated the problem concisely: "Gain I assert is their animating principle, as it is, in truth, more or less of all men. . . . A tremulous anxiety for the means of daily subsistence, precludes all leisure to contemplate the loveliness of justice, and properly to understand her principles."[7] Rather than belonging to a learned profession or a higher calling, Grayson suggested, lawyers were now embedded like everyone else in the marketplace. Self interest in an increasingly atomized society was the norm, and lawyers were no exception; in fact they seemed particularly susceptible to falling victim to corruption and luxury.

Third was the problem of independence in a republic that rejected forms of dependence and subordination. Lawyers were in an ambiguous position

[5] Petition of the Braintree Town Meeting, Sept., 1786.

[6] *Baltimore American*, Nov. 29, 1805 (italics in original).

[7] P. W. Grayson, "Vice Unmasked, An Essay: Being A Consideration of the Influence of Law upon the Moral Essence of Man, with other reflections" (New York, 1830).

or, perhaps, a double bind. On the one hand, lawyers represented others, clients, so the claim could be made that they were dependent on others for their business or that they were not independent producers, free of others, and self-sustaining. On the other hand, one of the aspects of republican lawyering could be construed as reserving to the attorney the right to make independent moral judgments about the virtue of the claims of clients on whom he depended for a livelihood. Would clients tolerate the substitution of the will of their attorney for their own will when clients thought that they were purchasing expertise and knowledge in the marketplace? Was the independence so prized by republican theorists fated to be eternally compromised by the social function of lawyering? And what about the perceptions of clients? In a society that valued independence, would clients resent being in the thrall of their lawyer, who possessed a grip on language and technicality? In a society that talked openly about the promise of equality, clients might chafe if they were placed under the protection of another person, dependent on his expertise.

It was equality, finally, that caused lawyers their most pressing ideological problem. Republicanism required selfless, educated, virtuous elites to lead and govern. Lawyers thought they were well suited to the task. They had forged connections or networks with other elites through marriage or kinship and also through business and economic transactions, which nevertheless contributed to the image of attorneys as dependent. Moreover, obsessive and risky land speculation led some lawyers into financial distress. Yet in a society that also valued the equality, individuality, and independence of its citizens, pretensions to leadership suggested pretensions to aristocracy and hierarchy. Lawyers had not been elected in their professional lives, though the charge was that they acted as if they were. (In Jacksonian America, this insight helped fuel the move to elect judges.) In their public lives they did often serve in elected political office, shaping public policy in part through their legal insights, not associating overwhelmingly with one political party or ideology.

Inevitably the bar's claims to elite status became caught up in the maelstrom of Jacksonian democracy. In 1832, Frederick Robinson jeered at lawyers' pretensions: "And although you have left no means unattempted to give you the appearance of Officers, you are still nothing more than followers of a trade or calling like other men, to get a living, and your trade like other employments, ought to be left open to competition."[8] Though his words were anti-monopolistic in tone, with implications for the educational

[8] Frederick Robinson, "Letter to the Hon. Rufus Choate Containing a Brief Exposure of Law Craft, and Some of the Encroachments of the Bar Upon the Rights and Liberties of the People" (1832).

and admissions process, the heart of the matter was equality of opportunity. Should the profession be less of a closed fraternity with the de facto right to exclude entry, particularly if the bar was associated with economic power? The common law was not supposed to be mysterious, but available to all. The Constitution was supposed to apply to all. So the legal profession should be open to all – though whether increasing the number of lawyers was a good idea or a bad idea seemed not to concern Jacksonian theorists, any more than the question whether simplifying the law through codification would cause lawyers to behave any differently once they were trained in the mysteries of the craft.

Though criticism of lawyers was widespread, it was not crippling. In some places, indeed, it seemed rather muted. Lawyers did not appear to be viewed as a particularly potent or threatening social or political force in Southern society. Their reputation, perhaps more myth than reality, placed them in a rather more genteel classification: well educated, well read, tied more closely to the planter elites and their culture, more interspersed in society, and often practicing law only when it suited them. Prosperous Southern lawyers often invested in land, plantations, and slaves, seamlessly blending with their culture rather than standing apart from it. Perhaps there was a lesson in their experience for other lawyers. Their major moral challenge was their involvement in a slave society, but most seemed to concern themselves simply with administering the system internally, coping with its contradictions and inconsistencies, rather than spending much time, at least at first, defending the system from external ideological attacks. They just acted like lawyers.

So both lawyers embracing republicanism and republican critics of lawyers helped shape the contested images that would follow the profession in various forms and elaborations throughout the century. Was it declining or was it rising? Was it a learned profession or a business? Was it selfless or self-interested? Was it public spirited or private oriented? Was it political or apolitical? Was it independent or dependent?

III. THE EDUCATION OF LAWYERS: THE SEARCH FOR LAW AS A SCIENCE IN A REPUBLIC

Apprenticeship

For most of the eighteenth and nineteenth centuries, the overwhelming majority of American lawyers were trained by other lawyers through what was known as the apprenticeship method, a method apparently conceived of as if its purpose was to train fledgling artisans in the mysteries of a craft or guild. Special knowledge and expertise were to be imparted by those solely in control of that knowledge to those wishing to enter a "profession" that was responsible for defining itself. Admission to the educational process was tantamount to admission to the profession, because the standards for bar admission were primarily established by the bar with occasional supervision by the courts. Those standards tended to prescribe a period of time "reading law" in an attorney's office, followed by only the most rudimentary examination by a judge. Whether one obtained a solid legal education was mostly fortuitous. There was not much method to the process, scientific or otherwise.

By necessity, therefore, almost all legal education was local. Potential students – often by dint of personal association or friendship, community, and family – enlisted in the offices of attorneys in their towns or metropolitan areas and agreed to pay a tuition of $100 or $200 (waived on occasion) to receive an "education." Though the education was decentralized, it was remarkably uniform. From the late eighteenth through the first quarter of the nineteenth century, law students began by reading primarily what their mentors had read before them. The process often started by reading general historical and jurisprudential works focusing on the feudal origins of law, or the law of nations or natural law. From the general, the educational program moved to the particular. The great advance in legal education at this time was provided by Blackstone's *Commentaries*, absorbed by generations of grateful law students. Arranged by systematic legal categories, the *Commentaries* provided complex yet concise insights and an overview into foundational legal principles. Blackstone also took the pressure off lawyers actually to teach, allowing them to carry on business (also using the cheap labor supplied by students), which the students might also observe.

After reading, students were expected to organize their own knowledge. They did this by compiling their own commonplace books, which distilled their readings into accessible outlines. Whether learning lessons from Blackstone (or St. George Tucker's later American version of Blackstone, or Kent's own *Commentaries*) or copying the writs, declarations, or answers of the attorneys in whose offices they read, the students, often unsupervised, in theory assiduously mastered the accrued lessons of the past filtered through the remarkably similar experiences of their teachers in the present. As a result, a certain regard for tradition, continuity, and timelessness was transmitted. Over time, the educational process was enhanced as judicial decisions became more available through case reports and legal treatises on more specialized subjects were published. Even then, a student's exposure to these materials was often at the mercy of the library of the law-office attorney.

A legal education could be haphazard, and as many students complained, it was almost always drudgery. At the dedication of the Dane Law School

(Harvard) in 1832, Josiah Quincy described the current form of legal education in need of reform. "What copying of contracts! What filling of writs! What preparing of pleas! How could the mind concentrate on principles." Books, said Quincy, "were recommended as they were asked for, without any inquiry concerning the knowledge attained from the books previously recommended and read. Regular instruction there was none; examination as to progress in acquaintance with the law – none; occasional lectures – none; oversight as to general attention and conduct – none. The student was left to find his way by the light of his own mind." The result was boredom, inattention, ignorance. "How could the great principles of the law . . . be made to take an early root . . . by reading necessarily desultory . . . and mental exercises . . . conducted, without excitement and without encouragement, with just so much vagrant attention as a young man could persuade himself to give. . . ." [9]

Reading law, therefore, was thought of as a practical education, technical learning by osmosis, but an education where acquiring the principles of the mysterious science was left to chance. There was much unhappiness with the methodology, but precious little change or thought about change. A prospective student understood that the critical step in the process was finding an office in which to read because, by rule or custom in most places, after three years or so of tedious endurance, bar admission would result. The bar decided who was worthy enough to enter the profession. The members of the bar were primarily a homogeneous group, and they generally rewarded those who were striving and seeking opportunity. To read law, one did not have to come from a wealthy family (merchants or planters), and though wealth helped a young man get accepted into a law office and pay his tuition, plenty of farmers' or ministers' sons found their way there. Also, having some form of undergraduate college education clearly helped – indeed, over time in some jurisdictions, the bar rules would require some formal education. But the search for organizing principles and alternative methods was only beginning.

University Law Professors

University law lectureships and professorships never really flourished in immediate post-Revolutionary America. Seeking to emulate Blackstone's success as Vinerian Professor of Law at Oxford, a small number of universities created professorships or chairs. The experiment began, thanks to Thomas Jefferson, with George Wythe's 1779 appointment at William and

[9] Josiah Quincy, "An Address Delivered at the Dedication of the Dane Law School in Harvard University, October 23, 1832."

Mary as professor of "Law and Police." (Wythe would be followed in the position by St. George Tucker.) Wythe's professorship, mostly because of his gifts and intellect, was to be the most successful of these attempts at legal education, but other examples abound in the 1790s – from the important law lectures of James Wilson at the University of Pennsylvania and James Kent at Columbia (though after the initial ceremonial lectures, interest and students seemed to wane), to David Hoffman's ambitious undertaking at the University of Maryland in 1814. Along the way Harvard, Virginia, and Yale began offering undergraduate law courses that over time evolved into university law schools.

In addition to signifying discontent with the apprenticeship custom, all these fledgling programs had one purpose in common. The lectureships stemmed from a conviction that law was to be a learned profession and that law, if not yet a science, was certainly one of the liberal arts essential to teaching and learning about the nature, place, and role of civic virtue in a newly minted republican society. If this society was to be self-governing, it needed to educate an elite that would understand the lessons of the past and devise institutions, legal or otherwise, to prevent the mistakes of the past from recurring. So, although there was some discussion of practical legal detail, the emphasis was on organizing knowledge about the law to establish an impact on the shape of society. Society would not be safe without republican lawyers.

Proprietary Law Schools

Proprietary law schools arose in the United States to fill a perceived vacuum. No one was teaching principles, and the grasp of the practical was assumed to flow seamlessly from observation and repetition. Lawyers also for the most part could superintend only a handful of students, and if no lawyer was available, a prospective student might have to travel or be inconvenienced. Monopolizing students might be frowned on, and so in some senses, it might be more efficient to form a school to attract a variety of students from a variety of places, particularly if the school could guarantee that they would be getting plenty of attention, organization, and books they might not find elsewhere.

Such was Tapping Reeve's insight and gamble when he founded the Litchfield Law School in a little corner of Connecticut in 1784. Reeve, eventually in partnership with James Gould, and finally Gould by himself, trained about one thousand lawyers (many of whom served in important positions in politics and law) before their doors closed in 1833, perhaps as a result of the competition emerging from university law schools, particularly Harvard.

Reeve and Gould offered rigor, supervision, and lectures. Over the course of fourteen months, students heard ninety-minute daily lectures organized around legal principles (not just the mindless rote of rules), recorded their lessons in notebooks, took weekly tests, and participated in forensic exercises. The measure of Litchfield's success is that though students were drawn primarily from the New England and mid-Atlantic states, the school's reputation was such that despite its relative isolation and Federalist proclivities about 30 percent of its enrollees were from the South, including John C. Calhoun.

Litchfield's reputation inspired other attempts by lawyers and judges to earn a living teaching law or to supplement their income by aggregating student apprentices. None of these efforts achieved the same level of broad acceptance and intellectual impact as Litchfield. But they appeared and then disappeared with various degrees of seriousness in localities in Virginia, North Carolina, New York, Massachusetts, and elsewhere. Their lack of infrastructure and financing, coupled with the slow reexamination of the ideas justifying the forms of legal education, eventually led some to believe that the place for the education of lawyers belonged in a university that could justify professional, as well as undergraduate, training.

University Law Schools

Joseph Story had such a vision. In 1829, beginning with the remnants of the endowed law professorship established at Harvard College more than a decade earlier, Story sought to transform the nature of legal education. A simple law professorship would no longer do; Litchfield showed that. Apprenticeship left too much to the risks of mentor inertia and student indifference. What was needed was systematic endeavor demonstrating that law was a science and belonged in a university. The question was, what kind of science. Story preferred to see law as a set of ideals, stressing universal principles of natural justice, spanning the ages and ever appropriate. Law was a moral science designed to guide human behavior. It was important, he thought, in a republic to develop a cadre of specially trained guardians, "public sentinel[s],"[10] to protect, as Lemuel Shaw had put it, against the excesses of democracy. Ever mindful of the spread of Jacksonian democracy, Story wanted to guarantee that lawyers would retain strong moral character. If lawyers could not control admission to the profession, they could at least control the content of a lawyer's education. Republican virtue must be perpetuated, sound principles enunciated clearly, governing standards declared. Training lawyers also meant sending them out into the world.

[10] Joseph Story, "Discourse Pronounced Upon the Inauguration of the Author as Dane Professor of Law in Harvard University (Aug. 25, 1829)."

Timothy Walker, who founded the Cincinnati Law School in 1835 in the image of Story and Harvard, was one. If they came to Harvard to learn, Story wanted them to populate the nation as missionaries.

Story's reach was national. Systemization of thought for him meant forming and shaping the general legal categories with which to organize a legal literature designed to tell lawyers how to believe or act. Story contributed greatly to his cause by writing innumerable legal treatises, ranging from *Commentaries on the Constitution* to various technical legal subjects. For Story, theory was practical. The success of Harvard Law School rose during Story's tenure and began a generation of decline on his death in 1845.

Not all who sought refuge in a university legal education shared Story's vision. Different ideas about the nature of legal education and legal science flowed from the rationality preached by the philosophers of the Scottish Enlightenment. Tied to what became known as Protestant Baconianism, which was rooted in natural theology and eventually the natural sciences, the recommended method was one of taxonomical classification that organized knowledge and the acquisition of knowledge from the bottom up around readily recognizable first principles, instead of from the top down, as Story advocated. The Baconian system of legal thought – espoused by lawyers and law professors like David Hoffman, David Dudley Field, George Sharswood, and, most ominously for Story, his colleague at Harvard, Simon Greenleaf – was supposed to be verifiable and vaguely empirical. This method, because it was more scientific, arguably had the virtue of being able to adapt better to social change. Story did not much like change, particularly political change. The loosely knit Protestant Baconians wanted to adapt law to American experiences (an idea that Story in theory was not opposed to) and to release it from its perceived dependence on pre-Revolutionary British common law. Law needed to be explained as a science, not simply as a faith. Seeking to train lawyers based on these principles, the Baconians saw lawyers more as specialists or experts, technocrats providing a service in the marketplace, though they retained concerns about the moral responsibility of lawyers. Story apparently was afraid that unless his method was used, the republic, founded under the stewardship of lawyers, would fade away, and that lawyers would no longer be part of a learned profession and noble calling. And indeed, the face of the profession was gradually changing, just as Story feared.

IV. THE GROWTH OF THE PROFESSION

Over the course of the nineteenth century, lawyers, in conjunction with courts, gradually lost whatever control they had over admission standards and practices. In 1800, fourteen of the nineteen states had requirements of between four to seven years of bar preparation. By 1840, only eleven of the thirty states insisted on prescribed periods of study. In jurisdictions like Massachusetts and New York, before the liberalization of rules governing admission, it might take a prospective lawyer up to a decade (including a fixed period of college education) to qualify for admission. By mid-century that had changed drastically. Good moral character with a shortened period of study or an examination became the standard in Massachusetts in 1836. New Hampshire in 1842 and Maine in 1843 required only evidence of good moral character, without any prescribed period of study. By 1860, just nine of the thirty-nine states insisted on any period of study. University legal education, which promised to help filter entry to the profession, was still slow to gather momentum, with about fifteen university law schools operating in 1850. These changes fed concerns about the composition of the bar that reignited disputes within the profession and the public over the proper place of lawyers in American society.

The bar was forced to open up under pressure from forces loosely associated with Jacksonian democracy that produced leveling arguments coupling equality of opportunity with suspicions about elites. The relaxation of admission requirements has often been bemoaned in the literature of the profession as a period of great decline. But it is difficult to determine the baseline against which to measure the fall from grace, or to assess precisely how many lawyers were entering practice, or who they were. The traditional view was that the bar was a meritocracy (thereby ensuring its status as an honestly earned craft or guild or elite). In 1841, St. George Tucker observed that "the profession of the law is the most successful path, not only to affluence and comfort, but to all the distinguished and elevated stations in a free government."[11] On the other hand, lawyers from John Adams onward had expressed concerns that increasing numbers of lawyers meant more unscrupulous, untrained pettifoggers clogging the courts, stealing clients, and leading the public to believe all attorneys were mendacious predators; and that, even worse, the practice of law had become a mere business.

There are very few reliable statistics on the number of lawyers in the United States between 1790 and 1850; most of the evidence is fragmentary, scattered, and anecdotal. Before 1850, there are limited data on the number of lawyers in some locations at some specific times. The federal Census of 1850, however, broke down occupations by location or state. It recorded just under 24,000 lawyers nationwide, almost half of them in only five states: Massachusetts, New York (with nearly 18 percent of the total alone), Ohio, Pennsylvania, and Virginia. And not surprisingly, by mid-century more lawyers were pushing west into Indiana, Illinois, and Wisconsin.

[11] [Henry St. George Tucker], *Introductory Lecture Delivered by the Professor of Law in the University of Virginia . . .* 8 (1841).

As to the number of lawyers as a proportion of the general population, "[b]etween 1850 and 1870, the ratio was fairly steady: 1.03 lawyers to every 1,000 population at the beginning and 1.07 at the end."[12] If one compares this data with numbers on the eve of the Revolution, it is clear that by 1850 many more men were entering the legal profession, and the relative number of lawyers in proportion to the general population had increased significantly. Indeed, lawyers in some places complained that the profession had become overcrowded and was degenerating into a mere business, while anti-lawyer critiques decried the "swarms" of lawyers. But in places like New York, the increased number of lawyers might have been a consequence of the accelerating pace of market expansion and trade, as well as the growing complexity of legal practice. And in any event, the impact of lawyers on public policy and political activity may have been disproportionate to their absolute or relative numbers. So, was the ubiquitous lament about the overcrowding and decline of the legal profession in part a complaint about who the new lawyers were?

Only a few brief demographic snapshots analyze data about lawyers' social class and status over the nineteenth century. The two most extensive studies are of Massachusetts and Philadelphia. For Massachusetts, Gerald Gawalt found that, of 2,618 trained lawyers practicing in Massachusetts and Maine between 1760 and 1840, 71 percent held college degrees. Admittedly, Massachusetts was hardly the frontier, but in a period when a college education was the exception and not the rule, this data seem scant evidence of the decline of the profession, at least in that state. Gawalt also found that over time most college-educated lawyers in Massachusetts and Maine came from professional families and often were the sons of judges and lawyers. It seems fairly clear that, at least for this period, Massachusetts lawyers retained the gloss of an educated elite, not necessarily upper class, but solidly grounded in the community. A narrower sample of lower federal court judges from 1829 to 1861 also indicates the judges were generally from the educated middle class. Western or frontier lawyers, drawn from a different cohort, seem to have been from more humble origins.

In Philadelphia, the story was a little different. From 1800 to 1805, 68 percent of Philadelphia lawyers were college graduates, and 72 percent came from elite families. By 1860, the number of college graduates in the profession had fallen to 48 percent. The pool of prospective lawyers, meanwhile, had expanded. Upper-class representation declined from 72 percent to 44 percent. Where middle-class families were only 16 percent of the

[12] Terence C. Halliday, "Six Score Years and Ten: Demographic Transitions in the American Legal Profession, 1850–1960," *Law & Society Review* 20 (1986), 53, 57. Incidentally, the ratio "rose steeply to 1.5 in 1900, but then contracted to 1.16 in 1920." *Id.*

sample in 1800–1805, now they were nearly half. Twenty-seven percent came from the artisanal and lower middle class. The lower-class group remained steady over time at 12 percent.

The appearance of a more heterogeneous profession where once there had been a more homogeneous legal community might explain some of the bar's rhetorical crankiness or anxiety about its status. However, agitation about lost status and lost community did not necessarily translate into reduced authority. The middle class was not preaching revolution, just access. This also meant that, as more individuals were engaged in an expanding economy, new markets for legal services would be created. One of the paths to enhanced market participation was to represent those touched by the same invisible hand. Most young lawyers sought entry to the profession to build their own lives, not threaten others.

In any case, there were clear limits to the bar's diversity. At this time, for obvious reasons, the profession remained overwhelmingly white, and male and Protestant. A handful of African Americans became lawyers before the Civil War. Only about six were admitted, beginning with Macon Bolling Allen in Maine in 1844. Allen left Maine within a year, apparently clientless, and was admitted to the bar in Massachusetts in 1845. Robert Morris, Sr., followed suit in Massachusetts in 1847, where he established a thriving practice, best remembered for his failed quest to desegregate the Boston public schools in 1848–1849 in *Roberts v. City of Boston*.

Women fared worse. There is some evidence that women on rare occasions appeared in court on their own or others' behalf, but no women were admitted to the practice of law before the Civil War. Belle Mansfield was admitted to practice in Iowa in 1869, and shortly thereafter, Myra Bradwell, fresh from having founded the *Chicago Legal News*, passed her bar exam, only to be denied admission, thereby starting the path to the constitutional decision barring her entry to the profession. At this stage, the weight of gender stereotypes was apparently too much to overcome.

By 1860, the bar was growing, with only a few cracks in its facade of social class. It was now a symbol of aspiration, and if indeed it was a higher calling, why would the bar complain about all those aspiring to enter? Anxious about losing status and professional control, the bar continued to fret. For all its concerns its hegemony over law never really seem threatened. However, immigrants, non-Protestants, racial minorities, women, and poorly educated supplicants were looming just over the horizon.

V. THE ORGANIZATION OF PRACTICE

Wherever a lawyer during this period might have been located – New England, Mid-Atlantic, Midwest, South, West, or the so-called frontier, Southwest, or eventually the Far West, urban or rural – the chances were overwhelming that he was a solo practitioner. And it was just as likely that he was a generalist, prepared to take any business that walked in the door. "In this country," one lawyer commented in 1819, "there is little or no division of labour in the profession. All are attornies, conveyancers, proctors, barristers and counselers.... It is this habit of practical labour, this general knowledge of business, which connects the professional man in this country with all classes of the community, and gives him an influence, which pervades all."[13] The realities of practice thus also determined the place of lawyers in American society.

A lawyer had to have some facility in pleading and litigation (though just exactly how much litigation actually went to trial is unclear), and the dimensions of a lawyer's expertise might be tested by where he practiced. For example, if a lawyer practiced on the frontier or the old Northwest, or parts of the South, or interior New England from 1790 to about 1820, unless he was anchored in a small metropolitan area, he probably rode circuit; that is, took his business on the road following the terms of the courts as they circulated throughout the jurisdiction. Thus, the typical lawyer faced a number of challenges. First, he probably did not know most of his clients until he met them. Second, he had to be a quick study, or at least capable of reducing the great mass of business into a routine processing mode (often just filing actions to preserve claims, particularly debt collections, or appearing to defend them). Third, he had to be nimble on his feet. He had to go to trial with little or no preparation, so some forensic ability might help, including an aptitude for shaping or developing a narrative – telling a good story. Rhetoric might or might not get in the way, although there is some evidence that the trial calendar was treated in some locations (rural as well as urban) as local theater or entertainment. Fourth, a lawyer's reputation was treated as a kind of roving commission: the success of his business depended on his perceived performance. Last, he had to be willing to travel with and develop a tolerance for a group of fellow lawyers and judges. In the absence of bar associations in most places, lawyers boarded and bonded with one another in all kinds of settings. There is a fair amount of bar and other literature heralding the brotherhood of lawyers – looking out for each other's business, for example. There are also accounts of boisterous and occasional violent confrontations between lawyers in the South and West, which sometimes are cited as evidence of their community.

As courts became more centralized, one shift in the method of practice over the century was the reduction of circuit riding, sometimes over the complaints of those who found it difficult geographically to gain access to courts. Though transportation networks were expanding, judges and

[13] Warren Dutton, "An Address Delivered to the Members of the Bar of Suffolk ... 1819," 6–7.

lawyers tended to withdraw from traveling, or at least circuit riding was no longer a central identifying feature for some of the bar. Over time in some places in Tennessee, Ohio, and Michigan, lawyers went to clients or physically searched for clients less often; rather the clients came to the lawyers. The market for services had changed.

Attorneys had another reason for choosing solo practice: there was not enough business to support more extensive office practices. Most lawyers made a decent enough living. Some struggled. A few became very rich. By 1830 Lemuel Shaw was earning between $15,000 and $20,000 annually, a great deal of money in those days. Alexander Hamilton, Daniel Webster, and others also made large sums of money. In New York and in some of the eastern seaboard cities from North to South, lawyers in practices tied to economic expansion and organization prospered by investing or by serving as corporate officers, bank directors, or trustees. Nonetheless, in 1856 John Livingston reported in his national survey of the bar that a lawyer's income averaged about $1,500 per year, less than most appellate judges' salaries at the time.

This general "sufficiency" does not mean the bar was not stratified. It was, not formally as in England, but by income. Age was one factor. In some places attorneys when first admitted were limited to practice only in lower courts for a probationary period. Young lawyers tended to move west to seek opportunity and avoid competition. The income hierarchy was differentiated further over time in some locales, like cities, based on what courts a lawyer practiced in – courts of criminal jurisdiction, for instance, as opposed to appellate practice. The primary marker of stratification, however, was the lawyer's clients. For a profession that valued its independence, it was remarkable to see a de facto classification of lawyers emerge based on whom they represented.

Closely examined, a simple debt transaction reveals the initial layers of the profession. On one side would stand the debtor, typically starved for cash. His lawyer would spend his time ascertaining the circumstances of the transaction, gathering the documents (probably limited and primitive), responding to pleadings (usually mechanical and rote), but often seeking to postpone the payment or judgment for as long as possible so his vulnerable client could remain afloat. The lawyer had few economic resources or legal strategies available, and he often negotiated or corresponded with the creditor's attorney from a position of weakness. His fee was likely to be small and difficult to collect. He scrambled for business and was fortunate if he could bargain with his opponents to renegotiate the terms of the transaction or arrange a settlement.

The creditor's lawyer, by contrast, operated in a much more stable environment. Legally protected in most circumstances, the creditor asserted his rights in the transaction from a position of strength. His lawyer behaved accordingly. He also evaluated the factual setting, counseled his client, negotiated on his behalf, and prepared the pleadings. But the underlying economic circumstances of the creditor were likely, though not always, to be better than the debtor's. Securing a debt for a relatively wealthy client was very different from scrambling to avoid paying a debt for a client with more limited resources. The creditor's lawyer, further, might have been specifically retained with fees to pursue the debt – mercantile firms or banks paid handsomely for lawyers' services, particularly in urban settings, and particularly as, over time, the transactions both in the original counseling and drafting phases became more complex and sophisticated. Thus, although lawyers might share a professional identity of sorts, on any given day, they might be doing very different things with very different consequences growing out of the same subject matter. The different forms of legal practice became segmented over time through repetition. They also became stratified as what the lawyer did increasingly reflected the wealth of the clients he represented.

Over the course of the century, the wealth of the client was more likely to be corporate, not individual. Here lay major engines of stratification – retention and repetition. An individual landowner might need an attorney occasionally for buying and selling land or arranging leases or easements. But what if a newly chartered railroad sought to take or cross his land? Suddenly the quiet enjoyment of his property became a major problem. Meanwhile his attorney – attuned to bread-and-butter miscellaneous disputes or minor property matters – might find himself confronting a new phenomenon, the retained railroad lawyer, professionally sophisticated and with substantial client resources at his disposal. The railroad attorney might have helped draft the legislative charter creating the enterprise (and lobbied for it politically with fellow lawyers), arranged and secured financing for the project (and drafted those documents as well), fended off the competing claims of other competitive roads or corporations (with their own retained attorneys), overseen the eminent domain or taking proceedings before nascent administrative bodies or the courts, negotiated complex deals, and generally dealt with a host of railroad-related matters. Hired railroad attorneys were very polished repeat players in the expansion of economic development projects. Landowners and their generalist lawyers were not. The enterprise or corporate lawyers tended to separate themselves from other strata of the profession through their specialization and economic success and, therefore, exercised more social and political power.

The emergence of a segmented and stratified profession was reinforced by social kinship and family networks. Bar elites cemented their social and political status and power by alliances with entrepreneurs: lawyers' families were often connected by marriage to fledgling industrial capitalists in New England, or to the owners of large manorial land holdings or mercantile interests in New York, or to banking or insurance interests in Philadelphia, or to planter elites in Virginia and South Carolina. Lawyers representing other constituencies tended to identify with them. Though its republican rhetoric asserted that the bar should have been monolithic, in practice it was not, giving rise to concerns about the profession's integrity.

Identification of lawyers with or by their clients had a ripple effect on contested views about ethical norms. If a lawyer had close social ties with his clients, zealous advocacy on their behalf could be assumed – it would seem to follow naturally from the perception that the moral universe or behavior of client and lawyer tracked each other. Hence there would be little need to question the acts of representation undertaken, thereby enhancing the lawyer's professional discretion. A lawyer who did not have the luxury of representing clients with whom he was economically or socially associated could not risk developing a reputation for less than complete devotion lest he endanger his future prospects. A lawyer who had to devote himself to a client to maintain that relationship or forge new relationships, that is, lacked discretion. Yet ultimately, whether a lawyer was comfortable representing interests he found congenial or was economically dependent on his client and therefore zealous, the organization of practice tended to inhibit the ethical standards of disinterested republicanism, or to inhibit the lawyer's appreciation of the tension in the marketplace that reduced their relevance.

During the century before the Civil War, social changes slowly occurred in the nature of practice. Partnerships emerged, though they were still the exception and not the rule, and may not have been very stable. Typically a partnership was composed of two attorneys who, because of the increased press of business, divided their responsibilities between litigation and office practices; the so-called office lawyers dealt with a growing diversification of practice, no longer just pleading, trial preparation, and jury work. Drafting instruments, planning transactions, and advising clients as to what was possible and what was not became the province of the office lawyer, who rarely entered a courtroom. Sometimes partnerships were formed between older and younger attorneys – the younger at first managing the office and preparing documents – somewhat akin to the apprenticeship relationship. The move toward partnerships tended to signal a recognition of the increased pace and complexity of practice.

Combining forces paved the way for another shift in practice, a subtle move toward specialization. There had always been pockets of specialization. The Supreme Court bar, composed of lawyers like Pinkney, Webster, and Wirt, was known for its oratorical skills in appellate advocacy. Trial lawyers like Rufus Choate or Lincoln were renowned for their forensic and rhetorical skills. But now specialties along the lines of specific areas of law began to emerge; they were technical, complex, and narrow. For example, bankruptcy law experts, still mostly solo, developed around the short-lived federal Bankruptcy Acts. Lawyers who might once have been generalists now devoted more of their time to one subject, where their talents and expertise could be honed more and more by repetition and familiarity. There were maritime lawyers, insurance lawyers, railroad lawyers, patent lawyers, finance lawyers, bank lawyers, factor and agent lawyers, and creditor lawyers – all primarily devoted to stoking the engine of economic development, and many focused on moving money as well as goods and services. In a number of ways, specialization fed the segmentation of the profession. As we have seen, the economic status of the client helped define the social and professional status of the attorney.

Increasingly, lawyers tended to cluster in cities. Eventually, particularly after the Civil War, the cities would become the home to larger law offices and law firms as demand for complex work across a variety of legal services exceeded the capacities of individual attorneys. Law practice was slowly forced to adapt to meet the multiple needs of clients in an interdependent world. Representing complex organizations in the various facets of their own corporate lives or in legal relationships with other complex organizations required more than one or two lawyers. The division of labor between litigation and office work was no longer sufficient: office work in particular could involve a whole new wave of planning and drafting demands, and integration with the world of commerce and enterprise.

Lawyers were skilled, if not always at shaping markets, at least in adapting to them. The organization and structure of practice moved fitfully toward life in the post–Civil War economy: more urban, less rural; more industrial, less agricultural; more expansive and interconnected, less local and isolated. Solo practitioners remained the backbone of the profession in numerous small communities, but the idea of the law firm was slowly taking shape.

VI. LAW AND LAWYERS

On one matter, most lawyers of any intellectual stripe between the Revolution and the Civil War could agree: law either was a science or should be a science. But exactly what the meaning of science was or what consequences flowed from law being a science was deeply contested. The critical question was the relationship of law as a science to civic virtue. The republican lawyers and their ideological descendants, the Federalist-Whig elites, strove mightily to capture the high road of the rhetoric of law as a science and, therefore, to seize and define the terms of the debate.

The Science of Law and the Literature of Law

For most republican lawyers, establishing legal science became a crucial organizing idea in the republican program, whether in legal education or political engagement. It was, they thought, the special responsibility and province of educated lawyers to ensure that private and public decisions were grounded in or sanctioned by the solid principles of law verifiable as a science. Precisely what this meant was a little unclear, but certain basic principles seemed generally accepted. First, law was a product of reason rather than passion, and therefore restrained the base or corrupt instincts of man. Second, law could be derived from principles that could be deduced in a systematic and orderly fashion from the mother lode of the common law, which was in turn derived from reported appellate cases. Third, law meant stability, order, certainty, and predictability as, over time, it developed culturally sanctioned norms or rules that tended to resist change, but were capable of slowly adapting to measured progress that would serve the greater public good. Others might have a different definition of the science of law. Jacksonians found the science of law to be a political science, grounded in positive law, the will of the people. Protestant Baconians found the science of law in natural theology filtered through the Scottish Enlightenment, preferring the methods of inductive natural science to deduction. But the republican vision of law dominated the debate, and every competing theory began by positing an alternative to it. Once generally embraced, how did the idea of legal science contribute to the formation of the literature of the law? The impact can be measured in three developments in the literature: law reports, legal treatises and commentaries, and legal periodicals.

The proliferation of American law reports was both a response to the demand from the profession for certifiably "decided" law and a result of its need for a reflective distillation of the rapidly increasing numbers of judicial decisions. The first reporters in the late eighteenth century were entrepreneurial actors meeting a perceived market; by the early nineteenth century the states and the federal government had begun to commission official law reports. Judicial reports satisfied the profession's demand for indigenous American law to reduce reliance on English precedents and to cope with the vast expansion in market activity that was a hallmark of the Early Republic.

In 1807, at the outset of the growth of law reports, a young lawyer named Daniel Webster, reviewing a volume of reports for a literary journal, made explicit the connection between case reporting and legal science:

> Adjudged cases, well reported, are so many land-marks, to guide erratick opinion. In America the popular sentiment has, at times, been hostile to the practice of deciding cases on precedent, because the people, and lawyers too, have misunderstood their

> use. Precedents are not statutes. They settle cases, which statutes do not reach. By reference to books, an inquirer collects the opinions and arguments of many great and learned men, on any particular topick. By the aid of these, he discovers principles and relations, inferences and consequences, which no man could instantaneously perceive. He has, at once, a full view of his subject, and arrives without difficulty, to the same conclusion, to which, probably, his own mind would in time have conducted him by a slow and painful process of ratiocination.[14]

In the canon of republican legal science, the identification of precedents from which followed order and stability was necessary to forestall incursions of "popular sentiment."

The second development in the literature of law was the appearance of commentaries and treatises, some as American versions of English editions, but increasingly over time, purely American volumes on various specific legal subjects. Blackstone had provided the model for the organization of legal knowledge for Americans, and he was emulated first in St. George Tucker's version of Blackstone in 1803, which sought to provide an American legal and political adaptation, and then by James Kent, whose four-volume *Commentaries* were published between 1826 and 1830. But the general classification of principles for study and application, though invaluable, needed supplementation as law practice became more varied and, in some manner, more technical. Lawyers wrote treatises covering in depth a range of subjects: water rights, corporations, insurance, evidence, contracts, damages, and international law. Most prominent among the treatise writers was Joseph Story, who wrote on the Constitution, equity, bailments, agency, partnership, promissory notes, bills of exchange, and conflict of laws. Each work in its own way conveyed Story's view of legal science, mining the common law and wider sources – if necessary the civil law or the law of nations – to derive legal principles from the historical foundations of law. In a sense, Story preempted the field of treatise writing as well as providing an American model. And he presided over a rejuvenation of legal writing, though it might be a conceit to call it a "literature." Between 1760 and 1840, almost 500 legal monographs (approximately 800 editions) were published in the United States, only about 90 of them (125 editions) in the period up to 1790. (The figure does not include case reports, codes, statutes, digests, legal periodicals, or most miscellaneous pamphlets like bar orations or discourses.) Lawyers were reaching out for guidance, and Story entered the field to ensure that the guidance conformed to his view of legal science.

[14] Daniel Webster [Book Review of 1 William Johnson, New York Supreme Court Reports], *The Monthly Anthology* 4 (1807), 206.

The third forum for writing about law was the legal periodical. Between 1790 and 1830 a total of twelve legal periodicals were published. In 1810, only one existed; in 1820 again only one; in 1830, five. In other words, early in the century very few legal periodicals generated enough interest or subscribers to survive. Between 1840 and 1870, in contrast, thirty-seven were formed, and more of them survived at least for the short term. They were an eclectic mix; most were utilitarian, printing early notices of decided cases, or book reviews of new treatises, or surveys of new statutes. But some, like *American Jurist and Law Magazine*, published in Boston between 1829 and 1843, the *Monthly Law Reporter* also published in Boston from 1838 to 1866, and the *Western Law Journal* published in Cincinnati from 1843 to 1853, had higher aspirations, publishing essays on subjects internal to the bar and on topics of general public concern to lawyers as well. The founding editor of the *Monthly Law Reporter*, Peleg Chandler, divulged to Joseph Story, his mentor at Harvard Law School, his reasons for beginning the journal: "A great deal is said in particular cases, even in arguments to the court, about what the law ought to be or might well be, but precious little *of what it is*." What was needed, Chandler insisted, was "to hold up before the profession and the public the decisions fresh from the court – to place before them the law as it comes from the dispensers of it – from those who are too far removed from the public to be easily affected by the changing fashions of the day. . . ." By so doing, his magazine would illustrate why "[n]oisy radicals are not men who have read intimately the reports and become acquainted with the intricate machinery, of which, if a part be disarranged, the whole may suffer. . . ."[15] Appealing directly to Story's understanding of legal science, Chandler sounded very much like Daniel Webster a generation before, applauding the arrival of law reports. He assumed that finding and stating "what it is" was a scientific undertaking.

As Chandler more than hinted, engaging in this pursuit of legal science had political consequences. Lawyers in a republic had a responsibility to be engaged in civic discourse, reasoning and arguing for the most effective legal rules in the public interest. Lawyers from the time of the Constitutional Convention in Philadelphia onward had gravitated toward the public, political arena, whether in legislatures, or state constitutional conventions, or executive offices. In Massachusetts from 1760 to 1810, just over 44 percent of all lawyers were elected to some public office; from 1810 to 1840, about a third of all Massachusetts lawyers were elected to public positions. (There is some evidence that lawyers served extensively in public positions throughout the nation.) Essays that Chandler published hence investigated the social, economic, and political implications of the scientific principles

[15] Peleg W. Chandler to Joseph Story, December 1, 1838.

of law they presented. To fulfill its mandate for civic virtue, a governing elite needed information and a forum to work out its arguments.

The legal science expounded in and by law reports, treatises, and periodicals also served an instrumental purpose, reinforcing the notion that only lawyers, scientifically and technically trained, could be trusted with law. Ironically, the anti-lawyer complaints that law was inaccessible and too complex might be true after all: only lawyers had sufficient command of arcane procedures and pleading, complex doctrine, and strange language. Through its literature, the bar justified its role to itself and the public by separating itself off – a special professional group, different from others in society. Law was the domain of lawyers. Their expertise, they argued, qualified them to administer the legal system and to resist the inroads of any non-scientific thought as they defined it.

The Common Lawyer and Codification

No technical issue of law reform so agitated the elite and academic lawyers in the nineteenth century as codification. At its core, the project of codification undermined the legal profession. By questioning the legitimacy of the common law and offering an alternative vision of law in a democratic society, codifiers challenged the central role lawyers played as guardians of the repository of law. As a result, there was much heated rhetoric on the subject. Whether the threat of codification was ever palpable is an interesting question, but at the very least codifying ideas was a political challenge to lawyers' control over the content of law.

The codifying impulse has a long history in America, beginning at least with the Puritans. Arguably the state and federal constitutions are examples of the art. So it is a little difficult to understand why the common lawyers were so upset at the appearance of arguments on the subject. Codification was never an organized movement. In fact, there were at least three distinct strands to the call for legal codes: a middle-class complaint about the common law, a social activist complaint, and a purely lawyerly complaint (with overtones of social activism). All criticisms focused on the perceived failings of the common law to provide responsive legal solutions to current social problems. Codifiers argued that the common law was bogged down by inaccessible technicalities derived from outdated British, not American, experiences and that lawyers manipulated the common law for their own self-interest, not the public's interest. In other words, law and lawyers were failing to deliver on promised republican virtue, and therefore, the making and administration of law should be returned to its true source in a democracy, the people, by having elected representatives in the legislature (who, ironically, might be lawyers) draft laws truly reflecting the will of the people. In the face of these charges, the common lawyers sought in effect to co-opt the arguments by transforming the debate into an internal legal discussion, rather than an ideological conflict.

The middle-class strand of codification drew its inspiration from prevailing anti-lawyer sentiment. The concerns expressed in the 1780s in Benjamin Austin's pamphlet, seeking abolition of the "order" of lawyers, slowly led to reconsideration of the nature of the law being practiced. In 1805, Jesse Higgins questioned the adequacy of the common law in a pamphlet entitled "Sampson against the Philistines; or, the Reformation of Lawsuits; and Justice Made Cheap, Speedy and Brought Home to Everyman's Door: Agreeably to the Principles of the Ancient Trial by Jury, before the Same Was Innovated by Judges and Lawyers." Higgins did not call for codification. Rather he thought lawyers made lawsuits expensive and time consuming and so suggested a system of arbitration to restore "cheap, speedy" justice, devoid of complexity. All that lawyers did, according to Higgins, was capitalize on people's distress and pull communities apart, rather than bind them together as republicanism required: "[T]he whole *body of common law*, the whole body of pleading, rules of evidence, &c. have no legislative vote to establish or even to define them. They depend wholly and entirely for their authority on notes taken by lawyers and clerks, about this very time, and hence the judges become the legislators." In addition, "all those laws which relate to property, . . . which are just and ought to be valid, are in every age and every country, the simplest rules, and fittest to the plainest capacities; . . . that any and every ignorant man . . . can decide any question agreeable to law, although he never heard a law read, or read one during his life."[16]

Higgins' middle-class lament was a central component of codification: Legislate, simplify the rules, state them clearly, make life easier, and reduce our dependence, financial and otherwise, on lawyers. Restore law to its roots in justice and reduce the power of lawyers.

The ideological origin of the common law was a distinct issue that attracted the attention of codifiers who had pursued an agenda of social activism, sometimes perceived as radical change. The social activists drew their criticisms from their causes: labor, antislavery, and religious tolerance. William Sampson, an Irish emigré attorney in New York, provides an example. His defense of New York City journeymen cordwainers in 1809 anticipated his more thorough-going call for codification in 1823 in his "Anniversary Discourse . . . on the Nature of the Common Law." Sampson attacked the nature of the cordwainers' indictment for conspiracy at common law for seeking to exercise their power as a nascent labor union.

[16] [Jesse Higgins], *Sampson Against the Philistines . . .* 16, 27 (1805).

Sampson's criticism of the common law was organized into four separate categories. He asserted that in America, at least formally under law, all men are or should be equal: "[T]he constitution of this state is founded on the equal rights of men, and whatever is an attack upon those rights, is contrary to the constitution. Whether it is or is not an attack upon the rights of man, is, therefore, more fitting to be inquired into, than whether or not it is conformable to the usages of Picts, Romans, Britons, Danes, Jutes, Angles, Saxons, Normans, or other barbarians, who lived in the night of human intelligence." Second, in England statutes were vehicles of inequality. "[T]he English code and constitution are built upon the inequality of condition in the inhabitants.... There are many laws in England which can only be executed upon those not favoured by fortune with certain privileges; some operating entirely against the poor."[17] Third, in America, statutes created equality; the common law was the source of inequality. Indictments at common law in the United States, therefore, were suspect because they were at variance with America's enlightened constitutional tradition. Finally, Sampson suggested that statutes were to be trusted because they had involved a process of filtration through the will of the people who were ever vigilant about equality. Codification, he added in 1823, would guarantee that "[o]ur jurisprudence then will be no longer intricate and thorny."[18]

The attacks that defenders of the common law found most difficult to deflect came from lawyers, many of them Jacksonian Democrats, who challenged the basic underlying political legitimacy of an uncodified law in a democracy. Robert Rantoul, tied to social reform movements and risking ostracism in Brahmin Boston, threw down the gauntlet in 1836. Judge-made common law, according to Rantoul, was simply judicial legislation. Judges had arbitrary power because the common law provided no certain and predictable rules. Law should be "a positive and unbending text," not maneuvered by lawyers in front of judges. "Why," asked Rantoul, "is an expost facto law, passed by the legislature, unjust, unconstitutional, and void, while judge-made law, which, from its nature, must always be expost facto, is not only to be obeyed, but applauded? Is it because judge-made law is essentially aristocratical?" This was a charge that republican lawyers like Joseph Story strangely might have found apt or congenial. An aristocracy, Rantoul suggested, that is indebted to the feudal barbarity of the dark ages for its power is inimical to the social needs and purpose of a modern nation.

[17] [Argument of William Sampson], "Trial of the Journeymen Cordwainers of the City of New York."

[18] William Sampson, "An Anniversary Discourse, Delivered Before the Historical Society of New York, on Saturday, December 6, 1823: Showing the Origin, Progress, Antiquities, Curiosities, and the Nature of the Common Law."

"Judge-made law is special legislation," and, according to Rantoul, "[a]ll American law must be statute law."[19]

If Rantoul supplied the ideological framework, it fell to David Dudley Field to shore up the theory and carry out the project and practice of codification. And he did so with relentless zeal, though only modest success, proposing code after code for New York and elsewhere. Field sought to demonstrate that codes rather than the common law were workable, expedient, and responsive, not inflexible and inexpedient. Codes devoted to specific legal subjects like civil procedure or criminal law would be comprehensive and transparent. Everyone would know what the law was; nothing would be mysterious. The advantage would be "the whole law brought together, so that it can be seen at one view; the text spread before the eyes of all our citizens; old abuses removed, excrescences cut away, new life infused." The "CODE AMERICA," as he put it, would contain "the wisest rules of past ages, and the most matured reflections of our own, which, instinct with our free spirit of our institutions, should become the guide and example for all nations." And for lawyers, "the great task is committed of reforming and establishing the law."[20]

Most of the academic lawyers who actually noticed the push against the common law were horrified and set about their own "task" of capturing the move for codification and reshaping it to their own ends. They were led by Joseph Story, Associate Justice of the U.S. Supreme Court and Dane Professor of Law at Harvard. In 1836, Story chaired a commission appointed by Governor Edward Everett of Massachusetts to determine the "practicality of reducing to a written and systematic Code the common law of Massachusetts, or any part thereof." Story set out to fend off codification by in effect rehabilitating the common law. In the process, he ended up either making concessions or engaging in contradictions, depending on how one assesses his arguments. Codes, Story argued, were cumbersome and inflexible. They could not by their very nature adjust quickly enough through the legislative process to changed social circumstances. "[I]t is not possible to establish in any written Code all the positive laws and applications of laws, which are necessary and proper to regulate the concerns and business of any civilized nation, much less of a free nation, possessing an extensive commerce. . . . "[21] But a limited form of codification could take place, one familiar and useful to lawyers and judges, a kind of digesting system

[19] Robert Rantoul, "Oration at Scituate, Delivered on the Fourth of July, 1836."

[20] David Dudley Field, "Reform in the Legal Profession and the Laws, Address to the Graduating Class of the Albany Law School, March 23, 1855."

[21] "Report of the Commissioners appointed to consider and report upon the practicality and expediency of reducing to a written and systematic code the Common Law of Massachusetts . . . ," reprinted in *American Jurist and Law Magazine* 17 (1837), 17, 30, 27.

consistent with Story's view of legal science, ordering categories and principles culled from cases and judicial decisions; in other words, the common law. Indeed, Story was already engaged in a version of this process through his prodigious treatise-writing efforts.

To reject codification, however, Story had to concede implicitly that Rantoul and others had a point. Once defended by him as stable, certain, predictable, universal, and the voice of experience, the common law was now described as flexible, changing, unfixed, and capable of growth. Ironically, uncertainty was now the common law's strength compared with positive law, which could not adjust as quickly to social change: "[T]he common law of Massachusetts is not capable of being reduced to a written and systematic Code; and . . . any attempt at so comprehensive an enterprise would be either positively mischievous, or inefficacious, or futile. . . . " Instead, he argued, "the common law should be left to its prospective operations in future (as it has been in the past) to be improved, and expanded, and modified, to meet the exigencies of society" by the application of its principles to new cases only rarely supplemented by legislation.[22]

Here then was the spectacle of common lawyers like Story defending the common law as flexible and capable of growth. Its flexibility was its strength. Once having brandished the common law as an unassailable citadel of stability and certainty, fixed in its derivation and application, the common lawyers now transformed it into a progressive science. To ward off the view that laws should exist in positive codes, Story was willing to risk admitting that judges make law. He did so because in his mind the greater danger to continuity, order, and stability was the old fear of democratic excess – the fear that the legislature, expressing the will of the people and taking the promise of equality too seriously, might readily undermine the carefully honed certainty and predictability of property rights. What Story was really afraid of was not that positive codes might fail to adjust quickly enough to changing circumstances, but that legislatures drafting codes would actually seek to change circumstances. Story was not opposed to the common law adapting to change grounded in recognized principles; he was opposed to changes in law he saw as derived from purely political motives.

The codifiers responded that if judges actually made law – if law was merely a matter of will – then let it be roped in, rendered consistent, and made by the legislature. For all of the debate among lawyers in elite circles, codification never obtained sufficient traction among lawyers who were focused on the more mundane issues of everyday practice. But the debates did reveal what the academic lawyers thought about what lawyers should be doing and the virtue of the law they were practicing.

[22] *Id.* at 31.

VII. THE REGULATION OF THE PROFESSION: ETHICAL STANDARDS, MORAL CHARACTER, CIVIC VIRTUE, AND THE ADVERSARY SYSTEM

In the face of widespread public criticism of the profession, lawyers faced a dilemma: how to regulate the conduct and behavior of their profession without at the same time conceding that their critics had a point. The problem was compounded by the fact that during the first half of the nineteenth century there was virtually no formal regulation of the conduct and behavior of attorneys. To the extent there was any supervision, it appeared to be self-regulation, but not self-regulation in a modern sense governed by codes of professional responsibility with rules or principles explicitly delineated. Rather regulation seemed to be left to the individual moral compass of each attorney perhaps reinforced by the norms of a professional culture. As long as the attorneys controlled the education and admission process, they could be vigilant about the moral character of aspirants to the bar, filtering by social class or critical observation the potential rogue attorney. Occasionally the handful of functioning local bar associations might enforce discipline or recommend action by a court. But courts had few guidelines as to appropriate conduct. When confronted with charges of unethical behavior, they had to rely on vague standards drawn from a lawyer's oath or duties as an officer of the court.

As the nineteenth century progressed, the ultimate question became what the social function of the profession was and what ethical guidelines would follow from it. Was it a profession whose legitimacy was grounded in its service to the public, with ethical rules to fit accordingly, or was the profession's primary responsibility to its clients, with rules adapted to the evolving practice of law in a market economy? The real task of the defenders of the role of the profession was to convince the critics, both internal and public, that law as a higher calling always had the interests of the community in mind and that the rhetorical posture of those participating in the debates over ethics was to forge standards that would foster, if not cement, the importance of providing legal services in a government of laws, and not men. The problem was that many more men were now practicing law, and it was probably going to be impossible to account for them or to testify as to their suitability. That anxiety helped feed discussion of what it meant to be an ethical lawyer.

Two figures predominate in America's antebellum discourse on the ethical conduct of lawyers, David Hoffman and George Sharswood. They embraced slightly different positions. Hoffman, a member of the elite Baltimore bar and a Federalist in the throes of anxiety for the lost republic, attempted to recast the profession in a fading republican vision in fifty "Resolutions in Regard to Professional Deportment," a kind of incipient code of professional responsibility appended to the second edition of his *A Course of Legal Study*, published in 1836. According to Hoffman, lawyers should be guided by their moral sentiments and judgments. They should exercise a critical analysis about the justness of their client's claims and refuse to participate in pursuing unfair or wrong causes, to engage in questionable tactics to vindicate the interests of clients, or to seek unfair advantage – in other words, lawyers should always behave as virtuous citizens. Hoffman stood in contrast to the notion asserted by Lord Brougham in England in the early nineteenth century that the lawyer's role was to pursue his client's interest zealously. In resolution after resolution, Hoffman meticulously laid out how lawyers confronted with difficult situations in practice should exercise their critical, moral judgment: "My client's conscience, and my own, are distinct entities: and though my vocation may sometimes justify my maintaining as facts, or principles, in doubtful cases, what may be neither one nor the other, I shall ever claim the privilege of solely judging to what extent to go."[23] As a trained elite, lawyers should reserve the right to express their independent moral judgment, not just their professional judgment derived from their special knowledge or skill. For Hoffman, professional judgment and moral judgment went hand in hand.

Hoffman's was a nostalgia for a lost age. Suspicious of open bar admission and unsupervised legal education (with law schools slow to develop), he believed that moral codes were necessary perhaps because the elites could no longer rely on lawyers to attend to the public good. By proposing ethical rules, Hoffman seemed to be conceding that private interests were now dominant and that what were really required were special standards for a world of zealous advocacy. If the bar could no longer control admission by ties of class and status, at least it could try to influence the character of those admitted by providing them with the ethical rules, guidelines, or prescriptions that formerly they might have been assumed to possess as second nature by dint of social upbringing. Lawyers now needed the rules spelled out explicitly, since the hustle and bustle of the marketplace had become the norm. Who did the lawyer owe his primary obligation to: the public or the client? Under republican theory, as one of Hoffman's allies remarked, the lawyer "feels that his first duties are to the community in which he lives"[24] and not necessarily to his client.

[23] David Hoffman, *A Course of Legal Study* (2nd ed., 1836), 755.

[24] Simon Greenleaf, "A Discourse Pronounced at the Inauguration of the Author as Royall Professor of Law in Harvard University (1834)."

Others were becoming less sanguine and more realistic about a lawyer's obligations. One was George Sharswood, a law professor at mid-century at the University of Pennsylvania, destined toward the end of the century to be Chief Justice of the Pennsylvania Supreme Court. In 1854, Sharswood published *A Compendium of Lectures on the Aims and Duties of the Profession of Law* (published in later editions as *An Essay on Professional Ethics*). Sharswood moved beyond Hoffman's moral imperatives. Though he was troubled by the idea of abandoning reliance on moral principles, Sharswood carefully tried to construct an ethical world that reflected law practice and yet, at the same time, constrained some of the perceived excesses of zealous advocacy. Perhaps shadowing debates in the legal periodicals of the time and justifying the value of a client-centered practice, Sharswood saw the contemporary ethical universe in shades of gray. A client should expect devotion from his attorney and an attorney must do everything he can for his client, within the law. As to distinguishing morality from law, Sharswood appeared reluctant to insist on rigid, moral stances. Lawyers might on occasion, depending on the situation, reserve the right to reject a client, but once a cause was accepted, zealous representation would follow.

Sharswood and others were in some senses on the horns of a dilemma, in part precipitated by the diverging demands of the republican tradition. Lawyers could be perceived as bastions of republican virtue by remaining independent of clients' interests and above the fray, though this was increasingly difficult in an expanding and interconnected market society, or they could embrace their clients' causes as their own and assert independence from others on behalf of their clients. Therefore, a lawyer could either evaluate from the outset whether justice was attainable in his client's cause or accept his clients more or less as he found them, and pursue justice as the client saw it, without assessing the consequences for the general community.[25]

Lawyers at mid-century were increasingly sensitive to charges that they were simply mercenaries. Over time, in professional journals and on other occasions, they took great pains to explain why zealous advocacy served everyone's interest, including the community. They were not entirely successful in convincing a skeptical public. They had better luck convincing themselves, but in doing so they ran the risk of conceding publicly either that the bar had a public relations problem, or that some of the charges were true, or that the profession, as perceived by elites, was in a period of decline. The risk, of course, was that if the bar recognized the legitimacy of

[25] A version of this point is made in Norman W. Spaulding, "The Myth of Civic Republicanism: Interrogating the Ideology of Antebellum Legal Ethics," *Fordham Law Review* 71 (2003), 1397, 1434.

the complaints, the next logical step would be calls for regulation, because self-regulation would be interpreted as unavailing or self-serving.

The trick for lawyers who were called on to justify the evolution of the professional norm of zealous advocacy was how to fit this norm within the warm rhetorical embrace of fading republicanism. For a profession and a public accustomed to hearing (if not as often believing) lawyers' attempts to justify the bar by invoking republican ideas about virtue and the public good, defending lawyers' own private interests was no mean task. In a democratic society concerned in theory with equality, convincing the public of the legitimacy of a self-described learned and educated elite took some doing. When it came to defending the ethical standards associated with zealous advocacy, the bar had only a few intellectual choices. It could admit that zealous advocacy was for private interest or gain. Or it could try to convince the public that zealous advocacy was yet another selfless act by lawyers serving their communities; that what lawyers were doing was consistent with republican virtue because lawyers were not acting in their own behalf, but selflessly for others; that the nature of legal representation had changed as society changed; and that lawyers were still meeting the needs of a public they had always served. Much of the anti-lawyer sentiment sought to strip away the veil of the public-spirited rationale of lawyers. The bar, attuned to the critique, tried to secure its place in society by reassuring its members that it was doing society's work and carving out ethical prescriptions to meet its needs.

CONCLUSION

In 1870, the nature and face of the profession were about to change. The end of the Civil War set in motion forces already gathering in antebellum America. The population was expanding, and the inexorable shift from rural to urban had begun. Immigrants and the children of immigrants added diversity to what once was a relatively homogeneous population. Former slaves, now free, had to cope with the ambiguous promise of freedom. Economic growth fueled by expanding railroads, developing interstate markets, and large industrial corporate organizations with proliferating labor requirements occurred in new and increasingly complex fashion.

The bar and the practice of law adjusted as well. The organization of practice slowly shifted. Though solo practitioners remained the backbone of the profession, and apprenticeship the main means of legal education, groups of lawyers with specializations began in increasing numbers, particularly in cities, to organize themselves into partnerships and then firms. As usual, the bar's elite remained concerned about who was admitted to practice. Bar associations, long dormant, were revived to maintain standards for entry and behavior. Lawyers also continued to participate in political life, safeguarding the Constitution and social order and never entirely losing sight of republican virtues.

The bar refocused and redoubled its efforts to cope with the demands that shifting demographics placed on admission and professional education, with alterations in forms and organization of practice, and with the reconfiguration and restatement of ethical norms. The pressure for change was in part resisted by recurring to the lessons of the past, a reliance on redesigned and redefined commitments to public citizenship as the true calling of the profession. Over the century from the Revolution to the Civil War, the profession changed subtly to avoid or rise above criticism, adopted educational practices to control access to the profession and professional knowledge, expanded the number of lawyers and variety of practices to create and serve markets for legal services, reshaped ethical and moral standards to fit the demands of modern markets, and confronted the nature of law itself to ensure that the state served society.

The bar's invocation of change, particularly its rhetoric, was not without its ironies, not the least of which was that, contrary to elite fears, the growth and expansion of the profession would lead to enhanced power and status in society. Opportunity and equality in the long run helped maintain the status of the bar as more people became lawyers, and the goals and norms associated with the hallmarks of professionalism and expertise reinforced rather than undermined social stability. When the ideas that animated professional legal identity came under pressure, lawyers sought to capture the shifting ideology, recast it in the bar's own image, and shape the ideology to serve the profession's own purposes. As a result, as America emerged from its shattering, destructive Civil War, attorneys, unlike almost any other professional group, were positioned to lead the country's reconstruction and beyond. Lawyers had survived and prospered, and they were prepared once more to direct their energy toward their understanding of what was necessary for the public good, even as what exactly the public good was would increasingly become contested.

Of the many figures born before the Civil War who sought immediately thereafter to escape the profession's earlier limitations, three in particular, in very different ways, foreshadowed the future. John Mercer Langston, one of the few practicing African American lawyers before the war, participated in Reconstruction America in the training of African American lawyers at the newly founded Howard University Law School in Washington, DC, heralding the embrace of newly found citizenship for some or, for others, the fulfillment of the meaning of citizenship. Myra Bradwell, pursuing a lifelong professional interest in law in Chicago, fought for admission to the bar, only to be rejected in her quest for formal professional identity by a

U.S. Supreme Court that could not allow her constitutional claim to escape their narrow views of a woman's proper role. And Christopher Columbus Langdell fled a Wall Street practice, beckoned by President Eliot of Harvard to reconstitute law as a science and reframe American legal education in the shape of the modern Harvard Law School. Langdell sought to professionalize the study of law and remove it from the dead hand of law office ritual and part-time university lecturers – all to prepare lawyers to meet the challenges of a new economic order increasingly remote from its roots. The question for the profession as it embarked on its new journey was whether it would inadvertently rediscover its past, or reject its past, or simply be condemned in new forms to repeat it.

4

THE COURTS, 1790–1920

KERMIT L. HALL

I. INTRODUCTION: COURTS AND DISTRIBUTIVE JUSTICE IN THE NINETEENTH CENTURY

With independence, Americans achieved one of the crucial goals of the Revolution: direction over their economic future. The process of economic transformation and the social and political changes that accompanied it quickened over the next century. Alexis de Tocqueville in the 1830s observed that the quest for "profit" had become "the characteristic that most distinguished the American people from all others." Signs of economic transformation dotted the landscape. By 1920, trains knitted the continent together; steamships plied the interior lakes and rivers and extended into international commerce; airplanes extended warfare to the skies; the telegraph and the radio provided unprecedented levels of communication; smoke belched from scores of new factories; cities such as Chicago and San Francisco thrived; and a great torrent of immigrants swept over the nation's borders. The personal, informal, and local dealings that typified the colonial economy yielded in the nineteenth century to an impersonal national and international market economy. Increased trading among private individuals for profit was one of the central developments of the period from the nation's beginning through the Progressive Era.

Social and political changes accompanied the nation's accelerating economy. At the middle of the nineteenth century slavery posed a massive contradiction to the underlying proposition that all men were created equal. Perhaps even more importantly, as the nation spread across the continent, slavery raised serious political questions about how free and slave labor could coexist. After the Civil War the nation had to wrestle with the fate of 4 million persons of African descent previously held in bondage. The war was also a struggle over the relationship of the states to the nation, the powers of the national government, and more generally the power that government at all levels should wield in dealing with issues of health, safety, morals, and welfare, the so-called police powers.

The exploding market economy had other consequences. The opportunity for economic gain lured millions of persons of foreign birth and often non-Protestant religions to America's shores. This unprecedented influx of human beings provided badly needed labor but it also undermined the traditional hegemony of white, Protestant America. Native Americans were driven increasingly from their original lands and eventually placed on reservations. Women and even children entered the labor market, the population shifted from rural to urban, and corporations arose as the primary means of conducting business.

The American political system had seen as much change as the economy and society. Political parties, disdained by the Founding Fathers, quickly emerged as a necessary means of providing unity to separated and divided governments constitutionally mandated in both the states and the nation. Parties then evolved into mass movements that broadened the base of politics, albeit without including women and African Americans. The parties themselves ultimately became a source of concern, and by 1900 a new reformist movement, the Progressives, emerged with the promise of corruption-free government founded on a scientific, non-partisan, and rational approach to governance. They challenged the prevailing political paradigm and, among other goals, urged that politics and law, courts and politicians, be divorced from one another.

Progressive criticism of the role played by courts and judges was as widespread as progressive criticism of the state of American politics. The concern was appropriate. Throughout the preceding decades both had helped to reshape the distribution of wealth that flowed from agreements reached among private individuals. But it would be a mistake to conclude that the results were expressly the work of judges in particular or lawmakers in general. As much as driving actions taken by merchants and bankers, lenders and borrowers, farmers and planters, and business people and laborers, courts reacted to them. Over the course of the nineteenth century, that is, simply adjusting existing legal rules to new economic realities became one of the chief contributions of courts, state and federal.

That said, legislators, state and national, did intervene in the economy with varying degrees of success. Hence, a constant interplay between judges and legislators over economic rights characterized the era. When legislators, for example, attempted to regulate the impact of economic change, courts sometimes struck their actions down as a violation of individual and corporate rights. Throughout the era courts tried to answer the critical question of how to allocate through law the costs, benefits, rewards, and risks associated with an increasingly acquisitive commercial market economy.

This meant, almost inevitably, that the question of distributive justice became one of the courts' most pressing concerns. In turn, a focus on distributive justice meant that the courts found themselves operating in a sometimes awkward embrace between law and politics. Tocqueville is once again helpful. He observed that in America eventually every political issue became a legal cause and the courts the forum for its resolution. The famed French visitor went on to explain that "the Americans have given their courts immense political power." Tocqueville's words offer an enduring insight into the interaction among politics, law, and courts, the rich brew from which distributive justice flows. Scholars and public commentators may debate the desirability of dispassionate and apolitical justice, but the historical reality of the courts in action, at all levels and in all places, underscores that they have generally been unable to escape shaping public policy, even when that might be their desire. Because, from the earliest days of the Republic, the courts have been embedded in and formed by politics, they have always been the subject of intense debate. Never was this truer than during the nineteenth century. The scope and substance of their dockets, how courts should be structured, staffed, and administered – every aspect of what they did was scrutinized intensively.

The courts addressed issues of distributive justice through a unique scheme of judicial federalism that matured during these years. America at its inception had two distinct systems of courts, one federal and the other state. Traditionally, the federal system generally and the Supreme Court of the United States in particular have commanded the lion's share of attention. This emphasis on the justices and their work calibrates the entire American court system by the actions of nine justices and gives exceptional weight to the federal courts. The perspective is not necessarily unreasonable; any account of courts in American history must pay serious attention to the Supreme Court and the lower federal courts. Indeed, the trend over the course of the century unmistakably recommends that attention. As America expanded geographically and burgeoned economically, so the stature of the federal courts grew with it. Especially in the wake of the Civil War and Reconstruction, a continental empire required a federal court system capable of bringing stability, certainty, and a national rule of law. Even so, during the nineteenth century the great body of day-to-day justice took place in the state trial and appellate courts, not the federal courts. Nor did growing federal judicial power necessarily come at the expense of state courts, which saw their importance and prestige increase too, as that of state legislatures decreased. When Americans became wary of their legislatures, it was to state appellate courts that they turned.

In short, as Tocqueville noted, Americans showed a tendency to place unprecedented faith in courts, whether state or federal. The story of the courts during these years is thus one of accelerating responsibility, of growing involvement in issues of distributive justice, and of increased importance in hearing, if not always settling, some of the century's thorniest political issues. It is also, on balance, one of an unwillingness to embrace equally those who did not already have power within the political system.

II. STATE COURTS AND JUDICIAL FEDERALISM

Americans tend to view the court system from the top down, although ironically they tend to live in it from the bottom up. From the nation's founding, the courts have been strongly local institutions. As the great legal historian James Willard Hurst explained, the colonial courts of general jurisdiction (civil and criminal) were laid out almost on a neighborhood basis: the geographic scope of a court was determined by the distance that a person could ride a horse in one day, which frequently coincided with the boundaries of a county. The first state constitutions followed this same pattern. One of the unique features of these courts was the overall independence they exercised over case flow, finances, and court administration. This emphasis on localism continued in most states well into the twentieth century and produced an often luxuriant crop of frequently parochial courts. As the political scientist Harry Stumpf points out, by 1920 the Chicago metropolitan area had more than 500 different courts.

Participants in the emerging commercial market economy, however, increasingly demanded that hierarchy, specialization, and professionalism be imposed on the courts. During the nineteenth century the courts gradually devolved from their initial three-tiered ordering (a variety of courts of limited jurisdiction at the bottom, state trial courts of general jurisdiction in the middle, and an appellate court at the top) into what was typically a five-layered system.

The bottom layer comprised justice of the peace or magistrate courts, the latter to be found largely in rural areas. The second layer grew out of the inadequacies of the first as, at the end of the nineteenth century, a few states began to establish municipal courts of limited jurisdiction, accompanied by specialized courts such as those devoted to juveniles. At the next, third, level one finds trial courts of general jurisdiction, which handled both civil and criminal matters. The fourth layer again emerged in the late nineteenth and early twentieth centuries, when many states created intermediate courts of appeals primarily in response to population growth and attendant rising rates of litigation and greater demands on the courts. Given the rapid expansion of judicial business, intermediate appellate courts were designed to filter cases on appeal and so reduce the workload of the fifth and final tier, the highest appellate courts, which were usually called supreme courts.

State Courts of Limited Jurisdiction

The bulk of the legal business in the United States was handled by the first two tiers of state courts, those of limited and specialized jurisdiction. These courts had the most direct impact on the day-to-day lives of citizens, whether rich or poor, native or foreign born. Taken together, these courts heard about 80 percent of all legal disputes and in almost all instances their decisions were final.

The courts of limited jurisdiction had a broad range of responsibilities and modest resources with which to exercise them. In criminal matters they dealt with minor offenses, such as petty larceny and burglary, and had the power to impose only limited punishments – fines, usually by 1920 no more than $1,000, and jail terms, usually not longer than 12 months. These offenses constituted the great majority of all criminal matters, which meant that most criminal justice was meted out by underfunded and understaffed courts in often hurried and uneven ways. Nor did courts at this level keep any comprehensive record of their proceedings. Many kept no record at all. The lack of records meant appeals were difficult and infrequent.

Until the first third of the twentieth century the judges of these courts had either little or no training in the law. Initially appointed from local elites, by the third decade of the nineteenth century the great majority of judges at the lowest levels were elected, most on partisan ballots, and held their offices for limited terms. When Tocqueville visited the United States, the practice of electing inferior court judges was sufficiently widespread that it drew his attention and wrath. Like more recent critics of judicial elections, Tocqueville concluded that election coupled with limited terms reduced the independence of judges and left them vulnerable to the prevailing political winds.

The judicial role itself was not well defined. In rural areas and small towns, judges often held other positions, serving, for example, as ex officio coroners. Numerous studies have revealed that judges of courts of limited jurisdiction tended to show a strong presumption about the guilt of those who appeared before them and, as a result, focused their attention not on questions of guilt or innocence but rather on the sentence to be imposed. They were usually compensated by fees rather than salary, which meant that their incomes varied according to the proportions in which those brought before them were adjudged guilty.

State Courts of General Jurisdiction

The trial courts of general jurisdiction formed the next layer. When Americans think of courts, it is these, which hear and decide civil and criminal matters at trial, that they generally have in mind. While similar in character they often varied in actual operation. For example, in many states, these courts heard appeals from lower courts of limited jurisdiction in addition to functioning as courts of original jurisdiction. In some states, the jurisdiction of these courts was divided into two divisions, one civil and the other criminal. Courts of general jurisdiction had an array of names, which could imply that similar courts enjoyed very different jurisdictional capacities: In California, for example, courts at this level were known as superior courts, in other states they were circuit or district courts, and in New York they were called supreme courts. (In that state, the highest appellate court became the Court of Appeals.) The judges of these courts of general jurisdiction invariably had formal legal training, were better paid than their counterparts on courts of limited jurisdiction, and enjoyed better facilities. After mid-century they too were almost always elected to office, for limited terms of service. Courts of general jurisdiction were also courts of record, which meant that taking appeals from them was far easier than with courts of limited jurisdiction.

Trial courts of general jurisdiction were the principal places in the legal system where grievances of the most serious kind were converted into formal legal disputes. Most of their business was civil rather than criminal – some 60 percent of the trials held in the United States during the nineteenth century involved civil, not criminal matters. Reliant in most instances on juries to render verdicts, the trial courts performed the vital function of taking complex grievances and addressing them through an adversarial process. This forced aggrieved parties to frame their disputes in formal, legal ways. For example, a person injured in a railroad accident would make a claim based on the emerging law of torts, a business person attempting to collect money would turn to the law of contract, and so forth. The legal framing of these disputes was important because the time and cost associated with doing so more often than not prompted a settlement without resort to a formal trial. As is true today, the pattern was for parties to settle their differences before having a jury do it for them. And, just as today, litigants with greater resources had a better chance of prevailing when they did go to trial.

These phenomena were not confined to civil litigation. Out-of-court settlements occurred in criminal trial courts where they were known as plea bargains. There too, defendants with money to buy the best legal counsel were at a major advantage. Most perpetrators of crimes in the nineteenth century were never caught, let alone brought to court. Those most likely to be caught and charged were persons committing the most serious crimes (rape, murder, theft, burglary); murder showed the highest rate of success. Property crimes were far less likely to be cleared. Overall, less than 2 percent of all reported crimes resulted in final settlement by trial and verdict. Instead, plea bargains, supervised and approved by trial court judges, were struck.

The courts of general jurisdiction bore the brunt of a surging population, an accelerating economy, and the inevitable recourse to law that accompanied both. The composition of their dockets mirrored the social and economic circumstances of industrialization. By 1890, civil trial courts in Boston, for example, had more than 20,000 plaintiffs a year. The courts were asked to address issues involving business relationships, real estate transactions, financial arrangements, and injuries associated with the growing complexity of urban life. The courts became safety valves of sorts, mediating conflicts among strangers stemming from business transactions or transportation accidents. The vast majority of these cases were cut-and-dried. Debt collection was the main theme: grocers, clothing stores, and doctors asked the courts to make their debtors pay. In 1873, Ohio's courts of general jurisdiction handed down more than 15,000 civil judgments worth more than $8.5 million. In December 1903, there were more than 5,100 cases on the dockets of Kansas City's courts, about 60 percent of them liability claims against companies.

As the civil business of the courts increased, the inability of the era's generally decentralized and unprofessional court system to deal with the results became ever more evident. In 1885, a special committee of the American Bar Association found that under then-existing conditions, processing a lawsuit all the way to decision took from one and a half to six years. In 1876, New Hampshire's county circuit courts had 4,400 cases continued on their dockets; 6,000 new cases were added the following year. Crowded dockets and delays were the norm. The rising professional bar demanded more courts and more judges. In the Progressive era, in some instances, the bar would have its demands answered.

State Appellate Courts

Business grew at the top of the hierarchy no less than everywhere else in the judicial system. By 1900 the work of the nation's appellate courts amounted to about 25,000 cases annually. These cases sustained more than 400 different series of case reports. New York's famous Court of Appeals, perhaps the most revered high court in the late nineteenth century, handed down almost 600 decisions a year. Between 1890 and 1920, the Illinois Supreme Court produced between 700 and 900 decisions annually. The California Supreme Court in 1860 published about 150 opinions. By 1890 that number had tripled. By 1920, however, organizational changes instituted by Progressive reformers had cut the court's output by more than half. One of the most important innovations adopted was establishment of an intermediate court of appeals designed specifically to relieve the workload of the high court. Other states soon joined California in this reform effort.

Intermediate courts of appeal had not existed through most of the nineteenth century. By the beginning of the twentieth century, however, they had emerged as an increasingly popular solution to the problem of rapidly expanding appellate dockets. By 1911, thirteen states had created intermediate appellate courts. A century later, forty-two states had done so. The reform clearly reduced the flow of cases going to the highest appellate courts. More important, by granting the judges of the highest appellate courts choice over the appeals they heard, they allowed state high courts to set their own agendas.

The diffuse nature of the American appellate courts reflected historical practices and traditions of the bar that varied from state to state, as well as differing assumptions among constitution writers about how best to fit courts to social needs. The confusing nomenclature of these courts makes the point. For example, the highest court of last resort in Maine and Massachusetts was called the Supreme Judicial Court; in Maryland and New York it was known as the Court of Appeals; in Ohio it was called the Supreme Court. In most states the intermediate appellate courts were separate entities, but in a few states, such as Texas beginning in 1891, these courts were formed into separate divisions for criminal and civil appeals.

Appellate courts had to contend with state legislatures jealous to preserve their own prerogatives from trespass by other branches of government. This meant, among other things, that initially in the nineteenth century they put judges on short leashes and limited judicial authority. Thus, in 1809 the Ohio Senate tried Judges George Tod and Calvin Pease for subverting the state constitution by undertaking as judges to pass on the constitutionality of an act of the legislature. Both trials ended with 'guilty' votes of a majority of the senators – one short of the two-thirds required for conviction.

Early in the Republic, many state legislatures continued the colonial practice of themselves acting as appellate tribunals, setting aside judicial decisions on their own authority. The willingness of the legislatures to do so suggests their inheritance from the pre–Revolutionary era of a certain distrust of courts, which were seen as arbitrary and coercive. The same distrust is evident in most state constitutions, which designed courts with blended common law and equity jurisdiction because of lingering fears about the discretionary powers of equity courts. Despite these difficult beginnings, between 1790 and 1920 state appellate courts acquired an increasingly greater level of authority and control over their dockets, a pattern that paralleled developments in the federal courts.

Notwithstanding their diversity, the state courts of last resort shared several similarities. On each court, appeals were heard by a relatively small number of judges (from three to nine) serving fixed terms (on average about seven years; a very few state judges, like their federal counterparts, enjoyed tenure during good behavior). State appellate judges were invariably active politically before their judicial service; after mid-century they reached their posts most frequently through popular, partisan elections. Appellate judges had formal legal training, typically during the nineteenth century by reading in the office of a lawyer or with a judge; by 1920 about 65 percent of appeals court judges had either attended or graduated from law schools. Increasingly, judges joining the courts came from less privileged backgrounds with fewer connections through birth and marriage to other lawmakers. Finally, every state court of last resort enjoyed final authority to determine the meaning of the state's constitution.

The highest state courts were kept generally busy throughout the century. Their sustained engagement in the legal affairs of the state meant that they were deeply implicated in shaping and maintaining the social order. In the pre–Civil War South, for example, these courts regularly heard cases involving slavery, ranging from the power of masters to discipline their slaves to the legitimacy of contracts made for the sale and transport of human chattel. Most slave justice occurred beyond the reach of the rule of law. From time to time, however, slaves and their masters came into the courtroom, even into the highest courts of appeal. Judge Joseph Henry Lumpkin of the Georgia Supreme Court in 1852 acknowledged the paradox of giving any expression to the idea of legal rights when it came to a slave. Lumpkin appreciated the humanity of the slave, but he accepted at the same time that the slave could never stand as an equal, either to his or her master or to the state of Georgia. Under such circumstances the court might have paternalistically protected the interests of the slave. For example, when Lumpkin considered an appeal by a slave convicted of rape, he noted that "a controversy between the State of Georgia and a *slave* is so unequal, as of itself to divest the mind of all warmth and prejudice, and enable it to exercise its judgment in the most temperate manner." That said, Lumpkin sustained the slave's guilty verdict and subsequent hanging. Other Southern judges took the slave's humanity into account. In *Ford v. Ford* (1846), Nathan Green of the Tennessee Supreme Court ordered a slave freed through a will despite the contention of his deceased master's family that a slave could not possibly sue in a court.

After the war these same courts had to address issues of racial segregation. In almost every instance they upheld the power of the state to discriminate. Nor was court tolerance of discrimination a peculiarity of the South. Racial groups outside the South won no more support from the highest appellate courts. The California Supreme Court refused to block the state legislature from imposing special liabilities on Chinese and Japanese immigrants, including limiting their rights to hold and use real property. Women fared little better. The Illinois Supreme Court, for example, in 1872 denied Myra Bradwell, who founded and published the *Chicago Legal News*, admission to the bar because she was a woman.

In every state economic change imposed heavy demands on the highest appellate courts of the states. From 1870 to 1900 more than one-third of the cases decided in these courts dealt with business matters, such as contract, debt, corporations, and partnerships. Another 21 percent involved real property. Thereafter, litigation patterns began to shift gradually away from business and property disputes and toward torts, criminal, and public law matters. By 1920, litigants were coming to realize that alternative ways of handling disputes, such as arbitration, were preferable to the courts, where outcomes were expensive, technical, and above all slow to eventuate.

We have seen that during the first half of the nineteenth century, state appellate courts found themselves confronted by legislatures anxious to constrain the encroachment of judicial authority on their own prerogatives. By the middle of the century, however, the authority of legislatures was coming under general attack, the outcome of growing public concern over corruption and the fiscal problems that legislative corruption imposed on the citizenry. The result was a tendency among constitutional reformers to add to the authority of state courts of last resort by providing for the popular election of their judges to limited terms of office. In 1832, Mississippi became the first state to make provision for election of state appellate judges, followed quickly by New York, Ohio, and several other states. Of twenty-one constitutional conventions held between 1842 and 1860, nineteen approved constitutions that allowed the people to elect their judges, often on partisan ballots. Only in Massachusetts and New Hampshire did delegates repudiate the concept, and in both instances voters rejected the delegates' work. On the eve of the Civil War, twenty-one of the thirty states had adopted popular election. While this reform is usually interpreted as an attempt to limit judicial authority, it was intended to do just the opposite. With the wind of popular election at their back, state appellate court judges began passing on the constitutionality of legislation at an unprecedented rate.

Before the Civil War, review of state statutes by state courts was "a rare, extraordinary event." Before 1861, for example, the Virginia Court of Appeals, the state's highest appellate court, had decided only thirty-five cases in which the constitutionality of a law was in question. Of these, the judges overturned the legislature on only four occasions. The Supreme Judicial Court of Massachusetts, one of the two or three most prestigious appellate courts in the nation before the Civil War (and one that to this day has appointed rather than elected judges), had by 1860 considered the constitutionality of sixty-two laws. It struck down only ten. Over the following sixty years, however, judicial review became an important practice in state courts of last resort and, if still controversial, an accepted feature of public life. The Virginia Court of Appeals, for example, found against one in every three of the statutes that came before it during the last third of the nineteenth century. Ohio's Supreme Court held 15 state laws unconstitutional in the 1880s, 42 in the 1890s, and more than 100 in the first decade of the twentieth century. The Minnesota Supreme Court in the period between 1885 and 1899 struck down approximately seventy statutes; the Utah Supreme court between 1893 and 1896 threw out eleven of the twenty-two statutes brought before it.

Judicial review went hand in hand with new legal doctrines designed to address the consequences of industrialization. One of the most important was the doctrine of "substantive due process," by which courts held it appropriate to judge the constitutionality of legislative action not simply according to procedural criteria of fairness but by examination of substantive outcomes. The *American Law Review* summed the matter up nicely at the end of the nineteenth century: "it has come to be the fashion . . . for courts to overturn acts of the State legislatures upon mere economical theories and upon mere casuistical grounds." The New York Court of Appeals set the doctrinal stage in the 1856 case of *Wynehamer v. People*, when it invoked substantive due process to strike down a law designed to regulate the liquor business. Thereafter the doctrine grew luxuriantly. The Iowa Supreme Court in 1900 nullified a statute that permitted the use of oil for lighting purpose only in lamps made by a particular manufacturer, but not in other lamps. The judges reasoned that any manufacturer capable of producing the required oil should be able to sell it to whomever they pleased.

By the early twentieth century, state courts were regularly striking down statutes based on their reading of state constitutions. Because state constitutions had become both longer and more code-like in character over the course of the nineteenth century, the courts of last resort found more and more grounds on which to act. Between 1903 and 1908, for example, state courts struck down more than 400 laws. Although the state appellate judiciaries generally held office for limited terms, judges claimed that election provided them sufficient popular support to legitimize their interventions.

The tendency to increased judicial activism needs to be kept in perspective. State appellate courts upheld the vast majority of economic regulatory legislation, leaving legislatures to apply state police powers broadly. Legislation that remained unquestioned included, for example, regulation of the professions, development of a system of occupational licenses, and limitations on the hours and conditions of labor. Still, appellate judges by 1920 had firmly established their right to decide conclusively what their state constitutions meant.

State Courts and Reform

The claim of judicial review drew the attention of Progressive reformers. State judges, they argued, exercised their powers of review indiscriminately; they campaigned for office by promising that once on the bench they would decide issues not on the merits but with particular, predetermined outcomes in mind. The American Judicature Society took steps to promote adoption of non-partisan judicial elections, as well as measures to force disclosure of the sources of contributions to judicial election campaigns, and to encourage greater judicial professionalization. The most important gains occurred in heavily urban states, such as New York, where judicial corruption and boss-driven politics were connected. The Society's greatest success would not come until the 1940s, however, when it pioneered the so-called Merit or Missouri Plan of judicial selection to reduce partisanship and electioneering in judicial selection.

The attack on accepted partisan forms of judicial election was one facet of a broader effort to rein in the direct impact of politics on the courts while elevating the professional administration of justice generally. Future Harvard Law School dean Roscoe Pound initiated this movement in 1906 when he authored a wholesale indictment of the shortcomings of state court systems. State courts, Pound charged, were rife with corruption and influence-peddling. They were also by and large completely incoherent in their approaches to law, notably at the lower levels of limited and general jurisdiction. As illustration of the state courts' shortcomings, Pound brought up the example of New York judge Albert Cardozo, father of future Supreme Court Justice Benjamin Cardozo, who some thirty years before had been convicted and jailed for taking bribes. Pound's report concluded that each state's courts should function as an integrated system in order to break down what Pound viewed as a destructive pattern of local autonomy. That meant, among other things, bringing greater administrative coherence to their operation, so that courts located beside one another would in fact know what the other was doing. The goal was to unify the court structure by consolidating and simplifying its management, budgeting, financing, and rule making. Pound's unification movement was only beginning to gather steam by 1920, and it has proceeded by fits and starts since then. For all of these reform efforts, the state courts remained very much creatures of the political cultures in which they operated.

Pound's call for reform blended with growing demands after the Civil War from the developing legal profession to improve the quality of state courts. As lawyers organized themselves as a profession, they expected judges to become more professional as well. First, new state bar associations, then the American Bar Association, founded in 1878, and then the American Judicature Society campaigned to improve municipal and metropolitan courts and to promote specialization of courts. For example, the movement to record proceedings in several major municipal court systems dates to the early twentieth century. Several states, following the model of the first juvenile court in Chicago in 1899, began to adopt statewide systems of specialized courts that provided consistency and predictability in application of the law. Growing concerns about the fate of juveniles were echoed in increasing doubts about the viability of the family and the adequacy of the existing court structure to deal with matters of adoption, divorce, and child custody. In 1914 Cincinnati pioneered the development of courts with jurisdiction over cases involving both children and families. Similar courts appeared shortly thereafter in other selected cities, including Des Moines, Iowa; St. Louis, Missouri; Omaha, Nebraska; Portland, Oregon; Gulfport, Mississippi; and Baton Rouge, Louisiana.

The rise of a class of consumers generated a new stratum of small claims courts, although they did not necessarily function to protect the buyer. The first small claims court in the United States was established in 1913 in Cleveland as the Conciliation Branch of the Municipal Court. The movement subsequently spread across the nation. Ironically, what was viewed at its inception as a reform designed to give the common person easy access to justice and to unclog the existing courts to deal with more serious matters often became instead a means for doctors, utility managers, and department store heads to collect debts owed by persons usually of modest income.

State courts formed the core of the new American legal system, dispensing justice over a broad area in increasingly greater numbers. To all intents and purposes, justice from 1790 to 1920 meant predominantly local justice meted out through local judges embodying the power of the state. This very localism was a source of considerable strength, but also, as Willard Hurst has observed, increasingly of limitation. As the Republic matured, as affairs of economy, society and state grew ever more complex and intertwined, state courts became increasingly vulnerable to incursions from the federal judiciary.

III. THE CONSTITUTION AND THE ESTABLISHMENT OF THE FEDERAL COURTS

The steady expansion of judicial power in nineteenth-century state courts was matched by similar developments in the federal judiciary. What emerged by 1920 was a uniquely American scheme of courts, characterized in particular by a substantially more powerful and influential federal court system than had been in existence at the nation's inception.

The federal Constitution crafted in 1787 was designed to bolster the authority of the national government through the establishment of an independent federal judiciary. While the debates in the Constitutional Convention gave relatively little attention to the issue of courts, the document that emerged sketched an entirely new court system, most fully realized in Article III, but with implications for the federal courts' structure and function scattered also through Articles I, IV, and VI.

Article III established "constitutional courts" based on "the judicial power of the United States," vested in "one Supreme Court, and in such inferior Courts as the Congress may from time to time ordain and establish." As in so many other instances, the framers drew on their state experience in establishing the federal judiciary. Most of them embraced the idea that the federal courts would curb popular excesses while preserving minority rights of property holders. James Wilson was a notable exception; he believed that the federal judiciary derived its authority as much from the people as did the elected members of the executive and legislative branches. The second most active voice in the Convention, Wilson insisted that the power of judges derived not just from their knowledge of the law but also from the direct grant of authority made by the people to them when the Constitution was created.

The federal courts drew intense scrutiny in the ratification debates, and they remained a source of controversy throughout the nineteenth century. Supporters of the new federal judiciary downplayed their importance. Alexander Hamilton insisted in *Federalist 78*, for example, that the courts would be "the least dangerous branch" because they had access to neither purse nor sword. According to Hamilton, the federal courts would exercise judgment instead of will, and law instead of politics. These together – probity and the rule of law – would become the bedrock of the federal courts' authority. Behind Hamilton's words lay a deeper understanding that the success of the American economy depended on federal courts strong enough to impose a national rule of law, one that would bring stability and order to the new nation's commercial and financial dealings.

Anti-Federalist opponents of the Constitution, on the other hand, viewed the federal courts as a threat to the sovereign rights of the states and even to the liberty of the American people. Robert Yates, of New York, insisted that the Congress, being accountable to the people, should be the final interpreter of the Constitution and that the role of the new federal courts should be strictly limited. He and other opponents of the federal Constitution argued that by making the courts and their judges "totally independent, both of the people and the legislature . . . [we] are . . . placed in a situation altogether unprecedented in a free country."[1]

Article III secured two great structural principles: federalism and the separation of powers. The Supreme Court became the nation's highest appellate court (it heard cases brought on appeal from other federal and state courts). The lower federal courts were to operate as the trial courts of the federal system, with special responsibilities initially in the areas of admiralty and maritime law. The strong nationalists in the Philadelphia Convention had wanted to specify the structure of the lower federal courts, since they feared that without doing so the already established state courts would dominate the interpretation of federal law. The strongest advocates of state power in the Convention, such as Yates, proposed precisely the opposite – that the task of interpreting the federal Constitution and conducting federal trials should be assigned to these same state courts.

The two sides settled their differences over the federal courts by deferring many issues to the first Congress and by leaving the key provisions of the Constitution dealing with the courts vague. This approach stood in contrast to state constitutional documents that typically spelled out in detail the structure of state courts. Article III did mandate the Supreme Court, but it left Congress to determine its size and the scope of its appellate jurisdiction. The Constitution granted the Supreme Court only a limited original jurisdiction in matters involving ambassadors, other public ministers and consuls, and those in which a state was a party. The Constitution was also silent on the question of the qualifications of the justices and the judges of the lower courts. For example, there was no constitutional requirement that a judge be an attorney, although throughout the history of the nation only persons trained in the law have served on the federal bench.

Finally, the Constitution failed to specify one of the federal judiciary's most important powers: judicial review, the practice by which judges declare unconstitutional acts of Congress and state legislatures. The framers certainly anticipated that judicial review would be exercised; the only unknown was its scope. Anti-Federalist Luther Martin, for example, observed during the convention that "As to the constitutionality of laws, that point will come before the Judges in their proper official character. In this character they have a negative on the laws." It did not follow, however, that they could

[1] *Essays of Brutus*, No. XI, reprinted in Herbert J. Storing, *The Complete Anti-Federalist* (1981), 2, § 2.9.135.

do what they wanted; delegates of every ideological stripe posited a sharp distinction between constitutional interpretation necessary to the rule of law and judicial lawmaking. "The judges," concluded John Dickinson, a Federalist, "must interpret the laws; they ought not to be legislators."

There was, however, a textual basis for the exercise of federal judicial review, especially of state laws. Article VI made the Constitution the "supreme Law of the Land," and in Article III the courts were named as interpreters of the law. The same conclusion can be reached by combining Article I, section 10, which placed certain direct limitations on the state legislatures, with the Supremacy Clause and Article VI. Simply put, judicial review of state legislation was an absolute necessity under the framers' compound system of federalism. Here too, nevertheless, the scope of the power remained to be defined. "The Framers anticipated some sort of judicial review," the famed constitutional scholar Edward S. Corwin observed. Of that, "there can be little question. But it is equally without question that ideas generally current in 1787 were far from presaging the present vast role of the Court."

Article III also conferred jurisdiction (the authority by which a court can hear a legal claim) in two categories. The first was based on subject and extended to all cases in law and equity arising under the Constitution, laws, and treaties of the United States, as well as cases of admiralty and maritime. The second category depended on the nature of the parties in legal conflict. This jurisdiction included controversies between citizens of different states, between a state and citizens of another state, between states, and between states and the nation.

Most of the delegates to the federal convention appreciated that the rule of law in a republican government required an independent national judiciary that would be only indirectly accountable. Thus, they granted the president authority to appoint federal judges with the advice and consent of the Senate. Once commissioned, these judges held office during good behavior, their salaries could not be diminished while in office, and they were subject to removal from office only "on Impeachment for, and Conviction of, Treason, Bribery, or other high Crimes and Misdemeanors."

More telling than the generalities of the Constitution itself, the single most important moment in the development of the federal courts was the Judiciary Act of 1789, a statute whose impact continues to this day. In debating what to do with the federal courts, the first Congress echoed the sentiments of the often conflicted delegates in Philadelphia. Critics of the federal courts in the first Congress continued to insist that they were not necessary, that their roles could be performed by state courts, and that they were, in any case, a "burdensome and needless expense." These debates remind us of the inherent localism of the American court system. Opponents claimed that federal judges would be remote and insensitive to state and local issues and that those persons charged with crimes would be hauled from their homes and tried in faraway places where they and their good characters would not be known. Proponents of a strong national government, led by Senator Oliver Ellsworth of Connecticut, prevailed, and in the Judiciary Act of 1789 Congress exercised its powers to create lower federal courts, just as the Federalists had desired. However, the Act lodged the new courts squarely in the states, a decision meant to placate Anti-Federalists. This politically acceptable compromise established a federal court organization that remained in broad terms unchanged for more than a century.

The 1789 act divided the new nation into thirteen districts and made the boundaries of the courts in these districts coterminous with those of the states. (Massachusetts and Virginia received two each, Rhode Island and North Carolina none because at the time they were still not members of the Union.) The act also divided the country into three circuits, in each of which a circuit court consisting of two justices of the Supreme Court and one district judge in the circuit would sit twice a year. The circuit courts, whose history was to be unsettled for more than a century, entertained appeals from the district courts below and held jury trials involving the most serious criminal and civil cases to which the federal government was a party. The Supreme Court itself was composed of five associate justices and a chief justice.

The act made Supreme Court justices into republican schoolmasters whose presence in the circuits symbolized the authority of the remote national government. Circuit riding, which persisted in various ways throughout the nineteenth century, also exposed the justices, in their capacity as trial judges, to local concerns. However, circuit riding was unpopular with the justices, for it exacted a heavy physical and mental toll. Justice William Patterson would complain bitterly that his travels through Vermont were so arduous that "[I] nearly went out of my head."

The 1789 act confirmed the power of Congress over the jurisdiction of the lower courts, and indeed over their very existence. Their allotted jurisdiction consisted of admiralty cases (given exclusively to the district courts) and cases concerning diversity of citizenship, with a limited appellate jurisdiction in the circuit courts over district court decisions. Federalists did succeed in section 25 of the act in allowing federal courts to review state court decisions involving federal laws and the Constitution, a provision that stirred heated debate until the Civil War. The new structure was notable because it actually withheld from the federal courts the potentially much broader power to hear all cases arising under the Constitution. As a result, for more than three-quarters of a century state courts played a distinctive role in interpreting the nation's ruling document and some of the laws associated with it.

While the creation of a federal court structure below the level of the Supreme Court had a strong nationalizing impact, the provisions of the 1789 act also recognized the strongly local quality of the courts. District judges, for example, not only lived among the people they served, but section 34 directed that on comparable points of law federal judges had to regard holdings in state courts as the rule of decision in their courts. Furthermore, district court judges were to be recruited from local political and legal backgrounds, and these lineages made them susceptible to the immediate pressures in the friends and neighbors who appear before them and whose lives were often directly affected by their decisions. These federal district courts and the judges that presided over them were a kind of hybrid institution, organized by the federal Constitution but sensitive to state interests. The upshot was that during the course of the nineteenth century the federal courts only gradually pulled even with the state courts in prestige and power.

IV. THE FEDERAL COURTS

As was true at the state level, the history of the federal courts from 1790 to 1920 shows consistent attempts to shape the courts' structure and jurisdiction in ways intended to produce a political and legal advantage for the majority in control at any particular moment. Over time, the federal courts grew more influential, more controversial, and, ironically, more widely accepted than at the time of the nation's founding.

The structure of the courts has generated political debate for more than two centuries. Throughout, the forces of localism, political influence, and administrative efficiency have tugged at one another. Circuit riding and the larger issue of the organization of the federal courts offer appropriate examples.

Circuit riding was one of the administrative weaknesses but political benefits of the new federal court structure established by the 1789 Judiciary Act. The first members of the Supreme Court were assigned not only to meet in the nation's capital (initially New York City) to hear and decide cases but also to hold courts in designated circuits. The practice, however, imposed often severe physical hardships on the justices, who faced the daunting task of traveling over poor roads and hazardous rivers. In 1793 the Federalist Congress bowed to pressure from the justices and made a minor change in the system by providing that only one justice rather than three had to serve in a circuit. More fundamental change took place in 1801, as the Federalist Party was going out of office. Congress in the Judiciary Act of that year abolished circuit riding altogether and created in its place an expanded circuit court system to be staffed by its own appointed judges. The change had the immediate political benefit of granting John Adams' outgoing Federalist administration the opportunity to appoint a host of politically loyal judges. A year later, however, newly elected President Thomas Jefferson and the Jeffersonian Republican majority in the Congress reintroduced a system of six circuits, to each of which one Supreme Court justice and one district court judge were assigned. The new federal circuit courts were abolished; not until 1869 were separate circuit court judgeships reestablished. The Jeffersonian Republicans were no fans of the federal courts in any case, and they took some delight in imposing circuit court riding duties on Supreme Court justices. The new circuits, which became essentially trial courts rather than courts of appeal, proved as unwieldy for the justices as they had before.

The justices found circuit riding increasingly oppressive, especially in the newly expanding western regions of the country. By 1838, for example, the number of federal circuits had risen to nine. In that year the justices reported to Congress that they traveled an average of almost 3,000 miles a year, an astonishing distance given conditions of travel. Justice John McKinley traveled more than 10,000 miles in his circuit, composed of Alabama, Louisiana, Mississippi, and Arkansas. He reported that he had been unable to hold court in Little Rock because of a combination of flooding and bad roads.

Until the Civil War, the organization of the federal courts changed little. The war and the post-war period of Reconstruction, however, profoundly accelerated the push toward a stronger national government and a more powerful federal judiciary to uphold it. In 1875, the Republican-controlled Congress adopted a new judiciary act that expanded the jurisdiction of the federal courts far beyond the modest bounds established in 1789. Republicans expected the act to permit newly freed slaves to circumvent the prejudice of state courts, but in practice the law most benefited interstate businesses. The most important change was a provision granting the federal courts original jurisdiction based on the "arising under the Constitution" provision of Article III, or under national treaties, provided the matter in dispute exceeded $500. This meant that a litigant could initiate a case in a circuit court based on the assertion of any federal right. As important, a defendant who was brought into a state court could have the case removed to the ostensibly more neutral national forum of a federal court. Either party, then, could remove a case to federal court. In addition, any and all diversity suits could be removed, even when one of the parties did not live in the "forum" state (that is, they were not resident in the state where the federal court proceeding was to be held). Most important, the act permitted removal of all suits raising a question of federal law. Collectively, these provisions effectively encouraged the removal of suits from state to federal courts, from local to national forums of law.

The Judiciary Act of 1875 became a milestone in the history of the lower federal courts' relationship to the business community. The statute responded to surging national commerce, in particular to railroad corporations seeking relief from state courts in cases involving foreclosure, receivership, taxation, and even injuries to person and property. Not only traditional cases based on diversity jurisdiction were now before the federal courts, but all actions involving federal laws. The act meant that for the first time a generalized federal question jurisdiction had been established – a jurisdiction that, as Justice Felix Frankfurter once observed, has come to be the indispensable function of the federal courts.

One of the consequences of this expanded jurisdiction was that the caseloads of the federal courts soared. For example, in 1870 the Supreme Court docket listed 670 cases. By 1880 the number had more than doubled. In 1870 federal district and circuit court dockets listed some 29,000 cases. By 1890 the number was more than 54,000. The lower federal courts grew in prestige and importance, emerging as "forums of order" in which interstate businesses could secure a hearing free from the local interests to which state courts presumably paid greater attention. That process had begun in 1842 when Justice Joseph Story's decision in *Swift v. Tyson* established a federal common law of commerce. It gathered momentum after the Civil War and continued unchecked into the New Deal of the 1930s.

A doubling of caseloads without an increase in the number of federal judges prompted delays not only in hearing but even more important in deciding cases before the federal courts. Although litigants were keen to turn to the federal courts, especially in matters involving the regulation of business by state and federal governments, they often encountered delays of years in having suits resolved. Growing demand and the increasing importance of the federal courts also meant rising costs. Between 1850 and 1875, the expense of operating the federal courts rose six-fold, from $500,000 to $3 million. By 1900 the figure had tripled, to $9 million. By 1920 it stood at $18 million.

In 1891, at the behest of a combination of corporate entities and the newly minted American Bar Association, Congress passed a further Judiciary Act to address these organizational problems. The 1891 act established a new and badly needed layer of federal courts just below the Supreme Court: the U.S. Courts of Appeal. Two new judges were to be appointed in each of the nine federal circuits that now stretched from coast to coast. The act also provided that a Supreme Court justice might serve as a third judge in each of the new courts, but did not make the justice's participation compulsory:

If required, a district court judge could take the justice's place. The act did not do away with the existing circuit courts. Rather, the U.S. Courts of Appeal were to review appeals from both federal district and circuit courts. The lack of clarity in the relationship between the new courts of appeal and the existing circuit courts meant a degree of jurisdictional confusion.

Most significantly, the 1891 act increased the Supreme Court justices' control over their own docket. Congress provided that decisions in the new circuit courts of appeal would be final, subject in most cases only to a writ of certiorari issued by the Supreme Court. This new authority gave the justices greater ability to order their agenda based on their assessment of the significance of a particular constitutional controversy. The new Judiciary Act had the added effect of underscoring for litigants the importance of the lower federal courts, since from that point on their decisions were given an increased finality.

Three additional steps taken in the first quarter of the twentieth century completed the transformation of the federal courts. First came the Judiciary Act of 1911, which finally abolished the federal circuit courts reconstituted by the 1802 repeal of the previous year's Judiciary Act. The 1911 act transferred the circuit courts' powers to the federal district courts. Second, congressional legislation in 1922 authorized the Chief Justice to oversee the federal courts generally and to provide for the assignment of district court judges where they were needed outside their own district. The act also created the Judicial Conference of the United States, composed initially of senior federal judges and expanded subsequently to include all federal judges. The mission of the conferences was to provide regular surveys of the business in the various federal courts with an eye to transferring judges between districts and circuits as caseloads demanded.

The third and most far-reaching step was the Judiciary Act of 1925, popularly known as the Judges' Bill. The outcome in good part of tireless lobbying by Chief Justice William Howard Taft, one of the leading figures in court reform during the twentieth century, the 1925 Judiciary Act clarified the jurisdiction of the federal courts and formalized their three-tier structure: district trial courts, courts of appeal, and the Supreme Court. The act established the federal district courts as the preeminent federal trial courts equipped with extensive original jurisdiction. The courts of appeal were identified as the final resting place in federal appellate jurisdiction, for the measure further broadened the Supreme Court justices' discretion in exercising review of lower court decisions under the writ of certiorari, which necessarily further narrowed access by litigants as a matter of right. As in previous instances of federal judicial reform, the 1925 act responded to corporations interested in a uniform administration of justice and to bar groups bent on improving the efficiency of federal (but not state) courts.

One of the critical roles filled by the district courts was the supervision of bankruptcy. Article I, section 8, of the Constitution authorized Congress to establish "uniform Laws on the subject of Bankruptcies throughout the United States." In 1841 Congress enacted its first attempt at comprehensive bankruptcy legislation, setting out voluntary procedures for individuals and largely ending imprisonment except in cases of fraud. Opponents considered the act too protective of debtors, and it was repealed the following year. A similar act was passed in 1867 and remained in effect for the next two decades before it too was repealed. Finally, in 1898, Congress agreed on a comprehensive bankruptcy statute setting out a body of law that would last for almost a century. The act designated the U.S. district courts to serve as courts of bankruptcy. It also established the position of referee, appointed by district judges, to oversee the administration of bankruptcy cases and to exercise limited judicial responsibilities under the guidance of the district court.

During the nineteenth century Congress also created other specialized tribunals to deal with matters falling outside the jurisdictional specifications of Article III. Among these tribunals, territorial courts were of particular importance. Territorial courts were temporary federal tribunals established by Congress to extend federal justice into areas that had not yet achieved statehood but were possessions (territories) of the United States. Territorial courts combined the roles of both district and circuit courts. Their judges, for the most part, had limited terms of office and were appointed by the president with the advice and consent of the Senate. Unlike Article III judges, territorial court judges could be removed for misfeasance without impeachment. In 1900 there were six territorial courts. These courts were implicated in a wide range of non-commercial issues. For example, in 1874, Congress passed the Poland Act in an effort to stem the practice of polygamy in Utah by bringing the weight of the federal government to bear. That law assigned jurisdiction of polygamy trials to federal territorial courts there and further provided for polygamy convictions to be appealable to the U.S. Supreme Court. In 1878 the Supreme Court of the United States, in *Reynolds v. United States*, sustained a Utah territorial court's decisions upholding the conviction of Brigham Young's private secretary, George Reynolds, and declaring polygamy unconstitutional.

In 1855 Congress created another special non-Article III court, the Court of Claims. Like the judges of the federal courts of general jurisdiction – the Article III courts – the three judges of the Court of Claims were nominated by the president, confirmed by the Senate, and served with life tenure during good behavior. The Court had jurisdiction to hear and determine all monetary claims based on a congressional statute, an executive branch regulation, or a contract with the U.S. government.

Prior to the court's creation, claims against the government were submitted through petitions to Congress itself. The 1855 act relieved Congress of the workload, but preserved its traditional control over the expenditure of all public monies by requiring the new court to report on its determination of claims and prepare bills for payments to successful claimants. In 1863, the Court of Claims gained authority to issue its own decisions rather than report them to the legislature, but the revised statute still required that the Treasury Department prepare an estimate of appropriations necessary to meet determinations made by the court before any money was distributed. In 1865, this resulted in a refusal on the part of the Supreme Court to hear appeals from the Court of Claims because its decisions were subject to review by an executive department. Within a year, Congress repealed the provision for review by the Treasury and specifically provided for appeals to the Supreme Court. Twenty years later (1887) Congress expanded the jurisdiction of the Court of Claims by making it the principal forum for all claims against the federal government. It is worth noting that until 1946 this court provided the only legal channel available for Native American tribes contesting violations of treaties with the United States.

V. THE U.S. SUPREME COURT

Since the Founding Era, the U.S. Supreme Court has been the single institution with national authority to develop a uniform national law. But although it sat atop the federal judicial pyramid in the nineteenth century, it only gradually earned the power to say conclusively what the Constitution meant. In its earliest years, indeed, the Supreme Court enjoyed little of the stature it would later accumulate. Among the first justices appointed by President George Washington, one declined to serve in order to take a more prestigious position as state supreme court judge; another, though accepting the position, failed to appear for a single session of the Court. The first Chief Justice, John Jay, pursued diplomatic interests as aggressively as he did his duties on the bench. Eventually he resigned altogether to become governor of New York.

Delegates to the Philadelphia convention had agreed on the necessity of establishing a Supreme Court, but they had reached no consensus on its duties. Led by James Wilson, they had debated at length the creation of a Council of Revision, consisting of the president and a number of federal judges (James Madison's Virginia plan) or cabinet officers (Charles Pinckney's proposal) to review federal (and perhaps state) legislation before it became law. That idea eventually gave way to the Supreme Court, the full scope of whose powers the delegates never defined fully. The president was given authority to appoint the justices, with the advice and consent of the Senate, and the members of the Court were to serve during good behavior, subject, like other Article III judges, to removal by impeachment of a majority in the House of Representatives and conviction by a vote of two-thirds of the members of the Senate. Of the 110 justices who have served on the high court to date, only one, Samuel Chase in 1804, has ever been impeached. Chase escaped conviction the following year.

Over the course of the nineteenth century the authorized size of the Court varied from six to ten, changing – in response both to the expansion of the federal circuit system and to political pressures – on no less than six occasions before 1869, when the present number of nine was established. Every justice appointed to the high court during these years (and indeed through 1967) was a white male.

The Supreme Court's original jurisdiction, as outlined in Article III, was modest. It was further limited early in the Court's career by the famous case of *Marbury v. Madison* (1803), in the course of which the Court itself decided that jurisdiction to issue writs of mandamus directed to other branches of government, as provided in the 1789 Judiciary Act, was unconstitutional. Cases heard under original jurisdiction, however, comprise only a tiny fraction of the Court's business, slightly more than 150 cases in the past two centuries. That jurisdiction extended only to "all cases affecting ambassadors, other public ministers and consuls, and those in which a state shall be a party." The Court, further, has never accepted that it has no discretion to refuse such cases; instead, it has declined to hear cases in its original jurisdiction unless there is compelling reason to do so. Through 1920, the cases that it did accept involved disputes over state boundary lines and water rights between two or more states.

By far the most important jurisdiction granted the Court was appellate. During the nineteenth century the justices steadily expanded that jurisdiction and by 1925, as we have seen, they had also gained significant control over their docket. Part of their motivation in doing so reflected the growing belief, as Tocqueville noted, that political matters were, for purposes of political stability, better managed through legal and judicial processes than by political branches alone. To an important extent, then, the power of the Supreme Court developed because Congress was willing for the sake of political expediency to leave difficult matters of public policy, such as the question of whether slavery could exist in the territories, to be shaped by the Court through law rather than politics. But the expansion of the Court's appellate jurisdiction was also prompted by Congress's belief, usually driven by demands from lawyers and the business community, that it would contribute to enhanced efficiency in the Court's operations and enhanced uniformity in federal law across the circuits and throughout the states.

Originally, cases were appealed most frequently to the Court based on a claim that an error had been committed in a court below. The justices, under this system, had little discretion over their docket. Thus, as the caseload of the federal courts grew, so too did the numbers of appeals. During its first decade, the Court heard fewer than 100 cases. By the mid-1880s the high court had more than 25,000 cases docketed, and it decided as many as 300 in a single year. Congress, however, has consistently given the high court greater discretion over its docket, with clear results. As it became more difficult for a case to reach the Supreme Court, the decisions of the justices became correspondingly more important, with public attention increasingly focused on them.

The history of the high court up to 1920 was the history of vital leadership. The justices played a decisive although often controversial role in public affairs, expanding their influence often while disavowing that they either wanted or should have such influence. For example, in addressing a directive from Congress to seat federal judges as pension claims commissioners, Chief Justice John Jay stated in *Hayburn's Case* (1793) that Congress could only assign judges to judicial and not administrative duties. The same year, Jay refused President George Washington's request for an advisory interpretation of the 1773 Franco-American treaty. By limiting the Court to actual cases and controversies, the early justices assured themselves that when they spoke they did so in ways that would have direct rather than imagined consequences, while also avoiding overt political and policy involvements.

Chief Justice John Marshall (1803–35) built on this early foundation by establishing the authority of the Court to interpret conclusively the meaning of the Constitution. He did so by confirming the Court's capacity to exercise judicial review – first for federal legislation in *Marbury v. Madison* (1803), in which the Court declared a portion of the Judiciary Act of 1789 unconstitutional; later for state legislation in such cases as *McCulloch v. Maryland* (1819), in which the Court voided a Maryland law imposing a tax on the Second Bank of the United States. The cost of this heightened judicial authority over constitutional interpretation was inevitably the judiciary's greater involvement in the political system.

Marshall's successors expanded the scope of judicial review and the prestige of the Court at the same time that they refused to adjudicate so-called political questions. In *Luther v. Borden* (1849), Chief Justice Roger B. Taney held that the question of which of two competing governments in Rhode Island was legitimate was entirely "political in nature." Therefore, Taney concluded, the political branches of the federal government, not the courts, could best determine whether Rhode Island or any other state had met the mandate of the Guarantee Clause of Article IV that each state have a republican form of government. The judiciary, Taney observed, had no role to play; its business was legal, not political.

Taney would himself succumb to the seductive influences of judicial power and in so doing provide a stark reminder of the costs to the high court of blurring the distinction between what was legal and what was political, between interpreting the law and making the law. In *Dred Scott v. Sandford* (1857), Taney spoke for a majority of the Court in attempting to settle the politically explosive issue of slavery in the territories by declaring that persons of African descent were not citizens of the United States and that they had no rights that white men were bound to respect. For good measure the Chief Justice made sure that incoming President James Buchanan, a supporter of slavery in the territories, knew of the Court's decision so that he could include an oblique reference to it in his inaugural address. Taney's opinion stirred outrage among free-state Republicans on the eve of the Civil War and sharply divided the public over how much power the justices should exercise. Similar outcries came when, in *Pollock v. Farmers Loan and Trust Company* (1895), a bare majority of the Court declared the federal income tax unconstitutional, a position that was not reversed until the ratification of the Sixteenth Amendment in 1913. A year later and with only one dissenting voice, *Plessey v. Ferguson* (1896) sustained segregation of the races based on the principle that separate but equal facilities met the requirements of the Equal Protection Clause of the Fourteenth Amendment.

The high court generally supported the regulatory efforts of both state and federal governments, but the justices learned that they too could employ substantive due process to block legislative action when it seemed appropriate to do so. In *Lochner v. New York* (1905), for example, a sharply divided court struck down a New York state law that prohibited bakers from working an excessive number of hours each week. The majority said that laborers should be free to strike whatever deal they could with an employer; Justice Oliver Wendell Holmes, Jr., in dissent insisted that the majority was merely reading an economic theory that favored business into the Constitution. Three years later, in *Muller v. Oregon*, the same court entirely ignored its *Lochner* precedent and decided to shine a paternal eye on women. A unanimous court held that the state of Oregon had power to regulate the conditions of labor of women because women were both emotionally and physically inferior to men. Progressive reformers argued that the Court needed to change and among the more aggressive suggestions was doing away with tenure during good behavior.

By 1920, both by design and circumstance, the purportedly apolitical Supreme Court had emerged as more than a court but less than a full-blown political institution. It was, in that regard, a metaphor for the entire American system of courts. What its history has repeatedly shown is a court that paradoxically functions of the world of politics without being directly in that world.

CONCLUSION: THE COURTS AND NINETEENTH-CENTURY CHANGE

Common law courts typically operate after the fact. They tend to respond to rather than anticipate change. The American court system between 1790 and 1920 exuded just such qualities. Litigants had to bring cases; lawyers representing them had to present arguments that squared precedent with new circumstances. But if continuity was a major chord, change and adaptation were certainly also present. Slavery, segregation, industrialization, massive influxes of foreign-born migrants, and the development of new technologies meant that courts could not simply do always as they had previously done. Nor did judges simply mirror the economic and social changes of the times through which they lived; they also attempted to shape the effects of change in allocating the costs, risks, and benefits of economic development while protecting individual property rights. In the process, they acquired new authority. By 1920 the courts exercised judicial review extensively, using that power to adjust the consequences of industrialization, sometimes by setting aside legislation and at other times by allowing it to stand. Even when they did not strike down a law, the simple fact that they were capable of exercising such a power made their capacity to limit legislative authority as important as the actual limits they imposed. The courts became better articulated with social and economic outcomes, and their judges more professional.

Courts' efforts to respond to the new industrial order were mixed, ambivalent, and even contradictory. They persisted to an extraordinary degree, even in states with elected judiciaries, in the belief that traditional property rights required continuing judicial protection. While judges were most often deferential to legislatures, they nevertheless recognized that property rights were sacrosanct. Breaking new legislative ground in matters of the rights of workers, African Americans, immigrants, or women was hence often beyond either their imaginative grasp or indeed their will to act. As the 1920s opened, nevertheless, there was no doubt that, for all of the diversity in the American system of judicial federalism, courts as a whole had established a firmer place in the American system of governance than they enjoyed at the nation's beginning.

5

CRIMINAL JUSTICE IN THE UNITED STATES, 1790–1920: A GOVERNMENT OF LAWS OR MEN?

ELIZABETH DALE

Histories of modern criminal justice are less studies of doctrine than they are examinations of the state, since it is generally assumed that the institutions of criminal justice – police, courts, and prisons – play an integral role in the process by which modern states maintain the order that advanced capitalist economies demand. But while most accounts of criminal justice in the modern West trace the way a formal, rational system of criminal justice based on the rule of law developed alongside a capitalist economy and a national state, the history of criminal law in the United States follows a different track. Although the long nineteenth century, stretching from ratification of the Constitution at one end to the close of World War I at the other, was marked by the emergence of an advanced, nationwide capitalist economy, it saw the development neither of a national state nor a national system of criminal justice.

Even as they position the United States outside the standard track of state development, histories of criminal law in the United States still trace its evolution along a parallel route, demonstrating that over the course of the long nineteenth century the country developed a *localized* state. It differed from the traditional state to the extent its scope was smaller, encompassing only the institutions of city, county, and state governments, instead of a national bureaucracy, and its operations were, as a result, on a smaller scale. But many have argued that its smaller scale was its greatest strength. Relative locality permitted a degree of popular participation unimaginable in a state based on national bureaucracies; the nineteenth-century American state encouraged popular sovereignty. The result, while not a traditional state in the Weberian sense, shared with the Weberian states an emphasis on law, criminal law in particular. Throughout the nineteenth-century United States (the slaveholding South is invariably the exception that proves the rule), the local state maintained order by channeling disputes into the state court system, which ruled according to locally understood norms, defined and applied by the people of the community. In addition to maintaining the discipline the national economy required, these local criminal courts offered opportunities for popular participation through service on juries, by means of private prosecutions, and by electing court judges. The breadth of participation was such that in much of the country (once again, the South was the exception) even those excluded from voting or holding office by reason of sex, race, or poverty could exercise some sovereignty through their involvement in the local courts.

The resulting history has been one of American distinctiveness, a unique, indigenous version of the rise of the state. But it has also been an extremely court-centered view. If the point of reference widens beyond the formal institutions of law, to consider what happened within the criminal justice system as part of what happened in the society outside the courts, the picture that emerges is no less distinctive, but considerably less uplifting. As we will see, the wider frame of reference raises serious questions about whether there ever was a state in the United States, even at the local level, during the long nineteenth century. Local governments, North and South, never developed the authority a state requires, with the result that they were never able to exercise a monopoly on violence or implement the certainty of a rule of law that state theory requires. Far from being instruments of popular sovereignty, local courts were all too often nothing more than tools of private justice, easily supplanted by extra-legal practices, while substantive law was ignored and unenforceable. Theories of punishment were undermined all too easily by private interests driven by a desire to make a profit rather than by theories of penology.

I elaborate on these contentions in what follows and, in so doing, construct an alternative history of criminal justice in the nineteenth-century United States. First, I revisit the ambiguous role that national government played in criminal law from the ratification of the Constitution to the Red Scare that came at the end of World War I. Then I turn to criminal justice at the local level. My exposition is arranged in the order of a criminal case: policing is followed by prosecution, and we end with a section on punishment. Each section canvasses local justice on a national scale, examining points of similarity and difference between the practices in the North and South; sections on formal institutions are balanced by considerations of informal practices. The picture that ultimately emerges is of a criminal justice system that rested on popular passions and pragmatic practices as much as on legal doctrine – a government of men, not laws.

I. A MARKET REVOLUTION WITHOUT A NATION-STATE

Shortly after the War of 1812, the United States began to develop a national market economy. By the 1840s, that economy was mature. While the various parts of the country participated in it differently – some through manufacture, some through the national and international sale of goods, others through the interstate sale of slaves – all had felt its effects long before the first shot was fired on Fort Sumter. So too, each experienced some impact of the economy's industrialization in the decades following the Civil War. Yet even as the economy achieved national scale, no nation-state arose in the United States.

The non-appearance of the nation-state was a consequence of repeated choices, not constitutional imperative. While the American Revolution may be read as resistance to efforts to bring the colonies into the variation on the nation-state that England was developing, and the Articles of Confederation as the codification of that extreme anti-state position, the subsequent ratification of the Constitution was a step back from an extreme anti-state position. How large that step had been was hardly a matter of consensus, as the endless antebellum debates over states' rights demonstrated. The impact of those debates was particularly felt in the area of criminal law. Just before the start of the Market Revolution, in 1812, the Supreme Court decided *United States v. Hudson and Goodwin*,[1] which declared that there could be no federal common law of crimes. The Court's conclusion that nothing in the Constitution permitted the federal courts to take on a general criminal jurisdiction stood in marked contrast to the concurrent development of a federal common law of commercial transactions, which the Court formally recognized in *Swift v. Tyson* in 1842 and which remained good law until 1938, when it decided *Erie Railroad v. Tompkins*.[2] Yet *Hudson* did not hold that the Constitution reserved the authority over criminal law for the states. Instead of framing the problem in terms of federalism, the Court's decision turned on its conclusion that the federal courts had only limited, rather than general jurisdiction, and could only act where Congress expressly gave them power to do so. While that ruling left open the possibility that Congress could pass an omnibus federal crime act, in the absence of congressional action the federal courts were not empowered to handle criminal cases.

Hudson actually resolved very little; its ambiguity was magnified by Congressional inconsistency. As early as 1789, Congress gave all federal courts the power to grant petitions of habeas corpus "for the purpose of an inquiry into the cause of a commitment." That act did not extend federal habeas protection to state court actions, but made clear that the protections existed for those held in federal custody. The next year, in the Federal Crime Act, Congress officially created some federal crimes, involving acts

[1] *United States v. Hudson and Goodwin*, 11 U.S. 32 (1812).
[2] *Swift v. Tyson*, 41 U.S. 1 (1842); *Erie Railroad v. Tomkins*, 304 U.S. 1 (1842).

or offenses against the U.S. government. In 1793, it passed the first Fugitive Slave Act, making it a federal crime to interfere with the capture of slaves; at the end of the decade, Congress created more federal crimes with the passage of the four Alien and Sedition Acts of 1798. Over the next sixty years, Congress passed several other substantive criminal laws: in the 1840s it prohibited postmasters from serving as agents of lotteries and banned the importation of "indecent and obscene" prints and paintings; in 1860, it passed a law intended to protect women who immigrated from seduction on board ship. Other acts of Congress in the 1820s and 1830s outlawed lotteries and dueling in the District of Columbia and criminalized the sale of alcohol in "Indian Territory." These laws represented only a part of the morals legislation Congress was asked to pass in the decades before the Civil War, but other efforts typically failed not as a matter of constitutional principle, but because Southern Congressmen were increasingly hostile to any sort of legislation that might provide a precedent for national regulation of slavery.

Even as regional interests effectively blocked efforts to pass federal criminal laws in the antebellum era, Congress expanded the federal role in criminal justice indirectly. A law passed in the early 1830s extended the federal habeas power, giving federal judges the authority to hear habeas corpus petitions brought by individuals imprisoned by state or federal authorities for "acts committed in pursuance of a law of the United States." At the end of the 1830s Congress expanded federal habeas power further, with a law providing that federal judges could hear claims by state or federal prisoners who were "subjects or citizens of a foreign state." Throughout the antebellum era, the federal government also created institutions of criminal justice. In the Judiciary Act of 1789, the first Congress created the office of U.S. Marshal and assigned one to each U.S. District Court. The marshals had the power to arrest and detain, and each was empowered to employ deputy marshals who could themselves deputize temporary deputies and summon a posse comitatus. Marshals also had the power to ask the president to call up the militia and order it to support the marshal, a power that one marshal exercised just three years later, during the Whiskey Rebellion in 1792. Toward the end of the antebellum era, violent disputes between pro- and anti-slavery forces led to a further increase in the marshal's powers. In 1854, in the wake of the disturbances in the Kansas-Nebraska territories, a ruling by the Attorney General of the United States expanded the marshal's power further by establishing that they had the authority to deputize the army as a posse.

Congress created other federal law enforcement agencies in the antebellum era, most notably in 1836, when it gave the postal service the power to hire inspectors to investigate postal crimes. Federal criminal jurisdiction expanded further during the Civil War. Military tribunals were created, initially to hear cases involving charges of treason and sabotage, which tried civilians in a variety of ways for a variety of offenses. But as time passed the jurisdiction of the courts expanded, and they ultimately heard cases involving crimes that ran the gamut from fraud against the government to morals offenses, such as selling liquor to Union soldiers. Federal law enforcement power increased in other ways as well. In 1861, Allen Pinkerton's detective agency, which had previously engaged in investigation for local and regional businesses (including the railroads), was hired to serve as the secret service for the Northern army. Its writ ran wide. The Pinkertons investigated businesses that defrauded the federal government, tracked and arrested those suspected of spying for the Confederacy, and also tried to monitor enemy troop strength. Two years later, in 1863, Congress established the Internal Revenue Agency and gave it the power to investigate and enforce tax laws. That same year, Congress authorized funds to pay for a private police force under the control of the Secretary of the Interior. In 1865, this force was made a permanent federal police agency – the Secret Service – under the control of the Secretary of the Treasury. From 1860 to 1877 the federal government had another "super" police force at its disposal in the shape of the U.S. Army, which performed police functions in the states of the former confederacy. In 1878, with the passage of the Posse Comitatus Act, Congress formally took the power to enforce criminal laws from the armed forces. But even after the passage of that act officially relinquished the power to the states and their National Guard units, the army was used during labor battles in the mining regions of Montana, and in 1894 in Chicago – over the objections of the state governor – during the strike by the American Railway Union against the Pullman Company.

The federal role in criminal justice expanded in other ways in the period after the Civil War. In 1873 the Comstock Act authorized postal inspectors to seize obscene materials (including information relating to contraception) sent in the mail. In 1908, the Justice Department, acting initially without Congressional approval, created an internal investigative unit, the Bureau of Investigation, which also had the power to arrest. The Narcotics section of the Internal Revenue Service was formed to enforce the federal drug regulations just before World War I; during the war, and the subsequent Red Scare of 1919–20, those agencies, along with the Secret Service, enforced the sedition and draft laws and began the practice of collecting dossiers on suspected subversives. In the period between the Civil War and World War I, Congress passed a series of laws on criminal matters as well, deriving its authority to do so from a variety of constitutional provisions. In the Judiciary Act of 1867, it expanded the scope of the federal Habeas Corpus Act, declaring that federal courts could issue the writ in "all cases where any person may be restrained of his or her liberty in violation of the constitution, or of any treatment or law of the United States." Congress used its powers under the Thirteenth and Fourteenth Amendments to pass the Civil Rights Acts of 1866 and 1875, both of which included criminal sanctions. In 1873, Congress relied on its constitutional authority to regulate the mail when it passed the Comstock Act. Congress passed several pieces of morals legislation, including the Lottery Act of 1895, which were based on its constitutional authority to regulate commerce, as was the Sherman Antitrust Act, passed in 1890, which established a range of criminal punishments for monopolistic behavior. Twenty years later, in 1910, Congress again relied on the Commerce Clause when it passed the Mann (White Slave) Act, which made it a felony to transport a woman in interstate commerce "for the purpose of prostitution or debauchery." In contrast, the Espionage Act of 1917 and the Sedition Act of 1918, omnibus laws criminalizing a range of activities relating to subversive activities and spying, were based on Congressional authority over the armed forces. The Volstead Act (1919), which gave the federal government the power to enforce prohibition, was passed pursuant to the Eighteenth Amendment.

In 1919, the Supreme Court affirmed convictions under the Sedition Act of 1918 in *Abrams v. United States* and *Schenck v. United States*.[3] But in the period between the end of the Civil War and the end of World War I, the Supreme Court's rulings in the area of the federal role in criminal law enforcement were marked by inconsistencies and confusion. The Court upheld the Lottery Act in *Champion v. Ames* in 1903, and the Mann Act in *Hoke v. United States* a decade later.[4] In yet another decision on the Mann Act, *Caminetti v. United States*, which was decided in 1917, the Court explicitly confirmed that Congress had the power to regulate individual morality.[5] Other Court rulings on federalism left the balance of state and federal authority unclear. In the *Civil Rights Cases* (1882), the Court struck down parts of the Civil Rights Act of 1875 on the ground that it infringed on the police powers of the states.[6] But in its decision on the Pullman strike, *In re Debs* (1895), the Court upheld a federal court contempt proceeding arising out of a federal injunction against the railroad boycott, and it justified the result with reference to Congressional authority to regulate the mail and interstate commerce.[7] The expansive federal power the Court recognized in *Debs* seemed at odds with the more limited view of federal commerce clause

[3] *Abrams v. United States*, 250 U.S. 616 (1919); *Schenck v. United States*, 249 U.S. 47 (1919).

[4] *The Lottery Cases*, 188 U.S. 321 (1903); *Hoke v. United States*, 227 U.S. 308 (1913).

[5] *Caminetti v. United States*, 242 U.S. 470 (1917).

[6] *Civil Rights Cases*, 109 U.S. 3 (1882).

[7] *In re Debs*, 158 U.S. 564 (1895).

power it articulated that same year with respect to the Sherman Antitrust Act, in *United States v. E. C. Knight*.[8]

Neither rhyme nor reason strung these rulings together, least of all police power theory. In *Adair v. United States* (1907) the Court declared the Erdman Act of 1898, which made it a federal offense for any employer in interstate commerce to blacklist or fire employees who joined a union, an unconstitutional infringement on state police powers.[9] In that case, the Court once again offered a narrow interpretation of Congressional authority to enact criminal legislation based on the Commerce Clause. But in *E. C. Knight* the Court declared the states' police powers were "essentially exclusive," which suggested that the federal government had some jurisdiction in that area. That same year, in *In re Debs*, the Court implicitly rejected the theory of *Hudson and Goodwin* that the federal courts were courts of limited jurisdiction, holding to the contrary that while the government of the United States was a government of enumerated powers, it had full sovereignty within those enumerated powers and could, therefore, use military force, the equitable powers of the federal courts, or the process of criminal contempt to protect its sovereignty. The Court's insistence in *Debs*, that its decision in no way replaced state court criminal jurisdiction, could not outweigh the importance of its ruling, since the result was to give federal courts the power to overrule the decisions of state authorities. Government by injunction, which greatly expanded the powers of the federal courts, continued through passage of the Norris-LaGuardia Act of 1932.

While many of its rulings in the area of criminal law were ambiguous and contradictory, the Supreme Court consistently refused to consider the possibility that the provisions of the Bill of Rights protected defendants in state court proceedings. In *Barron v. Baltimore* (1833) the Court had held that the Bill of Rights did not apply against the states, thus guaranteeing that states could determine what procedural protections defendants would be granted in criminal trials.[10] Invited, fifty years later in *Hurtado v. California* (1884), to reconsider that ruling in light of the intervening ratification of the Fourteenth Amendment, the Supreme Court once again denied that the Bill of Rights set any limits on state law enforcement officers or state court criminal trials.[11] The Court reiterated that point twenty years later, in *Twining v. New Jersey* (1908), where it held that the right against self-incrimination set out in the Fifth Amendment did not apply

[8] *United States v. E. C. Knight, Co.*, 156 U.S. 1 (1895).

[9] *Adair v. United States*, 208 U.S. 161 (1907).

[10] *Barron v. Baltimore*, 32 U.S. 243 (1833).

[11] *Hurtado v. California*, 110 U.S. 516 (1884).

in state court proceedings.[12] Although it modified that position modestly in the 1930s, it was not until the middle of the twentieth century that the Court agreed to extend the protections of the Bill of Rights to state court criminal proceedings.

The result, throughout the nineteenth century and well into the twentieth, was a national government whose ambivalent exercise of power either positively (by enacting and policing federal criminal laws) or negatively (by means of federal oversight of state court criminal processes) kept it from achieving the authority needed to establish a modern state. In the antebellum era, Tocqueville had suggested that the resulting localism created a distinctive American state that was a particular strength; writing at the end of the nineteenth century in his dissenting opinion in *Hurtado*, the first Justice Harlan was not so sure. Objecting to the Supreme Court's ruling that the Fifth Amendment did not apply to state court trials, he outlined both the benefit of the Fifth Amendment and the result of the failure to apply it to state proceedings: in "the secrecy of investigations by grand juries, the weak and the helpless – proscribed, perhaps, because of their race, or pursued by an unreasoning public clamor – have found, and will continue to find, security against official oppression, the cruelty of the mobs, the machinations of falsehood, and the malevolence of private persons who would use the machinery of the law to bring ruin upon their personal enemies." While Harlan's faith in the protections provided by the jury system was not entirely warranted, the history of the long nineteenth century bears out his perception that the vacuum that existed at the national level gave the United States a criminal justice system in which there was all too often neither state nor law.

II. FIRST FAILURES OF THE LOCAL STATE: POLICING SOUTH AND NORTH

Policing predates both capitalist economies and the modern state; law enforcement in a variety of forms existed in pre- and early modern Europe. This notwithstanding, studies of the state frequently tie the development of exclusive systems of police to the rise of the modern state. The history of policing in the United States raises several questions about that association. The sporadic efforts on the part of the national government to create police forces never established a significant police presence, and while local governments established a variety of policing agencies from 1780 to 1920, their authority was frequently checked and challenged by popular justice in a variety of forms.

[12] *Twining v. New Jersey*, 211 U.S. 78 (1908).

During the antebellum era, ironically, the strongest police forces arose in that part of the country most often considered anti-state. The English colonists to North America had brought with them traditional forms of policing – sheriff, constable, and night watch (a volunteer peacekeeping company drawn from the citizenry) – when they crossed the Atlantic. Before the American Revolution, those popularly based institutions provided the extent of policing for most of the colonies; the exception was those colonies in which the desire to control runaways and suppress slave insurrections prompted the creation of additional forces. The colonial government of South Carolina was one of the first to establish a special slave patrol, doing so in 1693. Other slaveholding colonies followed suit over the next century.

Patrollers' powers over blacks, free and enslaved, were considerable, but not unlimited. In South Carolina, for example, patrols could go into the dwellings of blacks (and white servants), seize contraband items, and arrest slaves, free blacks, or white servants. But they could not go onto white-owned property without the permission of the owner, and they could be, and often were, thwarted in their efforts to enforce pass laws and other restrictions on slaves by masters who refused to follow the laws. Notwithstanding the patrols' limitations, and perhaps because of them, toward the end of the antebellum era some elite whites in South Carolina argued that the jurisdiction of slave patrols should expand to include *white* poachers, trespassers, and vagabonds as well.[13]

By that point, fear of slave insurrection had already led Charleston, South Carolina, along with other Southern cities, to create armed, semi-military police forces. Charleston's police force, which had the power to arrest blacks and whites, was established as early as 1783; New Orleans established its own police department, modeled on Napoleon's *gendarmerie*, in 1805. There were some differences between these two models. Members of the New Orleans' force were uniformed and armed (at first with muskets, after 1809 with sabers) and served mostly at night, though some members were on reserve during the day. After 1836 the police in New Orleans moved away from that military model; its officers no longer wore uniforms or carried any weapons other than staves. By contrast, South Carolina consistently relied on the military model of policing. From 1806 on, Charleston had an appointed, uniformed guard whose members were paid a salary and armed with muskets and bayonets. Until 1821 members of this force patrolled the city streets in platoons of twenty to thirty men; in the aftermath of the abortive Denmark Vesey uprising, Charleston's patrol stopped wearing uniforms. While some accounts indicate Charleston's police squads continued to patrol the streets

[13] Minutes of the Beech Island (S.C.) Agricultural Club, 3 December 1859, pp. 130–131. South Caroliniana Library, University of South Carolina, Columbia, South Carolina.

at night, at least some guardsmen began to work assigned beats. The powers of Charleston's police expanded throughout the antebellum period: a horse guard was added in 1826 and a detective force in 1846. By 1856 the department had established a picture gallery of known criminals, as well as a classification system for recording arrests and convictions (to put this in perspective, Boston created its detective force the same year as Charleston, but New York had no detective squad until 1857 and did not organize a rogue's gallery until the end of the nineteenth century).

With more than 100 men in the department at the start of the Civil War, Charleston's police force was by far the largest in South Carolina. But by 1860 cities across the state, from Aiken to Yorkville, had active police forces. South Carolina's police, in turn, served as models for police forces in the major cities in Georgia, Alabama, and Virginia. Unique among antebellum Southern cities, New Orleans had several black officers on its police force from 1806 until 1830, but then had no African Americans on the force until 1867, when Reconstruction altered the balance of racial power in the city. During Reconstruction several other Southern cities, including Wilmington, North Carolina, modestly integrated their forces, and others experienced significant integration. By 1876 half the officers on Charleston's force were black. Reconstruction's end put a stop to that experiment, along with so many others, though there were still African American officers on the Tampa, Florida, police force in the 1880s; on the Wilmington, North Carolina, force as late as 1898; and in the Tulsa, Oklahoma, police department in 1917.

But the continued presence of black officers represented the remnants of the earlier pattern, rather than an established hiring practice. After its only black officer resigned, Tampa hired no black officers until 1922. Nor were the numbers of black officers ever particularly significant on police forces North or South, even when African Americans managed to obtain positions. In 1906 the police force in Atlanta had black officers, but they were confined to patrolling the black parts of the city; notwithstanding its thriving African American population, Tulsa's police force had just two black officers in 1919. The situation was no better above the Mason-Dixon line. Chicago hired its first African American police officer in 1873, but forty years later, when blacks represented 6 percent of the city's labor pool, they made up only 2 percent of its police force. And women, of course, fared far worse. North and South, city police departments had women serving as jail matrons before the Civil War, but the first policewoman in the country was not appointed until 1905.

While few in the South questioned the value of having squads of police to control the slave population, many opposed the creation of police forces in the North out of fear they posed too great a risk of increasing the size and power of local governments. Police were a problem precisely because they seemed a step toward the creation of a state. Philadelphia briefly established a day watch in 1833, but had no permanent force until the 1840s; Boston had established one only a few years earlier, in 1838. New York continued to have elected constables, complemented by appointed day marshals and a large force of night watchmen, throughout the 1830s. A commission appointed by the mayor in 1836 recommended that New York create a police force modeled on Sir Robert Peel's reforms establishing the London Metropolitan Police (1829), but its suggestion was ignored. There was a second effort to establish a police force in New York in 1844, when the state legislature recommended that the City create a "Day and Night Police" modeled on London's system and employing 800 men. The city government refused to go that far, but the mayor did appoint a uniformed police force of 200 men. That force lasted only as long as the mayor's term; when the new, Democratic administration took control of city administration the next year it implemented the state legislature's recommendation and created a department of 800 men. In contrast to the semi-military organization of the Southern police forces, officers in New York's newly created department, like their counterparts in Philadelphia and Boston, wore no uniforms and carried no weapons, though in New York each was given a special badge. It was only toward the end of the antebellum era that these Northern departments began to embrace a more militaristic model. In New York, members of the force were given uniforms in 1855 and officially allowed to carry guns in 1857; Philadelphia's officers had no uniforms until 1860, and Chicago's officers had to wait until 1863 for theirs. For the same reason, these cities also resisted creating centralized commands for their departments before 1860.

Just as a desire to suppress slave uprisings drove Southern cities to establish police departments, fear of riots and mobs finally led to their creation in the North. Boston's police department was created a few years after a riot that destroyed a Catholic girls' school; New York's efforts to establish a department began in earnest after three violent riots in 1843. Chicago established a police force after the Lager Beer Riot in 1855. While the creation of the police forces in the North had been limited by the fear that they might become a standing army, once created the forces in New York, Boston, Philadelphia, Chicago, and other major cities were untrained and subject to few legal restrictions. As a result, their successes were predictably limited, and their activities created disorder as often as they restrained it. In theory officers had authority to arrest anyone, but police typically were deployed against the lower classes and immigrant populations, their roles limited to breaking up fights and suppressing violence (especially riots). They were often unable to perform either role; throughout the antebellum period, city governments North and South often had to call in the militia, and several cities went further, forced to turn to private "volunteer militias" to supplement their police forces. Even that was not always enough. In antebellum Chicago and other cities property owners often hired private detective agencies to locate stolen property, and businesses hired private firms, such as the privately run Merchant Police, to patrol their premises. Sometimes, popular frustration with the failings of the police went further, prompting revolts against local government. In 1851, the Vigilance Committee took over San Francisco's government in response to its failures to maintain order. A few years later, in 1858, a Vigilance Committee protesting a similar problem in New Orleans seized control of both the state arsenal in that city and police headquarters. Unable to subdue the group, the mayor of the city declared its members a special police force. Several violent altercations followed, causing the mayor to be impeached, but the Committee disbanded when its party lost the next election. For others, self-help was a more straightforward, personal matter. Throughout the antebellum period men in New Orleans, New York, Philadelphia, and Chicago, as well as other cities, carried weapons for their own protection. Among elites, the weapon of choice was a sword cane until the creation of the revolver made that a more attractive option; men in the working class relied on knives and bare fists.

Efforts to strengthen the authority of the police and create a greater distance between governed and government increased after the Civil War. Local governments, particularly in the North, began to professionalize their departments in response to complaints that officers took bribes, displayed political or ethnic favoritism, and turned a blind eye to crime. Those complaints led most Northern cities to complete the move toward the military model of policing that had been favored in Southern cities before the Civil War, reorganizing their police departments under a centralized chain of command. Those developments did little to alter the basic perception that the police were corrupt and incapable of preventing crime or apprehending criminals, nor did they put an end to political influence on the police. Although centralization was intended to remove the police from political control that aim was undermined by the politicization of appointments to the central command. Other reform attempts, begun in New Orleans in the 1850s, to make merit the keystone of hiring and promotion decisions in police departments, were consistently blocked. It was not until the very end of the nineteenth century that most cities made police work part of the civil service and provided their officers with training. In 1888, Cincinnati created a police academy; New York implemented some informal training processes by the 1890s, but delayed creation of its own academy until 1909. Chicago established its training academy a year later.

Under such circumstances, as one might expect, popular forces continued to intersect with public policing, with frequently violent results. During South Carolina's Ellenton Riots in 1876, the local sheriff called in an all-white posse to help capture blacks suspected of aiding a wanted rapist. When the posse turned mob, it set off a weeklong race war. In 1888, a mob in Forest, Illinois, helped capture a young black man suspected of killing a white girl in Chicago and nearly lynched him in the process. Some suspects were not so lucky. In 1880, a mob in Northampton County, Pennsylvania, seized Edward Snyder, suspected of killing Jacob and Alice Geogle, and lynched him notwithstanding the protests of the local law enforcement officers. Police also were accused of doing nothing during moments of heightened tension. During the race riots in Chicago in 1919 and Tulsa in 1921, for example, the police were accused of standing by as white mobs attacked blacks and damaged their property. During the labor strikes of the era, some charged the police with attacks on striking workers and permitting strikers to be attacked, while others accused the police of aiding and abetting the striking workers.

III. THE ONGOING ROLE OF EXTRA-LEGAL JUSTICE

As all this suggests, well into the twentieth century different communities in the United States continued to use a variety of informal means to enforce norms. Those extra-legal processes, in turn, sometimes reinforced, but as often interfered with the formal processes of criminal justice, preventing local governments and police forces from claiming exclusive control over discipline or establishing a monopoly on violence.

Two forms of extra-legal justice, honor culture and lynch mobs, provide the bookends for the period. At the start of the antebellum era, honor culture's emphasis on personal response to assaults on reputation sanctioned the resort to violent means – duels, canings, or fights with fists and knives – by those who wished to punish everything from adultery to slander. But while reprisal was the preferred method of defending honor, violence, lethal or otherwise, was not the only means available. Notwithstanding that some studies assert that going to law was inconsistent with the defense of honor, Benjamin Perry, a lawyer who practiced in antebellum South Carolina, brought several lawsuits that he characterized as actions by young women brought in defense of their honor. Honor culture impinged on formal law in other ways as well. While some affairs of honor, including the duel in which Perry shot and killed his opponent, never resulted in prosecution, participants in other *rencontres* were arrested and tried. In many of these instances, the code of honor trumped, or at the very least modulated, the rule of law. In South Carolina in 1845, Charles Price shot Benjamin Jones because

Jones had called his (Price's) daughter a liar. A grand jury promptly indicted Price for murder, but at trial the petit jury as quickly rejected that charge, determining that Price was guilty of nothing more than manslaughter. An equally sympathetic judge then sentenced Price to just a year in jail.

Most histories associate honor with the South, but the culture of honor extended above the Mason-Dixon Line. In the 1840s and 1850s, merchants in St. Louis who had migrated to that city from New England held duels on a sandbar in the Mississippi known as "Bloody Island." In Philadelphia, young men of substance crept away to Delaware to kill one another in duels until well into the 1840s. Throughout the antebellum period, men from the middling and lower classes in cities like Philadelphia, New York, and Chicago defended their honor with knives and fist, and juries in the North were as willing as those in the South to excuse killings committed in the name of honor, either by acquitting outright or reducing the charges against the defendants. Young men North and South continued to fight and sometimes kill one another in the name of honor after the Civil War, and juries still treated them leniently when they were brought to trial. In 1887, a jury in Chicago acquitted Eugene Doherty, who was accused of killing Nicholas Jones in a fight outside a bar. In the course of reaching its verdict, the jury ignored the evidence that Doherty had been arrested at the scene minutes after the shooting, revolver in hand.

Even so, the close of the Civil War marked the beginning of the end of honor's influence as a form of extra-legal justice. But as honor suffered eclipse, other forms of extra-legal justice prevailed. From the evangelical backcountry of the antebellum South, to the predominantly Catholic mill towns of late nineteenth-century Pennsylvania, churches policed offenses committed by their congregants, judging and punishing a variety of wrongs including intemperance, adultery, and gambling. These punishments were seldom violent; shaming and shunning were the favored methods of reprimanding wrongdoers in most churches, although practice and participants varied from congregation to congregation. In some, women could be judged but were never permitted any sort of adjudicatory role; in others women judged and could be judged. In another informal process of investigation, adjudication, and punishment relating to morals offenses, women exercised greater authority. Sometimes their investigations of wrongdoing involved other women; other times women entered and enforced moral judgments against men. In either case, shame and social ostracism were the preferred means of punishing wrongdoers. These everyday courts of public opinion crossed class and regional bounds, functioning in communities of working-class women in antebellum New York and among elite white women in antebellum South Carolina. Similar processes were at work on shop floors among male laborers as well.

Men, aided by some women, practiced another form of community judgment that had a far more violent element. In antebellum New York, several of the riots that proved so difficult to control arose when mobs of working-class men attempted to police their own communities by driving out brothels and other establishments they considered immoral. Mob action was not confined to the working class. The San Francisco vigilantes of the 1850s and the New Orleans committee of roughly the same era were middle-class men who claimed they were enforcing community norms when they took law into their own hands. Once again, these informal practices continued well after the Civil War. In Chicago in the 1870s a mob in one neighborhood burned down a factory that they felt violated city laws and harmed their community; in 1887 women from the town of Ellsworth, Illinois, raided a local saloon. During the 1880s, mobs of men executed rough justice from South Carolina and Tennessee in the South to Indiana and Wisconsin in the North. Sometimes they formed to deal with a particular problem. In 1886, for example a mob in Irving Park, a Chicago neighborhood, drove a man suspected of taking indecent liberties with children out of the city. Other times, they policed general problems; in the 1880s mobs formed and beat men who whipped or abused their wives in both Indiana and South Carolina.

Informal vigilante efforts had organized counterparts in the Law and Order Leagues and other citizens associations that formed in the 1870s and 1880s. In Chicago in the 1880s, members of the Citizens Association monitored theaters for immoral shows and enforced liquor law violations. Officially, members of the organization tried to work through formal channels, relying on police officers to make arrests, but they were perfectly willing to make citizens arrests when they felt law enforcement officers were unwilling or unavailable. In 1901 in New York City, Judge William Travers Jerome led members of the City Vigilance League on raids of brothels and gambling dens, arguing that citizens had to enforce the laws because the police had failed to act.

New York's experience with vigilante justice suggests how often the efforts of law-and-order groups targeted vulnerable groups. From 1870 through World War I, New York's Anti-Saloon League shut down working-class bars; in roughly that same period the Society for the Suppression of Vice worked to suppress stage shows (and literature) its members deemed obscene, while the Committee of Fourteen, another private anti-vice society, focused on cabarets and saloons, venues particularly noted for racial mixing or homosexual clientele.

Some law-and-order groups tried to advocate for the excluded; a Committee of Public Safety, formed in New Orleans in 1881, monitored the arrests made by the police department, complaining about police brutality, particularly against blacks. Other times, minority groups took the law into their own hands as a form of self-help. In the aftermath of Chicago's race riot of 1919, blacks claimed that they had acted extra-legally to protect their lives and property because they could not trust the police to act. When the dust settled, it was clear that, throughout the riot, Chicago's police had been deployed to protect white property and white lives; not until the National Guard was brought in, at the tail end of the riot, had blacks received any official protection. Perceived failures of law in late nineteenth-century Chicago also led small manufacturing concerns and labor organizations to establish their own informal rules, creating systems by which they policed one another. Violations discovered by their informal courts were punished through strikes or violence. Both the law-and-order leagues and their less formal counterparts justified their actions on the ground that laws were being ignored, which easily became the argument that the legal system was itself unjust, or lawless.

That, of course, became the argument that Ben Tillman and other white supremacists in the South used to justify the creation of lynch mobs. In part because other forms of extra-legal justice conditioned both governed and government to mob violence, from the 1880s to the 1930s little was done to stop lynching. In that period, lynch mobs killed roughly 3,700 people, male and female, 80 percent of them black. As was the case with other forms of extra-legal justice, no region had a monopoly on this violence. While most of the reported lynchings occurred in the South, in the last half of the nineteenth century mobs killed men and women in a variety of Northern states, among them Wisconsin, Pennsylvania, and Illinois.

IV. THE POPULAR ROLE IN FELONY COURTS AND EFFORTS TO CHECK ITS INFLUENCE

In the first half of the nineteenth century, the forces of popular justice spilled out of the streets and into the felony courts, brought in most often by the juries that played roles at one stage of the proceedings or another. Throughout the antebellum era, many counties North and South followed English practice and relied on elected coroners to investigate unexpected deaths, with juries composed of "bystanders" selected from the neighborhood of the death. Toward the end of the century, these juries and the coroners who called them came under attack for their lack of professionalism. In 1877, Massachusetts replaced coroners with the medical examiner. But while newspapers in other parts of the country denounced coroners and their juries, pressing for their abolition throughout the 1880s, most jurisdictions did not follow Massachusetts' lead. New York had a coroner until 1915, and some counties in Wisconsin continued to rely on coroners until World War II.

Coroner's juries represented the first point of popular involvement in the legal system, and their role could be significant. They not only deliberated over the causes of unexpected death but often offered a preliminary determination of whether any crime had occurred. Coroner's juries could, and sometimes did, prompt a sheriff to initiate actions with a determination that a suspicious death needed to be the subject of prosecution, just as they could, and often did, forestall legal actions with a finding that nothing criminal had occurred. On more than one occasion their determinations were suspect; in 1907 a coroner's jury in Philadelphia found that a man found drowned in the Delaware River had committed suicide, notwithstanding the fact that he had been dragged from the water with his hands bound behind his back.

Because coroner's juries had to be composed of people from the scene of the crime, the juries were a popular institution, at least to the extent that they involved all classes of white men. (Slaves, blacks, and women, along with other marginalized groups, were rarely if ever members of coroner's juries, though they could provide testimony at an inquest.) In contrast, grand juries usually were composed of a community's elite. Notwithstanding that demographic difference, members of the grand jury were as willing as coroner's jurors to apply their own standards in determining what crimes should be prosecuted. Grand jury records from Philadelphia in 1839–59 show that the jury indicted in less than half the murder cases brought before it. The rate of indictments was higher in antebellum South Carolina, but even there grand juries entered indictments in only 63 percent of the cases they heard. Their unreliable nature brought grand juries under attack toward the end of the century; in the 1870s California began to substitute informations for indictments. No grand jury was ever called in cases that proceeded under an information. Instead there was a preliminary hearing before a magistrate, who bound a defendant over for trial if he felt there was evidence enough to proceed. This attack on jury power was relatively successful; by the end of the nineteenth century the federal government and many of the other states had borrowed the system from California and used it to sidestep their grand juries.

Even as the use of informations checked one source of popular influence on the prosecution of felony cases, the members of petit juries continued to play an important role in criminal trials. Andrew Hamilton's argument for the acquittal of John Peter Zenger, which may have been jury nullification's most famous moment, occurred in the eighteenth century, but the history of the practice extended into the twentieth. Such exercises of popular power were not without challenge. Shortly after the American Revolution, many state court systems tried to limit the jury's power, declaring that jurors were limited to finding facts while judges had the sole power to determine the laws, but these declarations did not have much impact. Juries in the antebellum South were notorious for deciding cases in accord with local values rather than the rule of law, with the result that in states like South Carolina conviction rates for many crimes, including murder, were less than 50 percent. But once again the phenomenon was not limited to the South. In antebellum New York City, less than a third of all men (defendants in murder cases were almost exclusively male) brought to trial for murder were convicted. In Philadelphia, in 1839–46, the grand jury indicted sixty-eight people for murder, but only 37 percent of those indicted were convicted once they were brought to trial. Although the numbers for that city changed after the Civil War – Philadelphia had a conviction rate for murder of 63 percent in the period 1895–1901 – the figures reflect the influence of plea agreements, rather than a shift in juror practice. Of the people convicted of murder in that city in 1895–1901, only thirty-four suffered that fate as a result of a jury verdict, while fifty-eight pleaded guilty. And in other parts of the country, conviction rates remained low after the Civil War. In late nineteenth-century Chicago the conviction rate for people brought to trial for murder was roughly 40 percent.

A number of reforms over the course of the nineteenth century sought to deal with the petit jury's power at trial; some were designed to expand that power, others to restrict its exercise. One early change, which took effect in the 1820s, increased the ability of jurors to convict by providing that jurors only need find that proof of guilt was beyond a reasonable doubt. While this standardized the burden of proof at a standard more stringent than that applied in civil cases, the standard was lower than the near certainty test that defense attorneys called for in the early national period. Another significant shift in jurors' powers came in the antebellum era, when many states, including New York, Tennessee, and Illinois, passed laws that gave juries the power to sentence as well as determine guilt.

Other, later reforms had an impact on the evidence that petit juries could hear. Before the Civil War, state courts typically followed English law, limiting defendants' ability to testify. Many restricted the defendants' right to testify under oath; some went further. As late as 1849, criminal defendants in South Carolina could make the final argument to the jury only if they presented no evidence on their own behalf. In 1867, Maine gave criminal defendants the right to testify under oath, and this innovation was quickly adopted in other states. Another change, made at roughly the same time, imposed restrictions on judges' ability to comment on the evidence.

A statute in Massachusetts barred judicial commentary in 1860; Mississippi limited judges to stating the law even earlier, in 1857.

In Chicago, one consistent influence on the low conviction rate was an Illinois statute that provided that jurors could substitute their own view of the law for the instructions given to them by the judge. The practice was so well established that jurors frequently received an instruction to this effect, most famously at the trial after the Haymarket Bombing in 1887. Jury nullification remained good law in Illinois even after the U.S. Supreme Court denounced the practice in *Sparf and Hansen v. United States* (1895).[14] In fact, the Illinois Supreme Court did not itself outlaw nullification until 1931.[15] But while Illinois and Maryland (where a provision in the state constitution permitted jurors to nullify[16]) were unusual in the degree to which they formally recognized that juries had the right to nullify, legal commentators from Arthur Train to Roscoe Pound complained that juries exercised that power informally through World War I.

Yet the evidence of the increased rate of plea bargains in late nineteenth-century Philadelphia reveals one force that checked the petit jury's power in felony courts. And that check on jury power was significant. In 1900 three out of four felony convictions in the New York county criminal courts resulted from plea agreements. Within a few decades the numbers in other cities were at least as dramatic. A study in 1928 determined that in 1920s Chicago, 85 percent of all felony convictions resulted from a plea, as did 78 percent of felony convictions in Detroit, 76 percent in Denver, 90 percent in Minneapolis, 81 percent in Los Angeles, 84 percent in St Louis, and 74 percent in Pittsburgh.[17] That shift had taken most of the nineteenth century to occur; Massachusetts courts had begun to take pleas in cases of regulatory crime (liquor offenses, for example) in 1808, and in 1845 a committee appointed by the Massachusetts House of Representatives endorsed plea agreements as a reasonable exercise of prosecutorial discretion. But plea bargaining was not quickly extended to cases involving other felonies. The first plea agreement in a case involving murder was not entered until 1848, and throughout the 1850s only 17 percent of all murder cases in Massachusetts were pleaded out. The trend changed in the decades after the Civil War; at the end of the 1890s 61 percent of all murder cases in Massachusetts were resolved with pleas. While the effect of the turn to plea agreements was to limit the power of the criminal court jury, the rise of plea bargaining was a result of indirect popular influence on

[14] 156 U.S. 51 (1895).
[15] *Illinois v. Bruner* 343 Ill. 146 (1931).
[16] Maryland Constitution, article 10, section 5.
[17] Raymond Moley, "The Vanishing Jury," *Southern California Law Review* 2 (1928), 97.

courts. In Massachusetts, which had an appointed judiciary throughout the century, judges resisted plea bargaining until caseload pressure forced them to do accept the practice at the end of the century. In contrast, in states where judges were elected, like Georgia (where judges controlled sentencing) and Indiana (where jurors sentenced), plea bargaining took hold in the antebellum era. In those states judges apparently used plea bargaining to control their caseloads and demonstrate their competence to the electorate.

Other reforms of the century were intended to increase the authority of the government in felony trials. To that end, by 1820 most states had created the office of public prosecutor, and in the antebellum era many states tried to use those prosecutors to consolidate their authority over criminal prosecutions by eliminating the old practice of private prosecution of crimes. But those efforts were not entirely successful. Governments did succeed in eliminating prosecutions initiated and often presented by private people, rather than by government lawyers, a practice that had allowed private people to use the courts for personal revenge. But they were unable, or unwilling, to bring to an end a second type of private prosecution, in which private attorneys were hired to assist state-supported prosecutors in presenting the case; that practice continued well into the twentieth century, subverting the claim that criminal prosecutions were undertaken on behalf of the state rather than for private revenge. The selective nature of this assault on private prosecution had a decided class aspect. While the first approach opened the courthouse door to the poor, letting them bring claims (even, of course, frivolous ones) against others at minimal expense, the second gave special advantages to the rich, who could hire the best lawyers to assist the state's attorneys.

The inequalities of criminal justice were more marked on the other side of the case. Wealthy defendants throughout the century went to trial with the best representation money could buy, but in most states criminal defendants charged with felonies were sorely pressed to get representation at all. As early as 1780, Massachusetts courts required that attorneys be appointed for indigent defendants charged with capital crimes, and by the end of the nineteenth century, defendants in New York and California had a right to free counsel in all felony cases. Toward the end of the century, courts in several jurisdictions, such as Chicago, asked attorneys to volunteer to represent indigents in capital cases, but in the same period courts in Florida refused to recognize that criminal defendants had a right to counsel. Concerted efforts to provide attorneys for indigent defendants did not begin until right before World War I. In 1914, Los Angeles became the first city in the country to create an office of public defenders. New York created a voluntary defenders organization three years later, but many jurisdictions waited until the late 1920s and early 1930s to provide for defendants who could not afford representation.

The rule of law often had little impact on felony trials, and appellate courts did little to remedy that problem. By 1840 most states permitted appeals from criminal convictions, although Louisiana did not do so until 1843. But while the right existed, the privilege was exercised rarely because few defendants could afford it. In Wisconsin, the state Supreme Court heard 27,000 appeals in the period from 1839 to 1959, but of those only 1,400 were appeals from criminal cases, and in other states appeals remained a relatively unimportant part of the criminal process through World War I. More popular, in both senses of the term, was the pardon, but for most of the period that was a decision left to the sole discretion of the elected governor, which meant it was a process tempered by political reality far more than by mercy or law.

V. GOVERNED WITHOUT GOVERNMENT, CRIMINAL LAW IN THE PETTY COURTS

The nineteenth-century criminal justice system also included petty courts, which heard the minor criminal cases, misdemeanors, and quasi-criminal cases and offered a different perspective on the extent of the power of the local state. In the colonial era these courts were often sites of neighborhood justice, run by justices of the peace who often had no legal training or experience and received no regular salary, instead collecting their pay in fees. Through the first half of the nineteenth century, these petty courts usually heard cases involving people from the surrounding communities, and the justices of the peace often ruled based on their personal knowledge of the parties before them, rather than any legal principle. In some petty courts, in particular those in Philadelphia, informality was reinforced by the standard practice of prosecution by private people. Without the requirement of lawyers, even people from the poorest neighborhoods felt free to go to the so-called alderman's court to get justice, recourse, or revenge. But to view all this as evidence that the petty courts were a mainstay of the localized state, where the people expressed a sovereign will, is to confound process with principle. By the middle of the nineteenth century, the Market Revolution created impersonal worlds full of strangers in place of the communities that had sustained these courts in the earlier period. Organized police forces put additional pressure on the petty courts, as arrests swamped them with cases. Under the pressure of increased use, judges subjected more defendants to summary punishment and were unable either to channel or direct popular notions of justice. Even as they failed to serve as instruments of the state, the petty courts also ceased to provide much in the way of sovereign power to the people who appeared before them. Contemporaries complained that those who brought claims to these courts, or appeared before them, saw them as nothing more than an arena for disputation, on a par with the dueling ground, the barroom floor, or the street corner. In the antebellum era, the petty courts neither offered the certainty of the rule of law nor preempted the resort to alternative (and even more violent) means of settling differences.

The situation only got worse after the Civil War. By 1880, petty courts had become assembly lines of punishment. Seventy percent of all the country's jailed inmates by 1910 were serving time for minor offenses, such as drunkenness, vagrancy, or disorderly conduct, and most of them had been sentenced by one of these petty courts. Process, from Pittsburgh to California, became increasingly summary; few defendants received a hearing that lasted more than a minute or two. Although the judges often had a legal background, there were few, if any, lawyers in these courts, and less law. Most defendants were sentenced to time served or fined a few dollars (which often was more than they could afford and resulted in further jail time as they worked off the fine), though justice frequently depended on who the defendant was and where the crime occurred. In Chicago from 1890 to 1925 the vagrancy laws were used against tramps from out of town. In Pittsburgh in that same period, young African American men from the community were imprisoned under the tramp laws in numbers far out of proportion to their numbers in the population, whereas whites were underrepresented. In Buffalo in the early 1890s, vagrancy laws were used to break strikes, which meant most of the men convicted under those laws were white laborers.

Some efforts were made to correct the problems of overcrowded courts. Faced with considerable hostility to its disorganized and lawless police courts, in 1906 Chicago collapsed them all into a centralized municipal court system. This new court heard petty crimes and handled preliminary hearings, as had the police courts before it. The difference lay in the way the new system handled those cases. Specialized courts were set up to hear particular matters; Morals Court, for example, heard all cases involving prostitution. Initially specialization reduced the number of cases before the court, which permitted the judges to devote more time and expertise to their cases. For a brief period after these reforms, the new courts were a place where working-class and poor men and women brought private prosecutions. But popular use of the new courts came with a cost. Staffed with a phalanx of social workers and social scientists trained in a variety of approaches (including, at least in the period around World War I, eugenics) who supported judges with the power to sentence people to indefinite probation, the municipal court system was no longer a place for parties to air out neighborhood problems and then go home. Women who filed claims against their husbands, parents who used the court to control their children, and any other defendant brought before the court in some other way found that it became a permanent part of their lives. Long after the initial cases had come to an end, judges, probation officers, and the court's support staff continued to track the parties. Chicago's Juvenile Court, created in 1899, had a similar impact on the lives of its charges and their families. Like the Municipal Court, the Juvenile Court favored ad hoc, personalized judgments; social science ideals, not law, influenced the court's decisions.

For all that they permitted extended intrusions into the lives of the people who appeared before them, the new municipal court systems were never creatures of an omnipresent state. Government underfunding meant that in its first decades, private individuals and institutions financed much of the work of Chicago's Juvenile Court and influenced its direction in the process. The Chicago Municipal Court was also subject to a variety of private influences, as reformers and social scientists played a role shaping its direction. Needless to say, reformers used the two courts as sites on which to pitch competing ideas. The result was that the government spoke not with a single voice, but with many voices. As much as overburdened dockets limited the police courts as a source of state authority, the competing and conflicting theories drifting out of the Juvenile and Municipal Courts weakened the ability of the state to use either as a source of authority as well.

VI. SUBVERTING THE SUBSTANTIVE LAW

Problems with the court systems were made all the more stark by the endless efforts, throughout the nineteenth century, to reform the substantive criminal law. Inspired by a variety of influences from the Enlightenment desire to make law more rational to a republican demand that law become more accessible to the public, in the early national period many states, most of them in the North, began to make crime a matter of statutory rather than common law. Pennsylvania began an extended effort to reform the criminal law in 1794, with the passage of a statute that split common law murder into two separate offenses. As other states followed its lead, many, often bowing to public pressure, added new crimes to their books, criminalizing behavior that had been frowned on, but legal before. Pennsylvania, which had passed its original blue laws in the colonial era only to see them fall into disuse in the 1740s, passed a law in 1779 that outlawed work and certain kinds of diversions on Sunday. Charleston, South Carolina, passed a Sunday closing law in 1801; toward the end of the antebellum era California passed two Sunday closing laws, one in 1855 that outlawed noisy amusements and a second in 1858 that closed stores and prohibited the sale of goods.

As time went on, other types of morals legislation joined the Sunday closing laws. In the 1830s, states as far apart as Maine and Michigan passed statutes prohibiting adultery, fornication, incest, and sodomy. That same decade Illinois passed a law prohibiting the sale of playing cards, dice, and billiard balls (as well as obscene materials), and temperance laws swept New England in the 1850s. Typically, these laws were intended to increase state control of behavior and were prompted by fears that urbanization was exposing people, particularly young men and women, to corrupting influences. To that end, enforcement often targeted particular groups; in St Louis during the 1840s, brothels were winked at, while prostitutes who rolled their tricks were charged. Notwithstanding selective enforcement, and often in fact because of it, many of these laws were subject to challenge, formal and informal, throughout the century. In 1833, a Jewish merchant from Columbia, South Carolina, prosecuted under a city ordinance that prohibited the sale or liquor or confections on Sunday, argued that the law deprived him of the religious freedom he was guaranteed by the state constitution. The trial court upheld the law on prudential grounds, concluding that custom and practice in the state declared Sunday to be the Sabbath and that the presence of large numbers of free blacks and slaves on leave in the city on Sunday necessitated laws that restricted temptation. A decade later, the Supreme Court of South Carolina heard a challenge to a similar law, this one brought by a Jewish merchant in Charleston who argued that his constitutional rights to religious freedom were violated by a Sunday closing law. Once again the court rejected that argument, on the ground that the state's police power gave it the authority to pass any law to punish behavior that shocked the conscience of the community. The court added that in South Carolina, conscience was Christian.

While Sunday closing laws and other morals legislation were typically passed as a result of pressure from groups interested in enforcing a morality based on Christian (usually Protestant) precepts, most state courts upheld Sunday closing laws on prudential, rather than religious, grounds. In 1848, the Pennsylvania Sunday closing law was upheld against a challenge by a Seventh Day Adventist. In its ruling the state supreme court noted that Sunday had become a traditional day of rest and tranquility and concluded that the law merely reflected that custom. A Missouri court upheld a Sunday closing law in the 1840s on similar grounds, noting that convention had declared that Sunday should be a day of peace and quiet. But while courts upheld Sunday closing laws, in practice they were dead letters in most places by mid-century. Attempts from 1859–67 to enforce a law in Philadelphia that prohibited the operation of horse cars on Sunday were unsuccessful; by 1870 New York's ban on public transportation on Sunday was a nullity; and popular defiance of California's Sunday closing laws led that state's supreme court to strike the law down in the early 1880s.

Efforts to use criminal law to control morality continued after the Civil War. Throughout the 1870s many states passed laws regulating obscenity, often modeling their laws on the federal Comstock Laws. Some states also criminalized the use of drugs or passed temperance legislation. Often these laws reflected considerable lobbying by reform groups, many of them dominated by women: the dispensary law that the South Carolina legislature passed in 1894 followed a decade and a half of efforts by the Women's Christian Temperance Union (WCTU) and other local women's groups. Attempts, only some of them successful, were made to regulate sexuality as well. In the 1860s and early 1870s, lawmakers in New York considered passing laws that would permit prostitution in the city but require all prostitutes to be licensed and subject to medical examinations. That effort failed, but St. Louis succeeded in passing a licensing law for prostitutes in 1870, although it was rescinded in 1874. Responding to shifts in medical knowledge, as well as pressures from doctors who sought to increase their professional authority by restricting the powers of midwives, the period after the Civil War was marked by a series of laws that made it a crime to perform abortions.

In that same period, fear that the young women who flocked to the nation's cities were inadequately protected against sexual predators led many states to pass statutory rape laws and raise the age of consent. The fate of those laws in the last decades of the century offered another example of how laws could be subverted, demonstrating the continued weakness of the local state. From Vermont to California, the reformers who pressed for passage of statutory rape laws hoped to protect young women from predatory older men, and in a few states, such as Vermont, those aims informed prosecutions until well into the twentieth century. But in California, the law was under attack from the first. Initially, arresting officers, judges, and prosecutors undermined the law, choosing to protect men who had sex with minors by refusing to arrest, prosecute, or convict them. After more judges more sympathetic to the law's aims were put on the bench, their efforts to enforce the law to protect vulnerable young women were complicated, and not infrequently thwarted, by parents who used the laws to try to regain control over their teenaged daughters. What began as a paternalistic effort to protect vulnerable young women by targeting a class that seemed to expose them to especial harm was transformed into an instrument to control the young women instead.

The problem of popular resistance was not confined to morals legislation. The Illinois Civil Rights Act of 1885 was intended to provide a state law remedy to blacks barred from places of public accommodation. The act had civil and criminal aspects, but by 1920 the combination of businesses that refused to comply with the law and failures of both public and private prosecution rendered both parts of the law a dead letter. Juries undermined other laws by refusing to enforce laws that were on the books. Just as they nullified when they refused to treat honor killing as murder, so too they nullified when they refused to enforce laws creating criminal defenses, such as insanity. The nineteenth century had seen the rise of the insanity defense, as most jurisdictions in the United States adopted the M'Naughton Rule. Yet while that law was intended to reinforce the concept of *mens rea* and provide greater protections for defendants, its guarantees were mostly honored in the breach. Arthur Train, a prosecutor in New York City at the turn of the century, reported that jurors systematically refused to follow the insanity defense, even in cases where the defendant was clearly insane. Rather than enter a finding of insanity, jurors preferred to sentence insane defendants whose killings did not seem outrageous to a number of years in prison, and sentenced other, equally insane defendants whose offenses seemed shocking, to death. Jurors outside of New York worked from a similar pattern, as popular opinion condemned insanity defenses as legalisms designed to subvert justice.

VII. PROFITABLE PUNISHMENT

The same reform movement at the end of the eighteenth century that resulted in the codification of substantive criminal law prompted reforms of punishment. Reformers argued that punishment was the key to criminal justice and that sentencing was a vital part of punishment. Particular emphasis was placed on making punishment fit the crime, with the result that many states sharply reduced the number of crimes they considered capital. In 1790, Pennsylvania passed a law declaring that several felonies, among them robbery and burglary, would no longer be capital offenses. Four years later, as part of its redefinition of murder, Pennsylvania declared that only first-degree murder was a capital crime. Over the next several decades, Virginia and most other states joined this process, significantly reducing the number of offenses they punished by death. By 1850 South Carolina had reduced the number of capital crimes it recognized to 22, down from 165 in 1813.

In 1779, Thomas Jefferson had argued that to deter crimes punishments had to be both proportionate to the offense and of determinate length. Progressive reformers at the end of the nineteenth century took the opposite approach, arguing that indefinite sentences were best suited to deterring crime and reforming those convicted. A focus on the difference in those arguments obscures the more important historical point – regardless of what the laws on the books required, for most of the nineteenth century a variety of practices made indeterminate sentencing the norm. In Massachusetts, as we have seen, the first plea bargain, in which a defendant exchanged a guilty verdict for a set sentence that was less than the possible sentence, was entered in 1808. A defendant charged with a violation of the state liquor license law pled guilty to one of four counts, in exchange for having the other three counts dropped. He paid a fine and suffered no other punishment.

As that original outcome suggests, those who entered into plea agreements might receive sentences that had little to do with the statutory punishment for their underlying crime. But even defendants who went to trial, and were sentenced in accord with statutory schemes, often served different periods of time. Pardons were used to reduce prison time and could be issued at the behest of a prison administrator, who might wish to reward good behavior or simply ease the pressures on an overcrowded jail. A related practice, the reduction of sentences for "good time" (good behavior), put the power to reduce sentences directly into the hands of prison administrators, though usually with some limitations as to the amount of time that a sentence could be reduced. A related variation on this process, parole, was a European invention that was adopted in U.S. prisons after the Civil War. It again gave prison authorities the power to release some inmates early, though in contrast to pardoned prisoners, or those whose sentences were reduced for good behavior, parole was a conditional release. Each of these practices helped to make the even the most specific sentence indeterminate, as did probation, which permitted convicted defendants to serve no sentence so long as they maintained good behavior. The practice was formally recognized in Massachusetts in 1836, but had antecedents in a variety of other practices; some, like the peace bond that dated back to the seventeenth century, were formally recognized by the courts, while others, like the practice of failing to hear charges against certain defendants so long as they behaved, had merely been informal processes. Supervision was another form of probation that was initially applied to juvenile offenders and then slowly transferred over to use with some adult prisoners.

The practice of indefinite sentencing was reinforced by the most significant reform of punishment in the nineteenth century, the creation of the penitentiary. During the Revolutionary Era, most states imprisoned convicted prisoners in rickety local jails, from which there were many escapes, though some states had prisons that were more like dungeons, where prisoners were manacled to the wall or floor of a communal cell. In 1790, the year that Connecticut converted an abandoned copper mine into a dungeon-like prison, Philadelphia remodeled its Walnut Street jail and sparked a major change in imprisonment in the United States.

The idea behind the new Walnut Street prison was twofold: prisoners who previously had been assigned to do public works on the streets of Philadelphia wearing uniforms and chains would henceforth be isolated from the populace (whether to protect the public from being corrupted by the prisoners or vice versa was subject to debate); in their isolation, prisoners would be given time and solitude in which to contemplate their offenses and repent. To those ends, inmates were isolated in individual cells and required to keep silent when they had contact with other prisoners during the day. Yet practice did not completely square with purpose. While prisoners were removed from contact with the public on the streets, they were not completely separated from the public gaze. For most of the antebellum era, Pennsylvania prisons admitted visitors for a small fee, in exchange for which they were allowed to watch the prisoners go about their daily lives. Nor did separate cells always breed the desired penitence; in 1820 a riot in the Walnut Street prison led to several deaths. That failure did not undermine Pennsylvania's enthusiasm for the general project. In the 1820s the state opened two penitentiaries, one, in Pittsburgh, known as Western State Penitentiary, and the other, in Philadelphia, known as Eastern State. Western State was beset by administrative problems for several years, but Eastern State quickly became a model for other states to follow. There, the scheme initially set up at Walnut Street Prison was modified so that prisoners no longer mingled with one another during the day. Instead, they remained in isolation for 23 hours out of 24, working and living in separate cells.

At roughly the same time that Pennsylvania was refining its penitentiary model, New York was experimenting with its own. It opened Auburn Prison in 1805 and for the next two decades experimented with living arrangements in an effort to achieve the perfect system. During the 1820s, prisoners at Auburn were also placed in isolation, but it was more extreme than the Pennsylvania version since the prisoners at Auburn were not given any work to occupy their time. In an effort to use loss of individual identity as a further means of punishment, Auburn's prisoners were assigned uniforms, shaved, and given limited access to family, friends, or lawyers. They marched to and from their cells in lockstep and always in ordered ranks, and they were supposed to be silent at all times. The result was a disaster. After several prisoners at Auburn committed suicide and several others attempted it; the prison administration concluded that the system was unworkable. In 1829, a modified system of punishment, which came to be known as the Auburn Plan, was put into effect. Under this scheme, prisoners worked together during the day (in contrast to the situation at Eastern State, where they worked in isolation) and then were confined to individual cells at night. This continued to be the general rule at Auburn until overcrowding in the middle of the century forced the prison administration to abandon the solitary cell.

Reformers in Pennsylvania and New York hoped that a regime of work, along with regimented lives, would teach prisoners self-discipline and self-restraint. But if reformers intended prison labor to be only one element of a holistic effort to restore inmates to virtue and industry, in the hands of prison administrators and state governments it became the driving force behind the new prisons. After administrators at Auburn claimed that their prisoners produced such a significant profit that the prison did not need to seek appropriations from the legislature, profits became the explicit goal of penitentiaries built in many states – Massachusetts, New Hampshire, Ohio, Kentucky, Alabama, Tennessee, Illinois, Georgia, and Missouri. The different states pursued profit in different ways and with different rates of success. Between 1800 and 1830 the penitentiary administrators in Massachusetts ran the prison industry, while in nearby New Hampshire the state sold its inmates' labor to private contractors, who employed inmates in shoemaking, stone cutting, and blacksmith work. Inmates in the penitentiary in Alabama also produced a range of goods, including clothing, shoes, farm equipment, and furniture, but in contrast to New Hampshire, their work was leased to a single individual who ran the prison as if it were a small manufacturing concern. Until 1853, Missouri leased its inmates out to private people. When public anxiety about escaped prisoners finally led administrators to abandon that practice, the state adopted a modified version of the Massachusetts model, building factories within its various prisons and having the inmates work in-house. In yet another variation on this theme, from 1831 to 1867 Illinois leased both its prisoners and the buildings they lived in to businesses.

The profits realized by the different states were as varied as their practices. Penitentiaries in Kentucky and Alabama turned steady profits in the decades before the Civil War, while the penitentiaries in Georgia usually did not. Studies of the Alabama and Kentucky prisons argue that they profited by dint of good management; other did not. The Massachusetts penitentiary turned a profit by bribing inmates to work; the penitentiary in Kansas made a profit, as did Michigan's, by taking in prisoners from other systems for a fee (Kansas took in prisoners from Oklahoma, Michigan took in federal prisoners). The result, at least in Kansas, was a severely overcrowded prison. Most prisons, in addition, relied on beatings and other forms of punishment to make sure inmates did their assigned work.

Whether it was because of outrage over financial shenanigans or merely the result of its famously contrarian mindset, South Carolina did not build a penitentiary until 1866, preferring to rely on its county jails to hold prisoners after they were convicted. Although North Carolina and Florida joined South Carolina in resisting the trend, most other states built penitentiaries before the Civil War and resumed the practice at war's end. Most states continued to seek profits from their prisoners into the twentieth century. Illinois maintained its modified convict leasing system until organized labor forced through a law barring prison work in 1903, Kansas kept up its struggle to make a profit by housing inmates until protests from Oklahoma stopped its practices in 1909, Missouri ran its prison as a profit center until 1920, and New Hampshire did not abandon the practice of convict leasing until 1932.

While the profit motive remained unchanged, methods did alter in some states in the aftermath of the Civil War. These states, which were mostly located in the South, began to lease prisoners out to private enterprises, much as Missouri had done in the antebellum period. Florida, which had tried and failed to make a profit on the penitentiary that it finally created in 1866, began to lease out its prisoners to turpentine farmers, phosphate mine owners, and railroad companies beginning in 1877. It continued the practice through World War I. Tennessee and Alabama leased their prisoners to coal mining concerns, and initially both states found the process quite lucrative. By 1866, each state was bringing in $100,000 a year from the prisoner leases, a sum that represented one-third of their respective budgets. But as time went on, problems arose. Tennessee in particular had difficulties when non-convict miners rioted and forced coal mining companies to release their prisoners and close down their mines. Alabama's experiment with convict miners was slightly more successful, and the state used convicts, particularly African Americans, in its mines for several years. But Alabama's system was subject to free labor protests as well and worked only so long as the mining companies were willing to give the convict miners pay and privileges. When that arrangement broke down, the convict miners refused to produce and the enterprise became less profitable.

Other Southern states, beginning with Georgia in 1866, shifted away from leasing out their inmates and instead put them on chain gangs to do public work. The chain gang was not a Southern invention; from 1786 to the opening of Walnut Street Prison in 1790, convicts in Philadelphia were assigned to gangs that did public labor on the streets of the city wearing a ball and chain. In the 1840s, San Francisco housed prisoners on a prison ship, the *Euphemia*, at night and assigned them to do public works in chain gangs during the day. Nor did the idea spring fully formed from the Georgia soil at the end of the Civil War. Initially, Georgia assigned misdemeanor arrestees to the chain gang and leased its felony convicts out to private enterprise. But time convinced the government of the benefits of having all its convicts work the chain gang to build public roadways, and in 1908 Georgia passed a law that prohibited convict leasing and put all its prisoners (including women, who served as cooks) to work in gangs. Other states, among them North Carolina and South Carolina, followed Georgia's lead, assigning some inmates to a variety of public works projects. The practice continued well into the twentieth century.

The years after the Civil War saw another development in imprisonment, as specialized prisons were gradually built to deal with specific populations. Once again, this was not an entirely new idea. The first house of refuge, a special institution for juvenile offenders, opened in New York in 1825, and other cities including Boston quickly launched comparable initiatives. Twenty years later, Boston offered a refinement on this principle when it opened the first reform school for boys. The first reform school for girls, the Massachusetts State Industrial School for Girls, did not open until 1856, and it was not until after the Civil War that other states, among them Wisconsin, Iowa, Michigan, and Kentucky, created similar institutions. They did not, however, all follow the same model. When the Louisville, Kentucky, House of Refuge opened in 1864, its inmates were boys and girls. In contrast, when the Girls Reform School of Iowa opened for business in 1866, it was, as its name implied, a single-sex institution. The Michigan Reform School for Girls, which opened in 1884, not only had an inmate population that was limited to young women but its entire staff was female as well.

While these institutions physically separated some young inmates from adult convicts, far more young offenders were housed with the general prison population. Even after the Civil War, offenders under 21 made up a portion, sometimes a significant one, of the populations in penitentiaries and county jails. In 1870, California state courts assigned boys as young as 12–15 to San Quentin and Folsom prisons. Of the 7,566 people assigned to Cook County Jail (in Chicago) in 1882, 508 were under 16 (one was no older than 8); 1,413 were under 21. Six years later, in 1888, Illinois executed 17-year- old Zephyr Davis for murder. In the 1890s, a Savannah, Georgia, newspaper reported that one-third of the people assigned to the local penitentiary were younger than 20, and 80 of them were less than 15 years old. Nor were juvenile offenders exempt from the profit motive that drove corrections. In Tennessee, juvenile offenders, who were not separated from adult inmates until the twentieth century, were expected to earn their keep by their labor, just as adult inmates were. The same was true for juveniles in jurisdictions that did separate them from the general prison population. Inmates in the New York House of Refuge were contracted out to private businesses or expected to do contract labor within House itself. Inmates at the Michigan Reform School were also contracted out to private businesses. The same held true at reformatories opened for women offenders. The Detroit House of Corrections, a reformatory for women, ran a successful chair manufacturing business in the early 1870s.

Reformers, particularly women, had lobbied states to create all-women cell blocks and to hire women as matrons for female prisoners as early as the 1820s. Some states built special reformatories for women prisoners in the middle of the century, but for much of the nineteenth century women were assigned to the same penitentiaries as men. Four women were incarcerated at Eastern State in 1831, all of them African American. Although there was a special cell block for women in that prison, at least one of the women, Ann Hinson, did not live in it, but rather occupied a cell in the most desirable block among male prisoners. Hinson enjoyed a special status because she served as the warden's cook and perhaps his mistress, but her situation, though extreme, was not uncommon. The Old Louisiana State Penitentiary, which functioned from the 1830s to 1918, held male and female prisoners (and a number of the prisoners' children) throughout most of its history. Illinois housed female inmates (less than 3 percent of its prison population) in the penitentiary at Joliet until it finally opened a women's prison in 1896. Few states took the situation of women inmates seriously in the late nineteenth century, Missouri appropriated money for a women's prison in 1875, but neglected to build one until 1926. Idaho created a women's ward in its penitentiary in 1905, but did not build a women's prison until 1974. In contrast to those states that assigned women to penitentiaries along with men, Massachusetts housed its women prisoners in the county jails until it created the Reformatory Prison for Women in 1875. One reason for the delays in creating separate women's prisons was economic. The prisons and prison industries relied on women to do their housekeeping.

The first completely separate prison for women (actually, a reformatory, not a penitentiary) opened in Indiana in 1873. A few years later, in 1877, the first reformatory for men 30 years and under opened in Elmira, New York. In theory, it was intended to rehabilitate younger prisoners by educating them and training them for useful work. To that end, its inmates were graded on their conduct and placed in different classes based on their behavior, with the idea of gradually conditioning them to return to the outside world. In practice, however, things were much as they were in the penitentiaries. Elmira's first director, Zebulon Brockway, had previously been director at the Detroit House of Corrections, where he had been noted for turning a profit with the prison's chair manufacturing business, and he brought the profit motive with him. Elmira inmates worked the entire day in the reformatory's several factories and spent only an hour and a half in the evening at lessons in the reformatory's carefully designed classrooms.

Although the reformatories boasted a range of services for their inmates, the greatest differences between the penitentiary and the reformatory were more basic. One had to do with sentences. Inmates in reformatories typically had indeterminate sentences so they could work themselves out of incarceration. In practice, however, as Samuel Walker notes, their sentences typically lasted longer. The other difference had to do with what brought the inmates to the reformatories in the first place. While some were imprisoned for committing crimes, many, especially women and children, were imprisoned on much more amorphous grounds – having drunken parents or being incorrigible.

Capital punishment was the exception to both the practice of indefinite sentencing and the desire to turn punishment into profit. Aside from the reduction in the number of capital offenses, capital punishment in the United States changed very little from the ratification of the Constitution to the end of World War I, although there were some efforts at reform in both halves of the century. In 1846, Michigan abolished capital punishment, and a handful of other states followed suit. Other states retained the death penalty, but set limits on it in other ways. By 1850, many states had passed laws or informally agreed to move executions to restricted venues, usually inside prison walls, mostly in an effort to emphasize the somber nature of the event and reduce the degree to which an execution was a public and popular spectacle.

But for all the rules that provided that executions should occur within the jail yard, rather than in front of an easily excited crowd, convicted murderers, like the victims of lynch mobs, continued to be hanged before enthusiastic mobs, whose members wangled tickets and passes to the event from sheriffs and local politicians or simply slipped in past the guards watching the gates. The pattern continued after the Civil War, as newspapers reported the executions in grand detail for those who could not make it to the hanging themselves. In Chicago, coverage of an execution typically began a day or so before, with extended stories of the last days, and then the final hours, of the convict. Those stories led up to accounts of the final scene, which reported on the manner in which the condemned approached death (whether with manly courage, cowardice, or dumb indifference), recounted the religious devotions, if any, that preceded the hanging, and recorded any last words that the defendant uttered before the drop. The hanging of particularly infamous criminals, such as the Haymarket defendants, provided Chicago's papers with at least a week's worth of stories, but even Frank Mulkowski, dismissed by most papers as nothing more than a brutish Polish immigrant, earned several days' worth of coverage prior to his execution in 1886.

The biggest change in the death penalty occurred in 1890 when, after several years of debate and considerable lobbying by the purveyors of electricity, the first death by electrocution was attempted at Auburn Penitentiary in New York. Described as quicker, surer, and less painful than death by hanging – which, in the hands of an inept hangman, all too often involved slow strangulation – the first electrocution was anything but. The condemned prisoner, William Kemmler, did not die until the second attempt and had to sit strapped to his chair convulsing uncontrollably for several minutes after the first attempt while the generator was restarted. Fortunately for those who favored the new approach, the next year New York successfully executed four men at Sing Sing using the electric chair. Although that execution quieted some who protested against the practice, opponents of the death penalty had some brief successes in this period. In 1907, Kansas abolished the death penalty, the first state to do so since before the Civil War. Within the next ten years, six other states followed suit; the last, Missouri, did so in 1917. But those successes were short lived. Two years after it passed the law abolishing the death penalty, Missouri reversed itself, reinstating the death penalty. By 1920, three of the other states that had just abolished the death penalty had reinstated it as well.

CONCLUSION

Standard, court-centered accounts of criminal justice in the United States over the long nineteenth century often have an unarticulated premise: that the country moved away from a localized system of criminal justice to embrace the European model of the nation-state, and in so doing abandoned its commitment to popular sovereignty. While some studies note the gains offered by this shift, particularly emphasizing the benefits of having the protections of the Bill of Rights apply to state court proceedings, others appear more concerned by the loss of an indigenous political tradition and the decline of community power. Framed as a narrative of declension, those histories gloss over the extent to which extra-legal violence, popular pressure, and exploitation shaped criminal justice in America during the long nineteenth century. They can do so only by ignoring the struggles that pitted governed against government in state court criminal trials, and the moments when different parts of the government battled one another. And when they do so, they forget the extent to which legal decisions depended more on who the parties were, or the passions of the moment, than on what the law required.

Contemporaries had a sharper understanding of what was going wrong and what needed to be done. The first Justice Harlan's laments in *Hurtado* were echoed by Roscoe Pound's complaints about popular influence on law.[18] Nor were those objections the product of some sort of post–Civil War decline. In the antebellum era, for every article that was published

[18] Roscoe Pound, "The Need of a Sociological Jurisprudence," *Green Bag* 19 (October 1907), 607.

praising the local courts when they rendered a verdict consistent with local ideas of justice, rather than the rule of law,[19] there was a second that deplored the same verdict as a sign of the nation's retreat into a jurisprudence of lawlessness.[20]

[19] *Philadelphia Public Ledger* 8 April 1843, 2 (verdict in Mercer trial).
[20] Anon., "The Trial of Singleton Mercer for the Murder of Mahlon Hutchinson Heberton," *New Englander* 1 (July 1843), 442.

6

CITIZENSHIP AND IMMIGRATION LAW, 1800–1924: RESOLUTIONS OF MEMBERSHIP AND TERRITORY

KUNAL M. PARKER

The paradigmatic function of a national immigration regime is to defend a territorial inside from a territorial outside. Access to and presence within this territorial inside are determined on the basis of whether one is a "citizen" or an "alien," where both terms are understood in their formal legal sense. All of the activities we associate with the contemporary U.S. immigration regime – exclusion and deportation, entry checkpoints, border patrols, detention centers, and the like – make sense in these terms.

Liberal American theorists have provided powerful moral justifications for this defense of the territorial inside from the territorial outside on the ground that it is only in this way that the coherence of a national community on the inside can be preserved and fostered. In this rendering, the coherence of the national community may not take the form of an oppressive *Blut und Boden* nationalism. Rather, the territorial inside must be a homogeneous space of rights enjoyed by all insiders. Although most of these insiders will be citizens, resident immigrants will be treated fairly and given a reasonable opportunity to become citizens. The very coherence of the territorial inside as a homogeneous space of rights justifies immigration restriction. Outsiders – who are imagined as citizens of other countries – have no morally binding claim to be admitted to the inside.

This theoretical rendering of the activities of the national immigration regime is the product of recent history. For the first century of the United States' existence as a nation (from the American Revolution until the 1870s), a national immigration regime that regulated individuals' access to, and presence within, national territory on the basis of their national citizenship simply did not exist. Even after such a regime came into existence in the 1870s, the idea of numerical restrictions on immigration emerged only slowly and was not comprehensively established until the 1920s.

More important, both before *and* after the establishment of a national immigration regime, there was simply no such thing as a territorial inside that was a homogeneous space of rights enjoyed by all those who were territorially present. Throughout American history, the territorial inside has always been rife with internal foreigners or outsiders who have – in a manner exactly analogous to the figure of the outsider of liberal immigration theory – found themselves restricted in their ability to negotiate the American national territory or otherwise inscribed with a lack of belonging. Indeed, the activities of the national immigration regime themselves appear inevitably to be accompanied by an often deliberate blurring of the distinction between inside and outside, citizen and alien.

To recover this history, it is necessary first to invoke the now-vanished world of contested non-national memberships and territorialities that prevailed in the United States until the Civil War. Even as it confronted mass immigration from places like Ireland and Germany, this was a world characterized by multiple internal foreignnesses – principally those applicable to native-born free blacks and paupers – that as such prevented the emergence of a national immigration regime that could direct its gaze outward on the external foreignness of aliens. Only after the Civil War, when national citizenship had been formally extended to the entire native-born population and national citizenship was tentatively linked to the right to travel throughout national territory, could a national immigration regime premised on the external defense of national territory emerge.

Although the core legal relationship between national citizenship and national territory was established for the first time as a result of the Civil War, the path to a national immigration regime of numerical restrictions and "illegal aliens" was neither automatic nor predetermined. Between 1870 and 1924, confronted with a vastly expanded immigration stream from Southern and Eastern Europe and Asia, the American immigration regime shifted from a strategy that sought to sift out limited numbers of undesirables from a basically desirable immigrant stream to a strategy based on the presumption that no alien could enter, and remain within, national territory unless explicitly permitted to do so. This shift took place in a set of overlapping contexts familiar from the writings of American historians – industrial capitalism, scientific racism, formal imperialism, expansion of the national government, and the rise of the administrative state. Yet each new restriction was beset with all manner of uncertainty. How precisely, for example, was one to define "whiteness" for purposes of naturalization law? How was one to determine country quotas for the new immigration regime? How was one to set boundaries between the power of immigration officials and the power of courts?

Notwithstanding the formal extension of national citizenship to the entire native-born population in the aftermath of the Civil War, various internal foreignnesses emerged as the national immigration regime sought to exclude certain kinds of aliens as undesirable. For every undesirable immigrant of a certain ethnic or national description, there corresponded a domestic minority subjected to discrimination and surveillance. Groups that had once found themselves on the inside as the result of a colonial or imperial acquisition of territory were reclassified to the "outside" and fell within the purview of the immigration regime. Conjoined to these new species of internal foreignness must be the legally sanctioned, formal and informal, public and private foreignness imposed on African Americans in the form of segregation – a closing off of public and private spaces analogous to the closing of the border to immigrants. Ironically, important parts of the battle against racial segregation in the urban North would be fought against European ethnic immigrants.

The object of historicizing aspects of the contemporary U.S. immigration regime is to emphasize that there is nothing immanent in national citizenship nor inevitable about its relationship to national territory that points toward the kind of immigration regime that currently subsists in the United States. It is also to show, through an examination of the long history of American citizenship and immigration, that the distinction between inside and outside, citizen and alien, is never clean.

I. EMERGING FROM THE EIGHTEENTH CENTURY (1780–1820)

It is essential to distinguish rigorously between the new category of U.S. citizenship that emerged in the aftermath of the American Revolution and the state-level legal regimes that governed the individual's rights to enter and remain within state territories. In the late eighteenth and early nineteenth centuries, the legal relationship between national citizenship and national territory did not undergird immigration restriction. Instead, U.S. citizenship as a category slowly infiltrated the state-level regimes.

During the Confederation period, the individual states moved to define their own citizenries and to establish naturalization policies. At the same time, however, there was a sense that the American Revolution had created a national politico-legal and territorial community that transcended state boundaries. This is reflected in the "comity clause" of Article IV of the Articles of Confederation, which reads in part as follows: "The better to secure and perpetuate mutual friendship and intercourse among the people of the different states in this union, the free inhabitants of each of these states (paupers, vagabonds, and fugitives from justice excepted) shall be entitled to all privileges and immunities of free citizens in the several states; and the people of each state shall have free ingress and regress to and from any other state." The clause sought for the first time to create something like a relationship between national membership and national territory through the imposition of the duty of comity on the individual states. (Admittedly, as James Madison pointed out at the time, the clause did so in a confused way by asking states to accord the "privileges and immunities of free *citizens*" to the "free *inhabitants*" of other states.[1]) However, what is especially revealing about the clause are the classes of individuals it excludes from the benefits of this obligation of comity; namely, "paupers, vagabonds and fugitives from justice."

With the formation of the United States at the end of the 1780s, the category of U.S. citizenship emerged for the first time as the legal category that would define membership in the new national political community. An important feature was the idea of voluntary, as distinguished from perpetual, allegiance. The English theory had been that subjects owed lifelong allegiance to the monarch. Not surprisingly, the notion that allegiance could be chosen – and hence cast off – was important in justifying the break from Great Britain.

Paradoxically, notwithstanding the new emphasis on the voluntary nature of allegiance, U.S. citizenship was extended among the native-born population by fiat. However, the question of what segments of the native-born population should count as U.S. citizens remained vague. As a sparsely populated country in need of settlers, the United States retained the basic *jus soli* or birthright citizenship orientation of English law. However, the principle of *jus soli* probably worked best only for native-born whites. At its moment of origin, the U.S. Constitution did not deal explicitly with the question of whether or not those belonging to other groups – free blacks, slaves and Native Americans – qualified as U.S. citizens by reason of birth in U.S. territory.

The U.S. Constitution was more explicit about the induction of aliens into the political community. Article I, Section 8 gave Congress the power to promulgate "a uniform rule of naturalization." In 1790, the first federal naturalization act limited naturalization to a "free white person" who had resided for two years in the United States, proved his "good character," and taken an oath "to support the constitution of the United States."[2] The naturalization period was increased to five years by the Naturalization Act of 1795 and has remained at five years ever since, with only one brief aberration in the late 1790s.[3]

The U.S. Constitution also revamped the comity clause of the Articles of Confederation. Article IV, Section 1 provided that "the Citizens of each State shall be entitled to all Privileges and Immunities of Citizens in the

[1] James Madison, *The Federalist*, No. 42. [2] Act of March 26, 1790 (1 Stat. 103).

[3] Act of January 29, 1795 (1 Stat. 414). The aberration was the short-lived Naturalization Act of June 18, 1798 (1 Stat. 566), which increased the naturalization period to fourteen years.

several States." The embarrassing, but revealing, reference to "paupers, vagabonds and fugitives from justice" in the "comity clause" of the Articles of Confederation was removed.

Despite the inauguration of the category of U.S. citizenship, however, Congress did not acquire the explicit constitutional authority to formulate a national immigration policy. Neither did it attempt to establish one in practice. If one had to identify the principal mode in which U.S. citizenship was wielded against aliens at the national level, it would make most sense to say that U.S. citizenship acquired meaning principally as a means of controlling the influence of aliens in the national political arena. Segments of the American national leadership repeatedly expressed fears about the capacity of aliens reared under monarchies or carried away by the excesses of the French Revolution to exercise republican citizenship in a responsible fashion. Evidence of these fears may be observed in the Constitutional Convention's debates over the qualifications for national political office and later, and more egregiously, in the Federalist anti-alien paranoia reflected in the passage of the Alien and Sedition Acts in the late 1790s.

The point, however, is that immigration policies – those everyday policies that determined outsiders' access to, and presence within, territory – remained in the hands of the states. State and local authorities regulated outsiders' access to their territories without relying on U.S. citizenship as providing the exclusive logic for distinguishing between insiders and outsiders.

For the most part, in the decades immediately following the American Revolution, the states continued colonial policies for regulating access to their territories. Colonial policies regarding the settling of British North America were influential in establishing an image of America that endured well beyond the Revolution. Hector St. John de Crèvecoeur's celebrated *Letters from an American Farmer*, which depicted America as a place where Europe's dispossessed could flourish, had in fact been written *before* the Revolution, although it was not published until the 1780s. Furthermore, a set of concerted British policies that had constituted America as something of a haven for European Protestants by the mid-eighteenth century fed directly into the post-Revolutionary national idea, first articulated in Thomas Paine's *Common Sense*, of America as "an asylum for mankind."

The actual legal structures regulating movement of peoples during the colonial period had always been distinct from the rosy vision of America as an "asylum." Colonial assemblies had adhered to the mercantilist idea that population equaled wealth. However, they had also repeatedly expressed misgivings about the specific kinds of people entering their territories as a result of British policies. These misgivings could be categorized as dislike of (a) the foreign (with a particular animus directed against Catholics), (b) the criminal, and (c) the indigent. Of these, it is the last that determined most unequivocally the logic of colonial territorial restriction.

What is especially noteworthy about colonial territorial restrictions is the seemingly indiscriminate way in which they mingled dislike of insiders and outsiders. The regulation of what was frequently labeled a "trade in persons" appears to have been an external manifestation of a highly articulated internal regime for regulating natives' access to territory. The governing logic of this comprehensive system of territorial restriction is to be found in American versions of the seventeenth-century English poor laws. The idea was that the poor were to be denied territorial mobility *as the poor*, because of the fear that they would impose costs on the places they entered, whether they entered such places from a place "beyond sea" or from a place just a few miles away.

It is particularly telling that local *poor relief* officials were entrusted with the responsibility for administering external and internal statutes regulating the territorial mobility of persons. In eighteenth-century Massachusetts, for example, shipmasters were required by a series of statutes to post a bond with local poor relief officials so that towns receiving "lame, impotent, or infirm persons, incapable of maintaining themselves . . . would not be charged with their support."[4] At the same time, townspeople were required in a series of "entertainment" statutes to notify local poor relief officials of individuals from other towns who were visiting them; failure to notify meant imposition of legal responsibility for any costs associated with such individuals on their hosts. Towns even provided their own legal residents with travel documents – species of internal passports – certifying that they would take them back in the event of illness or injury.

In the eighteenth century, in other words, "foreignness" was a polyvalent word. It denoted those who were outside the larger community of allegiance and blood, to be sure, but could also designate those who came from neighboring towns and colonies. National membership was not mapped onto territory in such a way that it carried with it rights of access to national territory conceived as such. Nor did territorial disabilities follow uniquely and unequivocally from a lack of national membership.

This sense that the poor were undesirable as the poor, and were to be denied territorial mobility regardless of their citizenship status, continued in full force after the American Revolution. As we have seen, the comity

[4] "An Act Directing the Admission of Town Inhabitants," in *The Acts and Resolves, Public and Private, of the Province of Massachusetts Bay*, 21 Vols. (Boston: Wright & Potter, 1869–1922), I, chap. 23 (1701).

clause of the Articles of Confederation excepted "paupers, vagabonds, and fugitives from justice" from each state's obligation to accord the "privileges and immunities of free citizens" to the "free inhabitants" of the other states. The native poor were thus rendered as internal foreigners to be denied territorial mobility.

Although states remained faithful to colonial poor relief models in most essentials, they also began incrementally and confusedly to insert new categories of citizenship into these models. But the legislation of this period does not appear to have distinguished meaningfully between U.S. citizenship and state citizenship. Furthermore, the disabilities imposed on natives and aliens were roughly comparable and were the result of a local politics. For example, under New York's 1788 "Act for the Better Settlement and Relief of the Poor," shipmasters were required to report the names and occupations of all "persons" brought into the port of New York and would be fined £20 for each unreported person, and £30 if such person was a "foreigner." The law further denied admission to "any person" who could not give a good account of himself to local authorities or was likely to become a charge to the city; such persons were to be returned "to the place whence he or she came."[5]

Massachusetts chose to refer to state citizenship, rather than U.S. citizenship, in its legislation. Thus, in the early 1790s, in a dramatic departure from colonial practice, Massachusetts made citizenship "of this or any of the United States" (but not U.S. citizenship) a prerequisite to the acquisition of "settlement" or "inhabitancy" in a town, thereby making it impossible for non-citizens to acquire legal rights to residence and poor relief in the town in which they lived, worked, and paid taxes. The same law also contained various provisions intended to make it difficult for citizens from other states and Massachusetts citizens from other towns to acquire a "settlement."[6]

Occasional statutory discriminations between citizens and aliens notwithstanding, indigent citizens might sometimes be worse off than indigent aliens. When cities and towns physically removed foreigners from their territories, they were far more likely to remove those who were citizens than those who were not, for the simple reason that it was cheaper to send someone to a neighboring state than to Europe. Connecticut's law of 1784 expressed an accepted principle of sound poor relief administration when it authorized the removal of all foreigners who became public charges, so long as the cost

[5] "Act for the Better Settlement and Relief of the Poor" (1788, chap. 62), *Laws of the State of New York Passed at the Sessions of the Legislature Held in the Years 1785, 1786, 1787, and 1788, Inclusive* (Albany: Weed Parsons and Company, 1886).

[6] "An Act Ascertaining What Shall Constitute a Legal Settlement of any Person in any Town or District Within this Commonwealth," Acts 1793, Chapter 34.

of transportation did not exceed "the advantage of such transportation."[7] Of 1,039 individuals "warned out" of Boston in 1791, 237 were born in foreign countries, 62 in other states, and 740 in other Massachusetts towns. Of course, "warned out" means only that these individuals were rendered legally subject to physical removal, not that they were actually physically removed. But evidence of actual physical removals out of state in late-eighteenth century Massachusetts points toward removals to New York and Nova Scotia, rather than to Europe or the West Indies.

The highly local understanding of the distinction between insider and outsider points to a central feature of systems of territorial restriction in the late eighteenth and early nineteenth centuries; namely, that even as territorial restrictions were promulgated at the state level and began to incorporate the new categories of U.S. and state citizenship, individual cities and towns rather than state authorities remained responsible in the first instance for the administration of poor relief and territorial restrictions. As immigration increased in the late eighteenth and early nineteenth centuries, seaports such as Boston, New York, and Philadelphia began to protest the injustice of having to bear the burden of supporting sick, poor, and disabled aliens. Tensions developed between state and local authorities; they would become more serious and would be resolved only through bureaucratic centralization at the state level by the middle of the nineteenth century.

In the late eighteenth and early nineteenth centuries, one other emergent system of internal territorial restriction should be mentioned: that applicable to free blacks. This system of territorial restriction was intertwined with that of the poor laws, but also distinct from it.

Slaves had always been subject to spatial and territorial restrictions as slaves. However, in the late eighteenth and early nineteenth centuries, the Northern abolition of slavery and the introduction of manumission acts in the South brought the problem of free blacks into sharp focus. Towns and localities all over the North expressed distaste for free blacks and sought to exclude and remove them from their territories through any means available. The important point here is that Northern towns and localities were expressing hostility not only toward blacks from the territorial outside (fugitive slaves or free blacks from the mid-Atlantic or Southern states; sailors and other migrants from the West Indies) but also toward individuals who had always been on the territorial inside (i.e., individuals who had been tolerated as town and local residents so long as they were slaves, but who had become repugnant with the coming of freedom). Freedom for Northern blacks brought with it, in other words, official, although ultimately unsuccessful,

[7] Quoted in Marriyn C. Baseler, *"Asylum for Mankind"; America, 1607–1800* (Ithaca, N.Y., 1998), 197.

efforts to render them foreign. As we shall see, this problem would become much more serious in the Upper South later in the nineteenth century. It is important, nevertheless, to establish that this distinct problem of internal foreignness began in the late eighteenth and early nineteenth centuries in the North.

II. TENSIONS OF THE ANTEBELLUM PERIOD (1820–1860)

From the perspective of the law of immigration and citizenship, the period from 1820 to 1860 was one of immense confusion. Although there was a marked development of a sense of national citizenship as implying certain rights with respect to national territory, this burgeoning national imagination coexisted with powerful – in the case of free blacks, increasingly powerful – internal foreignnesses. The result was two distinct sets of conflicts.

The first conflict occurred over the question whether the U.S. government or the states possessed the constitutional authority to regulate immigration. There was no immigration restriction at the national level. Nevertheless, between 1820 and 1860, as part of its developing Commerce Clause jurisprudence, the U.S. Supreme Court chipped away at the states' constitutional authority to regulate immigration. However, as long as slavery remained alive, the U.S. Supreme Court would not definitively rule that states had no constitutional authority to regulate immigration, because to do so would have stripped states – especially Southern states – of the power to regulate alien and native free blacks' access to their territories.

In this atmosphere of uncertainty surrounding the locus of constitutional authority over immigration restriction arose a second, distinct conflict: should the everyday regulation of outsiders' access to territory take place at the state or local level? Since the eighteenth century, the regulation of outsiders' access to territory had taken place at the local level. However, centralized state authority grew steadily throughout the antebellum period. Particularly as mass immigration into the United States picked up after 1820, state authorities increasingly became persuaded that the excessively parochial interests of local officials were obstructing the efficient regulation of non-citizens' access to state territories. By 1860, after decades of experimentation and conflict between state and local authorities, large state-level bureaucratic apparatuses had emerged to regulate immigration into state territories.

Federal-State Conflict and the Problem of Black Foreignness

As the Republic matured, there emerged the sense that *some* relationship must exist between national citizenship and national territory. This sense was conventionally expressed in terms of the rights that citizens of one state enjoyed with respect to the territory of another. In 1823, in the clearest antebellum attempt to elucidate the meaning of the "privileges and immunities" clause of Article IV of the U.S. Constitution, Justice Bushrod Washington declared that the "privileges" within the meaning of the constitutional text were those "which are, in their nature, *fundamental.*" One of these allegedly "fundamental" privileges was "the right of a citizen of one state to pass through, or to reside in any other state, for the purposes of trade, agriculture, professional pursuits, or otherwise. . . . "[8] However, one also encounters judicial pronouncements to the effect that *national* citizenship as such implied a right to travel throughout *national* territory. For example, in 1849, Chief Justice Taney's dissenting opinion in the *Passenger Cases* stated, "We are all citizens of the United States, and, as members of the same community, must have the right to pass and repass through every part of it without interruption, as freely as in our own States."[9]

The apprehension that there was some relationship between national citizenship and national territory continued to leave open the interrelated questions of (a) who belonged to the community of national citizens and enjoyed rights to enter and remain within every part of national territory and (b) which authority, the federal or the state governments, had the power to exclude and remove non-citizens from territory. We explore the second question before turning to the first.

The formal constitutional question was whether Congress possessed the power to exclude and remove non-citizens from national territory pursuant to Article 1, Section 8 of the U.S. Constitution, which gave it the authority "to regulate Commerce with foreign Nations, and among the several States," or whether the states possessed a corresponding power as part of their regular and residual "police" power to promote the health, safety, and welfare of their populations. The paradoxes of the antebellum legal representation of the movement of persons as "commerce" should not be lost. To begin with, the eighteenth-century "trade" in indentured labor had essentially died out by 1820. More important, however, to argue that the movement of "persons" was "commerce," and therefore that Congress could constitutionally regulate immigration, had anti-slavery implications. It opened the door for suggestions that Congress could constitutionally prevent the slave and free states from regulating the ingress of alien and native free blacks into their territories and even hinted, surreptitiously and by implication, that native free blacks might be U.S. citizens with the right to move throughout national territory.

Accordingly, it was the pro-slavery wing of the U.S. Supreme Court that argued most insistently that "persons" were *not* "articles of commerce" and

[8] *Corfield v. Coryell*, 4 Wash. C.C. 371, 380–81 (U.S.C.C. 1823).

[9] *Passenger Cases* (*Smith v. Turner; Norris v. Boston*), 48 U.S. (7 How.) 283, 283, 492 (1849).

that tended most often to invoke the figure of "the immigrant" as someone who exercised volition in coming to the United States. In his dissent in the *Passenger Cases*, for example, Justice Daniel argued indignantly that "the term imports is justly applicable to articles of trade proper, – goods, chattels, property, subjects in their nature passive and having no volition, – not to men whose emigration is the result of will"; it would be a "perversion" to argue otherwise.[10] For constitutional purposes, the invocation of the white immigrant as an actor capable of volition in movement served to secure the perpetuation of black slavery.

The tussle between the view that states could not constitutionally regulate immigrant traffic and the (pro-slavery) view that states could constitutionally regulate the influx of all non-citizens as a matter of state police power was never resolved before the Civil War. In 1837, in *Mayor of the City of New York v. Miln*, the U.S. Supreme Court upheld a New York law that required shipmasters to report passenger information and to post bonds for passengers who might become chargeable to the city.[11] In 1849, however, in the *Passenger Cases*, a deeply divided Court struck down New York and Massachusetts laws that involved the collection of head taxes on incoming immigrants.[12]

Beneath this formal constitutional debate lay the explosive question of whether free blacks were part of the community of U.S. citizens and, as such, whether they possessed the right to travel throughout national territory. Throughout the antebellum period, both free and slave states adamantly insisted on their ability to exclude alien and native free blacks. Even in states that saw themselves as bastions of anti-slavery sentiment, free blacks were unwelcome. In 1822, in a report entitled *Free Negroes and Mulattoes*, a Massachusetts legislative committee emphasized "the necessity of checking the increase of a species of population, which threatens to be both injurious and burthensome. . . . "[13] States further west sought to oblige blacks seeking residence to give sureties that they would not become public charges. In other instances, blacks were forbidden to move into the state altogether, sometimes as a result of state constitutional provisions.

The paranoia about the presence of free blacks was, of course, far greater in the slave states, where the presence of free blacks was thought to give a lie to increasingly sophisticated racial justifications for slavery. As the ideological struggle over slavery intensified, the situation of native free blacks in the South worsened. Slave state legislation usually barred the entry of free blacks

[10] *Passenger Cases* at 506.

[11] *Mayor of New York v. Miln*, 36 U.S. (11 Pet.) 102 (1837).

[12] *Passenger Cases.*

[13] Massachusetts General Court, House of Representatives, *Free Negroes and Mulattoes* (Boston, True & Green, 1822), 1.

not already residents of the state. However, over time, the states extended these prohibitions to their own free black residents who sought to return after traveling outside the state either to a disapproved location or to any destination at all. Slave states also often required that manumitted slaves leave the state forever, on pain of re-enslavement. Shortly before the Civil War, several slave states considered forcing their free black populations to choose between enslavement and expulsion, and Arkansas actually passed such legislation.

The U.S. Supreme Court repeatedly acquiesced in free and slave states' attempts to exclude native-born free blacks. For example, in 1853, in *Moore v. Illinois*, Justice Grier stated, "In the exercise of this power, which has been denominated the police power, a State has a right to make it a penal offence to introduce paupers, criminals or fugitive slaves, within their borders. . . . Some of the States, coterminous with those who tolerate slavery, have found it necessary to protect themselves against the influx either of liberated or fugitive slaves, and to repel from their soil a population likely to become burdensome and injurious, either as paupers or criminals."[14] The larger point here is that, in acquiescing in the states' efforts to exclude native-born free blacks, the Court was also taking a position on native-born free blacks' status as U.S. citizens. If Chief Justice Taney could state in the *Passenger Cases* that national citizenship implied a right to travel throughout national territory, to uphold states' rights to exclude native-born free blacks was tantamount to excluding native-born free blacks from national citizenship.

In general, native-born free blacks remained suspended between the status of citizen and alien. Northern courts trod carefully and hypocritically in this area, formally upholding *both* black citizenship and the discriminatory laws that impaired that status. Their conclusions were ultimately used to justify a denial of free blacks' national citizenship on the ground that no state actually recognized the full citizenship of free blacks and, *therefore*, that free blacks could not be members of the national community.

This position shaped the United States' willingness to recognize blacks as its own when they traveled abroad. U.S. Secretaries of State invoked blacks' lack of full citizenship in Northern states to justify their hesitation in issuing native-born free blacks passports attesting to their U.S. citizenship. In 1839, a Philadelphia black was denied a passport on the ground that Pennsylvania's denial of suffrage to blacks meant that its blacks were not state citizens, which implied that they could not be U.S. citizens. From 1847 on, the policy was to give blacks special certificates, instead of regular passports. The U.S. Supreme Court's tortured 1857 decision in *Scott v. Sandford* merely confirmed this suspension of native-born free blacks between the status of

[14] *Moore v. Illinois*, 55 U.S. (14 How.) 13 (1853) (Grier, J.).

citizen and alien. According to Justice Taney's opinion, blacks could not be U.S. citizens by reason of birth on U.S. soil (*jus soli*), birth to a citizen father (*jus sanguinis*), or naturalization.[15]

The legal decision to suspend blacks between citizen and alien status should not obscure the range of efforts, private and public, actively to represent native-born free blacks as "Africans" with a view to shipping them back to Africa. Here, the effort was not so much to deny blacks legal citizenship as quite literally to give blacks – but only those who were free – a *bona fide* foreign identity and place of origin to which they could be removed. Representing itself variously, as the occasion demanded, as both pro-slavery and anti-slavery, the American Colonization Society privately established the colony of Liberia in West Africa, to which it sought to encourage free blacks to return. Slaveholders all over the south conditioned manumission on their slaves' agreement to depart for Liberia, conditions that were legally upheld.

Considerable public support for colonization existed, particularly in the Upper South. Legislatures in Delaware, Maryland, Kentucky, Tennessee, and Virginia all appropriated moneys to facilitate colonization. Maryland's plan was the most ambitious. In the early 1830s, Maryland appropriated $200,000 to be spent over twenty years to "colonize" manumitted slaves. The legislature ordered county clerks to report all manumissions to a state-appointed Board of Managers for the Removal of Colored People, which instructed the Maryland State Colonization Society to remove the manumitted slave to Africa or any other place deemed suitable. Newly freed blacks wishing to remain in the state could choose re-enslavement or appeal to a county orphan's court. Those who were unable to obtain court permission and resisted the re-enslavement option might be forcibly transported. Of course, the draconian nature of these laws should not suggest an equally draconian enforcement: Baltimore became a center of free black life in the antebellum years.

Given this considerable investment in denying blacks' legal citizenship and in insisting on their foreignness, it is not surprising that at least some Southern state courts formally assimilated out-of-state free blacks to the status of aliens. This was hardly a common legal position (for the most part, states were satisfied simply to deny blacks' citizenship), but it is the ultimate illustration of the internal foreignness of native-born free blacks. In the 1859 decision of *Heirn v. Bridault*, involving the right of a Louisiana free black woman to inherit the property of a white man with whom she had been cohabiting in Mississippi, the Mississippi Supreme Court formally ruled that the woman could not inherit property *as an alien*. It offered the

[15] *Scott v. Sandford*, 60 U.S. (19 How.) 393 (1857).

following rationale: "[F]ree negroes [who were in Mississippi in violation of law] are to be regarded as alien enemies or strangers prohibiti, and without the pale of comity, and incapable of acquiring or maintaining property in this State which will be recognized by our courts."[16]

State-Local Conflicts Over Immigration

The constitutional conflict over whether the federal government or the states possessed the legal authority to regulate immigration created an atmosphere of legal uncertainty in which states were left to cope as best they could with the growing tide of immigrants. Antebellum immigration from Europe began in earnest in the 1820s and peaked between the late 1840s and mid-1850s as a result of the Irish famine migration. The migration of the first half of the nineteenth century was largely German and Irish and heavily Catholic. It was directly connected with, indeed indispensable to, the development of capitalism in the North. For the first time, it made sense to refer to an immigrant working class.

For the first time as well, there was a highly organized popular nativist movement. Antebellum popular nativism might be characterized as an attempt on the part of white working-class Americans at a time of bewildering change to combat what they perceived as their own increasing disempowerment. Fired by the fear of a vast Catholic conspiracy designed to subvert the Protestant Republic, nativists sought in the first instance to reduce immigrant participation in political life. Anti-immigrant tracts routinely called for lengthening the naturalization period so that immigrants would be properly educated in the ways of republican life before they could vote, checking fraudulent naturalizations, and safeguarding the integrity of the ballot box.

Throughout the surge of popular nativism, state-level immigration regimes remained oriented to the exclusion of the poor, although they also targeted immigrants with criminal backgrounds. However, important developments distinguished these state-level immigration regimes from their eighteenth-century predecessors. First, the modalities of territorial restriction were changing. Statutes that had once imposed restrictions on all incoming "persons" with only slight discriminations aimed at aliens gave way to statutes that targeted incoming "alien passengers" alone. Possibly the change registered a growing sense that the right to travel without undue impediment, at least for white Americans, was now one of the "privileges and immunities" secured them by Article IV of the U.S. Constitution. Whatever the reason, the local nature of territorial membership was giving

[16] *Heirn v. Bridault*, 37 Miss. 209, 233 (1859).

way to a sense that (a lack of) national citizenship implied (a lack of) rights to enter state territories. Second, states engaged in a strategic attempt to terminate resident immigrants' rights to remain in state territories. Although the applicable poor law regimes continued to provide for the removal of both in-state and out-of-state paupers to their localities or states of origin, the bureaucratic focus was increasingly on "alien paupers." The aim was explicitly to frighten immigrants into refraining from seeking poor relief for fear that removal would be a consequence of making demands for public assistance. The result was the beginning of a regular, if still small, transatlantic deportation process in the 1830s and 1840s.

The creation of a relationship between national citizenship and state territory was accompanied by a change in the *kinds* of disabilities placed on entering aliens. In the late eighteenth and early nineteenth centuries, shipmasters had been required to post bond in respect of incoming persons with local poor relief officials; these bonds would be acted on should such persons become chargeable to the localities they entered. However, local poor relief officials had often found it difficult to collect on the bonds. Immigrants often changed their names on arrival, which made them impossible to trace. In the 1820s, 1830s, and 1840s, accordingly, there was a shift to a system of outright taxation. In Massachusetts and New York, shipmasters had to pay a tax on all incoming immigrants and to post bond only for incoming immigrants with physical disadvantages. The tax revenues supported a vast network of services for paupers, both immigrant and native. When the *Passenger Cases* invalidated the Massachusetts and New York head taxes in 1849, states resorted to the stratagem of requiring a bond for all incoming immigrants and offering shipmasters the "option" of commuting bonds for a fee that was the exact equivalent of the head tax.

The relationship between national citizenship and state territory was inextricably bound up with the creation of centralized state-level bureaucratic structures that dislodged the local structures that had continued in force since the eighteenth century. Although this history must necessarily be faithful to the legal-institutional arrangements prevailing in the different states, the experience of Massachusetts is illustrative. There, the centralization of control over aliens' territorial rights and poor relief claims that took place between the late 1840s and mid-1850s was in an immediate sense a response to the Irish famine migration of the same period. But it was also the culmination of growing tensions between the state and the towns over matters of immigration and poor relief. Under the system of territorial restriction and poor relief that had prevailed since the eighteenth century, towns were required to bear the costs of supporting their own poor. However, they were also expected to administer poor relief to those who had failed to acquire legal residency in any town in the state, a category that included immigrants and out-of-state migrants, on condition of being reimbursed by the state. At the same time, town poor relief officials were entrusted with the responsibility of regulating outsiders' access to and presence within territory.

As immigrant pauperism increased throughout the 1830s and 1840s, Massachusetts sought to reduce the costs of supporting immigrant paupers by instituting a head tax on incoming immigrants and by generating discourses of citizenship that held the claims of immigrant paupers to be essentially illegitimate because they were the claims of aliens. However, the state's efforts to reduce the costs associated with immigrant pauperism were repeatedly frustrated by the actions of town poor relief officials. Town officials were notoriously lax in enforcing "alien passenger" laws because they knew that immigrant paupers would become the charge of the state rather than of the towns. They also showed a disturbing tendency to cheat the state in their request for reimbursements for supporting immigrant paupers by illegally inflating their reimbursement requests (the towns sought to shift the costs of supporting their own poor onto the state, often by representing native paupers as immigrant paupers). At the height of the Irish famine migration, state officials concluded that they simply could no longer afford the costs associated with town poor relief officials' excessively narrow view of their own interests that caused them to cheat the state or ignore its laws. The result was that Massachusetts centralized the regulation of immigrants' access to territory and the administration of poor relief to immigrants in the late 1840s and early 1850s.

The Massachusetts experience of centralization shows how the state-generated discursive link between national citizenship and state territory could be of little concern at the local level. One reason for this persistent local disregard of a state-generated connection between national citizenship and state territory – and of state discourses that sought to demonize the immigrant poor as aliens – was that national citizenship, understood in the sense of a right to poor relief and a right to reside in the community of one's choice, was still a relatively meaningless category when it came to the treatment of the native poor generally. So long as the native poor were disenfranchised and remained unable to travel throughout national territory as citizens – in other words, so long as the native poor were a species of internal foreigners – local officials would continue to ignore the state-level distinction between the native poor and the immigrant poor. They would treat native paupers much as they treated alien paupers, hounding them out of their towns and localities. Only with the replacement of local control by state control was this problem solved.

III. THE FEDERAL ERA (1860–1924)

In bringing slavery to an end, the Civil War removed the major impetus for states' insistence on the right to regulate access to their territories. State-level immigration regimes were declared unconstitutional shortly thereafter.[17] The Civil War also resulted in a clearing up of the variegated antebellum extension of citizenship to the native-born population. In 1868, expressly with a view to overruling the *Dred Scott* decision, Congress wrote the principle of *jus soli* or birthright citizenship into the Fourteenth Amendment to the U.S. Constitution, thereby fundamentally reordering the relationship between federal and state citizenship. U.S. citizenship was defined as a matter of a "person's" birth or naturalization in the United States, with state citizenship following from U.S. citizenship as a function of where U.S. citizens resided. Native-born blacks would never again be suspended between the legal status of citizen and alien or, worse yet, formally assimilated to the status of aliens in certain states.

The Architecture of the Federal Immigration Order

As U.S. citizenship was formally extended to the entire native-born population and the vestiges of state-level territorial control removed, it began to make sense to conceive of national territory as a space of and for the community of U.S. citizens in a more encompassing way than had been possible in the antebellum period. There were tentative moves toward constitutionalizing the right to travel throughout the nation's territory as an incident of U.S. citizenship. In 1867, the U.S. Supreme Court struck down a Nevada tax on persons leaving the state by means of public transportation on the ground that national citizenship encompassed the right to travel from state to state.[18] Although this decision did not attempt to bring state legal restrictions on the territorial mobility of the native poor to an end, it was the first significant constitutional pronouncement that set the stage for their long decline (a decline that would not be completed before the second half of the twentieth century[19]).

Such developments might be seen as contributing to the emergence of a national immigration regime that could turn its gaze exclusively outward on immigrants. But new forms of internal foreignness emerged coevally with the national immigration regime. Unlike in the antebellum period,

[17] *Henderson v. Mayor of New York*, 92 U.S. 259 (1876); *Chy Lung v. Freeman*, 92 U.S. 275 (1876).

[18] *Crandall v. Nevada*, 73 U.S. (6 Wall.) 35, 41 (1867).

[19] *Shapiro v. Thompson*, 394 U.S. 618, 89 S.Ct. 1322 (1969).

however, they did not get in the way of the development of the national immigration regime; rather, they were often its direct outcome. The targeting of immigrants by race, ethnicity, and national origin blurred the distinction between immigrants and domestic minorities, even as making U.S. citizenship a prerequisite to the enjoyment of various rights, privileges, and benefits introduced various kinds of discrimination into the lived community.

If the aftermath of the Civil War resulted in a national immigration regime and the creation of fresh internal foreignnesses, however, the constitutional legacy of the Civil War also, perhaps unwittingly, limited both the federal and state governments in ways that could sometimes redound to the benefit of immigrants. As national territory was consolidated as a space of and for U.S. citizens, it was also consolidated in theory as a homogeneous space of constitutional rights – transformed, as it were, into a coherent territorial inside. The nature of these constitutional rights was of course not always clear and would be the subject of struggle. Nevertheless, because the Fourteenth Amendment's language lent its protections explicitly to "persons," rather than citizens, immigrants on the territorial inside could invoke it against the state.

The structure of the new immigration regime is exemplified in the state's dealings with Chinese immigrants. Chinese had been immigrating to the United States since the late 1840s. Despite the small number of Chinese immigrants, anti-Chinese sentiment in California was intense. Organized white labor in particular saw in the Chinese a dangerous threat to its hard-won standard of living.

The question of Chinese access to U.S. citizenship was resolved early against the Chinese. In the aftermath of the Civil War, Congress had moved to amend the naturalization statute that had hitherto restricted naturalization to "free white persons" so as to make naturalization available to individuals of African descent. In 1870, Senator Charles Sumner of Massachusetts had proposed simply to delete references to "white" in the naturalization law, thereby opening up the possibility of citizenship to all immigrants, but Congressmen from the Western states had defeated his proposal on the ground that it would permit the Chinese to become citizens. Accordingly, naturalization was extended only to "aliens of African nativity and to persons of African descent."[20] Attorneys subsequently bringing naturalization petitions on behalf of Chinese immigrants argued that the term "white" in the 1870 naturalization law was poorly defined and should be interpreted to include the Chinese. The federal courts disagreed, however, on the ground that a white person was of the Caucasian race and that Chinese were of the

[20] Act of July 14, 1870 (16 Stat. 254).

"Mongolian race."[21] Nevertheless, the Fourteenth Amendment's embrace of "persons" in its birthright citizenship clause ensured that native-born Chinese would be U.S. citizens. In 1898, despite arguments from the government to the contrary (which suggests that the *jus soli* principle of the Fourteenth Amendment could be disputed even thirty years after its promulgation), the U.S. Supreme Court held as much.[22]

Despite the hostility to admitting Chinese into the national community, there had always existed a current of pro-Chinese sentiment growing from appreciation for Chinese labor, on the one hand, and the desire to increase commercial contact with China, on the other. In 1868, the United States and China had signed the Burlingame Treaty, which recognized reciprocal rights of travel "for purposes of curiosity, of trade, or as permanent residents."[23] However, anti-Chinese sentiment in California slowly seeped into national attitudes toward the Chinese. In 1875, as the very first piece of federal immigration legislation, Congress passed the Page Law, aimed at excluding "coolie labor" and Chinese prostitutes.[24]

As the move to restrict the entry of Chinese became a key issue in the national election of 1880, the United States renegotiated the Burlingame Treaty to give itself the right to "regulate, limit or suspend" the immigration of Chinese laborers whenever their entry or residence in the United States "affects or threatens to affect the interests of that country, or to endanger the good order of [the United States] or of any locality within the territory thereof."[25] Shortly thereafter, in 1882, Congress enacted the first of a series of Chinese exclusion laws suspending the immigration of Chinese laborers.[26] For the first time, the United States denied individuals the right to enter the country on the ground of race or nationality.

When the Chinese exclusion laws were challenged before the U.S. Supreme Court, the Court articulated for the first time in immigration law what was known as the "plenary power" doctrine. Although it acknowledged that the 1888 exclusion law under challenge was in fact in conflict with the treaty with China, the Court decided that it had no power to curb Congress's power to exclude aliens, regardless of the injustices inflicted on them. It expressed itself as follows: "The power of exclusion of foreigners being an incident of sovereignty belonging to the government of the United States, as part of the sovereign powers delegated by the Constitution, the

[21] *In re Ah Yup*, 5 Sawyer 155 (1878).
[22] *United States v. Wong Kim Ark*, 169 U.S. 649 (1898).
[23] Treaty of July 28, 1868 (16 Stat. 739).
[24] Immigration Act of March 3, 1875 (18 Stat. 477).
[25] Treaty of November 17, 1880 (22 Stat. 826).
[26] Act of May 6, 1882 (22 Stat. 58).

right to its exercise at any time when, in the judgment of the government, the interests of the country require it, cannot be granted away or restrained on behalf of any one."[27] Thus the source of the federal government's exclusion power – a power that had not been free from doubt as a matter of constitutional law for the entire period up to the Civil War – shifted from antebellum interpretations of the Commerce Clause to an invocation of "sovereignty" that had no explicit grounding in the constitutional text.

From its decision to immunize from substantive judicial review the federal power to exclude entering immigrants, the U.S. Supreme Court moved to immunize the federal power to deport resident immigrants. The 1892 Geary Act provided for the deportation of resident aliens. All Chinese laborers living in the United States were required to obtain a "certificate of residence" from the Collector of Internal Revenue within one year of the passage of the Act. Under regulations promulgated pursuant to the 1892 Act, the government would issue a certificate only on the "affidavit of at least one credible [white] witness." Any Chinese alien who failed to obtain the certificate could be "arrested . . . and taken before a United States judge, whose duty it [was] to order that he be deported from the United States."[28]

The Geary Act sparked a non-compliance campaign led by the Chinese Six Companies, the leading Chinese immigrant organization of the day. However, when the Six Companies set up a test case that reached the U.S. Supreme Court, they met defeat. The Court declared that "[t]he right of a nation to expel or deport foreigners, who have not been naturalized or taken any steps towards becoming citizens of the country, rests upon the same grounds, and is as absolute and unqualified as the right to prohibit and prevent their entrance into the country." Even worse, the Court ruled that deportation "is not a punishment for a crime," but only "a method of enforcing the return to his own country of an alien." The implication of interpreting deportation as a civil, rather than a criminal, sanction was that the deported alien was not entitled to the constitutional protections ordinarily applicable in criminal proceedings.[29]

The very harshness of the plenary power doctrine led to the invigoration of two different sets of legal principles that are a hallmark of modern immigration law; namely, the territorial inside/outside distinction and the procedure-substance distinction. With respect to the territorial inside/outside distinction, the U.S. Supreme Court made it clear that the Fourteenth Amendment to the U.S. Constitution protected all "persons" who

[27] *Chinese Exclusion Case (Chae Chan Ping v. United States)*, 130 U.S. 581 (1889).
[28] Chinese Exclusion Act of May 5, 1892 (27 Stat. 25).
[29] *Fong Yue Ting v. United States*, 149 U.S. 698 (1893).

happened to be on the territorial inside from certain kinds of actions by the federal and state governments (including discriminatory legislation by state governments that the Court deemed a violation of the Equal Protection Clause).[30] It is important to note, however, that this constitutional commitment to protecting all "persons" who happened to be inside U.S. territory did not reach the federal government's "plenary power" to exclude and deport on the basis of race.

The procedure-substance distinction was the subject of regular struggle between the federal government and Chinese immigrants. As the federal government's substantive power to exclude and deport aliens was progressively immunized from judicial review under the "plenary power" doctrine, Chinese immigrants' strategies focused increasingly on procedural issues. The battle between the state and Chinese immigrants over procedure is significant because it reveals how the state consistently sought, through manipulation of its emerging administrative forms, to blur the distinction between citizen and alien in its efforts to exclude and remove Chinese.

From the beginning, the Chinese community in San Francisco had been adept in seeking out judicial assistance to curb the excesses of overzealous immigration officials. Despite federal judges' stated opposition to Chinese immigration, they often tended to use their habeas corpus jurisdiction to overturn immigration officials' decisions to exclude Chinese immigrants, thereby leading to considerable tension between the courts and the bureaucrats, with the latter accusing the former of subverting the administration of the Chinese exclusion laws. The success of Chinese immigrants in using courts to curb the excesses of immigration officials eventually led Congress to pass laws that endowed administrative decisions with legal finality. Immigration restriction thus became one of the key sites for the emergence of the administrative state.

In 1891, dissatisfied with the state bureaucracies that had been administering federal immigration laws, Congress passed a new immigration law that abrogated contracts with state boards of immigration and created a federal superintendent of immigration who would be subject to review by the secretary of the treasury.[31] The 1891 act also made decisions of immigration inspection officers final. Appeals could be taken to the superintendent of immigration and then to the secretary of the treasury. Thus, judicial review of administrative decisions was eliminated for entering immigrants. In 1891, when a Japanese immigrant who was denied admission on the ground that she would become a public charge challenged the procedural

[30] *Yick Wo v. Hopkins*, 118 U.S. 356 (1886); *Wong Wing v. United States*, 163 U.S. 228 (1896).

[31] Immigration Act of March 3, 1891 (26 Stat. 1084).

arrangements of the 1891 act as a denial of due process, the U.S. Supreme Court dismissed her claims.[32]

The principle of judicial deference to administrators led to a blurring of the distinction between citizens and aliens, and thence to the constitution of the internal foreignness of Chinese immigrants. Of immediate concern to administrators was the strategy adopted by the attorneys of Chinese immigrants of taking admission applications of Chinese alleging to be native-born citizens directly to the courts – and thereby bypassing administrators – on the ground that the exclusion laws and the administrative remedies they envisioned were applicable only to aliens (and not to citizens). The U.S. Supreme Court weighed in for the government. In *In re Sing Tuck*, a case involving Chinese applicants for admission who claimed to be citizens, the Court ruled that such applicants must exhaust their administrative remedies as provided by the exclusion laws before being able to turn to the courts. Although the court refrained from deciding whether administrative officers had jurisdiction to determine the fact of citizenship, the dissenters recognized that the implication of the decision was to blur the distinction between citizen and alien and that the decision ultimately rested on a racialized notion of who might legitimately claim U.S. citizenship. As Justice Brewer put it, with Peckham concurring, "Must an American citizen, seeking to return to this his native land, be compelled to bring with him two witnesses to prove the place of his birth or else be denied his right to return and all opportunity of establishing his citizenship in the courts of his country? No such rule is enforced against an American citizen of Anglo-Saxon descent, and if this be, as claimed, a government of laws and not of men, I do not think it should be enforced against American citizens of Chinese descent."[33]

A year later, the Court went further. In *United States v. Ju Toy*, it held that the administrative decision with respect to admission was final and conclusive despite the petitioner's claim of citizenship. Justice Holmes stated that, even though the Fifth Amendment might apply to a citizen, "with regard to him due process of law does not require a judicial trial."[34] Not surprisingly, after the *Ju Toy* decision, habeas corpus petitions filed by Chinese applicants for admission in the Northern District of California dropped dramatically, from a total of 153 cases filed in 1904, to 32 in 1905, to a low of 9 in 1906. In subsequent years, after criticism of the Bureau of Immigration and its own decisions, the Court scaled back the harshness of the *Ju Toy* decision by requiring in the case of a Chinese American applicant

[32] *Nishimura Ekiu v. United States*, 142 U.S. 651, 660 (1891).

[33] *United States v. Sing Tuck*, 194 U.S. 161, 178 (1904).

[34] 198 U.S. 253 (1905).

for admission who alleged citizenship that the administrative hearing meet certain minimum standards of fairness.[35] However, this last decision appears to have had little impact on administrative practice.

The blurring of the difference between citizen and alien at the procedural level suggests one of the important ways in which the national immigration regime produced internal foreignness in the late nineteenth and early twentieth centuries. If the Fourteenth Amendment had made it impossible to take U.S. citizenship away from native-born Chinese as a matter of substantive law (albeit not for want of trying), immigration officials could do so as a matter of procedural law. In being denied judicial hearings, native-born Chinese were assimilated to the status of Chinese aliens. Bureaucratic prejudice could keep certain Americans from entering and hence residing in the country in which they had been born. This is perfectly consistent with the view of Bureau of Immigration officials, who viewed native-born Chinese as "accidental" or "technical" citizens, as distinguished from "real" citizens.

The denial of adequate procedure as a means of blurring the distinction between citizen and alien was only one of the ways of producing the internal foreignness of the Chinese. The harshness of the exclusion and deportation laws applicable to the Chinese and the general paranoia about the legality of the Chinese presence translated into a range of legal and administrative measures that forced the Chinese American community to live for decades in perpetual fear of American law enforcement officials. Anti-Chinese sentiment had, of course, resulted in various kinds of discrimination since the middle of the nineteenth century. But now the immigration regime itself spilled into the community. Starting in 1909, for example, all persons of Chinese descent – including U.S. citizens – were required to carry certificates identifying them as legally present in the country.[36] As deportation increasingly became a tool for regulating Chinese presence in the early twentieth century, Chinese communities all over the United States were repeatedly subjected to what has since become a tested method of ferreting out "illegal aliens" and of impressing on certain kinds of citizens their lack of belonging – the immigration raid, with all the possibilities of intimidation and corruption that it carried.

By 1905, the restrictionist focus had shifted far beyond the Chinese. However, the legal struggles of Chinese immigrants had brought about an articulation of the major principles of the federal immigration order. These might be listed as follows: racialized citizenship, plenary congressional power over the exclusion and deportation of immigrants as an incident

[35] *Chin Yow v. United States*, 208 U.S. 8 (1908).

[36] U.S. Dept. of Commerce and Labor, Bureau of Immigration, *Treaty, Laws, and Regulations* (1910), 48–53.

of "sovereignty," broad judicial deference to administrative decisions, and the legal production of the internal foreignness of disfavored immigrant groups.

Shaping the Community and Closing the Golden Door

In the 1870s and 1880s, domestic capital clearly recognized the advantages of unrestricted immigration in driving down wages and reducing the bargaining power of organized labor. Andrew Carnegie put it thus in 1886: "The value to the country of the annual foreign influx is very great indeed.... During the ten years between 1870 and 1880, the number of immigrants averaged 280,000 per annum. In one year, 1882, nearly three times this number arrived. Sixty percent of this mass were adults between 15 and 40 years of age. These adults were surely worth $1,500 each – for in former days an efficient slave sold for this sum."[37]

Organized labor had long been calling for immigration restriction to protect American workers from the competition posed by immigrant labor. However, because it was politically untenable to shut down European, as opposed to Asian, labor migration in its entirety, organized labor increasingly focused on the issue of "contract labor." In an ironic twist to the ideologies of freedom of contract that dominated the post–Civil War years, the immigrant who entered the United States with a transportation contract was represented as someone who had been "imported" by capitalists and, therefore, as someone who was less free and more threatening than the immigrant who came in without a contract.

Congress responded in 1885 with the first of the contract labor laws. The 1885 Act prohibited employers from subsidizing the transportation of aliens, voided transportation contracts, and imposed fines on violators.[38] The legislation, however, proved to be purely symbolic. In the first place, the practice of paying for the transportation of laborers, which had been prevalent in antebellum years when the need for skilled laborers was great, had largely died out by the late nineteenth century (when family-based migration served capital's need for fungible unskilled labor). Second, enforcement of the laws appears to have been cursory and ineffective. Between 1887 and 1901, at most 8,000 immigrants were barred under the alien contract labor laws out of a total immigration flow of about 6,000,000. In 1901, a congressional Industrial Commission concluded that the laws were "practically

[37] Andrew Carnegie, *Triumphant Democracy, or Fifty Years' March of the Republic* (New York: Charles Scribner's Sons, 1886), 34–35.

[38] Act of February 26, 1885 (23 Stat. 332). A second act provided for the deportation of any contract laborer apprehended within one year of entry. Act of October 19, 1888 (25 Stat. 566).

a nullity, as affected by the decisions of the court, and by the practices of the inspectors, and the administrative authorities."[39]

As the national immigration regime consolidated itself, the number of grounds of exclusion grew by leaps and bounds. The anxieties that the state expressed in its exclusion laws were typical of the punitive, moralizing, reformist, and eugenicist mood of the late nineteenth and early twentieth centuries. The exclusion of those "likely to become a public charge," a provision enacted in 1882 and based on antebellum state statutes, became the most important ground of barring entry into the United States.[40] Generations of immigrants learned to wear their finest clothes at the moment of inspection to convey an impression of prosperity. Closely related were the laws restricting the admission of aliens with physical and mental defects, including epileptics and alcoholics, which drove prospective entrants to attempt to conceal limps and coughs. There were also laws targeting individuals with criminal backgrounds (including those convicted of crimes involving "moral turpitude"), polygamists, and women coming to the United States for "immoral purposes."[41] Finally, after the assassination of President McKinley in 1901, the immigration laws began actively to penalize aliens for their political beliefs.[42]

However, the heart of the debate over immigration restriction in the early twentieth century lay not in the protection of the labor market, public finances, public morals, or the polity itself, but rather in something that stood in the popular mind for all of these together; namely the protection of the country's ethnic/racial stock. Increasingly, the race of immigrants was coming to do the work of "explaining" the class tensions, labor unrest, and urban violence that afflicted late nineteenth- and early twentieth-century America.

One should refrain from easy generalizations about the sources of the racial theories that were increasingly marshaled to demonize the new immigrants, who came increasingly from Southern and Eastern Europe, as well as more distant countries such as Japan and India. European Americans had access to their rich "internal" experiences with racialized others, to be sure, but also to earlier experiences with Irish and Chinese immigrants, not to mention to the fund of racial thinking that had accompanied the centuries-long European colonial experiences in Europe, Asia, Africa, and the Americas. All of these sources fed into the new "scientific" racial

[39] U.S. Congress, House, Industrial Commission, 1901, Vol. 15, p. lviii.

[40] Immigration Act of August 3, 1882 (22 Stat. 214).

[41] Act of March 3, 1875 (18 Stat. 477); Immigration Act of March 3, 1891 (26 Stat. 1084); Immigration Act of February 20, 1907 (34 Stat. 898).

[42] Immigration Act of March 3, 1903, (32 Stat. 1203, Section 2).

sensibilities and knowledges of the late nineteenth and early twentieth centuries.

The fear of the "race suicide" of "Nordics" resulting from the introduction of more prolific "inferior races," an idea propagated energetically by the Eastern-elite-dominated Immigration Restriction League, acquired considerable currency after 1900. The massive report on immigration submitted to Congress by the Dillingham Commission (1910–11) shared this general sensibility by considerately including a *Dictionary of Races or Peoples*. The *Dictionary* exemplified the new "scientific" understanding of race; in classifying immigrants "according to their languages, their physical characteristics, and such marks as would show their relationship to one another, and in determining their geographical habitats," the Commission identified dozens of carefully hierarchized "races" of immigrants.[43]

Predictably, the most virulent attacks were reserved for Asian immigrants in the West. By 1905, the Asiatic Exclusion League had been organized to bar the new immigration from Japan and India. Attempts to segregate San Francisco schools sparked a diplomatic crisis between Japan and the United States, resulting in the Gentlemen's Agreement of 1907, according to which Japan agreed voluntarily to restrict the immigration of Japanese laborers.

The Asiatic Exclusion League also lobbied fiercely for the exclusion of Indian immigrants, erroneously labeled "Hindoos." In the absence of any statutory provision explicitly prohibiting the entry of Indians, motivated administrators put generally applicable provisions of immigration law to creative racist ends. Immigration officials began to interpret the "public charge" provision to exclude Indian immigrants on the ground that strong anti-Indian prejudice in California would prevent them from getting a job, and thus render them "public charges." When this discriminatory use of the "public charge" provision was challenged in federal court, it was upheld.[44]

The increasing racialization of immigration law had especially adverse effects on female immigrants. In general, the immigration law of the period reinforced patriarchal ideas about gender roles. As an observer noted in 1922: "In the main, in the eyes of the law, a man is man, while a woman is a maid, wife, widow, or mother."[45] This made single or widowed female immigrants especially vulnerable to aspects of immigration law such as the

[43] Dillingham Commission Report, Vol. 5, *Dictionary of Races or Peoples*, Senate Document 662, Session 61–3 (Washington, DC: Government Printing Office, 1911), 2.

[44] *In re Rhagat Singh*, 209 F. 700 (1913). The U.S. Supreme Court eventually curtailed immigration officials' excessively broad interpretations of the "public charge" provision in *Gegiow v. Uhl*, 239 U.S. 3 (1915).

[45] "The Cable Act and the Foreign-Born Woman," *Foreign Born* 3, no. 8 (December 1922).

public charge provisions. But the consequences were worse yet for racialized immigrants. Chinese women had long experience with such attitudes. In a bow to patriarchal attitudes, the ban on Chinese immigration did not translate into a prohibition on the entry of wives. However, widespread American stereotypes about Chinese prostitutes made Orientalist markers of matrimony and class status – for example, bound feet suggesting the lack of need to work – crucial for a Chinese woman hoping to secure admission. Any evidence that the woman had worked might result in her classification as a crypto-laborer and her being denied entry. Fears about prostitution translated into greater interrogation and surveillance of Japanese, as well as Eastern and Southern European female immigrants. The Dillingham Commission devoted an entire volume to "white slavery" and sought to match its findings to the racial characteristics of the immigrant stream. Jewish women were seen as being especially vulnerable to the lure of prostitution once they had been admitted.[46]

In the early twentieth century, as the composition of the immigrant population changed, courts were compelled to confront once again the question of racial ineligibility for U.S. citizenship. Although the Chinese had been declared ineligible since the 1870s, there was considerable ambiguity as to whether Japanese, Indian, and other immigrants who entered the United States in the late nineteenth and early twentieth centuries fit within the black-white binary of naturalization law. Between 1887 and 1923, the federal courts heard twenty-five cases challenging the racial prerequisites to citizenship, culminating in two rulings by the U.S. Supreme Court: *Ozawa v. United States* (1922) and *Thind v. United States* (1923). In each case, the Court's decision turned on whether the petitioner could be considered a "white person" within the meaning of the statute.

Taken together, these decisions reveal the shortcomings of racial science. In earlier years, federal courts had relied on racial science, rather than on color, and had admitted Syrians, Armenians, and Indians to citizenship as "white persons." In *Ozawa*, the U.S. Supreme Court admitted that color as an indicator of race was insufficient, but resisted the conclusion that no scientific grounds for race existed. It avoided the problem of classification by asserting that "white" and Caucasian were the same and that the Japanese were not Caucasian and hence not "white."[47] However, in *Thind*, the Court was confronted with an Indian immigrant who argued his claim to eligibility to citizenship on the basis of his Aryan and Caucasian roots.

[46] Dillingham Commission Report, Vol. 37, pt. 2, *Importation and Harboring of Women for Immoral Purposes*, Senate Document 753/2, Session 61–3 (Washington, DC: Government Printing Office, 1911).

[47] *Ozawa v United States*, 260 U.S. 128, 197 (1922).

Now the Court found that the word "Caucasian" was considerably broader in scientific discourses than it was in non-scientific discourses. Rejecting the petitioner's claim to citizenship, it held that the words "white person" in the naturalization law were words of "common speech, to be interpreted with the understanding of the common man."[48] Racial science thus was summarily abandoned in favor of popular prejudice.

If U.S. citizenship was racialized during this period, it was also deeply gendered. Since the middle of the nineteenth century, male U.S. citizens had been formally able to confer citizenship on their wives. However, the law with respect to female U.S. citizens who married non-citizens had been unclear. In 1907, Congress decided to remove all ambiguities by legislating "that any American woman who marries a foreigner shall take the nationality of her husband."[49] In other words, female U.S. citizens who married non-citizens were not only unable to confer citizenship on their husbands, but in fact lost their own U.S. citizenship as a consequence of their marriage. In 1915, the U.S. Supreme Court upheld a challenge to this provision on the basis of the "ancient principle" of "the identity of husband and wife."[50] In the case of native-born Asian American female citizens, this law had the effect of rendering them permanently unable to reenter the community of citizens. Having lost their citizenship on marrying an alien, they became aliens racially ineligible for citizenship.

But quite in addition to being racialized and gendered, U.S. citizenship revealed that it had adventitious uses. It could be shaped and manipulated as a weapon of discrimination. As anti-immigrant sentiment mounted in the early twentieth century, state legislatures increasingly made U.S. citizenship a prerequisite to forms of employment and recreation, access to natural resources, and the like, thereby causing the meanings of U.S. citizenship to proliferate well beyond the sphere of the political (voting, political office, service on juries, and so on). Driven by the politics of race and labor, citizenship thus spilled into the social experiences of work and leisure in the lived community.

State attempts to discriminate on the basis of citizenship were typically dealt with as problems of "alienage law." The constitutional question was whether a state, in discriminating on the basis of citizenship, had gone so far as to intrude on the federal government's (by now) exclusive immigration power. In general, the U.S. Supreme Court held that a state could discriminate among citizens and aliens if the state was protecting a "special public interest" in its common property or resources, a category that was

[48] *Thind v. United States*, 261 U.S. 204, 215 (1923).

[49] Act of March 2, 1907 (34 Stat. 1228).

[50] *Mackenzie v. Hare*, 239 U.S. 299, 311 (1915).

interpreted over the years to include employment on public works projects, hunting wild game, and operating pool halls.[51]

The U.S. Supreme Court also upheld alienage distinctions that were aimed very clearly and directly at specific racialized immigrant groups. In the early twentieth century, resentment of Japanese immigrants on the West Coast increasingly centered on their success in agriculture. In response, Arizona, California, Idaho, Kansas, Louisiana, Montana, New Mexico, and Oregon attempted to restrict land ownership by aliens "ineligible to citizenship," a category carefully crafted to apply only to Asian immigrants, who were the only ones legally incapable of naturalizing. When the alien land laws were challenged, however, the U.S. Supreme Court upheld them.[52] The fact that the legislation only affected some racialized groups was not found to be a problem under the Equal Protection Clause of the Fourteenth Amendment because the law was framed in neutral terms of discrimination against non-citizens.

If the Chinese experience with citizenship had prefigured other Asian immigrant groups' experiences with citizenship, the events of the 1920s revealed that the Chinese experience with blanket immigration restriction also prefigured the experience of Asian *and* European immigrant groups. Significant restrictions on immigration occurred only with the xenophobic frenzy whipped up during World War I.

The context of suspicion fostered by the war enabled nativists to obtain in the Immigration Act of 1917 some of the restrictionist policies they had long advocated. A literacy test for adult immigrants was one of their most important victories. The 1917 law also submitted to the West Coast's demand for the exclusion of Indian immigrants. Hesitant to single Indians out for exclusion on the grounds of race, however, Congress created an "Asiatic Barred Zone" that included India, Burma, Siam, the Malay States, Arabia, Afghanistan, parts of Russia, and most of the Polynesian Islands.[53] In the end, it is unclear how much the literacy test affected European immigration, in part because of the spread of literacy in Europe during the same years.

[51] *Crane v. New York*, 239 U.S. 195 (1915); *Patsone v. Pennsylvania*, 232 U.S. 138 (1914); *Clarke v. Deckebach*, 274 U.S. 392 (1927). However, the U.S. Supreme Court did strike down an Arizona law that required any employer of more than five employees to employ at least 80 percent qualified electors or native-born citizens of the United States on the ground that it would be inconsistent with the exclusive federal authority to "admit or exclude aliens." *Truax v. Raich*, 239 U.S. 33 (1915).

[52] *Truax v. Corrigan*, 257 U.S. 312, cited in *Terrace v. Thompson*, 263 U.S. 197, 218, 221 (1923).

[53] Immigration Act of February 5, 1917 (39 Stat. 874).

By 1920, the war-boom economy had begun to collapse and immigration from Europe had revived, creating a propitious environment for greater restriction. Accordingly, in 1921, the logic of immigration restriction that had been formally applicable to almost all Asian immigrants since 1917 – exclusion – was extended to European immigrants, albeit in the form of quotas rather than complete restriction. The Quota Act of 1921 was described by the commissioner general of immigration as "one of the most radical and far-reaching events in the annals of immigration legislation."[54] Indeed it was, but what is of interest here is its arbitrariness.

The Quota Act limited European immigration to 3 percent of the number of foreign-born people of each nationality residing in the United States in 1910.[55] The aim was to give larger quotas to immigrants from Northern and Western Europe, and to reduce the influx of Southern and Eastern Europeans. By 1923, the commissioner general of immigration pronounced the Quota Act a success. He revealed that the percentage of Southern and Eastern European immigrants had decreased from 75.6 percent of the total immigration in 1914 to 31.1 percent of the total immigration in 1923. For the same years, as a percentage of total immigration, immigration from Northern and Western Europe had increased from 20.8 percent to 52.5 percent.

This change in the composition of the immigration stream did not, however, satisfy nativists. The Immigration Act of 1924 represented a compromise. It reduced the percentage admitted from 3 to 2 percent and made the base population the number of each foreign-born nationality present in the United States in 1890 instead of 1910. The Senate, balking at such gross discrimination, allowed the new quota provided that a new "national origins" test would be used beginning in 1927. The new national origins test was only superficially fairer. It placed a cap on the total number of immigrants, limiting admissions to 150,000 each year and using the 1920 census as the base. However, instead of using the number of foreign-born as its measure, as the earlier quota laws had done, the law set the quotas according to the proportion of each "national stock," including both native and foreign-born people. This favored "old stock" Americans over the new immigrant population, leaving to immigration officials the nightmare of calculating "national stocks."

The 1924 Act also furthered the exclusion of Asians. Though the law barred such aliens from entering the country as were, to use the euphemistic phrase of the time, "ineligible for citizenship," Japanese immigrants were

[54] Annual Report of the Commissioner-General of Immigration, 1921, 16.

[55] Act of May 19, 1921 (42 Stat. 5).

the real targets of the act because Chinese and Indian immigrants had already been excluded.[56]

Thus, in the 1920s, for the first time in the history of immigration restriction in the United States, the basic theory of exclusion shifted from a matter of the shortcomings of the individual immigrant (poverty, criminal background, health, etc.) to a matter of numerical restriction. Decisions to admit immigrants and the battles that accompanied them would take place in the abstract language of numbers. Of course, the grounds of exclusion for poverty, disability, criminal background, political opinion, and the like would continue in force, but these would henceforth serve to weed out individuals who had first to demonstrate that they fit within a national origins quota. The presumption that one could immigrate to the United States had shifted to a presumption that one could not immigrate to the United States. With this shift in presumptions came the figure of the "illegal alien" and a vast stepping up of border control and deportation activity. For the first time, Congress legislated a serious enforcement mechanism against unlawful entry by creating a land Border Patrol.[57]

Imperialism and Immigration

If the growth of the national immigration regime resulted in the production of the internal foreignness of American ethnic communities like the Chinese, the history of immigration from areas in which the United States had colonial/imperial involvements reveals how groups once treated as on the inside could progressively be rendered as on the outside and progressively brought within the purview of the immigration regime.

Although immigration statistics for the early twentieth century are notoriously inaccurate, scholars estimate that at least one million and possibly as many as a million and a half Mexican immigrants entered the United States between 1890 and 1929. Mexico has also been the single most important source country for immigration into the United States in the twentieth century. However, it is not simply the numbers of Mexican immigrants, but the peculiar history of Mexican immigration as one intertwined with colonialism that warrants separate treatment.

With the Treaty of Guadalupe Hidalgo in 1848, Mexico ceded to the United States more than half of its territory, comprising all or part of

[56] Immigration Act of 1924 (43 Stat. 153). Filipinos were the only Asians unaffected by the 1924 Act. As non-citizen U.S. nationals by virtue of their colonial status, Filipinos were exempt from the law. Their immigration to the United States became restricted in 1934.

[57] Act of February 27, 1925 (43 Stat. 1049).

present-day Arizona, California, Colorado, Kansas, Nevada, New Mexico, Oklahoma, Texas, Utah, and Wyoming. This treaty also transformed the lives of the estimated 75,000 to 100,000 Mexicans who lived in the ceded territories. It expressly provided that Mexicans could move south of the new international border or retain their Mexican nationality. If they had done neither within one year of the treaty's effective date, however, they would be considered to have "elected" to become citizens of the United States.[58]

The treaty's extension of U.S. citizenship by fiat to the resident populations of the ceded territories might have been the ironic consequence of a State Department bureaucrat's unsanctioned negotiations in Mexico City. However, Americans disturbed by the prospect of admitting their racial "inferiors" into the community of U.S. citizens (it should be recalled that the treaty was negotiated almost a decade before the *Dred Scott* decision) were comforted by the belief that the acquired territories were sparsely settled and would be transformed by white migration. Mexican Americans were confidently expected to disappear as a significant presence in the newly acquired area.

Massive white immigration into the acquired territories during the second half of the nineteenth century indeed had the effect of rendering Mexican Americans numerical minorities, even as they experienced a sharp loss in social, economic, and political power and became victims of racial discrimination as non-whites. By the end of the nineteenth century, however, this demographic situation began to change. A range of transformations – the extension of railway networks, the introduction of the refrigerated boxcar, the construction of irrigation projects, and so on – laid the foundation for explosive economic growth in the American Southwest, and hence for the region's seemingly limitless demand for agricultural and industrial labor. These changes took place just as conditions for Mexican peasants were worsening during the waning years of the nineteenth century. As a result, Mexicans began to pour into the Southwest.

At a time of rising nativism in the United States vis-à-vis European and Asian immigrants, it was precisely the colonial context of the acquisition of the Southwest and the rhetorical uses to which it was put by labor-hungry U.S. employers that saved Mexican immigrants, at least for a while, from being formal targets of U.S. citizenship and immigration laws. In 1897, a federal district court considering the question of Mexicans' eligibility for citizenship declared that "[i]f the strict scientific classification of the anthropologist should be adopted, [the petitioner] would probably not be classed as white." However, the constitution of the Texas Republic, the

[58] Treaty of Guadalupe Hidalgo, Article VIII.

Treaty of Guadalupe Hidalgo, and other agreements between the United States and Mexico either "affirmatively confer[red] the rights of citizenship upon Mexicans, or tacitly recognize[d] in them the right of individual naturalization." Furthermore, because these instruments had not distinguished among Mexicans on the basis of color, all Mexicans would be eligible to naturalize, regardless of color.[59] Thus, the United States' obligations to its colonized Mexican American population redounded to the benefit of Mexican immigrants.

Mexicans were also exempted from racial bars to immigration applicable to Asian immigrants and the quotas applicable to European immigrants from the 1920s on. Here, the reason seems to have been successful lobbying by Western and Southwestern interests to keep the border open. Once again, the history of Mexicans' relationship to the Southwest was invoked. By far the most influential arguments in favor of Mexican immigrants promoted the idea that history had rendered Mexican immigrants familiar – yet happily, temporary – sojourners in the United States. In 1926, Congressman Taylor of Colorado noted that Americans had become used to working with Mexicans after nearly a century of contact. "It is not at all like we were importing inhabitants of a foreign country. We understood each other. They have no influence whatever upon our habits of life or form of civilization. They simply want work.... Generally speaking they are not immigrants at all. They do not try to buy or colonize our land, and they hope some day to be able to own a piece of land in their own country."[60] The idea that Mexican immigrants were birds of passage was cited repeatedly to assuage nativists' fears that Mexicans might settle permanently in the United States.

Eventually, however, Mexican immigrants would also fall victim to the restrictionist tide, especially because Mexicans disappointed Americans by inconveniently remaining in the communities in which they labored. By the mid-1920s, a Mexican "race problem" had emerged in the Southwest. Although Congress was unwilling to impose quotas on Mexican immigration or to exclude Mexicans on racial grounds, it sought to restrict Mexican immigration by administrative means. U.S. consuls in Mexico began to enforce general immigration restrictions, refusing visas to Mexican laborers. At the same time, the formation of the Border Patrol in 1925 led to the first steps to curb Mexican illegal immigration. The official onslaught against Mexican immigrants reached its peak during the 1930s when officials of the U.S. Department of Labor, the Border Patrol, local welfare

[59] *In re Rodriguez*, 81 Fed. 337 (W.D. Texas, 1897).

[60] Ralph Taylor, in House Committee On Immigration, Immigration from Countries of the Western Hemisphere: Hearings, 1930, 237–38.

agencies, and other government bodies sought to secure the "voluntary" return to Mexico of Mexican immigrants and their U.S. citizen children. Scholars have estimated that between 350,000 and 600,000 individuals were thus repatriated to Mexico.

The other immigration streams shaped by an imperial context were those from the Philippines and Puerto Rico, territories acquired as a consequence of the Spanish American War in 1898. But the late nineteenth-century moment was very different from the mid-nineteenth-century moment of the acquisition of the Southwest. In the high noon of racial theory, there were real doubts about Americans' ability effectively to ingest these non-contiguous territories and their racially distinct populations.

Puerto Rico was clearly the more ingestible of the two; its population numbered less than one million. Accordingly, in the Jones Act of 1917, Congress enacted a bill of rights for Puerto Rico and granted U.S. citizenship to Puerto Ricans.[61] This was not the full membership enjoyed by Americans on the mainland. Nevertheless, as a consequence of the Jones Act, Puerto Ricans could move to the mainland United States and, on becoming state residents, claim the civil, political, and social rights enjoyed by other citizens.

The case of the Philippines was more troublesome. If American territorial acquisitions in earlier periods had been premised on territories' eventual admission to statehood, admitting the populous Philippine islands to statehood was unthinkable. The Filipino nationalist leader Manuel Roxas once remarked that statehood would have resulted in fifty Filipino representatives in Congress. Nevertheless, "benevolent" imperialism came with a price. If they were not U.S. citizens, Filipinos were at least "American nationals." As "American nationals," Filipinos were exempted from the quota acts and were able to enter and reside within the United States.

Not surprisingly, nativists in the 1920s sought to close the loopholes in immigration law that allowed Filipinos to enter the United States. However, because there was a sense in Washington that the anti-Filipino movement was merely a regional interest, Congress initially failed to act. Eventually, the desire to exclude Filipinos grew so great that exclusionists actually allied themselves with Filipino nationalists. They finally proved successful. The Tydings-McDuffie Act of 1934 granted the Philippines independence and stripped Filipinos of their status as "American nationals."[62] Filipino immigration became governed by the national origins quota legislation. A 1935 Repatriation Act sought to remove Filipinos from the United States by paying their transportation back to the Philippines on condition that they give up any right of reentry into the country.

[61] Act of March 1, 1917 (39 Stat. 951).

[62] Act of March 22, 1934 (48 Stat. 456).

CONCLUSION

The attempt by petitioners in *Ozawa* and *Thind* to obtain classification as "white" rather than as "African" for purposes of naturalization law reveals a great deal about how nineteenth- and twentieth-century immigrants, European and Asian, attempted to fit themselves into American racial hierarchies. Racial jostling on the part of immigrants has a long history, punctuated by dramatic and violent events such as the 1863 New York City draft riots when Irish immigrants lynched African Americans to protest their own conscription into the Union effort.

The rise of the national immigration regime was premised on the removal of the structural internal foreignnesses of the antebellum period and the constitution of U.S. territory as a homogeneous space of constitutional rights. It translated, as has been suggested, into a fresh set of internal foreignnesses as the immigration regime spilled over into the lived community in the form of immigration raids and heightened surveillance of American ethnic communities such as the Chinese.

However, the late nineteenth century also witnessed the emergence of another form of internal foreignness: legally sanctioned, public and private, formal and informal racial segregation. Perhaps this was not of the same legal order as the efforts of states in the antebellum period to exclude portions of the native-born population – free blacks – from their territories and to assimilate them to the formal status of aliens. The passage of the Civil War amendments had made such kinds of discrimination illegal. Nevertheless, in the decades that followed the Civil War, courts permitted other, newer kinds of discrimination and segregation through the reinvigoration of the public/private distinction or the spurious idea of "separate but equal."[63]

By the early twentieth century, then, a multitude of internal spaces in America – whether they involved shopping or transportation, residence or recreation, employment or education – were thoroughly fragmented, rendered open to some groups and closed to others. Closing off such spaces was especially significant because it was precisely in the variegated spaces of the new urban America that social membership would increasingly be instantiated and realized. Although immigrant groups such as Jews and Catholics, Asians and Latinos, were certainly victims of forms of segregation, its greatest impact was on African Americans.

The boundaries of spaces closed off to African Americans were actively patrolled through public laws and policies, judicially recognized private devices such as the racially restrictive covenant or the shopkeeper's absolute "right to exclude," the efforts of police and vigilantes, and the systematic

[63] *Plessy v. Ferguson*, 163 U.S. 537 (1896).

infliction of petty humiliation and violence. African Americans confronted borders – were made foreigners – as part of their everyday lives, but in paradoxical ways. Although they might not be permitted to purchase homes in certain neighborhoods, they were permitted to work there as domestics. Although they could not be guests in certain hotels, they could labor in hotel kitchens. Often, the object of segregation was simply to point to itself, as when African Americans in the south were required to sit in designated parts of public buses.

The irony of the struggle to desegregate residential and educational spaces in America, especially in the urban North between 1940 and 1980, was that it was often fought precisely against Jewish and Catholic immigrants and their immediate descendants who had come to occupy intermediate positions in America's ethnic and racial hierarchies, if they had not already become fully "white." To be sure, it was often precisely members of those immigrant groups who labored alongside African Americans, operated establishments that served them, and supported the African American struggle for civil rights. However, these immigrant groups also actively distanced themselves from African Americans – for example, American Jews who performed "blackface" – in order to negotiate their own social standing. It was in the struggles between African Americans and white ethnic Americans that one of the most egregious forms of twentieth-century internal foreignness (residential and educational segregation) was dismantled, even as it was simultaneously reconstituted in the form of suburbanization and an ongoing "urban crisis."

The African American experience in the United States, both before and after the Civil War, might be taken as a model for thinking about immigration. It suggests that foreignness has no intrinsic connection to whether one stands inside or outside territory. That boundary is simultaneously produced and transgressed, not least in the activities of the immigration regime itself. The model calls for a measure of caution when we designate those knocking at America's gates as outsiders from other countries to whom we owe nothing. American history tells us that the status of outsider has often, even paradigmatically, been conferred on those most intimately "at home."

7

FEDERAL POLICY, WESTERN MOVEMENT, AND CONSEQUENCES FOR INDIGENOUS PEOPLE, 1790–1920

DAVID E. WILKINS

In virtually every respect imaginable – economic, political, cultural, sociological, psychological, geographical, and technological – the years from the creation of the United States through the Harding administration brought massive upheaval and transformation for native nations. Everywhere, U.S. Indian law (federal and state) – by which I mean the law that defines and regulates the nation's political and legal relationship to indigenous nations – aided and abetted the upheaval.

The nature of U.S. Indian law is, of course, fundamentally different from the various indigenous legal and customary traditions that encompassed the social norms, values, customs, and religious views of native nations. These two fundamentally distinct legal cultures, and their diverse practitioners and purveyors, were thus frequently in conflict. Important moments of recognition, however, did take place, particularly the early treaty period (1600s–1800), and later, there were infrequent, spasms of U.S. judicial recognition. In *Ex parte Crow Dog* (1883) and *Talton v. Mayes* (1896), for example, the U.S. Supreme Court acknowledged the distinctive sovereign status of native nations by holding that the U.S. Constitution did not constrain the inherent rights of Indian nations because their sovereignty predated that of the United States.[1] Perhaps the period of greatest European acceptance occurred during the encounter era when indigenous practices of law and peace, particularly among the tribal nations of the Northeast, served as a broad philosophical and cultural paradigm for intergovernmental relations between indigenous peoples and the various European and Euro-American diplomats and policymakers with whom they interacted. Whether tribal, based in indigenous custom and tradition, or Western, based in English common law custom and tradition, law speaks to the basic humanity of individuals and societies. In both cases, it provides guidance for human behavior and embraces ideals of justice. Initially, therefore, law

[1] 109 U.S. 556; 163 U.S. 376.

was a powerful way for indigenous and non-indigenous leaders to forge well-founded diplomatic relations.

This state of multicultural negotiations, of treaties and mutual respect, would not be sustained. Gradually Euro-American attitudes of superiority – legal, political, religious, and technological – became uppermost. Tribal systems of law, policy, and culture came to be disrespected, displaced, and sometimes simply destroyed. Shunted aside into the corners as colonized peoples, native peoples seeking justice were required to use the same Anglo-American legal system that had devastated their basic rights.

Since the early 1800s, U.S. Indian law has only occasionally acknowledged the distinctive condition – tribal sovereignty – that structures every indigenous community's efforts to endure in their political and legal relationship with the federal government and the constituent states. The absence of genuine bilateralism – the lack of indigenous voice in law and politics despite the written diplomatic record – has plagued the political and legal relationship between tribal nations and the United States ever since. Here we focus on the creation of this situation.

The greatest absence in the study of American legal history and federal Indian law is the actual voice and presence of American Indians. That daunting silence enables Western law practitioners to act as if their vision and understanding of the law are all there is or ever was. Their presumption is contradicted by the ways in which the treaty relationship unfolded and in which indigenous peoples still struggle to practice their own legal traditions in the face of overwhelming pressure to ignore or belittle those very traditions. But the presumption is immensely powerful. How did U.S. law come so to dominate, directly and indirectly diminishing the inherent sovereign status of native nations and their equally legitimate legal traditions? The short answer is that the reluctance or unwillingness to acknowledge the legal pluralism of the continent stemmed from the inexorable drive of national and state politicians, the legal establishment, business entrepreneurs, and white settlers to ensure that nothing derail Euro-America's expansion from a fledgling national polity to an internationally recognized industrial state wielding unprecedented power, domestically and abroad.

The law, as defined and exercised by those in power in federal, state, and corporate offices, occasionally recognized indigenous sovereignty, resources, and rights. Far more often it was employed to destroy or seriously diminish them. Alexis de Tocqueville, one of the first commentators to note the almost fervid concern that Americans had with law and the legal process, observed its application to indigenous affairs. "The Americans," said de Tocqueville, in contrast to the "unparalleled atrocities" committed by the Spaniards, had succeeded in nearly exterminating the Indians and depriving them of their rights "with wonderful ease, quietly, legally, and philanthropically, without spilling blood and without violating a single one of the great principles of morality in the eyes of the world. It is impossible to destroy men with more respect to the laws of humanity."[2]

Coming to power during the bloody American Revolution and anxious to establish the legitimacy of their new state in the court of world and American settler opinion, U.S. policymakers, in constructing their framework for a democratic society, fervently supported a social contract that theoretically recognized the rights of virtually everyone. With sufficient flexibility of interpretation, the same contract allowed the oppression of basic human rights of women and minorities, indeed of any non-whites who lacked the proper skin color, class, and social connections to profit from the expansion of the state.

Native nations, because of their preexistence, political and economic independence, and early military capability, won a degree of respect from colonizing European nations and later the United States that African slaves and women could not obtain. Simultaneously, however, the American public stressed the tribal nations' allegedly inferior cultural, political, technological, and social status in relation to Euro-Americans. This schizophrenic mindset evidenced itself in U.S. Indian law in three distinctive yet interrelated paradigms or predispositions. The three are distinctive in the sense that their foundations lie in different sources, time periods, and motives. They are interrelated because underlying each is the same foundation of colonial and ethnocentric/racist assumptions. The three paradigms can be summarized by three keywords: treaties, paternalism, and federalism.

The treaty paradigm deems law the most effective instrument to ensure justice and fairness for aboriginal people. Here, the federal courts and the political branches formally acknowledged tribal nations as distinctive political bodies outside the scope of U.S. law or constitutional authority. The most basic assumption of this viewpoint was that treaty considerations (i.e., ratified treaties or agreements) were the only appropriate and legitimate instruments by which to engage in and determine the course of diplomacy between indigenous communities and the United States. As only nations may engage in treaties, the constituent states were reduced to being observers and could not interfere in the nation-to-nation relationship without federal and tribal consent.

When federal lawmakers and jurists acted in accordance with the treaty paradigm, as they did in enacting the Northwest Ordinance of 1787 and in cases such as *Worcester* v. *Georgia* (1831), *The Kansas Indians* (1867), and

[2] Alexis de Tocqueville, Democracy in America, vol. 1, edited by J. P. Mayer (Garden City, NY, 1969), 339.

Ex parte Crow Dog (1883),[3] the United States was formally acknowledging that tribes were separate and sovereign nations and that the treaties that linked the two sovereigns, much more than being mere contracts, were the supreme law of the land under Article VI of the Constitution. Under this disposition, the federal government's actions generally left indigenous nations free of the constitutional constraints applicable to the states and to the federal government itself. Early interactions under the treaty paradigm, then, granted both explicit and implicit recognition to legal pluralism, even though the language used in the various policies, laws, and cases still sometimes contained racist and ethnocentric discourse that perpetuated stereotypes about indigenous peoples.

The other two paradigms, of federalism and of paternalism, were far more commonly used throughout the period under examination – and beyond – to justify federal and state laws and court decisions that had devastating consequences for indigenous collective and individual rights. The consequences were so severe, in part, because neither of these frameworks gave any consideration whatsoever to native values, laws, or morals.

When the United States operated in accordance with the paradigm of federalism, the law was perceived as the prime mechanism for furthering the political and economic development and territorial expansion of the United States as a nation in conjunction with its constituent states. This view of the law was maintained notwithstanding the simultaneous presence on the North American continent – in fact and in law – of aboriginal nations, each intent on maintaining its own political and economic development and historic territories. The federalism paradigm was inward-looking, concentrating its gaze on the Euro-American political community. It treated tribal nations largely as obstacles to that entity's self-realization, otherwise unseen and unheard. This paradigm was very much in evidence prior to the Civil War.

When operating in accordance with the paradigm of paternalism, the United States tended to portray itself as a deeply moralistic, civilized, and Christian nation, virtually always above reproach. This view predominated from the 1860s into the 1930s, when the federal government inaugurated the Indian reservation program, established boarding schools, allotted Indian lands, and forcibly sought to acculturate indigenous peoples. Deeming Indian persons and nations culturally inferior, the law became an essential instrument in moving them from their uncivilized or "primitive" status to mature civility. The United States envisioned itself as a benevolent "guardian" to its naïve Indian "wards"; their cultural transformation was

[3] 31 U.S. (6 Pet.) 515; 72 U.S. (5 Wall.) 737; 109 U.S. 556.

considered inevitable. The only question was whether the process would be achieved gradually or rapidly.

Fundamentally, the various processes used by federal and state officials and corporate powers under the three paradigms brought about the cultural genocide, segregation, expulsion, and coerced assimilation of native peoples. Of these, coercive assimilation – the effort to induce by force the merger of politically and culturally distinctive cultural groups (tribal nations) into what had become the politically dominant cultural group (Euro-American society) – has been the most persistent process employed by U.S. lawmakers. The most vigorous and unapologetic manifestations of forced assimilation occurred during the latter part of the nineteenth century and into the 1920s. The Supreme Court sanctioned the denial of treaty rights, the confiscation of Indian lands, and a host of other coercive intrusions on the tribes by its creation of a new and wholly non-constitutional authority, Congressional plenary power, which it defined as virtually boundless governmental authority and jurisdiction over all things indigenous. While federal power is rarely wielded so crassly today, both the Supreme Court and the Congress continue to insist that they retain virtually unlimited authority over tribal nations and their lands.

The three paradigms or predispositions described here – treaties, federalism, and paternalism – have successively filled the imaginative field in which U.S. lawmakers and politicians operated during the nineteenth century and after and, to a real extent, in which they still operate today. Indigenous nations at the beginning of the nineteenth century were generally recognized by the United States as political sovereigns and territorial powers, even though they were usually deemed to be culturally and technologically deficient peoples. Between 1790 and 1920, tribal nations and their citizens experienced profound shifts in their legal and political status: from parallel if unequal sovereigns to domestic-dependent sovereigns; from relatively autonomous to removable and confinable entities, then to ward-like incompetents with assimilable bodies; and then, finally, to semi-sovereign nations and individuals entitled to degrees of contingent respect for their unique cultural, political, and resource rights, but only through the condition of attachment to land, which in turn meant continued subordination to an overriding federal plenary control.

These oscillations in the fundamental legal and political status of indigenous peoples confirm federal lawmakers' and American democracy's inability or unwillingness to adopt a consistent and constitutionally based approach to native peoples' sovereignty and their distinctive governmental rights and resources. The successive changes arise from Euro-American perceptions of aboriginal peoples – albeit perceptions with all too real consequences – rather than from the actualities of aboriginal peoples, how they "really are." They lead us to the conclusion that the United States has consistently refused to acknowledge the de facto and de jure legal pluralism that has always existed in North America. The federal government has still to live up even to the potential outlined in many treaties, the Constitution, and the Bill of Rights, far less the reality of what is written there.

As the discussion of the treaty paradigm will show, indigenous law and sovereignty occasionally have been recognized in U.S. law. They continue to play an important, if variable, role in structuring tribal political and economic relations with the United States and the several states. A number of commentators have observed that recognition and support of the indigenous legal and cultural traditions of tribal nations are critical if a democracy of law is ever to be achieved in the United States. Despite the remarkable efforts of tribal nations to retain and exercise essential components of their cultures and traditions, the political, legal, economic, and cultural forces wielded by non-Indians have made it impossible for tribes to act unencumbered. Yet their traditions remain "deeply held in the hearts of Indian people – so deeply held, in fact, that they retained their legal cultures in the face of U.S. legal imperialism, creating a foundation for a pluralist legal system in the United States today."[4] It is unfortunate that the Euro-American law that has occasionally supported tribal sovereignty has, so much more often, diminished it.

I. PARALLEL SOVEREIGNS: TRADE, TRUST, AND TREATY RELATIONS, 1790–1820

Cyrus Griffin, the President of Congress, announced on July 2, 1788, that the Constitution had been ratified by the requisite nine states. Federal lawmaking might then proceed. At that time, however, a significant body of law was already in existence, developed by Great Britain, France, Spain, Sweden, Russia, and Holland, and by the American colonies and by the Continental Congress, in their respective dealings with one another and with aboriginal nations. This body of multinational law incorporated many of the basic political and legal promises that the United States would later use to construct its relationship with indigenous governments. The United States had inherited the idea of using law in its dealings with tribes from predecessor European colonial governments.

Each of the colonial powers had exhibited distinctive political, social, and cultural traits in their interactions with the various indigenous nations they encountered, but certain principles and policies had been applied in common by the end of the eighteenth century and would be continued by

[4] Sidney Harring, *Crow Dog's Case* (New York, 1994), 24.

the United States. First was the doctrine of discovery, which had arisen in the fifteenth century from Catholic Papal bulls and European monarchical claims. The discovery doctrine held, in its most widely understood definition, that European explorers' "discovery" of lands gave the discovering nation (and the United States as successor) absolute legal title and ownership of the soil, reducing the indigenous occupants to mere tenants holding a lesser beneficial interest in their original homelands. Conversely, discovery also was defined as an exclusive and preemptive right that vested in the discovering state nothing less than the right to be the first purchaser of any lands the native owners might decide to sell. Here, discovery is a colonial metaphor that gave the speediest and most efficient discovering nation the upper hand in its efforts to colonize and exploit parts of the world hitherto unknown to Europeans. It was a means of regulating competition between vying European nations. Discovery also had symbiotic links to the doctrine of conquest: the acquisition of territory by a victorious state from a defeated entity in war.

Second came the trust doctrine, also known as the trust relationship. Like discovery, trust arose in the early years of European discovery and settlement of the Americas and can be traced back to Catholic Papal bulls. This doctrine holds that European nations and their representatives, as allegedly superior peoples, had a moral responsibility to civilize and Christianize the native peoples they encountered. Discovery and trust are fundamentally related concepts, with the "discoverer" having the "trust" obligation to oversee the enlightenment and development of the aboriginal peoples, since natives were not conceived as sufficiently mature to be the actual "owners" of their own lands.

Third was the application of a doctrine of national supremacy in matters of European (and later American) political and commercial relations with tribal nations. The regulation of trade and the acquisition or disposition of indigenous lands were to be managed by the national government and not left to constituent subunits of government, or to land companies or individuals.

Finally, because of the military and political capability and territorial domain controlled by the native nations, diplomacy in the form of treaties or comparable contractual arrangements was considered the most logical and economical method of interaction with indigenous peoples.

Endorsement of these important principles and policies – discovery, trust, federal supremacy, and diplomacy – was evident in several early actions by U.S. lawmakers. A first instance occurred in 1787, when the Confederation Congress enacted the Northwest Ordinance. The Ordinance defined a Northwest Territory in the Great Lakes region and set up guidelines for political and economic development of the region that would eventually lead to the creation of new states. Simultaneously, and adversely, Article 3 of the Ordinance contained a striking and unusual passage on the moral or trust relationship that the United States would follow in its dealings with Indian peoples. It reads in part:

> The utmost good faith shall always be observed towards the Indians, their lands and property shall never be taken from them without their consent; and in their property, rights and liberty, they never shall be invaded or disturbed, unless in just and lawful wars authorized by Congress; but laws founded in justice and humanity shall from time to time be made, for preventing wrongs being done to them, and for preserving peace and friendship with them ...[5]

The Northwest Ordinance, that is, embraced fundamentally contradictory policies. On the one hand, the United States sought to assure tribes that their lands and rights would be respected, except when "just and lawful wars" were fought. On the other hand, the lawmakers had already essentially distributed those same lands to the present and future white settlers, intent on continuing their inexorable march westward. The contradiction would endure.

The new federal Constitution was adopted two years later, in 1789. It contained four major constitutional clauses that directly implicated the indigenous/U.S. relationship: Commerce, Treaty-Making, Property, and War and Peace. These clauses affirmed that the national government – and Congress in particular – had exclusive authority to deal with indigenous nations in regard to trade and intercourse, diplomacy (to fight or parley), and land issues. While each would prove significant, the Commerce Clause, which empowers Congress to "regulate commerce with foreign nations ... states ... and with the Indian tribes," was the only source of explicit powers delegated to the legislative branch. In theory, the clause should not have extended to Congress any greater authority over tribes than it exercised over states. In both historical and contemporary practice, however, such has not been the case. As tribal dominion waned during the course of the nineteenth century, the federal government used the Commerce Clause to justify many new assertions of national authority over tribes. It also developed an entirely novel non-constitutional authority – plenary power – by which Congress, by definition, was granted absolute control over all indigenous affairs. By the latter part of the century, these legal tools enabled federal lawmakers to extend their reach over indigenous affairs to remarkably oppressive levels.

Beginning in 1790, at the behest of the president, the constitutional provisions most directly related to Indian affairs were given statutory expression

[5] 1 Stat. 50 (1789).

in a series of laws later codified in 1834 as the Indian Trade and Intercourse Acts.[6] The acts devoted considerable attention to maintaining peaceful relations with tribes by agreeing to respect Indian land boundaries and fulfill the nation's treaty and trust obligations to tribes. These comprehensive federal Indian policies also contained clauses requiring federal approval of any purchase of tribal land, regulated the activities of white traders in Indian Country through licensing, and imposed penalties for crimes committed by whites against Indians. Importantly, the laws were aimed at shoring up alliances with the tribes and evidenced respect for treaty rights by restricting states, traders, and private citizens from engaging with tribes on their own account. The Trade and Intercourse Acts mainly embodied Congress's legal and constitutional role as the primary agent in charge of overseeing trade and fulfilling the federal government's treaty obligations. They had very little impact on the internal sovereignty of indigenous nations.

In 1819, however, Congress stepped far beyond its designated role by adopting legislation explicitly designed to "civilize" Indian peoples. Appropriately entitled "An Act making provisions for the civilization of the Indian tribes adjoining the frontier settlements,"[7] the statute was significant for three reasons. First, it meant that Congress had officially decided to seek the cultural transformation rather than physical destruction of native peoples. Second, it signaled a bifurcation in Congress's responsibilities. While still charged with appropriating funds to fulfill the nation's treaty requirements to tribes considered as separate entities, it had now opted to pursue a parallel policy of civilization, assimilation, and absorption of the Indian into the body politic of the United States. Finally, Congress was assuming the power to legislate for persons who were not within the physical boundaries of the United States; the majority of native peoples still lived outside the demarcated borders of the United States.

The first responsibility, upholding treaty requirements, was constitutionally grounded in the Treaty and Commerce clauses. The second responsibility, or rather unilateral declaration, was an entirely different matter – embraced by Congress wholly gratuitously, without reference to the Constitution's definition of its capacities. The intersection between what Congress was legally required to do in relations with Indians and what it chose to do created a powerful tension that has affected the legal and political relationship of tribes and the United States since that time. What happens, for instance, when there is a conflict between the two sets of responsibilities? This is no empty question. As we shall see, tribes' treaty-reserved rights to designated communal land holdings, which it was Congress's responsibility to uphold, would be countermanded by the same Congress when it pursued

[6] 4 Stat. 729 (1834).

[7] 3 Stat. 516 (1819).

plans to "civilize" the community of land holders by allotting them those same lands (or a fraction thereof) as individual Indian property holders.

II. EARLY FEDERAL RESTRICTIONS OF TRIBAL PROPERTY AND SOVEREIGNTY: 1820s–1830

Even before the 1819 Civilization Act, Congress had signaled both in its ratification of certain treaties and its passage of particular statutes that indigenous peoples and their separate territories were within the reach of American citizenship and law. At this time, Congressional intent was couched in noncoercive terms to minimize the direct impact on tribal sovereignty. For example, Article Eight of the 1817 Treaty with the Cherokee – an early removal agreement – specified that those Cherokee who wished to remain on lands surrendered to the federal government were to receive a life-estate to a 640-acre individual "reservation" and also, if they desired it, American citizenship. The provisions were repeated in Article Two of the Cherokee Treaty of 1819.

In part because of the increasing numbers of whites moving onto tribal lands, Congress also expressed its intention to enforce a measure of federal criminal law inside Indian Country. An act of March 3, 1817, declared that interracial crimes involving Indians and non-Indians committed within Indian Country would be punished in the same fashion as the same offenses committed elsewhere in the United States. The statute gave federal courts jurisdiction over those indicted under its provisions. Importantly, it did not apply to intraracial (Indian on Indian) crimes. Tribes were assured that no extant treaty rights were to be adversely affected by the law.

Although U.S. Indian policy had been nationalized from the beginning of the American Republic, federal Indian law grew unevenly in the face of persistent legal wrangling between federal and state officials over which level of government would in fact control the nation's relationship with tribes. Several of the thirteen original states, especially Georgia and New York, homes to the powerful and politically astute Cherokee Nation and Iroquois Confederated tribes, respectively, viewed themselves as superior sovereigns both in relation to the indigenous nations residing within "their" borders and to the federal government. The politicians in these two states continued to negotiate treaties with the tribes as if the Commerce and Treaty clauses did not exist or simply did not apply to their actions.

This amalgam of states, with their expanding populations and economies; tribes, with their desire to retain their lands and treaty rights free of state and federal intrusion; and the federal government, with its contradictory impulse of supporting national and state territorial and economic expansion, but also responsible to tribes under treaty and trust obligations, proved a most volatile mix. By the end of the 1830s, the volatility in tribal-federal-state relations had worked out mostly to the detriment of the tribes: federal and state sovereignty were reinforced, territorial expansion encouraged, indigenous sovereignty and property rights weakened. Tribal rights and lands were not, of course, disregarded entirely. They were, however, sufficiently diminished that expropriation of Indian lands by land speculators, individual settlers, state governments, and federal officials could continue without letup. All of this was accomplished, in Alexis de Tocqueville's words, "in a regular and, so to say, quite legal manner."[8]

Tocqueville's "legal manner" – that is to say, the legal underpinnings of the indigenous/non-indigenous relationship – was largely the construction of the U.S. Supreme Court, led by Chief Justice John Marshall. Specific decisions were absolutely basic to the Court's achievement: *Johnson v. McIntosh* (1823), which dealt with tribal property rights; *Cherokee Nation v. Georgia* (1831), which determined tribal political status in relation to the federal government; *Worcester v. Georgia* (1832), which focused on tribal political status in relation to the states; and *Mitchel v. United States* (1835), which debated the international standing of tribal treaty rights. In fact, the cases would prove far more important for their long-run impact on tribal sovereignty as precedents and as legal rhetoric than for the specific issues each one addressed. At the time, and even as the national government's political branches were preparing to force the removal of native nations from their ancestral lands, the federal judiciary's rulings were supportive of as well as detrimental to indigenous rights.

In *McIntosh* (1823), the Court institutionalized a revised doctrine of discovery and engaged in a convoluted discussion of the doctrine of conquest. The results were oppressive to the sovereignty and proprietary rights of tribes. According to Chief Justice John Marshall, writing for the Court, not only had the discoverer gained the exclusive right to appropriate tribal lands, but the tribes' sovereign rights were diminished and their right to sell land to whomever they wished fatally compromised. Marshall acknowledged that both the discovery and conquest doctrines were self-serving, yet relied on them nonetheless. "However extravagant the pretension of converting the discovery of an inhabited country into conquest may appear," he ruled, "if the principle has been asserted in the first instance, and afterwards, sustained; if a country has been acquired and held under it; if the property of the great mass of the community originates in it, it becomes the law of the land, and cannot be questioned."[9] The Court transformed these extravagant theories into legal terms for largely political and economic reasons: the increasing indigenous resistance to land loss, uncertainty over what Spain,

[8] de Tocqueville, *Democracy in America*, 324.
[9] 21 U.S. (8 Wheat.) 543, 591.

France, and Russia's long-term intentions were on the continent, and its own desire to formulate a uniform American law of real property. Still, although it denied that tribes could alienate their lands to whomever they wished, the Court conceded that the Indians retained a right of perpetual occupancy that the United States had to recognize. It also determined that the federal government had to secure Indian consent before it could extinguish Indian occupancy title. In these respects the Court displayed a desire to adhere, at least in theory, to just and humane standards that recognized the prior existence of tribes and a measure of their property rights title, even as it embraced the ethnocentric view of the technological and proprietary superiority of Western nations.

In December 1823, some nine months after *McIntosh*, President James Monroe acted at the international level to solidify American hemispheric hegemony in a fashion that also confirmed the domesticated status of indigenous property. Monroe's message was propounded in his Annual Message to Congress, becoming what would be called the Monroe Doctrine. Drafted partially as a response to Russia's intention to extend its settlements southward from Alaska with an eye to joining with France, Austria, and Prussia in an attempt to force newly independent Spanish-American republics to return their allegiance to Spain, the Monroe Doctrine declared U.S. opposition to European meddling in the Americas. The political systems of the American continents were fundamentally different from those of Europe, Monroe warned. The United States would consider "as dangerous to our peace and safety" any attempt by European powers to extend their authority in the Western hemisphere. Reciprocally, the United States would not interfere with existing European colonies in the Americas or in the internal affairs of Europeans, or participate in European wars of foreign interests.

The combined effect of the *McIntosh* ruling and the Monroe Doctrine did not bode well for indigenous property or sovereignty. Meanwhile, Eastern states, clamoring for additional Indian lands and resources for their burgeoning populations and to rid themselves of an indigenous presence, gained a major ally when Andrew Jackson was elected president in 1828. The stage was set for a major test of American democracy, federalism, and the doctrine of separation of powers. The indigenous community that would bear the brunt of much of this concentrated attention was the Cherokee Nation of the Southeast.

III. THE CHEROKEE NATION, JOHN MARSHALL, AND THE LAW

The Cherokee were one of the first native peoples to succeed in fusing ancient tribal law ways with Anglo-American legal institutions. This acculturation process, in which the Western legal system was modified to Cherokee needs, was actually underway by the early 1820s. In that decade alone the Cherokee crafted a constitution loosely modeled after that of the United States, produced a written version of their language, and established the first tribal newspaper. In 1827, they formally announced their political independence, a fact already well understood by the federal government as evidenced by the fourteen ratified treaties signed with the tribe. The Cherokee emphatically declared that they were an independent nation with an absolute right to their territory and sovereignty within their boundaries.

The Cherokee declaration enraged Georgia's white population and state officials. Driven by the recent discovery of gold on tribal lands, but compelled even more by a conception of state sovereignty that precluded limitations imposed by the federal government, let alone a tribal people, Georgia legislators enacted a series of debilitating, treaty-violating laws designed to undermine Cherokee self-government. These acts parceled out Cherokee lands to several counties, extended state jurisdiction over the nation, and abolished Cherokee laws.

Cherokee appeals to President Jackson and Congress to intercede failed, and the tribe filed suit in the Supreme Court against Georgia, praying for an injunction to restrain Georgia's execution of the laws aimed at their legal dismemberment. Chief Justice Marshall rendered the Court's fragmented and ambivalent ruling on March 18, 1831 (*Cherokee Nation v. Georgia)*. A more fascinating case could hardly be imagined, Marshall noted. But first the Court had to ascertain whether it had jurisdiction to hear the case. Since the Cherokee were suing as an original plaintiff, the Court had to decide whether they constituted a "foreign state." After lengthy ruminations, Marshall held that the Cherokee Nation were not a foreign state and therefore could not maintain an action in the federal courts.

If they were not a foreign state, what were they? Marshall refused to accept either of the views of tribes available at the time – as foreign nations or subject nations. As "subject" nations, they would have been at the mercy of the states; as "foreign" nations, they would have been independent of federal control. Instead, Marshall generated an extra-constitutional political status for tribes by characterizing them as "domestic dependent nations." This diluted and ambiguous status has had a lasting effect on all tribes, even though technically it applied only to the Cherokee. First, the description precluded tribes from bringing original actions to the Supreme Court. And second, since they were denied status as "foreign nations," the tribes were effectively barred from benefits accorded to fully recognized sovereigns under international law.

Building on the legal construct of "discovery" that he had articulated in *McIntosh*, Marshall said that tribes occupied territory to which the United

States asserted a superior title. He then added extremely problematic wording that would prove highly detrimental to tribes. Tribes were "in a state of pupilage. Their relation to the United States resembles that of a ward to his guardian."[10]

Overall, the Court was highly fragmented. Six Justices (the seventh, Justice Duvall, was absent) presented four different sets of views on tribal status. Justice Johnson held that tribes lacked sovereignty but possessed an inherent political power that could mature into sovereignty later. Justice Baldwin simply said tribes had no sovereignty. Justices Thompson and Story believed that tribal status paralleled that of foreign nations. Justice McLean joined Marshall in his description of tribes as domestic dependent nations.

On the jurisdictional question the majority was thus against the Cherokee. On the merits, however, the Court divided four to two for the Cherokee. The Chief Justice, in fact, insinuated that he sided with the minority on the merits – he encouraged Justices Thompson and Story to write out their dissenting views. The Chief Justice even suggested a method of getting a case properly before the Court in the future.

Marshall would have the opportunity to reveal his innermost feelings sooner than he anticipated. *Worcester v. Georgia* (1832), the third of the Court's seminal Indian cases, is often hailed as the most persuasive and elaborate pronouncement of the federal government's treaty-based relationship with tribal nations. Interestingly, the Cherokee were not direct parties to this suit. And while *Worcester* is generally considered the strongest defense of tribal sovereignty, it may be understood more accurately as a case that supports federal sovereignty over state sovereignty. The principals in the case were Christian missionaries led by Samuel A. Worcester and Elizur Butler, and the State of Georgia. Georgia had enacted a law in 1831 that prohibited whites from entering Cherokee country without first securing a state license. Worcester and Butler had entered Cherokee territory without state authorization, but with tribal and federal approval. They were arrested and sentenced to four years in prison for violating state law. The missionaries immediately retained lawyers who brought suit against Georgia in federal court on the grounds that Worcester and Butler were agents of the United States. This raised the question of federal supremacy over state law. Here was the test case for which Marshall had been waiting.

Unlike his ambiguous opinion in *Cherokee Nation*, Marshall emphatically declared that all of Georgia's Indian laws violated the Constitution, federal statutes, and the treaties between the United States and the Cherokee. Lifting text almost verbatim from Justice Thompson's dissent in *Cherokee*

[10] 30 U.S. (5 Pet.) 1, 17.

Nation on the international status of tribes, Marshall held that treaties and the law of nations supported Cherokee sovereignty and independence, even though the Cherokee were no longer as powerful militarily as they had been and were now under the political protection of the federal government.

Worcester supposedly settled the issue of federal preeminence over state power regarding Indian tribes. The Chief Justice based much of his defense of federal power on his view of Indian tribes "as distinct, independent political communities."[11] He noted that the War and Peace, Treaty-Making, and Commerce Clauses provided the national government with sufficient authority to regulate the nation's relations with tribes. Marshall also attempted to rectify his previous equivocations on the doctrine of discovery, which he now said was nothing more than an exclusive principle limiting competition among European states that could not limit Indian property rights. He also clarified the Court's view of the actual political status of tribes. In *Cherokee Nation*, tribes were called "domestic dependent nations," not on par with "foreign" states. In *Worcester*, however, tribes were referred to as "distinct, independent communities," properly identified and treated as nations.

Although the Court overturned Georgia's actions and ordered Worcester's release, he remained in prison and was released only when a later deal was struck. More significantly and tragically, however, the majority of the Cherokee people and more than 100,000 other Indians representing more than a dozen tribes were eventually coerced into signing treaties that led to their relocation to Indian Territory west of the Mississippi River.

Three years later, in *Mitchel v. United States (1835)*, the Supreme Court issued another important opinion on indigenous rights. It has received little attention from legal and political commentators, in large part because most writers have concentrated their attention on the so-called Marshall trilogy – *McIntosh*, *Cherokee Nation*, and *Worcester*. In *Mitchel*, possibly because he was near retirement (he stepped down in July 1835), Marshall opted not to write the decision and assigned it to Justice Henry Baldwin.

Mitchel should be added to that short list of Supreme Court rulings that exhibit some support for tribal sovereignty and indigenous land rights. The Court's holding fundamentally contradicts, without expressly overruling, the doctrines espoused in *McIntosh*. The ruling asserted the following key principles: first, the doctrine of discovery lacks credibility as a legal principle; second, tribes are possessors of a sacrosanct land title that is as important as the fee-simple title of non-Indians; third, tribes have the right to alienate their aboriginal property to whomever they wish; fourth, the alleged inferiority of tribal culture does not impair aboriginal

[11] 31 U.S. (6 Pet.) 515, 559.

sovereignty; and fifth, tribes are collective polities and they and their members are entitled to international law's protections of their recognized treaty rights.

Tribes emerged from the Marshall era with a contradictory political status. They had been labeled both domestic dependent nations and distinct and independent political communities. The assertion that tribes were independent polities most closely approached their actual situation. But the cases' confused and contradictory analogies would prove highly problematic, resulting in persistent confusion about exactly where – if anywhere – tribal nations fit in the American constitutional landscape.

The long-term consequences of Marshall-era principles – discovery, the analogy of wardship, and domestic indigenous status – have been their distinct diminution of tribal sovereignty. Other Marshall era ideas – the supremacy of Indian treaties, the independence of tribal communities, the exposure of discovery, the exclusive jurisdiction of the federal government, and the sacredness of Indian title – offer tribes means to retain some measure of legal and political sovereignty.

IV. TRIBAL SOVEREIGNTY AND WESTERN EXPANSION, 1835–1860s

The three decades between *Mitchel* (1835) and the inception of the American Civil War (1861) were tumultuous years in American history, marked from the beginning as an era of massive Indian removal. These were the opening years of "Manifest Destiny," when the United States acquired political control of large parts of the Far West and, unexpectedly, encountered a new Indian frontier. The new territories included Texas (1845), Oregon (1846), more than one million square miles of the Southwest and West obtained from Mexico by the Treaty of Guadalupe Hidalgo (1848), and an additional 29,640 square miles acquired from Mexico in the Gadsden Purchase (1853). Within the span of a decade, the size of the United States had increased by 73 percent.

These vast conquests and purchases resulted in the physical incorporation into the United States of scores of previously unknown native nations. The inevitable cultural and territorial collision resulted in a Congressional policy of containment, specifically the establishment of Indian reservations. Between the 1830s and 1850s, the reservation policy remained in an experimental stage. It would not be implemented fully until the 1860s. In fact, treaties rather than Congressional legislation formed the basis of the law during this era of rapid expansion. That said, the broad outline of U.S. Indian policy – still visible – can be found in two comprehensive laws enacted by Congress, on June 30, 1834. The first measure was the final act in a series of statutes that regulated trade and intercourse with tribes.[12] The second, enacted the same day, provided for the organization of the Department of Indian Affairs.[13] By adopting these laws, Congress developed a set of institutions and procedures that clarified what had been a thoroughly ill-defined structural relationship between the United States and tribal nations.

By the late 1840s, two additional statutes had been enacted that were to have a lasting effect on tribes. The first amended the 1834 Non-Intercourse Act that had organized the Department of Indian Affairs.[14] The new measure made two significant changes in federal Indian policy. First, it stiffened and broadened preexisting Indian liquor legislation, which had long outlawed liquor in Indian country (a prohibition that would remain in effect until 1953). Second, it signaled a profound change in the manner and to whom the federal government would distribute moneys owed to native nations. Previously those funds were distributed to tribal chiefs or other leaders. Section 3 declared that moneys owed to Indian nations would instead be distributed directly to the heads of individual families and other individuals entitled to receive payments. Ostensibly designed to reduce the influence of white traders on tribal leaders, this amendment, in effect, gave federal officials tremendous discretionary authority on the question of tribal membership, insofar as the disposition of funds was concerned. According to legal scholar Felix Cohen, this was the first in a series of statutes aimed at individualizing tribal property and funds in a way that diminished the sovereign character of tribal nations.

The second act (1849) established the Department of Interior.[15] It contained a provision calling for the transfer of administrative responsibility for Indian affairs from the War Department to the new department. Supporters of this move believed, prematurely, that Indian warfare was ending and that responsibility for Indian affairs should therefore be placed in civilian hands. Congress retained constitutional authority to deal with tribal nations, but the legislature more often deferred to the president and the executive branch, especially in the sensitive area of Indian treaties, which were being negotiated by the dozens during this period.

Justice Roger Taney and Indian Law

Coinciding with the emergence of a more activist national state – legislative and executive – on tribal questions, the Supreme Court under Marshall's successor, Chief Justice Roger Taney, began to produce legal doctrines that confirmed the suppression of the treaty paradigm in favor of "federalism."

[12] 4 Stat. 729 (1834).
[13] 4 Stat. 735 (1834).
[14] 9 Stat. 203 (1847).
[15] 9 Stat. 395 (1849).

Taney enunciated the Court's embrace of this new perspective on tribal political status in *United States v. Rogers* (1846). Ironically, this unanimous decision, like the Marshall cases, also involved the Cherokee, even though they were not directly a party to the suit.

William S. Rogers, a white man residing within Cherokee Territory, had been indicted in a federal circuit court for the murder of Jacob Nicholson, also a white man. The crime had occurred in Cherokee Country. A confused circuit court sent the case to the Supreme Court on a certificate of division. Taney, writing for a unanimous court, dramatically rewrote the history of the legal and political relationship between tribes and the United States. Contrary to Marshall's fact-based *Worcester* opinion, Taney misrepresented the basis of Cherokee title to their lands, proposing that their lands had been "assigned to them" by the federal government and that they held title only with the "permission" of the United States. The Cherokee and the scores of other tribes then negotiating treaties with the United States were no doubt shocked to hear Taney use the discovery doctrine in a way that essentially denied any native proprietary rights at all. Removal, the Court implied, not only vacated any rights Indians thought they might have had in their original territories but it also offered them no substitute rights in the "Indian territory" to which they had been forced to move.

Rogers was also the first Indian law opinion to outline explicitly the Court's "political question" doctrine. Political question doctrine holds that it is not the province of the courts to render rulings on matters deemed essentially "political" in nature. These are matters best left to the legislative and executive branches. Describing Indians as an "unfortunate race," Taney stated that, even if Indians had been mistreated, "yet it is a question for the law-making and political department of the government, and not the judicial."[16] Along with the absence of land rights went the absence of conventional legal means of redress. The political question doctrine would continue to plague Indian legal efforts until it was formally disavowed in the 1980 Supreme Court ruling *United States v. Sioux Nation*.

Rogers is an appropriate representative of Supreme Court cases emphasizing the federalism paradigm, by which federal dominance over tribes was confirmed in virtually every respect – property, political status, and ethnic identity. It is worth noting that ten years after *Rogers*, Chief Justice Taney's infamous *Dred Scott* opinion (1857) would refer to Indians as historically "a free and independent people, associated together in nations or tribes" and treated as foreign governments "as much so as if an ocean had separated the red man from the white."[17] The description underscores the transformation to which *Rogers* had contributed.

[16] 45 U.S. (4 How.) 567, 572.

[17] 60 U.S. (19 How.) 393, 404.

The Taney Court's doctrines were particularly harmful to tribal sovereignty because that Court was much more concerned than its predecessor with protecting state authority within U.S. federalism. Historically, states' rights activists have generally been less supportive of tribal rights because of the geopolitical relationship between states and tribes (illustrated in Georgia's conflict with the Cherokee). Nevertheless, at this point most tribal nations existed outside the scope of Anglo-American law. Before mid-century, the law's impact had been felt mostly by the Eastern tribes whose experience with Euro-Americans dated to the pre-Revolutionary period. Western expansion would rapidly terminate this geographical isolation. The gradual encirclement of tribes by non-Indians, increased immigration, the Civil War and Reconstruction, and burgeoning industrialization – fueled in part by transcontinental railroads – all produced the circumstances in which the federalism paradigm would wreak legal havoc on native nations.

V. ORIGIN AND SCOPE OF FEDERAL PLENARY (ABSOLUTE) POWER: 1871–1886

From the late 1860s through the early twentieth century, the United States – Congress in particular – was openly bent on the destruction of native nations as identifiable cultural, sociological, and political bodies. The era of Congressional unilateralism vis-à-vis indigenous peoples began during Reconstruction; its clearest expression was a rider inserted in the Indian Appropriation Act of March 3, 1871, which provided "That hereafter no Indian nation or tribe within the territory of the United States shall be acknowledged or recognized as an independent nation, tribe, or power with whom the United States may contract by treaty."[18] Congressional unilateralism culminated in 1906 in systematic efforts to terminate the sovereign status of the Five Civilized Tribes in Indian Territory. Throughout, Congress wielded self-assumed and virtually unrestrained powers over Indians that could never have survived constitutional muster had they been asserted against American citizens.

The year 1871 is important for a second reason besides Congressional repudiation of formal treaty-making. In May of that year, two months after the repudiation of treaty-making, the U.S. Supreme Court ruled in *The Cherokee Tobacco* case[19] that the 1868 Revenue Act, which contained a provision imposing federal taxes on liquor and tobacco products in the United States, had implicitly abrogated an 1866 Cherokee Treaty provision by which Cherokee citizens were exempted from federal taxes.

[18] Stat. 566; Rev. Stat. § 2079, now contained in 25 U. S. C. § 71.
[19] 78 U.S. (11 Wall.) 616 (1871).

For tribes, the conjunction was catastrophic. The treaty repudiation rider effectively froze tribes in political limbo. They were no longer recognized as polities capable of engaging in treaty-making with the federal government, yet they remained separate sovereignties outside the pale of the U.S. Constitution. Meanwhile, Cherokees who were not then American citizens were now required to pay taxes to the federal government despite their noncitizenship, their express treaty exemption, and their lack of Congressional representation. Tribes and individual Indians were now bereft of legal or political protection. The federal government could explicitly or implicitly abrogate treaty provisions, and tribes had no recourse other than turn to the very Congress that had stripped them of recognition. Following *Rogers*, the Supreme Court deferred to the political branches on Indian matters, declaring in effect that Congressional acts would prevail as if the treaties were not even documents worthy of consideration.

In its 1871 rider, Congress had guaranteed the terms of treaties already negotiated. The *Cherokee Tobacco* decision almost immediately put that guarantee in doubt, announcing that treaty rights generally secured at the expense of significant amounts of tribal land and the loss of other valuable properties and freedoms could be destroyed by mere implication. The case established the "last-in-time" precedent (that is, later statutes may override earlier treaties) and also the rule that tribes are always to be considered "included" in Congressional acts unless they are specifically "excluded" in the language of the statute. And it disavowed the basic principle that specific laws, like treaties that generate special rights, are not to be repealed by mere implication of general laws.

With the treaty process essentially stymied and extant treaties now subject to implicit disavowal, and with white settlers and land speculators flooding into the far reaches of the West driven by powerful economic motives and a sense of racial superiority, federal lawmakers struggled with how best to support what they deemed the inevitable spread of capitalism and Protestantism while still providing some degree of respect and protection for tribal peoples and their dwindling lands. A loose coalition of individuals and institutions that would come to be called the "Friends of the American Indian," consisting of law professors, Christian leaders, reformers, leaders of the bar, and a few members of Congress, stood up against the powerful economic and political interests intent on destroying, or at least diminishing dramatically, the rights and resources of indigenous people. This loose alliance of native supporters, Petra Shattuck and Jill Norgren have written, "linked adherence to principles of rationality and morality with the pragmatic needs of manifest destiny. Their debates proved a forceful and convincing counterpoint to the popular clamor for the abrogation of the legal and moral commitments of the past."

The Friends of the American Indian may have helped ameliorate federal policy, but they did not alter its direction (nor did they wish to). Assimilation dominated federal Indian policy and law during the 1870s and into the first two decades of the twentieth century. It rested on consistent adherence to five basic goals: first, transform Indian men and women into agriculturalists or herders; second, educate Indians in the Western tradition; third, break up the tribal masses by means of individual allotment of tribal lands, in the process freeing non-allotted land for white settlement; fourth, extend U.S. citizenship to individual Indians; and fifth, supplant tribal customary law with Euro-American law. Save for the latter, these ideas had already been well in evidence, but their implementation had been spasmodic. From the 1870s on, with Indians essentially immobilized on reservations and rendered weak in the face of federal power by wars, alcohol, diseases, and displacement, the guardian-like U.S. government and allied institutions – notably the churches – could develop a more systematic and thorough approach to the increasingly ward-like status of indigenous peoples.

In the 1880s, federal efforts to assimilate Indians took a variety of forms. Prime among these were attempts to extend American law to reservations, subdivide the Indians' communal estate, and grant the franchise to individual Indians. First, let us consider the application of Euro-American criminal law to Indian Country.

Prior to the 1880s, as we have seen, relations between tribes and the United States were largely determined by treaties and the policies outlined in the trade and intercourse acts. Internal tribal sovereignty, especially crimes between Indians, was largely untouched by federal law. The idea of imposing federal criminal jurisdiction, however, slowly gained momentum as Western expansion led to the encirclement and permanent penetration of tribal lands by non-Indians. This "de facto" assimilation required a de jure response, said the quasi-political Board of Indian Commissioners in 1871. Indians had to be brought under the "domination of law, so far as regards crimes committed against each other" or the federal government's best efforts to civilize native peoples would be constrained.[20]

The first major case from the West involving the extension of Euro-American law into Indian Country arose directly as a result of the ever burgeoning numbers of whites settling on Indian lands. *United States v. McBratney* (1882)[21] involved the murder of one white man by another within the boundaries of the Ute Reservation in Colorado. The Supreme Court ruled that the equal footing doctrine – which holds that states newly

[20] United States Board of Indian Commissioners. *Annual Report* (Washington, DC, 1871), 432.

[21] 104 U.S. 621.

admitted into the Union were on an "equal footing" with the original states insofar as their political status and sovereignty were concerned – and the absence of explicit statutory language providing for federal rather than state jurisdiction regarding tribal lands gave state authorities jurisdiction over the crime. Ignoring Ute sovereignty and denying federal jurisdiction, the Court turned the *Worcester* principle of state non-interference in tribal territory on its head. Operating from its version of the federalism paradigm, it permanently transformed the tribal-state relationship by indicating that subject matter and identity, not geography, would determine questions of state jurisdiction.

The issue of Indian-on-Indian crime was next to arrive at the Supreme Court. The landmark case *Ex parte Crow Dog* (1883) dealt with a Sioux leader, Crow Dog, sentenced to death for the murder of a chief, Spotted Tail. The high court, using the treaty paradigm, unanimously held that the federal government lacked jurisdiction over crimes committed by one Indian against another. The decision was an important, if stilted, statement on tribal sovereignty. It served as the catalyst to jurisdictional changes advocated by those anxious to have federal law supplant tribal law, the final tipping-point toward a half-century of assimilation. A mere eighteen months later, Congress repudiated the treaty-based Court decision by attaching a legislative rider to the general appropriation act of March 1885 that extended federal criminal jurisdiction over Indians in matters involving seven major crimes – murder, manslaughter, rape, assault with intent to kill, arson, burglary, and larceny.[22]

Congress's direct attack on tribal sovereignty was not fatal to tribal self-determination, but enactment of the major crimes rider set a precedent for future Congressional intrusions. There was, however, some doubt as to the act's constitutionality. This became the central issue in *United States v. Kagama* (1886),[23] one of the most important Indian law decisions issued by the Court. Kagama was a Hoopa Indian (northern California) convicted of killing another Indian on the Hoopa Reservation. Kagama and his attorneys argued that the Major Crimes Act was unconstitutional and should be voided because Congress's Commerce Clause power did not authorize it to enact laws regulating Indian-on-Indian crimes occurring within Indian Country. The Supreme Court upheld the constitutionality of the Major Crimes Act, but rejected both the Commerce Clause and Property Clause arguments suggested by the government's lawyers. Instead, the Court denied tribal sovereignty by fashioning a set of arguments grounded in federalism and U.S. nationalism and steeped in ethnocentrism. The Court embraced geographical incorporation: because the United States "owned"

[22] 23 Stat. 362, 385 (1885).

[23] 118 U.S. 375.

the country, and because Indians lived within its boundaries, the United States could extend an unbridled power over Indians, based on the doctrine of discovery. The justices also embraced Indian wardship: Indian dependency and helplessness necessitated unlimited exercise of federal guardianship – what would later be termed "plenary" power. In other words, the Court determined that, based on its ownership of land, the federal government had virtually unfettered power over tribes. And in declaring Indians "wards of the nation," indigenous peoples had been rendered subject to a plenary Congressional authority to protect and defend its "dependents," exercised as Congress saw fit.

Ironically, in *Kagama* the Supreme Court held a federal statute applying to Indians to be constitutional while rejecting the only available constitutional clauses that would have rendered it constitutional. That the court could, in effect, step outside the Constitution to hold a law constitutional is quite a remarkable feat. Why it did so, however, is clear. It sought to legitimize the Congressional policy of coercive assimilation and acculturation of tribal citizens into the American polity. The Court developed the extra-legal sophistry of unbounded proprietary authority and wardship to further the assimilative process while at the same time acting to "protect" tribes from uninvited and intrusive state attacks on tribes and their dwindling resources.

Having addressed the subject of criminal jurisdiction, the federal government then acted on the question of extending federal citizenship to Indians. Many of the "Friends" – reformers and policymakers – believed that it was unfair to impose Euro-American norms of criminality and punishment without allowing Indians access to the full benefits and responsibilities accompanying American citizenship. Hence they advocated extending the franchise to Indians.

The first major test of whether the United States was prepared to follow the reformers' lead came in *Elk v. Wilkins* (1884).[24] John Elk had voluntarily emigrated from his tribe (his tribal affiliation was never mentioned) and moved to Omaha, Nebraska. After a time, Elk went to register to vote, claiming that the Fourteenth and Fifteenth Amendments gave him U.S. citizenship. His registration application was rejected by Charles Wilkins, the city registrar, on the grounds that Elk, as an Indian, was not a citizen of the United States. The case found its way to the Supreme Court, where Elk's constitutional claims were rejected. As an American Indian he belonged to an "alien nation." The majority maintained that, even if individual Indians met basic citizenship requirements, as Elk had done, they still could not be enfranchised unless Congress passed a law authorizing such a change in their legal standing.

[24] 112 U.S. 94.

Congressional reaction to *Elk* was swift, though ill focused. Some reform groups argued that the solution to the Indian "problem" was unfettered and immediate citizenship. Others declared that U.S. citizenship, a valid goal, should be a gradual process tied to individualized property ownership. The two camps compromised (at Indian expense) by embracing the allotment of much of Indian Country.

The General Allotment [Dawes] Act,[25] passed the year after the Supreme Court's *Elk* decision, intensified Congress's cultural and proprietary assault on indigenous peoples. Most observers suggest that this act – actually a detailed policy directive – and the multiple amendments and individual allotting agreements passed in its wake over the next two decades, constitute the single most devastating federal assault on indigenous nations. Most white philanthropists, and those federal lawmakers concerned to maintain the nation's position as a liberal and democratic polity, agreed that tribal social structures founded on common stewardship of land were the major obstacle to Indians' "progress" toward civilization. These "Friends" firmly believed in the need to break up the reservations, distribute small individual plots of land to tribal members, and then require the allotted Indian to adapt to Euro-American farming life. The allotments themselves were to be held in trust. For twenty-five years they could not be sold without express permission of the secretary of the interior. This was deemed a sufficient period for the individual Indian to learn the arts of a civilized yeoman farmer. U.S. citizenship accompanied receipt of the allotment. Tribal land not allotted to members was declared "surplus." This "extra" land was sold to non-Indians, whose settlement among the Indians, it was believed, would expedite their acquisition of white attitudes and behavior.

Tribal lands, already dramatically depleted through land cession treaties and agreements, were further reduced by the allotment policy and the subsequent individual allotting agreements. The allotment policy was, in the words of President Theodore Roosevelt, "a mighty pulverizing engine to break up the tribal mass." By 1934 when it was finally stopped, 118 of 213 reservations had been allotted, resulting in the loss of another ninety million acres of tribal land. What then ensued was in many ways even worse – removal of allotments from trust-protected status by forced fee patent, sale by both Indian landowners and the United States, probate proceedings under state inheritance laws, foreclosure, and surplus sale of tribal lands. Fundamentally, the entire allotment and post-allotment program had disastrous economic and cultural consequences for native peoples, which are still felt by both allotted tribes and individual Indians today.

[25] 24 Stat. 388 (1887).

VI. THE UNIQUE LEGAL STATUS OF THE PUEBLOS AND THE FIVE CIVILIZED TRIBES

Tribal nations are uniquely constituted social, political, and cultural entities. As we have seen, the consistent failure to recognize that reality has meant that federal efforts to develop a coherent and consistent body of legal principles to deal with the tribes were never very successful. But there were exceptions. Not all tribes were brought under the federal umbrella or were viewed the same way by the federal government. Two groupings of aboriginal peoples considered "exceptional" and who became the focus of a great deal of Western law thus merit specific discussion: the Pueblo Nations of present-day New Mexico (actually twenty-two distinctive indigenous communities) and the so-called Five Civilized Tribes[26] – the Cherokee, Chickasaw, Choctaw, Creek, and Seminole.

The Pueblos

The Pueblos are distinctive in part because of their particular culture and language and because of their long historical relationship with the Spanish and, later, the Mexican governments. Written agreements with Spain in the form of land grants, later acknowledged by the Mexican government, unquestionably affirmed Pueblo ownership, not just occupancy, of their lands. Pueblo land grants were both encompassed and recognized by the United States under the provisions of the 1848 Treaty of Guadalupe Hidalgo. One of the Hidalgo Treaty's provisions specified that Mexican citizens might choose either Mexican or U.S. citizenship. The Pueblo Indians, by choosing to remain in their homeland, were said by some federal commentators to have implicitly accepted U.S. citizenship. This federal citizenship status was first affirmed by the Supreme Court in *United States v. Ritchie*.[27]

Pueblo connections to previous Spanish and Mexican authorities, their apparently enfranchised status, and their generally peaceful demeanor toward American settlers and the federal government raised the question whether the Pueblos were to be considered "Indian tribes" within the meaning of existing federal statutes, such as the 1834 Trade and Intercourse Act, which were designed to protect tribal lands from white encroachment. Because of the Pueblos' ambiguous legal status and less confrontational

[26] The phrase "civilized" became part of the Five Tribes after their forced removal to present-day Oklahoma. Once they resettled, the members of these nations made tremendous social and political changes within their societies and were soon labeled "civilized" to distinguish them from the so-called wild tribes of the Western plains area.

[27] 58 U.S. (17 How.) 525 (1854).

comportment, increasing numbers of Mexican-American and Anglo-American settlers became squatters on Pueblo land grants. The Pueblos resented these intrusions and, with the support of their Indian agents and the federal government as their trustee, sought to have the trespassers evicted. The matter came before the Supreme Court in *United States v. Joseph* (1877),[28] in which the Court was asked to decide whether the Taos Pueblo constituted an Indian "tribe" under the meaning of the 1834 Intercourse Act. If they were, federal officials could expel the interlopers. If they were not, the government had no such authority, leaving the Pueblos to deal with the squatters as best they could by themselves.

The court found that the Pueblos were far more "peaceful, industrious, intelligent, honest, and virtuous" than the neighboring "nomadic" and "wild" Navajo and Apache Tribes. Therefore, they could not be classed with the Indian tribes for whom the intercourse acts had been passed. Being far too "civilized" to need federal guardianship, the Pueblos could decide for themselves who could live on their lands. The justices opted not to address definitively the issue of whether or not Pueblo individuals were American citizens, but they did acknowledge that the Pueblos' Spanish land grants gave them a title to their lands that was superior even to that of the United States.

In 1913, a year after New Mexico gained statehood, Pueblo status was dramatically reconfigured by the Supreme Court in *United States v. Sandoval*.[29] So long as New Mexico had only territorial status, the Pueblos had been of peripheral concern to the federal government. With statehood, the subject of intergovernmental relations and Pueblo status required clarification. Congress had provided in New Mexico's Enabling Act that the terms "Indian" and "Indian Country" were to include the Pueblos and their lands. These provisions were incorporated in the state's constitution as well.

Although a sizeable body of statutory and judicial law had held that the Pueblo were not to be federally recognized as Indians for purposes of Indian-related legislation, by 1913 the number of whites inhabiting Pueblo territory had increased strikingly, and federal policy was now focused on the coercive assimilation of all Indians. A general guardian/ward relationship had become the guiding policy assumption of many federal officials: all tribal people were viewed as utterly dependent groups in need of constant federal tutelage to protect them from unscrupulous whites and from their own vices.

In *Sandoval*, the Supreme Court found that the civilized, sober, and industrious Pueblo culture of its 1877 decision had somehow become "primitive" and "inferior" and utterly dependent on the U. S. government. Relying on

[28] 94 U.S. 614.

[29] 231 U.S. 28.

a legal paradigm steeped in paternalism and deferring to Congressional actions designed to protect the Pueblos from whites selling liquor, the Court went to extraordinary lengths to show that, although the Pueblo people remained "industrially superior" to other tribes, they were still "easy victims to the evils and debasing influence of intoxicants because of their Indian lineage, isolated and communal life, primitive customs and limited civilization." The Supreme Court proceeded to reconfigure Pueblo legal status, holding that their alleged cultural debasement necessitated federal trust protection of their lands from unscrupulous liquor traders.

The Five Civilized Tribes

As important as the Pueblo were in the development of Federal Indian law, the Five Civilized Tribes were even more significant. Each of the Five Tribes and members of those nations had figured prominently in the federal government's development of legal principles that enervated and devastated tribal sovereignty. The Cherokee Nation had been at the forefront of legal activity virtually from the outset – from the pivotal Marshall cases in the 1820s and 1830s to *United States v. Wildcat* in 1917[30] – but between 1870 and 1920, individual tribal members, particular tribes and combinations of the various five tribes were involved in far more federal cases than any other indigenous nation.

Because they were perceived as more "civilized" than all other tribes except the Pueblo, and because they had insisted on fee-simple title to their lands in Indian Territory through the treaties they had signed under the provisions of the 1830 Indian Removal Act, the Five Civilized Tribes were originally exempted from the Major Crimes Act of 1885 and the General Allotment Act of 1887. But although the exemptions were treaty-endorsed and extra-constitutional they would not last indefinitely: a multitude of interests – territorial and state governments, individual settlers and land speculators, federal policymakers, railroad companies, and others – were all clamoring for access to the Five Tribes' lands and resources and for control over the rights of the Tribes and their citizens.

From the late 1880s to the early 1900s, when the combined force of these interests finally brought about the legal dismemberment of the governments of the Five Tribes and the allotment and subsequent dispossession

[30] The Cherokee Nation or members of that tribe were involved in several important cases between these dates: *The Cherokee Tobacco*, 78 U.S. 616 (1871); *Cherokee Nation v. Southern Kansas Railway Co.*, 135 U.S. 641 (1890); *Talton v. Mayes*, 163 U.S. 376 (1896); *Stephens v. Cherokee Nation*, 174 U.S. 445 (1899); *Cherokee Intermarriage Cases*, 203 U.S. 76 (1906); *Muskrat v. United States*, 219 U.S. 346 (1911); and *Choate* v. *Trapp*, 224 U.S. 665 (1912).

TABLE 1. *Major tribal entities represented in federal court cases involving tribal sovereignty and plenary power (1870–1920)*

Tribes represented	Number of times tribes appear in cases
A. 5 Civilized Tribes	
Civilized Tribes (Collectively)*	6
Cherokee†	9
Cherokee & one other tribe	10
Creeks	6
Creeks & one other tribe	6
Chickasaw	2
Chickasaw & one other tribe	12
Choctaw	2
Choctaw & one other tribe	8
Seminole	2
Seminole & one other tribe	6
Total Five Tribes:	69
B. All Other Tribes	
Sioux (all bands)	11
Chippewa (all bands)	8
Osage	4
Shawnee	3
Yakima	3
Others	9
Total Other Tribes:	38
Total All Tribes:	107

* Collectively means that all Five Tribes were directly involved
† In the majority of these cases an individual member of a tribe is a party, rather than a tribe.

of much of their land, American law was deployed in ways that generally diminished but occasionally supported the nations' sovereignties. In *Cherokee Nation v. Southern Kansas Railway Company* (1890), for example, the Cherokee national government challenged an 1884 congressional law that had granted the Southern Kansas Railway a right-of-way through Cherokee territory. Drawing on its federalism and paternalism paradigms, the Supreme Court held that the Cherokee could not prevent the federal government from exercising its powers of eminent domain to take Indian lands. Justice John Harlan, relying on the wardship and dependency phrases established in previous Court rulings, held that their "peculiar" and "inferior" status deprived them of enforceable rights to their property. Even the fact that the Cherokee Nation held fee-simple title was "of no consequence" to the Court because the Cherokee were "wards of the United States, and directly subject to its political control."[31]

Although willing to dismiss the proprietary sovereignty of the Cherokee and to accommodate relentless Euro-American pressures for assimilation of Indians, when it came to certain practical effects of the twin forces of Westward expansion and federal plenary power the Court was willing to concede that the member nations of the Five Civilized Tribes might continue to exercise some degree of internal autonomy – internal criminal jurisdiction over their own members. In 1896, for example, on the same day the Supreme Court decided *Plessy v. Ferguson*,[32] establishing the "separate but equal" doctrine that sanctioned state Jim Crow laws, the court held in *Talton v. Mayes*[33] that the U.S. Constitution's Fifth Amendment did not apply to the Cherokee Nation because their sovereignty existed prior to the Constitution and was dependent on the will of the Cherokee people, not of the American public. Harlan was the lone dissenter (as he was in *Plessy*). Decisions like *Talton* were residues of the old treaty paradigm that affirmed tribal nations' political sovereignty, a status no other racial or ethnic minority group in the United States had ever possessed.

But *Talton* was an aberration, and it was countered by much more powerful forces aimed at the inevitable absorption of indigenous lands, resources, identities, and rights into the American body politic. Here the guiding principle was federalism: whether the states or the national government would be the dominant entity authorized to ignore or curtail Indian treaty rights or sovereign authority. Take, for example, yet another 1896 case, *Ward v. Race Horse*,[34] examining the state of Wyoming's claim to enact and enforce fish and wildlife laws curtailing the treaty-reserved hunting rights of the Shoshone-Bannock of the Fort Hall Indian Reservation. In a major states' rights decision, the Court ruled that Wyoming's game regulations superseded the Shoshone-Bannocks' 1868 treaty rights. Indian treaty rights were "privileges" that could be withdrawn or overridden by federal or state law. Specifically, Article Four of the 1868 treaty had been abrogated (implicitly) by Congress because it conflicted with Wyoming's Admission Act. If *Talton* appeared to acknowledge the old treaty paradigm, *Race Horse* dealt it a paralyzing blow, not only vacating earlier case law but also elevating state authority over tribes' vested rights and indeed over the federal government's vaunted guardianship of the Indians.

Having recast the juridical foundation for tribal-state relations and taking its cue from the coercive and absolutist tone of Congressional lawmakers, the Supreme Court moved to establish, clearly and unambiguously, the new reality of tribal-federal relations. The vehicle was *Lone Wolf v. Hitchcock*

[31] 135 U.S. 641, 657.
[32] 163 U.S. 537.
[33] 163 U.S. 376.
[34] 163 U.S. 504.

(1903), a suit brought by the Kiowa, Comanche, and Apache nations against the secretary of interior in an effort to avoid having their lands allotted without consent.[35] The tribes contended that allotment of their lands, as provided in legislation adopted by Congress in 1900, violated Article Twelve of the 1867 Treaty of Medicine Lodge. For the Court, Justice Edward D. White stated that the1867 treaty provision had been abrogated by the 1900 statute, even though he acknowledged that a purported agreement to modify the treaty provision on which the statute was loosely based lacked proper tribal consent.

Lone Wolf, often called the Court's second *Dred Scott* decision, was a near-perfect synthesis of the Court's "plenary power" and "political question" doctrines. White inaccurately stated that Congress had exercised plenary authority over tribes "from the beginning" and that such power was "political" and therefore not subject to judicial review. These statements were merely judicial rationalizations, but they were in line with the reigning policy toward Indians embraced by the federal government: Indians were dependent wards subject to a sovereign guardian – the federal government. White attempted to camouflage the blow by describing the government's actions as those of a "Christian people" confronted with the travails "of an ignorant and dependent race." Congress, he said, must be presumed to act "in perfect good faith" toward the Indians. But *Lone Wolf* was a devastating assault on tribal sovereignty. The Court's refusal even to examine Congressional acts that abrogated property rights established by treaty was particularly oppressive. *Lone Wolf* meant that treaties simply had no effect whenever Congress decided to violate their provisions. Yet, the hundreds of ratified treaties and agreements negotiated with the United States, nor the Federal Constitution, constituted the foundation for most indigenous rights.

In the company of so much else that had been transpiring in American law and policy, *Lone Wolf* confirmed a bitter reality: sporadically, Congress or the Court might acknowledge that their only legitimate powers vis-à-vis tribal nations were those expressly outlined in the Constitution or agreed on with indigenous peoples. But in practice no branch of the federal government recognized any real limit to its powers.

VII. PROGRESSIVISM, CITIZENSHIP, & INDIAN RIGHTS: 1904–1920

During the Progressive era, federal Indian policy, in particular those aspects overseen by the Office of the Commissioner of Indian Affairs, was increasingly managed by men who viewed themselves as dedicated guardians of

[35] 187 U.S. 553.

Indian peoples and their ever-decreasing property base. These individuals, however, were confronted with contradictory federal goals: adamant commitment to the full-tilt assimilation of Indians and their remaining resources predicated on the idea that indigenous peoples should be free of governmental supervision; and an equally adamant commitment to the maintenance of hegemonic guardian/ward relations with Indians, with attendant micromanagement of indigenous lands and resources, leaving Indians and tribal governments in an internally colonial relationship. That said, federal Indian policymakers were somewhat influenced by the Progressive ideals of social activism, elimination of economic and political corruption, and greater citizen involvement in governance, and consequently they offered qualified support for policies that recognized a degree of Indian self-rule and, as important, granted grudging respect for indigenous culture. Support for Indian education, in particular, enabled students to remain at home instead of being sent to distant boarding schools.

The first two decades of the twentieth century also saw sporadic outbursts of federal judicial and indigenous activism that, occasionally, resulted in protection for Indian treaty and property rights of both individual Indians and national tribes. These victories were achieved even though the paternalistic policy of assimilation remained entrenched. Still, the combination of staunch tribal resistance, federal officials willing to support a greater degree of tribal self-rule, and Indian students who had returned from boarding schools with ideas on how to improve their tribes' standing in relation to the federal government and American society formed the basic building blocks for developments in the 1930s and beyond that would enable native nations to recover some of their proprietary, cultural, and political rights.

During the Progressive period, the dominant federal themes of allotment, assimilation, guardian/ward status, and citizenship were supplemented by other ad hoc developments – affirmation of tribal sovereignty, protection of Indian treaty rights, and recognition of federal exclusive authority in Indian affairs. In 1904, for instance, the Supreme Court ruled in *Morris v. Hitchcock*[36] that the Chickasaw Nation, one of the Five Civilized Tribes, could lawfully extend its taxing authority over whites who resided on their lands. A year later, the Court handed down two very different but related opinions on Indian rights. First, in *In re Heff* (1905),[37] it held that Indian allottees became American citizens once their allotments had been approved. Therefore, federal laws that prohibited the sale of liquor to Indians were invalid – allotted Indians could buy and sell liquor as freely as any other American. The Commissioner of Indian Affairs admitted that the decision was "eminently logical," given prevailing federal Indian policy; he nonetheless

[36] 194 U.S. 384.

[37] 197 U.S. 488.

warned that it "places the ignorant, incapable, and helpless Indian citizens at the mercy of one class of evil doers."[38]

Congress reacted to *Heff* by passing the Burke Act, circumventing the *Heff* principle without entirely overthrowing it by withholding federal citizenship from allotted Indians for the duration of the twenty-five year trust period or until allottees secured a patent in fee (a certificate like a deed vesting legal ownership) to their allotment. The secretary of interior was granted authority to issue patents in advance of these statutory qualifications if, in his sole opinion, the Indian allottees were competent and capable of managing their own affairs. Congress presumably intended secretarial discretion to be used in a reasonable and not arbitrary fashion. In fact, the act led to the rapid alienation of much Indian allotted land. As Vine Deloria, Jr. and Clifford M. Lytle have put it, "Citizenship, thereupon became a function of the patent-in-fee status of land and not an indication that Indians were capable of performing their duties as citizens."

The second major ruling in 1905 was *United States v. Winans*.[39] This was the first case to arrive at the Supreme Court calling on the judiciary to interpret a common treaty provision reserving to a number of tribes in the Northwest their rights to fish at places of historical significance. The Court ruled (White dissenting) in support of tribal fishing rights reserved through treaty provisions. For the Court, Justice Joseph McKenna recited one of the more popular treaty rights doctrines – that treaties should be interpreted the way Indians would interpret them. A treaty must be construed as "that unlettered people" would have understood it since it was written in a foreign language and was drafted by a military power that was superior to that of tribes. Second, the Court dramatically reaffirmed federal supremacy over the states in certain areas and weakened the equal footing doctrine, which held that newly admitted states were on an "equal footing" with the original states in all respects, especially regarding sovereignty and political standing. The Court declared that it was within the power of the United States to preserve for native peoples their remaining rights such as fishing at their usual places, holding that this was not an unreasonable demand on a state. Third, and most important, McKenna announced the reserved rights doctrine, by which tribes retained all rights and resources not specifically ceded in treaties or agreements.

McKenna's opinion came a mere two years after the devastating *Lone Wolf* ruling in which the Court had clearly deprived tribes of their treaty-reserved property rights. How should this disparity be explained? A pragmatic reading of *Lone Wolf* suggests that the Court was implicitly acknowledging that

[38] United States Commission of Indian Affairs, *Annual Report* (Washington, DC, 1906), 28.
[39] 198 U.S. 371.

many whites had already established homesteads on the tribes' claimed lands. Relocating these non-native squatters, although perhaps the proper legal action, would have created massive political and economic problems for the state and the squatters, and also for the federal government (notably the president, who had already authorized settlement). In justifying Congressional confiscation of tribal reserved treaty lands, the Court had also baldly added that, once "civilized" and "individualized," Indians simply would not need all the land reserved to them.

Winans was much less threatening. It involved no major national political issues. No white had to be removed nor was the power of the president or of Congress at stake or even being challenged. At issue was the supremacy of a federally sanctioned treaty over a state's attempts to regulate resources covered by the treaty. First, the Court appeared to understand that fishing represented far more than a simple commercial enterprise for the Yakima Nation – in a very real sense it was their entire life. Second, to allow a state regulatory authority over activities guaranteed by treaty could have gravely injured the status of treaties as the supreme law of the land, in effect privileging state sovereign powers over those of the federal government. *Winans*, therefore, was a crucial and timely acknowledgment that a tribe's sovereign property and cultural rights, recognized and specifically reserved in treaties, warranted a measure of respect and would occasionally even be enforced by the federal government. In any case, there was no contradiction between the decisions in *Winans* and *Lone Wolf*. Both decisions underscored national authority. *Lone Wolf* reinforced the federal power to decide what was best for native people; *Winans* reinforced the supremacy of federal (and treaty) law over state law. But *Winans* does offer compelling evidence of a growing consciousness among some federal justices and policymakers – the continuing twin federal policy goals of land allotment and Indian individualization notwithstanding – that tribes were sovereign entities in possession of substantive property rights that were enforceable against states and private citizens, if not the federal government.

Three years later, in *Winters v. United States* (1908),[40] the reserved rights doctrine was extended – implicitly – to include the water rights of native peoples. *Winters* considered whether a white Montana landowner could construct a dam on his property that prevented water from reaching a downstream Indian reservation. The Supreme Court ruled against the landowner. First, the reservation in question had been culled from a larger tract of land that was necessary for "nomadic and uncivilized peoples"; second, it was both government policy and the "desire of the Indian" that native peoples be culturally and economically transformed and elevated from a "nomadic"

[40] 207 U.S. 564.

to an "agrarian" lifestyle; third, transformation could only occur if tribal lands were severely reduced in size, making them more amenable to agricultural pursuits (and precluding alternatives); finally, since the lands were "arid," they would be agriculturally useless without adequate irrigation.

The Court's four points were not enunciated as law, but they recognized the reality of history and indicated the Court's capacity to generate plausible arguments to protect precious tribal reserved rights. The court also cited the Indian treaty rule of interpretation, declaring that any ambiguities in the document should be resolved in the Indians' favor. The equal footing argument on which the landowner had relied was also dismissed, the Court noting that it would be strange if, within a year of the reservation's creation, Congress, in admitting Montana to statehood, would have allowed the Indians to lose their water rights, particularly since it was the government's policy to force Indians to adopt an agrarian lifestyle. In effect, the Court was saying that, when the United States entered into diplomatic relations with tribes or when it unilaterally created reservations, it appeared to be guaranteeing tribes the water necessary to provide for their needs, present and future.

In both *Winans* and *Winters* the federal government acted "on behalf of" or as the "guardian" of these two tribal nations. This was laudable in one sense, but also raised the important question of who actually "won" in these rulings: the federal government or Indian tribes? In addition to litigation for the protection of vital natural resources – fish and water – most Indian legislation and litigation of this period, much of it involving amendments and subsequent interpretations of those amendments to the General Allotment Act, arose from a powerful determination on the part of the federal bureaucracy to maintain a vague form of trust protection for Indian property. Rather than acknowledging and affirming complete Indian ownership of these still dwindling resources, Indians were treated as mere attachments to their lands, which meant that the Interior Department's policies and programs often conflicted with policies of the Congress aimed at facilitating Indian self-improvement.[41]

It should also be noted that Indians remained largely marginalized from the public policy process in virtually every era and arena thus far examined except one – claims against the federal government taken before the Court of Claims that had been established in 1855. Tribes had begun to file suits shortly after the court was established. In 1863 Congress amended the law to deny the right to file lawsuits to Indian tribes with treaty claims. It would not be until 1920 that a number of bills were introduced, at the behest of

[41] Vine Deloria, Jr., "The Evolution of Federal Indian Policy Making," in Vine Deloria, Jr., ed., *American Indian Policy in the Twentieth Century* (Norman, OK, 1985), 248.

individual tribes and friendly congressmen, that allowed some tribes to sue the government in the Court of Claims for monetary compensation over lands that had been taken or over treaty violations. However, tribes still had to secure Congressional authorization before they could file, which required a significant amount of lobbying and a sympathetic Congressional member or delegation to advocate on their behalf. Of course, tribes were virtually without any political or economic power during these years, and they were largely at the mercy of the Bureau of Indian Affairs' personnel who had dominated their lives and property since the 1880s. The Department of Interior itself frequently tried to prevent the introduction of Indian claims bills because it feared that the claims process would uncover evidence of rampant bureau incompetence and malfeasance then plaguing the agency. Eventually, Congress authorized an estimated 133 filings. In the actions that resulted, tribes won monetary recoveries in less than one-third of the cases.

While some individual tribes pursued tribal specific claims against the United States, broader intertribal and pan-Indian interest groups were also being formed in the early 1900s to pursue Indian policy reform, Indian religious freedom, and improvements in indigenous welfare. The Society of American Indians (SAI) was organized in 1911 at Ohio State University. SAI's founding was triggered by the experiences, both positive and negative, of Indian graduates of the federal government's boarding schools started in the 1870s. In its form, leadership, and goals, SAI was similar to contemporary white reform organizations and to the developing African American movements of the Progressive era. Its most dynamic leaders, including Charles O. Eastman and Arthur C. Parker, were largely well-educated middle-class Indians whose objectives included lobbying for a permanent court of claims, improving health care, promoting self-help, and fostering the continued assimilation of Indians while encouraging racial justice.

In Alaska, two gender-based native organizations were also born during this period – the Alaska Native Brotherhood, founded in 1912, and the Alaska Native Sisterhood founded in 1915. These were the first significant political and social intertribal organizations in Alaska before statehood. In their early years, the two organizations focused primarily on self-help and full American citizenship rights for natives. They also sought protection of their natural resources.

Two other indigenous movements affirmed the upsurge in Indian activism. First, peyote religion grew phenomenally from the late 1800s to the early 1900s. A truly intertribal faith, peyote use helped its practitioners improve their health and combat the ravages of alcohol. The Native American Church of Oklahoma was formally incorporated in 1918. Second, the Pueblo peoples of New Mexico continued their individual and collective struggle to protect their remaining lands from non-Indian squatters. The adverse effects of the *Sandoval* decision of 1913 had spurred their collective political mobilization, culminating in 1919 in formation of the All Indian Pueblo Council.

Citizenship

The issue of American citizenship for Indians bedeviled federal lawmakers during the Progressive years. As we have seen, the Supreme Court's ruling in *Heff* that Indian allottees automatically became U.S. citizens and thus were no longer subject to federal plenary authority had been legislatively thwarted by Congress with the enactment of the Burke Act in 1906. Subsequent Supreme Court rulings narrowed *Heff*, and it was finally expressly overruled, in dramatic fashion, in *United States v. Nice* (1916).

Nice affirmed what many federal lawmakers had been advocating for some years, namely that Indian citizenship was perfectly compatible with continued Indian wardship. According to Justice Willis Van Devanter, Congressional power to regulate or prohibit liquor traffic with Indians derived both from the Commerce Clause and from extra-constitutional sources, namely the dependency relationship that existed between Indians and the United States. It rested with Congress, said Van Devanter, to determine when or whether its guardianship of Indians should be terminated. "Citizenship," Van Devanter declared, "is not incompatible with tribal existence or continued guardianship, and so may be conferred without completely emancipating the Indians or placing them beyond the reach of congressional regulations adapted for their protection."[42]

Nice was decided three years before American Indian veterans of World War I were given the opportunity to attain U.S. citizenship in 1919, and eight years before Congress enacted the general Indian citizenship law of 1924, which unilaterally declared all remaining non-citizen Indians to be American citizens. Both the veterans' law and the general citizenship law provided that the extension of citizenship would not affect preexisting treaty-based Indian property rights. It became evident, however, that Indians were not full citizens, notwithstanding Congressional declarations to that effect. The citizenship they had secured, whether under prior treaty or later Congressional statute, was attenuated and partial. The provisions of both the 1919 and 1924 laws guaranteeing prior property rights of Indians as citizens of their own nations proved insufficient to protect the cultural, political, civil, and sovereign rights of individual tribal citizens. And since tribes, qua tribes, were not enfranchised, they remained beyond the pale

[42] 241 U.S. 591, 598.

of constitutional protection from the federal government. Paternalistic in tone and substance, *Nice* had mandated perpetual federal guardianship over citizen Indians, still considered incapable of drinking liquor without federal supervision and approval.

Nice was and remains a legal travesty. Indians were consigned to a continuing legal and political limbo: they were federal and state citizens whose rights were circumscribed by their status as "wards." For tribal members to receive any non-tribal rights or privileges as citizens, they often had to exhibit an intent to abandon tribal identity. At that point they might – though not necessarily – be considered worthy or "competent" to receive American political rights and privileges. The question of what precisely Indians gained with American citizenship and of whether the United States even had constitutional authority to declare Indians to be citizens unilaterally without their express consent remain problematic.

Meanwhile, Congress, ever the insistent guardian, acted in 1921 to formalize and provide a comprehensive funding mechanism for Indians, their seemingly perpetual wards. Prior to 1921, Congress and the Bureau of Indian Affairs had expended monies for Indians largely on the basis of treaty provisions or of specific statutes that addressed particular tribal needs. The Snyder Act,[43] however, granted general authority to the BIA under the Interior Department's supervision to spend Congressionally appropriated money "for the benefit, care, and assistance of the Indians throughout the United States." This money was to be used for a wide variety of purposes – health and education, resource projects such as irrigation, and so forth. This was the first generic appropriation measure designed to meet the tremendous socioeconomic needs of Indians wherever they resided.

The Indian Reorganization Act

Congress in the 1920s was unwilling to concede that its broad, variegated assimilation campaign was a failure, even though continual tribal complaints and white interest group criticism of federal Indian policies seemed to show otherwise. But events had already been set in motion that would culminate in a wholesale reordering of priorities, under the 1934 Indian Reorganization Act (IRA).[44] The IRA expressed Congress's explicit rejection of the allotment policy and the harsh coercive assimilation tactics that the BIA had used since the 1880s. The legislation was drafted by Felix Cohen under the supervision of John Collier, who had spent considerable time in New Mexico fighting for Pueblo land and water rights and who would later become Commissioner of Indian Affairs. The IRA had several

[43] 42 Stat. 208.

[44] 48 Stat. 984 (1934).

objectives – to stop the loss of tribal and individual Indian lands, provide for the acquisition of new lands for tribes and landless Indians, authorize tribes to organize and adopt a constitutional form of government and form corporations for business purposes, and establish a system of financial credit for tribal governments and individual business entrepreneurs – but was also beset by severe weaknesses. It did little to clarify the inherent political status of tribes. It failed to devise any real constraints on federal power, particularly administrative power, vis-à-vis tribal nations and their citizens. A critical, if uneven, attempt by the federal government to rectify some of the damage caused by the more horrific policies and laws it had imposed on native nations for nearly half a century, the IRA produced mixed results, which continue to affect tribal nations today.

Most dramatically, the IRA was effective in putting a halt to the rapid loss of indigenous land. It reminded all parties that tribal peoples were substantially different from other minority groups because they continued as cultural and political nations with inherent powers of self-governance and distinctive cultural and religious identities. But the IRA's avowed goal of energizing native self-rule was not fully realized. Some tribal nations took the opportunity to create tribal constitutions and establish bylaws. However, their documents had of necessity to include clauses that reminded tribal leaders of the discretionary authority of the secretary of the interior to dictate policy to tribes and overrule tribal decisions. Tribes that resisted efforts to institutionalize their governing structures along the constitutional lines suggested by federal officials were sometimes pressured to acquiesce by Collier and his associates.

Beyond the IRA

The conclusion of World War II and John Collier's resignation as Commissioner of Indian Affairs in 1945 signaled the beginning of another profound shift in federal Indian policy and law – from tribal self-rule to termination of the federal government's trust responsibilities toward a number of tribes. Termination was officially inaugurated as policy in 1953 by a joint resolution of Congress. Ironically, liberals supported termination as a means to free tribal peoples from racially discriminatory legislation and BIA regulations, whereas conservatives viewed it as a means to relieve Indians from the "retarding" effects of the IRA's policies, which were interpreted as hampering Indian rights as American citizens. American Indians had their own views on termination. Some tribes believed that it would mean full emancipation and would create opportunities for them to thrive politically and economically; others suspected that termination was a maneuver by which the United States would "legally" disavow its historic treaty and trust obligations, clearly violating the inherent rights of tribes and the federal government's commitment to the rule of law.

Termination was accompanied by a relocation program that sent thousands of reservation Indians to major urban areas. Congress also enacted Public Law 280, which authorized several states to extend criminal and some civil jurisdiction over Indians and Indian Country. All proved controversial. By the 1960s, grievances arising from termination, relocation, and the extension of state jurisdiction had combined with the influence of the broader civil rights movement and the environmental movement to fuel a surge in activism both in urban areas and on reservations. The resurgence of native pride, indigenous activism, the appearance of a generation of legally trained Indians, and shifts in personnel on the Supreme Court and in Congress brought a series of important political, legal, and cultural victories in native nations' struggle to regain a genuine measure of self-determination.

Much of the 1960s indigenous revival arose out of events like the fishing rights battles of the Northwest tribes, the ideas generated by Indian leaders at the American Indian Chicago Conference in 1961, the birth and subsequent rapid expansion of the American Indian Movement in 1968, the Alcatraz takeover in 1969, the Trail of Broken Treaties in 1973, and the Wounded Knee occupation, which also occurred in 1973. Congress responded to these developments by enacting the Indian Self-Determination and Education Assistance Act in 1975, among other laws. But these native victories engendered a vicious backlash among disaffected non-Indians and some state and federal lawmakers that led to Congressional and judicial attacks aimed at further abrogating treaties, reducing financial support for tribal programs, and other punitive responses. The Supreme Court also began to issue rulings that negated or significantly diminished tribal sovereignty, notably *Oliphant v. Suquamish* (1978), which directly limited the law enforcement powers of tribes over non-Indians committing crimes on Indian lands.

Since *Oliphant*, tribes have witnessed a parade of federal actions that at times have supported tribal sovereignty (the Indian Self-Governance Act of 1994) and at other times significantly reduced tribal powers, especially in relation to state governments (the Indian Gaming Regulatory Act of 1988). More distressing for tribes was the Rehnquist Court's fairly consistent opposition to inherent authority, which has been continued by the Roberts Court. Tribal governments have had their jurisdictional authority over portions of their lands and over non-Indians effectively truncated, and the federal trust doctrine has been defined very narrowly in a way that reduces U.S. financial obligations to tribal nations and their citizens. In addition, the Supreme Court's rulings have elevated state governments to a nearly plenary position in relation to tribal governments and the U.S. Congress itself, without dislodging or reducing the long entrenched federal plenary power over tribes and their resources.

Nevertheless, these have been dynamic times during which many native nations have made great strides in several arenas: cultural and language revitalization, land consolidation, and the development of more appropriate legal codes are notable examples. Gaming revenues have given tribes a small but seemingly secure foothold in the nation's political economy. Tribes have also proven willing, through increased electoral participation, to engage in state and federal political processes in an effort to protect their niche in the market.

CONCLUSION

Two centuries of contact between indigenous nations and the United States have caused profound and irrevocable changes in the proprietary, sovereign, cultural, and legal rights of tribal nations, just as it has meant massive changes in the laws, policies, and attitudes of Euro-Americans as well. Sustained cultural interactions between Europeans and indigenous peoples in North America began, we have seen, with a measure of cooperative military and economic respect. But both Europeans and later Euro-Americans generally acted from a perspective that denied the full proprietary rights and cultural sovereignty of tribal nations. So, despite the existence of dual legal traditions at the outset, and a diplomatic record that formally acknowledged the separate legal and political traditions of native nations, Euro-Americans soon began to act in ways that generally offered little respect for the customs and legal traditions of Indian peoples.

Euro-American legal traditions attained dominance over indigenous peoples in North America largely as a result of cultural ethnocentrism and racism. More instrumentally, Euro-American law facilitated U.S. westward expansion and settlement, as well as industrial development. The virtual exclusion of indigenous perspectives or customary legal traditions from U.S. legal culture after 1800 enabled American legal practitioners and policymakers to attain a hegemonic status vis-à-vis tribal nations. Nevertheless, federal lawmakers and Supreme Court justices have occasionally acted to recognize indigenous rights and resources, as evidenced in land claims, sacred site access, and co-management of certain vital natural resources.

The U.S. Supreme Court has tended to use one or some combination of three paradigms when called on to adjudicate disputes involving Indians: treaties, paternalism, and federalism. Not only the issues and tribes involved but also the diplomatic record, the relationship between the state and the federal governments, and ideologies of governance vis-à-vis native peoples have interacted to determine at each moment how the Court would decide any given case.

The relationship between tribes and the U.S. federal government continues to be without clear resolution. Further, because interracial and intercultural disputes are nearly always resolved in federal courts where legal principles like plenary power, the discovery doctrine, and the trust doctrine still lurk in the cases and precedents, tribes can never be assured that they will receive an impartial hearing. The United States has sometimes recognized and supported tribal sovereignty; at other times, it has acted to deny, diminish, or even terminate their sovereign status. Such indeterminacy accords imaginative tribal leaders and non-Indian leaders a degree of political and legal flexibility. Involved parties may successfully navigate otherwise difficult political terrain by choosing appropriate indigenous statuses that can benefit their nations and citizens. But it also deprives aboriginal peoples, collectively, nationally, and individually, of clear and consistent standing regarding the powers and rights they can exercise. Hostilities may have decreased, but cultural, philosophical, and political-legal tensions still cloud the relationship between tribal nations and the federal and state governments.

8

MARRIAGE AND DOMESTIC RELATIONS

NORMA BASCH

On the eve of the American Revolution, domestic relations law, as it would come to be called in the nineteenth century, encompassed a whole constellation of relationships between the male head of the household and the subordinates under his control. These included his wife, children, servants, apprentices, bound laborers, and chattel slaves, designated by William Blackstone as those in lifetime servitude. Although Blackstone did not create this conception of household relations, he incorporated it into his *Commentaries on the Laws of England*, the era's most influential legal primer, where it appeared under the rubric of the law of persons. Based as it was on a belief in the fundamental inequality of the parties and the subordinate party's concomitant dependency, the law of persons lay at the heart of subsequent challenges to domestic relations law in general and to marriage law in particular. By categorizing the law of husband-wife as analogous to other hierarchical relationships, it generated parallels that would become sites of contestation. According to the law of persons, both marriage and servitude were "domestic relations," and both mandated a regime of domination and protection to be administered by the male head of the household.

The law of persons cut a broad but increasingly anachronistic swath in the legal culture of the new republic and in the economic transition from household production to industrial capitalism. As a result, one change in domestic relations law over the course of the nineteenth century involved the gradual narrowing of the relations under its aegis. Whereas "family" had once comprehended the extended household profiled in the law of persons, by the time Anglo-Americans were reading the first editions of Blackstone, it tended to refer to a small kin group living under the same roof. Blackstone was in this instance already dated. The decline of apprenticeships, the increase in independent wage-earners, and the separation of home and work generated further changes. Although employers owned their employees' labor, their legal relationship to free laborers gradually slipped from the category of domestic relations. Slavery, of course, was eradicated as a legal category with the Civil War and Reconstruction. Yet, elements from the old paradigm of the extended hierarchical household continued to exert discursive power. The industrial employer drew on the preindustrial master's claim to his servant's personal services to buttress his own claim to authority over independent wage-workers. The correspondences between wifehood and servitude also remained popular. They were deployed not only by slaveholders eager to extol their benevolent dominion over their extended "families" but also by women's rights advocates intent on decrying the wife's degrading bondage. Still, in the long passage to legal modernity, domestic relations focused increasingly on marriage and parenting.

The other critical shift in domestic relations law over the course of the century consisted of inroads into the male-dominated corporatism of marriage. By the end of the century both wives and children enjoyed a greater measure of legal individuality, children came more frequently under the protection of their mothers or the state, and divorce was on the rise. At the same time, a belief in the sanctity of lifelong monogamy and in the husband's natural authority received renewed legal and rhetorical support while the drive to restrict birth control and abortion generated novel curbs on reproductive freedom.

The end-of-the-century picture of domestic relations law, then, is ambiguous. Although the principle of male headship was clearly compromised by the challenges of prior decades, it continued to resonate in the treatises, legislatures, and courtrooms of the nation. As the byproduct of diverse concerns, temporary coalitions, and economic exigencies, the changes in domestic relations law did not so much dismantle the principle of male headship as modify it, often in favor of the state. The changes, moreover, were complicated by jurisdictional diversity and doctrinal inconsistency. Thanks to federalism, the states controlled family governance, and in accord with Franco-Spanish legal models as well as the dominant English model, they created marital regimes that could differ dramatically from place to place.

Given the ambiguity, diversity, and inconsistency of state marital regimes, any effort to chart change nationally, much less assess its relation to the gender system, is fraught with problems. The web of affection and reciprocity that defined the marriage bond for most Americans did not encourage a hard calculus of gendered power. But although husbands and wives did not typically regard themselves as winners or losers in these deeply gendered legal regimes, it is entirely appropriate for us to sift and weigh the gendered distribution of marital power. The legal institution of marriage, after all, was one of the preeminent arbiters of gender roles, and it was reshaped by the same great political, economic, and social convulsions as other areas of law. Yet while revolution, industrialization, and the burgeoning marketplace left their impress on the contract of marriage as surely as on commercial contracts, the strict demarcation of marriage from other contracts made for very different results. In a century that elevated the concept of contract to unprecedented heights, marriage was a contract, as jurists were fond of pointing out, unlike any other. The emblem of harmony and stability in a shifting, competitive world, marriage was the irrevocable contract that made all other contracts possible.

The separation of the marriage contract from other kinds of contracts was critical to the legal formation of marriage as an institution. It not only enabled the state to dictate the terms of marriage to potential spouses as opposed to having them set their own terms, but it relegated marriage to a realm that was rhetorically distinct from the world of commerce and politics. The separation of the marriage contract, however, was never complete. Feminist critics of contractualism have argued that because the marriage contract silently underpinned the social contract, that mythical agreement marking the founding of modern civil society, it at once concealed and provided for the subordination of women to the political fraternity of men. Thus the classic story of the social contract, which is a story of freedom, repressed the story of the marriage contract, which is a story of subjection.

How, though, could a liberal democracy with its ethos of self-ownership and contractualism and its rejection of monarchy and arbitrary power continue to invest authority in the independent white, male head of the household at the expense of the persons deemed subordinate to him, including the person of his wife? In the long run, it could not. In the shorter run – over the course of the nineteenth century – it could do so, but only with strenuous cultural work and considerable legal innovation that masked and checked the challenges liberalism presented to the patriarchal family. The story of domestic relations law, in short, is one of the evolving tensions between male headship with its protections and constraints on the one hand and liberal individualism with its hazards and privileges on the other. We begin with the tensions unleashed by revolution.

I. MALE HEADSHIP, FEMALE DEPENDENCE, AND THE NEW NATION

In 1801 James Martin, the son of loyalist parents, sued the state of Massachusetts for the return of his deceased mother's confiscated property. During the Revolution his mother, Anna Gordon Martin, and his father, William Martin, had fled Boston for the British-held New York City, and with the defeat of the British in 1783, they moved their household to England. Their loyalty to the Crown, however, came at a price. Anna, the daughter of a wealthy Massachusetts merchant and landowner, had inherited real estate that was sold at auction under the provisions of the state's wartime confiscation statute. Because William Martin had served as an officer with the British forces, neither his allegiance to the Crown nor his defiance of the patriot cause was ever in doubt; he was listed by the state among persons who had joined the enemy. But the confiscated property had belonged to Anna, not William, and her defiance of the new political order was not as clear.

At issue in the case launched by the son was the time-honored principle of male headship and female subordination incorporated into the Anglo-American law of husband and wife. The case represented a pivotal moment in the post-Revolutionary redefinition of marriage. Was the principle of male headship, which comported with both the precepts of Christianity and the pre-Revolutionary gender system, altered in any way by revolution and war? Did Anna flee the country with William as a result of a wife's marital obligation to subject herself to her husband, or did she act as an independent sympathizer of the loyalist cause? Deeming the confiscation of the wife's property an improper and overly broad reading of the state's wartime statute, James Martin's attorneys supported the first scenario, which assumed the husband's coercive power over his wife. In the traditional view of marriage on which the core of their case rested, a wife's primary allegiance was to her husband, who mediated any relationship she may have had to the state and to the world at large. Anna, in this view, was without volition regarding her political options. If William had commanded her to leave, she had no choice but to obey him.

Attorneys for the state of Massachusetts working to validate the confiscation and sale of Anna's property supported an alternative scenario that assumed her independence in choosing to leave, thereby investing her with a direct relationship to the state. Their argument suggests the radical possibilities of applying anti-patriarchal ideology to the law of husband and wife. In Massachusetts, where the state also withheld dower, the so-called widow's thirds, from wives who had fled, the exigencies of revolution seem to have unsettled the common law unity of husband and wife, the reigning paradigm for marriage.

The Martin case, with its competing paradigms of marital unity and marital individuality, provides a framework for considering the contradictions unleashed by revolution and prefigures the pressures a nascent liberalism would exert on the patriarchal model of marriage. In the eyes of the law, the husband and wife were one person, and that person was the husband. This was the renowned legal fiction of marital unity from which the wife's legal disabilities flowed. Inasmuch as the wife's legal personality was subsumed by the husband, she was designated in the law-French of the common law as a femme covert, or covered woman, and her status in marriage was called her coverture. But in the eyes of the Massachusetts confiscation statute, husband and wife were two persons with individual choices regarding the Revolutionary cause. Since attorneys for the state along with the legislators who drafted the confiscation statute could envision wives as independent actors, we can see how the anti-patriarchal impulses of the Revolution might be directed toward marriage. That all four judges of the Massachusetts Supreme Judicial Court voted to sustain James Martin's claim against the state on the basis of his mother's coverture, however, exemplifies the widespread acceptance of the English common law model of marriage by post-Revolutionary jurists.

The English common law model of marriage as it was upheld by the Massachusetts judiciary and as it had been outlined in Blackstone's *Commentaries* was much more than an emblem of the patriarchal order. It encompassed those functions of marriage that judges and legislators would embrace long after the Martin case. These included the definition of spousal obligations, the regulation of sexual desire, the procreation of legitimate children, and the orderly transmission of property. But although such earthy and materialistic concerns have figured in family law from Blackstone's day to the present, Blackstone's reading of marriage was problematic for early nineteenth-century Americans, who were often uncomfortable with his rationales for its legal rules. His blunt insistence that the primary purpose of marriage was the creation of lawful heirs slighted the personal happiness they associated with matrimony and the harmonious influence they believed it exerted on the whole society. And while they affirmed the principle of male headship, they could no longer do so on precisely the same terms Blackstone had used in the law of persons.

The striking ambivalence in nineteenth-century responses to Blackstone's vision of marriage is instructive. Commentators could not accept him without qualifications and caveats, but neither could they reject him entirely. Editors writing glosses on the *Commentaries* and jurists creating new treatises expressed the need to unshackle marriage somehow from the harshest provisions of the common law. A growing interest in the welfare of illegitimate children, for example, was at odds with Blackstone's celebration of the common law's capacity to bar the inheritance of bastards. Those who were distressed with the wife's legal disabilities confessed incredulity at Blackstone's insistence that the female sex was a great favorite of the laws of England. Yet critics typically envisioned changes in the legal status of married women as exceptions to the provisions of coverture, which functioned as an enduring component in the definition of marital obligations. Blackstone's depiction of the law of husband and wife, then, continued to serve as a blueprint for understanding the rudiments of the marriage contract, and the rudiments of the marriage contract were strikingly unequal with regard to rights and responsibilities.

The wife's legal disabilities as outlined in the *Commentaries* were formidable. Any personal property she brought to marriage belonged to her husband absolutely while the management of her real property went to him as well. She could neither sue nor be sued in her own name nor contract with her husband, because to do so would constitute the recognition of her separate legal existence. Once married and under her husband's coercion, she was no longer even responsible for herself in criminal law. Indeed, the only crack in the bond of marital unity according to Blackstone lay in a theory of agency derived from the wife's capacity to act on behalf of her husband; because the husband was bound to supply her with "necessaries," she could contract with third parties in order to secure them.

The husband's responsibilities in this paradigm of male headship were no less formidable than the wife's disabilities. In addition to the support of the family, they included any debts his wife brought to the marriage. But while the husband's responsibilities were entirely in keeping with nineteenth-century notions of manliness, his corresponding power over the person and property of his wife was not easily reconciled with a companionate model of marriage. If the wife was injured by a third party, the husband could sue for the loss of consortium; she, by contrast, enjoyed no corresponding right since the "inferior" owned no property in the company or care of the "superior." Similarly, because a wife acted as her husband's agent, the husband was responsible for her behavior, and just as he had a right to correct an apprentice or child for whom he was bound to answer, so must he have a comparable right to correct his wife. Blackstone's insistence that wife beating was an ancient privilege that continued to be claimed only by those of the lower ranks could not have provided much solace to those who found it antithetical to the notion of marriage as an affectionate partnership.

Post-Revolutionary Americans responded selectively to this legal model of marriage in which the wife was obliged to serve and obey her husband in return for his support and protection. Some elements, like the husband's obligation to support and protect the wife, coalesced with the goals of an emerging white middle class devoted to a breadwinner ethos. Others, like the husband's right to chastise the wife, conflicted with enlightened sensibilities. And still others, like the wife's dower, her allotment from her husband's property if he predeceased her, emerged as an impediment to the sale of real estate and the flow of commerce.

As the problem of dower suggests, the provisions outlined by Blackstone for intestate succession, which spelled out custody rights as well as property rights and carried the logic of coverture into the end of marriage, could be controversial. If the wife predeceased the husband and had a surviving child, the husband continued to hold all her realty as a tenant by the curtesy of England, a right known as the husband's curtesy. As the natural guardian of the children, he was entitled to all the profits from her realty. The only circumstance in which the deceased wife's realty reverted to her family of origin while the husband was alive was if there were no living children. Although the husband's right to the custody of the children was automatic, a wife who survived her husband could lose custody by the provisions of his will. As for her interest in his property, her dower consisted of a tenancy in only one-third of his realty.

Still, even though dower was less generous than curtesy, it was one place where the common law vigorously protected the wife's right to some support. During the marriage, the wife's dower right loomed over the husband's realty transactions and provided her with some leverage. Because a portion of all the realty a husband held at marriage or acquired during the life of the marriage was subject to the wife's dower, he could not sell it without her consent and separate examination, a procedure designed to ensure she was not coerced into giving up potential benefits. Dower was a fiercely protected, bottom-line benefit of the English common law. A husband could exceed the terms of dower in his will, but if he left less than the traditional widow's thirds, the widow could elect to take dower over the will, a prerogative known as the widow's right of election.

Here in broad strokes was the model of male headship and female dependence embedded in the law of persons. The husband adopts the wife together with her assets and liabilities and, taking responsibility for her maintenance and protection, enjoys her property and the products of her labor. Giving up her own surname and coming under his economic support and protective cover, the wife is enveloped in a cloak of legal invisibility. Real marital regimes diverged significantly from this formal English model on both sides of the Atlantic before as well as after the American Revolution. Thanks to exceptions carved out in equity, some wives managed to own separate estates, and others enlarged the notion of agency beyond anything Blackstone could have imagined. Changes, however, did not always benefit the wife. Although dower in some jurisdictions expanded to include personal property, the separate examination, a potential source of protection, was increasingly ignored.

The deepest gulf between the Blackstonian paradigm and its post-Revolutionary incarnation pivoted on the narrow purpose Blackstone imputed to marriage, an institution viewed from the late eighteenth century onward as a good deal more than a conduit for the transmission of wealth. As James Kent, the so-called American Blackstone, put it in his own *Commentaries* in the 1820s, "We may justly place to the credit of the institution of marriage a great share of the blessings which flow from the refinement of manners, the education of children, the sense of justice, and the cultivation of the liberal arts."[1] Marriage, as Kent suggested, was a capacious institution, a source of both individual socialization and national improvement, and as it came to rest on a foundation of romantic love, its purpose began to include the emotional satisfaction of the marital partners. By the 1830s, middle-class Americans were celebrating marriage as the realization of an intimate and impassioned bond between two uniquely matched individuals who shared their innermost thoughts and feelings.

Coverture, an organizing principle in the post-Revolutionary gender system, was in conflict with the great expectations attached to marriage. A man's freedom to marry and become head of a household clearly defined his manhood, but a wife's dependency and subservience did not satisfactorily define her womanhood. The purpose of marriage always had included the procreation of lawful heirs, but thanks to a more intimate and egalitarian vision, it now encompassed the happiness and well-being of the husband and wife as well as the nurture and education of the next generation of citizens. Jurists, essayists, poets, and novelists idealized marriage as a loving and harmonious partnership that embodied core national values and required the participation of wives and mothers no less than that of husbands and fathers.

It is precisely because marriage embodied core national values and because the happy and orderly union of man and wife represented the happy and orderly union of the new nation that those forms of social organization regarded as threats to marriage were discouraged as a matter of public policy. This was true for Native American kinship systems, which accepted premarital sex, matrilineal descent, and polygamy and divorce. As white settlers drove Indians out from their ancestral lands in the course of westward expansions, the Bureau of Indian Affairs offered property and citizenship to "heads of households" who were prepared to give up their tribal affiliations and non-Christian marital arrangements.

Public officials could at least imagine assimilating Indians who embraced a Christian version of monogamy into the national polity; they did not extend that vision to African Americans. Although slaves often "married," their unions were devoid of recognition by state authorities because prospective spouses were regarded as without the capacity to consent. A master at any time could sell one partner away from the other and make a mockery of the Christian vow, "'til death do us part." Indeed, so at odds were slavery and the institution of marriage that a master's consent to a slave's legal marriage was deemed an act of manumission, an assumption that would make its way

[1] James Kent, *Commentaries on American Law*, 4 vols., 11th ed. (Boston, 1867), 2:134.

into arguments in the *Dred Scott* case. Moreover, although long-standing interracial unions existed, especially in the antebellum South, they did so informally and in the face of statutory bans on interracial marriages designed to keep the number of such unions small.

Changes in the legal and social construction of domestic relations after the Revolution were modest. As love and nurture and the needs of children assumed greater import, a modified conception of coverture that upheld the husband's responsibilities and respected the wife's contributions satisfied the needs of an emerging middle class. One radical consequence of severing the bonds of empire, as we will see, was the legitimization of divorce. At the same time, lifelong monogamy, a metaphor for a harmonious political union, was celebrated as the wellspring of public morality and national happiness. Coverture, which exerted enormous legal and discursive power, continued to sustain the gender order while the legal disregard for slave and interracial unions continued to sustain the racial order.

II. TYING AND UNTYING THE KNOT

What constituted a legitimate union and how and for what reasons could it be dissolved were questions impinging on the private lives of many couples who viewed marriage in more fluid terms than state authorities. These vexing questions made their way into the presidential campaign of 1828 when supporters of the incumbent, John Quincy Adams, accused his opponent, Andrew Jackson, of having lived with his wife, Rachel, in an illicit relationship. The Jacksonians dismissed the accusation as a petty legal misunderstanding that had been unearthed for purely partisan purposes. In their version of the story, Andrew Jackson had married Rachel Donnelson Robards in Natchez in 1791 on the presumption that she had been divorced from Lewis Robards by the Virginia legislature, only to discover that what they both believed was a formal divorce decree was merely an authorization for Robards to sue for a divorce in a civil court. Robards did not pursue this option until 1793 in the newly admitted state of Kentucky, which had previously fallen under the jurisdiction of Virginia. In 1794, after a final decree had been issued and the Jacksons came to understand they were not legally married, they participated in a second marriage ceremony. Now in 1828 their innocent mistake was being exploited by men so desperate to prop up the candidacy of the unpopular president that they were willing to collapse public/private boundaries and ride roughshod over the intimate recesses of the Jacksons' domestic life.

The Adamsites proffered a more sinister version of the so-called Robards affair, which they documented with Robards's Kentucky divorce decree. According to the decree, the defendant, Rachel Robards, had deserted the plaintiff, Lewis Robards, and was living in adultery with Andrew Jackson. Substituting the treachery of seduction for the innocence of a courtship undertaken in good faith, they accused Jackson not only of the legal lapse of living with his lady in a state of adultery but also of the moral lapse of being the paramour in the original divorce action. The stealing of another man's wife, a crime that violated the sexual rights of the first husband, was an indication of Jackson's inability to honor the most elemental of contracts. Raising the prospect of a convicted adulteress and her paramour husband living in the White House, the Adamsites equated a vote for Jackson with a vote for sin.

As debate in the campaign turned increasingly on the legitimacy of probing a candidate's intimate life in order to assess his fitness for public office, it also exposed the tensions between the private nature of marriage and the role of state intervention. The irregularity of the Jacksons' union raised a number of questions. Was their 1791 crime that of marrying and participating in bigamy or that of not marrying and living in sin? To what extent and with what degree of precision could the state define the making and breaking of the marriage bond? How could it enforce its definitions across a legally diverse and geographically expanding national landscape? And given the prevailing pattern of westward migration into sparsely settled and loosely organized territories, just how important was the letter of the law in legitimating a union like theirs?

The Jacksonian defense rested on the assumption that in the case of the Jacksons' union, an overly formalistic insistence on the letter of the law was unjust. Underscoring the frontier setting in which the pathological jealousy and emotional instability of Lewis Robards played out, Jackson supporters defended their candidate on the basis of his adherence to the spirit of the law if not the letter. Here was a man who in marrying a deserted and endangered woman showed he had the courage to do the right thing. In a pamphlet designed to demonstrate community approval for his "marriage," prominent neighbors and friends attested Rachel's innocence in ending her first marriage and the general's chivalry in saving her from Robards. The propriety of the Jacksons' union, as one Tennessee neighbor put it, was "the language of all the country."

But it was the letter of the law that concerned the supporters of Adams, who argued that if the Jacksons had married in Natchez in 1791, they would have produced proof of that marriage and provided it to the world. The Adamsite preoccupation with legal formalism was essential to their rationale for exposing the affair in the first place, and in their view the fault-based foundation employed by the law in adjudicating breaches of the marriage contract made it the perfect arbiter of the rules for conjugal morality. To permit marriage to end as a matter of individual inclination or even community approval was to threaten the entire social structure.

However important the Adamsites' reservations were, they were not enough to defeat the very popular Andrew Jackson. If the majority of the voters could tolerate the prospect of the convicted adulteress and her paramour husband living in the White House, it is probably because they refused to see the Jacksons in those terms. Legal records suggest that the irregularities in the Jacksons' matrimonial saga were not so rare. Legislative petitions indicate that numerous men and women tried to put a swift and inexpensive end to their unions by appealing to extra-legal community codes and turning to the legislature with the signed approval of friends and neighbors. Others simply walked away from their unions and began marriage anew. Court records of spouses who divorced themselves and "remarried" and subsequently ran afoul of the law probably constitute the tip of the very large iceberg of self-divorce and pseudo-remarriage.

Public debate over informal marriages and extra-legal divorces reflected the nagging contradictions between state intervention and contractual freedom, but even legal formalists who favored the closest possible state regulation of marriage understood that the rules for exiting marriage were far more important than those for entering it. As a result, when the legal system moved toward redefining marriage and defining divorce, the terms on which these parallel trends developed could not have been more different. Whereas American courts came to recognize a so-called common law marriage, a consummated union to which the parties had agreed, they were not about to recognize self-divorce. Common law marriage put the best face on an existing arrangement, legitimated children from the union, and brought the husband under the obligation of support. Self-divorce, or even too-easy divorce, menaced the social order.

Common law marriage originated in *Fenton v. Reed*, an 1809 New York decision validating a woman's second marriage so as to permit her to collect a Revolutionary war pension, although her first husband had been alive at the time of her remarriage. Elizabeth Reed's story was a familiar one. She claimed her first husband had deserted her, and hearing rumors of his death, she took a new partner. The decision, attributed to James Kent, held that although the second marriage was invalid until the first husband died, after his death no formal solemnization of the second marriage was required for its authenticity. Bigamy, which is what the second marriage was, may have been one of the least prosecuted crimes on American statute books until the Gilded Age. The innovation called common law marriage, moreover, which freed weddings from state control and even licensing, had little to do with the English common law and did not go unchallenged. Ultimately, however, it triumphed, and its triumph exemplified the judiciary's commitment to an instrumentalist approach to domestic relations in which the law functioned as a tool for socially desirable innovation, rather than as repository of inherited customs and precedents. Employing a distinctly contractarian ideology, courts and legislatures united to endorse a private construction of matrimony in order to ensure that the marriage was valid for those who wanted and needed it to be valid. In an effort to protect marriage as a public institution, the law endorsed a private and voluntary version of its legitimization.

Divorce was a different matter entirely. Resting as it did on the concept of a serious breach in the marriage contract, it warranted a far more determined use of state authority. Jurists could not advocate divorce by mutual consent much less by unilateral decision, because the underlying justification for rescinding an innocent spouse's marriage promise hinged on the assumption that the reciprocal promise had been broken by the guilty spouse. Fault played a pivotal role in the legal construction of divorce. Even the omnibus clauses in early divorce statutes, catchall phrases providing broad judicial discretion in decreeing divorces, assumed a fault that was too unique or elusive to be defined by statute, but that could be readily apprehended by the judiciary.

The statutory implementation of fault divorce (there was no other kind until well into the twentieth century) in the wake of the American Revolution had been swift and widespread. Colonies whose divorces had been overruled by the Privy Council in the political turmoil of the 1770s provided for divorce in their new state statutes. Other states followed suit, and by 1795 a disaffected spouse could end a marriage in a local circuit court in the Northwest Territory. Grounds varied widely, and some states limited decrees to the jurisdiction of the legislature. Nonetheless, by 1799 twelve states in addition to the Northwest Territory had recognized the right of divorce.

In instituting divorce in spare and simple statutes, it seems as if eighteenth-century legislators embraced a solution without fully understanding the problem. Not only did they neglect to address some thorny substantive and procedural issues, but they could not anticipate the number of spouses who would come to rely on the divorce process. Fault, the legal bedrock of divorce law, was difficult to prove and often contradictory to litigants' best interests. For those who wanted the terms of their marital dissolutions to be as easy as possible, mutual consent was appealing because it was swift and inexpensive and comported nicely with the pursuit of happiness. It is not surprising that nineteenth-century commentators, who were more experienced with the divorce process than their late eighteenth-century counterparts, read a great deal more into divergent legal grounds. The nineteenth-century advocates of a liberal divorce code argued that narrow grounds strictly construed encouraged both lying in petitions and extra-legal solutions. Their opponents countered that broad grounds liberally construed subverted the biblical one-flesh doctrine and marriage itself.

In retrospect it is evident that the decision to accept divorce in the first place regardless of its legal particularities constituted a paradigmatic revolution in marriage. The old common law fiction that the husband and wife were one and the husband was the one could no longer exert the same authority once a wife could repudiate her husband in a court of law. Perhaps because it was assumed that divorce would be rare, its initial acceptance proved less controversial than the working out of its particularities. In any case, on the threshold of the nineteenth century the notion that divorces could be decreed for egregious violations of the marriage contract had acquired statutory legitimacy, and it had done so with remarkably little opposition.

Divorce subsequently became the lightning rod for a wide-ranging debate about marriage and morals that reverberated through the nineteenth century and beyond. Jurisdictional diversity was a big part of the problem. As litigants shopped for more hospitable jurisdictions, interstate conflicts became inevitable. On the one hand, the stubborn localism of domestic relations law in the face of jurisdictional contests reflected a deep distrust of centralized authority over the family. On the other hand, the dizzying array of grounds and procedures embodied a disturbing range of moral choices. By mid-century, many states, especially those in the West and the area now called the Midwest, recognized adultery, desertion, and cruelty as a grounds, with cruelty and its shifting definitions remaining controversial. Also most states at this juncture, including new states entering the Union, provided for divorce in civil courts. Yet striking exceptions persisted. New York, for example, recognized only adultery as a ground, Maryland limited divorce to the jurisdiction of the legislature, and South Carolina refused to recognize divorce at all. Legislative decrees, which ebbed under the weight of mounting criticism and state constitutional prohibitions, did not disappear entirely from states providing for divorce in the courts, and residence requirements and their enforcement varied from state to state.

Legal disparities exposed American divorce as an incoherent amalgam of precepts and precedents based on the frequently conflicting foundations of the Judeo-Christian tradition and liberal contract theory. In a staunchly Protestant nation, albeit of competing sects, divorce represented the disturbing amplification and diversification of an action derived from the English ecclesiastical courts. At issue was which of the many divorce statutes reflected Protestant morality? The rules for ending marriage could run anywhere from South Carolina's decision to make no rules to Iowa's decision via an omnibus clause to abide by whatever rules the judiciary deemed appropriate. By the time Joel Prentice Bishop's 1852 treatise on marriage and divorce appeared, the breadth of that spectrum was problematic. As Bishop put it, at one extreme there was the view that marriage was indissoluble for any cause; it was favored in modern times as "a religious refinement unknown to the primitive church." At the other extreme, there was the view that marriage was a temporary partnership to be dissolved at the will of the two partners; it was held not only "by savage people, but some of the polished and refined."[2]

Migratory divorce, an action in which a spouse traveled out of state to secure a decree, demonstrated both the ease with which litigants could manipulate the divorce process and the readiness of the judiciary to uphold the sovereignty of local law. As a result, the divorce standards of a strict jurisdiction like New York were endangered by the laxity of a liberal jurisdiction like Vermont. The practice of migratory divorce, which emerged early in the century between neighboring states, only intensified as transportation improved. By the 1850s, Indiana, with its loose residence requirements and broad grounds, became a target for the critics of migratory divorce. Once railroad lines were united in a depot in Indianapolis, the clerk of the Marion County Court claimed he received at least one letter a day inquiring if a disappearing spouse had applied there for a decree. These roving spouses, husbands more often than not, became emblems for the hypocrisy of the divorce process and the immorality of its rules.

Migratory divorce, however, was nowhere near as important a check on each state's regulation of matrimony as the indifference or resistance of resident husbands and wives. State efforts to control marriage and divorce were not always successful in the face of a couple's determination to act as if they were free to govern their own marital fate. Some spouses agreed to end their marriages in ways that exhibited little reverence for the principle of fault; others participated in contractual separation agreements despite the antipathy of the judiciary; and still countless others walked away and started married life anew without any reference to or interference from the state. These widespread extra-legal practices confounded the tidy categories in the law of marriage and divorce. Yet legal constructions of marriage and divorce grew ever more important not only because they could help resolve property and custody conflicts and delineate the married from the unmarried but also because by mid-century they were emerging as compass points for the moral course of the nation.

[2] Joel Prentice Bishop, *Commentaries on the Law of Marriage and Divorce and Evidence In Matrimonial Suits* (Boston, 1852), chap. 15, sec. 268.

III. THE MARRIED WOMEN'S PROPERTY ACTS

When Thomas Herttell introduced a married women's property bill in the New York legislature in 1837, he supported it with an impassioned speech. In a year of financial panic marked by numerous insolvencies, one strand of his argument revolved around the instability of the antebellum economy. Long an advocate of debtor relief, Herttell addressed the trend toward boom-and-bust economic cycles and the problem posed by an improvident husband who wasted his wife's patrimony on high-risk speculation. Thanks to the husband's total control of marital assets, a wife's property, he averred, could be lost at the gaming table or spent on alcohol while she was immobilized by her contractual incapacity. The second strand of his argument, an assault on the anachronisms and fictions of the common law in general and on Anglo-American marital regimes in particular, was largely legal in its thrust. He warned that the married woman's trust, the equitable device created to bypass some of the restrictions of coverture and to protect the wife's property from the husband's creditors, was riddled with gaps and ambiguities. In an effort to garner support for his bill, he changed its title from an act to protect the rights and property of married women to an act to amend the uses, trusts, and powers provisions in the New York Revised Statutes.

Although debtor relief and trust reform undoubtedly met with some legislative approval, the third strand of his argument, a boldly rights-conscious diatribe against the wife's dependent status at common law, put him in radical territory. "Married women equally with unmarried males and females," he proclaimed in an appeal to the familiar triad of Anglo-American rights, "possess the right of *life, liberty*, and *PROPERTY* and are equally entitled to be protected in all three."[3] When Herttell asserted the "inalienable right" of married women to hold and control their property and insisted that any deprivation of that right was both a violation of the Bill of Rights and a symptom of the unjust exclusion of women from the political process, he was upending the gender rules of classical liberal theory. Liberal theorists from John Locke to Adam Smith never regarded wives as free as their husbands. On the contrary, they at once assumed and affirmed the wife's subordination and counted marriage together with the benefits of the wife's services among the rights of free men. Abolitionism, however, with its appeals to the self-ownership of free men generated notions about the self-ownership of married women that were antithetical to the principle of

[3] Thomas Herttell, *Argument in the House of Assembly of the State of New York the Session of 1837 in Support of the Bill to Restore to Married Woman "The Right of Property," as Guaranteed by the Constitution of this State* (New York, 1839), 22–23.

coverture. It was precisely this synergy between critiques of bondage and critiques of marriage that made its way into Herttell's remarks. Because the wife at common law was constrained to function as a servant or slave to her marital lord and master, he observed, she was herself a species of property. Only her husband's inability to sell her outright saved her from the status of unqualified slavery.

That Herttell made his remarks in a state that would launch the women's rights movement in 1848, the same year it passed a married women's property statute, illustrates how the nascent drive for women's rights converged with the reform of marital property. His speech, printed in a pamphlet financed by a bequest from his wife's will, became one in a series of ten popular pamphlets distributed by the women's movement in the years before the Civil War. But married women's property reform also represented narrowly economic motives as exemplified in early Southern statutes. The Mississippi statute of 1839, which preceded the first New York statute by nine years, insulated the slaves a wife owned at marriage or acquired by gift or inheritance from the reach of her husband's creditors. Mississippi's failure to give the wife independent control over her human property meant that the family remained a unified community of interests ruled by a male patriarch.

The desire to maintain the family as a male-headed community of interests was not limited to the South or to common law jurisdictions. In civil law jurisdictions like Louisiana, Texas, and California, which recognized marital assets as a community of property owned by both spouses, the control and management of the community typically went to the husband. The notion that the interests of husbands and wives were not the same or even worse antagonistic alarmed legislators across the nation, who tended to equate investing wives with legal and economic independence with introducing discord into the marital union. Wives who were competitive rather than cooperative were depicted as amazons in the marketplace who subverted the sacred bond of matrimony. In the first phase of reform, then, most states failed to give women explicit control over their property. The effect of these early statutes, which were focused on the property a woman acquired by gift or inheritance, was to transform the married woman's separate equitable estate into a separate legal estate. As a result, the statutes democratized an option once reserved for the wealthy and legally sophisticated by rendering it accessible, but they did not significantly alter coverture.

The second phase of reform encompassed a married woman's earnings and recognized the wife as a separate legal actor. The New York statute of 1860 extended the concept of a separate estate to include property from a wife's "trade, business, labor or services" and empowered her to "bargain, sell, assign, and transfer" it. The Iowa State of 1873 permitted a wife to receive wages for her "personal labor" and to maintain a legal action for it in her own name. Between 1869 and 1887 thirty-three states and the District of Columbia passed similar statutes. In moving beyond inherited property to include a wife's individual earnings and in empowering the wife to sue and be sued with regard to her separate property, the second phase of reform clearly undermined the common law fiction of marital unity.

Here again judicial hegemony over the law of husband and wife was evident, but in contrast to the earlier instrumentalism displayed in the recognition of common law marriage, the adjudication of the earning acts embodied a turn to formalism in which judges weakened or nullified a married woman's right to earnings by invoking old common law principles as self-contained, inflexible, and even scientific. At issue was the definition of the wife's separate earnings, which typically came from labor performed at home, such as taking in boarders, producing cash crops, raising chickens, and selling eggs. The judiciary persistently classified such activities as coming under the wife's traditional obligation of service. In a suit for tort damages brought two years after the Iowa earnings act, the court upheld a husband's right to all of his wife's household labor. Because the customary ways in which women earned money tended to be excluded from the reach of the earnings acts, a wife's labor at home on behalf of third parties fell within her obligation to serve as her husband's "helpmeet." When a husband takes boarders into his house or converts his house into a hospital for the sick, ruled the New York Court of Appeals in 1876, the wife's services and earnings belong to the husband. Even a wife's labor in a factory could be construed as belonging to the husband in the absence of evidence the work was performed on her separate account. Coverture, then, was challenged but far from eradicated by the second wave of legislation, in fact its legal authority remained formidable. As one member of the judiciary put it when he excluded rent from a wife's real estate from the category of a separate estate, "The disabilities of a married woman are general and exist in common law. The capabilities are created by statute, and are few in number, and exceptional."[4]

Because courts tended to treat the wife's legal estate, like her equitable one, as exceptional, they continued to place the wife under the husband's traditional power and protection. What were third parties – creditors, debtors, retailers, and employers – to assume? That in the absence of indications a married woman's property fit into this exceptional category, she came under the disabilities of coverture. There was also a quid pro quo behind the husband's continued authority. He enjoyed his marital rights by virtue of his marital duties, and the duty to support remained his, regardless of the amount of his wife's earnings or assets. Because he was the legally designated

[4] *Nash v. Mitchell*, 71 N.Y. 199 (1877), 203–4.

breadwinner and therefore responsible for his wife's "necessaries," he had a right to her services, earnings, and "consortium" (affection, company, and sexual favors). The breadwinner ethos grew ever more important in a market economy in which home and work were separated, the wife's household labor was devaluated, and her economic dependence was palpable.

The market yardstick of value, which afforded little room for recognizing the value of the wife's household services, was reinforced and updated in tort law. Wrongful death statutes, passed in the second half of the century, reproduced the model of husbands working outside the home for wages and wives remaining at home and economically dependent. Some states barred recovery of damages by a husband for his wife's wrongful death, thereby inverting the customary gender asymmetry of the common law. In states that permitted recovery by husbands, damages were limited since establishing the value of domestic services was more difficult than establishing the value of lost wages. Wifely dependency was the legal norm in torts as well as in property, and the prevailing ground for recovery in this nineteenth-century innovation in tort law was the wife's loss of her husband's support and protection. It is noteworthy that this change in tort law explicitly addressed and implicitly prescribed a wife's dependence at precisely the time wives were acquiring new forms of legal independence.

Coverture was transfigured in the second half of the nineteenth century, but the authority of the "superior" and the dependency of the "inferior" so prominent in the contours of Blackstone's law of persons remained a leitmotif in American marriage law. In a sanitized and sentimentalized Victorian incarnation, coverture continued to define what a man should be as a husband and what a woman should be as a wife. Yet one enduring legacy of the drive for married women's property rights was the conflicting visions of marriage it unleashed. Although the drive began as an effort to clarify debtor-creditor transactions, protect the family from insolvency, and recognize the waged labor of wives, it evolved into a contest that spiraled far beyond the provisions for marital property. And what made the contest so acrimonious was that every participant identified the legal construction of marriage as the foundation of the gender system.

Conservatives anxious to hang on to the traditional configuration of marriage underscored the protection and "elevation" it afforded women and the stability and prosperity it brought to the nation. Where conservatives saw protection, women's rights advocates saw subjection, which they regarded as a symptom of male depravity and the source of women's political exclusion. Giving husbands property rights in both their wives' assets and bodies, they reasoned, made marriage the key institution through which men established their authority over women. For utopian socialists, the problem with traditional marriage also pivoted on the evil of men owning women, but they viewed it not so much as a symptom of male depravity as a consequence of the whole unjust system of private property.

Liberal women's rights advocates like Elizabeth Cady Stanton, however, believed that property rights, which were part of the problem, could be part of the solution if they invested wives with the same self-ownership and independence society had granted to free, white men. No matter that self-ownership was in conflict with the protections afforded by coverture: it was difficult for the law to compel a delinquent husband to provide them. A woman with a good husband might thrive under his protection, but thanks to the codes of an androcentric legal system, a woman with a bad husband could find herself destitute. A wife's well-being, in short, should not depend on the benevolence of her husband.

Although this was an unsettling argument in the heyday of female domesticity and the breadwinner ethos, it invoked the rights associated with the modern liberal state. When women demanded property rights in the name of those private islands of self-ownership that were the hallmark of liberal individualism, they were not only rejecting the doctrine of marital unity, they were exploring and exposing the way provisions in the marriage contract excluded them from participation in the social contract. The radical challenge provided by using the argot of classical liberal theory to subvert the legitimacy of its own gender rules was not limited to women's rights pamphlets; it radiated into the mainstream of public discourse where it coalesced with the ideology of abolitionism and began to erode the moral authority of coverture.

IV THE BEST INTERESTS OF THE CHILD

The contractualism at the root of the marriage bond was more muted in the bond between parent and child. The ideal of self-ownership so evident in the women's rights movement could hardly be applied to children, who were in fact unavoidably dependent. Yet changing views of children contributed to the legal transformation of the family from a male-headed community of interests to a cluster of competing individuals. Children achieved a measure of legal individuality in a series of shifts that at once reflected and shaped the transition in their status from mere appendages of a father's will to discrete beings with special needs. Mothers, if they were morally fit and economically secure, were increasingly designated as the ones whom nature had endowed to meet those special needs.

The widely publicized 1840 *d'Hauteville* suit – a bitter contest over the custody of a two-year-old son – is a case in point. Characterizing the mother, the judge declared, "her maternal affection is intensely strong, her moral reputation is wholly unblemished; and . . . the circumstances of this case render her custody the only one consistent with the present welfare of her son."[5] Denial of Gonzalve d'Hauteville's challenge to Ellen Sears d'Hauteville's custody of their only child was by no means the only resolution available to the court. Given the wife's refusal to return to her husband's ancestral home in Switzerland after giving birth to their son in Boston, the ruling was incompatible with a father's presumptive right to custody, as well as the fault-based premise for custody in divorces and separations. Despite the ruling, the rights and entitlements of fathers were theoretically in force in 1840. A mother's voluntary separation from her husband without cause typically blocked her claim to custody, and fathers in most jurisdictions retained the right to appoint a testamentary guardian other than the mother. It is precisely because American family law in 1840 supported the principle of paternal authority that William B. Reed, Gonzalve d'Hauteville's attorney, built his case around the sovereignty of the husband as it was spelled out in Blackstone's *Commentaries*. Still, as Reed must have sensed when he reviewed the fluid, evolving nature of American family law, depending on the legal fiction that the husband and wife were one and the husband was the one was no longer enough in a culture that valorized relations based on affection and elevated the bonds of family to new emotional heights. Appealing to the tender ties of parenthood, Reed imbued Gonzalve d'Hauteville with a love no less vibrant or unselfish than that of the mother. No one can say, he argued, "with whose affections a child is most closely entwined, and whether the manly fibres of a father's heart endure more or less agony in his bereavement than do the tender chords which bind an infant to a mother's breast."[6]

Ironically, in using the image of an infant at its mother's breast in an effort to equate fathers with mothers, Reed was employing one of the most evocative tropes of the day and one that esteemed a mother's "natural" capacity for nurture at the expense of a father's traditional authority. The intensifying emphasis on a child's innocence and vulnerability and the Victorian conception of childhood as the critical stage in an individual's moral development contributed to the creation of new institutions, the most important of which was the common school. Others included orphan asylums, children's aid societies, and various homes of refuge all devoted to the cause of child welfare. The heightened focus on child nurture, which placed mothers at the very center of familial relations, found its way into the legal system. Although the father's common law rights were still presumed, as the *d'Hauteville* case with its judicial homage to motherhood indicates, that presumption was nowhere as strong at mid-century as it had once been.

[5] Samuel Miller, Jr., *Report of the d'Hauteville Case* (Philadelphia, 1840), 293.
[6] Miller, *Report*, 195.

Torn between applying the common law rights of the father and "the best-interests-of-the-child" doctrine, the judiciary moved toward favoring the mother in custody battles. On the assumption that children who were young or sickly were in particular need of a mother's care, maternal custody also rested on a tenet that came to be called "the tender years doctrine." Judges tied custody to gender as well as to age so that boys beyond a certain age might go to their fathers while girls of all ages tended to be placed with their mothers. Believing in fundamental differences between mothers and fathers, judges essentialized women as nurturers and, in so doing, were predisposed to place children in their care.

Legislatures also participated in the trend toward maternalism. Some states enacted statutes authorizing women to apply for a writ of habeas corpus to adjudicate the placement of a child, a move that turned custody from a common law right into a judicial decision. Notions of spousal equality associated with a loving and companionate model of marriage informed the statutory language used in the reform of custody. The Massachusetts legislature pronounced the rights of parents to determine the care and custody of their children as "equal." In 1860, largely as a result of sustained campaigns by women's rights advocates, the New York legislature declared a married woman the joint guardian of her children, with the same powers, rights, and duties regarding them as her husband.

Spousal equality and gender-specific roles were not mutually exclusive. In the drive for maternal custody, women's rights advocates mixed demands for equality with essentialist assertions of difference in almost the same breath. But as a decision rendered in the wake of the New York statute equalizing custody illustrates, neither arguments for equality or difference were effective when judges were determined to resist what they regarded as the excessive democratization of the family. When Clark Brook applied for a writ of habeas corpus for the return of his son from his separated wife, it was granted because she had left him without his consent and he had not mistreated her. In an appellate court ruling that relied on assumptions in the law of persons and avoided the language of Victorian maternalism, Justice William Allen insisted that the underlying quid pro quo in marriage had not been abrogated by the statute. Because a husband was bound to support his children, he enjoyed a right to their labor. If the new law had truly authorized the wife's custody, it also would have imposed on her the responsibility of support. Allen read the law as giving the wife a custody right she might exercise with her husband while she was living with him, but not away from him or exclusive of him.

The statute, which Allen claimed did not destroy the husband's traditional marital rights at the option of the wife, was repealed in 1862. That is not to say the courts reverted to paternal rights. On the contrary, the trend in decisions moved inexorably toward maternal custody. Maternal custody, however, was achieved not so much as a matter of maternal rights but as a matter of judicial discretion, which paved the way for enlarging state authority over the family. In the nineteenth century, courts replaced the father's absolute custody rights with their own discretionary evaluation of the child's welfare, thereby instituting a modern relationship between the family and the state. The common law was routinely cited and then frequently overruled in the name of "tender years" or "the best interests of the child." The ultimate authority over the family, however, was now the judiciary.

One exception to the purely discretionary nature of maternal rights was the changing law of bastardy, which gave custodial rights to the mother and improved the degraded common law status of the illegitimate child. At common law, as Blackstone noted, a bastard was fatherless as far as inheritance was concerned. He could inherit nothing since he was viewed as the son of nobody and was therefore called *filius nullius* or *filius populi*. To regard him otherwise, as the civil law did by permitting a child to be legitimized at any time, was to frustrate the main inducement for marriage: to have legitimate children who would serve as the conduits for the perpetuation of family wealth and identity. Those without property needed to marry and have legitimate children in order to fix financial responsibility and ensure that their offspring would not become public burdens.

American law departed dramatically from the common law provisions for bastardy. Over the course of the nineteenth century courts and legislatures alike designated the illegitimate child as a member of the mother's family and gave mothers the same custodial rights the common law had conferred on married fathers. Criminal punishment for producing an out-of-wedlock child disappeared, and although putative fathers were expected to support the child, they lost any claim to their custody. As a New Hampshire court ruled in 1836, the father could not elect to take custody of his child instead of paying for the child's support, an option that had been available in early America. Mothers of illegitimate children enjoyed a special legal status so long as they remained unmarried to the father and could provide support for their children. As a consequence of the legally recognized bond between mother and child, by 1886 thirty-nine states and territories provided the out-of-wedlock child with the right to share in a mother's estate. Yet the nineteenth-century American rejection of the common law stigma imputed to bastardy had its limits; in many jurisdictions an illegitimate child could not share in the estate of the mother's kin or defeat the claims of legitimate children. The judiciary, meanwhile, tried to legitimize as many children as possible by recognizing common law marriages and even marriages that were under an impediment. By 1900 more than forty states declared that children of voided marriages or marriages consummated after their births were legitimate.

The enhanced status of the mother of the illegitimate child and indeed the child could be undone by financial need. The close bond in the newly legalized family unit of mother and child, like the corporate unity in the traditional family, protected the family from state intervention only as long as there was economic support. Humanitarian attitudes toward all children – be they legitimate or illegitimate – could not prevent overseers of the poor from removing a child from the family and placing it in or apprenticing it to another family. This could occur at ages as young as four or five. Two contradictory impulses were at work in the legal construction of bastardy: one was the humanitarian and egalitarian desire embedded in Enlightenment thinking and spelled out in accord with Thomas Jefferson's plan in a 1785 Virginia inheritance statute to make all children equal in status; the other was the age-old concern for the taxpayer's pocketbook. It is not surprising that some elements of bastardy law reflected the anxiety of local taxpayers or that bastardy hearings revolved around the putative father's obligation of support. Putative fathers were often subject to arrest and property restraints until they agreed to provide support. And although some reformers argued for eradicating all distinctions between legitimate and illegitimate children, the fear of promiscuity and the threat it posed to the institution of marriage blunted the full realization of that goal. By the early twentieth century needy illegitimate children came increasingly under the purview of welfare agencies and social workers at the expense of the intimate bond between mother and child created in the Early Republic.

The other critical shift regarding children and their legitimacy was the mid-century formalization of adoption. Adoption law, in contrast to bastardy law, created a family devoid of blood ties. Adoption had taken place prior to statutory recognition through informal arrangements and private legislative acts. The Massachusetts adoption statute of 1851, however, which became the model for many other states, provided for the transfer of parental authority to a third party, protected the adoptee's inheritance, and conferred on adopters the same rights and responsibilities as biological parents. While the aim of that statute was to make the child's relationship to its adoptive parents the same as that of a biological child, not all states followed that precise pattern. Even in those that did, the judiciary often made distinctions between natural and adopted children.

In decisions that echoed the judicial distinctions regarding the inheritance rights of illegitimate children, judges frequently defeated the stated intent of statutes to make adopted and biological children equal. Though legislatures initiated formal adoption, it was the courts that monitored it and shaped it. In circumstances where the adoptive child competed for an inheritance with biological offspring, courts tended to favor the biological offspring, making the adopted child's status "special" rather than equal. Adoption, after all, was unknown at common law and was therefore subject to strict construction. And in the process of permitting artificial parents to take the place of natural ones and of making the judiciary the arbiter of parental fitness, adoption provided yet another pathway for the state to intervene in the family. Of course, most intact and self-supporting families avoided the scrutiny of the state. But in adoption, custody awards, and the law of bastardy, the doctrine of "the best interests of the child" transformed parenthood into a trusteeship that could be abrogated by the state through judicial decision making.

V. RECONSTRUCTION AND THE FREEDMAN'S FAMILY

Despite the growing authority of the state in specific areas of domestic relations, the paradigmatic legal unity of the family not only coalesced with the celebration of the household as a harmonious sanctuary from the outside world, but it did, in fact, serve as a buffer against government interference. Family unity, however, depended on the hierarchical ordering of its members. It is noteworthy that, before the Civil War, marriage and slavery were the two institutions that marked the household off from the state and identified its inhabitants as either heads of households or dependents. Given all the evocative analogies between slavery and marriage that dotted antebellum culture along with the shared foundation of the two institutions in the law of persons, it was difficult to consider slavery after the war without considering marriage or to address race without addressing gender. Although slavery was involuntary and marriage was contractual, both were domestic relations, and the parallels that had been invoked by feminists and slaveholders for their competing agendas re-emerged during Reconstruction. As the Reconstruction amendments revolutionized the relation between the states and the federal government, they turned the complex intertwining of race and gender into a permanent feature of American constitutional discourse. From Civil War pensions to the policies of the Freedmen's Bureau, moreover, the federal government began to demonstrate a growing presence in the institution of marriage.

The debate over the Thirteenth Amendment exemplifies the new confluence of gender and race at the constitutional level. When a Democrat in the House protested the amendment's failure to compensate slaveholders for the loss of their slaves, he reminded his colleagues of the prerogatives they enjoyed as husbands, fathers, and employers. A husband's right of property in the services of his wife, he insisted, is like a man's right of property in the services of his slave. In another appeal to patriarchal prerogatives, Senator

Lazarus Powell, Democrat of Kentucky, warned that the original wording in the amendment making all "persons" equal before the law would impair the powers held by male heads of households. Republicans also registered their concern with the gender-neutral language in the amendment, which Michigan senator, Jacob Howard, noted with alarm would make the wife as free and equal as her husband. When Charles Sumner, the Senate's staunchest abolitionist, withdrew his support from the inclusive language in the original draft, it signaled the Congressional commitment to the traditional contours of marriage.

Congress wanted only to extend the marriage contract as it presently existed to former slaves, a policy the wartime government had already put into place for the first slaves to reach the Union lines. Able at last to make labor contracts, freedmen and freedwomen were also able to make marriage contracts, a long-denied civil right that constituted a sweeping change in their status. In refusing to recognize the autonomy of the black family, slavery had rendered it open to disruption, separation, and the sexual whims of the master. As Harriet Beecher Stowe demonstrated to the world in *Uncle Tom's Cabin*, the separation of mother and child was one of slavery's most horrific transgressions. But it was fathers who were pivotal in the legal transformation embodied in the right to marry since implicit always in the male slave's degradation was his inability to control and protect the members of his own family. Thus it was to *freedmen* as heads of households that the Freedmen's Bureau directed its reforms, including its original plan to transform ex-slaves into property holders by giving them land.

In the summer of 1865, the Freedmen's Bureau issued "Marriage Rules," which authorized procedures for both dissolving and legalizing the unions of former slaves and declared an end to extra-legal unions. In the following year Southern states passed statutes and in some cases constitutional amendments that either declared the unions of former slaves legal or required their formal registration; extra-legal cohabitation was typically declared a misdemeanor punishable with fines. Legal marriage, however, was a radical departure from the norms of the antebellum plantation. Given the enforced instability of slave unions, the marital regimes devised by slaves often consisted of informal marriage, self-divorce, and serial monogamy. Because marriage was a civil right and a potential source of familial protection, many couples rushed to formalize their unions immediately after the war; in 1866 in North Carolina alone, where registration was mandated, more than 9,000 couples in seventeen counties attested their readiness to tie the knot officially. But defining which union was the legal one could be problematic, and disputes surfaced in the courts in the form of inheritance, bigamy, and divorce suits. Some freedpersons opted to resume prior unions rather than formalize their current union, whereas others simply failed to comply with either the rules or values of the new marital regimes. Those lower-class whites who like some Northern counterparts believed the partners in a union and not the state were in charge of their marital arrangements failed to comply as well.

Providing former slaves with the right to marry carried different meanings for different groups. For Reconstruction Republicans, as the agenda pursued by the agents of the Freedmen's Bureau indicates, it represented the formation of male-headed nuclear families and was inextricably linked to the party's paramount goal of turning former slaves into wage-workers. Accordingly the labor contracts drafted by the Bureau supported coverture by awarding a wife's wages to her husband even as it recognized the freedman's wife as a wage-worker. For freedmen, the right to marry was a mark of manhood and a symbol of citizenship, and their authority over the family unit carried the promise of insulating its members from outside interference. The new integrity that formal marriage conferred on the family became a legal tool for keeping children out of involuntary apprenticeships. Asserting their rights as heads of households, freedmen regularly went to court to block the implementation of apprenticeship provisions in Black Codes. For former masters, who had once counted slaves as members of their households, marriage was a way to assign economic responsibilities since the state had assumed the authority they had once held as slaveholders but not their obligations. Placing the unions of former slaves under the aegis of the state also afforded ex-Confederates a pathway for consolidating white power by instituting bans on interracial marriages.

As for freedwomen, who were urged to submit to the bonds of matrimony as they were liberated from the bonds of slavery, the right to marry was a mixed blessing. Those who gratefully accepted the privileges of white womanhood gave up full-time work for full-time wifehood and motherhood. For most, labor outside the household was an economic requirement and not a choice. Wifely subservience, however, was a choice, and marital contestations in county court records reveal that freedmen sometimes anticipated a deference their wives were not prepared to give. By virtue of their experiences as slaves, freedwomen were neither as acculturated to nor as accepting of the uneven distribution of marital power as middle- and upper-class white women. Yet to pursue a suit for domestic violence in legal regimes that still rested on the assumption that the husband represented the wife, they were compelled to cast themselves as helpless victims whose spouses had overstepped the farthest limits of patriarchal power.

The most pernicious constraints emanating from state control over the unions of freedpersons consisted in using marriage laws to uphold "racial purity," a policy that impinged on both sexes and prevailed in theory on both sides of the color line. Its real effect was to reinscribe racial hierarchies. Statutory prohibitions of "miscegenation," a word coined in 1864 that came to stand for any interracial sexual union, flew in the face of a contractual conception of matrimony and its attendant protections. Interracial couples battled anti-miscegenation laws by appealing to the Civil Rights Act of 1866 and the equal protection clause of the Fourteenth Amendment. Yet apart from two short-lived exceptions, they failed in all the fifteen suits to reach the highest state appellate courts. Marriage, intoned the Supreme Court of North Carolina in 1869, although initiated by a contract, was a "relation" and an "institution" whose ground rules had never been left to the discretion of the spouses. Inasmuch as whites and blacks alike faced the very same prohibitions, the court continued, such laws did not favor one race over the other. The court also defined marriage as a "social relation," thereby placing it beyond the ken of the rights enumerated in the Civil Rights Act and recognizing that full social equality between the races had never been a part of the Republican vision of Reconstruction.

Drawing on a national judicial trend to treat marriage as something of a hybrid, Southern courts quelled challenges to anti-miscegenation laws largely by defining marriage as a status. This was precisely the tack taken by the Texas Court of Appeals in 1877 when Charles Frasher, a white man wedded to a black woman, appealed his conviction on the grounds that such statutes were abrogated by the Fourteenth and Fifteenth Amendments and the 1866 Civil Rights Act. In defining marriage as a status, the court determined that the regulation of marriage was properly left to the discretion of the state of Texas. "[I]t therefore follows as the night follows day," it declared, "that this state may enforce such laws as she may deem best in regard to the intermarriage of whites and Negroes in Texas, provided the punishment for its violation is not cruel or unusual."[7] Similar bans, which were supported by an increasingly pseudo-scientific body of racist literature and were directed at intermarriage with Asians, appeared in Western jurisdictions and proliferated. By 1916, twenty-eight states and territories prohibited interracial marriage.

Marriage law also contributed to the debasement of African Americans through its systematic adherence to gender hierarchy. Although construing the family as a male-headed community of interests offered some protection to its members, female dependency provided a handy reference point for the disfranchisement of black men. Using the words "wives" and "women" interchangeably, senators reluctant to enfranchise African American men in the early days of Reconstruction invoked the constitutional status of white women as the perfect example for distinguishing the rights of citizenship from the political privilege of voting. Southern Redeemers, working state by state, did the work of disfranchising African American men and restoring

[7] *Frasher v. State*, 3 Tex. App. 263, 276–77 (1877).

white supremacy, but the move had been prefigured by senators underscoring the circumscribed political status of women as wives.

Despite the triumph of states' rights in the regulation of domestic relations, one lasting effect of Reconstruction was the federal government's intervention in marriage. There were already precedents. In 1855 Congress declared that a free, white woman of any nationality became a citizen automatically on marrying a male American citizen, and the child of any male American citizen was a citizen regardless of its birthplace. The Morrill Act of 1862, aimed at Utah Mormons, established the power of the federal government to regulate marriage in the territories. Reconstruction significantly amplified federal intervention in marriage. It was the federal government that took the lead in both offering marriage to freedpersons and distinguishing legal marriage from extra-legal unions, redefined as adultery and fornication. It was the federal government that reinforced the paradigm of wives as dependents in its pensions for Civil War widows and instituted governmental surveillance of the pensioners' marital qualifications. And it was the federal government's aggressive promotion of a narrowly traditional ideal of monogamy that set the stage for a full-scale assault on Mormon polygamy.

VI. POLICING MONOGAMY AND REPRODUCTION IN THE GILDED AGE

In the aftermath of the Civil War, a renewed commitment to the irrevocability of the federal union was bound up in public discourse with a renewed commitment to lifelong monogamy. As Abraham Lincoln had warned in a much-quoted domestic trope, "a house divided against itself cannot stand." Divorce, then, with its distinctly contractual foundations, its broadly divergent grounds, and its implicit acceptance of serial monogamy came under serious attack. Addressing a national divorce rate that was very low by current standards but clearly on the rise after the war, and decrying the seductions of secularism and modernity, conservative Protestants appended entire worldviews to "the divorce question."

The comments of Henry Loomis, a Connecticut clergyman, exemplify the way moral critics deployed lifelong monogamy as the critical marker for a Christian nation while equating divorce with national decay. Whereas true Christians viewed marriage as a divine institution and the foundation of civil society, Loomis observed, the "infidel or socialist" view of marriage was based on the idea that marriage should continue only at the pleasure of the partners. Given the historic ties between marriage and government, it was understandable, he conceded, that the nation's separation from England had nourished the acceptance of divorce. But now responsible Christians of the nineteenth century were reversing dangerous Enlightenment experiments, and the "infidel theory of the state" so popular at the time of revolution was giving way to a respect for divine authority. The infidels, the free-thinkers, and the free lovers, whom Loomis placed in direct opposition to anti-divorce Christians, belonged to a meandering stream of American radicalism that ran all the way from the Enlightenment anti-clericalism of a Tom Paine through the utopian socialism of a Robert Owen to the home-grown anarchism of a Steven Pearl Andrews. Yet the demarcation he created was too tidy by far since the infidel theory he condemned received its most ardent expression in the voices and practices of unorthodox Christians. Spiritualism's rejection of marital tyranny, the Church of the Latter Day Saints' devotion to plural marriage, and the Oneida Perfectionists commitment to "complex marriage" all challenged Loomis's definition of Christian marriage.

Loomis was joined in his anti-divorce sentiments by a host of local allies. Critiques by New England clergymen, including Theodore Woolsey, the president of Yale, became part of a larger campaign that evolved from an effort to eradicate Connecticut's omnibus clause into an organized legal crusade to make divorce less available. The New England Divorce Reform League, with Woolsey serving as president, became the leading edge of a movement for a uniform national divorce code. Its executive secretary, the Congregationalist minister Samuel Dike, took the League to national prominence by mixing clergymen, lawyers, and social scientists on the executive board. Dike then convinced Congress to fund a national survey on marriage and divorce, which was compiled by Secretary of Labor Carroll D. Wright and remains a remarkable statistical guide for the years between 1867 and 1902.

Dike's refusal to remarry a congregant whose divorce failed to meet his own religious scruples led to the loss of his church and became a catalyst for his reform activities. Denominational conventions often addressed the vexing theological dilemma of remarriage and the apparent gulf between secular law and the New Testament. Yet Christian precepts were central to Anglo-American marital regimes as illustrated by the casual verbal substitution of the biblical one-flesh doctrine for the legal fiction of marital unity. References to Scripture dotted discussions of divorce in state legislatures, and jurists and legislators alike assumed that the common law and Christianity (in its Protestant incarnation) were properly united in domestic relations and the union was in no way a violation of the disestablishment clause of the first amendment.

Those two assumptions, resting as they did on an exclusively monogamous view of marriage, with some denominational variations regarding its dissolution, help account for the government's success in pursuing polygamy in comparison to the relative failure of the drive to roll back divorce. Moral critics persistently linked both divorce and polygamy to the degradation of women and highlighted the ease and prominence of divorce in Utah. But while some states removed omnibus clauses and tightened residence requirements, most legislators were disinclined to retreat to an adultery-only standard for divorce; the divorce rate continued to rise, and a uniform, national divorce code never came to pass. Polygamy, by contrast, loomed as a much greater deviation from traditional Christianity, and Mormons soon discovered the extent to which conventional Protestantism trumped both their own reading of Christian marriage and their reliance on the protection of the First Amendment.

In the Gilded Age, eradicating polygamy became a defining feature of the Republican Party and a political substitute for the party's vaunted role in saving the Union. Republicans who had labeled polygamy and slavery "the twin relics of barbarism" before the war continued to compare plural wives to bond slaves after the war. Relying on patterns developed in Reconstruction, anti-polygamists demanded federal intervention in Utah. Enforcing the Morrill Act, however, which made bigamy in federal territories a crime punishable by imprisonment, had been foiled by Utah's failure to register marriages and by the recalcitrance of Mormon juries. After 1870, moreover, when Utah enfranchised the women of the territory, comparing Mormon women with bond slaves required a new kind of logic. When newly enfranchised plural wives endorsed polygamy at a series of mass meetings, critics suggested their complicity in their own enslavement.

The defeat of polygamy took place in a series of contests that placed the federal government in an unprecedented position of authority over marriage law. In an effort to enforce the Morrill Act, the Poland Act of 1874 empowered federal courts in the Utah territory to try federal crimes and empanel federal juries. As a result, a test case, *Reynolds v. United States*, emerged and reached the Supreme Court in 1879. The Mormons, who avowed plural marriage was a religious tenet that ordered their moral and social universe, also based their defense against the Morrill Act on the firmly established legal principle of local sovereignty over domestic relations. These arguments were no match for the anti-polygamy fervor of the era. Chief Justice Morrison Wait writing for the court in *Reynolds* designated polygamy too abhorrent to be a religious tenet, declared it "subversive of good order," and denounced it in a racial slur as the preserve of Asiatic and African people.

When polygamy persisted in the wake of the *Reynolds* decision, further federal action followed. Congress passed the Edmunds Act in 1882 disenfranchising polygamists, bigamists, and cohabitants and making it criminal to cohabit with more than one woman. In 1887 the Edmunds-Tucker Act disincorporated the Mormon Church, and in a strikingly indiscriminate provision, it also disenfranchised the women of Utah regardless of their religious affiliation or marital status. When the Mormons finally capitulated by officially abandoning polygamy, they set the stage for Utah's admission to the Union. And on the long path to capitulation, the government's aggressive campaign to eradicate this offensive local difference stood as a warning to other groups. Shortly after the decision in *Reynolds*, a group from Hamilton College gathered in upstate New York to oppose "complex marriage," an experimental regime that controlled reproduction, raised children communally, and prohibited exclusive pairings between men and women. When the Oneida Perfectionists gave up complex marriage in August of 1879, they noted in their newspaper that they could not remain blind to the lesson in the Mormon conflict.

Given the torrent of words and actions directed at deviations from monogamy, it is worth considering the common threat embodied in alternative marital regimes as well as in the serial monogamy unleashed by divorce. Part of the threat consisted in overturning the rules whereby men ordered their sexual access to women. The campaigns against polygamy and divorce typically extolled the Christian/common law model of monogamy for protecting the chastity of women while they obscured how the chastity of women represented male control of female sexuality. Campaigns against birth control revolved around a similar concern with regulating female sexuality and resulted in a growing governmental presence in reproduction.

The government's intervention in reproduction took place in the context of a dramatic demographic shift. Over the course of the nineteenth century white female fertility declined from a high of 7.04 to 3.56 children per family. In the absence of famine or catastrophic disease, we can only conclude that couples were voluntarily limiting the size of their families. One method when others had failed was abortion, which came under attack at mid-century from the newly founded American Medical Association. A decade later many states still had no provision making abortion a crime, and those that did relied on the old "quickening" rule of the common law, which permitted abortion so long as there was no discernible movement of the fetus. By the 1880s and 1890s, in the midst of a crusade for "moral purity," abortion, including those performed before quickening, became a crime in most states. Women who sought abortions were subject to criminal penalties along with the persons who provided them. Other forms of birth control generated federal intervention. Although separating sexual relations from reproduction was undoubtedly the goal of many men as well as women, it constituted a serious threat to the gender system by affording opportunities to women for risk-free sexual relations outside of marriage. Indeed, few advances held a greater potential for liberating women than reproductive freedom, which may account for why the resources for achieving it were defined as "obscene."

Anthony Comstock, a Christian fundamentalist, led the crusade against birth control. The 1873 federal bill bearing his name criminalized the use of the mails to disseminate "obscene, lewd, or lascivious" materials, including items for preventing conception and inducing abortion. Many states followed the federal lead with their own detailed statutes. Remarkably, Congress evinced no reservations about the scope or constitutionality of its assault on obscenity, and federal courts generally followed suit. Seven months after the bill's enactment, a federal district court in New York City upheld both the authority of Congress and the conviction of a physician for mailing powders with abortifacient and contraceptive properties. Three years later a federal court in Nevada used the law to penalize ambiguous advertising for contraceptive remedies.

The Comstock laws, which constrained the free flow of birth control information, were not strictly enforced, and they could not eradicate the impulse toward reproductive freedom that gathered force toward the end of the century. Yet although the quest for effective birth control acquired some respectability by the third decade of the twentieth century, abortion grew increasingly problematic. Abortions were still performed in significant numbers and were never equated with the crime of infanticide, but the women who sought them were no longer the middle-class wives of the mid-nineteenth century but instead single and working-class women. The criminalization of abortion not only deprived women of reproductive privacy and narrowed their options; it represented a significant departure from years of common law jurisprudence. The role of the federal government in enforcing uniform marriage standards was also a departure from the principle of local sovereignty that had reigned in the first half of the century. The most revealing feature in the crusade for moral purity and marital uniformity, however, was its devotion to pronatalism, which was directed at a society bent on limiting family size. Women – white, non-immigrant, properly married women of Northern European origin – were to serve American society by having more children. Here was maternalism with a vengeance, and with a distinctly nativist cast.

In the end, the devotion to maternalism played an equivocal role in reshaping American legal regimes. While Comstockery was placing new curbs on women's autonomy in the name of motherhood, motherhood was eclipsing fatherhood in custody awards in the courts, and the courts were exercising their authority at the expense of the male head of the household. The legal system now regarded wives primarily as mothers whose well-being was dependent on their husbands, and it regarded husbands primarily as wage earners for whom the state might act as substitute in limited and closely scrutinized circumstances. These updated legal constructions, although a far cry from Blackstone's extended patriarchal household, still retained some of its elements. They would make their way into the twentieth century to influence the welfare bureaucracies of the Progressive era and the provisions for Social Security.

CONCLUSION: THE LONG VIEW

One framework for viewing the long arc of nineteenth-century family law is to chart departures from the law of persons as it was outlined in Blackstone's *Commentaries*. Even though both the legal details and underlying rationale in Blackstone's blueprint for marriage and parenting were dated, it continued to serve as an outline for the rudiments of domestic relations law well into the nineteenth century. Blackstone, then, with his emphasis on the legal fiction of marital unity and its consequence of male headship, provides us with a convenient baseline from which to map out nineteenth-century innovations. Viewed from this perspective, the most striking trend in domestic relations law over the course of the nineteenth century was its shift toward the individuation of family members at the expense of the principle of male headship. A series of specific legal innovations chipped away at the old common law rules until the unified, hierarchical household of the Blackstonian model was a shadow of what it had been.

Nineteenth-century innovations took a variety of forms. One was clearly the legitimization of divorce, which unfolded amidst a growing commitment to romantic love and marital happiness. The recognition of divorce as a legal remedy, albeit on limited terms, not only compromised the legal fiction of marital unity that lay at the heart of the Christian/common law ideal of marriage but it also paved the way for the acceptance of serial monogamy. Another innovation took the form of giving wives the right to own property independently. Despite narrow legislative goals, the married women's property acts endowed wives as owners and earners with a legal identity apart from that of their spouses. In a culture that recast all family relations in affective terms, invested parenting with great emotional weight, and celebrated the innocence of childhood, legal innovations extended to parent-child relations as well. By endorsing a private construction of marriage, the juridical recognition of common law marriage resulted in insulating the children born in irregular unions from the disabilities of bastardy. In stark contrast to the English law of bastardy, nineteenth-century legal regimes also created a new, female-headed family in which unwed mothers enjoyed the same custodial rights as married fathers. As the notion of the child serving as a conduit of the father's will gave way to a concern for the child's best interests, mothers increasingly defeated fathers in custody contests, thereby eroding the father's presumptive right of custody. Similarly, by recognizing non-biological families, the formalization of adoption put another dent in the patriarchal foundations of Anglo-American family law.

It would be a mistake, however, to dismiss the limits of these reforms or ignore concerted efforts to undermine them. Although they point collectively to the democratization of the family, viewing them in an institutional framework provides a very different picture. Judicial hegemony over domestic relations reforms was as significant as the reforms themselves, and legislators undoubtedly came to expect judges to clarify, temper, and even reverse their more innovative forays. In discrete legal contests as opposed to generalized statutes, it was judges who tended to define the wife's separate estate narrowly, who hewed more often than not to the wife's traditional obligation of service, and who replaced the father's absolute right of custody with their own discretionary evaluation. As a result, many elements of coverture survived, and the judicial embrace of maternalism was always qualified. When judges awarded custody to mothers, they were standing in the traditional place of fathers and transforming themselves – not the mothers – into the ultimate authority over the family. Indeed, in custody, adoption, and the law of bastardy, the judiciary turned parenthood into a trusteeship that could be abrogated by the state. The role of the federal government in policing Civil War pensions, enforcing monogamy, and limiting reproductive freedom was another telling institutional development. It not only clouds the picture we have of women's increasing autonomy in the family but it also anticipates the ambit of the large welfare bureaucracies of the twentieth century.

How, then, are we to integrate these conflicting pictures of American family law? How are we to understand the tensions between the egalitarian and humanitarian impulses behind the legal reordering of the family on the one hand and the constraints, obfuscations, and reversals that accompanied it on the other? One way is to move beyond legal and institutional particulars to broader frameworks. If we place these tensions in a cultural framework, for example, we can read them as the agonizing contradictions between the destabilizing potential of romantic love and the regime of lifelong monogamy in which it was embedded and which the law modified. If we place them in a political framework, we can read them as the troublesome strains between liberalism and its patriarchal components. Admittedly the latter framework tells us more about what the law reveals than what it achieved, but what it reveals is a powerful and shifting dynamic between the legal construction of the family and the evolving gender system.

It is instructive to consider this dynamic in a specifically nineteenth-century American context. Although liberalism had the potential to disrupt all kinds of hierarchies, classical liberal theorists had assumed the wife's subordination and counted it among the rights of free men. Especially in the heyday of abolitionism, however, it was increasingly difficult to limit the rights of free men to men. To be sure, liberalism with its market yardstick of value and its failure to attribute value to the wife's household services may have proffered little to wives in the way of concrete remedies, but it always carried within its tenets a compelling challenge to their subordinate status. The credo of self-ownership and its corollary of bodily integrity so central to the crusade against slavery were threats to the gender order as well as the racial order and were understood as such by judges, legislators, and moralists. The anxieties unleashed by bringing the self-contracting, rights-bearing individual of liberalism to bear on the gender system by way of family law only intensified over the course of the century, culminating in novel restrictions on abortion and birth control that would make their way into the twentieth century.

Yet these were surely not the only legacy of legal change. The torrent of Gilded Age programs to police monogamy and sexuality was as much a manifestation of how the family had been transformed as an effort to restore it to traditional guidelines. And because the legal reordering of the family provided nineteenth-century women's rights advocates with a perfect field on which to deploy liberal political theory to subvert its own gender rules, it served as a catalyst for rethinking assumptions about marriage and parenting and for exploring and exposing their connections to the gender system. This too was a legacy that would make its way into the twentieth century and beyond.

9

SLAVERY, ANTI-SLAVERY, AND THE COMING OF THE CIVIL WAR

ARIELA GROSS

Enslaved African Americans who escaped to freedom wrote bitterly of the role of law in maintaining the institution of slavery. Harriet Jacob emphasized the law's refusal to act on behalf of slaves. The enslaved woman or girl had "no shadow of law to protect her from insult, from violence, or even from death." Frederick Douglass focused on the way law did act, turning human beings into property: "By the laws of the country from whence I came, I was deprived of myself – of my own body, soul, and spirit . . . " Whether through its action or inaction, slaves recognized the immense power of law in their lives.[1]

Law undergirded an economic system in which human beings were bought, sold, and mortgaged and a political system in which two sections of the United States coexisted profitably, one a slave society and one not. As we know, this coexistence did not last, and it is tempting to read back into the antebellum period an instability in the legal edifice supporting slavery that made its collapse inevitable. Yet, as both Douglass and Jacobs realized, the law worked remarkably well for a long period to subordinate human beings one to another, though not without considerable effort in the face of contradiction, internal conflict, and external challenge. Southern slaves and Northern abolitionists, in very different ways, posed a threat to the law of slavery, and it took work to overcome those threats. Ultimately, however, it was a bloody civil war, and not a legal process, that resolved the contradictions of human property.

Students of Southern history once supposed that law was largely irrelevant to African American culture, and to Southern culture in general. Most cultural historians of the nineteenth-century South have assumed that rituals

[1] Harriett Jacobs, *Incidents in the Life of a Slave Girl* (Cambridge, MA, 1987), 27; Frederick Douglass, "I Am Here to Spread Light on American Slavery: An address Delivered in Cork, Ireland, on 14 October 1845," *The Frederick Douglass Speeches, 1841–1846* (New Haven, CT, 1999).

of honor for whites and plantation discipline for blacks replaced law as the mechanisms to resolve conflict and punish wrongdoers. Thus, histories of white Southern culture emphasized duels, lynching, and master-slave relations. Literary sources, letters, and personal papers all painted a picture of a society governed primarily by what contemporary legal scholars would call "extra-legal norms." Studies of slave culture suggested that law had little influence on slaves' lives, because for most slaves, the master was the law. And so the legal history of slavery focused on the extraordinary situation – the fugitive to the North, the slave who killed her master – not slavery's everyday life.

But no longer. First, law was in reality pervasive in slavery – in the social construction of race, in the regulation of daily life, in the workings of the slave market, and in the culture of slaves, slaveholders, and non-slaveholding whites. Second, the great paradoxes of slavery and freedom in the antebellum republic were all framed precisely in terms of claims to legal rights: the right to property and the right to liberty. Slaves occupied a unique position in American society – as both human and property. In constitutional terms, slavery could be viewed simultaneously in terms of both liberty and property rights. Abolitionists emphasized the liberty of all Americans; slaveholders emphasized the property rights of all white Americans, including the right to own slaves. It is a distinctive feature of slavery in the American South – slavery embedded in a system of political liberalism – that its defense was full of the language of property rights. It was the legal-political language of property, indeed, that rendered slavery and liberalism compatible. Nor were the property rights arguments of slaveholders simply defensive; they were also used aggressively and expansively. Not only did they justify holding slaves in the South, they justified carrying them into the new territories to the West and North.

The language of rights was the only language most Southerners had available to define slavery. Thomas Reade Cobb's *Treatise on the Law of Negro Slavery* defined slavery in pure Lockean terms, as rights denied: "Of the three great absolute rights guaranteed to every citizen by the common law – the right of personal security, the right of personal liberty, and the right of private property, the slave, in a state of pure or absolute slavery, is totally deprived."[2] Through the denial of legal rights, the slave was put outside society.

Thus, we can see that law worked on two levels during the antebellum era: below the radar, law facilitated the routine functioning of the slave system and mediated the tensions among slaves, slaveholders, and

[2] Thomas Reade Cobb, *An Inquiry into The Law of Negro Slavery in the United States of America (1858)*, §86, 83.

non-slaveholders. Above the surface, law was the object of contest between Southern pro-slavery and Northern anti-slavery forces over the future of slavery in the Union. Through a succession of constitutional "crises" involving slaves who fled to free states and migrants who brought slaves to new territories, competing views of the legality and constitutionality of slavery increasingly came into direct conflict in legal as well as political arenas. As slaves who resisted their masters or ran away pushed difficult issues of human agency into the courtroom, they also pushed the anomalous constitutional status of slavery into the forefront of political debate, adding to growing Northern fears of an ascendant "Slave Power" conquering not only political institutions but also the Constitution itself.

Increasingly central on both of these levels of legal activity was the ideology of race. The power of race in the law was highlighted in the Supreme Court's affirmation, in the *Dred Scott* decision, that even free blacks had no claim to rights or citizenship, but it had been building for years. By the 1820s, slavery had become the South's "peculiar institution." It had been successfully regionalized by Northern abolition despite pockets of continuing enslavement that contravened official law, like the slavery Dred Scott experienced on Army bases in the Northwest Territories. The regionalization of slavery brought the issue of "comity" between free and slave states to the fore, highlighting the political issues involved in every legal determination about the status of slaves brought to free jurisdictions. Race held the potential to explain and justify the line between free and unfree; in the slave states it mobilized non-slaveholding whites behind the institution of slavery, and in the free states it created a counterweight to abolitionist compassion for the enslaved. On the local level, Southern jurists' increasing preoccupation with justifying slavery in their jurisprudence led not only to legislative crackdowns on the regulation of free blacks and on many of slaves' "customary" rights but also to a more self-conscious effort to make law "paternalist" and thereby to prove that slavery was the best possible condition for poor, childlike "negroes." Race was central to this new justificatory legal enterprise. Law became ever more the forum for telling stories about black character and, through it, white character.

The essential character of Southern antebellum society and its laws has been debated endlessly. Was it a pre-capitalist paternalist socioeconomic system inserted into a bourgeois capitalist world or a market society of profit-minded individuals pursuing individual gain? Was law an instrument of slaveholder hegemony, a facilitator of capitalist markets, an object of contest among many makers, an arena for battles over honor? Ultimately, these attempts at global characterization of either "the South" or "Southern law" are less useful to an understanding of the way legal institutions operated both as cultural forms and as technologies of power than close attention to the more mundane, daily ways that slaves and masters, slaveholders and non-slaveholding whites, buyers and sellers of slaves framed and waged their encounters with law. We can agree with Walter Johnson: "Neither structural contradiction nor hypocritical capitalism fully describes the obscene synthesis of humanity and interest, of person and thing, that underlay so much of Southern jurisprudence, the market in slaves, the daily discipline of slavery, and the proslavery argument."

I. THE EVERYDAY LAW OF SLAVERY

At the level of the day to day, in local trials, whites worked out their relationships with slaves and with one another *through* slaves. White men rarely faced criminal prosecution for striking slaves, but they quite often found themselves in court for civil suits regarding property damage to the slave of another. At trials, non-slaveholding whites had the chance to exercise power as jurors and as witnesses, telling stories about the character and mastery of defendants who were far more likely to be wealthy planters. Slaves had no officially sanctioned opportunity to exercise agency, but they too both consciously and unconsciously influenced outcomes in court, despite the dangers inherent in outright efforts at manipulation. Lawyers, finally, played the role of transmitters of culture as they traveled from town to town. They made their careers in the legal practice of the slave market and invested the fruits of their careers in the slave market. In all these ways, the institutions of slavery, law, and the market grew intertwined.

The growing power of race in Southern society shaped all legal confrontations; courts had the power to make racial determinations, and the stories told about racial character in the courtroom helped "make race." Despite the overdetermined quality of white Southerners' efforts to make the boundaries of race and slavery congruent, the indeterminacy of legal standards made some legal outcomes contestable. Courts, as arenas for shaping identities, lent some power to slaves.

Who Can Be a Slave? The Law of Race

By the early nineteenth century, it was well-settled law in every state that only a person of some African descent could be enslaved. One's appearance as a "negro" raised a legal presumption of one's enslavement, but this presumption could be rebutted by evidence of manumission, whiteness, or another claim to freedom. Most states passed statutes setting rules for the determination of "negro" or, more often, "mulatto" status, usually in terms of fractions of African "blood." Before the Civil War, most states also stipulated either one-fourth or one-eighth African "blood" as the definition of "negro." Yet even statutory definitions such as these could not resolve disputes about the racial identity (and hence, vulnerability to enslavement) of many individuals. Often, they just pushed the dispute back a generation or two as courtroom inquiry turned from the racial identity of the individual at issue to her grandmother. Still, the question remained: how could one *know* race?

In practice, two ways of "knowing" race became increasingly important in courtroom battles over racial identity in the first half of the nineteenth century, one a discourse of race as "science" and the other of race as "performance." During the 1850s, as the question of race became more and more hotly contested, courts began to consider "scientific" knowledge of a person's "blood" as well as the ways she revealed her blood through her acts. The mid-nineteenth century thus saw the development of a scientific discourse of race that located the essence of racial difference in physiological characteristics, such as the size of the cranium and the shape of the foot, and attempted to link physiological with moral and intellectual difference. Yet the most striking aspect of "race" in trials of racial identity was not so much its biologization but its performative and legal aspects. Proving one's whiteness meant performing white womanhood or manhood, whether doing so before the court or through courtroom narratives about past conduct and behavior. While the essence of white identity might have been white "blood," because blood could not be transparently known, the evidence that mattered most was evidence about the way people acted out their true nature.

Enslaved women suing for their freedom performed white womanhood by showing their beauty and whiteness in court and by demonstrating purity and moral goodness to their neighbors. White womanhood was ideally characterized by a state of legal disability, requiring protection by honorable gentlemen. In nineteenth-century legal settings, women of ambiguous racial identity were able to call on the protection of the state if they could convince a court that they fit this ideal of white womanhood. For example, in the "celebrated" freedom suit of Sally Miller, her lawyer sought to link white Southerners' confidence in the intangible but unmistakable qualities of white womanhood to identifiable acts of self-presentation and behavior his client performed:

"[T]he moral traits of the Quartronne, the moral features of the African are far more difficult to be erased, and are far more easily traced, than are the distinctions and differences of physical conformation," he informed the jury. "The Quartronne is idle, reckless and extravagant, this woman is industrious, careful and prudent – the Quartronne is fond of dress, of finery and display – this woman is neat in her person, simple in her array, and with no ornament upon her, not even a ring on her fingers."[3]

[3] Transcript of Trial, *Miller v. Belmonti*, No. 5623 (1845), Supreme Court Records, Earl K. Long Library, Special Collections & Archives, Univ. of New Orleans, La. "Quatronne" means person of one-fourth African ancestry, as in "quadroon."

The jury accepted the argument, and the Louisiana Supreme Court affirmed Sally Miller's freedom. Her case was covered heavily in local newspapers, and her trial narrative was repeated in novels and autobiographies by abolitionist ex-slaves, William Wells Brown and William Craft, as a dramatic representation of the power relations inherent in slavery, so little caring of the "sacred rights of the weak" that it could question even a fair, white maiden.

Men, on the other hand, performed white manhood by acting like gentlemen and by exercising legal and political rights: sitting on a jury, mustering into the militia, voting, and testifying in court. At trial, witnesses translated legal rules based on ancestry and "blood" into wide-ranging descriptions of individuals' appearances, reputation, and in particular a variety of explicit forms of racial performance: dancing, attending parties, associating with white people or black people, and performing civic acts. There was a certain circularity to these legal determinations of racial identity. As South Carolina's Judge William Harper explained, "A slave cannot be a white man." But this was not all that it seemed, for he also stated that a "man of worth, honesty, industry and respectability, should have the rank of a white man," even though a "vagabond of the same degree of blood" would not. In other words, "A slave cannot be a white man" suggested not only that status depended on racial identity but also that status was part of the essence of racial identity. Degraded status signified "negro blood." Conversely, behaving honestly, industriously, and respectably and exercising political privileges signified whiteness.[4]

Manumission and Free Blacks

As more and more people lived on the "middle ground" between slavery and freedom, black and white, they made it at once more difficult and more urgent for courts to attempt to draw those boundaries sharply and to equate race with free or unfree status completely.

By the 1830s, nothing had come to seem more anomalous to many white Southerners than a free person of African descent. Yet there was a substantial population of "free people of color" in the South, partly as a result of relatively lax manumission policies in the eighteenth and early nineteenth century. Legislatures hurried to remedy the problem, as free blacks were increasingly seen to be, with a plethora of laws governing manumission. Before Southerners felt themselves under siege by abolitionists, they had allowed manumission quite freely, usually combined with some plans for colonization. But by the 1820s serious colonization plans had died out in

[4] *State v. Cantey*, 20 S.C.L. 614, 616 (1835).

the South. In a typical Southern slave code of the latter decades of slavery, slaves could only be freed if they left the state within ninety days and if the manumitter followed other complicated rules. The rights of creditors were protected, and a substantial bond had to be posted for the care of the old or infirm freed slave.

Southern states also tightened restrictions on free blacks beginning in the 1830s and accelerating in the 1840s and 1850s. In part this was a reaction to the Denmark Vesey (1822) and Nat Turner (1831) insurrections, for Vesey was free, and Turner was a foreman, a near-free slave. But it was also part of the reaction, beginning in the 1830s, to anti-slavery sentiment in the North. In the late eighteenth century, most slaveholders spoke of slavery as a necessary evil – the Thomas Jefferson position. They were racists, but they did not pretend that blacks loved slavery; rather, they took the position that given current circumstances, slavery was the best that could be done. Blacks could not survive as free people in the United States – perhaps colonization would be a very long-range solution. By the 1830s, however, Southerners had developed a defense of slavery that pronounced it a positive good. For the most part, it was a racially based defense. According to Cobb and other pro-slavery apologists, blacks were inferior mentally and morally so that "a state of bondage, so far from doing violence to the law of his nature, develops and perfects it; and that, in that state, he enjoys the greatest amount of happiness, and arrives at the greatest degree of perfection of which his nature is capable."[5]

As Southerners articulated the positive-good defense of slavery more often in terms of race, they increasingly emphasized a dual image of the black person: under the "domesticating" influence of a white master, the slave was a child, a happy Sambo, as described by Cobb, but outside of this influence, he was a savage beast. As they strove to convince themselves and Northerners that slaves were happy Sambos, they more frequently portrayed free blacks as savages. With this emphasis on race, Southerners felt the need to draw the color line more clearly than ever. This placed the South's free people of color in an increasingly precarious position.

It is worth remembering that there were two quite distinct groups of free people of color. In the Upper South, where slavery was essentially dying out by the Civil War, and also in Maryland and Delaware, free black populations were largely the descendants of slaves manumitted during the Revolutionary era. As a group they were mainly rural, more numerous, and closer to slaves in color and economic condition than free blacks in the Lower South, who were light-skinned refugees from the San Domingo revolution, creole residents of Louisiana, and women and children freed as

[5] Cobb, *Inquiry into the Law of Negro Slavery*, 51.

a result of sexual relationships. Free blacks in the Lower South tended to be mixed racially; concentrated in New Orleans, Charleston, and a few other cities; and better off economically; some of them were large slaveholders themselves. The Upper South was more hostile to free blacks because they were more of an economic threat; in the Lower South, the cities recognized gradations of color and caste more readily.

Along with increased restrictions on manumission, the most important new limitations on the rights of free people of color were constraints on their freedom of movement. Free blacks were required to register with the state and to carry their freedom papers with them wherever they went. They were frequently stopped by slave patrols who mistook them for slaves and asked for their passes. If their papers were not in order they could be taken to jail or even cast into slavery. Mississippi required that, to remain in the state, free people of color be adopted by a white guardian who could vouch for their character. Increasingly, criminal statutes were framed in terms of race rather than status, so that differential penalties applied to free people of color as well as slaves, including banishment and reenslavement. In most of the new state constitutions adopted during the 1830s, free people of color were barred from testifying in court against a white person, voting, serving in one of the professions, or obtaining higher education. About the only rights that remained to them were property rights. Some managed to hold on to their property, including slaves. But by the eve of the Civil War, white Southerners had made every effort to make the line between slave and free congruent with the line between black and white. Free people of color and people of mixed race, both slave and free, confounded those efforts. It is no surprise that they were the target of so many legal regulations.

Slave Codes: "A Bill of Rights Turned Upside Down"

On paper, many aspects of slaves' lives were governed by slave codes. In practice, slaves were often able to carve out areas of customary rights contrary to the laws on the books. How, then, can we interpret the significance of the codes' detailed restrictions on every aspect of slave life? One way to read the statutes passed by Southern legislatures to regulate slavery, James Oakes has suggested, is as "Bill[s] of Rights [turned] upside down . . . a litany of rights denied." Slaveholders defined slavery in the terms they used to define freedom. Slaves had no right of movement, no right of contract, no right to bear witness in court, no right to own property.

The codes can also be read as timelines of every moment slaves resisted often enough to trigger a crackdown. The very specificity of the laws in Southern slave codes hints at this reading. Slaves were hiring out their own time and moving freely about towns frequently enough to merit a law; slaves were selling spirituous liquors, holding dances, and gaming frequently enough to merit a law. County court records in Natchez, Mississippi, reveal that the most frequent criminal prosecutions of blacks or whites were for selling spirituous liquors to a negro, selling spirituous liquors without a license, and gaming. It is often possible to track insurrectionary scares simply by reference to the legislative enactments of a particular region. For example, after Nat Turner's revolt, South Carolina passed laws against burning stacks of rice, corn, or grain; setting fire to barrels of pitch, tar, turpentine, or rosin; and other very specific prohibitions.

The slave codes reveal the hopes and fears of slaveholders. Particularly after the Vesey and Turner revolts, whites feared the power of black preachers, particularly free black preachers, to move slaves to rebellion. Many states passed laws dealing overtly with slave conspiracies, punishable by death. Other statutes prohibited slaves from gathering for religious meetings or dances and prohibited slaves or free people of color from preaching.

State courts established enforcement mechanisms that made these legislative prohibitions real. Slave patrols, appointed by county courts or militia captains, were supposed to "visit the negro houses . . . and may inflict a punishment . . . on all slaves they may find off their owner's plantations, without a proper permit or pass . . . " Slave patrols were also supposed to "suppress all unlawful collections of slaves," catch runaways, and punish slaves for other infractions. Eighteenth-century slave patrols had tended to involve a wide cross-section of the white community, but by the 1820s higher status whites in some areas appeared to think the work beneath them and relied instead on their overseers. In general, however, local white elites stayed active in patrolling. Control of the Southern labor force was too important for them to delegate to others, and slave patrols were useful adjuncts to slaveholders' authority. Similarly, while many masters chose to punish their slaves on their own farms or leave punishment to their overseers, some local governments provided whipping houses where slaves could be sent for the customary thirty-nine lashes. Runaway jails housed escaped slaves who had been recaptured.[6]

Marriage and Family

The slave codes illuminate another important aspect of slavery: control over the slave's sexuality and family life. Slaves could not legally marry. Nor could a black slave marry or have sexual relations with a white female. The codes did not mention relations between white males and black slaves; slave status followed the mother and not the father. Despite the laws, whites

[6] Edward Cantwell, *The Practice at Law in North Carolina* (Raleigh, NC, 1860).

routinely recognized slave marriages – often even in courtroom testimony or in judicial opinions. Yet when it came to testifying against one another in court or charging manslaughter rather than murder in the case of a man who had caught his wife in bed with another man, judges refused to recognize slaves' marriage. In his treatise on *Slaves as Persons*, Cobb justified the non-recognition of slave marriage in racial terms, advancing the myth that slaves were lascivious and their "passions and affections seldom very strong," so that their bonds of marriage and of parenthood were weak, and they "suffer[ed] little by separation from" their children.[7]

In fact, family was a source of autonomy and retention of African culture for enslaved people. Some of the best historical work on slavery has brought to life the ways that slaves retained their own values despite slavery by uncovering the survival of practices of exogamy – that is, not marrying first cousins. White Southerners married their first cousins, but black slaves did not and persisted in the practice. Efforts to maintain African culture are also in evidence in naming patterns that sustained African names alongside owners' imposition of day-names and classical names, such as Pompey and Caesar. Native-born populations of slaves appear to have had more success in self-naming – keeping kin names, especially those of fathers, in a system that legally denied fatherhood – than the first generation. This suggests that family was a source of strength in slave communities. It was also a source of resistance and a means of communication. Slaves ran away to get back to families and conducted "abroad" marriages with spouses on other farms, creating a larger community of African Americans.

The importance of family made it at the same time a source of vulnerability: family breakup was a powerful threat that enhanced slaveholders' control. It was a threat backed by experience – one-fourth to one-third of slave families were separated by sale. Family was also a powerful incentive not to run away, especially for slave women. Enslaved women who ran with their children could not get far; far more common was truancy, staying out for several days and then returning.

Unmarried or married, enslaved women lived with the fear of sexual assault. Sexual assault on an enslaved woman was not a crime. While Cobb suggested that "for the honor of the statute-book," the rape of a female slave should be criminalized, such a statute was passed in Georgia only in 1861 and was never enforced. Cobb reassured his readers that the crime was "almost unknown," because of the lasciviousness of black women.[8] In one Missouri case in the 1850s, the slave Celia murdered the master who had been raping her since she was a young teenager. Her lawyer brought a claim

[7] Cobb, *Inquiry into the Law of Negro Slavery*, 39.
[8] Cobb, *Inquiry into the Law of Negro Slavery*, §107, 100.

of self-defense, using a Missouri statute that gave "a woman" the right to use deadly force to defend her honor. But the court in that case found that an enslaved woman was not a "woman" within the meaning of the statute; the law did not recognize Celia as having any honor to defend.

Slave law and family law also intersected in the law of property and inheritance. The most basic property question regarding slavery, of course, was the status of the slaves themselves as human property – how would that status be inherited? By the nineteenth century, it was well-settled law that slave status passed on from mother to child, guaranteeing that the offspring of masters' sexual relationships with their slaves would become the property of the masters. In transfers as well, the master owned the "increase" of his human property: "When a female slave is given [by devise] to one, and her future increase to another, such disposition is valid, because it is permitted to a man to exercise control over the increase . . . of his property. . . . "[9] Furthermore, as one Kentucky court put it, "the father of a slave is unknown to our law. . . . "[10]

By refusing to recognize slaves' marriages or honor their family ties, Southern courts and legislatures inscribed the dishonor of slaves into law. It should be no surprise that, in the immediate aftermath of emancipation, many freed African Americans saw marriage rights as central to their claims of citizenship. A black corporal in the Union Army explained to a group of ex-slaves, "The marriage covenant is at the foundation of all our rights. In slavery we could not have *legalised* marriage: now we have it . . . and we shall be established as a people."[11] By identifying marriage as the foundation of citizenship, the speaker dramatized the way slavery's denial of family ties had served to put slaves outside society and the polity.

In the Criminal Courts

Slaves who fought back against the injustices of their lives – especially against masters who raped them, beat their children, or separated them from their families – ended up in the criminal courts of Southern counties. In the famous case of *State v. Mann*, Lydia ran away from her hirer, John Mann, who shot her in the back as she fled. The question in the case was the right of the slave to life – to be safe from cruel treatment. This was the one right Cobb had said the law allowed the slave. Yet, Judge Thomas Ruffin,

[9] *Fulton v. Shaw*, 25 Va. 597, 599 (1827). [10] *Frazier v. Spear*, 5 Ky. 385, 386 (1811).

[11] Letter from J. R. Johnson to Col. S. P. Lee, 1 June 1866, Unregistered Letters Received, ser. 3853, Alexandra VA Supt., RG 105, National Archives, reprinted in Ira Berlin et al., eds., *Freedom: A Documentary History of Emancipation, 1861–1867, Series II; The Black Military Experience* (Cambridge, MA, 1982), 672.

in a stark statement of the nature of slavery, held that courts would not interfere with the owner's authority over the slave: "We cannot allow the right of the master to be brought into discussion in the Courts of justice."[12] Discipline was to be left to owners – or, as Mann was, hirers – and trust placed in their private interest and benevolence.

Four years later, in *State v. Will*, the same North Carolina court overturned Ruffin's decision. In this case, Will, like Lydia, resisted his master and walked away from a whipping. Like Lydia, Will was shot in the back. But Will fought back, stabbing his owner three times with a knife. Will was put on trial for murder, but the presiding judge, William Gaston, decided that he was guilty of the lesser crime of felonious homicide. In doing so, he upheld the principle that there were limits to the master's authority over a slave and that a slave had the right to resist the master who overstepped the limits. Gaston wrote that "the master has not the right to slay his slave, and I hold it to be equally certain that the slave has a right to defend himself against the unlawful attempt of his master to deprive him of his life."[13] Oakes comments, "It is pointless to ask whether Ruffin or Gaston correctly captured the true essence of slavery." The two cases "reveal the divergent trajectories intrinsic to the law of slavery – the one flowing from the total subordination of the slave to the master, the other from the master's subordination to the state."

Ordinarily, when a white person was put on trial for abusing or killing a slave, the grand jury would simply refuse to issue an indictment or the jury would turn in a verdict of not guilty. Some doctors gave abhorrent testimony offering alternative theories as to the cause of death when a slave had been whipped to death – that she might have had a heart attack or a sudden illness and that her vicious character and angry passion would predispose her to such a seizure. But an owner could win damages from a hirer, overseer, or other person who abused his slave in a civil case for trespass. In these cases, juries were much more willing to find that cruelty had taken place in order to compensate the slaveholder.

Civil cases could be a big deterrent, but not to a master for mistreatment of his own slave. Neighbors of Augustus W. Walker testified that they had seen him "whip in a cruel manner his slaves and particularly a young girl 11 years old, whom he whipped or caused to be whipped at three different times the same day, eighty lashes each time and furthermore they said Walker overworked his negroes." Walker also locked his slaves in a dungeon and frequently inflicted "as many as one hundred licks to one boy at a time" with a "strap or palette." He made his slaves work from three-thirty

[12] *State v. Mann*, 13 N.C. (2 Dev.) 263, 267 (1829).
[13] *State v. Will*, 18 N.C. 121, 165 (1835).

in the morning until nine or ten at night, without meal breaks or Sundays off. In a criminal prosecution for "harsh, cruel & inhuman treatment towards his slaves," Walker was acquitted. The judge explained the flexible standard for punishment of slaves: "the master can chastise; the slave is entirely subject to his will; the punishment must necessarily depend on the circumstances . . . if the case is a grave one, the chastisement will probably be severe, if the slave is of a robust constitution, the chastisement may be increased . . . " In an accompanying civil case, in which Walker sued one Joseph Cucullu for selling him ten slaves "afflicted with serious maladies, diseases, and defects of the body." Cucullu argued that any problems with the slaves could be attributed to Walker's harsh treatment. However, the Louisiana court found for Walker in the civil case as well, above all because he did not "strike . . . at random with passion or anger," but had a *system* for plantation management and discipline. The most important thing was that a master should have a regular system of "rules" that he "imposes on him[self]."[14]

Criminal prosecutions of slaves like Will exhibit a trend toward greater procedural guarantees for slaves. The greatest unfairness slaves faced were white juries and the exclusion of slave testimony against a white person. Unfortunately, slave testimony was allowed against a black person, and it was not uncommon for slaves to be convicted on the basis of the testimony of other slaves. Yet slaves received real defenses, often by prominent lawyers, and their appeals and writs of habeas corpus were heard all the way up the state court systems. Procedural guarantees were grudgingly conceded by men who feared their consequences, but saw them as necessary to slavery in a liberal system. The conflicts between Lydia and Mann, Will and Baxter, Ruffin and Gaston, exemplified the problem of slave resistance in such a society. When slaves resisted, they forced the law to deal with them as people.

Slavery and Commerce

The courthouse was one of two institutions central to Southern culture., The other was the slave market. Civil trials involving slaves were routine events that brought townsfolk and planters together to fight over their human property and, in the process, to hash out their understandings of racial character. Through rituals invested with all the trappings of state authority, both white and black Southerners again and again made the journey from one institution to the other, slave market to courthouse.

[14] *Walker v. Cucullu*, No. 326 (1866), Louisiana Supreme Court Records, Earl K. Long Library, Special Collections & Archives, Univ. of New Orleans, La.

The slave markets that provided so many lawyers with their livelihoods – both as litigators and as slaveholding planters – did a vigorous business in the antebellum Deep South. Although importation of foreign slaves ended in 1808 as a result of constitutional prohibition, throughout the antebellum period the states of the Deep South continued to import slaves from the Upper South in ever greater numbers. Slave traders brought slaves from Virginia, Kentucky, and Tennessee to sell at the markets in Charleston, Natchez, and New Orleans. Overall, more than a quarter of a million slaves came into the Deep South from the Upper South each decade from the 1830s on. Local sales also accounted for a substantial part of the trade, probably more than half. Individual slaveholders sold slaves to one another directly or used local traders as intermediaries. And slaves were sold by the sheriff at public auction when a slaveholder or his estate became insolvent. In South Carolina, one state for which solid numbers are available, insolvency sales amounted to one-third of all slave sales.

Southern states periodically banned domestic importation, as Mississippi did, for example, from 1837 to 1846. Bans appear to have been prompted by both economic and security considerations: sectional tensions between older, established areas that had no need of more slaves and newer areas; temporary economic panics; and reactions to well-known slave insurrections. The bans, however, were always overturned and in any case made little impression on the trade. Mississippi was the first state to develop another form of regulation in 1831, again in reaction to the Turner rebellion in Virginia; it required imported slaves to register a "certificate of character" from the exporting state, guaranteeing that the slave was not a runaway or thief. This requirement was also quite simple to circumvent, as one trader explained: all one had to do was "to get two freeholders to go along and look at your negroes. You then tell them the name of each negro – the freeholders then say that they know the negroes and give the certificates accordingly."

Prices for slaves rose throughout the antebellum period, with the exception of the panic years of the late 1830s and early 1840s. "Prime male field hands" in the New Orleans market sold for about $700 in 1846; their price had more than doubled by 1860 to upward of $1,700. To own slaves was to own appreciating assets, as important as capital as for the value of their labor. Slaveholders were an economic class whose slave property was their key asset; they moved around frequently, investing little in towns or infrastructure. Even the high level of land speculation in Mississippi and Alabama suggests that slaveholders were not particularly attached to their land. Slaves were their most important form of capital.

Slaves were also the cornerstone of the Southern credit economy, for they were highly desirable as collateral for loans. Credit sales of slaves ranged from a high of 37 percent of all slave sales (1856) to a low of 14 percent (1859), averaged 20 percent, and rarely had terms longer than twelve months; land mortgages lasted two to five years. Thus, slaves were the ideal collateral for debts. A complex web of notes traded on slaves existed, though it could, and often did, fall through in years of financial panic and high land speculation.

Other segments of the Southern economy also depended on slaves. Hiring, or leasing, provided an important way for both individuals and corporate entities, especially towns and cities, to obtain labor without making the major capital investment in slaves. Slave hiring may have involved as much as 15 percent of the total slave population. Hiring relationships also took place among private parties. Slaves, in fact, were fragmented property, with so many interest-holders in any particular slave that there was no such thing as a simple, unitary master-slave relationship for most slaves and most masters.

Market transactions, credit relations, and hires all led to disputes that had the potential to land the parties in court. In cases of hire, some owners sued hirers for mistreating a slave. More often, these cases resembled warranty suits in that hirers sued owners when the leased slave turned out to be "unsound," died, or ran away. In either situation, the trial revolved around the question of who should assume responsibility for the condition and character of the slave.

Most sales anticipated litigation at least indirectly by including an express warranty by the seller that a slave was "sound in body and mind and slave for life." Form bills of sale used by slave traders generally included spaces for the sex, name, and age of the slave and for the warranty, but left the language blank to allow variation. Some bills of sale explicitly excluded certain aspects of that particular slave's condition or character from warranty.

When slave buyers were dissatisfied with their purchases, they tried to recover for the problems directly. Usually this meant confronting the seller with a demand that he take back the slave and return the purchaser's money. Slave traders were more likely to settle such cases out of court than were private individuals. In their private writings, planters wrote of their frustration with the legal system. Benjamin L. C. Wailes, a prominent doctor and planter of Natchez, became embroiled in litigation when the life estate-holder of his plantation Fonsylvania sold and mortgaged a number of slaves without permission. After an unsuccessful suit for eight slaves sold through Miles and Adams, New Orleans commission merchants, he wrote in his diary: "Note. Never engage in a law suit if to be avoided or have anything to do with lawyers without a written agreement as to terms and compensation."[15]

[15] Benjamin L.C. Wailes, Diary, Sept. 2, 1859, available at Duke University Archives.

Buyers, sellers, owners, and hirers of slaves most often brought their disputes to the circuit courts of their county. They went to court primarily to win monetary damages. Their suits dominated the dockets of circuit courts and other courts of first resort at the county level. In Adams County, Mississippi, about half of the trials in circuit court involved slaves, mostly civil disputes among white men regarding the disposition of their human property. Of these civil disputes, a majority were suits for breach of warranty – for example, 66 percent of the appealed cases in the Deep South and 52 percent of the trials in Adams County. Suits based on express warranties could be pled as "breach of covenant" or as "assumpsit," both actions based in contract. In Louisiana, suits of this type were especially common, because the civil law codified consumer protections under the category of "redhibitory actions." One could obtain legal relief for the purchase of a slave who was proven to have one of a series of enumerated "redhibitory" vices or diseases, including addiction to running away and theft.[16] Although professional traders preferred cash sales or very "short" credit (notes payable in six months or one year), a significant number of buyers in local sales paid at least part of the slave's price with notes, some of them with much longer terms. In those cases, breach of warranty might be a defense to a creditor's lawsuit to collect the unpaid debt. Over the course of the antebellum period, litigation increased in the circuit courts because of the growing population and economy, but slave-related litigation increased grew even more quickly, indicating the rising economic centrality of slaves.

Commercial law appeared to be the arena in which the law most expected to treat slaves as property – in disputes over mundane sales transactions. When slave buyers felt their newly acquired human property to be "defective" physically or morally, they sued the seller for breach of warranty – just as they would over a horse or a piece of machinery. In these and other commercial disputes, the parties brought into question and gave legal meaning to the "character" and resistant behavior of the enslaved, who persisted in acting as people. Take as an example *Johnson v. Wideman* (1839), a South Carolina case of breach of warranty, in which the buyer (Wideman) defended his note against the seller by claiming that the slave Charles had a bad character. According to Wideman, Charles was everything that struck terror into a slaveholder's heart: he owned a dog (against the law); he was married (unrecognized by law); he tried to defend his wife's honor against white men; he not only acted as though he were equal to a white man, he *said he wished he was a white man*; he threatened white men with

[16] "Of the Vices of Things Sold," La. Civ. Code, Bk. III, Tit. 7, Chap. 6, Sec. 3, arts. 2496–2505 (1824).

violence; he refused to work unless he wished to; and he did not respond to whipping.[17]

The plaintiff-seller's witnesses told a different story. According to them, Charles was a drunkard and an insolent negro only when he lived with Wiley Berry, a "drinking, horse-racing" man himself (from whom Johnson bought Charles). As one witness explained, "He had heard of [Charles's] drinking. He had borne the character of an insolent negro: but not in the time he belonged to the Johnsons." Others testified that Charles was humble and worked well, that when Johnson owned him, "he was not so indolent as when he belonged to Berry." Berry had exposed him to spirits and had whipped him frequently. Johnson's case rested on the contention that Charles was a good slave when managed well, and the only evidence of his insolence came from his behavior under Berry and under Wideman himself.

Judge John Belton O'Neall, Chief Justice of the South Carolina Court of Errors and Appeals, who presided over the trial on circuit, explained that he had instructed the jury as follows: "Generally, I said, the policy of allowing such a defence might be very well questioned. For, most commonly such habits were easy of correction by prudent masters, and it was only with the imprudent that they were allowed to injure the slave. Like master, like man was, I told them, too often the case, in drunkenness, impudence, and idleness." O'Neall's "like master, like man" theory of slaves' character led him to find for the seller in this case.

Thus, even a court that wanted to exclude moral qualities from implied warranty, as did South Carolina's High Court of Errors and Appeals, still heard cases where the moral qualities of a slave were put on trial. In *Johnson v. Wideman* we see the range of behaviors and qualities permissible in a skilled slave. For example, when Charles confronted his first master, Wiley Berry, about Berry's behavior with his wife, he convinced Henry Johnson that he was in the right in this dispute with Berry. This case also offers a strong judicial exposition of a common theory of slave vice: "like master, like man." Johnson's argument, largely accepted by the trial judge and Justice O'Neall, was that Charles's misbehavior could be attributed to the freedom Berry gave him and the bad example Berry set. This theory removed agency from the slave, portraying the slave as the extension of his master's will.

By painting slaves as essentially malleable in character, courts could lay the responsibility on masters to mold the slave's behavior. Thus, sellers emphasized malleability and exploited the fear of slaves' deceitfulness to do so. Slaveholders constantly feared that slaves were feigning illness or

[17] *Johnson v. Wideman*, 24 S.C. L. 325 (Rice 1839).

otherwise trying to manipulate their masters; a good master was one who could see through this deceit and make a slave work.

Southern courts confronted the agency of slaves in other kinds of litigation arising out of commercial relationships as well, most commonly actions for trespass and other actions we would categorize today as "torts." Owners brought lawsuits against hirers, overseers, or other whites who had abused their slaves or to recover the hire price for slaves who had fallen ill or run away during the lease term.

All of the explanations of slave character and behavior outlined above – as functions of slave management, as immutable vice, as habit or disease – operated in some way to remove agency from enslaved people. Reports of slaves who took action, such as running away on their own impulse and for their own rational reasons, fit uneasily into these accounts. Yet because slaves did behave as moral agents, reports of their resistance persistently cropped up in court. At times, witnesses provided evidence of slaves acting as moral agents; on other occasions, the nature of the case required acknowledgment of slaves' moral agency.

Occasionally the courts explicitly recognized slaves' human motivations as the cause of their "vices." More often, these stories were recorded in the trial transcripts, but disappeared from the appellate opinions. Just as judges were reluctant to recognize slaves' skills and abilities, they feared giving legal recognition to slaves as moral agents with volition, except when doing so suited very specific arguments or liability rules. Recognizing slave agency threatened the property regime both because it undermined an ideology based on white masters' control and because it violated the tenets of racial ideology that undergirded Southern plantation slavery in its last decades.

Judges outside of Louisiana recognized slave agency most directly in tort cases, in which a slaveholder sued another for damage to a slave when under the other's control. Most commonly, the defendant in such a case was an industrial hirer or a common carrier, usually a ferry boat. Common carriers were generally held responsible for damages to property on board, which they insured. In *Trapier v. Avant* (1827), in which Trapier's slaves had drowned crossing in Avant's ferry, the trial judge tackled the question of "whether negroes, being the property damaged, they should form an exception to the general rule of liability in the carrier." He determined that slaves should not be an exception. "Negroes have volition, and may do wrong; they also have reason and instinct to take care of themselves. As a general rule, human beings are the safest cargo, because they do take care of themselves." According to the judge, the humanity of the slaves did not present enough of a problem to alter the general property rule. "Did this quality, humanity, cause their death? certainly not – what was the cause? The upsetting of the boat. who is liable fore the upsetting of the boat? The ferriman; there is an end of the question." The dissenting judge, however, pointed out the problem created by slaves' human agency: if the slaves had run away or thrown themselves overboard before the ferryman had a chance to reach them, then holding Avant responsible would amount to converting his contract into a guarantee of the slaves' "good morals and good sense."[18]

In effect, not recognizing slaves as agents with free will meant holding all supervisors of slaves strictly liable for their character and behavior; recognizing slaves as agents, conversely, meant that supervisors were not required to "use coercion" to compel slaves' behavior. The first option created the equivalent of a warranty of moral qualities in the tort context, with all of its attendant difficulties. The second option threatened anarchy.

In the commercial, criminal, and family law contexts, courts wrestled with the dilemmas posed by human property. Lawyers and judges confronted slave resistance by promoting stories about the origins and development of slave character and behavior that removed rational agency from slaves. In this way, the law created an image of blackness as an absence of will, what Patricia Williams has called "antiwill."

Because the conflicts so often devolved into a debate over mutability or immutability of character, the focus inevitably shifted from slaves to masters. Mastery and the character of masters came into question directly under the dictum of "like master, like man," but indirectly as well in every decision about a slave's character that reflected in some way on her master's control, will, or honor. Northern abolitionists always said that the worst thing about slavery was how it depraved white men's character. Slaveholders defending slavery tried in various ways to disprove this accusation and even to show that white men improved their character through governing. By the final decades before the Civil War, most Southern slaveholders were keenly aware of the relationship between their role as masters and their character. The courtroom was one arena in which slaveholders and other white Southerners worked out their hopes and fears for themselves and their future.

II. SLAVERY, ANTI-SLAVERY, AND THE CONSTITUTION

Just as slavery was fundamental to the culture and economy of the South, slavery was pivotal to the compromises and conflicts of national politics throughout the early nineteenth century, and it was the central issue in the administration of a federal legal system. The constitutional compromise reached in 1787 did not hold. Increasingly, runaway slaves pressed

[18] *Trapier v. Avant*, Box 21, 1827, S.C. Sup. Ct. Records, South Carolina Department of Archives and History.

the legal system to confront the constitutional basis of slavery just as territorial expansion forced the political system to reckon with the conflict between slave labor and free labor. Pro-slavery and anti-slavery constitutional theories clashed as their advocates used the legal system to forward their political goals. The irreconcilability of their visions resulted in the ultimate constitutional crisis, civil war.

Anti-slavery constitutionalism faced an uphill battle in the American legal and political arena. From the controversy over anti-slavery petitions in Congress in the 1830s through the debates over fugitive slaves in legislatures and courts, radical abolitionist positions on the Constitution were increasingly marginalized. The contest over slavery became ever more the struggle of Northern whites to head off the "Slave Power's" threat to their own freedoms.

The Abolitionist Movement

The era between the American Revolution and the 1830s was the first great period of the abolitionist movement. The first white abolitionists were a group of Quaker lawyers in Pennsylvania who formed the Pennsylvania Abolition Society in 1775. These anti-slavery advocates were elite white men who worked within the political and legal system to achieve the gradual abolition of slavery. They used a variety of tactics, including petitioning state legislatures and Congress regarding specific issues, such as the domestic slave trade and slavery's westward expansion, and litigating cases of kidnapped free blacks or runaway slaves.

Although the lawyers who defended fugitives tried to work within existing law, rarely making broad arguments about the constitutionality of slavery, their legal strategies did lay the groundwork for a broader attack on the institution. Through such litigation, as well as campaigns for the rights of free blacks in the North, anti-slavery lawyers developed the legal and constitutional arguments that became the basis for abolitionism after 1830.

The Pennsylvania Abolition Society lawyers hoped that a buildup of judicial victories, not landmark cases, would eventually result in the national obstruction of slavery. Numerous complaints from African Americans concerned about kidnapping drove the Society's legal strategy, which initially targeted loopholes and technicalities in Pennsylvania's own Gradual Abolition Act in order to free slaves within and outside the state. A number of legal mechanisms were available to protect black people within the state's borders. The most important writ in the anti-slavery arsenal was the "great writ" of habeas corpus. The writ de homine replegiando was also used to win the release of captured fugitives and to gain jury trials for them. These writs required the recipient to "deliver the body [of a detainee] before" a legal official. The writ de homine replegiando was even more useful than habeas corpus, however, because it required the fugitive to be released from custody until the resolution of the legal process. Abolitionist lawyers used these writs to fight for the freedom of individual slaves, case by case.

By contrast, black abolitionists developed strategies that sharply diverged from the legal activism of the early white abolitionists. Black anti-slavery activists used the early media, including pamphlets and newspapers, to appeal directly to the public, rather than merely lobbying and petitioning legislators. They also relied on social organizations such as churches and benevolent societies to disseminate information and build popular support. To further these activities, the American Society for the Free Persons of Color was formed in 1830, holding its first meeting in Philadelphia to discuss national tactics for combating racial prejudice and slavery.

By directly confronting the underlying racism of the colonization movement and demanding an end to slavery as well as rights for free blacks, black abolitionists spurred the advent of immediatism. White abolitionists in Massachusetts, especially William Lloyd Garrison and Amos Phelps, joined together with black activists to advocate "immediate" abolition and integration. Abolitionism stormed onto the national scene in the 1830s with the birth of a new national organization, the American Anti-Slavery Society. Two calls to action heralded the rise of militant anti-slavery: David Walker's 1829 *Appeal to the Colored Citizens of the World* and the first issue of William Lloyd Garrison's *Liberator*, on January 1, 1831. Walker's appeal exhorted African Americans to take up arms if necessary to fight slavery. In the inaugural issue of the *Liberator*, Garrison proclaimed, "I will not equivocate – I will not excuse – I will not retreat a single inch – AND I WILL BE HEARD."

The *Liberator* targeted all schemes for gradual emancipation, especially colonization. As criticisms of colonization's hypocrisy became more prevalent in the 1830s, many abandoned the movement and devoted themselves to immediatism: not only Garrison but Arthur and Lewis Tappan, Sarah and Elizabeth Grimke, Salmon P. Chase, Gerrit Smith, Theodore Dwight Weld, and many others. Black abolitionists had called for immediate abolition before the 1830s, but it was the trends among white abolitionist leaders in that decade that made immediatism a force in national politics.

The new wave of abolitionists fought for an end to segregated schools and other institutions within Northern states – winning important victories in Massachusetts – and began calling for mass action against slavery in the South. They drew in blacks and whites, women and men, establishing for the first time in an integrated movement. This new strategy of mass action revolutionized the legal work and legislative petitioning of early abolitionists. While abolitionists continued to represent fugitive slaves and to petition legislatures, they refused to obey "political roadblocks or legal limitations" as their predecessors had. Instead they "used the people to circumvent the obstacles to abolition." Huge crowds of citizens who showed up at a trial might successfully keep a fugitive slave from being retried or "upset the cool course of the law [by] making an 'audience' for the judge and lawyers to contend with."[19] The American Anti-Slavery Society grew quickly in the 1830s, establishing 1,600 auxiliary branches by 1837 and collecting more than 400,000 signatures during the following year on anti-slavery petitions to Congress.

Southerners took the groundswell of 1830s abolitionism seriously. In response to the flood of anti-slavery petitions arriving on Congress's steps, Southerners responded with their own fierce legal and extra-legal action. A mob in Charleston, South Carolina, seized mail sacks containing American Anti-Slavery Society literature and burned them. John C. Calhoun endorsed a bill to prohibit the mailing of any publication "touching on the subject of slavery" to anyone in a slave state. These efforts to squelch free speech regarding slavery culminated in the "gag rule" controversy, in which Calhoun introduced numerous resolutions attempting to force the Senate's refusal of anti-slavery petitions.

Yet only a few years later, in 1840, the American Anti-Slavery Society split into factions, the political abolitionists forming the Liberty Party to directly effect their anti-slavery aims through political means and the Garrisonians continuing to insist that change could best be effected through public opinion. "Let us aim to abolitionize the consciences and hearts of the people, and we may trust them at the ballot-box or anywhere," declared Garrison.[20] During the 1840s, three anti-slavery groups emerged from the schism within the abolitionist movement, each with a different constitutional theory.

Pro-Slavery and Anti-Slavery Constitutional Theories

Of all of the constitutional theories of anti-slavery, the one that had the most in common with Southern perspectives on the Constitution was that of the ultra-radical William Lloyd Garrison. Southerners made the sound constitutional argument that the compact would never have been made if it did not recognize and support slavery; that the freedom of whites had been based on the enslavement of blacks, and that the Constitution protected property rights in slaves. Garrison declared the Constitution to be "a

[19] Richard S. Newman, *The Transformation of American Abolitionism: Fighting Slavery in the Early Republic* (Chapel Hill, NC, 2002), 144–45.

[20] *The Liberator*, March 13, 1840.

covenant with death, an agreement with hell" precisely for the reason that it *did* sanction slavery. Garrisonians, including Wendell Phillips, believed that slavery could not be overthrown from within the legal and constitutional order; extra-legal means would be required. Beginning in the 1840s, Garrison moved from his anti-political perfectionism to a constitutional program of disunion through secession by the free states and individual repudiation of allegiance to the Union.

Garrison's remained a minority perspective among abolitionists, but it was in some ways the most prescient view. Political and legal action within the constitutional system continued to be a dead end for abolitionists, who were continually put on the defensive by ever more aggressive and overreaching pro-slavery political forces wielding dubious theories of "nullification" – that the Constitution was a compact between states, which could "nullify" or withdraw from the compact whenever they chose.

The political appeal of the Southern rights argument to Southern nonslaveholders depended on several linked ideas, some of which also had resonance in the North, notably the notion of white man's democracy – that having a black "mudsill" class made possible greater equality among whites. Other Southern arguments, however, confronted the North and West with what looked like implacably expansionist claims, based in part on fear of what the South would be like without slavery – the threat that without the ability to expand its socioeconomic system into the territories, the South would be doomed to second-class citizenship and inequality in a Union dominated by an alliance of Northern and Western states. Under these conditions, Northerners for their part grew fearful that an expansionist octopus-like "Slave Power" would overwhelm and consume the free-labor North.

Within anti-slavery politics, radical constitutional abolitionists such as Frederick Douglas and Lysander Spooner began to argue after 1840 that, rather than endorse slavery, the Constitution in fact made slavery illegitimate everywhere, in the South as well as in the territories. Theirs was a minority position that relied on a textual reading of the Constitution, arguing that the document nowhere explicitly sanctioned slavery and that the "WRITTEN Constitution" should not be "interpreted in the light of a SECRET and UNWRITTEN understanding of its framers." The radicals argued that the federal government should abolish slavery in the states because it violated the Fifth Amendment due process guarantee, the Article IV guarantee of republican government, and other clauses of the Constitution. Spooner and Douglas also made originalist arguments about the founders' intentions to have slavery gradually wither away. They claimed that the slavery clauses of the Constitution had been written in such a way as to offer no direct support to the institution, even while satisfying its supporters in the short term. According to this view, the Constitution had become perverted by acquiescence in pro-slavery custom, but its anti-slavery character could be redeemed by federal action: "The Constitution is one thing, its administration is another. . . . If, in the whole range of the Constitution, you can find no warrant for slavery, then we may properly claim it for liberty." Finally, the radicals relied on a natural law interpretation of the Constitution, insisting that it had to be read side by side with the Declaration of Independence and given the meaning that best expressed the ideals of the Declaration.[21]

The most popular anti-slavery position, held by moderate abolitionists like Salmon P. Chase, posited that the federal government lacked power over slavery, whether to abolish it where it existed or to establish it anew anywhere. Drawing on Lord Mansfield's famous decision in *Somerset's Case* (1772), they argued that slavery was established only by positive law and only existed in those places (the South) where it had been so created. The political theory that went along with this constitutional theory was that of "divorcement," the idea that slavery was dependent on support by the federal government and would wither away if separated from it. By 1845, divorce had given way to Free Soil, which in effect fully applied *Somerset* to American circumstance. This was the idea embodied in the Wilmot Proviso of 1846; it eventually became the Republican Party platform and the argument of Lincoln in his debates with Stephen Douglas. It was opposed by Douglas, whose theme of "popular sovereignty" held each new state could decide for itself whether to be slave or free. The Compromise of 1850 and the Kansas-Nebraska Act of 1854 embodied popular sovereignty's emphasis on state-by-state decision making, leading to terrible civil wars in the territory of Kansas between rival pro-slavery and anti-slavery governments, each with its own constitutions.

All of these constitutional theories came into direct conflict in a series of legal confrontations involving two sets of issues: the fate of fugitive slaves in free states and territories and the future of the territories themselves. The first set of controversies, regarding fugitive slaves, came to a head largely in state legislatures and courts, as Northern legislatures sought to protect fugitives and both Northern and Southern courts wrestled with the interpretation of those statutes and of the Fugitive Slave Laws passed by Congress to implement the Constitution's Fugitive Slave Clause. The second set of dilemmas, regarding the status of slavery in the Western territories, played out in Congress and in presidential politics in a series of short- (and

[21] Frederick Douglass, "The Dred Scott Decision: Speech at New York, on the Occasion of the Anniversary of the American Abolition Society," reprinted in Paul Finkelman, ed., *Dred Scott v. Sandford: A Brief History with Documents* (New York, 1997), 177, 181.

shorter) lived compromises. The two sets of controversies culminated and merged in the dramatic and infamous Supreme Court case of *Dred Scott v. Sandford* (1857), which represented the ultimate constitutionalization of political conflict – a case that the Supreme Court meant to resolve the conflict conclusively, but instead helped pave the way for war.

Personal Liberty Laws and the Rights of Fugitives in the North

Many slaves ran away, some with help from whites and free blacks; the so-called Underground Railroad had an estimated 3,200 active workers. It is estimated that 130,000 refugees (out of 4 million slaves) escaped the slave South between 1815 and 1860. By the 1850s, substantial numbers of Northerners had been in open violation of federal law by hiding runaways for a night. By running away, slaves pushed political conflict to the surface by forcing courts and legislatures to reckon with the constitutional problems posed by slaves on free soil. Later, during the war, slave runaways would again help force the issue by making their own emancipation militarily indispensable.

Southern slaves in the North – whether visiting with their masters or escaping on their own – raised a difficult issue of comity for the courts to resolve. Even so-called sojourning slaves could be considered free when they stepped onto free soil. The question of whether the Northern state should respect their slave status or whether the Southern state should bow to the rule became a heated issue throughout the states.

The state courts reached different answers to the question. The best precedent from the abolitionist standpoint was a Massachusetts case decided by Chief Justice Lemuel Shaw in 1836, *Commonwealth v. Aves*. Citing *Somerset's Case*, Shaw wrote that slavery was "contrary to natural right and to laws designed for the security of personal liberty." Therefore, any "sojourning" slave who set foot on Massachusetts soil became free; fugitives were the only exception. But *Aves* represented the peak of anti-slavery interpretation of comity. By the end of the 1830s, any agreement in the North about the obligations of free states to return slaves to Southern owners had dissipated. States had given divergent answers on the questions of whether legislation was necessary to secure the rights of masters and whether states could or should provide jury trials to alleged slaves.[22]

From the 1830s until 1850, many Northeastern states tried to protect Northern free blacks from kidnapping by slave catchers and to provide some legal protections for escaped slaves who faced recapture in the North. In most of New England, New York, New Jersey, and Pennsylvania, legislatures

[22] 35 Mass. 193 (1836).

passed personal liberty laws to limit the recovery of fugitive slaves from within their boundaries by forbidding the participation of state authorities or the use of state property in the capture of a fugitive. Other laws gave alleged runaway slaves procedural protections in court and created various obstacles to recovery by owners.

Some state statutes, such as that of Massachusetts, tied anti-kidnapping provisions to the writ of habeas corpus. One such law was the Pennsylvania personal liberty law, which gave rise to the famous Supreme Court case, *Prigg v. Pennsylvania* (1842). *Prigg* was a test case arranged by Pennsylvania and Maryland to determine the constitutionality of Pennsylvania's personal liberty law. For the Court, Justice Joseph Story held the Fugitive Slave Act of 1793 to be constitutional and therefore concluded that a Pennsylvania law prohibiting local collaboration with slave reclaimers was also unconstitutional. He read the Constitution with the assumption that the fugitive slave clause had been necessary to the compromise that secured the Union and the passage of the Constitution. Therefore, "seizure and recaption" of fugitive slaves was a basic constitutional right, and states could not pass laws interfering with that right. But *Prigg* left open important questions, some of which Story purported to answer only in dicta: Could states enact laws to obstruct recapture or provide superior due process to captured slaves? Did *Prigg* enshrine in American law, as Story later claimed, the *Somerset* principle that slavery was only municipal law? Justice Story's opinion argued that the power to pass legislation implementing the fugitive slave clause resided exclusively in Congress. Congress proceeded so to act in 1850, as part of the Compromise of 1850. For his part, Chief Justice Taney – concurring in *Prigg* – argued that the states, while they could not legislate to hinder recaption, could always enact measures to aid the rights of slaveholders to recapture fugitives.

Abolitionists were furious over the outcome in *Prigg*. Garrison wrote: "This is the last turn of the screw before it breaks, the additional ounce that breaks the camel's back!"[23] Yet many anti-slavery advocates used the essentially pro-slavery *Prigg* decision for their own purposes in the 1840s, picking up Story's hint that it could be read, or at least mis-read, to bolster the *Somerset* position, and insisting that free states must do nothing to advance slavery.

Northern states passed a new series of personal liberty laws in part out of increased concern for the kidnapping of free blacks given the lack of procedural protections in the 1850 federal Fugitive Slave Act, but also out of a growing defiance against the "Slave Power." For example, a new Pennsylvania Personal Liberty Law of 1847 made it a crime to remove a

[23] *The Liberator*, March 11, 1842.

free black person from the state "with the intention of reducing him to slavery" and prohibited state officials from aiding recaption. It reaffirmed the right of habeas corpus for alleged fugitives and penalized claimants who seized alleged fugitives in a "riotous, violent, tumultuous and unreasonable manner."[24] The Supreme Court overturned these laws in the consolidated cases of *Ableman v. Booth* and *United States v. Booth* in 1859, in an opinion by Justice Taney upholding the constitutionality of the 1850 Act and holding that a state could not invalidate a federal law.

Increasingly, slaveholding states specified that slavery followed a slave to free jurisdictions, whereas free states made the distinction between temporary sojourns, during which a slave retained slave status, and transportation to a free state or territory with the intent to remain, in which case the slave was emancipated. However, under the 1850 Fugitive Slave Law, blacks in any state, whether free or not, were in danger of being accused of fleeing from bondage. The law empowered court officials to issue warrants allowing alleged runaways to be turned over to any claimant with convincing evidence that the prisoner was a slave, without a trial. The law greatly enhanced slaveholders' power to recover their property anywhere in the country by annulling attempts by states to protect fugitives from recapture. Furthermore, the law allowed marshals to summon "bystanders" to help them, commanded "all good citizens" to "assist in the prompt and efficient execution of this law," and provided officials with an extra reward for determining the accused to be a fugitive.[25] Gangs of bounty hunters began kidnapping African Americans to sell southward. Captured blacks' opportunities to defend themselves were severely eroded. As many as 3,000 free blacks, fearing enslavement, headed for Canada, by the end of 1850. No longer could one be certain that free states were truly free; it now seemed to many Northerners as though the tentacles of the "Slave Power" reached to the Canadian border.

Comity – recognition of the validity of the laws of one state by the sovereign power of another – had seemed for a time to be a stable compromise between the rights of property and of liberty. Joseph Story wrote in 1834 that comity was rooted in "a sort of moral necessity to do justice, in order that justice may be done to us in return." Similarly, Cobb believed comity was necessary to "promote justice between individuals and to produce a friendly intercourse between the sovereignties to which they belong."[26] But that accommodation dissolved under the pressure of sectional conflict. Both

[24] Pennsylvania Session Laws, 1847, 206–08, "An Act to Prevent Kidnapping . . . and to repeal certain slave laws."
[25] 9 U.S. Statutes at Large 462–65 (1850), at 463.
[26] Joseph Story, *Commentaries on the Conflict of Laws* (Boston, 1846), 39–45; Cobb, 174.

Southern and Northern courts became increasingly aggressive. In *Lemon v. People* (1860), for example, New York's highest court freed a number of slaves who were merely in transit from Virginia to Texas on a coastal vessel and had docked briefly in New York City's harbor to refuel. Similarly, the Missouri Supreme Court, in *Scott v. Emerson* (1852), explained, "Times are not as they were when the former decisions on this subject were made. Since then not only individuals but States have been possessed of a dark and fell spirit in relation to slavery. . . . Under such circumstances it does not behoove the State of Missouri to show the least countenance to any measure which might gratify this spirit."[27] Missouri's refusal to apply principles of comity to the slave Dred Scott was ratified by the U.S. Supreme Court five years later.

Territorial Expansion

Just as the problem of fugitives increasingly brought sectional tension to the surface, so did the seemingly inevitable march of territorial expansion. Westward expansion of the United States raised the political question of whether slave or free states would dominate the Union. The Missouri Compromise of 1820 had decreed one new free state for each new slave state; Southerners worried about the balance of power in Congress between slave and free states. The succeeding decades saw a sequence of "compromises" struck, each lasting a shorter time than the previous one.

The Missouri Compromise admitted Maine as a free state and Missouri as a slave state and drew a line at the 36th parallel – all new states formed north of the line would be free, and all south would be slave. This was the most stable compromise of the antebellum period. It was upset by the annexation of Texas in 1846. Just three months after the start of the Mexican-American War, Congressman David Wilmot proposed an amendment to a military appropriations bill, which became known as the Wilmot Proviso. It would have barred slavery in all of the territories acquired from Mexico. Although the Proviso failed to pass, it marked the beginning of the Free Soil movement. Free Soilers wanted to check Southern power and keep slavery out of new territories to protect the "rights of white freemen" to live "without the disgrace which association with negro slavery brings on white labor." The Free Soil Party formed in 1848 to fight for free labor in the territories. Although the new party failed to carry a single state in the 1848 election, it did quite well in the North.

In the 1850s, "settlements" of the slavery question came fast and furious – each one settling nothing. The Compromise of 1850 resulted in the

[27] *Scott v. Emerson*, 15 Mo. 576, 586 *1852).

admission of California to the Union as a free state, while the other parts of the Mexican Territory came in under "popular sovereignty"; the slave trade was abolished in the District of Columbia; and the new, more stringent Fugitive Slave Law was passed. Under the 1850 law, suspected fugitives were denied the right to trial by jury and the right to testify in their own behalf.

In 1854, Senator Stephen Douglas introduced a bill to organize the Kansas and Nebraska territories on the basis of popular sovereignty, officially repealing the Missouri Compromise. Douglas hoped that the Kansas-Nebraska Act would focus the Democratic Party on internal expansion and railroad building. Instead, the passage of the act split the Democratic Party along sectional lines and led to the formation of the Republican Party, which was a coalition of Northern Whigs, dissident Democrats, and Free-Soilers who first came together in Michigan and Wisconsin. The Republicans emphasized a platform of free soil and free labor for white men.

In 1856, violence broke out in Kansas: the "sack of Lawrence" by pro-slavery forces was followed by the civil war that became known as "Bleeding Kansas" and John Brown's massacre of slaveholders at Pottawatamie. Preston Brooks' near-fatal caning of abolitionist Senator Charles Sumner on the floor of the Senate coincided with the Lawrence attack. All these events convinced free-soil Northerners that the "Slave Power" had grown impossibly aggressive. Likewise, Southerners began to believe that abolitionists' tentacles were everywhere.

It was in this overheated atmosphere that the Supreme Court decided the *Dred Scott* case in 1857. Chief Justice Roger Taney apparently hoped that his opinion might settle these roiling constitutional controversies. Instead, he probably hastened the resort to armed conflict.

The Dred Scott Case

Dred Scott v. Sandford addressed a question of comity that was similar to but not the same as that raised by *Prigg v. Pennsylvania*. In *Dred Scott*, the issue was not the fate of a fugitive to a free state, but rather of a sojourner in a free territory. Territorial expansion raised the new question of whether slaves who moved into new territories should be presumed slave or free. Chief Justice Roger Taney's infamous decision in *Dred Scott v. Sandford* represented only the second time to that point that the Supreme Court had overturned an act of Congress, and it was seen by many at the time as the first shot fired in the Civil War. It was in reaction to the *Dred Scott* decision immediately following the Kansas-Nebraska Act that Abraham Lincoln declared, "A house divided against itself cannot stand."

The case's long legal odyssey began when Dred Scott's owner, John Emerson, took Scott out of Missouri, a slave state, to Illinois, a free state, and then to Minnesota Territory, a free territory. Emerson was an Army physician successively transferred to different stations. Scott's daughter was born somewhere on the Mississippi River north of Missouri, in either a free state or territory. Scott and his daughter returned to Missouri with Emerson, who died, leaving his wife a life interest in his slaves. Scott then sued for his freedom; he won in lower court in Missouri on comity grounds, supported by earlier Missouri precedent that a master voluntarily taking a slave for permanent residence in a free jurisdiction liberated the slave. However, in 1851, the Supreme Court decided *Strader v. Graham* (in an opinion by Taney), ratifying a turnaround in conflict-of-laws doctrine, whereby courts were to prefer the policy of the forum state – a holding first applied in Northern courts as anti-slavery doctrine, but one that Southern courts could use too.

When the Dred Scott case arrived at the Missouri Supreme Court, the Court applied Missouri law and found Scott to be a slave, noting that "[t]imes are not as they were when the former decisions on this subject were made." Sectional conflict had made comity impossible. Dred Scott found a new master, John Sanford (brother of the widow Emerson) and, in a collusive suit, sued for freedom from his new master in another state through a diversity suit in federal court. The federal district court found that Scott's status should be determined by Missouri law, which had already upheld his status as a slave, and he therefore remained a slave. Dred Scott appealed to the U.S. Supreme Court in December 1854, and the case was argued in February 1856. Interestingly, no abolitionist lawyers argued Scott's case. His attorney, Montgomery Blair, was a Free-Soiler concerned with the spread of slavery into the territories. George T. Curtis, who joined Blair for the December 1856 reargument of the case, was a political conservative opposed to anti-slavery but fearful that the Taney Court might overturn the Missouri Compromise and exacerbate sectional conflict.

The case presented two important questions. First, was Scott a citizen for purposes of diversity jurisdiction? Second, was Scott free because he had been taken into a free state and free territory? A third question, which could probably have been avoided, was whether Congress had the power to prohibit slavery in the territories. In other words, was the Missouri Compromise constitutional? In an era in which the Supreme Court usually strove for unanimity, there was little agreement on the Court on any one of these questions. The Court issued nine separate opinions in the case, including numerous overlapping concurrences and dissents, and many have argued that Taney's well-known opinion spoke for a majority of one. The opinions of Justice Daniel and Justice Campbell were, if such a thing is possible, even more extreme than Taney's. Nevertheless, Taney's high-handed effort to "settle" the sectional conflict on Southern terms certainly had a far-reaching influence.

The most infamous part of Taney's opinion was the first section, in which he held that Scott was not a citizen, because neither slaves nor free blacks could claim the privileges and immunities of citizenship. To reach this conclusion, Taney made an originalist argument that blacks were "not included, and were not intended to be included, under the word 'citizens' in the Constitution.... On the contrary, they were at [the time of the framing of the Constitution] considered a subordinate and inferior class of beings, who had been subjugated by the dominant race." In fact, blacks were "so far inferior that they had no rights which the white man was bound to respect." Even if some states, like Massachusetts, had bestowed rights on them, their state citizenship did not confer U.S. citizenship on them.

Taney might have stopped there, finding that Dred Scott had no right to sue in federal court and sending him back to Missouri court. Judge Nelson's concurrence argued more conservatively that slavery was a state question that should be (and had been) decided by the state of Missouri. But Taney was determined to answer the final question in the case, namely whether Congress could make a territory free by federal law. Taney held that the Missouri Compromise was unconstitutional and that the federal government lacked power over slavery except to protect property rights in slaves. He claimed that Article IV Sec. 3 of the Constitution, authorizing Congress to legislate for the territories, applied only to the public lands as they stood in 1789. According to this logic, the Northwest Ordinance was constitutional, but Congress had no power to legislate for the territories once people were able to legislate for themselves, reaffirming the "popular sovereignty" principle of the Kansas-Nebraska Act. A blistering, sixty-nine page dissent by Justice Benjamin Curtis attacked each and every one of Taney's premises. Curtis painstakingly recreated the history of free blacks in the late eighteenth century, showing that in a number of states, free blacks had been voters and citizens at the time of the founding. Curtis also argued forcefully that Congress had the right to regulate slavery.

Taney had hoped that his decision would lay to rest the political debate over slavery. He was not the only one to harbor this hope. In his inaugural address delivered just two days before the announcement of the decision, Democratic President-elect James Buchanan observed pointedly that the issue of slavery in the territories was "a judicial question, which legitimately belongs to the Supreme Court of the United States," to whose decision he would "cheerfully submit."[28] Many observers saw this agreement between Taney and Buchanan as more than happenstance – in fact, as a conspiracy.

[28] James Buchanan, Inaugural Address, March 14, 1857, in James D. Richardson, ed., *A Compilation of the Messages and Papers of the Presidents* (New York, 1897), 6:2962.

In his opening campaign speech to the Illinois Republican convention in 1858, Lincoln pointed to the fact that the *Dred Scott* decision was

> held up . . . till *after* the presidential election . . . Why the *outgoing* President's felicitation on the indorsement? Why the delay of a reargument? Why the incoming President's *advance* exhortation in favor of the decision? . . . We can not absolutely *know* that all of these exact adaptations are the result of preconcert. But when we see a lot of framed timbers, different portions of which we know have been gotten out at different times and places and by different workmen – Stephen, Franklin, Roger and James, for instance – and when we see these timbers joined together . . . in *such* a case, we find it impossible to not *believe* that Stephen and Franklin and Roger and James all understood one another from the beginning, and all worked upon a common *plan* or *draft* . . . [29]

Of course, the decision could not have had less of the effect Taney hoped for it. Frederick Douglass declared that his "hopes were never brighter than now," after the decision came down, because he believed it would incite the North to take a firmer stand against slavery. *Dred Scott* almost certainly contributed to the election of Abraham Lincoln in 1860 and the onset of the Civil War the following year.

Dred Scott was never overruled by the Supreme Court, although the Thirteenth and Fourteenth Amendments, passed by Congress in 1865 and 1868, ended slavery and guaranteed civil rights for African American citizens. Justice Frankfurter was once quoted as saying that the Supreme Court never mentioned *Dred Scott*, in the same way that family members never spoke of a kinsman who had been sent to the gallows for a heinous crime.

CONCLUSION

On the eve of the Civil War, slavery was a system that functioned quite smoothly on a day-to-day level. Law helped the institution function – enforcing contracts, allocating the cost of accidents, even administering sales. Slaves who fought back against their masters could sometimes influence the outcome of legal proceedings, and their self-willed action posed certain dilemmas for judges who sought to treat them solely as human property. But the legal system developed doctrines and courtroom "scripts" that helped erase evidence of slaves' agency and reduce the dissonance between what the ideology of white supremacy dictated relations between slaves and masters ought to be and what had actually transpired among slaves, slaveholders and non-slaveholders to bring them into the courtroom.

[29] Abraham Lincoln, Illinois State Journal, June 18, 1858, reprinted in Paul M. Angle, *Created Equal? The Complete Lincoln-Douglas Debates of 1858* (Chicago, 1958), 1–9.

Ultimately, it was politics that destroyed slavery. Slaves helped push sectional conflict over slavery to the surface by running away. Fugitive slaves forced the legal system to confront the issue of comity as well as the problem of territorial expansion. And because, in the United States, all major political conflict is constitutionalized, although slavery did not lead to a crisis in law, it did create a crisis for the Constitution. The Civil War was the constitutional crisis that could have ended the brief experiment of the United States. Instead, it led to a second American Revolution, a revolution as yet unfinished.

10

THE CIVIL WAR AND RECONSTRUCTION

LAURA F. EDWARDS

The Civil War and Reconstruction utterly transformed American society. Historians argue over the nature and extent of the changes wrought during the period, but there is little disagreement over the importance of the period as such: if nothing else, the sheer volume of scholarship establishes that point. Textbooks and college-level survey courses usually break with the Civil War and Reconstruction, which provide either the ending for the first half or the beginning of the second half. Books debating the causes of the war and its implications line the library shelves and are fully represented in virtually every historical subfield: party politics, ideology, religion, the economy, slavery, race and ethnicity, the status of women, class, the West, the South, religion, nationalism and state formation, as well as law and the Constitution. Other historical issues dating from the American Revolution to the present are linked to this period as well – historians look back to the nation's founding for the war's roots and then trace its effects into the present.

Rather than focusing on the war years or their immediate aftermath, legal historians have tended to concentrate on matters linked to it, before and after. Particular emphasis has been given to the perceived limits of the U.S. Constitution in diffusing the issues that led up to war and to the changes that occurred in federal law afterward, although a considerable body of work examines the legal implications of policy changes in the Union during the war as well. The first group of professional historians to consider these issues had been raised in the bitter aftermath of the war, and their work reflected that background. This group – influenced by the Dunning school, after its intellectual mentor, William A. Dunning, a professor at Columbia University – deemed Reconstruction an unmitigated failure. Although the work of Dunning school historians ranged widely in focus, they singled out legal changes at the federal level – specifically, the Thirteenth, Fourteenth, and Fifteenth Amendments – for particular opprobrium. Open apologists for white supremacy, these historians argued that the amendments constituted an illegal usurpation of state authority and led the country to the brink of chaos: by imposing the will of a radical minority and granting rights to African American men who were incapable of exercising them, the results destroyed the South and jeopardized the nation's future. Inflammatory today because of its open racism, Dunning School scholarship actually reflected a reconciliation among whites, North and South, at the beginning of the twentieth century. It assumed a consensus on racial issues in all sections of the country. The war and, particularly, its aftermath could thus be characterized as an avoidable aberration, the work of radical elements in the North who captured the national stage and forced their wild schemes on an unsuspecting populace.

The Dunning school has had a remarkably long purchase on the scholarship of the period, including legal history. The aftershocks of World War II, when the scope of the Holocaust was revealed, dealt a final blow to its overtly racist props. But its themes continued to define the basic questions about legal change: Was the Civil War inevitable, within the existing constitutional framework? To what extent did postwar policies alter fundamentally the legal order of the nation?

Later historians writing in the shadow of the civil rights movement addressed those questions by focusing on Reconstruction's promise of full civil and political equality to African Americans. One strand of the scholarship has emphasized the failures. A combination of judicial foot-dragging and political maneuvering turned back the clock nearly to where it had been before the war. Not only were white Southerners allowed to regain control, they were also allowed – even encouraged – to ignore new federal law and to create a new racial system that closely resembled slavery. To make matters worse, federal courts then turned to the Fourteenth Amendment to buttress the position of corporations at the expense of labor, creating new inequalities from the very laws that were intended to promote greater equality.

Where some historians have seen a glass half empty, others have seen it half full. Federal policy, particularly the Fourteenth Amendment, was a "second American revolution" that provided the constitutional basis to fulfill at last the promises of the first. Progress came slowly, culminating only in the mid-twentieth century with the civil rights movement. But those changes never would have been realized at all had it not been for the policies of the Reconstruction era.

The tendency to see Reconstruction as an era that promised great legal change has spilled over into the scholarship on the Civil War. Recent histories have treated the war as if it were inevitable, a fight that had to be waged to clear the way for what came next. They characterize the conflict as the collision of two distinct social orders, each with different conceptions of individual rights, the role of law, and the reach of the state. Only one could survive. One body of scholarship has focused on the dynamics leading up the war, with an eye toward explaining why conflicts reached the point where the existing institutional order could no longer contain them. This work has pointed to inherent weaknesses attributable to the Constitution, particularly the lack of authority at the federal level, which short-circuited the development of a strong, effective nation-state. Those weaknesses not only contributed to the outbreak of the war but they also presaged problems that the reconstructed nation would need to address afterward. Another body of scholarship has looked to the war years more directly as a precursor to Reconstruction, examining wartime policies within the Union and the Confederacy to contextualize postwar policies and reactions to them. This work has tended to emphasize change rather than continuity by showing how the war, itself, took the nation in new legal directions.

Most work undertaken within the field of legal history has focused on the national level, exploring mandarin policy debates and then tracing the effects through the states and, from there, to people's lives. This scholarship treats causation as a process that works from the top down, with the most momentous changes emanating from the three branches of the national government. Lately, though, a body of work has emerged that not only expands the field of vision to include law at the state and local levels but also locates the sources of change outside the federal government. Not all of this work falls within the field of legal history, at least as traditionally conceived: it is to be found in women's, African American, labor, and Southern history and is inspired by the approaches used in social, cultural, and economic history. Nevertheless, this body of scholarship both engages questions that have been central to legal history and highlights the legal component of issues not usually considered in that field. As this work shows, the war opened up a series of debates about the location of legal authority and the daily operation of law. It also reveals that legal change flowed from below as well as above, directed by the actions of ordinary people in all sections of the country who confronted questions about law in the course of the war and its aftermath. The theoretical implications of federal law filtered through the courts, but the practical application occurred in local areas, both North and South. That dynamic drew ordinary Americans further into conflicts about the operation of law, its scope, and its ends.

Here, I unite the traditional work of legal history with the new approaches that contemplate law from the perspective of social, cultural, and economic history. I develop one central argument: the Civil War forced the nation to confront slavery. The implications of that confrontation reached beyond the status of former slaves to transform law and legal institutions in ways that affected all the nation's citizens. I begin with the Civil War itself, focusing on changes during the war years that took the nation in new legal directions afterward. In both the Union and Confederacy, many wartime policies addressed immediate concerns and were not intended as reforms to law or the legal system. Yet, whether explicitly intended to change law or not, wartime policies laid the groundwork for profound changes in the legal order afterward.

The second section turns to Reconstruction, but takes the analysis beyond the brief formal span of that period and into the last decades of the nineteenth century. Here I trace the legal difficulties presented by emancipation, which necessitated the integration of a formerly enslaved population into the legal order. I look beyond federal cases resulting from the Reconstruction amendments and other national legislation for signs of what Reconstruction meant at the state and local levels. An exclusive focus on the federal level can understate the extent of change in this period by characterizing the problem as one of establishing and implementing the civil and political equality of African Americans *within* the existing legal order. As difficult as that was, the issues become more problematic when considered in the context of states and localities. Events at these levels reveal that the extension of rights to African Americans required structural change in the logic and institutions of law. The implications reached out in unpredictable directions, involving issues seemingly unconnected to the war and people whose legal status was not directly affected by Reconstruction policies.

I. THE CIVIL WAR

From the outset, questions about law, particularly the location of legal authority, were central to the Civil War. Secessionists, of course, asserted state sovereignty over most legal issues. At the outbreak of the war, debates over states' rights had become inextricably tied to sectional differences connected to slavery. Those claiming to represent "the South" advocated an extreme states' rights position, whereas their counterparts from "the North" predicted the end of the Union should such a view prevail. Yet the polarized rhetoric overstated the differences between the two sections. It also oversimplified the underlying issues by conflating questions about governing structures with disagreements over the content of the resulting decisions. Those issues centered on federalism – the relative balance of legal authority between states and the federal government. Federalism had not always divided the nation into opposing geographic sections. At the time of the nation's founding, for instance, Southern slave holders were among those advocating a stronger federal government. In 1832, during the Nullification Crisis, most Southern political leaders still rejected the extreme states' rights position of South Carolina radicals. Even in subsequent decades, as states' rights became a lightning rod for sectional differences, the rhetoric did not accurately describe federalism's practical dynamics, to which the balance of state and federal authority was as much a means as an end. Political leaders shifted back and forth, depending on the particular issue. Stances on the Fugitive Slave Act (1850) and the U.S. Supreme Court's decision in *Dred Scott* (1857) are representative. Many Northerners opposed both as illegitimate encroachments on states' established purview over the legal status of those who lived within their borders. Many Southerners supported them as necessary means to uphold property rights, as established in their own states and threatened by other states' laws. However heated, debates remained possible as long as both sides accepted the legitimacy of the existing legal order. The breaking point came when Southern political leaders rejected that order. Political leaders remaining in the Union did not, nor did they seek fundamental change in it.

Yet, change is what resulted, on both sides of the conflict. Recent research has focused on the Union, particularly the dramatic increase in federal control over issues that previously had rested with states, local areas, and individuals. Scholars have shown how the evolution of policy in the Union during the Civil War laid the groundwork for the dramatic legal changes of Reconstruction. Their analyses also tend to echo the terms of contemporary debate, namely that centralization would remove law from the people. Yet, tracing the implications beyond the federal arena suggests additional layers to the issue. In daily life, the results of increased federal authority were more ambiguous, altering people's relationship to law in unforeseen ways. In those areas occupied by the Union Army, for instance, federal presence actually had democratizing tendencies. In other policy realms traditionally considered as attempts to increase opportunities for ordinary Americans – such as the transcontinental railroad and the opening of Western lands – federal policies had very different effects.

Historians have not considered Confederate policies to have had the same kind of long-term impact on the nation's legal order as those of the Union. That conclusion is understandable, in the sense that Confederate laws were fleeting products of a short-lived political experiment. Even so, their implications were still lasting, because states' rights led in two, contradictory directions that left deep trenches in Southern soil. Conducting a war to establish states' rights required a centralized, federal government. By the end of the war, the Confederate national government actually had assumed far more authority than the U.S. government ever had, at least on paper. In practice, however, the continued commitment to states' rights undercut the central government's legitimacy and tied it up in controversy. The upheaval of war, which was fought primarily on Confederate soil, further undermined the legitimacy of government at all levels. It was not just the war, moreover, that produced conflicts over law. Different people had long defined law in their own terms: the dislocation of wartime provided opportunities for those differences to emerge. The result was a radical decentralization of legal authority that went far beyond what states' rights advocates ever imagined or desired. The end of the war may have led to the collapse of both the Confederate government and the legal order that it tried to create. But the conflicts generated by that government and its policies defined the postwar years.

The Union

In mobilizing to defend the existing legal order, those in the Union ended up changing it. As often has been the case in U.S. history, war went hand in hand with an increase in federal authority. Abraham Lincoln began using the open-ended nature of presidential war powers almost immediately in his efforts to hold the border states of Maryland, Kentucky, and Missouri in the Union. He suspended civil rights, threatened martial law to force votes against secession, and then forestalled further conflict through military occupation. Lincoln continued to make liberal use of presidential powers throughout the war. In 1862, he announced that anyone who resisted the draft, discouraged others from enlisting, or was deemed disloyal to the Union war effort would be subject to martial law. That meant dissenters would be tried in military courts rather than in state or local courts, where juries might be more sympathetic. He also suspended constitutional guarantees, such as the writ of habeas corpus, thereby closing off the means by which those arrested through executive order could contest imprisonment. Executive authority expanded in other directions as well, particularly through the draft and the War Department. While the draft represented a major encroachment by the federal government on the rights of its citizens, the War Department became a model for modern bureaucracy, as it developed an elaborate structure to manage those drafted into the military and to oversee occupied areas.

Congressional Republicans followed suit, extending the federal government's reach to wage war more effectively. Funding the army's operations required the complete overhaul of the nation's financial structure and the centralization of authority over it. Congress also enhanced federal power by expanding the scope of the judiciary. Concerns about dissent led to the Habeas Corpus Act of 1863, which enhanced the power of federal officials vis-à-vis the states and expanded the jurisdiction of federal courts. That same year, Congress also created the Court of Claims to settle claims against the U.S. government, which formerly had been settled in Congress. Claims multiplied exponentially as a result of the war.

Not all wartime initiatives, however, were connected to the war. Many were part of the Republican Party's political agenda, which advocated more federal involvement in the nation's economy. What Republicans hoped to accomplish was an extension of the existing economic and legal order to encompass the generality of the population. Their goal was evident in the party's slogan, "free soil, free labor, free men," evoking a polity based on independent producers along the lines of the Jeffersonian ideal. In that ideal, male farmers and artisans owned the means of production (land or the tools of their trade), which allowed them to direct their own labor and that of their families. Male economic independence then grounded the legal order, because it entitled men to rights: access to the legal system through full civil rights as well as the ability to alter and create law through political rights. Economic independence thus secured the entire nation's future by ensuring a responsible, engaged citizenry, who were equal before the law.

Like most ideals, this one was more consistent in theory than in practice. Despite the rhetorical emphasis on equality, inequality was integral to it. By the 1850s, most adult white men could vote and claim the full array of civil rights on the basis of their age, race, and sex. But for others, age, race, and sex resulted in inequalities. The legal status of male, independent producers, for instance, assumed the subordination of all domestic dependents – wives, children, and slaves – to a male head of household and the denial of rights to them. Free African Americans were included in theory but not in practice. The free black population had increased in the decades following the Revolution, with abolition in Northern states, the prohibition of slavery in many Western territories, and individual emancipations in the South. State and local governments had responded by replacing the disabilities of slavery with restrictions framed in terms of race. Even for free white men, the ideal of economic independence and legal equality had never fully described reality. For many, economic independence had been difficult to achieve. Their situation deteriorated as capitalist economic change intensified in the antebellum period, for those changes eroded the link between economic independence and legal rights as state legislatures uncoupled claims to rights from the ownership of productive property. Numerous legal restrictions still attached to those without visible means of support and even those who performed menial labor.

The theoretical link between economic independence and legal rights nonetheless persisted. If anything, its symbolic significance acquired more importance over time, as the Republican Party's popularity suggests. The notion of a republic of independent producers resonated widely and powerfully, even among those who did not enjoy its promises in their daily lives. Placing those promises at the center of its platform, the Republican

Party hoped to use federal power to create more independent producers and promote their interests.

Secession gave Republicans a decisive majority in Congress and the opportunity to act on this agenda, which they did, even as the war raged around them. With the 1862 Homestead Act, they opened up settlement of Western lands that had been tied up in sectional controversy. The act made land more readily available to individual farmers than previously. It also prohibited slavery, which Republicans deemed incompatible with the interests of independent producers. To encourage farmers' success, Congressional Republicans provided for the development and dissemination of new agricultural methods through the Land-Grant College Act and a new federal agency, the Department of Agriculture. Then they tied all these individual farms together in a national economic network with the Pacific Railroad Act, which subsidized construction of a transcontinental railroad. To bolster manufacturing, Congressional Republicans passed protective tariffs. Financial reforms that helped fund the war effort figured prominently as well. Many of those changes, including the creation of a unified national currency and a central bank, did for finance what the railroad did for transport, facilitating capital transfers and economic exchanges across the nation's vast expanses.

At their most idealistic, Republicans hoped that these economic programs would enhance individual rights, particularly those of free white male household heads. Yet, with the exception of Western settlers, few ordinary farmers, artisans, and laborers benefited from Republican economic programs. Republican initiatives instead fueled a competitive, national economy that swallowed up small, independent producers. Railroad corporations gained the most directly, pocketing millions of acres of public land and other federal incentives. Those who did own their farms or shops were no longer the kind of independent producers posited in the ideal. Cornelius Vanderbilt, for instance, hardly fit the category although he owned his own railroad "shop." But, then, neither did farmers who presided over large, mechanized enterprises, sold most of what they produced, and bought most of what they consumed.

The Republican economic future was one of wage labor, not independent producers. That created unforeseen contradictions, because the Republican legal order was still based on independent producers, not wage work. Wage laborers were included among the "free men" of Republican rhetoric, in the sense that they owned their own labor, could sell it at will, and could enjoy whatever they earned in doing so. If they were adult, white, and male, they also could claim full civil and political rights, at least in theory. But in practice, they were legally subordinate to their employers, who enjoyed rights as independent producers that wage workers did not. Property rights gave employers extensive authority over their factories. Those rights extended over laborers while they were on the job, where they could do little to alter working conditions on property that was not their own. In this context, the legal equality that wage workers theoretically enjoyed as citizens could actually compound their subordination: in law, Vanderbilt and his employees were equal, preventing legal intervention on employees' behalf; while as a property owner, Vanderbilt could do whatever he wished with his property, preventing legal intervention on employees' behalf.

Many Republicans' reluctance to expand federal authority beyond its traditional bounds compounded these problems. They were comfortable using federal power to promote economic growth, the principle of equality before the law, and the Union. But they were unwilling to use it to address the inequalities that resulted in practice, whether economic or legal. Doing so, they argued, pushed centralization too far and threatened individual liberty.

That stance shaped popular perceptions of the federal government during the Civil War. Despite Republican intentions to distribute existing economic opportunities and legal rights more broadly, at least among the free white male population, most ordinary Northerners actually experienced federal authority through the draft, taxes, and military service. Those encounters were not always positive, even for those who supported the war effort: the federal government did not give; it took – resources and lives. It offered little in return, other than rhetorical promises of freedom and equality. That situation only reinforced existing suspicions of centralized authority and limited possibilities for its future use.

Slaves and the Future Legal Order of the Union

The Republican Party's reluctance to use federal authority to rectify inequalities among individuals carried over into slavery. Although most Republicans opposed slavery, not all advocated its abolition in those areas where it already existed. Only a small minority favored the extension of full civil and political rights to former slaves – and many of those were free blacks who identified with the Republican Party but could not vote because of racial restrictions on suffrage in their states. Many Republicans considered any intervention in slavery to be a dangerous projection of federal authority onto the states and a fundamental violation of individual property rights. That the federal government might go further, mandating the legal status of free blacks or anyone else, was not on the political horizon in 1860. Echoing the Republican Party's platform, Abraham Lincoln opposed only the extension of slavery in Western territories at the time of his election. Otherwise he promised to leave the regulation of slavery, where it already existed, to the states.

From the war's outset, free blacks in the North tried to turn the war for Union into one for the abolition of slavery and the legal equality of all free people, regardless of race. So did slaves in the Confederacy. Even before the states of the upper South seceded, slaves along the South Carolina coast began fleeing to U.S. naval vessels. By August 1861, several thousand were camping with General Benjamin Butler's army at Fortress Monroe, Virginia. Permanent U.S. posts in North Carolina, South Carolina, and Georgia early in the war made it possible for more African Americans to seize their freedom. Wherever Union troops went, slaves found them and followed them. They did so at great risk. Runaways faced execution if recaptured by Confederates and an uncertain future if they remained in Union camps.

African Americans' actions slowly pushed the military to intervene in slavery. At first, commanders did not really understand that escaped slaves expected freedom once they made it to Union lines. Many considered slaves either too stunted by the institution of slavery or too inferior racially to understand the concept of freedom, let alone to act so decisively to obtain it. Nor did Union officers know what to do with these refugees, since their own commander-in-chief, President Abraham Lincoln, still insisted that nothing would be done to interfere with slavery. In fact, the Fugitive Slave Law mandated that all runaways be returned. Existing law and Republican policy statements, however, did not anticipate the situation facing the Union armies. With thousands of African Americans crowding into Union camps and following federal troops, military officials had no choice but to adapt. Union commanders also saw the strategic benefits of harboring the enemy's slaves and were quick to appreciate the value of a ready labor supply for themselves. The specific policies, though, were uneven and ad hoc, because they were formulated by individual officials as part of their command. The use of federal authority thus resulted in a devolution of policy, allowing commanders the same discretionary power over slavery as they had over their troops and the areas they occupied.

Slavery collapsed far more slowly in federal law than it did in the areas occupied by federal troops. Forced to explain his decision to harbor slaves in legal terms, General Butler defined runaways as "contraband": property seized as a consequence of war. In August 1861, Congress validated Butler's position in the first Confiscation Act, which allowed for the seizure of all property used in support of the rebellion. But that designation also underscored the tenuous legal position of runaway slaves, who were still property, even behind Union lines. It was not until the spring of 1862, with the second Confiscation Act, that Congress recognized escaped slaves' freedom, declaring "contraband" to be "forever free." That act, however, also had distinct limits. It freed only specific individuals, as a temporary accommodation to the military crisis. As such, it did not imply fundamental change in slavery's legal status within the Union.

In 1862, Congressional Republicans moved closer to that kind of change, outlawing slavery in the District of Columbia and federal territories. But the Emancipation Proclamation, issued immediately afterward, stopped short of full abolition. It allowed slaveholders in the Confederacy to keep their slaves if their states returned to the Union within 100 days. If that did not happen, all slaves within the Confederacy would be free. Obviously, slaves had to leave to enjoy their freedom, since the Confederacy did not recognize U.S. authority. The Emancipation Proclamation thus encouraged slaves to do what they had been doing already. It solidified the freedom of those who escaped to Union lines. It also escalated the terms of the conflict, moving beyond the battlefield and making war on the Confederacy's basic social structures. But it left the institution of slavery legally in place. Slavery would retain its status in the United States until the passage of the Thirteenth Amendment, after the end of the war.

The legal status of former slaves remained even more ambiguous than that of the institution they fled. Wartime enactments that established their freedom did not specify what rights were included, but existing laws suggested definite limits on them. In 1862, Congress did pass a new Militia Act that allowed African Americans to serve in the military. Free blacks had lobbied hard for military service, seeing that as a key step in establishing full civil and political rights. But racial inequality followed them into the military. Nor did military service alter existing legal restrictions that proliferated in state and local laws. Following hard on the heels of abolition in Northern states, these measures reflected an enduring connection between racism and abolition. In the logic of the time, African Americans should not be enslaved, but their racial nature still made them inferior to whites and incapable of exercising civil or political rights responsibly, so restrictions were necessary to police them and to protect the larger public. In *Dred Scott*, the U.S. Supreme Court pushed the argument one step further, denying all people of African descent citizenship in the nation. The implications of *Dred Scott* were unclear, precisely because questions about the specific civil and political rights of citizens previously had been left to the states. It was also controversial for the same reasons. But all those ambiguities resulted in the continuation of existing restrictions on free blacks, not the dismantling of them.

In occupied areas, the military took over where states left off. The rights that escaped slaves could claim varied widely, depending on the specific commander, but military policies that applied to all commands significantly circumscribed the range of possibilities. The system of compulsory labor was particularly important. Military officials considered such a coercive system consistent with free labor in the sense that former slaves entered into contractual agreements and were compensated for their labor. The logic reflected fundamental assumptions about the individual rights of wage workers within a free labor system more generally: freedom was not measured in terms of either the circumstances that brought a person into a labor contract or the terms of that contract, but in the ability to contract. Advocates of free labor, moreover, expected force in establishing such a system: people unused to it would have to be coerced into labor contracts and subjected to harsh contractual terms, until they understood its dynamics and accepted its benefits. Racism tended to narrow this vision still further. Many free labor proponents in the Union believed that former slaves might eventually internalize the values that made reliable, manual workers, if instructed properly and carefully. But until then, they needed to be kept in line – by whatever means necessary. In fact, some doubted that former slaves would ever learn and saw legal coercion as an essential, permanent component of freedom.

Most people in the Union did not expect the Civil War's outcome to be abolition or the structural legal changes that came with it. When the federal government mandated the end of slavery, it extended its authority over all states in the Union, not just those in the former Confederacy. Republicans had proposed greater use of federal authority to promote economic growth. They also accepted the necessity of federal power to conduct the war effort. But abolition upset the legal order far more, bringing the federal government into issues of individual rights, an area that formerly had been left to the states. Abolition also opened up more questions than it resolved about both the status of former slaves and the extent of federal authority over all the nation's citizens. Would the changes represented by abolition be temporary or permanent? A return to the terms that existed before the war would give Confederate states the ability to define and direct their postwar social order. Yet many on the Union side were reluctant to extend the scope of federal authority. They had gone through the war to preserve, not to change the polity they had known.

The Confederacy

Unlike those who remained in the Union, Confederates rejected the nation's existing legal order. Rejection, however, did not necessarily imply radical change. Perhaps the most graphic example is the Confederate Constitution, which duplicated much of what it purported to replace. The Confederate Constitution did limit the authority of the Confederate federal government in key areas by sanctioning slavery and forbidding Congress from making protective tariffs or launching internal improvements. But those limitations addressed substantive issues in the sectional conflict; they did not change the basic governing structures. Its guarantee of states' rights – by allowing for nullification along the lines claimed by South Carolina in 1832 – did constitute such a change, but that measure sat uneasily in a document otherwise identical to the U.S. Constitution and included the same open-ended balance between states and federal government.

Conflicts over the extent of federal authority, reminiscent of those within the United States before secession, emerged almost immediately. The demands of war complicated the conflicts, creating a situation particularly ill suited to a decentralized governing structure. The Confederacy lagged far behind the Union in almost every material measure of the ability to wage war – population, transportation, agricultural acreage, and manufacturing capacity. To marshal limited resources, the Confederate government, under President Jefferson Davis, extended federal authority in unprecedented directions, going well beyond what the Union ever did. The Confederacy enacted a national draft that forced most adult white men into military service. It gave its officials the right to appropriate private property for the war effort, stripping farms of livestock and provisions. That appropriation extended to slaves, whom Confederate officials impressed at will, often over their masters' protests. The Confederate government nationalized key segments of manufacturing and transportation to coordinate the military's movement and supply. Federal control extended to finance as well, where the Confederacy instituted national taxes and a national currency so that it could print what it could not collect from its citizens. Toward the end of the war, the Confederate Congress even approved a measure that would have enlisted and armed slaves in exchange for their freedom.

But the national government's power existed largely on paper. Its critics, who continued to stand by the principle of states' rights, were numerous and strident. Nor did they stop at words. State officials, notably Governors Joseph Brown of Georgia and Zebulon Vance of North Carolina, openly obstructed federal policies. Widespread popular perceptions of the national government's inefficiency and inadequacy intensified its precarious hold on authority. It failed to curb inflation, end scarcities, forestall the encroachment of Union troops, or otherwise justify the sacrifices it was demanding. Perhaps the most dramatic illustration of its lack of legitimacy was desertion. As the war dragged on, thousands of Confederate soldiers simply voted with their feet and went home. Efforts to force them back failed miserably. Confederate military officials who rode through the countryside hunting down the Confederacy's own citizens and pressuring women and children to reveal the whereabouts of neighbors and kin accomplished little other than the further erosion of faith in their government.

It was not just the national government that failed to establish its authority. The Confederacy descended into a chaos of competing governing bodies, in which everyone claimed to be in charge and no one could actually do much to resolve the crisis. Federal, state, and local officials levels fielded an endless, escalating series of complaints, few of which they were able to remedy. The respectful deference of early requests gave way to anger and contempt, as ordinary people lost confidence in the ability of government to hold society together or administer its rules fairly. Counties and municipalities provided some of the most important services, including poor relief and the resolution of most legal conflicts. But at the point when people needed those services the most, local governments literally crumbled. Not only were there no resources to distribute, there were not even enough men to fill the necessary positions and to keep up the semblance of order.

As the legal system ceased functioning, people took law into their own hands. The result was not always lawlessness. Instead, people acted on their own notions of justice, grounded in local values and suited to the situation at hand. People sheltered deserters and kept their whereabouts secret. They set up an underground economy invisible to outsiders, particularly those who wanted to collect taxes. They redistributed property to those who did not have enough, pilfering and in some cases openly appropriating goods. Poor whites moved onto lands abandoned by slaveholders who fled the approach of Union troops. Slaves who escaped or remained behind when their masters left also took over plantations, with the expectation of running them on their own.

But with no identifiable center of authority, conditions did degenerate into lawlessness. Guerilla war broke out in many areas of the Confederate home front, as ordinary people battled for the authority that the government could no longer command. In some places, the lines of demarcation were between Unionists and Confederates. In other places, though, opportunistic mobs ransacked the countryside, taking what they could and doing as they wished, regardless of political affiliation.

The collapse of slavery precipitated an equally profound legal crisis. In law, slavery was part of a system of governance that linked individuals to the state and defined their legal rights through their positions within households. Heads of household assumed moral, economic, and legal responsibility for all their domestic dependents, including African American slaves, white wives, and children. They also represented their dependents' interests in the public arena of politics. The position of household heads thus translated directly into civil and political rights. The exemplary household head was an adult, white, propertied male. As the logic went, these were the only people capable of the responsibilities of governance, whether in private households or public arenas. By contrast, white women and children and all African Americans were thought to require the protection and guidance of white men, because they lacked self-control and the capacity for reason. When slaves ran to Union lines they threatened the structural logic of this legal order. If masters could not control their dependents and dependents could leave at will to direct their own lives, the entire system was destabilized and the basis of all white men's rights undermined.

Aware of those dynamics and fearing the outcome, some Confederates demanded that troops be pulled from the front and stationed in local areas. Barring that, they asked that more white men be left on the home front. Although raising the specter of bloody slave revolts, these concerned Confederates also emphasized the basic connection between the maintenance of slavery and the Confederate social order. The Confederate government, however, privileged battles with the Union army over the battles with its own citizens unfolding on Southern plantations.

The Confederacy ended up losing in both arenas. Many die-hard Confederates had difficulty accepting General Robert E. Lee's surrender to General Ulysses S. Grant. But at least that side of the war did have an identifiable end. The other side of the war – the one that tore through the Confederate home front and ripped it apart – did not. Unresolved and largely relegated to a secondary position during the military conflict, those issues and their legal implications became the central focus in the next phase of the war.

II. RECONSTRUCTION

The end of slavery opened more questions than it resolved. The surrender of the Confederacy did not answer how those states would be rejoined to the Union. The collapse of the Confederate government did not erase memories of conflicts over the exercise of law in that region. The end of hostilities did not clarify whether the wartime authority acquired by the federal government would be kept or scaled back. Nor did emancipation define African Americans' status as free people.

These questions hung in the air, unanswered, at the time of Confederate surrender. Unknown, also, was how they would be resolved – specifically, how that would be done within the existing legal order and at which level. Ultimately, the integration of a formerly enslaved population into the polity required changes in the basic relations between the federal government and the states, as well as the legal status of all citizens, regardless of race. Even the Black Codes, the first infamous efforts to deal with the legal status of former slaves, entailed major legal alterations, although they were intended to duplicate elements of slavery. The Fourteenth and Fifteenth Amendments and other federal legislation went further, not only establishing the civil and political rights of former slaves but also recasting the rights of all citizens and the relationship between states and the federal government. At the same time, important legal continuities, evident in and accentuated by the war, ultimately limited the extent of these changes. So, too, did their implementation. In this sense, changes at the federal level constitute only the tip of the iceberg, although legal historians have tended to focus their attention there. Federal law opened the possibility for change only in theory. Reconstruction was not just an incomplete legal revolution, in the sense of awaiting a full interpretation and application of the law in the federal courts, as other historians have argued. It was incomplete in a more profound sense. As much as the new laws promised, they required the active participation of ordinary people to make the promises concrete – and that process was far more difficult than the passage of laws or even their legal interpretation in appellate decisions.

Re-Creating the Union

The specific rights of former slaves depended on the relation between the former Confederate states and the Union. According to Lincoln, the Confederate states technically remained in the Union during the war, because secession was legally impossible. The relationship between those states and the Union remained the same as it had always been. By this logic, the Confederate states would retain authority over the status of all those living within their borders, including former slaves.

Lincoln also maintained that decision-making power over the states of the former Confederacy lay with the president, in his capacity as commander and chief. Republican leaders in the U.S. Congress saw the issue differently. They argued that Confederate leaders had negated their states' relationship to the Union when they seceded and declared war. Now that the Union had defeated the rebellion, there were no longer states in that area, as there once had been. The Confederacy was instead defeated territory, under federal control. By this logic, then, the federal government could exercise extensive authority over the status of former slaves and that of everyone else in the former Confederacy as well. As the legislative body in the federal government, Congress would direct the project. Congressional Republicans' willingness to use federal authority signaled they embraced a more expansive vision of Reconstruction than Lincoln. For them, it was about the internal reconstruction of the former Confederate states, not just national reunion.

These questions were still being debated at the time of Lincoln's assassination, when Vice-President Andrew Johnson assumed the presidency. With the nation in turmoil and Congress in recess, Johnson moved unilaterally. Acting on the basics of Lincoln's logic, he tried to return the Union to what it had been before the war, with as few changes as possible. Specifically, he readmitted the states of the former Confederacy, once they had passed the Thirteenth Amendment, negated the ordinances of secession, and created new state constitutions in accordance with those principles. He did disfranchise high-ranking Confederate officials, but allowed for amnesty if they applied for it personally.

In the summer of 1865, while Congress was still in recess, the former Confederate states began reorganizing under Johnson's plan. The resulting state constitutions did withdraw the secession ordinances and abolished slavery, but otherwise left their states' basic structures of governance in place. They also included provisions that denied former slaves civil and political rights. Although the specific restrictions varied, African Americans had few rights beyond the ability to enter into contracts and gain access to the criminal and civil courts. Most states excluded them from juries, limited their testimony against whites, and required them to work, to carry passes from their employers, and to obtain permission when buying and selling property. The terms used to refer to African Americans are also suggestive. They were "negroes," "persons of color," men and women who were "lately slaves," and "inhabitants of this state." Although free, African Americans were not to be confused with other citizens. That fall, the Confederate states' new representatives took their seats in the U.S. Congress. In many instances, they were the same men who had been heading the Confederacy just a few months before. By Johnson's standards, the results were a success. National reunion was accomplished quickly and without radical change. By the standards of others within the Union, Johnson's plan was a disaster. The entire situation seemed like a blatant attempt to deny the outcome of the war: the same political leaders who had led their states out of the Union now guided them back, along paths largely of their own choosing.

As opposition mounted, an explosive political battle ensued between Congressional Republicans and President Johnson. Congressional Republicans ultimately wrested control over Reconstruction, nearly impeaching Johnson in the process. In 1867, they negated Johnson's plan, divided the former Confederacy into military districts, and placed them under federal authority. Confederate states would be reconstituted and readmitted to the Union only if they accepted major changes in their legal order, as mandated by Congressional Republicans. In addition to abolishing slavery and the nullification ordinances, those terms included the extension of full civil and political rights to African Americans. Specifically, the former Confederate states had to ratify the Fourteenth Amendment, which prohibited legal distinctions on the basis of race, religion, or previous servitude. Then they had to square their constitutions and their laws with those principles. The delegates charged with making these changes to their state constitutions had to be selected by an electorate that included African American men and excluded all high-ranking Confederate officials. Suffrage would be extended to others involved in the Confederacy only after they had sworn loyalty oaths. The Fifteenth Amendment, which protected political rights more specifically, was ratified soon thereafter, in 1868 when the newly reconstructed states were part of the Union.

At the same time, Congressional Republicans also shifted more authority to the federal courts, increasing their jurisdiction to counter the decisions of recalcitrant state courts that impeded the Reconstruction process. Building on the Habeas Corpus Act of 1863, Congress significantly extended the practice of "removal" in a series of measures culminating with the 1871 Voting Rights Act. Removal was a key weapon that Congressional Republicans used to combat Johnson's Reconstruction plan: it literally permitted the "removal" of cases languishing in obstructionist state courts of the former Confederacy to federal courts. Once the elements of Congressional Reconstruction were in place, removal provided the means for enforcing federal oversight of civil and political rights guaranteed in the Fourteenth and Fifteenth Amendments. Congressional Republicans buttressed removal with the 1867 Habeas Corpus Act, which expanded federal power by transforming the concept of habeas corpus into an open-ended writ that gave federal officials the broad authority to intervene in cases being tried in state court at any stage of the process.

Within the former Confederate states, the legal ramifications of Congressional Reconstruction also involved central questions about the institutional location of legal authority. In the slave states, the denial of civil and political rights to slaves had depended on their position within households. When emancipation formally released them from that relationship, it shattered both the conceptual logic and the material foundations of authority in these states. As free men, African American men could, theoretically, take on the role of household head with all its legal rights and public privileges. Similarly, African American women could now claim the rights previously reserved for white women as dependent wives and daughters. The implications extended to white men, who faced the loss of their property and, in the case of slaveholders, most of their dependents as well. Not only did the borders of their households shrink but the very basis of their authority there was called into question, a situation that also undermined their exclusive claims to legal rights and political power. The emancipation of slaves and the extension of rights to them formed an equation with two sides: changes for African Americans entailed changes for whites as well.

The results took concrete form at the constitutional conventions mandated under Congressional Reconstruction, where delegates created some of the most democratic state governments in the nation. In addition to extending full civil and political rights to African Americans, they opened up the legal system and government at both the state and local levels to whites of poor and moderate means. Over the next few years, the dynamics of governance were literally upended in the states of the former Confederacy. African Americans and poor whites prosecuted cases and sat on juries, participating directly in formal legal arenas. They elected local officials, such as sheriffs and magistrates, who played crucial roles in the administration of law. They also selected representatives to their legislatures, which solidified and built on the democratic changes in their states' constitutions. The extension of suffrage to African American men, in particular, turned former Confederate states with large black populations into Republican strongholds, supporting further legal change at the state and federal level in keeping with the spirit of Congressional Reconstruction – sometimes more so than in states that had remained in the Union.

African Americans and poor whites in the former Confederacy were not simply passive recipients of rights. They pushed the process of Reconstruction along locally by challenging the existing legal culture of their states. African Americans did so during the Civil War, when they ran from slavery to Union lines with the intent of defining their own lives as free people. They continued to do so under Johnson's Reconstruction plan, even though the Black Codes formally restricted their rights. The legal importance of their actions is not always obvious: mostly what they did was undertaken in pursuit of the ordinary business of daily life. But African Americans' actions acquire legal significance when seen against the backdrop of slavery, where slaves were denied "rights" so basic and so assumed by most white Americans that they did not seem to rise to the level of "rights" at all. The law did not recognize slaves' marriages, their claims to their own children, or their ownership of any property, including the clothes on their backs. The law mandated where slaves could go, requiring written permission for them to move beyond the bounds of their owners' land and prohibiting assembly not supervised by whites. It even regulated slaves' interactions with their masters and other whites, specifying that they show due deference, excusing violence against them if they did not, and barring the use of force to defend themselves, even when their lives were in danger. Of course, legal prohibitions did not mean that slaves had no belongings, families, or lives outside their masters' control. But it did mean that all these things were "privileges" that masters could revoke at any time, leaving slaves with no recourse beyond what they could muster on their own.

Given that backdrop, even the simplest acts took on larger, legal meanings, particularly in the first few years following emancipation. Even before they obtained full civil and political rights in law, African Americans were working to solidify their new legal status: they brought scattered families together under one roof, they kept their children from being apprenticed by former slaveholders, they demanded pay for the work that they did, and they withheld the deference they were once obligated to give. In all these ways African Americans rejected their former legal position as dependents within households headed by whites. Both whites and African Americans understood such behavior for what it was: an overt challenge to the existing legal order.

After the former Confederate states were reorganized under Congressional Reconstruction, African Americans and poor whites took advantage of their new access to political institutions and the legal system. The most obvious examples are those of men participating in the political process – voting for state and local officials as well as occasionally filling such positions themselves. But both women and men also participated in legal deliberations, testifying in court and prosecuting cases, in an effort to make the rights guaranteed in law a concrete presence in their lives. Many of these incidents, which usually stayed in local courts, did not result in profound judicial pronouncements: a black male worker prosecuted his white employer for assault or a poor woman filed rape charges against her more respectable neighbor in cases that were resolved with relative dispatch and little fanfare in local venues. Such cases nonetheless extended the meaning of new state and federal laws in important ways, making them central to the operation of the legal system and giving them concrete meanings. Southerners who had once been excluded from legal arenas insisted on their right to make use of law and to bend it to their own interests. Their very presence in the legal system countered the goals of conservative whites, who sought to limit access to rights and legal institutions on the basis of race, gender, and class. Nor did these people merely mouth Republican Party principles or work within existing channels. Instead, they turned the courtroom into their own public forum, demanding recognition of concerns ignored in party politics and advancing interpretations of their rights that were far more radical than those in any party platform. They sought to rework social and economic relations in practice, not just in the letter of the law.

The Limits of Federal Authority

Although the legal changes of the Reconstruction period represented an enormous watershed for the nation, important continuities also placed defined limits on the outer edges of change. Many Congressional Republicans were reluctant to change the relationship between states and the federal government, although not quite as reluctant as Johnson had been. They supported the extension of federal power to reconstruct the states of the former Confederacy through the Congressional Reconstruction plan. After that, though, many Republicans and their Northern constituents began to question the further use of federal authority. The Fifteenth Amendment, which clarified the Fourteenth Amendment by specifically securing political rights to all men, encountered much more opposition than its predecessors.

One reason for foot-dragging was that change did not just affect the former Confederacy. The Fourteenth and Fifteenth Amendments, for instance, theoretically altered the legal status of everyone in the Union and moved questions about the rights of citizens from the states to the federal government. They negated legal restrictions on free blacks in Northern states just as they did in Southern states. In addition, the amendments opened up a series of troubling questions about the extent of federal authority over state laws regulating civil and political rights as well as individuals' ability to appeal to the federal government to protect their rights. Additional legislation to extend the federal government's ability to apply and enforce those measures was not particularly popular among white Northerners, who were more interested in punishing Confederates than they were in remaking the nation's legal order. In fact, the Fourteenth and Fifteenth Amendments might never have been approved had not Congress required former Confederate states to adopt the Fourteenth and had not Republican-dominated Southern states led approval of the Fifteenth.

Congress largely left the enforcement and implementation of federal policy to states and localities in the South. In 1865, Congressional Republicans had set up the Bureau of Freedmen, Refugees, and Abandoned Lands to oversee the transition from slavery to free labor and to address other wartime dislocations in the former Confederacy. The Freedmen's Bureau, as it came to be called, became one of the first federal social service agencies. Its agents moved to local areas to explain the concept of wage labor, to supervise the signing of labor contracts, to mediate disputes, and to make sure that wages were paid. They dealt with a wide range of other issues as well, including the distribution of aid to indigent whites and blacks, the reunion of families that had been separated by slavery or the war, the establishment of schools, and even legal aid. The Bureau's effectiveness varied widely, depending on the commitment of local agents. It nonetheless provided a potentially stabilizing presence in an area that had been torn apart by war and was undergoing a wrenching social transformation. Congress, however, phased out the Bureau between 1867 and 1868, as soon as the former Confederate states rejoined the Union. As the logic went, a federal presence was no longer necessary or justifiable once states had been reconstituted. Such matters reverted to the states.

Some Republicans, particularly those from the South, did advocate continued federal involvement. After the states of the former Confederacy rejoined the Union, conflicts raged within them over the control of state and local government. Violent and bloody, they were as much an extension of the internal battles that had ravaged the Confederacy during the war years as they were a conventional contest between two political parties for votes and offices. The Democratic Party, opposed to all the changes instituted under Congressional Reconstruction and Republican rule, did what it could to seize political power and control over law. When intimidation and fraud failed to produce the desired results at the ballot box, party loyalists turned to violence. Supported by a range of paramilitary groups including the Ku Klux Klan, they targeted Republican leaders as well as prominent African Americans whose success challenged notions of racial inferiority that white Democrats embraced with the religious fervor of true believers. The Klan and other groups looted, burned homes, destroyed crops, and terrorized entire families with ritualized forms of rape, torture, and murder. In some areas, violence ended in horrific massacres. Violence also bore results, delivering control of state government to Democrats in most states during the 1870s.

Once they gained control of their state governments, Democrats began working around federal law and, sometimes, defying it outright. In 1874, Mississippi set the standard with the "grandfather clause." Instead of denying suffrage explicitly on the basis of race or previous servitude, which was prohibited by the Fifteenth Amendment, Mississippi Democrats decreed that anyone whose grandfather had not voted in 1860 could not vote either. That, of course, excluded all African Americans and many poor whites as well. Strictly speaking, though, the grandfather clause fell within the letter of the law, if not its spirit. When Congress remained silent and federal courts upheld the clause, Democrats elsewhere in the South followed Mississippi's lead, restricting civil and political rights on the basis of everything but race or previous servitude. Federal courts generally upheld these efforts because the laws themselves did not make racial distinctions and the real effects of the laws lay beyond their purview.

Some Republicans did favor the use of federal authority to achieve substantive change in the legal order. Republicans from the South and their Northern allies also repeatedly begged Congress to intervene militarily, but to no avail. Some Congressional representatives and political commentators dismissed reports of violence, even when they came in the form of sworn testimony at the Ku Klux Klan hearings. How could they believe ignorant, rural African Americans who had so recently been slaves, when respectable whites denied the charges? Republicans did manage to pass legislation that gave the federal government greater enforcement power in the Civil Rights Act of 1875. The legislation affirmed existing federal measures, an important statement, given the context. It also extended the scope of federal involvement, banning segregation and allowing for more aggressive enforcement.

The decisions of federal courts, however, did not support the efforts of Congressional Republicans or answer the pleas of African Americans and their white Republican allies in the South. They went in the opposite direction, limiting the implications of the Reconstruction amendments and related federal legislation. Ironically, the federal courts had the ability to do so, precisely because of the increased powers granted to them during the Civil War and Reconstruction: they used their increased jurisdiction to decline to use it. The *Slaughterhouse Cases* (1873) brought the U.S. Supreme Court to this fork in the road, a fact suggested by the multiple, somewhat ambiguous meanings of the decision, which historians continue to debate. *Slaughterhouse* was not about the immediate issues of Reconstruction, namely the civil rights of African Americans. It involved white, mostly Democratic butchers in New Orleans, who had been denied licenses to practice their trade through regulations enacted by the Republican government of Louisiana. Their lawyers used the Fourteenth Amendment to contest the regulations, arguing that the butchers' rights, in general terms, had been abridged as citizens of the United States and that the regulations also violated the due process clause of the Fourteenth Amendment. The second claim rested on a broad reading of the due process clause, in substantive rather than procedural terms, as the collection of rights vested in individuals that could not be contravened arbitrarily. The U.S. Supreme Court decided against the butchers in a decision that affirmed a narrow reading of the Fourteenth Amendment. The result limited the amendment's power to uphold all citizens' civil rights by defining its reach only in terms of protecting former slaves and by affirming the states' purview over the rights of their citizens.

The Court pushed the same logic further in *The Civil Rights Cases* (1883), which not only struck down the Civil Rights Act of 1875 but also further limited the use of existing federal law to uphold individuals' civil and political rights. Rather than protecting African Americans' equality, the Court found that federal intervention in such matters affirmed African Americans' inequality before the law: it amounted to special treatment that undercut their legal status. By 1883, the *Civil Rights Cases* affirmed in federal law what was already a reality in legal practice in many states. In 1876, as part of the settlement in the disputed presidential election of that year, national political leaders agreed to withdraw the federal government from the Reconstruction process and to respect home rule. Governance over people within states, in other words, would remain with the states. Nonetheless, the *Civil Rights Cases* made it that much more difficult to contest the implications of home rule.

The same limited vision of federal power, perpetuated through the authority granted to federal courts, also enabled segregation to flourish.

The *Civil Rights Cases* set the stage by striking down measures in the 1875 Civil Rights Act that included equal access to public transport and other accommodations as a central element of civil rights. These measures were included in the 1875 act because informal practices of segregating the races were already being sanctioned at the state and local level in the South. The practice of segregation had a certain legal ambiguity, because it involved private as well as public property and did not always have a direct relationship to clearly defined, legally recognized civil rights. By contrast, the laws mandating segregation usually referred to race directly, thus violating federal legislation prohibiting legal discrimination on the basis of race. Such laws nonetheless proliferated in the states of the former Confederacy in the years following the Civil War, as Republicans lost their hold on political power and Democrats took over both state and local governments. First appearing in local ordinances, segregation ultimately made its way into state law as well, if only in the form of affirmations of the legitimacy of such practices.

African Americans routinely mounted challenges, with uneven results and ambiguous legal implications. Often, they had difficulty obtaining a legal hearing in these matters. When they did, they could not always convince judges that segregation constituted a violation of civil rights. They nonetheless continued to challenge segregation in a series of cases that culminated in *Plessy v. Ferguson* (1898). *Plessy* has achieved iconic status in the scholarship, largely at the expense of the cases leading up to it and the existing legislation and legal practice that it merely affirmed. The most famous aspect of the decision is the "separate but equal" doctrine, which held that the separation of the races did not necessarily imply inequality or a violation of Fourteenth Amendment rights. In one sense, the logic confounded rulings in prior civil rights cases, which had focused on the letter of the law and not the results. In another sense, though, it extended the earlier logic by ignoring the results of segregation, which clearly did produce racial inequality. Equally important was the affirmation of state control over issues relating to individuals' civil and political rights. In *Plessy*, the U.S. Supreme Court cast race relations as a domestic matter best interpreted and addressed at the state level. The language invoked long-standing legal precedents that gave household heads authority over their domestic dependents and their private property, free from outside interference. *Plessy v. Ferguson* returned African Americans to a position similar to the domestic dependency of slaves, although this time they were the metaphoric dependents of Democratic officeholders in state government, instead of the actual dependents of individual slaveholders. African Americans now had rights in theory, which they did not have as slaves. But, just like the situation in slavery, they had no legal recourse to contest decisions outside the domestic realm, now cast as the states.

The Limits of Law

The limits of legal change in the Reconstruction era, however, were defined not only by the decisions of judges and legislators. They were defined also through a broader legal culture, in which deeply ingrained practices were entwined so thoroughly with each other as to be almost impossible to disentangle. The effects of race and slavery, for instance, were difficult to separate from other relationships and issues in law, such as marriage and labor relations, all of which reinforced each other. That legal culture characterized the North as well as the South, making change difficult to realize within the existing system.

Often, the implications of federal Reconstruction policies are seen as a peculiarly "Southern" issue, at least until the courts began using those measures to redefine economic issues and relations later in the century. Yet there were distinct parallels between the slave states and the rest of the nation in legal matters. The legal handling of race relations within the states of the former Confederacy laid the groundwork for an emerging nationwide legal order that enabled many Americans to see all people of color as marginal, to countenance extreme inequalities in economic status, to exclude women from the rights that supposedly were extended to all citizens, and to characterize legal change in the Reconstruction period to achieve civil and political for African Americans as the "excesses" of racial radicals.

The distance between the Black Codes and Congressional Reconstruction was not as great as might seem at first glance. The fallout between President Johnson and Congressional Republicans tends to map the sectionalized rhetoric of that conflict onto the substance and outcome of Reconstruction policies. Outraged critics of Johnson saw his Reconstruction plan as a crass attempt to ignore the Union's victory. They found the racial restrictions in the former Confederate states' new constitutions a particularly egregious example of that. Dubbed the "Black Codes," they became representative of the underlying problems of Johnson's plan more generally: winking at President Johnson while passing the Thirteenth Amendment, the former leaders of the Confederacy then snuck slavery in through the back door with his assent. The interpretation stuck. In one sense, it was accurate. The same delegates who passed the Black Codes also debated their secession ordinances and the Thirteenth Amendment as if they still had a choice in the matter.

Yet, elements of the Black Codes differed from law in other states only in degree. At the close of the Civil War, only a minority of Americans actually exercised full civil and political rights. Most people occupied legal positions on a very broad middle ground, removed from slavery but still distant from the legal rights that defined the opposite pole. No free woman of any race, married or single, could claim the full array of individual rights. Many men found themselves on that same middle ground as well, although their places there were different from those of women. Free blacks, in particular, enjoyed very limited rights: many states that remained in the Union had laws nearly identical to those in the Black Codes. The citizenship of free blacks also remained uncertain, clouded by contradictory laws within individual states and the U.S. Supreme Court's controversial decision in *Dred Scott*. Johnson's Reconstruction plan evaded these questions, handing them to conservative lawmakers in the states of the former Confederacy instead. Drawing on the laws that had applied to free blacks in both the North and the South, former Confederates attempted to codify a new, extremely limited legal status for African Americans in their own states. In many ways, both the approach and the results revealed as much about the legal dynamics of race in the nation as it did about those in the South.

More than a regional aberration, the Black Codes also anticipated subsequent policies under Congressional Reconstruction in other ways. Among the most important commonality was the emphasis on marriage and its connection to individual civil and political rights. The Black Codes mandated the legal marriage of all formerly enslaved couples. As slaves, African Americans' marriages had not been recognized in law, and emancipation did not alter that situation. Some states simply declared couples then living together to be married, whereas others required registration as validation of those unions. Although saturated in the morality of the Victorian age, these policies were more about structure than sentiment. Marriage extended so deeply into the legal order as to be nearly impossible to extract without radical renovations. Outside marriage, for instance, there were no legally recognized fathers. Without fathers, there were no legally recognized parents, since mothers had no formal rights to their children at this time. That posed serious problems for the state, which depended on the legal bonds that tied family members together and made fathers and husbands economically responsible for dependent wives and children. Children born outside legal marriages became wards of the state. Their economic support fell to counties, as did that of women who could not make ends meet on their own and whose extended families could not or would not provide for them. The last thing that conservative white delegates wanted was to acquire responsibility for formerly enslaved women and children. They thought freedpersons should take responsibility for their own family members. Given skepticism about African Americans' capacity for freedom, delegates also thought that legal compulsion would be necessary to accomplish that assumption of responsibility. Marriage provided the means, by placing families in a legal structure that made men into household heads, with enforceable, legal obligations to their dependents.

The legal importance of marriage extended beyond these economic practicalities as well. Marriage also determined the distribution of civil and political rights, conferring them on heads of household and denying them to dependents. Unlike children, women retained legal rights outside of marriage. They controlled their property, their wages, and their ability to contract, instead of surrendering rights to their husbands. The prospect of self-supporting, self-governing women then called the allocation of other rights into question as well. Male heads of household enjoyed rights in their own names and represented the rights of their wives and children because they were liable for them. Within the existing governing structures, those people who were supposed to be dependents had few rights; in theory, they did not need them. Without marriage, the rationale for this situation also evaporated. The Black Codes resolved that issue. Placing formerly enslaved women within households as wives, the Black Codes affirmed the existing legal order in which men could claim individual rights and women could not. At the same time, though, the Black Codes also opened the dangerous possibility that African American men, as heads of household, might claim individual rights, along with obligations for their families. The Codes' elaborate lists of limitations on freedpersons' rights read as extended repudiations of that possibility.

Later federal legislation that overturned the Black Codes' racial restrictions still determined individuals' rights through the position they were supposed to occupy within households. Women's rights activists did try to alter that situation. Many had been active in the abolition movement and brought a similar critique to the position of women. After the Civil War, they hoped that the nation would address gender as well as racial inequality. Despite their involvement in the Union war effort, close ties to Republican legislators, and active lobbying on behalf of both women and African Americans, they were disappointed. Congressional Republicans refused to include women, arguing that the extension of civil and political rights to them was politically impossible and would only undermine efforts to obtain those rights for African American men.

Granting rights to women also would have undermined the logic of extending them to African Americans. Under the Black Codes and afterward, African Americans had used men's legal status as husbands, fathers, and heads of household to gain a purchase on other rights as well. Using fathers' parental rights, they reclaimed children who had been apprenticed to local planters and put to agricultural labor in the fields. They also found husbands' legal prerogatives useful in shielding women, as wives, from the abuse of employers and other whites. Republicans also drew on that same logic, emphasizing men's differences from women and their responsibilities for their families in justifying the extension of rights to them. Like white men, African American men served as soldiers in the military, demonstrating their fitness for freedom. Now that African American were free and expected to take care of their families and represent their interests, they needed the civil and political rights to do so.

The decision to extend rights to men only turned the traditional legal relationship between household position and rights into a wholly gendered relationship: all men could, at least in theory, claim those rights, but no woman of any race could. The denial of rights to women became a "natural" result of their very being, rather than a consequence of their structural position within society. Arguing in a neat circle, the U.S. Supreme Court upheld the denial of civil rights to women in *Bradwell v. The State of Illinois* (1873) on that basis: women were different by nature than men; men were citizens with claims to full civil and political rights; therefore, the rights guaranteed to all citizens by the Fourteenth Amendment did not extend to women. This decision and others limited the implications of the Fourteenth Amendment, excluding half of the nation's citizens from its protections. Legitimating women's inequality through nature also conveniently placed the issue beyond the ken of mere humans. If anything, it made the possibility of change that much more remote.

The Republicans' decision to abandon women's rights split the women's movement in two, with one side supporting racial equality for African American men and the other criticizing those efforts. The critics, most of whom were white, expressed their dissatisfaction in overtly racial terms, using negative characterizations of African Americans. They did so to question the logic that enshrined manhood as the standard for claiming civil and political rights. Why should civil and political rights be the prerogative of men, simply because they were men? What made men more deserving of those rights and more capable of exercising them than women? Specifically, why could poor, ignorant black men of questionable morals exercise those rights more responsibly than wealthy, educated, respectable white women? Yet the content of their rhetoric both drew on and reinforced deeply rooted racial biases that justified the denial of rights in terms of race. That racial strain continued to mark the feminist movement in the late nineteenth and early twentieth centuries, not only severing questions of gender from race but also casting gender inequality in racial terms (as involving primarily white women) and racial inequality in gendered terms (as involving primarily African American men).

Although white feminists played the race card to express their opposition, those same racial biases also informed the policies they opposed. After the Civil War, prominent white Republican leaders supported the extension of full civil and political rights to African American men because they rejected the notion that race determined human capacity or the content of individual character. But they were in the minority. Most white people in the nation believed that race mattered a great deal and made all African Americans innately inferior to all whites. How they acted on those ideas, however, differed. Where conservative whites in the former Confederacy believed that laws were necessary to single out African Americans and keep them in their place, many white Republicans thought the situation would take care of itself. Even the elimination of racial distinctions in law would not result in actual equality between the races, because nothing would alter African Americans' racial destiny. They would sink to the lowest segments of society, where existing laws would be sufficient to keep them in line. Those sentiments, which lay just beneath the surface of federal policies, suggested distinct limits in Congressional Republicans' policies. Equality in law did not necessarily translate into a commitment to racial equality in practice. To the contrary, legal equality was a political possibility at this time precisely because so many assumed that it would not result in racial equality.

The failure to acknowledge, let alone address, the legal status of wage labor magnified those underlying inequalities. Labor law also constituted another key link between Congressional Reconstruction and the Black Codes. The Black Codes framed these restrictions in terms of race, with the intent of forcing free African Americans into agricultural wage labor, supervised by whites. Contemporary critics and later historians rightly saw these laws as creating a labor relation akin to slavery. To be sure, the restrictions on black workers moved them very close to the position of slaves. They also faced constraints that white workers did not. Yet the laws were not just a throwback to slavery. In many instances, they restated existing laws that already applied to free white laborers. Like the Black Codes, existing laws cast the labor relationship as an unequal relationship between "master" and "servant." Employees surrendered rights just by entering into the wage contract: they could not leave until the end of the contract, they could forfeit all their wages and face criminal penalties if they left, and they had virtually no legal recourse in conflicts with their employers. The terms of the contract could limit workers rights even further. Employers wrote in all sorts of restrictions regulating their employees' dress, place of residence, hours of labor, recreation, and their demeanor. Other than refusing the work, which carried the possibility of vagrancy charges, there was nothing workers could do about the terms demanded by their employers. Some states intentionally extended the application of labor legislation beyond African Americans by passing a separate set of laws that applied to all wage workers. But even legislation framed in racial terms did not negate existing laws that already applied to whites. In the perverse logic of the time, such duplication was legally necessary because the Black Codes categorized freed slaves as a separate category of people, governed by a different set of laws.

Subsequent federal policies prohibited restrictions that applied only to African American workers. But the inequalities in the labor relation never drew the fire or the attention that racial inequalities did. In fact, the elimination of racial distinctions had the effect of extending those inequalities in labor law to all workers, regardless of race. Nor was the situation much different elsewhere in the nation. Regardless of political affiliation or place of residence, many of the nation's leaders believed those kinds of laws to be necessary. As they saw it, people should be able to enter into contracts to sell their labor and should receive compensation for it. All propertyless people, though, needed some coercion to direct them into steady labor and to keep them working to support themselves. At the very end of the Civil War, some Republicans did advocate the confiscation and redistribution of plantations, with the goal of turning former slaves into the kind of independent producers who occupied such a central place in the party's rhetoric and who would not need to work for wages at all. Those proposals foundered on the shoals of property rights, which were also central to Republican political rhetoric and the legal foundation of independent production. Even so, these proposals completely sidestepped the problematic place of wage laborers in the legal order.

The limitations begun by Black Codes continued under Republican regimes in the former Confederate states, although Republicans did infuse the labor relationship with some progressive aspects of Northern free labor ideology. Most states, for instance, strengthened workers' ability to collect their wages through laborers' lien laws. But Republicans did not change the hierarchical structure of the labor relationship. Quite the opposite. Laborers' lien laws generally restrained workers' mobility and their right to determine the terms of the labor relationship by specifying that the lien applied only if the laborer had worked the contract's full term and fulfilled its other specifications. A few states, South Carolina among them, granted laborers' liens without such restrictions and established procedures for mediating contract disputes. This legislation allowed workers to bring their complaints to mediators who could force employers to meet contractual obligations and made labor-related issues a matter of public debate. Even more than laborers' liens, contract mediation held the potential for remaking labor relations by allowing workers legal recourse. Still, the effects were limited because the mediation process affirmed the very inequalities that had subordinated laborers as domestic dependents. Laborers brought themselves to white, elite mediators at great personal risk, facing fines and imprisonment if they were judged to have broken their contracts' provisions. At a time when contracts regularly demanded such things as obedience and respect from workers, the burden of proof clearly rested with the workers.

Under Republican rule, the states of the former Confederacy also expanded the category of common labor to include "sharecroppers." During the antebellum period, no Southern state except North Carolina recognized a distinction between sharecroppers and renters. All were tenants, who retained legal rights over their labor and its product when they rented land. Even in North Carolina, where the law placed sharecroppers under the direct supervision of their landlords and denied them property rights in the goods they produced, the legal definition was not always observed in practice. But such independence, whether legal or customary, became problematic for landlords after emancipation. White planters first assumed that former slaves would work for them as wage laborers. Then credit shortages, poor crops, and the resistance of freedpersons themselves closed off this possibility. As African American laborers began to work for a share of the crop on specific plots of land, the courts denied them the legal rights granted tenants, turned them into sharecroppers, and lumped them into the same category as common laborers. Although sharecroppers might exercise some authority over their labor and its product in practice, they had no legally established rights to either.

The restrictions in Southern labor law remained particularly extreme, but they were not completely out of line with the direction of labor relations in the nation as a whole. Throughout the United States, more people entered the ranks of wage labor. They sold their labor and received wages for it, but had no claim on the products of their labor. With few options, they were forced to sign contracts that demanded the surrender of a range of rights to their employers and to work in dangerous conditions over which they had little control. Northern workers registered their dissatisfaction in a series of strikes that rocked the North and Midwest during the last decades of the nineteenth century. Beginning in the late 1870s, labor unrest not only overlapped with Reconstruction in the South but also picked up on issues central to the process of change there. Workers also worked through the courts, trying to use Fourteenth Amendment rights to alter the balance of power at the workplace. Drawing, in part, on the elements of the arguments rejected in *Slaughterhouse*, the courts consistently used the Fourteenth Amendment against them, maintaining that the ability to contract was a protected right. Any measure that undercut it by dictating the contracts' terms and taking the decision out of individuals' hands was a violation of the Fourteenth Amendment. At the same time, the courts recognized corporations as legal persons and extended Fourteenth Amendment rights to them. The results only magnified workers' inequality, making them theoretically equal to corporations that only grew in size and power as the century wore on and refusing intervention that might equalize that situation.

CONCLUSION

All these limits, however, did not signal the absence of change, but the outer reaches of new terrain opened up as a result of the Civil War and Reconstruction. The period was one of crisis, which forced a wide range of Americans to debate the relationship between people and law with a degree of openness and readiness for innovation that has been rare in the nation's history. The results, for good and for ill, reached beyond the status of Confederate states, slavery, and even the legal status of former slaves to touch the lives of all Americans and to reshape the institutional structures of the legal order that underpinned the U.S. government. Not all Americans benefited in equal measure, but even those who did not still had the promises of Reconstruction on which to draw for both inspiration and practical legal ammunition. They continued both to refer to and, often, stretch the meaning of the era's laws: women demanded full civil and political rights; African Americans kept working through legal channels to end segregation, to abolish voting restrictions, and eliminate other constraints on their constitutionally guaranteed rights; workers kept emphasizing the legal inequalities inherent in the labor relation; and, as new groups of ethnic minorities entered the nation, they would also reach for these legal principles to solidify their claims to citizenship and its rights. In fact, historians have referred to the period as an "unfinished journey" or a second but incomplete revolution. Those phrases also underscore the difficulty of realizing promises – even fairly well-defined legal ones – in a nation in which law extends to the people and involves them. Extending rights and integrating new groups of people into the polity are not just top-down propositions, a matter of spreading existing laws more broadly; they entail fundamental changes in the legal order – an ongoing process that has to keep moving and is always just beyond reach precisely because people themselves keep redefining the meaning and purpose of the laws.

11

LAW, PERSONHOOD, AND CITIZENSHIP IN THE LONG NINETEENTH CENTURY: THE BORDERS OF BELONGING

BARBARA YOUNG WELKE

The Declaration of Independence and the preamble to the U.S. Constitution express a powerful vision of the fundamental right of all individuals to freedom, liberty, and equality. Looked at one way, that vision was incrementally transformed into lived reality for a broader and broader number of Americans over the course of the long nineteenth century. The American Revolution transformed subjects into citizens; between the 1820s and 1840s property qualifications for voting were removed, extending the franchise to most white men; the 1860s brought freedom to the roughly four million Americans held in chattel slavery and a constitutional revolution in individual rights; married women's property reform and ultimately the franchise in 1920 gave women a fuller individuality; and millions emigrated to America's shores and became citizens. One can look at this history and believe in some fundamental way in America's liberalism.

And yet, taking the story as a whole, one cannot escape a different narrative. White male legal authority was fundamental to the very nature and meaning of nineteenth-century American law in both conceptual and constitutive terms. It created law's borders and boundaries. From the outset, personhood, citizenship, and nation were imagined to belong within gendered and racialized borders: white men alone were fully embodied legal persons, they were America's "first citizens," they were the nation. The universal human legal person imagined by liberalism was in fact highly particularized. More important, however much change there was on the surface over the course of the long nineteenth century, the borders of belonging never escaped their initial imagining. Racialized and gendered identities – simply assumed at the beginning as the source of rights – came to be self-consciously embraced, marked in law, and manipulated as the fundamental bulwarks for keeping white men within these borders and others outside, not simply up to the Civil War but after it as well. In turn, the founding assumptions that imagined legal personhood and from it citizenship and nation as white and male in the long nineteenth century fundamentally shaped the development of the American legal and constitutional order for the twentieth century.

Legal individuality – or as I have termed it, the "borders of belonging" – over the course of the long nineteenth century (from the Revolutionary era to the1920s) provides the frame for this narrative. I use the terms "borders" and "belonging" in both a spatial (physical and geographic) and figurative sense. The term "borders" refers here to the borders of the nation and to the relationship between the states and the federal government. It refers equally to physical and psychic personhood (self-ownership) and to the legal consequences assigned to gendered or racialized elements of individual identity. Likewise, I use the term "belonging" to mean self-ownership or belonging to oneself, as well as to mean "membership" or "participation" as in citizenship. But the term also connotes less positively the realities of "belonging to," as in legal relationships of authority and subordination (e.g., master/slave, master/servant, husband/wife). This story requires looking across law, region, and time. It draws on law regulating immigration, naturalization, and citizenship; on law regulating labor, access to professions, and vagrancy; on property and tax law, the law of domestic relations, and on law regulating reproductive freedom, race, and civil rights; and on criminal law, Indian law and policy, and the structure and institutions of law itself. I do not trace in full any of these areas of law; many are recounted more fully in other chapters of this volume. Rather, I seek to elucidate patterns, to capture something of the scope and power of law in giving shape to legal individuality.

The chapter proceeds analytically rather than chronologically. In Part I, I trace what often remains least examined: the capacities that law gave white men as persons and as citizens. Law gave white men a superior claim to the land and defined nation in their image; white men held on to their privilege with resilience and tenacity in the face of dramatic social, political, and economic change. Part II focuses on the operation and consequences of law's exclusion of women and racialized others from the borders of belonging and then turns to their pursuit of right. Finally, Part III traces the way these borders were patrolled through the structure of the American legal system, the multiplicity of sites of law, the role of ideology, and the fundamental fact that white men made, interpreted, and enforced law. Racialized and gendered power, I argue, were critical in shaping the twentieth-century American state.

Each section of the chapter traverses the entire era so that subjects considered in one section are revisited in others from a different vantage point. The goal ultimately is that by laying the argument out as a series of overlays we emerge with a clearer sense of the chronology of personhood, citizenship, and nation in the long nineteenth century.

I. LAW'S PRIVILEGING OF WHITE MEN

"As to your extraordinary Code of Laws, I cannot but laugh . . . Depend upon it, We know better than to repeal our Masculine systems." (Letter, John Adams to Abigail Adams, 1776)

"Rightly considered, the policy of the General Government toward the red man is not only liberal, but generous. He is unwilling to submit to the laws of the States and mingle with their population. To save him from this alternative, or perhaps utter annihilation, the General Government kindly offers him a new home, and proposes to pay the whole expense of his removal and settlement." (President Andrew Jackson, Second Annual Message, 1830)

"We do not regard [slavery] as an evil, on the contrary, we think that our prosperity, our happiness, our very political existence, is inseparably connected with it . . . We will not yield it." (Inaugural Address, John A. Quitman, Governor of Mississippi, 1850)

"I am willing to admit that all men are created equal, but how are they equal? . . . . I do not believe that a superior race is bound to receive among it those of an inferior race if the mingling of them can only tend to the detriment of the mass." (Peter Van Winkle, Republican Senator, West Virginia, Debate re Amending Naturalization Law, 1866)

"Well, sir; it is to protect a man in his business. . . [and] for the accom'odation of the passengers generally, the white people. . . . the traveling public." (Explanation of object of racial segregation, John G. Benson, Master, *Governor Allen*, 1878)

"A man's self is the sum, is the sum total of all that he CAN call his, not only his body and his psychic powers, but his clothes and his house, his wife and children . . . his reputation and works, his lands and horses, and yacht and bank-account." (William James, *Principles of Psychology*, 1890)

Self-Ownership and Citizenship

Although it well could have been otherwise, law in the New Republic accorded full personhood and belonging to white men only. Law protected a man's real and personal property through the law of property, his reputation through the law of slander and libel, and his "property" in his wife through the law of coverture, in his children through the law of patriarchy, and in his human chattel through the law of slavery. The American Revolution carefully shielded these apparent inconsistencies in a republic founded on Enlightenment principles and accorded white men a key additional privilege: citizenship.

The white male citizen took form in a die cast by the dependency and subjectness of women, slaves, free blacks, and Indians. Indians were excluded from the constitutional order; slaves became ballast in the delicate balance between North and South, a property right with constitutional sanction. And while a few states might recognize free blacks as citizens, the nation's first Naturalization Law passed in 1790, with its provision limiting naturalization to "free, white persons," testified to the assumption that the United States was in fact and would remain a white nation. In revolutionary rhetoric, traits defined as female represented the antithesis of the good republican, coded male. A man's independence – the key qualification of the citizen-voter – was secured through family headship and property ownership.

The new Constitution did not define who was a citizen. Rather, citizenship like personhood was given shape and meaning largely by state law. And, here law preserved regimes of dependency constructed over a century and a half of colonial development. No regime was more fundamental to preserving the established social and political order than the law of coverture. In his *Commentaries on the Law of England*, Sir William Blackstone defined men's and women's relative rights and obligations in the following terms: "By marriage, the husband and wife are one person in law; that is, the very being or legal existence of the woman is suspended during the marriage, or at least is incorporated and consolidated into that of the husband."[1] Children born to their union were his, not hers. The obligation to obey was hers, the right to discipline his. His place of residence became hers because a married woman could have no settlement separate from her husband. Women's loss of personhood under the law of coverture augmented men's; her dependence defined his independence. So too, the mantle of white men's U.S. citizenship extended over their wives and children. In 1855, Congress mandated that any woman who by virtue of marriage to a U.S. citizen and who might be naturalized under existing laws (in other words, who was free and white) "shall be deemed a citizen."[2] Until 1934, a legitimate child born abroad was a birthright citizen only if its father was a citizen who had resided in the United States before the child's birth.

Debate in the Philadelphia convention did not address the contradiction that women's legally enforced dependence under coverture posed in a nation fundamentally premised on independence. Slavery was debated and preserved, even provided constitutional protection. What greater evidence could there be of law's power than slavery? Through it human beings were transformed into property, chattel owned by other men for working the land. But the economic interest in slavery extended far beyond the master class to the white men who leased slaves, insured human chattel, ran slave markets, bought cotton, and ran the inns and taverns that serviced the slave trade on market days, Court Week, and so on. In the sense that a court of

[1] Sir William Blackstone, *Commentaries on the Laws of England* (Chicago, 1979) 1:430.
[2] Act of Feb. 10, 1855, 10 Stat. 604.

equity would use the term, all had unclean hands. Moreover, slaves represented more than a pool of unfree labor; they became, quite literally, the coin of the realm. Easily convertible to cold cash, they were the best collateral a man could offer or ask for. In this regard, commercial law complemented the law of slavery; indeed, the commercial law of slavery made up as much as half of the business of circuit courts in the antebellum South. The market in slaves held another benefit as well: it held out the promise that even the most marginal of white men might yet acquire a slave and thus secure their independence, full citizenship, and inclusion in the master class.

Where white men's property rights in blacks lacked (or lost) legal sanction, states reinforced white men's supremacy through the extension of universal white male suffrage coupled with the disenfranchisement of free blacks, bars on black testimony in cases against whites, and bans on immigration of free blacks. The compromise over slavery in the Constitution provided a text from which Chief Justice Roger B. Taney could conclude in *Dred Scott v. Sandford* (1857) that slave or free, blacks were not "constituent members of the sovereignty." Not only could they never be citizens of the United States, they were "so far inferior that they had no rights which the white man was bound to respect."[3]

Emancipation dissolved, without compensation, property in human chattel – a momentous transformation through law in the right to personhood and the right to property – but it did not end white men's dominion over black Americans. New legal tools took up the law of slavery's work. After the Civil War, Southern legislatures passed Black Codes – draconian measures intended to tie black labor to the land. Congress forced the repeal of the codes, but in the name of "freedom of contract" bound blacks in service to white landowners under labor contracts. In the years after Reconstruction in the South, sharecropping coupled with vagrancy laws, convict labor laws, disfranchisement, and others ensured not just a pool of unfree black labor at white hands, but white mastery.

In a context in which white men's ownership of their own labor was redefined as the foundation of their independence, "free labor," the role of law in defining other labor as unfree – not just slave labor, but also Chinese contract labor, Indian child indentured labor, and women's reproductive and other labor – became increasingly essential. Indenture acts passed by Western states blurred the line between free and slave states. Under California's law passed in 1850, "citizens" were given the right to take custody of an Indian child and place him or her under apprenticeship. When coupled with the state's vagrancy law that authorized law enforcement

[3] 19 How. 407.

officials to arrest and hire out to the highest bidder Indians found loitering, drunk, or "guilty" of any number of other offenses, the result was that as many as 10,000 Native Americans were held in virtual slavery. Peonage laws in Utah and New Mexico (in effect in New Mexico until 1867 when Congress moved to enforce the Thirteenth Amendment's prohibition against servitude) and the importation of thousands of Chinese contract workers in the 1850s similarly assured white men of both their own freedom and a pool of unfree labor. Later in the century, the power to mobilize as citizens and voters to prevent further immigration of Chinese laborers both protected white men's "free labor" and attested to their enfranchisement.

White men's legal authority over others in the nineteenth century was complemented by their expanded right of self. Over the course of the nineteenth century, state courts created an American doctrine of self-defense that sharply repudiated the English common law doctrine that one must retreat "to the wall" at one's back before legitimately killing in self-defense. In its place, American courts adopted the rule of "no duty to retreat." The American doctrine was shaped in cases involving white men; it presumed and further fostered an independence that only they had under the law. The black slave and the married woman had no right to resist with deadly force a master's or husband's physical assault. Indeed, what a man did to his wife within the marriage relation was, in large measure, defined by law as private. So complete was a husband's dominion over his wife and home that a corollary of the law of self-defense extended to a man who killed on discovering his wife with a lover, provided he acted in the heat of the moment. The slave's only protection were not the hollow proscriptions written into law, but a master's economic self-interest.

The law of self-defense was an American innovation on an established principle in the common law. But there were vast areas of common law newly forged in the nineteenth century in response to industrialization and changing forms of capitalism that presumed self-ownership, including the law of accidental injury, wrongful death, contract law, and the law of corporations. Both tort and contract law presumed capacity that in fact only white men had under the law. The founding assumption of the law of negligence was that the actor was, in fact, "his own master and judge, of what was, and was not prudent."[4] Courts and legal commentators explained the standard of conduct against which that of the actors was judged as that of the "reasonable man." Wrongful death statutes, a response to the growing death toll from industrial accidents, effectively defined men as providers and women as dependents. A majority of American states limited wrongful death actions to cases involving the death of a man. So too, the law of

[4] *Chicago, Burlington and Quincy R. R. v. Hazzard*, 26 Ill. 373 (1861).

contract was premised on self ownership. Contract doctrines like caveat emptor ("buyer beware") rested on an assumption of capacity that only white men had.

Whiteness itself was property. "How much would it be worth," asked Albion Tourgee, Homer Plessy's lawyer in *Plessy v. Ferguson*, "[t]o a young man entering upon the practice of law, to be regarded as a white man rather than a colored one?" Wasn't reputation for being white "not the most valuable sort of property, being the master-key that unlocks the golden door of opportunity?"[5] Uninterrupted by the end of slavery, legalized discriminations rendered whiteness the "master-key." But what Tourgee assumed must be made explicit: whiteness was a form of property when *coupled with* manhood.

Laying Claim to the Land and the Space of the Nation

At the heart of building and preserving white men's status as America's "first citizens" was the project of laying claim to the land and, more broadly, the space of the nation. At its founding, the United States was a mere foothold on the eastern edge of a vast continent. Within a couple of decades, the building of what Thomas Jefferson had derided as an oxymoron – "a republican empire" – was set in motion by none other than now-President Jefferson's purchase of the Louisiana Territory. By the middle of the century, the territory of the United States spanned the continent from the Atlantic Ocean in the East to the Pacific Ocean in the West. The nation expanded through law; and through law, in equal parts affirmative and negative, it ensured that the United States would be a white man's nation. From the beginning, law operated negatively, effectively according white men a superior claim to the land by denying others' access to it. Law provided a tool for divesting Native Americans of their claim to the land, protecting it from claims by women and African Americans, and defining the borders of the nation to exclude racialized others, like the Chinese and Japanese or, where not excluded, to limit their access to property.

The story of the steady and relentless white dispossession of Indian land is a well-known one. What is most important to highlight here is the fundamental fact that dispossession was authorized by and legitimated through law. One of the first official acts of the federal government on behalf of the new nation was to claim ownership of all the land east of the Mississippi River, forcing in turn the undefeated tribes into treaties yielding their

[5] Tourgee-Walker Brief, pp. 9–10, *Plessy v. Ferguson*, in *Landmark Briefs and Arguments of the Supreme Court of the United States*, vol. 13, Philip B. Kurland and Gerhard Casper, eds. (Arlington, VA, 1975).

claim to the land. That Indians were peoples outside the borders of the new nation was affirmed in the new U.S. Constitution adopted in 1789, giving Congress the power "[t]o regulate Commerce with foreign Nations, and among the several States, and with the Indian Tribes."[6] The tension of Indian nations "outside" the Republic yet within the physical borders of the United States increased with each phase of westward expansion and white settlement. Yet, for a full century U.S. Indian policy focused on keeping Native Americans outside the boundaries of the nation. Under this policy, Indians were pushed physically ever farther westward onto increasingly marginal lands until there was literally nowhere else to go.

The other side of dispossession was the seeding of the West with white settlers. Without exception the push came from demand for access to land for white settlement. From the treaties with individual tribes following the Paris Peace Accord of 1783, to the Indian Removal Act of 1830, to the forced removals to reservations following the Civil War, to the opening of Indian Territory in western Oklahoma, to non-Indian homesteading in 1889, America's native inhabitants were forced to make way for white settlement. One of the most far-seeing provisions of the Constitution was the provision that new states would enter the union with the same status as the original thirteen. Yet, from the outset, law provided that statehood rested on settlement by white men. Under the terms of the Northwest Ordinance (1783), settlers could elect their own legislature only when their numbers reached 5,000 free adult white men; admission to statehood depended on the number of "settlers" – not Indians – growing to 60,000 and adoption of a republican constitution. The Homestead Act (1862) made settlement of the West by white yeoman farmers national policy. Thus, law assured that white men would hold the reins of power as the nation expanded.

In the last quarter of the nineteenth century, U.S. policy – long predicated on an assumption of separation of white and Indian peoples – changed course. The legal foundation for the change was laid in 1871 with Congressional abrogation of the treaty system. Henceforward, Congress could simply legislate changes in Indian land ownership without securing tribal approval. It did just that in the Dawes Severalty Act in 1887, which gave the president of the United States authority to divide tribal lands, giving 160 acres to each family and smaller plots to individuals. Many factors and many constituencies, including white "friends" of the Indian, supported passage of the Dawes Act. While the Dawes Act did not lead immediately to white dispossession of huge tracts of Indian land, it is impossible to imagine its passage without its tantalizing promise of some 80 million "surplus" acres of land that would be freed for white settlement – a

[6] U.S. Constitution, Art. 1, sec. 8.

promise that was more than fulfilled. Later amendments to the law easing "protections" in the act that had limited Indians' ability to alienate their allotments further marginalized Indians' claim to the land. In less than two decades, the flood of white settlers into South Dakota and Oklahoma left Indians a dispossessed minority on lands once wholly theirs. In just over a century, from the policy of separation through the policy of "assimilation," and through the wars and massacres to which these policies gave license, the white man had effectively supplanted Native Americans' legal claim to the land.

Where white men used law and the force it legitimated to erase Native Americans' claim to the land through dispossession, they used law and the force it legitimated to prevent women, blacks, and other racial minorities from making claims to the land through possession. Men's full personhood provided the foundation of their superior claim to the land. Fathers passed land to sons because only they were fully empowered under law to devise and bequeath, to contract and reap the benefits of the land's riches. The law of coverture protected men's superior claim to the land. Under the law of coverture, at marriage, a husband not only took ownership of all his wife's personal belongings, but on the birth of a child, he assumed the status of "tenant by courtesy" over his wife's real estate and with it the right to rent out those lands, cut timber on them, or otherwise collect profits from them until they passed to her heirs. He could not sell the land, but then neither could she. Beginning with modifications of lands subject to dower in the years of the Early Republic, states tempered the law of coverture, and by the end of the nineteenth century every state had passed married women's property and earnings laws. Industrialization brought the threat of business failure to an emergent middle class and with it a desire on the part of male legislators to protect property inherited by daughters from husbands' losses. Industrialization also led to the creation of new kinds of "paper" property such as stocks that did not fit neatly into established categories of "real" and "personal" property. And most fundamentally, even before the Revolution market capitalism transformed land into a commodity that like any other needed to be free for exchange, something that women's inheritance rights under coverture ("dower") impeded. In other words, the expansion of women's rights through married women's property reform was, in important respects, the product of a need to liberate land and men from the encumbrances of coverture. The reforms granted families power in the market, but they did little to free women from their dependence on men or to disrupt the importance of women's dependence in the construction of men's independence. Men's self-ownership continued to be defined in law and social theory in terms that included sovereignty over a wife.

The law of slavery in place in every state in the Union at the time of the American Revolution constructed blacks as property to be claimed by whites just as whites claimed the land itself. Moreover, as property, blacks were barred, under the law, from themselves acquiring property. Like the relationship to the Indians, the Founding Fathers wrote chattel slavery into the U.S. Constitution. With abolition, whether in the North in the early nineteenth century or the South with the Civil War, came new legal measures safeguarding white claims to the land. Northern states' abolition of slavery in the early decades of the nineteenth century "created" a population of free persons of color in the North (and through individual manumissions in the same time frame, in the South). The end of slavery in the North was vigorously coupled with other legal measures to ensure that whites retained their claim to the land. Every Northern state considered, and many states, especially border states including Illinois and Indiana, enacted laws prohibiting the immigration of free blacks; others, like Ohio required blacks entering the state to prove their free status and post a bond guaranteeing their good behavior. Newly admitted Western states, like Missouri and Oregon, came into the Union with state constitutional bans on black immigration. That the laws largely went unenforced did not remove their power or their border-setting message. They testified that in freedom, as under slavery, the land and through it the nation itself belonged to whites.

In the American South following emancipation, laws safeguarding whites' claim to the land and creating a pool of immobile, black agricultural laborers were as vital to safeguarding white men's superior claim to the land as slavery had ever been. The Black Codes adopted by states of the former Confederacy in 1865 and 1866 bound blacks to white-owned land. Mississippi's Black Code, for example, required all freedmen, at the beginning of each year, to have written evidence of their employment contract for the coming year and made any freedman leaving that employment subject to arrest. The law went so far as to forbid freedmen from even renting land in rural areas. Other states' Black Codes imposed similar restrictions. Republicans assailed the Black Codes as a return to slavery and yet, in their place, gave freedmen "contract freedom," with no right to opt out and be unemployed. There were important differences between the regime of contract and slavery, but at its core there was a fundamental continuity: after the Civil War, as before, whites owned the land.

The end of Reconstruction brought a vigorous backlash against even the modest freedoms and economic independence that Southern blacks had achieved in the years since the Civil War. In any number of particulars these laws consolidated whites' claim to the land and their claim to black labor at the same time that they worked to undermine the fragile hold on economic independence that some African Americans had gained. Following Redemption, Southern state legislators rolled back the substantial property taxes that landowners had faced for the first time during Reconstruction, adding taxes that pointedly targeted kinds of property owned by blacks. Former slave states enacted laws exempting from taxation machinery and implements used on plantations while at the same time taxing mules and tools used by black sharecroppers. So too, they enacted laws cutting off customary rights such as hunting and fishing on private property that had provided blacks and poor whites with a vital margin of economic independence. These laws borrowed provisions from state Black Codes passed during Presidential Reconstruction that had defined hunting and fishing on private property as vagrancy and had imposed taxes on dogs and guns – essential tools for hunting – owned by blacks. Black Codes provided a template as well for state criminal code revisions following Redemption that sharply increased penalties for petty theft.

Anti-miscegenation and Jim Crow laws passed at century's end were equally critical in reclaiming and safeguarding white property claims. State miscegenation laws reached full flower in the years after Reconstruction, amidst Western expansion. Newly admitted Western states extrapolated on the original white/black racial binary of Southern miscegenation laws by prohibiting intermarriage between whites and a plethora of racial others – blacks, Indians, Chinese, and Japanese. Although there were stunning examples of variation on a theme, the bottom line remained the same: racialized others could themselves intermarry, but they were not to muddy the white side of the color line. Marriage between whites and non-whites put white claims to the land at risk. Miscegenation laws proved a vital tool enabling white relatives of deceased white men to claim for themselves property or inheritance that otherwise would have passed out of white hands to the surviving spouse.

Jim Crow, too, secured white claims to the space of the nation. Jim Crow transit laws included a positive grant, a source of new rights: the legal right to occupy a space from which blacks, traveling in their own right, were excluded. In every state in the South, beginning with the passage of Jim Crow transit laws and continuing into the 1930s and 1940s, whites brought and won damage suits against common carriers for violating state law by allowing black passengers to ride in the same rail coach or eat in the dining car at the same time as whites. Jim Crow, in essence, granted whites a temporary property claim by virtue of a contract for passage. And that right and with it the power of Southern states, whatever the formal restraints of federalism, extended across state boundaries.

Despite passage of state anti-discrimination laws following the U.S. Supreme Court's invalidation of the Civil Rights Act of 1875 in *The Civil*

Rights Cases (1883), Jim Crow was practiced widely and in places codified in the North and West. Jim Crow operated in law and practice throughout the country in everything from public schools; to welfare benefits; to housing; to public swimming pools, restaurants, movie houses; and to town and residential property lines. So, for example, in the early twentieth century local officials in the Southwest and North denied mother's pensions, the first state-mandated child support benefit, to black and Mexican mothers. And across the West and Southwest in the late nineteenth and early twentieth centuries, states relied on constitutional precedents like *Plessy* in passing their own laws and ordinances imposing segregated school systems for Mexicans, Asians, and Native Americans. Where law proved a stumbling block – as in the case of Mexicans – school boards could fall back on the segregated landscape, locating schools in "white" or "Mexican" neighborhoods; gerrymandering school district lines where necessary; and, finally "explaining" segregation not by resort to race, but to racially coded criteria, such as language, morals, and disease.

Even more pervasive were the discriminations that "private" property ownership made lawful. In cities and suburbs across the nation beginning in the early twentieth century, white property owners entered into "restrictive covenants" barring sales of property to an array of racial and religious minorities including blacks, Chinese, Japanese, and Jews. A unanimous U.S. Supreme Court in *Corrigan v. Buckley* (1926) gave white property owners free rein to do what it had held in *Buchanan v. Warley* (1917) that cities could not constitutionally do: protect residential segregation. What individual homeowners lost in terms of the right to freely convey their property was compensated for by essentially expanding their rights beyond their own property lines. Restrictive covenants ran with the land and gave white homeowners a property right in perpetuity to a white neighborhood. Given the pervasiveness outside the South of "sundown towns" – jurisdictions that excluded African Americans (and in some areas other racial minorities and Jews) by ordinance, signs, word of mouth, and violence – in the decades after 1890, one might question the need for racially restrictive covenants as much as the power of the Supreme Court.

Exclusion was not limited to residential ownership. Private property gave license to discriminate. Through the first half of the twentieth century and beyond, the legal right of owners of a broad array of "private" businesses – restaurants, hotels, beauty parlors, bars, theatres, dining clubs, and colleges – to discriminate among patrons on the basis of race and gender held firm. "Whites only" signs or their negative, "No ___ allowed," dotted establishments in towns and cities across the nation. All that differed was the targeted other – Indians in Minnesota and the Dakotas; Chinese and Japanese in California, Oregon, and Washington; Mexicans in Arizona, New Mexico, California, and Texas; blacks throughout the South, Southwest, and even areas in the North; and women in establishments across the nation. In the eyes of most white Americans, whites were the public, and in the eyes of most white men, certain spaces were simply the domain of men.

Through the first three-quarters of the nineteenth century, the focus of nation building was largely on internal borders. In the last quarter of the century, Americans trained their sights on protecting white claims to the land from the periphery. Beginning with the Page Act of 1875 and culminating with the National Origins Act of 1924, the United States strained the flow of immigration through ever finer sieves. The first targets were Chinese women, then Chinese laborers, then Japanese, then idiots, polygamists, anarchists, and a bevy of others singled out by personal characteristics; and finally, immigrants who did not match America's "native stock." By ignoring non-white, non-European peoples in defining the nation's native stock, the trickle of continued immigration permitted under the immigration acts of 1921 and 1924 privileged European countries, further bolstering the restrictions that made America a white nation. And to protect whites' claims to the land against the tiny Asian population in the United States, Western states passed alien land laws prohibiting property ownership by those ineligible for naturalized citizenship. As the path of American empire extended at century's end to lands separate from the continent, the United States carefully protected the borders of belonging. The two poles were represented by Hawaii and the Philippines. Whereas Hawaii could be envisioned as part of the nation someday, the Philippines would occupy an entirely new legal status – "unincorporated possession": a site for U.S. assumption of the white man's civilizing burden, but most certainly not one from which future U.S. citizens would come.

In Defense of Mastery

The chronology of the long nineteenth century reveals a pattern of challenge and adaptation. Every successful incursion on privilege was met by a consolidation, so that in some fundamental way the century did not "progress" at all.

To say that the borders of belonging were from the outset defined in gendered and racialized terms does not mean that white men all enjoyed the same legal status in nineteenth-century America. The United States was born a nation in which all white men did not even share political equality under the law. The assumption that republican government depended on an independent citizenry and that independence demanded property ownership meant that every state carried over property qualifications for suffrage from colonial law. The effect, of course, was that for the first thirty to fifty years of the new nation, most "citizens" – men as well as women – could not vote.

Yet, as an immediate matter, that exclusion was not especially significant. First, at the outset the right to vote was not freighted with the political and social significance it would acquire as the century progressed; the rights of citizens were yet in the making. Second, there were so many other particulars in which the law protected white men's superior rights. The law of coverture was brought wholesale into the new nation's legal structure. The Founders wrote slaves' subordinate status into the Constitution, and state laws relating to slavery, in turn, were reenacted in the Revolution's wake. The physical, that is national, borders of belonging seemed secure. Land was plentiful. Native Americans were peoples apart. Naturalization was limited by law to "free white persons."

But forty years after the founding of the Republic the borders of belonging were on the verge of their first fantastic upheaval. The Jacksonian era, often seen as a moment of contradiction because of its simultaneous expansion and contraction of rights, was not a contradiction at all. It was simply the first test. The challenges came from literally every direction.

First, there was the challenge embedded in the nation's very founding principles. There was nothing inherent in the principles espoused in the Declaration of Independence that limited their imagining or their application to white men. Nor were the nation's Founding Fathers blind to the hazards or possibilities to which their revolutionary rhetoric gave rise. As James Otis asked in 1764, "Are not women born as free as men?"[7] Nor were women's rights the most glaring contradiction to the nation's founding principles. In the wake of the Revolution, the pressure for abolition – domestically and internationally – was intense. By 1830, every Northern state had abolished slavery, whether through legislative enactment, judicial decision, or constitutional revision. Yet, slavery's abolition in the North was not simply the product of principle. Slavery was abolished in the North because principle coincided with an economic transformation that marginalized slavery's economic importance and because, in relative terms, the property interest at stake was limited; that is, slaves were few. And even so, "disowning slavery," in terms of actual practice in the North, was of far longer duration. Where principle conflicted with economic demands as it did in the South, economic demands prevailed, thinly veiled by rationalization.

[7] James Otis *The Rights of the British Colonies Asserted and Proved* (Boston, 1764).

Massive white migration "west" in the 1820s and 1830s brought Americans into direct conflict with Indian tribes at the same moment that the destabilizing impact of industrialization began to sweep many white men into a new subordinate wage-earning class. American courts drew the new hired labor into the rubric of master/servant doctrine – a sleight of hand, if you will, in which "free labor" in fact represented a dramatic extension of a relationship of subordination. The fiction of the hireling's independence provided the foundation for common law doctrines, such as assumption of risk, the fellow-servant rule, and contributory negligence, that furthered the hireling's subordination.

Nor was industrialization's destabilizing force limited to the wage-earning class. In the boom-and-bust economy of the early industrial order, business failures multiplied exponentially. Furthermore, industrialization freed a growing group of white, "middle-class" women, urged on by the teachings of the Second Great Awakening, to pursue a sense of moral obligation beyond the household. More yet, a small elite among women began to see the contradiction between their legal and cultural subordination and the principles for which the Revolution had been fought. First privately and then publicly, in part inspired by activism in the abolitionist movement, they began to resist their own subjection.

Reflecting on the forces at play, what stands out in Jacksonian America is that the stakes of gendered and racialized privilege suddenly increased. This was the context in which states moved to repeal common law restrictions barring aliens from land ownership and extended universal white male suffrage. Once seen in this context, these reforms were not the first steps in a progressive broadening of land ownership and suffrage – a realization of the liberal ideal – but rather were but two elements in a collection of responses intended collectively to resist the first major threat to the borders of belonging. The Indian Removal Act of 1830; the tightening of the law of slavery in the South; adoption of laws in Northern states barring free blacks from immigrating to the state, from voting, and from property ownership; universal white male suffrage; even married women's property laws – all reinforced the boundaries that revolutionary principle, Northern abolition, industrialization, religious revival, and Western expansion had begun to threaten.

Pressures on the borders would only increase over the next two decades. In the summer of 1848, women gathered at Seneca Falls, New York. Their demands for full and equal rights as individuals and citizens, including the right to vote, sparked the first women's rights movement. The Mexican-American War vastly expanded the territory of the United States, but also guaranteed by treaty the rights of "citizens" to the Mexicans who lived on that land. Political upheaval and economic disaster abroad fed a growing tide of European and, for the first time, Chinese immigration. As the numbers of Americans grew, pressures for Western expansion and white access to Indian lands increased. And with each new state admitted to the Union, the long-term viability of the delicate balance over slavery that had been struck at the framing was increasingly questioned on both sides.

The Civil War has long been recognized as a dividing line in the history of the United States, but why and with what consequences for our understanding of American history? The final collapse of the compromise over slavery divided the nation between those who claimed supremacy for state's rights and those who claimed the supremacy of union. Slavery was the combustible element. In these terms – that is, the forging of "nationhood" – the Civil War was indeed a second American Revolution and makes sense as a dividing point for surveys in American history. Henceforward, it would be "the United States," not "these United States."

But that dividing line has served to obscure a more fundamental continuity in the nature of the American Republic. The Civil War tested the borders of belonging – of person, citizen, and nation – as never before, but afterward they continued to be defined fundamentally as before, through the gendered and racialized beings of white men. This is not to deny the significance of freedom for the four million held in chattel slavery. It is intended to suggest that understanding how freedom could be so hemmed in by constraint requires placing the end of slavery in the broader context of the long nineteenth century, as well as grasping the incremental, other-directed path that led to freedom.

Freedom for the four million held in slavery in the South began as a byproduct of Northern victories, was fed by enslaved men and women's pursuit of freedom, was formalized into military strategy by a desperate president – Lincoln's "threat" of emancipation directed to the rebellious South – and was incorporated into the Constitution in the Thirteenth Amendment in the resolve that the nation would not again be torn asunder by slavery. Section 2 of the Fourteenth Amendment was never intended by most as a guarantee of freedmen's right to vote. The end of slavery washed away the critical balance between North and South embodied in the three-fifths clause of Article I of the Constitution. Section 2 of the Fourteenth Amendment restored that balance: if granted the right to vote, freedmen would no doubt vote Republican; if denied the right to vote, they would at least not count toward the number of representatives Southern states could send to Congress. For most white Americans, North and South, the end of slavery was never about equality as we would recognize that term today. There was certainly no expectation that putting an end to slavery would undermine white men's prerogatives as America's first citizens. Indeed to many whites, an end to slavery was vital to safeguarding the boundaries that created a white man's republic.

What rights African Americans gained in law and enjoyed in fact in the years of Reconstruction were the product of continued Southern white intransigence, which inflamed Northern opinion, and the reality that Republican political power depended on Southern blacks. Republicans were determined not to have won the war only to lose political power. Too often we read Section 1 of the Fourteenth Amendment, with its guarantees of birthright citizenship, due process, and equal protection and its prohibition of state denial of the privileges and immunities of citizenship, as though it stands alone. Section 1 did indeed represent a dramatic reconfiguration of state and federal power in protection of civil rights, but, for our purposes here it is important to recall the other sections too. And, more, it is vital that we not lump all the "Reconstruction Amendments" together as though they were passed and ratified as one. The three amendments spanned five long, politically tumultuous, and violent years. Each amendment was itself a response to events on the ground.

The bounds of freedom are not easily constrained of course. Like the American Revolution a century before, the Civil War unleashed the expectations of women and racial minorities. African Americans embraced Lincoln's Emancipation Proclamation, seeing in it and in the Thirteenth, Fourteenth, and Fifteenth Amendments and the Civil Rights statutes a commitment to equality and justice for all. Women pressed for inclusion in the Republic as full rights-bearing individuals and citizens.

Supposing the demands for freedom, equality, and full citizenship could have been limited to freedmen and freedwomen and to white women, they would still have represented a fundamental threat to white men's status. The threat was all the greater because the demands could not be limited. In 1866, Senator Charles Sumner began what would evolve into a four-year battle to eliminate the racial prerequisite to naturalization by demanding that Congress strike the word "white" as a requirement for naturalization. In that time period, Congress would pass the Civil Rights Act of 1866 and the Fourteenth and Fifteenth Amendments to the Constitution. And, yet, on July 4, 1870, the Senate – dominated by Republicans – overwhelmingly rejected Sumner's amendment.

To allow the Civil War, and especially the end of slavery to become the fundamental dividing line of the nineteenth century – the terminus of a nation "half slave and half free" – is to obscure other exclusions even then in the making, as well as the opportunity the war itself offered for safeguarding white men's superior claim to self-ownership, citizenship, and nation. For example, the limited control over reproduction that abortion accorded women was under attack even before the war. The American Medical Association's successful crusade to make abortion illegal at every stage of pregnancy began in 1857 and had achieved success in every state in the nation by 1880, spanning the war years. The war provided the opportunity for passage of the Homestead Act (1862), the explicit purpose of which was to seed the West with white settlers, and for adoption of a Reservation Policy (1867) dispossessing Native Americans of all Western land except for two areas in the Dakotas and Oklahoma territories. Treating the Civil War and Reconstruction as the end point of an era ignores the ugly continuities between slavery and the at best stunted freedom enjoyed by the vast majority of African Americans in the South at century's end.

At the end of the century, industrial capitalism brought further threats to white male privilege. Massive immigration, like a flood of currency, devalued hirelings' labor; inadequate wages pulled their wives and children into the labor force. Legal reform made the state rather than the individual man as husband and father the arbiter of children's and women's labor. So too, the criminalization of birth control, like the criminalization of abortion, protected the racial and gender hierarchy not by increasing men's traditional patriarchal authority over the women in their households, but by giving the state itself the power to police women's bodies.

The pursuit of border enforcement was so intense in part because the boundary lines themselves were unclear and shifting. Massive new waves of immigration at the end of the nineteenth century added to the pressure that emancipation coupled with industrialization created for embodying formal ways of policing the color line in law. Law could prohibit intermarriage of whites and persons of color, it could mandate racial separation in public transit and education, it could limit naturalization to white persons, and so on. But this, it would become clear, was not a sure fix. Racial categories were variable from state to state. And in a given state, by administrative necessity, what was "white" and what "colored" depended on legal context. The myriad definitions of color in a single state's statutes were eloquent testament to the constructed quality of race. Law itself destabilized the racial order, for who was white and who was colored, and how to know the difference, invited challenge and subversion.

In its turn, immigration restriction beginning in the 1880s must be paired with the final assault on Native American sovereignty. Immigration restriction imposed increasingly fine filters limiting entrance to the nation; dissolution of Native American sovereignty sought to end the contradiction of nations within a nation. The one operated by exclusion, the other by inclusion; both were calculated to protect and, in fact, did protect whites' claim to the land and with it the space of the nation.

II. TO BE "OTHER" IN LAW

> *"By the laws of the country from whence I came, I was deprived of myself – of my own body, soul, and spirit."* (Frederick Douglass, *Narrative*, 1845)

> *"To think that all in me of which my father would have felt a proper pride had I been a man, is deeply mortifying to him because I am a woman."* (Elizabeth Cady Stanton, Letter to Susan B. Anthony, 1855)

> *"The land of the Dakotas was once large and covered with buffalo and grass," Red Cloud began. But then, "white people poured into our country" and began to "divide up our land and tell us what part they would give us."* (Red Cloud, 1878, in Ostler, *Plains Sioux*, 123–24)

> *"[S]hould a colored person endeavor, for a moment, to lose sight of his disability, these staring signs would remind him continually that between him and the rest of mankind not of his own color, there was by law a great gulf fixed."* (Charles H. Chesnutt, *The Marrow of Tradition*, 1901)

> *"I'm not interested in being a citizen because . . . I would be a citizen in name only – with no privileges or considerations. I would still be a 'dirty Mexican.'"* (Special Survey of the Mexican Colony at Hick's Camp, CA, Jan. 1940, in Gutiérrez, *Walls and Mirrors*, 89)

> *"I was no longer Charles Choy Leong, but Charles Choy Wong, a tainted person with an illegal family history and a fractured identity. I was not who I thought I was: the fragile wholeness of my desired 'All American' identity was now cracked into pieces, like Humpty Dumpty."* (Charles Choy Wong and Kenneth Klein, "False Papers, Lost Lives," *in Origins and Destinations: 41 Essays on Chinese America*, 1994)

Subject Identities

One of the most fundamental and far-reaching consequences of the law's imagining of "people" as white men was the impoverishment of individual identity for everyone else. Women and racial others were "subject" in at least two senses of the word. First, they were quite literally "subject to" white men's authority and right. Second, whatever their formal citizenship status, they remained subjects, rather than full and equal members of the nation.

The American Revolution tested the gendered hierarchy ingrained in the common law; the gendered hierarchy held. In one particular after another, the Revolutionaries crafted law to uphold the principle that a husband's right to the loyalty of his wife took precedence over her loyalty to the state: loyalty oaths were required only of adult males, not females; confiscation acts excluded dower portions from seizure; married women were routinely granted the right to "cross enemy lines" to join their husbands; and married women who had joined husbands were assumed to have been subject to their husband's will and thus able to reclaim property following the Revolution.

The refusal, of the revolutionary generation to adapt married women's legal status to the ideals for which the Revolution was fought was a critical marker of the conservatism of the Revolution itself.

In turn, from the beginning of the New Republic, women were constrained to enjoy the rights and protections of self-ownership and citizenship through men. Women's legal subordination was marked in the first instance by the requirement that at marriage a woman take her husband's surname. Married women exercised legal rights only through their husbands. In cases of accidental or intentional injury, a woman's husband, not the woman herself, had the right to bring suit. With only the narrowest of exceptions, the injury was to his rights, not hers – his right to her body, services, and lost wages. All that the law treated as personal to or belonging to her was her pain and suffering. Even women's citizenship was subject to their husbands' and defined in terms of obligation to one's husband. Men did not risk losing their citizenship through marriage; women did. Under the Expatriation Act of 1907, Congress provided that American women who married aliens lost their citizenship even if they continued to reside in the United States. The Cable Act (1922) safeguarded the citizenship of only those female citizens who married foreigners eligible for citizenship. American-born women who married Asian men still lost their citizenship, and those who married men eligible for citizenship but then resided abroad for two years were themselves treated as naturalized citizens who lost their citizenship. In other words, citizenship for women remained contingent.

The two reforms that have been taken most often as evidence of women's increased status in the nineteenth century – married women's property law reform and the trend toward granting divorced women custody of young children – capture, in fact, women's continued legal subordination. On paper, married women's property reform effected a broad transformation, including granting to a married woman the right to sue in her own name, to enter into contracts, and to inherit property. In practice, state courts interpreting the laws largely eviscerated gains that the statutes otherwise might have yielded. Courts narrowly interpreted provisions, such as a married woman's right to her earnings, to limit the laws' application to wages earned in workplaces outside the home. Married women's egg money, money from boarders or taking in laundry, even wages earned in industrial "homework," and most emphatically a woman's household labor all remained her husband's by law.

Likewise, grants of child custody to women meddled at the margins of women's subject identity. Under the common law, a woman in an untenable marriage faced a bitter choice: to leave her marriage was to lose her children. Courts' gradual embrace of a new doctrine under which women might gain custody of their children – the "best interests of the child" doctrine – was, in this sense, an advance for women. But the doctrine did not recognize in women the same unequivocal legal right to their children in the case of separation or divorce that men had historically held. A judicial patriarchy replaced the husband's patriarchy. Women who gained custody of their children under the "best interests" doctrine raised their children at the sufferance of male judges. Mothers' custody of their children depended on a set of assumptions about women as mothers and conditioned that right on a woman meeting a male judge's standards of what it meant to be a "good mother" not simply at the moment, but for life.

And women were to be mothers. By 1880, the campaign begun by the AMA two decades earlier had made abortion – legal under the common law before quickening – illegal in every state. The law imposed maternity in other ways as well. The federal and state Comstock laws denied women access to information relating to abortion and birth control by banning it from the mails as "obscene" and forcibly closing birth control clinics. Denial of access to professions and "protective" labor legislation effectively precluded women from securing the economic independence without which they were bound to remain subject to men's will. Judicial decisions incorporated this subject identity into constitutional doctrine: in *Bradwell v. Illinois* (1873) the U.S. Supreme Court held that the right to practice a profession was not protected by the Privileges and Immunities Clause of the Fourteenth Amendment, leaving states free to bar women, as Illinois had, from the practice of law; in *Muller v. Oregon* (1908) the Supreme Court held that state legislation limiting women's working hours did not violate the Fourteenth Amendment.

As the example of women should suggest, subjectivity was structured and guarded as much by inclusion as exclusion. But this tension went beyond gender. The border of belonging was never just one between those who could claim citizenship and those who could not. Women were citizens from the beginning of the New Republic. Mexicans incorporated into the United States under the Treaty of Guadalupe Hidalgo were guaranteed under the treaty's terms all the rights of U.S. citizenship. Section 1 of the Fourteenth Amendment recognized the birthright citizenship of freedmen and freedwomen. As the U.S. Supreme Court recognized in *Wong Kim Ark* in 1898, Asians born in the United States also held birthright citizenship under the terms of the Fourteenth Amendment. The Dawes Act acknowledged the claim to citizenship of some Native Americans, and the Indian Citizenship Act of 1924 extended U.S. citizenship to all Native Americans. Yet none of these groups enjoyed full membership in the nation. Moreover, with the exception of the largely symbolic gesture of amending the naturalization law in 1870 to include "persons of African nativity or African descent," naturalized citizenship remained limited to white persons.

Elaborate administrative regimes were put in place to assert and assure the subject status of racial others. Having relegated Native Americans to reservations, "knowing" the Indian population – in the sense of being able to assign a fixed identity to each Indian – became an essential prerequisite to the assertion of U.S. sovereignty. Censuses provided a tool that allowed for the imposition of disciplinary and administrative control in matters ranging from food rations and annuity goods to punishment for crime. Similarly, following passage of the Chinese Exclusion Act white immigration officials' inability to distinguish one Chinese person from another by appearance led to the creation of increasingly elaborate regimes of paper identification.

At the same time, the very creation of categories of illegality among racialized others like Chinese and later Mexicans, coupled with white inability to distinguish among them, led to the labeling of entire groups as outside the borders of belonging. The Chinese Exclusion Laws rendered all Chinese in the United States at risk of being falsely identified and deported. But the pattern had been set earlier than this: following passage of the Fugitive Slave Act of 1850 – and compounded by the act's provisions barring the fugitive from giving testimony – no black in a free state was safe.

The extension of citizenship and other rights too operated as tools for assuring the subject status of racial others. For example, freedmen and freedwomen long denied the right to marry under slavery found themselves bound to middle-class white norms defining the marital relationship. Freedmen and freedwomen who had long lived as husband and wife suddenly discovered that cohabitation without legal marriage was now a crime. A number of Southern states passed laws simply recognizing ex-slave couples living together at a certain date as legally married regardless of the intention or desires of the individuals. When these men or women sought out partners who had been sold under slavery, they found themselves charged with bigamy and leased out to whites under convict labor laws. So too, under the Dawes Act, Native Americans found their citizenship dependent on adopting "civilized" (i.e., white) living practices.

What escape there was from subject identities under the law privileged men over women regardless of race and across time. From the British promise of freedom to slaves who joined the British cause in the American Revolution, to slaves' purchase of their own freedom, to the escape from slavery via the underground railroad, to male slaves who enlisted in the Union Army during the Civil War, black men benefited, however marginally, by virtue of their gender over black women. It was manpower in fighting a war that the British and, in turn in the Civil War, that the North sought. In turn, black men trained in blacksmithing, carpentry, and other skilled men's crafts far more than black women had the opportunity to accumulate money to purchase their freedom. So too their gendered experience of slavery gave them greater knowledge of the land beyond their own master's property holdings and fewer close ties to children that impeded individual escape.

Access to citizenship and even immigration similarly privileged men over women. In the wake of emancipation, freedmen, not freedwomen, gained the right to vote, to sit on juries, and to hold elective office. It was no accident that the federal agency established to oversee the path to freedom was titled the "Bureau of Refugees, Freedmen, and Abandoned Lands"; in shorthand parlance, the "Freedmen's Bureau." The path to citizenship for Native Americans also privileged men. Whereas Native Americans had been pointedly excluded from birthright citizenship under the Fourteenth Amendment through the clause "and subject to the jurisdiction thereof," the Dawes Act (1887) opened a limited path to citizenship. Under the act, allotment, as well as citizenship, assumed a white family structure, providing a one-quarter section "to each head of a family" and granting citizenship to "every Indian . . . who has voluntarily taken up . . . his residence separate and apart from any tribe of Indians therein, and has adopted the habits of civilized life. . . ."

Immigration law too privileged men over women. In some cases gendered privilege was incorporated into the law by singling out occupations that men or women, but not both, were understood to hold. For example, the first limitations and exemptions on Chinese immigration were fundamentally gendered. The Page Law (1875) prohibited immigration of individuals entering the country for "lewd or immoral purposes" and was intended to prevent the immigration of primarily Chinese women who were assumed to be prostitutes. The Chinese Exclusion Act of 1882 exempted merchants, students, and teachers – all occupations held by men – from its provisions. Other immigration provisions, such as the exclusion of those "likely to become a public charge," were not on their face gendered, but reflected a larger concern that independent female migration represented a danger, and operated in practice to exclude unaccompanied women. In this way, immigration restriction reinforced the gendered hierarchy of male providers and female dependents.

While escape from subject identities opened opportunities, it exacted a high cost. For Native Americans, the law and the courts' interpretation of the Fourteenth Amendment in cases like *Elk v. Wilkins* (1884) made renunciation of Indian life and culture the cost of citizenship. Even then Native Americans did not fully shake their "subject" identity. Under the terms of the Dawes Act, Indians did not hold full title to their allotment; rather, the federal government held the deed in trust. The decision whether an Indian had made the necessary transformation in identity rested not in his own determination but in the hands of white men.

For African Americans and Chinese, there was a different path: passing. For African Americans, passing was limited to those who by virtue of skin coloring would not be identified as black. Passing opened the doors that came with property in whiteness; privately it required a sundering of family ties and made them something of a fugitive from justice in every interaction where racial separation was mandated by law or custom. And, daily, there came the threat of being unmasked. For most Chinese, through what is called the "Exclusion Era" (1882–1943), immigration itself depended on a form of passing: the assumption of "paper lives" – elaborate fictions that included not only assuming a new name but also memorizing a new past to pose as a member of the exempt classes. Nor could illegal Chinese immigrants drop their paper identities once they had immigrated. Under the Exclusion Act, the Immigration Service was authorized to deport anyone who entered the country illegally, no matter how many years had passed.

Inclusion within the borders of belonging in any one particular for a given group often came at the cost of further subordination of others and, more troubling still for the future, tended to reinforce the legitimacy of the stunted narrative of personhood, citizenship, and nation with which the century began. In their effort to retain their fragile hold on the land, the Cherokee in early nineteenth-century Georgia reshaped their lives according to white governance and custom in matters ranging from gender roles, to the ownership of black slaves, to a constitution. And yet in the 1830s, the Cherokee were forced west. In the aftermath of the Civil War, many freedmen asserted their freedom, their manhood, by claiming property in the person of their wife. Yet ultimately freedmen's property claim in their wives was as incomplete as their property claim in their own labor. For one of the glaring inconsistencies of freedmen's freedom of contract was that they were not free to refuse to contract. Freed slaves who did not enter labor contracts found themselves classed as vagrants and punished through compulsory labor.

Ultimately, the most fundamental expression of women's and racialized others' subjectivity was their erasure, by law's operation, from the historical record. Slaves were denied even the most fundamental expression of personhood: a legal name. The fact of their existence was memorialized only by the thriving market in human chattel that recorded their exchange for a price. Until 1870, the U.S. Census recorded only heads of household. Coverture erased whole lives. Debates over legal rights in and beyond courtrooms easily elided the voices and the interests of those whose claim to belonging was most tenuous.

Daily Indignities, Daily Lives

One of Frederick Douglass's earliest memories as a child was of his master ordering his Aunt Hester into the kitchen where he stripped her from neck to waist, bound her hands together and stretched her arms high over her head where he tied them to a hook in a ceiling beam, and beat her until the blood dripped on the floor. Why begin with violence? Because although we like to think of violence as an exception or even as lawlessness, violence – sanctioned, enabled, and hidden by law – was central in the daily lives of women and racialized others. Slaves did not have to be beaten themselves to know that a master *could* beat them to within an inch of their lives, indeed, kill them, without suffering legal penalty. Hearing of a neighbor woman's cruel treatment at the hands of her husband, in June 1792, the New England midwife Martha Ballard recorded in her diary, "O the wretch. He Deserves severe punishment."[8] But he was not punished. Neighbor women were left to talk among themselves of the wrong and perhaps celebrate their own good fortune in not having a husband who would ill use them, but the law offered them no sanction to assist her and little recourse should they find themselves in a similar position. Law placed wives, like slaves, in harm's way. As Elizabeth Cady Stanton would note, the "care and protection" that men gave women was "such as the wolf gives the lamb, the eagle the hare he carries to the eyrie!!"[9]

Law licensed the "private" exercise of violence in part by defining the household as private, but law equally sanctioned public violence. Colonial laws authorizing the death, whipping, branding, castration, dismemberment, and ear-slitting of runaway slaves were carried over into state law in the Early Republic and were given additional sanction and federal scope by the Fugitive Slave clause of the Constitution and the Fugitive Slave Acts of 1793 and 1850. Rarely are the incentives of law so naked in expression as in the Fugitive Slave Act of 1850: $5.00 to the commissioner if he determined that the black was not a runaway; $10.00 if he awarded the certificate of rendition. Rarely are the protections of the accused so non-existent: owners and agents were licensed by law to seize an alleged fugitive with or without legal process, and on their word alone rested the fate of the alleged fugitive. "Chinese catchers" – special agents trained to find and arrest Chinese in the United States in violation of the Chinese Exclusion laws – mimicked the role of the fugitive slave catcher of slavery days. When the Seventh Cavalry finished its "disarming" operation at Wounded Knee in December of 1890, 170 to 200 of the 270 to 300 dead or mortally wounded were women and children, slaughtered as they fled or sought hiding. A final example: "Judge Lynch." Legalized violence framed daily life.

In the light of lived experience, the idea of law offering protection of property, life, or even dignity rang hollow. When Cornelia Wells Bailey, a young black woman, was assaulted by two drunken white men – the

8 Laurel Thatcher Ulrich, *A Midwife's Tale: The Life of Martha Ballard, Based on Her Diary, 1785–1812*, 130.

9 "Address Delivered at Seneca Falls and Rochester, New York" (1870).

"Hale boys" – on a train in Glasgow, Kentucky, in 1894 and brought suit against the railroad, everyone in the courtroom must have enjoyed the legal charade as the railroad's lawyer questioned Bailey's father. "Did you have these boys arrested and prosecuted for mistreating your daughter?" "No sir." "Didn't swear out any warrant against them?" "No sir." "They both lived here close to Glasgow?" "Yes sir." "Never tried to have them prosecuted at all?" "No sir."[10] Suing the railroad was the Baileys' best bet, but even there it was a black woman's word against that of the white conductor and brakeman as to what happened on the train that day, and they denied ever seeing Bailey before and insisted that since "the law" had been in effect – requiring separate coaches for white and black passengers – they had never put or allowed a white passenger to go into the "colored" compartment.

The sequestering of racial others by force of law in public transit, education, and reservations; the racial exclusivity practiced through restrictive covenants; and the exclusion of women from public life physically marked women's and racial others' lives as outside the borders of belonging. As Charles Chesnutt expressed it, "Should a colored person endeavor, for a moment to lose sight of his disability, these staring signs would remind him continually that between him and the rest of mankind not of his own color, there was by law a great gulf fixed."[11] By the terms of state laws, accommodations in public transit were required to be equal *and* separate. Experience taught a different lesson. "Did you ever see a Jim Crow waiting room?" W. E. B. Du Bois began a description of Jim Crow travel in his 1921 *Darkwater: Voices from Within the Veil*. His description took in the lack of heat in winter, the suffocating lack of air in summer, the smell, the dirt, the crowding, the indignity undifferentiated by season. On reservations, Indians often waited months for "treaty" rations to arrive. When annuities finally arrived they were often of inferior quality, purposely unsuited to Indian life. Indian women stood in long lines only to have "treaty" rations thrown to them "as if they were dogs."[12]

Making illegal conduct that otherwise would have been legal did not change the need to engage in the conduct or the sense of a right to do so. The criminalization of abortion did not end the demand for abortion. The criminalization of Chinese immigration did not affect the push and

[10] Testimony of Perry Wells (father of Cornelia Wells Bailey), *Bailey v. Louisville & Nashville R. R. Co.*,44 S. W. 105 (1898), Supreme Court Records Case No. 341, Kentucky Department for Libraries and Archives (Frankfort, KY).

[11] Charles Chesnutt, *The Marrow of Tradition* (1901), 56.

[12] Jeffrey Ostler, *The Plains Sioux and U.S. Colonialism from Lewis and Clark to Wounded Knee* (New York, 2004), 132.

pull factors that led to immigration. Instead, in these and other examples, criminalization contributed to the devaluing or loss of respect for law, fed corruption, and increased both costs and hazards. With ports of entry closed to them, Chinese laborers resorted to risky, expensive border crossings from Mexico and Canada. Illegality whether in immigration or abortion created underground networks and economies. Ferreting out criminal conduct licensed its own forms of violence – physical as well as psychic. Interrogations of Chinese immigrants at Angel Island could last hours or days, included exhaustive searches of luggage, and for a time included invasive, humiliating physical examinations. The investigative procedures in abortion cases too constituted a form of punishment and control calibrated to warn doctors, humiliate women, publicly expose their transgressions, and force them to become, even in death, a witness against their abortionists.

As the boundaries of legality changed, so too did the nature of or possibility for community. Again and again, Native Americans found themselves bound by treaties signed by those acknowledged to act by U.S. government officials, not by the tribes themselves. Enforcement of laws often depended on defections from within subject communities. Chronicling his escape from slavery, Frederick Douglass questioned the term "free state," burdened as it was by the Fugitive Slave Act. Following passage of the Chinese Exclusion Act, informants from within the Chinese community exposed illegal Chinese to authorities. Moreover, criminalization of conduct rendered those denied the privileges extended to white males vulnerable to other abuses in the shadow of the law. Illegal and undocumented Chinese, for example, like illegal immigrants today, had little recourse against exploitation by oppressive employers, extortion or blackmail by corrupt government bureaucrats and other Chinese, or violent crime.

Being subject meant a narrowing of life's horizons. One story speaks for many. New England midwife Martha Ballard's life, like those of the women she was midwife to, spanned momentous changes in the life of the nation – the American Revolution, the formation of a new nation, the transformation of subjects to citizens. Martha Moore married and became Mrs. Ballard with all that that entailed under the law of coverture before the Revolution. Her diary, written after the Revolution, attests as nothing else can to the absence of a revolution in women's legal rights. Her references were unself-conscious, generally unquestioning expressions of life as she knew it. As the entries and silences in Martha Ballard's diary suggest, hers was a world in which women had no role in public life, in which wives, like houses and cows, belonged to men. By the end of the nineteenth century, with the criminalization of abortion as a tool discrediting midwives, male doctors would be well on their way to supplanting even the niche that had given Martha Ballard's life so much of its meaning, which had provided, in fact, the reason for the diary that allows us to know of her life at all.

In Pursuit of Right

Writing in the wake of emancipation, a South Carolina educator and minister noted, "The Negroes are to be pitied. They do not understand the liberty which has been conferred upon them."[13] He could not have been more mistaken. His statement ignored, first, that the subjugation all African Americans – free and slave – had experienced during slavery offered a school like no other in exactly what was at stake in the word "liberty." His statement ignored as well freedmen's and freedwomen's agency in their own liberation. Yes, President Lincoln had signed the Emancipation Proclamation, but well before he did thousands of slaves had abandoned their masters and headed for Union lines. Their flight undermined slavery as much as their service to the Union buoyed the Northern cause. In turn, their embrace of self-ownership in the wake of emancipation, quite literally, embodied liberty. That their liberty was all too quickly constrained by law should not be allowed to eclipse the moment of freedom. For every individual and every group discussed in this chapter the pursuit of right, like subjection itself, was shaped by historical contingencies that related to that individual life and that particular group. This they had in common: what liberty they had was theirs by their demand, their pursuit of right waged against the defense of mastery, and they well understood its meaning. Liberty, by definition in this new American Republic, was secured, not conferred.

Most actions in pursuit of right remain invisible to us – hidden behind a veil constructed by law. Every story of a slave learning to read, fleeing bondage, feigning illness, or striking back is a story of resistance. For every story that we know, we must apply a multiplier of some unknowable number. In a world that depended on concealing the inhumanity of slavery, the slave narrative represented resistance of the most profound sort. The narrative thread of resistance ran through acts as public as Elizabeth Stone's refusal to take her husband's name on marriage and as private as a married woman claiming a right of self in the marital bed. In the late nineteenth century, after abortion had been made illegal in every state in the nation, hundreds of thousands of women continued to have abortions every year. The narrative thread of resistance ran through every illegal border crossing and the life of every Chinese immigrant.

[13] Eric Foner, "Rights and the Constitution in Black Life during the Civil War and Reconstruction," *Journal of American History* 74 (1987), 869.

There is a synergy between individual resistance and collective resistance and pursuit of right. But unlike individual resistance, the collective pursuit of right requires the coalescence of a whole series of elements. Subjection must be understood for what it is; it must be understood as shared, that is as resting on characteristics that one individual shares with others and on which subjection rests. There must be a language of right to call on, and tools of communication, including literacy or an ability to associate, must be accessible. The American Revolution had articulated a new language of universal, God-given, unalienable rights, expressed most fully in the Declaration of Independence. Although directed to the relation of king and subject, this language of right opened the way for reconsideration of relationships of domination and subordination more generally.

Abolitionism took root in the fertile ideological soil provided by Enlightenment ideas incorporated in the American Revolution. The American Revolution, though, did not immediately spark a broader revolution. Abolitionist sentiment was centered in the North and embraced most enthusiastically by Quakers and the small population of Northern blacks. The vast majority of slaves lived in the South – their urgent and persistent desire for freedom thwarted by geography, illiteracy, bondage, and the U.S. Constitution. And with the abolition of slavery in the North, the legal bonds of slavery tightened in the South.

Among elite white women there were those who understood that the Revolution opened questions about women's relationship to government and even more fundamental questions that went to the heart of familial relations. Yet their challenges remained private, voiced as in Abigail Adams' famous correspondence with her husband John or in correspondence within small circles of women. Women's Revolutionary era petitions to Congress remained individual supplications. Women's subjection remained jumbled together with any number of other relations of inequality and dependence, complicated by the very relation that underpinned women's subordination: marriage. Moreover, the act of association, so fundamental to identity formation, was still in the future, to be spawned as much by forces and institutions tangential to law – the religious revival of the Second Great Awakening, the beginning of the Industrial Revolution in America, even the press – as by law itself.

Most Native American tribes that saw themselves as part of the revolutionary moment at all had staked their independence on defeat of the Revolution. Other tribes' inclusion within the formal boundaries of the nation awaited territorial expansion and the westward surge of white settlement. This was true of the tribes of the Great Plains and the Pacific, whose most enduring goal was not inclusion at all, but tribal sovereignty. The boundaries of Mexico subsumed territory that would only later become the American Southwest. The beginnings of Chinese and other Asian immigration remained well in the future, a product itself of Western expansion.

For each of these groups, exclusion fostered identity and community, which became critical support structures and training grounds for the pursuit of right. White women first acted collectively as women in the 1830s, not in pursuit of the rights of women, but in moral reform, temperance, and abolition. In the antebellum North and West, excluded from white churches, schools, political assemblies, and organizations, black Americans established their own associations. Similarly, in the wake of emancipation, African Americans, long denied by law the freedom to associate, deliberately began the project of association building. During the years of Reconstruction and even more so after, black community organizations provided the foundation for black challenges to the borders of belonging. In the American Southwest, discrimination and exclusion led Mexican Americans to begin to articulate an ethnic consciousness that combined their Mexican heritage and their status as Americans, providing a foundation by the 1920s for challenges to segregated education and discrimination in public accommodations and on juries and for voter registration drives and anti-poll tax campaigns.

Across time, it was the denial of rights in the face of rights or entitlements extended to others that rankled. With each successive expansion of suffrage – first to white men and then to African American men – the inequity of the denial of suffrage to women became increasingly hard to bear; the importance of suffrage to citizenship itself became increasingly clear. Had suffrage been insignificant, the claim underlying the Fifteenth Amendment that freedmen needed the franchise to protect their rights, even their persons, and that this need justified separating the black man's exclusion from women's equal exclusion would not have been made. Chinese in the 1880s understood that it was they alone who were denied the right to immigrate, while at least for a time, others continued to immigrate freely.

Perhaps the most striking commonality across time was the consistency with which pursuit of right took form in law. In *Cherokee Nation v. Georgia* (1832), the Cherokee resisted the state of Georgia's incursions on Cherokee sovereignty, bringing suit as a "foreign state" and insisting that individual states had no authority over Indian tribes and that the Constitution mandated that relations be regulated by federal treaty. How different and yet how alike was the forum shopping less than ten years later of Ellen D'Hauteville – the unhappily married daughter of a Boston Brahmin, who was determined to leave her marriage but keep the only child, a son, of her union with a Swiss count. Unable to resolve their differences short of law, she allowed herself to be "found" and suit instituted for custody in the state that offered the greatest promise of keeping her child. As one Southern legislature after another moved toward adoption of Jim Crow transit, leading black men formed statewide committees to lobby against passage of the laws and, once they were passed, planned constitutional challenges in the state courts. Indeed, every group – Native Americans, women, African Americans, and Chinese – turned to the Constitution in pursuit of right. In significant part, their suits reflected the transformation that the Fourteenth Amendment especially worked in the constitutional order.

And when constitutional challenges were exhausted, women and racialized others took the tools of their subordination and made them into platforms for the pursuit of right. The word "male" had been deliberately inserted in Section 2 of the Fourteenth Amendment to make it clear that it did not prohibit the denial of the right to vote to women. Women instead focused on Section 1 of the Fourteenth Amendment as the foundation of their claim that as birthright citizens they already had the right to vote. Relegated to reservations, Native Americans took the goods the U.S. government intended to promote "civilization" and adapted them to their own ways of life. In the same temporal context, African Americans took separate coach laws – long seen by historians solely as tools for enforcing black oppression – and wielded them in pursuit of individual right. In lawsuits brought across the South from the 1880s through the modern civil rights movement of the twentieth century, African Americans challenged inequality in accommodations, the failure of railroad employees to keep whites out of black coaches, and assaults by carrier employees against blacks in enforcement of the laws.

Why, borrowing Audre Lorde's words, use the "master's tools" to attempt to "dismantle the master's house"?[14] Perhaps first and most important was the recognition that the United States was, in Frank Michelman's evocative, double-edged phrase, "Law's Republic."[15] There was also the remarkable exhibition of law's power: after all, had not the inconsistency of slavery been eliminated through the rule of law? And, finally, there was the power of law's words: the Declaration of Independence; the ringing phrase "We the people" in the Constitution's preamble; the pregnant promises of Article IV guaranteeing the "citizens of each State . . . all privileges and immunities of citizens in the several states," and guaranteeing every state "a republican form of government"; and the Fourteenth Amendment to the Constitution with its guarantees of birthright citizenship, equal protection, and due process of law. Yet, as we ponder Lorde's skepticism that the master's tools could dismantle the master's house, we are left to wonder why the two most

[14] Audre Lorde, "The Master's Tools," in Cherrie Moraga and Gloria Anzaldua, eds., *This Bridge Called My Back: Writings by Radical Women of Color* (New York, 1983).
[15] Frank Michelman, "Law's Republic," *Yale Law Journal* 97 (1988), 1493.

dramatic transformations in right – the formation of the new nation itself and the end of chattel slavery – took form in the context of rebellion not law.

III. WHAT IS THIS THING CALLED LAW?

Tapping Reeve, *The Law of Baron and Femme, Parent and Child, Guardian and Ward, Master and Servant, and of the Powers of the Courts of Chancery* (1816)

"An Act to Provide for the Allotment of Lands in Severalty to Indians on the Various Reservations, and to Extend the Protection of the Laws of the United States and the Territories over the Indians, and for Other Purposes." (Dawes Act, 1887)

Judge Hunt: *"The court must insist – the prisoner has been tried according to the established forms of law."*

Susan B. Anthony: *"Yes, your honor, but by forms of law made by men, interpreted by men, administered by men, in favor of men, and against women. . . ."* (Remarks at end of trial for illegal voting, 1873)

"*[T]he child in question is a white, Caucasian child . . . abandoned . . . to the keeping of a Mexican Indian, whose name is unknown to the respondent, but one . . . by reason of his race, mode of living, habits and education, unfit to have the custody, care and education of the child."* (*New York Foundling Hospital v. Gatti*, U. S. Supreme Court, 1906)

"Not all or nearly all of the murders done by white men during the past thirty years in the South have come to light, but the statistics . . . show that during these years more than 10,000 Negroes have been killed in cold blood without the formality of judicial trial and execution." (Ida B. Wells, *The Red Record*, 1895)

"Gentlemen's Agreement" (Japanese exclusion, 1907)

The Masks of the Law

The structure of law itself masked the breadth and depth of white male privilege as well as the subordination of racial and gendered others. But law was neither autonomous nor the product or instrument of a master conspiratorial plan. Events and processes buffeted and overtook law, local issues shaped national policy, events in one venue spilled over to influence law and policy in others, coincidental simultaneity influenced the reading of and legal response to events in far-flung fields, and individuals marshaled law in pursuit of their own narrow ends while others mobilized law to fight for a more inclusive polity. Perhaps most fundamentally, American ideals – from the vision of republican liberty in the Early Republic, to the celebration of America as a nation of laws, to liberalism, to equality, justice, and liberty for all – alternately sanctioned, masked, and delegitimized racialized and gendered limitations of the borders of belonging.

The federal system – and beyond that the physical structure of laws and ordinances itself – operated to mask, at the same time that it assured, law's privileging of white men. There was not only the U.S. Constitution but also each state's constitution; not only federal but as well each state's or territory's statutes, administrative laws, and common law; and beyond these the ordinances of cities, towns, and villages across the full sweep of America. To take just one of the venues, a state's statutes, laws were not grouped together under a heading "Laws to Ensure the Happiness and Privilege of White Men." Rather, the evidence – like the experience of privilege and subordination – was scattered among hundreds and thousands of statutory provisions.

Compilations of these laws of privilege and subordination were not written as such. Treatises on domestic relations, such as Tapping Reeve's *The Law of Baron and Femme* (1816), put the reader on notice through title alone that they were expressing the natural, proper order of things. Thomas R. R. Cobb's, *An Inquiry into the Law of Negro Slavery* (1858), the only Southern treatise on slave law, defended slavery as dictated by natural law. The only collection of states' laws on race published in the early twentieth century – Gilbert T. Stephenson's, *Race Distinctions in American Law* (1910) – was intended to defend, not expose, race distinctions in law.

Even going to those individual statutes or common law precedents, one did not see privilege and subordination baldly cast. In critical respects, the legal construction of whiteness and male privilege was masked because it was achieved through laws that did not, on their face, positively privilege whiteness or manhood. In the first instance, laws created the space in which white men exercised freedom and authority by barring others from that physical and figurative space.

Outright privilege often was masked by inclusive statutory language. State Jim Crow laws providing for segregated public transit had titles like "An Act to promote the comfort of travelers on railroad trains, and for other purposes" (North Carolina, 1899). So too, the state laws and constitutional provisions that effectively disfranchised African American men beginning with Mississippi's new constitution in 1890 were on their face racially neutral. Nowhere was race mentioned, yet almost every particular was carefully calculated to stop black men from voting. The titles of major federal enactments relating to other groups were similarly obfuscatory. The formal title of the 1887 Dawes Act was positive: "An Act to Provide for" and "to Extend the Protection of." State alien land laws simply provided that aliens ineligible for citizenship could not own land. They never mentioned race in their terms, yet in intent and effect they imposed a racial prerequisite/prohibition to land ownership. The National Origins Act of 1924 never mentioned race. There is no language here of taking or subordination or denial of identity.

Not until the 1930s, 1940s, and 1950s would collections of federal, state, and local laws, ordinances, and judicial decisions charting racial distinctions in law – such as Charles S. Mangum, Jr.'s *The Legal Status of the Negro* (1940), Charles S. Johnson's *Patterns of Negro Segregation* (1941), and Pauli Murray's *States' Laws on Race and Color* (1951) – capture the national scope of legal discrimination with a view to eradicating racial privilege from law. And not until the 1970s would state commissions on the status of women begin to document the overwhelming, legally imposed disabilities under which women labored and lived. With the exception of just a few earlier voices, it was only in the 1970s that a new generation of historians and legal scholars, one that included women, African Americans, Native Americans, and Asians, systematically began to unmask the gender and racial bias of legal structures.

Courts and lawmakers dressed subordination in the language of privilege and protection. The asserted public policy goal of state anti-abortion laws passed between 1860 and 1880, was the protection of women. "Man is or should be woman's protector," wrote Justice Joseph P. Bradley in his concurrence to the U.S. Supreme Court's 1873 decision in *Bradwell v. Illinois*. Separate coach laws, like Indian removal, were described in terms of offering protection and safety to blacks and Native Americans. The distant echo of these laws resound in current legislation, such as California's "Civil Rights Initiative," states' "Women's Right to Know" laws, and the federal 1996 "Personal Responsibility and Work Opportunity Act."

Courts and lawmakers insisted that difference was part of God's ordained order to which law must yield, helpless to do otherwise. In *Bradwell*, Justice Bradley's opinion was a paean to motherhood. "[T]he paramount destiny and mission of woman are to fulfill the noble and benign offices of wife and mother," he declared. "This is the law of the Creator. And rules of civil society must be adapted to the general constitution of things." Only a few years earlier, in the 1867 case *West Chester and Philadelphia R. R. v. Miles*, Justice Agnew of the Pennsylvania Supreme Court wrote that God had created the races "dissimilar" to effect his intent that they not "overstep the natural boundaries He has assigned to them." Anticipating William Graham Sumner's classic argument, the U.S. Supreme Court in *Plessy v. Ferguson* concluded, "Legislation is powerless to eradicate or to abolish distinctions based upon physical differences." In Sumner's words, "legislation cannot make mores," or more tersely, "stateways cannot change folkways."[16]

The rhetoric of equality shielding the deliberate construction of privilege and disability ran deeper than common law decisions or legislative enactments. The "American" ideal of independence, mastery, and the self-made man has long had a cherished place in the Republic's lexicon of ideals. In fact, the claim that identity rests outside law is and always has been a closely guarded, jealously protected fiction. This mythic ideal gained new, powerful adherents in the wake of emancipation and in the midst of burgeoning industrial capitalism. From Horatio Alger, to Frederick Jackson Turner, to Andrew Carnegie the ideology of individualism cast failure at the feet of the individual. Writing for his brethren in *The Civil Rights Cases* (1883), in which the court struck down the central provision of the Civil Rights Act of 1875, Justice Bradley insisted that "[w]hen a man has emerged from slavery . . . there must be some stage in the progress of his elevation when he takes the rank of a mere citizen, and ceases to be the special favorite of the laws, and when his rights, as a citizen or a man, are to be protected in the ordinary modes by which other men's rights are protected."

The Lawmakers

The structure of the legal system reflected the authority of white men. How could it have been otherwise in a society in which white men were the makers, interpreters, keepers, and enforcers of the law and from which racial others and women were systematically and brutally excluded? White men steadfastly guarded their power over every aspect of the legal system. Through the first half of the nineteenth century, their authority largely went unchallenged. Law was the domain of white men. The right to hold office was limited to those who could vote, and only white men had the suffrage. Jurors were selected from electors; judges from the ranks of lawyers and other prominent men. The entire structure of the legal system was premised on a reasoning world of white men separate from the emotional world of women and racialized others.

The formal structure of lawmaking in turn produced a world of white manly interaction that sealed the bonds of men's authority and loyalties. Judge, juror, legislator, lawyer, legal scholar were themselves heads of household – they shared the benefits and obligations of the structured dependencies of husband/wife, father/child, and for many master/indentured servant, apprentice, slave. In the course of a lifetime of legal practice, it was common

[16] William Graham Sumner, *Folkways: A Study of the Sociologicol Importance of Usages, Manners, Customs, Mores, and Morris* (Boston, 1911), 77.

for a lawyer in the antebellum South to become slaveholder and planter and in turn judge. Judges and lawyers formed deep personal bonds riding circuit together. The circle was broadened to include jurors and witnesses in individual cases as the male legal actors traveled to accident scenes and shared authority in the courtroom. Whether it was the charge, "Gentlemen of the jury," or the elucidation of legal standards – as for example, Oliver Wendell Holmes's description of the "reasonable man" in *The Common Law* – these relationships bore tangible fruit in the law.

White men jealously guarded their preserve against intrusion. In slave states, as well as many Northern and Western states, white men's words and actions were protected against contradiction by bans on slave (or free black) testimony against whites. Ex-slaves confirmed the power the bans placed in white men's hands, seeing in the bans the ultimate guarantee of their disempowerment. Can we wonder that Reconstruction – the one moment in which African American men held substantial legislative and judicial power in the American South – was vilified through the first half of the twentieth century as pervasively corrupt, as the imposition of "black rule" on the white South?

Those looking for evidence of corruption would do well to consider the systematic, brutal expulsion of black men from positions of elected and appointed office, and even suffrage, jury service, and lawyering, in the wake of Reconstruction. From a pitiful high of 24 black lawyers in Mississippi in 1900, black lawyers were driven out of practice and even out of the state, so that by 1935 there were only 5 black lawyers in the entire state. Perhaps most damning of all, the racism that colored the entire legal, social, economic, cultural, and political order meant that black lawyers could hope for little justice for themselves or their clients.

Nor could African Americans, women, Asians, or others hope for justice from a jury of their peers. Despite the Supreme Court's 1880 holding in *Strauder v. West Virginia* that the Fourteenth Amendment's Equal Protection Clause made it unconstitutional for a state to limit jury service to "white male persons," the fact of the matter was that, after the end of Reconstruction, and in many places well before, blacks were systematically barred from juries. White women fared poorly as well. Through the nineteenth century, access to law's inner chamber as legislator, judge, and even voter or juror was limited not only to whites but to white men. Women were constrained to act as petitioners. Women seeking licenses to practice law beginning in the 1870s faced ridicule, condescension, and patronization in equal parts. But behind it all was a steadfast commitment to retain the bar as man's domain. Even in states that allowed women to practice law, women found the doors largely barred by new standards of professionalization that made law schools the foundation for the practice of law, but legally excluded women from them. Those who were licensed were relegated to the margins of legal practice. The right to serve on juries did not, in most states, "come" with suffrage or follow naturally after ratification of the Nineteenth Amendment. Indeed, through most of the twentieth century, women's exemption from jury service was one of those exclusions masked as a privilege.

A final "lawmaker" stood outside the formal legal system: throughout the long nineteenth century violence was the right-hand man of law. White violence was a tool. You can make a list: Sand Creek, Colorado; Snake River, Oregon; Wilmington, Delaware; Rock Springs, Wyoming; Wounded Knee, South Dakota; Manila, the Philippines. These and hundreds of other less celebrated acts of terror and violence, including, most important, lynching, prepared the ground for legal sanction – not limiting the sphere of action of whites, but limiting that of those marked as racial others. White violence led other whites to see the necessity of reinforcing the borders of belonging. It legitimated separation and exclusion of racial others, whether by corralling Native Americans onto reservations away from white settlement, excluding Chinese laborers under the Chinese Exclusion Act, implementing Jim Crow and black disfranchisement, or denying rights of American citizenship to Filipinos. And it led these groups of racial others to accept, in some measure, their legally sanctioned separation and exclusion, for the measure of protection it afforded.

Racialized and Gendered Power in the Making of the Twentieth-Century American State

The founding assumptions that imagined legal personhood, citizenship, and nation as white and male in the long nineteenth century fundamentally shaped the development of the American legal and constitutional order for the twentieth century as well. The construction of the modern administrative state was ineluctably linked to defense of the white male republic. The favored interpretation of the rise of the modern administrative state has long been tied to industrial capitalism. Cherished pride of place as America's first permanent administrative agency has belonged to the Interstate Commerce Commission created under the Interstate Commerce Act (1887). In this interpretive scheme, the administrative state emerged as a response to industrialization, an effort to control the leviathan to protect the interests of the individual. The Interstate Commerce Commission serves as stepping-stone to other administrative agencies intended to police industry and corporate power and ultimately to the New Deal. Even as scholarly work pushes the beginnings of the modern state well back into the nineteenth century, exemplified in the U.S. Postal Service and the management of government lands, it retains the hallmark of the earlier interpretation: race regulation and gender regulation are outside, before, or peripheral to the birth of the modern legal order.

It is less comfortable but more accurate to recognize that Americans first embraced the apparatus and enforcement mechanisms that characterize the modern administrative state as tools in defense of the white male republic. It is a measure of how completely we have defined the Indian as outside the nation that we do not recognize the Indian Office as one of America's first administrative agencies. Well before the ICC, the Bureau of Indian Affairs was administering U.S. reservation policy. The class action lawsuit brought in 1996 for mismanagement of the "Indian Trust Fund" – the huge fund that grew out of the allotment of tribal land to individual Indians – attests like nothing else can to the "permanence" of this federal regulatory structure. The Fugitive Slave Act of 1850 offers one of the first examples of administrative courts focused on an exclusive subject matter. More generally, the Civil War, Congressional Reconstruction, and the Bureau of Refugees, Freedmen, and Abandoned Lands were the first large-scale federal experiments in administrative governance.

In significant respects, the modern regulatory state was born out of the demand for belonging. At the state level, had African Americans in the wake of the Civil War simply accepted their "customary" exclusion from public transit – in other words, had they not insisted that freedom by definition included equal access to public transit – there would have been no need for state-mandated Jim Crow. Had prospective Chinese immigrants and existing Chinese residents in the United States responded to the growing hostility to their presence by not immigrating, or if in the United States by returning to China, there would have been no need for the complex administrative machinery of the Bureau of Immigration. In both cases, formal statutory law took authority out of the hands of state and federal courts that had proved susceptible to rights arguments.

A critical component of the new regulatory order included the criminalization of individual conduct that had formerly been legal. One can see it in state laws criminalizing abortion; state and federal laws banning the distribution of birth control literature and devices; state laws and city ordinances making it a crime for white and black passengers to share the same space in a railroad or streetcar; the spread of state laws barring marriages between whites and racial others; immigration restriction making immigration by certain individuals a crime; and the restriction of work beyond a certain number of hours, after certain hours, or in violation of certain prescribed conditions.

By no means was every enactment criminalizing conduct in these years calculated to preserve white men's hegemony. Gilded Age and Progressive era enactments included public health measures that prohibited the sale of illuminating oil prone to "flash" below certain temperatures, outlawed spitting in public to prevent the spread of tuberculosis, and required the inspection of meat products. They included, as well, laws that eroded men's patriarchal privileges by criminalizing child labor and requiring birth certificates without which child labor legislation would have been unenforceable. All of these laws rested on the state police power to protect the health, safety, and public welfare of its citizens. That laws protecting white men's gender and racial prerogatives were part of a larger regulatory transformation, however, should not be allowed to distract us from realizing that such laws fundamentally defined the era, and more, that the modern state took shape through them.

The new regulatory regime mobilized individuals and non-governmental agencies to serve as agents of the state. The newly organized American Medical Association itself spearheaded the movement to criminalize abortion and throughout the 100-year history of criminal abortion laws remained a vital organ of the state in securing their enforcement. Others were less willing state agents. Doctors, fearing prosecution themselves, conditioned their treatment of women patients suffering from botched abortions on obtaining what were called "dying declarations" from their patients informing on their abortionists. Railroads fought enactment and enforcement of Jim Crow at every step of the way, not out of any commitment to racial equality but rather to retain their own autonomy of action. They too were mobilized by the criminal sanctions provided against both railroads and conductors under separate coach laws to act as state agents in enforcing the laws: under every state's Jim Crow laws, a railroad conductor who failed to separate white and black passengers faced criminal prosecution, as did railroad companies and their executives for failure to enforce the statutory mandate of Jim Crow. State miscegenation laws imposed criminal penalties not only on the couple, but as well on the minister who ratified their interracial union. Government-imposed fines on shipping companies that brought "undesirable immigrants" forced companies to screen passengers at ports of embarkation. What all these laws recognized was that the "state" in its formal institutions and personnel was really helpless to enforce these laws. The only way to realize the laws' intent was to target "service providers" – railroads, doctors, ministers, and others as the case may be – and make them, through threat of prosecution and/or promise of individual gain, agents of the state.

Even as these laws usurped rights, they created new individual rights that through private legal actions legitimated state power and action and reinforced the racialized and gendered borders of belonging. For example, in suits brought by white and black passengers, courts recognized that separate coach laws gave individual passengers a legal right to occupy space in a railroad car from which intrastate travelers of the opposite race were excluded, for the failure of which railroads were liable in damages. Yet, as black women's suits challenging violations of state Jim Crow laws document, this new right simultaneously enforced the racial order. Having long resisted conductors' attempts to force them to ride in colored compartments or smoking cars, black women in their lawsuits during the Jim Crow era replaced the gendered qualifier "who is a lady" following a woman's name by a racial qualifier, "she being a colored woman." White relatives invoked state anti-miscegenation laws in lawsuits to ensure that property from interracial marriages remained in their, that is, white, hands. One of the motivations behind the AMA's drive to criminalize abortion was to push midwives (women) out of the practice of medicine so that male doctors could have the field of obstetrics and gynecology free from female competition. Racially restrictive housing covenants gave whites a legally enforceable right to a white neighborhood.

The modern American state was built, in significant measure, on a supreme faith in statistics, yet Americans seemed oblivious to how fundamentally the borders of belonging shaped the numbers. Return immigration to China was higher because Chinese exclusion laws, anti-miscegenation laws, prohibitions on alien land ownership and on naturalization, and a myriad other legal and extra-legal discriminations against the Chinese made the United States a hostile land. Black travel was lower because many blacks who could afford to travel stayed home rather than face the dangers and indignities of Jim Crow transit. Deaths from abortion were higher because of criminalization. So too was the death rate for Native Americans because of poverty and inadequate health care on reservations.

CONCLUSION

In November 1869, as the Fifteenth Amendment to the Constitution hung in the balance, *Harper's Weekly* cast itself firmly on the side of ratification with a political cartoon by Thomas Nast titled "Uncle Sam's Thanksgiving Dinner." The cartoon imagined an inclusive America. Seated at a large oval table – a table that by its very shape insisted America was a nation of equals – was a diverse collection of people: a white woman, a black man and his family, a Chinese family, an American Indian, a Russian family, an Irishman, and many more. As a frontiersman-like figure carved the turkey, the others engaged in what appears to be lively conversation. And should there be any question of the rights enjoyed by those seated at the table, the words on the centerpiece read "self government" and "Universal Suffrage," and flanking the table and the main title were the phrases, "Come One Come All" and "Free and Equal." Completing the image were portraits of Presidents Lincoln, Washington, and Grant, with statues of justice and liberty between them, a draped American flag, and a landscape scene titled "Welcome." In this idealized imagining of America, all were equals, all full members individually and in the collectivity. America could be, must be, Nast argued, a nation where there were no borders of belonging marked by distinctions of race, gender, class, or ethnicity.

Another look at Nast's image reveals that, even at this extraordinary moment, the argument for a nation without borders of belonging rested on elisions and stereotype and was itself transitory. The Indian was seated at the table, his claim to the land equal rather than prior and hence superior to the others. The erasure of history was reinforced by the landscape painting hanging on the wall. It showed ships approaching a developed shoreline. There was nothing here of white settlers being greeted by native inhabitants of the land. The diversity of membership in the nation was captured in racially and ethnically stereotyped caricatures, re-inscribing the very characteristics that had provided a foundation for a hierarchy of belonging. Nast seated the Japanese, Chinaman, woman, and African American next to each other at the near end of the table, somewhat larger than the rest by virtue of perspective. The choice seems deliberate – an acknowledgment that they in fact loomed larger at this historical moment. Interestingly, the only way Nast could embody full personhood in a woman iconographically was to picture a racially white woman seated at the table alone. The nation itself was cast in male terms – it is "Uncle Sam's" Thanksgiving dinner. The white frontiersman remained in a way, the first citizen, with the honor of carving the turkey.

Nast himself would have been unlikely to draw the cartoon a few years later. Nonetheless, the Thanksgiving Dinner was an extraordinary image. It tried hard to embody the ideals of freedom, liberty, and equality set forth in America's founding documents, ideals that it had taken a Civil War and emancipation to make truly imaginable in their fullest sense to at least a few, for at least a time. The Civil War was a watershed: as a moment of possibility for reshaping the borders of belonging, its importance is impossible to overstate. And yet it has misled us. The confusion is imbedded in Abraham Lincoln's historic words – "I believe that this government cannot endure, permanently, half slave and half free." The institution of slavery, the abolitionist challenge to it, had bequeathed to Americans a narrow, limited vision of freedom, liberty, and equality. Looking at America prior to the Civil War, one sees not a nation half slave and half free, but a nation in which a central condition of freedom and belonging for the few was varying levels of unfreedom for the majority of Americans. Freedom was defined by a set of overlapping, binary oppositions – man/woman, white/Native American, white/black – in which one side of the opposition enjoyed greater freedom by virtue of the other's relative unfreedom.

The freedom of the few and the unfreedom of the many were constructed through and safeguarded by law. Even as the Civil War brought an end to slavery, there came both before it and fast on its heels a dramatic redrawing and reenforcement through law of the borders of belonging not simply in the American South but across the nation, not simply for African Americans but for a whole range of individuals based on categories of race, gender, ethnicity, and class. With lasting consequences for millions of individual lives and for the nation as a whole, the universal human legal person in the liberal ideal took the highly particularized form at the end of the long nineteenth century as it had at its beginning, of the white male.

12

LAW IN POPULAR CULTURE, 1790–1920: THE PEOPLE AND THE LAW

NAN GOODMAN

Law has been a source of popular interest for centuries. From tabloid journalism to serious news coverage to everything in between, legal conflicts and controversies have been capturing the public's imagination ever since the nation's inception and, arguably, before. With the advent of movies, radio, and television in the twentieth century, popular representations of law have become commonplace, but even before these technologies were invented, the law had considerable popular appeal. Unable to appreciate the spectacle of courtroom justice via satellite from their homes, people in the nineteenth century satisfied their curiosity about recent legal developments by attending trials in person and by keeping up with the flood of newspaper and magazine articles devoted to legal events. Helping fuel an unquenchable demand for law-related stories, book publishers like Beadle and Adams churned out thousands of dime novels whose plots revolved around crimes, while artists and craftsmen made their own contributions in the form of public statues, coins, paintings, and medallions devoted to legal themes. Virtually no area of life was unaffected by the popular obsession with the law. During the infamous trial of the preacher Henry Ward Beecher for adultery in 1875, for example, the law even found its way into a popular playground rhyme that "testified" to the preacher's integrity: "Beecher, Beecher is my name – Beecher till I die! I never kissed Mis' Tilton – I never told a lie!"

In spite of, or perhaps because of, the law's widespread appeal as a topic of lurid as well as serious concern, the relationship between law and culture, both high and low, remains obscure. Widely represented in the novels and rhymes that we associate with popular culture, the law tends to be seen more as a source of entertainment than as an integral and constitutive part of our culture. In part this misunderstanding can be traced back to an Enlightenment view of the law as something that lay entirely outside the realm of culture. Culture was the province of anthropology – the myths, traditions, and customs of a society. It was associated exclusively with "primitive" peoples and treated as an index of a society's disorder and mutability. Law, by contrast, was seen as an expression of maturity and civility – it embodied a society's unified regulation. Later, in the nineteenth century, when the idea of culture was redefined by Matthew Arnold as "the best which has been thought and said in the world," the law was given a place within culture. But the move only confirmed a long-standing suspicion that the law was an aspect of high culture, not of the culture of the people.

Recent scholarship on the relationship between law and popular culture has done much to challenge this view. The suggestion has been made that far from being an isolated discipline, the law exists – and has always existed – in a state of interdependence with other aspects of the culture around it. Often the law exerts a dominant, censorious influence on the cultural life of a society; this version of the relationship between law and culture is understood fairly well. But just as often the law shapes itself in the image of preexisting social and cultural movements, or as a result of a negotiation with people and their various forms of cultural expression, it represents a compromise in the form of a statute, say, that is honored in the breach or that depends for its definition on local custom. But how does this process of interpenetration work, and what aspects of the cultural life of nineteenth-century Americans entered into such a relationship with the law?

To answer this question we must look to certain elements of that culture, including the myriad representations of the law in the artifacts of the time, especially in its literary fictions. But to understand how and why such artifacts figured in the life of the people and of the law, we must also look beyond them to the movements and expressions – the rise of a public sphere and the sources of popular protest, including slavery and women's independence – that characterized public opinion and made possible a connection between law and culture in the first place. In examining these subjects we will encounter an alternative to the usual top-down view of how law was made and functioned in the lives of ordinary men and women in the nineteenth century.

I. THEORIES OF LAW AND POPULAR CULTURE

Two fallacies have been largely responsible for confusion over the law's relationship to popular culture. The first arises from the designation of the law as an autonomous and unified regulator of social behavior. To appreciate the extent to which the law has figured in American popular culture, we must see it in its many complex and often contradictory forms. It is no longer possible to view the law as a discrete realm of activity or as a source of objective truth. Nor is it possible to understand the sources of law as composed entirely or even primarily of unimpeachable written codes. According to the legal historian, Lawrence Friedman, the law includes a series of systems that "society defines as 'non-legal,' that is, as economic, social, cultural, or political." Legal culture is not simply a product of the institutions that make and promulgate the law, but of the mindset of the people who interact with it.

The second fallacy concerns the idea of culture. Once identified only with the artifacts produced specifically for high or low audiences – opera for the elites, soap opera for the masses – culture now includes the books, paintings, and music of those classes, and their norms and values as well. Moreover, culture embraces not only what is written or painted but also the act of writing and painting, as well as a host of other activities that put those norms and values into place – informal meetings, associations, protests, parties, and parades. Within the realm of popular culture, there has been further definitional confusion: do the artifacts and values of the people function as a form of control by ruling classes or as an authentic expression of underclasses' own beliefs and attitudes? The question itself suggests the problem, for it is no longer possible to see popular culture as either control or expression; it is instead an arena of social conflict in which political expression of all sorts gets played out in an ever expanding field of human interaction. This is also why representations of culture as distinctly "high" or "low" are outdated. Far more profitable are models, like Frederic Jameson's, which contend that in capitalist societies high and low cultures depend on and reinforce each other. But it is only with a clear sense of how law and culture became fixed in their separate spheres and then were gradually set free from them that we can understand just how intertwined they were in the long nineteenth century.

Law: A Redefinition

The relationship between law and popular culture has long been thought of as unidirectional and hierarchical. The law has been viewed as a source from which popular culture takes its cue, and popular culture, as it deals with "law" in its turn, appears a mere reflection of or reaction to the law's pronouncements. But these assumptions are rooted in a misunderstanding of the law as autonomous and exclusively rule oriented. For centuries, Western civilization was prey to the idea of law as rules imposed from above. In Europe, law had been the preserve of an elite, "kept secret," the novelist Franz Kafka wrote, "by the small group of nobles who rule us." This view reinforced the idea that, while law determined the lives of average subjects or citizens, it was not in any way determined by them. Influential theories about the law have endorsed this view. The language philosopher and pragmatist, J. L. Austin, equated the law with the positive or visible command of a sovereign power. Even in regimes that were not clearly monarchical or absolutist, the law was considered ubiquitous and all powerful. Michel Foucault pointed out the disciplinary nature of an often invisible and unknowable law in his association of law with the image and institution of the panopticon, the Benthamite design on which so many modern prisons were built. The panopticon, in which prisoners were positioned in cells so as to be visible at all times to each other and to a central tower the inhabitants of which they themselves could not see, was an emblem, according to Foucault, of a legal order in which the illusion of power was sufficient for the maintenance of power itself.

But new ideas about law and culture have made it possible to see beyond the law's disciplinary dimension. One recent approach has come from an unlikely source: an acknowledgment by lawyers and legal scholars that there are sources of discipline in culture other than the law. As the legal theorist Robert Ellickson puts it, "governments do not monopolize the control of misconduct."[1] In their willingness to include within the ambit of law not only court decisions and legislation but also law-like activities, legal scholars have turned to the study of social norms as a way of supplementing their understanding of how the law operates in society. Norms – informal rules that include everything from "don't shove" and "don't cut in line" to "be a team player" and that keep certain segments of society in check not by the threat of criminal or civil punishment but by the threat of humiliation and shunning – are seen as working in tandem with official law to control behavior.

With this in mind, we can begin to appreciate how social norms operated in quasi-legal ways in the nineteenth century. In the case of prostitution, for example, one of the nineteenth century's most intractable legal problems, reformers discovered that the humiliation of a prostitute's white, male, middle-class patrons – a norm-based mode of punishment – was a far more effective tool in eliminating the practice than the jailing of the prostitutes themselves.

Another new approach to the study of law and culture moves the study of law away from the study of discipline altogether. Scholars who take this approach see law as something that not only punishes but also creates. As Rosemary Coombe explains, "legal discourses are spaces of resistance as well as regulation, possibility as well as prohibition, subversion as well as sanction."[2] An example of this dual function in the nineteenth century can

[1] Robert C. Ellickson, *Order Without Law: How Neighbors Settle Disputes* (Cambridge, MA, 1991), 4.

[2] Rosemary J. Coombe, "Contingent Articulations: A Critical Cultural Studies of Law," in Austin Sarat and Thomas R. Kearns, eds., *Law in the Domains of Culture* (Ann Arbor, MI), 35.

be seen in the operation of contract law, which created new and productive relationships (between bargaining partners) and severely limited others (between employer and employee). Seen from this perspective, law and popular culture reinforce each other. Far from being a series of incontrovertible, black letter pronouncements, the law, according to legal philosophers like H. L. A. Hart, is more like a set of rules approved, evaluated, and acted on in intelligent ways by the populace.

Acknowledging that the law and culture are interactive allows us to identify manifestations of the law in a wide range of practices, including the practices of everyday life. It was with this in mind that in 1985 the legal historian Hendrik Hartog turned his attention to the practice of pig keeping in nineteenth-century New York. What he found was that despite a local court decision of 1819 that prohibited the keeping of pigs in the streets – they were considered a health hazard and a nuisance – the working poor continued to do so for decades. The law, as stated by the court, seemed to have had little significance for the New Yorkers who continued to engage in an age-old practice that provided them with an emergency source of food and an effective and reliable means of ridding their otherwise neglected neighborhoods of garbage. In this, a new cultural practice that was tantamount to law was created. "People's imagination of what the law says may shape the expressive activities through which cultural meanings are created," writes Coombe.[3]

Culture: A Redefinition

The inability to acknowledge the fluidity between law and popular culture is a result not only of reified theories of the law but also of antiquated views of culture. Matthew Arnold's distinction between high and low culture depends on a notion of literary and artistic works as self-sufficient wholes. More recent theories insist that the artistic productions of the higher classes are not the timeless texts they were once taken to be, but rather the historically situated articulations of their authors. Thus, literature and other forms of artistic expression are treated as sharing properties with discourses as varied as the law, science, and advertising. In addition, the low or popular culture that was once attributed exclusively to less civilized societies is now known to be an aspect of the most developed societies as well.

The emphasis of recent theories on shared discourses has particular relevance to the interconnections between law and literature. James Boyd White has emphasized the extent to which both law and literature are "compositional activities," disciplines devoted to the composition of texts that interpret, legitimate, and even regulate empirical data through narrative

[3] Coombe, "Contingent Articulations: Critical Cultural Studies of Law," 55.

descriptions: in the case of literature, a novel, poem, popular song, or even nursery rhyme; in law's case, a trial transcript or a judge's opinion.[4] In the Beecher-Tilton trial, for example, in which key elements of evidence – including personal letters and eyewitness testimony – were known to the court, spectators, and reading audience by belletristic epithets like "The Letter of Contrition," and the "Pistol Scene," even this distinction between literary and legal styles of narrative begins to unravel. In translating official legal jargon into the Victorian language of sentiment, the Beecher-Tilton trial not only found its way into the popular imagination, but also exhibited its own consciousness of that popularity, blurring the line between storytelling, both legal and fictional, inside and outside the judicial system.

The compositional or constructed nature of law is a further reminder of its place within the larger culture. For Owen Fiss, the judicial act reveals the extent to which the law is, like literature, "neither a wholly discretionary nor a wholly mechanical activity . . . [but rather] a dynamic interaction between reader and text."[5] Similarly for Ronald Dworkin, literary and legal paradigms are comparable mixtures of critical and creative acts. Dworkin offers a notoriously odd but apt metaphor for the legal process, claiming that the law is like a chain novel, "each judge . . . a novelist in the chain."[6] But the possibilities afforded in viewing law and literature as interpretive partners are nowhere more apparent than in the work of Robert Cover, who describes them as coequal narratives in a normative world. "No set of legal institutions or prescriptions," Cover writes, "exists apart from the narratives that locate it and give it meaning."[7] In this Cover ascribes to literature and, by extension to other forms of cultural expression, the kind of normative potential that we typically ascribe only to law. The law alone, Cover suggests, is only part of a larger world of narrative myths, a lexicon of normative action that surrounds it in the form of critiques, utopian aspirations, apologies, and fictions. But these fictions, Cover explains, cannot easily be distinguished from the rules that constitute the law itself, for even these incorporate and cannot exist without the expression of their own alternatives. "Law may be viewed as a system of tension," he writes, "or a bridge linking a concept of a reality to an imagined alternative."[8]

[4] James Boyd White, *Heracles' Bow: Essays on the Rhetoric and Poetics of the Law* (Madison, WI, 1985), 107.

[5] Owen Fiss, "Objectivity and Interpretation," in Sanford Levinson and Steven Mailloux, eds., *Interpreting Law and Literature: A Hermeneutic Reader* (Evanston, IL, 1988), 229.

[6] Ronald Dworkin, "Law as Interpretation," in W.J.T. Mitchell, ed., *The Politics of Interpretation* (Chicago, 1983), 263.

[7] Robert Cover, "Nomos and Narrative," in Martha Minow, Michael Ryan, and Austin Sarat, eds., *Narrative, Violence, and the Law: The Essays of Robert Cover* (Ann Arbor, MI, 1992), 95–96.

[8] Cover, "Nomos and Narrative," 101.

II. AMERICA'S EXAMPLE

The metaphor of the bridge articulates a dynamism that is inherent in American law and culture. Heir to the English tradition, American law diverged from English law from the start. The most important difference was the most obvious: in America there was no king. The absence of a monarch gave the law a prominence it otherwise would not have had. "In America," Thomas Paine noted, "the law is king."

In Revolutionary America the rule of law was meant to answer the tyranny of monarchy. Built into the law of the Revolutionary period was the very resistance and distaste for monarchical constraints that catapulted American law into a unique relationship with popular culture. In the translation across the Atlantic from monarchy to republic, the law had undergone a metamorphosis, from the product of a sovereign power to the expression of the people's will. "In the United States," Alexis de Tocqueville wrote, "everyone is personally interested in the law . . . not only because it is the work of the majority, but because it is his own, and he regards it as a contract to which he is party." One of the most significant elements of Tocqueville's view is that it pertained to all Americans, regardless of class. In America, people were so consumed with the law, he observed, that it became not just a topic of common conversation but a lingua franca, or in his words, "a vulgar tongue."[9]

Some Americans, however, feared that the absence of a sovereign or central power, theoretically poised to address the people's needs, would impede the smooth functioning of government. Paradoxically, their fear ensured that ongoing exchange would occur between the legal and cultural spheres. In America, it was possible to see the influence not only of the law on the people, but of the people on the law. Through their representatives the people spoke directly to the government, while the representatives, in turn, reported back to the people. While the law helped shape public behavior, public opinion exerted a comparable pressure on the law by shaping the perceptions and thoughts of elected officials. "A popular government without popular information, or the means of acquiring it, is but a prologue to a Farce or a Tragedy or, perhaps, both," wrote James Madison.[10]

The open channels of communication between the people and the government subjected the law to public review and in particular to the influence of public morality. The popular support shown for the law in the antebellum period, in spite of a pervasive anti-lawyer sentiment, was one subtle indication of the intimacy between law and morality. Anti-lawyer sentiment reinforced the general consensus that the law should be accessible to the

[9] Alexis de Tocqueville, *Democracy in America*, vol. I (New York, 1945), 257, 290.

[10] James Madison, *James Madison: Writings: Writings 1772–1836* (New York, 1999), 790.

general population without a professional bar. The importance placed on the "reasonable man" as a standard for legal and social conduct was another. To the hypothetical "reasonable man" – the composite personality against which a particular individual was to be judged – was ascribed behavior that was considered customary for the community at a given time, thus ensuring that social norms would be brought to bear in the evaluation of criminal and civil responsibility.

In the early years of the nineteenth century, the easy intercourse between law and popular culture was still largely an artifact of the Revolution. But as the century progressed, the rationale for the bond renewed itself. In the Jacksonian middle decades of the century, for example, the idea of a law informed by the people was the cornerstone of the promise of democracy. Elected president in 1828 and reelected in 1832, Andrew Jackson ushered in a period in which popular opinion, in its mythical generality, was elevated above the law, in its official capacity. Regardless of whether Jackson made good on his promise of equality for all Americans (he organized a brutal genocide against the Indians, among other atrocities), he was the first truly popular president, embraced as a man of the people and affectionately known as Old Hickory, a nickname that echoed the popularity of frontier figures like Daniel Boone. Moreover, his rhetoric of the many against the few and his war against privilege shaped notions about popular contributions to government for a long time to come. Government's "true strength," Jackson wrote in 1832, "consists in leaving individuals and States as much as possible to themselves."[11] Jackson's laissez-faire model became a foundation for the kind of citizen participation in the law that ran the gamut from voting to serving on juries; actively lobbying legislators; keeping pigs; staging protests, riots, and strikes; and writing magazine editorials, dime novels, and newspaper graphics. Under his presidency the public sphere – defined by Jurgen Habermas as "... a realm of our social life in which something approaching public opinion can be formed"[12] – grew in size and scope, extending the location, both real and imagined, where popular culture and the law were intertwined.

III. PROTEST AND THE PUBLIC SPHERE

Popular engagement with the law in the nineteenth century often took the form of protest, which must be seen not only as an expression of

[11] Andrew Jackson, "Veto Message Regarding the Bank of the United States; July 10, 1832," *The Avalon Project at Yale Law School, 1996–2005*.

[12] Jurgen Habermas, Sara Lennox, and Frank Lennox, "The Public Sphere: An Encyclopedia Article, 1964," *New German Critique* 3 (1974), 49–55.

dissatisfaction with the law, but as the creation of an alternative to it. Protests are common to every period in history, but protests in nineteenth-century America were typically more sustained than those that preceded them (lasting in some cases for months or years) and marked by a wide-ranging participation that was made possible by an expanded public sphere. In turn, protests allowed people to form communities of conduct, custom, and expression that functioned like the law or in law-like ways. Protests took place in drawing rooms as well as on the streets and led to changes in social etiquette as well as in civic behavior. Often designated as illegal at the time, some protest movements nevertheless led to systemic legal reform. In a century punctuated by the national cataclysm of civil war, protest proved a telling local counterpoint, a key to what many ordinary people thought about the law's effect on their lives.

The public sphere in Jacksonian America was resonant with voices from a range of socioeconomic classes, due in large part to universal suffrage (which, though limited to white men, was a vast improvement over many European suffrage systems) and the two-party system. Add to this the sheer number of people (including thousands of immigrants who came in waves throughout the century), as well as the expanding material environment, and the recipe for popular legal activism was in place. Eager to play a bigger part in the creation of public culture, people had already discovered the virtue of public display in the form of organized parades, which typically included committees of artisans, fraternal orders, and militias as well as more explicitly political groups. Much of the democratic public culture of the Jacksonian period celebrated America's achievements in the unveiling of monuments to former presidents and major battles, as well as in chauvinist displays of ethnic and patriotic pride, such as the declaration of holidays to honor St. Patrick and the Fourth of July.

It was but a stone's throw from parade to protest. Throughout the nineteenth century people clamored for legal redress of social and political ills. Notices for public meetings of all sorts – conventions of workingmen, Jacksonian Democrats, and Locofocos (alternative radical democrats in 1830s New York), among others – began to displace news items in the newspapers and drew hundreds of supporters every night. People met in a variety of makeshift locations, in public halls, saloons, public squares, street corners, and private homes to discuss their causes and to air their complaints. Topics ranged from the anti-rent movement (a protest against the Old Dutch patroon system that made farmers pay rent to rich landlords in the Hudson Valley in New York), Indian removal, and immigration in the first half of the century to the railroad and oil monopolies and steel strikes of the second half. Countless broadsides, newspaper and magazine articles, and popular novels recounted these struggles throughout the century, including

Helen Hunt Jackson's *Ramona* (1884), about Native Americans in Southern California, and Frank Norris's *The Octopus* (1901), about the railroads.

But two sources of protest were of particular note: labor conditions, because they remained a vital concern throughout the century, and slavery, because, more than any other issue in the nineteenth century, slavery affected the way people thought of and responded to the possibility of justice in the United States.

Wage Labor

Public response to poor working conditions that included sixteen-hour days, smoke- and gas-filled factories, meager quantities of food, and child labor, took aim at the ideologies behind the two most rapidly developing and influential areas of the law in the nineteenth century, contract and tort. It was the new, industry-friendly contract and tort law of the nineteenth century that underwrote the factory system and allowed unconscionable practices to take place.

Under nineteenth-century contract law, contracts were no longer subject to a fairness review, as they had been in the eighteenth century. Formerly, contract disputes had been adjudicated according to a community's sense of fairness, which in most if not all cases tended to favor the interests of the working classes as opposed to those of the commercial classes. But by the nineteenth century the tide had turned, and contract law required only that the parties agree – that there be, in the language of the law, a "meeting of the minds." Under this interpretation, contracts were considered to be an expression of the free and independent wills of the contracting parties (nineteenth-century contract law was known as the will theory of contracts), regardless of what general principles of equity might dictate. Removed from popular control, however, contract law too often veiled a relationship of inequality and obligation. In the employment arena, where contracts were used to establish relations between master and servant, with obviously unequal degrees of bargaining power, there was virtually no free contract at all. In the largest category of cases affected by the new theory of contract, for example, workers who had agreed to work for a certain length of time – typically a year – were barred from receiving compensation for any time less than the whole. Where the tenets of fairness would, in the past, have brought about a decision in their favor, especially in those cases where workers were killed or disabled on the job, nineteenth-century contract law refused to "rewrite" the original agreement. From the workers' perspective, contracts were too often used to disguise the coercion that compelled their consent.

Even more oppressive than the will theory of contracts in the workplace were the uses to which tort law, in particular the developing doctrine of negligence, were put. The doctrine of negligence is crucial to an understanding of the nineteenth century because it, more than any other area of the law, altered the story that the culture told itself about blame and responsibility. Before the changes that took place in the first third of the nineteenth century, the law held that the responsibility for compensating someone for an accident fell absolutely or strictly on the individual who caused the injury. But the doctrine of negligence redirected the inquiry to the issue of fault. Unless an individual was identified as blameworthy, the accident victim bore the cost of the harm. The anti-compensatory thrust of negligence law served as a license to entrepreneurs who were often the defendants in tort litigation. Thousands of workers were injured on the job, but their injuries went uncompensated and ignored. Of all the employers, the railroad, the literal and figurative engine of nineteenth-century progress, was perhaps the worst offender in this regard.

Where the law was confused or, as in many new settlements in the West, non-existent, workers provided their own counterparts to it. An example of how custom filled the void and served as a template for civil regulation can be seen in the mining codes that sprang up all over the Western mining camps. These unofficial codes "were little bodies of law adopted as binding customs" that established rough but workable rules and processes for recording miners' claims, for deciding the precedence of claims, for settling disputes among claimants, and for enforcing the decisions of the miners' courts. Mining clubs were often protectionist and corrupt in themselves, but they sometimes succeeded where official law had failed.

In places where established courts found in favor of employers who continued to avoid taking responsibility for the victims of unfair contracts and unsafe conditions, however, the trade union movement grew, as did one of the unions' favorite tactics, the strike. Strikes, like boycotts and pickets, occupied an unusual position in the link between popular culture and the law in that they were legal, but from the standpoint of the legal hierarchy of courts and company lawyers, highly undesirable. They were, then, a good example of how the people's culture (the culture of the striking workers, that is) could test and eventually reshape the limits of officially enshrined law. Small groups such as laundry workers and garment workers used the strike to gain power, especially in times of economic depression in the 1850s, 1870s, and 1890s.

One group that thrived in a period of depression, the early 1870s, was the Mollie Maguires, disgruntled mineworkers in the anthracite coal region of eastern Pennsylvania. Organized as a labor union, the Mollies worked for years in total secrecy to overthrow the mining companies' management. Composed primarily of recent Irish immigrants, the Mollies had a labyrinthine hierarchy that included local chapters with body masters, district organizations, and an overarching union that received new passwords on a weekly basis from England. Through these chapters, the Mollies protested low wages, long hours, and ill health among the men who worked the mines, but they also functioned as welfare societies for members who could not find work (often because of strikebreakers) or who were disabled. In the end, through the efforts of an undercover Pinkerton agent who lived with them for years, several of the Mollies were accused and convicted of perpetrating the violent murders of coal mine operators, bosses, and superintendents. Nineteen were hanged in what was the largest public execution since the burning of the "witches" in Salem in 1692. The verdict, however, did little to staunch the flow of public opinion about the Mollies and their goals.

In an early instance of the crossover of legal and popular audiences, the transcripts of the witnesses testifying at the Mollies' trial were reprinted in newspapers and pamphlets. In addition, in the Spring of 1876 three newspapers, *The New York Weekly*, the *Saturday Journal*, and *The Fireside Companion*, ran serial novels about the Mollies. In 1877, Allan Pinkerton, of the detective agency that had brought them to trial, published his novel, *The Mollie Maguires and the Detectives*, the sixth installment in his popular detective series. With the exception of the Pinkerton novel, all of the popular literature inspired by the Mollies was, despite their violent tactics, sympathetic to their cause.

If the violence of the Mollies put the *legality* of their movement into doubt, it did little to diminish their *legitimacy* in the public's eye. The Mollies were generally perceived as addressing grave social injustices and as being driven by and reflecting the popular will. Moreover, the violence displayed by groups like the Mollies was in line with official policy that sanctioned violent methods on the part of law enforcement, a policy that accounts in part for many of the similarities between official law and outlaw culture and, by extension, between official law and popular culture. In the case of the Mollies, for example, the miners' violence was met in equal measure by the violence of the Pennsylvania Coal and Iron Police who were sent by the state to control them.

Unprecedented violence also marked the Haymarket riot of 1885. On the evening of May 4 of that year, anarchist leaders of the Central Labor Union, the parent organization for twenty-two unions, called a meeting in Haymarket Square in Chicago to discuss events of the previous day when police had fired into a crowd of strikers. Everything remained relatively peaceful among the three thousand people who had assembled in the square until a bomb exploded in the crowd, killing seven policemen and wounding more than sixty others. Evidence disclosing who planted the bomb was never uncovered, but four anarchist labor leaders (only one of whom was present at the scene) were hanged, another committed suicide, and three were imprisoned. In the wake of the hangings, protests sympathetic to the strikers spread throughout the world.

In Western America, where the law that regulated labor and land acquisition remained unclear, official law and unofficial law often merged in the form of a violence known as vigilantism. Vigilance committees were formed in the 1850s in San Francisco, California, Carson, Nevada, and Denver, Colorado. Composed primarily of men from the merchant classes, these committees took the law into their own hands, hunting down so-called criminals, trying them in courts of their own creation, and lynching them as they saw fit. Even after the vigilance committees disbanded, there were periodic lynchings and other manifestations of vigilante "justice" in almost every state of the union. In some instances representatives of the official legal culture – elected officials of a municipal government, for example – allied themselves with unofficial groups of bandits, as in the case of the Ku Klux Klan in the South.

The clash of violent tactics used by both the legal establishment and the workers that characterized the century's approach to labor unrest came to a head in the Pullman strike of 1894. In this strike, workers who manufactured George Pullman's famous sleeping railway cars and who lived in the town of Pullman, a wholly owned subsidiary of the company located in what is now the southern part of Chicago, were driven to strike when the company, which had cut their wages several times in the 1880s and early 1890s, refused to reduce their rent to a similar degree. Workers struck on May 11, 1894, and by late June railroad workers throughout the nation sympathetic to their cause began to boycott all trains carrying Pullman cars. When President Grover Cleveland called in federal troops to keep the trains moving, violence and looting in Chicago ensued. The federal government declared victory in August when the strikers were either laid off or forced to return to work, but the bitterness of the strike served as an incentive to the business and labor leaders of the Chicago area to find a less one-sided solution. The result of their efforts was the Chicago Civic Federation, composed of representatives from the public, organized labor, and capital. The Civic Federation worked outside the law and yet within its general parameters for reform. Many state reforms resulted, including the passage of numerous laws that required safety inspections in factories, revised tort law to allow for greater compensation for injured workers, and regulated wages and working hours.

Strikes among meat packers, as well as the publication of *The Jungle* (1906), an influential novel by Upton Sinclair about the abuses of that industry in Chicago, also led to sweeping reforms. Just six months after Sinclair's novel was published to great acclaim and with unprecedented publicity, including front-page notices in all the major newspapers, Congress passed the Pure Food and Drug Act and the Beef Inspection Act. In the following months and years, federal reforms, which typically followed on the heels of state and local reforms, addressed the regulation of the railroads and the telephone and telegraph industry, turning many of the workers' demands voiced through protest into law.

Slavery

The practice of keeping slaves in nineteenth-century America engendered endless debate about its constitutionality. Laws and judicial decisions (the Fugitive Slave Law of 1850 and the *Dred Scott* decision of 1857, to name just two) reinforced the institution of slavery, but slavery was repeatedly challenged by slave revolts, runaways, and ultimately by civil war. From the late eighteenth century on, however, protesters and abolitionists waged a quieter and in many ways more successful campaign to put an end to slavery. By putting pressure on legislators, organizing within their communities, and changing people's attitudes toward people of African ancestry, abolitionists did more to change the view of slavery in the popular mind and imagination than any other group concerned with slavery at the time.

Abolitionists recognized the importance of changing the laws on slavery directly, and they worked hard to rewrite the legislation that sanctioned slavery in the years leading up to the Civil War. But their less explicitly legislative efforts were often more noteworthy and more successful. The Underground Railroad, the unofficial conduit to freedom made up of houses known as safe havens for runaway slaves, was the most celebrated of these popular efforts to abolish slavery, but others should not go unnoticed. Self-proclaimed abolitionists, as well as those who did not necessarily consider themselves political, met in prayer groups to remind themselves and others about the evils of slavery. Others held fairs and bazaars to raise money to help slaves escape. Still others, as agents of organizations like the American Anti-Slavery Society, toured the country giving lectures on the evils of owning slaves.

In terms of its place within nineteenth-century popular culture, the abolitionist movement is remarkable in two respects. The first is its all-inclusive class membership. The call to end slavery found supporters from all socioeconomic classes, from the elites, to the middle-classes, to the working poor. The fact that anti-slavery sentiment transcended class difference, even in an increasingly class-conscious society, indicates just how powerful certain popular movements were in forming coalitions and alliances that the law, as such, could not promote. Not surprisingly, most of the charitable work within anti-slavery organizations was done by people from the upper and middle classes – people who had the leisure to devote their time and energy to helping others and the authority to make a difference when they did. But the working classes were typically aligned with them (at least until they were conscripted as soldiers and forced to leave their jobs and sacrifice their pay).

The second attribute that makes the abolitionist movement an important link in the analysis of nineteenth-century law and popular culture was its appeal to popular morality. In its association of slavery with inequality, abolitionists targeted the widespread moral and religious underpinnings of their society, arguing that slavery violated Christianity's precept to "love your neighbor as yourself."

One of the most influential documents in the abolitionists' arsenal was Harriet Beecher Stowe's best-selling novel about slavery, *Uncle Tom's Cabin* (1852). By addressing slavery through a domestic paradigm (the novel is rendered as the story of several families, both masters and slaves), rather than writing a political tract, Stowe hoped to change not legal reasoning but popular sentiment. That Stowe chose the novel form to voice her opinion also says a great deal about how important popular culture was to the abolitionist strategy. Aspiring to alter popular opinion as a way of altering the law, radical abolitionists saw the power of narrative's ability to move a reader emotionally, to keep the suffering of the slave's existence in focus at all times. Frederick Douglass's tremendously popular *Narrative of the Life of Frederick Douglass, An American Slave* (1845) also follows this strategy by presenting a series of carefully chosen scenes of the gruesome whippings to which he and other slaves were subject.

Abolitionists also quickly recognized the importance of graphic images in their struggle to influence popular opinion. At least one anti-slavery society passed a resolution to endorse the use of "pictorial representations" of slaves "so that the speechless agony of the fettered slave may unceasingly appeal to the heart of the patriot, the philanthropist, and the Christian."[13] Others soon followed suit, and images of slaves being torn from family members, being sold at auction, or being whipped and branded appeared in broadsides, newspapers, and books throughout the antebellum period. One image of a male slave in chains, fashioned by Josiah Wedgwood in England and distributed widely in America by Benjamin Franklin as early as 1787, was particularly influential. Of this image, Franklin wrote to Wedgwood: "I am persuaded it may have an Effect equal to that of the best written pamphlet, in procuring favour to those oppressed People."[14] As was the case with the printed graphics, images like Wedgwood's were

[13] *Proceedings*, First Anti-Slavery Convention of American Women (New York, 1837), 14.
[14] Franklin is quoted in Alison Kelly, *The Story of Wedgwood* (New York, 1963), 42.

widely reproduced and manufactured for cameos, coins, and medals. Similar images of both male and female slaves in chains decorated the needlework – the pincushions, bags, pen-wipers and card-racks – made by women in anti-slavery sewing circles.

Of course, images of slaves in the nineteenth century were not always disseminated in the service of the abolitionist cause. In the antebellum and postbellum minstrel show, whites put on blackface in a complex gesture of racial hatred and admiration. Staged primarily for the working classes in the popular theaters of the day, the minstrel vogue catered to workers whose class status, regardless of their skin color, made their place in society insecure. Seeing the minstrel's buffoonery – his incompetence in the face of modern innovations like the razor blade and bicycle – allowed the white workingman to feel superior. But a more subtle connection between the minstrel show and working-class culture emerges in the observation that these shows often served to familiarize the working classes with the new technologies and urban dangers of their own world. In this, blackface was an unusual acknowledgment that whites could learn from blacks, if only from their mistakes. Considered a debased form of black culture by luminaries like Frederick Douglass, minstrelsy has also been seen as a tribute to the pervasiveness of the contributions slaves made to American music and dance. The minstrel show thus underlined the cross-racial nature of popular culture even before the Civil War and the unclassifiable way in which popular images appropriated for one purpose might serve another. Inscribed in the artifacts and amusements of family life was the ambivalence of popular opinion.

IV. WOMEN'S SPHERE

As a space marked off from business, political, and legal affairs, popular culture in the nineteenth century was identified as often with women's concerns as it was with men's. Commonly viewed as mentally and physically inferior to men, although just as commonly put on a pedestal, middle-class women inhabited a domestic sphere that was thought to be a haven from official burdens and responsibilities. So pervasive was the ideology of separate spheres for men and women that even working-class women, who did not have the luxury of staying home, were considered essentially domestic creatures.

Once married, William Blackstone wrote, women were "civilly dead." But they were not dead with respect to the growth of culture. To the extent that popular culture, as opposed to legal or civil culture, was fostered in the home, through the customs and conduct of family life, women were its main producers and purveyors. They were also expert at recognizing the possibilities for using the private, domestic sphere to influence and alter behavior in the public sphere. Exerting their will from behind the scenes, using the sentimental, religious, and moral discourse of the nineteenth century to their advantage, women worked the legal and political realms from two directions: they manipulated the official, legal sphere through their influence on the men who controlled it, and they claimed the right to vote, to serve on juries, and to have laws tailored, especially in the areas of marriage and childbearing, to their own ends.

Sentimental Power

Examining the documents left by women in the nineteenth century – their novels, diaries, wills, letters, manuals, deathbed confessions, and gravestones – historians like Ann Douglas and literary critics like Jane Tompkins have uncovered evidence of their powerful influence on the popular sphere. Never straying far from their domestic roles, women developed a discourse about human duties and decency that served as a viable alternative to the official, patriarchal discourse of rights and privileges that excluded them. Examples of their duty-oriented rhetoric informed everything from household manuals written for women, to advice columns in *Godey's Lady Book* (the most popular female periodical of the mid-nineteenth century), to the lessons taught at Catharine Beecher's Hartford Female Seminary, where girls were trained as helpmeets for men. In promoting this discourse, Douglas notes, women capitalized on the expression of a rigorous Calvinism that had previously characterized the discourse of ministers and, by extension many of their male parishioners, in the seventeenth and early to mid-eighteenth centuries. But instead of parroting Calvinist exhortations to self-restraint and self-abnegation, women successfully made them their own by infusing them with a feminine slant, a genteel Christianity that evinced sympathy and sentimentality. Rooted in religion, the sentimental aspects of this new rhetoric became widespread among women of the middle classes and led to the adoption of a language that stressed nurture, generosity, and acceptance or what John Stuart Mill called a "culture of the feelings."

Given a liberty to express themselves in sentimental terms that eluded them in all other spheres of life or rhetoric, women quickly established themselves as the bearers of morality, and it was as the culture's moral conscience that they participated in many of the great legal, political, and social issues of the day. Of course, not all women had the same progressive impulses and aims; there were as many, if not more, women in favor of slavery as against it. Nor were they all conscious of their arguably inferior status in society. But the persistent efforts of reformers among them to expand the public sphere for women and to make women active rather than passive members of popular culture ensured that they, rather than those women contented with the status quo, took the initiative. In this way, the power of sentiment could take on a distinctly reformist cast.

In the first two decades of the century, female reformers performed charitable activities predominantly of a religious sort, providing general relief to poor widows, wayward children, and orphans. In New England, "cent societies" sprang up in which women collected donations for foreign and domestic religious missions. But as the century wore on, women's charities – the Loyal Women's League, the Female Benevolent Society, the Female Guardian Society, and the Female Moral Reform Society, among others – grew more formal and women's activities within them more all-inclusive. Thus, by the end of the first third of the nineteenth century the issue of gender equality inspired the vast majority of women's reform groups, and gender became a fixed feature of the law and popular culture equation. A burgeoning gender consciousness among women had the effect of making gender a more compelling basis for popular affiliation than class. The influential novelist and reformer, Lydia Maria Child, articulated the virtue of this cross-class affiliation by criticizing middle-class women for separating themselves from their less fortunate sisters when she said that each woman was "a hair's breadth" away from the other."

Child's statement singled out domesticity as the best foundation for forging ties that ultimately linked women and their concerns to the public arena. The result was a large and vocal community of women urging new policy and legal reform in many areas, including married women's property rights, temperance, equal access to institutions of higher learning, equal pay for equal work, prostitution, divorce, and suffrage. Of these, the last three reveal the most about women's relationship with the law.

A law making it easier for married couples to divorce would have given women greater control over their property, their children, and their general well-being. But in terms of women's contribution to popular culture, the more significant effect of such a law would have been to protect them from the accusation of adultery, at least in cases where women, denied a divorce and otherwise forced to live as celibates, chose to live with another man. Although most courts throughout the nineteenth century refused to grant divorces except in cases of extreme physical or mental abuse, and then only with a prohibition against remarriage, divorce, or actions simulating divorce, remained a popular aspiration. And despite the torrid warnings against liberal divorce law that appeared frequently in popular periodicals (divorce liberalization was even the subject of a famous novel by William Dean Howells, *A Modern Instance*, published in 1882, which took a conservative stand against it), large numbers of people continued to choose the blatantly illegal alternative of remarrying before a spouse's death or of living adulterously in a happy union made illegal only by their original, unhappy marriage.

Not infrequently, unofficial adulterous unions resulted in the murder of one or another partner; typically, it was the "wronged" husband who killed the man who had "seduced" his wife. Many of these cases made it to trial and became major media sensations. Entire trial transcripts were published in newspapers or in pamphlet form, and opening and closing arguments by defense attorneys were made widely available. In 1869–70, for example, the country was transfixed by the McFarland-Richardson trial, in which Daniel McFarland was accused of killing Albert Richardson, the seducer of McFarland's wife, Abby. The law required that the defendant be acquitted only if the killing were in the heat of the moment, but if premeditation was evidence of the murderer's culpability in theory, it did not figure as such in practice. So strong was the bias against women's marital independence in these years that even obvious signs of a murderer's premeditation did not end in his conviction. Consider the following facts: after intercepting a love letter in 1867 from Richardson to his wife, McFarland shot and wounded Richardson. A year later, after Abby successfully obtained a divorce (after establishing residency in Indiana, one of the few states with a liberal divorce policy), McFarland shot Richardson again in New York, this time killing him. Even a law granting women divorce was clearly not enough to contest the popular male perception that rights for women meant a loss of rights for men, revealing just how inextricable the relationship between law and popular culture could be.

Cases upholding the authority of husbands over wives had a ripple effect on another issue of particular concern to women in this period: prostitution. To the extent that overly restrictive divorce laws kept people in bad marriages, prostitution continued to thrive. To be sure, prostitutes serviced large numbers of single men, as well as otherwise happily married men who were enjoined by Victorian mores to maintain an unrealistic sexual restraint at home. Moreover, before 1820, most venues for prostitution were concentrated in working-class neighborhoods or near the docks, so the link between middle-class family mores and prostitution was not always visible. But by mid-century, there were houses of prostitution within upper- and middle class neighborhoods as well. To curb the practice, police arrested prostitutes, and legislatures in San Francisco, New Orleans, and New York passed laws criminalizing their behavior, going so far as to prohibit a woman from "standing on the sidewalks in front of premises occupied by her" or from "soliciting by words, gestures, knocks any person passing or being on a public street."[15]

[15] Mary P. Ryan, *Women in Public: Between Banners and Ballots, 1825–1880* (Baltimore, 1990), 91.

But if these laws temporarily controlled the outward manifestation of prostitution, they fell far short of providing any long-term solution. Women reformers understood far better than their male counterparts that the more effective attack on prostitution would come from reshaping the private attitudes that would eventually affect public behavior. Implicit in the female approach to prostitution was the recognition that even women of the middle classes were capable of prostitution fantasies. Among the pornographic materials that flooded the presses in the 1830s and 1840s were novels like George Lippard's *Quaker City; or the Monks of Monk Hall* (1844) and George Thompson's *Fanny Greeley; or Confessions of a Free-Love Sister* (c. 1853), both of which portrayed otherwise genteel women as nymphomaniacs and masturbators. With this insight in mind, female reformers chose to target not the prostitutes themselves, but the institution of prostitution and its male patrons. To this end, women reformers developed a two-pronged approach: to educate their own husbands and sons about the sin of sexual promiscuity and to paint prostitutes as victims of male dominance, an all too familiar form of oppression. Blinded at times by a sentimental approach to the problem that saw prostitutes as victims rather than criminals (some women chose a career in prostitution rather than one in factory work, for example), middle-class reformers also clearly saw the political and legal advantages of sisterhood over class rivalry. Clara Cleghorne Hoffman of the National Women's Christian Temperance Union made a direct connection between the prostitutes who were paid for their services and women of the more respectable classes. "Hundreds go forth to swell the ranks of recognized prostitution," she wrote in 1888, "but thousands more go forth to swell the ranks of legalized prostitution under the perfectly respectable mantle of marriage."[16] The image of the female victim, long a staple of the literary approach to prostitution and seduction in such novels as Hannah Foster's *The Coquette* (1797) and Stephen Crane's *Maggie* (1893), became a rallying point for cross-class affiliation that involved more women in popular legal reform.

Of the three areas of reform discussed here – divorce, prostitution, and suffrage – the last was the least family oriented; yet even here the link between women's entrance into the public sphere and their moral and emotional powers, traditionally reserved for the family, was prominent. Capitalizing on their ostensible birthright of intuition and sensitivity, women's sentimental rhetoric was invoked as a counterpart to the male discourse of rights. The "Declaration of Sentiments," adopted at the women's right convention held in Seneca Falls in July of 1848, made reference to women's special

[16] Clara Cleghorne Hoffman, speech in *Report*, International Council of Women, assembled by the National Women Suffrage Association (Washington, DC, 1888), 283–84.

emotional and moral endowments. Modeled directly on the "Declaration of Independence," this document resolved that "it is the duty of the women of this country to secure to themselves their sacred right to the elective franchise" and "that the same amount of virtue, delicacy and refinement of behavior that is required of women in the social state should also be required of man. . . . " Advocates of equality, like Margaret Fuller, who was never a vocal supporter of suffrage per se, made a point of grounding their arguments for equal rights for women on the qualities – the intuition, the "electrical" or "magnetic" element, as she called it – traditionally attributed to them.[17] Even when the New Woman movement took hold later in the century, women's equality included an appeal for a specifically feminine power that was not tied to childbearing, but was gendered nonetheless. This appeal was given dramatic power by Edna Pontellier's campaign not to be a "mother-woman" in Kate Chopin's *The Awakening* (1899). Despite the claims of many men that the female in possession of a "masculine mind" was an aberration, women reformers found ways to venture into the public sphere without becoming vulnerable to the charge that they had lost their femininity.

Consumer Power

Experienced in making their desires known through their influence, women found the world of commerce and consumerism especially conducive to their designs. Through the articulation of their needs within the domestic sphere, women transformed themselves into ideal consumers and became the primary targets of commodity culture in the nineteenth century. This had the dual and somewhat paradoxical effect of bringing them into the public sphere and of making the public sphere more domestic. Women's roles in commodity culture served on a literal level to open up more public space to them and on a figurative level to turn a stereotypically feminine activity, shopping, into a public and political forum.

As the century progressed, certain public places – ice cream parlors, banks, libraries, art galleries, public gardens, and parks – began to welcome women, but nowhere were women made to feel more at home than in the department store. When A.T. Stewart opened the first American department store in New York in 1846, he had a specifically female clientele in mind. Designed with wide rotundas, large halls, and a ladies' parlor lined with giant mirrors, Stewart's provided a safe version of the outside world to women who were only just beginning to venture out of their homes. Inside

[17] Margaret Fuller, "Woman in the Nineteenth Century," in Mary Kelley, ed., *The Portable Margaret Fuller* (New York, 1994), 285.

the store, women could stroll as they might on the streets, but without incurring the dangers – male stares, provocations, filth, noxious smells – that lurked there. Gradually, as more stores like Stewart's were built, women began to dominate the space not only inside but outside the stores as well, until, in 1860, a twenty-block stretch of Broadway filled with shopping emporia became known as the "Ladies Mile." In this way, women like Nellie Wetherbee, a devoted diarist, could spend an entire day out of doors. "I bought black silk dress and silk morning dress," she notes cursorily in one entry. "Then around to Mrs. Burdett's and ordered my underclothes . . . out shopping all day" she writes in another.[18]

Although there were drawbacks to this consumer presence – endless consumerism appeared dreary to many women and dangerously attractive to others – shopping remained an accessible and manageable way for many women to appear in public. It not only broke up the confinement and monotony of their otherwise housebound lives but it also presented an opportunity for self-expression. *Sister Carrie* (1900), Theodore Dreiser's story of a young girl from a poor, Midwestern background who parlays good looks and spunk into stardom, describes the effect of a shopping trip on the still "undiscovered" Carrie, as a "relief": "Here was the great Fair store with its multitude of delivery wagons about, its long window display, its crowd of shoppers. It readily changed her thoughts, she who was so weary of them. It was here that she had intended to come and get her new things. Now for relief from distress, she thought she would go in and see."[19] The explicitly political undertones of consumer behavior were not lost on many of the century's most outspoken female reformers. In her *Reminiscences*, Elizabeth Cady Stanton recalls an incident in which she once urged a Congressman's wife to buy a new stove in her husband's absence:

> "Why," [her friend] replied, "I have never purchased a darning needle, to put the case strongly, without consulting Mr. S., and he does not think a new stove necessary." "What, pray," said I, "does he know about stoves, sitting in his easy-chair in Washington? If he had a dull old knife with broken blades, he would soon get a new one with which to sharpen his pens and pencils, and, if he attempted to cook a meal – granting he knew how – on your old stove, he would set it out of doors the next hour. Now my advice to you is to buy a new one this very day!"[20]

In clothes and other consumer activities women found an outlet for wresting control over their lives from men, and working girls were in the

[18] Nellie Wetherbee, *Diary*, Bancroft Library, January 9, December 22, 1860.
[19] Theodore Dreiser, *Sister Carrie* ((New York, 1970), 51.
[20] Elizabeth Cady Stanton, *Eighty Years and More; Reminiscences 1815–1897* (New York, 2003–2006), 98.

vanguard in this respect. Unable to spend an entire day shopping, working girls nevertheless made their mark on consumer culture and cultivated a number of public places like gardens, picnics spots, theaters, and dance halls that increasingly catered to their needs. One species of working girl, the "bowery g'hal" (the female counterpart of the bowery b'hoy), took her name from a street in New York, the Bowery, where the working classes socialized. Dressed in the fashionable "polka," a tightly fitted jacket, bowery "g'hals" carved out a niche for themselves in the public sphere. If fashion, in its appeal to what is timely and trendy at once, is, by definition, an expression of collective, rather than individual interests, then working girls, outfitted in their "polkas," made an explicitly political statement, calling attention to themselves as a group that needed to be reckoned with.

Middle-class women soon adopted their own uptown version of working-girl style. In demanding clothing that allowed them greater freedom of movement, they made fashion into a system of protest and reform. Their independence in this respect did not escape men's notice. The Reverend John Todd, one of mid-century's most popular male writers, put it this way when discussing the virtue of bloomers, one of the newest fashion fads: "Some have tried to become semi-men by putting on the Bloomer dress. Let me tell you in a word why it can never be done. It is this: woman, robed and folded in her long dress, is beautiful. . . . Take off the robes, and put on pants, and show the limbs, and grace and mystery are all gone."[21] But once they had started down the path of consumer expression, women did not want to stop. They used their presence as consumers to inaugurate all sorts of trends, from bike riding to tennis playing to occupational equality, often masking substantial gains in liberty as mere fashion. Nowhere, however, did they have more to say than as the primary consumers of novels, in whose pages much public expression about the law was conducted.

V. FICTION

Literature offers an especially compelling example of how law in the nineteenth century operated in a popular, extra-legal sphere. Serialized in newspapers, pamphlets, and dime novels throughout the century, popular (in the sense of widely consumed and appreciated) fiction was particularly conducive to the airing of social concerns because, like the judicial system, it could be structured in adversarial terms – the classic struggle between good and evil – but also because, unlike the law, it could contain the social and political contradictions that were the lifeblood of popular culture as a whole. But literature functioned in a parallel way to law most obviously

[21] Howard Zinn, *A People's History of the United States* (New York, 1980), 119.

because it shared law's mandate to represent: to give a presence and voice to Americans in all their individuality and diversity. The cultural equivalent of representative government, literature had many of the same aspirations and fulfilled many of the same purposes as the law.

That American literature had a special obligation to represent a diverse population was acknowledged relatively early in the century by writers like Ralph Waldo Emerson who, in his essay "The Poet" (1844), explicitly called for an American spokesperson who could assimilate the voice of every man. "The breadth of the problem is great," he wrote, "for the poet is representative. He stands among partial men for the complete man, and apprises us not of his wealth, but of the common wealth."[22] Emerson lamented the American poet's failure to appear ("I look in vain for the poet whom I describe"), but, in fact, his call was answered many times over. Self-consciously styling himself "the American poet," Walt Whitman, for example, wrote to Emerson's specifications, embracing in his poetry the common man and the common culture. "Walt Whitman, a kosmos, of Manhattan the son/Turbulent, fleshy, sensual, eating, drinking and breeding/No sentimentalist, no stander above men and women or apart from them."[23]

Not only poets, but novelists and storywriters rededicated themselves to the problem of representing the common man in literature. Authors in this category typically revealed a keen awareness of class divides and of the difficulties of writing about people who, for the most part, did not write themselves. Among these are such innovative works as *Life in the Iron Mills* by Rebecca Harding Davis (1861), and *The Silent Partner* by Elizabeth Stuart Phelps (1871). But perhaps no work grappled more famously with the questionable ability of literature and the more obvious inability of the law to give expression to the plight of the working classes than Herman Melville's "Bartleby, the Scrivener" (1853). In this story, a meek and mild-mannered man named Bartleby accepts a position as a copyist, or scrivener, in a law office only to find that, after several weeks of working productively, he now "prefers not to." Bartleby's expression of inertia – what could be called his passive resistance or civil disobedience – represents a serious problem for his employer, who offers many incentives for Bartleby to return to work or alternatively, to leave the workplace, all to no avail. Bartleby remains a cipher, refusing not only to work but also to give any reason for his refusal but the repetition of the maddeningly polite phrase – "I prefer not to." Although seemingly inscrutable to all around him, the phrase itself is a reflection of the oppressive environment in which Bartleby works – an

[22] Ralph Waldo Emerson, "The Poet," in Stephen E. Wicher, ed., *Selections from Ralph Waldo Emerson* (Boston, 1957), 223.

[23] Walt Whitman, *Leaves of Grass* (New York, 1968), 52.

environment in which legality, civility, gentility, and even charity mask the inequalities that people like Bartleby suffered.

Though it is notable that writers like Emerson, Whitman, and Melville were concerned about the mass of men, it is important to remember that they were not read by many of them. The working classes preferred different kinds of stories, typically with more salient plots. To cater to their needs a booming industry of pulp fiction developed, made possible by a newly invented printing technology that facilitated the mass production of affordable fiction. Following on the heels of the penny press in the early 1830s were trial reports, yellow-covered pamphlet novels, and the orange-covered dime novels (strategically priced at ten cents rather than the typical twenty-five cents) that saturated the market. Between 1860 and 1890 alone, there were countless dime novel publishing ventures, including Beadle's "Dime Novels," which lasted for 321 issues; Beadle's "New Dime Novels," which issued 309 reprint volumes; Munro's "Ten Cent Novels"; and Frank Tousey's "Wide Awake Library." Moreover, a tradition safeguarding freedom of the press ensured that people's tastes would dictate demand. The result was a heavy emphasis on sensationalism, stories that were, because of their scurrilous content or graphic descriptions, excluded from the genteel press. Two genres of sensationalist literature prevailed: crime and adventure.

Crime

Nineteenth-century crime fiction was an offshoot of the true-crime narratives of the eighteenth century that, as the literary scholar Karen Halttunen explains, were themselves an outgrowth of the execution sermons of the seventeenth century. From the colonial period forward, narratives of gruesome murders, taken from court records and then embroidered, appealed to people's interest in hearing about evil first hand, in coming to know and perhaps learning to exorcise their own human impulse to sin. But if we accept that it was possible for fiction not only to reflect but also to ease social tensions, we can begin to see how these fictions also helped people grapple with the anxieties and fears engendered by a surge in violence that the law failed to contain.

An obsession with the kind of evil that law enforcement might fail to notice, or prevent, fueled the extraordinary output of gothic fiction in the late eighteenth and early nineteenth centuries. Ventriloquism, necrophilia, hereditary insanity, and psychological trauma motivated the irrational actions (suicide, serial murders, confessions) of the characters in Charles Brockden Brown's *Wieland* (1798), Louisa May Alcott's "A Marble Woman," (1865), and John Neal's *Seventy-Six* (1823). Even in narratives not intended as gothic, like *New York by Gas-Light* (1850) by George Foster, where illegality never rises above the mundane level of pick-pocketing or petty thievery, crime was a haunting and ghastly thing. "What a task we have undertaken!" Foster writes in the first of his gaslight sketches. "To penetrate beneath the thick veil of night and lay bare the fearful mysteries of darkness in the metropolis. . . ."[24]

Crime haunted popular fiction because it haunted the people who read it. In the increasingly crime-ridden nineteenth century, people began to feel that it was up to them to do what the law and its enforcers could not do: police themselves. The murder mysteries and detective fiction that began to appear in the early to mid-nineteenth century served as a way to reevaluate evidence that had resisted earlier detection. Thanks to the marvel of literary mass production, which included factories not only for the physical reproduction of books but also for the writing of the novels themselves, true-crime stories like Lizzie Borden's 1892 murder of her parents in the sleepy town of Fall River, Massachusetts, received multiple fictional renditions, a sorting through and teasing out of the facts in ways official legal narratives could not.

Adventure

Nineteenth-century adventure stories deployed many of the same social strategies as crime stories. They simultaneously fanned and tamed popular tensions over the rising tide of violence. Narratives that the literary historian, David Reynolds, designates as "Dark Adventure" tales offered readers the chance to dismiss the violent nature of mass culture as outlandish. In twisted and unrealistic tales of pirates and corsairs, strange sea monsters, and exotic wars, these books offered their readers escapes from a variety of threats, including immigration and American imperialism. According to Reynolds, these tales charted the trajectory of illicit and immoral behavior without trying to moralize about it.

By contrast, another group of narratives that Reynolds identifies as "Moral Adventures" did, as the name suggests, engage in problem solving and self-censorship. In Horatio Alger's *Ragged Dick* series, for example, Alger's boy-hero starts out earning his keep by shining shoes, but comes, through sheer determination and a healthy dose of rugged individualism, to rule over a shoeshine empire. In this series, written primarily for boys, Americans came to terms with a society made oppressive by laws that favored the ruling classes; but they learned, by Dick's example, to cope with that system

[24] George G. Foster, *New York by Gas-Light, and Other Urban Sketches* (Berkeley, CA, 1990), 69.

by bending if not breaking the law and becoming the exception, not the rule. Alger's pull-yourself-up-by-your-own-bootstraps philosophy provided a necessary, albeit temporary, fix for a legal system that, despite its claims to egalitarianism, did not recognize the underclasses.

Other stories, like the late-century pulp fictions of authors like Harold Titus, Frank Packard, and Herbert Ward, rehearsed the terrors of railroad accidents, a common occurrence in a country ruled by the iron giant. Stories like "The Night Operator" and "The Semaphore" addressed themselves to specific legal issues – whether to compensate workers for injuries on the job or how to assign blame for accidents between railroads and motorists or pedestrians – thus supplementing the law by suggesting resolutions to conflicts the law had less time to explore.

Two sub-genres of the adventure story deserve special mention: the tall tale and the Western. Like all adventure stories, these sub-genres dealt with the extremities of American life in the nineteenth century and used the vernacular, the speech of the common man (denied a presence in official law), to stage the multiplicity of human voices. In the tall tales of the Southwest that featured likable but brazen rascals, pranks take the place of violent crime and allow readers to linger without fear in a world of potential dangers. In these stories, humor is both a weapon for and defense against the unpredictable. In George Washington Harris's *Sut Lovingood Papers* (1854–58), lying, cheating, and disrespect are the order of the day. For example, when Sut rides his own father, like a horse, into the fields, the overriding effect of the role reversal (of father and son, as well as of father and animal) is absurd, but there is a lingering sense that if it were required by circumstance, such an upheaval of social order could be accomplished. Similarly, in the Davy Crockett almanacs published between 1835 and 1856, humor makes of the real-life Davy Crockett, who died heroically at the Alamo, a larger-than-life figure capable of adapting to society by virtue of his excesses alone.

The Western's counterpart to these comical figures is the outlaw who, more than any law-abiding citizen, embodies effective solutions to the constant savagery and competing claims of life on the edge of civilization. For example, Davy Crockett's more serious analogue was Daniel Boone who, in John Filson's narrative of his adventures (1784), the first of many accounts of Boone's life, appears as the self-sufficient man who is *a law unto himself*. The hunter/trapper who, by dint of his skill alone, survives in the wilderness was an enormously attractive image even for readers in the urban centers of the Northeast, far removed from the frontier.

The strongest and earliest incarnation of the outlaw hero was the highly affable, and yet socially inept, Natty Bumppo, the literary creation of James Fenimore Cooper on whom all subsequent cowboys and outlaws were based.

Cooper's Leatherstocking Tales narrate the adventures of the honest and heroic Natty, a white man who, having been raised by the Indians, finds himself at odds with white settler society. Although the books that recounted Natty's adventures were not dime novels, they sold very well, leaving not only a persistent mythology of Western heroism in their wake, but a readership that could be constituted and reconstituted throughout the century for the consumption and distribution of popular fiction. Natty precedes figures like Davy Crockett and Daniel Boone, tales of Buffalo Bill and Calamity Jane, and dime westerns by Edward Wheeler, Ned Buntline, and Edward Ellis. The plot of Cooper's novels also anticipates the repetitive formula adopted by the dime novelists – capture, flight, and pursuit. But the far more interesting parallel is the way in which Cooper's hero, like the dime western heroes that followed, navigated a lawless world by accepting the possibility of law while at the same time resisting it. In *The Prairie* (1827), a now elderly Natty gives voice to his lifelong ambivalence: "The law – 'Tis bad to have it, but, I sometimes think, it is worse to be entirely without it. Age and weakness have brought me to feel such weakness, at times. Yes – yes, the law is needed, when such as have not the gifts of strength and wisdom are to be taken care of."[25]

An early adopter of frontier methods, Natty, like Deadwood Dick and all his dime novel heirs, feels free to challenge or uphold the law when necessary. This flexible posture is the perfect response to a liminal West where law does not anticipate social change, but rather lags far behind it. Natty also represents the difficulties of men who, in an age of brutal competition – waged with guns in the West and with money in the East – needed to find a way to adhere to the Victorian definition of masculinity while at the same time defining a new masculinity that acknowledged occasional lapses into defiance of the law or the accepted moral order. Finally, the western helped counterbalance a law that actively reviled the Native Americans by showing how whites could live in close proximity to them (as they were forced to do on the frontier), and yet avoid the ostensible taint of doing so. For all his Indian ways, Natty is forever proclaiming his status as a pure-bred white man, in his words a "man without a cross."

Natty's heroism and singularity informed popular fiction throughout the nineteenth and twentieth centuries. The image of the Natty-like cowboy riding off into the sunset, leaving a semblance of order and a blur of identity behind him, is a fixture of westerns like Owen Fister's *The Virginian* (1902), and Zane Grey's *Riders of the Purple Sage* (1912). But it is also present in the work of the central fiction writers from these centuries. As Reynolds points out in *Beneath the American Renaissance*, we need only think of the solitary

[25] James Fenimore Cooper, *The Prairie* (New York, 1987), 27.

and west-bound Ishmael in Melville's *Moby Dick* (1850) to see the features of the popular western hero of Cooper and the dime novel. Hawthorne's high-brow fiction offers traces of the gothic horrors that enthralled tens of thousands of readers. But perhaps the most enduring legacy of popular fiction in the nineteenth century is the way it profitably blurred the lines between popular and high culture and proved fertile ground for writers like Edgar Allan Poe, Louisa May Alcott, and Mark Twain who, by recognizing and incorporating the powerful images spawned in popular fiction, defy categorization as either popular or elite.

CONCLUSION

Oliver Wendell Holmes, Jr., wrote that "the life of the law has not been logic: it has been experience."[26] Not quite the argument presented here – that the law can be found in novels and parades, as much as in cases and statutes – Holmes nevertheless saw clearly much of what was important about the relationship between law and popular culture in the nineteenth century. Above all, law in the nineteenth century was experience: the experience of ordinary people as well as of the elites, of lawyers, judges, street hawkers, and factory workers. If the law was the product of older legal traditions, especially the common law tradition of England, the logic of legal theorists and jurists, and sheer necessity (the coming of the railroad, for example, meant that there had to be railroad laws), it was also the product of people's understanding of it and their responses to it.

Understanding the law in this way, however, does not make the link between law and popular culture crystal clear. It is always difficult to see how the outlook of any given individual at any given time (comfortably ensconced in his or her living room or taking a lunch break on the job) intersects with the law at all. But what popular culture in the nineteenth century teaches us is that, even in an age of supreme individualism, individuals did not think or act alone. Popular culture in the nineteenth century came about as a result of concerted effort, of individuals responding to each other. Nor were these encounters always familiar. As the urban and industrial displaced the rural and the agricultural, people often shared a bond not of knowledge but, strangely enough, of anonymity. The nineteenth century may have been witness to the closing of the frontier, as Frederick Jackson Turner has argued, but it was also witness to the opening of the public sphere. A growing population with a growing income led to a bigger built environment that included spaces like halls, museums, amusement parks, sidewalks, and streets in which people could gather. Technological

[26] Oliver Wendell Holmes, *The Common Law* (New York, 1991), 1.

innovations – the steam engine, the slaughterhouse, the corset, and the gas range – meant new ways of seeing and of behaving in public and new ideas about distance and the value of human life. These ideas, in turn, gave rise to new customs and new norms.

What were the norms and values of the people in the nineteenth century? Even now, after cataloguing numerous examples, it is difficult to say. But the constant public displays – the shopping, parades, and protests; the newspapers, magazines, and books; the statues, needlepoint, and clothing – demonstrate that popular culture was nothing if not diverse. There were people who defended slavery and others who fought against it, people who welcomed industrialization and others who felt victimized by it. Popular culture was not univocal. Nor was it only popular, in the sense of working class. An interest in legal issues, Tocqueville reminds us, was not confined to the members of any one class. Everyone in nineteenth-century America was interested in the law, and thanks to the extraordinary advances in printing technology that made the years from 1790 to 1920 the age of newspapers, everyone could read about it.

To some of these norms, the law responded with open arms, writing them into official existence. The doctrine of negligence was a judicial response to the norms exercised by factory owners that made their employees responsible for work-related injuries. Others norms and attitudes were dismissed initially and only entered the annals of official law after the nineteenth century had come and gone; the passage of workers' compensation laws, for example, a corrective to the negligence doctrine, had to wait until the early twentieth century. Still other norms and customs existed just below the law's radar throughout the century, but were no less effective for it, supplementing, and in some cases substituting for established law. But whether any given norm or value crossed the line from popular legal culture into official legal culture is less important than the recognition that these norms served to foster the interpenetration of popular culture with the law. They are best seen as conduits whereby two social systems, official law and unofficial law, spoke to each other. The patterns established in the nineteenth century for this kind of cross-cultural and cross-class communication would light the way for the century to come.

13

LAW AND RELIGION, 1790–1920

SARAH BARRINGER GORDON

In 1830, the chronicler Alexis de Tocqueville wrote of the extraordinary power of religion in the young American nation. The enduring vigor of religious expression and its influence at all levels of society have indeed been remarkable. Equally important, however, the growth and increasing importance of religion in American life have occurred in a nation without formal religious establishments. In the 1790s, the beginning of the period covered by this chapter, religious life in the United States was relatively lackluster.

The eventual intersection of religious freedom and religious commitment surprised even many Americans. Certainly most nineteenth-century Europeans assumed that established religion was the only way to ensure faith and morality in any country. In the New World and in the new country, Americans learned that the absence of most formal legal protections for religion did not necessarily mean the absence of religion. This lesson was learned over time, and with much backing and filling. Nor has separation of church and state been stable or even comfortable for many believers. Yet any examination of law and religion must begin with the paradox that astounded Tocqueville and has become such a central feature of American life – faith, multiple faiths, have flourished in a country that has an increasingly powerful government but no official faith.

The story behind that paradox begins just after the crest of the great constitution-making years of the 1770s and 1780s, with the ratification of the Bill of Rights by the states in 1791. Most important for our purposes are the Establishment and Free Exercise Clauses of the First Amendment, which state "Congress shall enact no law respecting an establishment of religion, or prohibiting the free exercise thereof." Judges, scholars, and commentators have long debated the meaning and sweep of the religion clauses; the history of the Founding Era has been central to this often contentious battle. Supreme Court jurisprudence, especially, has been grounded in interpretation of the Framers' intent as a means of understanding and implementing the constitutional commands of the religion clauses.

The rhetorical warfare over what the religion clauses mean has become especially virulent over the last half-century. A religious revival of massive dimensions, sometimes dubbed "the Fourth Great Awakening" in reference to prior American revivals, has burned across many sectors of American society in recent decades. In the same period, the Supreme Court has expanded and retracted the sweep of the federal religion clauses, alternately infuriating and pacifying opposing camps. In the early twenty-first century, the relationship of religion and law is everywhere in politics, and political argument about law is everywhere in religion. In such an era of jangled nerves and passionate commitment, interpretation of law is guided as much by ideology and belief as by any dedication to principle.

The riven quality of debate has colored historical analysis, transforming any attempt at overview into a politicized undertaking. Yet it is possible to make scholarly progress despite the minefields if one pays close attention to religious as well as legal history and resists generally the temptation to see each and every development as confirmation or refutation of one or another theory. It is also vital to accept that the First Amendment is only one piece of the puzzle throughout the period, often hardly a presence at all. The central question, in 1790 as in 1920 and 2008, is how religious people of varying faiths can form a polity that is both respectful of and yet never identical with religious commitments – in other words, how have Americans resolved the quandary of religious freedom in an ostensibly secular state?

If the question has been relatively constant, the answers are not: they are necessarily tentative and have changed over time. The approach taken here tackles a variety of topics in ways that treat historical developments across the long nineteenth century as every bit as important as the Founding Era. The breadth of possible topics in this extraordinarily rich field means that many worthy developments are treated cursorily, if at all. Personalities or more localized events in either religion or law are left to others. Rather, I concentrate on developments in religious and legal doctrine and activity with clear national import – matters of significance at the highest level. This approach makes broad substantive interpretation possible, but at the expense of detail and thorough coverage of many minor and even some major events.

I begin with the drafting and ratification of the First Amendment, moving to the law of religion in the states, including both freedom of worship and disestablishment and their effects on believers and religious institutions. I also treat the growth of non-mainstream Protestant groups across the country, including imports such as Catholicism and Judaism that traveled with European immigrants as well as home-grown faiths such as

Mormonism, and the many effects such dissenters had on the law of religion. Differences within Protestantism, too, especially over vital questions of legal and religious import such as the validity of slavery, augmented an already growing diversity by splintering important denominations in the Civil War era, generating a whole new law of church property. I then turn to the push to reform society in a Christian mold that dominated questions of law and religion in the postwar decades, drawing believers into active engagement with government and increasing ecumenical cooperation among different denominations – even across the traditional Protestant-Catholic and Christian-Jewish divides.

Although many proposed reforms were unsuccessful, temperance was a reform that the vast majority of Protestants, at least, could support. They were joined by smaller but nonetheless key supporters from other faiths, as well as scientists, politicians, and doctors. Prohibition, long sought by reformers of religious as well as secular stripe, was finally enacted into national law by constitutional amendment in 1919. By erasing alcohol from society, reformers were convinced they could cleanse and nourish individuals as well as families and the broader society, eradicating most violence, poverty and many diseases. These hopes faded over time, but Prohibition accomplished more than many popular histories would have us believe.

Yet, many more traditional Protestants resisted the pull of ecumenicism and politics, even of the reformist kind. Instead they recommitted themselves to the "fundamentals" of their faith, including biblical literalism and rejection of the new sciences that challenged concepts as basic as the authorship of the Bible, the age of the Earth, and God's creation of humans. Such conflicts among believers over the embrace of modernity would become more important in the later twentieth century, especially in legal battles over education, school prayer, public displays of faith and religious symbols, and more. Their beginnings are treated here because the fissures that have divided "liberal" and "conservative" members of many religions trace their roots in America to the first controversies over science and education in the Progressive era. By 1920, many conservative Protestants felt the first stirrings of a new relationship to government – an uncomfortable and disturbing sense that a once benign political order had been captured by those whose mission was to inculcate secularism, especially in public education.

On this note of doubt and division the period closes, bracketing the subjects treated in the chapter. If we begin with the high-flown but inconclusive words of the First Amendment, we end with the deep and controversial involvement of believers in reform as well as in critique of reform and its embrace of science, modernism, and secularism. In between, of course, much had happened that has made the law of church and state fascinating and deeply frustrating to the advocates on all sides of the debates that rage into the twenty-first century. Understanding the broad trajectory of this story is key to navigating the field.

I. THE FEDERAL RELIGION CLAUSES

It is difficult to settle on a unified interpretation of the religion clauses of the First Amendment, especially one that is reliably supported by historical research. The simplicity of the language has lured scholars and advocates nonetheless; their attempts have not yielded any consensus. In part, this is because the motivations for supporting the amendment in the first national Congress in 1789 and at subsequent state ratifying conventions were themselves varied and even contradictory. Equally important, the Congressional debates yield little evidence that the Framers themselves thought a great deal about the niceties of interpretation or that some of them even thought the first amendments to the new national Constitution would be of any lasting importance. Debates between Federalist supporters of the Constitution and Anti-Federalist opponents were resolved in large measure when Federalist James Madison honored a campaign promise in 1789 to draft a series of amendments, but many in Congress showed little enthusiasm for working out what such amendments would mean in real terms. Just to give one example, there is no dependable definition of the word "religion" as it is used in the Constitution, a question that has vexed American jurisprudes for many decades. Some have even proposed that religion means something different when considered in light of the Establishment Clause than it does for the Free Exercise Clause, even though it is clear that the constitutional text presumes a single meaning; the word "religion" appears only once in the two clauses. In this as in many other areas of lively debate, the Framers of the religion clauses gave no explicit guidance.

Such is the importance attached to historical interpretation, however, that lack of direct evidence has not stanched the flow of ink on the question, much of it dedicated to proving one or another politically motivated stance. Most prevalent are works that address the question whether the Establishment Clause was designed to produce "a wall of separation between church and state," a phrase drawn from Thomas Jefferson's 1803 Letter to the Danbury Baptists, much used and also much criticized in Supreme Court decisions and scholarly arguments. In fact the concept of separate spheres for religion and government was already well known in the seventeenth and eighteenth centuries and has a long history in American dissenting traditions, including but not limited to Baptists and Quakers.

Equally important, the religion clauses were themselves aimed explicitly at the federal government, preserving states' power to deal with religion as they saw fit. Only Congress, not state governments, was prohibited from enacting laws "respecting an establishment of religion or prohibiting the free exercise thereof." The Supreme Court, doing only what all those educated in constitutional structures anticipated it would do, made it clear in the nineteenth century that it would not consider challenges to the laws of the states that were grounded in the religion clauses.[1] Not until the mid-twentieth century were the Establishment and Free Exercise Clauses "incorporated" by the Supreme Court and applied to states as well as the national government through the Due Process Clause of the Fourteenth Amendment. Thus, in addition to working with an inconclusive historical record for the eighteenth century, interpreters of the religion clauses labor in an environment in which constitutional clauses directed explicitly at the federal government are now applied to states and local governments. The resulting confusion and contention have made the law of religion among the most unpredictable and tangled in all of constitutional law.

II. THE STATES AS BATTLEGROUNDS IN LAW AND RELIGION

Clearly, twenty-first century battles over the meaning of the religion clauses do not occur in a historical vacuum. Although debates over the First Amendment do not reflect sustained thought on the relationship of law and religion, American history is replete with conflict over religion in public and private life. Some episodes are better known than others; but the record is full and instructive. For much of the period, developments in state rather than national law were at the cutting edge.

In the late colonial and Revolutionary eras, religious diversity became a fact of political life at the local level. Yet religious establishments were the rule and were widely assumed to be up to individual jurisdictions to determine. By the late eighteenth century, most colonies (and then the new states) moved from support of a single denomination to a more general levy in support of religious groups. Such an approach did not create a true "establishment" of all religions, because government largesse did not flow everywhere – certainly not to radical groups or to minority communities, such as Jews or Native Americans. Yet support was scattered across a significant assortment of Protestant groups, reflecting the great variety of religious commitments in the Early Republic.

The first "Great Awakening" of the middle decades of the eighteenth century had prepared the ground by increasing religious diversity. Religious enthusiasm deepened denominational differences and even split existing denominations. In addition, new emphasis on individual conscience and the

[1] *Barron v. Baltimore*, 32 U.S. (7 Pet.) 243 (1833); *Permoli v. New Orleans*, 44 U.S. (3 How.) 589 (1845).

concomitant erosion of ecclesiastical authority battered religious hierarchies throughout the colonies. Congregational churches in New England, Quakers in Pennsylvania, and the Episcopal Church in the South all remained formally or informally established, but none commanded the strength and unity of allegiance necessary to the maintenance of real sectarianism. Immigration and population growth further undermined homogeneity and introduced new sects, leading some to a pragmatic tolerance (and even acceptance) of diversity. Enlightenment rationalism and the tolerant gnosticism known as "religious indifference" further eroded the commitment to tax support for religion, especially in Mid-Atlantic states.

In this atmosphere of change and innovation in religion as well as politics, Thomas Jefferson introduced legislation to the Virginia House of Burgesses in 1779 that proposed abolishing Virginia's weak yet tenacious Anglican establishment. Jefferson's "Bill for Establishing Religious Freedom" was debated for more than five years. Eventually, it passed with the support of Virginia Baptists as well as aristocratic Deists and those suspicious of the dominant Anglican clergy. James Madison joined with Jefferson in defense of disestablishment; both drew heavily on the theory that civil and religious liberty are two sides of the same coin. This position was already familiar from the work of John Locke, whose Letter on Toleration (1689) deeply influenced American political thinkers.

Virginia's debates and eventual disestablishment, especially the work of Jefferson and Madison, have been widely cited and relied on as the key to understanding the proper relationship of church and state in America, even in the twentieth and twenty-first centuries. In state legislatures and in political pamphlets and newspapers printing the words of participants in Virginia, full debate on the meaning of disestablishment seems accessible in ways that are denied to those researching the federal religion clauses. The temptation to rely on Virginia as the model is understandable, but its limitations have been shown by scholarly analyses of the complex motives and behind-the-scenes negotiations that characterized Virginia's disestablishment, as well as by the inherent inequity of relying on the experience of one state as the stand-in for all others.

And indeed, disestablishment happened gradually and in different ways in different places across the new country. It would be a mistake to conclude that Jefferson's long-standing anti-clericalism was the sole or even primary motivating force behind separation of church and state in the Early Republic. In fact, many clergymen concluded that they and the churches they served would reap rewards from disestablishment. Separation from this point of view was designed both to reduce government power to regulate and to support religion, freeing churches to pursue their own concerns after separation from Great Britain as well as liberating them from domestic state oversight. In this sense, religious liberty is indeed the partner of political liberty, and the "wall of separation" preserves freedom on both sides of the divide.

The movement toward increased toleration and decreased establishments was well underway in many states by 1787 when the Federal Constitution was drafted. Virginia was the first, but by no means was it alone in practicing toleration or debating the proper support that should flow from government to religious institutions. Given that the states were the important decisionmakers in the late 1780s, the paucity of evidence from the federal Framers becomes less surprising. Many of them thought that there was no need for explicit protection for religious liberty in the national Constitution. Religious coercion was on the wane everywhere in the new country. Further federal action arguably would be nugatory, given that in the federal system states rather than the national government were presumed to be the proper source of regulation or deregulation of religion.

The various states differed substantially in both heritage and practice. The middle states, including Pennsylvania and New York, both large and important jurisdictions, had long-standing traditions of respect for liberty of conscience, and they embraced separation without substantial difficulty or dissension. Other states struggled longer and harder. Virginia, of course, actively disestablished first, but the Anglican church was more or less formally established throughout the Southern states. These establishments were weak indeed and constantly subject to rumors that the clergy wanted secretly to install an Anglican bishop and create an establishment more closely resembling that of Britain. This politically charged suspicion was paired with the discontent of religious dissenters, especially Baptists, whose enthusiasm inspired them to challenge the authority of the elite Anglicans. By the end of the eighteenth century, Southern establishments had followed Virginia's lead.

In New England, Congregationalists resisted longer. Dissenters were vigorous, however, especially when forced to pay taxes in support of the local church or jailed for failure to pay. They embraced the Republicanism of Thomas Jefferson, if not his social radicalism, and attacked the top-down elitism of the Congregational establishment. But the Congregationalist "Standing Order" was politically as well as socially important, and many clergy were also town magistrates. Connecticut's establishment lasted until 1818; Massachusetts was the last of all the states to disestablish, in 1833.

The remaining benefits of establishment evaporated for the Standing Order when the Massachusetts Supreme Judicial Court imposed democracy on the core process of Congregational governance, the calling of a minister. In Dedham in 1818, the more liberal Unitarians comprised a majority of the voting men of the town and voted to call a minister of their own persuasion.

The covenanted members of the church (those who had experienced evidence of their own salvation that was confirmed by the rest of the congregation and were thus admitted into full membership) objected that a liberal was by no means their choice. They were charged, they said, with preserving the orthodoxy of the church and its surrounding parish. The court, however, held that the payment of taxes, rather than the purity of a Calvinist faith, was key to the power to vote in the election of the town minister, as it was in other municipal elections.[2] With doctrinal disputes resolved decisively against them, the old order gave way, despite their deep distrust of a secular state.

It would be a mistake to assume that Baptists, Unitarians, Presbyterians, Quakers, and their fellow liberal travelers – North or South – advocated total separation, however much they might embrace absolute inviolability of individual conscience as a religious and political goal. In this sense they differed from the Enlightenment rationalism of Jefferson and Madison. Most assumed that some kind of Christian identity was essential to the flourishing of political as well as social life. To understand this liberal religious perspective, it is vital to distinguish between separatism and secularism. Indeed, eighteenth-century deism and secularism were the subject of withering attacks on "infidelity" – originally a religious rather than a sexual term – by the late 1790s. Evangelical as well as more orthodox Christians saw themselves as battling the forces of unbelief, led by Thomas Jefferson, the "arch-infidel, the Virginia Voltaire," and his sidekick Thomas Paine, "that filthy little atheist." Jefferson, who long sought to temper religious dimensions of official acts, refused while president to follow the Federalist tradition of proclaiming national fast and thanksgiving days. These and other evidences of disrespect for the authority of religion made Jefferson many enemies among the clergy and traditional Protestants generally.

The anti-clerical, free thought tradition exemplified by Jefferson loomed large in the anxieties of churchmen of the Early Republic. Resistance to disestablishment in America frequently found its most articulate spokesmen in those who claimed that Jefferson's own wickedness was at the root of calls to separate church and state. The French Revolution, they argued, was the logical result of such secularism, which unleashed debauchery, violence, free love, and all manner of "licentiousness." Trenchant predictions of political and social danger flowing from religious skepticism effectively discredited the deism and secularism that were frequently associated with the Enlightenment. Most Americans remained suspicious of infidelity and skepticism and consequently rejected the more radical implications of disestablishment. Despite the secular aspirations of the philosophes and the

[2] *Baker v. Fales*, 16 Mass. 492 (1820).

natural rights tradition they espoused, then, the process of disestablishment did not generally erode religious commitments or undermine the political power of religious institutions.

Indeed, many commentators believed that disestablishment actually increased religious fervor. In 1837, the influential Congregationalist minister Lyman Beecher recalled his deep misgivings at the prospect of disestablishment in Connecticut two decades earlier. As he acknowledged, he need not have worried. Instead of unraveling the social fabric, disestablishment paved the way for an extraordinary and long-standing religious revival. Across the spectrum, Protestants in the opening decades of the nineteenth century dedicated themselves anew to a revived and reconfigured sense of religious mission. Instead of embracing a sectarian commitment to one truth available only through adherence to a given group's doctrine, Americans developed a generally harmonious and successful plan for living together and respecting religious differences in a pragmatic compromise dubbed "denominationalism" by historians of religion. By the time Tocqueville wrote in 1830, the revival was already decades old. The era of religious establishments was over, that of religious politics had begun.

III. THE NEW "MARKET" FOR RELIGION

Denominationalism and the religious vigor unleashed by the Awakening in the early nineteenth century allowed most Protestant groups to agree that they need not follow precisely the same practices or doctrines, yet they could still share a core set of Christian commitments that identified all as belonging to the same essential faith. With disestablishment creating a voluntaristic approach to faith and worship – that is, one could no longer be coerced financially or physically to attend services or affirm faith – Protestant denominations quickly adapted to an atmosphere in which they competed with one another for adherents, yet respected the right of others to exist and even to save souls. Competition created a new "market" for religion, replicating in the religious arena the social and political competition taking root in the rest of the country. The spectacular growth of groups (notably Methodists and Baptists) that took advantage of the new popularly based system to attract adherents taught others how to appeal to their audiences as well.

The early nineteenth-century revivals were based in this popular appeal, rather than in doctrinal niceties. In general, theology took a back seat to enthusiasm, prompting some conservatives to bemoan the lack of intellectual depth and sophistication in the new religious feeling. The phenomenally successful Charles Grandison Finney, for example, made no apologies for appealing directly to the emotions of his audience. Finney, who had been a lawyer before experiencing a searing spiritual awakening, boasted that he sought to convince his listeners as he would a jury and that his client was none other than Jesus Christ. Although some observers deplored Finney's theatrical style, none could argue with his popularity and influence. Astute observers noted the coalescence of religious enthusiasm with toleration among Protestants.

This "Second Great Awakening" and its concomitant respect for conscience had significant limitations, as well as broad implications for law and politics. First, although Protestants often congratulated themselves on their perfect toleration and their commitment to disestablishment, they imposed strict boundaries on both concepts. To most political as well as religious leaders, Christian faith remained an indispensable ingredient of political stability. Without the authority of God to back them up, they believed, the less potent earthly magistrates could not ensure the obedience of citizens. Outgoing President George Washington stressed in his 1796 farewell address that the "security for property, for reputation, for life" all rested on "religious principle," and congratulated the country on sharing the "same Religeon."

A shared sense of religious commitment did indeed sustain what some scholars have called a "de facto" Protestant establishment across the nineteenth century, one that allowed for widespread and varied observation of religious practice while retaining a distinctly Protestant moral and social vision for the nation. Primarily through voluntary associations, American Protestants created and sustained a variety of benevolent organizations with aspirations for national moral regeneration. A portion of these organizations were themselves ecumenical, at least among mainstream Protestant groups, and married an emphasis on social and moral improvement with a distaste for the sorts of doctrinal wrangling that had been a favorite sport of many eighteenth-century apologists. Instead, the nineteenth-century believer was more likely to be a social activist, dedicated to deploying Christian fervor in the service of missionary, temperance, and/or other reforms, of which anti-slavery would prove the most incendiary. Such endeavors were by no means officially sponsored or supported in direct ways. Yet many Americans assumed that their governments (local, state, and national) reflected and even embodied religious values and basic morals of an undefined yet undeniably Protestant sort.

When pressed on the matter, especially after the Civil War by Catholics arguing that their educational and service organizations deserved support from state and local governments, many states passed constitutional amendments named after Republican Congressman James G. Blaine. Blaine had hoped to amend the Federal Constitution in 1875 by modifying the religion clauses to prohibit control of any national funds by a "religious sect." He was unsuccessful. At the state level, however, numerous so-called Blaine Amendments were passed prohibiting government funding for religious institutions anywhere in the state. Widely criticized as founded in religious, especially anti-Catholic, prejudice, in the early twenty-first century Blaine Amendments are still in effect in thirty-seven states. Certainly, defense of public education and of broadly phrased yet frequently imprecise "American freedoms" against assumed Catholic incursions has a long and often unsavory history in American history. The Blaine Amendments enacted by states as varied as California, New York, Texas, and Pennsylvania all were motivated by the desire to ensure that a particular vision of religious freedom and disestablishment was maintained even in the face of religious diversity, immigration, and the growth of state governments and their systems of public education.

IV. THE BOUNDARY BETWEEN LIBERTY AND LICENSE

Assumptions about the benevolent relationship between government and religion – especially religion of the Protestant sort – were supported and sustained in law and legal commentary. Many judges and lawyers, while they celebrated disestablishment, made it plain that religious tolerance did not require countenancing anti-Christian behavior. Equally important, they argued, democratic principles meant that the faith of the majority was entitled to special respect. Thus, the law of religious liberty, as it was developed in antebellum America, dovetailed comfortably with Protestant principles, much to the annoyance of Thomas Jefferson and other rationalists.

The first salvo in the debate came in 1811 from James Kent, soon to become the foremost treatise writer of the antebellum period, then Chief Justice of the New York Court of Appeals. Kent upheld the blasphemy conviction of John Ruggles, for "wickedly, maliciously and blasphemously" shouting "*Jesus Christ* was a bastard, and his mother must be a whore." In England, such "profane ridicule" was treated as a common law crime. In New York, however, a state without an established religion, Ruggles' lawyer argued that there could be no criminal punishment because Christianity had no formal legal status. Kent replied that the good people of New York were themselves Christian, and the offense lay against their sensibilities, rather than an established religion. For the same reason, he continued, "attacks upon the religion of *Mahomet* or of the grand *Lama*" were not punishable, because "the case assumes that we are a christian people, and the morality of the country is deeply engrafted upon christianity, and not upon the doctrines of worship of those imposters."[3] In this way, Christianity "in

[3] *People v. Ruggles*, 8 Johns. 290, 291, 294–295 (1811).

its enlarged sense" (rather than any doctrinal particulars) was known to and protected by law. Indeed, Kent stressed, the Christian religion was the basis of public decency and respect for all of law. Without protection for this generalized Christianity, liberty would degenerate into license, corroding the legal system and undermining social peace. Only openly defiant and indecent behavior would be punished under this approach, leaving private opinion untouched and absolutely free while controlling anti-Christian action. Liberty of belief was strictly bounded in law, therefore, by firm limits on dissenting behavior.

Other courts followed suit, declaring, for example, that Christianity was part of the common law of Pennsylvania and other states that had never maintained an establishment, as well as those that had. Such decisions were broadly popular and helped sustain the comforting sense that religious liberty was sustained and even nourished by religious principles, all based on the common heritage and beliefs of the American people. State legislatures, too, enacted blasphemy statutes to supplement common law decision making.[4]

Jefferson and the anti-clerical wing of the Democratic party, alarmed by the coalescence between popular religious prejudices and legal doctrine, fought back cogently but ultimately ineffectively. In 1824, Jefferson charged that state judges had undermined democracy "in their repeated decision, that Christianity is a part of the common law." This was the first step down the path to "burning witches" as in England, he argued, the sure end of a process that began with the blending of law with religious belief. Jefferson had always been concerned that federal courts would hold that Christianity was part of the national common law; he seems to have supported the inclusion of the religion clauses in the First Amendment in part as a means of derailing any such predilection. His distrust of the judiciary and its common law powers found confirmation in the *Ruggles* case and other blasphemy prosecutions.

Yet Jefferson's conviction was never widely shared, and jurists countered his claims that the law would be turned to strike at harmless differences among Christians. Indeed, Jefferson's own sympathy for the French Revolution colored his campaign against conservative judges with a tinge of atheism and blasphemy. According to one judge writing in an important blasphemy case after Jefferson had published his attack on such prosecutions, Christianity was the key to freedom, rather than the tool of oppression.

[4] Such statutes, while some are still on the books, are now widely assumed to be unconstitutional. Yet they were common throughout the nineteenth and the first half of the twentieth century. One case only has held such a statute unconstitutional; see *Maryland v. Irving K. West*, 9 Md. App. 270, 263 A.2d 602 (Md. App. 1970).

The cautionary lesson of France proved that Jefferson's own prescription for freedom would lead to "tears and blood."[5]

Joseph Story, Associate Justice of the U.S. Supreme Court and an eminent treatise writer, also attacked Jefferson's argument as an attempt "to contradict all history" and corrode the liberty and social order that depended on Christian principles of liberty of conscience tempered by respect and restraint. Yet Story and others like him, although they never advocated separation of religious principles from government, were deeply opposed to a formal union of church and state. In other words, the dominant nineteenth-century position rejected Jeffersonian secularism while embracing a vigorous disestablishmentarianism. Story summarized the majority view by explaining that the goal of toleration was "to exclude all rivalry among Christian sects" for government largesse and approval. But to leap from such an institutional disentanglement to outright secularism, as Jefferson did, was too much. To "countenance, much less to advance mohametism, or Judaism, or infidelity, by prostrating Christianity" would erode public and private virtue, exposing the country to disorder and decay. Disestablishment, by contrast, encouraged virtue by allowing individuals to follow their beliefs, and equally important, by allowing churches to appeal directly to conscience without government meddling and the destructive rivalry that government support caused between churches.

The difference between protection of Christian principles and an outright establishment is aptly illustrated by Story's careful opinion for the Supreme Court in the famous "Girard Will" case of 1844. The Enlightenment rationalist Stephen Girard, French emigrant and fabulously wealthy financier in the Revolutionary and Early National periods, left his estate to the City of Philadelphia, and ordered the city to establish a school for the education of young white male orphans between the ages of 8 and 18. In addition to providing for their instruction in morality and maintenance free of charge, Girard directed that "no minister" ever be allowed to teach at the school. Girard's aggrieved relatives challenged the will as an inherently anti-Christian document. When the case was appealed to the Supreme Court, Story upheld the will in a decision that was both deferential to religion and to the democratic principles that distinguished American disestablishment from European patterns of government. The new Girard College was not founded on anti-religious principles, Story emphasized, because it directed that students be instructed in morality, which could only and always be traced back to Scripture. In this view, the absence of ministers was no real hindrance to faith, because any good Protestant knows that he can read the Bible for himself. Students at Girard College, therefore, would be trained

[5] *State v. Chandler*, 2 Harr. 553, 567 (Del. 1837).

in the basic and timeless lessons of faith transmitted by Gospel. And while it was true, as the challengers said and Story conceded, that Christianity was part of the common law, the relationship was one that did not dictate adherence to all Christian precepts as a matter of law. Rather, Christianity was peculiarly important in rules governing the family and marriage, Story stressed, serving as moral background and guiding force in the most intimate of all human relationships. Anything else would be to enforce tyranny at the expense of liberty.

Story's was by far the more popular way to think about religious liberty. In contrast to Jefferson's secularism, Story and most other legal thinkers gradually reinterpreted the source and meaning of disestablishment. Instead of a pragmatic concession to diversity, by the mid-nineteenth century Protestants congratulated themselves that they had deliberately created a place for truly voluntary faith. Religious fervor and the extraordinary level of religious commitment among Americans, they claimed, were corollaries of disestablishment, not just a happy coincidence. Apologists answered European critics by explaining that America was a "Christian nation" because of, rather than in spite of, religious freedom. Good government, based on solid Protestant values, had finally "solved" the vexing question of the proper relationship of church and state. Voluntarism in both realms – democracy and liberty of conscience – protected and respected the individual citizen while preserving the essentially Christian character of government.

V. RELIGIOUS DISSENT AND THE LIMITS OF LIBERTY

The cozy equation between Protestantism and American democracy was based on more than just opposition to Jefferson, of course. By embracing democratic principles in religion as well as politics, judges and commentators also implicitly attacked non-democratic theologies. In the Early Republic, Roman Catholicism was the primary object of such attacks. Local decision making, majority rule, and a minister's accountability to his congregation rather than to a remote and hierarchical authority all distinguished Protestantism in American "nativist" theory from foreign, "papist" Romanism. Attacks on secretive, primitive, imported religion stoked prejudice as well as national pride.

Thus in a world defined in part by anti-Catholicism, separation of church and state took root and flourished. A small Catholic population in 1800 grew dramatically over the course of the nineteenth century, sharpening Protestant barbs and quickening their sense that homogeneity – at least the kind that existed in the big Protestant tent – was essential to the vision of cooperative voluntarism that underlay their vision of a "Christian nation."

Catholics were only part of the problem. The growth of radical dissenting groups from within the Protestant fold was even more threatening, especially from the perspective of those who relied on an unregulated Protestantism to maintain and augment the moral fiber of the country. The Second Great Awakening – and the atmosphere of change and mobility that followed independence and continued with westward expansion – spawned new faiths as well as invigorating older, more familiar ones. As many Americans learned, even Christian belief was unpredictable in a land of such diversity and size.

Religious enthusiasm provided the essential support for the mainstream Protestant understanding of church and state. It also led new believers in entirely new directions, however, and often onto divergent spiritual paths. Even as apologists for the new American system claimed that it produced harmony and singleness of purpose within diversity, dissenters sprouted like mushrooms from within the Protestant fold. Upstate New York, where Charles Grandison Finney preached to congregations quivering with excitement, was so susceptible to the fires of religious enthusiasm that it became known as the "Burned-over District."

Among the new dissenting groups, Shakers and Oneida perfectionists, both of whom formed separate communities based on reinterpretations of the family and sexuality, sparked extensive comment and condemnation. Both groups saw their share of legal problems, as disgruntled members sought to recover property they had donated to the Shakers, and John Humphrey Noyes, founder of the Oneida community and advocate of "group marriage," fled to Canada to avoid prosecution for adultery in New York. But no single group triggered controversy or generated legal action at a level comparable to the Church of Jesus Christ of Latter-day Saints, popularly called the "Mormon" church after its new scripture, the Book of Mormon. This new faith, which has appropriately been labeled a new religious tradition, so alarmed many Americans that they refused to concede even that latter-day faith was itself Christian. For their part, the Latter-day Saints condemned the religious diversity and social confusion they saw around them. They insisted that theirs was the true Christian church, and claimed that Protestants were apostates, while the Catholic Church was the "Mother of Harlots." Despite their very different theology and self-understanding, Mormons and Mormonism were also deeply related to the nineteenth-century American religious experience. They challenged basic assumptions of Protestant homogeneity and the relative safety of disestablishment in a democracy.

Most important, Mormons and their church were at the center of a firestorm over the relationship of church and state. Just over a decade after the church was formed in 1830, founder and first prophet Joseph Smith, already a well-known and controversial figure, received a revelation from God, commanding him and other Mormon men to practice polygamy – or plural marriage as they called it. So incendiary was this revelation that Smith kept it from all but a few trusted followers until his death at the hands of a lynch mob in 1844, and his successor Brigham Young only acknowledged the practice in 1852 after he led the faithful westward to the Great Basin and established a latter-day theocracy on land that was later organized as Utah Territory.

In response to the outrage that greeted Young's announcement, Mormons claimed that they had the right to determine their own religious preferences and domestic practices in their own territory. Although the precise question had never been resolved with certainty, they had substantial reason for thinking that they were right. Territories were not states, but they were presumed to be states in formation, and to have significant powers of self-government. Some even argued that the only qualification for statehood was a population of fifty thousand or more.

In the 1850s, however, the status and sovereignty of territories became a topic of debate at the highest levels. Mormons were a significant part of this process, but the primary focus of conflict was slavery and its expansion into new areas. The Compromise of 1850, which organized the Utah Territory as well as enacting a new and especially controversial fugitive slave law, heightened rather than diffused tension over the spread of slavery. It would be too much to say that anti-slavery agitation and feeling were exclusively religious impulses. But there can be no doubt that humanitarian sympathies excited by Christian conviction were central to the growth of opposition to slavery, and especially important in the articulation of reasons why slavery should not be tolerated in the "Christian nation" so dear to Northern Protestant hearts. Some passionate abolitionists even argued that slavery contravened a "higher law" than any a state or federal power could enact. Such claims were, of course, generally unanswerable by government and certainly unwelcome to most statesmen.

Religion was also important to pro-slavery arguments; apologists pointed to the benefits of Christianization for Africans, the Bible's apparently unquestioning acceptance of slavery, and more. In the end, of course, bloodshed rather than religious argument resolved the debate over slavery. Yet it would be a mistake to discount the importance of such concepts as expiation of sins, millennialism, sacrifice, rebirth, and martyrdom to the interpretation of a fratricidal civil war and its place in national history. Many Americans understood their own national history cosmologically; that is, they saw the unfolding of God's plan for humanity on U.S. soil. The "Battle Hymn of the Republic," written by Julia Ward Howe during the darkest year of the Civil War, ably captured this concept of God's special interest in the conflict over slavery and freedom, integrating political and religious concepts in ways long familiar to many Americans, but with new intensity in a time of profound conflict and devastating sacrifice.

Legal resolution of the status of territories and the role of Christian humanism initially raised by slavery came only after the Civil War in a decades-long conflict over polygamy in Utah. Congress first outlawed polygamy – often called slavery's "twin" by Northern reformers and defended in similar terms by Southern conservatives (that is, as a local practice not subject to national oversight) – in 1862 after the South had seceded. In law, then, plural marriage had been abolished at the beginning of the Civil War. Yet because of widespread Mormon resistance combined with the ineffective procedural measures attached to the initial legislation, a conviction for polygamy was not obtained until the mid-1870s. Inevitably it was appealed. When George Reynolds' appeal was heard by the U.S. Supreme Court, it became the first of the Court's religion clause decisions. The decision rejected the notion that religious belief gave the believer an excuse for violation of the criminal law.

Reynolds v. United States is remarkable in two ways, both of which tie federal jurisprudence to state law. First, Chief Justice Morrison Remick Waite's opinion for the Court relied heavily on Virginia's experience, and especially on Jefferson's interpretation of that experience, to determine the meaning of the federal religion clauses. The lessons of state history, the Court held, were directly applicable to the First Amendment. It was in *Reynolds* that the Court first quoted Madison's Memorial and Remonstrance and Jefferson's Letter to the Danbury Baptists. The Virginia legislature had explicitly prohibited polygamy shortly after disestablishment, Waite also emphasized. This showed that nobody had ever thought religion could trump the state's commitment to monogamy.

The opinion also drew on the substantive law of religion as it was developed in the states. If one were to allow religious belief to excuse socially harmful actions, the Court stressed, all of government would crumble, for every man would become a law unto himself. Like Kent, whose treatise was cited favorably in *Reynolds*, Waite distinguished between belief (a rough analog to conscience in much legal commentary) and action, which regulation validly controls. As in state blasphemy cases, therefore, *Reynolds* sharply limited the range of dissent. The decision was broadly popular, a reflection of the deep dismay and outrage provoked by polgygamy and its Mormon practitioners. The few critics of the decision focused on the narrowness of the Court's holding. While protection for belief should not be undervalued, the language of the First Amendment (which is couched in terms of "free exercise," after all) seems to run counter to such a crabbed reading. Instead of creating a new – and possibly more expansive – jurisprudence for the federal religion clauses, the Supreme Court adapted state precedent to national issues.

Reynolds unleashed a barrage of anti-polygamy legislation that followed the Court's lead in applying principles of state law to a resistant Mormon population, which by the late 1870s had spread beyond the bounds of Utah and into adjoining territories and states. Congress imposed familiar rules from the states, especially laws relating to husband and wife, including additional protections for monogamy; punishment of adultery, incest, and fornication; and marital property provisions. Unprecedented levels of enforcement through criminal prosecutions of thousands of Mormons – sometimes called the "Americanization" of Utah – resulted in a legal regime that effectively created a more thorough-going and sustained Reconstruction in the West, in contrast to the partial, relatively short-lived Reconstruction of the South.

This second Reconstruction left a deep mark in law, as well as on the people of Utah. A dozen major Supreme Court decisions dealt with multiple aspects of the Constitution's protection for religion. While some were victories for Mormons, all followed the path laid out in *Reynolds*: religious belief cannot excuse criminal behavior, provided there is a plausible secular reason for the definition of the behavior as criminal. Widespread disapprobation of Mormonism, popular outrage at Mormon leaders' practice of polygamy, and broad Protestant support for anti-polygamy legislation and criminal punishment of polygamists all obscured the constrictions that the national government, like the states, had placed on the power of religion.

The effects of this constriction would become more obvious in the second half of the twentieth century. It is fair to say that in the nineteenth century few outside Utah and its orbit saw the danger lurking in the doctrine. By the closing decades of the nineteenth century, "religious liberty" meant roughly that Protestant faiths competed on a level playing field, paving the way for extraordinary ecumenicism within the Protestant fold. This cooperative ethic translated into significant cultural, social, and political power. Yet the flip side of the coin was equally powerful. Real religious difference, whether homegrown or imported with the waves of immigration that rolled across the Atlantic and Pacific alike after the Civil War, was exposed to increasingly powerful and peremptory state and federal governments whenever it crossed the evanescent barrier between "belief" and "action."

Limitation on the scope of protection cannot be gainsaid. But it is also undeniable that within the realm of protection, and in the cracks left between the power to punish and the will to expend the energy on punishment, significant religious vitality and creativity survived. Just to name a few of the more important examples of religious vigor – the founding and growth of the Native American Church with its unique blending of native sweat lodge and peyotism with more traditional Christian elements, the development of a distinctive form of American Catholicism, and the founding of American Reform and Conservative Judaism – all testify to the capacity for religious innovation and enthusiasm in American life, even in a period when substantially greater restrictions on religious freedom were the rule.

VI. LEGISLATION AND THE PRIVATE LAW OF RELIGION

Also important was the growing body of private and public but non-constitutional law that sculpted the day-to-day interactions between religious organizations and the political orders in which they found themselves. The law of charitable donations, pew rents, rights of incorporation, ministerial licensing, and the like generated a substantial case law throughout the period. For much of the time and for most disputes, conflicts over such matters were the sort of quotidian dispute that involve litigants in lawsuits that have little to do with religion. Yet in many areas, law that began as legislative or even common law mandates acquired constitutional dimension as both sides discovered that religious liberty was implicated in such everyday statutes as tax exemptions for religious property, Sunday closing laws, public education, and more.

A hedge of unique laws surrounding religion set it aside from other legal areas in key ways. Most laws were protective of religious interests, but by no means all. Although there were significant variations from state to state, for example, it is worth noting that many states set limitations on the amount of land a religious corporation could own. Often the limit was $50,000 in real estate and two, twenty, or forty acres – all relatively small amounts even in nineteenth-century terms. Other provisions limited the rights of religious organizations to benefit from bequests made within a short period (generally six months or one year) before the death of the testator. Both sorts of limitation can be classified as "mortmain" statutes; that is, restrictions on religious institutions designed to limit the acquisition of wealth along the lines of pre-Reformation Britain. Maryland even went so far as to include in its constitution a provision that required each purchase of real property by a religious organization to be approved by the legislature. Although such restrictions may have been inherited from English law, they generally were interpreted in ways that allowed religious corporations substantial latitude, even though they imposed some inconvenience. Mortmain statutes understandably fell out of favor in the early twentieth century.

Other laws, such as those governing tax exemption for religious property, have had more staying power, even though they have been subject to relatively continual criticism. In some states, of course, property belonging to an established church would by definition have qualified as public property and thus would naturally be exempt. When dissenters were granted the right to direct their taxes to their own churches, those, too, became recipients of funds raised by taxation, and thus logically tax exempt. With the end of establishment, however, the rationale for exemption ceased to exist. Legislatures responded to challenges by obeying what one court called "the almost universal, innate promptings of the human heart" and passed exemption statutes.[6] Many states then followed up such legislative action with constitutional amendments, some commanding and others allowing tax exemption for religious property. As one commentator noted in the early twentieth century, the practice of granting exemptions is "as old as the oldest of the thirteen colonies" and has continued unbroken despite the evaporation of the justification that had sustained the tradition.[7]

Sunday closing laws, also traceable to the days of establishment but continued long after and in places where no established religion had ever held sway, faced similar logical problems. But they also enjoyed widespread popular and legislative support. After all, it would make no sense to tax the people to support the local church and then not provide the means for them to attend. Legislatures routinely enacted and reenacted such protections for Christian worship, commonly explaining their action as simply providing workers with a day of rest. This secular explanation for the existence of Sabbatarian restrictions was so pervasive that the California Supreme Court, which held the new state's Sabbath legislation unconstitutional in 1850, admonished the legislature for having given an explicitly Christian justification for the law. Sure enough, the successor statute, which assured judges and the broader public that California's new Sunday closing law was simply designed to give workers a well-deserved break from their labors, was duly upheld by the state supreme court two years after the original opinion.

Religious teaching, including Bible reading, moral instruction based on religious principles, and prayer in the public schools, varied significantly from place to place and time to time, but could generally be described as ubiquitous in most jurisdictions. Controversy erupted in several states in the nineteenth century when Catholics objected to the King James Bible as the default Scripture. Indeed, many Protestants simply assumed that the King James Version was the "true" Bible and that its use in schools was an ecumenical exercise. For their part, Catholic educators, although they certainly did not countenance Protestant Scripture as an educational tool,

[6] *Howell v. Phila*, 1 Leg. Gaz 242, 8 Phila 280 (1871).

[7] Carl Zollman, *American Civil Church Law* (New York, 1917), 239; *Walz v. Tax Commission*, 397 U.S. 664 (1970) upheld the constitutionality of exemptions from property taxes.

were also deeply opposed to any system that did not ground children in the community and practice of the Catholic faith. The Cincinnati school board went so far as to attempt to pacify Catholic objections to the public school system by banning Bible reading in 1869. The ban survived a legal challenge, because Ohio judges held that local school boards had substantial autonomy. In his argument on behalf of the plaintiffs in the case, future U.S. Supreme Court Justice Stanley Matthews stressed that Christianity was the true source of disestablishment, proving that America was actually more Christian than its European critics could understand.

Scholars disagree about the effectiveness of religious instruction in public schools and even about its prevalence. Yet it is clear that the default rule assumed that religious instruction was a part of any educational system. Jefferson's Virginia notwithstanding, American educators included one or more forms of religious practice and teaching – almost always of a Protestant sort despite Catholic objections – throughout the nineteenth and early twentieth centuries. Even in Cincinnati after the ban on Bible reading, for example, teachers regularly used textbooks that included Christian poetry and prose, as well as biblical passages and entire Psalms. Only in the twentieth century did the Supreme Court hold that school prayer, Bible reading, and all other forms of explicitly religious exercise in public schools violated the Establishment Clause of the Federal Constitution.[8]

Most important of all areas of private law affecting religion over the nineteenth century, and revealing especially of the intricate and intimate relationship between religious and political structures even in an officially disestablished regime, is the law of church property. In 1871 the Supreme Court decided *Watson v. Jones*, a property dispute growing out of the rupture of the Presbyterian Church. In 1837, when Southern and Northern Presbyterians found themselves unable to harmonize their beliefs about slavery and its place in a Christian community, they split. Each branch claimed to be the true and only successor to the prior unified church. Other important denominations experienced similar schisms – the Methodists (1844) and

[8] Significant political controversy over education has often been tinged with religious undertones. Public funding for education at private schools, especially Catholic parochial schools, has been debated with more or less vitriol at several periods from the mid-nineteenth century onward. One episode bears mentioning here, although the legal arguments focused on protection for parents and business, rather than religion. In *Pierce v. Society of Sisters* 268 U.S. 570 (1925), the Supreme Court unanimously struck down a 1922 Oregon statute that required the state's schoolchildren to attend public schools. The statute itself was clearly supported by anti-Catholic groups, most infamously the Ku Klux Klan. The Supreme Court held that no state may destroy valuable business interests (private schools) or interfere with the rights of parents unless extraordinary circumstances justified the intrusion.

Baptists (1845) also split. These sectional splits have been called a prelude to the crisis of the Union, and they surely exacerbated tension and suspicion. They also raised vital questions about how to treat internal disputes in a postestablishment world. Massachusetts's decision in *Baker v. Fales* (1820) had of course imposed democratic rule on tax-supported churches, but the Supreme Court in *Watson* retreated from such an overtly political management policy. Instead, the Court held that the duty of judges was to defer to the structures of authority within the denomination itself. That is, courts were to determine how the procedural rules of the denomination dictated the case should be decided and then enforce that decision, even if only a minority of former members supported the outcome. In this sense, courts conceded that religious organizations were in some senses sovereign entities, with the right to determine and direct internal affairs (even if such affairs were not conducted democratically), and to invoke the power of the state in aid of such enforcement.

The relationship of government power to religious affairs arose again directly in the unusual case, *Church of the Holy Trinity v. United States*, which was decided by the Supreme Court in 1892. This case, which is known today primarily for its directives to lower courts on how to interpret statutes, required the Court to analyze an 1885 statute that was designed to keep out impoverished immigrants, primarily those from China, who were brought over by their employers after signing work contracts. When the elite Church of the Holy Trinity in New York called the Anglican divine E. Walpole Warren to its fashionable pulpit and paid for his transportation across the Atlantic, the statute seemed to apply directly. "The law is no respecter of parsons," quipped the *New York Times*. But the Supreme Court held otherwise, announcing that it would not presume that Congress intended to restrict the right of Holy Trinity or any other church to employ the minister of its choosing. "This is a Christian nation," wrote Associate Justice Joseph Brewer for the Court, and the contract labor statute could not be extended to exclude the Reverend Warren without trampling on the basic assumptions behind all national legislation – that impinging on Christian observance was inimical to religious freedom.[9]

Brewer's "Christian nation" language and the evident hope for and satisfaction with a (relatively) homogeneous religious character that lie behind it have been widely cited in the century and more since the decision. The case itself is something of an anomaly in the law of the religion clauses as well as the statutory law of religion, given that it carves out an exception for religion in an otherwise neutrally phrased statute. Even more unusual is the Court's explicit invocation of a religious character for the country as

[9] *Church of the Holy Trinity v. United States*, 143 U.S. 457, 471 (1892).

a whole. Although Justices of the Supreme Court, including Joseph Story, had long presumed the benevolence of the national government toward Christian belief and practice in speeches and treatises, and the Mormon cases sustained punishment of a polygamous system widely presumed in the nineteenth century to be "un-Christian," *Holy Trinity* was the most explicit dictum on the subject from the Court itself. The case stands as a high (or low, depending on the perspective of the observer) watermark in jurisprudence, arguably a reflection of confidence in the capacity of religion to define and sustain an American national character. In the late nineteenth century, Supreme Court Justices were themselves Protestant, with varying degrees of commitment and practice. The Justices' presumptions arguably sustained their understanding of the scope of religious liberty as well as the essentially Christian character of the American nation.

VII. SECULARISM, SCIENCE, AND REGENERATION THROUGH REFORM

It has frequently been remarked that Protestants turned after the Civil War from advocating the possibility of human self-improvement through religion, to imposing legal duties to improve on all comers, believers and otherwise. "Morals" legislation is the term often deployed to describe the flexing of Protestant political muscle in the later nineteenth century, by which is meant not only laws respecting Sabbath observance but also obscenity, pornography, prostitution, sex with underage girls, and of course temperance. None of these reforms was really new in postbellum America, but it is certainly true that Protestant involvement in nationwide political reforms grew in tone and volume. Religious historians traditionally viewed this period as the last gasp of Protestant hegemony, an era of increasingly desperate and even despotic attempts to stay at the forefront of social and cultural life. The reformers' many failures, and even some of their successes, were as notable for their effects within the Protestant fold as for their impact on law and legislation, not to mention the question of their capacity to change people's behavior.

More recent scholarship on the question of the power and effectiveness of Protestant activists in the late nineteenth and early twentieth centuries is sharply divided. These divisions often are traceable to the hot button question whether American people and especially their government have ever been (or should be) "secular." While few scholars criticize the Founders, this later period is widely considered fair game. Scholars frequently locate the roots of contemporary theory and practice in the late nineteenth century, raising the temperature of the debate over the character and worth of the period's jurisprudence of religion. Focus on rival scholarly treatments of legal developments must be balanced, however, with careful attention to changes in religious thought and practice. Many of the most interesting and sustained changes in the relationship of religion to law occurred outside the courtroom. In newer venues, especially in advocacy for reform and in missionary work, believers created new tissues connecting church and state. Equally important – although very different in outcome – intellectual and scholarly events profoundly affected religious thought and even belief. Aftershocks of revolutions in social and natural science have been felt not only internally in religious life but also in the kinds of conflict between believers and government that came to courts and legislatures, especially in the twentieth century.

Traditionally, legal scholars assumed that "secularization" – or a gradually increasing separation of church and state paired with an erosion of religious and especially clerical influence in public life – began in earnest after the Civil War and triumphed in the early decades of the twentieth century. One newer school agrees that the state, especially the national government, secularized significantly after the Civil War. In this revisionist interpretation, however, Protestant (rather than secular) politicians carefully circumscribed the reach of religion and were scrupulous always to give secular reasons for political and legal actions. Claims that Sunday closing laws were motivated by the desire to ensure that all laborers had one day of rest a week and that closing on Sunday was merely a coincidence with the Christian Sabbath rather than an establishment of religion, for example, were ubiquitous. Protestant politicians engaged in such sleight of hand not because they wished to curtail the influence of Protestantism in public life, but because they assumed that separation of church and state worked to the benefit of a broad-based Protestant commitment to individual liberty and personal moral responsibility.

In one reading, these assumptions were based in virulent anti-Catholicism. There can be no doubt that many Protestants congratulated themselves that they had overcome centuries of Catholic oppression, but it is too much to ground all of secular reform in reactions to Catholicism, even allowing for the disdain and dislike for Irish, German, and Italian immigrants who poured across the Atlantic in the late nineteenth century. After all, Jews from Eastern Europe, Chinese from Asia, Native Americans throughout the West, and the hated Mormons in Utah all excited fear and animosity in many quarters. If secularization in law and politics did indeed increase in the late nineteenth century, and if there is a plausible argument for assuming secularization was actually motivated by religious prejudice, it would be as reasonable to assume that it was intended to discredit and defang all sorts of religious difference, not just Catholics.

Another school of thought sees Protestant reform activity in the late nineteenth and early twentieth centuries as a massive attempt to stamp out sin and limit the reach of individualism by government fiat. From this perspective, "social control" was designed to make the world safe for Protestants by curtailing personal liberties to sin through legal restrictions on gambling, drinking, sex outside marriage, and reading pornography – pretty much anything that felt good was on the list. Much of the time, Protestant activists were unsuccessful, and even when their reforms were enacted officials tended overwhelmingly to give secular reasons for the legislation. Even the reformers' most notable success, Prohibition (which is described more fully later), falls into this category, because it was a majoritarian rather than a biblically based reform. In other words, most people wanted to ban alcohol, and that is why the Volstead Act (1919) was passed. In this view, reformers worked hard to increase their power in the national state, but it remained secular despite a determined onslaught. Contrary to the vision of secularism as rooted in anti-Catholic prejudice, this school sees secularism as predating the nineteenth century, but surviving only after teetering precariously on the verge of a Protestant theocracy. For all their differences, both schools base their interpretation on a "paranoid style" or "anxiety of influence" paradigm long familiar to historians.

A third approach, more varied and arguably more nuanced, rejects the idea that one can point to an increasing "secularization" among judges and legal theorists in the late nineteenth century; nor, for that matter, can one plausibly argue that they resisted wide-ranging pressure to incorporate new religiously based ideas into law. Instead, the broad secularism of the American state remained more or less what it had ever been – a government deeply imbued with Protestant values of personal integrity and responsibility, which dovetailed more or less comfortably with nineteenth-century law and politics. Yet this relationship frayed at the edges as science and scientific progressivism cut into cozy notions of a person's ability (and duty) to overcome his upbringing and environment even if both were wretched. If anything, Protestant sophistication and dedication to active involvement with the world ensured a deep and persistent relationship between law and religion across the long nineteenth century, changing to suit new environments and different places. The adaptability of many American believers was matched by their energy and drive.

It is this commitment to reform and renewal at the political and bureaucratic levels that characterizes much of late nineteenth- and early twentieth-century law and religion. From the perspective of government as well as religious organizations, there was much to be gained from the relationship, even though there was never a time that religious and secular aspects of

American life fit together seamlessly. Scores of religious organizations filled essential functions in education, health, and more by the latter decades of the nineteenth century. "Faith-based initiatives," in this sense, are nothing new. It is also important to note, however, that while much of the action in religion and law in this period occurred outside the courtroom and the traditional venues of legal thought and action, it paved the way for intense and often rancorous legal confrontations by the middle decades of the twentieth century. To appreciate the background of battles over evolution, just to take one example, it is essential to understand how science and scientific thinking affected believers in the decades before the Scopes "Monkey Trial" rocketed onto the national scene, further dividing and embittering those who had once thought of themselves as allies.

Central nineteenth-century assumptions, including (but not limited to) the divine authorship of the Bible, the age of the Earth, and human origins, were assailed by the higher biblical criticism and evolutionary biology emanating from universities. Well before 1924, when Clarence Darrow put his erstwhile friend William Jennings Bryan on the witness stand in Dayton, Tennessee, many believers found themselves torn between advances in human knowledge and the traditional commitments of their faith. Many adapted and adjusted, but many others refused to compromise. And so the seeds were sown for twentieth-century legal battles, of which conflict over teaching evolution in public schools has been among the most poignant and persistent.

In addition to natural sciences such as geology and biology, which frequently are blamed for causing all the ruckus, Progressive social science and the Social Gospel movement that traveled alongside it generated real and lasting challenges to the ostensibly secular values of nineteenth-century mainstream Protestantism. Environmental determinism, for example, made the imposition of personal responsibility for behavior seem like gratuitous cruelty. It is easy, however, to overestimate the effects of this challenge. For all that professional social workers and psychologists appeared as real figures in courtrooms and prisons around the country in the twentieth century, it is still the case in the twenty-first that criminal responsibility, to take just one example, rests on the individual – a full century after archaeology, anthropology, biology, and environmentalism first nibbled at the edges of timeless Protestant certainties about freedom of will.

It is also vital to emphasize that many Protestants of reformist stripe embraced the new scientism, welcoming the opportunity to connect empirical study and scientific insight with a compassionate social conscience. Adapting to new circumstances, "liberal" (meant in the theological as well as the social and political sense of that word) Protestants began the long and painful journey away from their conservative brethren, a process that has become much clearer in hindsight than it ever was to those who lived it. These liberals also gradually made common cause with several groups, not excluding Jews and Catholics, who understood all too well the effects of prolonged poverty and deprivation. In this sense, the institutions that formed to effect reform (rather than the reformist impulse itself) and their grounding in religious as well as secular impulses were the new story in the very late nineteenth and early twentieth centuries. In ecumenical and professional settings, Progressives of varying faiths met and grappled with social problems, such as crime, disease, poverty, and more. The possibilities of combining faith with scientific and professional expertise and then deploying government to carry out reforms on a massive scale were all but irresistible to those who saw around them a teeming and chaotic world in need of betterment.

Even with these enthusiasms in mind, it is possible to appreciate that quietism, the active discouragement of involvement in public and political life as a manifestation of religious conviction, could appeal to those less accommodating of the lightning pace of scientific and economic development and the modernist impulses that accompanied them. The inclination to dive into the world, to improve it and shepherd it, rested fundamentally on the conviction that the world was indeed susceptible to improvement, as well as the concomitant belief that faith-driven intervention was the key to real improvement. The rush to embrace the world in newly scientific ways – to organize and rationalize and professionalize Christian service to the world – horrified and alienated many more conservative Protestants. They preferred to separate themselves from the world and often from the more intrusive government that had once seemed a reliably supportive if largely ineffective and distant presence. Quietism in this sense did not by any means imply lack of commitment; conservatives eventually fought back when they felt themselves threatened directly. Their appeal, as we now know, was far more widespread than supercilious critics and scholars once assumed.

As modernist liberals shifted ground and emphasis in the early twentieth century, the "fundamentals" seemed endangered to those who refused to compromise with a world run amok. Although the gradual separation of those who still clung to the literal truth of the Bible from more liberal Protestants has generally been presumed to have occurred in the South, both Northern and Southern fundamentalists rejected the new scientific explanations for life and the ways we should understand and interpret it. In this sense, a brewing controversy over dogma that would divide Protestants legally and politically as well as religiously in the later twentieth century lurked in the interstices of the new science and its rejection by conservative religious circles. Dogmatic controversy hovered in the background at the turn of the century in deep and important ways not seen since the early eighteenth century. In the twentieth century, many of those controversies played out in legal as well as cultural arenas.

For those who welcomed the new world and the chance to get their hands dirty, however, rampant industrialization, immigration, expansionism (and its kissing cousin imperialism), and more created a rich field for labors at home and abroad with little concern for more conservative believers left behind. Such was the influence of Progressive activists, that for decades scholars virtually assumed that they were the only important religious figures of their age and that intelligent men of God met the new world head on, dug in, and started helping. They especially worked for human rights, wherever they perceived them to be threatened. In some cases, passion for the work overwhelmed the original vocation. In China, for example, missionaries were as eager to halt the practice of binding the feet of girls as they were to make new converts. The Young Men's Christian Association (YMCA), which began in the mid-nineteenth century as an evangelical mission to men who had migrated to the new industrial centers, became a series of community centers with a vaguely sheepish sense of an overtly religious past by the middle years of the twentieth century. Even the fast-growing Salvation Army focused first on the outer man, pointing out that material food was necessary before a soul could turn to spiritual sustenance.

Such profound commitments to material betterment as the key to the advancement of the faith eroded denominational differences among mainstream Protestant groups and spurred the development of new and large-scale organizations to tend and guide those working in new fields. This process has frequently been labeled bureaucratization, a loaded term that implies a bloated structure separated by layers of apparatchiks from those in real need. In fact, the new rationalization and systematization, particularly when viewed in light of the massive challenges presented by burgeoning concerns posed by entire new populations of immigrants and urban poor, seemed to offer hope of truly effective management and efficacious delivery of assistance. The administrative state, in which agencies and committees and rule-making dominated legal change and debate by the 1930s, derived much of its moral fervor and energy from the reformist impulse that powered mainstream Protestants in earlier decades to embrace politics and social science as they pushed for legal change.

New aid agencies and ecumenical programs immersed believers in governance, necessitating a close and sustained working relationship between politicians and government officials on the one hand, and the believers whose faith in improvement galvanized them to action on the other. By the early twentieth century, child labor, education of adults as well as children, temperance, prostitution, gambling, pornography, charitable hospitals, orphanages, immigration, civil service, wage and hour reform in particular and labor missions in general, Sabbatarian observance, and more all drew reformers' attention at both the state and federal levels. The combination of a more traditionally religious reform impulse with a newer emphasis on scientific thought and rational techniques reconfigured the relationship of church and state as partners in the analysis of problems and the delivery of services.

Many such reform efforts required legislation and administrative apparatus as well as means of reporting violations and providing support that drew government officials and religiously motivated activists closer in working terms. Some observers, disturbed by the new relationship, claimed that it violated the mandate for separation of church and state. Government support of religious organizations that delivered medical and educational services in federal territories, for example, were challenged in the late nineteenth century as violations of the Establishment Clause. The Supreme Court sustained such programs, holding that the Roman Catholic faith of a hospital's founding order did not taint the secular services provided there.[10] From this perspective, government support for the charitable arms of religious organizations is as much a product of the Social Gospel of the late nineteenth and early twentieth centuries as of a repoliticized Christian Right a century later.

Of all the many reforms that blended religious and secular concerns in law, the Volstead Act and the Eighteenth Amendment stand as both zenith and, from some viewpoints, the nadir. The "dry crusade," as it was called, blended humanitarian and social concerns in a deliciously traditional yet innovative package. Temperance movements since the 1830s had united campaigns for political and personal reform, usually under a religious banner. The creation of the Anti-Saloon League and the Prohibition Party in the late nineteenth century cemented the links. Progressives and Populists warmed to a rhetoric that combined individual and social reform in tangible ways. The Social Creed of the Churches, the Social Gospel's equivalent of a party platform, was amended in 1912 to advocate protection of "the individual and society" from the "economic and moral waste" of alcohol. The "great experiment" was officially launched in 1919 – a dramatic and powerful cooperative effort by religious, social, and political forces to eliminate what they saw as the primary cause of political corruption, industrial accidents, and individual moral turpitude.

After Prohibition's repeal in 1933, scholarly interpretation focused overwhelmingly on the sanctimonious quality of religious reformers' support for temperance. In more recent decades, however, scholars have recovered both

[10] *Bradfield v. Roberts*, 175 U.S. 291 (1899).

the Progressive elements of the crusade and its embrace of a scientific remedy for the ills of industrial society. Frances Willard, for example, the venerable head of the Woman's Christian Temperance Union, brought a distinctly evangelical concern with the health of women and families to the crusade, representing a broad and often overlooked political constituency critical to the success of the reform. Indeed, to many liberal and even some more conservative religious leaders and their political allies, Prohibition looked like a valid and compassionate alternative to socialism, given the widespread conviction of a deep and abiding relationship between liquor and corruption at work as well as in the home. Equally important, the movement may have been dominated by Protestants, but it had important non-Protestant elements, such as the Catholic Total Abstinence Union. Temperance also appealed to the new "social scientists," many of them trained as clerics, who pioneered the academic fields of sociology, psychology, and economics, bolstering their religious conviction and political inclination with empirical research.

With such broad and varied sources of support from within religious communities, it is undeniable both that faith was integral to the passage of the Eighteenth Amendment and that the resulting reform was conceived as a means of cleansing all aspects of society as well as politics. Supporters of the amendment often blamed corruption in politics and government on alcohol and assumed that Catholics were susceptible to both. Yet they generally phrased their support for legal action in more neutral terms, emphasizing public good rather than private prejudice.

With such comfortable presumptions about the unity of purpose between religion and good government, Protestants constructed the early twentieth-century version of their long-standing "de facto" establishment of religion – they also tackled enormous and seemingly intractable problems in all of society. It is inaccurate, in other words, to dismiss dry crusaders as interfering busybodies preoccupied with personal morality at the expense of the critical issues presented by industrialization and urbanization. In fact, they were after all three – they hoped and predicted that Prohibition would simultaneously ameliorate suffering and inefficiencies of all kinds, but especially those produced by corruption, violence, and despair.

CONCLUSION

It seems appropriate to leave the Crusaders at the close of our period in 1920, at the start of the Prohibition interlude with their hopes and aspirations intact. As historians have documented in more recent work on the effects of the Eighteenth Amendment, Prohibition was more successful than popularly believed, nor was enforcement as ineffective as the era's images of bumbling "keystone cops" would suggest. Failure was grounded in other disillusionments, especially in the realization that the religious and political reforms espoused by Social Gospel Progressives and the social engineering they touted were apparently powerless to prevent the all-out economic collapse and resulting Depression in the 1930s.

Equally devastating to the more conservative, literalist wings of the Protestant mainstream was the highly publicized Scopes trial, which erupted onto the national stage in 1924, but had antecedents earlier in the century when Protestants began to split into liberal and conservative theological camps in their approach to modernism in general and science in particular. The trial itself degenerated into a spectacle, complete with a Southern rural location, a small army of journalists who covered the event, and the celebrated tourney between the trial's famous legal adversaries. The event turned deep and serious questions about the capacity of scientific theories to challenge religious commitments – and the role of government in mediating the dispute between the two – into a carnivalesque inversion of the debate. The trial; H. L. Mencken's vitriolic attacks on Bryan in the Baltimore newspaper, the *Evening Sun*; and especially the play and subsequent film, *Inherit the Wind*, that painted opponents of evolution as unreflective and even oppressive, tarred literalists with an anti-intellectual, unsophisticated brush that lasted for decades.

The result was not the disappearance of resistance to evolutionary theory or the abandonment of biblical literalism. Instead, conservative Protestants tended to avoid the limelight, flying underneath the radar of national media and even most national politicians, all the while maintaining strong educational and denominational institutions. The political division between right and left-leaning Protestants was not entrenched until the later twentieth century, when conservative Catholics and Jews made common cause with traditional Protestants in opposition to what they viewed as an increasingly secular state. Liberals, who by the 1930s had embraced a vision of religious pluralism that accommodated secular reasoning and scientific methods, overlooked the persistent doubts voiced offstage by their more traditional brethren.

Yet by 1920 the fault lines for the two major and enduring questions of religion and law that would dominate the remainder of the twentieth century had already been laid. First, government support for the provision of educational, medical, and social services by religious institutions was in place in both state and federal programs. Second, the interference of a growing and more powerful state in the religious lives of its citizens had already caused substantial friction. Although neither was yet a significant issue of national constitutional jurisprudence, by 1920 both had gained sufficiently defined edges to achieve lasting import. Once the Supreme Court "incorporated" the religion clauses of the First Amendment in the 1940s, submerged but long-simmering debates about religion and government rocketed to the surface, where they have remained ever since.

In light of both the high-flown yet imprecise language of the religion clauses with which we began and the profound divisions over both religion and government with which we conclude, it is clear that, whatever the motivation behind the religion clauses when they were enacted, America has never been the "Christian nation" that some proponents argued it should be nor the secular behemoth that others feared it had become. The place where religion and law meet has also been the place where believers' highest hopes for their country meet their darkest fears. And it has been the field of combat between rival faiths. Predictably – in retrospect at least, if not in lived experience – the combination of encounters has produced a tangled, unsettled, and contentious law of religion. Understanding the history of the relationship between religion and law in American life makes the tangle seem not only understandable but almost unavoidable. The significant religious vitality that has been nourished as well as bounded by the law of religion is the extraordinary story; the confusion of the law itself seems far less important when viewed in this larger and more historically grounded context.

14

LEGAL INNOVATION AND MARKET CAPITALISM, 1790–1920

TONY A. FREYER

Legal innovation in certain fields of property, contract, tort, and corporate law did much to constitute a distinctively American capitalist market economy from 1790 to 1920. British and continental European capitalist systems were characterized by dependence on larger state bureaucracies, whereas American market capitalism resolved social conflict through an adversarial judicial process. "Until I went to the United States," wrote Matthew Arnold in 1888, "I had never seen a people with institutions which seemed expressly and thoroughly suited to it." A half-century earlier, Alexis de Tocqueville had contrasted the egalitarian ideology of American democracy with the peoples' trust that difficult and contentious public issues were best left to judges. These comments suggest that the process of judicial dispute resolution did much to legitimate American society's changing conception of liberty. Paradoxically, however, enduring conflicts over liberal economic rights created divergent market statuses for free Americans and unfree "others." In this chapter we examine, first, how the changing constitutional order shaped a producer-oriented political economy; second, the property and contract law promoting that outcome from 1790 to 1860; third, how changes in the constitutional order fostered corporate capitalism from the Civil War to the Progressive era; and fourth, the new economic rights claims that emerged during those same decades. A conclusion suggests that Supreme Court Justice John Marshall Harlan embodies the strengths and weaknesses of American liberal capitalism throughout the entire period.

I. A POLITICAL ECONOMY FOR PRODUCERS

During the 1790s, Americans strenuously debated not only the implementation of their new constitutional and legal institutions but also the character of market relations. The alternatives were clear. By funding the national debt, establishing a sound currency, creating a national bank, and forming a free national market for internal commerce, Alexander Hamilton and the Federalists created a mercantile image of republicanism. Thomas Jefferson's and James Madison's Democratic-Republicans envisioned, by contrast, a republic based on small producers, especially yeoman farmers.

At the crux of these economic and political issues were the constraints that governmental centralization imposed on property and contract rights. Americans did not live in an ideal competitive economic order guided by an invisible hand. Instead, a producer way of life prevailed within relatively self-contained local markets dominated by small to medium-sized farmers or planters and a few modest-scale artisans or merchants. Industry in the form of small workshops, mills, and factories emerged along streams serving limited communities. Larger merchants handled the distribution of British textiles and other quality imports, and Southern planters sold agricultural staples in transatlantic trade. More generally, however, the market for manufactured goods and foodstuffs rarely extended beyond regional limits. Notwithstanding the conspicuousness of Hamilton's economic program and the corresponding image of mercantile republicanism, the states exercised the most direct influence on the majority of American small-scale producers.

Contract and property rights shaped, accordingly, the initial stages of market diversification and specialization that sustained small free and slaveholding producers. Whites defined liberty by distinguishing their free status from unfree others. One may grant that by the 1790s slavery was dying in the North; strin unfree status comprehended, in varying degrees, married women, Native Americans, and the dispossessed in general.

The Whiskey Rebellion of 1791 dramatized the contest for republican identity. Hamilton had resorted to a special tax on liquor in part because the South had blocked a direct federal tax on property, including slaves. For Southerners, the issue concerned not only the security of property rights but also the political advantages they enjoyed as a result of the Constitution's three-fifths clause. The property rights that the whiskey rebels claimed were more limited but no less significant. Moonshine was the farmer's response to market imperatives: it cost less to distill produce as liquor for sale in local markets than to transport it in bulk over poor roads. Enforcing the federal tax threatened the independence of backcountry subsistence farmers – their republican liberty based on local control of property rights.

The Virginia and Kentucky Resolutions also challenged Hamilton's conception of republican liberty. Madison and Jefferson claimed that the Constitution was a compact of states, and Jefferson intimated that the compact theory justified nullifying the Sedition Act of 1798. The republican authority that the Resolutions asserted rested, in turn, on the English doctrine of police powers. In its original feudal formulation, the government's "policing" authority embraced virtually all actions of civil officialdom. As the police power doctrine evolved in America its meaning narrowed to encompass legislation or judicial decisions pertaining to health, welfare, and morality. Thus, by the 1790s the states' police powers defined the nature of free and slave labor, the content and enforcement of mercantile market regulations, the bounds of married women's limited autonomy within coverture, and other rights of property and contract.

The states' exercise of police powers implemented republican attachments to local control. After independence, Americanization of police powers followed the passage of "reception" laws that selectively adapted English legal process, statutes, and common law in each state. Despite persistent condemnation of aristocratic English legal forms, the state legislatures and courts incorporated into the police powers the essentials of English procedure, including the jury, the grand jury, writs, written pleadings, and oral testimony. The divergence between slave and free labor systems, the limitations that different states imposed on married women's autonomy under coverture, conflicting interstate mercantilist market restrictions, and preferences that states gave to local over foreign residents in property and debtor-creditor disputes all indicate that republican ideology facilitated creative uses of the police power to benefit local interests. The Federal Constitution itself affirmed the police power principle in the Commerce, Contract, Fugitive Slave, and Privileges and Immunities Clauses, as well as in the Ninth and Tenth Amendments.

The tensions attending the reception process facilitated innovation in property law. William Blackstone's classic statement of English law taught Americans that numerous shared claims among debtors and creditors, widows and children, landlords and tenants, real estate owners and community officials limited the abstract principle of unfettered dominion. Thus, by the end of the eighteenth century the states had generally replaced the feudal English rules of primogeniture and entail with an American principle of partible inheritance distributed among family members. Also, more so than in England, a locally controlled assessment process was required for the taking of property through eminent domain. In some states police powers limited the husband's primacy within coverture by conferring on wives property title through trusts and prenuptial agreements. Employing police powers, many states expanded the *femme sole* trader laws inherited from England so that a woman could conduct business affairs in her husband's absence. Other American variations were the mechanic's lien benefiting small suppliers and artisans and the tenancy in common liberalizing land transfers.

The process of innovation fostered conflicts over title to property within and between states. In the North states required property transfers to be publicly recorded in the county courthouse; where the recording system prevailed, a registered deed generally triumphed over another claim. Throughout the Southern states the registry system had a weaker hold, and those states normally did not enforce a registered deed's priority. The sectional divergence was complicated by territorial expansion. The Northwest Ordinance of 1787 instituted the registry system, ensuring that the states established north of the Ohio River would maintain the priority of the registered deed. By contrast, property title disputes were a conspicuous fact of life after North Carolina and Virginia approved the formation of Kentucky and Tennessee; the persistence of Native American treaty rights within these states and Georgia further aggravated property claims.

Innovation in debtor-creditor law benefited debtors, the nation's most conspicuous financial losers. Americans' pervasive dependence on credit resulted in a more tolerant view of indebtedness and business failure than that prevailing in Britain. Although the short-lived federal bankruptcy act of 1800 incorporated some strict English doctrines, its implementation was more beneficial to debtors than was the case in England. Similarly the state laws enforced republican values by favoring defaulting debtors. Since many voters were also debtors, the states' laws were more egalitarian than their English counterparts and ameliorated the vulnerability of smaller producers to the risks of capitalist market relations.

A suspicion of pro-capitalist contract doctrines was inherent in Americans' initial approach to corporations. In eighteenth-century Britain and America, the law of corporations did not operate on the principle that individuals and corporations possessed the same legal personality and thus the same contractual obligations. Instead, people sought corporate charters from the King or the state legislature because under English doctrine, in return for operating in accordance with the public interest, the corporation received the authority to assert specific claims before the courts. The potential for expanding corporate identity nonetheless existed. The American republican discourse that conferred ultimate lawmaking legitimacy on the popular will sanctioned the claim that the people could authorize special privileges for corporate charters in state laws or enumerated provisions of constitutions. James Wilson and Alexander Hamilton made that very argument in defense of the Bank of North America and its stockholders when the Pennsylvania legislature repealed the Bank's charter. Their effort failed in the face of countervailing assertions that republican power could be affirmed on behalf of the commonwealth against the special privilege of a few capitalists. According to Wilson's and Hamilton's theory the Constitution's Article I § 10 forbidding state impairment of contracts could not be so construed, but their advice was not heeded.

Such tensions fostered the creation of the federal judiciary. State constitutions affirmed an independent judiciary under the separation of powers principle. During the 1780s and 1790s state high courts attempted to assert that principle more than twenty times in an effort to overturn legislative interference with property and contract rights. State legislatures successfully defied the state judges, however, and protected local factions. The federal judiciary, by contrast, had a stronger constitutional position. Two-fifths of the delegates to the Constitutional Convention had been involved with judicial bodies established under the Articles of Confederation. The most active of this group included James Wilson and Oliver Ellsworth, who in Philadelphia helped shaped the Constitution's Article III instituting a separate federal judiciary. As a senator, Ellsworth was the primary draftsman of the Judiciary Act of 1789, establishing the federal judicial system; both Ellsworth and Wilson were Supreme Court Justices during the law's initial operation. Such men well understood the arguments for a federal judiciary insulated from local control.

The federal judiciary made attempts to balance national and state authority. In *Calder v. Bull* (1798), for example, the Supreme Court narrowly construed the Constitution's prohibition against the enactment by states of laws that retroactively interfered with property rights. But federal courts also upheld federal taxes as in the Whiskey Rebellion and sustained the federal treaty power protecting transatlantic commercial contract rights. The exercise of federal judicial power in *Chisholm v. Georgia* (1793) resulted in states' rights advocates winning passage of the Eleventh Amendment, curtailing federal jurisdiction in diversity actions brought against states. The federal judges' enforcement of the Sedition Act of 1798 fueled Jefferson's and Madison's claims in the Virginia and Kentucky Resolutions. Meanwhile, the Justices failed to clarify the basis for claims that the courts enjoyed powers of review over legislation – whether natural law or the Constitution's enumerated powers underpinned a theory of judicial review. Such constitutional and legal disputes concerning the meaning of republican liberty jeopardized the Union's very existence.

Following the "revolution of 1800" the interaction between legal innovation and market relations became still more contested. Courts and legislatures reconstituted property and contract rights within a republican ideological frame that, emerging from the Jeffersonian defeat of the Federalists, was hardly consensual. One strand of post-1800 republicanism clearly sanctioned federal and state governmental activism led by a disinterested "monied gentry" represented by Jefferson, Madison, and the memory of George Washington on behalf of virtuous, liberty-loving republican citizens seeking the public interest through their acquisition and use of property. In opposition, self-described "Old Republicans" exploited culturally coded fears of conspiracy to argue that such activism – particularly by the federal government – threatened liberty and property, including Southern slavery.

Jacksonian Democracy would transform this second strand into a dominant liberal ideology espousing freer market relations, limited but essential federal action – especially providing the constitutional framework for territorial expansion – individual liberty, and state sovereignty. In its turn, the national mercantilism identified with Henry Clay's American system and the Whigs reshaped the first strand of republican liberty to maintain liberal market relations under the rubric of a "harmony of interests." Republicans identified Clay's activist government with the Northern states' defense of free labor from a slaveholders' conspiracy that endangered the Union. Chief Justice John Marshall proved adept at exploiting all these tensions to confirm an unparalleled constitutional legitimacy for an independent judiciary and judicial review. As Tocqueville observed, the resulting American state and federal courts became the most powerful judiciaries in the world.

Meanwhile, property and contract rights constituted a market economy distinguished by pervasive dependence on credit. Even marginal and isolated farmers, herdsmen, or artisans confronted the risks and opportunities that credit provided. Indeed, the Americans' extensive reliance on judicially enforceable commercial credit contacts among networks of family members and other personal associates was distinctive. On an unparalleled scale, the American credit system fostered relatively easy entry into and exit from innumerable small and medium-sized undertakings, as well as larger corporate and mercantile enterprises. Accordingly, small farmers, artisans, and shopkeepers could prosper alongside wealthy financiers and big slaveholding planters. Clearly the latter possessed market power and influence, but they were not dominant. In addition, the states' use of public credit to promote transportation, banking, and manufacturing corporations embodied the divergence between republican and liberal political discourse sanctioned by constitutional limitations imposed by the Supreme Court and state high courts on corporate charters. In Britain, by contrast, capital funding came primarily from banks.

Legal sanction of the credit system promoted associational as well as capitalist market relations. Despite the growth of state-chartered banks – especially after Andrew Jackson's destruction of the second Bank of the United States – small producers relied on personal contacts to procure credit. In 1830 only nineteen county and ten city banks existed in Pennsylvania, and although the number steadily increased, state-incorporated banks did not displace private contractual sources of credit. During the depression of 1839–43 the Whiggish *Hunt's Merchants' Magazine* repeatedly affirmed the virtues of associational over entrepreneurial market values. Admittedly, local community rivalry for internal improvements encouraged bank incorporation, but the initial beneficiaries of such expenditures were local builders, teamsters, and unincorporated enterprises. In other cases, the long-term credit that such banks and larger merchants extended throughout local communities benefited farmers whose mortgages were protected from default proceedings by lax debtor-creditor laws.

When it came to enforcement of associational credit relations among women and ethnic groups the law was equivocal. The loosening of rules binding together husband and wife through coverture, as well as the cultural stereotyping of some immigrants, etched economic activity with a free/unfree opposition that defined the bounds of republican liberty and liberal market relations for producers and capitalists alike. The exploitation of women and ethnic minorities nonetheless coexisted with their growing entry into the market economy. Even before states began enacting Married Womens' Property Acts following the panic of 1837 and the depression of 1839–43, wives often managed business property and served as guarantors of contractual credit obligations because of their husband's moral deficiencies – such as intemperance – or bankruptcy. These market relations resulted from women's central place within the kinship networks on which credit contracts relied, suggesting that the permeability of the separate public and private household spheres extended beyond women's involvement in reform movements. Private credit reports revealed that ethnic stereotypes underpinned commercial contracts; credit was forthcoming for "hardworking Germans," but extended cautiously to Jews who were "hard to rate." Despite concerns about the intemperance of Irish men, the reports expressed respect for the superior morality and business "brains" of their wives.

The status of free blacks within associational credit contracts indicated the law's ambivalence. Southern "old republicanism," which sanctioned slavery, imposed pervasive racial discrimination on free blacks. Within local Southern communities, however, the actual enforcement of commercial credit contracts and property rights could subordinate racist exploitation to associational market relationships. Southern society's widespread yet silent acceptance of interracial sexual exchanges embraced thousands of free people of color who escaped poverty to become property-holding members of the producer economy. These interracial exchanges often were part of larger kinship relationships that included Jews and Native Americans. Such networks among "outsiders" were, in turn, central to complex webs of debtor-creditor obligations that invariably were tested in state courts. In keeping with the cultural quiescence legitimating interracial familial bonds, moreover, Southern judges generally enforced these obligations to the benefit of free people of color. Whereas Southern judges vigorously upheld the societal assumptions underpinning slavery, their enforcement of debtor-creditor rights among whites and free people of color was more interstitial, maintaining the ties of cultural silence. These decisions contrasted sharply with the discriminatory treatment that Southern law afforded free blacks.

Blacks in the North faced a similarly conflicted free/unfree situation. Free Soilers opposed the spread of slavery into the territories, but they and Northern Democrats favored excluding free blacks from residence in various Midwestern states and resisted granting them limited citizenship rights in New York and other Northern cities. In addition, even abolitionist havens like Boston permitted racially segregated public schools. Following the Supreme Court's affirmation in *Prigg v. Pennsylvania* (1842) of federal supremacy in the enforcement of the fugitive slave law, Northern states began enacting personal liberty laws. The Republicans used the *Somerset* doctrine of 1772 to enact personal liberty laws that undercut a slaveholder's right to reclaim slave property by strengthening police power guarantees of due process. These rules, in turn, replaced the exclusion of free blacks with formal equality before the law. As a result, the North's personal liberty laws sanctioned for whites as well as for free blacks the contract and property rights underlying liberal market relations and the Republicans' free labor ideology. This outcome was consistent with the Massachusetts legislature's overturning of racial discrimination in Boston's public schools in 1855.

The changing ideology legitimating the legal profession reinforced the law's ambivalences. During the first half of the nineteenth century, many state legislatures opened the legal profession to any adult male possessing "good moral character." Lawyers and judges nonetheless attempted to impose professional standards by formulating a code of honor and neutral expertise that should govern lawyers and judges. Tocqueville and others asserted that this made the bench and bar an American aristocracy of merit; it also subjected the discovery of supposedly neutral legal principles in litigation and judicial decision making to the contingencies of the adversarial process. From the 1830s on, popular and elite journals and religious commentators repeated the criticism that adherence to the adversarial process subordinated equitable results to the imperatives of judicial process. Thus, abolitionists such as Harriet Beecher Stowe condemned the law's apparent moral relativism, demanding instead legal rules that encompassed natural justice. As energetically, slavery's Southern defenders like Louisa McCord used publication channels to affirm a separation between law and morality and the absolute defense of slavery as a neutral principle.

The contest over legal rules was reproduced in the changing relationship between American judges and the jury. State constitutions placed the jury on a level with the electoral franchise itself as an expression of the community's popular will. The social class composition of the jury confirmed its democratic character. Philadelphia's jury lists for the 1840s included 144 male taxpayers listed by occupation. A near majority (49 percent) were self-employed artisan/mechanics, such as carpenters, bricklayers, and plumbers; merchants or small wholesalers constituted 25 percent, whereas farmers comprised 10 percent. The remainder included seven laborers, six service people or professionals, and three individuals identified as "gentlemen." In rural areas jurors were drawn from the ranks of farmers and small-town artisans. In civil cases concerning property and contract rights, to be sure, antebellum American courts gradually adopted the rule pioneered by the eighteenth-century British judge Lord Mansfield making the jury responsible for the facts while the judge controlled the law. Even so, moderate advocates of codification such as Joseph Story recognized that America's selective reception of English evidence rules increased the influence of lawyers' advocacy before juries and appellate courts. Indeed, the procedural basics of evidence became increasingly complex largely because Americans were more anxious about centralized power than were the British.

These changes highlighted the social dynamics of judicial dispute resolution. On the level of evidentiary procedure, for example, the American business entry rule gave juries access to records made in the regular course of business, although technically they were hearsay. In commercial cases the American rule opened the private affairs of business people to the public view of jurors whether they were large capitalists, small producers, women, or free people of color. In addition, American state trial and appellate judges remained less bound by precedent than their English counterparts. Trials thus constituted a process of conflict mediation depending on effective lawyer advocacy and the discretion of judges. The proliferation of elected state trial and appellate judges strengthened local community control, but in the small towns and rural areas where most American lived, law firms of just a few lawyers possessed considerable influence with local judges and juries. The American bench and bar pioneered, too, the contingent fee system, which was illegal in England. In 1856 a critic writing in *Hunt's* blamed the common failure of juries to reach a verdict in commercial litigation on a "foreign" threat.

Across the nation, the conception of an institutionally autonomous judicial process was debated in the light of contrasting impressions of American party politics. Commentators of all political party persuasions published articles popularizing the tension between law and morals inherent in the adversarial process. By contrast, ministers representing opposing conservative and evangelical Protestant faiths; political economists serving Jeffersonian Democratic-Republicans, Jacksonian Democrats, Whigs, and Republicans; and such popular writers as James Fenimore Cooper distinguished the purportedly neutral expertise identified with the legal profession and the judicial process from the power struggles of party politics driven by corruption and vested interests. Elite lawyers and leading judges succeeded in establishing the dominance of judicial dispute resolution by re-imagining the popular belief in the constitutional ideal that all power should be responsive to and limited by power beyond itself. Thus, lawyer arguments and judicial decisions claimed to extract from constitutional and common law texts neutral principles that could be decoded to have extra-legal meaning depending on the institutional, political, and cultural context.

II. LEGAL CHANGE

Prior to the Civil War, developments in several fields of law exemplified how the legal process channeled social conflicts. Bankruptcy law was a case in point. Tocqueville expressed surprise at the "strange indulgence that is shown to bankrupts." He observed that, "the Americans differ, not only from the nations of Europe, but from all the commercial nations of our time." Concerned about the market vulnerability of small producers as well as capitalist entrepreneurs –including widows who were left destitute or in possession of encumbered property – by the 1830s reform activists had generally succeeded in abolishing imprisonment for debt. State laws and the short-lived federal Bankruptcy Act of 1841 enabled debtors as well as creditors to initiate bankruptcy proceedings. Moreover, the legislation left administration of the law to the discretion of judges, who usually construed it in favor of bankrupt debtors. This pro-debtor stance reinforced the associational credit networks that characterized the nation's independent proprietors. A study of those who benefited from the federal law found that 45 percent achieved "successful" market independence and proprietary autonomy during the rest of their business lives. Throughout the same period 15 percent maintained precarious independence. The rest lost their proprietary independence, joining the growing ranks of free wage-earning workers or the white-collar, salaried middle class.

The threat of failure permeated debtor-creditor relations. From 20 to 50 percent of independent proprietors entered default proceedings at some point between 1800 and 1860. The cycle of recessions and panics exacerbated market uncertainty. Repeatedly, capitalists engaged in interstate trade lobbied Congress for a federal bankruptcy law, but succeeded only in winning passage of the pro-debtor Act of 1841. Meanwhile, in *Sturges v. Crowninshield* (1819) and *Ogden v. Saunders* (1827) the Supreme Court generally upheld state control of debtor-creditor relations. As a result, states periodically passed stay laws that established moratoriums on debt collection. States grappled further with debt default as they adopted the mechanic's lien giving artisans a claim against the land and improvements of property holders when they failed to pay. Technically, the mechanic's lien gave artisan bills first claim against the debtor's estate. Even so, the lien law undoubtedly aided the more numerous small artisans most because their credit dependency put them in the greatest risk of failure should a debtor default.

In American contract law the trend was to promote easy access to credit, but changes in that area of law were far broader. During the first half of the nineteenth century the English intentionalist theory embodying the principle of caveat emptor gradually prevailed in American contract law, indicating the decline of property assignments as the dominant mode of market exchange. The change in the lease from a document of property tenure to a basic commercial contract in which the tenant's rights eclipsed those of an English-style landlord suggested the broad trend. Even so, the necessity of expanding credit transfers was so fundamental that American lawmakers developed legal rules to govern negotiable commercial paper instruments, bankruptcy, leases, and corporate charters more fully than for ordinary sales contracts or free-labor wage agreements. At the same time, the federal judiciary and the Supreme Court enlarged the reach of the Contract and Commerce Clauses, repeatedly confronting political pressures pitting entrepreneurial market relations against the states' police power. Thus, although the decision in *McCulloch v. Maryland* (1819) upheld federal authority to incorporate a national bank, Jackson's veto of the recharter of the second Bank of the United States affirmed the states' local control. In the *Alabama Bank* cases of 1839, moreover, the Court established the comity principle permitting states to enact protectionist credit policies.

Americans especially depended on negotiable commercial contracts. The fragmented state banking structure meant that bank notes depreciated beyond local markets, making private merchants and small storekeepers the principal sources of credit. Since specie was scarce, the nation's medium of exchange constituted innumerable local, interstate, and international credit transactions among private individuals in the form of bills of exchange and promissory notes. To facilitate the transfer of these commercial paper contracts, the mercantile law inherited from England rigorously enforced the legal principle of negotiability. In Britain, however, banks were not politically objectionable so they rather than individuals dominated credit exchanges. American banks, by contrast, were neither politically nor economically secure. As a result, lawmakers enlarged access to credit by creating forms of negotiable paper, such as municipal bonds, bank certificates of deposit, bills of lading, checks, chattel notes, and negotiable instruments payable in "good merchantable" commodities, including whisky. Innovations were resisted, especially in the form of accommodation loans that involved no actual exchange of a valuable consideration. Particularly controversial was a bankrupt debtor's use of accommodation paper to prefer certain creditors over others.

The proliferation of negotiable contracts benefited small producers. Tocqueville noted that the greater abundance of small undertakings was more impressive than the conspicuousness of big enterprises. Large mercantile creditors nonetheless urged rigorous enforcement of the intentionalist theories underlying caveat emptor on the basis of a federal commercial code as in Britain and continental Europe. They particularly demanded federal regulation of accommodation loans. States' rights politics and republican ideology defeated, however, the movement for federal debtor-creditor laws. Indeed, in regard to accommodation loans, women, free people of color, or wage workers often prevailed over capitalists. Meanwhile, the Supreme Court's institution of a federal common law governing commercial contracts in *Swift v. Tyson* (1842) created a dual credit market: federal judges enforced interstate credit transactions, whereas the state authorities maintained local control of associational credit relations.

The law of free-labor wage contracts also underwent critical development. Southerners defended their "peculiar institution" as morally preferable to the "wage slavery" that by 1860 characterized growing numbers of Northern industrial workers who had lost their market autonomy and had become dependent on wage contracts. Between forms of independent contracting and unfree compulsion, industrial workers in the Northern states occupied a middle market space. Even American slaves could accommodate fear of punishment and the master's ultimate labor dependency to negotiate some limits on the amount of work they were forced to accomplish.

Similarly, within free-labor markets employment-contract law increasingly facilitated bargaining. Courts in Massachusetts and elsewhere shifted the burden of evidence from workers to employers in conspiracy cases, granting workers a broad right to withhold their labor except where employers could prove an express intent to fix wages – a high standard to meet. Exactly what constituted an unlawful labor conspiracy differed among the states, but on the whole, free labor possessed wide freedom to associate in order to strengthen its bargaining position. Most significantly, American law rejected the English rule imposing criminal sanctions for failure to perform a labor contract. In addition, various state court decisions and statutes limited or removed altogether the employer's power to withhold wages to compel service.

Easy credit and sympathy toward failed debtors fostered a producer identity, rather than a working-class consciousness. The modest scale of industrial enterprises was attributable to reliance on commercial credit contracts and the omnipresence of bankruptcy proceedings, which in turn suggested the fluidity of market entry and exit. In conjunction with the liberal labor conspiracy doctrine and the restrictions imposed on the employer's power to compel contract compliance, debtor-creditor law indirectly enhanced the bargaining position of Northern industrial workers. Symbolic of this pro-producer outcome was the tendency of small shopkeepers – who might have themselves risen from the wage earner's ranks – to provide strikers easy credit. Nevertheless, the uneven outcomes within and between states undercut the formation of a wage earner or employer consciousness, especially given that even many bankrupts who lost their proprietary independence became white-collar, salaried employees rather than industrial "wage slaves."

The law favoring debtors coincided with market realities that further weakened class consciousness. Importantly, wage workers remained a minority within the Northern free-labor economy. Although America was the world's second-ranking industrial country by 1860, in the nation's leading industrial center of Philadelphia, just 17.5 percent of the workforce was employed in industrial pursuits. In addition, except in New England where larger industrial firms emerged, most Northern textile mills, coal mines, gunpowder works, and flour mills were of small or medium size, employing fewer than sixty workers usually under the supervision of an owner/operator. Outside New England, too, most industrial enterprises were not incorporated, heightening the associational market vulnerability and interdependency between employers and wage workers. In the textile mills of Pennsylvania and elsewhere, moreover, workers and owners alike embraced the common evangelical Protestant opposition to slavery. Throughout the Mid-Atlantic region occupational mobility was limited, although it did occur. Significantly, wage rates for those at the bottom of the region's urban populations may have increased by as much as 82 percent between 1820 and 1856. Thus the means for acquiring possessions and sustenance were fairly widespread, even if upward mobility was not.

Agricultural producers confronted a similar degree of risk and opportunity under debtor-creditor law. The homestead exemption, a Texas innovation, spread throughout the nation. Agriculture depended on mortgage debt. Since the colonial era, American legislatures had lightened the threat of foreclosure by broadening the procedural claims for delay. Even so, widespread distress resulting from the depression of the early 1840s led numerous Midwestern states to enact laws that virtually prevented creditors from foreclosing on existing or future mortgages. In *Bronson v. Kenzie* (1843) the Supreme Court overturned Illinois' protective law as a violation of the Contract Clause. The decision also upheld, however, a wide range of intermediary procedures under the states' stay laws that permitted lengthy delays. The pervasiveness of shaky credit also fostered multiple property claims in states created out of territories taken from Native Americans or won in treaties with foreign nations. The claims pitted squatters, "adverse possessors," against non-resident, speculator owners. During the Jeffersonian Democratic-Republican era, legislative majorities in Kentucky and Tennessee defended the rights of adverse possession, successfully defying Supreme Court decisions favoring the non-resident claimants. Eventually, the federal Preemption Act of 1841 supported the squatters' right to settle unoccupied public land that they could then purchase at the minimum price.

Innovation in credit-based land titles was matched in other areas of property rights. Marshall's decision in the Cherokee Nation cases holding that Native Americans were neither U.S. citizens nor foreign nationals but "wards" whose land claims were within the control of the federal government enabled President Jackson to favor Georgia's citizens, forcing the Cherokee to remove westward. Meanwhile, federal and state judiciaries repeatedly affirmed that under the police power slaveholders could use slave property for credit and other market transactions in much the same way that non-slave property was employed in the free-labor states. The police power's wide scope also promoted the erosion of coverture by the Married Women's Property Acts, which spread steadily throughout the Union, especially after the Seneca Falls convention of 1848.

On a more prosaic level, American lawmakers simplified the transfer of property title, reducing the intricate English doctrines of conveyancing to two basic forms: the warranty deed and the quitclaim deed. States further reformed property rules by which lawyers might test land titles by replacing the maze of technical English land actions with the single action of ejectment. Boston merchants pioneered the dynastic trust, which on the basis of the "prudent investor" rule gave a trustee long-term discretionary authority to change capitalist portfolio investments more easily than was possible in the rest of the United States or Britain.

Stock laws further highlighted American distinctiveness. Although colonial Americans rejected the English rule requiring livestock owners to fence in their animals, by the early nineteenth century Northern states increasingly adopted the English practice. Southern states, however, maintained the original American stock laws, imposing on property holders the obligation to construct fences around land to keep wandering stock out. The South's stock laws gave landless herdsmen a vast public domain that supported their republican independence by maintaining their large herds of animals at little direct cost. Mississippi, Georgia, and Alabama courts held even the railroads accountable to the herdsmen's rights.

Similarly, riparian property law diverged regionally – in this case between the arid West and the more plentiful rainfall area east of the Mississippi River. Broadly, the Eastern states followed the English common law doctrine, which apportioned the claims of up- and downstream users according to the standard of "reasonable use." Throughout the region of more plentiful rainfall there was diversity in the state courts' construction of mill laws, as some judges favored entrepreneurial market uses, whereas others gave greater weight to the property owner's "quiet enjoyment." The general regional outcome affirmed, however, that riparian property rights were fought over within a "reasonable" balance of market interests. The status of riparian rights was different in the arid West where the first developer of water power – especially mining industries – had a riparian right of prior appropriation against all subsequent users.

A striking permutation of contractual relations was the emergence of tort law governing accident liability. Under the common law, accident claims required a showing of proof that fit within various pleading categories, representing the legal fiction that a residual contractual duty of care existed between the parties. Accordingly, Blackstone did not refer to tort law; instead, for purposes of litigation he described how the pleading rules should be used to join the issue so that the jury could determine liability as a matter of both law and fact. Moreover, a strict liability standard was distinguishable in certain English cases according to which liability existed for pernicious conduct without fault. Not until the early nineteenth century did judges develop a negligence principle to assert authority over the law, leaving the facts to the jury's judgment. Proving a moral cause of injury or damage resulting from some fault became central to the negligence standard of liability. Thus theoretically, a "pure" accident might happen in which there could be no recovery because fault could not be proven. But, whereas the old pleading rules left the standard of liability to the jury's determination, the new principle of negligence circumscribed the jury's discretion within a judicially prescribed boundary.

The emergence of tort law as a significant doctrinal category occurred primarily within a moralistic frame. During the nineteenth century accidents became a common subject of popular fiction, journals, and the burgeoning mass distribution news medium known as the "penny press." The antebellum American legal profession, however, acquired its understanding of negligence doctrines through court decisions presented in the multitude of legal treatises and journals concerning railroads and related specialized areas of law. Permeating the negligence doctrines was the same evangelical Christian moralism abroad in the wider cultural discourse. By the 1830s this Christian moralism spread beyond an elite "American gentry," penetrating the producer economy of small towns and larger urban centers, including the growing working classes and salaried middle class. Moral absolutism inspired evangelicals, North and South, with an earnest purposefulness combining a belief in self-reliance, self discipline, and individual obligation. In sum, it instilled what evangelical Protestants called "character." Individuals possessing such character needed no reminders to do their duty; an internal sense of obligation made them reliable. Moreover, a society constituted of such virtuous citizens required only the limited government identified with the "old republican" and Jacksonian liberal ideologies. Tying individual liberty to moral conviction in private life promoted a concern for the general welfare consistent with the Whigs' and anti-slavery Republicans' advocacy of free labor and the "harmony of interests."

Equivocal outcomes in American tort cases reflected the intersection of Christian moralism and political ideology. Clearly, plaintiffs could lose under such doctrines as contributory negligence and the fellow servant rule. During the antebellum period some judges applied these and related negligence doctrines according to a liberal market ideology that benefited developers and employers, whereas other judges used the doctrines to assert humanitarian standards that held employers to the community's perception of moral accountability. Statistical studies reveal that, when accident cases reached trial, plaintiffs usually won. Appeals were exceptional, but when they did occur, the outcomes divided evenly between defendants and plaintiffs. The somewhat greater likelihood of defeat encouraged defendants to settle without litigation, a trend that became increasingly significant.

Reports of railroad accidents and of appellate cases suggested the meaning of these outcomes. Early on, New Jersey required railroads to make annual accident reports. Totals from five annual reports of three different roads between 1852 and 1858 showed that twelve passengers were killed and nineteen were injured, twenty-four "strangers"(such as trespassers) were killed and twenty-six injured, and nine employees were killed and eleven injured. A sample of forty negligence cases decided by the Delaware, Maryland, New Jersey, and Pennsylvania high courts from 1845 to 1860 indicated that 40 percent of the accidents involved property, 22.5 percent concerned passengers, 15 percent crossings, 12.5 percent livestock, 0.05 percent employees, and 0.05 percent nuisances. Overall, the railroad won as often as it lost, but the breakdown by category revealed a pattern. Passengers won 70 percent of the time, and the courts upheld property rights over the railroad's interests in 56 per cent of the cases. The railroad won whenever a collision occurred with livestock, and the cases split evenly when strangers died crossing tracks. Employees lost their cases, whereas in neither nuisance case did the railroad win.

The pattern indicates that moral accountability prevailed over express liberal market imperatives. Clearly, the four states' appellate courts upheld the jury's broad presumption that railroads were liable when passenger safety was at issue. The dominant concern for passenger welfare was further affirmed in the few accident cases involving interstate stagecoach companies or railroads that the federal judiciary decided. The view of antebellum legal commentators – and railroad managers themselves – was that most courts did not employ harshly the rule of contributory negligence and related negligence doctrines, leaving juries wide discretion to decide for the plaintiff as a "mixed question" of law and fact. Even so, state appellate cases concerning property litigation perhaps revealed most directly the meaning of the courts' application of negligence doctrines. The railroads lost three of five cases resulting from non-fire damage to real estate and two suits concerning the loss of livestock freight; cases involving harm to mills or the death of slaves split evenly. Railroads won three of four cases when locomotives sparked fires and had to pay a father for the lost labor of his son. From a litigator's point of view, the odds of plaintiffs' winning such cases, while not as high as those involving passengers, were still good enough to constitute a market for legal services in which the prevailing negligence doctrines enforced Christian and republican community values over liberal market individualism.

The outcomes suggested the limits of judicial-dispute settlement. Courts clearly applied the fellow servant rule against workers. Despite the increasing danger of the industrial workplace, litigation in worker accidents was exceptional. In the four Mid-Atlantic states textile manufacturers and railroads often continued to employ injured workers in menial tasks; when employees died the companies provided some support for widows and children. At least in the case of the railroads, the largest industrial employer, an explanation for this paternalism was that American managers unlike their British counterparts did not possess a state-sanctioned discipline program. Britain's Railway Act of 1840 authorized criminal indictment of workers who violated the private firm's regulations; American managers generally lacked such authority. Moreover, workers as voters and jurors acquiesced in narrowly focused legislation or court decisions that punished only negligent, accident-causing conduct. Perhaps railroad employees feared that greater politicization of the safety issue might result in an English-style discipline system. Conversely, lacking state-backed coercive power over workers, managers had incentives to adhere to Christian moralism and republican communitarianism when dealing with accidents. Indeed, most managers followed the lead of Henry Varnum Poor's *American Railroad Journal* in advocating reasonable safety legislation. Even when courts applied the fellow servant rule, diversity prevailed. Some Midwestern states limited the doctrine; Southern policy held that managers were liable for accidents involving slave workers.

These results were consistent with the broader constitutional accountability the Supreme Court imposed on corporations. The Court's decision in *Dartmouth College v. Woodward* (1819) interpreted the Constitution's

Contract Clause to establish the principle that for purposes of legislative action corporate charters were contracts. Even so, the divergence between Marshall's majority opinion and Story's concurrence created some uncertainty in liberal corporate relations. Marshall's leading opinion upheld the constitutional principle that state legislatures could expand the use of corporations beyond Blackstone's narrow definition. Accordingly, American capitalists exploited the Contract Clause's constitutional principle in order to promote "internal improvements," such as roads, canals, and railroads. In addition, New England entrepreneurs adopted the corporate form to larger business purposes – such as textile manufacture – which contrasted with the smaller, more common unincorporated producer enterprises found to the south. Justice Story's concurring opinion championed the broader use of incorporation for business purposes. Story nonetheless expanded on other federal court decisions that had reinterpreted English phraseology to grant the legislature authority to reserve wide-ranging regulatory powers at the point legislators first enacted or subsequently renewed corporate charters. Story's "reserve" regulatory power thus clawed back some of the protection Marshall's opinion granted corporate capitalists.

Throughout the antebellum era the Supreme Court both promoted and imposed accountability on corporations. A study found that between 1804 and 1849 the Supreme Court decided thirty-eight cases involving corporate law; of these, banks were litigants in twenty, transportation companies in seven, insurance companies in three, and industrial or mercantile firms in two. This number was small compared to the hundreds of suits concerning unincorporated enterprises in debtor-creditor litigation representative of the producer economy. But like the more famous decisions establishing the constitutional boundaries between federal authority and the states' police power, the Supreme Court's corporate law opinions shaped the limits within which states and to a lesser extent federal lawmakers re-imagined corporate capitalism. The Taney Court – beginning with its invalidation of implied monopolies in *Charles River Bridge v. Warren Bridge* (1837) – employed the reserve principle to promote the state legislature's regulatory authority under the police power. The Taney Court also extended its predecessor's corporate law precedents in the application of the Commerce Clause to promote the states' regulatory uses of taxes or licensing agreements. Accordingly, it enlarged on the police power regulations that the Marshall Court had implied in *Gibbons v. Ogden* (1824), *Brown v. Maryland* (1827), and *Willson v. Blackbird Creek Marsh Company* (1829).

Constitutional limitations shaped public discourse about the politics of corporate capitalism. Until the 1820s road, canal, and railroad promoters employed the rubric of "internal improvements" to advocate state and federal activism on behalf of virtuous, liberty-loving republican citizens seeking the public interest through individual initiative. Whigs and Republicans maintained these values until the Civil War. Local officials and courts resourcefully manipulated the ideas to maintain corporate accountability through eminent domain proceedings. But Jacksonian Democracy and the depression of 1839–43 fostered the rising liberal ideology in which state or federal promotion of "soulless" corporations was identified with political opportunism and factional conspiracies.

The basic ideological imperatives nonetheless concerned the *degree* of government involvement and policies favoring the general welfare. Some states actually built their improvements, whereas others primarily subsidized the private developers' risk through generous capital allocations and grants of special privileges. Politicians applied the constitutional authority of the police power, however, to confer corporate privileges only in return for guarantees of sufficient tax or toll income to support public welfare. In Baltimore, for example, toll taxes from the Baltimore & Ohio Railroad and other lines funded city schools. Similarly, states used corporate taxes to limit the tax burden on agricultural interests. New Jersey was perhaps most adept at implementing such a policy: in return for a monopoly on all goods transported between New York and Philadelphia, the Camden & Amboy Railroad and Canal Company paid a transit tax that by the 1850s funded about 90 percent of the government's operations.

Lawmakers imposed further public accountability through rules of corporate governance. Throughout the antebellum era state and local governments held large blocks of stock in many corporations, enabling them to control the boards of directors. Since private investors generally purchased shares to avoid rather than establish operational control over corporations, public stockholders tended to be more active than private shareholders. The Taney Court's decision in *Dodge v. Woolsey* (1856) encouraged shareholder litigiousness by establishing the derivative lawsuit. Even so, state judges generally upheld public stockholders over corporate directors. Meanwhile, state and federal courts developed the business interest rule that directors acting in good faith and with due care were not liable for losses resulting from bad decisions. These directors were nonetheless subject to the ultra vires doctrine – investigating whether their activities were within the scope of the corporation's chartered authority – and to quo warranto proceedings, which primarily determined whether an act was lawful. Not until the Civil War did the B&O and Pennsylvania railroads manage to turn these legal and political constraints to their advantage. In return for increased and continuing tax income, legislators in Maryland and Pennsylvania agreed to surrender the public shareholding interest, leaving directors relatively free. From then on the states' influence over corporate decision making declined, increasingly displaced by a liberal market ideology favoring capitalist entrepreneurship.

The limits of corporate accountability shaped the uses of incorporation for other business purposes. Although unincorporated enterprises dominated at least 60 percent of the national market, the steady growth of wage workers and a salaried middle class indicates the expanding proportion of corporate capitalist pursuits. Even so, mercantile firms diversified into insurance through incorporation; companies such as Aetna exploited the legal advantages that incorporation offered to insure Southern slave masters against the loss of their human property. Still, such entrepreneurial capitalism did not displace the producer economy's reliance on easy credit relations maintained under debtor-creditor laws. Similarly, some small-scale industrial producers procured general incorporation laws from legislatures that formalized the powers and obligations imposed under the reserved powers doctrine. Particularly in the industrializing communities of New York and the Mid-Atlantic states, such laws gave small firms more routinized access to judicial dispute resolution. Nevertheless, legislatures enacted general incorporation laws sporadically, and lawmakers did not necessarily permit firms already incorporated through special charters to adopt the general laws. Also, because Congress limited the federal judiciary's jurisdiction, corporations rarely benefited from the *Swift* doctrine. Before 1860, accordingly, among producers the inroads of entrepreneurial corporate capitalism, though important, were constrained.

III. THE RISE OF CORPORATE CAPITALISM

The antebellum Republic died in the Civil War. Enormous wartime expenditures established lasting, more expansive government activism. In 1790 state and local government spending had been about 3 percent and federal expenditures less than 2 percent of the national income. By 1900, total local, state, and federal expenditures had increased to about 7 percent of national income. During the same postbellum decades, the proportion of local governmental spending rose roughly 55 percent and that of the states just 10 percent, whereas the proportional increase in federal spending was 35 percent. Thereafter, the proportion of peacetime federal spending rose gradually until World War I.

The Civil War also altered the channels of legal innovation, compelling a reconstitution of market relations. The postwar decades saw the free/unfree opposition underlying the property and contract rights of all Americans since the foundation of the Republic transformed, though not resolved. For Southerners, the Thirteenth Amendment's abolition of slavery represented an extraordinary taking of human property without compensation. The subordination of market imperatives to the abolitionists' humanitarian impulse did not, however, prevent the South from imposing on the freedman a discriminatory status of citizenship, including unfree contract and property rights under exploitative Black Codes. By the 1876 election, the Republican-controlled federal government's failure to enforce the Fourteenth and Fifteenth Amendments confirmed the South's triumph. The Supreme Court's restrictive decisions limiting these amendments – especially the narrow construction of the Privileges and Immunities Clause in the *Slaughterhouse Cases* (1873) – sanctioned the same result.

The Populist movement of the nineteenth century's closing decades was a third signal of massive change. The independent agricultural, mercantile, and artisan producers of the antebellum Republic were now a minority. The disruption of the producer's predominantly rural way of life was particularly pronounced during the 1880s. The rural population grew by nearly five million, but the urban population jumped by eight million; the proportional decline of rural Americans from 72 to 65 percent between 1880 and 1890 was greater than in any census period in the nation's history. This dislocation – in conjunction with pronounced price deflation and market depressions in 1873–76 and 1890–92 – aggravated popular anxieties concerning lost opportunities and threatened national identity. Increasingly, male and female wage workers occupied the industrial sectors that giant corporations exploited. Urban consumers comprised another vulnerable group. The producer economy controlled by small-scale, unincorporated enterprises gave way to a form of corporate capitalism in which owners and operators were separate and managers became the principal decision makers.

The changing place of women engendered social conflict channeled through the legal process. Between the Civil War and the adoption of the Nineteenth Amendment in 1920 the formal constitutional equality of citizenship advocated by the Seneca Falls reformers was to a certain degree attained. The demise of legally enforced coverture in favor of women's greater control of property and contract rights altered the permeability of separate public and domestic spheres. Corporate capitalism's displacement of the producer economy imposed on women and men alike an exploitive market dependency. Yet for women, physical removal from the domestic sphere into the workplace did not end their identification with the ideal of domesticity; instead, lawmakers recast the discourse of liberty into an identity embracing women's special vulnerability to changing market relations and dangers. The most conspicuous field of law in which lawyers argued for and judges and juries generally upheld this new identity against the claims of corporations involved accidents. Southern courts tried to ameliorate the dangers facing women of color, and Southern officials used the gendered protective policy in part to justify instituting racially separate access to railroads, street cars, and steamboats. In other cases, women's rights organizations and growing numbers of women voters joined reformers to win passage of laws restricting the hours women could contract to work, limiting child labor, and imposing temperance-inspired constraints on the property rights of alcoholic beverage manufacturers and distributors. Progressive lawyers such as Louis Brandeis employed protectionist discourse to win judicial sanction for such laws.

The conception of American liberty was altered by a spreading legal discourse of "otherness." The destruction of slavery compelled a legal reconstruction of liberty that aspired to virtually universal possessory individualism, even for the exploited. Women's struggle for equal citizenship centered to a considerable extent on expanding their liberty to control property and to enter into contracts. Similarly, Booker T. Washington eloquently asserted the benefits that African Americans gained from possessing land or independent businesses. After the defeat of the Plains tribes, reformers and conservatives alike divided over whether Native Americans could become incorporated into the mainstream American way of life, defined in terms of private property and freedom of contract. Similarly, the Chinese who had immigrated under labor contracts to work for the mining industry and the railroads faced opposition within Western states over claims to pursue certain trades. In each of these cases, the rights claims were contested through the judicial process, resulting in outcomes that upheld the "other's" rights as a matter of constitutional principle and legal doctrine; at the same time, however, lawmakers subjected those claims to an inferior status.

W. E. B. DuBois was perhaps the sharpest observer of the complex interdependence between Americans' attachment to economic liberty and legalized "otherness" and inferiority. In *The Souls of Black Folk*, he identified the "peculiar . . . double consciousness" that African Americans possessed, "this sense of always looking at one's self through the eyes of others. . . . One ever feels his two-ness, – an American, a Negro . . . two warring ideals in one dark body." DuBois respected Washington for stressing the value of economic liberty, but he rejected Washington's faith that widespread property ownership among blacks was attainable within the South's Jim Crow system. It was, DuBois exclaimed, "utterly impossible, under modern competitive methods, for working men and property-owners to defend their rights and exist without the right of suffrage." The South's vicious "crop-lien system" resulted in part from "cunningly devised laws" that were "made by conscienceless men to entrap and snare the unwary," making "escape . . . impossible, further toil a farce, and protest a crime." The "ignorant, honest Negro" buying land through installment loans was particularly vulnerable to the "enterprising Russian Jew" who sold it, "pocketed money and deed and left the black man landless, to labor on his own land at thirty cents a day." Thus, DuBois asked rhetorically, "Can we establish a mass of black laborers and artisans and landholders in the South who, by law and public opinion, have absolutely no voice in shaping the laws under which they live and work?"

The Great Merger Wave of 1895–1904 was the climax of the long postwar redefinition of market relations. The transformation had deep institutional origins. The Civil War and Reconstruction – as well as the war against the Native American Plains tribes – heightened public opposition to the twin evils of corrupt government and unrestrained corporate capitalism. The struggle between reformers and defenders of big business weakened and divided political parties. The resulting political fragmentation increased public reliance on lawyers' advocacy and judicial dispute resolution. Led by the railroads' predatory practices and a trust agreement pioneered by Standard Oil, corporate capitalists exploited the diffusion of public authority to adopt anti-competitive arrangements. These contracts bound firms too loosely to survive state prosecution. In 1889, however, New Jersey enacted the first law permitting corporations to own stock in other corporations, creating managerially centralized holding companies. In the *Sugar Trust* decision of 1895 the Supreme Court held that the Sherman Act of 1890 did not prevent holding companies that concentrated manufacturing and production within a single state, promoting unparalleled numbers of mergers. Shortly thereafter the Court began repeatedly to invalidate cartel arrangements among corporations doing interstate business. This reinforced the merger wave until the Court finally limited the holding company in 1904. According to Alfred Chandler, the Supreme Court's sanction of mergers compared to its invalidation of interstate cartel practices fostered modern managerial capitalism.

Market transformation and dislocation aggravated anxieties about otherness. Though most Americans still lived in rural areas and small towns, they steadily lost connection with the producer's identity rooted in agricultural society. As producers confronted the proliferation of large corporations, their attempts to form viable political party coalitions foundered on conflicting ethno-racial and class conceptions of otherness, paralleling the Southern Populists' inability to prevail against appeals of white supremacy in their attempts to espouse market regulation based on class unity. Similarly, small businessmen opposed not only big corporations but also labor unions. Relying on a contorted interpretation of antitrust laws they won the labor injunction from the courts, which they used to attack unions, often employing ethnically coded images of foreign radicalism and socialism. By contrast, Samuel Gompers' "Americanized" union movement found a few big business leaders, such as Andrew Carnegie, and those involved in the National Civic Federation more willing to accept compromise concerning labor's demands. Many reformers, despite lauding small enterprises, embraced a homogeneous consumer identity that prized market efficiency above all. "Bigness" per se was not a problem, they proposed. The distinction was instead one between good and bad firms and could be policed by regulatory agencies. Reformers' embrace of regulation was not confined to the market. They often pushed otherness images to the point of supporting anti-democratic restrictions on ethnic groups and the perpetuation of racial segregation.

The institutional channels of social conflict resolution became increasingly fragmented with the rise of regulatory bureaucracies. Populists, Progressives, and other reform groups attacked court litigation as the primary method of resolving property and contract disputes resolution, urging instead that legislative control of social welfare and economic policy was more democratic. Many reformers, however, preferred the delegation of regulatory authority to administrative agencies staffed by experts with the necessary technical skills. New York's increased spending for regulatory agencies was indicative: expenditures rose from $50,000 in 1860 to $900,000 in 1900. During the same period the state's spending for social welfare and health increased from $263,000 to $6,500,000.

The railroad industry was the first leading market sector subject to the regulation of administrative agencies. Beginning with Massachusetts in 1869, state after state created railway commissions. The federal structure of state regulation nonetheless ensured a contradictory pattern of strong and weak commissions that undercut policy effectiveness and increased compliance costs. After years of legislative deadlock, the Supreme Court's *Wabash* decision of 1886 prompted Congress to pass the Interstate Commerce Act of 1887, which created a federal regulatory agency, the Interstate Commerce Commission (ICC). During the 1890s, the Supreme Court limited the ICC's powers through narrow interpretation; a decade later, however, the Court sustained the enlarged authority that Progressives had won for the commission.

Although reformers did not overcome judicial supremacy, activist lawyers turned the litigation process to reform purposes. Increased market diversification and specialization created a dual clientele for legal services. Lawyers representing the corporate economy developed large "factory" firms possessing the skills needed to advise corporations on the business uses of law, to defend corporations in court, and to lobby for corporations within political parties and state and federal governments. Paralleling the emergence of this specialized corporate defense bar was the rise of trial lawyers who employed contingency fee contracts to defend the rights of weaker groups. Perhaps the most famous reform attorney was Louis Brandeis, "the People's

Lawyer," whose clientele tended to come from ethnic minorities, modest-sized enterprises, and the dispossessed "others." He also lobbied legislatures for stronger regulatory agencies. Throughout the nation, the plaintiffs' bar kept pace with the growing demand for corporate accountability.

Increasingly, the federal courts became the leading forum for social conflict resolution. In 1875 Congress started to extend federal jurisdiction to the fullest level possible under the Constitution, including the right to remove cases from state to federal court on a showing that local prejudice prevented a fair hearing. Reform-minded lawyers and their counterparts among groups from the Consumer League to the National Association for the Advancement of Colored People attacked the federal judiciary for protecting corporate giants. The reformers achieved some Congressional victories limiting the growth of federal jurisdiction; more importantly, they challenged the meaning of American liberty, using federal jurisdiction to win rights claims on behalf of small businesses, workers, women, and other weaker groups. Contentious issues included the relation of liberal property and contract claims to the states' police power and the federal government's constitutionally enumerated powers, the labor injunction, and the inequitable advantages for corporations arising from the federal judiciary's expanded administration of the *Swift* doctrine.

Adversarial legal resolution of disputes converged with ideological conflicts. The destructiveness of the Civil War encouraged widespread popular acceptance of the remorseless Social Darwinism identified with William Graham Sumner's philosophy and liberal laissez-faire political economy. Neither school of thought, however, dominated bureaucratic policy or judicial decision making. Producer ideologies, meanwhile, remained common only among certain farm and labor groups; both liberal Christian Social Gospel ideas and trust in professional expertise associated with Thorstein Veblen gained influence. Reform-minded lawyers, judges, and bureaucrats pragmatically blended these ideas to attack "formalism," which they believed sustained corruption and the abuse of market power. The intense interest group competition of the period is also attributable to fragmented political ideologies in which reform wings emerged within each party to be challenged by conservatives and third parties.

Overall, then, the contested meanings of republican liberty inherited from the antebellum era were reshaped by lawyers through adversarial processes conducted before judges, juries, and increasingly administrative agencies. The end of slavery compelled a reconstruction of liberty that included the universality of liberal property and contract rights, but coexisted with the commensurate claim of limited market freedom for society's "others." The free/unfree status underlying economic rights claims continued in new forms, in other words, accentuating the central paradox of American liberty.

IV. NEW CLAIMS TO ECONOMIC RIGHTS

Between the Civil War and World War I the constitutional order reconstituted economic rights claims. The Republicans' Homestead Act of 1862 opened the last of the federal territories to free labor, distributing the land without cost on the basis of squatter's rights. The Morrill Land Grant Act of the same year established agricultural science in state colleges and created the Department of Agriculture. Also during the Civil War the Republicans established a national banking system, which achieved its most effective institutional structure in the Federal Reserve Act of 1914. As a result, farm mortgages came under the control of "foreign" banks and insurance companies domiciled in a few Northeast, Midwest, and West Coast cities. State bankruptcy laws and federal legislation culminating in the national Bankruptcy Act of 1898 nonetheless continued to protect farmers, and many states created the "spendthrift trust" doctrine, which further extended the property beneficiary's protection from creditors. Generally, too, rules favoring charitable trusts and tenets over landlords were standardized.

From the Civil War on, the married women's property laws extended coverage to include wages earned under employment contracts. Female wage earners were becoming increasingly common as the producer economy gave way to managerial capitalism. The subjection of the separate spheres to market imperatives transformed property rights claims. Uniformly, women's wages for comparable work were less than those for men; at the same time legislatures enacted and courts sustained police power policies that defined the liberty of women as different from that of men. In *Muller v. Oregon* (1908), the Supreme Court unanimously upheld Brandeis's argument, a procedural innovation subsequently known as the Brandeis Brief, defending a law that restricted the number of hours women could contract to work in laundries. For purposes of shifting the burden of proof, the Court accepted Brandeis's "social facts" demonstrating the unique physiological characteristics of and demands on women as familial nurturers, so justifying the state's intervention on their behalf. The protectionist outcome nonetheless further undercut the wage earnings of women.

Similarly, the Supreme Court's construction of the Thirteenth and Fourteenth Amendments affirming the guarantee of free labor sanctioned the liberal property rights of freedmen and their descendants. But the Court's holding that the police power permitted the South's system of racial segregation ensured discrimination in the administration of those rights. Judicial challenges to Jim Crow as in *Buchanan v. Warley* (1917) suggested the unintended consequences resulting from the enforcement of such conflicting rights. In this case the Court upheld the NAACP's argument that state-imposed racial discrimination in residential housing violated the property rights and economic liberty protected by the Due Process Clause of the Fourteenth Amendment and the Civil Rights Act of 1866. But the victory resulted in the use of private restrictive contracts to prohibit the sale of residential property to Jews and African Americans. The Progressives' residential zoning plans, first enacted in New York City in 1916, also benefited wealthier property owners over poorer groups; the former especially used the rules against blacks and Jews.

The Court's rejection of liberal property rights for Native Americans had similarly contentious results. Following the military defeat of the Plains tribes, reformers and conservatives argued over what place, if any, the conquered people had within the nation. Conservatives thought that tribal Indians would eventually die out. The dominant group of reformers, by contrast, advocated a program of assimilation based on the granting of property rights to Native Americans willing to leave the reservations. While cynicism and exploitation clearly guided the assimilation program in practice, its ideology of liberty symbolized the reformers' faith in the civilizing benefits of the right to possess private property. Under treaties, however, the federal government had created and the Supreme Court had sustained the reservation system that included communal property rights. This principle the Supreme Court affirmed in *Ex Parte Crow Dog* (1883). The Court's unanimous decision upheld the autonomy of tribal law over both criminal procedure *and* communal property rights. The decision shocked the reformers into strengthening the assimilation program, but the Court's sanction of communal property helped keep most Native Americans on the reservations, despite impoverished living conditions.

California's effort to destroy the property rights of the Chinese in San Francisco was similarly contentious. By the 1880s Chinese immigrants – mostly resident aliens running laundries or producing cigars – comprised approximately 10 percent of the population. Fearing competition, proprietors from European immigrant backgrounds got the city to pass a licensing ordinance. Local officials' administration of the ordinance clearly discriminated against the Chinese. Lawyers representing Chinese business owners argued that the law's purpose and enforcement violated the liberty guaranteed in the Fourteenth Amendment, as well as the rights of aliens granted under treaties. The state claimed that the law was a legitimate exercise of the police power. The Chinese lost in the state courts, but won before the Supreme Court. Unanimously, the Court held that the city's discriminatory enforcement violated the liberty to use property and make contracts. Even so, Congress eventually restricted further Chinese immigration.

Commerce Clause and economic due process doctrines fostered innovation in regard to other property rights. The Court's sanction of the states' police power favored consumer demands for lower gas and electric prices through local control of public utilities, but in the name of those same consumers it upheld interstate chain stores and drummers over local retailers. Regarding bus and truck industries the courts sustained regulations encouraging competition. The Supreme Court aided the temperance crusade, allowing states to regulate – even prohibit – alcoholic beverages despite the interstate nature of the business. Also, after the Court's decisions upheld the rate-setting power of the ICC, federal and state commissions used the power – despite opposition from bigger railways – to subsidize small roads at the expense of larger ones.

Populists, Progressives, and other reform advocates kept state and federal property tax rates lower than those existing in Europe. The Supreme Court struck down a federal income tax in 1895, but the Sixteenth Amendment established the authority, which Congress used to tax wealthy individuals and big corporations. The reformers expanded corporate taxation beyond those tolls and taxes imposed on banks and transport companies prior to the Civil War, a policy that prevailed over corporate resistance. Large planters and insurance companies overcame herdsmen's resistance to pass livestock laws closing the open range, bringing an end to this property right. The right of eminent domain became more disputed, as states attempted to remove from local appraisers the power to determine what constituted "just compensation." Even so, the Court's incorporation of the Fifth Amendment's Taking Clause to apply to the states through the Due Process Clause of the Fourteenth Amendment often, though certainly not always, strengthened the appraiser's authority because federal rules governing just compensation were more solicitous toward the property holder's interests.

The reshaping of property rights through the legal process extended debtor-creditor relations. The antebellum policy that state and federal bankruptcy proceedings generally favored debtors received validation with the Bankruptcy Act of 1898. The law finally created a permanent federal process governing failed debtors; it excluded corporations; extended the right of voluntary bankruptcy; gave priority to protecting wages due male and female workers, clerks, or servants; and did not end the most important state exemptions. Creditors could not force bankruptcy proceedings on a "wage earner or a person engaged chiefly in farming or the tillage of the soil." The worker-friendly provisions contrasted sharply with the policy of other nations that tied bankruptcy to criminal prosecution and imprisonment. The South, however, did adapt the system of racial apartheid along lines approximating foreign practices. Local law enforcement officials and planters exploited Southern debtor-creditor laws and the crop-lien system to entrap African Americans and poor whites in a virtually inescapable cycle of debt. Progressives condemned the system as a form of slavery, the federal government prosecuted it as a violation of national statutes against peonage, and – with the secret support of Booker T. Washington – the federal courts declared the system invalid in *Bailey v. Alabama* (1911). Custom, however, maintained the cruel practices.

Contract rights claims changed still more. Prior to the Civil War, for example, the Wisconsin Supreme Court had heard disputes that involved land, the sale of livestock, marketing the wheat crop, credit and finance matters arising from surety agreements, and relatively simple labor contracts. By the turn of the century, the laws in those areas had become sufficiently standardized that they no longer were the primary source of litigation. Instead, specialized enterprises such as real estate brokers suing for payment of commissions dominated the Wisconsin court's docket. Even so, litigation over negotiable bills and notes, which had been central to preserving the market opportunity of small-scale producers before the Civil War, only gradually declined in importance. The federal government's banking and currency policies displaced the average person's dependence on negotiable credit contracts as a medium of exchange. Lawmakers nonetheless continued to create new forms of negotiable commercial paper, especially municipal bonds. Beginning with the Supreme Court's expansion of the *Swift* doctrine in the decision of *Gelpcke v. Dubuque* (1864), these bonds were the subject of about 300 cases in which pro-debtor local governments resisted national and international creditors. The creditors finally prevailed during the 1890s. By 1916 nearly all states had adopted the Uniform Negotiable Instruments Law prepared by experts associated with the Conference of Commissioners on Uniformity of Law.

Trade and professional licensing was another particularly contentious form of standardized contract. The Supreme Courts held in *Munn v. Illinois* (1877) that public interest doctrine empowered state and local governments to regulate occupational licensing in order to protect consumers; the doctrine also enabled trade and professional groups to restrict entry on the basis of technical expertise. Even so, the doctrine invited repeated litigation testing the meaning of liberty for those excluded from trades and professions. The Court in 1873 upheld Illinois' right to exclude Myra Bradwell from the legal profession expressly because of her gender. Two decades later, however, public interest doctrine had loosened sufficiently within the states that women were slowly being admitted to the practice of law, as well as other professions and trades. In addition, the *Munn* doctrine permitted Northern as well as Southern public officials to develop racially segregated markets of licensed practitioners, though in keeping with the emergence of Jim Crow, Southern authorities maintained the separation more vigorously than their Northern counterparts. Similarly, the Court's holding in the *Civil Rights Cases* (1883) that the Fourteenth Amendment's Equal Protection Clause applied only to states and not to racial discrimination imposed by state-licensed private accommodations gradually was less enforced in the North but remained virtually absolute in the South.

The spread of consumer marketing contracts encountered opposition as well. The efficiencies claimed by big corporations arose in large part from managers' competing on the basis of advertising more than price. Branding was essential to national advertising strategies, and as growing numbers of brands reached the market, manufacturers attempted to impose price agreements on wholesalers, distributors, and retailers. Such practices often depended on the technological monopoly guaranteed under patent and copyright provisions. Brandeis, ever the adamant foe of the "curse of bigness," opposed allowing large corporations to monopolize these practices, arguing that if small firms could enter into and have the courts enforce such cartel practices, they could attain the same economies of scale that larger firms claimed as their main justification. Along with the Fair Trade League he employed arguments that criticized giant corporations' threats to personal and small business independence, accountability, and local control on which participatory democratic citizenship depended. His appeals sought to win judicial support for small firms to enforce price-fixing contracts and patent-licensing agreements, applying a rule of reasonableness as did the British courts. Ultimately, however, the Supreme Court rejected Brandeis's argument.

Among the less conspicuous innovations in contact law was the third-party beneficiary rule permitted by the Field Codes that states increasingly adopted after 1860. Also, many state and federal judges loosened the rules limiting recovery in breach of contract suits. While the jury retained primary authority over damages, the courts began incorporating into the cost calculations such considerations as "natural consequences," damages that contracting parties may have been expected to foresee and thereby should have reasonably attempted to avoid. Exceptions abounded, but plaintiffs' lawyers managed to exploit suspicions of evil corporations to win larger damage judgments.

Similarly, state legislatures rewrote regulations to limit the advantages that defense lawyers achieved for insurance companies in the negotiation of contracts. Initially, the companies exploited the right to remove cases from state to federal court in order to benefit from the *Swift* doctrine by imposing "ruinously" discounted settlements on vulnerable policy holders. By the 1890s, however, Supreme Court decisions helped plaintiffs' lawyers defeat the purposes of the removal by requiring application of state law, including subjecting the insurance companies to higher damage awards.

Another innovation weakened the doctrine of caveat emptor. During the final decades of the nineteenth century, the rise of a national market accentuated the demands of consumer groups, particularly small traders and farmers. Again, conceptions of liberty were reworked through the legal process until most courts accepted a doctrine advanced in an 1888 treatise on sales that favored the concept of *implied warranty* over the "buyer beware." Selling products by sample "implied" a warranty that the sample was representative of the whole. If the reasonable presumption of conformity proved false, the buyer could sue and win damages because the implied warranty was breached. Initially, the doctrine developed in conjunction with sales contracts for manufactured goods; eventually it facilitated the standardization of sales contracts throughout the entire distribution system.

During the Progressive era, New York judge Benjamin Cardozo's opinion in *McPherson v. Buick Motor Co.* (1916) employed the implied warranty theory to expand corporate damage liability. Cardozo creatively reshaped warranty theory to deny privity of contract, making the manufacturer liable to the buyer for harm resulting from the defective product. The decision suggested a transformation already underway. Following the Civil War, American society's dependence on the adversarial process and the negligence system in accident cases grew apace, testing more than ever the meaning of liberty. The most vulnerable groups were women and workers. In state and federal courts, plaintiffs' lawyers presented arguments that stressed that women's special domestic status and gendered liberty were threatened by machinery that caused pain and death. Given the power of such arguments, corporations enlarged the resources devoted to seeking settlements, which generally were less expensive than the costs of litigation. In many cases, however, litigation was unavoidable. Once in court, plaintiffs won more often than they lost; in the exceptional case that went to appeal, plaintiffs won about half the time, even in the South where race complicated matters. Indeed, during the initial decades following Reconstruction, Southern state and federal courts decided so many accident cases in favor of free women of color that the issue encouraged legislatures to impose even greater racial segregation.

Conflicting conceptions of liberty enforced through the negligence system also undermined the fellow servant rule. English courts often applied the fellow servant rule narrowly, leaving managers more liable for the injuries of employees than did many American courts. But inconsistency prevailed. From the 1860s on, the Supreme Court expanded the discretionary authority that federal judges applied on the basis of the fellow servant rule. During the 1880s and 1890s a majority on the Court shifted between Justice David Brewer who opposed the English policy and Stephen J. Field who generally favored it. In 1892 Brewer won a majority in *B. & O. R.R. v. Baugh*. Soon after, however, many federal judges creatively began distinguishing the precedent in order to declare the English policy. The success of gendered appeals gradually facilitated the adoption of the strict liability principle in workers' compensation legislation. The Progressives won passage of the bureaucratically managed restriction of the fellow servant and assumption of risk doctrines in the Federal Employers' Liability Act of 1908. After the Court struck down an initial law, it upheld a stricter version as a legitimate exercise of the Commerce Clause. Beginning in 1910 the states also began enacting worker's compensation, despite opposition from conservatives and even Samuel Gompers, who wanted the issue to be resolved through collectivc bargaining.

Ultimately, judicial dispute resolution subjected corporations to piecemeal accountability. Progressive reformers attacked the Supreme Court's notorious "liberty of contract" decisions in *Lochner v. New York* (1905) and *Hammer v. Dagenhart* (1918). Clearly, federal and state judges' use of such doctrines exploited workers because they accepted the underlying premise that employees and employers possessed equal liberty within the marketplace, when in fact the latter dominated. The effectiveness of the reformers' attacks was undercut in part because the Supreme Court and its state counterparts used the contested conceptions of liberty to affirm more state or federal regulations than they invalidated, upholding licenses or taxes ensuring the quality of oleomargarine, phosphorous matches, and drugs, as well as laws intended to protect workers engaged in hazardous industries such as mining or maritime shipping. In addition, the reformers could not agree on how to defeat the judicially imposed labor injunction and replace it with bureaucratically coerced collective bargaining. Similarly, persistent confrontations over diversity jurisdiction and the *Swift* doctrine divided Progressives. Even the outcome regarding child labor was equivocal since the Supreme Court did not prevent Northern protective legislation; the South, by contrast, continued to exploit children because they were black.

Gradually the judicial reconstruction of liberty benefited corporate managers once the separation between owners and managers prevailed within the national market. The Supreme Court's *Northern Securities* (1904) decision made holding companies vulnerable to antitrust challenge. Then, in breaking up Standard Oil and American Tobacco in 1911, the Court established the "rule of reason" to guide its administration of antitrust law: only combinations and contracts unreasonably restraining trade were subject to action under antitrust law; size and monopoly power per se were not illegal. In marked contrast to the laws of other nations, cartel practices continued to be prohibited. Indulgence toward mergers and looser forms of anti-competitive cooperation fostered managerial centralization through merger. Despite the protests of Brandeis, most Progressives agreed that bigness was not in and of itself bad. The tension in antitrust policy reflected the contested American image of liberty, combining moralistic concerns about individual accountability with faith in market efficiency. As a result, antitrust policy reshaped a precarious balance within American capitalism by preventing the complete monopolization of single firms, but promoting instead oligopolistic competition among a few managerially centralized giant corporations.

Other technical examples are indicative of the contrary outcomes attained through judicial dispute resolution. The widespread adoption of "par value" laws, for example, outlawed the sale of watered stock to innocent investors. Yet courts construed these and related laws to hold corporate managers to a "good faith" standard adopted from the antebellum business interest rule, which defined fiduciary duty in terms of "reasonableness"; most state and federal courts interpreted reasonableness to enlarge managerial autonomy. The old doctrine of ultra vires underwent a similar decline: as general incorporation spread, American lawmakers construed the general grant of corporate powers so broadly that the right to void a manager's transaction because it exceeded the terms of the charter became irrelevant. When, finally, corporations failed, federal courts pioneered the railroad equity receivership, which again relied on strengthened managerial responsibility for maintaining the rights of investors.

CONCLUSION

Justice John Marshall Harlan suggests the paradox of American liberty enforced through judicial accountability. A Kentucky Whig slaveholder whose support of Republican policies during the Civil War and Reconstruction won him appointment to the Supreme Court, Harlan embraced Hamilton's mercantile capitalism and the abolitionists' opposition to "unfree" economic rights. He became famous for dissents favoring reform principles in a host of cases – the *Civil Rights*, *Plessy*, *Sugar Trust*, *Lochner*, the first *ICC*, *Income Tax*, and others. Like most Populists and Progressives, Harlan equated the giant corporation's burgeoning "money getting" market dominance with slavery. Through his dissents, Harlan alerted his fellow citizens that the judicial process could cripple federal and state defense of liberty against the dangers posed by corporate capitalism.

Harlan, however, also authored or joined in some of the Court's anti-labor and pro-railroad decisions. Thus he refused to allow the federal government to interfere with yellow dog contracts because the law deprived workers of the liberty to sell their labor much as slaveholders had denied that right to slaves. Similarly, Harlan's opinion for a unanimous Court in *Santa Clara County v. Southern Pacific Railroad* (1886) held that the Fourteenth Amendment's Equal Protection Clause protected the corporate shareholder's fair return on investment from discriminatory taxation.

In Harlan's view, the new slavery that corporate capitalism represented, just as much as its predecessor that had caused the Civil War, threatened to destroy the promise of free and equal labor guaranteed by the Declaration of Independence, the Constitution, and the Bill of Rights. But regulation was, potentially, a new slavery too. Only the federal judiciary led by the Supreme Court, it seemed to him, had the constitutional independence to realize individual liberty. To do so, Harlan thought, it had to strike a balance of power between activist government and the new slavery, whatever form it took.

15

INNOVATIONS IN LAW AND TECHNOLOGY, 1790–1920

B. ZORINA KHAN

Law and technology are both critical for understanding the evolution of American society. As such prominent commentators as Thomas Paine and Alexis de Tocqueville have pointed out, U.S. policy has always been distinguished by the central role of law and the judiciary. Meanwhile, its citizens stand out for their innovativeness and willingness to adopt new technologies, to such an extent that some have even characterized the United States as a "republic of technology." This favorable view of invention and innovation was matched by the readiness of the judiciary to accommodate the radical transformations caused by innovations. Some modern observers contend, however, that technology in the twenty-first century is so radically different from previous experience that technological change today threatens the viability of the conventional legal system as a means of regulation or mediation.

The notion that our own era is unique displays a limited appreciation of the cumulative impact of such innovations as the telegraph, steam engine, railroad, radio, hydroelectric power and commercial air travel on American society in the nineteenth and early twentieth centuries. Unprecedented technical progress during that period brought about discrete and measurable changes in the lives, lifestyles, and livelihoods of Americans that, arguably, exceed those of our own time. Less dramatic advances in knowledge and their applications also significantly promoted social welfare. For example, the diffusion of information about hygiene and common medical technologies among households extended life expectancies and improved the standard of living. Technological innovations also affected the scope and nature of the law. Competition policy, medical malpractice, nuisance, trespass and torts, the allocation of riparian rights, and admiralty law all reflected turmoil wrought by technical changes. Advances in forensic science and technology transformed the enforcement and adjudication of criminal law. Organizational innovations influenced the nature of property rights, employment contracts, and liability rules.

Technological change was not limited to domestic issues, for it also facilitated more numerous and more rapid transactions with other nations during peace and war. Indeed, the very boundaries of maritime sovereignty were set by existing technology – the three-mile territorial limit was determined by the maximum distance of a cannon shot. Innovations like submarines, underwater international cables, and manned airplane flights created jurisdictional and third-party effects among nations that the legal system had to address. The legal implications of naval blockades and sanctions changed as newer ships and submarines developed, and the law of agency and bottomry incorporated developments in communications that meant ships at sea were no longer completely cut off from their owners on land. When firms like Singer Sewing Machine and Standard Oil became multinational enterprises, their corporate transformation raised issues of taxation, jurisdiction, and other far-ranging legal dilemmas.

Here we focus on the period between 1790 and 1920. Clearly, technological change was not unknown before this time, but the innovations of the nineteenth century were significantly different from those of previous centuries because their sphere of influence was so much larger. For the first time in American history, innovations in transportation extended the practical boundaries of markets and social interactions, making national and international transactions routine. Moreover, the expansion of communications networks introduced time as a central feature of such interactions and facilitated productivity changes through greater intensity of work and leisure. As a result of both factors, nineteenth-century technologies not only engendered conflicts between transactors but they created a world in which the pace, scale, and scope of third-party effects were potentially much larger. This in turn raised the policy question of how to ensure that technological progress increased net social welfare without causing unrestrained market power or undue redistributive effects.

Although our concern here is the relationship between the law and technology, it is important to realize that legal institutions comprised only one element in a complex network of institutions that functioned as complements or as substitutes to the law. In certain contexts social norms or familial ties served as the most effective moderators of behavior, independently of state-enforced rules, whereas circumstances that required little discretionary decision making were dealt with at least cost through administrative bureaucracies. As Montesquieu and Adam Smith both pointed out, markets can be self-regulating, since the pursuit of self-interest in market-related transactions may be sufficient to ensure that participants in a civil society cooperate in a manner that promotes the common good. Courts in the seventeenth and early eighteenth centuries performed a comprehensive regulatory function that encompassed both the private and public realms. They monitored and enforced dominant moral and religious codes and imposed restrictions on commerce through price controls, licensing, enforcement of contracts, and property rights. Soon after the first decade of the eighteenth century, as the scale of market activity increased, a division of labor across institutions led to caseloads in civil courts that primarily involved economic transactions to enforce debt contracts. At the outset, therefore, the legal system was well prepared to accommodate the new economic challenges of the nineteenth century.

By the end of the period under review, legal institutions still formed an integral part of American life, but their responsibilities had altered because their domain had been supplemented by an array of associative and administrative institutions. This process of bureaucratization, perhaps because it was more visible than the decentralized decision making of the court system, led some observers to highlight regulation as a twentieth-century innovation. But economic activity in the United States has always been subjected to the public interest: the major change has been in the type of institution that accomplished this task. Indeed, which particular institution prevails – norms, legal system, bureaucratic regulation, government, or market – may be less important than the degree of flexibility exhibited, for institutions that do not respond to social evolution will necessarily become irrelevant. As Thomas Jefferson noted,

> I am not an advocate for frequent changes in laws and constitutions. But laws and institutions must go hand and hand with the progress of the human mind. As that becomes more developed, more enlightened, as new discoveries are made, new truths discovered and manners and opinions change, with the change of circumstances, institutions must advance also to keep pace with the times. We might as well require a man to wear still the coat which fitted him when a boy. . . .

The Framers of the American Constitution had been certain that social welfare would be maximized through the "progress of science and useful arts." They felt that this would be best achieved through a complementary relationship between law and the market. The Constitution and early statutes were carefully calibrated to ensure a democratic, market orientation toward invention. The wish to further technological innovation through private initiative created a paradox: to promote diffusion and enhance social welfare, it would first be necessary to limit diffusion and to protect exclusive rights. Thus, part of the debate about law and technology has always centered on the boundaries of the private domain relative to the public domain. Innovations in printing and publishing added to the complexity of the issue by introducing constitutional questions of freedom of speech. Effective policies toward furthering innovations, whether by statute or common law, required a balancing of costs and benefits that was far more subtle than a monolithic promotion of the interests of any one specific group in society.

Legal institutions exerted a significant influence on social and economic interactions; technology was no exception. Patents and copyrights, as the subject of federal law, exhibited greater uniformity than if under state jurisdiction and thus facilitated the development of a national market. Intellectual property law had a direct effect on the rate and direction of inventive activity and cultural innovations. As the creators of the intellectual property system recognized, inventors would be motivated to address important needs of society if they were able to appropriate the returns from their efforts. Patent laws ensured the security of private property rights in invention. The attitudes of the judiciary were also relevant, because if courts were viewed as "anti-patent" this would tend to reduce the expected value of patent protection. Legal rules and doctrines influenced who became inventors and the nature of their inventions. For instance, relatively low patent fees served to encourage ordinary citizens to invest in creating new discoveries, whereas an examination system increased the average technical value of patents, fostered a market in inventions, and encouraged the diffusion of information. Technology was also shaped by other areas of property law, as well as by rules regarding contract, torts, crime, and constitutional issues.

The relationship between law and technology was reciprocal for, just as law shaped technology, technical innovations significantly influenced legal innovations. How and why the common law changed constitutes a standard debate in political and legal histories. A classic source of dissension relates to the arguments of scholars who agree that American legal institutions were flexible, but contend that the judiciary was captured by the interests of a small group in society. Morton Horwitz, in particular, admits that the antebellum legal system played a key role in the nascent industrialization of the United States, but argues that judges were biased in favor of capitalists and industrialists, whom they regarded as key to the promotion of economic development. The judiciary reinterpreted existing legal rules in property, torts, and contracts in an instrumentalist fashion to place the burdens of expansion on workers and farmers. In so doing, judicial decisions led to outcomes that subsidized the efforts of industrialists, regardless of the statutes and of legal precedent. Judges assumed the role of legislators to the extent that "judge-made law" should be viewed as a derogatory term. This "ruthless" transformation meant that the economically progressive classes were able to "dramatically . . . throw the burden of economic development on the weakest and least active elements of the population."[1]

[1] See Morton J. Horwitz, *The Transformation of American Law, 1780–1860* (Cambridge, MA, 1977), 101.

The specifics of the subsidy hypothesis have been challenged, but it has proven to be a resilient interpretation of the American experience. Its most recent incarnation is in the form of a mathematical model whose creators claim that regulation in the Gilded Age was an optimal response to the failures of the legal system. Edward Glaeser and Andrei Shleifer argue that large-scale corporations wielded excessive power in the courts, "routinely bribed" judges and juries, and engaged in other legal and illegal tactics to ensure outcomes that were biased in their favor. Consequently, the legal system "broke down." This "subversion of justice" proved to be inappropriate for the needs of the time and was replaced by regulatory agencies, which they allege were less susceptible to the same corrupting influences.

New technologies in the nineteenth century raised questions about the relevance of existing legal rules and ultimately caused changes in the law, albeit with a lag. Since the judiciary is by its nature conservative and technology is dynamic, the legal system potentially could have functioned as a significant bottleneck to innovation. Instead, the common law was sufficiently flexible to cope with new discoveries. This flexibility did not occur because of any preconceived bias toward any particular group in society. Indeed, the United States remained a largely agrarian society well into the nineteenth century, and industrialization depended on an efficient agricultural sector. Instead, we can identify five different mechanisms through which technological change had an impact on the law: technical innovations affected existing analogies, altered transactions costs, increased the speed and scope of transactions, influenced norms and expectations at both the industrial and societal levels, and changed judicial and legislative conceptions of the most effective means to promote the public interest.

In the first instance, courts attempted to mediate between parties to disputes that related to the incursions of new technologies through a process we can regard as "adjudication by analogy." Early on, the law was stretched to accommodate discrete changes by attempting to detect some degree of equivalence across technologies, either by form or by function. Second, however, inappropriate analogies tended to increase the frequency of legal conflicts or appeals, which served as a signal that revisions were insufficient. Under these circumstances, inappropriately reasoned rulings increased the cost of transacting and made it necessary for legal doctrines and legislation to change to encompass the new innovations. The third mechanism was activated by technologies, such as major advances in transportation and communications, that led to a more rapid pace of activity and thereby produced pressures for rapid responses in the legal system. Fourth, judicial decisions attempted to enforce community standards and expectations, which were a function of the current state of technology. Finally, the judiciary recognized that, to increase overall social welfare, the law must evolve to allow citizens the most effective way of taking advantage of new technological opportunities.

It is undoubtedly true that, as the proponents of the subsidy thesis pointed out, a number of changes in the common law during the nineteenth century benefited corporations, and some decisions were harsh toward frail widows and worthy workers. However, the tendency was not monolithic, and some scholars have even produced evidence in support of the notion that judges interpreted contract law so as to protect employees. Other doctrinal developments, such as the abolition of privity of contract, served to increase, rather than decrease, manufacturer liability. Procedural innovations that benefited low-income plaintiffs included the adoption of contingency fees and class action suits. Moreover, it was also true that overall social advantages could result from outcomes that might seem to be unduly favorable to one party. For instance, advantages to the general public accrued when federal statutes prohibited a few creditors from using state laws to bankrupt a national railroad that was undergoing temporary difficulties during a recession. In the face of such varying outcomes, economic logic may allow us to understand better the general tenor of legal decisions, even though it is obvious that the motivation for legal doctrines or decisions was not limited to economic reasoning.

Technology extends into every facet of our lives, from reproduction to death. So does the legal system. In this chapter, we use investigation of two significant issues to stand for the whole interaction. First we assess the intellectual property laws that the founders authorized in the very first section of the Constitution, indicating the central role they ascribed to law and technology in the future of the nation. The United States created the first modern patent system by statute, and its effectiveness was reinforced by a federal judiciary that ensured property rights were secure and inventors were able to appropriate the returns from their efforts. Copyright law illustrated the difficulties and dilemmas that the legal system experienced in dealing with such new technologies as mimeographs, flash photography, cinematography, piano rolls, phonographs, radio, and "information technology," including the stock ticker and the telegraph. Even the preliminary decision about whether these technologies fell under the subject matter to be protected by the law created deep conflicts that were complicated by constitutional questions about freedom of speech and the needs of a democratic society. Second, we analyze the effect of new technologies – steamboats and canals, railroads, telegraphy, medical and public health innovations, and the automobile – on the common law itself. Technological innovations led to legal innovations, changed the relative importance of state and federal policies, and ensured a continual debate about the effectiveness of judicial as opposed to bureaucratic regulation.

I. INTELLECTUAL PROPERTY LAWS

The United States from its inception as a nation had the option of drawing on European precedents for its intellectual property system, but chose to pursue very different policies toward both patents and copyrights. The American patent system was distinguished by its favorable treatment of inventors and the inducements held out for inventive activity; the copyright regime was hedged about with caveats and restrictions. The first Article of the U.S. Constitution included a clause to "promote the Progress of Science and useful Arts, by securing for limited Times to Authors and Inventors the exclusive Right to their respective Writings and Discoveries." George Washington issued a plea to highlight its importance, and Congress quickly complied in 1790 by passing separate patent and copyright statutes.

Patents

The American patent system was based on the presumption that social welfare coincided with the individual welfare of inventors. Accordingly, legislators emphatically rejected restrictions on the rights of American inventors and ensured that the legal system facilitated the operation of a free market. Working requirements or compulsory licences were regarded as unwarranted infringements of the rights of "meritorious inventors" and incompatible with the philosophy of U.S. patent grants. Fees were deliberately kept among the lowest in the world, patentees were not required to pay annuities to maintain their property, there were no opposition proceedings, and once granted a patent could not be revoked unless there was evidence of fraud. As a result, the annals of American invention were not limited to the wealthy, corporate entities, or other privileged classes, but included a broad spectrum of society. In an era when state policies prohibited married women from benefiting from their economic efforts, federal patent laws did not discriminate against women and other disadvantaged groups.

The initial establishment of an examination system was replaced by the 1793 model in which patents were awarded through registration, with disputes being resolved in the district courts. When this system was reformed by statute in 1836, the United States created the world's first modern patent institution. The primary feature of the American system was an examination of patent applications for conformity with the laws. In particular, the 1836 Patent Law formally established a Patent Office that was staffed by trained and technically qualified employee examiners. The French had opposed examination in part because they were reluctant to create positions of power that could be abused by officeholders, but the characteristic American response to such potential problems was to institute a policy of judicial checks and balances. To constrain the ability of examiners to engage in arbitrary actions, the applicant was given the right to file a bill in equity to contest the decisions of the Patent Office, with the further right of appeal to the Supreme Court of the United States.

The historical record indicates that the legislature's creation of a uniquely American system was a deliberate and conscious process. The basic parameters of the U.S. patent system were transparent and predictable, in itself an aid to those who wished to obtain patent rights. In addition, American legislators were concerned with ensuring that information about the stock of patented knowledge was readily available and diffused rapidly. The Patent Office itself was a source of centralized information on the state of the arts. As early as 1805, Congress stipulated that the Secretary of State should publish an annual list of patents that were granted in the preceding year, and after 1832 it also required the publication in newspapers of notices regarding expired patents.

Technology policy was conducted at the national level, which contributed to the rapid development of a national market for innovations. The designers of the American system of intellectual property envisioned that the federal legal system would be closely integrated with every phase of the life of patents and copyrights from the initial grant, its defense and trade, through to possible extensions. It is interesting to speculate why legal oversight of intellectual property rights was not relegated to the state legislatures, since many of the colonies had passed patent and copyright laws in the eighteenth century. Property rights are worth little unless they can be legally enforced in a consistent, certain, and predictable manner. The value of patents was enhanced because patent issues were litigated at the federal and not the state level, with a right of appeal to the Supreme Court, which contributed to uniformity and certainty in intellectual property. Federal courts from their inception attempted to establish a store of doctrine that fulfilled the intent of the Constitution to secure the rights of intellectual property owners. The judiciary acknowledged that inventive efforts varied with the extent to which inventors could appropriate the returns on their discoveries and tried to ensure that patentees were not unjustly deprived of the benefits from their inventions.

Courts explicitly attempted to make decisions favorable to the promotion of social and economic development through technological change.[2] The

[2] *Ames v. Howard*, 1 F. Cas. 755 (1833).

attitudes of the judiciary were primarily shaped by their interpretation of the monopoly aspect of the patent grant. In *Whitney et al. v. Emmett et al.* (1831), Justice Baldwin contrasted the policies in Britain and America toward the patent contract. English courts, he pointed out, interpreted the patent grant as a privileged exception from the general ban on monopolies. Apart from this proviso, the judiciary had total discretion in interpreting and deciding the ends that would promote public welfare. The patent was seen as a trade-off, a bargain between the inventor and the public with a negotiable outcome. In contrast, in the United States the patentee was not recognized as a monopolist per se, and judges had little discretion other than to fulfill the explicit intention of the Constitution.[3] Numerous reported decisions before the early courts declared that, rather than unwarranted monopolies, patent rights were "sacred" and to be regarded as the just recompense for inventive ingenuity. Supreme Court Justice Joseph Story, the acknowledged patent expert of the antebellum courts, indicated in *Lowell v. Lewis* (1817) that "the inventor has a property in his invention; a property which is often of very great value, and of which the law intended to give him the absolute enjoyment and possession . . . involving some of the dearest and most valuable rights which society acknowledges, and the constitution itself means to favor."[4]

The 1840s saw an increase in the number of patentees resorting to courts of equity to obtain temporary or permanent injunctions against unauthorized users of their inventions. Preliminary injunctions could also be obtained pending common law litigation, if patentees stood to suffer severe losses. But judges were alert to the possibility of unwarranted harm to the defendants whose enterprises could be broken up. Oliver Parker's request for a wholesale injunction against 100 mill owners was disallowed because his patent was within weeks of expiring. The judge was reluctant to issue an injunction that would adversely affect so many enterprises, when the patentee received no benefit from closure of the mills and would later be compensated by the payment of damages if it were indeed proven that the patent was infringed.[5] In the absence of antitrust statutes, equity provided a more flexible channel for mediating between the inventor's exclusive rights and a general monopoly. The plaintiff in *Smith v. Downing* (1850), an assignee of telegraph promoter Samuel F. B. Morse, sought a permanent injunction against the defendants, who operated a telegraph under assignment from Royal E. House. After a detailed exposition of the incremental nature of the development of the telegraph, the court refused the injunction. Exclusive

[3] *Whitney et al. v. Emmett et al.*, 29 F. Cas. 1074 (1831).
[4] *Lowell v. Lewis*, 15 F. Cas. 1018 (1817).
[5] See, for instance, *Parker v. Sears*, 18 F. Cas. 1159 (1850).

patent rights allowed the inventor to benefit from the acknowledged property in his improvement; at the same time, such property did not extend to the entire field, because this would grant the marginal improver a monopoly that would halt general progress in the area. House's telegraph was not only different from Morse's, but technically superior; hence to mandate an estoppel against his ingenuity and the defendants' enterprise would have been an "extraordinary" measure.[6]

One of the advantages of a legal system that secures property rights is that it facilitates contracts and trade. Partly as a result, an extensive national network of licensing and assignments developed early on: in 1845 the Patent Office recorded 2,108 assignments, which can be compared to the cumulative stock of 7,188 patents that were still in force in that year. By the 1870s the number of assignments averaged more than 9,000 per year, and this number increased in the next decade to more than 12,000 contracts recorded annually. Assignments provide a straightforward index of the effectiveness of the American system, since a market for patented inventions would hardly proliferate if patent rights were uncertain or worthless. The secondary market in patent rights was based on the legally valid assumption that the patent embodied some intrinsic technical value. The English system, which initially offered no protection to purchasers who were deceived into buying false patents, encouraged unproductive speculation and deterred the development of trade. In contrast, American legal rulings voided promissory notes and other contracts for useless or fraudulent patents as part of a policy of protecting and securing legitimate property rights.

The judiciary was willing to grapple with other difficult questions, including the appropriate measure of damages when patent infringement likely lowered prices, disputes between owners of valid but conflicting patents, and the problem of how to protect the integrity of existing contracts when the law changed. One such question revolved around the criteria for patentability. The terms of the 1836 Patent Act authorized the grant to "any person or persons having discovered or invented any new and useful art, machine, manufacture, or composition of matter, or any new and useful improvements on any art, machine, manufacture, or composition of matter, not known or used by others before his or their discovery or invention thereof, and not, at the time of his application for a patent, in public use or on sale." The patent statutes required that inventions should be new and useful, but the judiciary treated the utility requirement as merely nominal, since it was the function of markets, not courts, to determine the utility and value of patents. Infringers who tried to undermine the validity of the

[6] *Smith v. Downing*, 1 Fish. Pat. Cas. 64 (Mass. 1850).

original patent on the grounds of utility were reminded that their very use of the item overturned any allegation of lack of utility. Instead, the major issue in any patent lawsuit related either to the novelty of the invention or the extent to which it promoted the progress of useful arts.

To nineteenth-century courts, patentable technology incorporated ideas and discoveries that were vested in tangible form, and "a mere abstract idea" or processes independent of a means of realization could not be treated as the exclusive property of any one person, for doing so would limit diffusion and learning without any measurable social return. When patents were granted for inventions that seemed to be for contracts or business methods, they were uniformly overturned by the courts, unless the idea or principle could be construed as vested in a tangible medium. The Patent Office granted an 1891 patent to Levy Maybaum of Newark for inventing a "means for securing against excessive losses by bad debts," which he assigned to the U.S. Credit System Company. The patent covered a method of computing the industry norm for operating losses and constructing tables that allowed comparisons relative to the industry average. When the owners of the patent brought an infringement claim before the courts, the patent was dismissed as "a method of transacting common business, which does not seem to be patentable as an art." In litigation regarding the validity of an invention for "time limit" transfer tickets for use by street railways, the defendants sought to decry the patent as "a method of transacting business, a form of contract, a mode of procedure, a rule of conduct, a principle or idea, or a permissive function, predicated upon a thing involving no structural law." The Circuit Court admitted that if the defense claim were true, then the patent would have to be invalidated. As another judge had expressed it, "Advice is not patentable." However, it was decided that though "the case is perhaps near the border line, we think the device should be classed as an article to be used in a method of doing business," and as an item to be manufactured, the ticket was patentable.[7]

In *Earle v. Sawyer* (1825) Justice Story rejected the argument that patents required inventive inputs or efforts that went beyond those that could be produced by an artisan who was skilled in the arts. Story was not persuaded by the "metaphysical" notion of patentability, for the standard "proceeds upon the language of common sense and common life, and has nothing mysterious or equivocal in it. . . . It is of no consequence, whether the thing be simple or complicated; whether it be by accident, or by long, laborious thought, or by an instantaneous flash of mind, that it is first done. The law

[7] See *Cincinnati Traction Co. v. Pope*, 210 F. 443 (1913); *Hotel Security Checking Co. v. Lorraine Co.*, 160 F. 467 (1908); *United States Credit System Co. v. American Credit Indem. Co.*, 53 F. 818 (1893).

looks to the fact, and not to the process by which it is accomplished."[8] This commonsense standard was entirely appropriate for an era in which ordinary non-technical craftsmen and women could make valuable innovations based on simple know-how. A departure from this approach occurred when *Hotchkiss v. Greenwood* (1850) proposed that "unless more ingenuity and skill in applying the old method... were required in the application of it... than were possessed by an ordinary mechanic acquainted with the business, there was an absence of that degree of skill and ingenuity which constitute essential elements of every invention. In other words, the improvement is the work of the skilful mechanic, not that of the inventor."[9]

The frequency of citation indicates that the Hotchkiss ruling long remained an isolated decision, but after the 1870s it became the reigning precedent for decisions that invalidated patent grants on the grounds of non-obviousness and later for the absence of a "flash of genius." Although the purist will view the move toward the more stringent non-obviousness criterion as not strictly in keeping with a democratic orientation, the heightened standards likely functioned as a more effective filter in view of the great increase in technical qualifications and patenting rates occurring among the population during the postbellum period. Another change occurred because early judicial optimism about the coincidence between private and public welfare had begun to wane by the second half of the century. By then, the courts had experienced the tactical use of litigation by patentees and their assignees to protect national monopolies. Justice Woodbury was prompted to dictate, "The rights of inventive genius, and the valuable property produced by it, all persons in the exercise of this spirit will be willing to vindicate and uphold, without colorable evasions and wanton piracies; but those rights on the other hand, should be maintained in a manner not harsh towards other inventors, nor unaccommodating to the growing wants of the community."[10]

The United States differed from the rest of the world in terms of its treatment of foreign inventions and foreign inventors. Most countries had simple registration systems and allowed patents of importation, which allowed their residents to appropriate and obtain patents for discoveries made by residents of other countries. American laws employed the language of the English statute in granting patents to "the first and true inventor." But, unlike in England, the phrase was used literally to grant patents for inventions that were original in the world, not simply within U.S. borders. Although the treatment of foreign inventors by the United States varied over time, its policies were much more favorable toward aliens than those

[8] *Earle v. Sawyer*, 8 F. Cas. 254 (1825). [9] *Hotchkiss v. Greenwood*, 52 U.S. 248 (1850).
[10] *Woodworth v. Edwards*, 30 F. Cas. 567 (1847).

of other countries. The earliest statutes of 1793, 1800, and 1832 restricted rights in patent property to citizens or to residents who declared an intention to become citizens. As such, although an American could not appropriate patent rights to a foreign invention, he could freely use the idea without any need to bear licensing or similar costs that would otherwise have been due if the inventor had been able to obtain a patent in this country. Nevertheless, numerous foreign inventors (presumably of higher valued discoveries) were able to obtain U.S. patent protection through appeals to Congress. In 1836, the stipulations on citizenship or residency were removed, but were replaced with discriminatory patent fees that retaliated for the significantly higher fees charged in other countries: foreigners could obtain a patent in the United States for a fee of $300, or $500 if they were British. After 1861 patent rights (with the exception of caveats) were available to all applicants on the same basis without regard to nationality. Liberality to foreign inventors was obtained at low cost since, for most of the nineteenth century, the number of foreign patents filed in the United States was trivial relative to the total.

By the end of the nineteenth century, the United States was directing its efforts toward attaining international uniformity in intellectual property rights laws. A significant motivating factor was the success of American patentees in penetrating foreign markets. Americans inventors were also concerned about the lack of protection accorded to their exhibits in the increasingly prominent World's Fairs. Internationally, the impetus for change occurred as part of an overall movement to harmonize legal policies, because the costs of discordant national rules became more burdensome as the volume of international trade in patents and industrial products grew over time. The first international patent convention was held in Austria in 1873 at the suggestion of U.S. policymakers, who wanted to be certain that their inventors would be adequately protected at the International Exposition held in Vienna that year. The conventions also yielded an opportunity for the United States to protest provisions in foreign laws that discriminated against American patentees.

By the beginning of the twentieth century, the United States had become the most prolific patenting nation in the world. Many major American enterprises owed their success to patents and were expanding into international markets; the U.S. patent system was recognized as the world's most successful. It is therefore not surprising that the harmonization of patent laws implied convergence toward the American model, which was viewed as "the ideal of the future," despite resistance from other nations. Countries such as Germany were initially averse to extending equal protection to foreigners because they feared that their domestic industry would be overwhelmed by American patents. Ironically, because its patent laws were the most liberal, the United States found itself in a weaker bargaining position than nations who could make concessions by changing their protectionist provisions. This likely influenced the U.S. tendency to use bilateral trade sanctions rather than multilateral conventions to obtain reforms in international patent policies. The movement to create an international patent system demonstrated very clearly that intellectual property laws did not exist in a vacuum, but were part of a bundle of rights that were affected by other laws and policies, as well as by the scale and scope of economic activity.

Copyright and Allied Rights

Despite their common source in the intellectual property clause of the U.S. Constitution, American copyright policies provided a marked contrast to the patent system. The subsidy argument is quite implausible in accounting for the differences between patent and copyright doctrines. Copyright differed from patents precisely because the objective of both systems was to maximize social welfare, which led to an underlying rationale that was consistent with economic reasoning. The political rhetoric of copyright has always centered on the creative individual, but then (as now) copyright enforcement was largely the concern of commercial interests. The fraction of copyright plaintiffs who were authors (broadly defined) was initially quite low and fell continuously during the nineteenth century. By the start of the twentieth century less than 10 percent of all plaintiffs in copyright cases were the creators of the item that was the subject of the litigation. Instead, by the same period, the majority of parties bringing cases were publishing enterprises and other assignees of copyrights. Although the judiciary attempted to ensure that the rights of all parties were fairly considered, their major concern was not to benefit publishing companies, but to protect the public interest in learning.

Like other forms of intellectual property laws, the copyright system evolved to encompass improvements in technology and changes in the marketplace. Copyright decisions illustrate how adjudication by analogy economized on legal inputs, but this area of the law also indicates the extent to which judge-made policies were constrained by the statutes. Many of the technological innovations of the nineteenth century were sufficiently different from existing technologies as to make judicial analogies somewhat strained, and they ultimately required accommodation by the legislature. As the Supreme Court pointed out, "From its beginning, the law of copyright has developed in response to significant changes in technology. Indeed, it was the invention of a new form of copying equipment – the printing press – that gave rise to the original need for copyright protection. Repeatedly, as new developments have occurred in this country, it has been the Congress that has fashioned the new rules that new technology made necessary."[11]

The earliest federal statute to protect the product of authors was approved on May 31, 1790, "for the encouragement of learning." This utilitarian objective meant that, unlike European doctrines that enshrined the inalienable rights of authors, in the United States copyrights were among the most abridged in the world. The primary focus was on widespread access in order to enhance public welfare, and incentives to copyright owners were viewed only as a secondary motive. Registration secured the right to print, publish, and sell maps, charts and books for a term of fourteen years, with the possibility of an extension for an equal term. Major issues in copyright law primarily related to subject matter, duration, and enforcement, all of which expanded significantly during the course of the nineteenth century. The statutes were substantively revised in 1831, 1870, and 1909. The statutory extension of copyrights to musical compositions and plays was quite straightforward, as was the grant of property rights for engravings and sculpture. By 1910 the original copyright holder was granted derivative rights, including translations into other languages, performances, and the rights to adapt musical works. The burgeoning scope of copyright protection that technological advances required raised numerous questions about the rights of authors and publishers relative to the public, and courts continually were confronted with the need to delineate the boundaries of private property in such a way as to guard the public domain.

Although musical works were not protected by the first copyright act, the 1831 statute allowed protection for musical compositions, at that time limited to sheet music. The creation of mechanical means of reproducing music, such as the player piano and the phonograph, raised questions about the relevance of existing copyright rules, in part because the analogy between sheet music and these mechanical inventions appeared remote. *Stern v. Rosey* (1901) dealt with the question of whether an injunction should issue against a manufacturer of phonograph records who had used copyrighted music. The court rejected the notion that copyright protection for music extended to such a different technological transformation. *Kennedy v. McTammany* (1888), which was argued in the Massachusetts Federal District Court, was brought by the copyright owner of a song entitled "Cradle's Empty, Baby's Gone." Judge Colt failed to accept the plaintiff's argument that McTammany's perforated piano rolls infringed on the copyright for the

[11] *Sony Corp. of America v. Universal City Studios, Inc.*, 464 U.S. 417 (1984).

music, because he could "find no decided cases which, directly or by analogy, support the position of the plaintiffs." In 1908 the Supreme Court affirmed this position when it considered the claim brought by a music publishing company against the manufacturer of player-piano rolls.[12]

In 1909 Congress responded by revising the copyright law to give composers the right to the first mechanical reproduction of their music. However, after the first recording, the statute permitted a compulsory license to issue for copyrighted musical compositions: that is to say, anyone could subsequently make his or her own recording of the composition on payment of a fee that was set by the statute at two cents per recording. In effect, the property right was transformed into a liability rule. The prevalence of compulsory licenses for copyrighted material (unlike patents) is worth noting for several reasons: licenses underline some of the statutory differences between patents and copyrights in the United States, they reveal economic reasons for such distinctions, and they demonstrate the use of political compromises among the various interest groups in the music industry.

The advent of photography created a new form of "authorship" that was granted copyright protection in 1865. Photography also offered a ready means of copying books, paintings, and engravings that led to copyright infringement litigation. *Rossiter v. Hall* (1866) dealt with photographic copies that had been taken of a copyrighted engraving of Washington's house that the statutes protected against unauthorized reprints. The defendant argued unsuccessfully that, since photography had not been invented at the time of the statute, it followed that this form of copying was not prohibited.[13] Although the judiciary was reluctant to appropriate the task of Congress and create new policies, at times judges were able to adjudicate cases relating to new technologies by stretching an existing analogy. This was apparent in the development of litigation surrounding movies not long after Edison obtained his 1896 patent for a kinetoscope. The lower court rejected Edison's copyright of moving pictures under the statutory category of photographs, but this decision was overturned by the appellate court:

> To say that the continuous method by which this negative was secured was unknown when the act was passed, and therefore a photograph of it was not covered by the act, is to beg the question. Such construction is at variance with the object of the act, which was passed to further the constitutional grant of power to "promote the progress of science and useful arts. . . . " [Congress] must have recognized there would be change and advance in making photographs, just as there has been in making books, printing chromos, and other subjects of copyright protection.[14]

[12] *Stern v. Rosey*, 17 App. DC 562 (1901); *Kennedy v. McTammany*, 33 F. 584 (1888); *White-Smith Music Pub. Co. v. Apollo Co.*, 209 U.S. 1 (1908).

[13] *Rossiter v. Hall*, 20 F. Cas. 1253 (1866).

[14] *Edison v. Lubin*, 122 F. Cas. 240 (1903).

Technological innovations created new cultural properties to be protected, but many of these also facilitated infringement through mechanical means of reproduction that lowered the costs of duplicating copyrighted works. Congress responded to the creation of new subject matter by expanding the scope of the copyright laws. The legislature also repeatedly lengthened the term of copyright, arguably to support the value of copyright protection in the face of falling costs of infringement. In 1790 the duration of copyright protection comprised 14 years from registration, with the possibility of renewal for a further 14 years; after 1831 the maximum term was 28 years from time of registration with the right of renewal for 14 years; whereas the 1909 statute allowed 28 years plus extension for a further 28 years if the author were still alive. Nevertheless, it is worth repeating that the largely utilitarian rationale of the American statutes ("to promote learning") precluded perpetual grants, and the term of copyright protection in United States was among the most abbreviated in the world. Similarly, the United States offered the most liberal opportunities in the world for unauthorized use of copyrighted material if copying qualified as "fair use."

Technological innovations that facilitated unauthorized copying heightened the tension between public welfare and private interests, leading some to question whether the fair use doctrine and copyright itself could endure. However, it is vital to understand that fair use was not formulated simply as a function of technologies that influenced the ability to monitor use, nor was it limited because courts recognized the (moral or other) rights of authors. Even if monitoring costs were zero and all use could be traced by the author, fair use doctrines would still be relevant to fulfil the ultimate function of property rights in cultural products. Without fair use, copyright would be transmuted into an exclusive monopoly right that would limit public access and violate the Constitution's mandate to promote the progress of science. In short, according to American legal doctrines, fair use was not regarded as an exception to the grant of copyright; instead, the grant of copyright was a limited exception to the primacy of the public domain.

The need to balance public welfare against the right of authors is partly why copyright, according to Justice Joseph Story, belonged to the "metaphysics of the law." It was Story who first outlined the American fair use doctrine in *Gray v. Russell* (1839) and then again in the more frequently cited *Folsom v. Marsh* (1841).[15] Fair use allowed unauthorized use of some portion of a copyrighted work, although exactly how much copying was permissible constituted (and remains today) "one of the most difficult points that can well arise for judicial discussion." Story offered several guidelines in Folsom: "we must often, in deciding questions of this sort, look to the

[15] *Gray v. Russell*, 10 F. Cas. 1035 (1839); *Folsom v. Marsh.*, 9 F. Cas. 342 (1841).

nature and objects of the selections made, the quantity and value of the materials used, and the degree in which the use may prejudice the sale, or diminish the profits, or supersede the objects, of the original work." The fair use doctrine thus illustrates the extent to which policymakers weighed the benefits of diffusion against the costs of exclusion. If copyrights were as strictly construed as patents, it would reduce scholarship, prevent public access for non-commercial purposes, increase transactions costs for potential users, and inhibit the learning that the statutes were meant to promote.

Current and increasingly polarized debates about the scope of patents and copyrights often underestimate or ignore the importance of allied rights that are available through other forms of the law, such as contract and unfair competition. The distinction is important for at least two reasons. First, such allied rights as contract or misappropriation doctrines are likely to be limited to the parties directly involved in a specific exchange, whereas copyright gives the owner broader rights against society; second, private rights are less subject to public oversight. A noticeable feature of nineteenth-century case law is the willingness of the judiciary to extend protection to non-copyrighted works under alternative doctrines in the common law, although the judicial mind in 1915 balked at the thought of extending free speech protections to commercial productions such as movies. More than 10 percent of "copyright" cases were decided using concepts of unfair competition, in which the court rejected copyright claims but still protected the work against unauthorized users using fair trade doctrines. Some 7.7 percent dealt with contracts, which raised questions such as ownership of photographs in cases of "work for hire." A further 12 percent encompassed issues of trade secrets, misappropriation, and the right to privacy.

The development of the right to privacy is especially interesting, since it illustrates the creation of a new legal concept at common law to compensate for the potential of new technologies to infringe on third-party rights. Samuel Warren and Louis Brandeis, in what has been touted as the most effective law review article of all time, argued that "modern enterprise and invention" subjected the ordinary individual to unwarranted suffering that could not be alleviated through existing laws of copyright, tort, trespass, slander, and libel. Instant photographs and "numerous mechanical devices" led to the "evil of invasion of privacy." The concept of a legal right to privacy immediately entered into litigated arguments, and the New York Supreme Court, in *Schuyler v. Curtis et al.* (1891), quoted directly from the law review article, but distinguished between private individuals and public figures who by implication ceded the right to privacy. In a Massachusetts case three years later the wife of the great inventor George H. Corliss tried to enjoin the publication of a photograph of her late husband. The court rejected the plea because her husband was "among the first of American inventors, and he sought recognition as such," permitting thousands of his photographs to be distributed at the Centennial Exposition in Philadelphia.[16] In 1903, the New York legislature passed a statute that levied criminal and civil liability for the unauthorized use of the "name, portrait or picture of any living person" for "advertising purposes, or for the purposes of trade," and several other states did the same. The first unambiguously successful application of the right to privacy, *Pavesich v. New England Life Insurance Co* (1905), along with some thirty other lawsuits prior to 1920, dealt with allegations that unauthorized commercial use of the plaintiff's photograph violated a right to privacy.[17]

The legal records of patent and copyright disputes yield valuable insights into nineteenth-century society. The significant differences in international patent and copyright laws in particular illustrate the extent to which these policies were market oriented. The United States was a nation of artificers and innovators, both as consumers and producers, and its citizens were confident of their global competitiveness in technology and accordingly took an active role in international patent conventions. Although they excelled at pragmatic contrivances, Americans were advisedly less confident about their efforts in the realm of music, art, literature, and drama. As a developing country, the United States was initially a net debtor in exchanges of material culture with Europe. The first copyright statute implicitly recognized this when it authorized Americans to take free advantage of the cultural output of other countries and encouraged the practice of international copyright piracy that persisted for a century. The tendency to reprint foreign works was aided by the existence of tariffs on imported books that ranged as high as 25 percent

Throughout the nineteenth century, proposals to reform the law and to acknowledge foreign copyrights were repeatedly brought before Congress. Prominent American and European authors and their publishers supported the movement to attain harmonization of U.S. copyright policies with international law, but their efforts were defeated. From the American perspective, the public interest was not limited to the needs and wishes of a cultural elite. It was not until 1891 when American literature was gaining in the international market that U.S. laws granted copyright protection to foreign residents in order to gain reciprocal rights for American writers and artists. However, the statute also included significant concessions to printers' unions in the form of manufacturing clauses. First, a book had to be published in the United States before or at the same time as the publication date in its country of origin. Second, the work had to be printed here or

[16] *Schuyler v. Curtis et al.*, 15 N.Y.S. 787 (1891); *Corliss v. Walker Co.*, 64 F. 280 (1894).
[17] *Pavesich v. New England Life Insurance Co.*, 50 SE 98 (1905).

printed from type set in the United States or from plates made from type set in the United States. Copyright protection also depended on conformity with stipulations such as formal registration of the work. These clauses resulted in the failure of the United States to qualify for admission to the international Berne Convention until 1988, one hundred years after the initial accord.

II. INNOVATIONS AND THE LAW

American society at the start of the nineteenth century was still overwhelmingly agrarian, but by 1920 the United States had become the world's foremost industrial power. The advent of industrialization and more extensive markets created conflicts between the rights of farmers and mill owners, mill owners and their workers, and enterprises and consumers, all of which required legal mediation. Technological advances and legal change had reciprocal and mutually reinforcing effects. Property laws and contracts attempted to define rights and allocate liability within a changing context. In particular, tort law developed as a distinct body of thought independently of property and contract law, because new technologies, urbanization, and more frequent exchanges among strangers were associated with more accidental injuries and higher transactions costs. At the same time, the costs of injuries created incentives for inventors to direct their attentions to safety devices, such as steam gauges, safety elevators, and more effective railroad couplers, air brakes, and crossing signals. In the entire period before 1860, only 771 patents mentioned safety in the specification, but during the decade of the 1860s some 1,940 patents did so, and in the following decade this number increased to more than 3,021 patents. The courts responded by quickly altering the standards of due care to incorporate existing technological options as long as they were cost effective. Here I consider such changes in legal institutions in relation to specific innovations, including canals, railroads, the telegraph, medical devices, public health systems, and automobiles.

Canals and Railroads

The development of cheap and efficient internal transportation was a prerequisite for economic development in a country as vast as the United States, so it is not surprising that transportation comprised a key element of state policy and private initiative. By 1830, even though state involvement was largely limited to the grant of charters, investors and entrepreneurs had privately funded an extensive network of turnpikes in the Northeast. After the state of New York financed the building of the hugely successful Erie

Canal, numerous other public and private canal ventures were undertaken throughout New England, the Middle Atlantic, and Midwest. The United States also possessed ready access to natural bodies of water, and advances in steamboat technologies increased their importance as a conduit for commerce. Between 1830 and 1860 national steamboat tonnage increased by a factor of ten, and shipping rates on upriver transport fell dramatically. As a result of these technical and price savings, the effective distance between towns and markets was reduced significantly.

In the antebellum period some 650 reported cases involved canals; another 468 dealt with steamboats. Transportation along water routes raised many of the issues that the railroads later would confront, including the nature of state charters, the role and effectiveness of canal commissioners, compensation for injuries to passengers and workers, takings and just compensation, discriminatory prices, taxation, and financing. In the era of canal-building mania, the courts provided well-needed ballast to the airy financial schemes of canal boosters. For instance, *Newell v. People* (1852) held that a New York state statute, which authorized the debt for the Erie Canal Enlargement and the building of the Genesee Valley and Black River Canals to be paid from future canal revenue surpluses, was unconstitutional.[18] Many states, beginning with New York, altered their constitutions to restrict debt financing at both the state and municipal levels, because of their unhappy experience when financial panics adversely affected the funding of canals.

Some of the lawsuits involved conflicts between different cohorts of technologies: could canals and turnpikes block railroads because their charters were drawn up earlier and implicitly conferred exclusive rights that could not be eroded by later technologies? The famous Charles River Bridge decision in 1837 rejected this view because if earlier charters ensured monopoly profits the benefits from subsequent competition and technological change would be reduced or eliminated. Progress also meant that already existing property rights might have to be defined more narrowly. Thus, the old common law rule that property rights in land extended upward and downward without limit no longer applied, and courts allowed railroads and bridges the right to cross privately owned waterways and turnpikes.

New technologies required a balancing of the benefits to be derived from their applications against the harm that is associated with their use. They brought the possibility that economic and social advances could be blocked by hold-outs or by individuals with conflicting interests who threatened to make the transactions costs associated with innovations prohibitively high. The use of eminent domain played an important part in the promotion

[18] *Newell v. People*, 7 N.Y. 9 (1852).

of turnpikes, canals, railroads, and telegraphs by reducing or eliminating such costs. The U.S. Constitution advocated the right of eminent domain to ensure that private property could be taken for public use, as long as just compensation was offered. This clause raised questions about the security of private property, what comprised public use, and how just compensation was to be determined in a non-consensual, non-market exchange.

In the nineteenth-century transportation cases, just compensation for takings was ascertained through mutual agreement, by commissioners in an administrative process, or by a jury. Legislatures determined the extent and constraints of "public use." Their decisions were straightforward in the specific case of canals for transportation or railroads that, though privately owned, offered valuable common carrier services to the general public. In other instances, the benefits to the public were less direct, but this did not entirely rule out the application of the doctrine of eminent domain. In 1832 Jasper Scudder brought a case in equity against the Trenton Delaware Falls Company, which had been incorporated to create water power for some seventy manufacturing mills. Scudder's counsel argued that the corporation was created only for private purposes since the benefits of the water mills would derive solely to private individuals; thus it was inappropriate to allow the use of eminent domain. The Chancellor rejected this viewpoint because manufacturing enterprises, though admittedly private, contributed to employment and general economic prosperity and indeed promised to generate far larger communal benefits than some turnpikes actually produced.[19]

To an even greater extent than canals, railroads quickly gained public approval and became a symbol of American progress. Economic historians rightly caution against an inflated assessment of the role of locomotives in the nineteenth-century economy, given the existence of viable alternatives, but it is undoubtedly true that the significance of railways increased over this period in terms of use, employment, and social impact. Justice Caruthers of the Tennessee Supreme Court lyrically wrote in 1854 that "the common dirt road for wagons is superseded by turnpikes, and these again by the railroad. . . . Blessings innumerable, prosperity unexampled, have marked the progress of this master improvement of the age. Activity, industry, enterprise and wealth seem to spring up as if by enchantment, wherever the iron track has been laid, or the locomotive moved."[20] Other courts demonstrated a similar readiness to ensure that the common law kept up with innovations in transportation.

Approval of any new technology is never universal, however, and many balked at their influence. One such controversy related to the policy of the

[19] *Scudder v. Trenton Delaware Falls Company*, 1 N.J. Eq. 694 (1832).

[20] *Louisville & N. R. Co. v. County Court of Davidson*, 33 Tenn. 637 (1854).

railroads to rationalize the norms for reckoning time. More than 188 railroads adopted standard time on November 18, 1883, and a large number of cities did likewise. However, standard time was not formally recognized by the federal government until 1918, even though Congress adopted standard time for the District of Columbia in 1884. Given the lack of consensus, it is not surprising that a significant number of lawsuits arose to settle the different interpretations of time. Southern courts in particular evinced some hostility to the railroad interests and felt that, according to one Georgia judge, "to allow the railroads to fix the standard of time would be to allow them at pleasure to violate or defeat the law." Similarly, a Texas court quoted "from the American and English Encyclopedia of Law (volume 26, p. 10) as follows: 'The only standard of time recognized by the courts is the meridian of the sun, and an arbitrary standard set up by persons in business will not be recognized.'" As late as 1899, an appellate court upheld the view that solar rather than standard time should be applied.[21]

A more enduring legal legacy arose after the number of tort lawsuits brought against the railroads mounted rapidly after the Civil War. In 1890 more than 29,000 individuals were injured in railroad accidents and 6,335 persons were killed; in 1913 injuries attained the quite astonishing level of 200,308, with almost 11,000 fatalities in that one year alone. Legal historians have attributed the development of tort law in the nineteenth century to disputes regarding the injuries and negative externalities that the railroads generated. Such a claim has to be modified somewhat because both the harms and the legal issues were not entirely unprecedented. The benefits from all improvements in internal transportation came at a higher risk if only because of the growth in the number of transactions. Steamboats proved to be especially hazardous because of fires from sparks and accidents when high pressure boilers exploded. This led to the passage of federal statutes in 1838 and 1852 that attempted to regulate safety and assigned the burden of proof in negligence cases to steamboat owners and captains.

In the debate over the impetus for the imposition of regulations and their efficacy, some economists have argued that, although regulatory policies succeeded in generating and funding useful research, improvements in safety were predominantly due to private initiatives that would have proceeded in the absence of federal regulation. Figure 15.1 shows the annual number of patents granted for railroad safety and for safety-related inventions in general, expressed as a percentage of all patents. The two series are pro cyclical and behave very like each other until World War I. After this period, railroad traffic was reduced significantly, and patents for railroad safety fell relative to overall safety patents. Both series suggest that investments in

[21] *Henderson v. Reynolds*, 84 Ga. 159 (1889); *Parker v. State*, 35 Tex. Crim. 12 (1898).

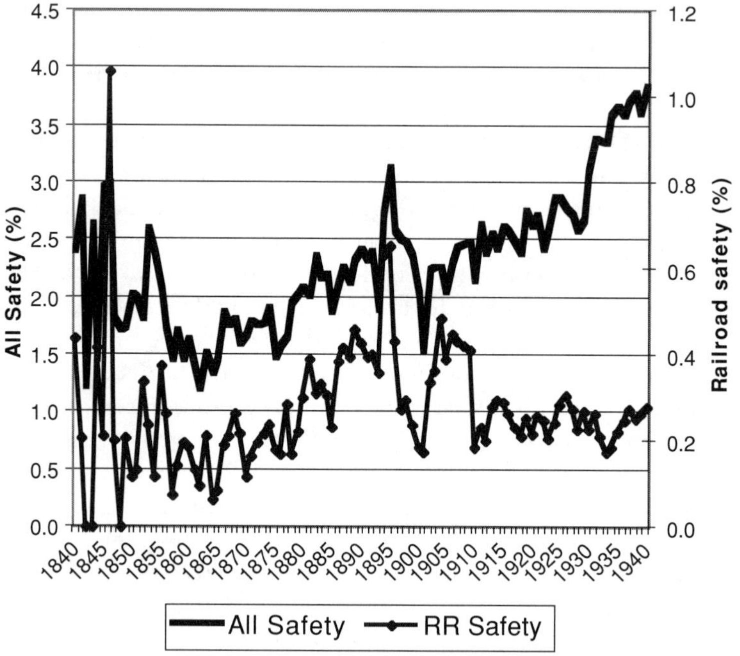

FIGURE 15.1. Safety-Related Inventions in Railroad and All Sectors, 1840–1940 (percent of all patents). Source: U.S. Patent Office Reports, 1840–1940. Notes: Inventions are considered to be safety related if the patent specification includes two or more appearances of variations of the word "safe." Changing the frequency affects levels, but does not substantively affect the patterns.

safety-related innovations were primarily responding to the market rather than to regulation. In particular, Interstate Commerce Commission oversight of the railroads from 1887 and the introduction of federal railroad safety legislation in 1893 do not seem to be associated with spurts in railroad safety patents when compared to safety patents in general. These data bear out the conclusions of researchers who find little impact of regulation on the adoption of such devices as air brakes and automatic couplers. When government intervention succeeded in generating the development of automatic train controls, the innovation proved to be ineffective on both technical and cost bases. The patent data suggest that we should not underestimate market incentives for enterprises to invest in safety and to self-regulate. Railroads were not opposed to safety-related legislation, but they rejected provisions mandating specific devices that might be incompatible with other forms of equipment and might become obsolete quickly.

A number of scholars view legal tort doctrines as presumptively biased against workers and favorable toward employers and enterprises. Such a claim is not entirely supported by economic analysis or the preponderance of evidence. The common law for unintended torts adhered to four rules in deciding liability: industry norms, the fellow servant rule, contributory negligence, and the assumption of risk. The judiciary held enterprises to a standard of care that comprised the norm for the industry and only punished deviations away from the norm. The industry norm criterion, by relying on established community standards, economized on information gathering by the judiciary. The fellow servant rule was first upheld in a railroad case in 1842, which absolved the railroad from liability due to contributory negligence on the part of another employee.[22] A rule of contributory negligence created incentives for workers to monitor each other. This made sense in contexts such as railroad operations in which workers were mobile and had a great deal of discretion: first, many injuries occurred because workers acted without due care; and second, monitoring and enforcement costs for employers were high. Railroads that tried to introduce rules to alter hazardous but convenient habits encountered resistance from workers. After the Civil War several state legislatures limited the use of the fellow servant rule in railroad accidents, and in 1908 the Federal Employers' Liability Act abolished it entirely.

The assumption of risk rule involves the idea that rational individuals will weigh the costs and benefits of their actions, so an employee will engage in a risky activity only if he is compensated for the expected harm either through insurance or through a higher wage premium. Thus, economic analysis supports the nineteenth-century policy that, as long as the employer was not negligent or deficient in safety standards, there was little need for judicial intervention when employees in risky jobs were injured in the normal course of employment. However, it should be noted that this approach depends on the assumption that workers have many alternatives from which to choose and that wages will adjust to reflect a risk premium. The empirical evidence

[22] *Farwell v. Boston & W. R. R. Corp.*, 45 Mass. 49 (1842). Liability rules give incentives for precautionary behavior and also have implications for informational and administrative costs: negligence rules give both parties incentives for efficient precaution, but have higher informational and administrative costs; whereas, a rule of strict liability toward enterprises minimizes transactions costs, but creates little incentive for victims to invest in precaution. If firms are held strictly liable and consumer demand is not very responsive to price changes, firms can increase prices, implying that the cost of injuries will be borne by consumers in general. If consumer demand is responsive to price changes, shareholders in the firm will bear the costs of injuries in the form of lower net earnings, and the firm will tend to overinvest in resources to reduce harm.

on this point is hard to assess because of data inadequacies, but suggests that wages were indeed higher to compensate for risk, although workers were not perfectly compensated for risk-bearing. Moreover, workers who chose to engage in risky activities may have had few alternative opportunities. However, we can further examine the extent to which variation of standards comported with economic logic in the case of passengers and freight.

Although employees might be held to have assumed the risk inherent in railroad or other industrial occupations, this was not true of passengers. Hence, railroads were held to higher standards of care for passengers than for employees, and if a passenger was injured, the burden of proof was on the railroad to show why it should not be held liable. The argument has been made that judges protected passenger safety and the interests of the propertied class above those of the railroads, and it may be expected that, even if this were not so, juries would be more inclined to favor passenger plaintiffs over corporate defendants. In the case of goods to be transported, once the items were conveyed to the train they were completely within the control of the shipper; hence, railroads were strictly liable for freight. Slave passengers could not be viewed in the same liability context as freight, for the "carrier cannot, consistent with humanity and regard to the life and health of the slave, have the same absolute control over an intelligent being endowed with feelings and volition, that he has over property placed in his custody."[23] In short, the legal records do not support the notion that the judiciary was biased in favor of any single party and instead suggest a genuine attempt to generate outcomes that were equitable in every sense of the term.

Improvements in transportation and communications created a national market in which state laws were increasingly discordant and discriminatory. These questions were faced on waterways, when federal admiralty laws were applied to steamships engaged in interstate commerce, but Figures 15.2 and 15.3 highlight the role of railroad litigation in providing the impetus toward federalization.

Some states refused to honor charters of "foreign railroads" that were granted in other jurisdictions; others tried to add to their coffers by taxing interim transactions or imposing restrictions on rates and operations, even though the final destination was in another state. As the figures indicate, the disproportionate appeal to federal courts relative to state courts comprised an integral part of the policies of the railroad companies well into the twentieth century. Their victories in the Supreme Court changed the interpretation of the Constitution, in particular the Commerce Clause, the

[23] *Wilson v. Hamilton*, 4 Ohio St. 722 (1855), discussing *Boyce v. Anderson*, 2 Pet. R. 150 (1829).

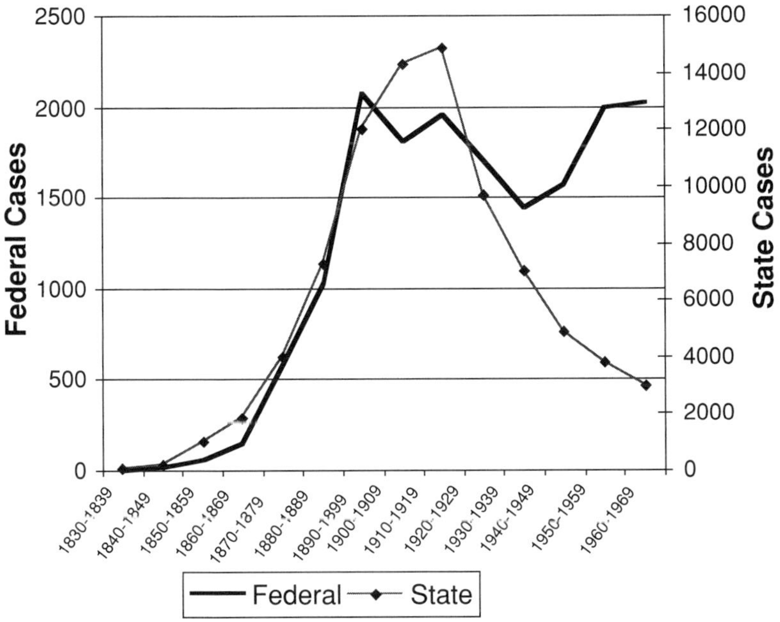

FIGURE 15.2. Railroads: State and Federal Litigation, 1830–1970. Source: Lexis-Nexis database of state and federal reported cases.

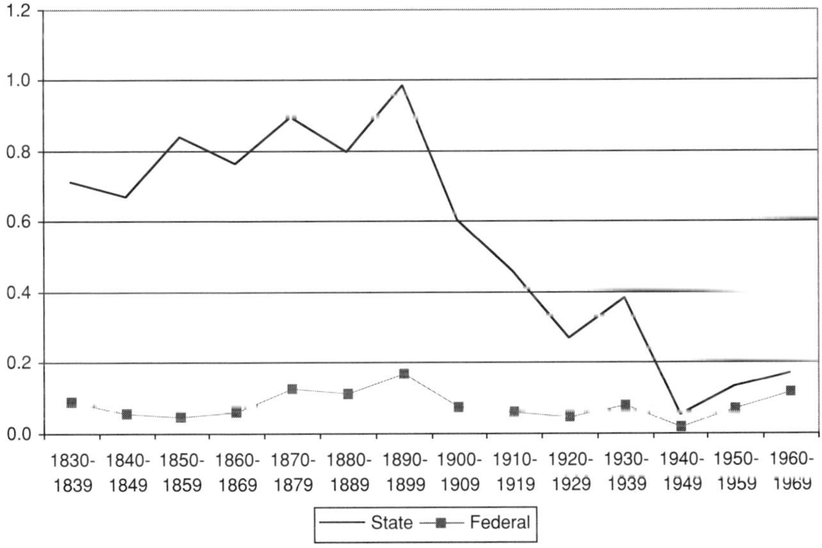

FIGURE 15.3. Railroads: State and Federal Lawsuits Relative to Usage, 1830–1970 (per million miles traveled). Notes and Sources: Usage reflects millions of passenger miles traveled, from the *Historical Statistics of the United States*, series Q274–312.

prohibition of lawsuits against state governments in the Eleventh Amendment, and the Due Process Clause of the Fourteenth Amendment. Railroad companies ultimately succeeded in obtaining legal recognition that the public interest was not consistent with constraints on market expansion that benefited narrowly partisan local interests.

This recognition did not occur instantaneously, but through a long process of appeals. Railroads questioned state regulation of rates in the Granger cases of 1877, but were defeated. The judiciary hesitated to apply the Due Process Clause of the Fourteenth Amendment and conceded the right of the states to regulate rates for undertakings that affected the public interest. However, in the *California Railroad Tax Cases* of 1882, the court agreed that a local tax violated the railroad's due process rights and further was inconsistent with the equal protection provision because the railroad was taxed differently from other enterprises.[24] In 1890, the U.S. Supreme Court ultimately upheld the view that state policy regarding rates was within the jurisdiction of the courts under the "substantive due process" clause of the Constitution. In the 1890s 41 federal cases involved questions of due process that were raised in connection with the railroads; the following decade there were 87, and by the 1920s the number had increased to 449 cases. These decisions enabled the federal judiciary to overrule state policies and allowed them to support private property rights that the state actions would have constrained. Although the Supreme Court abandoned the use of substantive due process to protect private property in the 1930s, the concept endured in other contexts, especially in the struggle to promote civil liberties. The railroads won a second victory with similar long-term implications, this time with respect to interpretations of the Eleventh Amendment that barred federal lawsuits against the states or state officials. In *Ex Parte Young* (1908), the Supreme Court ruled that federal courts could prevent state officials from enforcing policies that conflicted with the Fourteenth Amendment. The decision would have lasting implications for the movement to end racial segregation in schools.[25]

Several other significant legal doctrines were influenced by the public interest nature of the railroads, most noticeably in bankruptcy and reorganization. Federal bankruptcy legislation was intermittent and largely unenforced for much of the nineteenth century until the passage of the National Bankruptcy Law of 1898. State rulings initially followed the English bias toward the rights of creditors, who were generally allowed to levy against and sell distressed property on a first-comer basis. This created perverse incentives for creditors to race to force the firm into bankruptcy even when the corporation might be viable in the long run. Clearly, sectional interests

[24] *Railroad Tax Cases*, 13 F. 722 (1882).

[25] *Ex parte Young*, 209 U.S. 123 (1908).

were not necessarily mutually consistent or appropriate for dealing with interstate enterprises like railroads. The result was a legislative vacuum that became especially problematic during the panic of 1873 when almost a fifth of railroad operations failed. Federal courts were reluctant to grant individual creditors the right to dissolve national corporations at the cost of losing the public benefits of a functioning interstate railroad. Instead, court-appointed receivers kept the railway operating during bankruptcy while the firm was reorganized and financially restructured. Strikes were not tolerated while the railroad was under receivership, and lawsuits could not be brought against receivers during restructuring, although equity courts tried to ensure that existing management did not unduly skew outcomes in their own favor. This gradual shifting of bias toward the rights of debtors was consolidated in the 1898 federal legislation that was enacted after the great depression of 1893. However, railroads themselves were not covered by federal bankruptcy statutes until 1933, when equity receiverships became redundant.

The process of railroad consolidation accelerated after the Civil War and at the same time exacerbated the tensions between state and federal oversight of commerce. As discussed above, railroads appealed to federal courts to mediate, but the figures indicate that the major forces acting on railroad concerns remained at the state level until the end of the century. In 1887 the Federal Interstate Commerce Act superseded many elements of state policies, as did several other federal acts up to passage of the Transportation Act of 1920. At this point, federal regulation influenced content, access, ownership, safety, pricing, consolidations, and operations, not only in the railroad industry but also in other key enterprises, such as electric utilities and the telephone. Despite the rhetoric that accompanied the introduction of federal regulatory commissions, it is worth repeating that regulation had a long common law tradition vested in court rulings toward natural monopolies and other enterprises that involved the public interest. Moreover, judicial oversight was not made redundant by the advent of regulation; instead, regulatory enforcement depended heavily on court decisions. Although much of the historical focus has been on state and federal regulation, we should also speculate about the incentives for firms to self-regulate. Indeed, some have argued that federal regulation was instigated by railroads and electric utilities as a means of reducing competition.

Telegraphy

The telegraph, although not quite a "Victorian Internet," emerged in the 1840s as the first commercially viable means of interstate electronic communication. Telegraphy diffused so rapidly that by 1851 the Bureau of the

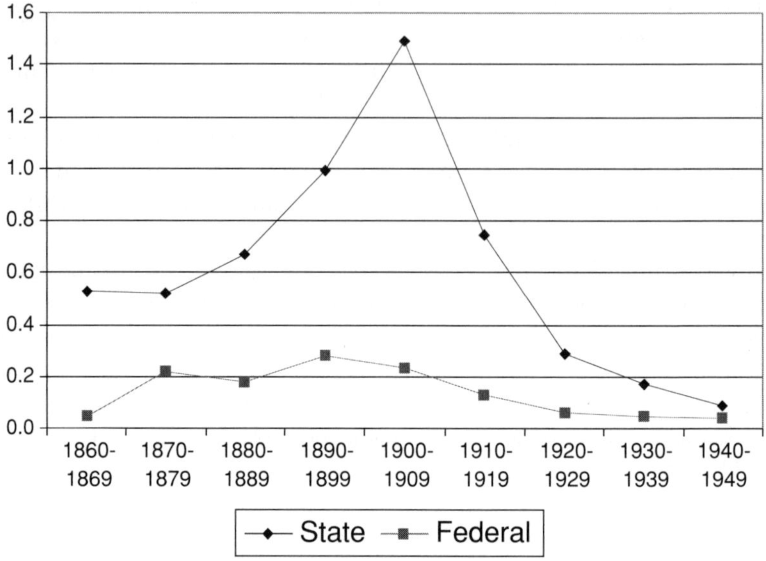

FIGURE 15.4. Telegraph: State and Federal Lawsuits Relative to Usage, 1860–1950. Notes and Sources: Lexis-Nexis state and federal lawsuits. Usage data (millions of messages sent) are from *Historical Statistics of the United States*, series R46–70.

Census reported that 75 companies with more than 20,000 miles of wire were in operation. These small-scale enterprises proved to be inefficient, and a series of consolidations and exits ultimately resulted in the domination of Western Union. In 1870 Western Union alone operated almost 4,000 offices and handled more than 9 million messages. By 1890, its 19,382 offices were dealing with approximately 56 million messages. Diffusion of this form of communication was impressive, but like the twenty-first-century Internet, the applications were predominantly among businesses rather than consumers. Perhaps as a result of this business orientation, the law did not draw an analogy to newspapers or other print media, nor did it raise First Amendment questions about freedom of speech. Instead, the courts and legislature stressed a comparison with postal roads, turnpikes, and railways. The Post Roads Act of 1866 designated telegraph companies as common carriers who were granted privileges including rights of way on public lands and waterways, access to free timber and resources, and recourse to eminent domain. In return, the telegraphs assumed the public interest duties of common carriers analogous to the transportation enterprises.

As the pattern in Figure 15.4 suggests, several common legal issues affected transportation and communications technologies. The Supreme

Judicial Court of Massachusetts argued that, while the telegraph was undoubtedly a valuable means of communication, "Its use is certainly similar to, if not identical with, that public use of transmitting information for which the highway was originally taken, even if the means adopted are quite different from the post-boy or the mail coach. It is a newly discovered method of exercising the old public easement, and all appropriate methods must have been deemed to have been paid for when the road was laid out."[26] It was fortunate for telegraph companies that courts supported the idea that the previously granted rights of use also extended to the newer technology: "If this were not true . . . the advancement of commerce, and the increase in inventions for the aid of mankind would be required to adjust themselves to the conditions existing at the time of the dedication, and with reference to the uses then actually contemplated."[27] An atypical award of $2,500 in damages given for use of a narrow plot of land illustrates the high costs that would have resulted if owners of the telegraph lines had had to contract new bargains with holders of public easements. In states that rejected such analogies, including California, Illinois, Maryland, Mississippi, and Missouri, property owners were able to sustain costly injunctions and compensation for trespass or reductions in the value of their land.

A second consequence was that the most significant doctrines in telegraph cases related to the duties of common carriers. English legal decisions dating back to the Middle Ages raised questions of a duty to serve the public and to charge just rates in so doing, especially in the case of monopolies. According to the Supreme Court of California in 1859,

> The rules of law which govern the liability of telegraph companies are not new. They are old rules applied to new circumstances. Such companies hold themselves out to the public as engaged in a particular branch of business, in which the interests of the public are deeply concerned. They propose to do a certain service for a given price. There is no difference in the general nature of the legal obligation of the contract between carrying a message along a wire and carrying goods or a package along a route. The physical agency may be different, but the essential nature of the contract is the same.[28]

As common carriers telegraph companies were not held vicariously liable for criminal transactions and in some cases were not permitted to refuse messages even if the sender was engaged in suspected illegal transactions.

Telegraph companies that accepted the designation of common carrier and its benefits were obligated to charge reasonable, non-discriminatory rates. This stipulation allowed judicial oversight over competition policy

[26] *Pierce v. Drew*, 136 Mass. 75 (1883). [27] *Magee v. Overshiner*, 150 Ind. 127 (1898).
[28] *Parks v. Alta California Tel. Co.*, 13 Cal. 422 (1859).

well before the antitrust statutes were enacted. Courts adopted an economic definition of discrimination, rejecting charges of anti-competitive behavior if the differences in price were justified in terms of difference in costs. For instance, in *Western Union Tel. Co. v. Call Publishing Co.* (1895), the court held that the telegraph company had not engaged in "unjust discrimination" because it faced different circumstances and costs in meeting the needs of a morning newspaper relative to an evening newspaper, which explained the differential tariffs charged.[29] However, courts varied in their support for quantity discounts, some arguing that this pricing policy suppressed competition and encouraged the creation of monopolies.

The established telegraph law for much of the nineteenth century accepted the common carrier analogy, but quite early on some noticed that the comparison was somewhat strained. The common carrier designation had an important implication for the telegraph company because it implied assumption of liability for the "goods carried." Railroads as common carriers were strictly liable for freight entrusted to their care and thus could be viewed as insurers of goods consignments. Under this doctrine, the liability of telegraph companies for their messages could be enormous, since an error in the transmission of a buy or sell order could amount to many thousands of dollars. At the same time, unlike the value of consignments on railroads or turnpikes, clearly the intrinsic value to the telegraph company of any message was significantly lower than its value to the sender and receiver of the message. To insure against mistakes, the telegraph company required that the message should be repeated at a cost of half the regular rate or else liability was limited to the cost of the transmission. The courts were confronted with disputes that challenged the right of companies to limit their liability in this way, since common carriers were supposed to assume that risk themselves. The stakes increased when businesses began to use abstruse codes or ciphers to protect their confidentiality and to reduce the cost of sending lengthy messages. Cotton exporters who wished to convey the message, "We make firm bid two hundred bales of fully middling cotton at 43–4d twenty-eight millimeters, January and February delivery, shipment to Havre" instead required Western Union to send the words "Holminop, New Orleans, Galeistraf, dipnoi, Granzoso, Liebsesin Dipnoi liciatorum, diomus, grapholite, Gradatos and Texas." In another case, the telegraph operator transmitted the word "chatter" rather than the "charter" of the ciphered message, and the difference between the letter "r" and the letter "t" cost the sender about $1,000, leading to an action against the telegraph company for $1,054 in damages.

[29] *Western Union Tel. Co. v. Call Publishing Co.*, 44 Neb. 326 (1895).

In response, the analogy to common carriers was ultimately rejected. The Supreme Court in the landmark decision, *Primrose v. Western Union* (1894), ruled, "Telegraph companies resemble railroad companies and other common carriers. . . . *But they are not common carriers*; their duties are different, and are performed in different ways; and they are not subject to the same liabilities."[30] Instead of common carriers, some courts treated telegraph messages as bailments. Bailees were not expected to act as insurers, but only to hold to reasonable standards of diligence in completing their task, with damages generally limited to the price of their services. Certainly, in the case of coded messages, it was impossible for the telegraph company to determine the relative importance of the communication and to regulate the amount of care it took accordingly. Western Union was justified in charging higher rates for important messages by requiring that they should be repeated, since "it does not exempt the company from responsibility, but only fixes the price of that responsibility, and allows the person who sends the message either to transmit it at his own risk at the usual price, or by paying in addition thereto half the usual price to have it repeated, and thus render the company liable for any mistake that may occur."[31] This was simply the liability standard that had been set in the classic 1854 English case of *Hadley v. Baxendale*, but its application to the telegraph industry was delayed because of the common carrier analogy.

The advent of the telegraph introduced several other interesting questions in the area of contract law. Previous methods of communication had depended on physical delivery through the postal service, whereas telegraph transmissions could be received within minutes. Time was therefore introduced as an important part of a contract conveyed by telegraph, and charges of negligence were related to slight delays or errors in transmission. Other cases determined that a telegraph message could be regarded as a valid form of contract even if it was not signed in handwriting by both parties. As the California Supreme Court expressed it in 1900, "Any other conclusion than the one here reached would certainly impair the usefulness of modern appliances to modern business, tend to hamper trade, and increase the expense thereof."[32] The development of international cable services further increased market efficiency and the ability to monitor agents engaged in distant transactions. At least one outcome of this was to reduce the autonomy of agents at sea, for the first time constraining their ability while at sea to enter into contracts that would bind the owners of the ship without the owners' previous consent.

[30] *Primrose v. Western Union*, 154 U.S. 1 (1894), my emphasis.
[31] *Camp v. Western Union Tel. Co.*, 58 Ky. 164 (1858).
[32] *Brewer v. Horst & Lachmund Co.*, 127 Cal. 643 (1900).

As with other technologies, conflicts arose because of nuisance and trespass, including claims that electrolysis destroyed water pipes and that the high-voltage electric lines of urban tramcars interfered with telegraph and telephone transmissions. Again, courts avoided assigning fault and instead tried to determine the lowest cost avoider, given the existing state of the arts. The opinion in an 1890 lawsuit between a telephone company and an electric railway effectively described the role of technological advances in determining the standards of liability:

In solving these questions, we are compelled to bear in mind the fact that the science of electricity is still in its experimental stage; that a device which to-day may be the best, cheapest, and most practicable, may, in another year, be superseded by something incomparably better fitted for the purpose. It is quite possible, too, that the legal obligations of the parties may change with the progress of invention, and the duty of surmounting the difficulty be thrown upon one party or the other, as a cheaper or more effectual remedy is discovered.... the question of his liability will depend upon the fact whether he has made use of the means which, in the progress of science and improvement, have been shown by experience to be the best; but he is not bound to experiment with recent inventions, not generally known, or to adopt expensive devices, when it lies in the power of the person injured to make use himself of an effective and inexpensive method of prevention.[33]

Public Health and Medical Technologies

Legal doctrines about public health and medicine drew on metaphors that echoed policies toward transportation and communications technologies. Advances in steamboats, railroads, and the telegraph and telephone were presented as the natural object of public policy because they were integral to broad-based economic and social growth. Numerous other innovations such as the water closest or faucets were extolled with less rhetorical flair, but could be interpreted as no less significant to social welfare and thus fell within the proper scope for state law and judicial intervention. Innovations that affected the quality and length of life fell into this category, including those that improved hygiene, sanitation, pollution, and medical techniques and devices. Medical and health issues in particular were at the forefront of contentious legal decisions that related to private disputes and public laws.

In the early nineteenth century it is likely that cures were regarded, as one judge put it, as "in the hands of Him who giveth life, and not within the physical control of the most skillful of the profession."[34] Doctors tended to be trained informally, were unattached to medical networks or hospitals,

[33] *Cumberland Telephone and Telegraph Co. v. United Electric R'y Co.*, 42 F. 273 (1890).
[34] *Grindle v. Rush*, 7 OHIO 123 (1836).

and were accorded little respect. Another judge was reported to have said that, "if there was any kind of testimony not only of no value, but even worse than that, it was, in his judgment, that of medical experts."[35] By the 1890s, however, medicine was regarded as an eminent calling, doctors had acquired significant authority, and even general practitioners appealed to current findings in both science and technology. Health care had become specialized and organized within institutions, and the laboratory comprised an important unit in hospitals as well as for doctors in private practice. The industrialization of medicine occurred partly because of technological advances that provided doctors with a formidable array of new diagnostic tools. By the end of the nineteenth century these included the stethoscope, ophthalmoscope, laryngoscope, microscope, X-ray machine, spirometer, neurocalometer, blood pressure gauge and electrocardiograph. Medical instruments facilitated tests and treatment for notorious diseases like tuberculosis, typhoid, cholera, and diabetes and encouraged the professionalization of nascent specialties such as chiropractic.

Medical malpractice suits became more prevalent relative to population during the period of early industrialization because of shifts in demand and supply factors. Technological innovation affected medical malpractice through its impact on both the demand side and the supply side. The demand for legal redress was partly related to social expectations that were raised by the achievements attained in medical technology and by the diffusion of such knowledge among lay persons. The supply of disputes likely increased because more doctors were available to offer second (and different) opinions and alternative services and because of the rapid adoption and more extensive usage of medical devices. Impersonal mechanical diagnoses and laboratory tests quickly became the gauge of effective treatment, regardless of their actual efficacy. To observers from other countries, American medicine had ironically lost sight of the patient in its obsession with technological advances. This assessment was complicated by the desire of patients themselves for more technological inputs in their medical care regardless of their proven efficacy, so that the battery of tests that comprised the physical check-up became an annual routine early in the twentieth century.

Technological innovations in the field of medicine had varying effects on the propensity to litigate. It was true that they could facilitate more accurate diagnoses and improve the treatment of patients, but it was also possible that innovations led to more uniform standards of treatment that made defective practices more measurable and manifest. It might be expected that some doctors would be accused of malpractice because they were less proficient with new devices or less up-to-date and that current technologies

[35] Supreme Court of Illinois, *Rutherford v. Morris*, 77 Ill. 397 (1875).

might lead to unrealistic expectations. The application of X-rays in medical litigation illustrates the role of new technologies in such disputes. Wilhem Conrad Roentgen first published his discovery of "a new kind of ray" at the end of 1895 in the *Proceedings of the Würzburg Phisico-Medical Society*. Only a few months later the use of X-rays was introduced in the United States and related patents were filed, but ordinary citizens were also captivated by the discovery. Doctors who failed to use the machines, despite the dangers of burns to patients, risked being accused of incompetence and a violation of their fiduciary duty. Less than two years after the invention was introduced, a Midwestern jury was instructed to draw conclusions from X-ray photographs that were entered into the records. Patients retained the services of expert witnesses who used X-ray evidence to prove their case, and doctors countered with their own proofs.

As with other technologies, the law varied its standard of what was acceptable according to current understandings of proper medical care. The courts considered malpractice as a physician's breach of the fiduciary duty to offer competent services through negligence, ignorance, or lack of due care. The physician was initially held to a standard of competence that took into consideration the type of community in which he practiced. In 1824 a dispute in the remote village of Lubec, Maine, involved a patient whose local doctor had allegedly botched treatment of a dislocated joint. The judge felt that it was not to be expected that a doctor in a small rural town would possess the same degree of skill as a European-trained specialist in Boston. Later courts argued that doctors should be held to a nationally accepted standard because improvements in transportation and communications had created a national market, with equality of access to information. Despite this, the locality standard proved to be enduring and was still the norm even in the early twentieth century.

The endogeneity of legal doctrines to technological changes was evident in cases that dealt with medical malpractice, but the converse was also true – that is, medical practice changed according to what was legally acceptable – as witnessed by rules about abortion. In 1849, the Supreme Court of New Jersey outlined the development of the law toward abortions and pointed out that legal precedent uniformly was in agreement that it was acceptable to procure an abortion before the point of "quickening" in the pregnancy. The opinion quoted Blackstone's view that "life begins in contemplation of law as soon as an infant is able to stir in the mother's womb."[36] Even after quickening the removal of the unborn child was deemed to be a misdemeanor rather than murder. In the decades after the Civil War abortion at any stage was outlawed by statute throughout the country and criminalized

[36] *State v. Cooper*, 22 N.J.L. 52 (1849).

as a felony. However, in several states an abortion was still held to be acceptable at any point in the pregnancy if there were valid medical reasons for the procedure to save the mother's life or to prevent serious bodily injury. Thus, the legality of each abortion depended heavily on the interpretation and state of medical knowledge regarding its alleged therapeutic necessity, itself a function of current diagnostic technology.[37]

Public health likewise had long been considered a legitimate concern of the state. From the earliest years of settlement, local governments regulated the provision of food and sanitation, enacted laws to prevent nuisances, and called on formidable police powers to deal with perceived dangers to community welfare. Measures to counter infectious diseases could lead to especially draconian measures, including lengthy quarantines, forcible entry and the seizure or destruction of private property, criminal prosecution, and imprisonment. In 1796 Congress pledged federal support for state measures to ensure effective quarantines. In 1809 Massachusetts introduced the first law to require vaccination against smallpox. In an age of widespread danger of epidemics, many towns used funds from their treasury to pay for preventative measures. For instance, in 1828 the Connecticut town of Salisbury paid $50 to local physicians to inoculate its residents with the cowpox bacillus. Similarly, the Philadelphia City Council in 1798 commissioned the eminent engineer Benjamin Henry Latrobe to design a public water system, to counter fears that contaminated water was responsible for outbreaks of yellow fever. The owners of targets of quarantine – ranging from merchant ships to tenements – were just as likely, however, to find themselves forced to underwrite the expenses.

Public health policy in the nineteenth century was closely aligned with sanitation technology and engineering. The police power of the state to ensure the health and safety of the public was used to enforce the provision of running water and the use of water closets in private properties. These measures led to protests, such as occurred when the City of New York passed an act in 1887 that required tenement houses to provide running water on all floors because of health and safety reasons. The owners of one such tenement (oddly enough, a church) claimed that the costs of installing such facilities were so high as to constitute a taking of private property. And indeed, estimates suggested that the cost of improved sanitation and fittings in homes increased the cost of house construction by $15,000 in the period between 1850 and 1900. The takings argument was rejected by the appellate court, which pointed out that "hand rails to stairs, hoisting

[37] In 1899, medical justifications for abortion included Bright's disease of the kidney, cancer of the womb, and malformation of the pelvis, among others See *Wells v. New England Matrial Life*, 191 Pa. 207 (1899).

shafts to be inclosed, automatic doors to elevators, automatic shifters for throwing off belts or pulleys, and fire escapes on the outside of certain factories. . . . Under the police power persons and property are subjected to all kinds of restraints and burdens in order to secure the general comfort and health of the public."[38]

The U.S. Supreme Court tended to support state health officials acting in the public interest to the extent that it was argued that the state did not have to provide evidence to justify its public health policies as long as they were in accordance with "common beliefs." The dangers of such unfettered powers were illustrated in the eugenics movement that developed toward the end of the nineteenth century. At that time genetic science, studies of evolutionary biology and heredity, and biostatistics and sociology combined to reach the conclusion that the genetic composition of the population should be regulated by statute. These supposedly scientific rationales provided an impetus for policies that ranged from restrictive immigration laws to the forced sterilization of individuals with allegedly undesirable genetic characteristics. In 1896 Connecticut restricted the ability of epileptics and mentally disabled persons to marry, and similar laws were enacted in more than twenty states, including Kansas, New Jersey, Ohio, Michigan, and Indiana. In New York, *In Re Thomson* (1918) examined the constitutionality of a 1912 law passed to permit the sterilization of mentally disabled adults in its institutions. The court ruled that the statute violated the Equal Protection Clause of Fourteenth Amendment, noting that a similar law had been declared unconstitutional by the Supreme Court of New Jersey. Although a number of state judges joined in restricting or overturning such laws, the U.S. Supreme Court affirmed these policies on the grounds of public interest. Advances in medical technology meant that sterilization could be effected readily and safely in males by vasectomy and in females by salpingectomy, rather than by more drastic invasive measures. The Court's approval of compulsory sterilization drew on the public health analogy of compulsory vaccination, which served the public interest as well as the interest of the parties directly involved irrespective of their individual wishes.[39]

[38] *The Health Department of the City of New York, Appellant, v. The Rector, Church Wardens and Vestrymen of Trinity Church in the City of New York*, 145 N.Y. 32; 39 N.E. 833 (1895).

[39] Oliver Wendell Holmes wrote, "The public welfare may call upon the best citizens for their lives. It would be strange if it could not call upon those who already sap the strength of the state for these lesser sacrifices, often not felt to be such by those concerned, in order to prevent our being swamped with incompetence. It is better for all the world, if instead of waiting to execute degenerate offspring for crime, or to let them starve for their imbecility, society can prevent those who are manifestly unfit from continuing their kind. The principle that sustains compulsory vaccination is broad enough to cover cutting the fallopian tubes. Three generations of imbeciles are enough." Only Justice Butler dissented. *Buck v. Bell*, 274 U.S. 200 (1927).

Automobiles

The automobile for some is the icon of the American way of life. As early as 1917 the United States accounted for 85 percent of the world's motor cars. In 1920 only 1 percent of American homes had central heating, but 26 percent owned automobiles; by 1930 this number had increased to 60 percent. The automobile, to an even greater extent than the railroad or other transportation innovations, changed patterns of work, crime, leisure, and residence. As early as 1906, the author of a legal treatise pointed out that, although "many of the cases merely have called for the application of established rules of law, in dealing with the motor vehicle," it was also true that "many branches of the law are being affected by the horseless carriage figuring in litigation. Where the automobile's permeating influence will stop is beyond prophesy. It is certain, however, that the motor car, including everything connected with it, is bound to be the subject of a vast amount of litigation in the future."[40] By 1931, the same treatise ran to twenty volumes, reflecting the rapid increase in both state and federal litigation.

Although litigation increased markedly, the data indicate that federal courts did not play a major role in the public policies that developed toward motor vehicles. We may speculate whether this would have been the case if the interstate highways had been constructed more rapidly or whether the decentralized nature of motor vehicle ownership necessarily encouraged state governance. The common carrier concept was applied to commercial motor vehicles, but analogies from the era of the railroads proved to be of limited relevance and the doctrine was modified almost beyond recognition. Rate regulation of common carrier motor vehicles was viewed as redundant, because the number of alternative modes of transportation ensured that competition protected the public from exorbitant prices. States established commissions to issue licenses or "certificates of public convenience and necessity" that regulated the numbers of carriers, their routes, modes of operation, and ownership issues, such as whether railroads should be allowed to offer vehicular common carrier service. As with all licensing, an argument can be made that, despite the stated objectives, the end result was to limit competition rather than uphold standards that benefited public safety or convenience.

The case of the automobile illustrates the ambiguities of attitudes toward overt constraints on individual behavior as opposed to regulations that affected enterprises in the name of the public. The dual standard toward regulation was evident in responses to measures to deal with automobile torts, which were far more costly than those associated with railroads or mining. The increased use of motor vehicles was accompanied by a disproportionate

[40] Xenophon P. Huddy, *The Law of Automobiles* (Albany, NY, 1906), vi–vii.

growth in harm: in 1920 automobiles caused some 11,000 deaths (half of whom were children); in 1924 this number more than doubled, over 700,000 injuries were sustained, and property damage was substantial. The fatality rate for automobile accidents rose from below five deaths per million persons in 1906 to seventy-two deaths per million a decade later. Fatalities were highest in urban areas, and in 1920 the largest number of fatalities relative to population occurred in Los Angeles, followed by Buffalo, both of which experienced rates that exceeded 200 per million. New York injury rates in 1920 were approximately 25 times that of fatalities, and Boston alone recorded 21,182 injuries in the same year. The majority of automobile accidents were caused by human error rather than mechanical flaws, and terms such as "speed maniac" or "road hog" had already entered the public lexicon at the turn of the century.

Public policy was again required to mediate among competing claims. Efforts included the passage of legislation to provide rules and regulate behavior, appeal to the courts, and enable third-party means of compensating those who were harmed. Safety measures that regulated behavior – drivers' tests and licenses, vehicle registration, age limits, and traffic regulations – were introduced in a slow and haphazard fashion. In the 1920s and 1930s states imposed an inconsistent jumble of regulations on driver behavior, but enforcement was lax and such legislation was not at the forefront of policies toward automobiles. Instead, the state courts were rapidly clogged with disputes brought by victims of "jitneys," taxicabs, trucks, and privately operated vehicles.

As in all tort cases, the issues centered on liability and on compensation. When conflicts appeared between existing and former technologies, judges refused to assign unilateral blame and instead ensured that the lowest cost outcome prevailed. For instance, more than 900 lawsuits dealt with the harm caused by horses frightened by cars. In *Macomber v. Nichols* (1876), the judge declared, "Persons making use of horses as the means of travel or traffic by the highways have no rights therein superior to those who make use of the ways in other modes. . . . Horses may be, and often are, frightened by locomotives in both town and country, but it would be as reasonable to treat the horse as a public nuisance from his tendency to shy and be frightened by unaccustomed objects, as to regard the locomotive as a public nuisance from its tendency to frighten the horse."[41] The standard of the time required the driver of the car to defer to horses, since the latter were more common. When automobiles became the norm, however, the standard shifted to reflect that fact.

A significant legal development occurred when courts overturned the privity of contract doctrine to take into account the circumstances of

41 *Macomber v. Nichols*, 34 Mich. 212 (1876).

automobile manufacture and the complexity of the vehicle structure. Before 1906 there were no cases involving manufacturer's liability except when the item was held to be inherently dangerous: "The general rule is that a contractor, manufacturer, vendor or furnisher of an article is not liable to third parties who have no contractual relations with him for negligence in the construction, manufacture or sale of such article."[42] In *Johnson v. Cadillac Motor Co.*, the plaintiff was seriously injured by a defective tire on his automobile, which had been sold by a retail dealer. The court held that no contractual relationship existed between the driver and the manufacturer and dismissed the complaint. Judge Coxe, in his dissent from this decision, implied that the buyer of complicated new mechanisms of new technologies could not readily judge their safety as well as the manufacturer:

> The principles of law invoked by the defendant had their origin many years ago, when such a delicately organized machine as the modern automobile was unknown. Rules applicable to stagecoaches and farm implements become archaic, when applied to a machine which is capable of running with safety at the rate of 50 miles an hour. I think the law as it exists to-day makes the manufacturer liable if he sells such a machine under a direct or implied warranty that he has made, or thoroughly inspected, every part of the machine, and it goes to pieces because of rotten material in one of its most vital parts, which the manufacturer never examined or tested in any way. If, however, the law be insufficient to provide a remedy for such negligence, it is time that the law should be changed. "New occasions teach new duties"; situations never dreamed of 20 years ago are now of almost daily occurrence.[43]

Coxe's argument was similar to the decision in *MacPherson v. Buick Motor Co.* (1916), which stated that a manufacturer had a duty of care even to third parties who were not directly involved in contractual relations with the firm. Cardozo rejected the privity of contract defense because the standard approach had to change with the times:

> The maker of this car supplied it for the use of purchasers from the dealer. . . . The dealer was indeed the one person of whom it might be said with some approach to certainty that by him the car would not be used. Yet the defendant would have us say that he was the one person whom it was under a legal duty to protect. The law does not lead us to so inconsequent a conclusion. Precedents drawn from the days of travel by stagecoach do not fit the conditions of travel to-day. The principle that the danger must be imminent does not change, but the things subject to the principle do change. They are whatever the needs of life in a developing civilization require them to be.

[42] *MacPherson v. Buick Motor Co.*, 217 N.Y. 382 (1916).
[43] *Johnson v. Cadillac Motor Car Co.*, 261 F. 878 (1919).

The point was affirmed by the appellate court in Johnson. Drawing on a shaky analogy to a principle that had always been accepted by the common law, the court likened the automobile manufacturer to a producer of poisonous drugs or "imminently dangerous articles" who had a duty of care to the public. However, Cardozo correctly highlighted the extent to which harm could be foreseen: "foresight of the consequences involves the creation of a duty."

Predictability of outcomes was also emphasized in *Chittenden v. Columbus* (1904).[44] When the court imposed a fine of $25 on a motorist who was exceeding the town speed limit of seven miles per hour, the plaintiff protested that the law illegally discriminated against automobiles, since street cars were allowed to go faster. The court disagreed because, unlike automobiles, streetcars ran on set tracks and could thus be avoided more easily by others. If injury could be foreseen, efficiency required that the law offer incentives to avoid such harm by placing liability on those who could avoid it at lowest cost. As Coxe had presciently pointed out, the automobile was such a complicated mechanism it was unlikely that the ordinary driver could detect a structural deficiency, whereas it was readily within the capability of manufacturers to test each part and ensure that it was safe. A corollary of this doctrine was that the federal courts later upheld General Motors' right to stipulate that their dealers should use only GM replacement parts: exclusive contracts of this sort did not lessen competition but ensured quality control, since any defects would have adverse effects on the company's reputation and liability.

Automobiles influenced the rise of enterprise liability and led to legal doctrines that absolved users from responsibility for their actions on the grounds that technology had outpaced their understanding. However, the majority of automobile accidents did not occur because of tortious actions by enterprises, but involved harms caused by negligence on the part of drivers or pedestrians. Several legal innovations were a response to the falling prices for the new technology, which encouraged its diffusion throughout the population. The first automobile owners were wealthy individuals who were likely to hire chauffeurs, which led to legal questions of agency that could be subsumed in the existing law of master and servant. The law of agency had to be modified when the price of cars fell to the point at which ordinary families could afford to purchase vehicles that they drove themselves. The family agency doctrine took into account the likelihood that other family members would be just as likely to drive the car as the owner, and courts held the owner (generally the father) vicariously liable for the actions of the rest of the family. This holding encouraged the owner

[44] *Chittenden v. Columbus*, 5 Ohio C. C. 84 (1904).

of the vehicle to monitor and regulate the actions of family members to ensure that their behavior was consistent with safe use.

Another result of automobile ownership by ordinary families was that insurance comprised an important public policy issue. Plaintiffs, even if successful in obtaining a judgment for damages, were often unable to collect their dues because the impecunious automobile owner had purchased the vehicle on an installment plan and was financially unable to pay. Early insurance companies lacked information to compute and rate risks effectively, so the majority chose to avoid universal coverage and limited their policies to specific contingencies such as theft or fire. The problems for insurance writers, worried that mistaken assumptions about risks would lead to payouts exceeding their revenues, were compounded by inconsistent state and municipal regulations. In some states, insurance liability only applied to commercial vehicles or major urban centers, and some cities like Los Angeles and Cleveland passed local ordinances independently of state laws. Safety advocates turned to the analogy of workers' compensation to lobby for state-sponsored automobile insurance or regulation of the insurance industry. After 1910 the National Workmen's Compensation Service Bureau computed rates for liability and property damage insurance for automobiles. However, lobbyists for state-sponsored insurance plans along the lines of workers' compensation failed to achieve their objectives, and states continued to vary in their treatment of insurance. The major public policy toward automobile torts remains that of third-party insurance or compensation for harm done, rather than incentives for self-insurance or limitations on use.

CONCLUSION

We live in interesting times; but so did the population of the nineteenth and early twentieth centuries. The elevation in standards of living during this period was associated with the rapid diffusion of inventions that transformed the daily lives of ordinary citizens. Technological change was not uniformly benevolent, and it is appalling to modern observers to assess the costs in terms of injuries, mortality, morbidity, and environmental damage. Innovations also had redistributive effects, such as interference with existing water rights, the fall in returns to railroad stockholders when automotive vehicles substituted for passenger and freight transportation, or even the increased benefits to personal beauty that resulted from the rise of service-oriented occupations. The incentives to invent and innovate were influenced by the rules and standards of social and economic exchange, and in turn those rules had to accommodate the new technologies: "the great inventions that embodied the power of steam and electricity, the railroad and the steamship, the telegraph and the telephone, have built up new customs and new law."[45]

Here I have suggested that one of the reasons for the relative success of the United States during the long nineteenth century was its dependence on an array of institutions that proved to be sufficiently flexible to provide incentives for the creation of technological innovations and also the means to manage their use and consequences in the public interest. These institutions included (but clearly were not limited to) the private market, the political process vested in the legislature, administrative regulation, insurance, and the legal system. I have deliberately highlighted the role of the market economy and that of the common law. President Theodore Roosevelt did likewise in his 1908 address to Congress, noting that "for the peaceful progress of our people during the twentieth century we shall owe most to those judges who hold to a twentieth century economic and social philosophy and not to a long outgrown philosophy, which was itself the product of primitive economic conditions." In short, the democratic market orientation of the American legal system played a key role in the advances of this era.

The United States benefited from the talents of the extraordinary cadre of individuals who comprised the judiciary. Courts confronted a continuous stream of disputes that arose as humankind went about the commonplace business of life and from these unpropitious materials created decisions that were based on analogies drawn from historical experience, logic, and the attempt to serve the community in general. An analysis of law reports supports the notion that the judiciary objectively weighed costs and benefits, and ultimately the decisions that prevailed promoted social welfare rather than the interests of any single group. As Benjamin Cardozo expressed it, "the final cause of law is the welfare of society."[46] American judges understood that one of the best means to protect the rights of customers and to constrain the power of corporations was through market competition. The legal system formed a decentralized method of dispute resolution that was continuously calibrated to the changes that affected society, technological or otherwise. This is not to say that every judge was of the caliber of Joseph Story or Benjamin Cardozo, but a system of appeals assured that "the tide rises and falls, but the sands of error crumble."[47]

Regulation, on the other hand, is too often a function of a unique cataclysmic event – a stock market crash, a fire or train collision that results in much loss of life, a single epidemic or terrorist attack, the sinking of a ship – that grips the public imagination and provides the political impetus for

[45] Benjamin N. Cardozo, *The Nature of the Judicial Process* (New Haven, CT, 1921), 62.
[46] *Ibid.*, 66.
[47] *Ibid.*, 177.

policies that might have been appropriate for that event but subsequently are likely to prove to be ineffective guides for future actions or outcomes. Regulation and "protective" legislation typically came about as a result of political interests, rather than economic understanding, and often constituted a veiled attempt at raising barriers to entry or increasing the costs of competitors and of disdained social groups. Regulatory provisions were most effective when they simply codified the historical tendencies of the common law and ultimately depended on enforcement from the federal legal system. Administrative bodies such as the ICC and the FTC at times were headed by legal practitioners: Brandeis is credited (or blamed) for the establishment of the FTC and SEC, and Cooley was the first ICC Commissioner. Rather than substitutes, the legal system was a valuable and necessary complement to state and federal regulatory systems, but their relative importance varied with time and circumstance.

Although the nineteenth century is frequently characterized as the heyday of untethered competition, one can be impressed with the extent to which new technologies were both enabled and constrained by common law holdings to conform to prevailing conceptions of social welfare. The major innovations considered here – the railroad, the telegraph, medical technologies and public health strategies, and the automobile – were regarded as integral to social progress. Because they were vested with a public purpose, private enterprises were conscripted to serve the needs of the community. It is therefore not surprising that judges such as Cardozo saw the ultimate objective of law to be the promotion of "social utility." From this perspective, neither is it surprising that courts ensured the protection of railroad passengers, consumers, children, debtors, and other classes of society at the same time that they were attempting to provide incentives for the growth of private enterprise.

The advent of each new technology created uncertainty about how the law would be interpreted, which analogies would be applied, and what the prevailing standard would be. This uncertainty likely accounts, at least in part, for the increase in the number of lawsuits that initially occurred, even after adjusting for the scale of use. The courts were typically at the forefront of policies toward technology in the nineteenth century and provided a gauge of legislative needs. Legislation encountered the technologies of the day with a lag and tended to follow signals emanating from the conflicts before the courts. Thus, legal decisions, although statute-bound and based on historical experience, were to some extent forward looking. We can only speculate about the subsequent decline in litigation rates that all of the figures exhibit, but the number of litigated disputes likely fell because of learning by all parties involved, greater certainty about standards, the introduction of new legislation that resolved outstanding issues, or in some instances as a result of a shifting of oversight from the courts to other institutions.

Patents and (to a lesser extent) copyrights were regarded as fundamental to industrial and cultural progress and protected as such at the federal level from the very beginning of nationhood. As a result, interstate markets developed early on with extensive trade in rights and subdivided rights. Inventors were regarded as public benefactors, because (unlike monopolists) they contributed new improvements that expanded the frontiers of production and consumption. Therefore the law was quite unambiguous in its objective of protecting legitimate patent rights in order to provide incentives for inventive activity and diffusion. However, it was necessary for judges in equity jurisdiction to thwart patent owners who attempted to extend their rights beyond their just bounds to obtain monopoly control over the entire industry. Copyright, on the other hand, provided weaker incentives for new expression and risked reducing public access to knowledge. New technologies presented further dilemmas because they increased the scope and duration of copyright protection and had potentially deleterious effects on the public domain. In the attempt to protect public welfare, legal innovations expanded beyond traditional copyright doctrines to noncopyright holdings under unfair competition, trade secrets, and the right to privacy.

In the context of technological innovations, market integration ran up against the constraints of individual state policies that inhibited standardization and increased the costs of transacting. The first national enterprises – the railroads and the telegraph companies – appealed to the federal courts to apply provisions of the Constitution. Had they failed, the consequences would have been harmful not just for big business and market integration, but for the attempts of social reformers who wished to override the political biases of state legislatures in areas as disparate as racial segregation and abortion. While federalism was a prerequisite for market integration, the converse did not necessarily hold, since general market integration did not preclude state oversight, especially for technologies whose use was predominantly local. During the period under review, roads were largely intrastate and unconnected, making long-distance travel prohibitively costly for most purposes. This comprised at least one reason why the law toward automobile users was predominantly state oriented, and relatively few federal questions arose in the courts. Instead, federal policies were mainly directed toward resolving free-rider problems among states by matching state funding to construct interstate highways.

The automobile industry quickly made important contributions to law, economy, and technology. Despite its prominence, few historians have addressed the legal implications of the automobile, an omission that is all the more noticeable when compared to the attention accorded to other major innovations such as the railroad. Although the transportation function of both railroads and automobiles was the same, few legal analogies were drawn between them. It might be argued that the railroad's significance in legal scholarship owed to the public need for mitigation of the harms to consumers and workers from accidents and the need to regulate monopolistic railroad strategies. Yet, third-party effects associated with automobiles, in the form of injuries to children and other bystanders, were far greater than in the case of railroads. We may speculate that the different scholarly treatment owes to the difficulty of integrating the automobile into a theoretically coherent model of legal and technological change. The railroad was relatively easy to characterize because it encouraged the development of big business, was conducive to polarized class-based interpretations, and encouraged the growth of federal oversight and administrative regulation. In contrast, even with growing market integration, the automobile was associated with decentralized consumer use, harms to ordinary citizens by other ordinary citizens, few interstate issues, and increased oversight by states and municipalities. The decentralization of activities that occurred with widespread automobile ownership meant that the public would have had to bear the consequences of pervasive regulation. Instead of legal or regulatory measures to significantly limit private use, the scale of harms afflicted by automobile users motivated an institutional shift toward private insurance. Policymakers were reluctant to follow the vaccination analogy that allowed incursions into the private sphere of consumer activities in the name of the public interest.

Effective policies toward innovations required a social calculus that was far more subtle than the promotion of the interests of any one specific group in society. Technological advances altered the costs and benefits of transacting within a particular network of rules and standards, and institutions proved to be sufficiently flexible to encompass these changes. We can gain some insights into the effectiveness of American legal institutions from the experience of developing countries today. In many nations political elites have captured institutions to further the narrow self-interest of these privileged groups. Institutional scleroses, the prevalence of inefficient regulatory bureaucracies, corruption, and inadequate legal systems have resulted in widespread poverty, despair, and the absence of incentives for increased productivity. If the subsidy thesis is correct, and the American legal system early on was captured to promote the interests of a favored few, it is quite unlikely that the United States would have experienced more than a century of relatively democratic economic growth and technological progress. In short, since the founding of the Republic, institutions have altered as the scale and scope of market and society have evolved, but the central policy objective of promoting the public interest has remained the same. That is, after all, one of the chief virtues of a society that is bound and enabled by prescient constitutional principles.

16

THE LAWS OF INDUSTRIAL ORGANIZATION, 1870–1920

KAREN ORREN

The period from 1870 to 1920 was a time of profound challenge for the American legal system. During these years, an indecisively connected country of small producers became a centralized industrial nation, and a legal system devoted to regulating the affairs of independent farmers and businessmen and their few employees had to adapt to the increasingly complex relations entailed in the finance and operation of large corporate enterprises. The dimensions of the project are indicated by the growth in railroading, the defining industry of the age. At the start of the Civil War, the United States contained 30,626 miles of railroad track; in 1916, the year when track mileage reached its historical apogee, there were 254,251 miles. Roughly 60 percent of this increase had come before the turn of the century. In 1870, the railroads employed 160,000 workers, by 1900 this figure was 1,040,000, and by 1920 it would rise to 2,236,000. Growth was comparable in construction, mining, and manufacturing. With more employees came more workers' collective actions. By the outbreak of World War I, the number of yearly strikes nationally had increased by a multiple of five; in the interim, major labor-business confrontations were directly linked to several crucial political events – passage of the Interstate Commerce Act, for instance, and the presidential election of 1896.

Under these circumstances, it is not surprising that social issues and conflicts have eclipsed the more strictly legal aspects of what judges decided in available accounts. The emphasis is reflected in the period's nickname, "Lochner era," after *Lochner v. New York* (1905), in which the U.S. Supreme Court struck down as unconstitutional a state statute mandating a ten-hour working day for bakery workers. It has also outlasted a major revision in Lochner era scholarship. Older Lochner era scholarship mounted a caustic morality play – small producers against corporations, business against workers, courts against legislatures – and attacked a rigidly formal "classicism" for its indifference to disparities in power. The revisionist narrative is redemptive: judges strove mightily on behalf of what they considered founding commitments to personal liberty, to society without classes, to a neutral, "night watchman" state tested by new and disruptive forms of association. If earlier Lochner era scholarship regarded legal rules mainly as a smokescreen for the suppression of lower orders, the revisionist telling has them an endangered species in a rear-guard defense of higher purposes.

Both interpretations are supported by ample evidence and, looked at more closely, are not so much inconsistent with one another as they are mirror images. One highlights policy results, debunking the reasons judges offered for their decisions; the other extols the judges' reasons, downplaying the impact on society of what they decided. As such, they are able to offer the identical purchase on future legal development: repudiation, by the New Deal Court, of policy results and reasoning together. Still, none of this squares with something else we know, which is that many reform landmarks of Progressive lawmaking – railroad regulation, antitrust statutes, protective food and drug statutes, industrial accident statutes, and others – survived judicial scrutiny at state and federal levels, according to the same (bogus) formalisms and the same (misplaced) constitutional ideals. Neither repudiated nor significantly weakened, these programs carried on as bulwarks of the American welfare state for the next half-century. On its face, this continuity challenges leading interpretations of the Lochner era at the same time as it raises questions about the historical contours of law under the New Deal.

To explain the anomaly and to provide a more open-ended analysis of the jurisprudence of the period, this chapter places legal principles and rules rather than social conflict at the center of inquiry, and situates their application in the Lochner era within the longer chronology of Anglo-American legal development. The discussion concentrates on three closely related principles. The first is *jurisdiction*, the idea that whoever finally determines the substance of law in any particular instance must have legitimate warrant in advance to do so. Most commonly, jurisdiction refers to the authority of different courts to adjudicate particular disputes between individuals or groups in society. More generally, and as it is used here, jurisdiction expresses the authority of government officers, including judges but also legislators and others in public stations, to – literally – say what the law is. The ultimate locus of jurisdiction is a fundamental problem in any legal process; it was a major conundrum for the framers of the U.S. Constitution. During the years under examination here, it was arguably the most strenuously contested of all legal questions.

The second principle is *precedent*: the requirement that the law imposed on parties in dispute be the same law that was imposed previously, in analogous cases. Precedent is the mainspring of common law procedure, bringing together the requirements of predictable law and equitable administration.

Among government officers, legislators are distinguished by their freedom from precedent in matters under their jurisdiction; the discretion they exercise in this regard distinguishes them from judges. The robustness of common law as an important foundation for American government and of the judiciary as an independent body was tied closely to adherence to precedent. "Legislation by the judiciary" is a term of opprobrium, signifying constitutional disorder; it has been applied to "Lochnerisms" of all hues and vintages.

The third principle is *rights*, claims that one person may legitimately make on the person or actions of another, enforceable in a court of law. Although rights are often asserted on philosophical or constitutional grounds, their distribution in society at any given moment is determined by the ongoing processes of the legal system as a whole. Citizens have – may successfully assert – rights against other citizens and against public officers; public officers have rights against other officeholders and against citizens. The revisionist interpretation of Lochner era jurisprudence proposes that judges were less concerned with rights than their predecessors had been and were more interested in the proper alignment of government powers. Here I suggest that a better way of grasping the transition at issue is through the increasing tendency of the law to recognize collective as well as individual rights, both in private life and in government.

In the late nineteenth and early twentieth centuries, these three principles took on, as in all periods, a distinctive content. The argument below builds on a single observation: during the period from 1870 to 1920, American judges administered one set of rules to determine jurisdiction, precedent, and rights when the subject matter of the dispute before them was commerce – production and trade of goods and money – and another set when the subject matter of the dispute before them was labor – relations between master and servant and employees' collective action. In theory, the three principles ought to be tied together: the location of jurisdiction should be the deciding factor in whether or not precedent applies and whether, given the facts of the case, there is a right under the law. But in the cases on industrial organization during these years the connection is incomplete. In disputes where they took jurisdiction, judges sometimes adhered to precedent and sometimes not. These decisions and whether or not the plaintiff's assertion of a legal right prevailed were patterned by the subject matter – commerce or labor – of the litigation.

To account for rather than merely uncover this division, it is necessary to situate the discussion in its broader history. This may be accomplished by means of three historical markers. The first is the reception of English law into the United States. By the early decades of the nineteenth century, the national government and every American state and territory except

Louisiana incorporated the common law and statutes of England into their own laws as of a certain date – the founding of the colony, national independence, admission to statehood, and so on. Next only to the framing of the U.S. Constitution, this reception was the single most influential event in the history of American law. Not every English law was received; statutes on royalty and the church, for instance, were excluded, as were those pertaining to particular English locales. But laws that were applicable to society generally, including those regulating commerce and labor, were absorbed and routinely relied on as authority in American judicial opinions. Although technically English cases and statutes more recent than the stated date of reception were only advisory, they too were frequently cited.

The second marker is the imprint of England's commercial revolution on the constitution of English government. From Parliament's revolt against the monarchy over the question of monopolies in the seventeenth century and continuing on through the eighteenth, final authority – jurisdiction – over commerce moved steadily to the legislature, where commercial interests and their allies held sway. Parliament in turn increased the authority of the courts of common law, giving them jurisdiction over the great body of commercial rules not covered by statutes, largely at the expense of the courts of Admiralty. Considered as a historic turning point, these events paralleled changes pursuant to England's religious upheaval in the sixteenth century, in which the King's authority was increased relative to the bishops and the authority of the secular courts relative to their ecclesiastical counterparts. These changes illustrate the course of Anglo-American legal development, in stages, by which authority over discrete activities in society is relocated, from jurisdictions characterized more by hierarchy and rules to jurisdictions characterized more by equality and innovation, from institutions that operated more like courts to institutions that operated more like legislatures.

With specific regard to the legal system, this transition resulted over time in judges who, at least in some circumstances, behaved like legislators. Consider the career of the dominant juridical figure of the middle decades of the eighteenth century, who would have such formative influence on the United States: William Murray, Lord Mansfield, Solicitor General of England, Attorney General, leader of the House of Commons, and for over thirty years Chief Justice of Kings Bench. If Chief Justice John Marshall is the high priest of American law, Lord Mansfield is its patron saint. Mansfield is credited with bringing the international law merchant and the commerce-friendly rules of equity into the common law courts; revising laws in banking, negotiable instruments, promissory notes, and marine insurance; and shaping English commercial law overall into the purposeful, expansive, pragmatic instrument that embodied the spirit of its age, the law on which American lawyers and judges cut their teeth. Mansfield's actions were highly controversial. Junius, his anonymous political enemy, spoke for the opposition when he leveled the charge that "in contempt of the common law of England you have made it your study to introduce into the court where you preside, maxims of jurisprudence unknown to Englishmen. . . . King's Bench becomes a court of equity; the judge, instead of consulting the law of the land, refers only to the wisdom of the court and the purity of his conscience."[1]

The third historical marker is that portion of the English law that remained unaffected by these changes. This included the common law of master and servant, which, two centuries after the start of the commercial revolution, was still administered in its ancient form by local justices of the peace, an office entrusted with that duty in the reign of Edward III. The few labor statutes appearing on the statute rolls were understood to be clarifications of older common law provisions. Along with the law of other "private relations" listed by Blackstone – husband and wife, parent and child, guardian and ward, and corporations – master and servant law was received into the legal systems of the United States just as it existed in England, unaffected by theories of Parliamentary sovereignty. A survey of English statutes cited as authority by American judges prior to 1820 offers dozens of pages on commercial subjects but only a handful of references to labor, and most of these are to the Elizabethan Statute of Apprentices, which was regarded in England as a redaction of earlier common law.[2]

Transposed into America, which had written constitutions and a stronger demarcation among government branches, this disjointed state of affairs assumed, if anything, greater stability than before. Excepting laws concerning the commerce in slaves, which was eliminated in an upheaval of its own, it persisted in the United States unchanged following the Civil War. We encounter the American judiciary in the late nineteenth century as a system in full flower, its operatives professional and self-confident, its activities at the center of American culture and politics. What will appear later as confused and inequitable behavior was the product of decisions arrived at according to well-rehearsed routines, along established guidelines. In major part, it was an artifact of judges being called on to administer not one law of industrial organization between 1870 and 1920, but two.

To indicate the range of controversies in play, this chapter takes up several of the most prominent issues of industrial organization over which parties struggled. To demonstrate the essential unity between federal and state

[1] C. H. S. Fifoot, *Lord Mansfield* (Oxford, 1936), 183.

[2] Elaine Gaspar Brown, *British Statutes in American Law, 1776–1836* (Ann Arbor, MI, 1964).

rulings, it examines decisions of both the U.S. Supreme Court and the higher courts of New York. Placing these issues within the development of Anglo-American law and concentrating on their specifically legal features do not cause the social content of these years to disappear; on the contrary, the substance of individual cases sets the patterns that emerge in successive litigations. These patterns are important for their continuity from and into different eras, including our own, and into subject matters other than those in which they first took shape. Both movements comprise the legal significance of any age.

I. JURISDICTION

Blackstone likened the forms of action at English common law in the eighteenth century to a gothic castle, its approaches winding and forbidding. The American law of jurisdiction after the Civil War resembled nothing so much as a house of mirrors, its corridors irregular and dizzying. One step in any direction produced altered, many-sided views. Officeholders could be personally penalized and their decisions reversed because another officeholder found an exercise of authority to be within the jurisdiction of yet a third officeholder (or subset of officeholders) or that it was prohibited altogether. Citizens might pursue actions through the serpentine turns of state and federal law only to learn at the last that they had started in the wrong place. Jurisdictional decisions comprise the best evidence for the opinion that during 1870–1920 the American judiciary ran amok, bent on aggrandizing its own jurisdiction at the same time it favored already privileged private interests. A more circumspect analysis reveals that judges assumed markedly different postures when the suit concerned the interests of commerce than when it concerned the interests of labor, thus calling into question the judicial aggrandizement thesis as a whole.

The disparity may be indicated first of all with regard to the statutes regulating either commerce or labor that were passed by Congress during 1870–1920 and struck down by the U.S. Supreme Court. By this time, the Court's jurisdiction to decide whether a given subject matter was within constitutional bounds of Congressional authority either under the Commerce Clause or some other provision was well established. Therefore it is impressive that, of the hundreds of statutes regulating commerce that Congress passed during these years, the Court struck down as unconstitutional a grand total of four. The four stand out against a record of legislative innovation that included, among other statutes, the Interstate Commerce Act, the Sherman Antitrust Act, the Pure Food and Drug Act, the Federal Trade Commission Act, and the Federal Reserve Act. Each of the Court's four decisions was based, in whole or in part, on the absence of Congressional jurisdiction.

By absence of jurisdiction the Court did not mean the truism that no government officer or agency has authority to do what is unconstitutional or illegal. Rather, the Court rested its opinion expressly on Congress either having presumed an authority that under the Constitution it did not possess when it passed the statute, or that Congress had left the question of its presumed authority ambiguous in the statute itself.

All four instances occurred before the turn of the twentieth century. The first, *United States v. DeWitt* (1870), arose on an indictment in Michigan for the federal crime of mixing and selling oil with naphtha, a prohibition left over from an old revenue statute that otherwise had been repealed. The Court held that, standing alone, the prohibition was a "regulation of police . . . relating exclusively to the internal trade of the States" and therefore was unconstitutional.[3] The second decision, *United States v. Fox* (1877), declared a section of the Bankruptcy Act that made it a federal offense to defraud anyone of goods within three months prior to commencing state bankruptcy proceedings to be a usurpation of state authority and also an ex post facto law.[4] The third decision, *The Trade Mark Cases* (1879), invalidated a statute that revised the federal law of copyrights and patents to include trademarks. In its decision, the Court applied a new canon of statutory construction: all penal statutes must be worded in sufficiently definite language as to admit of no uncertainty as to their reach. Because the new statute said nothing about being limited to interstate and foreign commerce or to the District of Columbia, the Court found it was unconstitutional. Finally, *Monongahela Navigation Co. v. United States* (1893) overturned a section of the 1888 River and Harbor Appropriation Act on the grounds that its provision for Congress to determine "just compensation" violated due process guarantees of the Fifth Amendment, "just compensation" being a question within the jurisdiction of the judiciary.[5]

None of these decisions is widely remembered. The first two are garden-variety police power decisions familiar in American law since the era of *Gibbons v. Ogden* (1824); the second and third decisions reflect the judiciary's heightened attention to due process protections after the passage of the Fourteenth Amendment. The fourth decision raised the knotty matter of the overlapping functions of Congress and the judiciary. This had come to a boil only twice before the Civil War – in *Marbury* (1803) and *Dred Scott* (1857) – but would take on greater urgency in the succeeding decades. Nothing, however, underscores the anomaly of these few holdings among the great body of commercial decisions as does a comparison with the Court's treatment of disputes that arose under Congress's contemporaneous

[3] 76 U.S. 41, at 45.

[4] 95 U.S. 670.

[5] 148 U.S. 312.

labor legislation. The number of times in which the Court invalidated labor statutes on constitutional grounds was also four. Each statute had been a basic plank in the labor movement's national program, and together they made up the lion's share of its Congressional gains. Like the commercial statutes that were overturned, each labor statute faltered, in whole or in part, for reasons of jurisdiction.

All four labor decisions occurred after the turn of the twentieth century. First, the *Employers' Liability Cases* (1908) struck down a 1906 law that imposed liability on employers for injuries to employees on interstate railroads; the Court said that the statute's word "employees" could be read to cover employees working for interstate railroads but not personally engaged in interstate commerce, thereby violating the Commerce Clause. *Adair v. United States* (1908) invalidated Section 10 of the Erdman Act of 1898, making it a federal crime for railroads to discriminate against or discharge an employee for union membership or for refusing to promise not to join a union ("yellow dog contract") as a condition of employment. The Court found that these provisions violated the railroads' rights of contract and due process under the Fourteenth Amendment and also that the act of employing a worker did not bear a sufficiently direct relationship to interstate commerce to bring the subject under Congress's jurisdiction. *Hammer v. Dagenhart* (1918) overturned a 1916 statute prohibiting interstate shipment of factory products made by children under 14 years of age; the Court held that the statute illegally interfered with manufacturing located inside individual states and thereby under their sole jurisdiction. Finally, *Knickerbocker Ice Co. v. Stewart* (1920) reviewed a statute that amended the Judicial Code to cover maritime workers under state workers' compensation laws. The Court held that Congress had unconstitutionally delegated its admiralty jurisdiction under Article III to the states.

This preliminary brief for a jurisdictional division between commerce and labor based on negative outcomes under judicial review is supported by a corresponding division in the reasons the Court gave for its decisions when reviewing Congressional statutes in the two areas, outcomes notwithstanding.[6] Consider, as a first example, litigation under the Sherman

[6] The foregoing pattern is confirmed in state adjudication as well, in which the period 1870–1920 covers the high point of the police power. A review by the author of 106 laws legislated in New York during these years on the subjects of commerce and labor and challenged in the state's highest court on constitutional grounds indicates that 79 percent of the commercial statutes were upheld and 53 percent of the labor statutes were struck down. Closer analysis reveals a change in the court's behavior around 1907. Prior to 1907, only two labor statutes of a total of nine (22 percent) were upheld. Both were successfully defended as health measures. The first, in 1873, required the licensing of pilots steering steamships in or out of New York ports; the other, in 1904, imposed a

Antitrust Act, passed in 1890 and arguably the most far-reaching commercial statute of the late nineteenth century. The Sherman Act criminalized "every contract, combination in the form of trust of otherwise, or conspiracy, in restraint of trade or commerce" among the states or with foreign countries; further, it invested authority in the U.S. Circuit Courts to prevent and restrain violations of the statute on petition by the local U.S. Attorney. In all of the major disputes before the Supreme Court, the principal argument was over whether the circuit court below had taken appropriate jurisdiction – that is, whether the trust or combination in question was within Congress's authority under the Commerce Clause – in which event the Supreme Court might proceed to examine the legality of the lower court's order; or, alternatively, whether the dispute concerned dealings strictly among local businessmen that were under the jurisdiction of the respective state, in which event there was nothing further to decide unless and until the state court's order was appealed on a writ of error.

Over a period of fifteen years the Supreme Court expanded the reach of federal antitrust policy to create broadened national authority at the expense of the jurisdiction of the states. In *United States v. E.C. Knight* (1895) the Court held that manufacturing was not commerce in the meaning of the Sherman Act, but upheld the constitutionality of the act as interpreted. In *U.S. v. Trans-Missouri Freight* (1897) and *U.S. v. Joint Traffic Association* (1898) – opinions prohibiting pooling arrangements by interstate railroads – the Court held that by "every" restraint of trade, the Congress meant all, without exception. In *Standard Oil Co. of New Jersey v. U.S.* (1911) and *U.S. v. American Tobacco Co.* (1911) the Court decided that by "every" restraint Congress meant every "reasonable" restraint. Put differently, with these rulings, the Supreme Court permitted the Sherman Act to stand as written while steadily widening the jurisdiction of the federal officeholders who administered and enforced it.

The Court accomplished this feat without ever seriously questioning the Sherman Act's constitutionality and by deferring to Congress in other ways. In *Knight*, the justices preserved the statute by drawing the legal boundaries of the law to coincide with their interpretation of Congress's jurisdiction under the Commerce Clause itself. The Commerce Clause did not embrace manufacturing; therefore the Sherman Act did not include a monopoly in manufacturing among its prohibitions. In *Joint Traffic Association*, they tarried with the issue of constitutionality only long enough to

ten-hour maximum on the labor of bakers. After 1907, the number of statutes upheld rose to five of six (83 percent). Although not complete, these figures also suggest that for this last interval, the New York Court of Appeals' sanction of labor legislation alongside commercial legislation led the U.S. Supreme Court by nearly three decades.

agree with the decision in *Knight*. As a consequence, while opinions debated what precisely the legislature intended, Congress's authority expanded and contracted apace. Whether Congress had stayed within or exceeded the common law was questioned, but not its discretion to act either way. That Congress could not have been so unreasonable as to have meant "every" contract in restraint of trade was originally the dissenting position on the Court; ultimately that argument prevailed. The Court applied and ignored rules of statutory construction to suit. Mindful of its "duty to restrict the meaning of general words whenever it is found necessary . . . to carry out the legislative intent," for instance, it did not regard the word "every," which it first narrowed and then liberalized, as unconstitutionally vague. Justices argued fiercely about the meaning of "restraint of trade," but they never invoked the rule that penal statutes must be worded unambiguously, nor was the Sherman Act unconstitutional for failing expressly to exempt from its purview commerce carried on purely inside a state. The Court altered its justification of Congress's jurisdiction, from plenary authority under the Commerce Clause in *Trans-Missouri Freight* to authority constrained only by the Fifth Amendment in *Standard Oil of New Jersey*, but it never doubted the legislature's authority per se.

In addition to their deference to Congress, a second feature of the commerce decisions is their pragmatism, their mood of flexibility, of rule-as-you-go. The opinions invoked the categories and "nice distinctions" attributed to the "classical" jurisprudence of the Lochner era: manufacturing versus commerce, direct versus indirect, objectives versus means, necessary versus incidental. But these distinctions never determined outcomes. The category of manufacturing that protected the national sugar monopoly in *Knight* did not subsequently protect the production of pipe, tile, or cigarettes. Commission-fixing for transporting cattle to and from the stockyard hub of Kansas City had only an "indirect" relation to interstate commerce and was exempt from the Sherman Act.[7] Transactions to control cattle prices paid in Midwestern stockyards were part of a "current of commerce" and "direct" and therefore were covered by the act.[8] Key concepts regularly changed their meaning. For instance, no antitrust prosecution was successful in the absence of a finding that the parties intended to restrain trade. In *Knight*, however, intention referred to the parties' objectives, and "indirect" meant "unintended."[9] In later cases, intention is proved by showing that restraint was the "necessary effect" of a contract; in *Addyston Pipe and Steel Co. v. United*

[7] *Hopkins v. United States*, 171 U.S. 578, 591 (1898).
[8] *Swift and Company v. United States*, 196 U.S. 375, 397, 398–99 (1905).
[9] 156 U.S. 1, 17.

States (1898), the Court affirmed a circuit court opinion holding that, where there was a necessary effect, the design behind a contract was "immaterial."[10]

Some cases emphasized "means." Justice Brewer joined the majority for dissolution in *Northern Securities Company v. United States* (1904) for the reason that the trust at issue resulted from a preexisting plan and not from decisions made by individual investors.[11] *Standard Oil* sees the combination at issue to be a product of "ruthless" methods. *American Tobacco* finds evidence of intention to restrain trade in the warehouses acquired from competitors.[12] Every justice opposed excessive rigidity in procedure. When, in the cattle price-fixing case, plaintiffs complained that the facts and charges of the indictment were imprecise, Justice Holmes, no classicist, answered as follows: "Whatever may be thought concerning the proper construction of a statute, a bill in equity is not to be read and construed as an indictment would have been read and construed a hundred years ago. . . . The scheme alleged is so vast that it presents a new problem in pleading."[13]

No allowance for modern times characterizes the labor decisions. It is not possible to examine a series of labor cases like the litigation under the Sherman Act because none exists. There were indeed Sherman Act suits against unions, but opinions in those cases ask only whether the unions' actions obstructed interstate commerce as defined in that law; they do not link that question to the law of master and servant. On the other hand, the four labor statutes that the Supreme Court declared unconstitutional provide the relevant contrast. The first difference is the justices' careful weighing of constitutionality, which in the labor decisions is consistently found wanting. Second is its correlate: the Court's unwillingness to defer to Congress, even in arguable cases. Far from drawing statutory boundaries to coincide with Congress's jurisdiction under the Commerce Clause, as it did with the Sherman Act, the Court makes no effort to interpret labor legislation in any manner that would save it. Its opinion in *First Employers' Liability Cases*, for instance, notes that the wording of the statute offers no

[10] 85 F. 271 (1898); aff'd 175 U.S. 211. The circuit court opinion was written by William Howard Taft, already an influential judge.

[11] 193 U.S. 197, 362.

[12] This open-ended situation was corrected in the Clayton Act, passed by Congress in 1914, enumerating specific unlawful conduct that was unlawful restraint of trade and that would by itself constitute violation of the act absent proof by the accused of some legal justification. Meanwhile, intention continued as an important factor in behavior not covered. In 1920, in *United States v. United States Steel*, 251 U.S. 417, the Court held that bigness, absent any intent to stifle competition, was not a violation of the Sherman Act.

[13] 196 U.S. 375, 394–5.

disclaimer as to intrastate employers, and on that basis it holds that Congress exceeded its authority. In *Adair* the majority remarks, "in passing," that, while the Erdman Act works to protect union members from discriminatory treatment, it provides no similar protection for non-members.

As in its Sherman Act decisions, the Court in its labor opinions draws lines and categories, but now rigidly respects them. In reading Section 10 of the Erdman Act in *Adair*, it might have invoked a current-of-commerce metaphor, linking union membership to smooth operations in interstate railroads. Instead, while agreeing that statutes requiring safe brakes and equipment and imposing liability on the company for injuries had "direct" reference to interstate commerce, it found that neither the hiring and firing of workers nor membership in a labor organization had, logically or legally, "any bearing upon the commerce with which the employee is connected by his services."[14] The opinion goes further, deploying the Fifth Amendment to erect a barrier between Congress's jurisdiction under the Commerce Clause and businessmen's liberty and property rights against Congress' interfering in contracts with employees. In *Knickerbocker Ice*, the majority expressly adheres to the "rule of formality" in striking down the applicability of state workers' compensation laws to maritime employees, opining that Congress's admiralty jurisdiction constructs a barrier against the states that supersedes its ordinary authority to legislate.[15]

In the labor decisions, the barriers held. Partway through this chronology, in *Wilson v. New* (1917), the Court upheld the Adamson Act, which reduced the railroad workday from ten to eight hours, at the same pay, on grounds of national emergency – a threatened strike on the eve of American entry into war – and on the statute's provision for a trial period before taking final effect. The opinion also recalled that in 1893 it had sanctioned a sixteen-hour law for train workers in pursuit of safer public transport, and in 1913 a second law, the Second Employers Liability Act, drafted to allay constitutional qualms about its predecessor.[16] But its next labor decision, *Hammer v. Dagenhart*, dispelled any hopes this conciliatory posture might be permanent. In an effort to sidestep the Court's protection of employers' contracts with their employees under the Fifth Amendment, and relying on both its Commerce Clause jurisdiction and its authority under the police power to preserve public health, Congress prohibited transport across state lines of all products made in factories that had, within the previous thirty days, employed persons under the age of fourteen or between the age of fourteen and sixteen, and working more than eight hours a day or more than six days a week or between 7 P.M. and 6 A.M.

[14] 208 U.S. 161, 178.
[15] 253 U.S. 149.
[16] 243U.S. 332, 349.

In *Hammer*, the several lines by which the Court determined national and state jurisdiction in labor cases become a cross-hatch: between manufacturing and commerce; between goods harmless in themselves (child-made products) and those intrinsically evil (liquor, lotteries, prostitution); between powers delegated to the Congress and those reserved to the states under the Tenth Amendment; and between the Commerce Clause and the Fifth Amendment. The intense strain between the national branches, moreover, is visible in the open rejection of Congress's motives, exactly contrary to the attitude adopted in reviewing commercial statutes. The act was "repugnant" to the Constitution; it did "not regulate transportation among the States, but aims to standardize the ages at which children may be employed in mining and manufacturing among the States."[17]

That the motives or purposes of a statute ought to be the primary element in determining Congress's Commerce Clause jurisdiction had been the Court's view in the early nineteenth century. In *Gibbons v. Ogden* (1824) Chief Justice Marshall wrote that, when the City of London enacted quarantine laws affecting commerce, it did not mean that London had concurrent authority with Parliament to grant a monopoly for navigating on the Thames; if, under color of a health law, "enactments should be made for other purposes, such enactments might be void."[18] This position, however, proved impractical in allocating the many commercial activities steadily undertaken within the federal system, and in 1851 the Court adopted the doctrine of "concurrent powers": commercial matters of national concern would fall under the authority of Congress and those of a local concern under the jurisdiction of state legislatures.[19] Subsequently, it held that Congress might enact regulations under its Commerce Clause jurisdiction not for reasons of commerce itself but for reasons of morals or health or the requirement of a nationally uniform policy, as with liquor and lottery sales and the movement of prostitutes.

The majority in *Hammer* realized it was backtracking from this earlier position. Acknowledging it had neither "authority or disposition" to question Congress's motives, it nonetheless insisted that what it suspected Congress intended to do – that is, regulate child labor within the states – would in any event be a "necessary effect" of the statute. And if Congress could regulate local matters by prohibiting the movement of commodities in interstate commerce, "all freedom of commerce will be at an end . . . our system of government practically destroyed."[20] Compare this with the majority opinion in *Northern Securities* in which Justice Harlan asks whether it was constitutional for Congress to prescribe that the system

[17] 247 U.S. 251, 271–2.
[18] 22 U.S. 1, 25.
[19] *Cooley v. Board of Wardens*, 53 U.S. 299.
[20] 247 U.S. 251, 276.

of competition be enforced on all commerce among the states: "As in the judgment of Congress the public convenience and the general welfare will be best subserved when the natural laws of competition are left undisturbed by those engaged in interstate commerce, and as Congress has embodied that rule in a statute, that must be, for all, the end of the matter if this is to be a government of laws, and not of men."[21]

The Court's rigidity in reviewing labor statutes, so different from its flexibility in its commerce decisions, is evident, finally, in *Knickerbocker Ice*. To circumvent common law rules that prohibited employees from suing their employers for damages, and to enable injured seamen and their survivors to collect preset amounts from state workers' compensation funds, Congress had amended the Judiciary Act of 1789, which gave the federal courts exclusive jurisdiction over "all civil cases of admiralty and maritime jurisdiction, saving to suitors, in all cases, the right of a common-law remedy where the common law is competent to give it," by adding the phrase, "and to claimants rights and remedies under the workmen's compensation law of any State."[22] This legislation was intended to reverse an earlier holding in *Southern Pacific Railroad v. Jensen* (1917) that such an award by the New York Court of Appeals to the estate of a deceased stevedore was unconstitutional under Article III, which gave the federal courts jurisdiction over all maritime and admiralty cases; states might pass additional regulations, but not to an extent that "interferes with the proper harmony and uniformity of that law in its international and interstate relations."[23] The Court held these limitations were fundamental to the Constitution, much as the Commerce Clause and Congress's acts under it preempted state statutes that erected analogous obstacles.

Knickerbocker Ice decided that Congress's amendment of the Judiciary Act violated the uniformity essential to the nation's freedom of navigation. Justice McReynolds for the majority found ballast in an opinion written by Justice Bradley shortly after the Civil War, in which the latter said it was unquestionable that the Constitution contemplated a maritime law "coextensive with, and operating uniformly, in the whole country," beyond the disposition of individual states. Justice Holmes dissented. He cited federal admiralty decisions validating state statutes that restructured titles to land under navigable waters, provided liens for material and labor on the property of defaulting ship owners, regulated fisheries, and imposed liability for accidental deaths of crew and passengers on colliding ships. As for the parallels with the Commerce Clause, Holmes referred to the Court's recent overruling of arguments supporting national uniformity when it

[21] 193 U.S. 197, 338.

[22] See below, on liability rules.

[23] 244 U.S. 205, 216.

upheld the Webb-Kenyon Act, which delegated Congress's authority over the importation of liquor to the states, describing the arrangement as in the very nature of "our dual system of government."

The majority in *Knickerbocker Ice* argued that liquor was "exceptional." It had a point, especially insofar as neither liquor nor the other subject matters mentioned in Holmes's opinion involved the relation of master and servant, the issue in the decision at hand. The relation was not spoken of directly, but Justice McReynolds alluded to the matter when he opined that the implementation of workers' compensation in maritime affairs would undermine Congress's aims to encourage investment in ships. Justice Holmes himself also recognized its relevance, venturing the observation that "somehow or other" common law rules of liability between master and servant had come to be applied in admiralty cases. In any case, in striking down the statute the majority adhered rigidly to what it described as admiralty's primordial preference for uniformity. Justice Holmes, for his part, called the Court's reasoning "mechanical." Earlier, writing the Court's opinion in *Jensen* he had denied that admiralty was a *corpus juris* at all, describing it as simply a loose grouping of customs and ordinances of the sea and famously asserting, "The common law is not a brooding omnipresence in the sky but the articulate voice of some sovereign that can be identified."[24] *Knickerbocker*, however, and the Court's other decisions striking down Congress's labor statutes proved that for the time being and for all practical purposes Holmes was mistaken.

II. PRECEDENT

The critique of the legal realists, that late-nineteenth- and early-twentieth century jurisprudence was attentive to the law in books and not to the law in action, that it emphasized the integrity of legal processes at the expense of legal consequences, came down in the end to the accusation that American courts relied, mechanically or opportunistically and often both, on outmoded precedent. Precedent was frequently the reason for a plaintiff's choice between suing in federal or state court. It was the gist of Justice Story's 1842 opinion in *Swift v. Tyson*: since the rulings of state courts were "at most, only evidence of what the laws are, and are not, of themselves laws," the instruction to federal judges in Section 34 of the Judiciary Act – that they rest decisions at common law on the "laws of the several states" – meant only statutes and not judge-made law, with the effect of freeing federal judges from state court precedents.[25] Story's notion of a higher or "general" common law, with greater authority than locally decided cases, was the notion

[24] 244 U.S. 205, 222.

[25] 41 U.S. 1, 18–19.

that Justice Holmes later ridiculed in *Jensen*, as "a brooding omnipresence in the sky."

The relations of federal and state courts aside, scholars have discerned a continuing tension in American law between "Mansfieldian" and "Blackstonian" schools of precedent; that is, between law guided by precedent but ultimately based on reason and law based exclusively on precedent; or, put differently, between the reformist, natural law of the American Revolution and the orthodox, black letter law of the professionalized bar. In these terms, based on its reputation, the judiciary in the late nineteenth century would seem to have been a carrier of the second tendency. Whatever the validity of such a view, the patterns of adherence and non-adherence to precedent point to the historical disjunction between commerce and labor that is evident in cases on jurisdiction. It is significant that Lord Mansfield's storied creativity – his refusal to be bound by precedent when he deemed it unwise – was largely confined to his commercial decisions and that it was in commercial disputes, not labor disputes, where Justice Story in *Swift v. Tyson* saw a general common law at work.

Judges' review of legislation complicates the question of legal precedent, reducing it to a second-order inquiry subordinate to jurisdiction. Precedent comes into play only when the venue is courts, not legislatures. On the other hand, consideration of precedent as an independent issue can reinforce the findings on jurisdiction presented above. It is a fair inference from the U.S. Supreme Court's separate treatment of commerce and labor statutes under judicial review that the justices were not, or were not only, following provisions of the Constitution in establishing jurisdiction, but were acting according to rules dictated by Anglo-American history at the point English law was received into the United States. The position of precedent was affected by these same historical circumstances. The move of commercial affairs to Parliament accommodated new interests spawned by the commercial revolution; Parliament did not turn around and broaden the authority of the common law courts at the expense of Admiralty to hog-tie their commerce decisions with ancient restraints. The rise of Equity under Lord Mansfield's leadership was in the same spirit – the freedom of commercial activities from obstacles in the old law, that is to say, precedent. As was the case with jurisdiction, however, these innovating spirits did not infuse the regulation of master and servant.

The analysis of precedent below shifts the focus to judges' treatment during the same period of non-constitutional disputes that arose from conflict within the two major institutions of industrial organization: the workplace and the business corporation. Both institutions were still regulated mainly by non-statutory law administered by the judiciary; both had centuries of precedent behind them. Given that ultimate legal jurisdiction over their activities was shared among constitutional branches, the judiciary might have been expected to act preemptively to protect its domain, to be most adaptive to pressures to change in those disputes where it had cause to be anxious about the legislature's encroachment on its authority, and to be less free-wheeling where the legislature already had a wide berth to rewrite the law. In the event, it did the opposite: faced with new variations on old themes of master and servant, judges acted Blackstonian and clung to precedent, whereas in commercial disputes, Mansfieldian reason was the order of the day. Henry Campbell Black's 1912 treatise on precedent rehearses this program with respect to *Swift*: in master-and-servant disputes federal courts must follow precedents of the states where they occurred; in commercial disputes – including such venerable topics as contracts, negotiable instruments, and personal liability – they were at liberty to exercise their independent judgment.[26]

To show that discontinuity between labor and commerce occurred in state as well as federal law during the period, the examination of precedent turns to the courts of New York, a leading venue for litigation on both subjects. A first window may be opened on the New York decisions concerning industrial accidents. Precedent in that vexed body of law reduces to the operation of three common law rules. The first rule was that an injured employee (or his or her survivor) could maintain a suit against a master for injuries only if he or she could plausibly claim the master was personally at fault. This rule was often formulated in terms of the master's duty under the contract to provide a safe workplace, including adequately skilled workers, and tools and machinery in good working order; the rule's application rested heavily on proof of the master's preexisting knowledge of dangerous conditions. The second rule permitted the injured employee to collect damages only if he or she could not be shown to share fault for the injury, however slightly ("contributory negligence"), in which case the master was not liable. The third rule immunized the master from liability for injury caused an employee through the misconduct or mistake of another person working for the same company ("the fellow servant rule"); the only exception to the fellow servant rule was when the master could be shown to have hired or retained employees he knew were incompetent or otherwise unsuitable.

The provenance of these rules points up an important element in the application of precedent in labor disputes of the period more generally. Each refers to the same 1837 English case, *Priestly v. Fowler*, in which an injured laborer unsuccessfully sued his master for ordering him to ride in

[26] Henry Campbell Black, *Handbook on the Law of Judicial Precedents or the Science of Case Law* (St. Paul, MN), 535, 611, 626, 639.

an overloaded van. Because the laborer did not claim in his original declaration that the master knew the van was overloaded, the barons of the Court of Exchequer found the master had no legal duty from the mere existence of a valid contract between the parties; indeed they opined that only absurd consequences would flow from holding a master responsible for matters of which he was unaware.[27] *Priestly v. Fowler* was a landmark case in the burgeoning law of negligence (or "torts") because prior to 1837 there is no record of any injured worker ever, on any occasion, having sued his master for causing an injury. This vacuum in turn points to the rule before this time, one much older than the nineteenth century, that masters were protected against such suits by the voluntary nature of the labor contract and by the doctrine of assumed risk, expressed in the maxim *volenti non fit injuria* (loosely translated, "there is no legal injury to a person who willingly places him/herself at risk.") This older or "shadow" precedent, of masters' absolute unsuability for injury, itself emanating from an originary, time-out-of-mind, pre-inscribed conception of the master-servant hierarchy, hovers over the proceedings of labor litigation in the so-called Lochner era. Following logically from the character of the master-servant relation in itself, no citations were necessary for its authority. Another example in master and servant law of such a shadow precedent is the master's authority to discipline the worker. From 1835 on, there are American decisions to the effect that the master may not discipline the worker by physical punishment.[28] But the ground-level rule that the master might impose discipline in other ways goes without saying; it is one of the master's rights, its origins likewise lost in time, intrinsic to workplace governance.

Seemingly simple, the law of industrial accidents did not operate without wrinkles. Consider the fellow servant rule: from the 1870s on, the New York courts formulated a variation of the rule under which the master was liable for employees' injuries caused by other employees, of whatever rank, if the latter were performing tasks required of the master as his own legal duty. Sometimes known as the "vice-principal doctrine" and pertaining to corporations as well as to privately owned companies, this was an important change during an era of increasingly large and impersonal enterprise. On the other hand, perhaps for these same reasons, judges were hesitant to apply it. In *Cregan v. Marston* (1891) for instance, the New York Court of Appeals, the state's highest court, reversed a holding by a lower ("supreme") court that the master was liable for the death of a worker who was killed when a frayed rope caused a bucket of coal to fall and crush him. Under common law, the master had a duty to provide safe materials, and the defendant employer had deputized an engineer to make sure all ropes were in sound

[27] 150 E.R. 1030.

[28] *Matthews v. Terry*, 10 Conn. 455 (1835).

condition. The court, however, held that the vice-principal rule did not apply to everyday defects that could be observed and repaired by ordinary workmen using materials on hand.[29] In *Neagle v. Syracuse, Binghamton, and New York Railroad* (1906), the court held that the vice-principal rule did not avail a fireman killed when his locomotive went off the track as it pushed a snowplow over impacted patches of ice. The master had hired a crew to remove the ice, but the regular track-walker in the normal performance of his duties should have observed where the track remained unsafe; the injury was caused through a "detail of the work," attributable to the negligence of a fellow servant and not the master.[30]

The law of industrial accidents troubled everyone concerned. Its hair-splitting seemed arbitrary. Because so much depended on who knew exactly what about which unsafe condition, perjury was a constant temptation to both sides. As exhausting as they were demoralizing, workers' injuries were reported to consume, in the first decade of the twentieth century, roughly one-quarter of the New York judiciary's workload. In 1910, by which time judges as well as legislators publicly appealed for reform, New York became the first state to pass a workers' compensation statute requiring the participation of employers. Indeed, the Court of Appeals, when it struck down that law as unconstitutional, assured the public of its "desire to present no purely technical or hypercritical obstacles to any plan for the beneficent reformation of a branch of our jurisprudence in which . . . reform is a consummation devoutly to be wished." Yet when all was said and done, these judges could not bring themselves to turn their back on precedent, particularly one precedent that they said had always been "the law of the land": that no man without fault was liable to injuries sustained by another.[31] Not until 1918, after the New York constitution was amended to provide that the costs of industrial accidents would henceforth be borne not by individuals but by the public, in the price they paid for products and services, did the same court finally uphold a compulsory workers' compensation scheme.

A second group of disputes in which precedent figures prominently during the period concerned collective actions – union strikes, picketing, and boycotts. As in other states, judges in New York rested their collective action decisions variously on holdings of English courts, the U.S. Supreme Court, and other state courts. Unlike workers' injury cases, cases on collective action can be tracked back in court records for many centuries based on the ancient action against enticement; that is, the wrong of inducing a master's employee to abandon his employment, no matter the reason.

[29] 126 N.Y. 568.

[30] 185 N.Y. 270.

[31] *Ives v. South Buffalo Ry. Co.* 201 N.Y. 271 (1911).

The enticement action was grounded in the same paradigmatic order of the workplace already discussed, now highlighting the master's right to exercise his authority free of interference by outsiders. In New York court decisions between 1870 and 1920, enticement sometimes appears in its own name; more often it travels under more up-to-date aliases like interference with the master's rights to use of his property as he might see fit, depriving employers of their freedom to run their businesses, and preventing workers from obtaining or continuing work. By this time in history, American workers were free to quit work, even in a group, as long as they did not do so at the inducement of anyone else.

Before 1893, New York labor decisions relied heavily on collective action precedents from other states. That year, after a first state supreme court refused to prevent striking cigar makers from using methods ordinarily proscribed (picketing, unfair lists, a strike fund) on the grounds that the New York judiciary had never itself, independently, endorsed the rule against enticement, a second supreme court, in *Curran v. Galen*, rose to the occasion. *Curran v. Galen* (1893) upheld a charge of conspiracy against local brewery workers who had obtained the plaintiff's dismissal for refusing to join their union, based exclusively on New York law. By this time, there were two applicable New York statutes, one permitting workers to "cooperate" for the purpose of securing or maintaining wages and another making it a crime to prevent the exercise of any lawful calling by "force, threats, intimidation" or interfering with the use of property. *Curran v. Galen* acknowledged that workers in New York had a "perfect right" to unite with others to quit work, but not "to insist that others should do so."[32] With this case as precedent, state judges restrained and punished collective actions without inhibition, whenever actual force, threats, and intimidations were involved and also in situations that were entirely peaceful but might well pose a "menace to any timid person" working or shopping at a targeted company.[33]

The resilience of precedent in labor disputes and its close relation, the reluctance of judges to innovate, can be seen finally in a widely heralded pro-union New York decision that failed to blaze a new path. Following state constitutional reform and a progressive turn in judicial appointments, the Court of Appeals in 1902 decided *National Protective Association of Steam Fitters v. Cumming*, which said striking workmen had "an absolute right to threaten to do that which they had a right to do." *National Protective Association* was a secondary boycott decision that held it was legal for the union to tell three construction companies that they would face a general

[32] 22 N.Y.S. 826. The earlier decision was *Rogers v. Evarts*, 17 N.Y.S. 264 (1891).
[33] *Searle Manufacturing Co. v. Terry*, 106 N.Y. S. 438 (1905).

strike unless employees belonging to a different labor organization were discharged. In its opinion, the court described English labor law as "hostile to the statute law of this country {and} to the spirit of our constitution." It announced no new rule, however, hinging its position instead on the reasoning that workers had no remedy for injuries caused by incompetent members of other unions. The secondary boycott, involving persons outside the immediate relation of the parties, all but invited the judges to depart from the enclosed world of the enticement action and take notice of wider community interests. But the opinion in *National Protection Association* kept matters enclosed; the concurrence took pains to say that *Curran v. Galen* was not overruled.[34] The result was that *Curran v. Galen* was relied on by New York courts as before, only now with *National Protective Association* as additional authority.[35]

Bossert v. Dhuy (1917) provided another opportunity. In *Bossert*, the Court of Appeals refused to restrain permanently the carpenters' union from notifying builders, architects, and contractors who were the plaintiff's customers that if they purchased supplies from his non-union mill they could expect labor troubles of their own. The opinion rested on *National Protective Association* and cited dicta in a U.S. Supreme Court decision that refused to restrain the same union in similar circumstances on grounds that a private plaintiff could not bring an injunction action under the Sherman Antitrust Act.[36] *Bossert*, likewise, provided no new rule. Less than two years later, New York appellate judges returned to *Curran v. Galen* as precedent in *Auburn Draying Co v. Wardell* (1919), which enjoined the Teamsters union from going further than the carpenters in *Bossert* by placing the plaintiff on an "unfair list" distributed throughout the working community. The Court noted the "aggressiveness" of such a move, summarized earlier cases, including *Bossert*, and explained, "What we have written declares sufficiently the clear and inescapable distinction between the facts and legal principles involved in this case."[37]

A different pattern characterizes the role of precedent in New York courts' commercial decisions. As a first illustration, consider the cases on ultra vires, a doctrine implementing the idea that corporations acted illegally if, in making contracts, they strayed outside the boundaries established by

[34] 170 N.Y. 315, 329, 332, 334.

[35] *Schwarcz v. International Ladies' Garment Workers' Union*, 124 N.Y.S. 968 (1910); *Auburn Draying v. Wardell*, 165 N.Y.S. 469 (1917); *S.C. Posner Co. v. Jackson*, 223 N.Y. 325 (1918).

[36] 221 N.Y. 342, at 359–60. The U.S. Supreme Court opinion referred to is *Paine Lumber v. Neal*, 244 U.S. 459 (1917).

[37] 227 N.Y. 1, 12.

their charters or enabling statutes. The doctrine had been announced in the United States for the first time by *New York v. Utica Insurance Co*, which was decided by the state supreme court in 1818. There, a corporation chartered to provide insurance was indicted for issuing bank notes, in violation of a state statute permitting banking operations only to those "persons" granted charters for that specific purpose. The court's opinion was in keeping with the theory then prevalent that corporations were "fictions," artificial creations of the legislature, incapable of committing a legal wrong. However, "so far as they travel out of their grant, they act as a company of private persons and become a mere association doing business without any express authority by law."[38]

By the time of the Civil War, the ultra vires doctrine had been curtailed significantly. In 1860, for example, the New York Court of Appeals turned away the argument that two consolidated railroad corporations could not be guilty of causing an injury to a passenger because they had no right under their charters to consolidate. The opinion ventured as to how the fictional perfection of business corporations was a notion that would convert those beings into "malicious monsters," in contact with "almost every member of the community," few of whom could be expected to know anything about their charters: "in laying down rules of law which are to govern such relations, we should avoid a system of destructive technicalities."[39]

Between 1870 and 1920, New York judges took steady strides away from ultra vires and from the fictional theory of the corporation with which it was paired. In *Whitney Arms Co. v. Barlow* (1875), they held that plaintiffs who had received benefits under a contract could not later plead ultra vires to avoid fulfilling their side of the bargain. From here on, corporations in the state could sue for perfomance on unfulfilled contracts ("executory contracts") even when they were ultra vires. In *Whitney Arms*, concerning the sale of railroad locks, the court permitted collection of what was owed, over the defendant corporation's claim that the seller company was chartered to manufacture munitions and had no lawful business in locks.[40] In 1891, this waiver was extended to promissory notes issued for an ultra vires purchase of stock in another company and, in 1896, to an ultra vires lease of property. The explanations given for these decisions were eminently practical: the safety of business transactions required that contracts be enforced, any other policy would encourage fraud, and the contract had not harmed the public at large. By the end of the period under study here, the sole vitality left

[38] 15 Johns. 358, 381.

[39] *Bissell v. The Michigan Southern and Northern Indiana Railroad Companies*, 22 N.Y. 258, 264, 278.

[40] 63 N.Y. 62.

in the earlier doctrine consisted in allowing stockholders and government (but only them) to intervene when an ultra vires contract had been executed on both sides and, when neither party had performed, in refusing judicial enforcement altogether. By 1916 New York had adopted the position that the corporation was "real" enough to be guilty of moral offenses – specifically slander – and, by 1920 in a libel case, to be punished for malice by punitive damages.[41]

Lest this progression seem a lingering if imperfect adherence to an old doctrine, rather than the steady abrogation of inconvenient law, it should be noted that ultra vires was itself a narrowing of the rule prevalent during earlier centuries, when corporations of all types were chartered by the Crown and were answerable only to the Crown's own actions. In England, the first loosening of that doctrine is attributed to an eighteenth-century decision in which a man was imprisoned for altering a bank note, despite evidence that the original was invalid, having been signed by an officer of the issuing company who lacked authority to affix his name. Later in the century the unraveling was furthered by Lord Mansfield, who devised a special action of assumpsit to circumvent obstacles that ultra vires presented to the efficient administration of wills. To be sure, there is a legal consistency in the rule of precedent followed in the commercial decisions: adjustment to the practices of business. If it is the case that "shadow" precedents returned master and servant litigation to the setting of an earlier age, the precedents in commercial litigation seem to goad the parties into a mode of "flash-forward."

This last feature is especially marked in the settlement of disputes that occurred inside individual corporations. A case in point is *Colby v. Equitable Trust* (1908), in which a stockholder sued to enjoin a merger that was accomplished through the transfer of the entire assets of the company by the board of directors on a majority vote of the stockholders. Some years prior to the suit, but after the plaintiff purchased his stock, the New York legislature became one of the first to allow directors such latitude. Under the older rule, directors were authorized by their charters or enabling statutes to conduct routine business with majority assent; however, non-routine matters like mergers required unanimous stockholder approval to be legal. This was also the rule at common law, reaffirmed several times since the Civil War. That said, there had been considerable slippage in the definition of routine, as courts upheld management's authority, over minority stockholder dissent, to issue preferred stock, to declare a dividend to pay for a merger, and to purchase property from one of the board's own directors.

[41] *Kharas v. Collier*, 171 A.D. 388 (1916); *Corrigan v. Bobbs-Merrill*, 228 N.Y. 58 (1920).

The *Colby* ruling relied on an earlier decision holding that the legislature had authority to change the stockholder unanimity rule, and it quoted a warning in another opinion that if judges did not restrain themselves "upon mere opinion" from interfering with the will of majority stockholders they would soon be called on "to balance probabilities of profitable results . . . [which was] no business for any court to follow." Considering that directors of the two companies were now intermingled, the court determined to do just that. Calculating the worth, in rounded dollars, of the merger to stockholders, the judge determined that the plaintiff would be disadvantaged by the proposal, but weighing in the prospects of likely future earnings the court could see great benefits down the line. "On balance" it was not "so clear" that the agreement was "so unfair" as to justify intervention. The plaintiff had pointed to precedents supporting the injunction; the court answered in another flash-forward. Two-thirds of the stockholders of the new entity must assent to the merger; since it was only tentative, many of the precedents cited did not apply.[42]

The proleptic style of the commerce opinions was not confined to issues of unanimity. For instance, as early as 1832, New York courts permitted individual stockholders to file "derivative" actions against corporate officers and agents for fraud or mismanagement, without waiting for management to sue in the company's name or to announce they declined to sue, which was the older rule. In 1880, this recourse was effectively countermanded by the Court of Appeals' announcement, in *Hun v. Cary*, of the "business judgment" rule. The business judgment rule shielded directors from liability even if they were proven to have damaged the company or its stockholders or otherwise violated the law, as long as their actions could not be shown to have been intentionally negligent or fraudulent or lacking in ordinary knowledge or prudence. In eighteenth-century English law, a similar rule was applied to charitable corporations. In the United States, it had been extended to those companies whose detailed charters already subjected them to suits for ultra vires. *Hun* concerned the liability of bank trustees, doing business under general legislation, and the effect of the decision was to extend the rule to include business corporations of all kinds. From here on, the standard of legality would become whether a prudent and diligent man might have taken the same action under similar circumstances.

During litigation, but also before their actions landed them in court, parties in the labor cases could rely with some degree of certainty on existing law, if only law from the distant past. Under the business judgment rule, parties in the commercial cases could only imagine what judges and juries might consider reasonable or prudent behavior at some indeterminate

[42] 124 A.D. 262, 267–72.

viewpoint in the future. For stockholders, this was an especially high hurdle, even when they were successful in bringing directors to trial. By its nature, the business judgment rule raised the question of the defendant's intent, something difficult to prove, and in any case it was an inquiry discouraged by flash-forward logic's inhibition of second guessing. In labor cases, under the enticement precedents, intent was a forbidden inquiry. That said, the violence and other harm assumed to flow from workers' collective actions under the shadow precedent of ancient work relations meant that the benefits of legal certainty were equally lopsided in their distribution.

III. RIGHTS

Rights – enforceable claims that one person may legally make on the actions or person of another, including officers of the law – are already implicated in these remarks. The question of which officer or agency has jurisdiction over a particular dispute and whether or not legal precedent is followed in a court's holdings will have a direct bearing on the remedy, which in turn expresses substantive rights of the parties and of similarly situated persons in the future. Remedy aside, the decision on jurisdiction and the rulings the judge makes as the trial proceeds express substantive rights of the judge and due process rights of the parties. A citizen's right under the U.S. Constitution to be heard in one jurisdiction ("forum") rather than another was addressed by the Supreme Court in 1878 and largely shelved until well into the twentieth century; the right to have one's case decided according to precedent has never been argued before the Court.[43] Especially in the decades following the passage of the Fourteenth Amendment, debate over rights was as energetic as it was inevitable. The litigation swirling around changing industrial activity was often, in the minds of all concerned, as importantly about rights as about facts, as much about the rights of businessmen and unions in the future as of the parties in court. What is not debatable on this record is that the rights of parties in commercial disputes were of a different character from the character of rights of parties in labor disputes.

Colby v. Equitable Trust, already discussed, may stand for the commercial cases as a group. From the viewpoint of rights, what is significant is less the outcome than the self-described process of balancing by which the court reaches its result. The plaintiff, other minority stockholders, majority stockholders, directors, the legislature – all are seen to have rights, but rights as it were in abstract rather than arising from the situation in the case at bar. The rule of unanimity offers no privileged position. The fact that the court

[43] *Pennoyer v. Neff*, 95 U.S. 714.

acknowledges that the law was unfair to the plaintiff does not strengthen the case for his protection; the judge notices how few shares he owns and worries about the long-term consequences of allowing a small minority stockholder to thwart the majority's will. It is unclear what right of the plaintiff is being balanced, since placing majority stockholders' rights on the scale by definition negates the principle of unanimity, as well as the purposes within the corporation to which it was applied.

Judges in New York in these years sometimes spoke of an "adjustment of rights" in deciding commercial cases. Never did they use that phrase with reference to their labor decisions and with good reason. Compare *Colby v. Equitable Trust* with *Auburn Draying v. Wardell*, also already discussed. Like *Colby*, *Auburn Draying* concerned an injunction, sought by a trucking company, ordering a local branch of the Teamsters union to refrain from including the company's name on a publicly circulated "unfair list" as a means of forcing it to employ only union labor. Having gone on for some seventeen months without violence or threats of violence, this tactic had been successful in causing the company's customers to quit shipping goods on its trucks. The court's opinion took notice of rights possessed by everyone involved: the company and other employers, employees both organized and unorganized, the plaintiff's customers, and the public at large. It deemed "beyond question" the rights of the Teamsters to associate, to recruit members, and, through the "solidified power" of association, to secure better wages and working conditions. The only qualification was that they not attempt to bring about the plaintiff's general "exclusion and isolation" or, by controlling the acts of third parties who enjoyed "natural freedom and civil rights" of their own, cause the "negation and destruction" of employers' right of property.

By granting the injunction, *Auburn Draying* places the plaintiff employer in precisely the preemptive position it denied the plaintiff stockholder in *Colby*. This position was inherent in the static, hierarchical, one-on-one relations between master and servant – the opinion calls them "reciprocal rights" – and in particular in the master's right against enticement. Solicitude for the plaintiff's "isolation" is in ironic contrast to the legal impenetrability of the workplace that runs through the labor cases of the period as a constant theme. In this regard, the emblematic decision is *Hitchman Coal & Coke v. Mitchell* (1916), in which the U.S. Supreme Court enjoined a nationally directed non-violent campaign to organize miners in West Virginia. The opinion narrates the activities of owners, supervisors, employees, local organizers, and national union leaders, which are not balanced as to their rights but arrayed in formations of "insiders" and "outsiders." The latter come from other states, keep secret lists, and speak in foreign tongues in opposition to the "universally recognized right of action for persuading an employee to leave his employer."[44] Two years before, in 1914, Congress had passed the Clayton Act. Section 20, which prohibited federal injunctions in "any case between an employer and employees [in] . . . dispute over terms or conditions of employment" and declared that neither persuading a worker to strike nor traveling to a place where workers were located for the purpose of conducting organizing activity violated any law of the United States. *Hitchman Coal and Coke* does not acknowledge the Clayton Act's existence.

The increasing prominence of the federal labor injunction between 1870 and 1920 registers the broader movement of lawmaking and law enforcement in industrial affairs to the national government. It also signals a movement toward greater government cohesion at all levels. An inheritance from England, authority under the U.S. Constitution and state constitutions as well was organized by the common law rights of individual officers – legislators, judges, commissioners, and so on – who, like all other rights holders, were liable for their actions in court. At this time, however, the system was undergoing modification, in large part in response to the greater reliance on collective organization in industry. Legally, the tendency was manifest in a multitude of ways, including greater use of the injunction, which could only be issued by an equity judge – in the United States, he was the same judge, but presiding, that is to say, exercising his rights "in equity" – in the absence of a jury and often outside the presence of the defendant, and free of a number of common law restrictions on his behavior. The authority of other officers advanced apace. *In Re Debs* (1895) upheld the right of the U.S. Attorney General to seek an injunction against strikers in the great railroad strike against the Pullman Palace Car Company, based on the national administration's "plenary authority," despite all precedent requiring a property interest. Similarly, in the area of criminal prosecution of business corporations, the New York Court of Appeals in *People v. Ballard* (1892) upheld the right of the state's Attorney General to bring an action for corporate malfeasance in the name of the state without, as precedent required, a stockholder as co-plaintiff. Judges themselves for the most part became immune from suit, even when they acted in excess of their jurisdiction or from malicious motives. U.S. Supreme Court Justice Joseph Bradley provided a suitable corporate rationale: any other decision would endorse "the weakness of judicial authority in a degrading responsibility."[45]

The farthest shore of this development was the U.S. Supreme Court's discovery of "sovereign immunity," lodged in the Eleventh Amendment and adhering to all officeholders as a barrier against suits in federal court. Prior

[44] 245 U.S. 229, at 252.

[45] *Bradley v. Fisher*, 80 U.S. 335, 347 (1871). The only requirement was that the subject matter be such that the judge might have had jurisdiction in a proper case.

to this time, government officers were liable in their own names to citizens' suits for damages and injunctions and to remedy injuries they caused to statutory, common-law, or constitutional rights; the last category became important after the passage of the Civil War constitutional amendments, particularly the Fourteenth Amendment. The new doctrine appeared in a series of actions initiated by bondholders seeking to collect on securities that had been repudiated in various ways by their issuing states. Although the nominal defendants were tax collectors and other state revenue officers, the Court said the suits were undertaken with the intention of coercing the state, the only party able to grant effective relief, and for that reason were unconstitutional. Suits on this general model pepper the American legal record from *Marbury v. Madison* (1803) onward; suits against state officers in federal court are usually tracked to *Osborne v. National Bank* (1824). Under the doctrine of sovereign immunity, they became illegal. The Court's initial decisions having protected state officers against suits by citizens from other states, which roughly corresponded to the purposes of the Eleventh Amendment as written, "sovereign immunity" was extended in 1890 to ward off suits by citizens of their home states as well, although the rule was riddled with exceptions.

Again, as instructive as these developments are for the changing distribution of rights, they are at least as interesting for what they indicate about the changing character of rights as such, becoming more fluid and receptive to innovation. In this perspective, the rights of officers bear a strong resemblance to the rights of parties in commercial disputes: changes in the rights of officers often occurred in commercial settings. Characteristically, one of the most important of the Supreme Court's decisions on sovereign immunity of this period, *Ex Parte Young* (1908), does not uphold the principle but abrogates it. *Young* was a habeas corpus suit brought by the Attorney General of Minnesota (Edward Young), who was held in custody for disobeying a federal court order that he not pursue enforcement of a state law providing for maximum railroad rates against the Northern Pacific Railroad. The order was issued when two of the railroad's stockholders asked that the railroad be forbidden to continue charging customers the prescribed rates in compliance with the law. The statute had imposed extremely high fines for every ticket sold in violation of the prescribed schedule. After a hearing, the federal judge deemed the law confiscatory and the law unconstitutional and issued his injunction. Young was arrested for contempt when he sought a writ of mandamus from the state court to enforce the act.

Since the circumstances of the case did not fall under any of the exceptions to the doctrine of sovereign immunity, Young claimed the district court's order was unconstitutional on that ground. The Court could also have overturned the lower court's order because the stockholders had not shown the common law tort necessary under existing law to bring such a suit. Nevertheless, it upheld the decision of the lower court and denied Young release, based on the theory that when a state officer attempts to enforce an unconstitutional statute he is stripped of his official status and cannot carry the immunity of the state. The decision had the effect of reinstating suits against officers for injunctive relief; it would have a long life, into the twentieth century's Rights Revolution. Justice Peckham's opinion for the majority has a familiar ring, starting with the disclaimer that the decision "is not free from doubt." Explaining why the Court will take jurisdiction, rather than wait and allow state judges to examine the constitutionality of the statute in the course of criminal proceedings, Peckham imagines the impacts of his choice on the possible actions and capacities of various participants in the dispute, now and in the near future: on Young himself, stockholders of the "eleven thousand million" dollar corporation, the district court judge, the state court judge, the jury hearing the criminal charges against Young in state court, and the officer in charge of Young's custody. After this consideration, Peckham comes, on balance, to his decision.[46]

In terms of creativity, the doctrine of "substantive due process" rivals the doctrine of "sovereign immunity," but on the side of citizens, not government. Intended as the legal antidote to a rapidly expanding national police power, substantive due process had its origins in the Due Process Clause of the Fourteenth Amendment. It designated a set of personal rights, related to property or to "liberty of contract," which could not be impaired by legislation without violating the meaning and spirit of justice under free government. The idea was not unheard of in prior American law; *Dred Scott* (1857), for example, protected slave owners' "vested right" of property in slaves, all other rights claimants notwithstanding. Substantive due process first appeared in its own name in the dissenting opinions in *The Slaughterhouse Cases* in 1873, in which a majority of the U.S. Supreme Court upheld a Louisiana monopoly on butchering livestock as a valid exercise of the police power of the state. The doctrine reached its apotheosis in *Lochner v. New York* (1905), striking down a statute providing maximum hours for bakery workers as an unconstitutional infringement on "liberty of contract."[47]

Cases like *Lochner* illustrate the important function that substantive due process performed in the context of labor. At a time when master-servant relations were legally a "domestic relation" under the sole jurisdiction of the

[46] 209 U.S. 123, 142–68.

[47] 83 U.S. 36; 198 U.S. 45.

states, and collective actions were an affair of state law even when numerous "outsiders" were involved, substantive due process under the Fourteenth Amendment added the constitutional element necessary for federal jurisdiction. Review in federal court opened the possibility of defeating a statute that survived judicial review in its home state, as the maximum-hours statute in *Lochner* had, in New York. Also, a decision in the U.S. Supreme Court extended to all forty-eight states. When, for example, the Court, on grounds of substantive due process, struck down Kansas's law against the yellow dog contract in *Coppage v. Kansas* (1915), it swept away fourteen other similar state statutes at the same time. On the other hand, in statutory review and run-of-the-mill collective action cases in state court, and on issues other than jurisdiction in federal court, substantive due process was redundant. Whether the right was called "liberty of contract" or something else, the decision almost always came down in the end to the master's rights to hire and fire without interference; the limited judicial imagination evident in these cases was devoted to that maneuver.

Consider the example of *Truax v. Raich* (1915), an unusual case that juxtaposes the rights of an employee under substantive due process and the rights of a government officer under sovereign immunity. In *Truax*, the Court heard an action to restrain the Attorney General of Arizona from enforcing a statute that required employers with more than five employees at any one time to engage at least 80 percent of them from among qualified electors or native-born citizens. The Court came easily to the conclusion that the law unconstitutionally denied foreign-born persons equal protection under the Fourteenth Amendment and that, based on *Young*, the suit was not against the state in violation of the Eleventh Amendment. The obstacle to securing the injunction, however, was the plaintiff, a foreign-born cook in a restaurant, who was threatened with dismissal if his employer was forced to obey the law. As a legal immigrant, the cook's right to pursue his calling was protected by the Fourteenth Amendment, but as an at-will employee he could be dismissed at any time and could not be reinstated by the Court over the rights of the employer; therefore his dismissal did not provide the property interest required for equity jurisdiction. Nor could a servant legally plead the cause of a master. That said, the Court issued the injunction. In an opinion less circumspect but no less ingenious than *Young*, it concluded, "The employee had a manifest interest in the freedom of the employer to exercise his judgment without illegal interference or compulsion and, by the weight of authority, the unjustified interference by third persons."[48] Through a novel interpretation of a vicarious right in the

[48] 239 U.S. 33, 38.

plaintiff, the case proceeded and the statute went down; the time-honored principle of enticement survived, as undiluted by competing principles as before. *Truax v. Raich* would shortly appear as authority for *Hitchman Coal & Coke v. Mitchell.*

In this light, it is interesting to ask to what extent the right to substantive due process in the context of the commerce cases successfully mimicked the action of enticement, attempting to afford businessmen the same unapproachable high ground that the right against enticement afforded employers. The evidence offered earlier, on jurisdiction, indicates the rarity with which the U.S. Supreme Court struck down federal statutes regulating commerce, based on substantive due process or any other ground. But federal statutes are not the only test; the reputation of substantive due process as a legal obstacle to the development of the American welfare state is based largely on successful rollbacks of public regulation after agencies were set in place. Once again, viewing the commerce cases separately from the labor cases adds considerable nuance to this view. Here too, this question is best answered within a longer perspective than 1870–1920 and must be paired with the history of the expanding boundaries of the police power, against which the rights of substantive due process were deployed.

The starting point here is the animus toward government grants of monopoly that was a fixture of the common law since the seventeenth century; this animus existed alongside the uncontested government authority to regulate social activities in the interest of public health and safety. This animus made its way into American constitutionalism via the Commerce and Contract Clauses, although like other commercial articles of faith, it was often balanced with public purposes to yield legislation later upheld as constitutional. By the same token, the legal status of monopolies that did not involve government grants but that businessmen formed independently under charters or, later, under general incorporation statutes remained unclear; on this subject, the English cases were oblique and antebellum practices in the American states inconsistent. This question presented itself with great urgency after the Civil War, as business activities increasingly assumed corporate and other joint methods of organization. Many subjects in addition to monopoly power were contested, but they were skirmishes to the side of the major action.

Once formulated under the Fourteenth Amendment, the prospect that substantive due process might shield burgeoning enterprise from the tentacles of the police power held great expectations. That proposition, however, was precisely the one that the U.S. Supreme Court declined to endorse in *Munn v. Illinois* (1877). *Munn* upheld the constitutionality of an Illinois statute that provided a schedule of maximum rates for storing grain.

The statute was passed to block operations of what the Court said was a "virtual monopoly" consisting of a combination of large warehouse companies doing essentially the same thing, but privately, for all grain shipped through Chicago.[49] *Munn* was a momentous holding; next to outright confiscation, setting maximum prices came closest to epitomizing the common law prohibition against taking from A to benefit B. In fact, this ground was never relinquished. Its most famous progeny prior to 1920 was the Court's refusal to permit the pooling of rates in the railroad industry, even with the imprimatur of the ICC; its farthest concession was to the "rule of reason" in decisions enforcing the Sherman Act.

The circumstances that justified the Court's decision in *Munn* are critical for assessing the achievements of substantive due process. If one overlooks that state-controlled rates set by a publicly appointed commission displaced privately controlled rates set by private businessmen, then much that happens afterward seems a retreat from a once-vigorous police power in the face of an increasingly robust doctrine of substantive due process. If one recalls the facts of *Munn*, on the other hand, what followed seems to be a widening movement by federal and state agencies into the zone only recently claimed as business's own by right. Consider the several heralded court-administered blows to public regulation: rates set by commissions were subject to review by the federal courts, both as to facts and law[50]; rate-making was not sanctioned by the judiciary until specifically authorized by legislation[51]; rates that provided no profit whatever or that did not account for investment values were treated as confiscatory[52]; some rates arguably inoffensive to existing rules were disallowed[53]; and state commissions could not order regulated companies to provide below-rate train tickets or services free of charge.[54] These, like most other commercial decisions for two centuries, were accommodations to what businessmen and justices agreed were needs of trade. They pale against the premise that government might rightfully legislate prices.

Munn relied on a phrase of Lord Chief Justice Hale's: business "affected with a publick interest." By this, Hale, writing in the seventeenth century, meant business that imposed a "common charge" on the public, unmediated by competition; he gave as an example ownership of a lone wharf in

[49] 94 U.S. 113.

[50] *Chicago, M. & St. P. Ry. v. Minnesota*, 134 U.S. 418 (1890); *I.C.C. v. Alabama Midland R.R.*, 168 U.S. 144 (1897).

[51] *I.C.C. v. Cincinnati, N.O., and Texas Pacific Ry.*, 167 U.S. 479 (1897).

[52] *Reagan v. Farmers' Loan and Trust Co.*, 154 U.S. 362 (1894).

[53] *Smyth v. Ames*, 169 U.S. 466 (1898).

[54] *Louisville and Nashville Railroad Company v. Central Stock Yards Co.*, 212 U.S. 132 (1909); *Missouri Pacific Railroad Co. v. Nebraska*, 217 U.S. 196 (1910).

a busy port or the only wharf licensed by the queen to collect customs. "Affected with a public interest" became one of the proverbial categories of the "classical" style of Lochner-era judges, discarded by a later generation of jurists as useless.[55] But just because a category is not endlessly expansive does not on that account make it useless. For instance, in *Brass v. North Dakota* (1894), with no monopoly on the horizon, virtual or otherwise, the Court rebuffed a substantive due process claim of a rural warehouse owner who was penalized for refusing to store grain grown on an adjoining farm at legislatively set rates. The Court proceeded by analogy: if it was valid in *Munn* for a state legislature to control the price of storing grain in one region, "it follows that such power may be exerted over the same business when carried on in smaller cities and in other circumstances . . . "[56]

This reasoning was not exceptional; it signifies a permanent advance in the line of government authority under the police power to regulate prices in a wide swath of railroads, stockyards, fire insurance, and other private non-monopoly enterprises.[57] The opinion in *Brass* shows the familiar earmarks of decisions on commerce in the Lochner era and of the decisions on commerce in the century before: flexibility, adaptability, deference to legislation, and reasoning by analogy; the idea that the maximum rates may be imposed "in other circumstances"; and hints of cases that can be expected to arise beyond the one presently in court. To be sure, *Brass* was a 5–4 decision: a dissenting justice was Justice Field, one of the first champions of substantive due process. All American legal doctrine must run the gauntlet of shifting majorities on the Supreme Court. Given the prevailing approach, the rigors and absolutes of substantive due process were discordant. In the critical area of prices, the substantive due process decisions left the rights of business diminished.

The administration of substantive due process rights in the labor cases caused no comparable erosion of baselines. Defeats for organized labor during the period were profound. Conflicts were clamorous and widely publicized. Injunction orders frequently ended in the jailing of strike leaders for contempt and the destruction of union treasuries through heavy fines. All of this shored up the legal status quo rather than altering it. There were isolated legislative gains under the police power: state statutes on maximum working hours for miners and women, federal statutes on safety brakes, maximum hours for railroad employees, and payment of wages in money rather than scrip. These were not extended by analogy to "other

[55] *Nebbia v. New York*, 291 U.S. 502 (1934).

[56] 153 U.S. 391, 403.

[57] In addition to cases already discussed, see *German Alliance Insurance v. Kansas*, 233 U.S. 389 (1914).

circumstances." By and large, the law that regulated rights between the great body of American employers and American employees stood exactly where it had been in 1870.

IV. CONCLUDING REMARKS

Any conclusions rest on the central finding, which is that between 1870 and 1920 there were two laws of American industrial organization, each administered with its own principles and rules. The two coexisted in separate but parallel time frames. The law regulating labor extended as far back in Anglo-American history as there are case records; the law regulating commerce was a creature of the seventeenth and eighteenth centuries. Each bore the imprint of its origins. Much of what has been written about the rigidity and obstructionism of American law during the era and about its remoteness from a changing society is halfway correct. The opposite description, that the law of the period was highly adaptive, respectful of Congress, and mindful of divergent interests, is also halfway correct.

Enough has been said by now about the specifics of both laws to permit a few observations about them together. The first concerns the legal stability of these years. During the half-century examined, and presumably also during the sixteen years remaining before the "switch in time" on the New Deal Court in 1936, the judiciary at both the national and state levels administered a dual system of justice that in retrospect can be seen as profoundly contradictory, in letter and, perhaps most importantly, in spirit, with little noticeable slippage, despite appeals for relief from the relevant constituencies in society. Businessmen and their allies in the legal community sought refuge from the accommodative instincts of the courts in the doctrine of substantive due process; organized labor and its allies in the legal community asked to be treated with the same flexible attitude and according to the same principles as commerce. By itself, these strategies attest to the strength of legal traditions and rules against outside pressures. It is also striking that the head-on conflict between Congress and the Supreme Court did not occur earlier than it did. A conflict of this kind ushered in the period, in 1868–99. Even considering that the Court did not strike down Congress's labor legislation until after the turn of the century, there was still a long wait until 1936, and through an especially turbulent time.

The causes of constitutional calm during these years are no doubt bound up closely with party politics and with the onset of World War I. Still, it is interesting to speculate how the Court's divided jurisprudence may have been an element in the mix. It is easy to imagine that the steady assault by the law of master and servant on organizations claiming to represent a significant segment of American society would have been less politically sustainable without the accommodative posture toward business. More to the point, except for the largely deferential attitude assumed by the Court toward important legislation regulating commerce, including the Sherman Act and the Interstate Commerce Act and others, the cost to the institutional position of the Court of *Adair*, for instance, and *Employers' Liability Cases* might have been far higher.

A second observation concerns the reputation of law during these years for being pro-business. This was both true and untrue. The law was unambiguously favorable to masters over employees, and masters were usually businessmen. But in the case of commerce, accommodation to new business enterprise frequently entailed the disparagement of the rights of other businessmen standing in the way, just as accommodation to new enterprises in the eighteenth century entailed the same thing. That was the deeper meaning of *Standard Oil v. United States* (1911). The "business judgment rule" presumed the abridgment of some businessmen's rights, at least to the degree that stockholders in corporations are businessmen; so, for that matter did the "derivative" suit for stockholders. The law was facilitative to new forms of business organization, but the fluid, balanceable nature of the rights at stake did not promote the consistency of results necessary for easy historical characterization.

Thirdly, the divided nature of American law between 1870 and 1920 has important implications for the historical status of the New Deal Court. Again, notwithstanding the sixteen years intervening, to the extent that prominent legal features associated with the New Deal Court – deference to Congress, for instance, the process of "balancing" rights, and others – are not simply foreshadowed but already fully operational in the commerce decisions of the former period, the relationship is one of unimpeded continuity, not disruption. This continuity changes historical assessments in both historical directions. In the same way that it causes 1870–1920 to appear more modern and less reactionary, it causes the "switch in time" in 1936 to appear less revolutionary and creative. Labor relations were, so to speak, folded into the precepts of a law already in place. The New Deal Court elaborated no novel doctrines to bolster labor's new position. "Representatives of their own choosing," the replacement for "liberty of contract" as the motto of the new order in labor relations, is a phrase taken from the Wagner Act.

Finally, a few observations on connections between the laws of industrial organization during 1870–1920 and the present era are in order. In recent decades, critics on different ends of the political spectrum have detected "New Lochnerisms" in U.S. Supreme Court opinions, rights that are not mentioned in the Constitution but that are imagined by the justices, so to speak, based on other provisions and claimed to be protected against legislative abridgment in a manner resembling rights under substantive due process. This depiction is hurled back and forth along the political spectrum, against rights ranging from privacy and freedom of the Internet to commercial speech and standards of tort reform. The study of 1870–1920 adds perspective on the source and timing of these accusations.

It was suggested above (in Section III, "Rights") that the doctrine of substantive due process was, at bottom, an attempt to provide a permanent ground of resistance against the forward momentum and deference to the legislature in the Court's decisions under the police power, in the same way that the enticement action functioned against legislation in the sphere of labor relations. When the law that regulated labor was abandoned as a separate division of jurisprudence and was, as it were, absorbed into the legal routines and rationales of the law that regulated commerce, it happened through the Court's disavowal of common law generally as a basis of rights under the Constitution. Although it would take some time for this move to play itself out in other areas of society once governed by common law rules, it had the effect of bringing all constitutional rights under the regimen of adaptability and balance that before then had applied only to commerce. For instance, in family relations, it would become increasingly clear over time that the common law privileges of husbands had been removed along with the common law privileges of employers. But if the resulting legal benefits to wives and women, for instance in reproduction rights and family relations generally, were to become permanent, enforceable rights and not just a default position, vulnerable to legislation, something creative, indeed "Lochnerian," was unavoidable.

Understanding that in 1870–1920, and indeed for centuries before, there was more than a single American law leads to an appreciation of the fact that this is no longer so, that the Constitution is now a legally unified instrument, and to that extent it is thoroughly modernized. In this light, many of the devices of modern law, from "strict scrutiny" to "original intent," can be seen as an effort by judges and parties in society to find stable and defensible ground in a setting that resists permanent rules. In 1911, Justice Harlan, dissenting from the Court's decision in *Standard Oil v. U.S.* and in particular from the "rule of reason" by which the case was decided, found himself "compelled" to observe that "there is abroad, in our land, a most harmful tendency to bring about the amending of constitutions and legislative enactments by means alone of judicial construction."[58] Some eight

[58] 221 U.S. 1, 100, 105.

decades later, Justice Scalia could not have said it better. The same criticism has been constant since the eighteenth century; witness Junius's diatribe against Lord Mansfield. Justice Harlan preferred the refuge of statutes; his colleagues, the administration of rights by judges trained and appointed for that purpose. Each side insists the other exercises too much discretion. The search goes on.

17

THE MILITARY IN AMERICAN LEGAL HISTORY

JONATHAN LURIE

The subject of the military in American history has attracted considerable attention, both scholarly and popular. Every major war in our history has been the subject of sustained historical analysis. The American Civil War, for example, continues to generate more scholarship than any other event in American history. When it comes to legal history, however, the military suddenly falls into a deep, dark hole. What explains this inconsistency?

The paucity of interest in the intersection of law and the military is puzzling, given that the military has long been an integral part of American civil society. Successful military commanders (Washington, Jackson, Grant, and Eisenhower) have all been elected and reelected president by impressive majorities. Less distinguished generals have also been elected president (Harrison, Taylor, Hayes, and Garfield). At least two others (McClellan and Hancock) ran but failed to win. Far from an impediment, a successful military career has sometimes been of inestimable political value to one seeking elected office.

Military culture, too, has never been totally absent from American life. To a great extent, especially after our major wars, American life has become suffused with a popular nostalgia for military experience. In the half-century after World War II, with the intriguing exception of the Vietnam War period, nostalgia for military culture reached levels that would have been unimaginable a century before. As a result, American militarism, with its emphasis on preparedness, patriotism, and the supposed "superiority" of military values, has had a sustained impact on American culture. Indeed, if cultural norms are a valid indication, the United States has become in the early twenty-first century the most militarized of any Western society, if not the entire world community; and this in a country that has had no military draft for more than a generation. Some of this popular obsession with things military has expressed itself as interest in military law. Since World War II, for example, several films have dealt with law in a military context: *A*

Few Good Men (1992), *The Court-Martial of Billy Mitchell* (1955), and *The Caine Mutiny* (1954) immediately come to mind. So does a television series that dealt in a highly improbable fashion with the office of the Navy Judge Advocate General, entitled *JAG*.

Yet, popular cultural interest in matters military has not extended to military justice and military legal history in any lasting fashion. Occasions have arisen, as we shall see, during which popular attention has focused on a specific incident, but such attention has been episodic and not frequent in character. Rather, since the nineteenth century military law and military justice have been regarded as arcane matters that involved complicated and alien concepts, policies, and practices. The gulf is reciprocated by military law's practitioners: one can sense in surveying the history of American military justice their determination to keep the process as free as possible from civilian oversight. Why has this characteristic emerged, how can it be explained, and wherein lies its significance?

These questions become more intriguing when attention is called to a variety of important developments within the history of American law that have been well researched by historians – legal formalism, codification, sociological jurisprudence, legal realism, due process, and judicial activism, to mention only a few. With some justification, one could claim that these familiar developments have little relationship to the "separate sphere" of military justice. In fact, as this chapter argues, military justice has indeed felt the effects of these "external" trends in American law, albeit through a process that has been haphazard and irregular. The explanation, both for the separation of military justice from the development of American law and its incompleteness, lies in characteristics of American military justice that originated as long ago as the Revolutionary Era, but have nevertheless continued to affect its practices ever since.

I. THE LEGACY OF THE REVOLUTION

Certain key characteristics of the situation of the military within the American Republic were established by the American Revolution and persisted thereafter. They included, first, a resolute rejection of a standing army – and when that proved impossible to sustain, insistence on retention of only a small military establishment always subordinated to civilian political control; second, supremacy of the concept of the citizen soldier; third, a military that would be separate from the rest of the American polity; and fourth, the evolution of a body of laws governing both the military and military conduct separate from state and federal statutory development. Over time, these characteristics have, ironically, lessened the effectiveness of the most important of these principles: civilian political control.

The Revolutionary generation took a consistent position against standing armies in general, emphasizing instead that military conflict was both an immediate and temporary, rather than permanent phenomenon. Once the war with England had been resolved, the Confederation Congress reluctantly approved a small peacetime standing army of barely 700 men. Fears of a permanent military establishment notwithstanding, the problems of an expanding frontier, the challenge posed by Indians, and issues of foreign policy all mandated a standing army. None other than Thomas Jefferson, the first president known for anti-military and limited government views, approved creation of the U.S. Military Academy at West Point. Jefferson was less concerned with strengthening the military than with reform of the Army and, more broadly, of the political establishment, which he deemed necessary for the survival of his Republican administration. Despite the new military academy and with the significant exception of the Civil War the U.S. Army has remained extremely small. At the end of the eighteenth century, it took up less than 15 percent of the federal budget; one hundred years later (1897), the figure was barely 13 percent.

The Army's limited size and its presence out of sight on the frontier rather than in major urban centers both help explain the lack of significant American interest in either the military or military culture. Further, emphasis on civilian control was evident from the start, as well as the idea that civilian political leadership was not at all incompatible with temporary military involvements. The conception of a military separate from the civilian society from which its members might be drawn was not a legislative innovation but a ratification of what was in fact the case. Over time, however, a military apart from the civilian world, and replete with its own system of military justice – as mandated by Congress in the Articles of War – came to be seen as appropriate and positively desirable. There were, however, drawbacks in the legal field. As federalism and a system of state appellate jurisprudence evolved, military justice also aged – but it did not mature.

Within a generation after the Revolution, regulations governing the American military had been fixed by Congress. The Articles of War, enacted during the conflict, established detailed rules and practices of military justice for the Army. They were to remain in place without major alteration until after World War II. A second enactment, the Act to Govern the Navy, more accurately described as "Rocks and Shoals," endured as long. The two federal statutes explained regulations, forbade certain practices, established penalties, and provided for court-martials. Military trials were in fact among the earliest (and may have been the first) federal judicial proceedings in American legal history.

Until the post–World War II era, military law was not concerned with what might be called due process. From the eighteenth century to the present, there has always existed a tension between the administration of military justice and its relationship to the overall purpose of the military establishment. Acceptance of the premise of "victory" as the single purpose for the military has resulted in the insistence that military justice procedures should never be permitted to impede or delay attainment of that goal. The justification of "military necessity" nestles with real difficulty within the operative norms of military justice. As we shall see, when these have collided, invariably the norms of due process have given way.

The context in which military justice operated differed from its civilian counterpart, introducing further dissonance. A fixed courtroom often had to give way to a ship or a theatre of war, either of which might relocate in a matter of hours. The roles assigned the various participants were established by custom as much as by law. Thus the commanding officer was given the authority to select the members of a court-martial, all of whom were usually subordinate to him in rank. Nor was the commander bound by the verdict. He could instruct the court's members "to reconsider." This might result in a harsher verdict, which in turn the commander could lessen either as a sign of mercy or possible redemption on the part of the accused.

With the possible exception of the Judge Advocate General, trained lawyers rarely participated in court-martials. The Judge Advocate General was charged with somehow protecting the "rights" of the accused even as he prosecuted the same individual. From its earliest years, the military justice system assumed that outside civilian counsel was not necessary. Nor was there any formal appeals process in the sense that it was applied in the civilian world. As Commander in Chief, the president could review the decisions and penalties meted out by court-martials, but the effectiveness of the process was inevitably circumscribed by time limitations. Given all the demands on a president's time as the office evolved and became more politicized, it became impossible to survey the record of a court-martial, especially a lengthy one, in any manner comparable to the process followed by civilian appellate courts.

The authority of the Chief Executive in matters of military justice was in any case somewhat circumscribed. He might not approve the sentence, he might order the record returned "for correction of errors," or he might issue a pardon, but he could not reverse a conviction or expunge the proceedings altogether. It becomes clear, then, why to some mid-nineteenth-century observers the procedures and practices of military justice seemed anomalous. On the one hand there existed a healthy state and federal system of civilian appellate jurisprudence and, on the other, a system of military justice anchored in ritual, tradition, obedience, and a desire for rapid resolution. This system had emerged with minimal Congressional oversight and a growing tradition of minimal civilian involvement in military justice matters.

This anomalous military justice system had evolved not so much from American experience as from English antecedents. The origins of military law go back to the fifth century, but the first mention of it in English legal history appears to have been in 1218–19, when the Rolls of the Justices in Eyre for Yorkshire recorded that one male had "lost his hand in the war by judgment of the marshal of the army for a cow which he stole in a churchyard." The first constitutional enactment, as opposed to various institutional edicts, appears to have been the Mutiny Act of 1689, passed by Parliament shortly after the Glorious Revolution. Based on a famous incident in which a Scots regiment refused to obey orders from the new Protestant monarchs, William and Mary, the Mutiny Act expressed Parliament's determination that "Soldiers who shall Mutiny or Stirr up Sedition, or shall desert Their Majestyes Service be brought to a more exemplary and speedy punishment than the usuall Forms of Law will allow." One can see a direct link between the 1689 statute and the words of F.W. Maitland two hundred years later when he wrote that "a standing army could only be kept together by more stringent rules and more summary procedure than those of the ordinary law and the ordinary courts."

It is easy to understand why, by the time of the American Revolution, it was logical to adopt the British Articles of War. The colonists had retained the English language and the common law, as well as the basic British institutions of "representative government" on the national, state, and county level. After four separate colonial wars against the French, colonial military officials, including George Washington, were familiar with the British military system. When, in 1776 with the Revolutionary War underway, Washington requested a more rigorous military code, John Adams knew where to look. Assisted by Thomas Jefferson, they engrafted the British Articles of War "totidem verbis" onto the American counterpart. The results remained essentially intact for nearly two centuries.

Civil-military dualism provides the context for understanding the tension between military justice and its civilian counterpart. Supposedly separate, on occasion they interacted with some intriguing results. Two examples provide illustration. The first involves somewhat unusual interplay between an obscure federal judge and General Andrew Jackson, later to become a more popular president – if less revered – than George Washington. It featured military action against a civilian. The second offers an early sample of public debate concerning military justice. It concerned severe civilian criticism for conduct of a naval captain while at sea.

The General and the Judge

The climax of the War of 1812 came after the treaty ending hostilities between England and the United States had been signed, but before word of the agreement reached Washington. Prior to the Battle of New Orleans and with strong support from the city fathers, Andrew Jackson had placed the notably cosmopolitan city under martial law. His resulting victory against a much larger force made Jackson a national hero. Although hailed as the city's savior, for two months Jackson declined to lift martial law until he had received official word of the treaty. Many city residents in New Orleans chafed under martial law. One editorial noted, "We do not feel much inclined through gratitude, to sacrifice any of our privileges, and less than any other, that of expressing our opinion of the acts of his administration."[1] Like military justice in general, Jackson's response was rapid, rigorous, and – from his vantage point – free of legal niceties.

Through means that remain uncertain but may well have involved threats and intimidation, Jackson obtained the name of the editorial's author. The critic in question turned out to be one Louis Louailler, who was also a member of the Louisiana Legislature. Arrested by a unit of troops on Jackson's orders for spying and inciting a mutiny, Louailler apparently yelled to a crowd around him that he was being kidnapped. A lawyer offered his services and rushed to the home of Federal Judge Dominick A. Hall, who promptly issued a writ of habeas corpus, returnable in open court the next morning. Just as promptly, Jackson ordered the arrest of Judge Hall for "aiding, abetting and exciting mutiny within my camp." The next day found the unfortunate editorial writer not before Judge Hall, but rather confined in the same barracks with him.

Jackson convened a court martial to try Louailler, who quickly challenged its authority on the grounds that he was neither a member of the army nor of the militia. As to the charge of spying, what spy would go to the trouble of publicizing his views through a newspaper editorial? The court dismissed the charges, whereupon Jackson dismissed the court – something that, under existing military law, he had every right to do – and ordered Louailler confined anew. In fact it was far from clear whether the Articles of War applied to a civilian. What Jackson needed – a military tribunal with authority to try civilians accused of military offenses – had not yet evolved. During the Mexican War and after, the military commission would emerge as the military's quasi-judicial body to undertake such prosecutions. Its most notorious use may well have been the trial of eight

[1] Jonathan Lurie, *Arming Military Justice: The Origins of the U.S. Court of Military Appeals* (Princeton, N.J., 1992)

civilians, including one woman, for the assassination of Abraham Lincoln in 1865.

Himself a former lawyer and judge, Jackson knew better than to try Judge Hall by court-martial. Instead he ordered that Hall be marched out of the city "to prevent you from a repetition of the improper conduct for which you have been arrested and confined."[2] One day later Jackson received official word of the peace treaty. He immediately revoked martial law, freed Louailler, and permitted Hall to return to New Orleans. The judge's response was not long in coming.

Possibly Jackson realized what might be facing him, for in acknowledging one of the multiple plaudits heaped on him in the wake of the war, the general referred indirectly to the recent period of martial law. When fundamental rights were threatened by invasion, certain privileges might "be required to be infringed for their security. At such a crisis, we have only to determine whether we will suspend for a time, the exercise of the latter, that we may secure the permanent enjoyment of the former."[3] The General had no doubt that "laws must sometimes be silent when necessity speaks." Here, Jackson echoed Thomas Jefferson. The author of the Declaration of Independence had also noted that obedience to written constitutions and statutes was a high duty of citizenship. "But it is not the highest. The laws of necessity, of self preservation, of saving our country when in danger, are of a higher obligation.... To lose our country by a scrupulous adherence to written law, would be to lose the law itself, with life, liberty and property ... thus absurdly sacrificing the ends to the means."[4] Indeed, the contention has resonated throughout subsequent American military legal history. Lincoln reiterated "necessity" during the Civil War, military officials repeated it as they forcibly "relocated" American citizens of Japanese origin during World War II, and commanders in Vietnam used it to explain conduct during the Vietnam War. Necessity reappears in the published statements of U.S. Attorney General John Ashcroft in the aftermath of the World Trade Center Towers attacks in 2001.

In general, the federal courts have responded to "announcements of military interests with supine deference."[5] No such "supine deference," however, could be attributed to Judge Dominick Hall. On March 21, 1815, he

[2] *Correspondence of Andrew Jackson*, ed. John S. Bassett, vol. 2 (Washington, D.C., 1927), 189, 367.

[3] Robert Remini, *Andrew Jackson and the Course of American Empire, 1767–1821* (New York, 1977), 310.

[4] In Arthur M. Schlesinger, Jr., *War and the Constitution: Abraham Lincoln and Franklin D. Roosevelt* (Geffysburg, PA, 1988), 11.

[5] Comment, "Free Speech and the Armed Forces: The Case Against Judicial Deference," *New York University Law Review* 53 (1978), 1123.

issued a show cause order for Jackson to appear before him, to explain why he should not be held in contempt of court. Three days later, surrounded by a crowd of admiring spectators, the victorious general did indeed appear.

The proceedings, which extended over two court sessions, are of interest for several reasons. Never before had a federal judge initiated contempt proceedings involving himself against a famous general of the U.S. Army. Moreover, neither man was inclined to excuse the actions of the other. When Jackson sought to submit a lengthy justification for his actions built on military necessity, Hall refused to hear it. He agreed with the government attorney who attributed Jackson's "arbitrary proceedings" not to "his conviction of their necessity," but rather to the "indulged infirmity of an obstinate and morbidly irascible temperament, and to the unyielding pride of a man naturally impatient of the least show of opposition to his will." Jackson then refused to answer a number of interrogatories, because Hall "would not hear my defense." Hall held Jackson in contempt of court and fined him $1,000 – a sum promptly raised by several of Jackson's supporters.

Further fame and continued controversy awaited Jackson, but this incident rankled in his memory. Late in his life, when he was in financial difficulty and failing health, Congress revisited the episode. Jackson's supporters urged that the fine be repaid. Another former president, Congressman John Quincy Adams, a man whose admiration for Jackson was less than excessive, opposed the proposal, but Congress endorsed it, and granted Jackson $2,732.90 (including interest). The elderly general welcomed reversal of the fine imposed by "the vindictive and corrupt Judge Hall" and found vindication as well as financial remuneration to be a fitting and satisfying conclusion.

In terms of insights into both American military legal history and policy, the results were much less satisfying. The real issue – whether Jackson had been justified in detaining Hall and disobeying the writ – received no definitive resolution. In part, Hall must bear much responsibility for this fact. His refusal to hear Jackson's explanation is hard to justify, all the more as in no way would it have limited Hall's future options in the case. Moreover, his decision to proceed at all in a matter involving himself raised, at the least, a question of judicial impropriety. On the other hand, Hall's action indicated that he had never assumed that Jackson might be somehow immune from a federal writ or that a citizen could be denied due process by a general any more than by another government official. Jackson's decision not to pursue any appeal deprived a federal appellate tribunal of a great opportunity to consider the question. Finally, the entire incident indicated that, in the American experience, civilian control of the military cannot always be separated from the political process, rendering – as always – such control less effective than might otherwise be the case.

The Captain, the Midshipman, and the Somers

Even as the Jackson-Hall matter reached a conclusion, another incident involving military justice came to public attention. Unlike the earlier dispute, which faded from public consciousness between 1816 and 1842, the second incident attracted the attention of one of the most popular nineteenth-century American writers, James Fenimore Cooper. It caused sustained public debate between 1843 and 1844, as well as a call for judicial intervention. The episode did not involve the Army but rather the Navy; the participants included a captain described by one author as a "sanctimonious, humorless, vain, moralistic . . . and above all, vastly inhuman" and a young midshipman, a "lonely, defiant outcast of eighteen," whose father happened to be the Secretary of War.[6]

In December 1842, the U.S. Navy Brig *Somers*, commanded by Captain Alexander Mackenzie, arrived in New York with news that some fifteen days before three young crew members had been executed for a mutiny that had never occurred. Apparently convinced that the three were scheming to take over the ship, Mackenzie had ordered their arrest on a charge of intended mutiny, as contrasted with either attempted or actual wrongdoing. No actual occurrence of a mutinous nature appeared to have taken place, but this had not prevented Mackenzie from convening a court of officers that, under pressure from the Captain, met in secret and recommended that the three be executed.

At no time did the court hear from the accused; they were not permitted to confront any witnesses, nor to "procure testimony on their behalf," nor were they permitted to attend at any time, nor even informed that a trial was in progress. Mackenzie acknowledged that he had pushed for Spencer's execution because he was sure that Spencer's father would make such a step impossible, once the *Somers* had returned to the United States. After both a court of inquiry as well as a court-martial, the Navy refused to find Mackenzie guilty of any wrongdoing. Those who supported his conduct emphasized that the military justice system had provided the captain of a small ship at sea with a swift and effective method of discipline.

Several interested observers, including Supreme Court Justice Joseph Story, took the position that Mackenzie had been justified in what he did, based on "the circumstances which created a reasonable ground of fear for his life," as well as for the security of his ship. This argument, of course, was not very different from Andrew Jackson's claims of necessity. Others, especially James Fenimore Cooper, were very critical of the captain's written

[6] See Frederic F. Van De Water, "Panic Rides the High Seas," *American Heritage* 12 (1961), 22–23.

apologia concerning his conduct. Cooper described Mackenzie's report as a "medley of folly, conceit, illegality, feebleness and fanaticism." The captain, he fumed, reasons that "if there be a doubt of [the prisoner's innocence,] hang him."[7]

Cooper believed that the conduct of both Mackenzie and the Navy exposed a serious flaw in the American legal system as it had evolved by the mid-nineteenth century. An officer had taken the lives of three of his subordinates "without a trial . . . without a hearing – without any overt act of mutiny, violence, or resistance even in the face of death." If "the name of an American citizen cannot be a warranty that life will not be taken without the accusation, hearing and condemnation, required by the law, of what are our boasted rights?" Here, Cooper confronted – even if he could not contextualize – the difference between military law and its civilian counterpart and found it offensive and unacceptable. How could American citizens be executed without a hearing? What basic rights relating to citizenship did they abandon on joining the armed forces?

Cooper proposed what for the times was a radical change in existing procedure. The trial of cases such as that of Spencer should be put "exclusively, except in those beyond the reach of such tribunals, into the hands of the civil courts." In this trial, "professional prejudices had more to do with some of th[e] votes, than professional knowledge." Cooper refused to credit Mackenzie's claim that he had sought merely to save the ship, his own life, and those of his associates. "The act was, unquestionably, one of high moral courage, one of the basest cowardice, one of deep guilt, or one of lamentable deficiency of judgment."[8] Cooper drew four conclusions. First, civilian tribunals might well be more knowledgeable and thus preferable to military courts; second, in certain military cases such as this one, there should be some sort of role for a civilian court; third, the abusive command influence exercised by Mackenzie violated fundamental law; and fourth, Navy officials had much to answer for in their conduct of the case.

With the possible exception of the founding of the U.S. Naval Academy at Annapolis, no immediate results appear to have come from the *Somers* affair. But indirectly, echoes of the case were heard. By 1850, a cousin of one of the officers on the *Somers* had achieved some success as an author. In his fourth book, *White Jacket; or the World in a Man-of-War*, published that year, Herman Melville did not mention the Spencer tragedy directly, but he denounced the harshness of military discipline and indirectly of military

[7] Harrison Hayford, *The Somers Mutiny Affair* (Englewood Cliffs, N.J., 1959), 76; *Letters and Journals of James Fenimore Cooper*, ed. James F. Beard, vol. 4 (Cambridge, Mass., 1964), 358.

[8] *Letters and Journals of James Fenimore Cooper*, 344.

justice. The Articles of War were simply "an importation from . . . Britain, whose laws we Americans hurled off as tyrannical, and yet retained the most tyrannical of all." Echoing Cooper, Melville noted that the necessities of the military might "warrant a code . . . more stringent than the law that governs the land . . . [but] that code should conform to the spirit of the political institutions of the country that ordains it. It should not convert into slaves some of the citizens of a nation of freemen."[9]

The infliction of harsh penalties based on claims of necessity, so important to the rationale for military discipline, continued to trouble Melville. The contention that capital punishment should be abolished in the American military did not arise, if only because from the Revolution to the present the concept that in the military one follows orders even if they result in one's death remained a given. It was fully appropriate that in the "lawful" conduct of war, death could be imposed for numerous offenses. Throughout the remainder of Melville's life, however, debate over capital punishment in civilian society continued. In a poem published after the Civil War he warned of the possibility that those responsible for Lincoln's murder would be executed. "Beware the people weeping," he wrote, "when they bare the iron hand." Surely the term "iron hand" could be applied to military justice, especially during the nineteenth century. As we shall see, the term held particular validity for the treatment meted out to the eight civilians accused of Lincoln's assassination.

Melville's most intriguing meditation on military justice and the harshness of what was justified by "necessity," written during the last years of his life, remained concealed within his papers and was not published until 1924. Set on board a British man-of-war during the Napoleonic Wars, Melville's novella, *Billy Budd*, centers on the apparent compulsion of a legal system to execute an innocent human being, even as those ordering such a course acknowledged his innocence and confess the injustice. It remains unclear exactly what prompted Melville to return to military justice in his final work. Perhaps he still remembered the tragedy of Philip Spencer. Perhaps in *Billy Budd*, he intended to attack capital punishment. Perhaps he wanted to question the morality of legality when placed in a context of immoral military or political necessity.[10] Whatever the motivation, there is a definite link between Cooper's comments and Melville's later works.

It took almost a century, but the points raised by Cooper ultimately contributed to major changes in American military justice. These changes centered on the creation of an appellate process, replete with civilian judges. In

[9] Herman Melville, *White Jacket; or, The World in a Man-of-War* (New York, 1850), 172.

[10] Robert Cover, *Justice Accused: Antislavery and the Judicial Process* (New Haven, CT, 1975), 249–52.

the long interim, meanwhile, one other similarity between the Jackson-Hall imbroglio and the *Somers* incident should be noted. Neither matter was referred to a federal appellate court. Not until the era of the American Civil War did this change. It was symbolic of the lack of a legal interest in matters military that the U.S. Supreme Court did not consider such a case until 1858.

II. MILITARY JUSTICE, 1858–66

Although, as the Civil War well revealed, the scope of American federalism had hardly been resolved, civilian control of the military at least had become a well-established doctrine by mid-century, as had the function of state and federal appellate tribunals in civilian courts. The president was Commander in Chief of the armed forces, but they were created, clothed, armed, housed, fed, regulated, and paid by Congress. That, however, was as far as it went. Some presidents might review an occasional court-martial, but for the most part military justice remained a thing in and of itself. Did civilian control apply to review concerning military justice decisions? To put it another way, did a federal appellate court have jurisdiction over a military court? The answer to this (thus far unasked) question appeared to be "no."

On the other hand, the Constitution itself was silent on the issue. Nor had Congress – beyond adopting the Articles of War and the Act to Govern the Navy – clarified the position. Military justice had thus far developed free from civilian surveillance, but as if by default. And if the special mission of the military seemed to recommend an independent system of military justice, such incidents as the tragedy on board the *Somers* served as reminders that some sort of appellate review was warranted. But where, and by whom it should be applied, and on what body of appellate law could it be based?

In 1858, the U.S. Supreme Court considered the case of *Dynes v. Hoover*. It involved an actual member of the armed forces, as opposed to a civilian in trouble with military authorities, and it offered the justices an important opportunity to define some parameters between civilian and military jurisdiction. The plaintiff was charged with desertion from the Navy, but was convicted of "attempting to desert." He filed suit, arguing that the court-martial lacked jurisdiction to try him for this offense because he had not originally been so charged and because "attempting to desert" was not a listed offense "within the cognizance of a naval court martial."[11]

On behalf of the government, Attorney General Caleb Cushing conceded that attempted desertion was not a specified offense within the statute. But the point was irrelevant. Section 32 of the Act to Govern the Navy provided

[11] *Dynes v. Hoover*, 20 How. 65, 15 L. ed., 845 (1858).

that "all crimes committed by persons belonging to the navy which are not specified in the foregoing articles, shall be punished according to the laws and customs in such cases at sea." For both Cushing, and later the Court, this provision resolved this case. It not only barred the plaintiff from prevailing but also essentially blocked the Court from any consideration of the merits in the dispute.

By a vote of 8-1, with no formal dissent submitted, Justice James Wayne stated that a court-martial verdict "when confirmed . . . is altogether beyond the jurisdiction or inquiry of any civil tribunal whatever." As for Section 32, Wayne acknowledged that the language was vague. Nevertheless, its "apparent indeterminateness" notwithstanding, the provision "is not liable to abuse, for what those crimes are, and how they are to be punished, is well known to practical men in the navy and army, and by those who have studied the law of courts-martial."

Although Wayne had emphasized that if a military tribunal went beyond its jurisdiction a different procedure might be warranted, his glib assertion that punishment "according to the laws and customs of the seas" is not liable to abuse" warrants brief discussion. Pre-Civil War jurisprudence took a much narrower view of due process than would be true in the twentieth century, especially for the military. And as we have seen, in both England and the United States after 1783 the military justice system was isolated from civil influence. It is not relevant whether this isolation was intentional or not, although there is virtually no evidence that in the United States it was; to find for plaintiff in *Dynes* would make the civil courts "virtually administer the Rules and Articles of War."

The holding appeared to bar civilian judicial intervention in military justice cases involving a member of the armed forces. But what if the accused was a civilian, who had no military connection whatsoever? The cases of *Ex Parte Vallandigham* (1864) and *Ex Parte Milligan* (1866) provided contradictory answers to that question and well illustrate the tendency for American constitutional law sometimes to reflect an intriguing amalgam of principle and expediency.

An antiwar politician and former Congressman seeking the 1863 Democratic gubernatorial nomination in Ohio, Clement Vallandigham denounced the ongoing war as "wicked, cruel, and unnecessary." Promptly arrested by military authorities, Vallandigham was tried, convicted, and sentenced to prison by a military commission. Possibly uncertain as to how the civil courts might rule, President Lincoln did not wait for the outcome of Vallandigham's plea for a writ of habeas corpus from a federal court. Instead, he ordered the prisoner transported behind enemy lines and there released from custody. The president strongly desired both liberty and Union, but when push came to shove, Union would be first. His former law partner commented that, in cases such as this one, Lincoln "would keep them in prison a while to keep them from killing the Government."[12]

In 1864, the Supreme Court rejected Vallandigham's plea for a federal writ. Again the decision was written by Justice Wayne. He might have used the occasion to reflect on the jurisdictional differences between a military commission and a court-martial. Both were composed of officers, but the former was limited to civilians accused of criminal acts in time of war, whereas the latter was limited to dealing with members of the military involved in specific offenses as defined by a written statute, such as the Articles of War. Vallandigham's case, dealing with a civilian tried by a military commission, represented an opportunity to distinguish it from the *Dynes* holding, which had involved a member of the Navy tried by court-martial. Instead Justice Wayne, this time for a unanimous court, merely reaffirmed *Dynes*. He held that a military commission was *not* in fact a court; thus it was not a tribunal over which the Constitution authorized high court appellate review. Wayne admitted that a military commission was exactly like a court in that it had "discretion to examine, to decide and sentence," but it did so through a "special authority" not reviewable by a federal judicial tribunal.[13]

While the decision can be seen more as an example of judicial avoidance than sound jurisprudence, such judicious caution becomes understandable in the context of wartime. Why confront the Union Army – at that time the largest standing army in the Western world – over the case of a notorious Ohio malcontent, all the more as the Commander in Chief had already taken final action in the case? Further, using lack of jurisdiction as the basis for the decision avoided the much more difficult question of a military commission's jurisdiction over a civilian accused of a non-military offense. Yet this underlying issue may well have troubled lawyers and judges in a society where even in wartime the military had never been dominant.

Two years after *Vallandingham*, the Court decided a similar case, with what appeared to be very different results. Like Vallandingham, Lambdin P. Milligan was a militantly antiwar and anti-Lincoln civilian who had been arrested, tried, convicted, and sentenced by a military commission. At that point, however the similarity ended. Milligan had been sentenced to death, but Lincoln ordered the record returned for certain "errors." Before he could reexamine it, the president was assassinated. President Johnson not only approved the sentence, but actually set a date for the execution – May 19, 1865 – whereupon Milligan's lawyers (who included such luminaries as

[12] Charles Fairman, "The Law of Martial Rule and the National Emergency," *Harvard Law Review* 55 (1942), 1284.

[13] *Ex Parte Vallandingham*, 1. Wall., 243, 243–54 (1864).

David Dudley Field and Jeremiah Black) sought judicial intervention from the federal Circuit Court, sitting in Indianapolis. Before hearing argument, the two judges sitting on the case, one of whom was Supreme Court Justice David Davis, addressed a confidential letter to President Johnson. Urging that the execution be postponed, they informed Johnson that Milligan had been sentenced "by a new tribunal unknown to the Common Law." Moreover, a number of lawyers "doubt its jurisdiction over citizens unconnected with the military," a point that "is not clear of difficulty." If Milligan were executed and the Court later found military jurisdiction to be lacking, "the government would be justly chargeable with lawless oppression . . . ," and "a stain on the national character would be the consequence."[14]

The two judges may have been aware of the criticism that had accompanied the very recent trial of the Lincoln conspirators by military commission. Described by one critic as a court "of officers too worthless for field service, ordered to try, and organized to convict," military commissions had been employed during the war on several occasions, even though the civil courts in Washington were open and functioning. There could be no doubt that, in the Southeast at least, the war was over. Why then, was it appropriate to try seven men and one woman by military commission? Lawyers had challenged the commission's legality to its face; the issue had not been resolved, and yet the eight Lincoln conspirators had been found guilty and four executed. Now, here was another civilian facing a military commission death sentence. One can understand why the judges were concerned.

Five days after receiving the letter, President Johnson commuted Milligan's sentence to life imprisonment at hard labor. But he ignored the underlying issue raised by the two judges – that the question of unlawful imprisonment be resolved *before* implementation of a sentence. Thus Milligan's case went forward and in due course reached the Supreme Court. Although the justices heard and decided the case early in the spring of 1866, the formal opinions were not filed until December, about a year and a half after cessation of hostilities. Justice David Davis, author of the decision and one of the two judges who had written to Johnson, hinted at the reasons for the delay. With "public safety" now assured, the issues raised in the case "can be discussed and decided without passion or the admixture of any element not required to form a legal judgment."[15] In other words, with the Union Army dramatically diminished in size, there was now enough judicial confidence in military obedience to the Court's mandate to justify a ruling contrary to the military viewpoint.

[14] National Archives, Papers from the Office of the Judge Advocate General: Indiana Treason Trials.

[15] *Ex Parte Milligan*, 4 Wall. 2, 109 (1866).

Justice Davis held that a proceeding by military commission was beyond the power of law when applied to a civilian where the civil courts were operating and governmental control remained unchallenged, as was true in Indiana. "No usage or war could sanction a military trial there for any offense whatever of a citizen in civil life, in nowise connected with the military service." Certainly the appropriate authorities could proclaim martial law, but the necessity for such a step "must be actual and present; the invasion real, such as effectively closes the courts and deposes the civil administration." None of these conditions applied to Milligan's situation nor, presumably, to the earlier case of Vallandigham – a decision that Davis completely ignored, even though he had voted against him.

Although the Court was unanimous in denying jurisdiction for a military commission in *this* case, there was marked dissent concerning a second point of the decision. To find that one military commission had acted contrary to law in a specific instance was far from saying that Congress could never establish such tribunals with authority over civilians under any circumstances. Davis so held, however, and prevailed by the slimmest of majorities, a 5-4 split.

The dissenters insisted that Congressional power to establish military commissions represented a fundamental exercise within the legislative purview. That conditions in Indiana had not warranted such a step could not deprive Congress of such a right in other circumstances, the determination of which was strictly a matter of legislative discretion. The legislature had not authorized military commissions in Indiana; hence Milligan had to be released. But Congress possessed such power on a plenary basis. Should it have chosen to act, protections offered civilians by the Bill of Rights would not apply.

Because *Ex Parte Milligan* has often been cited as a landmark decision in the area of civil rights, it should be understood in its context. The decision did not bar imposition of martial law. Moreover, it appeared to apply only to states where civil courts and governmental administration were in normal operation. The case involved a civilian, and by emphasizing this fact as he repeatedly did, Justice Davis reiterated a point made in previous cases: that military commanders, when dealing with military personnel, were beyond the reach of federal courts. As far as concerned supervision of military justice by civilian appellate courts, the case established nothing.

On the other hand, the decision indicated that, when the High Court wished to do so, it could and would intervene in a case involving military justice. To be sure, in strictest legal terminology, a military commission was not a court-martial. However, the rules of court-martial governed trials before the commission. One wonders then, why the Court refused jurisdiction in the *Ex Parte Vallandigham* case, but willingly assumed it in 1865 in *Milligan*. The facts in each case were essentially identical. Perhaps the Court was affected more than it liked to admit by the shifting tides of war.

Little changed in military justice between the Civil War and World War I. Legal education, scholarship, and research, however, were transformed during this time. With Langdell's innovations in law school instruction well underway, in 1889 an obscure retired colonel named James Fry proposed something that had been hinted at by James Fenimore Cooper almost a half-century before. Reflecting his times, Fry argued that "the science of military law is progressive," as "is the science of civil law to a greater degree." Progress in the civil field "in principles or modes of procedure which are essential to the ascertainment of truth" cannot be "at variance with the objects of the military code [the Articles of War], and they ought to be applied to it."[16] Here was one instance that could have provided a telling example of the possible interplay between ongoing legal scholarship and military justice. It concerned appellate military justice.

Noting, correctly, that the president and Congress were the only sources of appeal from a court-martial, Fry found that many "cases are reopened which were supposed to be closed, and are retried by tribunals without legal power and without judicial modes of procedure." These practices resulted from too great an emphasis on rigor and rapidity in military justice cases. Less speed and more "unquestionable judicial proceedings" were necessary. Fry's solution was a proposed military court of appeal, a sort of "Supreme Court-martial." Such a judicial tribunal would be much better equipped to ascertain the truth than either Congress or the president.

Existence of such a court might well obviate both the temptation and the necessity for Congressional or presidential intervention in the first place. Indeed, Fry may have been less concerned about the quality of military justice than with minimizing opportunities for civilian interference by the executive or legislative branches of the federal government. His proposed innovation was a military court of appeals, not a court of military appeals. The distinction represented much more than a question of semantics. A military court of appeals would be within the military justice system, whereas a court of military appeals would be outside, civilian in character, and presumably more independent in its judgment.

Nothing came of Fry's proposal for more than a half-century. At a time of major intellectual ferment within legal education and procedure, it was simply ignored. Given the obscurity of the journal in which it appeared, this is not surprising. Nor should one be surprised that no one within the military appears to have publicly endorsed the suggestion. But in fact Fry's ideas were merely dormant. Ultimately Congress created an appellate

[16] James B. Fry, *Military Miscellanies* (New York, 1889), 183.

system for the military that included several tribunals both within and outside the military. Developments between 1917 and 1948 paved the way for this legislative innovation. Although Fry's insights received no apparent acknowledgment, in fact they are reflected in these events.

III. WORLD WAR I

In 1919, an experienced JAG officer recalled that on the eve of World War I, as for most of the nineteenth century, the Army remained small and compact and for the most part removed from urban centers. There was, added William Rigby, "but little public interest, either in the army itself or in military affairs."[17] American entry into World War I permanently altered this perception. In April 1917 the JAG department consisted of seventeen officers. By December 1918, its commissioned officers numbered more than 400. The rapid expansion of the Army caused a number of strains arising from the influx of thousands of new officers "unschooled in Army traditions, unacquainted with each other and the men under them, and unaccustomed to command." When detailed to sit on court martials, they displayed "ignorance of military law and traditions, uncertainty of themselves, undue fear of leniency . . . and a tendency to avoid responsibility" by handing out severe penalties along with recommendations for clemency, thereby attempting "to shoulder onto higher authority the responsibility of determining the proper quantum of punishment."[18]

Some commanders welcomed an opportunity to appear in the role of the merciful leader, one willing to lessen a harsh penalty and thus giving the accused soldier a chance for redemption. Other officers, including Acting Army JAG Samuel Ansell, argued that the system itself rather than command discretion contained ample authority for "revisory and corrective power." Ansell pointed to a very short statute, originally enacted during the Civil War, but still retained as law in the Revised Statutes (Section 1199) in 1917: "The Judge Advocate General shall receive, revise, and cause to be recorded the proceedings of all courts-martial, courts of inquiry, and military commissions." These words, Ansell believed, authorized some sort of appellate review. By 1917, within American legal scholarship there was no lack of understanding the nature of appellate review. It was simply a process of informed judgment, unhurried and deliberative.[19] But how could such

[17] William C. Rigby, Draft of Report on Court Martial Procedures, in *Records of the Judge Advocate General*, NARC, RG 153, entry 26, box 30 (1919).

[18] Rigby, Draft of Report on Court Martial Procedures.

[19] Daniel J. Meador, *Criminal Appeals: English Practices and American Reforms* (Washington, D.C., 1973), 162.

a process be compatible with military justice? One took time, the other required speed; one called for a formal appellate procedure, whereas the other did not even have a formal appellate process.

Ansell's superior, Army Judge Advocate General Enoch Crowder, had already justified the lack of appellate procedures in the military. His words are reminiscent of the 1689 English statute we have already encountered: "In a military code there can be, of course, no provision for courts of appeal. Military discipline and the purposes which it is expected to subserve will not permit the vexatious delays incident to the establishment of an appellate procedure."[20] Crowder added that because the commanding general, advised by his legal officer, had to "approve every conviction and sentence before it can become effective," such action "effectively safeguard[ed] the rights of an accused."

Nevertheless, in October 1917, Ansell reversed the verdicts in several court-martials, objecting both to procedural flaws and to excessive punishment. However, he did not recommend reversal to the Secretary of War, as was the traditional practice. Rather he acted unilaterally, citing Section 1199 as his authority. Army officers could not accept the idea that a member of the JAG department could rescind an action ordered by a commander. In a formal brief submitted to Secretary of War Newton Baker, Ansell insisted that revise was equivalent to review, and review could only mean the ability to reconsider, reexamine, and correct, if warranted, a previous legal decision. This power was vested in the office of the Judge Advocate General. Not surprisingly, Army JAG General Enoch Crowder rejected this position, arguing that revise and review had separate and distinct meanings. He could find no instance where the power to revise had been interpreted to mean exercising appellate judicial review. Nor could he find any evidence to show that the JAG had on his own authority ever reversed a court-martial.

Baker supported Crowder's claims, noting that "the extraction of new and large grants of power by reinterpreting familiar statutes with settled practical construction is unwise."[21] Yet Ansell persisted and in early December 1917 submitted another brief to Crowder and Baker. This time, he went further and, contrary to well-established military doctrine, insisted that a court-martial was not an instrumentality of the executive branch. In fact, it was a judicial proceeding that had been authorized by Congress, under constitutional authority vested in that body. But the leading authority on military law, William Winthrop, had held that, although court-martials were judicial tribunals and "their legal sanction is no less than the federal

[20] Wiener, 19.

[21] "Trials by Courts-Martial," in *Hearings before the Committee on Military Affairs*, United States Senate, 65th Cong., 3rd sess., 1919), 29.

courts," they were not courts "in the full sense of the term." According to Winthrop, this was so because of penultimate authority exercised by the president as Commander in Chief. Although several Supreme Court decisions had found that court-martials were judicial in character, these holdings were more concerned with issues of jurisdiction than with the origins of court-martial authority.

Although Crowder conceded that some sort of review might indeed be appropriate, he insisted that it had to be based on recommendations given to the convening authority by the JAG department. Ansell had argued that the sine qua non for real reform of military justice was a reviewing power, located in the JAG office, but independent of and binding on the convening officer. "What reason can there be," he asked, "to require this office to review for errors of law and then be denied the power of correction?"[22] To solve this difficulty, Ansell proposed a court of military appeals to be located within the JAG department and to consist of three judges "learned in the law." They would be selected by the president, would be confirmed by the Senate, and would serve with life tenure. Each judge would have all the emoluments of a U.S. circuit judge.

Crowder maintained that the president should act as a sort of supreme court of review in all military cases, "with ample authority to revise, reverse, modify or set aside any sentence of a court martial." He was unable to conceive of any appellate procedure for military justice except at the hands of the president. Hence, according to the Army Judge Advocate General, Congress could not establish any sort of appellate court because it might interfere with powers belonging to the Commander in Chief. Apparently, if one sought an appellate tribunal independent of military command, the only way to attain it was through the highest ranking military commander. Moreover, if the president opted to create such a body, how could it be independent of the military influence when it would be administered by lower ranking military functionaries?

The Ansell-Crowder disagreement became public in 1919, and once again the subject of military justice received much attention from the media. Ansell's recommendations and Crowder's rebuttals were discussed and debated by Edmund Morgan and John Wigmore, both serving in the Army JAG Corps and destined for distinguished careers as legal scholars. But with the war over, little came from the dispute except lasting enmity between the JAG of the Army and Ansell, who resigned from the military in July 1919. While Congress ultimately enacted some minor changes in the Articles of War in June 1920, his proposed court was not among them. Instead, a new article, 50½, created a board of review within the JAG

[22] "Trials by Courts-Martial," in *Hearings before the Committee on Military Affairs*, United States Senate, 65th Cong., 3rd sess. (1919), 68.

department, consisting entirely of officers serving in an advisory capacity only. It was far from an appellate court.

The Ansell-Crowder controversy was significant as a harbinger of things to come. For the first time the Army seriously debated the issue of a military justice appellate procedure. While the war was being fought, it seemed undesirable to tamper with the Articles of War. With its victorious conclusion there no longer seemed any necessity for change. Yet the proposal for a court of military appeals turned out to be only dormant, rather than deceased. After passage of thirty years and a second world war, a proposed court of military appeals again was submitted to Congress, and Samuel Ansell lived to see it enacted into law.

IV. AFTERMATH OF WORLD WAR II

Several noteworthy criticisms were levied against military justice during World War I. First, wide discrepancies existed in punishment for the same offense. Second, the rights of the accused were not protected during a court-martial. Third, defense counsel were often incompetent. Edmund Morgan had observed that defendants in court-martials were often prosecuted by "officers of low rank who wouldn't know a law book from a bale of hay, and as frequently are defended by a chaplain who is hardly able to distinguish between a rule of evidence and the Apostle's Creed."[23] Ill prepared to cope with the relatively brief American involvement in World War I, the potential for abuse in an essentially unreformed system was all the greater during the three and a half years of World War II.

By 1945, the U.S. Army had expanded to more than 8,000,000 personnel, and the size of the Navy had doubled. At least 12,000,000 Americans were subject to military justice. At the height of the war, more than a half-million court-martials were convened each year. More than 1,700,000 trials were held, more than 100 executions were carried out, and at the end of the war in 1945, some 45,000 members of the U.S. armed forces were incarcerated. Given these numbers, along with extensive war press coverage and important advances in communications, such as radio and motion pictures, to say nothing of the greater numbers of attorneys in the military, one can understand why severe criticism of the military justice system recurred. Again, Congress investigated, and again hearings resulted that included a number of critical references. At least seven different studies of military justice for the Navy were conducted between 1943 and 1947, and two for the Army between 1943 and 1946. The same problems that

[23] John Wigmore Papers (Northwestern University), clipping from the *New York World*, April 4, 1919.

had been noted during the Ansell-Crowder dispute were cited anew, but the military still adhered tenaciously to tradition and remained resistant to change.

Unlike the aftermath of World War I, however, two significant developments suggested more hopeful prospects for reform. First, the emergence of the Cold War meant no sustained respite from military preparedness. Second, the armed services were now unified, under a new Secretary of Defense. The appearance of what became known as the "Defense Establishment" made the continuation of separate and duplicate systems of military justice – the Articles of War (Army) and the Act to Govern the Navy – impractical. Finally, lingering differences within Congress over partial reforms based on several of the earlier reports indicated that a new comprehensive approach might be more successful.

Early in May 1948, the chairman of the Senate Armed Services Committee wrote to Secretary of Defense James Forrestal urging that legislation be prepared that would "provide a uniform system of military justice applicable alike to all three services." Forrestal agreed and shortly established within his office two interrelated committees. The first was an ad hoc committee of three civilian undersecretaries from the three military services, with a chairman to be named. The second was a separate working committee comprising one military representative selected by each member of the main panel together with several lawyers and civilian researchers within Forrestal's office. The working committee's job was to examine and evaluate all the previous reports and recommendations, compare and contrast the existing rules and procedures, and finally to produce a working draft of each article for a new uniform code of military justice, applicable to every branch of the armed services. Each article in turn would be submitted to the main committee for modification, rejection, or ultimate final approval.

V. ENACTMENT OF THE UNIFORM CODE OF MILITARY JUSTICE, AND THEREAFTER

In the early summer of 1948, one of Forrestal's aides, Marx Leva, was given the task of selecting a chairman for the ad hoc committee. A former naval officer and graduate of Harvard Law School, Leva had become Forrestal's first General Counsel in 1948 and an assistant Secretary of Defense. Leva considered several possibilities, among them Owen Roberts, a former justice of the Supreme Court who had recently been made dean of the University of Pennsylvania Law School, as well as several distinguished lawyers who had chaired the various committees that had produced previous reports on military justice. Ultimately, however, Leva and his assistant Felix Larkin concluded that the chair ought to be an outsider who had not been involved in the previous proceedings. Leva settled on one of his former teachers at Harvard, the same Edmund Morgan who had served in the JAG corps during World War I and strongly supported Ansell during the 1918–19 controversy. Long retired from the JAG corps, Morgan had taught at Harvard Law School for almost a quarter-century. Well aware of Morgan's pro-Ansell position, Forrestal assured him that "the part which you played in connection with the necessity for reforms in the military justice system at that time should be an asset rather than a liability."[24] On July 29, 1948, Morgan was duly appointed as "expert advisor" on the military justice study being undertaken within Forrestal's office.

Even before Morgan accepted the appointment and the instructions (or the precept) had been prepared for his committee, Larkin persuaded Forrestal to adopt a different approach to the committee deliberation and decision making. Larkin had become very familiar with all the recent reports on military justice and was well aware of their usual fate. On completion, they were returned to the originating department for review and reaction. For the most part they never reappeared. Larkin had no desire to undertake a major comparative study and draft a comprehensive new code of military justice for submission to Congress only to have the various JAGs "review it, and have it interminably debated and nothing ever happen."[25] He emphasized to Forrestal that the armed services were represented on both the working group and Morgan's primary committee. Indeed, each undersecretary could draw on whatever legal military expertise from within his own service that he deemed appropriate. Therefore, he urged, once Morgan's committee had agreed on its recommendations, the resulting decision should not be reviewed again by any of the services, nor even by Forrestal's office, but should be final. Only in those – it was hoped, very few – instances in which Morgan's committee did not agree could Forrestal have the last word. The Secretary of Defense approved Larkin's plan, with the result that the great majority of the proposed uniform code's more than 140 articles were submitted to Congress in the form decided by Morgan's panel. Unlike earlier recommendations, the military in 1948 could discuss and debate the reforms, but could not derail them. This time, impetus for reform and its ultimate shape would come from the office of the Secretary of Defense.

From the outset, Morgan's committee faced serious challenges. Within a limited time frame, barely six months, his panel had to consider the need for uniformity that would ensure due process for the military without impeding the central function of the armed services, the key differences between the three services in administration of military justice, and the political

[24] Edmund M. Morgan Papers (Vanderbilt University), July 24, 1948.

[25] Felix Larkin, Interview with author, December 17, 1987.

preferences already indicated by Congress, to whom the finished product would be submitted. These challenges notwithstanding, the committee was able to construct a complex statute with many articles and that required Forrestal's intervention in only in a few instances. In each case where consensus eluded the committee, Forrestal accepted the position taken by Morgan.

The two major areas of disagreement encountered during the proceedings were, first, over the role of the "law member" in a court-martial and, second, over the nature of the review/appellate process in military justice. The first matter addressed whether the law member should function strictly as a judge or retire to deliberate with other members of the court but not actually vote on the case. Those who supported this practice pointed out that if the law member had to give instructions in open court, they would have to be drafted to withstand legal challenge. If, on the other hand, the law member retired with the rest of the court members, he could explain the law in lay terms, increasing the chances for a legally acceptable verdict. The Air Force representative on the working committee denied that errors were committed by the law member. Typically, several questions were raised, "which he answers, and we don't have the errors in law." Larkin responded that what went on in conference was off the record. Thus, there was no way of knowing even what instructions were actually given, let alone whether or not they were legally appropriate. The Army representative emphasized that "the glory of the court martial system has been its freedom from technicalities." Here, agreement eluded the panel.

The greater challenge to consensus for Morgan's committee was posed by the new uniform code's central innovation, a system for appellate review. Unlike the other articles, which were usually channeled from the working group to the Morgan panel, the initial proposal for an appellate system came from Morgan himself. Drawing heavily on what Fry had hinted at and on what Ansell had first proposed in 1918, the chairman called for a tripartite process, beginning with the convening authority, the military official who had initiated the court-martial. The entire record of trial was to be examined by his staff judge advocate or legal officer. If the accused remained unhappy with the resulting action or lack of action taken by the commander, Morgan's second stage involved review by a board that would be established in the JAG office for each service. Unlike contemporary military practice these panels would exercise plenary review authority. They would weigh evidence, judge the credibility of witnesses, and determine controverted questions of fact. They might affirm or set aside verdicts in whole or in part, dismiss charges, or require that the case be reheard.

At the apex of Morgan's appellate structure would be what he called a "judicial council." As originally proposed, it was to include three lawyers who would be nominated by the Secretary of Defense to the president, who in turn would appoint them to this "court." Subject to Senate confirmation, they would receive a stipend equal to that of U.S. circuit judges, and their terms would "be long, probably for life." Morgan gave this council virtually the same appellate functions as the intermediate panel and jurisdiction in three areas: any case in which the penalty was death or in which the sentence affected a general officer; any case referred by the JAG for final appellate review; and cases in which the council determined that the petitioner had demonstrated reasonable grounds that injustice had been done to the accused, or where one review board's decision conflicted with another, or where "the best interests of the service will for some reason be furthered by a review."

As originally drafted, Morgan's tripartite appeal plan represented a dramatic change from current practice. In addition to its basic design of one uniform system applicable to all three services, his proposals limited the influence, if not control, that JAGs had long exercised over military justice. The findings of his intermediate Board of Review could not be altered and required no approval from JAGs before being implemented. At the highest level of appellate review, he had taken the "judicial council" out of the JAG's office entirely and opened its membership to civilian lawyers with life tenure. With understandable understatement, the Army representative to Larkin's working group deplored "any diminution of the position of the Judge Advocate General."

Ever the realist, Morgan was prepared to see major modification to his proposal. What ultimately resulted was just that. At the apex, instead of a judicial council appointed through the office of the Secretary of Defense for extended terms, was a panel of judges serving fifteen-year terms. Life tenure was denied them, even though they had all the usual perquisites of federal appellate jurists. Second, the panel's authority was reduced. As enacted by Congress the judicial council, now renamed the Court of Military Appeals, lost authority to weigh evidence, judge the credibility of witnesses, or determine controversial questions of fact. These functions were vested exclusively in the intermediate Boards of Review, which were to be appointed entirely by the JAG of each service and would serve at his or her pleasure. The Court of Military Appeals, however, retained the power to rule on matters of law, as well as the broad discretionary ability to decide what cases to hear.

Whatever Morgan's actual feelings on the matter, he well understood the realities of a newly united military establishment and its requisite command structure. Nor could he have forgotten the ultimate rejection of Ansell's proposed court. A Court of Military Appeals, albeit of limited scope, was surely better than none at all. The new Uniform Code of Military Justice (UCMJ) had to have at least tacit acquiescence from the military, if not outright approbation, to gain enactment. This required numerous "adjustments" that would not have been acceptable had the code been drafted by a committee of civilian lawyers.

The Uniform Code of Military Justice was submitted to Congress in the spring of 1949. Congress had its own priorities, and so the bill did not receive final legislative approval until the spring of 1950. To the end, the JAGs remained unhappy with the Court of Military Appeals, even though life tenure for its members had been dropped. The military also objected to the power of reversal granted to the Boards of Review, as well as the proposal to bar the law officer of a court-martial from voting with other members. Morgan's comments to the Senate Committee considering the UCMJ on these points may well have persuaded the senators not to alter them. During World War I, he recalled, commanders had not even wanted lawyers as members of a court-martial because of their fear that lawyers "would bitch up the thing by telling them some law." As to the need for an appellate authority to review and reduce sentences, Morgan emphasized that excessive sentences had resulted in major criticisms of military justice. He had sat for a time as chairman of the clemency committee, "and I know we remitted 18,000 years in 6 weeks."

The Senate's changes to the UCMJ as it had passed the House were minimal, except in one regard. Unlike the House, the Senate declined to grant the judges of the new court life tenure, opting instead for a term of eight years and ultimately accepting fifteen. Senator Wayne Morse warned his colleagues that limiting tenure in this manner might well cause individuals with outstanding qualifications to decline appointment. More important, he chided his colleagues for inconsistency. The Senate wanted the new court to be on a par with U.S. Courts of Appeal, yet it declined to give the judges the security of tenure that their federal counterparts enjoyed. Morse's comments were prescient, as the history of the new court would demonstrate. Nevertheless, enactment of the UCMJ in 1950 redefined American military justice for the remainder of the twentieth century and beyond. Never before had Congress created a civilian appellate court especially for the military.

Unfortunately, the new code failed to provide clear demarcation between the JAGs and the court concerning ultimate supervising authority over military justice. In the minimal Congressional debate that had preceded final passage of the UCMJ, the new tribunal had been labeled "the supreme court of the military." It would not be unreasonable for such a court to claim for itself some sort of supervisory role in military justice administration. Yet, the UCMJ made no reference to the court as an overseer of the system. On the contrary, it was the JAGs who were specifically mandated to undertake "frequent inspections in the field in supervision of the administration of military justice" (Article 6). While the new legislation mandated cooperation between JAGs and judges, in a real sense it had also built tension if not actual conflict into the relationship.

Nor, although trumpeted by its sponsors as on a par with all other federal appellate courts, was it clear whether the new Court of Military Appeals was in fact similar to those other tribunals. Was this court to be considered part of the executive branch or, as with other federal appellate courts, within the judicial branch? Was it some sort of administrative agency or a bona fide appellate court? From the outset, the court – formally known as the U.S. Court of Appeals for the Armed Forces (USCAAF) – received no consistent answers to these questions. The explanation for this lack of clarity may be found in what appear to have been inconsistent, if not contradictory, actions by Congress. Unlike any other federal tribunal before or since, the court was housed within the new defense establishment for "administrative purposes only." Supreme Court Justice Antonin Scalia observed in 1997, "the [UCMJ] does not specify the court's 'location' for non administrative purposes."[26] Nor has either the High Court or Congress ever clearly defined what "for administrative purposes only" actually means. Life tenure, another concomitant of the federal judiciary, has deliberately and consistently been denied the USCAAF. The benefits of regular availability of appointments have, of course been obvious to Congress since 1950. Approximately one-third of USCAAF judges have either been members of Congress or served as staff members to various Congressional committees.

The USCAAF differs in other ways from other federal courts. Its appellate review jurisdiction is limited only to cases arising from military tribunals. Unlike any other federal appellate bench, its judges may be removed by the president for neglect of duty, misconduct, or mental or physical disability.[27] Similarly, only the judges of this court have been mandated by statute to meet with the various JAGs and other personnel appointed by the Secretary of Defense to survey and assess the operation of the military justice system. Congress has also declined to place the new tribunal under the Administrative Office of the U.S. Courts, again unlike all other Article III federal courts. Thus it seems clear that while Congress has repeatedly emphasized that USCAAF is in terms of salary and similar perquisites just like any other federal appellate body, its actions have belied its rhetoric.

The problem of where to locate USCAAF's functions never went away. In 1997 Justice Scalia had no doubt that the court was within the executive branch.[28] There is some evidence in the court's history to justify the claim. In October 1951, only a few months after it started to operate, the Civil

[26] *Edmond v. United States*, 520 U.S. 651, 664 (1997).
[27] UCMJ, 10 U.S. C, Article 142. [28] *Edmond v. United States*.

Service Commission determined that the court fell within the executive, rather than the judicial branch of government. This meant that, contrary to most federal courts, appointment of court personnel would come within the purview of the Civil Service Commission, with the judges unable to make appointments purely as they saw fit.

In 1954, the District of Columbia Circuit Court of Appeals ruled that USCAAF was a court and not an administrative agency, but this conclusion was not without its own ambiguity. The court "with the entire hierarchy of tribunals which it heads, may perhaps be considered as being within the military establishment: perhaps, whether or not this is so, it is properly to be viewed as a specialized legislative court. . . . " In any view, this new tribunal "appears to us to be a court in every significant respect, rather than an administrative agency."[29] It is not clear whether this holding definitely resolved whether USCAAF was within the military establishment. The words used by the Circuit Court of Appeals indicated some doubt in the matter.

More than twenty years later, USCAAF revisited the issue, albeit indirectly. In 1977, Chief Judge Albert Fletcher, Jr., obtained an advisory ruling from the Civil Service Commission (CSC) that reversed its earlier determination. Now the Commission concluded that USCAAF was "beyond a doubt, a "proper component of the judicial branch of government." Moreover, "we now consider your agency outside the Commission's purview, subject only to your own personnel [sic] authority."[30] Although the court had long advocated this view, it had acquiesced in the earlier finding. Consequently most of its staff had been under CSC administration. Unwilling to accept the possible and sudden abandonment of civil service classifications, as well as protection, a number of court staff filed suit against the judges.

The CSC had based its 1977 ruling on a federal statute enacted in 1968 that had made some changes in the administration of military justice. When the Justice Department considered the staff's pending suit, it found that the legislative history of the statute contained "no express discussion of the civil service status" for court employees. Indeed, "there is no indication whatsoever that the Congress either contemplated or intended" to change such a status. Thus there could be no justification or legal basis to litigate the issue. Faced with the conclusion that the position now taken by the Civil Service Commission's staff could not be "successfully defended," the case was resolved quickly and quietly by a simple return to the status quo ante.

[29] *Shaw v. United States*, 209 F. 2d 311 (1954).

[30] Civil Service Litigation File, undated. Papers, U.S. Court of Appeals for the Armed Forces.

There is, then, evidence to justify Justice Scalia's claim that USCAAF, although indeed a legitimate federal appellate tribunal, remains an "Executive branch entity." Questions about its own legitimacy and functions have been an ongoing part of USCAAF's history from its inception. In the absence of Congressional action they remain difficult to resolve.

Problems of a different nature, dealing with the Korean War and other domestic challenges, occupied President Truman as the Uniform Code of Military Justice became law. He did not get around to selecting the first three judges of the new court for yet another year. When he did, he chose lawyers who had been involved in each of the three services. Robert Quinn, a former governor of Rhode Island, had served in the Navy, George Latimer, a member of the Utah Supreme Court, had been in the Army, whereas Paul Brosman, then dean of Tulane Law School, represented the Air Force. Even before they took their oaths of office, the question of the court's role in administering appellate review of military justice surfaced. At their very brief appearances before the Senate Armed Services Committee in an unusual Saturday morning session, its chair Senator Richard Russell alluded to this concern. He remarked, correctly, that "this court is something new in anything I know of in the judicial system" and that "I personally had misgivings about the creation of this court." Willing to concede that there were several cases within the military in which individuals had not even received decent treatment, let alone adequate justice, Russell still insisted that "any abuse of the powers of this court will be disastrous to this Nation. . . . " The chair further put the three nominees on notice: "I am sure that you gentlemen will in your duties temper justice with that knowledge that this will indeed be a court of military justice[,] and will not be an agency that will be damaging to the observance of discipline in the armed services." Three days later, with minimal debate and without even a voice vote, the three were confirmed unanimously.

Russell's uneasiness has been repeated throughout USCAAF's history in several different forums, always implying the same point: military justice was somehow always subordinate to military discipline. Whether this unease has been warranted and whether it has impeded the perceived independence of this court remain unclear. The concern, however, has been an essential component of the court's history. It may well have been detrimental to rigorous civilian-judicial scrutiny of military appellate justice, even as supporters of the system within the military have applauded its operation.

It is worth noting that, especially in the early years of the court's history, the JAGs did not cooperate with it enthusiastically. Although they had certainly influenced the final drafting of the UCMJ, in several instances their sentiments had not been controlling – as in the establishment of the court itself. From their perspective, it could be seen as an institution forced by outsiders on a system of military justice that had prevailed for more than 150 years and had seen the American armed forces through to victory in two world wars. That military justice system had revolved around the JAGs. Without them the entire military justice system could not operate. They, not the members of a court-martial, were expected to demonstrate technical and expert knowledge of the law; a panel of officers disregarded their legal advice at its peril. And so it was – until 1951.

A verdict from the new civilian USCAAF in favor of a defendant, whatever the specific grounds might be, could be seen as a condemnation of a JAG practice or procedure. The JAGs could conclude, and with some justification, that establishment of this court was, in reality, a reflection of their inability to provide what the civilian legal order now deemed to be acceptable standards of military appellate review.

Yet, even the most conservative JAG, and the military is a notoriously conservative institution, recognized political reality. The new code and court were not going to go away. Cooperation if not open consultation was more than an operational necessity. It was now a federal mandate. For better or worse, appellate judges and JAGs had become partners in the process. In a real sense, as the JAGs ultimately realized, the more effective, thorough, and "just" their operations were, the less work of correction there would be for the new court.

For more than a half-century then, the relationship between these two major participants in the administration of military justice has ranged from ill-concealed antagonism, to grudging acceptance, to even an occasional spasm of approbation. However, it has always been guarded. From time to time, the JAGs have sought to curb the influence or authority of the court, either by limiting its jurisdiction, altering its composition, or seeking Congressional and/or civilian pressure to force a change in its decisions. Whether intentionally mandated by Congress or not, the tension between JAG and the judges has been a dominant theme in the court's history and one that has not yet been played out. In fact, it may be incapable of ultimate resolution.

The same might be said for the court's relationship to the General Counsel's office within the greater Department of Defense. Before 1976–77, there had been little, if any, friction between the court and civilian Pentagon officials – even though the court has always been a part of that entity "for administrative purposes only." Indeed, for the first twenty-five years of the court history, the office of the General Counsel had demonstrated minimal interest in USCAAF. The annual appearances by Chief Judge Robert Quinn or his colleague, former Senator Homer Ferguson, before the Senate Appropriations Committee to justify annual budgetary requests reflected a similar lack of external concern. The very brief sessions were characterized by a tone of conviviality between the former governor and the few senators usually in attendance.

All this changed during the era of Albert Fletcher, Jr., as chief judge. Appointed to the court by President Gerald Ford in 1975, Fletcher steered the tribunal in a direction of greater activism within appellate military justice, as well as greater judicial aggrandizement for his court. A few statistics illustrate the new trend. In 1975, shortly before Quinn's final illness and resignation, the court granted fewer than 6 percent of petitions for review. Barely eight months into Fletcher's term almost 17 percent had been granted. In 1974, less than half of USCAAF decisions had favored the accused. By the end of 1975, that number had risen to almost 69 percent. What one observer called an "energetic resurgence" was obvious to all court watchers. From the military viewpoint, this was a disturbing trend.

It became apparent that Fletcher's court had concluded that military justice was too important to be left solely to military commanders. The balance between military justice and military discipline, noted by Senator Richard Russell a quarter-century before, was shifting. Considerations of justice were to be given greater emphasis. The commander might retain his disciplinary prerogatives, but his judicial functions were to be lessened. Absent regular Congressional scrutiny – always possible, but usually improbable – Fletcher had determined that his court was the only institution capable of bringing to the military justice system the type of constant leadership and supervision he deemed necessary.

The JAGs, of course, disagreed. It was one thing to remove a commander from exercising judicial functions because of his disciplinary authority. It was quite another to hold that his interest in discipline "should play no part in judicial determinations." They also pointed out that the UCMJ had specifically designated supervisory authority over military justice to them, and not to Fletcher's court. Unfortunately for all concerned, Fletcher combined judicial activism with a less than judicious arrogance. In November 1977, in a widely circulated interview, he emphasized that "we don't serve the military. The civilians created us. We have no responsibility to the military. Our responsibility is to the civilian community called Congress . . . not to the Judge Advocates General."[31]

By 1978, antagonism between Fletcher and the office of General Counsel in the Defense Department had also surfaced, resulting in another departure from its earlier history. In contrast to earlier years of the court, that office now became actively involved in an effort to coordinate JAG criticism of Fletcher, if not of his court. The General Counsel, a Washington-based attorney, Deanne Siemer, was informed by an assistant that the Army and Navy JAGs "are separately to attack" the court in speeches before a forthcoming

[31] *Army Times*, November 28, 1977, 30.

ABA meeting and that "these speeches were reviewed and approved in our office this week." The speeches would criticize the USCAAF "as an activist court bent on mandating changes in military jurisprudence through judicial decisions which contravene the expressed will of Congress. . . . " Never before had the office of the General Counsel allied itself with senior JAG officials in preparing public criticism of the USCAAF. Issues of propriety aside, it was clear that this office had evolved to a point in 1978 where it could actively pressure a civilian court to render decisions more in conformity with the military's desires.

Siemer went even further. On April 3, 1978, she leaked a proposal to abolish Fletcher's court and to move its jurisdiction over to the Fourth Circuit Court, sitting in Richmond, Virginia. She later claimed that the most effective way to force the JAGs to consider "whether they really wanted this Court was to propose that we get rid of [it.]" Such a tactic may have persuaded the JAGs that her alternative was worse than what they had grown used to in the past quarter-century, and it may have pushed the court to modify some of the doctrinal positions that had generated such controversy, which it did. Ultimately Siemer orchestrated the selection of a new chief judge and Fletcher's removal from that post, although he continued to sit as a judge until 1985.

Taken together, the concerns voiced by Senator Russell in 1951, the consistent refusal of Congress to grant life tenure, and the unprecedented tactics of the General Counsel all reiterate the fundamental question that dogged the court from the outset – whether it has been, can, and should be truly independent of the military. They also invite some consideration of the relationship between the military justice system and the larger civilian community from which the military is drawn. No one can deny that military justice operates within and reflects a distinct internal legal culture. From the Revolutionary Era to the present, this culture has evolved in a separate form and, with few exceptions, virtually independent of the civilian world. Whether the Constitution's Framers intended this to occur is less important than that it has occurred.

As the military has become a more professional organization, less sympathetic to and less dependent on a civilian based force, this tendency may have been exacerbated in large measure by the silent acquiescence of the external legal community. Several indications of acquiescence can be identified. First, there has been a consistent and, in the last four decades, an exacerbated tendency for the U.S. Supreme Court to abstain from intervention in military justice appeals. When it has involved itself, it has always sustained the military position, with only one exception. That exception, *O'Callahan v. Parker* (1969), was summarily overruled in 1987.[32] Of these kinds of cases,

[32] *O'Callahan v. Parker*, 395 U.S. 258 (1969); *Solario v. United States*, 483 U.S. 435 (1987).

Chief Justice William Rehnquist insisted that "courts must give great deference to the professional judgment of military authorities concerning the relative importance of a particular military interest." "Judicial deference," he added, "is at its apogee when legislative action under the congressional authority to raise and support armies and make rules and regulations for their governance is challenged."[33] Rehnquist's claims to the contrary, it is difficult if not impossible to ascertain any specific Congressional intent that the Supreme Court exercise such deference.

A second consequence of this historical lack of civilian judicial interest in military justice is the similar lack of interest on the part of American law schools. For the most part, military law has been absent from the major law reviews. The subject has not been considered appropriate for inclusion in the usual curriculum, with the exception of an occasional offering at a time of public awareness of the military – as in, for example, the early 1970s when controversy over the Vietnam War was at its height. The last forty years have seen few graduates from the elite law schools go into careers in military law.

As in American law in general, so in military justice, historical change has been generated more often by reaction rather than innovation. Military culture tends to be conservative in character, and military justice has reflected this tendency. Because it mirrors a military culture and the military legal culture within it, significant change has been slow to occur. When it has, most often it has resulted from Congressional fiat rather than military initiative. Congressional insistence forced the military to welcome women into the service academies, and Congressional interplay with a presidential proposal resulted in the adoption of the "don't ask-don't tell" approach to homosexuality in the military. The insistent claim that military justice must be separate from its civilian counterpart, as well as the consistent assertion that the primary purpose of the military is victory rather than misplaced reliance on judicial norms, dominates the history of American military law and justice. As we have seen, such domination, with very few exceptions, has occurred with the acquiescence of the American judiciary, particularly in times of war when the judiciary has consistently deferred as well to executive branch assaults on civil liberty. Its perpetuation illustrates the fundamentally unsolvable dilemma of military justice in a civilian society.[34]

Yet, American military justice has been transformed to a remarkable extent. A brief comparison between two of the most notorious American army court-martials in the twentieth century illustrates how far the system

[33] *Goldman v. Weinberger*, 475 U.S. 503 (1986); *Roster v. Goldberg*, 453 U.S. 57 (1981).

[34] An excellent example of this trend is the 1942 case of the German saboteurs, *Ex Parte Quirin*, 317 U.S. 1 (1942).

has come since 1945. One arose out of World War II, the other from the Vietnam War. One involved a private convicted of desertion, the other a lieutenant convicted of involvement in the murder of some 500 Vietnamese during the My Lai massacre in Vietnam. One admitted he had run away from his unit, the other admitted no wrongdoing. One was tried under the old Articles of War, the other under the Uniform Code of Military Justice.

Only one soldier has been executed for desertion by the American military since 1864. Other members of the armed forces had been sentenced to death for the offense, but only Edward Slovik was actually executed. He had no attorney to assist in his defense. His "assigned counsel" went into business after the war. How much he knew about rules of evidence and criminal procedure may be imagined. He made no objection to any members of the court, called no witnesses on Slovik's behalf, declined to cross-examine four of the five government witnesses, and did not even make a closing statement as the court-martial concluded. The proceeding must have been one of the shortest on record. It began at 10:00 A.M. on November 11, 1944, and was completed – verdict rendered, death sentence imposed – by 11:40, not even 1 and 3/4 hours in length. From arrest and confinement on October 9, 1944 to execution on January 31, 1945, the entire process of military justice for Slovik took a little more than three months.

On March 16, 1968, Second Lieutenant William Calley led Charlie Company of the Army's first battalion, 20th Infantry in the murder of approximately 500 Vietnamese civilians. On September 5, one day before he was due to be discharged from the Army, Calley faced charges for the multiple murders of "Oriental human beings." The pretrial investigation began on November 23. Calley's actual court-martial began on November 17, 1970, more than two years after the incident at My Lai. Calley had as his lead counsel a former judge of the USCAAF, George Latimer. Convicted on March 29, 1971, Calley was sentenced to life imprisonment at hard labor. His court-martial lasted 45 days, making it one of the longest in American history, and it may be contrasted with Slovik's, which took less than two hours. Further appeals, as well as presidential interference, extended the Calley case into 1976, when the U.S. Supreme Court refused to hear his appeal. Actually, Calley spent only a few months in jail. The Vietnam War had ended before the case was concluded.

There are important differences between these two court-martials. One was secret; the other occurred in the midst of major publicity, antiwar agitation, and a presidential scandal resulting in Richard Nixon's resignation from the Presidency. One was efficient, rapid, and rigorous, the other drawn out and controversial. Calley had well-trained counsel, and the benefit of the due process procedures set forth in the Uniform Code of Military Justice, to say nothing of the opportunities for appellate review. Slovik did not, even though according to military law in effect in 1944, the treatment meted out to him was legal. Taken together, these two court-martials well illustrate what military justice had been and what it had become.

CONCLUSION

All the underlying fears for the fate of civil liberties in a time of war, whether declared or not, have reappeared since the terrorist attacks of September 11, 2001. On November 13, 2001, President George Bush issued an order calling for military commissions to try those who had somehow provided assistance for the attacks. Taking a cue from Franklin Roosevelt's ill-advised order in 1942, Bush barred any exercise of judicial review "in any court of the United States, or any State thereof." It soon became clear, however, that the administration, speaking through its very conservative Attorney General John Ashcroft, intended the executive order to apply primarily to foreign nationals who might be residing in the United States or abroad. Essentially but not exclusively, the order would operate outside the United States. Apparently, if one was suspected of being a foreign terrorist, one did not deserve – let alone require – constitutional rights.

Ashcroft appeared to consider it unnecessary to prove that one was such an individual. Presumably, such a determination requires "fact finding and procedural protections of an independent court capable of distinguishing between the guilty and the innocent." These characteristics are usually not attributed to military tribunals, which Michal Belknap describes as "an expeditious way of determining guilt and meting out sentences, particularly the death penalty." American military legal history reflects the fact that "historically such tribunals have functioned as instruments for punishment, not exoneration."

On March 21, 2002, in the wake of severe criticism from diverse quarters, the Defense Department issued detailed procedures for the new military commissions, some of which moved in the direction of greater due process protection. Judicial review was still excluded, although officials acknowledged that "it's not within our power to exclude the Supreme Court from the process." More to the point, of course, is the High Court's inclination to exercise this power on its own, with similar results. Possibly with such awareness in mind, on February 10, 2003 the American Bar Association adopted a four-part resolution. Brief discussion of its provisions seems an appropriate way to conclude this account of American military legal history. History, recalled Mark Twain, does not repeat itself, but it does sometimes rhyme.

The ABA called for those detained within the United States as "enemy combatants" to be afforded "meaningful judicial review," albeit employing a standard appropriate both to the needs of the detainee and the requirements of national security. It asked that such individuals not be denied counsel, subject again to the standard just noted. It suggested that Congress in coordination with the executive branch "establish clear standards and procedures governing the designation and treatment of U.S. citizens, residents, or others who are detained within the United States as 'enemy combatants.'" Finally, the ABA urged that in setting such policy, "Congress and the Executive Branch should consider how the policy adopted by the United States may affect the response of other nations to future acts of terrorism." In the context of the 2003 War with Iraq, such a suggestion takes on added importance.

American military legal history, as I noted at the outset, has been dogged by conflicting principles that indeed may be incapable of resolution. How far should due process be observed if the system that insures it is itself under attack? To what extent should open criticism be permitted when its expression might, as Lincoln feared during the Civil War, undermine the system of representative government that protects it? To what extent should the military justice system rather than the civil courts be given responsibility for answering these questions? If our legal history does not provide clear, concise answers, perhaps one can find clues in our past. For better or for worse, our military legal history may best represent a synthesis of principle and expediency. To see evidence of its continuing presence, it is necessary only to look around.

18

THE UNITED STATES AND INTERNATIONAL AFFAIRS, 1789–1919

EILEEN P. SCULLY

The United States did not join the ranks of great powers until after the Spanish-American War and did not become a decisive force in global affairs until World War I. This apparent trajectory from isolated insularity to great power stature has generated the myth that until the "imperial thrust" of the late 1890s, Americans enjoyed a certain "free security," from George Washington's presidency to Theodore Roosevelt's, afforded by the fortuitous combination of geography and European preoccupations. Yet, from the earliest days of the Republic, competition and consolidation among European states – projected to every part of the globe – shaped the hemispheric and international context for America's continental expansion, economic ascent, and evolving constitutional order. In the first decades after the ratification of the Constitution, the nascent Republic pushed up against British, Spanish, French, and Native American holdings, and it truly was hostage to great power rivalries. Successive territorial acquisitions, the migration of Americans and their enterprises to all areas of the world behind the forward European advance, the end of formal European empires in the Americas, and the establishment of virtual U.S. regional hegemony in the Caribbean all unfolded in an interstate and increasingly capitalist world system. While modern state-building projects generated and naturalized the boundary between "domestic" and "foreign" affairs, expansion, transplantation, porosity, and transcendent founding principles confounded the complex construction of the "United States" as a distinct, fixed, concrete territorial nation-state.

To think about the history of law in America with regard to international affairs from 1789 to 1919 thus requires a vantage point beyond presidential administrations, successive foreign policy doctrinal enunciations, and the sequential eras periodizing conventional domestic history. Also inadequate are the high federalism and legalistic formalism evident in accounts that take the modern world order as a given, then track the United States as if it had been from the start the constructed, territorially bounded, uniformly sovereign nation-state envisioned by international relations models, with a clear "inside" and "outside" and discernible (though contested) "national interests" pursued by an executive properly deferred to by other branches of government.

More historically accurate is the international landscape of the long nineteenth century, bracketed by the Seven Years War and establishment of the United States on the one side and by World War I and the Treaty of Versailles on the other. Encompassed within are political and social upheavals stretching from the Americas across Europe through to Russia, China, and Japan; transnational industrial and commercial revolutions; systems of slavery expanded, intensified, and then abolished; nation-states formed and forged; colonies invented, administered, and resisted; international law envisioned, expanded, colonized, and universalized; the Great War and previous lesser wars; and then – finally – the peace talks outside Paris and creation of the League of Nations. Sounding the close, with the Bolshevik Revolution in Russia and the unequal, unworkable bargains struck at Versailles, comes the first upsurge of twentieth-century epistemological challenges to the paradigmatic orderings of European hegemony.

What most sharply brings into a single conceptual frame the long nineteenth century's myriad comings and goings, conflagrations and coalescences, is the emergence, solidification, and internationalization of Europe's "Westphalian system" of secular, territorially bounded, fictively equal, sovereign nation-states expanding beyond their core regions into what consequently became the colonial world. The signposts of the long nineteenth century thus look to the construction of the modern international system as a world of territorial, sovereign, secular nation-states, arrayed in a racialized hierarchy of empires and colonies, small powers, great powers, and hegemons and legitimized by a repository of evolving international law and customary norms. A problem-centered analysis looks to the creation of central states, their penetration of hinterlands to attain "national sovereignty," struggles over what constitutes the "inside" and "outside" of these states, and the simultaneous coalescence of Euro-American states into a "family of nations" as against deficient sovereigns bound to the system through "unequal treaties" and economic dependency.

From the vantage point of the long nineteenth century, American history is appropriately merged into the history of this Westphalian system, this panoply of territorial nation-states and absolute sovereigns, colonies and empires, international law and customary practices, just wars and ephemeral peacetimes, diplomacy and *realpolitik*. Though it blurs details and crosscuts presidential administrations, this *longue durée* is nonetheless essential to understanding the relative speed, complex causation, and collective consciousness associated with the transformation of the United States from those beleaguered thirteen colonies hugging the Atlantic coast to that great power at Versailles whose president was pushing and persuading all others into a promised new world order. In the creation, internal development, territorial expansion, and near global ascendancy of the United States by 1919, the two meta-narratives of the Westphalian long nineteenth century are inextricably intertwined: the one – revolutions, wars, colonies, and empires; and the other – an evolving language and logic of power and participation in the world of nation-states, territorial sovereigns, and a notional "international rule of law."

I. THE WORLD OF WESTPHALIA

Although scholars disagree about the extent to which the Peace of Westphalia (1648) actually inaugurated a new epoch in international affairs, there is broad consensus that the arrangements called for by the signatories tended to secularize international relations, give sway to a more decentralized international order, elevate the sovereign territorial state as the primary unit of diplomacy, emphasize the balance of power as the principal avenue for stabilizing the system, and encourage a self-helping, minimalist approach to the "rules of the game." The terms of the agreements, and the Congress of Westphalia through which they were reached, laid the foundations for both realist and idealist visions of world order, the one view supposing that stability was best achieved by autonomous states pursuing self-interests and the other, that peace and mutuality might be brought by supra-national norms and structures.

The defining attributes of the Westphalian system include the primacy of territorial sovereign nation-states, international law as an instrument for preserving nation-states and regularizing relations among them, theoretical equality and mutual non-intervention among qualified sovereigns, force as a legitimate recourse for state interests, and the use of alliances and treaties to prevent the domination of any one power over all others. The contrasting "Charter conception" of world affairs in the era of the United Nations recognizes non-state actors, such as individuals and transnational organizations; views international law as a proper vehicle for achieving global parity and well-being; posits that binding obligations are incurred by membership in the world community, rather than solely by a sovereign's consent; and seeks to narrow the legitimate occasions for the use of force.

The original signatories to the 1648 Treaty of Westphalia ending the Thirty Years War had emerged as modern monarchies by the eighteenth century, secular nation-states by the time of the American Civil War, and highly organized, intensely nationalistic imperial rivals by the start of the twentieth century. Founding Westphalian orderings of sovereignty, diplomacy, and a supra-national but non-binding code of conduct were given philosophical and doctrinal coherence by Enlightenment suppositions about transcendent natural rights, the social contract, and the law of nations. They were infused with concern for individual liberties and national self-determination by the American and French Revolutions. The violence of the latter, and the ensuing Napoleonic Wars, pushed aside naturalist visions of international law as a higher order, bringing in the first full wave of narrower positivist assertions that explicit agreements and customary usages are all that bind sovereigns. Beginning with the Congress of Vienna's (1815) post-Napoleonic reordering of Europe, these regional-cultural norms and protocols were then stabilized through successive multilateral congresses and institutionalized by variegated conventions. Marked by the Congress of Berlin (1885), Westphalian norms were racialized through late nineteenth-century developmental theories and extended beyond Europe through colonialism and informal imperialism. They were redeemed in some measure as democratizing, equalizing mechanisms in human affairs when the League of Nations expanded and institutionalized membership in the "family of nations."

European expansion and ascendance organized Westphalia, and Westphalia in turn shaped not only the international environment but also the internal governance of members, would-be members, and dominated regions. As the American Framers well understood, moving out of the ranks of colonies, protectorates, and imperial holdings ultimately required adoption and institutionalization of the "Westphalian mechanics" that facilitated mutual dealings among secular, territorially bounded, fictively equal, sovereign nation-states. Acceptance as a peer, even if still a rival, meant demonstrating the attributes of a modern state – an effective, functionally secular central government exercising a monopoly over the means of violence, discernible and defensible national boundaries, a legal system upholding the "standard of civilization" if not for all than at least for resident foreigners, rules for demarcating insiders and outsiders, and an openness to international trade.

In Westphalian states, the expansion of representational governance and electoral mobilization of populations generated an "imperial citizenship" for sojourning members, extending politics to global dimensions. Extraterritorial jurisdiction over and diplomatic-military interventions on behalf of individuals and their enterprises on the basis of nationality became an expectation, entitlement, and instrument of state. Greater travel and commerce led to more frequent clashes between governments over the activities and status of resident foreigners. Sojourners became ever more the embodiment of national power, making each such clash a question of "national honor." Resident foreigners were hypothetically subject to local laws and were required to exhaust local remedies before invoking diplomatic protection. However, the stipulation that local remedies ought to conform to the "standard of civilization" transformed potential equity and accommodation into informal imperialism and commercial penetration.

Colonial powers inflated and zealously guarded the rights of their own nationals residing in non-Western areas, deploying a gunboat legalism that combined coercive force with invocation of international law and customary norms. Using treaties and diplomatic protection conventions as the support beams of an informal imperialism in which indigenous central governments were kept in place to maintain local order, pay off loans and indemnities, and enforce unequal treaties required the foreign powers to compel their own nationals to conform to the letter of these treaties. As nationality-based claims proliferated, each requiring expenditure of state resources and incurring some degree of risk, central governments adopted ever less consensually based definitions and determinations of nationality status and moved to monopolize and scrutinize the movement of individuals across boundaries, as seen in the expansion of passports in Western Europe beyond their original purpose of policing vagrancy and the comings and goings of particular groups. Municipal laws and policies making nationality exclusive, discernible, and demonstrable were reinforced by presumptive expatriation mechanisms and regulations pertaining to the status of spouses and offspring.

The norm of absolute territorial sovereignty meant subordinating or subsuming all contending sovereignties in the realm, and it recommended a strong executive hand to guide the "ship of state." To be a sovereign among sovereigns mandated a discernible demarcation between internal governance and external relations, such that a state has an inside and an outside, with known ways of distinguishing between insiders and outsiders. Enlightenment-era critiques of mercantilism as a violation of an inherent right of nations to trade freely were reformulated so that refusal to trade or to open local markets for commerce was contrary to international law, and hence proof of deficient sovereignty. Comity among fellow sovereigns required enforcement of agreed-on terms within the internal realm, shaping laws regarding resident aliens, immigration, commerce, and later, religious minorities. Positivism narrowed the sources of obligation binding sovereigns to expressions of consent, as in treaties and customary practice; electoral politics in Westphalian states complicated the meaning and shortened the duration of sovereign consent, whereas governments not qualified to join the "family of nations" seemed perpetually bound. Taken together, sovereignty, nationality, diplomatic protection, state responsibility, and treaties formed an "international property regime," enforced among equals through comity and on deficient sovereigns through gunboat legalism.

II. THE UNITED STATES AND WESTPHALIA

At both elite and popular levels, Americans demonstrated a historic and continuing ambivalence toward the Westphalian system of power politics and European-configured international norms as an edifice made for artifice – what Jefferson termed, "the workshop in which nearly all the wars of Europe are manufactured." From those emissaries sent out by Secretary Jefferson wearing "the simple dress of an American citizen" to the less conspicuously attired American delegation at Versailles, there was a conviction that Westphalia could be at once used and redeemed; in the right hands, the law of nations could be put to higher purposes than imperial aggrandizement and the balance of power. Disputes about whether to acquiesce to Westphalia or raise it to more transcendent heights shaped the origins of the first party system in the 1790s, as Hamiltonians and Jeffersonians debated the wisdom and implications of neutrality in war between France and Britain. The Hamiltonian-Jeffersonian divide on foreign policy delineated clear and enduring philosophical differences, conventionally juxtaposed as realism versus idealism. Yet the two traditions were transversely joined through the physics of power and expansion. Expansion would push Europe back to its own hemisphere while securing and enlarging the sphere of republican liberty; liberating trade would create a virtuous, productive citizenry at home and improve the lives of peoples in less fortunate parts of the world.

Resisting the baneful effects of Westphalia meant, paradoxically, an ever fiercer embrace of its central precept – absolute sovereignty. From President Washington's farewell cautions to his countrymen to Woodrow Wilson's doomed, life-draining fight to get America into the League of Nations, the conviction prevailed that expanding and protecting the empire of liberty required a free hand in international affairs. This in turn meant resisting any arrangement that might compromise U.S. sovereignty or circumscribe constitutional provisions, such as the role of Congress in declaring war, the Senate's treaty ratification power, and the invented right of presidents to enunciate and enforce foreign policy doctrines for this or that part of the globe. The climb from nascent republic to regional hegemon seemed only to amplify this indulgent national sense of being alone in the world, untainted by the mix of ends and means this ascendance had required.

For most jurists, legislators, public figures, and ordinary citizens, there was a "foreign" foreign policy, enacted "out there" in the world, probably best not undermined by constitutional stickling and partisan bickering. Bifurcated from this somewhat intangible realm was a "domestic" foreign policy, made immediate and real through clashes on immigration, resident aliens, profits and wages in business and manufacturing, periodic foreign extradition demands, and reports from out there about insults to particular Americans or imminent threats to some mix of concrete and abstract "American interests." Always, there was a suspicion of entangling alliances, multilateral organizations, and supra-national designs, a disposition infused with that much remarked-on sense of national exceptionalism.

Territorial and commercial expansion, although reconciled by James Madison's innovative reasoning about how a republic might become an empire of liberty, nonetheless brought the United States more fully into the trajectory of Westphalian powers. Continental conquest and obliteration of indigenous cultures and land rights intersected first with early enunciations of modern international law as justifying war to gain territory not yet productively and fully put to profitable use. Following paths carved out by Britain, Spain, and France, American commercial and religious groups staked their claims within territories and societies rendered vulnerable by the "deficient sovereignty" of traditional rulers. While invoking transcendent norms and urging a liberalization of international law, private American commercial and cultural enterprises in Latin America, Asia, Africa, and the Ottoman Empire – never as substantial or far-reaching as European concerns in those regions before 1920 – gained the shelter of the international "rule of law," through most favored nation clauses in unequal treaties that the U.S. government concluded on European victories in colonial wars. In Latin America, the vision of a hemisphere of free republics robustly sheltered from old worlds inspired the 1823 unilateral pronouncement that only much later came to be known as the Monroe Doctrine. Originating from well-founded fears of European reconquest of the Americas after the first wave of successful independence struggles, President James Monroe's hemispheric "off limits" warning to old world monarchs gambled correctly that British naval supremacy could be counted on to hold back the rivals of free trade. Some seven decades later, various "corollaries" transformed the Monroe Doctrine into a declaration of American hemispheric suzerainty, backed by growing U.S. military, economic, and political force.

Over the course of the long nineteenth century, Westphalia's gravitational imperatives and incentives inscribed on the distinctive American system all of the standard markings of modern nation-states, bringing it into far closer structural and philosophical convergence with its foreign counterparts than the Framers first envisaged. The centralizing push of Westphalia intersected with the centralizing logic of federalism, with power gravitating to the national government vis-à-vis the states and to the executive branch over the legislative and judicial. This was an uneven and contested process, with the outcome unclear until the tumultuous end of the nineteenth century and start of the twentieth. Then, propelled by industrialization and globalizing forces, the American state grew more surely into the Westphalian template of large modern militaries, funded through national systems of revenues, all administered by centralized, pervasive bureaucracies and overseen by governments voted in by politically mobilized populations.

Nationwide labor strikes, massive immigration from Southern and Eastern Europe, corporate competition and consolidation, ever more volatile boom-bust cycles, and a round of international crises seemed to shift the dynamic and direction of American politics. To borrow Walter LaFeber's striking metaphor, the American constitutional order underwent "a centrifugal-centripetal effect: as American military and economic power moved outward, political power consolidated at home," bringing forth a train of "[i]mperial presidencies, weak congresses, and cautious courts."[1] Here again, the context was international. Late nineteenth-century globalization accelerated events and linked peoples up in activities and ideas crossing boundaries even while multiplying and constructing differences. Across the world, governments, power holders, and rivals undertook state-building projects built on some form of hyper-national identity; multinational empires remade themselves through new technologies of mass mobilization and surveillance. Sovereignty came ever more to signify the successful consolidation of control over delineated lands and mobilized populations.

III. WESTPHALIA AND THE CONSTITUTIONAL ORDER

Across presidents, policies, parties, chief justices, and eras, there were four core and interconnected areas in which American law and legal understandings were shaped most decisively over the long nineteenth century by this jagged, resisted convergence with Westphalian language, logic, and realities: (1) political sovereignty, as shared and divided between state and national governments under federalism and arrayed across the three branches of government through checks and balances; (2) constitutionalism and territoriality, as the Framers' conjoined imperatives for a government kept limited in authority and reach; (3) volitional allegiance, as the origin and continuing basis for citizenship and its extra-territorial extension into nationality; and (4) the "international rule of law," as aspiration, premise, weapon, and hindrance in America's dealings abroad.

In each area, Westphalian dilemmas generated solutions that preserved some core elements of the founding vision while surrendering others. As well, each evolved through ad hoc arrangements given force and coherence only under the pressure of a series of converging crises in the 1890s. The

[1] Walter LaFeber, "The Constitution and United States Foreign Policy: An Interpretation," in David Thelen, ed. *The Constitution and American Life* (Ithaca, NY, 1988).

tensions within federalism came to mandate a divided "internal sovereignty" and a unitary "external sovereignty," leading one later Justice to claim that the Framers had successfully "split the atom" of sovereignty. External sovereignty became extra-constitutional and was concentrated in the federal government, the executive branch most particularly. Constitutionalism and territoriality were ruptured, as the Supreme Court discerned in all previous expansion a sanction for executive and legislative branch arrangements for America's new imperial holdings wherein the Constitution did not follow the Flag. American nationality was nearly severed from domestic citizenship, becoming the property of the national government to apportion, define, and retract, ever more like an adoption agreement than John Locke's social contract. The international "rule of law" frayed under the late nineteenth-century imperial scramble, leading to a surge of internationalism and competing visions of what might best bring equity and stability to world affairs. Wilsonianism emerged as a middle way between reactionary militarism and revolutionary internationalism.

Federal courts were instrumental and central to the uneven, contested convergence of Westphalia and the American constitutional order, but in quite complex ways. Judicial decisions pertained largely to the areas of immigration, bilateral treaty obligations, and local enforcement of international law – especially regarding the status of resident aliens, extradition demands, and the domestic moorings of international trade. At the same time, the incorporation of international law into the Constitution meant that federal courts had always to look at the United States from the outside in, revisiting time and again the perceived tensions among national territorial sovereignty, government by consent, and federalism's power-sharing configurations. Most Justices throughout the period shared the premise expressed so much later by Felix Frankfurter in *Harisiades v. Shaunessy* (1952): "It is not for the Court to reshape a world order based on politically sovereign states."[2] Such stoicism veils the historical reality that – if not quite present at the creation – the Court helped carve out and shore up this Westphalian world order. In mediating claims on the Constitution's ambiguous promises, jurists reified the categories thus employed: sovereignty, jurisdiction, citizenship-nationality, the standard of civilization, state responsibility, and territorial boundaries.

Complicating judicial assaying was the broader shift in contemporary understandings of international law, particularly on questions of how sovereigns may be bound. Jeremy Bentham's origination of the term "international law" in the 1780s had crystallized a distinction struggled over since the mid-seventeenth century between, on the one hand, obligations arising

[2] 342 U.S. 580, 596, Frankfurter, concurring.

out of treaties, precedents, and customs and, on the other, transcendent rights and responsibilities inhering in human nature and incumbent on sovereigns as participants in a social contract by which nations are joined in a moral community. In the mid-nineteenth century, the more bounded (positivist) understanding of international law gained momentum, seeming to pull Westphalia ever further from naturalist moorings. As Bentham stood between two worlds, though, so too did Americans straddle the natural law vision of nations as moral beings brought together in a social contract and the less ethereal view of international law as obligations agreed on by independent, fictively equal sovereigns whose overriding moral imperative was the preservation of their own territorial nation-state. Integrating the law of nations into the Constitution had not been mere pragmatism, but an article of faith among the Framers; to paraphrase first Chief Justice John Jay, when the United States took its place "among the nations of the earth," it became "amenable to the law of nations." Sovereignty in and of itself required this amenability. At the same time, the Constitution invests Congress with the authority "to define offenses against the law of nations," underscoring an appreciation that some truths were not as self-evident as others. Assigning this definitional power to a representative body placed the "law of nations" in an enduring tension with state and federal interests, both directly subject to the unpredictable will of those who have consented to be governed.

These changing conceptions of the "consent of the sovereign" marked the gradual ascendance of positivism in international law over the late nineteenth century. Yet, American thinking did not envision positivism as devoid of naturalist morality. There was no simple Jeffersonian-Hamiltonian juxtaposition in American thought between the social contract among nations envisioned by Grotius and Vattel and the "consent of the sovereign" view of obligations gaining ground among Westphalian states. The equation of "consent of the sovereign" to "consent of the people" offered a synthesis of the two, rather than seeming to force a choice. Leading American jurists, legal commentators, and diplomats envisioned a positivist grounding for international law as an absolute prerequisite for an international system built on social contract principles, where "the people" might stand as the only legitimate source of international obligations.

IV. FEDERALISM AND WESTPHALIAN SOVEREIGNTY

Westphalian territorial and national sovereignty meant above all negating or subsuming competing sovereignties within the land. In the United States this was a process evident not only around state prerogatives, but even more starkly so in the Marshall Court's relegation of Native American nations to the status of "domestic dependent nations," subsequently determined by Congress to lack the requisite capacity to conclude treaties with the government. Continental expansion through the nineteenth century brought regions and peoples into different legal relations with the federal government, producing a rich mix of competing sovereignties and defining America as an extended polity with variegated and competing jurisdictional assertions that challenged constitutionalism and territoriality. The intersection of regionalism, states rights precepts, and federally sanctioned slavery slowed and complicated the process of nation building.

Judicial decisions locating "national sovereignty" in the Congress sanctioned federal foreign affairs preeminence vis-à-vis the states and initially tilted the balance within the federal government toward legislative predominance. Rulings that put treaties on a par with legislation provided Congress a foreign policy role beyond the Senate's designated "advise and consent" ratification authority; the Court's "later in time" rule enabled Congress to amend or void treaties, in ongoing response to political currents of the day. Undertaken with the authority derived from constitutional text and "original intent," judicial activism brought treaty obligations and international law to bear on the whole of the American legal system down through every locality. Before *Erie Railroad Co. v. Tompkins* (1938) rejected the practice, courts applied customary international law, if not embodied in legislation and statute, as a variant of domestic, non-federal common law; they did not include it within the "supreme law of the land" and so did not take state violations under judicial review. Enacting legislation needed to effect this court-mandated alignment between domestic and international law, Congress was brought into state realms once thought shielded by constitutional cartography.

Both federalism and consensual governance, each raising questions about the location of American sovereignty, thus greatly complicated assertions of external sovereignty as among other sovereigns. For Justice Wilson, in *Chisholm v. Georgia* (1793), "[t]o the Constitution of the United States the term sovereign is totally unknown." A more Westphalian rendering came in Chief Justice Marshall's much-cited dictate in *Schooner Exchange v. M'Faddon* (1812), which at once defined territorial sovereignty and acknowledged obligations accruing by virtue of membership in a "world . . . composed of distinct sovereignties, possessing equal rights and equal independence, whose mutual benefit is promoted by intercourse with each other." Here, consent was tacit, signified by the claim to sovereignty among equals, with a nation's jurisdiction within its own territory being "necessarily exclusive and absolute . . . susceptible of no limitation not imposed by itself."[3]

[3] 2 U.S. 419, 454; 11 U.S. 116, 136.

For most of the nineteenth century, however, the establishment of national sovereignty was complicated by the intersection of expansion and slavery. The doctrine of popular sovereignty, invoked most notably by Stephen Douglas on the extension of slavery to the new Mexican cession and the remaining Louisiana Territory, challenged the legality of Congressional authority over the governance of these regions. The Marshall Court had read as a broad grant Article IV § 3 of the Constitution, empowering Congress to "make all needful Rules and Regulations respecting" the territories. Opponents held up the Ordinance of 1787 as a charter, and – failing that – looked to the law of nations regarding acquisition and governance. Congress had vitiated the Ordinance in response to violent disorder in the Ohio region; the Court effectively voided it in 1850, declaring that it had been superseded by the Constitution. By Reconstruction, it had rejected entirely the idea that the reach of Congress was not contiguous with U.S. borders.

Among the principal avenues available for federal courts to nationalize sovereignty was the constitutional incorporation of international law and treaties into the "supreme law of the land." This left it to federal courts vitalized by the invention of judicial review – to assign relative weights to the constituent elements of this supreme law, including written and unwritten international law, specific treaty obligations, and Congressional legislation. The Constitution's own blend of transcendent naturalism and more circumscribed provisions was evident in judicial decisions on the relationship between the law of nations and the American political-legal order. *United States v. Palmer* (1816) gave federal circuit courts criminal jurisdiction over piracy, not directly on the basis of international law, but because it was a crime that violated the "peace and dignity of the United States."[4] The formula that international law is to be enforced only insofar as it has a basis in U.S. law seemed to reconcile territoriality with obligations to prevent or prosecute violations against the law of nations.

International law impinged on U.S. law through canons of construction: Marshall's dictum in *Murray v. Schooner Charming Betsy* (1804) was, "An act of Congress ought never to be construed to violate the law of nations, if any other possible construction remains."[5] Here, other possible constructions did intrude, as the meaning of the law of nations narrowed to treaties and customary usages. The implications were quickly manifested on the question of slavery. Classic naturalist theory resounds in Justice Story's Circuit Court opinion in *US v. The Schooner La Jeune Eugenie* (1822): "every doctrine, that may be fairly deduced by correct reasoning from the rights

[4] 16 U.S. 610.

[5] 6 U.S. 64, 118.

and duties of nations, and the nature of moral obligations, may theoretically be said to exist in the law of nations; and unless it be relaxed or waived by the consent of nations, which may be evidenced by their general practice and customs, it may be enforced by a court of justice, whenever it arises in judgment."[6] Yet, Story's acknowledged exceptions – consent as evidenced by general practice and customs – became a basis for Marshall's distinction in *The Antelope* (1825) between "whatever might be the answer of a moralist" and the "legal solution" jurists must seek "in those principles of action which are sanctioned by the usages, the national acts, and the general assent, of that portion of the world of which he considers himself a part, and to whose law the appeal is made." This was further narrowed in Justice Taney's *Dred Scott* precept that, "there is no law of nations standing between the people of the United States and their Government, and interfering with their relation to each other."[7]

As with slavery, transcendent laws of nature and the code of honor among sovereigns ran counter to the consent of the governed when treaty obligations penetrated the domestic foreign policy realm, rather than requiring something somewhere "out there." For Chief Justice Marshall at the start, a treaty was first and foremost a contract between sovereigns. A treaty may be self-executing or may require enabling legislation from Congress. In cases pitting individual interests over the national good of adhering to contracts signed, the latter must always prevail. Adherents to the doctrine of *pacta sunt servanda* envisioned states as moral beings and sovereigns bound by honor, fearing that breaches of faith among nations could only return the society of nations to Hobbesian primitivism. However, late nineteenth-century courts consistently upheld the federal policy of Chinese exclusion, notwithstanding the Burlingame Treaty promising reciprocal treatment of nationals. Anticipating Justice Sutherland's incidents of sovereignty reasoning by almost fifty years, the *Chinese Exclusion Case* (1889) affirmed that sovereignty, rather than the Constitution itself, invests Congress with full authority over immigration matters and the full discretion to interpret relevant treaty provisions. *Fong Yue Ting v. U.S.* (1893) included deportation and exclusion of particular individuals or groups as integral components of the "inherent and inalienable right of every sovereign and independent nation, essential to its safety, its independence and its welfare."[8]

The "later in time" rule devised by Justice Benjamin Curtis and fully sanctioned in *Cherokee Tobacco* (1870), put treaties on a par with legislation, thus subject to repeal and amendment. The "political question" doctrine served as an adjunct, allowing the Court to nullify all or parts of treaties,

[6] 26 F. Cas. 832.
[7] 23 U.S. 66, 121; 60 U.S. 393, 451.
[8] 130 U.S. 581; 149 U.S. 698, 703, 706.

defer to Congress, and turn over management of the consequences to the "political branches." *The Head Money Cases* (1883) affirmed that a treaty is "primarily a compact between independent nations" that "depends for the enforcement of its provisions on the interest and the honor of" those parties, and breaches may be negotiated or become precipitants to war.[9] The distinction between self-executing treaties and those requiring enabling legislation provided a further avenue for Congressional assertion of foreign policy powers. At the same time, Senate discretion as to which category treaties might fall into then brought enabling legislation into the realm of divided and overlapping prerogatives with the House of Representatives. The treaty power was marked as an exclusive federal power, beyond the reach of the Tenth Amendment, by *Missouri v. Holland* (1920). States were declared utterly irrelevant "[i]n respect of our foreign relations generally," in *U.S. v. Belmont* (1937).[10] The end of the Cold War, however, has revised questions about the place of the states in U.S. international relations.

Yet, locating sovereignty in one body of the people's representatives, the Congress, obligated federal courts to wrest it from others, state governments. Along the federal-state axis of power division and sharing, a consensus had emerged early on for federal preeminence in what the Founding generation understood as diplomacy, such as treaties and alliances; what remained contested throughout the nineteenth century was whether preeminence meant exclusivity and what "foreign affairs" included. The Framers put off-limits to the states that range of prerogatives then understood as "foreign affairs," including making treaties and alliances, conscripting and maintaining national troops and warships, taxing imports and exports, coining money, and granting letters of marque and reprisal. Yet the Constitution neither grants the federal government nor denies to the states full and sole purview over American international dealings, leaving the way open for concurrent federal-state powers in various areas. It was thus not foreordained that federal supremacy should become federal exclusivity; that is, the effective preemption of the states from a realm grown to include all aspects of immigration, naturalization and resident alien status, all diplomatic intercourse, the full range of extradition, expatriation, passports and travel, and all commerce deemed "foreign," even as it washed up on state shores and passed through intermediaries standing unmistakably on state soil.

The logic of federalism that propelled federal preeminence seemed reinforced by understandings of original intent discerned in the Framers' historical moment, recalling not only the self-evident vulnerability of the nascent Republic to geographically proximate foes with starkly different purposes

[9] 18 F. 135, 141.

[10] 301 U.S. 324, 331.

but also the specific deficiencies in the Confederation framework discussed at the Constitutional Convention and identified in *Federalist* essays. On a continent occupied by European powers and home to Indian nations still deemed foreign sovereigns, the prospect of state governors and legislators grown bold and querulous through diplomatic coups and impasses gave special urgency to that prescriptive sentiment heard all the way from Madison's *Federalist* 42 through the nineteenth century and beyond: "If we are to be one nation in any respect, it clearly ought to be in respect to other nations." Then and later, those who contemplated a more decentralized federalism were pushed to compromise by the invocation of threats to "national security." Over the nineteenth century and through the twentieth, presidents consistently used this same tactic to expand beyond recognition the executive power to respond to immediate threats by deploying troops on Southern borders and into other sovereign realms.

Over the nineteenth century, judicial deference and landmark decisions incrementally but steadily subordinated state prerogatives and powers to federal priorities in foreign affairs, quite broadly defined. State governments resisted in the interrelated areas of immigration, resident aliens, treaty obligations, extradition, and commerce; until the passage of the Seventeenth Amendment in 1913, states using legislative appointment of Senators benefited from the judicial endorsement of Congress as the seat of "national sovereignty." Chief Justice Marshall's deployment of the "dormant foreign Commerce Clause" in *Brown v. Maryland* (1827) brought state import-licensing requirements into "foreign commerce."

The struggle played out most dramatically on matters of extradition and resident alien status, as they inspired judicial demarcations between and among sovereignty-based federal prerogatives, constitutional stipulations regarding state-federal relations, interstate rendition protocols, internal state police powers, and cross-border management practices in a nation expanding up against contiguous sovereigns to the North, South, and West. The executive branch and the Senate eschewed international extradition arrangements until compelled by the energies of border states in the Union and the demands of international reciprocity; at mid-century, this internal push and external pressure prompted the Supreme Court to put extradition squarely under federal monopoly.

Similarly, the ultimate federal monopoly over immigration came by virtue of a combined, bottom-up push by coastal states, once courts had overruled passenger laws and associated ordinances by which New York, Boston, and San Francisco had managed arrivals numbering in the hundreds of thousands each year. Competing pressures on Congress from groups on both sides of the question produced compromise legislation, listing "undesirable" groups theoretically barred as immigrants, yet omitting funding and enforcement mechanisms. Economic depression in the early 1890s, combined with mounting popular anxieties about a loss of national identity, culminated in a federal assertion of sovereignty – addressed to both internal and external audiences: sovereignty is the ultimate power and authority to say who may cross into, and who must depart from, a demarcated territorial realm.

By the 1890s, federal control over immigration was complete, judicially sanctioned as a legitimate subordination of state concerns to a larger national interest in maintaining good relations with other nations and balancing the rival interests of domestic constituencies. With few exceptions, individual and particular groups of would-be immigrants had no right to invoke constitutional provisions or protections, until the 1890s. *Yick Wo v. Hopkins* (1886) extended Fourteenth Amendment protections to resident aliens targeted by state regulations. An emergent "alien rights tradition" was marked by the transfer of cases involving deportation and alien rights from the venue of immigration law to the criminal justice system. Landmark decisions separated immigration controls from deportation proceedings, construing the latter as punishment and thus amenable to the Due Process Clause. Cases up through the 1960s on state laws pertaining to resident alien inheritance demonstrate resistance to the interlocking logics of federalism and Westphalia.

Once located in the federal government, national sovereignty then gravitated from Congress to the executive branch, culminating in the "sole organ" theory of extra-constitutional executive power articulated in the 1930s in *Curtiss-Wright* (1936). Within the federal government, the checks and balances among the three branches, particularly between the Congress and the executive, open the way for each political generation to shift the balance in the exercise of foreign relations powers. In the phrase of presidential historian Edward S. Corwin: "The Constitution . . . is an invitation to struggle for the privilege of directing American foreign policy." To Congress comes purview over taxation, the common defense, interstate and foreign commerce, naturalization, treaty ratification, and criminalization of offenses against the law of nations. Executive branch power centers on the president as Commander in Chief, with the performance of that function subject to Congressional oversight. The other explicit foreign policy power assigned by the Constitution specifically and only to the president is the authority to receive foreign ambassadors. Beyond this, the president and Senate share power to make treaties and to appoint U.S. ambassadors, ministers, and consuls.

This "invitation to struggle" over where constitutionalism meets foreign affairs was seized from the start, contributing to the emergence of the first party system around Hamiltonian and Jeffersonian principles. Beginning with Secretary Hamilton himself, the triumvirate of presidential primacy, federal exclusivity, and foreign affairs exceptionalism seemed absolutely mandated by complex and manifest realities. Beyond mere survival, the measures and maneuvers required to propel the Republic into continental and commercial empire recommended an executive branch constrained only by "the exigencies of the nation and the resources of the community." In its double-entry bookkeeping for "domestic" and "foreign" realms, and its broad construction of "national interests" as intrinsically just, Hamiltonianism anticipated the mid-nineteenth-century shift in international law and diplomacy from naturalist invocations of transcendent moral imperatives to positivist views of sovereigns as absolute in their own realm and bound to other sovereigns only by retractable consent.

Early Jeffersonians envisioned the Constitution's foreign affairs powers as fully subject to checks and balances and state prerogatives, with Congress a full, and even dominant, partner. Yet, even before President Jefferson abandoned narrow constructionism to expand the empire of liberty by way of the Louisiana Purchase and in compliance with higher "laws of necessity, of self-preservation, of saving our country when in danger," Secretary Jefferson had already insisted that "[t]he transaction of business with foreign nations is Executive altogether." In the conflict with Hamilton over the treaty with France, the purposes and implications of neutrality, and President Washington's deployment of the modest diplomatic recognition power in the imbroglio over the arrival and activities of revolutionary France's new diplomatic envoy, Citizen Genet, Jefferson's calculations were no less directed to expedience and national interests than were Hamilton's. Historians discern a convergence after the War of 1812 of Jeffersonian and Hamiltonian visions of a commercial empire of liberty, with Jeffersonian agrarian republicanism periodically resurfacing when expansion seemed to serve plutocratic over populist interests.

Diverging on so many fundamentals around domestic federalism, Hamiltonians and Jeffersonians found common ground on the foreign policy dimensions of Hamilton's insistence in *Federalist* 80: "The peace of the whole ought not to be left at the disposal of a part." In its original invocation, this was quite clearly directed at the states, but almost immediately came to include individual citizens, when Secretary of State Jefferson shepherded through Congress the (Logan) "Act to Prevent Usurpation of Executive Functions" by individuals with the "temerity and impudence" to "interfere" in presidential dealings with other sovereigns. More gradually, and certainly against greater resistance, though, the subordination of the "parts" to the "peace of the whole" argument transformed Congress into merely elected representatives of "the parts," incapable of seeing beyond their electoral bargains to behold the national interest.

Federal courts gave Hamiltonianism the greater impetus from the start, cumulatively sanctioning both federal supremacy in foreign affairs and, more haltingly, executive branch primacy over the legislative and judicial branches. Deference to the other two branches on foreign affairs came through the political question doctrine and the act of state doctrine, each demarcating certain areas as not amenable to judicial resolution. Legal scholars see in this deference an understanding that giving way on foreign policy questions afforded the judiciary a surer foothold in the domestic sphere. So too, however, whereas the Federalist orientation of early jurists ebbed and flowed beyond the Marshall Court on domestic issues, its hold was more abiding on questions arising around federalism and international affairs.

In unanticipated ways, judicial affirmations of Chinese exclusion as an exercise of a "plenary power" growing out of sovereignty, apart from and above the Constitution, equipped the executive branch with both the motive and the doctrinal precedents for the post-1900 push for presidential primacy in American international affairs. The "large policy" advocates of the Republican "System of '96," some genuinely concerned about the advance of Japan toward Hawaii and the Philippines and the tempting vulnerability of Central America, were hemmed in by divided legislators and stalled initiatives on tariff reciprocity, as well as by the ever more problematic disjuncture between U.S. protection of its sojourning nationals and violence against resident aliens in the United States. Westphalia's premise of the unitary sovereign, speaking and acting for the nation in a moment and forever, seemed now far more compelling and useful than divided and overlapping powers across three counterpoised branches of what was, after all, the same tree of liberty.

In re Nagle (1890) brought forth the Court's declaration that the president has implied powers: "the rights, duties, and obligation growing out of the Constitution itself, our international relations, and all the protection implied by the nature of the government under the Constitution."[11] Courts had earlier endorsed the executive's ultimate authority to determine the degree of force needed to handle and resolve an external difficulty. By the close of the century, jurists had fully sanctioned the expansion of that "modest implied power" authorizing Executive Orders and Executive Agreements, viewing the latter as treaties and hence as "the law of the land," despite the intended circumvention of the Senate; of the 2,000 or so international agreements the United States entered into from 1789–1939, only 800 were through the treaty process. Here was the inspiration for Theodore Roosevelt's "stewardship" theory of the presidency, expanded

[11] 278 F. 105, 109.

by Justice Sutherland in *Curtiss-Wright* in anointing the executive "the sole organ of the Federal government" in foreign relations. Elected by the people to assert, defend, and protect, a "national sovereignty" transferred directly from the erstwhile colonial master Great Britain to the new national government, the executive thus owed more to Westphalia and London than to the excruciations at Philadelphia.

In between *In re Nagle* and *Curtiss-Wright* came a succession of "imperial presidents," some more obviously so than others, but all exercising far more unilateral authority in American foreign relations than afforded to or even imagined by their nineteenth-century predecessors. President Theodore Roosevelt's "stewardship theory," that the president may do anything not explicitly forbidden by constitutional law to benefit the country's interests, was Hamiltonian at the core. It recalled the first Secretary of the Treasury's insistence that the only limits that mattered were "exigencies" and "resources." In its turn-of-the-century iteration, this "imperial presidency" was the cockpit of empire, as executive agreements on trade and tariffs took on an aura of constitutionality, and U.S. military interventions multiplied under the direction of the executive as Commander in Chief. Yet, here too, Hamiltonianism and Jeffersonianism were transversely joined in an expansion and extension of the "empire of liberty."

V. CONSTITUTIONALISM AND TERRITORIALITY

Americans left the eighteenth century firmly wed to territoriality and constitutionalism as principles and strictures essential to preserve individual liberty and government by consent. Having experienced collectively the coercive side of imperial protection and perpetual allegiance, the Framers envisioned an American government whose jurisdiction and authority were constrained, first, by the (expanding) geographic boundaries of the "United States of America" and, second, by the Constitution itself. In the abstract, conjoined territoriality and constitutionalism were consistent with the understandings of sovereignty that the founding generation derived from Emmerich Vattel's *The Law of Nations*, written during the Seven Years War and their principal source of inspiration on such matters. Sovereigns absolute in their domain, as against other sovereigns, meshed with the American idea that territorial proximity trumped all other claims; anticipating the right of other sovereigns to intervene on behalf of their own aggrieved subjects on American soil, the Alien Tort Claims Act (1789) had opened up federal courts to resident foreigners invoking rights based on international law. Original exceptions to territoriality were twofold: first, State Department maritime jurisdiction for crew on American flag ships, and, second, as provided for by the Crimes Act of 1790, federal authority over U.S. citizens abroad in cases of treason, piracy, slave trading, and counterfeiting.

This perceived congruity among territoriality, constitutionalism, and sovereignty is evident in Thomas Jefferson's quite straightforward statement on the rights and responsibilities of Americans abroad: the "persons and property of our citizens are entitled to the protection of our government in all places where they may lawfully go." Each element of the formulation speaks from Vattel. Citizens are entitled to protection for themselves and their property in reciprocation of allegiance. Sovereigns are obligated to protect and avenge citizens harmed in the territory of another sovereign, for otherwise "the citizen would not obtain the great end of the civil association, which is, safety." In Jefferson's "all places where they may lawfully go," may be heard Vattel's injunction that "[t]he foreigner cannot pretend to enjoy the liberty of living in the country without respecting the laws: if he violates them, he is punishable as a disturber of the public peace, and guilty of a crime against the society in which he lives: but he is not obliged to submit, like the subjects, to all the commands of the sovereign."[12]

Abstract congruity ran aground in the multiplication of American nationality as the basis for claims in foreign domains not reachable through territoriality and the division of those domains into members and non-members of the "family of nations." Here in Westphalian algebra, then, was where positivism constricted the Jeffersonian natural law vision – not in the "consent of the sovereign" basis of obligation, but in the gradations of sovereignty that transformed the world beyond the Appalachian Mountains into places and people more or less deserving of mutuality. When "nation" and "state" and "sovereign" are culturally inflected, Vattel's succinct and lucid precepts about non-interference, restraint, and mutuality among states as moral beings acquire an ambiguity he did not intend.

The rudiments of inflected Vattel came readily to hand when the United States concluded treaties embodying some degree of extra-territorial jurisdiction over its nationals in Morocco (1787), Algiers (1795), Tunis (1797), and Tripoli (1805). Independence had brought the loss of British protection against piratical attacks by the Barbary States on American vessels. Rulers of these city-states, under the nominal control of the Ottoman Porte, had developed a profitable trade in ransoming captured American crewmen. The treaties, and the Barbary Wars in 1801, gave the United States the same privileges in these areas enjoyed by other Western powers. However, until mid-century there was no identifiable American community residing in these areas, and in practice these privileges translated simply into consular jurisdiction over seamen on U.S. public and private vessels.

In terms of protecting Americans abroad, one legacy of the Barbary crisis was the meshing of interests in free trade, unencumbered neutrality, and

[12] Emmerich de Vattel, *The Law of Nations*, ed. Joseph Chitty (Philadelphia, 1861), Book II, Chapter VIII, §108.

equally emotive rhetoric in the "domestic" foreign policy realm about fellow citizens victimized by barbarous authorities beyond the Westphalian pale, and hence clearly outside the "family of nations." These early treaties opened the way for others in the 1830s with the Sublime Porte, giving Americans extra-territorial immunities from local authority in Turkey and Egypt. Seeking to get out from under the British Levant Trading Company and its required "consular protection" fees, the United States also hoped to challenge British and French dominance. The treaty allowed American navigation in the Mediterranean and through the Dardanelles and the Bosporus Straits; it also gave access to the Black Sea and markets of southern Russia.

In the inflected Vattel of American diplomacy and extension of nationality-based jurisdiction there were three distinct tiers. The first comprised relations with perceived legal and cultural equals, Western Europe in particular; the second, interactions in the Americas, the Pacific islands, and certain African areas; and the third, dealings with non-Western sovereigns who had ceded resident foreigners varying degrees of self-governance. In both the first and second spheres, resolution of conflicts over sojourning nationals occurred through invocation of international law, arbitration, bilateral treaties, and power politics. The defining difference between the two realms lay less in the exercise of formal diplomacy than in the impact of U.S. attitudes and decisions on the less powerful underdeveloped countries of Latin America, the Pacific, and Africa. What occurred as "comity" in U.S.-European relations translated into "hegemony" in the second realm, most especially in Central America.

In its diplomacy with Westphalian nations, although not yet a great power itself, the United States exerted the liberalizing influence – so clearly recalled by later generations – on issues of neutrality, free trade, individual rights antecedent to both nationalities and states, volitional allegiance and free expatriation, non-intervention by European powers in newly independent Latin American republics, international copyright and property standards, and regional conventions on communications and transportation. U.S. European conflicts typically centered on European governments' efforts to lay claim to the military services of their nationals who had become naturalized U.S. citizens. Confrontations with Britain over its impressments into military duty of sailors on American flagships brought together in the War of 1812 issues of volitional allegiance, U.S. sovereignty as extended to American ships, and the rights of neutrals.

What became official U.S. policy was first enunciated by Secretary of State James Buchanan in 1848, that no distinction should be drawn between native-born and naturalized Americans sojourning abroad when considering requests for diplomatic protection. Buchanan's approach gained ground in the 1850s, as the Democrats wooed German-American constituents, a group particularly concerned to be able to visit and even settle down in their places of birth. Attorney General Jeremiah Black issued an 1859 opinion characterizing American naturalization as "a new political birth" that erects a "broad and impassable line" between the new citizen and his native country. Reconstruction-era amendments and legislation creating federal citizenship and defining its privileges erased this native-naturalized distinction in American nationality.

After decades of periodic incidents and imbroglios, the United States and Western European powers reached a modus vivendi, settling competing claims on the basis of "comity," meaning a broad agreement among perceived legal and cultural equals about the rules of the game. Here, the norm became *par in parem non habet imperium* or "an equal has no power over an equal." While adhering to different membership models, *jus sanguinis* and *jus soli*, Western governments concluded bilateral treaties by way of preempting mutual conflict over the actions, circumstances, or fate of particular individuals. In terms of criminal jurisdiction, similar notions of due process, concern for reciprocity, and relative social and political stability allowed U.S. officials to pursue what has since been termed the "global due process" approach to diplomatic protection and extra-territorial interventions. In practice, this meant that an American citizen abroad charged with a crime in a "family of nations" member was turned over to local authorities, with the proviso that the individual would be treated humanely and get what most would considered a fair trial; official American responsibility was to obtain basic due process for an individual, less because of U.S. citizenship but more because common humanity demanded it.

In the second tier, territoriality as a limit on federal jurisdiction and the reach of American laws translated into empire, hegemony, and exploitation. In North America, settlers and entrepreneurs well preceded the state in defining what was to be the United States. The state followed and asserted jurisdiction over grand swaths of territory, incorporating residents into subjects and then citizens. The hope that expansion would fuel the empire of liberty became a driving imperative by the 1820s, slowed by sectionalism, race, and slavery. Diplomacy, treaties, wars, purchases, and incorporation – all defined and extended American sovereignty. The ultimate boundaries of the United States were marked where jurisdiction became subject to Westphalian protocols of diplomatic protection, intervention, and mutual recognition of competing sovereignties.

International boundaries changed Americans on the move into citizens on the one side and sojourning resident aliens on the other. New republics in Central America sought to encourage development by promising land to would-be immigrants. Learning from the template of Texas-Mexico, as Americans moved into Nicaragua, Costa Rica, Honduras, Guatemala, and El

Salvador, they thought to bring their American nationality with them and through assertion of diplomatic protection claims established autonomous enclaves resistant to fiscal and political control by native authority; sections of Honduras become such refuges for about 2,000 Americans around 1892, and concession holders took virtual control of the Mosquito Coast. While federal officials tended to defer to local authority in Latin America in cases involving an individual brought up on criminal charges, they energetically defended the physical safety and property rights of these concession-holding sojourners. In this setting, with a power ratio shifting decisively in America's favor, U.S. insistence that beyond American territory its citizens came under local authority gave free rein to soldiers of fortune, entrepreneurs, and would-be despots. Exemplifying the type was "filibuster" William Walker, who died by a firing squad in Honduras after leading mercenaries in three separate invasions of Central America and agitating among Southern slaveholders to annex the area. Deploring the lawless behavior of Walker and others of his ilk, the U.S. government nonetheless pursued the larger strategy of gunboat legalism, consolidating and capitalizing on gains made by individuals and businesses claiming American nationality.

Westphalian states reached across boundaries on behalf of the persons and property of their own nationals, using diplomatic protests, sanctions, and gunboats. Resident foreigners were subject to local laws and were required to exhaust local remedies before invoking diplomatic protection. However, the stipulation that local remedies ought to conform to a "universal standard of justice" transformed these apparently equitable and reciprocal agreements into informal imperialism and commercial penetration. At a minimum, the universal standard required basic due process. As well, municipal authorities had to provide a plausible and explicit reason for any infringement on a resident foreigner's person or property; such takings required a transparent legal process with equitable, prompt compensation. There was continuing disagreement about state responsibility in instances in which the wrong had been caused in the course of official efforts to suppress rebellion or by the actions of rebels themselves.

Local unrest and violence brought forth claims by foreigners for personal and property damage; resulting indemnities or blockades exacerbated the fiscal instability of central governments, inspiring efforts to extract taxes or payments from resident foreigners. These efforts provoked diplomatic interventions, feeding local unrest and violence. France established a monarchy in Mexico in the early 1860s, having arrived to collect debts; Spain incorporated Santo Domingo and launched war against Peru and Chile; a decade after its victory over Mexico and acquisition of the Mexican Concession, the United States led the assault and destruction of Greytown, in Nicaragua, after a U.S. consul was set on by a local mob, and the legality of this recourse was sanctioned in *Durand v. Hollins* (1854). In response to this coercive property regime, many Latin American countries incorporated into constitutions, treaties, contracts, and laws so-called Calvo clauses, requiring foreigners to relinquish recourse to diplomatic protection claims in contract disputes as a precondition for residence or business operations. While the United States looked to cement commercial ties through Pan-Americanism conventions on commercial affairs, such as copyright, customs duties, and communications, when the conferences began producing resolutions on diplomatic protection, nationality-based claims, and coercive collection of debts, the Senate had to step into the breach each time with a refusal to endorse the documents.

It was in the Asia-Pacific region that the second tier blended into the third; that is, the realm of non-Western sovereigns who had (often involuntarily) ceded resident foreigners varying degrees of self-governance. Before the Opium Wars of the 1840s, the few Americans who found their way to China were subject to local jurisdiction and assumed the risks involved as a trade-off, part of the costs of doing their own or their god's business. Britain's victory in the Opium War opened the way for the first Sino-American treaty, incorporating various privileges through the most-favored-nation (MFN) clause. Historically, this MFN multiplier, whereby "ends" seem to come without complicity in "means," reinforced the conviction evident from the time of the Founders that the United States could conform to and gain by Westphalian precepts and power politics without being corrupted in the process. Consistent with Jacksonian attitudes toward westward expansion and "obstacles" in the way, China and Japan were not simply other countries operating by different cultural and political mores; they were places en route, however slowly and ambivalently, to civilization, not unlike this or that Western territory headed for statehood among equals in the American Union. Expansion – territorial, commercial, and juridical – meant the transplantation of clear property rights, recognized forms of law and order, and free access to internal markets.

These same provisions and perceptions served as the model for subsequent similar arrangements in Siam (Thailand) in 1856, Japan (1858), and Korea (1856). The United States exercised extra-territoriality ("extrality") in varying degrees in these colonial areas and for the most part followed the European lead. In the Ottoman Empire, American extrality was shaped largely by preexisting Ottoman-Western arrangements. The model for consular jurisdiction in non-Christian regions was the "capitulations" that Westerners enjoyed in the Ottoman Empire until World War I, their grant dating to the twelfth century. When the Ottoman Turks conquered Constantinople in 1453, they expanded and regularized a system already in use in the Mediterranean, that of issuing letters of protection to non-Muslim migratory merchants. (The evocative term "capitulations" derives from the *capitula*, or chapters, in these documents). Quite different, though, were bilateral, postwar, state-to-state contracts, such as the 1842 Treaty of Nanking (Nanjing) opening China, the 1850 agreements opening Japan, and the revised treaties conceded to by Ottoman rulers. These nineteenth-century unequal relationships derived their destructive dynamic from an irreversible shift in the balance of power in favor of Western Europe and an effort by increasingly centralized Westphalian governments to incorporate colonial sojourners into the national polity.

American extra-territorial jurisdiction ultimately reached its most extensive and elaborate form in treaty port China, with the U.S. government reserving full jurisdiction over civil, criminal, and administrative cases involving American defendants; a range of rights and influence in Sino-American cases with Chinese defendants; and application of American, rather than Chinese, laws. At its peak in the 1920s, the American extra-territorial justice system in China comprised sixteen consular courts and the higher U.S. Court in Shanghai, all applying a mix of Anglo-American common law, federal statutes, territorial codes (such as the Alaska Code), and local bylaws enacted by foreigners in the various open ports. The U.S. Court for China, abolished after 1943 when the United States ceded its extra-territorial rights in China, was granted original jurisdiction in most civil and criminal cases in which Americans were defendants, as well as appellate jurisdiction over cases decided first in consular courts; in the early 1930s, the court was shifted to Department of Justice purview. Extra-territorial and consular courts came under the rubric of "treaty or legislative courts" not fully subject to the founding Judiciary Act or the Constitution itself; cases could be (and periodically were) appealed from consular courts through the ninth circuit court in California and thence (rarely) up to the Supreme Court.

Yet, while domestic courts endorsed extrality, and the executive branch comprehended its utility, Congress found State Department consular jurisdiction unconstitutional, philosophically anathema, and fiscally unwarranted and so balked at passing enabling and reform legislation. In the words of one senator, invoked approvingly a century later by the Warren Court: "If we are too mean as a nation to pay the expense of observing the Constitution in China, then let us give up our concessions in China and come back to as much of the Constitution as we can afford to carry out." Though approving sporadic reforms, until 1906 Congress consistently rejected more systemic legislation; even at time of general civil service reform, there was insufficient support for successive bills drafted by the State Department for the establishment of a superior court in Shanghai.

Thus, across the century, federal authorities had cobbled together varying measures of territoriality and constitutionalism for "anomalous zones" in the District of Columbia and Hawaii and for extraterritorial "consular districts" in Asia, North Africa, and the Ottoman Empire. The Supreme Court's 1891 decision in *Ross v. U.S.* that the Constitution has no application beyond the territory of the United States affirmed the original decision of the State Department consular court in Yokohama in 1880, a court set up under "unequal treaty" provisions. At the start of the twentieth century, as Congress followed the executive branch into war and occupation in Central America and the Philippines, it was the Court that determined – neither unanimously nor forever – the bounds of the American "constitutional community," as the Justices discovered in the *Insular Cases* where precisely territorial and commercial expansion changed from conquest and incorporation of "the frontier" to acquisition and administration of "the empire." In both instances, the physical or jurisdictional extension of the United States was coterminous with the expansion of progress, civilized justice, and individual liberty.

Among the collected *Insular Cases*, *Downes v. Bidwell* (1901) divided the Court into four dissenters, including the Chief Justice, asserting that the Constitution attaches to American sovereignty always and everywhere. The remaining Justices arrived at the "Constitution does not follow the flag," but through different reasoning. One view held that the Constitution follows Congress, drawing on Chief Justice Marshall's reading of Article IV §3 giving Congress the power to govern and legislate for territories, including the decision as to the applicability of the Constitution. The alternate path was through incorporation, whereby the applicability of the Constitution depends on the original agreement by which the territory entered the compact. Incorporated territories are understood as en route to statehood and thus covered by the Constitution; unincorporated are anomalous and are under U.S. jurisdiction, with inhabitants owed protection in exchange for allegiance, but U.S. governance not subject to constitutional requirements.

The differences were submerged in the authority of the decision for all extra-territorial jurisdiction arrangements. Constitutionalism and territoriality were coupled, as twin precepts with no binding force on the federal government, a precedent reaffirmed and expanded up through the late 1950s. The Court's dictate spawned a broad array of anomalous zones, in which the United States demanded allegiance from its sojourning nationals and indigenous subject peoples, but exercised its jurisdiction not subject to constitutional restraints. Extra-territorial jurisdiction had never fully adhered incorporated constitutional liberties and due process rights, but this was now formalized and judicially sanctioned. Indeed, when the

Theodore Roosevelt administration established the U.S. Court for China in 1906, the theory proposed was that court officers were to act not as officers of the federal government in some proximate distance to the Constitution, but as agents for the Chinese government, with the latter's consent as expressed in treaty, and to redress China's own deficient sovereignty, evident in its inability to maintain good order on its own.

VI. VOLITIONAL ALLEGIANCE

To be a sovereign among sovereigns mandates a discernible demarcation between internal governance and external relations, such that a state has an inside and an outside, with known ways of distinguishing between insiders and outsiders. Nationality, understood as an extension of citizenship across territorial boundaries, created "outside insiders" of a sort, a parallel to resident aliens who were "inside outsiders." Westphalian nationality combined earlier ideas that migratory subjects belonged to the sovereign with Enlightenment views that states are formed to protect members and enable each individual to enjoy the "rights of man." Whether states subscribed to "perpetual" or "volitional" allegiance as the basis for the relationship between sovereign and citizen-subject, understandings of nationality cohered around remnants of feudal fealty, expectations of social contract reciprocity, and prerogatives of territorial sovereigns absolute in their own domains.

To pour this mix into a mold of "American nationality" was alchemy. The enactment of reciprocity between a government by consent and those consenting to be governed inevitably and invariably became entangled, crossing over the invented demarcation between the inside and outside of a constitutional community. The original understanding of expatriation as an inherent right growing out of volitional allegiance seemed to anticipate only "domestic" foreign policy concerns, primarily those occasioned by perpetual allegiance demands from distant sovereigns on new arrivals to American shores. Not foreseen were the complexities of allegiance, expatriation, constitutionalism, and territoriality as "foreign" foreign policy dilemmas arising through the entirety of the nineteenth century, as native and naturalized Americans across the globe redeemed claims on the Constitution and conferred valorized nationality on offspring, spouses, enterprises, property, and useful locals.

In the decades after the American Revolution, Federalist domination of Congress and the courts translated into laws and precedents emphasizing individual obligation to the whole. Successive laws in the 1790s made citizenship more difficult to obtain, more demanding to possess, and more complicated to throw off. Jeffersonian Republicans emphasized the individual's right to expatriate himself from his native land and resisted Federalist efforts to narrow this right of expatriation through heightened government scrutiny of immigrants and increased residency requirements for naturalization; so too, they feared the partisan abuse of expanded federal powers over individuals and states in the name of "the peace of the whole." Yet, the fault line in evolving American understandings of how one allegiance might be severed and another taken up – and what rights and responsibilities were abandoned and assumed – was not the Hamiltonian-Jeffersonian divide, but was instead that bifurcation of "domestic" foreign policy and "foreign" foreign policy underlying the whole of American thinking about the United States and world affairs. Laws and precedents within the "domestic" foreign policy realm apprehended expatriation and migration rights from within an expanding receiver country generally open to newcomers, concerned to ensure that, once abandoned, an allegiance inscribed at birth was wholly dissolved by "the baptism" of American naturalization. Rendered in these terms, the Revolution was rekindled each time news arrived from afar of an outrage committed against a naturalized American who had ventured back into the realm of his original sovereign.

Where expatriation-volitional allegiance became more complex, thus marking the boundary between the bifurcated realms, were cases in which the wronged sovereign was the U.S. government itself. Early on, this dilemma inspired Justice Ellsworth's support for perpetual allegiance in the *Isaac Williams* case before the Connecticut District Court, leading to a jail sentence for an individual who had left the United States several years back, had been naturalized and settled in France, and then fought for the French against England. Jeffersonian and Hamiltonian orientations converged on a less onerous "conditional allegiance," grounded in the conviction that "the parts" must not be permitted to endanger "the whole," a doctrine endorsed in judicial precedents of the 1790s. *Talbot v. Janson* (1795) held that the natural right of free expatriation does not include the right to injure the country of one's native allegiance. Echoing this precept, the Pennsylvania circuit court's rendering in *Henfield's Case* (1793) acknowledged expatriation as a natural right, but one counterbalanced by the "part" of every individual's "contract with society" to abide by "the will of the people" as expressed in law.

In the "foreign" foreign policy realm, complexities and compromises urged American nationality policy into unmistakable Westphalian contours. Transplanted to Westphalian soil, initial and comparatively modest concessions to constitutional balancing multiplied into continuous incremental constrictions of volitional allegiance in favor of a more state-centric consensualism. *Talbot*'s insistence that every citizen is bound by an official proclamation of neutrality was amplified many times over in Justice

Taney's *Kennett v. Chambers* (1852) dictum that "every citizen is a portion" of American sovereignty and is thus "equally and personally pledged" by agreements entered into by the United States.[13] The process culminated in the doctrine of presumptive expatriation, by which federal officials might infer from circumstances that an individual had, in effect, given up American nationality; judicial second thoughts came in the late 1960s, beginning with *Afroyim v. Rusk* (1967).

In the 1850s, the State Department and Congress established policies and laws regarding the extension of nationality to non-resident dependents of American citizens. The 1855 Nationality Act adapted general Westphalian views of marriage as both conferring and erasing female nationality; the female "derivative nationality" approach endured until Congress passed the Cable Act in the early 1920s. The 1855 act also stipulated that American nationality could not pass to offspring born abroad to naturalized American fathers who themselves had never resided in the territorial United States. This latter provision was inspired by the frequency with which State Department consuls across the world found that valorized American nationality had been handed down through two or three generations, having been originally obtained for that purpose.

Congress had been stymied by successive expatriation bills in 1813 and 1818, as the effort to codify the right and stipulate conditions and procedures presented a federal-state sovereignty issue and even raised the question as to whether the U.S. government was the proper object of individual allegiance, given that the Constitution was a compact between states and the federal government. While the Constitution gave the legislative branch authority over naturalization, it was not clear that expatriation was an implied or necessary power growing out of that original grant. Legal sanction for expatriation came only in the 1860s when the Fourteenth Amendment, through its judicial renderings in the *Slaughterhouse Cases* (1873), and Reconstruction-era Congressional legislation enshrined expatriation as an inherent right and incorporated into the definition of citizenship an entitlement to American diplomatic protection when outside of U.S. territory. In an act inspired by ongoing conflicts with Britain regarding two Irish-Americans in custody, and over the Civil War-era *Alabama* claims for damage to Northern properties by British-built Confederate ships, Congress bound the executive branch henceforth to employ all means short of war on behalf of "any citizen of the United States [who] has been unjustly deprived of his liberty by or under the authority of any foreign government."

When Reconstruction-era statutes and case law construed diplomatic protection as an inherent right of citizenship and then this new entitlement

[13] 55 U.S. 38, 50.

was transplanted to "foreign" foreign policy, the predictable result was a proliferation of free-riding individuals acquiring valorized American nationality for functional over affective motives. With diplomatic protection now an entitlement of citizenship redeemable through nationality-based claims, the State Department crafted a complex, quite unwieldy protocol for "presumptive expatriation" to manage the day-to-day dilemmas of a "constitutional community" with near-global dimensions. The executive branch sought to do through administrative procedure what Congress would not allow it to do legislatively. Case by case, the State Department constructed an extraterritorial citizenship regime for sojourners, a bureaucratic rationale for the dispensation or withholding of diplomatic protection and recognition of status.

Underlying these various efforts was the drive by federal officials to make diplomatic protection the government's discretionary right, not the individual's legal entitlement. In contrast to 1790s expatriation cases, such as *Henfield's Case* and *Talbot v. Janson*, the question in these later instances thus became not whether an individual could freely expatriate himself under any circumstances, but whether a government could assume (and thus effect) expatriation from an individual's actions and circumstances. Outside of female derivative nationality, Congress rejected explicitly and repeatedly the notion of presumptive expatriation, by which federal officials might infer from circumstances that an individual had, in effect, given up American nationality. However, presumed expatriation was the preference for federal officials, proceeding on the executive branch view that "the correlative right of protection by the Government may be waived or lost by long-continued avoidance and silent withdrawal from the performance of the duties of citizenship as well as by open renunciation." The gradual appropriation of diplomatic protection as the property of the U.S. government, although wholly consistent with Westphalian customary norms, was a notable departure from much earlier American understandings, as in the Logan Act's preservation of the right of individual Americans to pursue claims against foreign governments.

The legal and conceptual analogy linking the status of resident aliens in the United States with that of American nationals abroad had been almost fully obscured by the insistent bifurcation of "foreign" foreign policy versus "domestic" foreign policy. Federal courts voided state legislation and state court decisions to protect the rights of aliens guaranteed by international law. Yet, this federalization did not resolve the fundamental lack of parallelism in expectations and demands regarding sojourning Americans and those obtaining for resident foreigners in the United States. When "alien rights" meant the status and treatment of sojourning Americans, for example, U.S. officials invoked this four-pronged argument: "sovereignty" by definition meant the wherewithal to control all people and things in the realm; this control could be gauged by the security of foreigners and their property; when such harm occurred, "state responsibility" was not diminished either by the existence or absence of particular laws or by internal power arrangements and constraints; and a "denial of justice" to the aggrieved foreign national was best judged by the outcome of local adjudication proceedings.

However, when such questions arose around resident aliens in the United States, the American response to the complaining government typically invoked "federalism" as an obstacle to intrusion into state matters and shifted from outcomes to process, asserting that "state responsibility" had been met simply by giving aliens access to a justice system that conformed to the "standard of civilization" sanctioned by international law. On occasions when the United States did accept responsibility for mob violence against aliens, the culpability was explained as a failure to do for aliens what it would have done for its own citizens. Presidents turned to the device of cajoling Congress into appropriating funds for victimized resident aliens, forwarded to diplomatic representatives or home governments for disbursement; outrages against Chinese in Washington, Montana, Alaska, and California were "resolved" in this way. However, the executive branch stipulated in all such instances that these funds came out of American generosity and humanity and were not concessions of culpability or precedent for future incidents.

The multiplication of difficulties and embarrassments in the 1890s around the obvious lack of parallelism between American immigration and resident alien management and U.S. intervention on behalf of its nationals abroad prompted executive branch initiatives to "bring Westphalia home," as successive presidents urged the automatic federalization of cases involving "state responsibility" issues of international law. Federal courts leaned in this same direction, although the outcome was less the internalization of Westphalia than the near-complete domestication of immigration and alien resident cases as matters covered by "due process" issues of criminal procedure. State laws punishing aliens in the United States illegally, as well as federal deportation proceedings, were judicially reviewed for conformity to constitutional protections. As noted earlier, resident aliens were brought under Fourteenth and Fifteenth Amendment provisions, put on par with U.S. citizens in this regard.

These developments prompted several initiatives from the Roosevelt administration on the extra-territorial governance of sojourning Americans. At hand were the Supreme Court's 1891 decisions in *Ross v. U.S.* and the various *Insular Cases* that the Constitution has no application beyond the territory of the United States. Those decisions effectively disaggregated the constituent elements of republican citizenship – territoriality, constitutionalism, and consensualism – and refashioned them as discretionary elements of sovereignty: jurisdiction, allegiance, nationality, and protection. This enabled federal officials, now with judicial endorsement, to parcel out varying proportions of each element to different groups and case by case. Hence, Americans coming under the jurisdiction of the U.S. Court for China did not have the right to jury trials, but they could, and did, appeal civil and criminal cases all the way up to the Supreme Court; Chinese and other non-American complainants in this court gained access to the American federal court system, such that extra-territoriality could function as a virtual extension of the Alien Tort Act judicial machinery within the United States.

The fundamental shift in the premises and precepts of American nationality became apparent only over the next several decades, as new legislation and precedents took hold. Between 1902 and 1911, the United States signed nationality-naturalization agreements with Haiti, Peru, Salvador, Brazil, Portugal, Honduras, Uruguay, Nicaragua, and Costa Rica; in 1913, President Taft formally endorsed the presumptive denationalization provisions in the 1906 Rio de Janeiro Pan-American Conference. From 1910 through the 1920s, American international law practitioners and specialists took up the project of enunciating and organizing what became U.S. doctrine up through the advent of international human rights conventions after World War II. Nationality was, first and foremost, not fully consensual and was less like an Enlightenment social contract than an adoption agreement. Second, American nationality was not necessarily or always equivalent to U.S. citizenship. As in the anomalous zones demarcated by *Ross* and the *Insular Cases*, allegiance and jurisdiction did not automatically bring one fully into the constitutional community.

Third, assertion of nationality-based claims and the rendering of redress must be considered state-to-state obligations; while the aggrieved national was a beneficiary in the process, the state itself was the injured party and was bound to seek redress for the violation of its right not to have any portion of its patrimony mistreated or disrespected. Fourth, while American nationals must submit to local jurisdiction and exhaust all recourses open to them within a foreign state, they were entitled to seek diplomatic protection earlier in the process when residing in states not meeting the "minimum standard" of justice recognized among "civilized" societies."[14]

By the eve of World War I, then, the Framers' untested notion of nationality as an organic extension of volitional citizenship beyond domestic boundaries had gravitated into sovereign-centered consensualism by which

[14] Edwin Borchard, "The 'Minimum Standard' of the Treatment of Aliens," *American Society of International Law, Proceedings of the Thirty-third Annual Meeting* (1939), 49–74.

nationality might be recognized, bestowed, negotiated, and retracted by federal officials. A little-noted precedent for this approach to subject-nationality was Secretary of State William Marcy's 1855 instruction to U.S. consuls in Latin America about a particular claim made against Mexican authorities for property destruction and wrongful incarceration; in view of *Dred Scott*, American-born "persons of African descent could not be regarded as entitled to the full rights of citizenship," but if such individuals could be certified by the consul as free and born in the United States, "the government would regard it as its duty to protect them, if wronged by a foreign government."[15]

When war began in Europe, official U.S. neutrality became entangled with the rights of American companies to trade with and loan money to belligerents and the freedom of American nationals to travel on British passenger ships across the path of German U-boats. Ensuing events inspired divergent lessons on the "rights of the parts" and "the peace of the whole." For President Calvin Coolidge, speaking in 1927, "the person and property of a citizen are a part of the general domain of the nation, even when abroad" and thus required full and active intervention if threatened or harmed. From philosopher John Dewey came lamenting wonderment at Westphalia's fantastical anthropomorphism of states into persons with "a touchy and testy Honor to be defended and avenged."[16]

VII. A NEW INTERNATIONAL "RULE OF LAW"

By the 1890s, waves of anti-Americanism crested in Central America, the Caribbean, and China. Successive Pan-American conventions now became a forum to protest those Westphalian conventions that so regularly resulted in bombardments, customs house seizures, and other debt collection forays by the U.S. and European governments. Although resisting infringements on diplomatic protection-intervention rights, the Anglo-American rapprochement in the 1890s, evident in Britain's handling of the Venezuela crisis and repudiation of claims on a future isthmian canal, shifted executive branch views about what constituted legitimate bases for foreign intervention. Secretary of State Richard Olney's declaration at mid-decade that "the United States is practically sovereign on this continent," together with America's acquisition of an "insular empire" through victory in the

[15] William Marcy, Secretary of State to U.S. Consul, Matamoras, 18 Jan. 1855. Dispatches from U.S. Consuls in Matamoras, Mexico, 1826–1906. Microfilm-281. National Archives and Records Administration, College Park, MD.

[16] Joseph Ratner, ed. *Intelligence in the Modern World. John Dewey's Philosophy* (New York, 1939), 471.

Spanish-American War, suggested a future role for the United States as bill collector for European interests, as a function of hemispheric "sovereignty." In 1905, President Roosevelt endorsed the Drago doctrine against forcible collection of public debts; however, the United States and other powers would agree to Drago precepts only if debtor governments would guarantee binding arbitration, and the latter was understood as an infringement of sovereignty.

In China, the Boxer crisis revealed the tenuousness of "treaty port imperialism," and the deployment of troops to relieve the legation quarter raised the prospect of the powers dividing China up into territorial spheres of influence. William McKinley and Theodore Roosevelt recognized that. while America's strategic interests in China were minimal, the Republican Party relied on the "open door constituency" of outward-looking commercial and secular reform groups interested in a "large policy" generally and, more particularly, in the pursuit of China as a market for surplus production and redemptive Progressivism. Actual American investment in China was, from the perspective of this constituency, disappointingly low, but its members were vocal advocates of preserving a long-term option on the China market, in the main by preventing any one nation or combination of powers from closing the open door.

Although the United States was by no means a major player in the "great game" of East Asian politics at the time of the Boxer crisis, it was ultimately the American-inspired, British-run, Open Door system that emerged to fill the void. Secretary of State John Hay's circular Open Door Notes to the treaty powers called for the preservation of China's territorial integrity and political sovereignty while also proposing that China be kept open for business, on "a fair field and no favor" basis, with no spheres of influence. This was the "open door imperialism" noted by historians, designed to prop open markets for outsiders on an equal opportunity basis, preserve the central government if possible so as to avoid chaos or great power division of the spoils, and liberalize imperialism to keep the door open from within, as against anti-foreign violence and anti-imperialist agitation.

Even as the United States was building an extra-territorial empire, combining possessions and political-economic hegemony, it thus became part of a broader movement among the Westphalian powers toward less visibly coercive international laws and protocols. These projects did not displace gunboats, but signaled some recognition that the coercive deployment of treaties, sovereignty, and nationality-based protective interventions had diminished the efficacy and normative force of international and customary law. Both the high-minded and pragmatic sought to salvage, at the very least, some notion of "international society" and a "law of nations." The challenge became, to borrow the pungent metaphor of one contemporary, to "weave a net of international law with meshes small enough to give the little people a chance to hold on."[17]

Earlier initiatives in support of arbitration and third-party conflict resolution included Senate resolutions from the 1850s that the United States secure, when practicable, provisions in treaties for arbitration in advance of aggression; one such call in the 1870s suggested the establishment of an international tribunal invested with sufficient authority to preclude war as a legitimate response to conflict and ensuring that "a refusal to abide by its judgment" would be understood as "hostile to civilization." State legislatures in Vermont and Massachusetts in the 1830s to the 1850s called for peaceful resolution of international disputes and for a congress of nations convened to establish an international tribunal for such purposes. In the 1890s, several state bar associations joined international groups to urge the creation of a permanent international tribunal for arbitration, an idea proposed by the International Law Institute in the mid-1870s.

These initiatives came to fruition in the late 1890s, with the advent of the "Hague system," a series of Hague Conferences aimed at limits on particularly destructive weapons and prevention of war through negotiation, inquiry, mediation, conciliation, arbitration, and adjudication. The inaugural gathering was the 1899 Peace Conference called by the Czar of Russia to reduce arms spending, bringing together twenty-six of the fifty-nine governments then claiming to be sovereign nations, including Germany, Austria-Hungary, China, France, Britain, Italy, Japan, Mexico, Turkey, and Russia. The 1899 meeting adopted the Convention for the Pacific Settlement of International Disputes (through good offices, mediation, inquiry commissions, and non-mandatory arbitration). American delegates, most notably Seth Low and Alfred Thayer Mahan, rejected limits on the types and use of weapons as impractical and counterproductive, arguing that "the more costly and destructive are wars, the more protracted are periods of peace." Mahan, known most famously for his work on "sea power and the state," asserted that the United States was well below suggested quotas both in terms of gross comparison and relative to territorial size and population. More generally, the American position expressed "cordial interest and sympathy," for "all movements that are thought to tend to the welfare of Europe," but insisted on "carefully abstaining from anything that might resemble interference."

The second Hague Conference, in 1907, produced a draft of the Permanent Court of International Justice, a declaration, and thirteen conventions, including limitations of the use of force for recovering contract debts and

[17] *American Society of International Law, Proceedings of the Nineteenth Annual Meeting* (1925), 91–92 (Albert Bushnell Hart commenting).

laws of war, peace, and neutrality. In the creation of the Permanent Court, the United States sought a tribunal more like the Supreme Court of the United States, a permanent body generating case law, as opposed to a bench convened for specific cases. Compromise became possible when arbitration was stipulated as voluntary, and delegates agreed to a permanent council and judges and acceptance of a Code of Procedure for appeals. Also, the United States was able to exclude certain issues, such as international conventions relating to rivers and various monetary matters, from a proposed list for compulsory arbitration. Still, true to form, the U.S. delegation presented a declaration that "nothing contained in the convention should make it the duty of the United States to intrude in or become entangled with European political questions or matters of internal administration, or to relinquish the traditional attitude of our nation toward purely American questions."

Among international lawyers and specialists, positivism took on the promise of a "science of law" that might serve higher causes. James Brown Scott, co-founder of the *American Journal of International Law* and State Department legal counsel, represented the humanitarian edge of this movement. Reacting against the Austinian view of international law as merely positive morality, Lassa Oppenheim and others turned back to the Grotian vision of a society of nations, seeing now how such an association might function when experts could identify and codify the "what actually is" of international precedent, practice, and conventions. However high-minded, such ambitions were found fully consistent with U.S. nation-building in Cuba and the Philippines.

In his inaugural address on March 4, 1897, President McKinley had declared arbitration as "the true method of settlement of international as well as local differences," its efficacy demonstrated in labor-management relations in the United States and "extended to our diplomatic relations by the unanimous concurrence of the Senate and House of the Fifty-first Congress in 1890." Yet, revitalizing international law meant short-term concessions, greatly resisted by Congress not only on constitutional grounds but also out of concern to keep separate "foreign" foreign policy and "domestic" foreign policy. Senate vetoes of arbitration treaties and sharp divisions in Congress on all matters related to the new "insular empire" translated not only into a proliferation of Executive Agreements and Executive Orders but also a bipartisan "bargain" on American territorial and commercial expansion: hegemony in preference to occupation or incorporation; if occupation, then liberal governance undertaken as a civilizing mission; and if incorporation, then subject status for inhabitants, not full citizenship. Intervention was not precluded, as there were sixty-plus American interventions in Central America and the Caribbean between 1900–30. The goal of U.S. occupation, however long or short, was to leave behind a state that could conform to the international property regime and in which there was sufficient stability to reassure investors.

The intensification of international competition for markets in the first decades of the twentieth century made the U.S. government more responsive to the needs of American businesses seeking markets and investments throughout Latin America and Asia. New government bureaus collected information on trade, and Congress provided legislation designed to give companies every advantage in foreign markets by not holding them to domestic strictures, marking the advent of questions about the "extra-territorial application" of legislation. The issue of nationality-based diplomatic protection came to the fore, but in unexpected ways. Although Taft-era "dollar diplomacy" seemed more congenial to Americans abroad and the interventionist impulse stronger, the situation from the perspective of sojourners was more ambiguous.

"American interests" had a new portfolio, organized around the strategic encouragement and support of private bank loans to unstable governments, with these loans being accompanied by U.S. financial advisors; bringing these countries onto the gold standard was a first step in the creation of a New York-based "dollar bloc" meant to challenge Britain's sterling bloc. For Wilsonians too, the embrace of commerce was leavened by suspicion toward particular businesses. In Mexico, China, and Costa Rica, for example, President Wilson withheld support from particular firms and banks; he initially refused to endorse an international banking consortium in China, changing his mind only with assurances of broader participation. Washington now accelerated the elimination of sojourners' "special privileges," supporting only equality of treatment toward Americans and America through MFN provisions in treaties.

From Theodore Roosevelt to Woodrow Wilson, the executive branch assumed "stewardship" over American international relations and did so with shared premises, even if choosing different tactics. Historians describe these premises in terms ranging from "open door imperialism" to "liberal developmentalism." The underlying logic was that the United States could break from nineteenth-century imperialist interventionism and coercive treaties to "grow" the rule of law, authentic sovereignty, and democratic capitalism by implanting structures and protocols and cultivating local elites using the "policy of attraction" that William Howard Taft crafted for the Philippines. In China, where giving up unequal treaties would put the United States at a disadvantage among rivals, extra-territorial jurisdiction became a way to "showcase" American justice and fair dealing. Made more urgent by what war left behind and took, expanded, and enriched by "national self-determination," "open covenants openly arrived at," "collective security," and a "society of nations," this was the vision that Woodrow Wilson brought to Versailles.

CONCLUSION

Just after the end of the long nineteenth century were the great League of Nations international law codification projects, initiated when it became clear that Western powers could no longer dictate international law and custom to weaker countries and that the latter had greater leverage to negotiate their own participation in the "rules of the game." Indeed, codification meetings became so many forums for new and earlier dissenting ideas, made more urgent than academic when Mexico and the Soviet Union began pursuing unilateral expropriation and nationalization as development strategies and social mobilization programs. Geography, size, and the disposition of its powerful neighbor curtailed Mexico's experimentation, whereas the (former) Soviet Union had a longer run at holding the international economy at bay.

The 1930 Conference on the Codification of International Law at The Hague brought together forty-seven governments, with prior agreement that among "ripe questions" for standardization were nationality and the responsibility of states for harm to the person or property of foreigners in their territory. Despite (or perhaps because of) several years of preparatory work among League committees, the gathering devolved into an unsettling amplification of irreducible conflicts of interest, divergent cultural norms, and irreconcilable narratives about the whys and wherefores of wealth and poverty among nations. On nationality, beyond a broad consensus about the dangers of stateless persons unreachable by national laws, representatives ultimately concluded that the definition, acquisition, and conditionality of citizenship lay at the heart of domestic politics and so could not be yielded to the indifferent, perhaps mischievous hands of an international body. Delegates Richard W. Flournoy and Ruth B. Shipley conveyed the U.S. government's refusal to accede to terms that included female derivative nationality and expatriation by permission of the erstwhile sovereign. Shaped by Latin American and Chinese representatives, proposals on state responsibility called for virtual naturalization of foreign owners of property within a state for purposes of assessing rights and duties, with liability for injuries limited to the actions of designated central-level officials and no penalties attached to the failure of states to enact laws embodying customary international obligations.

Hopes for international law codification faded, soon overtaken by the worldwide Great Depression. Japan's 1931 seizure of Manchuria and the resurgence of German aggression within Western Europe gave the lie to the vision of collective security, by which disparate peoples had been pledged to come to the aid of strangers in the name of a common humanity. Peace at any price proved quite costly, and the ambiguity of lessons derived was then enshrined in the Charter of the United Nations, the Preamble of which begins, "We the Peoples of the United Nations. . . . " In 1945, the meaning was clearly "we the populations of the nations united," whereas different translations had emerged by the dawn of the twenty-first century, when the web of institutions and conventions comprising the United Nations had come to be seen by many as a nascent, viable global government.

Visionaries and re-visionaries are ever more prone to recount as a great captivity narrative the emergence and coalescence of Westphalian sovereign states, with the demise of that system predictably projected to liberate the human race from global feudalism and its legitimizing illusions of freedom and mobility. Triumphant narratives of progress and pluralism are increasingly displaced by an odd scholarly nostalgia for the world before Westphalia, as if the way ahead to cultural multiplicity and sustainable, equitable livelihoods lies back in time, when communitarian ethics had not yet been silenced by Enlightenment rationality and the globe had not yet been segmented into self-involved national polities. Almost forgotten, it seems, is that over the span of 100-plus years, nation-states and national identities provided the means by which, around the world, populations of several million unrelated strangers were compelled and induced to tolerate one another and then to surrender by degrees before an "us" more inclusive, diverse and reciprocal than any of them would have settled on if left to their own devices and desires.

19

POLITICS, STATE-BUILDING, AND THE COURTS, 1870–1920

WILLIAM E. FORBATH

As the last federal troops departed the South in the late 1870s, hundreds were sent west to repress a strike by the workers on Jay Gould's newly consolidated railway lines. The "Southern question," a Virginia newspaper observed, had been put to rest. Now, the "trust question" and "the relation of labor and capital" would dominate the nation's politics. The dislocations and discontent produced by new national corporations, national markets, and burgeoning industrial centers brought forth a welter of new legislative responses and new uses of state power, including experiments in administrative state-building at both state and national levels. Not only nation-spanning railroads and manufacturing firms but also mass immigration from abroad and increasingly bitter inequalities and class conflict at home presented new challenges that made America's pre-Civil War traditions of local self-government and Jacksonian laissez-faire seem inadequate and antiquated.

When Europeans spoke of the "statelessness" of nineteenth-century America, they had in mind the absence of a powerful central administration and of a national "state elite" to run it. "Administration" and "bureaucracy" were foreign-sounding terms. They seemed antithetical to the American system of government, which had been born in revolt against just such a modern state. Instead, antebellum America possessed a small, unassuming national government, which left most tasks to state lawmakers, local officials, and the courts. The leaders of bar and bench were, in Tocqueville's famous phrase, America's "high political class"; they were the rough equivalent of Europe's administrative state elites. Common law judges hammered out and administered a remarkable portion of the important rules of social and economic life. Even at the state level, America had little "administration" beyond local officials; not high administrators but judges supervised the work of local officialdom.

But war is "the health of the state"; from big wars, central states emerge stronger and more centralized. The Civil War and Reconstruction had brought a national draft, a national income tax, national monetary controls, and a national welfare and educational agency for former slaves. They had brought national citizenship and a vast expansion of federal court jurisdiction. With the end of Reconstruction, however, came the end of virtually all of these new national institutions, swept aside with the return of Southern Democrats to Congress and the return of national politics to localism, racism, and laissez-faire. National citizenship endured in legal conflicts over political-economic policy, but precious little else.

Only the greatly enlarged powers of the national judiciary remained to oversee the creation of a new American state in the late nineteenth and early twentieth century. As a result, the elites of bench and bar would become, to a quite extraordinary extent, key actors in the battles and decisions over the design of governance. At stake were the most basic questions about the future of industrial America and the role of the state in economy and society. Would the giant new corporations be dismantled to preserve a more decentralized economic order or viewed as creatures of the state subject to extensive public regulation; or would they be "naturalized" and treated as though they were rights-bearing private individuals or "persons," protected against undue state interference? Would the creation of nation-spanning firms occasion the building of a powerful national administrative state to oversee and regulate them, or would oversight and regulation remain with the courts? Would the common law rules regulating industrial employment give way to more "collectivist" or "social" minded legislation? And how far would these and other social relations, hitherto regulated by local officialdom, courts, and common law, fall under the sway of more central, administrative state institutions? The administrative agency was not only a new "fourth branch" of government, making and applying public policy in new and seemingly "lawless" ways, it also embodied a new form of governmental knowledge and expertise: not legal but economic and social "science" informed and validated its decisions, and leading practitioners often were harsh critics of courts and common law. Would the nation's judiciary make way for this "fourth branch"? Would the old elites of bar and bench shape the new world of "administration" and "bureaucracy" in their image?

Two general outlooks prevailed in these battles. One was a conservative philosophy that dubbed itself "Liberalism," after the classical liberal tradition. Popularly known as "laissez-faire," it arose in response to the legislative victories and administrative state-building of postbellum reformers and spawned the era's most famous Supreme Court decisions, like *Lochner v. New York* (1905); legal historians call it classical legal liberalism. The other was "Progressivism," which defined itself in opposition to laissez-faire. If classical legal liberalism stood for limited (and decentralized, dual federalist) government, a "neutral" night watchman state, and the primacy of courts and common law and traditional legal and constitutional niceties, Progressivism stood for social science and social reform legislation, redistribution, and administrative state-building. We can understand much about the modern state that emerged during these decades by analyzing it as the product of conflict and accommodation between the new liberalism of Progressive reformers and the classical legal liberalism of the "*Lochner* Constitution."

Administration would win a large and enduring place in American government. But the modern state America got was not the free-wheeling and autonomous, expert-led central administrative state envisioned by many Progressives outside the legal fraternity but one limned by more cautious legal Progressives, who positioned themselves to mediate between the old liberalism and the new. As vast as the twentieth-century American state became, it retained, in certain crucial and distinctive ways, their classically liberal and legalist stamp. But much state-building also eluded the liberal dialectic of new state authority and new legal limits on state authority. Mass immigration, Westward expansion, and imperial adventures all prompted major experiments in administrative state-building and new exertions of governmental authority, raising fundamental questions about the scope and power of the American state and the boundaries of the community constituted by the U.S. Constitution. Many of the answers that Congress and the Executive gave were bluntly racist and illiberal, but the courts responded by cutting swathes of governance and regulation free from any significant liberal-legal-constitutional control.

I. CLASSICAL LEGAL LIBERALISM

After the Civil War, reformers began making unprecedented demands on government, calling for redistributive rules and regulations and foreign-looking "bureaus" and "commissions" to enforce them. Modest by European standards, this spate of reform initiatives broke with received notions of legitimate public purposes and received ways of doing public business. They called forth a conservative response, which styled itself "Liberalism." Republican lawyers and jurists, businessmen, academics, and journalists were the leaders of this conservative reform movement of the 1870s and 1880s. During the Civil War and early years of Reconstruction, these same men had etched out a new conception of an active democratic state to undergird the expanded powers of the federal government and the project of Radical Reconstruction. Now they were appalled to hear the language of popular sovereignty and active democratic government appropriated by labor and agrarian agitators denouncing "property rights rulership" and "wage slavery." As plebeian reformers began to demand and gain "eight-hour day" laws and rigid railroad rate regulations, elite Republican opinion-makers like the famous editor of the *Nation*, Edwin Godkin, lamented the emergence of a "politics of class feeling." The disenchantment with federal intervention and "Black Republicanism" in the South that ran through the pages of Godkin's *Nation* and other Northern journals by the mid-1870s was bound up with the desire of these "liberals" to curb the clamor for "class legislation" at home in the industrializing North.

Although they were renouncing one activist democratic outlook, many new liberals could feel they were returning to an older democratic reform tradition: the first expressions of laissez-faire doctrine – the first systematic protests against state activism in America – arose from the Jacksonian campaigns against national bank and state corporate charters, against government-created "monopolies" that privileged the few over the many. Likewise, the first judicial opinions striking down "class legislation" in the name of a laissez-faire reading of state constitutions were not the late nineteenth- and early twentieth-century cases condemning maximum hours laws and other labor reforms, but antebellum decisions by Jacksonian jurists overturning legislative favors for a privileged class of entrepreneurs or corporate entities. Now, ironically, the new liberals seemed to be transforming the Jacksonian vocabulary into a defense of the few against the many.

But if they assailed labor's and farmers' experiments with state power, the liberals were no less alarmed by capitalists seeking "state favors," "abusing the taxing power," and clamoring for "tariff schemes, subsidy schemes, internal improvement schemes." The "aggrandizement of capital by law," they warned was the "parent" and inspiration of labor's "socialism." The state and the law had to be reclaimed from capture by private interests, whether of labor or capital. Not only capital's state subsidies but the unprecedented power of the emerging large corporation itself troubled these men. The common law was replete with doctrines and ideology hostile to corporate expansion. Late nineteenth-century liberal jurists often wielded them vigorously.

To be ambivalent about corporations' effects on individual freedom, free markets, and republican government was to remain alive to the classical liberal view of corporations as artificial, carefully hedged creatures of the state. Perhaps none felt this ambivalence more than the liberal reformers who were also corporate attorneys – like David Dudley Field, the brother of Supreme Court Justice Stephen Field. In their work and speeches as law reformers, men like Field extolled a legal order that protected a free and competitive marketplace, equal rights, and equal opportunities. But as leading attorneys for the new corporations, they strove to undercut and supplant the very legal concepts and doctrines that sought to keep corporations within the framework of competitive individualism that their liberal legal reform ideology prized. They were at once foes and agents of the "aggrandizement of capital by law."

The prominence of elite attorneys in new liberal circles and the emerging ideology's counter-majoritarian bent help explain why in government the new liberalism won most support in the judiciary. But the explanation runs deeper. It goes to a convergence of the larger political scene and more particular intellectual and professional developments. Just as the clamorous reform politics of postbellum, industrializing America seemed to call for a revival of classical liberalism among elite reformers generally, the particular professional situation of the legal elite was calling forth an effort to put the common law and the authority of the elite bar on firmer intellectual and ideological foundations. The legal profession faced new rivals in the form of new professionals – economists, social scientists, and others – who formed new academic departments and professional associations and claimed scientific expertise in the government of social and economic affairs. The old challenge of maintaining the authority of common law governance over hasty, amateurish democratic legislation was joined by the new challenge posed by rival would-be governing elites. The old claim of bar and bench to infuse the common law with wise rules of conduct based on the profession's superior virtue and learning no longer seemed up to meeting these challenges.

A new approach was needed, and the postwar legal elite provided it, resting the disinterested, objective quality of legal discourse and expertise on more systematic, "scientific" grounds. The leading judges and legal scholars who fashioned this new mode of legal thought – classical legal liberalism – no longer claimed to supply wise rules of conduct for life's myriad circumstances. Instead, these legal thinkers used highly general and abstract legal principles (above all, freedom of contract and security of private property), precedents, and reason to specify the conditions under which people, or lawmakers, were free "to behave as they pleased." The object of legal science and learning was to draw clear boundary lines around these zones of private and public action. Courts' power and duty lay in patrolling these boundaries. Liberal jurists claimed to do this in a neutral, non-coercive fashion by treating all (adult, male) persons as legal equals and deriving all legal obligations from exercises of will – either the will of private individuals or the will of the state. In either case, the courts could be said to impose obligations or sanctions on individuals solely as agents of someone else's will. In private law, this meant no liability without contract or fault. By the turn of the century, as classical legal liberalism became fully elaborated, private and public law principles were integrated in an elegant formal system. Common law rights and duties derived from the general principles of freedom of contract and security of private property; constitutional law ensured that the legislature and executive never trenched on these same principles except in fulfillment of a legitimate exercise of the state police power or of one of the enumerated powers of Congress, likewise conceived as bounded zones or spheres. The systematic, integrated quality of classical legal liberalism is worth bearing in mind because it helps one understand the confidence and even militancy with which courts expanded and defended their powers over the nation's political economy and as arbiters of the state's role therein. The very same classical liberal legal principles and methods that ensured a fair and objective system of courts and common law adjudication were the ones that secured the general liberal goal of a system of lawmaking free from class domination by the rich few or the property-less many.

The first systematic exposition of the new laissez-faire liberalism was a constitutional treatise. In 1868, Thomas M. Cooley, then Chief Justice of the Supreme Court of Michigan, published *A Treatise on the Constitutional Limitations Which Rest Upon the Legislative Power of the States of the Union.* Cooley's political odyssey was richly typical of the new laissez-faire liberals: he was a radical Jacksonian in his youth, an abolitionist, a Free Soil Party organizer and Republican Party founder who broke with the Republicans during the Grant administration, and finally an independent Mugwump, or new liberal reformer and jurist. His judicial opinions exemplified the highly abstract yet deeply felt fusion of abolitionist and laissez-faire meanings of "discrimination by the state." Cooley's *Treatise* would enjoy greater sales and circulation and more frequent citation than any other treatise of the latter half of the nineteenth century. In it he wrote that the "sacred right" to private property stood as "the old fundamental law" prior to the Constitution, and through it popular sovereignty was limited. Like his judicial opinions, Cooley's *Treatise* assailed "class legislation" in all its forms, from the use of the taxing power to subsidize private enterprise to the segregation of schools by race, to the enactment of maximum hours laws on behalf of workers. The critical task for courts, wrote Cooley, lay in distinguishing laws that answered genuine public-regarding purposes from those that merely served a private class interest. The police powers of the states were ample, on his account, to address public health and welfare, safety, and morals. But they could be abused.

In the 1870s and 1880s, it was not federal but state high courts that proved most willing to take up this task of patrolling the constitutional boundaries of state power. The statutes that provoked the most judicial ire were labor reforms aiming to redress the weak bargaining power of workers. Thus, for instance, in its 1886 *Godcharles v. Wigeman* ruling, the Pennsylvania Supreme Court struck down a measure requiring manufacturing and mining corporations to pay their workers in cash rather than scrip from the company store. The court condemned the law as "degrading and insulting" to the workers, for it attempted "to do what cannot be done; that is, [to] prevent persons who are *sui juris* from making their own contracts." Then, echoing the language of Justice Field's famous *Slaughterhouse* dissent, in which Field had quoted Adam Smith on the just liberty of workingman and employer, the state high court declared that the worker "may sell his labor for what he thinks best, whether money or goods, just as his employer may sell his iron or coal."[1]

Over the next several decades, courts gradually etched out a universe of labor reforms they were willing to uphold as valid police power measures. Factory or mine safety laws always passed muster. Hours laws for women and children generally (but not always) were upheld, on the theory that they were distinctly vulnerable, legal dependents, not *sui juris*, and also the "mothers [or the future] of the race," giving the state a public-regarding rationale for such laws. Likewise, beginning in the 1890s, courts began to uphold maximum hours law for men in trades thought especially dangerous like mining.

But as *Lochner v. New York* (1905) illustrates, in the 1900s, and beyond, state and federal courts continued to strike down labor laws whose purpose was seen simply to be a redistribution of bargaining power and, with it, wealth or workplace authority. *Lochner* involved a ten-hour law for bakery workers, which the state defended on the ground that long hours by hot ovens ruined workers' health. Therefore, the law fitted within a traditional category of police powers regulation. The *Lochner* majority found this specious. The work of bakers seemed to them no more or less unhealthy than countless other trades. To uphold this law would be to invite hours legislation in any line of work, merely because a majority in the legislature thought this desirable. Indeed, the Court suspected that the "real purpose" of this statute was nothing more than that: it was really "a labor law, pure and simple," meaning redistribution "pure and simple." As such, it could not stand. And neither could state or federal measures aimed at enhancing workers' bargaining power by protecting workers from being fired for joining a union or by modifying the harsh common law restraints on strikes and boycotts.

What explains the special willingness of Lochner era courts to strike down labor laws such as this? First, labor was at the heart of the era's bitterest contests over state power and social organization. That the United States saw no mass socialist or labor party did not diminish the violence of industrial conflicts nor the demands for legislation to redress growing inequalities

[1] *Godcharles v. Wigeman*, 113 Pa. 431 (1886).

between labor and capital. Hours and wages legislation and laws protecting labor organizations seem modest enough reforms. But many of their working-class and populist champions hoped they would help legislate away the industrial capitalist order itself – what they dubbed "wage slavery" and "property rights rulership" – in favor of a "Cooperative Commonwealth."

Jurists, however, were disturbed not only by the radical rhetoric and reform vision animating this brand of "class legislation." The reforms themselves subverted the basic classical legal liberal tenets of constitutional governance as much of the legal elite had come to understand them. For legislatures to redraw the most basic terms of what had become the most pervasive and important of contractual relations, the employment contract, and for them to authorize unions to share power and control over industrial property against the will of the property owners meant there was no core of categorically private economic rights but only the changing whims of political majorities and the possibility of boundless statism. Unless one held fast to the idea that the common law precepts at the heart of the courts' outlook were fair and neutral, defining a baseline of private rights that the state could not trammel, the promise of classical legal liberalism to ensure principled limits on government and state power unraveled. That would mean the end of economic order and prosperity, the end of liberalism, and the end of the primacy of judge-made law. No wonder the classical liberal jurists did not give up without a fight.

II. PROGRESSIVISM AND THE LEGAL PROGRESSIVES

Progressivism emerged in the 1890s and 1900s. Its leaders often defined the movement in terms of opposition to Lochner Court laissez-faire individualism and legal formalism. The classical liberal scheme met with working-class and Populist critics from its inception. By the 1890s, however, it also found middle-class and professional critics arrayed against it. As "persons" such as U.S. Steel and Standard Oil began to claim the standard package of "equal rights," middle-class Progressives concluded that the agrarian and working-class critics were correct: legal equality of rights – to make contracts, to own property – was no guarantee of equal citizenship in industrial America. Giant corporations were arrogating to themselves the tools of industry, transportation, communication, and finance. They were not only "enslaving the worker" but also "driving the farmer, small tradesman, artisan and manufacturer to the wall" and undermining the proprietary, competitive capitalist order on which the inherited ideals of "equal rights" and "equal opportunity" had hinged.

Some Progressive reformers – Louis Brandeis, Robert LaFollette – carried into the early twentieth century an older reform vision of a decentralized

America: vibrant regional economies of small producers, medium-sized firms, and cooperatives. Most, however, made their peace with many features of the modern corporate order. Their solutions to the problems of economic domination, poverty, and exploitation was not dismantling the giant corporations but building up new governmental organizations – bureaus, commissions, and administrative state apparatus – to regulate them and adapt their business-like organizational achievements to the tasks of governance and social provision.

As state-builders, the Progressives aimed to supplant the "state of courts and parties" with a modern regulatory and administrative state and to secure political and constitutional legitimacy for the new state's managerial and bureaucratic forms of governance – forms designed to ameliorate the social world of corporate capitalism and also to wrest power from plutocrat-, boss- and (immigrant working-class) "machine"-ridden party politics. They championed "direct democracy" measures like the direct primary, the initiative, referendum, and recall to thwart the corruption of party politics and to forge a new democratic public in urban-industrial America.

Socially, Progressivism remained, at heart, a middle-class movement, uniting members of the old middle class – shopkeepers, business proprietors, and skilled workers – with legions from the new professions and their penchant for bringing scientific, managerial, and professional "expertise" to bear on social problems. Progressivism was also a women's movement. Excluded from the suffrage and party politics, women entered public life through the movement's countless reform organizations – from urban settlement houses to such national associations as the Consumers' League, which drafted child labor, wage and hour, and worker and consumer safety laws and lobbied and litigated on their behalf. Enlightened leaders of big business and the corporate bar also loomed large. Who better to tame the giant new corporations than the men who constructed them?

No wonder Progressive reform's vocabulary was varied. The old anti-monopoly outlook stood alongside modern reformers' emphasis on expertise, which infused the Progressives' administrative state-building ambitions. Equally pervasive was the theme of the "social" nature of human experience and human problems. The contrast between a dogmatically individualistic liberal "legal" understanding of justice and a truer and deeper "social" understanding was everywhere in Progressive thought. When Progressives spoke of social versus legal justice, they meant a conception of fairness and right that looked beyond legal forms and legal equality to address the actualities of wealth and poverty, power, and powerlessness in industrial America.

Social justice demanded a legislative overhaul of the common law rules regulating the labor market, the employment relation, and the prerogatives of capitalist property. To a great extent, Progressives also demanded that common law adjudication itself be discarded. The abstract categories of common law contract and property rules were not only veils for the courts' class biases; they also could not capture the particularities of social and economic life and the specific problems of concrete social groups, which needed specialized agencies, rules, and regulations to deal with them.

For many of the most influential Progressive thinkers outside the legal fraternity, the critique of the individualism and formalism of classical legal liberalism extended to a wholesale critique of courts, constitutionalism, and liberal rights generally. Herbert Croly, leading Progressive pundit and founding editor of the *New Republic*, offered a pungent version of this critique. "In the beginning," wrote Croly, "the American democracy could accept an inaccessible body of [judge-made] Law," because in pre-industrial America "the Law promised property to all." This was the Constitution's "original promise": economic opportunity and a republic of freeholders secured by limited government and equal rights to own and hold property. But in an industrialized America, legal equality left American workers "exposed to exploitation" and "economically disenfranchised." Courts were incapable of safeguarding the old ideals of liberty and equality in a modern age. So, it was essential to "end the benevolent Monarchy of the courts and the Constitution." It was time to abolish judicial review, as well as judicially crafted rules of economic life: "Government should no longer be subject to the Law." A "permanent expert administration," Croly prophesied, soon would substitute for a "permanent body of law" as the American state's main source of "stability and continuity."[2]

Other Progressives, like Theodore Roosevelt, Woodrow Wilson, Frank Goodnow, and Allen Smith, decried the separation of powers between legislature and the executive for stymieing responsible and coordinated governance. They lambasted the courts' and political culture's ingrained hostility to administration. Administration and bureaucracy must cease to be seen as "foreign excrescences." The American state needed to be "Prussianized," Wilson declared. We must build up competent and autonomous bureaucracies while making them "breathe American air" to fit with our more liberal and democratic ideals and institutions. All these reforms demanded constitutional change, and almost every prominent Progressive agreed that the Constitution had to become more changeable: the amending clauses had to be amended. Roosevelt's vision of constitutional reform became the centerpiece of his 1912 run for the White House. Roosevelt inveighed against "local legislatures attempting to treat national issues as local issues . . . [and] still more [against] the overdivision of governmental powers." Not only

[2] Herbert Croly, *Progressive Democracy* (New York, 1914) 119, 121, 125, 358.

must constitutions state and federal be made readily amendable to usher in the "New Nationalism" but if "the American people are fit for complete self-government," then they must be able not only to amend but also "to apply and interpret the Constitution." So, state high court decisions ought to be subject to review by the people through referendum, enabling "the people themselves . . . to settle what the proper construction of any Constitutional point is."[3]

Abolition of judicial review, popular recall of judicial decisions, "government no longer subject to law," and administration insulated from judicial accountability – these were reckless, revolutionary, and dangerously illiberal notions to even the most Progressive members of the legal elite. Far better to reform the courts, the common law, and Constitution from within than to suffer them to be dismantled from without. Far better for the judiciary to accommodate the rise of an administrative state than to be swept away by it. It fell to legal Progressives like Brandeis, Roscoe Pound, and Charles Evans Hughes to introduce Progressive insights into legal scholarship and common law and constitutional doctrine. Thus, for example, Brandeis nudged the Supreme Court to consider liberty of contract cases and the proper scope of police power regulation in light of "social facts," rather than outmoded individualist ideology. Pound criticized the ways that courts construed statutory reforms as though lawmakers were ignorant and meddlesome tinkers and the common law rules of property, tort, and contract were sacrosanct.

Likewise, legal Progressives urged the courts to give administrative rule-making and adjudication a chance to prove its mettle. "But yesterday the courts played the chief role in the . . . conduct of affairs"; now, "[e]xecutive [as opposed to judicial] justice is what commends itself to a busy and strenuous age," and courts risked having "nothing of any real moment left to them." "Executive justice," Pound warned, was "justice without law." But "justice without law" was a "necessary evil," so Pound lectured the elite bar associations in the 1900s. America had become "law-ridden." "What in other lands was committed to administration and inspection and executive supervision, [nineteenth century America] left to courts." A season of "justice without law" was inescapable, in Pound's view, because American courts "paralyz[ed] administration" by routinely "enjoining" and "interfering with" even the most trivial bits of executive decision making.

In reaction, the states seemed determined to take away "judicial review of administrative action" or to cut it down to "the unavoidable minimum."

[3] Theodore Roosevelt, "The New Nationalism," in *The Works of Theodore Roosevelt* (New York, 1926) 19–20; Theodore Roosevelt, "A Charter of Democracy – Address Before the Ohio Constitutional Convention," *Outlook* (1912), 390, 391, 399.

Americans were putting their faith in organs of government that delivered "positive action" in a swifter, more summary fashion, in ways that comported not with lawyers' notions of due process but with "lay notions of fair play." State commissions, administrative boards, and other new bureaucratic organs of public authority seemed to be burgeoning along with the industrial cities and their mass immigration, mass poverty, massive numbers of industrial accidents, and other labor and social problems, which the new commissions tallied and publicized. Not only the protracted, procrastinating procedures of the courtroom but also the individualistic categories of common law causation, fault, and liability seemed an unjust and inefficient way to address the staggering toll of industrial accidents and other everyday losses and misfortunes in a modern mass society. Small wonder that Pound, Hughes, and other law reformers feared that the building up of a law- and lawyer-less bureaucratic state apparatus might be unstoppable, unless the elite bar and bench shifted from reaction to reform.[4]

III. MODERNIZING THE COURTS: JUDGES AS STATE-BUILDERS

Historians too often tell a story of state-building in which legal Progressives and legal conservatives (classical liberals) simply clashed over the creation of modern governmental bureaucracies. This overlooks the many ways legal Progressives like Pound proved consummate elite reformers, tacking and mediating between the old liberalism and the new, striving to make social reform and the new administrative state safe for the courts and the common law, the inherited Constitution, and the social and political authority of the elite bar and bench, and vice versa. The story of clashing liberalisms also overlooks a state-building arena where these adversaries combined forces. Advancing their competing agendas, both sides contributed to the modernization, bureaucratization, and governmental expansion of the judiciary itself.

One hallmark of successful modern state-building is increasing the capacity of state institutions to gain autonomy from private interests and local institutions in order to implement nationwide policies. A second hallmark is the construction of bureaucratic routines and authority to oversee and direct social and economic life across such far-flung domains. Of all the branches of government, courts seem the least adapted to either broad-gauged policymaking or the construction of bureaucratic hierarchy. But

[4] Roscoe Pound, "Organization of Courts," *Journal of the American Judicature Society* 11 (1927), 69, 70, reprinting "An address delivered before the Law Association of Philadelphia, January 31, 1913."

consider the institutional development of the American judiciary from the 1870s to the 1910s.

Begin with the federal judiciary and with legal-doctrinal and jurisdictional changes. In 1875 the Reconstruction Congress endowed the federal courts for the first time with general "federal question" jurisdiction. Enacted as part of Congress's effort to protect the civil rights of African Americans and white Republicans in the Reconstructed South, this new fount of power greatly enhanced federal courts' supervisory authority over state and national regulatory initiatives. As Progressive economist John Commons observed, the Supreme Court became in these decades the "nation's authoritative political economist," making national policy in everything from utility rate regulation to corporate expansion to industrial employment. But there had to be ways to give broad effect to the Court's authoritative rules and standards governing the metes and bounds of public regulatory and private capitalist power. Thanks to this expansion of federal jurisdiction, constitutional challenges no longer had to be raised as defenses. They could be framed as suits for injunctive relief and became a feature of "government by injunction."

Alongside the constitutionalization of matters like the proper formulas for rate regulation, the expansion of federal common law was a generative source of national judicial policymaking. Common law prevailed wherever statutes did not, and the larger that the domain of federal (as opposed to state) common law became, the greater was the extent of uniform, nationwide judge-made substantive law. The core of federal common law was "general commercial law," in Justice Story's classic antebellum formulation. For the federal judiciary to make commercial law for the entire nation seemed consistent with the national government's authority over interstate commerce. What changed in the late nineteenth century was the expansion of federal common law into the common law realms of torts and contracts, hitherto a state court preserve. Thus, on one hand, the federal judiciary forbade Congress from exercising its lawmaking power over such issues as the liability rules affecting manufacturing employment or intrastate business transactions; those were matters of state law. Yet, at the same time, the federal judiciary boldly inserted itself into those very matters, criticizing and supplanting state common law rules in the name of the "general common law" as the federal courts fashioned it – and fashioned it, as the elite bar and bench candidly explained, with a more even handed solicitude for corporate defendants than one found in the more "popular" and "plebeian" state tribunals.

Another 1875 jurisdiction-expanding measure enabled federal courts to give broad application to the expanded federal common law. That year, Congress enlarged the right of out-of-state defendants sued in state court to "remove" the suit to a federal trial court, and in 1877 the Supreme Court construed the new "removal" statute to embrace "non-resident" corporations. Now the bulk of suits brought by or against a corporation could be heard by a federal judge administering the federal common law. Thus, the new federal common law and the manifold expansion of federal jurisdiction vastly enlarged the reach of federal courts into hitherto state and local domains. Other institutional changes, most notably the creation of the Circuit Court of Appeals ninety years later in 1891, brought the federal courts themselves under more centralized oversight, properly outfitting the Supreme Court as a national policymaker, able to supervise and control the lower courts by making review by the Court a discretionary matter for the first time. State judiciaries followed suit. Thus, both the national and state supreme courts began to choose cases with a self-conscious eye toward policymaking and wrote longer opinions that did just that.

At the end of the day, as with all chains of bureaucratic command, it was the lower trial judge who had to implement the policies made on high. Here, the jury was an impediment so far as state-builders were concerned. By the mid-nineteenth century, courts had discarded the earlier view that juries could decide law as well as facts. Judges kept questions of law for themselves. Nevertheless, jury trials continued to vex the judge as regulator of complex social and economic problems. Moreover, the remedial arsenal of a jury-tried case was limited almost entirely to damages. So, the advantages of equity for state-building were many. Sitting in equity, the judge was freed of juries; he could order discovery, which provided far more information than common law pleading, he could select and appoint subordinate officials such as receivers, and his remedial arsenal was vastly enlarged.

From the 1890s onward, "government by injunction" became a much-noted aspect of American life. The labor injunction marked a new era of rapidly expanding regulation – and suppression – of strikes and boycotts. Superseding the authority of local government, state and federal equity judges enacted detailed decrees to govern almost every really large strike or boycott; they tried workers and union officials accused of violations and meted out punishment. But the labor injunction was only the most prominent use of this equitable remedy. Surveying the injunction's varied uses, political scientists concluded it was the only effective means of executing "the will of the state" in many other matters like prohibition (of alcohol), where, as with labor conflict, the "popular feelings of the localities" ran counter to the command of a central state authority. Even more striking was the late nineteenth-century innovation of using the equity receivership as a crucial governmental vehicle for restructuring railroads and other large corporations burdened with high fixed costs and expansion plans gone awry. More than 30 percent of the nation's large railroads were taken into such "friendly receiverships," so called because the federal judges adopted the reorganization plans and often the personnel proposed by the railroads' managers. Here, as we will see, federal courts made into public policy the creation of national systems of management and control and dramatically remodeled receivership law to enable the policy to go forward.

State-building judicial initiatives like the labor injunction and railroad receivership were the work of judicial conservatives. But Progressives had their own transformative achievements in expanding, centralizing, and bureaucratizing the exercise of judicial authority. Appropriately enough, legal Progressives' most impressive state-building-via-the-courts took place in the realm of "social problems." While they assailed "government by injunction," legal Progressives led the creation of vast new municipal courts in major cities across the country in the 1900s and 1910s. Much as the labor injunction brought an unprecedented degree of active state regulation and involvement in labor conflicts, the new municipal courts began to wield governmental power over realms of everyday urban life in which public officialdom and state-made norms hitherto had been largely absent.

From the most business-minded to the most radical reformers, in board rooms and settlement houses, Progressives agreed that existing urban governments were unequal to the task of governing the cities. Poverty, crime, disorder, and disease seemed rampant; the cities were vast metropolises governed by hopelessly archaic, ineffectual, and corrupt institutions. Party patronage and private charity stood as the sole welfare agencies, and amateur Justices of the Peace and policemen on the beat, the only embodiments of law and order that the new "urban masses" encountered. Like the jury, the JP court or "justice shop" was more an extension of civil society than a proper organ of state power. Many reformers looked abroad and found models of public administration and welfare provision. The legal Progressives had a better idea. Rather than supplant the old urban courts, the goal should be to modernize them. Professionalize the decision makers, replacing the party-appointed JP with a judge screened and chosen by the elite bar; centralize the dispersed neighborhood JP courts in an imposing new downtown court building; rationalize the informal "justice shop" proceedings and the endlessly time-consuming pleadings and appeals system of higher urban courts; create a single, bureaucratically organized hierarchy of courts under the command of a single "Chief Judge"; and specialize the courts themselves, creating new juvenile courts, new family courts, and other new "social" courts. This vast new system of social policing operated as one branch of the new judicial-administrative bureaucracy and entrusted broad, almost autocratic power to judges who acted under vague standards through a small army of probationary, medical, and mental health officials. Here was court-based state-building *par excellence*, melding legal and social science expertise and enlisting the new professionals under the command of the old professional state elite. Here too, the line between judicial adjudication and bureaucratic administration – between what Pound called judicial justice and "executive justice" or "justice without law" – blurred beyond recognition.

This was exactly the line that classical legal liberalism insisted on patrolling so vigilantly in the name of individual liberty and the "rule of law." Indeed, the same elite lawyers who invoked those classic conservative values to condemn administrative regulation of corporate affairs often smiled progressively on the rise of administration in this realm, where the lives and affairs of poor and plebeian Chicagoans and New Yorkers were governed. Ironically, it fell to old-fashioned liberal jurists elected by plebeian voters in Chicago, New York, and elsewhere vainly to invoke due process norms against some of the darkest and most coercive aspects of Progressive state-building in the criminal justice and penal systems.

For better and worse, then, Progressive state-building scored its greatest successes at state and municipal levels, whereas conservative, pro-corporation liberal jurists built up the administrative and governmental capacities of the federal courts. But, as we shall soon see, the legal Progressives also did much to temper and "modernize" federal judge-made law and pro-big business legal discourse in the 1910s, helping the conservative federal bench and legal elite preserve and even expand their authority while the modern state was under construction.

IV. THE TRUST QUESTION

In the early twenty-first century we take the large corporation for granted, but its legitimacy was hotly contested from the 1870s until World War I. Giant corporations were arrogating to themselves the tools of industry, transportation, communication, and finance. These vast concentrations of wealth and power appeared to be "enslaving the worker" in one conservative jurist's words, "driving the farmer, small tradesman, artisan and manufacturer to the wall," and undermining the proprietary, competitive capitalist order on which inherited ideals of "equal rights" and "equal opportunity" hinged.

Elsewhere, consolidators of manufacturing plants and railway lines submitted their plans to the scrutiny of high administrative officials and central state bureaucracies. Here the rise of large-scale enterprise proceeded under state, not federal, incorporation statutes, and the main substance of public regulation stemmed from judge-made law. Even as the "trust question" prompted wide-ranging debate, bitter conflict, and new antitrust legislation, the key issues remained under judicial rule.

From the 1880s onward, Congress faced many competing constituencies clamoring for different legislative responses to the trust question, and federal lawmakers crafted statutory language that deferred many hard policy choices to the federal judiciary, where old liberal hostility to consolidation remained strong until the end of the century. Meanwhile, however, corporate attorneys and corporate boodle would succeed in undoing crucial state-statutory-based constraints on corporate expansion, and a new generation of pro-bigness legal thinkers would supply new liberal rationales for undoing old liberal doctrinal constraints. At the end of the day, a shift in judicial opinion in favor of bigness combined with popular attachment to a decentralized legal and constitutional order and distrust of central-state-building to enable the new corporate elite and the new private leviathans to prevail.

Popular attention was first riveted on the question of industrial concentration by the publication of Henry Demarest Lloyd's muckraking articles on monopoly. The first, "The Story of a Great Monopoly" (1881), assailed the Standard Oil Company, detailing the firm's ruthless predatory practices as it swallowed up competitors, commandeered transportation routes, and forced independent dealers and producers to the wall. Standard Oil also became the first actual "trust" in 1882 when that firm's legal counsel conceived of the trust form as a route to corporate consolidation that avoided state corporation laws' bans on one corporation holding stock in another. Five other nationwide trusts were organized during the 1880s, including the Whiskey and Sugar trusts. While the "Trusts" often brought down or left unaffected the costs of goods to consumers, their power over the economy – as well as their exploitive labor practices and penchant for buying and selling lawmakers – were ominous.

The search for profits and control motivated this movement of expansion and consolidation. In many industries, new technologies and new ways of organizing production yielded economies of scale, which advantaged large firms. Bigness, however, magnified the costs of sharp increases in the price of materials, market downturns, or "ruinous competition" brought on by new market entrants and the "overproduction" of goods. Some firms sought to manage these hazards through vertical integration; others through horizontal arrangements. Horizontal arrangements involved agreements among producers of a given good to limit production and/or maintain prices; these could take the simple form of a contract or the more complex and tighter form of a cartel, or, finally, a merger among competing firms.

Conservative (classical liberal) jurists were not hospitable to any of these forms of combination and consolidation. During the eighteenth and early nineteenth century, a business could incorporate only by negotiating for a special charter with the state, and the charter was viewed as granting the incorporators a special privilege, often linked to a monopoly on some particular trade. Thus, the common law distinguished sharply between the property rights of "natural" persons and the rights enjoyed by the "artificial person" embodied in the corporation. The latter were carefully circumscribed, and the taint of "special privilege" lingered even after the Jacksonian era ushered in "free incorporation" and general incorporation statutes. Common law doctrines as well as state incorporation statutes preserved many limitations on corporate conduct that applied solely to the corporation, still viewed as an "artificial" entity, a creature of the state.

State statutes set limits on capitalization, common law ultra vires doctrine forbade leasing corporate property to other corporations or transferring stock to a holding company, and common law doctrine also demanded unanimity among shareholders to authorize sales of corporate assets. What's more, many states had laws forbidding "foreign corporations" from doing business within their borders – a prohibition that seems to us to run afoul of the Constitution's protection of interstate commerce and its guarantee of equal treatment of out-of-state citizens. But until 1910, the Supreme Court hewed firmly to the doctrine that the corporation was a "mere artificial being" of the state of its creation, entitled to no legal recognition outside its borders. The legal and constitutional legitimization of the large-scale corporation thus involved uprooting much old law.

During the last decade of the nineteenth century, important economists and public intellectuals began to ponder whether the large-scale enterprise was not "unnatural" but instead "inevitable." Prevailing economic wisdom still held that competition was the natural order of economic life, except for the rare case of the "natural monopoly" like the railroad. But now economic thinkers like Henry C. Adams, chief statistician for the newly formed Interstate Commerce Commission, began to see the railroads as just one of many industries "which conform to the principle of increasing returns [to scale], and for that reason come under the rule of centralized control." In Adams' view, since competition was destined to vanish and no "laws compelling competition" could bring it back, "the only question" was "whether society shall support an irresponsible, extra-legal monopoly, or a monopoly established by law and managed in the interest of the public."

Contemporaries called this reform vision "regulated monopoly"; it contrasted not only with "unregulated monopoly" but also with another emerging reform vision dubbed "regulated competition." Theodore Roosevelt would become the most prominent spokesman for the first reform outlook, Louis Brandeis for the second. Brandeis shared with the old classic liberal thinkers on the bench the view that giant enterprise injured inherited liberal and republican values and that competition among smaller and middling sized firms could be reinvigorated; but like Roosevelt and other

Progressives, Brandeis embraced the need for sophisticated regulation and innovative uses of state power to achieve his vision of a decentralized and democratic modern economy.

While they spurned Adams' and, later, Roosevelt's prescriptions, the new titans of industry echoed their diagnosis: concentration was inevitable, and the trust was a natural product of economic "evolution." The courts demurred. In the late 1880s, six different states brought suits to revoke the charters of corporations that had become constituents of the great trusts, contending, successfully, that state corporation law and ultra vires doctrine forbade them. True, said the New York Court of Appeals in the celebrated Sugar Trust case, "an individual having the necessary wealth" could legally have bought up and consolidated all the sugar refineries joined in the Trust. But it was "one thing for the State to respect the rights of ownership . . . and the business freedom of the citizen." It was "quite another thing" for the State to "create artificial persons" and allow these corporations "with little added risk" to "mass their forces . . . vastly exceeding . . . in their power over industry any possibilities of individual ownership."[5] So, the large corporation still seemed far away from being a "natural" entity, enjoying equality of rights with the individual entrepreneur.

The new Wall Street corporate law firms were undaunted. And the federal system came to their aid. Several corporate attorneys drafted an amendment to New Jersey's corporation law to permit incorporation "for any lawful business or purpose whatever." Among other things, this handily allowed one corporation to own the stock of another. The state legislature obliged the Wall Street attorneys, leading to the reorganization of almost all the nation's Trusts as New Jersey corporations. Soon, the state legislatures of Delaware and New York followed suit, eliminating or weakening key restraints on corporate growth and consolidation. Corporations hobbled by other states' more traditional legal regimes easily reincorporated in the liberalized jurisdictions.

Despite these severe limitations of state law, most members of Congress and the federal bench would continue to view state government as a primary locus of authority over the trusts. So, when Congress took up the Trust Question in 1888–90, the division of federal versus state authority loomed large in debates. Senator John Sherman, as chair of the Senate Finance Committee, saw clearly the inadequacies of state regulation. His first antitrust bill envisioned direct federal control over corporate structure, authorizing federal courts to dissolve all agreements or combinations "extending to two or more states" and "made with a view or which tend to prevent full and free competition" in goods "of growth, production, or manufacture," much as

[5] *People v. North River Sugar Ref. Co.*, 76 N.Y. 582, 24 N. E. 834, 840 (1890).

state officials could "apply for forfeiture of charters." Sherman's bill, however, ran afoul of the constitutional scruples of colleagues on the Judiciary Committee, who saw it as usurping power belonging to the states not the national government. The latter redrafted Sherman's bill, so the statute as enacted omitted all reference to "growth, production, or manufacture" and simply condemned "every contract, combination in the form of trust or otherwise, or conspiracy in restraint of trade or commerce" and also outlawed monopolization of any part of interstate commerce.

The 1890 Congress left it to the courts to determine what specific forms of business conduct and combination violated the common-law-based language of the act, but for two decades neither the courts nor commentators could agree whether the new federal statute simply codified common law norms or enacted stricter prohibitions. The common law distinguished between "reasonable" and "unreasonable" restraints on trade, condemning only the latter, but the statute contained no such distinction. Congress had preferred ambiguous statutory language so that it could please competing constituencies: the agrarian and populist public demanding restoration of some form of proprietary capitalism versus the metropolitan business interests favoring continued development of the new giant corporations under enhanced oversight. Broad public political battles thus were channeled onto legal-interpretive terrain, and the antitrust decisions of the Fuller and White Courts, from the 1890s through the 1910s, generated as much public attention and controversy as would the Warren Court's civil rights decisions.

The Supreme Court pursued a jarring course. From 1897, when it decided the *Trans-Missouri* case through the end of Chief Justice Fuller's tenure in 1910, a majority of the Court, led by Justices Peckham and Harlan, insisted that the Sherman Act went further than the common law, condemning *all* restraints of trade. "Competition, free and unrestricted" was the rule, they declared, casting the Court as guardian of the "independent business man" at risk of becoming a "mere servant." To fold the word "reasonable" into the statute would be the worst kind of "judicial legislation." This view met ridicule and alarm in powerful dissents by Justices Holmes and White, in lower court opinions, and in speeches by political leaders, including Roosevelt. Holmes accused the majority of enacting a literal ban on combination and with it "a universal disintegration of society." Future Chief Justice White decried that, in the name of free competition, the majority had opened the door to limitless governmental power to restrict contractual freedom and the fundamental right to sell one's property, all in disregard of modern technology and business conditions, which entailed a substantial measure of consolidation. The Court's divisions were heated partly because the majority's views on the Sherman Act rubbed against the grain of statutory and common law developments in the state and lower federal courts. In the wake of New Jersey's and other states' new statutes, the turn-of-the-century merger movement took off. As long as state law now sanctioned the creation of corporations without limits on powers or capital, it seemed to follow that within their chartered rights, the corporations had the same power to acquire property as an individual. Confronted by the mass migration of corporations to New Jersey, state high courts grew resigned: corporations, in fact, could do anything they wanted; the elegant new "inevitability" theory corresponded to gritty reality. In this climate, corporate attorneys tore through the remaining statutory and doctrinal impediments to mergers, and an increasingly pro-bigness bench welded onto the corporation a rights-bearing identity akin to the old liberal individual's freedom from state interference in the realms of contract-making and property acquisition.

Roosevelt had no truck with the pro-bigness conservatives' notions about corporations' "natural rights," but he was no less persuaded that consolidation and giant corporations were inevitable – and, potentially, progressive. Still, as president, he did initiate proceedings against two of the most notorious trusts, James M. Duke's American Tobacco Company and John D. Rockefeller's Standard Oil Company. The government prevailed against both in the lower courts, and in 1911, with the Supreme Court's rulings imminent, antitrust doctrine seemed to stand at a crossroads. The doctrinal question – whether the common law "rule of reason" was a feature of the Sherman Act – translated in public discourse into the broader question of whether the nation's antitrust law would continue to condemn all trusts or only "bad" ones. If the doctrine of unrestricted competition persisted, every corporate consolidation would be vulnerable to the charge of diminishing the free play of competition and depriving the country of independent dealers. The corporate reorganization of the nation's economy probably would continue, but beyond the pale of federal law!

The new Chief Justice marshaled a majority of eight behind his opinion declaring that the common law's "rule of reason" was the "guide" to interpreting the Sherman Act. In a lone dissent that riveted public attention, Harlan assailed the Court for betraying what he saw as Congress's populist purpose in 1890: to outlaw all trusts along with "the slavery that would result from aggregations of capital." By abandoning its initial reading of the Sherman Act, the Court was indulging in "judicial legislation" for the rich and powerful. President Taft stood by his Chief Justice and declined to call for any amendment to the Sherman Act. Indeed, doctrinally, Taft read the decisions as foreclosing little and pursued an active policy of antitrust prosecutions against major corporations. Progressives in Congress, however, heeded Harlan's call and denounced the Court for reading into the

Sherman Act just the phrase that the trusts wanted to see in it. Public confidence in the nation's antitrust law virtually vanished. New legislation seemed inevitable. Should Harlan's doctrine be revived? Should the trust problem be taken from the courts and put under the ongoing regulation and supervision of some new national administrative agency, as in Europe?

The three-way race for the White House in 1912 put these questions on the public docket. In 1912 Roosevelt challenged Taft for the Republican nomination, based on the proposition that Taft had drifted toward a stand-pat conservatism. Exhibit A was Taft's defense of the judiciary, contrasted with Roosevelt's advocacy of a powerful new regulatory state and a sharp diminution of judicial authority. Losing the Republican nomination, Roosevelt helped create and then ran on the Progressive Party platform, which promised national corporation law and national regulation of industry and big business, including a powerful national bureau to monitor and separate the "good Trusts" (with their greater efficiency and economies of scale) from the "bad" (with their predatory business practices and their purely opportunistic and anti-competitive welding together of firms). For his part, candidate Wilson echoed his advisor Louis Brandeis in decrying the "curse of Bigness." Bigness in this view was generally a bad thing in itself. The Brandeisian reform vision evoked the hope of restoring a more decentralized political economy in which smaller firms continued to flourish. Together, Roosevelt and Wilson garnered three votes to every one for Taft. Greater legislative and administrative intervention in the new corporate economy seemed irresistible.

In 1914, President Wilson signed into law two new antitrust measures, the Federal Trade Commission (FTC) and the Clayton Acts. The first created a regulatory commission with power to identify and proscribe "unfair methods of competition" and "deceptive business practices." The second outlawed particular unfair business methods: price discrimination, tying contracts, and some kinds of interlocking directorates. But the language was sufficiently qualified and ambiguous to leave room for the more conservative Court of the 1920s to construe most of the acts' provisions as no more than codifications of inherited judge-made rules.

Combined with pro-bigness common law developments, the "Rule of Reason" decisions had gone far toward settling the trust question, pushing it from the center of national politics. Congress had chosen modest reform embodied in the 1914 statutes, spurning the bolder Progressives' statist vision of a national commission with power to issue and revoke national corporate charters and to supervise corporate pricing, accounting, and capitalization and investment policy. This proved a bridge too far in the direction of centralized administrative state-building. Combined with Congress's modesty, the Court's common-law-inspired handiwork helped assure the high degree of autonomy from party politics and state command that private managerial and financial elites would enjoy in the new corporate economy of the twentieth century. By 1920, the giant nation-spanning corporation had become what the late nineteenth-century courts declared it could never be: a natural, rights-bearing actor on the legal-constitutional stage, endowed with all the "rights and business freedom of the citizen" or individual proprietor. No concomitant national administrative state apparatus had arisen to oversee and regulate the corporation. Instead, the elite bar and bench continued to preside over regulatory conflicts and choices, large and small, about the shape and governance of the industrial firm.

V. THE RAILROADS, THE ICC, AND THE COURTS: THE FIRST GREAT BATTLE OVER NATIONAL ADMINISTRATIVE STATE AUTHORITY

One nineteenth-century industry did witness creation of a path-breaking federal regulatory agency: the railroads. Here in 1887, a little more than a decade after completion of the transcontinental railroad, Congress created the Interstate Commerce Commission. The "roads" were not only the prototype of the large corporation; they were the infrastructure of the new industrial economy, and the rates they charged farmers, merchants, and manufacturers shaped the fortunes of whole swathes of the country. Overbuilt, overcapitalized, and burdened by excess capacity and ruinous rate wars, their enormous power demanded a harness: all sides clamored for regulation. Railroad rate regulation, in turn, occasioned some of the era's most important contests over state power. How far and on what terms could the state regulate and constrain the new giant corporations? And how far would the nation's judiciary make way for a new "fourth branch" of government, taking over functions that belonged to the legislatures and the courts? The administrative agency was not only a new branch, claiming power over property rights and economic liberty the courts held dear. It also embodied a new form of knowledge and expertise: not legal but economic "science" informed and validated its decisions, and leading practitioners, like ICC chief statistician Henry C. Adams were harsh critics of classical legal liberalism and laissez-faire policies. As they clashed over public versus private and judicial versus administrative powers, lawmakers, jurists, and new administrative regulators also participated in a dramatic conflict between two markedly different visions of industrial America.

The roads sought regulation to avert ruinous rate wars. Shippers and merchants sought it to halt rate discrimination between short- and long-haul shipping and between points where the railways competed and those where one road enjoyed a monopoly. The latter's Populist and Progressive champions hoped to encourage balanced regional economic development, averting what they saw as the "forced centralization" of the nation's manufacturing and market geography. For as railroad managers and financiers like Jay Gould bought up competing and connecting lines and joined them into nationwide railway systems, they grew hell-bent on securing long-haul, high-volume traffic at any price. Thus, they paid large rebates to large, long-haul shippers and cross-subsidized long-haul competition with monopoly rents from short-haul traffic. Such efforts to centralize trade in a few dominant locations devastated interior markets, cities, towns, and regions throughout the country. Congress and State Houses resounded with calls for an end to the railroads' autocratic dominion over trade and development and their "destructive system of forced combination and centralization" and "forced concentration of capital and work." The national roads responded with their version of the inevitability thesis. Long-haul, high-volume traffic between far-flung cities was the only way to achieve the economies of scale needed to reckon with huge fixed costs. But regionalists in Congress and the railroad industry pointed out that well-run intraregional lines also achieved economies of scale, met fixed costs, and generated profits. Transportation efficiency depended on the size and distribution of the markets the railways served, and this geography was under construction; it was the heart of the politics of rate regulation. Through anti-discrimination provisions like those in the Interstate Commerce Act of 1887, regulators sought parity for smaller and shorter hauls.

If market geography was politically constructed, so were fixed costs, not only in Congressional battles over financial policies but also in federal courts. Again and again, system builders like Gould found themselves overextended and exposed to the rights of creditors to dismantle the interregional consolidations. In advance of default, consolidators found safe harbors in federal receiverships. Federal judges generally bought the story that only the incumbent managers could run the roads and only their national-system-building strategies made economic sense. In scores of cases, the rights of investors, the structure and level of railroad capital costs, and the authority of managers were all at stake. The upshot was a series of doctrinal innovations buttressing the system managers' prerogatives and also lowering their fixed costs an average of 25–30 percent by stripping bondholders' rights. Managers gained vast power to reconstruct capital costs to match the contingencies – and disadvantage the rivals – of their consolidation strategies.

Protests against rate discrimination began in the 1860s, and reform movements in the Midwestern states produced the first rate regulation laws ("Granger Laws") in the 1870s. Named after a movement of agrarian reformers, some of the statutes created state commissions to establish "just and reasonable" rates; others codified detailed maximum rates directly. They were assailed by the new laissez-faire-minded liberals as legalized theft and "brigandage," born of blind popular animosity toward the new railroad corporations. The first constitutional challenge under the Fourteenth Amendment came to the U.S. Supreme Court in *Munn v. Illinois* (1877). Like the *Slaughterhouse* decisions a few years earlier, *Munn* was a resounding affirmation of the state's police power. The states, said the Court, had "inherent authority" to set maximum rates. Harking back to the earliest railroad corporation charters in the 1850s, which had carried maximum rate provisions, and further back, to English and colonial practice to fix maximum charges for "ferries, common carriers, hackmen" and the like, the Court held that private property might be regulated when "affected with a public interest." Confronted by railroad counsel's argument that the roads were entitled to judicial review of the reasonableness of the maximum rates, the Court concluded that the question was not a judicial one. This was too much for Justice Field, who objected that the majority had opened the door to "practical confiscation" of corporate property under the guise of regulation. The reasonableness of rates could not be left in the hands of elected or executive officials; otherwise, the "property interests of shareholders" would be forever insecure.[6]

As with *Slaughterhouse*, so with *Munn*, Field's dissenting views became majority opinions in little more than a decade. Confronted by the states' and then Congress's first significant experiments in administrative regulation of an industry at the heart of the emerging national economy, the Court refused to sanction this new kind of government authority. The commission was not, in fact, a radical agrarian idea, at all, the railroads preferred the commissions and their economist-experts to the more populist legislatures as rate-makers. Indeed, the economists and other professionals who staffed the commissions saw themselves as saving the private economy from the impulsiveness of American democracy. But in the *Minnesota Rate Cases* (1890) the Court struck down the statute creating that state's railroad commission and giving it final authority to set maximum rates. Relying on *Munn*, the state reasoned that if the substantive fairness or reasonableness of legislatively determined maximum rates did not present a judicial question, then neither did the commission's rate-making. In dissent, Justice Bradley agreed: "Due process does not always require a court. It merely requires such tribunals and proceedings as are proper to the subject in hand." But the Gilded Age Court was not about to cede such authority to these untested tribunals and proceedings. The Minnesota statute was infirm for not expressly mandating notice, hearings, and the opportunity for the companies to be heard, and

[6] *Munn v. Illinois*, 94 U.S. 113 (1876).

in any event, the "question of the reasonableness of a rate of charge for transportation" was "eminently a question for judicial investigation."

Perhaps, some day, the Court would cease demanding de novo judicial determinations of facts and law. The Court might weary of serving as the country's authoritative railroad accountant and settle for a more tolerant measure of judicial supervision. In the 1890s and 1900s, however, the federal judiciary's militancy against the state agencies only grew. Not only did the roads enjoy a substantive right to a judicially determined fair return. The sanctity of that right, federal judges decided, demanded that it become a sword as well as a shield. The 1890s, after all, were the decade of the Populist campaign and the Pullman and Homestead Strikes, when Justice Brewer promised to magnify the federal judiciary's "office" to "safeguard the Nation." Nurtured by the Supreme Court, the rate regulation injunction became as central an instrument of federal judicial governance as the more notorious labor injunction.

The Court also forced Congress into action. During the 1870s the Court had upheld states' authority to reach interstate rates, but in 1886 it withdrew that authority. This created a vacuum where the states could not regulate and Congress had not regulated. Within a year of the 1886 ruling, Congress acted: the Interstate Commerce Act (1887) firmly asserted federal jurisdiction over interstate railroading, established the Interstate Commerce Commission (ICC), and outlawed pooling and short-haul/long-haul discrimination. Drawing on old common law doctrine that common carriers' rates must be "reasonable and just," the act authorized the ICC to investigate complaints and to set aside "unjust" rates, but nowhere expressly authorized it to set new ones. It made carriers liable for injuries from violations, but nowhere specified standards or procedures for judicial review. A tentative and experimental piece of legislation, the act was thus shot through with compromises and uncertainties. Yet, it marked a new age in statecraft; for the first time Congress enacted a national scheme providing for potentially broad control over a vital industry and committed regulation to a virtually untested institution, an independent regulatory commission.

Congress's ambiguous offering of statutory authority was just sufficient for an able commission to hammer out a cogent set of policies, rules, and procedures for this grand experiment. One cannot imagine a more able or appropriate first ICC Chair than Thomas Cooley, whom we first encountered as the leading treatise writer and architect of laissez-faire constitutionalism. In the 1860s, when he authored *Constitutional Limitations*, Cooley held in traditional Jacksonian terms that the greatest threat to "equal rights" lay in state power captured by private interests. By the 1880s, Cooley had grown more leery of the private power of large corporations and more willing to use state power to achieve the values – broad proprietorship, substantive equality of opportunity, and market decentralization – at the roots of his earlier laissez-faire outlook, values that also animated the Interstate Commerce Act's anti-discrimination provisions. Cooley's background as a Michigan Supreme Court justice, first dean of Michigan Law School, and receiver for Jay Gould's bankrupt Wabash Railroad hardly presaged a radical or anti-court commission. But his appointment of Henry Carter Adams as the commission's economist signaled Cooley's changing views of the role of the state in the industrial economy. Like Adams, Cooley envisioned a middle ground between laissez- faire and European statism, mindful of the railroads' dual identities as private enterprises and public highways and of the Congressional mandate to end rate discrimination.

Under Cooley, the ICC set about the enormous task of establishing, in his words, "a new body of administrative law for inland transportation." Working out general rules after deciding many individual cases, in good common law fashion, it developed a doctrine of regulated competition that not only subjected private rate-making to public norms but also fashioned terms on which the regionalists' claim to parity and the railroads' claim to a legitimate return could be mutually served. For the first several years of its administration, the ICC could fairly claim that many of the nation's railway lines were finding that the long-haul/short-haul clause as the ICC construed it had put a healthful restraint on reckless rate wars and more broadly that regulated competition was making traffic "more evenly remunerative," even as it relieved it "from the weight of [unjust] burdens."

The statute's anti-pooling provision was a hard nut for the Commission to crack. Sophisticated economists like Adams had argued, unavailingly, to Congress that pools publicly monitored by commissioners with access to the roads' costs and finances were the only way to ensure fair rates for shippers while allowing the roads to avert the rate wars that forced them either to bankruptcy or to gouging the shippers on non-competitive portions of their lines. How, then, to construe the act's anti-pooling clause? Under Cooley, the ICC looked on benignly as cartels adjusted their policies to meet the letter of the law, abandoning practices like designating shares of tonnage and instead attempting to achieve the same ends through the publication of prices, which the act and the ICC required. A member losing market share could petition the pool for a price adjustment, which, once granted, would be registered publicly with the ICC. At the same time, most of the major pools voluntarily began to abide by the Commission's long-haul/short-haul rules.

The Supreme Court, however, was having none of this state-nurtured public/private cooperation. Using cases brought by recalcitrant roads during the late 1890s, the Court rejected every important aspect of the ICC's construction of the act and gutted every portion of its fact-finding, adjudicatory and policymaking authority.

The Court spurned the new agency's construction of its own powers. As with the Sherman Act, there was controversy about whether the Interstate Commerce Act altered the common law from which key statutory language derived. Common law authorized courts to set aside unjust and unreasonable rates; but courts had never claimed authority to set new ones. Well-regarded state railway commissions, however, which the ICC took as models for its own powers, had done so. They would not set rates in the first instance, but having voided an unreasonable rate, they would set a reasonable one. The Commission adopted this practice. But after a decade, the Court rejected it: if Congress wished to confer rate-setting power, it would have to do so expressly. Meanwhile, as Justice Harlan noted in dissent, the ICC was "shorn, by judicial interpretation, of authority to do anything of an effective character." Not only enforcement but also fact-finding authority was shorn.

A veteran defender of due process values, Cooley boldly lectured the Court on the need to overcome the equation of due process with courts. Administrative tribunals must be respected. The ICC, as he had fashioned it, provided notice, opportunity to be heard, decisions on the record, as well as technical expertise. So, Cooley insisted, federal courts should defer to both the ICC's findings of fact and its administrative rulings based on "discretion and sound judgment" in technical matters. This domain stood apart from what a reviewing court properly ought to address: pure questions of law and assurance that the ICC observed its own procedural rules. Unless courts came to recognize these different domains of due process, the ICC's value as a board of experts would be destroyed.

And so it was. The Supreme Court bluntly declared that reviewing courts would not be bound by the Commission's fact-finding, any more than by its rulings or policy determinations; they would conduct hearings de novo at which parties could submit new evidence.

By 1900, then, the ICC was no more than a hollow symbol of government concern for the railroad problem, and neither farmers, nor merchants, nor the railroads themselves were happy about it. The roads reverted to rate wars and raised rates at non-competitive intermediate points to subsidize the cuts. Rate stability finally returned with wholesale mergers. Investment bankers and judicially furnished receiverships and reorganizations supplied what was not available from regulation. Legal parity for regional trade had to wait another decade before Congress finally upheld rules like those Cooley's ICC had fashioned and the Court had struck down. By then, however, the regionalist vision had been practically defeated. The railroads had become the backbone of a national market landscape dominated by nation-spanning firms and centralized national commerce.

The ICC would finally emerge in 1920 as the signal triumph of Progressive state-building. The agency gained powers hitherto dispersed among the states, Congress, the courts, and the executive. Brought on by Progressive era and wartime presidential initiatives, the ICC's revival was heralded as vindication of the independent commission over the narrow interests of logrolling lawmakers and the usurpations of jealous judges. A key moment was Teddy Roosevelt's White House tenure. Unable to make the Bureau of Corporations into an omnibus regulator of the corporate economy, TR did succeed in rekindling the nation's one experiment with administrative regulation of big business by pushing through Congress the Hepburn Act of 1906. That statute expressly granted the ICC the rate-making power Congress previously had omitted and the Court denied. Even this was not easily won. The price of support from the Republican Old Guard was scrapping language that sharply limited judicial review. In its place, the statute provided that "if upon such hearing as the [circuit] court may determine to be necessary, it appears that the order [of the commission] was regularly made and duly served, and that the carrier is in disobedience of the same, the court shall enforce obedience." Thus, as often before, the resources of statutory ambiguity enabled all sides to claim victory.

This time, however, the Court did not exploit those resources to claim the broadest possible judicial power. The Court upheld the grant of rate-making power and also declined to read into the Hepburn Act continued de novo review of the substance of ICC rulings or continuation of the practice of allowing new evidence on appeal. Instead, the Court read the statute as providing for limited judicial review, restricting appeals courts largely to questions of law and procedure. In *ICC v. Illinois Central* (1910) the Court declared it would not assume (any longer) that the administrative body acted in "crude" or "inexpedient" ways and so, would desist from "invok[ing] the exercise of unwarranted judicial power to correct assumed evils." Judicial review, henceforth, would ordinarily attend only to the "power to make the order" and not the wisdom of it. Thus, while reserving for the courts the power "in proper cases" to engage in more substantive review, the Court engaged in a showy act of self-restraint on behalf of administrative authority. More than two decades after its creation, the ICC finally gained a secure sphere of regulatory power and a measure of deference from the courts.

Experience with the ICC had altered the perceptions of conservative jurists. Given competent and fair-minded ICC decision makers, the federal bench began to feel that vigorous substantive oversight of *state* commission findings was burden enough. Federal judges noted the court-like procedures that Cooley and his successors had installed and the ample opportunities the ICC's administrative hearing officers afforded railroad counsel to present evidence and defend their rates. If, at last, the Court was prepared to agree that due process did not always require a court, that was partly because the ICC had judicialized key administrative processes. Nor did the Court ever give up the power or occasional practice of substantive review. The threat of resuming de novo fact-finding and rate determinations remained real and reassuring to conservatives. This pattern of newness greeted by overbearing judicial oversight and familiarity breeding judicial accommodation and administrative autonomy would repeat itself with the next generations of new federal regulatory agencies: the Federal Trade Commission in the 1910s, and the New Deal agencies in the 1930s and 1940s.

Most deeply revealing of the dialectics of American state formation was the way in which the ICC itself became court-like. To gain autonomy from the courts the American administrative state made itself in their image. Cooley is emblematic. A conservative innovator, he changed his views about the proper role of the state in economic life, but designed much of the new state apparatus around a judicially modeled conception of due process. Few future administrative state-builders were as imbued with old liberal, common law values as Cooley, but every federal regulatory agency would be brought into this mold. To this day, comparative scholars underscore that "adversarial legalism" – lawyer-dominated, court-like regulatory procedures – are the singular, defining attribute of the American administrative state.

Throughout the industrial capitalist world of the late nineteenth and early twentieth century, liberal thinkers worried, with reason, about the deep tension between rule of law values and mounting bureaucratic regulation of business and industrial life. Some, like Britain's Dicey, claimed that "administration" was intrinsically at war with the rule of law. Unconstrained by legal precedent or procedure, administrators ruled by edict, by lawless discretionary judgments about what was sound policy for the time being. Only the common law and the courts, said Dicey, could safeguard individual rights. But in Britain, and on the Continent, well-established administrative state elites fought back. In England, high civil servants pointed to their own liberal consciences, to Parliament's watch over the state apparatus, and to the English courts, which had review power over administrative actions. But with no tradition of constitutional review, the deference of English courts toward high administrative acts became legend in this era. Thus, England's administrative and welfare state-builders confronted no Diceyan moment that compared with the American 1890s–1900s. And only America constructed its national railroad commission and other business-regulatory bodies in so common-law- inspired, court-like fashion.

Progressive thinkers like Roosevelt, Wilson, and Herbert Croly envisioned a more European future for the American state, with a new caste of high civil servants making and implementing public policy free from private, political, or judicial intermeddling. But that was not to be. The long conflict between the old liberalism and the new, and the preeminent role of bar and bench in the battle, would give America a "bureaucracy" that remained far more beholden to the courts and the private bar than Progressive and, later, New Deal state-builders had envisioned, putting an indelible adversarial legalist stamp on the American version of the "modern administrative state."

VI. THE LABOR QUESTION

In ways we can barely imagine today, the labor question roiled American politics in the decades around the turn of the twentieth century. Many of the main dramas in the history of law and the modern American state revolved around it. The nation's ideal of republican self-government had always demanded citizens with a measure of material independence and authority in their work lives. Yet by the 1870 Census, the bulk of the nation's "producers" were neither slaves nor farmers nor petty proprietors, but property-less wage earners, dependent on the industrial labor market. America in the 1870s saw the nation's first industrial depression and mass unemployment, its first mass strikes and boycotts. Over the next decades, industrial conflict mounted, strikes grew more violent, and thoughtful Americans of all classes feared the nation was on the brink of a second civil war – between labor and capital.

The place of organized labor in the nation's legal order and political economy would remain unsettled for decades. The courts governed the labor market and the employment contract, and the courts in the industrializing North had made a great investment in the ideal of "free labor." Along with lawmakers, politicians, and pundits, antebellum jurists had lauded the "free labor system" over Southern slavery. The hallmark of the free labor system was the liberty of every workingman to sell his labor. Given equality of rights, Abe Lincoln often declared, the industrious workingman enjoyed great opportunities; he soon ceased being a hireling and became a proprietor, with young hirelings of his own. Even as a wage earner, the Northern workingman was deemed by jurists to be a robust, free-standing agent who looked out for himself. Affirming the workingman's individual autonomy and his boundless social mobility, this free labor outlook proved enduring. It helps explain the fiercely individualistic rhetoric one finds in Gilded Age judicial opinions condemning labor laws as "paternalistic" and "insulting and degrading" to the "personal independence" and "dignity" of the individual workingman. Unions, strikes, and boycotts also challenged this free labor individualism, since they rested on the premise that the individual industrial worker was powerless to improve his lot. What's more, by using their collective economic power to enforce "fair" wages and union rules and standards across a given city or industry, trade unionists announced themselves to be rival lawmakers, supplanting the courts' common law governance of contract and property relations with norms of their own.

One might expect that this legal regime was one of laissez-faire, protecting the freedom of contract and the rights of property from turbulent legislative majorities and ill-considered reforms, but otherwise leaving the employment relationship severely alone. In fact, the nineteenth-century common law of employment was one of hierarchy and subordination, of illiberal fixed status as much as liberal free contract. While the United States developed into a burgeoning industrial nation, employment law remained lodged in the master's household, in legal treatises on "domestic relations." Courts mingled free-contract principles with the older doctrines of master and servant. The common law of employment, treatise writers conceded, bore the "marks of social caste." The master's relation to his servant was one of governance, discipline, and control. In judges' minds, the felt necessity of governing the industrial workplace, of disciplining an unruly workforce, often recently arrived from rural settings overseas, and of subduing a trade union movement intent on challenging employers' authority all made the old common law of master and servant resonate with modern times. So courts continued to recognize an employer's property interests in his employees' or servants' labor, his right to their loyalty and obedience, and his right to enjoin and unleash state violence against their organizing efforts.

The allowable boundaries of workers' collective action changed little from the beginning of the nineteenth century until the second and third decades of the twentieth. In 1900, strikes to improve wages and working conditions at a particular workplace were clearly legal, as they had been virtually throughout the century. Boycotting of almost all kinds – both producers' and consumers' – was becoming a tactic that could not legally be urged or carried out. Before the 1890s, courts had barely considered the legal status of many kinds of boycotting activities. However, by the early twentieth century, common law and federal antitrust doctrine condemned in needlepoint detail virtually the whole spectrum of peaceful secondary actions aimed at "unfair" (non-union) goods and materials. Likewise, organizing activities and sympathy strikes fell under an increasingly thorough ban.

Not the substantive law but its application changed dramatically in the late nineteenth century. The rise of larger and more durable labor organizations combined with city-wide and regional boycotts and new and broader strike ambitions to stoke judicial hostility and prompt a change in the characteristic form of legal intervention. Conspiracy prosecutions did not disappear, but they gave way in importance to the labor injunction. By 1920, the nation had seen roughly 2,200 anti-strike decrees, only a fraction of the total number of strikes, but a number that grew with each decade and included a substantial share of larger strikes, organizing campaigns, and secondary actions. The rise of "government by [labor] injunction" richly illustrates three key features of the drama of law and modern state formation in pre-New Deal America: how courts built up remarkable new governmental capacities, trumping traditional local authorities as well other rival state-builders; how judicial review worked in both subtle and obvious ways to help undercut dramatic departures from judge-made law; and how much legal intervention and state violence were needed to support the courts' conceptions of the free market and private liberty.

The labor injunction was born in the railroad strikes of 1877 with which this chapter began, issuing from federal courts that held the struck railroad companies in receiverships. As the massive strikes unfolded, many federal judges with roads under their equitable receivership authority reasoned that the strikes presented a new necessity for "extending our administrative capacities" over roads that were, after all, "public authority for the time being." Because mayors and governors often sympathized with the strikers and would not call out local or state police when strikers disrupted freight traffic, the irate federal judges took matters in their own hands, ordering their marshals to deputize volunteers or calling out federal troops to put down the strikes. Strike leaders were arrested for contempt, and their convictions marked the first contempt sanctions against persons who were neither parties to nor named by court orders. Soon, the anti-strike decree found use in strikes against non-bankrupt lines, and prison terms were meted out to strike leaders whose followers were not disrupting but merely refusing to work on struck roads. Even primary strikes were deemed violations of the new Sherman Antitrust Act's bar on combinations in restraint of interstate trade.

Over the course of the 1880s and early 1890s the main elements that would make up the role of the federal judiciary in the 1894 Pullman Strike were put into place: decrees against strikes and boycotts on non-receivership lines, long experience of collaboration with railroad management and attorneys, precedents for summoning troops over the heads of state authorities, the preference for summary proceedings over jury trials, and the transformation of the federal courtroom into "a kind of police court," in then Circuit Court Judge William Howard Taft's words. Swayed by Pullman's ruthless wage cuts and intransigent refusal to confer with his employees, a new union of railroad workers led by Eugene Debs allowed itself to be led into a showdown. In the legal elite's view, the union's web of sympathetic boycotts of Pullman sleeping cars embodied the most disturbing development of class-based unionism. Judge Taft issued and administered one of the scores of federal injunctions against the boycotts, prohibiting Debs' union and others from threatening or conspiring to quit work in any fashion that would embarrass the railways' operations and from refusing to handle the Pullman cars. A genial man, Taft's response to the strikers was savage. "Until they have much bloodletting [by federal troops enforcing the court decrees]," he wrote his wife, "it will not be better. . . . They have killed only six of the mob as yet. This is hardly enough."

With *In re Debs* (1895) the Supreme Court lent its imprimatur to the federal judicial role in railway strikes and the new use of equity in industrial conflicts. The Court suggested that the alternative to "government by injunction" was anarchy. In fact, other national policy and state-building paths appeared. At the ICC, Chairman Cooley tried to encourage the new agency to become an active arbiter in railway labor, disputes but his fellow commissioners rebuffed his proposals. Some federal judges offered another alternative. They refused to enjoin strikes called by workers protesting court-appointed receivers' efforts to reduce wages, change schedules, and dismiss men without conferring with the workers' representatives. Instead of enjoining the strikes, the judges directed the recalcitrant line to confer with its workers and provided that the old rules, wage rates, and work schedules would remain in force until the workers agreed otherwise or the receivers proved they were "in excess of a fair, just, and reasonable compensation." Thus on the eve of the Pullman Strike, these judges demonstrated that courts could use their equitable powers to etch out an arbitral rather than a repressive governmental role, on which Congress might have built.

In re Debs swept these alternatives aside. It also helped assure the injunction's luxuriant growth outside the railroad industry. One might think the railroads were a special case, but during the 1880s and 1890s, "government by injunction" flourished in the dramatically different setting of city-wide and national boycotts of goods made by "unfair" firms. Arraying entire working-class communities or national organizations against a single employer, boycotts lent unions much greater power – and rubbed more abrasively against judges' individualism – than did the ordinary wage strike. "Their action," as one court remarked, "in the language of the times, was purely sympathetic." So, injunctions began routinely to issue against boycotts, as well as strikes for union recognition, enforcement of work rules, or refusals to transport or work on "unfair" products. Hundreds of equity decrees forbade "whomsoever" doing "whatsoever" to carry out a strike or boycott the courts had condemned. Each decree resembled a tailor-made criminal code outlawing quitting "in concert," picketing, holding meetings, singing union songs, supplying funds or food or other support to strikers, and publishing the names of "unfair" employers. And punishment for defying labor injunctions was meted out by the injunction judge himself, avoiding juries as well as the discretion of locally elected prosecutors. Often, too, where a particular mayor, sheriff, or other local official tolerated picketing, a judicial decree could prod him to change policies. Thus, by the 1900s, major strikes and boycotts were met with judicial decrees outlawing labor's most powerful weapons and prized forms of collective protest.

Because skilled workers were well organized in many of the nation's great cities and industrial regions and because "sympathy" ran strong, the outcomes of the sharpest clashes between unions and employers very often were determined by the state. The courts, in turn, very often determined the state's posture, trumping other state actors' perspectives. From the courts' perspective, the unions were rival lawmakers seeking to impose their own rules and standards on employers whose property rights protected them from just such interference.

For their part, most Progressive lawyers and jurists had no use for employers' assertions of broad property rights-based protection against workers' economic power, but they were nonetheless often hostile to the cartel-style self-rule that craft unions and allied (usually small to medium-sized) employers sought to impose on the markets. Thus, legal Progressives like Brandeis supported reforming "government by injunction" and loosening the judge-made restraints on collective action, but shunned the collective laissez-faire for peaceful economic action that trade unionists thought was their due. Brandeis favored a broad freedom of collective action for organized labor. By repealing repressive judge-made law and instituting legislative policies supporting that broad freedom, Brandeis and other Progressives aimed to undergird unions with substantial economic power. Only then would employers assent to collective bargaining. In return, Progressives demanded that unions recognize the state's legitimate authority to determine the metes and bounds of "responsible unionism." Progressives had no more use for abstract, categorical claims of liberty by labor than by capital. There had to be some form of public, legal accountability on labor's part for unwarranted forms of economic injury, and what kinds of injuries or strike or boycott objectives were unwarrantable was not a determination Progressives thought could be made once and for all at a high level of generality. If it was blind formalism when courts treated the individual worker as the legal equal of the corporate employer, it also was blind formalism to ignore the differences between individual and collective marketplace action on workers' part. This Progressive viewpoint won favor with a handful of state courts and a handful of left-leaning unions. But most courts and most unions had no truck with it, clinging instead to their deep mutual mistrust and to their respective versions of laissez-faire.

From the 1890s through the 1920s, organized labor prevailed on legislatures to pass many "anti-injunction statutes." The states and Congress passed roughly forty court-curbing measures during these decades – reversing substantive labor law doctrines, instituting procedural changes, and narrowing, and, in some instances, flatly repealing equity jurisdiction over labor. At least twenty-five of these statutes were voided on constitutional grounds, and most of those not struck down were vitiated by narrow construction.

Most important and instructive from the point of view of governmental development was the fate of the labor provisions of the Clayton Antitrust Act. Beginning in the 1890s, firms whose products moved in interstate commerce found some lower federal courts prepared to grant decrees condemning strikes and boycotts as conspiracies and combinations in restraint of trade, in violation of the new federal antitrust law. Other lower courts disagreed, but not the Supreme Court, which ruled in the *Danbury Hatters Case* (1908) that the Sherman Act covered union activities, and, ominously, also made trade unionists liable for treble damages for losses occasioned by boycotts against "unfair" firms. When Woodrow Wilson signed the Clayton Act into law in 1914, AFL chief Samuel Gompers hailed its labor provisions as "the Magna Carta" of organized labor. These provisions declared that "[n]othing contained in the anti-trust laws . . . forbid[s] the existence and operation of labor . . . organizations" and listed ten "peaceful" and "lawful" labor activities (including strikes and boycotts) that injunctions could not forbid; they also made some procedural reforms in contempt cases arising from injunction suits. Gompers publicly interpreted these provisions as granting organized labor all it had asked from Congress, but other public commentators at the time insisted that the statute fell far short of granting labor immunity from antitrust law or of repealing "government by injunction." To William Howard Taft, in private practice and president of the American Bar Association at the time, the labor provisions did nothing more than state "what would be law without the statute."

Certainly, the language of the Clayton Act's labor provisions was ambiguous, and most historians agree that the ambiguities were deliberate. The act bore the imprint of powerful lobbying by unions and employers alike and of compromise among lawmakers with conflicting views about the proper scope of labor's freedom. Labor's state of semi-outlawry had made for more violent industrial conflicts, narrower constituencies, and less middle-class support. Also, in the give-and-take of legislative bargaining, labor's advocates were confronted with a double bind. Yes, we could include more unambiguous language, stripping the courts of equitable jurisdiction over any industrial conflicts or clearly immunizing secondary actions, but that language already has been tried in earlier state statutes – and the courts uniformly have struck it down! Thus, the courts had already dealt the Congressional conservatives a handful of trumps for their negotiations with labor's representatives; in practical effect Congress chose to leave the power to determine the bounds of labor's freedom of action largely where it had been – with the courts.

Duplex Printing Press Co. v. Deering (1921) offered the Supreme Court's first interpretation of the Clayton Act's labor provisions. Members of a machinists' union had refused to set up printing presses built by the one manufacturer in their industry that would not recognize their union. This was not, then, a broad sympathy strike or general boycott – the kind of action courts condemned as class-based animosity lacking any basis in economic self-interest – but rested squarely on the defendants' interest in maintaining their union contracts. Justices Brandeis, Holmes, and Clarke agreed that this was precisely the kind of peaceful boycott that the Clayton Act was meant to safeguard. But the majority read the act as Taft had predicted. Nothing that the federal courts had previously outlawed had become legal. *Duplex* contrasted starkly with antitrust decisions involving corporate conduct. The White Court's "rule of reason" had legitimated vast combinations like U.S. Steel. Yet, federal antitrust law deemed the machinists union's Lilliputian attempt to coordinate the efforts of workers at a handful of printing press makers an illegal restraint of trade. The judiciary that modernized antitrust law to accommodate the giant corporation remained wedded to a deeply authoritarian view of the rights of employers and their "servants." Until the social upheavals and massive political realignments of the 1930s, the constellation of national political power left the courts as the state's effective arbiters of labor, as they were of corporation policy.

VII. THE SOCIAL QUESTION AND THE PECULIARITIES OF THE AMERICAN WELFARE STATE

The labor question opened on to the "social question": how to secure citizens of a newly industrialized society (or enable them to secure themselves) against the inevitable hazards of accidents, illness, unemployment, and old age? Americans addressing the question in the late nineteenth and early twentieth century were engaged in a lively transatlantic conversation with reformers throughout the industrial nations of Europe. Everywhere, a similar array of solutions vied with one another. Trade unionists tended to favor unions and workers' voluntary associations as providers of mutual aid; and in the United States, as in England, thousands of workers' cooperative insurance organizations emerged. Middle-class reformers like the Progressives and their European counterparts leaned in favor of public social insurance. As high civil servants, social scientists, or professional reformers, they were the pioneers in welfare-state-building. Finally, everywhere, enlightened large employers, usually in collaboration with commercial insurance companies, created their own workers' insurance programs, which, in the United States, went under the rubric of "welfare capitalism."

The first important American efforts in the arena of social provision for individual misfortune arose in response to industrial accidents. The United States saw an epidemic of industrial accidents during the decades bracketing the turn of the last century. New state labor bureaus and commissions and Progressive social scientists tallied and publicized the staggering numbers of workplace injuries and deaths. Industrial accidents were no accident, the new statistics-wielding experts proclaimed, but inevitable and devastating, not only to the victim but also to his or her dependents. In that light, the protracted procedures of the courtroom and the individualistic categories of common law causation, fault, and liability seemed unjust and inefficient. So, several American states set about adopting workers' compensation schemes, based on the English model, making employers strictly liable for workplace accidents, making insurance compulsory, and replacing common law adjudication with administrative tribunals and fixed schedules of compensation.

The novelty of the new statutes lay in their statistical approach to thinking about accidents. The word "statistics" itself, which derives from the word "state" and describes the science of gathering facts bearing on the condition of the state, did not appear until the late eighteenth century; indeed, it was the new central state institutions of Europe that first generated an "avalanche of printed numbers" treating human events like life, death, illness, and accidents as predictable, law-like regularities of social life. Thinking in terms of probabilities, rather than particularities, made possible the actuarial calculations underpinning the development of insurance systems.

As states inaugurated workers' compensation commissions and crafted insurance programs, social insurance seemed unstoppable. State commissions from Ohio to New York to Tennessee linked workers' compensation to the problems of "unemployment, sickness ... old age and death." Theodore Roosevelt's Progressive Party platform called for compulsory health insurance; and soon the leadership of the American Medical Association – later a steadfast opponent – was endorsing health insurance as the "next step" in social insurance policy.

In the United States the constitutional question hung over workers' compensation laws, to say nothing of minimum wages and the other kinds of social insurance, which rubbed more abrasively against the old liberal Constitution's anti-redistributive grain. Even workers' compensation schemes seemed perilously close to the classical legal liberal line separating allowable accident cost allocations from impermissible redistribution of property from A to B. As state workers' compensation commissioners gathered, constitutional law "was the most carefully discussed problem." Concerns about breaching the constitutional baseline led reformers to draft the early statutes with opt-out provisions and to limit coverage to so-called hazardous industries. Such modest early statutes vexed the very commissioners and social insurance experts who lobbied on their behalf.

Still, the other shoe dropped. In *Ives v. New York* (1911), New York's high court struck down that state's landmark workers' compensation statute. As historian John Witt points out, the statute had embodied the critical move from "individualized common sense [common law] causation" to "actuarial causal tendencies." With this, the modern administrative state seemed equipped to socialize and redistribute any number of risks – poverty, old age, unemployment, sickness – on the basis of their causal links to employment. In the name of "personal responsibility" and "political equality," the New York Court of Appeals aimed to block this move, when it declared the statute to be an unconstitutional taking of employers' property, an illegitimate legislative redistribution of wealth, such as the U.S. Supreme Court condemned in *Lochner*.

Ives, like *Lochner*, would be reversed – *Lochner* by the Court itself a little more than a decade after the decision, *Ives* by a state constitutional amendment. But neither reversal left a broad opening for social citizenship and administrative state-building to unfold anew; sharp constitutional constraints remained. Neither reversal could turn back the clock, and in policy and state formation, timing is crucial.

The U.S. Supreme Court upheld workers' compensation statutes, but it did so in stages. And it held that the statutes' constitutionality under the due process clause hinged, partly, on whether they afforded employers a quid pro quo for the imposition of strict liability. The courts also imposed sharp federalism limits on workers' compensation, forcing the creation of many work accident systems; this patchwork of different legal regimes consumed decades of effort on the part of social insurance advocates. In addition to workers' compensation, a handful of states also enacted modest old-age pension programs, all of them voluntary. By the 1920s, several state legislatures had passed minimum wage legislation and created boards like England's, but all these laws and agencies were declared unconstitutional. Ernst Freund, Joseph Cotton, and other constitutional lawyers also warned that workers' compensation was different from health or unemployment insurance. No common law baseline of already existing employer liability existed for the hazards of illness or joblessness; therefore, any state-mandated employer contribution seemed likely to run afoul of the courts.

While America's Progressive social insurance proponents found themselves stymied, other players and other risk-spreading solutions began to occupy the field. Other lines of policy and institutional development began to unfold. In the domain of accidents outside the workplace, private insurance companies and the plaintiffs' bar – the much-reviled "ambulance chasers" and their "runners" – set up shop, settled accident cases by the tens of thousands, and, in the process, fashioned actuarial tables to determine the average "value" of given injuries, creating a decentralized system of private administration that resembled the bureaucratic machinery of publicly administered social insurance elsewhere. Similar developments unfolded in old age and health insurance. Private employers and employers' associations in tandem with insurance companies took the lead in fashioning plans. In all these areas of social policy, the plaintiffs' bar, private commercial insurance companies, and private employers' associations were the "first movers," as political scientists would say, and first movers enjoy large advantages over those who would displace them when a new crisis reopens the door to reform, as it would in the 1930s.

Over the first half of the twentieth century, all industrial nations would socialize and bureaucratize the world of risk, injury, and vulnerability. Unlike the other nations in this transatlantic conversation, which went a long way toward creating broadly inclusive systems of public social insurance, America kept administration in private hands. Compared to Britain, and even more sharply to the capitalist democracies of continental Europe, America's *public* welfare state remained a paltry and partial affair. Still, during those same decades, a large portion of American working people came to enjoy a robust measure of privately constructed job security, pension rights, and private health insurance – a *private* welfare state that surpassed England's and Western Europe's public systems along several dimensions.

America ended up administering a remarkable swath of twentieth-century social policy through new private organizations and old nineteenth-century institutions of government. And where new public officials gained administrative authority, as with industrial accidents and workplace safety, America judicialized the way these public officials exercised administrative power, creating legions of administrative law judges. A good part of the reason for these divergent paths of welfare state development lay in the ways that the longstanding power of bar and bench was bolstered by the absence of a well-established administrative state elite in the early twentieth-century United States, in America's deeply entrenched and judicially enforced traditions of federalism, and in the authority American courts enjoyed in striking the balance between the old liberalism and the new.

VIII. FORGING THE MODERN ILLIBERAL STATE: RACE, NATION- AND STATE-BUILDING, AND THE DOCTRINE OF PLENARY POWERS

The new Progressive or "social" brand of liberalism assailed the inequalities and violence of classical legal liberalism's governance of the nation's political economy. It offered a corrective comprising redistribution, social provision, and administration. Classical legal liberalism, in turn, offered critical resources for those aggrieved by new governance, regulation, and redistribution, including, occasionally, those at the bottom aggrieved by new forms of social policing. Along with expanding and centralizing state power, there emerged an expanding array of individual rights, in the rubric of classical legal liberalism. But this liberal constitutional dialectic of new state authority and new limits on state authority does not capture all the state-building afoot in the late nineteenth and early twentieth centuries. Much central state-building, including important new administrative agencies, arose beyond the pale of liberal constitutional constraints and exerted power over people whom the courts left rightless.

Mass immigration, westward expansion, and imperial ambition prompted Congress and the executive branch to embark on dramatic, unprecedented expansions of central state power; these, in turn, raised fundamental questions of sovereignty and statehood – of defining the nation-state's members, its powers, and its social and territorial boundaries. Many of the answers that Congress and the Executive gave these questions were bluntly illiberal in everyone's eyes, including the Justices'. Yet, in cases adjudicating the metes and bounds of national authority over immigrants, Indian tribes and tribal lands, and colonial territories and colonized peoples, the majority of the federal judiciary and of the U.S. Supreme Court stepped away from the precepts of classical legal liberalism. In these domains, individuals had no rights and governmental power no limits that the courts were bound to recognize and enforce.

In sharp contrast to the state-building arenas canvassed so far, where robust judge-made substantive and procedural rules held sway, here the Supreme Court declared that Congress had "plenary power" to construct new administrative apparatus and determine the substantive scope and procedural forms of assertions of national power just as Congress saw fit, immune from judicial review. Remarkably, these "plenary power" cases remain good law, and significant law, in terms of twenty-first-century America's treatment of "territories" like Puerto Rico, of Native Americans, and of immigrants.

Immigration: State-Building and Nation-Making at the Gates, Keeping Out "Unassimilable Aliens"

The plenary power doctrine was first elaborated in *Chae Chan Ping v. United States* (1889), known as the Chinese Exclusion Case. At issue were the exclusion laws of the 1880s, which halted the immigration of Chinese laborers to the United States. This was among the first significant federal immigration restrictions enacted since the short-lived Alien and Sedition Acts of 1798 and the first occasion in which the nation barred immigration based on the would-be immigrant's race or nationality. The particular provisions at issue also worked to exclude a Chinese laborer who had resided in the United States for twelve years and returned with a federal certificate authorizing his reentry. None of the laborer Ping's objections was availing, however. Congress's power to exclude "foreigners" was an "incident of sovereignty," wrote Justice Field for a unanimous Court, "to be exercised for protection and security." "If Congress considers the presence of foreigners of a different race in this country, who will not assimilate with us, to be dangerous to [the nation's] peace and security, . . . its determination is conclusive upon the judiciary."

In earlier cases, the Court had found Congress's power over immigration to reside in the foreign commerce clause. On that basis the postbellum Court wrested control over immigration from the states and began nudging and prodding Congress to take over the administration of the nation's borders – an instance of judicially forced central-state-building that resulted in the 1891 creation of the federal Immigration Bureau, just as the Court had prodded Congress to enact the Interstate Commerce Act a few years earlier by denying the states' railroad commissions power over interstate railroad rates.

Having forced the states to give up and Congress to assume the task of regulating and administering immigration, the Court now saw the power to exclude would-be immigrants as one inhering in national "sovereignty" and deemed it essential to protecting the nation from foreign aggression. Foreign invasions could take forms other than a military attack. They could stem from the cumulative acts of individual aliens, which the Court described as "vast hordes . . . crowding in upon us." The combined sense of spatial and racial peril in the Court's words was advertent. Sovereignty meant more than control of borders. It also implied power to construct an "American people" and American nationhood.

Field's notion of the state as a sovereign exercising jurisdiction over territory was not a novel one. It ran through international law and American jurisprudence since its founding and animated such classic late nineteenth-century jurisdiction cases as *Pennoyer v. Neff* (1877). Likewise, the proposition that national statehood implies a power to control the national territory's borders was well entrenched in international law. It seems inevitable, and right, that as mass immigration burgeoned, the Court would find that the Constitution equipped the national government with this gate-keeping authority. Quite otherwise was the plenary power idea: that the power to exclude was unlimited and unchecked by judicial review or by any limitations on federal power located elsewhere in the Constitution. Casting the power as a feature of sovereignty and statehood in the world of nations, rather than as an aspect of the power to regulate foreign commerce, pushed against a strong judicial role for it linked immigration control to national security and foreign affairs, where judicial deference already had a long pedigree.

Even after the Court abjured authority to review the substance of federal immigration laws, there remained questions about the reviewability of administrative officials' decisions applying the new immigration statutes. We have seen how the Supreme Court refused to allow emerging administrative agencies to make legal or even factual determinations free from searching judicial oversight, thus for instance hobbling the ICC by denying its decision-making autonomy until the 1910s. Not so with the Immigration Bureau; its exclusion and deportation decisions also affected basic liberties, but in sharp contrast to the ICC, the Immigration Bureau's decisions promptly gained what administrative lawyers call legal "finality," or freedom from judicial review. The Bureau was thus an early bloomer, and an anomaly, in the emergence of the modern American administrative state.

Of course, the Court could not have ushered in such administrative autonomy single-handedly. The issue first arose in the 1880s, prior to the creation of the federal Bureau, when immigration decisions were still in the hands of state officials at ports like New York and San Francisco. The harsh summary proceedings through which California decided Chinese laborers' bona fides (as either returning resident aliens or returning birthright citizens) under the federal exclusion laws prompted the leading Chinese merchants of San Francisco to mount a concerted litigation campaign involving hundreds of habeas challenges. No foes of the general principle of Chinese exclusion, federal trial judges nonetheless proved receptive to hundreds of petitioners like the laborer Ping, alleging long years of U.S. residence or, in many cases, U.S. birth and birthright citizenship, and seeking a judicial hearing before banishment. So, when burgeoning European immigration combined with the Court's voiding of New York's regulatory regime to lead Congress to draft federal immigration legislation and create a national Immigration Bureau, it was lawmakers from California, enraged by judicial interference with their state machinery of Chinese exclusion, who called for a rule of administrative finality and a bar on judicial review.

Although the rule of finality was contained in the general immigration statute of 1891, the first challenges all involved Asians and Asian Americans. The view that Asians were an "unassimilable race" "without morality" who would only exploit the nation's legal process combined with the spectacle of Chinese laborers "clogging" the federal courts with hundreds of habeas actions to help sway the Supreme Court to uphold Congress's grant of administrative finality. Thus, the Court applied the new plenary power doctrine to the procedural as well as substantive dimensions of immigration law, even though the universe of claimants included Chinese American citizens as well as aliens and would-be immigrants from Europe as well as Asia. "[W]ith regard to him," wrote Justice Holmes in a 1905 case involving a Chinese laborer claiming birthright citizenship against a threatened deportation, "due process of law does not require a judicial trial."[7] Ernst Freund, the pioneer administrative law scholar, reacted philosophically: "Hard cases make bad law."

Over the next century, the Court granted the would-be immigrant little more due process protection. Well-placed advocates and pro-immigrant Secretaries of Commerce and Labor nudged the Bureau to adopt internal procedural reforms, making its administrative tribunals more court-like, but to this day, judicial review of immigration decisions remains exceedingly deferential and immigration bureau tribunals remain harsh and summary. When political tides turn against immigrants, as they have in the early twenty-first century, courts still offer them almost no shelter from Kafkaesque bureaucratic arbitrariness. Plenary power and administrative finality over vulnerable "aliens" proved not only bad but enduring law.

Native Americans: The Bureau of Indian Affairs and the Indian as Indigenous Outsider and "Ward of the State"

In some measure, the law's harsh and illiberal treatment of the alien at the gates seemed to spring from his anomalous position in relation to the nation-state concept of a territory and a people occupying and belonging to it. He was figured as neither a member of the American state nor a person within its borders; rather, he stood outside the border, a citizen elsewhere and, presumably, safeguarded in his rights by some other sovereign in that other place. An outsider to our law here, he was an insider there. These reassurances could not explain the illiberal treatment accorded Native Americans and residents of America's new Caribbean and Pacific colonial possessions. In both the Indian and the possession cases, the indigenous peoples were neither aliens nor non-residents. Yet, despite their birth and residence on U.S. soil and the Fourteenth Amendment's rule of birthright citizenship, the Supreme Court refused to include them in the circle of citizenship rights. As Congress and the executive branch constructed colonial administrations and a vastly expanded and professionalized Bureau of Indian Affairs, the form and substance of their coercive powers were left free from judicial restraints, along the lines of the alien cases and the plenary power doctrine. Rather than recognizing them as rights-bearing members

[7] *United States v. Ju Toy*, 198 U.S. 253, 263 (1905).

of the national community, the federal courts cast these peoples as internal aliens, "inside outsiders" in historian Kunal Parker's apt phrase.

Beginning in 1877, the great civil service reformer and state-builder, Secretary of the Interior Carl Schurz used his office to transform the Bureau of Indian Affairs (BIA) into a modern bureaucracy staffed by social scientifically trained professionals, centralizing authority away from state and territorial governors and undertaking unprecedented kinds of governance and powers over Native Americans. From Jackson's presidency until Grant's, state policy had consisted in forcing Indians to move west of the Mississippi and forcing them onto reservations. In the 1870s began the "assimilationist era." A coalition of Western land interests, Christian reformers, and professional "friends of the Indian" in the Bureau assailed the old policy of forced segregation on semi-sovereign tribal reservations in favor of a new one of destroying the Native Americans' tribes, cultures, lands, and institutions and, in the words of one Commissioner, "assimilating the Indian into citizenship with the masses of the Republic."

Two new policies were the key to the assimilationist project. One was abolishing customary tribal law by ending tribal jurisdiction over civil and criminal matters and imposing "American Anglo-Saxon" law. The second was the forced division of tribal lands, held in common, into severalty and its allocation to individual Indians. For Western land interests, the object of the new policies was opening hundreds of thousands of acres of property to new settlement and cultivation and railroads. But for the BIA's professional "friends of the Indian," the object was nothing less than the "civilization" of the Indian soul, the transformation of Native Americans from primitive communalists into modern individualists, making them say "mine" instead of "ours." For his part, Theodore Roosevelt would later acclaim the 1888 Congressional statute dividing tribal lands into individual allotments a "mighty pulverizing engine to break up the tribal mass." And so it was. But the next decade saw the opposite of liberal autonomy and enlightenment: Indians lost 75 percent of their lands, what was left was desert, and Indians grew ever more exposed to poverty and dependency as well as spiritual demise.

While Congress and the Bureau may have meant to pulverize and remake Native Americans into classical liberal rights-bearing individualists and citizens, neither they nor the federal judiciary endowed them with citizens' ordinary civil and political rights. In the thick of the government's brutal citizen-making exercises, the Supreme Court ruled that the citizenship clause of the Fourteenth Amendment ("All persons born or naturalized in the United States, and subject to the jurisdiction thereof, are citizens of the United States . . . ") did not confer citizenship on Native Americans born under the jurisdiction of a tribe, even those who had separated from their tribe and now dwelt "among white citizens." Nor would Congress's dismantling of tribal jurisdictions change this.

For much of the nineteenth century, Congress regulated affairs with Indian tribes by way of treaties. Conceiving governance of Native Americans as somewhat akin to relations with foreign nations supported assertions of plenary federal power, just as in the alien cases. But ironically, the Court announced the application of the plenary power doctrine to Native Americans in a series of cases upholding statutes that set about ending the treaty system, abrogating treaty rights, displacing tribal law with U.S. law, and forcibly redistributing Indians' property. If Native Americans were to be treated no longer as members of separate nations and polities, but as citizens instead, what warranted holdings that they had no enforceable rights and that Congress's and the Bureau's powers over them and their lands were plenary?

The Court's answer lay in the condition of dependency to which Indians had been reduced, but not only in that. "[R]emnants of a race once powerful, now weak and diminished in numbers," the Indians' "very weakness and helplessness" imparted to Congress "the duty of protection, and with it the power" to subject them to measures the Court would have deemed unconstitutional if they applied to "the white man" and his "superior," fully "civilized race." By contrast, the "red man" was not a citizen but a "ward" of the national government; Congress's plenary authority over him rested no longer on his membership in another polity, but rather (by analogy to the common law of ward and guardian) on his still uncivilized, child-like state of property-less savagery. Native Americans were "in a state of pupilage," and Congress and the Bureau were free to lift their Indian children to the adulthood of liberal individualist, fee-simple civilization in almost any manner they saw fit.

"Race," then, or, more specifically, a keen conception of racial hierarchy, buttressed by much "modern" social science and legal scholarship, was key to the law's treatment of Native Americans and supplied a link to the other major sites of illiberal state-building in the decades bracketing the turn of the last century. Anthropology, ethnology, and eugenics emerged in these decades as new professional disciplines. Congress and newly created federal bureaus and commissions enlisted many of the new disciplines' leading lights to survey and gather up-to-date scientific knowledge about the ever-increasing array of "inferior races" falling under national state authority. No wonder. As historian Mark Weiner has shown, law, liberty, and liberal legal institutions were central concerns for all these disciplines, and directly or indirectly, all spoke to current dilemmas of governance and statecraft. These and other social "sciences" arrayed the "races" of humankind along an evolutionary ladder; all saw legal development as a – and in many cases *the* – central marker of racial progress and civilization. And all agreed that only races at or near that top rung had the capacity for sustaining and living under liberal legal institutions. Inner dispositions, habits of heart and mind that we understand as "cultural" these disciplines viewed as "racial." Good governance hinged on knowing that a certain few races – variously dubbed "Anglo-Saxon," "Aryan," or "Nordic" – gave the world the liberal tradition of rule of law and limited government; even more important was that only those few races came already equipped with the inner self-control and aptitude for "abstract thinking" and the racially determined "moral and intellectual character" suited to liberal legal institutions.

The implications of all this racial knowledge for governing immigration, Native Americans, and colonial subjects seem plain enough, and we have glimpsed justices using them to underpin applications of the plenary power doctrine: illiberal rules for preliberal people. If America was to be a modern, global power, it had to regulate and govern many races, and it would be perilous, as well as sentimental and backward-looking, for constitutional doctrine to clothe those without the racial ingredients of liberal legal civilization with legal rights they were unfit to exercise or enjoy.

As with any complex body of "modern" ideas and knowledge, however, there were significant, open-ended debates, which also found expression in legal discourse and state policy. Thus, for example, there was a rift across these disciplines about whether inferior or primitive "racial traits" and "capacities" were fixed and hard-wired or changeable in response to changing environments, new social experience, and "tutelage," as the anthropologists and other professionals in the BIA believed. The latter outlook reflected a Lamarckian conception of racial inheritance, and it was vague enough to support both sanguine and glum views of the pace and possibilities of "racial progress" and "assimilation" for groups like Native Americans or Southern European peasant/immigrants.

State-Building and Empire: Colonialism and the Liberal Constitution

When the curtains opened on American empire in the 1890s, the glummer and more deterministic view of "inferior races" played the leading role. Empire meant competition for global markets and global power, overseas possessions in the Pacific and Caribbean, trade outposts and coaling stations en route to Asian ports, and a place on the world stage among the Great Powers. Imperial battlegrounds abroad also offered opportunity for unity at home, helping heal Civil War wounds by providing a common cause around which a shared (white) national racial identity might be renewed and deepened. Nowhere was the enthusiasm for administrative state-building stronger than among leading imperialists who hoped to build up a powerful and far-flung state apparatus in the name of colonial administration.

The Spanish-American War seemed to deliver all this, as it brought Cuba, Puerto Rico, and the Philippines into America's hands, the latter two as colonies, forcing the construction of new administrative bureaucracies at home and abroad and with them the question of imperial rule. In public political debate that question was nicely framed under the heading: "Does the Constitution follow the flag?" Did the Constitution's guarantees of individual rights and its limits on the forms and uses of state power apply to the way America would govern the new overseas possessions and their peoples?

The prominent young Republican Senator from Massachusetts, Henry Cabot Lodge had no doubts. Educated in legal history at Harvard by Henry Adams (his was among the first doctoral degrees in history in the nation), Lodge brought his learning to the Senate floor, where he expounded on the (in)capacities of the "Filipinos" and their "Malay" racial stock. "You can follow the story of political freedom and representative government among the English-speaking people back across the centuries until you reach the Teutonic tribes emerging from the forests of Germany and bringing with them forms of local self-government which are repeated today in the pure democracies of the New England town meeting." According to this influential "story" of American legal institutions and their racial origins, widely shared among the turn of the century's legal elite as well as the new professional historians and social scientists, "the individual freedom and highly developed form" of republican self-rule that were Anglo-Americans' racial legacy were products of "the slow growth of nearly fifteen hundred years." "You can not change race tendencies in a moment," Lodge warned his colleagues. "[The] theory [of more sanguine racial thinkers, like the 'assimilationists' in the Bureau of Indian Affairs], that you can make a Hotenntot into a European if you only took possession of him in infancy and gave him a European education among suitable surroundings, has been abandoned alike by science and history as grotesquely false."

An outspoken advocate of American expansion during the McKinley administration, Lodge won the president's ear, helping persuade him to go to war against Spain and to gain the new island colonies. Lodge's fellow New England Republicans, Hoar of Massachusetts and Hale of Maine, were bitter Senate opponents of Lodge's imperial designs, contending that overseas empire-building would undermine American constitutionalism and the nation's core liberal and republican commitments. If America was not prepared to welcome the Philippines (and Puerto Rico and any other such new territories) to statehood – and all the Senate's anti-imperialists agreed it should not – then the nation could not hold and rule over these territories as colonies and their inhabitants as colonial subjects without violating the Constitution and the nation's founding principles.

The debate reached the Court in the *Insular Cases* of 1901–04. The narrow issue, which opened onto large questions, was the legality of a duty imposed by federal law on imports from the newly acquired Puerto Rico. The Constitution requires that duties be "uniform throughout the United States." But was Puerto Rico part of "the United States," notwithstanding that no one in power had any intention of granting it statehood? Or was Puerto Rico still a "foreign country," notwithstanding that it was an American possession with a civil government constructed by Congress and the president? All sides agreed that the decision about Puerto Rico would govern all the new possessions. All agreed, as well, that the question whether the uniformity clause constrained Congress in governing the new possessions was bound up with the broader question whether all or any of the Constitution's rights-bearing provisions and constraints on government power extended (or "followed the flag") to the new American territories. Behind these questions was the problem of civic identity. Were the people of the insular territories, born on American soil and subject to the jurisdiction of the United States, to be citizens and members of the nation bound together by a common commitment to live under liberal constitutional principles and entitled to their protection? Or were they to have a legal status not easily reconciled with liberal republican principles – not citizens, but colonial subjects?

The Court was intensely divided, but opinions broke along two basic lines, which one contemporary commentator shrewdly dubbed "fundamentalists and modernists." The modernist majority agreed to a broad constitutional allowance for colonial administration; the four dissenters refused. Dissenting were not only Justice Harlan but also Justices Brewer, Peckham, and Fuller, authors of *Debs* and of *Lochner*, "fundamentalists" here – as there – on the question of judicially enforced constitutional safeguards, and willing to force the nation either to forsake dreams of overseas territories or pay the price of admitting the territories and their inhabitants into the national community and constitutional fold. These were no racial egalitarians. They acknowledged that many races were "unassimilable" and "could not with safety . . . be brought within the operation of the Constitution." But for them, the only sensible conclusion was for America to shun the imperialists' invitation to take up the "world's work" and the "simple and strong" tasks of "administration" it entailed. A liberal constitutional state could not also be an imperial state.

Announcing the judgment of the Court, Justice Brown affirmed that Congress had plenary power over the new territories. His was a "modernist" perspective as well as an imperialist one because it grasped that constitutional precepts were historically contingent, and it took account of the modern exigencies of a liberal nation administering imperial outposts inhabited by less advanced, pre-liberal peoples. Under such circumstances, Justice Brown reasoned, to insist that Congress abide by constitutional limitations "might be fatal to the development of what Chief Justice Marshall called the American Empire." New and "distant possessions" like the Philippines would be "inhabited by alien races, differing from us in religion, customs, law . . . and modes of thought," Brown observed. The "administration of government and justice according to Anglo-Saxon principles may for a time be impossible." Brown was, after all, the author of *Plessy* and its reliance on the "modern" race science of the 1890s. To those "many eminent men" like Hale and Hoar who feared that "an unrestrained possession of power on the part of Congress may lead to unjust and oppressive legislation," Brown had a response, which also sounded in a racial key. It was unnecessary, as well as unwise, to look to the Constitution for restraints on America's imperial governors, because restraint would be assured by the "principles of natural justice inherent in the Anglo-Saxon character, which need no expressions in constitutions or statutes to give them effect." Race, in other words, justified dispensing with constitutional limits, and race would guarantee a just administration.[8]

The plenary power doctrine signified the judiciary's most generous accommodation – or abdication – to modern state-building and the claims of administrative autonomy. In these arenas, lawmakers and state-builders responded to some of the most fundamental and enduring questions of twentieth-century statecraft: the boundaries of membership and the limits of state power in relation to the variety of humankind and the lure of empire. The answers they gave were fundamentally illiberal. Occasionally, judicial stalwarts of classical liberalism protested in dissent, but the federal courts, which elsewhere hedged in the new administrative state and defended the precepts of liberty and limited government so vigorously, fell into line and marched to the imperial drumbeat.

IX. WARTIME STATE-BUILDING AND PEACETIME DISMANTLING

"War," Randolph Bourne wrote in 1918, "is the health of the State." America's preparation for and entry into World War I brought a remarkable expansion of national authority and federal bureaucracy. The national

[8] *Downes v. Bidwell*, 182 U.S. 244 (1901). See also *DeLima v. Bidwell*, 182 U.S. 1 (1901) and *Dorr v. United States*, 195 U.S. 138 (1904).

government briefly became a pervasive and powerful presence in everyday life, claiming unprecedented powers over private property and local affairs. It ran the railways and the avenues of communication, directed industry and regulated the price of foodstuffs, and operated a vast propaganda and censorship machine. All this called forth constitutional challenges, but the Court largely spurned them, upholding national authority with greater consensus than fifty years before, during the last great wartime expansion. With Wilson at the helm, leading Progressives hoped that wartime state-building, public administration of economic life, and extensive public-private cooperation would create institutions that could be adapted to peacetime management of social progress. New federal agencies like the National War Labor Board, the War Labor Policies Board, and the War Industries Board inspired plans and proposals for a peacetime federal "reconstruction council," a "peace industries board," a national "labor relations tribunal," and so on. Wartime experience could overcome traditional fears of statism, collective action, and centralized power.

But wartime state expansion proved temporary, at the level of both institution building and legal doctrine. In sharp contrast to the plenary power doctrine, the judge-made law authorizing these enlargements of the administrative state was short-lived.

Congressional "preparedness" in 1916 authorized the president to take over the nation's railways in event of war. Takeover included rate-setting for all classes of service, intra- as well as interstate, denying state regulatory commissions power over any government-operated line. North Dakota disagreed, and when its case reached the Court, thirty-seven states filed an amicus brief. Speaking through Chief Justice White, the Court upheld the government in *Northern Pacific Railway Co. v. North Dakota* (1919). The president, said White, had not acted under the commerce clause but under the government's war power, which was "complete and undivided" and reached what ordinarily were local and state affairs as far as necessary to meet the emergency. Similar decisions upheld the national government's takeover of telephone and telegraph lines and its power to conscript citizens to serve in the military overseas and to control agricultural prices.

With armistice, Congress swiftly set about dismantling the administrative machinery of national economic management. Peacetime variants of the new executive branch agencies were not to be countenanced. Even Wilson divorced himself from the Progressive "reconstruction planners" in his administration and urged that readjustment problems could be left to the individual efforts of "spirited businessmen and self-reliant laborers."

A Republican Congress, after 1918, and a Republican White House, after 1920, presided over postwar America, and they had no truck with reform-minded statist notions like the continuation of nationalized railways or of the wartime federal safeguards for trade unions and collective bargaining. But other institutional innovations of wartime endured. Congress authorized a continuation of many kinds of government-fostered combination and cooperation among business firms. Industrial and trade associations sought and received new legal toleration and government support. Executive departments like Commerce, Agriculture, and Interior began to function as coordinators and clearinghouses for these private associations.

For its part, the 1920s Supreme Court under Chief Justice William Howard Taft would enact its own rather sophisticated "return to [antebellum] normalcy," reinvigorating many important Lochner era safeguards against redistribution and public administration of private economic life while interring others. Thus, the Taft Court resurrected the old judicial hard line against union organizing, strikes, and boycotts, ushering in a decade of the most intensive use of the labor injunction the country ever saw. Indeed, the 1920s Court declared that employers had a constitutional right to anti-strike and anti-boycott decrees, which neither Congress nor the state legislatures could substantially abridge.

Overall, the Court was not committed, unambiguously, to laissez-faire. But it put firmly to rest the wartime notion that *any* important economic activity could be deemed by Congress or state lawmakers to be "affected with a public interest" and thereby subject to public regulation. Only a handful of private pursuits warranted that label; for the rest, price and wage regulation were beyond the constitutional pale. At the same time, the 1920s Court not only abandoned the old antitrust precepts against "bigness" in the "rule of reason" cases but it also opened a new and broad berth for business associations to exchange information and collaborate on standardizing products and practices without running afoul of the Sherman Act. Thus did the postwar Court selectively build on wartime experience, and thereby modernize and strengthen the late nineteenth- and early twentieth-century legal framework of a political economy steered and regulated largely by the nation's courts and private corporate and business elites. The more adventurous wartime experiments in public regulation and redistribution of economic power would endure as precedents for the 1930s, when private solutions and private elites once more seemed inadequate.

CONCLUSION

By 1920, the foundations of the modern regulatory and welfare state had been laid. Yet, the courts were more powerful than ever. Courts yielded a significant measure of power and authority to the administrative agencies they deemed worthy and "responsible" – from the ICC (after its decades-long judicial tutelage) to the Immigration Bureau and other federal, state, and local agencies engaged in policing the new immigrant working classes and other racial "others" in the teeming cities, out West, and beyond. But courts remained the nation's "authoritative political economists" and the final arbiters of the substantive and procedural boundaries of state power. Courts struck the balance between old (classical, individualist) and new (social, collectivist) liberal values and continued to define and redefine the rules and standards governing much of social and economic life, leaving many areas of twentieth-century social policy and social provision that other nations were assigning to public bureaucracies in the hands of common law judges, attorneys, and private bureaucratic institutions, like employers and insurance companies.

Congress did not fail to address the leading problems of the day: the trusts, the railroads, the pervasive conflict between labor and capital. However, the clash of increasingly well-organized competing interests combined with the newness of national legislation in these areas to yield studiously ambiguous and common-law-laden statutes. Thus, more often than not, Congress left the hard, deeply contested questions where it found them – in the judiciary's hands. Judicial authority also found a boost from popular attachment to a decentralized constitutional order and popular distrust of bold central-state-building visions like Roosevelt's.

Meanwhile, under the varied leadership of conservatives, moderates, and Progressives, the elite bench and bar "magnified [their] office," building up and centralizing the judiciary itself, expanding the courts' own regulatory powers and capacities, and infusing new administrative agencies with court-like, adversarial processes. They produced a modernized judiciary and a judicialized lawyer- and common-law-dominated administrative state that, for better and worse, remains with us today.

Many important developments in administrative state-building and judicial governance unfolded outside the liberal dialectic of new state authority and new legal limits on state authority. Equal rights and liberty were not for everyone, because not everyone had the minimum moral and mental capacities for self-rule, the human stuff on which liberal legal regimes had to rest. Racial hierarchies grew more complex and hardened in these decades. The hierarchy included the immigrant "races" arriving from Asia and, by the millions, from Southern and Eastern Europe to form a new industrial proletariat, the new colonial subjects in the Philippines, along with the old racial others, Native and African Americans. In popular and high-brow public discourse, all these "races" were arrayed on an evolutionary scale, and, in varying degrees, all fell short of "old stock" white Americans; none were thought fully equipped for living under liberal legal rule.

Fashioning and upholding illiberal laws for pre-liberal peoples came easily. Trade unionists (like African American and women's rights advocates) invoked classical liberal rights and legal equality to challenge pre-liberal, quasi-feudal forms of subordination inscribed in common law doctrines of master and servant. But the judiciary built up "government by injunction" largely around such doctrines. Also unfettered by liberal legal restraints were the major experiments in administrative state-building prompted by mass immigration, westward expansion, and imperial adventures abroad. These experiments raised fundamental questions about the scope and power of the American state and the bestowal of membership in the community constituted by the U.S. Constitution. The answers that Congress and the executive gave were bluntly racist and illiberal, but the courts responded by cutting swathes of governance and regulation free from any significant liberal-legal-constitutional control, creating constitutional black holes that also remain in the twenty-first-century American state.

BIBLIOGRAPHIC ESSAYS

CHAPTER 1: LAW AND THE AMERICAN STATE, FROM THE REVOLUTION TO THE CIVIL WAR

MARK R. WILSON

General

There are few broad comparative studies that would allow us to better understand early American political development from a transnational or global perspective. One valuable overview is Michael Mann, *The Sources of Social Power, Volume II: The Rise of Classes and Nation States* (New York, 1993). One source for a concise account of the British case in the mid-nineteenth century is the chapter titled "The Nature of the State," in K. Theodore Hoppen, *The Mid-Victorian Generation, 1846–1886* (Oxford, 1998), 91–124. Especially in the United States, social scientists' interest in the autonomous capacities of the state increased starting in the 1980s. This was evident in the essays collected in Peter Evans, Dietrich Rueschemeyer, and Theda Skocpol, eds., *Bringing the State Back In* (New York, 1985). More recently, theorists have warned against attributing too much coherence and power to formal state organizations: see George Steinmetz, ed., *State/Culture: State-Formation after the Cultural Turn* (Ithaca, 1999) and Joel S. Migdal, *State in Society: Studying How States and Societies Transform and Constitute One Another* (New York, 2001). A stimulating discussion of the deficiencies of conventional notions of state power may be found in Peter Baldwin, "Beyond Weak and Strong: Rethinking the State in Comparative Policy History," *Journal of Policy History* 17 (2005), 12–33.

We know a great deal about party politics and the courts in the early United States, but much less about governmental administration. The richness of the literature on party politics is evident in one recent synthesis: Sean Wilentz, *The Rise of American Democracy: Jefferson to Lincoln* (New York, 2005). One essay by a leading historian of party politics that begins to discuss the state explicitly is Ronald P. Formisano, "State Development in the Early Republic: Substance and Structure, 1780–1840," in Byron E. Shafer and Anthony J. Badger, eds., *Contesting Democracy: Substance and Structure in American Political History,*

1775–2000 (Lawrence, KS, 2001), 7–35. A rich survey of the era, which is especially interested in the decline of the gentry, is Robert H. Wiebe, *The Opening of American Society: From the Adoption of the Constitution to the Eve of Disunion* (New York, 1984). The standard surveys of American legal history, which are attentive to developments in the Early Republic, are Lawrence M. Friedman, *A History of American Law* (2nd ed., New York, 1985) and Kermit Hall, *The Magic Mirror: Law in American History* (New York, 1989). The standard overview of federal administration, often overlooked, remains the multivolume account by Leonard D. White: *The Federalists: A Study in Administrative History* (New York, 1948); *The Jeffersonians: A Study in Administrative History, 1801–1829* (New York, 1951); and *The Jacksonians: A Study in Administrative History, 1829–1861* (New York, 1956).

Ironically, the notion that the early United States was governed by "a state of courts and parties," which influenced many historians and political scientists starting in the 1980s, came from a study that concentrated on the *late* nineteenth century: Stephen Skowronek, *Building a New American State: The Expansion of National Administrative Capacities, 1877–1920* (New York, 1982). A similar perspective is provided in Charles Bright, "The State in the United States During the Nineteenth Century," in Bright and Susan Harding, eds., *Statemaking and Social Movements: Essays in History and Theory* (Ann Arbor, 1984).

By the end of the twentieth century, a second generation of state-centered interpretations of early American political history challenged the idea of a "state of courts and parties," arguing that the early American state was complex and robust. Among the most important articulations of this view are Richard R. John, "Governmental Institutions as Agents of Change: Rethinking American Political Development in the Early Republic, 1787–1835," *Studies in American Political Development* 11 (1997), 347–80 and Ira Katznelson, "On Rewriting the Epic of America," in Ira Katznelson and Martin Shefter, eds., *Shaped by War and Trade: International Influences on American Political Development* (Princeton, NJ, 2003), 3–23.

Population

The standard history of the U.S. Census is Margo J. Anderson, *The American Census: A Social History* (New Haven, 1988). Anderson's work may be supplemented with James H. Cassedy, *Demography in Early America: Beginnings of the Statistical Mind, 1600–1800* (Cambridge, MA, 1969), Patricia Cline Cohen, *A Calculating People: The Spread of Numeracy in Early America* (Chicago, 1982); and Paul Schor, "Statistiques de la Population et Politique des Categories aux États-Unis au XIXe Siècle: Théories Raciales et Questions de Population dans le Recensement Américain," *Annales de Démographie Historique* (2003), 5–21.

Two important surveys of the politics and law of American citizenship, which discuss the early nineteenth century at length, are Rogers M. Smith, *Civic Ideals: Conflicting Visions of Citizenship in U.S. History* (New Haven, 1997) and Alexander Keyssar, *The Right to Vote: The Contested History of Democracy in the United States* (New York, 2000). Studies that trace the treatment of population and citizenship in the various state constitutions include Rowland Berthoff, "Conventional Mentality: Free Blacks, Women, and Business Corporations as Unequal Persons, 1820–1870," *Journal of American History* 76 (1989), 753–84; Marc W. Kruman, *Between Authority and Liberty: State Constitution Making in Revolutionary America* (Chapel Hill, NC, 1997); and Laura J. Scalia, *America's Jeffersonian Experiment: Remaking State Constitutions, 1820–1850* (DeKalb, IL, 1999).

Discussions of church and state in the early United States include Daniel R. Ernst, "Church-State Issues and the Law: 1607–1870," in *Church and State in America, A Bibliographical Guide: The Colonial and Early National Periods* (New York, 1986), 331–64; John M. Murrin, "Religion and Politics in America from the First Settlements to the Civil War," and John F. Wilson, "Religion, Government, and Power in the New American Nation," both in Mark A. Noll, ed., *Religion and American Politics: From the Colonial Period to the 1890s* (New York, 1990), 19–43, 77–91; John G. West, Jr., *The Politics of Revelation and Reason: Religion and Civic Life in the New Nation* (Lawrence, KS, 1996); Daniel L. Driesbach, "Thomas Jefferson, a Mammoth Cheese, and the 'Wall of Separation' Between Church and State," and Jon Butler, "Why Revolutionary America Wasn't a 'Christian Nation'," both in James H. Huston, ed., *Religion and the New Republic: Faith in the Founding of America* (Lanham, MD, 2000), 65–114, 187–202.

Major studies of slavery, politics, and the law include Paul Finkelman, *An Imperfect Union: Slavery, Freedom, and Comity* (Chapel Hill, NC, 1981) and Don E. Fehrenbacher, *The Slaveholding Republic: An Account of the United States Government's Relations to Slavery* (New York, 2001). Two instructive short essays on the subject are Robin Einhorn, "The Early Impact of Slavery," and Michael F. Holt, "The Slavery Issue," both in Julian E. Zelizer, ed., *The American Congress: The Building of Democracy* (Boston, 2004), 77–90, 189–200. Short but suggestive discussions of whiteness in the early United States may be found in Noel Ignatiev, *How the Irish Became White* (New York, 1995) and Matthew Frye Jacobson, *Whiteness of a Different Color: European Immigrants and the Alchemy of Race* (Cambridge, MA, 1998). Early immigration law is described in Gerald L. Neuman, *Strangers to the Constitution: Immigrants, Borders, and Fundamental Law* (Princeton, NJ, 1996) and Aristide R. Zolberg, *A Nation by Design: Immigration Policy in the Fashioning of America* (Cambridge, MA, 2006).

Three outstanding studies of family law and the changing legal status of women are Norma Basch, *In the Eyes of the Law: Women, Marriage, and Property in Nineteenth-Century New York* (Ithaca, 1982); Michael Grossberg, *Governing the Hearth: Law and the Family in Nineteenth-Century America* (Chapel Hill, NC, 1985); and Nancy Isenberg, *Sex and Citizenship in Antebellum America* (Chapel Hill, NC, 1998).

Economy

There is an extraordinarily rich literature dealing with law and political economy in the early United States. General essays on the subject include those in James Willard Hurst, *Law and the Conditions of Freedom in the Nineteenth-Century United States* (Madison, 1956); Harry N. Scheiber, "Federalism and the American Economic Order, 1789–1910," *Law and Society Review* 10 (1975), 57–118; Richard Sylla, "Experimental Federalism: The Economics of American Government, 1789–1914," in Stanley L. Engerman and Robert E. Gallman, eds., *The Cambridge Economic History of the United States, Volume II: The Long Nineteenth Century* (New York, 2000), 483–541; and Richard R. John, "Farewell to the 'Party Period': Political Economy in Nineteenth-Century America," *Journal of Policy History* 16 (2004), 117–25. For all the strengths of the literature in this field, many historians have overlooked basic questions about comparative public finance. Helpful in this area are Paul B. Trescott, "Federal-State Financial Relations, 1790–1860," *Journal of Economic History* 15 (1955), 227–45; Paul B. Trescott, "The United States Government and National Income, 1790–1860," in *Trends in the American Economy in the Nineteenth Century* (Princeton, NJ, 1960), 337–61; Charles Frank Holt, *The Role of State Government in the Nineteenth Century American Economy, 1820–1902: A Quantitative Study* (New York, 1977); John B. Legler, Richard Sylla, and John J. Wallis, "U.S. City Finances and the Growth of Government," *Journal of Economic History* 48 (1988), 347–56; and Robin L. Einhorn, *American Taxation, American Slavery* (Chicago, 2006).

An influential study that stresses the abundance of local regulation throughout this era is William J. Novak, *The People's Welfare: Law and Regulation in Nineteenth-Century America* (Chapel Hill, NC, 1996). This work may be usefully balanced with Helen Tangiers, *Public Markets and Civic Culture in Nineteenth-Century America* (Baltimore, 2003). On municipal governments and their changing relationships with the states, major studies include Jon C. Teaford, *The Municipal Revolution in America: Origins of Modern Urban Government, 1650–1825* (Chicago, 1975); Hendrik Hartog, *Public Property and Private Power: The Corporation of the City of New York in American Law, 1730–1870* (Chapel Hill, NC, 1983); and Eric H. Monkkonen, *America Becomes Urban: The Development of U.S. Cities & Towns, 1780–1980* (Berkeley, 1988); also helpful are Jon Teaford, "City Versus State: The Struggle for Legal Ascendancy," *American Journal of Legal History* 17 (1973), 51–65 and Robert M. Ireland, "The Problem of Local, Private, and Special Legislation in the Nineteenth-Century United States," *American Journal of Legal History* 46 (2004), 271–99. Two valuable accounts of urban politics and government at mid-century are Amy Bridges, *A City in the Republic: Antebellum New York and the Origins of Machine Politics* (New York, 1984) and Robin L. Einhorn, *Property Rules: Political Economy in Chicago, 1833–1872* (Chicago, 1991).

An essential study of the courts and capitalist enterprise during this era is Morton J. Horwitz, *The Transformation of American Law, 1780–1860*

(Cambridge, MA, 1977). For a detailed counter-narrative, see Peter Karsten, *Heart Versus Head: Judge-Made Law in Nineteenth-Century America* (Chapel Hill, NC, 1997). The early legal history of American business corporations is described in James Willard Hurst, *The Legitimacy of the Business Corporation in the Law of the United States, 1780–1970* (Charlottesville, VA, 1970) and Ronald E. Seavoy, *The Origins of the American Business Corporation, 1784–1855* (Westport, CT, 1982). Two wide-ranging studies of labor law during these years are Robert J. Steinfeld, *The Invention of Free Labor: The Employment Relation in English and American Law and Culture, 1350–1870* (Chapel Hill, NC, 1991) and Christopher L. Tomlins, *Law, Labor, and Ideology in the Early American Republic* (New York, 1993).

On banking, one classic study is Bray Hammond, *Banks and Politics in America: From the Revolution to the Civil War* (Princeton, NJ, 1957); more recent overviews include John B. Legler, Richard Sylla, and John J. Wallis, "Banks and State Public Finance in the New Republic: The United States, 1790–1860," *Journal of Economic History* 47 (1987), 391–403 and Howard Bodenhorn, *A History of Banking in Antebellum America: Financial Markets and Economic Development in an Era of Nation-Building* (New York, 2000). Important studies of early national communications policy include Richard R. John, *Spreading the News: The American Postal System from Franklin to Morse* (Cambridge, MA, 1995) and Paul Starr, *The Creation of the Media: Political Origins of Modern Communications* (New York, 2004).

There is a vast literature on internal improvements. Among the studies written in the wake of the New Deal that stressed positive state interventions in the economic sphere before the Civil War were Oscar Handlin and Mary Flug Handlin, *Commonwealth: A Study of the Role of Government in the American Economy: Massachusetts, 1774–1861* (Cambridge, MA, 1947); Louis Hartz, *Economic Policy and Democratic Thought: Pennsylvania, 1776–1860* (Cambridge, MA, 1948); and Milton Heath, *Constructive Liberalism: The Role of the State in the Economic Development of Georgia to 1860* (Cambridge, MA, 1954). Influential surveys of this work include Robert A. Lively, "The American System," *Business History Review* 29 (1955), 81–96; Carter Goodrich, "Internal Improvements Reconsidered," *Journal of Economic History* 30 (1970), 289–311; and Harry N. Scheiber, "Government and the Economy: Studies of the 'Commonwealth' Policy in Nineteenth-Century America," *Journal of Interdisciplinary History* 3 (1972), 135–51. Important newer contributions to this field included Harry N. Scheiber, *Ohio Canal Era: A Case Study of Government and the Economy, 1820–1861* (Athens, OH, 1969); L. Ray Gunn, *The Decline of Authority: Public Economic Policy and Political Development in New York, 1800–1860* (Ithaca, 1988); John Majewski, *A House Dividing: Economic Development in Pennsylvania and Virginia before the Civil War* (New York, 2000); and Sean Patrick Adams, *Old Dominion, Industrial Commonwealth: Coal, Politics, and Economy in Antebellum America* (Baltimore, 2004). Valuable studies of internal improvements from a national perspective include Carter Goodrich, *Government Promotion of American Canals and Railroads, 1800–1890* (New York, 1960); Laurence J. Malone, *Opening the West: Federal Internal Improvement before 1860* (Westport, CT, 1998); John Lauritz Larson, *Internal Improvement: National Public Works and the Promise of Popular Government in the Early United States* (Chapel Hill, NC, 2001); and Stephen Minicucci, "Internal Improvements and the Union, 1790–1860," *Studies in American Political Development* 18 (2004), 160–85.

For a comparative view of internal improvements in the United States and Europe, one influential study is Colleen A. Dunlavy, *Politics and Industrialization: Early Railroads in the United States and Prussia* (Princeton, NJ, 1994); this book should be read together with James M. Brophy, *Capitalism, Politics, and Railroads in Prussia, 1830–1870* (Columbus, 1998). Developments in France and Britain are considered in Henry Parris, *Government and the Railways in Nineteenth-Century Britain* (London, 1965); Reed G. Geiger, *Planning the French Canals: Bureaucracy, Politics, and Enterprise Under the Restoration* (Newark, DE, 1994); and R. W. Kostal, *Law and English Railway Capitalism, 1825–1875* (Oxford, 1994).

Major studies of the rise of public schooling include Lawrence A. Cremin, *American Education: The National Experience, 1783–1876* (New York, 1980); Carl F. Kaestle, *The Evolution of an Urban School System: New York City, 1750–1850* (Cambridge, MA, 1973); Carl F. Kaestle, *Pillars of the Republic: Common Schools and American Society, 1780–1860* (New York, 1983); and Carl F. Kaestle and Maris A. Vinovskis, *Education and Social Change in Nineteenth-Century Massachusetts* (New York, 1990). Some comparative statistics are provided in Albert Fishlow, "Levels of Nineteenth-Century Investment in Education," *Journal of Economic History* 26 (1966), 418–36.

The development of criminal law, criminal courts, and the emergence of uniformed police forces is described in several remarkable studies, including Roger Lane, *Policing the City: Boston, 1822–1855* (Cambridge, MA, 1967); Wilbur R. Miller, *Cops and Bobbies: Police Authority in New York and London, 1830–1870* (Chicago, 1977); Michael Stephen Hindus, *Prison and Plantation: Crime, Justice, and Authority in Massachusetts and South Carolina, 1767–1878* (Chapel Hill, NC, 1980); Allen Steinberg, *The Transformation of Criminal Justice: Philadelphia, 1800–1880* (Chapel Hill, NC, 1989); and Theodore Ferdinand, *Boston's Lower Criminal Courts, 1814–1850* (Newark, DE, 1992). The most influential history of early American prisons is David J. Rothman, *The Discovery of the Asylum: Social Order and Disorder in the New Republic* (Boston, 1971); an overview by the same author is "Perfecting the Prison: United States, 1789–1865," in Norval Morris and David J. Rothman, eds., *The Oxford History of the Prison: The Practice of Punishment in Western Society* (New York, 1995), 111–29. Our knowledge of early jails remains limited, but one suggestive survey is J. M. Moynahan and Earle K. Stewart, *The American Jail: Its Development and Growth* (Chicago, 1980). On poor relief, the standard history is Michael B. Katz, *In the*

Shadow of the Poorhouse, A Social History of Welfare in America, (New York, rev. ed. 1996).

Territory

Bartholomew H. Sparrow is the author of two short but suggestive essays on this subject: "Territorial Expansion," in Julian E. Zelizer, ed., *The American Congress: The Building of Democracy* (Boston, 2004), 168–86, and "Empires External and Internal: Territories, Government Lands, and Federalism in the United States," in Sanford Levinson and Sparrow, eds., *The Louisiana Purchase and American Expansion, 1803–1898* (Lanham, MD, 2005), 231–49. A wide-ranging study of the Louisiana Purchase may be found in Peter J. Kastor, *The Nation's Crucible: The Louisiana Purchase and the Creation of America* (New Haven, 2004). More specialized studies, which focus on constitutional law and international relations theory, respectively, are Gary Lawson and Guy Seidman, *The Constitution of Empire: Territorial Expansion and American Legal History* (New Haven, 2004) and Scott A. Silverstone, *Divided Union: The Politics of War in the Early American Republic* (Ithaca, 2004).

Political and legal historians have often overlooked the early American military. One important call to address this deficiency was issued in Ira Katznelson, "Flexible Capacity: The Military and Early American Statebuilding," in Ira Katznelson and Martin Shefter, eds., *Shaped by War and Trade: International Influences on American Political Development*, (Princeton, NJ, 2003), 83–110. Among the essential histories of the army during this era are Marcus Cunliffe, *Soldiers & Civilians: The Martial Spirit in America, 1775–1865* (Boston, 1968); Edward M. Coffman, *The Old Army: A Portrait of the American Army in Peacetime, 1784–1898* (New York, 1986); William B. Skelton, *An American Profession of Arms: The Army Officer Corps, 1784–1861* (Lawrence, KS, 1992); and Samuel J. Watson, "Professionalism, Social Attitudes, and Civil-Military Accountability in the United States Army Officer Corps, 1815–1846," PhD diss., Rice University, 1996.

Studies that trace the role of the military in early national exploration and technological innovation include William H. Goetzmann, *Army Exploration in the American West, 1803–1863* (New Haven, 1959); Merritt Roe Smith, *Harpers Ferry Armory and the New Technology: The Challenge of Change* (Ithaca, 1977); and Robert G. Angevine, *The Railroad and the State: War, Politics, and Technology in Nineteenth-Century America* (Stanford, 2004). On scientific research, major surveys include A. Hunter Dupree, *Science in the Federal Government: A History of Policies and Activities to 1940* (Cambridge, MA, 1957) and Robert V. Bruce, *The Launching of Modern American Science, 1846–1876* (New York, 1987).

The essential overview of the relationship between the American state and Native Americans is Francis Paul Prucha, *The Great Father: The United States Government and the American Indians* (Lincoln, NE, 1984). One book-length study of the Supreme Court's rulings in this area is David E. Wilkins, *American*

Indian Sovereignty and the U.S. Supreme Court: The Masking of Justice (Austin, TX, 1997).

Concise discussions of land and land policy include the introductory chapter in Howard Roberts Lamar, *Dakota Territory, 1861–1889: A Study of Frontier Politics* (New Haven, 1956) and Jeremy Atack, Fred Bateman, and William N. Parker, "Northern Agriculture and the Westward Movement," in Stanley L. Engerman and Robert E. Gallman, eds., *The Cambridge Economic History of the United States, Volume II: The Long Nineteenth Century* (New York, 2000), 285–328. A detailed general survey is Paul Wallace Gates, *History of Public Land Law Development* (Washington, 1968); a more focused discussion of the early nineteenth century is provided in Daniel Feller, *The Public Lands in Jacksonian Politics* (Madison, 1984). Brief but suggestive essays on the American approach to land are provided in James C. Scott, *Seeing Like a State: How Certain Schemes to Improve the Human Condition Have Failed* (New Haven, 1998) and David E. Nye, *America as Second Creation: Technology and Narratives of New Beginnings* (Cambridge, MA, 2003). The standard history of the Land Office is Malcolm J. Rohrbough, *The Land Office Business: The Settlement and Administration of American Public Lands, 1789–1837* (New York, 1968).

We have several outstanding studies of the relationship between military veterans and land policy, including James W. Oberly, *Sixty Million Acres: American Veterans and the Public Lands Before the Civil War* (Kent, OH, 1990); John Resch, *Suffering Soldiers: Revolutionary War Veterans, Moral Sentiment, and Political Culture in the Early Republic* (Amherst, 1999); and Laura Jensen, *Patriots, Settlers, and the Origins of American Social Policy* (New York, 2003).

An essential survey of Western history that pays considerable attention to law and the state is Richard White, *"It's Your Misfortune and None of My Own": A History of the American West* (Norman, OK, 1991). Studies of government and the courts on the frontier include Robert M. Ireland, *The County Courts in Antebellum Kentucky* (Lexington, KY, 1972); John R. Wunder, *Inferior Courts, Superior Justice: A History of the Justices of the Peace on the Northwest Frontier, 1853–1889* (Westport, CT, 1979); and Malcolm J. Rohrbough, "The Influence of Government and Law on the Settlement of the Trans-Appalachian West, 1775–1830," in Janusz Duzinkiewicz, ed., *States, Societies and Cultures, East and West: Essays in Honor of Jaroslaw Pelenski* (New York, 2004), 921–40.

Antebellum territorial policy and its relationship to the outbreak of the Civil War are discussed in many works, including David M. Potter, *The Impending Crisis, 1848–1861* (New York, 1976) and Michael A. Morrison, *Slavery and the American West: The Eclipse of Manifest Destiny and the Coming of the Civil War* (Chapel Hill, NC, 1997).

Civil War

The standard one-volume history of the immediate antebellum years and the Civil War is James M. McPherson, *Battle Cry of Freedom: The Civil War Era*

(New York, 1988). The end of slavery and the war's effects on the Constitution are considered in Harold M. Hyman, *A More Perfect Union: The Impact of the Civil War and Reconstruction on the Constitution* (New York, 1973) and Michael Vorenberg, *Final Freedom: The Civil War, the Abolition of Slavery, and the Thirteenth Amendment* (New York, 2001).

A comparative analysis of the wartime states in the South and the North is presented in Richard Franklin Bensel, *Yankee Leviathan: The Origins of Central State Authority in America, 1859–1877* (New York, 1990). Political economy in the wartime North is discussed in Heather Cox Richardson, *The Greatest Nation of the Earth: Republican Economic Policies During the Civil War* (Cambridge, MA, 1997) and Mark R. Wilson, *The Business of Civil War: Military Mobilization and the State, 1861–1865* (Baltimore, 2006).

One influential survey of the postwar period is Morton Keller, *Affairs of State: Public Life in Late Nineteenth Century America* (Cambridge, MA, 1977). The importance of the Civil War pension system in the postwar political economy is described in Theda Skocpol, *Protecting Soldiers and Mothers: The Political Origins of Social Policy in the United States* (Cambridge, MA, 1992).

CHAPTER 2: LEGAL EDUCATION AND LEGAL THOUGHT

HUGH C. MACGILL AND R. KENT NEWMYER

Though dated, the most comprehensive and thoroughly documented account of American legal education for the nineteenth and early twentieth centuries is Alfred Z. Reed, *Training for the Public Profession of the Law* (New York, 1921), supplemented by Alfred Z. Reed, *Present-Day Law Schools in the United States and Canada* (New York, 1928). See also Josef Redlich, *The Common Law and the Case Method in American University Law Schools* (New York, 1914). The best study is William P. LaPiana, *Logic and Experience: The Origin of Modern American Legal Education* (New York, 1994), which contains an excellent bibliography of primary and secondary sources. A useful overview is Robert Stevens, *Law School: Legal Education in American from the 1850s to the 1980s* (Chapel Hill, NC, 1983). Steve Sheppard, ed., *The History of Legal Education in the United States: Commentaries and Primary Sources* (Pasadena, CA, 1999) collects numerous hard-to-find primary sources. J. Willard Hurst, *The Law Makers* (Boston, 1950) has worn well. The *Index to Legal Periodicals* lists hundreds of articles dealing with this period under the heading "Legal Education." Morris L. Cohen, *Bibliography of Early American Law*, 6 vols. (Buffalo, NY, 1998) is an essential tool for the earlier period. The *National Union List of Manuscripts*, prepared by the Library of Congress, is the definitive guide to manuscripts of leading figures in legal education. The *Journal of Legal Education*, commencing in 1947, contains relevant articles and book reviews. Its predecessor, *The American Law School Review*, vols. 1–6 (1904–1920), is extremely helpful, containing (sometimes in excerpted form) papers presented at meetings of the AALS and the ABA and considerable informal data on academic appointments in a formative period. For the antebellum period the *American Jurist and Law Magazine* (1829–1843) contains much useful information. See also *American Law Review*, vols. 1–62 (1866–1929), Association of American Law Schools, *Proceedings*, vols. 1–19 (1901–1920), and American Bar Association *Reports*, vols. 1–45 (1878–1920).

There is no comprehensive study of apprenticeship legal education. One suggestive essay is Charles McKirdy, "The Lawyer as Apprentice: Legal Education in Eighteenth Century Massachusetts," *Journal of Legal Education* 28 (1976), 124. The availability of materials for the study and practice of law in the Early Republic is discussed in Jenni Parrish, "Law Books and Legal Publishing in America, 1760–1840," *Law Library Journal* 72 (1979), 355 and Herbert Johnson, *Imported Eighteenth-Century Law Treatises in American Libraries 1700–1799* (Knoxville, TN, 1978). Given the highly individualistic nature of apprenticeship learning, it is not surprising that much relevant material is contained in biographies and published private papers of individual lawyers and judges. Especially useful in this regard is Alfred S. Konefsky and Andrew J. King, eds., *The Papers of Daniel Webster: Legal Papers* (Hanover, NH, and London, 1982), I. For a later period, one might consult Martha L. Benner and Cullom David, eds., *The Law Practice of Abraham Lincoln* (DVD-ROM; Champaign, IL, 2000). See also W. Hamilton Bryson, *Legal Education in Virginia 1779–1979: A Biographical Approach* (Charlottesville, VA, 1982).

Among the studies of leading legal educators are R. Kent Newmyer, *Supreme Court Justice Joseph Story: Statesman of the Old Republic* (Chapel Hill, NC, 1985) and his "Harvard Law School, New England Culture, and the Antebellum Origins of American Jurisprudence," *Journal of American History* 74 (1987), 814. Also see Alonzo T. Dill, *George Wythe: Teacher of Liberty* (Williamsburg, VA, 1979); Charles T. Cullen, *St. George Tucker and Law in Virginia 1772–1804* (New York and London, 1987); and Paul D. Carrington, "Law as 'The Common Thoughts of Man': The Law-Teaching and Judging of Thomas McIntyre Cooley," *Stanford Law Review* 49 (1997), 495. For Theodore W. Dwight at Columbia, see Staff of the Foundation for Research in Legal History under the Direction of Julius Goebel, Jr., *A History of the School of Law, Columbia University* (New York, 1955), 33–132. There is as yet no biography of C. C. Langdell, but several excellent recent articles by Bruce A. Kimball fill much of the gap: Bruce A. Kimball, "'Warn Students That I Entertain Heretical Opinions, Which They Are Not to Take as Law': The Inception of Case Method Teaching in the Early Classrooms of C. C. Langdell, 1870–1883," *Law and History Review* 17 (1999), 57; Kimball, "Young Christopher Langdell, 1826–1854: The Formation of an Educational Reformer," *Journal of Legal Education* 52 (2002), 189; Kimball, "The Langdell Problem: Historicizing the Century of Historiography, 1906–2000s," *Law and History Review* 22 (2004), 277; Kimball and R. Blake Brown, "'The Highest Legal Ability in the Country': Langdell on Wall Street, 1855–1870," 29 *Law and Social Inquiry* (2004), 39; and Kimball, "Langdell on Contracts and Legal Reasoning: Correcting the Holmesian Caricature," *Law and History Review* 25 (2007), 345. References to the extensive literature on Langdell's premises, methods, and influence are contained in the general sources previously cited; a representative sampling might include Thomas C. Grey, "Langdell's Orthodoxy," *University of Pittsburgh Law Review* 45 (1983), 1; John H. Schlegel, "Langdell's Legacy, or, The Case of the Empty Envelope," *Stanford Law Review* 36 (1984), 1517; M. H. Hoeflich, "Law and Geometry: Legal Science from Leibnitz to Langdell," *American Journal of Legal History* 30 (1986), 95; Paul Carrington, "Hail! Langdell!", *Journal of Law and Social Inquiry* 20 (1995), 691; and Howard Schweber, "Before Langdell: The Roots of American Legal Science," in Steve Sheppard, ed., *The History of Legal Education in the United States* (Pasadena, CA, 1999), II: 606. Anthony Chase, "The Birth of the Modern Law School," *American Journal of Legal History* 23 (1979), 329 places Langdell's reforms in the context of Eliot's transformation of Harvard as a whole. On the latter, see Lawrence Veysey, *The Emergence of the American University* (Chicago, 1965), and Alain Touraine, *The Academic System in American Society* (New York, 1974). The definitive treatment of parallel developments in medicine and medical education is Paul Starr, *The Transformation of American Medicine* (New York, 1982).

Histories of individual law schools tend more toward the celebratory than the cerebral; see Alfred S. Konefsky and John Henry Schlegel, "Mirror, Mirror on the Wall: Histories of American Law Schools," *Harvard Law Review* 95 (1982), 833. Exceptions include Charles Warren, *History of the Harvard Law School*, 3 vols. (New York, 1908) and The Staff of the Foundation for Research in Legal History under the direction of Julius Goebel, Jr., *A History of the School of Law, Columbia University* (New York, 1955). William R. Johnson, *Schooled Lawyers: A Study in the Clash of Professional Cultures* (New York, 1978) is both a history of legal education in Wisconsin and an excellent monograph of broader scope. Another study dealing with legal education in the Midwest is Frank L. Ellsworth, *Law on the Midway: The Founding of the University of Chicago Law School* (Chicago, 1977). For the early years of the University of Virginia Law School see the informal but informative book by John Ritchie, *The First Hundred Years: A Short History of the School of Law of the University of Virginia for the Period 1826–1926* (Charlottesville, VA, 1978). For proprietary law schools during the antebellum period, see Creed Taylor, *Journal of the Law School, and the Moot Court Attached to It; at Needham, in Virginia* (Richmond, 1822) and Marlan C. McKenna, *Tapping Reeve and the Litchfield Law School* (New York, 1986). The early years of law at Yale are discussed insightfully in two essays by John Langbein in Anthony T. Kronman, ed., *History of Yale Law School* (New Haven and London, 2004).

Legal education is closely tied to the evolution of the legal profession itself. Relevant studies include Charles Warren, *A History of the American Bar* (Cambridge, MA, 1912); Maxwell Bloomfield, *American Lawyers in a Changing Society,*

1776–1876 (Cambridge, MA, 1976); Gerald W. Gawalt, *The Promise of Power: The Emergence of the Legal Profession in Massachusetts, 1760–1840* (Westport, CT, 1979); and Gerald W. Gawalt, ed., *The New High Priests: Lawyers in Post-Civil War America* (Westport, CT, 1984). Useful essays are collected in Kermit L. Hall, ed., *The Legal Profession: Major Historical Interpretations* (New York and London, 1987). Anton-Hermann Chroust, *The Rise of the Legal Profession in America*, 2 vols. (Norman, OK, 1965), though generally uncritical, contains some useful material. On the affinity between emerging corporate firms and the new model law school graduate, see Wayne K. Hobson, *The American Legal Profession and the Organizational Society, 1890–1930* (New York and London, 1986); Robert T. Swaine, *The Cravath Firm and its Predecessors, 1819–1947*, 2 vols. (New York, 1946), II; and Otto E. Koegel, *Walter S. Carter, Collector of Young Masters, or The Progenitor of Many Law Firms* (New York, 1953).

For the concepts of profession and professionalism in higher education, see Burton H. Bledstein, *The Culture of Professionalism: The Middle Class and the Development of Higher Education in America* (New York, 1976). The theme is analyzed more closely in Magali S. Larson, *The Rise of Professionalism: A Sociological Analysis* (Berkeley, CA, 1977) and developed in a legal context in Theodore Schneyer, "Professionalism as Politics: The Making of a Modern Legal Ethics Code," and Eliot Freidson, "Professionalism as Model and Ideology," both in Robert L. Nelson, David M. Trubek, and Rayman L. Solomon, eds., *Lawyers' Ideals/Lawyers' Practices: Transformations in the American Legal Profession* (Ithaca and London, 1992) at 95 and 215, respectively. Two essays by Robert W. Gordon should also be consulted: "Legal Thought and Legal Practice in the Age of American Enterprise, 1870–1920," in Gerald L. Geison, ed., *Professions and Professional Ideologies in America* (Chapel Hill, NC, 1983), 70 and "Corporate Law Practice as a Public Calling," *Maryland Law Review* 49 (1990), 255.

CHAPTER 3: THE LEGAL PROFESSION

ALFRED S. KONEFSKY

In 1986, Olavi Maru observed that "[t]here is no adequate broad, general historical study of the legal profession in the United States": *Research on the Legal Profession: A Review of Work Done* (2nd ed., Chicago, 1986), 1. Not much has changed in the intervening years since Maru's assessment, though there are now a number of useful studies that focus more narrowly on issues facing the American bar between the Revolution and the Civil War. The three standard workhorses remain Charles Warren, *A History of the American Bar* (Boston, 1911); Roscoe Pound, *The Lawyer from Antiquity to Modern Times* (St. Paul, MN, 1953); and Anton-Hermann Chroust, *The Rise of the Legal Profession in America* (Norman, OK, 1965). Each has substantial interpretive shortcomings, though each contains the occasional nugget of valuable information. For example, Chroust provides raw data, amassed from a variety of sources, on the number of lawyers in seventeenth- and eighteenth-century America. The most incisive study of the bar remains James Willard Hurst, *The Growth of American Law: The Law Makers* (Boston, 1950). Though only about a third of the book (and even less for the antebellum period) is devoted to the legal profession, the analytical categories, methods, and questions are as important today as they were when Hurst wrote more than a half-century ago. Lawrence Friedman cogently summarizes a variety of sources in his chapter on the bar in his *A History of American Law* (2nd ed., New York, 1985). Readers will also want to consult Michael Burrage, *Revolution and the Making of the Contemporary Legal Profession: England, France, and the United States* (New York, 2006).

Some very good studies place the profession more broadly in the history of wider professional culture. Daniel H. Calhoun, *Professional Lives in America: Structure and Aspiration, 1750–1850* (Cambridge, MA, 1965) contains a very perceptive study of lawyers in one Tennessee county, and Samuel Haber, *The Quest for Authority and Honor in the American Professions, 1750–1900* (Chicago, 1991) has particularly useful accounts of legal culture in this period for Cincinnati and Memphis. Perry Miller attempted to locate the legal profession in its wider intellectual context. Though somewhat idiosyncratic, when used with caution, it still has a distinctive voice and much to contribute. The chapters on "The Legal Mentality," in *The Life of the Mind in America: From the Revolution to the Civil War* (New York, 1965), are still stimulating, as are the distilled edited versions of some of the primary sources he used in *The Legal Mind in America: From Independence to the Civil War* (New York, 1962). Along these lines, but within a slightly wider cultural view, Robert Gordon's comments on the Federalist-Whig legal elites are very insightful. See his essay "Legal Thought and Legal Practice in the Age of American Enterprise, 1870–1920," in Gerald L. Geison, ed., *Professions and Professional Ideologies in America* (Chapel Hill, NC, 1983). Further attempts to cast the bar in a wider ideological environment include Russell G. Pearce, "Lawyers as America's Governing Class: The Formation and Dissolution of the Original Understanding of the American Lawyer's Role," *University of Chicago Law School Roundtable* 8 (2001), 381; Gerald W. Gawalt, "Sources of Anti-Lawyer Sentiment in Massachusetts, 1740–1840," *American Journal of Legal History* 14 (1970), 283; and James W. Gordon, "The Popular Image of the American Lawyer: Some Thoughts on Its Eighteenth and Nineteenth Century Intellectual Bases," *Washington & Lee Law Review* 46 (1989), 763. Maxwell Bloomfield, *American Lawyers in a Changing Society, 1776–1876* (Cambridge, MA, 1976) contains a number of essays on problems confronting the bar in the nineteenth century as well as portraits of aspects of the careers of individual attorneys. See also Alfred S. Konefsky, "Law and Culture in Antebellum Boston," *Stanford Law Review* 40 (1988), 1119.

There is some very good work as well on the legal professional cultures of individual states. See, in particular, for Virginia, A. G. Roeber, *Faithful Magistrates and Republican Lawyers: Creators of Virginia Legal Culture, 1680–1810*

(Chapel Hill, NC, 1981), F. Thornton Miller, *Juries and Judges Versus the Law: Virginia's Provincial Legal Perspective, 1783–1828* (Charlottesville, 1994), and E. Lee Shephard's two articles: "Lawyers Look at Themselves: Professional Consciousness and The Virginia Bar, 1770–1850," *American Journal of Legal History* 25 (1981), 1 and "Breaking into the Profession: Establishing a Law Practice in Antebellum Virginia," *Journal of Southern History* 48 (1982), 393; for Maryland, Dennis R. Nolan, "The Effect of the Revolution on the Bar: The Maryland Experience," *Virginia Law Review* 62 (1976), 969, and Jeffrey K. Sawyer, "Distrust of the Legal Establishment in Perspective: Maryland During the Early National Years," *Georgia Journal of Southern Legal History* 2 (1993), 1; for New Hampshire, see John Phillip Reid, *Controlling the Law: Legal Politics in Early National New Hampshire* (DeKalb, IL, 2004); for Kentucky, see James W. Gordon, *Lawyers in Politics: Mid-Nineteenth Kentucky as a Case Study* (New York, 1990).

On the so-called frontier lawyers, see William F. English, *The Pioneer Lawyer and Jurist in Missouri* (Columbia, MI, [1854] 1947); Joseph G. Baldwin, *The Flush Times of Alabama and Mississippi* (New York,1853); Howard Feigenbaum, "The Lawyer in Wisconsin, 1836–1860: A Profile," *Wisconsin Magazine of History* 55 (1971–72), 100; Frances McCurdy, "Courtroom Oratory of the Pioneer Period," *Missouri Historical Review* 56 (1961), 1; Elizabeth G. Brown, "The Bar on a Frontier: Wayne County, 1796–1836," *American Journal of Legal History* 14 (1970), 136; Gordon M. Bakken, *Practicing Law in Frontier California* (Lincoln, NE, 1991); Michael H. Harris, "The Frontier Lawyer's Library: Southern Indiana, 1800–1850, as a Test Case," *American Journal of Legal History* 16 (1972), 239; A. Christopher Bryant, "Reading the Law in the Office of Calvin Fletcher: The Apprenticeship System and the Practice of Law in Frontier Indiana," *Nevada Law Journal* 1 (2001), 19; and the various studies of Abraham Lincoln cited here.

There are very few general studies of Southern lawyers. Brief reflections on the subject appear in Paul Finkelman, "Exploring Southern Legal History," *North Carolina Law Review* 64 (1985), 73; James W. Ely, Jr., and David J. Bodenhamer, "Regionalism and the Legal History of the South," in D. Bodenhamer and J. Ely, eds., *Ambivalent Legacy: A History of the South* (Jackson, MS, 1984); and Kermit Hall, "The Promises and Perils of Prosopography – Southern Style," *Vanderbilt Law Review* 32 (1979), 331. See also Gail Williams O'Brien, *The Legal Fraternity and the Making of a New South Community, 1848–1882* (Athens, GA, 1986); Ariela J. Gross, *Double Character: Slavery and Mastery in the Antebellum Southern Courtroom* (Princeton, 2000); Paul Finkelman, "Thomas R. R. Cobb and the Law of Negro Slavery," *Roger Williams Law Review* 5 (1999), 75; and Alfred L. Brophy, "Humanity, Utility, and Logic in Southern Legal Thought: Harriet Beecher Stowe's Vision in Dred: A Tale of the Great Dismal Swamp," *Boston University Law Review* 78 (1998), 1113. Most of the material must be gathered from biographies of political and judicial figures.

For studies of legal education for this period, see the primary sources collected in Steve Sheppard, ed., *The History of Legal Education in the United States: Commentaries and Primary Sources* (Pasadena, CA, 1999) and Michael H. Hoeflich, ed., *The Gladsome Light of Jurisprudence: Learning the Law in England and the United States in the 18th and 19th Centuries* (Westport, CT, 1988). For apprenticeship, see Alfred S. Konefsky and Andrew J. King, eds., *The Papers of Daniel Webster: Legal Papers, Volume 1, The New Hampshire Practice* (Boston, 1982), and for an interesting attempt to rehabilitate the reputation of some forms of "elite" apprenticeships, see two essays by Daniel R. Coquillette: "The Legal Education of a Patriot: Josiah Quincy Jr.'s *Law Commonplace* (1763)," *Arizona State Law Journal* 39 (2007), 317, and "Justinian in Braintree: John Adams, Civilian Learning, and Legal Elitism, 1758–1775," in Daniel R. Coquillette et al, eds., *Law in Colonial Massachusetts 1630–1800* (Boston, 1984). On the Litchfield Law School, see Marion C. McKenna, *Tapping Reeve and the Litchfield Law School* (New York, 1986); Andrew M. Siegel, Note, "'To Learn and Make Respectable Hereafter': The Litchfield Law School in Cultural Context," *New York University Law Review* 73 (1998), 1978; and Lawrence B. Custer, "The Litchfield Law School: Educating Southern Lawyers in Connecticut," *Georgia Journal of Southern Legal History* 2 (1993), 183. For university law professorships and university law schools, see R. Kent Newmyer, "Harvard Law School, New England Culture, and the Antebellum Origins of American Jurisprudence," *Journal of American History* 74 (1987), 814; Daniel R. Coquillette, "'Mourning Venice and Genoa': Joseph Story, Legal Education and the *Lex Mercatoria,*" in Vito Piergiovanni, ed., *From Lex Mercatoria to Commerical Law* (Berlin, 2005); William P. LaPiana, *Logic and Experience: The Origin of Modern Legal Education* (New York, 1994); Ronald L. Brown, ed., *The Law School Papers of Benjamin F. Butler: New York University School of Law in the 1830s* (New York, 1987); Steve Sheppard, "Casebooks, Commentaries, and Curmudgeons: An Introductory History of Law in the Lecture Hall," *Iowa Law Review* 82 (1997), 547; Mark Bailey, "Early Legal Education in the United States: Natural Law Theory and Law as a Moral Science," *Journal of Legal Education* 48 (1998), 311; Craig Klafter, "The Influence of Vocational Law Schools on the Origins of American Legal Thought, 1779–1829," *American Journal of Legal History* 37 (1993), 307; Thomas L. Shaffer, "David Hoffman's Law School Lectures, 1822–1833," *Journal of Legal Education* 32 (1982), 127; and a series of articles by Paul Carrington, among them, "Teaching Law and Virtue at Transylvania University: The George Wythe Tradition in the Antebellum Years," *Mercer Law Review* 41 (1990), 673; "The Revolutionary Idea of University Legal Education," *William & Mary Law Review* 31 (1990), 527; "The Theme of Early American Law Teaching: The Political Ethics of Francis Lieber," *Journal of Legal Education* 42 (1992), 339; and "One Law: The Role of Legal Education in the Opening of the Legal Profession Since 1779," *Florida Law Review* 44 (1992), 591. On the early history of law at Yale, see John Langbein's interesting chapters in Anthony T. Kronman, ed., *History of the Yale Law School* (New Haven, 2004). And, finally, for a very suggestive and insightful analysis of antebellum legal education, see Howard Schweber, "The Science of Legal Science: The Model of the Natural Sciences in Nineteenth-Century American Legal Education," *Law & History Review* 17 (1999), 421.

For the social structure of the profession, there are two excellent studies. Gerald W. Gawalt's work is rich with careful detail and thoughtful analysis, as well as a strong sense of what is occurring in Massachusetts legal culture generally: *The Promise of Power: The Emergence of the Legal Profession in Massachusetts, 1760–1840* (Westport, CT, 1979). A more narrowly focused but very interesting account is Gary B. Nash, "The Philadelphia Bench and Bar, 1800–1861," *Comparative Studies in Society & History* 7 (1965), 203. Additional prosopographical data may be found in the following works by Kermit Hall: "The Children of the Cabins: The Lower Federal Judiciary, Modernization, and The Political Culture, 1789–1899," *Northwestern University Law Review* 75 (1980), 432; "240 Men: The Antebellum Lower Federal Judiciary, 1829–1861," *Vanderbilt Law Review* 29 (1976), 1089; "Social Backgrounds and Judicial Recruitment: A Nineteenth-Century Perspective on the Lower Federal Judiciary," *Western Political Quarterly* 29 (1976), 243; and *The Politics of Justice: Lower Federal Judicial Selection and the Second Party System, 1829–1861* (Lincoln, NE, 1979). For valuable demographic data, see Terence C. Halliday, "Six Score Years and Ten: Demographic Transitions in the American Legal Profession, 1850–1960," *Law & Society Review* 20 (1986), 53, and Mark W. Granfors & Terence C. Halliday, "Professional Passages: Caste, Class and Education in the 19th Century Legal Profession," ABF Working Paper #8714 (1987). For information on the handful of African American lawyers in the antebellum period, see J. Clay Smith, Jr., *Emancipation: The Making of the Black Lawyer 1844–1944* (Philadelphia, 1993) and Joseph Gordon Hylton, "The African American Lawyer, The First Generation: Virginia as a Case Study," *University of Pittsburgh Law Review* 56 (1994), 107; on the absence of women in the profession at this time, see Virginia G. Drachman, *Sisters in Law: Women Lawyers in Modern American History* (Cambridge, MA, 1998) and Karen Berger Morello, *The Invisible Bar: The Woman Lawyer in America 1638 to the Present* (New York, 1986).

The best source of information on the organization and operation of legal practice on an everyday basis is contained in several sets of the published legal papers of prominent lawyers: L. Kinvin Wroth and Hiller B. Zobel, eds., *The Legal Papers of John Adams* (Cambridge, MA, 1965); Julius Goebel, Jr., ed., *The Law Practice of Alexander Hamilton* (New York, 1964–1981); Alfred S. Konefsky and Andrew J. King, eds., *The Papers of Daniel Webster: Legal Papers* (Hanover, NH, 1982–1989); James W. Ely, Jr., and Theodore Brown, Jr., eds., *The Legal Papers of Andrew Jackson* (Knoxville, 1987); and Martha L. Benner and Cullom Davis, eds., *The Law Practice of Abraham Lincoln* (DVD-ROM, 2000; selected letterpress edition forthcoming). In addition, one volume of *The Papers of John*

Marshall has material related to Marshall's law practice: Charles F. Hobson, ed., *Selected Law Cases, 1784–1800, Volume 5* (Chapel Hill, NC, 1987). See also Daniel R. Coquillette and Neil Longley York, eds., *Portrait of a Patriot: The Major Political and Legal Papers of Josiah Quincy Junior* (Boston [Charlottesville], 2005–2007).

Though there have been a number of editorial projects related to lawyers' papers, very few lawyers' biographies exist for this period. Many political and judicial biographies have the obligatory introductory chapter on the subject's legal education and early legal career before ascending to political office or the bench. One of the best of these in terms of integrating the judge into the legal culture of the time is R. Kent Newmyer, *Supreme Court Justice Joseph Story: Statesman of the Old Republic* (Chapel Hill, NC, 1985). Leonard W. Levy, *The Law of the Commonwealth and Chief Justice Shaw* (Cambridge, MA, 1957) contains some information on Shaw's early practice; Timothy S. Huebner, *The Southern Judicial Tradition: State Judges and Sectional Distinctiveness, 1790–1890* (Athens, GA, 1999) has material on Southern judges and legal culture; and Robert R. Bell, *The Philadelphia Lawyer: A History, 1735–1945* (Selinsgrove, PA, 1992) has profiles of some antebellum lawyers; see as well Donald M. Roper, "The Elite of the New York Bar as seen from the Bench: James Kent's Necrologies," *New York Historical Society Quarterly* 56 (1972), 199. For a while, there was a cottage industry in studies of Lincoln's law practice: Albert A. Woldman, *Lawyer Lincoln* (Boston, 1936); John J. Duff, *A. Lincoln: Prairie Lawyer* (New York, 1960); John P. Frank, *Lincoln as a Lawyer* (Urbana, IL, 1961); and Paul Carrington, "A Tale of Two Lawyers," *Northwestern University Law Review* 91 (1997), 615, which compares Lincoln with Charles Sumner. They all, of course, would have benefited from the recent compilation of the Lincoln Legal Papers. Some of that work has begun; see Mark E. Steiner, "Lawyers and Legal Change in Antebellum America: Learning from Lincoln," *University of Detroit Mercy Law Review* 74 (1997), 427, as well as Steiner's more comprehensive book, *An Honest Calling: The Law Practice of Abraham Lincoln* (DeKalb, IL, 2006), Brian R. Dirck, *Lincoln the Lawyer* (Urbana, IL, 2007), and Allen D. Spiegel, *A. Lincoln, Esquire: A Shrewd, Sophisticated Lawyer in His Time* (Macon, GA, 2002). For Jefferson, see Frank L. Dewey, *Thomas Jefferson, Lawyer* (Chicago, 1986) and Edward Dumbauld, *Thomas Jefferson and the Law* (Norman, OK, 1978). For Webster, see Robert W. Gordon, Book Review, "The Devil and Daniel Webster," *Yale Law Journal* 94 (1984), 445, and Hendrik Hartog, Book Review, "'The Significance of a Singular Career," *Wisconsin Law Review* (1984), 1105. See also John Witt's elegant chapter on James Wilson in John Fabian Witt, *Patriots and Cosmopolitans: Hidden Histories of American Law* (Cambridge, MA, 2007). In a more specialized manner, G. Edward White, *The Marshall Court and Cultural Change, 1815–1835* (New York, 1988) has a number of very deft portraits of members of the Supreme Court bar that focus on their practices before the High Court. And for evidence about legal practices and attitudes in the debtor/creditor worlds, see Bruce H. Mann, *Republic of Debtors: Bankruptcy in the Age of American Independence* (Cambridge, MA, 2002), and Edward J. Balleisen, *Navigating Failure: Bankruptcy and Commercial Society in Antebellum America* (Chapel Hill, NC, 2001). There is some very helpful material in Elizabeth Baker, *Henry Wheaton* (Philadelphia, 1937) and Paul S. Clarkson, *Luther Martin of Maryland* (Baltimore, 1970); and more recently, in Jerome Mushkat and Joseph G. Rayback, *Martin Van Buren: Law, Politics, and The Shaping of Republican Ideology* (DeKalb, IL, 1997) and Maurice G. Baxter, *Henry Clay the Lawyer* (Lexington, KY, 2000). A more dated study is John T. Horton, *James Kent: A Study in Conservatism, 1763–1847* (New York, 1939). A number of good doctoral dissertations have found their way into print, including Charles T. Cullen, *St. George Tucker and Law in Virginia, 1771–1804* (Charlottesville, 1987); Robert Ireland, *The Legal Career of William Pinkney, 1764–1822* (New York, 1986); Walter Hitchcock, *Timothy Walker, Antebellum Lawyer* (New York, 1990); and Robert K. Kirtland, *George Wythe: Lawyer, Revolutionary, Judge* (New York, 1986). In addition, the doctoral thesis of Joseph Burke, *William Wirt: Attorney General and Constitutional Lawyer* (PhD diss., Indiana University, 1966) is useful. But the best lawyer's biography is Jean V. Matthews, *Rufus Choate: The Law and Civic Virtue* (Philadelphia, 1980).

I have not included any examples of the enormous literature generated by the bar itself, the deep pool of primary sources like memoirs, recollections, bench and bar compilations, addresses, eulogies, memorial bar proceedings, life and letters, etc. They are too numerous to mention, though some of them have found their way into the secondary sources mentioned and quoted herein, particularly the edited collections of Miller (for the Field, Grayson, Quincy, Sampson [Anniv. Discourse], and Story quotations), Hoeflich (for the Greenleaf quotation), and Howe (for the Rantoul and Sampson [Argument] quotations); the Gawalt article (for the Braintree and Robinson quotations) and book (for the Dutton quotation); as well as the Bloomfield book (for Chandler's letter to Story).

The best substantive essays on legal literature are John H. Langbein, "Chancellor Kent and The History of Legal Literature," *Columbia Law Review* 93 (1993), 547; Ann Fidler, "'Till You Understand Them in Their Principal Features': Observations on Form and Function in Nineteenth-Century American Law Books," *Papers of the Bibliographical Society of America* 92 (1998), 427; Susanna L. Blumenthal, "Law and the Creative Mind," *Chicago-Kent Law Review* 74 (1998), 151; and G. Edward White, "The Chancellor's Ghost," *Chicago-Kent Law Review* 74 (1998), 229. Also helpful is Michael H. Hoeflich & Karen S. Beck, eds., *Catalogues of Early American Law Libraries: The 1846 Auction Catalogue of Joseph Story's Library* (Austin, 2004). On early American law reporting, see Morris L. Cohen and Sharon Hamby O'Connor, *A Guide to the Early Reports of the Supreme Court of the United States* (Littleton, CO, 1995); Craig Joyce, "The Rise of the Supreme Court Reporter: An Institutional Perspective on

Marshall Court Ascendancy," *Michigan Law Review* 83 (1985), 1291; Daniel R. Coquillette, "First Flower – The Earliest American Law Reports and the Extraordinary Josiah Quincy, Jr. (1744–1775)," *Suffolk University Law Review* 30 (1990), 1; Alan V. Briceland, "Ephraim Kirby: Pioneer of American Law Reporting, 1789," *American Journal of Legal History* 16 (1972), 297; and Erwin C. Surrency, "Law Reports in the United States," *American Journal of Legal History* 25 (1981), 58. For a listing and compilation of the existing monograph sources, see Jenni Parrish, "Law Books, and Legal Publishing in America, 1760–1840," *Law Library Journal* 72 (1979), 355; and for a statistical summary of information on legal periodicals, see Bloomfield. The most invaluable and comprehensive resource is the multivolume edition of Morris L. Cohen, *Bibliography of Early American Law* (Buffalo, 1998, 2003). For the codification movement, see Charles M. Cook, *The American Codification Movement: A Study in Antebellum Legal Reform* (Westport, CT, 1981), and also two very interesting book reviews of Cook: Andrew J. King, "Book Review," *Maryland Law Review* 41 (1982), 329, and, particularly, Robert W. Gordon, "Book Review," *Vanderbilt Law Review* 36 (1983), 431. Mark DeWolfe Howe's sourcebook, *Readings in American Legal History* (Cambridge, MA, 1952), also contains suggestive primary materials on the subject. On legal ethics, see a thorough survey of the field and a call for a revisionist account in Norman W. Spaulding, "The Myth of Civic Republicanism: Interrogating The Ideology of Antebellum Legal Ethics," *Fordham Law Review* 71 (2003), 1397. See also Michael H. Hoeflich, "Legal Ethics in the Nineteenth Century: The 'Other Tradition,'" *Kansas Law Review* 47 (1999), 793, and Fannie Farmer, "Legal Practice and Ethics in North Carolina, 1820–1860," *North Carolina Historical Review* 30 (1953), 329.

CHAPTER 4: THE COURTS, 1790–1920

KERMIT L. HALL

Courts and Distributive Justice

Scholars of the courts in the nineteenth century have devoted considerable attention to the distributive economic consequences of the law. Much of that emphasis is due to the work of James Willard Hurst, whose pioneering studies of the American legal system retain vitality today. Hurst offered the enduring insight that judges, along with legislators, played central roles in allocating the costs, benefits, and rewards of economic development throughout American history. No other scholar has had as great an influence as Hurst. His *The Growth of American Law: The Law Makers* (Boston, 1950) analyzed the ways in which public and private law themes worked their ways through a host of institutions, including the courts. Hurst made the additional important point that courts, while significant, did not and could not act alone in fashioning the uniquely American scheme of distributive justice. Constitutional conventions, legislatures, and regulatory agencies, among other institutions, were also important.

It was the variety of these lawmaking bodies that actually made the courts, and the rising practice of judicial review and the development of separation of powers, so important. Hurst analyzed these developments, along with broad changes in American society, through a portfolio of scholarship unprecedented for its rigor, fairness, and cogency. These works included *Law and the Conditions of Freedom in the Nineteenth-Century United States* (Madison, 1956), *Law and Economic Growth: The Legal History of the Lumber Industry in Wisconsin, 1836–1915* (Madison, 1964), and *Law and Markets in United States History: Different Modes of Bargaining Among Interests* (Madison, 1982). Hurst concluded that courts played a vital and generally even-handed role in distributing the bounty of American economic expansion in the nineteenth century, a theme that he addressed in *Law and Social Order in the United States* (Ithaca, 1977).

The best analysis of Hurst's impact on thinking about law, courts, and economic change is in Harry N. Scheiber, "At the Borderland of Law and Economic History: The Contributions of James Willard Hurst," *American Historical Review* 75 (1970), 744–56. A summary of all of Hurst's scholarship, including that dealing with courts, can be found in "The Works of James Willard Hurst," *Wisconsin Law Review* (1997), 1205–10. The implications of Hurst's scholarship are explored in "Symposium, Law and Society in American History: Essays in Honor of J. Willard Hurst," *Law & Society Review* 10 (1975–76), 9–333.

Hurst's essentially consensual view of law and legal institutions has come under increasing attack from scholars who believe that judges were far from fair in managing the distribution of wealth. These arguments are summarized by Scheiber in "Book Review," *Yale Law Journal* 107 (1997), 823–60. As Scheiber notes, some leading "Critical Legal Studies" scholars began to argue in the 1970s that courts were "instrumentalist" in their decisions, seeking to transform the law of torts, property, and contracts in such a way as to redistribute wealth from the agricultural to the "entrepreneurial" classes. They did so successfully and in a way that was highly exploitative, especially of the interests of labor and frequently the common good. One key work is Morton J. Horwitz, *The Transformation of American Law, 1790–1860* (Cambridge, MA, 1977); he extended this analysis into the twentieth century in *The Transformation of American Law, 1870–1960: The Crisis of Legal Orthodoxy* (New York, 1994). However, much of Hurst's writing was critical of the failure of nineteenth-century law – and of courts generally – to operate in a rational and accountable way. Horwitz has himself been the subject of attack by Peter Karsten, *Heart Versus Head: Judge-Made Law in Nineteenth Century America* (Chapel Hill, NC, 1997), who argues that judges were deeply concerned with fairness and equity in their rulings and that they often based their decisions on such qualities rather than, as Horwitz and others have suggested, ruthlessly redistributing wealth to corporations. Even though written before Horwitz's latest book and Karsten's study, Tony Freyer's "Reassessing the Impact of Eminent Domain in Early American Economic Development," *Wisconsin Law Review* (1981), 1263–84 persuasively argues that the role of courts in distributing the consequences of economic change requires further investigation.

Whatever the correctness of Horwitz's arguments, there is no doubt that courts were important to nineteenth-century economic development. Two important works are Zorina Khan, *The Democratization of Invention: Patents and Copyrights in American Economic Development, 1790–1920* (Cambridge, MA, 2005) and James W. Ely, Jr., *Railroads and American Law* (Lawrence, KS, 2001).

Explanations of the role of courts in American history frequently draw on the insights of Alexis de Tocqueville. One of the best analyses of his work can be found in Mark Graber, "Resolving Political Questions Into Judicial Questions: The Tocqueville Thesis Revisited," *Constitutional Commentary* 21(2004), 485–546. In the case of the Supreme Court, the argument is advanced into the nineteenth century by Richard Pacelle, *The Role of the Supreme Court in American Politics: The Least Dangerous Branch?* (Boulder, 2002) and even more directly in Howard Gillman, "How Political Parties Can Use the Courts to Advance Their Agendas: Federal Courts in the United States, 1875–1891," *The American Political Science Review* 96 (2002), 511–24. Another excellent book that draws on this theme and connects the nineteenth- to the twentieth-century experience in matters of racial justice is Michael J. Klarman, *From Jim Crow to Civil Rights: The Supreme Court and the Struggle for Racial Equality* (New York, 2004).

State Courts and Judicial Federalism

Scholars of courts have too often begun their analysis with the top of the judicial pyramid, notably the Supreme Court. This "high court bias" in American legal history has until recently shaped views about the role of courts, ignoring the impact of local and state courts on the day-to-day lives of Americans. This point was made by Hurst in *The Lawmakers*, but it has subsequently been advanced by other scholars. The best starting point for understanding the role of courts in American history generally is Lawrence M. Friedman, "Courts over Time: A Survey of Theories and Research," in Keith O. Bynum and Lynn Mather, eds., *Empirical Theories About Courts* (New York, 1983), 44–47. The structure and design of these courts as a part of state constitutional systems are carefully detailed in G. Alan Tarr, *Understanding State Constitutions* (Princeton, NJ, 2000). Also important is the extraordinary essay by Robert A. Kagan et al., "The Business of State Supreme Courts, 1870–1970," *Stanford Law Review* 30 (1977), 121–56, which traces changes in the behavior of state appellate courts and industrialization of the nation. It is complemented by the essay by Stanton Wheeler, Bliss Cartwright, Robert A. Kagan, and Lawrence M. Friedman, "Do the "Haves" Come out Ahead? Winning and Losing in State Supreme Courts, 1870–1970," *Law & Society Review* 21 (1987), 403–46 and by Lawrence M. Friedman, Robert A. Kagan, Bliss Cartwright, and Stanton Wheeler, "State Supreme Courts: A Century of Style and Citation," *Stanford Law Review* 33

(1981), 773–818. The place of state courts in the American federal system is the subject of Michael E. Solimine and James L. Walker, *Respecting State Courts: The Inevitability of Judicial Federalism* (Westport, CT, 1999). The tie between the states and the Supreme Court of the United States is analyzed provocatively in Eric N. Waltenburg and Bill Swinford (1999), *Litigating Federalism: The States Before the U.S. Supreme Court* (Westport, CT, 1999).

The work of nineteenth-century state trial courts is analyzed in Lawrence M. Friedman, *A History of American Law* (3rd ed., New York, 2005). Friedman makes the telling point that through most of the nineteenth century lower courts gradually became professionalized as both the procedures that they followed and the qualifications of their judges improved. As Friedman notes, however, lay judges continued to pay an important role in local courts well into the twentieth century. Friedman also charts the rise of criminal courts in the nineteenth and early twentieth centuries in *American Law in the Twentieth Century* (New York, 2002) and with Robert V. Percival in *The Roots of Justice: Crime and Punishment in Alameda County, California, 1870–1910* (Chapel Hill, NC, 1981). Michael Stephen Hindus addresses the earlier era in a very helpful comparative study that is especially helpful on the evolution of the justice of the peace. See Hindus, *Prison and Plantation: Crime, Justice, and Authority in Massachusetts and South Carolina, 1767–1878* (Chapel Hill, NC, 1980). On matters of gender and sex, see George Robb and Nancy Erber, eds., *Disorder in the Court: Trials and Sexual Conflict at the Turn of the Century* (New York, 1999).One of the best introductions to the history of lower courts and their evolution in the nineteenth century is by a political scientist. See Harry P. Stumpf, *American Judicial Politics* (2nd ed., New York, 1997).

One important development was the rise of juvenile courts. On their development see Anthony M. Platt, *The Child Savers: The Invention of Delinquency* (2nd ed., Chicago, 1977) and Sanford J. Fox, "Juvenile Justice Reform: An Historical Perspective," *Stanford Law Review* 22 (1970), 1187–1239. The role of local courts in the Progressive era and the interplay of social change and crime are the subject of Michael Willrich, *City of Courts: Socializing Justice in the Progressive Era* (Cambridge, MA, 2003), which places the development of courts in Chicago within the larger social history of the city. The role of courts in nineteenth-century Chicago and their roles as regulators are creatively analyzed in William J. Novak, *The People's Welfare: Law and Regulation in Nineteenth-Century America* (Chapel Hill, NC, 1996). On matters of the development of race and state and local courts, see the fine book by David Delaney, *Race, Place, and the Law, 1836–1948* (Austin, TX, 1998). A more traditionally historical approach with considerable insight about the role of courts is Donald Nieman, *Black Southerners and the Law, 1865–1900* (New York, 1994). Nieman's book is helpful in sorting through the actions of local and state courts in dealing with the growing regulation of black-white relations in the years leading up to Jim Crow.

There has been considerable writing on the history of highest state courts of appeal, almost always termed supreme courts. For example, Charles Sheldon, *The Washington High Bench: A Bibliographical History of the State Supreme Court, 1889–1991* (Seattle, 1992) delivers far more than its prosaic title suggests. James W. Ely, Jr., ed., *A History of the Tennessee Supreme Court* (Knoxville, 2004) traces the development of one state high court and the political, social, and economic pressures that figured in its development. One of the important features of state courts is the differing cultures in which they function. Those differences and their consequences for American law during these years is highlighted in Kermit L. Hall, "Progressive Reform and the Decline of Democratic Accountability: The Popular Election of State Supreme Court Judges, 1850–1920," *American Bar Foundation Research Journal* (1984), 345–70. The role of state courts in the American system of law and governance is skillfully addressed in Helen Hershkoff, "State Courts and the 'Passive Virtues': Rethinking the Judicial Function," *Harvard Law Review* 7 (2001), 1833–1941. There is no doubt that these high courts were busy in the nineteenth century and deeply implicated in the society. In the antebellum South, for example, slavery was a constant issue before the courts, often framed around issues involving contracts, torts, and even criminal law. Timothy S. Heubner's *The Southern Judicial Tradition: State Judges and Sectional Distinctiveness, 1790–1890* (Athens, GA, 1999) makes this important point, but it also demonstrates the important role that state judges played in developing the law outside the context of slavery both before and after the Civil War. In the American West in the nineteenth century, territorial judges, appointed by the federal government, played a role similar to that of state supreme courts. These little-studied courts were critical in carrying legal culture to the frontier, which turned out to be more sophisticated that scholars had believed, a conclusion reached in John D. W. Guice, *The Rocky Mountain Bench* (New Haven, 1972). Melvin Urofsky, "State Courts and Protective Legislation during the Progressive Era: A Reevaluation," *The Journal of American History* 72 (1985), 64- 91 is a seminal work that undermines the argument that state appellate judges were legal Neanderthals willing to overturn blindly all efforts to deal with the consequences of industrialization. While they initially blocked some of it, most such legislation eventually passed judicial muster.

Still, there is no doubt that state courts began increasingly active in exercising their power to strike down legislative acts. Judicial review was a central feature in the growth of power of state courts, a subject that is skillfully addressed in Theodore Ruger, "A Question Which Convulses a Nation: The Early Republic's Greatest Debates About the Judicial Review Power," *Harvard Law Review* 117 (2004), 826–96. Also valuable in understanding the political struggle over judicial review and judicial organization in the federal courts of the Early Republic is Mary K. Bonsteel Tachau, *Federal Courts in the Early Republic: Kentucky 1789–1816* (Princeton, 1978). Margaret Nelson, *A Study of*

Judicial Review in Virginia, 1789–1928 (reprint ed., New York, 1947), while dated, makes this important point, one echoed by Friedman, *A History of American Law*.

In fact, the state courts at all levels had become so active by the end of the nineteenth century that they were the subject of major reform efforts. That effort is detailed by Roscoe Pound, one of the leading figures of American court reform in the Progressive era. Pound's *Roscoe Pound and Criminal Justice* (reprint edition, New York, 1965) connected changes in the courts to improvement in the criminal justice system. These same developments are tracked by Michal Belknap, *To Improve the Administration of Justice: A History of the American Judicature Society* (Chicago, 1992).

The Constitution and the Establishment of the Federal Courts

The literature on the history of the federal courts is extensive and largely focused on the Supreme Court of the United States. Nevertheless, there are several excellent introductions to the creation and growth of the lower courts in the nineteenth century. There are two good staring points for analyzing these courts. The first is Erwin C. Surrency, *History of the Federal Courts* (2nd ed., New York, 2002), which contains an enormous amount of detail about the development of the courts. A more analytical and evaluative approach is taken by Maeva Marcus, ed., *Origins of the Federal Judiciary: Essays on the Judiciary Act of 1789* (New York, 1992), which offers broad-ranging essays on every feature of the early development of the lower federal courts.

The Federal Courts

Until twenty years ago the lower federal courts were little studied and even less understood. Since then there have been numerous scholarly treatments of individual courts, although we have nothing like a synthesis. The roles of federal and state judges as advisors are the subject of Stewart Jay, *Most Humble Servants: The Advisory Role of Early Judges* (New Haven, 1997). Among other notable works are Tony A. Freyer, *Forums of Order: The Federal Courts and Business in American History* (Greenwich, 1979); Jeffrey Brandon Morris, *Federal Justice in the Second Circuit: A History of the United States Courts in New York, Connecticut & Vermont* (New York, 1987); Robert J. Kaczorowski, *The Politics of Judicial Interpretation: The Federal Courts, Department of Justice and Civil Rights, 1866–1876* (New York, 1985); Kermit L. Hall and Eric W. Rise, *From Local Courts to National Tribunals: The Federal District Courts of Florida, 1821–1990* (New York, 1991); Christian G. Fritz, *Federal Justice in California: The Court of Ogden Hoffman, 1851–1891* (Lincoln, NE, 1991); Peter Graham Fish, *Federal Justice in the Mid-Atlantic South: United States Courts from Maryland to the Carolinas, 1789–1835* (Washington, DC, 2002); and Edward A. Purcell, *Litigation and Inequality: Federal Diversity Jurisdiction in Industrial America, 1870–1958* (New York, 1992). The connection between political change and the recruitment of federal judges is analyzed in Kermit L. Hall, *The Politics of Justice: Lower Federal Judicial Selection and the Second Party System, 1829–1861* (Lincoln, NE, 1979). A particularly good study of the interaction of race and the criminal justice system in the federal courts is Lou Falkner Williams, *The Great South Carolina Ku Klux Klan Trials, 1871–1872* (Athens, GA, 1996). The business and administration of these courts and the role of the Progressive movement and William Howard Taft in particular are the subjects of Peter Graham Fish, *The Politics of Judicial Administration* (Princeton, 1973).

The U.S. Supreme Court

No court has received more sustained attention than the U.S. Supreme Court. A good introduction to the Court and its evolution during the nineteenth century into one of the major organs of government is Robert G. McCloskey and Sanford Levinson, *The American Supreme Court* (4th ed., Chicago, 2004). There are essays on the most important cases decided by the justices during these years along with broad conceptual essays about the Court in Kermit L. Hall, James W. Ely, Jr., and Joel Grossman, eds., *The Oxford Companion to the Supreme Court of the United States* (2nd ed., New York, 2005). The Court's history is also the subject of Bernard Schwartz, *A History of the Supreme Court* (New York, 1995). The early history of the Court and its relationship to state courts are treated especially well in Maeva Marcus, et al., *The Documentary History of the Supreme Court of the United States 1789–1800*, 7 vols. (New York, 1989–2004) and Scott Douglas Gerber, *Seriatim: The Supreme Court Before John Marshall*, (New York, 1998). For an overview of the main issues driving the Court in the nineteenth century see William H. Rehnquist, "The Supreme Court in the Nineteenth Century," *Journal of Supreme Court History* 27 (2002), 1–13.

The business of the Court, like the business of the federal courts a whole, changed dramatically over the course of the nineteenth century. Felix Frankfurter and James Landis, *The Business of the Supreme Court: A Study in The Federal Judicial System* (reprint ed., New York, 2006) summarizes these developments.

The Court in the Early Republic is the subject of William R. Castro, *The Supreme Court and the Early Republic: The Chief Justiceships of John Jay and Oliver Ellsworth* (Columbia, 1995). Of special value in understanding the origins and impact of judicial review is William E. Nelson, *Marbury v. Madison: The Origins and Legacy of Judicial Review*, (Lawrence, KS, 2000). Other worthwhile studies of the Supreme Court in the nineteenth century are David P. Currie, *The Constitution and the Supreme Court: The First Hundred Years, 1789–1888* (Chicago, 1985); Don E. Fehrenbacher, *The Dred Scott Case: Its Significance in American Law and Politics* (New York, 1978); Julius Goebel, Jr., *History of the Supreme Court of the United States, Volume 1, Antecedents and Beginnings to 1801* (New York, 1971); George L. Haskins and Herbert A. Johnson, *History of the Supreme Court of the United States, Volume 2, Foundations of Power: John Marshall, 1801–1815* (New York, 1981); Harold M. Hyman and William M. Wiecek, *Equal Justice*

Under Law: Constitutional Development 1835–1874 (New York, 1982); Carol B. Swisher, *History of the Supreme Court of the United States, Volume 5, The Taney Period, 1836–1864* (New York, 1974); and G. Edward White, *History of the Supreme Court of the United States, Volumes 3–4, The Marshall Court and Cultural Change 1815–1835* (New York, 1988).

The Court became an increasingly important player in the post-Civil War era. That change is traced in Stanley I. Kutler, *Judicial Power and Reconstruction Politics* (New York, 1968) and John Semonche, *Charting the Future: The Supreme Court Responds to a Changing Society, 1890–1920* (Westport, CT, 1978). The impact of the Court on American federalism is the subject of Michael Les Benedict, "Preserving Federalism: Reconstruction and the Waite Court," *Supreme Court History* (1978), 39–79 and Benedict, "Laissez Faire and Liberty: A Re-Evaluation of the Meaning and Origins of Laissez-Faire Constitutionalism," *Law and History Review* 3 (1985), 293–331. For a detailed analysis of the Court during Reconstruction see Charles Fairman, *History of the Supreme Court of the United States, Volumes 6–7, Reconstruction and Reunion, 1877–1917* (New York, 1971). Two particularly valuable biographies of chief justices during the Progressive era are Walter F. Pratt, *The Supreme Court Under Edward Douglass White, 1910–1921* (Columbia, 1999) and James W. Ely, Jr., *The Chief Justiceship of Melville W. Fuller, 1888–1910* (Columbia, 1995). There are many other biographies of members of the Court, but a particularly rewarding and engaging approach to placing in perspective the Court and some of its most interesting justices, such as Oliver Wendell Holmes, Jr., is G. Edward White, *The American Judicial Tradition: Profiles of Leading American Judges* (rev. ed., New York, 2006). Two other notable biographies of major high court figures by R. Kent Newmyer are *John Marshall and the Heroic Age of the Supreme Court* (Baton Rouge, LA, 2002) and *Supreme Court Justice Joseph Story: Statesman of the Old Republic* (reprint ed., Chapel Hill, NC, 1986).

CHAPTER 5: CRIMINAL JUSTICE IN THE UNITED STATES, 1790–1920

ELIZABETH DALE

The State and the Rule of Law in the Long Nineteenth Century: The backdrop for the chapter is the Weberian thesis that associates modernity with the state monopoly on violence and therefore with the rise of the state. Most histories of criminal law in the United States tie developments in the criminal justice system to the rise of the local state after the Founding Era: see, for example, Samuel Walker, *Popular Justice: A History of American Criminal Justice* (2nd ed., New York, 1998); Lawrence M. Friedman, *Crime and Punishment in American History* (New York, 1993); Allan Steinberg, *The Transformation of Criminal Justice: Philadelphia 1800–1880* (Chapel Hill, NC, 1989); and Kermit Hall, *The Magic Mirror: Law in American History* (New York, 1989). This view of the criminal justice system is reinforced by studies of the nineteenth century that link the creation of a distinctively American legal system designed to mix social control and market capitalism: Charles Sellers, *The Market Revolution: Jacksonian American 1815–1846* (New York, 1991); Morton J. Horwitz, *The Transformation of American Law, 1780–1860* (Cambridge, MA, 1977); and William E. Nelson, *The Americanization of the Common Law: The Impact of Legal Change on American Law, 1760–1830* (Cambridge, MA, 1975).

When they link the rise of the state to criminal law, these histories of the nineteenth century assume the rule of law, noting its absence as an anomaly to be explained as a phenomenon particular to a region or culture: see, for example, Michael Hindus, *Prison and Plantation: Crime, Justice and Authority in Massachusetts and South Carolina, 1767–1878* (Chapel Hill, NC, 1980) and Edward Ayers, *Vengeance and Justice: Crime and Punishment in the Nineteenth-Century American South* (New York, 1984). In this respect as well, histories of criminal law are not much different from American legal history, which typically dates the establishment of the rule of law to the writing of the Constitution, if not before. Consider, for example, John Phillip Reid, *Rule of Law: The Jurisprudence of Liberty in the Seventeenth and Eighteenth Centuries* (DeKalb, IL, 2004).

This chapter offers an alternative theory, influenced by scholarship that calls the various parts of that story into question. Some of these works assert that the authority of the rule of law was contested throughout the nineteenth century: see, for example, Christopher Tomlins, *Law, Labor and Ideology in the Early American Republic* (Cambridge, 1993), which traces the significance of "the police" as an alternative to the rule of law in the first half of the nineteenth century, and Elizabeth Dale, *The Rule of Justice: The People of Chicago versus Zephyr Davis* (Columbus, OH, 2001), which argues that even at the end of the nineteenth century the rule of justice was often subordinated to popular notions of justice. Others demonstrate that for much of the nineteenth century the very idea of the state was challenged by notions of popular sovereignty: see, for example, Larry Kramer, *The People Themselves: Popular Constitutionalism and Judicial Review* (Oxford, 2004), focusing on popular constitutionalism across the United States through the 1830s; Philip Ethington, *The Public City: The Political Construction of Urban Life in San Francisco, 1850–1900* (New York, 2001), examining popular challenges to state power in California during the vigilante era in the second half of the nineteenth century; Stephen Kantrowitz, *Ben Tillman and the Reconstruction of White Supremacy* (Chapel Hill, NC, 2000), which examines the claims of popular (white) authority to act in place of the courts in late nineteenth-century South Carolina; and Mary Ryan, *Civic Wars: Democracy and Public Life in the American City During the Nineteenth Century* (Berkeley, 1998), describing the powers of popular forces over government across the nineteenth century. Taken together, these studies reveal the strength of non-state forces for much of the long nineteenth century, raising questions of the limits and alternatives to state power that this chapter touches on and that studies of criminal law will need to consider in greater detail in years to come.

A Note on Organization and Sources

The historiography on criminal law divides neatly into three types: national surveys, regional studies, and local sources. There are two major histories of criminal law across the United States; each spends considerable time examining the nature of criminal law in the nineteenth century: see Samuel Walker, *Popular Justice: A History of American Criminal Justice* (2d ed., 1998), and Lawrence M. Friedman, *Crime and Punishment in American History* (1993). In addition, these overviews of American legal history devote space to criminal law in the period covered by this chapter: Lawrence M. Friedman, *American Law in the Twentieth Century* (New Haven, 2002); Kermit Hall, *The Magic Mirror: Law in American History* (1989); and Lawrence M. Friedman, *A History of American Law* (2nd ed., New York, 1985).

National histories of criminal law in the United States face a serious problem, for throughout most of the nation's history (and throughout the nineteenth century) criminal law was a local matter. Not unexpectedly, there is a strong presumption that regional differences led to regionally distinctive systems of criminal law. This theory has had its greatest hold with respect to the South. In 1940 Charles Sydnor, "The Southerner and the Laws," *Journal of Southern History* 6 (1940), 3, argued that a combination of economic, religious, and cultural characteristics made the legal culture of the antebellum South distinctive. In the years since, historians have offered variations on that theme: Christopher Waldrep, *Roots of Disorder: Race and Criminal Justice in the American South, 1817–1880* (Urbana, IL, 1998; race relations create distinctive legal culture); Peter Bardaglio, *Reconstructing the Household: Families, Sex and the Law in the Nineteenth-Century South* (Chapel Hill, NC, 1995; the combination of honor culture and gender norms created a unique Southern legal system until the late antebellum era, when economic shifts brought the legal system more in line with that of the North); Edward L. Ayers, *Vengeance and Justice: Crime and Punishment in the 19th Century American South* (New York, 1984; religion and honor culture created a unique system of justice); and Bertram Wyatt-Brown, *Southern Honor: Ethics and Behavior in the Old South* (New York, 1982; patriarchy and honor culture created a specifically Southern system of law). In contrast, histories of the West have tried to challenge the idea that the West was uniquely lawless frontier. *See* Clare V. McKanna, Jr., *Race and Homicide in Nineteenth-Century California* (Reno, NE, 2002); John Phillip Reid, *Protecting the Elephant: Property and Social Behavior on the Overland Trail* (reprint edition, San Marino, CA, 1997); and Robert D. McGrath, *Gunfighters, Highwaymen, and Vigilantes: Violence on the Frontier* (Berkeley, 1984).

In addition to the regional studies, a number of studies look at criminal law in particular states or cities during some or all of the nineteenth century. Examples of this type of study are Eric Monkkonen, *Murder in New York City*

(Berkeley, 2000); Roger Lane, *Violent Death in the City: Suicide, Accident and Murder in Nineteenth-Century Philadelphia* (Columbus, OH, 1999); Allen Steinberg, *The Transformation of Criminal Law: Philadelphia 1800–1880* (Chapel Hill, NC, 1989), Lawrence M. Friedman and Robert V. Percival, *The Roots of Justice: Crime and Punishment in Alameda County, California, 1870–1910* (Chapel Hill, NC, 1981); Michael Hindus, *Prison and Plantation: Criminal Justice and Authority in Massachusetts and South Carolina* (Chapel Hill, NC, 1980), which is, as its title suggests, a comparative work; and Jack Kenny Williams, *Vogues in Villainy: Crime and Retribution in Ante-bellum South Carolina* (Columbia, SC, 1959). Some of these studies, for example Williams, *Vogues in Villainy*, reinforces the idea of regional distinctiveness; others, such as Lane, *Violent Death in the City* and Monkkonen, *Murder in New York*, both of which found honor culture in Northern cities, seem to undermine it.

Not surprisingly, given its local flavor, much of the literature on the history of criminal justice is found in journal articles, many published by social historians and printed in journals devoted to the history of a particular state or a particular region. I have deliberately cited a number of those articles below to give a sense of the research hidden in these less familiar journals. To make it more accessible for those who wish to use this bibliographic essay as a resource for future research, I have organized this essay around the structure of a criminal prosecution. The first two sections deal with policing and crime, the third and fourth with trials and court processes, the fifth section considers punishment, and the sixth the role of extra-legal justice.

I. Policing

Police departments were first established, and then significantly reformed, during the course of the nineteenth century. As a result there are a number of studies of police forces in the nineteenth century. Sally Hadden, *Slave Patrols: Law and Violence in Virginia and the Carolinas* (Cambridge, MA, 2000; comparing the policing of slaves in several Southern states); Wilbur R. Miller, *Cops and Bobbies: Police Authority in New York and London, 1830–1870* (2nd ed., Chicago, 1999); and Richard C. Lindberg, *To Serve and Collect: Chicago Politics and Police Corruption from the Lager Beer Riot to the Summerdale Scandal, 1855–1960* (Carbondale, IL, 1998); Dennis C. Rousey, *Policing the Southern City: New Orleans, 1805–1889* (Baton Rouge, LA, 1996; generally about New Orleans, though the book discusses policing in other Southern cities); Eric H. Monkkonen, *Police in Urban America, 1860–1920* (Cambridge, 1981); David R. Johnson, *American Law Enforcement: A History* (Wheeling, IL, 1981); Roger Lane, *Policing the City: Boston, 1882–1885* (Cambridge, MA, 1971); and Sam Bass Warner, Jr. *The Private City: Philadelphia in Three Periods of its Growth* (Philadelphia, 1968; policing in Philadelphia during the antebellum era in Chapter 7).

Because of the nature of police work, policing is also a subject that comes up in urban histories, labor histories, and studies of immigration and race relations. There are, for example, glimpses of the reorganization of the Chicago police department in the late nineteenth century in Richard Schneirov, *Labor and Urban Politics: Class Conflict and the Origins of Modern Liberalism in Chicago, 1864–1897* (Urbana, IL, 1998) and discussions of the first African American officers on Chicago's police force in Christopher Robert Reed, *Black Chicago's First Century: Volume 1, 1833–1900* (Columbia, MI, 2005). But more could be done on the integration of blacks, immigrants, and women into police forces. Women were hired onto some police forces in the late nineteenth and early twentieth centuries: see Mary Jane Aldrich-Moodie, "Staking Out Their Domain: Women in the New York City Police Department, 1890–1935" (PhD diss., University of North Carolina, 2002); Doris Schargenberg, "'The Division Has Become a Necessity,'" *Michigan History Magazine* 86 (2002), 76 (women in Detroit police department, beginning in 1920); and Samuel Walker, "The Rise and Fall of the Police Women's Movement, 1905–1975," *Law and Order in American History* (1979), 101. However, there are few studies that explore female police officers' experiences or their impact.

Given the significant role that the police play in the criminal justice system, more could be done to explore nineteenth-century policing at the local level. At the same time, the studies by Miller, Rousey, and Hadden suggest the value of considering policing in comparative context. A recent essay by Clive Emsley, which reviews the literature on nineteenth-century policing in several European countries (notably England, France, Italy, and Prussia), sets out a typology of policing that might be fruitfully applied to future studies of police departments in the American setting: Clive Emsley, "A Typology of Nineteenth-Century Police," *Crime, Histoire & Sociétés* 3 (1999), 29.

II. Crimes

Murder: The nineteenth-century United States had high murder rates compared to countries in western Europe, and this fact has preoccupied quite a few historians. Roger Lane, *Murder in America: A History* (Columbus, OH, 1997) is a general study that examined murder rates throughout the United States, but most studies focus more narrowly. Many consider murder rates in particular cities – Lane, *Violent Death in the City: Suicide, Accident, and Murder in Nineteenth-Century Philadelphia* (Columbus, OH, 1999); Monkkonen, *Murder in New York*; and Jeffrey Adler, *First in Violence, Deepest in Dirt: Homicide in Chicago, 1870–1920* (Cambridge, MA, 2006) – or in counties: William Lynwood Montell, *Killings: Folk Justice in the Upper South* (Lexington, KY, 1986; a county at the Kentucky-Tennessee border). In a recent book, Gilles Vandal compared homicide rates in cities and rural areas in Louisiana: Gilles Vandal, *Southern Violence: Homicides in Post-Civil War Louisiana, 1866–1884* (Columbus, OH, 2000). Clare V. McKanna, Jr. took a similar approach in another study, looking at homicide rates in the state of California from 1850 to 1900: *Race and Homicide in Nineteenth-Century California* (Reno, NE, 2002). A quick glance at the works reveals little agreement about why homicide rates in the nineteenth century were so high. The various theories are set out in two forums on murder in America: *American Historical Review*, 111 (2006), 75 et seq. and *Social Science History* 25 (2001), 1 et seq.

Morals legislation: While there are a few exceptions – see, for example, Robert M. Ireland, "The Problem of Concealed Weapons in Nineteenth-Century Kentucky," *Register of the Kentucky Historical Society* 91 (1993), 370 – most of the other work on crime in the nineteenth century has focused on what Lawrence M. Friedman called the Victorian Compromise, the ambiguous relationship between stricter regulation of morality through criminal law and actual enforcement of those laws. Not surprisingly, many of these studies have focused on sex crimes and crimes arising from sexual relations. See. for example, Julie Novkov, "Racial Constructions: The Legal Regulation of Miscegenation in Alabama, 1890–1934," *Law and History Review* 20 (2002), 225; Leslie J. Reagan, *When Abortion was a Crime: Women, Medicine and Law in the United States, 1867–1973* (Berkeley, 1997; the criminalization of abortion), Timothy J. Gilfoyle, *City of Eros: New York City, Prostitution, and the Commercialization of Sex, 1790–1920* (New York, 1992; regulation of prostitute and prosecution of vice); Mary E. Odem, *Delinquent Daughters: Protecting and Policing Adolescent Female Sexuality in the United States, 1885–1920* (Chapel Hill, NC, 1995); and Joel Best, *Con trolling Vice: Regulating Brothel Prostitution in St. Paul, 1865–1883* (Columbus, OH, 1998).

There are also a number of works that consider the rise of blue laws in the nineteenth century: Peter Wallenstein, "Never on Sunday: Blue Laws and Roanoke, Virginia," *Virginia Cavalcade* 43 (1994), 132; Joseph B. Marks and Lisa J. Sanders, "The Blue Laws Debate: A Sacramento Shopkeeper's Story," *Western States Jewish History*, 25 (1993), 211; Raymond Schmandt, "The Pastor of Loretto, Pennsylvania, versus the All-American Game of Baseball," *Western Pennsylvania Historical Magazine*, 69 (1986), 81; Arnold Roth, "Sunday 'Blue Laws' and the California State Supreme Court," *Southern California Quarterly* 55 (1973), 43; Vernon Lestrud, "Early Theatrical 'Blue Laws' on the Pacific Coast," *Rendezvous* 4 (1969), 15 (blue laws in California, Oregon, and Washington); Maxine S. Seller, "Isaac Leeser: A Jewish Christian Dialogue in Antebellum Philadelphia," *Pennsylvania History* 35 (1968), 231 (Leeser's activities against blue laws); Harold E. Cox, "'Daily Except Sunday': Blue Laws and the Operation of Philadelphia Horse Cars," *Business History Review* 39 (1965), 228; and J. E. Ericson and James H. McCrocklin, "From Religion to Commerce: The Evolution and Enforcement of Blue Laws in Texas," *Southwestern Social Science Quarterly* 45 (1964), 50. And a third group of studies looks at efforts to pass temperance legislation: Ray Cunningham, "Virtue and Vice in Homer: The Battle for Morals in a Central Illinois Town, 1870–1890," *Illinois Heritage* 7 (2004), 14; Dale E. Soden, "The Women's Christian Temperance Union in the Pacific Northwest: The Battle for Cultural Control," *Pacific Northwest Quarterly*, 94 (2003), 197; Richard Hamm, *Shaping the Eighteenth Amendment: Temperance*

Reform, Legal Culture, and the Polity, 1880–1920 (Chapel Hill, NC, 1995); and Donald Pitzer, "Revivalism and Politics in Toledo: 1899," *Northwest Ohio Quarterly* 41 (1968–1969), 13.

While most of these studies are focused on state-level efforts to legislate morality, others trace the way that morals legislation became a federal issue: Gaines Foster, *Moral Reconstruction: Christian Lobbyists and the Federal Legislation of Morality, 1865–1920* (Chapel Hill, NC, 2002); Mara Keire, "The Vice Trust: A Reinterpretation of the White Slavery Scare in the United States, 1907–1917," *Journal of Social History* 35 (2001), 5; and Hamm, *Shaping the Eighteenth Amendment: Temperance Reform, Legal Culture, and the Polity*.

Most books on morals legislation explore the role of reform networks, though more could be done to bring the insights of social movement literature, particularly *national* social movement literature, into the history of criminal law. See Michael P. Young, "Confessional Protest: The Religious Birth of U.S. National Social Movements," *American Sociological Review* 67 (2002), 660 (examining antebellum temperance and anti-slavery movements as social movements on a national scale) and Alan Hunt, *Governing Morals: A Social History of Moral Regulation* (New York, 1999). But several of the works, Foster's book in particular, suggest another aspect of criminal law that deserves more study: the significance of religion. While a few books, notably Susan Jacoby's *Wild Justice: The Evolution of Revenge* (New York, 1983), have suggested the influence that particular theological beliefs had in shaping attitudes toward punishment, more could be done to examine the impact of religious ideas and religious groups on American theories of crime.

III. Procedures and Courts

Practice and process: There are few histories that deal with criminal procedure or consider the roles of jurors, judges, or attorneys in criminal trials in the nineteenth century, and those that do so typically are focused on individual states. Alan Rogers traced changes in criminal trials and procedure in Massachusetts in "Murder in Massachusetts: The Criminal Discovery Rule from *Snelling* to Rule 14," *Journal of American Legal History* 40 (1996), 438, and he looked at the history of court-appointed lawyers representing capital defendants in that state in "'A Sacred Duty': Court Appointed Attorneys in Massachusetts Capital Cases, 1780–1980," *American Journal of Legal History* 41 (1997), 440. James Rice considered the increasing role of lawyers in criminal trials in Maryland in another article, "The Criminal Trial Before and After the Lawyers: Authority, Law, and Culture in Maryland Jury Trials, 1681–1837," *American Journal of Legal History* 40 (1996), 455, while Robert Ireland explored the ongoing significance of private prosecutions in "Privately Funded Prosecution of Crime in the Nineteenth-Century United States," *American Journal of Legal History* 39 (1995), 43.

Several other works provide significant glimpses at the nineteenth-century criminal trial in the course of a larger study. Jack Kenny Williams described felony trials in his study of crime in antebellum South Carolina, *Vogues in Villainy*, while Allen Steinberg sketched the changes in Philadelphia's criminal justice system in *The Transformation of Criminal Justice*. Less has been done with the rules of evidence and proof. Barbara Shapiro's study of Anglo-American rules of evidence, *Beyond "Reasonable Doubt" and "Probable Cause": Historical Perspectives on the Anglo-American Law of Evidence* (Berkeley, 1991), is complemented by some studies of particular rules: see, for example, Alan G. Gless, "Self-Incrimination Privilege Development in the Nineteenth-Century Federal Courts: Questions of Procedure, Privilege, Production, Immunity and Compulsion," *American Journal of Legal History* 45 (2001), 391; G. S. Rowe, "Infanticide, Its Judicial Resolution, and Criminal Code Revision in Early Pennsylvania," *Proceedings of the American Philosophical Society* 135 (1991), 200; David McCord, "The English and American History of Voluntary Intoxication to Negate *Mens Rea*," *Journal of Legal History* [Great Britain], 11 (1990), 372; and Jeffrey K. Sawyer, "'Benefit of Clergy' in Maryland and Virginia," *American Journal of Legal History* 34 (1990), 49 (tracing the doctrine's demise in the early nineteenth century). But aside from those works and a few specific case studies that treat evidentiary and procedural rules – see, for example, M. Clifford Harrison, "Murder in the Courtroom," *Virginia Calvacade* 17 (1967), 43 ("reasonable doubt" standard in relation to a 1912 murder trial) – little has been done in this area. The only comprehensive study of the procedural and evidentiary shifts in criminal law is Michael Millender's unpublished dissertation, *The Transformation of the American Criminal Trial, 1790–1875* (PhD diss., Princeton, 1996).

Likewise, the history of the insanity defense and its influence on the nineteenth-century criminal justice system have been the subject of a number of studies. They trace its rise, Alan Rodgers, "Murders and Madness: Law and Medicine in Nineteenth-Century Massachusetts," *Proceedings of the Massachusetts Historical Society* 106 (1994), 53; the problems it caused, Charles E. Rosenberg, *The Trial of the Assassin Guiteau: Psychiatry and the Law in the Gilded Age* (Chicago, 1968) and Robert M. Ireland, "Insanity and the Unwritten Law," *American Journal of Legal History* 32 (1998), 157; and efforts to reform it, Janet E. Tighe, "'Be it Ever So Little': Reforming the Insanity Defense in the Progressive Era," *Bulletin of the History of Medicine* 57 (1983), 395.

Courts: There are a number of studies of specific criminal courts, most notably the juvenile justice system. Eric Schneider examined juvenile justice across the nineteenth century in his monograph *In the Web of Class: Delinquents and Reformers in Boston, 1810s–1930s* (New York, 1992). Other studies look at the rise of the distinctive juvenile court system at the end of the nineteenth century: David Tanenhaus, *Juvenile Justice in the Making* (New York, 2004); David Wolcott, "Juvenile Justice Before Juvenile Courts: Cops, Courts and Kids in Turn-of-the-Century Detroit," *Social Science History* 27 (2003), 109; and David Wolcott, "'The Cop Will Get You': The Police and Discretionary Juvenile Justice, 1890–1940," *Journal of Social History* 35 (2001), 319. And a few studies have looked at misdemeanor and police courts. Steinberg's *Transformation of Criminal Law* describes the declining power of those petty courts in Philadelphia. His study ended in 1880, roughly the moment when *Roots of Justice*, the study of felony and police courts in Alameda County, California by Lawrence M. Friedman and Robert Percival, picked up. Michael Willrich looked at Progressive Era Chicago's experiment with a municipal court, intended as a replacement for the corrupt police court system and as a means of social control, in *City of Courts: Socializing Progressive Era Chicago* (Cambridge, 2003). See also Lynne M. Adrian and Joan E. Crowley, "Hoboes and Homeboys: The Demography of Misdemeanor Convictions in the Allegheny County Jail, 1892–1923," *Journal of Social History* 25 (1991), 345.

More work could be done to examine "other" criminal justice systems. Of the few that have been done, most of these studies deal with the criminal justice system for slaves and free blacks in the antebellum era: James Campbell, "'The Victim of Prejudice and Hasty Consideration': The Slave Trial System in Richmond Virginia, 1830–1861," *Slavery and Abolition* 26 (2005), 71; Thomas D. Morris, *Southern Slavery and the Law, 1619–1860* (Chapel Hill, NC, 1999); Mary E. Seematter, "Trials and Confessions: Race and Justice in Antebellum St. Louis," *Gateway Heritage* 12 (1991), 36 (trial of four free blacks for murder and arson); Philip J. Schwartz, *Twice Condemned Slaves and the Criminal Laws of Virginia, 1705–1865* (Charlottesville, 1988); William Cinque Henderson, *Spartan Slaves: A Documentary Account of Blacks on Trial in Spartanburg, South Carolina, 1830–1865* (PhD diss, Northwestern University, 1978); Daniel Flannigan, "Criminal Procedure in Slave Trials in the Antebellum South," *Journal of Southern History* 40 (1974), 537; John C. Edwards, "Slave Justice in Four Middle Georgia Counties," *Georgia Historical Quarterly* 57 (1973), 265; Robert McPherson, ed., "Georgia Slave Trials, 1837–1841," *American Journal of Legal History* 4 (1960), 257; and E. Merton Coulter, "Four Slave Trials in Elbert County, Georgia," *Georgia Historical Quarterly* 41 (1957), 237. In contrast, there is hardly any work on the criminal justice systems that applied to Native Americans in the nineteenth century, Brad Asher, *Beyond the Reservation: Indians, Settlers and Laws in the Washington Territory, 1853–1889* (Norman, OK, 1999), or the processes by which those legal systems were created. See Blue Clark, Lone Wolf v. Hitchcock: *Treaty Rights and Indian Law at the End of the Nineteenth Century* (Lincoln, NE, 1994).

Plea bargains: Trials were not, of course, the typical experience of defendants in the twentieth-century criminal courts, where most cases were pled out. This practice had its beginnings in the nineteenth century. Summary jurisdiction, a practice that let magistrates try some minor criminal matters without a jury (or an indictment), offered one means of processing cases with little or no process. See, for example, Bruce Phillip Smith, *Circumventing the Jury: Petty Crime and Summary Jurisdiction in London and New York City, 1790–1855* (PhD diss. Yale University, 1997). The development of plea bargaining allowed even felony cases to be resolved in summary fashion: see David J. Bodenhamer, "Criminal Sentencing in Antebellum America: A North-South Comparison,"

Historical Social Research [West Germany], 15 (1990), 77 (finding plea bargains North and South before the Civil War). Several studies have demonstrated the development's impact on conviction rates: see Lane, *Violent Death in the City* and Monkkonen, *Murder in New York*. Another collection of studies explore the relation between the rise of plea bargaining and the growth of state power: George Fisher, *Plea Bargaining's Triumph: A History of Plea Bargaining in America* (Stanford, 2004); Mary Vogel, "The Social Origins of Plea Bargaining: Conflict and Law in the Process of State Formation, 1830–1860," *Law and Society Review* 33 (1999), 161; and Mike McCanville and Chester Mirsky, "The Rise of the Guilty Pleas: New York, 1800–1865," *Journal of Law and Society* 22 (1995), 443.

IV. Criminal Trials

Published criminal trial transcripts were popular literature in the nineteenth century – Karen Halttunen, *Murder Most Foul* (Cambridge, MA, 1998) and David Ray Papke, *Framing the Criminal: Crime, Cultural Work and the Loss of Critical Perspective, 1830–1990* (Hamden, CT, 1987) – and an entire historical genre has arisen around the study of individual criminal cases. Robert Darnton called these works, which trace repercussions of murders, scandals, riots, and catastrophes through the social order, "incident studies": Darnton, "It Happened One Night," *New York Review of Books* (June 24, 2004), 60. In an earlier essay, William Fisher called it New Historicism after Stephen Greenblatt's work: William Fisher, "Texts and Contexts: The Application to American Legal History of the Methodologies of Intellectual History," *Stanford Law Review* 49 (1997), 1065.

Regardless of the name given to it, these studies illuminate the workings of the criminal justice system in the long nineteenth century, tracing the ways in which law intersected with social, moral, and political forces in all sorts of trials. One of the articles Fisher cited as an example of the approach was a misdemeanor trial – a prosecution for keeping a pig in New York City: Hendrik Hartog, "Pigs and Positivism," *Wisconsin Law Review* (1985), 89. All sorts of crimes have been the subject of these histories, including assassination – Charles E. Rosenberg, *The Trial of the Assassin Guiteau: Psychiatry and the Law in the Gilded Age* (Chicago, 1968); murder – Patricia Cline Cohen, *The Murder of Helen Jewett* and Dale, *The Rule of Justice*; manslaughter – Regina Morantz-Sanchez, *Conduct Unbecoming a Woman: Medicine on Trial in Turn-of-the-Century Brooklyn* (New York, 1999); lynching – Mark Curriden and Leroy Phillips, *Contempt of Court: The Turn-of-the-Century Lynching that Launched a Hundred Years of Federalism* (New York, 1999); adultery – Richard Wightman Fox, *Trials of Intimacy: Love and Loss in the Beecher-Tilton Scandal* (Chicago, 1999); aiding runaway slaves – Gary Collinson, "'This Flagitious Offense': Daniel Webster and the Shadrach Rescue Cases, 1851–1852," *New England Quarterly* 68 (1995), 609; and rebellion – Arthur Scherr, "Governor James Monroe and the Southampton Slave Resistance of 1799," *Historian* 61 (1999), 557 and Winthrop Jordan, *Tumult and Silence on*

Second Creek: An Inquiry into a Civil War Slave Conspiracy (Baton Rouge, LA, 1993).

V. Punishment

Imprisonment: The long nineteenth century marked the shift from physical punishments (whipping, the stocks, executions) to incarceration of prisoners in penitentiaries, and a number of books and articles focus on that shift and its causes. The start of the penitentiary movement, at the beginning of the nineteenth century, is described in two monographs: Adam J. Hirsch, *The Rise of the Penitentiary: Prison and Punishment in Early America* (New Haven, 1992) and Michael Meranze, *Laboratories of Virtue: Punishment, Revolution and Authority in Philadelphia, 1760–1835* (Chapel Hill, NC, 1996). For most of the nineteenth century, penitentiaries were a Northern phenomenon; Southern states resisted it throughout the antebellum era – see Ayers, *Vengeance and Justice* and Williams, *Vogues in Villainy* – and turned to convict labor during Reconstruction: Karin Shapiro, *A New South Rebellion: The Battle Against Convict Labor in the Tennessee Coalfields, 1871–1896* (Chapel Hill, NC, 1998); Gavin Wright, "Convict Labor After Emancipation: Old South or New South?" *Georgia Historical Quarterly* 81 (1997), 452; and Alex Lichtenstein, "Good Roads and Chain Gangs in the Progressive South: 'The Negro Convict as a Slave,'" *Journal of Southern History* 59 (1993), 85.

It was not until the end of the century that Southern states finally embraced the penitentiary; see Matthew J. Mancini, *One Dies, Get Another: Convict Leasing in the American South, 1866–1928* (Columbia, SC, 1996); by that point some Northern states had begun to experiment with reformatories: see Paul Keve, "Building a Better Prison: The First Three Decades of the Detroit House of Corrections," *Michigan Historical Review* 25 (1999), 1; Mark Colvin, *Penitentiaries, Reformatories, and Chain Gangs: Social Theory and the History of Punishment in Nineteenth-Century America* (New York, 1997); Alexander W. Pisciotta, *Benevolent Repression: Social Control and the American Reformatory Movement* (New York, 1994); and Robert G. Waite, "From Penitentiary to Reformatory: and Alexander Maconochie Walter Crofton, Zebulon Brockway, and the Road to Prison Reform: New South Wales, Ireland, and Elmira, New York, 1840–1870," *Criminal Justice History* 12 (1991), 85.

As that suggests, this is another area where the literature emphasizes regional difference; see David J. Bodenhamer, "Criminal Sentencing in Antebellum America: A North–South Comparison," *Historical Social Research* [West Germany], 15 (1990), 77. Much of the work, however, focuses on imprisonment in individual states or regions: Theresa Jach, "Reform Versus Reality in the Progressive Era Texas Prison," *Journal of the Gilded Age and Progressive Era* 41 (2005), 53; Keith Edgerton, *Montana Justice: Power, Punishment, and the Penitentiary* (Seattle, 2004); Jeffrey Koeher and Walter L. Brieschke, "Menard: Development of a Nineteenth-Century Prison," *Journal of the Illinois State Historical Society* 96 (2003), 230; Jayce McKay, "Reforming Prisoners and

Prisons" Iowa's State Prisons – Their First Hundred Years," *Annals of Iowa* 60 (2001), 139; Vivien M. L. Miller, "Reinventing the Penitentiary: Punishment in Florida, 1868–1923," *American Nineteenth Century History* [Great Britain] 1 (2000), 82; Larry Goldsmith, "'To Profit by His Skill and to Traffic in His Crime': Prison Labor in Early 19th-Century Massachusetts," *Labor History* [Great Britain], 40 (1999), 439; Timothy Dodge, "Hard Labor at the New Hampshire State Prison," *Historical New Hampshire* 47 (1992), 113; Gary Kremer, "Politics, Punishment and Profit: Convict Labor in the Missouri State Penitentiary, 1875–1900," *Gateway Heritage* 13 (1992), 28; Martha Myers, and James Massey, "Race, Labor, and Punishment in Postbellum Georgia," *Social Problems* 38 (1991), 267; Donald Walker, *Penology for Profit: A History of the Texas Prison System, 1867–1912* (College Station, TX, 1988); Paul Knepper, "Converting Idle Labor into Substantial Wealth: Arizona's Convict Lease System," *Journal of Arizona History* 31 (1990), 79; and Glen A. Gildemeister, *Prison Labor and Convict Competition with Free Workers in Industrializing America, 1840–1890* (DeKalb, IL, 1987). Yet a glance at the literature suggests the profit motive cut across state borders; see William Staples, "In the Interests of the State: Production Politics in the Nineteenth-Century Prison," *Sociological Perspectives* 33 (1990), 375. This suggests that more work could be done to test the comparative assumptions and examine whether and when trends in imprisonment crossed regions and state boundaries.

There are other possibilities for comparative study. In an article written in 1985, Nicole Hahn Rafter urged more work be done to learn about women prisoners: Rafter, "Gender, Prisons and Prison History," *Social Science History* 9 (1985), 233. Before she wrote, there had only been a handful of articles examining the experiences of women in prison: see Robert Waite, "Necessary to Isolate the Female Prisoners: Women Convicts and the Women's Ward at the Old Idaho Penitentiary," *Iowa Yesterdays* 29 (1985), 2 and W. David Lewis, "The Female Criminal and the Prisons of New York, 1825–1845," *New York History* 42 (1961), 215. Since then, a handful of studies have looked at the special experiences of women prisoners; Mara Dodge has written several articles on this subject, including "'The Most Degraded of Their Sex, if Not of Humanity': Female Prisoners at the Illinois State Penitentiary at Joliet, 1859–1900," *Journal of Illinois History* 2 (1999), 205 and "'One Female Prisoner is of More Trouble than Twenty Males': Women Convicts in Illinois Prisons, 1835–1896," *Journal of Social History* 32 (1999), 907. Other historians have followed suit: Leslie Patrick, "Ann Hinson: A Little-Known Woman in the Country's Premier Prison, Eastern State Penitentiary, 1831," *Pennsylvania History* 67 (2000), 361; Joan Jensen, "Sexuality on a Northern Frontier: The Gendering and Disciplining of Rural Wisconsin Women, 1850–1920," *Agricultural History* 73 (1999), 136; Nan Wolverton, "Bottomed Out: Female Chair Seaters in Nineteenth-Century New England," *Dublin Seminar for New England Folklife* 23 (1998), 175; and Anne M. Butler, "Still in Chains: Black Women in Western Prisons, 1865–1910," *Western Historical Quarterly* 20 (1989), 18.

These works invite comparisons, either exploring the ways in which male and female prisoners were treated or examining the different ways that women experienced imprisonment.

The articles by Patrick and Butler, which deal with the particular situation of black women, are complemented by other works that look at the intersection of race, prison, and punishment in the nineteenth century. Again, many of these studies are local; for example Mary Ellen Curren, *Black Prisoners and their World, Alabama, 1865–1900* (Charlottesville, VA, 2000); Lynne M. Adrian and Joan E. Crowley, "Hoboes and Homeboys"; and Michael S. Hindus, "Black Justice Under White Law: Criminal Prosecutions of Blacks in Antebellum South Carolina," *Journal of American History* 63 (1976), 575. Some are regional: Matthew J. Mancini, *One Dies, Get Another: Convict Leasing in the American South, 1866–1928* (Columbia, SC, 1996) and McKanna, *Homicide, Race, and Justice in the American West, 1880–1920*. Still others are comparative: Henry Douglas Kammerling, *'Too Much Time for the Crime I Done': Race, Ethnicity, and the Politics of Punishment in Illinois and South Carolina, 1865 to 1900* (PhD diss. University of Illinois, 1999). There are also studies that examine how ethnicity influenced punishment: Brad Asher, "'Their Own Domestic Difficulties': Intra-Indian Crime and White Law in Western Washington Territory, 1873–1889," *Western Historical Quarterly* 27 (1996), 189; Linda S. Parker, "Statutory Changes and Ethnicity in Sex Crimes in Four California Counties, 1880–1920," *Western Legal History* 6 (1993), 69; and David Beesley, "More Than People v. Hall: Chinese Immigrants and American Law in Sierra Nevada County, 1850–1920," *Locus* 3 (1991), 123. Once again, the body of literature invites serious study of whether, and how, imprisonment was applied to members of different groups.

More could also be done regarding the imprisonment of minors. There are some studies that trace the treatment of young convicts back to the beginning of the nineteenth century; see, for example, Gary Shockley, "A History of the Incarceration of Juveniles in Tennessee, 1796–1970," *Tennessee Historical Quarterly* 43 (1984), 229; Christopher Span, "Educational and Social Responses to African American Juvenile Delinquents in 19th Century New York and Philadelphia," *Journal of Negro Education* 71 (2002), 108; and Eric Schneider, *In the Web of Class: Delinquents and Reformers in Boston, 1810s–1930s* (New York, 1992). There are also studies that look punishment of juveniles at the end of the nineteenth century: David Tanenhaus, *Juvenile Justice in the Making* (Oxford, 2004); David Wolcott, "Juvenile Justice Before Juvenile Courts: Cops, Courts and Kids in Turn-of-the-Century Detroit," *Social Science History* 27 (2003), 109; David Wolcott, "'The Cop Will Get You': The Police and Discretionary Juvenile Justice, 1890–1940," *Journal of Social History* 35 (2001), 319; Randall G. Shelden, "A History of the Shelby County Industrial and Training School," *Tennessee Historical Quarterly* 51 (1991), 96; and Mary R. Block, "Child-Saving Laws of Louisville and Jefferson County, 1854–1894: A Socio-Legal History," *Filson Club History Quarterly* 66 (1992), 232.

A recent group of articles look specifically at girls imprisoned in the juvenile justice system: Sharon E. Wood, "Savage Girls: The 1899 Riot at the Mitchellville Girls School," *Iowa Heritage Illustrated* 80 (1999), 108 and Georgina Hickey, "Rescuing the Working Girl: Agency and Conflict in the Michigan Reform School for Girls, 1879–1893," *Michigan Historical Review* 20 (1994), 1. Once again, this wealth of material points to a need for studies that look across these different groups, testing for commonalities and differences. In addition, more work might be done to consider the role of class in the process of imprisonment. Progressive era reformers, like John Peter Altgeld of Illinois, worried about the age, class, and gender of prisoners in their attacks on the criminal justice system: John P. Altgeld, *Our Penal Machinery and Its Victims* (Springfield, IL, 1884). Some studies have matched their focus: see, for example, Georgina Hickey, "Rescuing the Working Girl," but there is room for additional work.

Other forms of punishment: Of course, not all defendants convicted of crimes were imprisoned. Some were executed. The major study of capital punishment in the nineteenth-century United States is Louis Masur, *Rites of Execution: Capital Punishment and the Transformation of American Culture, 1776–1865* (New York, 1991), but there are other studies that have looked at capital punishment in particular states: Philip B. Mackey, *Hanging in the Balance: Anti-Capital Punishment Movement in New York State, 1776–1861* (New York, 1982) and Negley Teeters, *Scaffold and Chair: A Compilation of Their Use in Pennsylvania, 1682–1962* (Philadelphia, 1963).

Those convicted of crimes could be punished in other ways as well. Until the 1840s, white men found guilty of bastardy in South Carolina might be sold into servitude to pay for their child's upkeep, Richard B. Morris, *Government and Labor in Early America* (New York, 1942), and whites from that state who were convicted of other crimes could be whipped until that punishment was limited to blacks in the 1840s: Williams, *Vogues in Villiany*. California relied on whipping as punishment until the end of the Civil War – Gordon Bakken Morris, "The Courts, the Legal Profession, and the Development of Law in Early California," *California History*, 81 (2003), 74 – and Virginia did so through the end of Reconstruction: William A. Blair, "Justice versus Law and Order: The Battles over the Reconstruction of Virginia's Minor Judiciary, 1865–1870," *Virginia Magazine of History and Biography* 103 (1995), 157. Whipping remained Kentucky's required punishment for many petty crimes until the end of the nineteenth century: Robert M. Ireland, "The Debate over Whipping Criminals in Kentucky," *Register of the Kentucky Historical Society* 100 (2002), 5. The literature suggests there was a racial dimension to the punishment chosen, but more could be done to explore this issue.

Insanity: David Rothman's study considered insane asylums as well as prisons, and other scholars have echoed this argument, particularly emphasizing the degree to which both types of institution were viewed as a necessary means of social control: for example, Marvin E. Schultz, "'Running the Risks of

Experiments': The Politics of Penal Reform in Tennessee, 1807–1829," *Tennessee Historical Quarterly* 52 (1993), 86. The connections between the institutions go far deeper; in many states for much of the antebellum era those judged insane for any reason were housed in jails: see Frank Narbury, "Dorothy Dix and the Founding of Illinois' First Mental Institution," *Journal of the Illinois State Historical Society* 92 (1999), 13. Reformers, notably Dorothy Dix, began to challenge that in the 1840s and 1850s, and by the start of the Civil War there were special asylums for the insane in a number of eastern states, as far west as Illinois and even in southern states like Alabama: see Bill L. Weaver, "Establishing and Organizing the Alabama Insane Hospital, 1846–1861," *Alabama Review* 48 (1995), 219. More states followed in the period after the Civil War: see, for example, William D. Erickson, "'Something Must be Done for Them': Establishment of Minnesota's First Hospital for the Insane," *Minnesota History* 53 (1992), 42 and Russell Hollander, "Life at the Washington Asylum for the Insane, 1871–1880," *Historian* 44 (1982), 229. Studies of the creation of these institutions provide a means of tracing shifts in understandings of punishment, incarceration, and rehabilitation, a point suggested by some works: Andrew T. Scull, "Madness and Segregative Control: The Rise of the Insane Asylum," *Social Problems* 24 (1977), 337 and Schultz, "Running the Risks of Experiments," in Ellen Dwyer, ed., *Homes for the Mad: Life Inside Two Nineteenth-Century Asylums* (New Brunswick, NJ, 1987; comparing Utica, founded in 1843, and Willard, founded in 1863), but more could be done to engage these relations and explore their consequences.

Cultural influence: One question in the literature on homicide is whether particular cultural forces led to the high rates of homicide and low rates of punishment in the United States. See the forum on homicide in *American Historical Review*, 111 (2006), 75 et seq. Studies of punishment explore a variation on this issue, looking at the reason why some crimes of violence were punished and some were not. Many follow Wyatt-Brown, *Southern Honor*, attributing responses to violence North and South to honor culture; see, for example, Lane, *Homicide in America* (noting the existence of plebian honor culture among the working class in the North). But others ascribe failures to punish violence to other forces: William Lynwood Montell, for example, argued that the lawless violence he traced in late nineteenth-century Kentucky had its roots in a combination of whiskey, the heritage of guerilla fighting during and after the Civil War, and an intense localism caused by an underdeveloped economy: Montell, *Killings: Folk Justice in the Upper South* (Lexington, KY, 1986). Fitzhugh Brundage in *Lynching in the New South: Georgia and Virginia, 1880–1930* (Urbana, IL, 1993) found that economic differences gave rise to the different lynching rates in Georgia and Virginia between 1880 and 1930 and that changes in economic circumstance helped reformers bring lynching to an end.

A number of other studies, focusing on the so-called unwritten law cases of the late nineteenth and early twentieth century, complicate these arguments by suggesting the different ways that gender norms dictated reactions to killings that punished seductions: see Hendrik Hartog, "Lawyering, Husband's Rights, and 'the Unwritten Law' in Nineteenth-Century America," *Journal of American History* 84 (1997), 67; Martha Merrill Umphrey, "The Dialogics of Legal Meaning: Spectacular Trials, the Unwritten Law, and Narratives of Criminal Responsibility," *Law and Society Review* 33 (1999), 393; and Gordon M. Bakken, "The Limits of Patriarchy: Women's Rights and 'Unwritten Law' in the West," *Historian* 60 (1998), 702.

VI. Extra-Legal Justice

As the work on cultural influences on law suggests, the formal workings of criminal law in the nineteenth century were shaped by popular forces that functioned outside the courts and often outside the law, but only a few works explore this area of criminal law. Studies of popular justice have typically emphasized its extra-legal and violent aspects, looking particularly at duels, vigilante groups, and lynching. See, for example, Wyatt-Brown, *Southern Honor*; McGrath, *Gunfighters, Highwaymen, and Vigilantes*; Michael Pfeifer, *Rough Justice: Lynching and American Society, 1874–1947* (reprint ed., Urbana, IL, 2006); W. Fitzhugh Brundage, *Lynching in the New South*; and Richard Maxwell Brown, *Strains of Violence: Historical Studies of American Violence and Vigilantism* (New York, 1975).

But while those familiar manifestations of popular justice are important, they are not the only means by which popular forces acted to judge wrongdoing, impose punishment, or otherwise influence criminal justice in nineteenth-century America. Elite gossip networks could be used to judge misconduct and punish wrongdoers, as Peggy Eaton and Andrew Jackson learned to their chagrin in the 1820s: see John F. Marszalek, *The Petticoat Affair: Manners, Mutiny, and Sex in Andrew Jackson's White House* (New York, 1997). Workers used shaming and shunning punishments against strike breakers in antebellum Philadelphia and late nineteenth-century Tampa: Feldberg, *Philadelphia Riots* and Nancy Hewitt, *Southern Discomfort: Women's Actions in Tampa, Florida, 1880s–1920s* (Urbana, IL, 2001). And church groups disciplined those who violated congregational norms: Henry Stroupe, "'Cite Them Both to Attend the Next Church Conference': Social Control by North Carolina Baptist Churches," *North Carolina Historical Review* 52 (1975), 156. See generally Elizabeth Dale, "A Different Sort of Justice: The Informal Courts of Public Opinion in Antebellum South Carolina," *South Carolina Law Review* 54 (2003), 627.

But again we can go further. There were instances when nineteenth-century popular justice mirrored the state, punishing acts that the formal law recognized was wrong. There were also moments when popular justice went beyond the scope of law, punishing those who committed acts that the formal rules did not define as criminal. Historians of crime and criminal law need to do more to consider when violence, shaming, or shunning are expressions of popular justice and what they tell us about justice and informal processes of law. And we can also do more to consider *when* the popular will was expressed. The obvious place to start is with the jury system. Why, and how often, did grand juries take matters into their own hands? What about petty juries? Studies suggest that jury nullification had come to an end with the rise of judicial review before the Civil War; see, for example, Nelson, *The Americanization of the Common Law*; Kramer, *The People Themselves*; and Clay S. Conrad, *Jury Nullification: The Evolution of a Doctrine* (Chapel Hill, NC, 1998). However, jury nullification was not formally outlawed on the federal level until the decision in *Sparf and Hansen v. United States* (1895), remained a right in Illinois until *People v. Bruner* (1931), and continues to be a constitutional right to this day in Maryland. More could be done to explore its extent in the nineteenth century and to test its influence.

And how else did popular influence come into the courts? Did the end of private prosecutions mark the point at which private influence no longer determined who could be prosecuted and for what? Or were their other ways that individuals or groups could influence what crimes would be prosecuted and who would be tried? There were any number of ways private people could be involved even at the earliest stages of the criminal justice process: they could be bounty hunters, Stuart H. Traub, "Rewards, Bounty Hunting, and Criminal Justice in the West, 1865–1900," *Western Historical Quarterly* 19 (1988), 287 (tracing the way that bounty was used to involve private citizens in the criminal process) or participate in raids by citizens leagues like the preventive societies of New York: Gilfoyle, *City of Eros* (preventive societies opposed to vice that formed from 1865 to 1880). How did those popular forces interact with the formal processes of law, and when or why did they supplant them? See generally Craig B. Little and Christopher P. Sheffield, "Frontiers and Criminal Justice: English Private Prosecution Societies and American Vigilantism, in the Eighteenth and Nineteenth Centuries," *American Sociological Review* 48 (1983), 796 (arguing that English extra-legal processes were appendages of criminal justice, while American extra-legal activities were often alternatives to formal law). Finally, since all these processes seem to be part of the larger whole, we need to develop some theoretical perspectives from which to evaluate these extra-legal forces in comparison to one another. An article written in 2000 by Benoît Garnot provides a typology of popular justice that could serve as a starting point: Garnot, "Justice, infrajustice, parajustice et extrajustice dans la France d'Ancien Régime," *Crime, Histoire & Sociétés* 4 (2000), 103.

CHAPTER 6: CITIZENSHIP AND IMMIGRATION LAW, 1800–1924

KUNAL M. PARKER

Inevitably, any account of the legal history of citizenship and immigration from 1800 to 1924 must acknowledge the impossibility of taking adequate stock of the vast literature associated with the somewhat separate field of immigration history. Nevertheless, scholars interested in the legal history of citizenship and immigration should acquaint themselves with immigration history not only because of its richness and density but also to avoid some of its pitfalls.

In much U.S. immigration history, immigration is ontologized as spatial movement between already constituted political-territorial entities: the immigrant comes "to" America "from" another country. This is revealed in the titles of such different immigration histories as Oscar Handlin's *The Uprooted* (Boston, 1952), Ronald Takaki's *Strangers from a Different Shore* (New York, 1989), and Roger Daniels' *Coming to America* (New York, 1990). In thus conceiving of the ontology of immigration, U.S. immigration history often unwittingly naturalizes the work of the modern immigration regime. After all, it is precisely the activities of the post-1870 national immigration regime – with its proliferation of documents, inspections, and controls – that produce "the immigrant" as a figure traveling "to" America "from" another country, a figure who may be denied rights of access and presence on the basis of his or her citizenship. Not surprisingly, much U.S. immigration history has been focused on the post-1870 period. There is a relative disregard of the varieties of pre-1860 "immigration restriction" covered in the chapter.

In large part, U.S. immigration history's relative disregard of the extended legal history of immigration restriction has to do with the field's origins in the early twentieth-century "Americanization" movements that sought to manage America's resident immigrant populations. In its initial academic rendering, U.S. immigration history set for itself the classic early twentieth-century social scientific "problem" of the "traditional" European immigrant's assimilation into "modern" American society – the object was not to theorize the state forms that produced foreignness in the first place. Early immigration histories, such as William Thomas's and Florian Znaniecki's *The Polish Peasant in Europe and America*, published in five volumes between 1918 and 1920 (Chicago), established the terms for what followed. See, for example, John Daniels, *Americanization Studies: America via the Neighborhood* (New York, 1920); William M. Leiserson, *Americanization Studies: Adjusting Immigrant and Industry* (New York, 1924); Robert E. Park, *Americanization Studies: The Immigrant Press and Its Control* (New York, 1922); Peter E. Speek, *Americanization Studies: A Stake in the Land* (New York, 1921); and Winthrop Talbot ed, *Americanization* (New York, 1920).

After the Immigration Act of 1924 had effectively brought immigration to a close, U.S. historians turned quite self-consciously to the archives to create immigration history as a sub-discipline. Whether they gave immigration history a Whiggish cast or a tragic inflection, however, they retained the focus on the problem of assimilation. Every aspect of immigrant life – labor, gender and family, ethnic and religious affiliation, public dependency, political participation, and so on – could be accounted for within this rubric. Naturally, the rubric permitted for vigorous debates, as suggested by the neat mirroring of the titles of Oscar Handlin's *The Uprooted* and John Bodnar's *The Transplanted* (Bloomington, IN, 1985).

Even as immigration historians were preoccupied with the problem of assimilation, the emergence in the early twentieth century of the related phenomenon of multiculturalism – something to which American Jewish (often immigrant) intellectuals contributed significantly – lent immigration history a certain "ethnicized" cast. Beginning in the immediate post-World War II decades, immigration historians began to focus on the assimilation experiences of particular national immigrant groups – Poles, Norwegians, Italians, and so on – that were often the groups from which they themselves might claim a certain descent. This scholarly trend has had an extended life, giving rise to journals such as the *Journal of American Ethnic History*. See, for example, Thomas H. Archdeacon, *Becoming American: An Ethnic History* (New York, 1983); John Bodnar, *Immigration and Industrialization: Ethnicity in an American Mill Town, 1870–1940* (Pittsburgh, 1977); Kathleen N. Conzen, *Immigrant Milwaukee, 1836–1860: Accommodation and Community in a Frontier City* (Cambridge, MA, 1976); Dino Cinel, *From Italy to San Francisco: The Immigrant Experience* (Stanford, 1982); Donna R. Gabaccia, *From Sicily to Elizabeth Street: Housing and Social Change Among Italian Immigrants, 1880–1930* (Albany, 1984); Jon Gjerde, *From Peasants to Farmers: The Migration from Balestrand, Norway to the Upper Middle West* (New York, 1985); Susan A. Glenn, *Daughters of the Shtetl: Life and Labor in the Immigrant Generation* (Ithaca, 1990); Ewa Morawska, *For Bread with Butter: The Life-Worlds of East Central Europeans in Johnstown, Pennsylvania, 1890–1940* (New York, 1985); Rudolph Vecoli, *Chicago's Italians Prior to World War I: A Study of Their Social and Economic Adjustment* (PhD diss., University of Wisconsin, 1962); and Virginia Yans-McLaughlin, *Family and Community: Italian Immigrants in Buffalo, 1880–1930* (Ithaca, 1977). It is noteworthy how many of the titles listed have a "from"/"to" structure.

It was not long, however, before the social upheavals of the 1960s compelled immigration historians self-consciously to take into account something that they had hitherto excluded – race (with related categories such as gender and sexuality, each with its own distinct intellectual genealogy). Beginning in the 1970s, but especially in the last two decades, we have witnessed an explosion of immigration history thematized around questions of race and its relationship to ethnicity and "whiteness." Immigration historians who once focused on ethnicity began to write about race. At the same time, the focus on assimilation has lifted as scholars have begun to problematize nationhood and study diasporic imaginations. In this regard, immigration history has proved no exception to the general trend sweeping American social history. See, for example, Rudolph J. Vecoli, "Are Italian Americans Just White Folks?" in A. Kenneth Ciongoli and Jay Parini, eds., *Beyond the Godfather: Italian American Writers on the Real Italian American Experience* (Hanover, NH, 1997). Vecoli is the author of an important article criticizing Handlin's *Gemeinschaft/Gesellschaft* thesis in *The Uprooted* and hence a participant in the earlier assimilation/ethnicity literature: Rudolph J. Vecoli, "*Contadini* in Chicago: A Critique of *The Uprooted*," *Journal of American History* 51 (1964), 404.

The literature on race and whiteness in the context of immigration is vast and cannot be cited here exhaustively. See, for example, Thomas A. Guglielmo, *White on Arrival: Italians, Race, Color, and Power in Chicago, 1890 –1945* (New York, 2003); Noel Ignatiev, *How the Irish Became White* (New York, 1995); Mathew Frye Jacobson, *Whiteness of a Different Color* (Cambridge, MA, 1998); Desmond King, *Making Americans: Immigration, Race, and the Origins of the Diverse Democracy* (Cambridge, MA, 2000); and David Roediger, *The Wages of Whiteness: Race and the Making of the American Working Class* (New York, 1991). On immigrant diasporic imaginations, see Mathew Frye Jacobson, *Special Sorrows: The Diasporic Imagination of Irish, Polish and Jewish Immigrants in the United States* (Cambridge, MA, 1995).

The newer critical focus on race and gender and nationhood as something *produced* has in general made it easier to bring in legal discourses (see below). Nevertheless, immigration historians' understanding of the ontology of immigration as a movement "to" America "from" another country often persists. The understanding of immigration as the activity of a state policing an international border makes it possible even for sophisticated immigration historians to claim that there was very little immigration restriction before the emergence of the federal immigration regime. For example, in a recent book, the historian Erika Lee states: "*Beginning in 1882*, the United States stopped being a nation of immigrants that welcomed foreigners without restrictions, borders, or gates": Erika Lee, *At America's Gates: Chinese Immigration During the Exclusion Era, 1882–1943* (Chapel Hill, NC, 2003), p. 6 (emphasis added).

Having highlighted some of the blind spots of immigration history, let us turn to the literature on which the chapter builds. The discussion that follows is necessarily selective. To begin with, the reader should consult general histories of American immigration policies. See, e.g., Marion T. Bennett, *American Immigration Policies: A History* (Washington, 1963) and Robert A. Divine, *American Immigration Policy, 1924–1952* (New Haven, 1957). An invaluable guide to immigration legislation is E. P. Hutchinson, *Legislative History of American Immigration Policy, 1798–1965* (Philadelphia, 1981).

Modern scholarship draws our attention repeatedly to the profoundly inegalitarian ways in which U.S. citizenship was granted to or withheld from the native population in the late eighteenth and nineteenth centuries. James Kettner's *Development of American Citizenship* (Chapel Hill, NC, 1978) offers a penetrating account of the seventeenth-century English ideas that informed American citizenship, dwells at length on late eighteenth- and early nineteenth-century debates about voluntary allegiance and the forms of citizenship instantiated at the state and federal levels, and then traces the tortured development of

U.S. citizenship up to the catastrophic *Dred Scott* decision in 1857. Although its account ends in the mid-nineteenth century, it remains the best – and most elegant – single treatment of U.S. citizenship as a history of ideas. Rogers Smith's monumental *Civic Ideals* (New Haven, 1997) owes more to social history and covers a larger terrain. It emphasizes the twinning of liberalism and ascriptive inegalitarianism in the unfolding of American citizenship over the course of the nineteenth and early twentieth centuries. The authoritative work on the racialization of citizenship in the post-1870s naturalization context is Ian Haney Lopez's *White by Law: The Legal Construction of Race* (New York, 1996). The work of Linda Kerber, Nancy Cott, Candice Bredbenner, and Martha Gardner traces the deeply gendered and racialized nature of citizenship. See Linda K. Kerber, *No Constitutional Right to be Ladies: Women and the Obligations of Citizenship* (New York, 1998); Candice Bredbenner, *A Nationality of Her Own: Women, Marriage, and the Law of Citizenship* (Berkeley, 1998); Nancy Cott, *Public Vows: A History of Marriage and the Nation* (Cambridge, MA, 2000); and Martha Gardner, *The Qualities of a Citizen: Women, Immigration, and Citizenship, 1870–1965* (Princeton,NJ, 2005).

While the historiography of American citizenship repeatedly underscores its inegalitarian extension on grounds of race and gender, it should be emphasized that this historiography is sometimes plotted along liberal and nation-centered lines. Rogers Smith exemplifies this species of writing. While Smith bemoans the ascriptive aspects of nineteenth- and early twentieth-century citizenship in *Civic Ideals*, in an earlier work, he has called for an alteration of the Fourteenth Amendment's *jus soli* provision to deny birthright citizenship to the U.S.-born children of "illegal" immigrants on the ground that such "illegals" have entered the community without its "consent." In other words, Smith laments the egregious history of citizenship and immigration, but without joining that history to the equally oppressive – albeit formally non-ascriptive – ways in which citizenship operates in the contemporary exclusion, deportation, and welfare contexts. This is also true of other scholars who have written historical/theoretical works on American citizenship. See Peter H. Schuck and Rogers M. Smith, *Citizenship Without Consent: Illegal Aliens in the American Polity* (New Haven, 1985). See also Judith N. Shklar, *American Citizenship: The Quest for Inclusion* (Cambridge, MA, 1991) and Peter H. Schuck, *Citizens, Strangers, and In-Betweens: Essays on Immigration and Citizenship* (Boulder, CO, 1998). Following Bernard Bailyn's work on the peopling of British North America – *The Peopling of British North America: An Introduction* (New York, 1986 – some of Bailyn's students have published fine studies of the British policies that governed migration to North America in the eighteenth century. Marilyn Baseler's *"Asylum for Mankind": America, 1607–1800* (Ithaca, 1998) details eighteenth-century British policies regarding the settlement of displaced European Protestants, paupers, and convicts in North America. She also traces the beginnings of American dissatisfaction with British shipments of convicts after the American Revolution. See also Alison Games, *Migration and the Origin of the English Atlantic World* (Cambridge, MA, 1999).

However, to expand what "immigration restriction" meant in the eighteenth century and early nineteenth centuries, we must turn to other historiographies. Historians of colonial New England have offered rich accounts of the complicated system of "internal" territorial restriction applicable to native paupers. Douglas Lamar Jones' work on vagrancy and pauperism is indispensable in this regard: see Douglas Lamar Jones, "The Transformation of the Law of Poverty in Eighteenth Century Massachusetts," in Daniel Coquillette, ed., *Law in Colonial Massachusetts, 1630–1800* (Boston, 1984). Ruth Herndon's *Unwelcome Americans: Living on the Margin in Early New England* (Philadelphia, 2001) is a valuable edition of documents detailing the prosecutions and "warnings out" of Rhode Island paupers. On the restrictions applicable to free blacks in the late eighteenth century, the reader should consult Joanne Melish's *Disowning Slavery: Gradual Emancipation and "Race" in New England, 1780–1860* (Ithaca, 1998). Kunal Parker canvasses late eighteenth- century efforts to assimilate emancipated slaves to the status of foreigners with a view to making explicit the connections between African American history and immigration history: see Kunal M. Parker, "Making Blacks Foreigners: The Legal Construction of Former Slaves in Post-Revolutionary Massachusetts," *Utah Law Review* 75 (2001).

Historians had long been aware of state-level immigration regimes in the antebellum period. However, Gerald Neuman's important and thoroughly researched article, "The Lost Century of American Immigration Law, 1776–1875," *Columbia Law Review* 93 (1993), 1833, was the first in recent years to draw legal scholars' attention to the plethora of regimes of territorial restriction – internal and external – that flourished in antebellum America and preceded the national immigration regime. Neuman exhaustively details regimes applicable to the poor, the criminal, the sick, and free blacks. Building on Neuman's work, Kunal Parker focuses on the experience of Massachusetts, tracing the shift from a local to a state-level immigration regime between 1780 and 1860 and drawing attention both to the new and negative uses of citizenship in antebellum America and to the willful blurring of the distinction between citizen and alien, native and immigrant, when it came to dealing with the poor: Kunal M. Parker, "State, Citizenship, and Territory: The Legal Construction of Immigration in Antebellum Massachusetts," *Law and History Review* 19 (2001), 583. Mary Sarah Bilder examines antebellum Commerce Clause jurisprudence related to immigration and provides a thorough account of the connections between slavery and the trade in indentured persons: Mary Sarah Bilder, "The Struggle Over Immigration: Indentured Servants, Slaves and Articles of Commerce," *Missouri Law Review* 61 (1996), 743. The reader should also consult the vast literature on antebellum nativism directed against Irish and Catholic immigrants. See R. A. Billington, *The Protestant Crusade, 1800–1860:*

A Study of the Origins of American Nativism (New York, 1938) and Kerby A. Miller, *Emigrants and Exiles: Ireland and the Irish Exodus to North America* (New York, 1985).

Although most studies of African Americans in the antebellum period do not explicitly characterize the legal regimes applicable to free blacks as a species of immigration restriction, they may certainly be read that way. The authoritative and indispensable work on free blacks in the antebellum south is Ira Berlin's *Slaves Without Masters: The Free Negro in the Antebellum South* (New York, 1975). Leon Litwack's *North of Slavery: The Negro in the Free States, 1790–1860* (Chicago, 1961) outlines Northern efforts to regulate and restrict the entry and presence of free blacks. P. J. Staudenraus's *The African Colonization Movement, 1816–1865* (New York, 1961) is a factual history of antebellum efforts to endow free blacks with their own geographical origins in Africa – a place they were allegedly "from" and "to" which they could be returned

Much of the work on the legal history of immigration has focused on the activities of the post-1870 national immigration regime. The best recent work on the emergence of the immigration regime has often focused on the contests between immigrants and the emerging federal immigration order. A seminal work in this area is Lucy Salyer's *Laws Harsh as Tigers: Chinese Immigrants and the Shaping of Modern Immigration Law* (Chapel Hill, NC, 1995). Focusing on the late nineteenth and early twentieth centuries, Salyer traces how the efforts of Chinese immigrants to use the judicial system provided the impetus for concentrating power in the hands of immigration officials and for the curtailment of judicial review. Salyer offers us, in other words, a brilliant account of immigration as one of the major sites of the emergence of the American administrative state. Mae Ngai's *Impossible Subjects: Illegal Aliens and the Making of Modern America* (Princeton, NJ, 2004) carries the story forward, offering a complex account of the intertwining of race and nationality in the passage of the quota legislation of the 1920s and then tracing the emergence of the figure of the "illegal alien." Ngai continues with a discussion of the connections between immigration and America's colonial policies, ending with an analysis of post-World War II immigration reform. The second half of the chapter draws heavily from Salyer and Ngai.

In addition to these monographs, it is important to consult the work of immigration scholars based in law schools. Linda Bosniak and Hiroshi Motomura have offered us penetrating accounts of the modern doctrinal distinctions between "immigration law" and "alienage law," on the one hand, and the difference between procedure and substance, on the other hand: see Linda Bosniak, "Membership, Equality, and the Difference That Alienage Makes," *New York University Law Review* 69 (1994), 1047 and Hiroshi Motomura, "The Curious Evolution of Immigration Law: Procedural Surrogates for Substantive Constitutional Rights," *Columbia Law Review* 92 (1992), 1625.

There are several possible thematizations of the legal history of immigration, of which I mention two. First, there is the vast body of scholarship inaugurated by John Higham's book *Strangers in the Land: Patterns of American Nativism, 1860–1925* (2nd ed., New Brunswick, NJ, 1988), still an authoritative work on American nativism. Much of the newer work on race and gender can be set in relationship to Higham's work. As stated above, it often draws on legal discourses. Scholars of Asian Americans in particular have given us highly detailed accounts of the legal experiences of gendered and racialized Asian immigrants in the late nineteenth and early twentieth centuries. Insofar as such accounts detail the efforts of the state to police Asian immigrants and communities, they underscore the internal foreignness imposed on Chinese immigrants by a hardening immigration regime and will be useful to the legal historian of immigration, civil rights, and discrimination generally. On Asian American, the reader should consult, inter alia, the works of Angelo Ancheta, Sucheng Chan, Lucy Cheng, Roger Daniels, Bill Ong Hing, Erika Lee, Charles J. McClain, Mae Ngai, Gary Okihiro, Lucy Salyer, Alexander Saxton, Nayan Shah, and Ronald Takaki.

Scholars of Mexican Americans, likewise, have drawn attention to the range of formal and informal processes through which Mexican immigrants were admitted, removed, and subjected to discrimination. On Mexicans, the reader should consult the works of David Gutierrez, Francisco Balderrama and Raymond Rodriguez, Pierrette Hondagneu-Sotelo, Arnoldo de Leon, and George Sanchez. Martha Gardner's work, cited above, deals with both Asian and Mexican immigrant women.

Second, there are important overlaps between immigration history and labor history. The early work of the sociologist Kitty Calavita traced the relationship between immigration law and capital-labor relations in the nineteenth century, focusing in particular on the administration of the contract labor laws. Calavita has since produced detailed studies of the Bracero program and of the role of the modern immigration regime in the production of illegal immigration: see Kitty Calavita, *U.S. Immigration Law and the Control of Labor, 1820–1924* (London, 1984) and *Inside the State: The Bracero Program, Immigration, and the I.N.S.* (New York, 1992). Gunther Peck's important work blurs boundaries among immigration history, labor history, ethnic history, and the history of the American West in showing how the state simultaneously impeded and enabled the efforts of early twentieth-century Italian, Greek, and Mexican immigrant labor bosses to recruit and exploit immigrant labor; Peck focuses in part on the administration of the alien contract labor laws: see Gunther Peck, *Reinventing Free Labor: Padrones and Immigrant Workers in the North American West, 1880–1930* (New York, 2000). Scholars have also focused on related aspects of immigration law such as the public charge provisions and the anti-radical and anti-anarchist provisions. For an entry into the literature on labor migration from Europe to America, the reader should consult the work of Dirk Hoerder. For a study of the public charge provision, see Patricia R. Evans, *"Likely to Become a Public Charge": Immigration in the Backwaters of Administrative Law, 1882–1933* (PhD diss., George Washington University, 1987). For the suppression of dissent, see William Preston, *Aliens and Dissenters: Federal Suppression of Radicals, 1903–1933* (Cambridge, MA, 1963).

Finally, to extend the reach of the chapter to the internal foreignness imposed on African Americans during the century following the Civil War, it would be important to focus not only on the late nineteenth-century rural to urban – and northward – migration of Southern blacks but also on the rich literature on segregation and desegregation in the North and South. It is hardly a coincidence that the overtly discriminatory aspects of citizenship and immigration law, on the one hand, and segregation, on the other hand, were dismantled at the same time – as the United States sought to win world approval and domination in the context of the Cold War. See James R. Grossman, *Land of Hope: Chicago, Black Southerners, and the Great Migration* (Chicago, 1989); William H. Chafe, *Civilities and Civil Rights: Greensboro, North Carolina and the Black Struggle for Freedom* (New York, 1980); John Dittmer, *Local People: The Struggle for Civil Rights in Mississippi* (Urbana, IL, 1994); Arnold Hirsch, *Making the Second Ghetto: Race and Housing in Chicago, 1940–1960* (Cambridge, 1983); John T. McGreevy, *Parish Boundaries: The Catholic Encounter with Race in the Twentieth-Century Urban North* (Chicago, 1996); Jonathan Rieder, *Canarsie: The Jews and Italians of Brooklyn Against Liberalism* (Cambridge, MA, 1985); Thomas J. Sugrue, *The Origins of the Urban Crisis: Race and Inequality in Postwar Detroit* (Princeton, NJ, 1996); and Mary L. Dudziak, *Cold War Civil Rights: Race and the Image of American Democracy* (Princeton, NJ, 2000).

CHAPTER 7: FEDERAL POLICY, WESTERN MOVEMENTS, AND CONSEQUENCES FOR INDIGENOUS PEOPLE

DAVID E. WILKINS

The nexus between indigenous peoples and the expansionary forces of the United States – including the actions and policies of the federal government, the states, corporate interests, and private parties – is suffused by a host of geographic, demographic, sociological, psychological, political, environmental, intergovernmental, technological, and cultural factors. Each of these is critical to understand how and why events unfolded as they did. But overarching, intertwining, and underlying them all is the force and power of the law that, as Felix Cohen once said, dominates indigenous affairs in all aspects in a way not duplicated in any other segment of American society.

In the early years of sustained contact and interaction, the various indigenous legal traditions coexisted, albeit uneasily, alongside the Western legal traditions of the various European powers vying for a position of power in the hemisphere. The diplomatic record that ensued – treaties, accords, tribal-specific and nation-specific indigenous policies, and indigenous responses to these policies – reflected this uneasy and ad hoc intersection of legal customs and traditions.

Vine Deloria, Jr. and Raymond J. DeMallie's two-volume account, *Documents of Indian Diplomacy: Treaties, Agreements, and Conventions, 1775–1979* (Norman, OK, 1999) is an outstanding work that fills the gaps in history and indigenous perspective that previously plagued anyone seeking to learn a more complete account of the diplomatic processes that actually developed among indigenous peoples and between native nations and the various European nations and the United States. Robert A. Williams, Jr., *Linking Arms Together: American Indian Treaty Visions of Law and Peace, 1600–1800* (Oxford, 1997) provides a solid account of indigenous treaty understandings and shows how an indigenous vision of law during the encounter era formed the essential philosophical and cultural paradigm that guided relations between these two sets of disparate peoples, a view that fundamentally contradicts the stereotypical view of American history that asserts that European and later American law dominated aboriginal people from the very beginning.

Rennard Strickland's *Fire and the Spirits: Cherokee Law From Clan to Court* (Norman, OK, 1975) discusses how and why the Cherokee Nation went about modifying its traditional customary legal system to incorporate elements of Western law and the ramifications this had on the community and their political relations with the State of Georgia and the federal government. A more recent compilation of essays edited by Oren Lyons and John Mohawk, *Exiled in the Land of the Free: Democracy, Indian Nations, and the United States Constitution* (Santa Fe, NM, 1992) contains eight essays that, on the one hand, argue how indigenous legal and customary tradition influenced the genesis of the American Constitution, and on the other hand, poignantly show how subsequent interpretations of this very same document have served to destabilize and diminish the sovereignty and resources of indigenous peoples.

Frank Pommersheim's *Braid of Feathers: American Indian Law and Contemporary Tribal Life* (Berkeley, CA, 1995) is a solid treatment of the evolution of tribal court systems and the distinctive political and structural constraints they face as they struggle to carry out their responsibilities as the crucible of indigenous self-determination. Finally, G. Peter Jamison and Anna M. Schein edited a recent study, *Treaty of Canandaigua 1794: 200 Years of Treaty Relations Between the Iroquois Confederacy and the United States* (Santa Fe, NM, 2000) that contains a number of essays demonstrating the value of Indian treaties from an indigenous perspective.

Of course, while these developments were transpiring, advocates of Western law, believing in its inherent superiority, continued their efforts to gain control of tribal lands and resources and to transform native identity. A strong account of the ancient intellectual roots of this dominant Western approach is Robert A. Williams, Jr., *The American Indian in Western Legal Thought: The Discourse of Conquest* (Oxford, 1990). This volume documents that the Western legal conquest tradition dates back to the Crusades' medieval discourses and, the author asserts, continues to the present time.

Several other works by prominent legal writers and social scientists also give substantial treatments of how colonial law, constitutional history, and Supreme Court rulings and federal Indian policy elevated the United States to a controlling position vis-à-vis the indigenous nations; they include Russel Lawrence Barsh and James Youngblood Henderson, *The Road: Indian Tribes and Political Liberty* (Berkeley, 1980); Petra T. Shattuck and Jill Norgren, *Partial Justice: Federal Indian Law in a Liberal Constitutional System* (Providence, RI, 1991); Jill Norgren, *The Cherokee Cases: The Confrontation of Law and Politics* (New York, 1996); John R. Wunder, *"Retained by the People": A History of American Indians and the Bill of Rights* (New York, 1994); Vine Deloria, Jr. and Clifford M. Lytle, *American Indians, American Justice* (Austin, TX, 1983); Vine Deloria, Jr. and David E. Wilkins, *Tribes, Treaties, & Constitutional Tribulations* (Austin, TX, 1999); David E. Wilkins, *American Indian Sovereignty & the U. S. Supreme Court* (Austin, TX, 1997); David E. Wilkins and Tsianina Lomawaima, *Uneven Ground: American Indian Sovereignty and Federal Law* (Norman, OK, 2001); Tim Alan Garrison, *The Legal Ideology of Removal: The Southern Judiciary and the Sovereignty of Native Nations* (Athens, GA, 2002); and P. G. McHugh, *Aboriginal Societies and the Common Law: A History of Sovereignty, Status, and Self-Determination* (New York, 2004).

Charles F. Wilkinson has been an active chronicler of the legal struggles of native nations, and although his views on Congressional plenary power, the constitutional status of American Indian peoples, and his quixotic view of the law as the most vital and positive force for the protection of indigenous rights are disputed by a number of native scholars and activists, his contributions, most notably his study, *American Indians, Time, and the Law: Native Societies in a Modern Constitutional Democracy* (New Haven, CT, 1987), furnishes a worthy overview of contemporary federal law as it has been applied to native peoples.

Likewise, Francis P. Prucha, a historian, has written extensively on federal Indian policy and the treaty process. His works contain useful data, although the perspective he uses serves to reinforce what he perceives as a diminished political and legal status for tribal nations and their treaty rights. The major two-volume account, *The Great Father: The United States Government and the American Indians* (Lincoln, NE, 1984) and *American Indian Treaties: The History of a Political Anomaly* (Berkeley, 1994) are examples of his approach in the field. Frederick E. Hoxie, *A Final Promise: The Campaign to Assimilate the Indians, 1880–1920* (Lincoln, NE, 1984) is another useful account of a crucial historical period that also contains some legal analysis.

The subject of claims against the federal government, both indigenous and non-indigenous, has been the focus of three treatments to date. Edward Lazarus focused on the efforts of the Sioux Nation for legal redress in *Black Hills/White Justice: The Sioux Nation Versus the United States, 1775 to the Present* (New York, 1991). Larry C. Skogen concentrated on the little known but very important depredations claims that allowed white settlers to file suits in federal courts in an effort to collect against tribal funds for property losses they were alleged to have endured at the hands of tribal peoples. His study, *Indian Depredation Claims, 1796–1920* (Norman, OK, 1996) is a treasure trove of information about a particularly problematic and heretofore largely ignored set of legal cases.

Last, Michael Lieder and Jake Page's *Wild Justice: The People of Geronimo vs. the United States* (New York, 1997) examines the Chiricahua Apache's legal and political struggles in the wake of their imprisonment in the late 1800s and their forced exile to eastern lands.

John R. Wunder has edited a six-volume study, *Native American Law and Colonialism, Before 1776 & 1903; Constitutionalism and Native Americans, 1903–1968; The Indian Bill of Rights, 1968; Recent Legal Issues for American Indians, 1968 to the Present; Native American Cultural and Religious Freedom*; and *Native American Sovereignty* (New York, 1990s), that broadly examines how the federal government sought to forcibly integrate indigenous peoples into the national legal framework. The volumes also contain indigenous responses to these forced assimilative attempts.

Several specific Supreme Court cases have received book-length treatment because of their historical and precedential importance for or against tribal sovereignty and treaty rights. Lindsay G. Robertson's *Conquest by Law: How the Discovery of America Dispossessed Indigenous Peoples of Their Lands* (New York, 2005) is a detailed account using previously unknown historical documents to trace the details of the seminal Indian property rights case, *Johnson v. M'Intosh* (1823). Blue Clark's *Lone Wolf v. Hitchcock: Treaty Rights and Indian Law at End of the Nineteenth Century* (Lincoln, NE, 1994) synthesizes legal analysis that is historically and politically grounded in time with the culture and traditions of the Kiowa Nation. *Ex parte Crow Dog*, a portentous 1883 case that affirmed the inherent sovereignty of the Sioux Nation to try and punish their own citizens free of federal interference, was deftly analyzed by Sidney L. Harding in *Crow Dog's Case: American Indian Sovereignty, Tribal Law, and United States Law in the Nineteenth Century* (New York, 1994). And the landmark 1908 Indian water rights case, *Winters v. United States*, has been analyzed by John Shurts in *Indian Reserved Water Rights: The Winters Doctrine in its Social and Legal Context, 1880s–1930s* (Norman, OK, 2000).

Finally, and not surprisingly, several excellent essays have been written by social scientists, law professors, and legal historians that detail key aspects of this important historical era. Vine Deloria, Jr.'s "Laws Founded in Justice and Humanity: Reflections on the Content and Character of Federal Indian Law," *Arizona Law Review* (1989), 203–24 provides an striking overview of the subject area, with an emphasis on the inherent contradictions rampant in federal law and judicial opinions. Milner Ball, in "Constitution, Court, Indian Tribes," *American Bar Foundation Research Journal* (1987), 1–140 and Nell Jessup Newton, "Federal Power over Indians: Its Sources, Scope, and Limitations," *University of Pennsylvania Law Review* (1984), 195–288 detail the genesis and evolution of major Supreme Court doctrines like plenary power, trust, and the discovery doctrine, that have been invoked to curtail the sovereign nature of tribal nations. George S. Grossman, "Indians and the Law," in C.G. Galloway, ed., *New Directions in American Indian History* (Norman, OK, 1988), 97–126 and Nancy Carol Carter, "American Indian Law: Research and Services," *Legal Reference Services Quarterly* (1984/1985), 5–71 are two good bibliographic sources that identify useful material for readers who wish to explore the nuances of this subject matter.

This essay would be remiss if it did not contain at least a few references to one of the leading writers on the legal status and intergovernmental relationship between indigenous peoples and the federal government – Felix S. Cohen. While he is most noted for his classic account, *Handbook of Federal Indian Law* (Washington, DC, 1942), which is still the standard reference book on this topic, Cohen also wrote several incisive essays examining specific angles of indigenous legal status: "The Spanish Origin of Indian Rights in the Laws of the United States," *Georgetown Law Journal* (1942), 1–21; "Indian Rights and the Federal Courts," *Minnesota Law Review* (1940), 145–200; and "Original Indian Title," in *The Legal Conscience: Selected Papers of Felix S. Cohen* (New Haven, CT, 1960), 273–304, to name but a few.

CHAPTER 8: MARRIAGE AND DOMESTIC RELATIONS

NORMA BASCH

Anyone approaching the legal evolution of marriage and domestic relations in nineteenth-century America needs to begin with Michael Grossberg's comprehensive *Governing the Hearth: Law and the Family in Nineteenth-Century America* (Chapel Hill, NC, 1985); for understanding the emergence of the history of family law as a scholarly field, see his essay, "Crossing Boundaries: Ninete-Century Domestic Relations Law and the Merger of Family and Legal History," *American Bar Foundation Research Journal* 4 (1985), 799–847. For the South and an emphasis on Southern exceptionalism, see Peter W. Bardaglio, *Reconstructing the Household: Families, Sex, and the Law in the Nineteenth-Century South* (Chapel Hill, NC, 1995). On the very public nature of marriage including early federal intervention, see Nancy F. Cott's *Public Vows: A History of Marriage and the Nation* (Cambridge, MA, 2000). For emphasis on legal institutions and practices as well as a nuanced reading of the role of coverture, see Hendrik Hartog, *Man and Wife in America: A History* (Cambridge, MA, 2000). Still useful, especially for state-by-state details and divergences, is George E. Howards's *A History of Matrimonial Institutions*, 3 vols. (Chicago, 1904).

Another route into the history of family law is through nineteenth-century American legal treatises, including critical comments on the "law of persons" in the numerous American editions of William Blackstone's late-eighteenth-century *Commentaries*. Some important American works published over the course of the century include in chronological order: Tapping Reeve, *The Law of Baron and Femme* (New Haven, 1816); James Kent, *Commentaries on American Law*, 4 vols. (New York, 1826–1830); Joseph Story, *Commentaries on Equity Jurisprudence*, 2 vols. (Boston, 1839); Joel Prentice Bishop, *Commentaries on the Law of Marriage and Divorce and Evidence in Matrimonial Suits* (Boston, 1852), a work that marks family law as the focal point of specialized treatise writing; and James Schouler, *A Treatise on the Law of Domestic Relations* (Boston, 1870), a title far more modern than Reeve's Anglo-Norman "Baron and Femme."

Because a broadly Western perspective is important for understanding the family as a social institution, I include here a sampling of European and comparative works on the social history of the family in addition to American works. On the American side see Steven Mintz and Susan Kellog, *Domestic Revolutions: A Social History of American Family Life* (New York, 1988); John Demos, *Past, Present, and Personal: The Family and Life Course in American History* (New York, 1986); Arthur W. Calhoun, *A Social History of the American Family from Colonial Times to the Present*, 3 vols. (Cleveland, 1919); Ellen K. Rothman, *Hands and Hearts: A History of Courtship in America* (New York, 1984); Carl Degler, *At Odds: Women and the Family in America from the Revolution to the Present* (New York 1980); Karen Lystra, *Searching the Heart: Women, Men, and Romantic Love in Nineteenth-Century America* (New York, 1989); and Mary Ryan, *Cradle of the Middle Class: The Family in Oneida County, New York* (Berkeley, 1981). For a European and comparative perspective see Lawrence Stone, *Family, Sex, and Marriage in England, 1500–1800* (London, 1977); John Gillis, *For Better, For Worse: British Marriages, 1600 to the Present* (New York, 1985); Jack Goody, *The Development of the Family and Marriage in Europe* (Cambridge, 1983); Jacques Donzelot, *The Policing of Families* (New York, 1979); Ralph Trumbach, *The Rise of the Egalitarian Family* (New York 1978); and Edward Shorter, *The Making of the Modern Family* (New York, 1975).

On the problematic nature of the wife's allegiance in the Revolution and the potential for the renegotiation of gender roles, see Linda K. Kerber, "The Paradox of Women's Citizenship in the Early Republic: The Case of *Martin vs. Massachusetts*, 1805," *American Historical Review* 97 (1992), 349–78 and Kerber, *No Constitutional Right to be Ladies: Women and the Obligations of Citizenship* (New York, 1998); see also Joan R. Gunderson, "Independence, Citizenship and the American Revolution," *Signs* 13 (1987), 59–77, which argues that dependency acquired a gender-specific meaning in the Early Republic; on dower and inheritance see Carole Shammas, Marylynn Salmon, and Michel Dahlin, *Inheritance in America from Colonial Times to the Present* (New Brunswick, NJ, 1987); for the status of wives in the Early Republic see Cornelia Hughes Dayton, *Women Before the Bar: Gender Law and Society in Connecticut, 1639–1789* (Chapel Hill, NC, 1995) and Marylynn Salmon, *Women and the Law of Property in Early America* (Chapel Hill, NC, 1986). On subsequent tensions between coverture and female citizenship, see Candice Lewis Bredbenner, *A Nationality of her Own: Marriage and the Law of Citizenship* (Berkeley, 1998).

Carole Pateman exposes the pivotal but hidden role played by the marriage contract in the proverbial social contract in her path-breaking *The Sexual Contract* (Stanford, 1988); see also Gordon J. Schochet, *Patriarchalism in Political Thought* (New York, 1975); Mary Lyndon Shanley, "Marriage Contract and Social Contract in Seventeenth-Century English Thought," *Western Political Theory* 32 (1979), 79–91; and Susan Moller Okin, *Women in Western Political Thought* (Princeton, 1979). Jay Fliegelman delineates the anti-patriarchal impulses of the Revolution in *Prodigals and Pilgrims: The American Revolution Against Patriarchal Authority, 1750–1800* (New York, 1982) as does Melvin Yazawa in *From Colony to Commonwealth: Familial Ideology and the Beginning of the American Republic* (Baltimore, 1985) as well as Jan Lewis, "The Republican Wife: Virtue and Seduction in the Early Republic," *William and Mary Quarterly* 44 (1987), 689–721 and Norma Basch, "From the Bonds of Empire to the Bonds of Matrimony," in David Konig, ed., *Devising Liberty: Preserving and Creating Liberty in the New American Republic* (Stanford, 1995).

On the Robards affair and political contestations over the union of Rachel and Andrew Jackson, see Norma Basch, "Marriage, Morals, and Politics in the Election of 1828," *Journal of American History* 80 (1993), 890–919 and Harriet Chappell Owsley, "The Marriages of Rachel Donelson," *Tennessee Historical Quarterly* 37 (1977), 479–92. On common law marriage and extra-legal marriage, in addition to Grossberg's aforementioned *Governing the Hearth*, see Ariela Dubler, "Governing Through Contract: Common Law Marriage in the Nineteenth-Century," *Yale Law Journal* 107 (1998), 1885–1920; Stephen Parker, *Informal Marriage, Cohabitation, and the Law* (New York, 1990); Stuart Stein, "Common Law Marriage: Its History and Certain Contemporary Problems," *Journal of Family Law* 9 (1969), 277–97; John E. Semonche, "Common Law Marriage in North Carolina: A Study in Legal History," *American Journal of Legal History* 9 (1965), 324–41; Otto E. Koegal, *Common Law Marriage and its Development in the United States* (Washington, DC, 1922); Timothy J. Gilfoyle, "The Hearts of Nineteenth-Century Men: Bigamy and Working-Class Marriage in New York City, 1800–1890," *Prospects* 19 (1994), 135–160; and Hendrik Hartog, "Marital Exits and Marital Expectations in Nineteenth-Century America," *Georgetown Law Journal* 80 (1991), 95–129. On desertion, see also Paula Petrik, "If She Be Content: The Development of Montana Divorce Law, 1865–1907," *Western Historical Quarterly* 18 (1987), 261–91.

The literature on divorce is extensive and ranges from comprehensive overviews to local studies based on county courts records. Roderick Phillips provides a sweeping and multifaceted treatment of divorce in *Putting Asunder: A History of Divorce in Western Society* (Cambridge, 1988). See also Lawrence Stone, *Road to Divorce: England, 1530–1987* (New York, 1990) and William J. Goode, *World Changes in Divorce Patterns* (New Haven, 1993). Studies of American divorce include Norma Basch, *Framing American Divorce: From the Revolutionary Generation to the Victorians* (Berkeley, 1999); Richard H. Chused, *Private*

Acts in Public Places: A Social History of Divorce in the Formative Era of American Family Law (Philadelphia, 1994); Glenda Riley, *Divorce: An American Tradition* (New York, 1991); Lawrence M. Friedman, "Rights of Passage: Divorce Law in Historical Perspective," *Oregon Law Review* 63 (1984), 649–69; Merril D. Smith, *Breaking the Bonds: Marital Discord in Pennsylvania, 1730–1830* (New York, 1991); Robert L. Griswold, *Family and Divorce in California, 1850–1890)* (Albany, NY, 1982); Michael S. Hindus and Lynne E. Withey, "The Law of Husband and Wife in Nineteenth-Century America: Changing Views of Divorce," in D. Kelly Weisberg, ed., *Women and the Law: A Social Historical Perspective*, 2 vols. (Cambridge, MA, 1982), 2:133–53; Gale W. Bamman and Debbie W. Spero, *Tennessee Divorces, 1797–1858* (Nashville, TN, 1985); Elaine Tyler May, *Great Expectations: Marriage and Divorce in Post-Victorian America* (Chicago, 1980); Richard Wires, *The Divorce Issue and Divorce Reform in Nineteenth-Century* Indiana (Muncie, IN, 1976); and William L. O'Neill, *Divorce in the Progressive Era* (New Haven, 1967).

For divorce in the South, see Janet Hudson, "From Constitution to Constitution, 1868–1895: South Carolina's Unique Stance on Divorce," *South Carolina Historical Magazine* 98 (1997), 75–96; Jane Turner Censer, "'Smiling through Her Tears': Antebellum Southern Women and Divorce," *American Journal of Legal History* 25 (1981), 24–47; and Lawrence B. Goodheart, Neil Hanks, and Elizabeth Johnson, "'An Act for the Relief of Females': Divorce and the Changing Legal Status of Women in Tennessee, 1716–1860," *Tennessee Historical Quarterly* 44 (1985), 318–39, 402–16. On the Early Republic, see Nancy F. Cott, "Divorce and the Changing Status of Women in Eighteenth-Century Massachusetts," *William and Mary Quarterly* 33 (1976), 586–614; Sheldon S. Cohen, "'To Parts of the World Unknown': The Circumstances of Divorce in Connecticut, 1750–1797," *Canadian Review of American Studies* 11 (1980), 275–93; and Thomas R. Meehan, "'Not Made out of Levity': Evolution of Divorce in Early Pennsylvania," *Pennsylvania Magazine of History and Biography* 92 (1968), 441–64. On statutory divergences and conflicts of law, see Michael M. O'Hear, "'Some of the Most Embarrassing Questions': Extraterritorial Divorces and the Problems of Jurisdiction before *Pennoyer*," *Yale Law Journal* 104 (1995), 1507–1537 and Neil R. Feigenson, "Extraterritorial Recognition of Divorce Decrees in the Nineteenth Century," *American Journal of Legal History* 34 (1990), 119–67. On expanding grounds and the cultural transitions that underpinned them see Robert L. Griswold, "The Evolution of the Doctrine of Mental Cruelty in Victorian American Divorce, 1790–1900," *Journal of Social History* 20 (1986), 127–48 and Griswold, "Law, Sex, Cruelty and Divorce in Victorian America, 1840–1900," *American Quarterly* 38 (1986), 721–45. On cruelty see also Elizabeth Pleck, *Domestic Tyranny: The Making of Social Policy Against Family Violence from Colonial Times to the Present* (New York, 1987). On the analogies constructed by liberal women's rights activists between the bonds of marriage and the bonds of slavery, see Elizabeth B. Clark, "Matrimonial Bonds: Slavery and Divorce in

Nineteenth-Century America," *Law and History Review* 8 (1990), 25–54 and Clark, "Self-Ownership and the Political Theory of Elizabeth Cady Stanton, *Connecticut Law Review* 21 (1989), 905–41.

Comprehensive coverage of the married women's property acts is complicated by federalism and the same state-by-state divergences that plague other aspects of American family law. Marylynn Salmon provides a formidable and geographically broad foundation for understanding the legal status of wives before the advent of formal married women's property statutes in *Women and the Law of Property in Early America* (Chapel Hill, NC, 1986). Overviews of the statutes and their adjudication include Reva B. Siegel, "Home as Work: The First Women's Rights Claims concerning Wives' Household Labor, 1850–1880," *Yale Law Journal* 103 (1994), 1073–1217 and Siegel, "The Modernization of Marital Status Law: Adjudicating Wives' Rights to Earnings, 1860–1930," *Georgetown Law Journal* 82 (1994), 2127–2211, which should be read in conjunction with Jean Boydston, *Home and Work: Housework, Wages, and the Ideology of Labor in the Early Republic* (New York, 1990); Richard H. Chused, "Married Women's Property Law: 1800–1850," *Georgetown Law Journal* 71 (1983), 1359–1425; and Chused, "Late Nineteenth-Century Married Women's Property Law: Reception of the Early Married Women's Property Acts by Courts and Legislatures," *American Journal of Legal History* 29 (1985), 3–35; Linda Speth, "The Married Women's Property Acts, 1839–1865: Reform, Reaction, or Revolution?," in D. Kelly Weisberg, ed., *Women and the Law: A Social Historical Perspective*, 2 vols. (New York 1982), 2:69–91; Carole Shammas, "Re-assessing the Married Women's Property Acts," *Journal of Women's History* 6 (1994), 9–30; and Elizabeth Bowles Warbasse, *The Changing Legal Rights of Married Women, 1800–1861* (New York, 1987).

Regional, state, and local studies of marital property reforms include Norma Basch, *In the Eyes of the Law: Women, Marriage and Property in Nineteenth-Century New York* (Ithaca, NY, 1982); Suzanne Lebsock, *The Free Women of Petersburg: Status and Culture in a Southern Town, 1784–1860* (New York, 1984); and Lebsock, "Radical Reconstruction and the Property Rights of Southern Women," *Journal of Southern History* 43 (1977), 195–216; Peggy A. Rabkin, *Fathers to Daughters: The Legal Foundations of Female Emancipation* (Westport, 1980); Catherine B. Cleary, "Married Women's Property Rights in Wisconsin, 1846–1872," *Wisconsin Magazine of History* 78 (1994–1995), 110–37; Kathleen Elizabeth Lazarou, *Concealed Under Petticoats: Married Women's Property and the Law of Texas, 1840–1913* (New York, 1986); and Dianne Avery and Alfred S. Konefsky, "The Daughters of Job: Property Rights and Women's Lives in Mid-Nineteenth-Century Massachusetts," *Law and History Review* 10 (1992, 323–56. On marital property and female homesteading on federal territory, see Richard H. Chused, "The Oregon Donation Act of 1850 and Nineteenth Century Federal Married Women's Property Law," *Law and History Review* 2 (1984), 44–78. John Fabian Witt delineates new asymmetries between husband and wife in wrongful death actions in "From Loss of Services to Loss of Support: The Wrongful Death Statutes, the Origins of Modern Tort Law, and the Making of the Nineteenth-Century Family," *Law and Social Inquiry* 25 (2000), 717–55.

Norma Basch analyzes the political ramifications of recognizing married women's property rights in "Equity versus Equality: Emerging Notions of Women's Political Status in the Age of Jackson," *Journal of the Early Republic* 3 (1983), 297–318.

Mary Ann Mason provides an overview of the history of child custody in *From Father's Property to Children's Rights: A History of Child Custody in the United States* (New York 1994) while Michael Grossberg elegantly charts the trend toward maternalism through a single case in *A Judgment for Solomon: The D'Hautevelle Case and Legal Experience in Antebellum America* (New York, 1996). See also Grossberg, "Who Gets the Child? Custody, Guardianship, and the Rise of a Judicial Patriarchy in Nineteenth-Century America," *Feminist Studies* 9 (1983), 83–95 and Jamil S. Zainaldin, "The Emergence of a Modern American Family Law: Child Custody, Adoption, and the Courts, 1796–1851," *Northwestern University Law Review* 73 (1979), 1038–89. Although focused on the modern sealing of adoption records, E. Wayne Carp, in the process of outlining an earlier ethos of openness, provides an excellent introduction to the history of adoption in *Family Matters: Secrecy and Disclosure in the History of Adoption* (Cambridge, MA, 1998). See also Yasuhide Kawashima, "Adoption in Early America," *Journal of Family Law* 20 (1982), 677–96; Joseph Ben-Or, "The Law of Adoption in the United States: Its Massachusetts Origins and the Statute of 1851," *New England Historical and Genealogical Register* 130 (1976), 259–69; Stephen B. Presser, "The Historical Background of the American Law of Adoption," *Journal of Family Law* 11 (1971), 447–86; Leo Albert Huard, "The Law of Adoption: Ancient and Modern," *Vanderbilt Law Review* 9 (1956), 743–77; and Julie Berebitsky, *Like Our Very Own: Adoption and the Changing Culture of Motherhood* (Lawrence, KA, 2000). On the treatment of orphans, see Linda Gordon, *The Great Arizona Orphan Abduction* (Cambridge, MA, 2001).

Reconstruction is a watershed of sorts in family law not only because of the ties between marriage and slavery, which were both "domestic relations," but because of new federal policies regarding both the marriage of freedpersons and the administration of military pensions. Critical to understanding the limits and hazards of contractual freedom in the wake of Reconstruction is Amy Dru Stanley's *From Bondage to Contract: Wage Labor, Marriage, and the Market in the Age of Slave Emancipation* (New York, 1998).The literature on debates over the Fourteenth Amendment is vast, but on the desire of Congress to sustain state control over domestic relations other than slavery, see William E. Nelson, *The Fourteenth Amendment: From Political Principle to Judicial Doctrine* (Cambridge, MA, 1988). Megan J. McClintock details the federal intervention in marriage through the administration of federal pensions in "Civil War Pensions and the Reconstruction of Union Families," *Journal of American History* 83 (1996),

456–80. On freedmen, freedwomen, and marriage, see Laura P. Edwards, "'The Marriage Covenant is at the Foundation of All Our Rights': The Politics of Slave Marriages in North Carolina after Emancipation," *Law and History Review* 14 (1990), 81–124; and Edwards, *Gendered Strife and Confusion: The Political Culture of Reconstruction* (Urbana, 1997); Katherine M. Franke, "Becoming a Citizen: Reconstruction Era Regulation of African American Marriages," *Yale Journal of Law and Humanities* 11 (1999), 251–309; Donald Nieman, *To Set the Law in Motion: The Freedmen's Bureau and the Legal Rights of Blacks, 1865–1868* (Millwood, NY, 1979); and Herbert Gutman, *The Black Family in Slavery and Freedom, 1750–1925* (New York, 1976). For "miscegenation" and interracial marriage see Martha Hodes, *White Women, Black Men: Illicit Sex in the Nineteenth-Century South* (New Haven, 1998); Emily Field Van Tassel, "'Only the Law Would Rule between Us': Antimiscegenation, the Moral Economy of Dependency, and the Debate over Rights after the Civil War," *Chicago-Kent Law Review* 70 (1995), 873–926; Diane Miller Sommerville, "The Rape Myth in the Old South Reconsidered," *Journal of Southern History* 61 (1995), 481–518; Peter Wallenstein, "Race, Marriage and the Law of Freedom: Alabama and Virginia, 1860s-1960s," *Chicago-Kent Law Review* 70 (1994), 371–438; and Peggy Pascoe, "Miscegenation Law, Court Cases, and Ideologies of 'Race' in Twentieth-Century America, *Journal of American History* 83 (1996), 44–69.

Sarah Barringer Gordon expertly dissects the federal government's unremitting assault on polygamy in *The Mormon Question: Polygamy and Constitutional Conflict in Nineteenth-Century America* (Chapel Hill, NC, 2002); see also Douglas Parker, "Victory in Defeat: Polygamy and the Mormon Legal Encounter with the Federal Government," *Cardozo Law Review* 12 (1991), 805–19; Carol Cornwall Madsen, "'At Their Peril': Utah Law and the Case of Plural Wives," *Western Historical Quarterly* 2 (1990), 425–43; Carol Weisbrod and Pamela Sheingorn, "*Reynolds v. United States*: Nineteenth-Century Forms of Marriage and the Status of Women," *Connecticut Law Review* 10 (1978), 1828–58; and Orma Linford, "The Mormons and the Law: The Polygamy Cases," *Utah Law Review* 9 (1964–1965), 308–70, 543–91.

For a general history of American sexual attitudes, see John D'Emilio and Estelle B. Freedman, *Intimate Matters: A History of Sexuality in America* (New York, 1974). On Comstock and comstockery, see Nicola Beisel, *Imperiled Innocents: Anthony Comstock and Family Reproduction in Victorian America* (Princeton, 1997); Helen Lefkowitz Horowitz, "Victoria Woodhull, Anthony Comstock, and Conflict over Sex in the United States, *Journal of American History* 87 (2000), 403–34; and Horowitz, *Sex Battles over Sexual Knowledge and Suppression in Nineteenth-Century America* (New York, 2002). On contraception and abortion, see Andrea Tone, *Devices and Desires: A History of Contraception in America* (New York, 2001); Janet Farrell Brodie, *Contraception and Abortion in Nineteenth-Century America* (Ithaca, NY, 1994); Leslie Reagan, *When Abortion Was a Crime: Women, Medicine and the Law in the United States, 1867–1973* (Berkeley, 1997);

James C. Mohr, *Abortion in America: The Origins and Evolution of National Policy, 1800–1900* (New York, 1978); James Reed, *From Private Vice to Public Virtue: The Birth Control Movement in American Society Since 1830* (New York, 1978); and Linda Gordon, *Woman's Body, Woman's Right: A Social History of Birth Control in America* (New York, 1974).

CHAPTER 9: SLAVERY, ANTI-SLAVERY, AND THE COMING OF THE CIVIL WAR

ARIELA GROSS

Primary Sources

Some of the best resources for the study of law and slavery are the cases themselves. A terrific guide to cases involving slaves is Helen Catterall, *Judicial Cases Concerning American Slavery and the Negro* (New York, 1968). In five volumes, Catterall collected brief excerpts of every reported state supreme court case in which a slave is mentioned and indexed them by subject. Many state archives and libraries retain the trial records of these cases in their collections; some county courthouses still have the trial records from lower courts as well.

There is a wonderful collection of manumission suit records on the Web site of the St. Louis Circuit Court Historical Records Project, http://stlcourtrecords.wustl.edu.

Few treatises were written on the law of slavery, but they are fascinating ideological documents. Thomas R.R. Cobb, *An Inquiry into the Law of Negro Slavery in the United States of America* (reprint ed., New York, 1968) is the first volume of an intended two-volume set, which is an apology for the institution. John Belton O'Neall, *The Negro Law of South Carolina* (Columbia, SC, 1848) was disavowed by the State of South Carolina after it commissioned the work because it was too reformist. Other compendia of laws regarding slaves were written by abolitionists: William Goodell, *The American Slave Code in Theory and Practice* (New York, 1853) and *The Law of Freedom and Bondage in the United States*, 2 vols. (Boston, 1858), and George M. Stroud, *A Sketch of the Laws Relating to Slavery in the Several States of the United States of America* (reprint ed., New York, 1968). The only book written as an actual resource for lawyers was Jacob D. Wheeler, *A Practical Treatise on the Law of Slavery* (reprint ed., New York, 1968).

Also useful for the student of slavery and the law are ex-slaves' narratives, including Charles Ball, *Fifty Years in Chains, or, The Life of An American Slave* (Detroit, 1969); John W. Blassingame, ed., *Slave Testimony: Two Centuries of Letters, Speeches, Interviews, and Autobiographies* (Baton Rouge, LA, 1977); John Brown, *Slave Life in Georgia: A Narrative of the Life, Sufferings, and Escape of John Brown, Fugitive Slave* (Savannah, GA, 1972); William and Ellen Craft, *Running a Thousand Miles for Freedom* (reprint ed., New York 1969); Frederick Douglas, *The Frederick Douglas Papers* (New Haven, CT, 1979); Frederick Douglas, *My*

Bondage and My Freedom (New York, 1969); Harriet Jacobs, *Incidents in The Life of A Slave Girl* (reprint ed., New York, 1988); Gilbert Osofsky, ed., *Puttin' on Ole Massa: The Slave Narratives of Henry Bibb, William Wells Brown, and Solomon Northrup* (New York, 1969); and Terry Alford, *Prince Among Slaves* (New York, 1977).

Everyday Law of Slavery

Much of the discussion of the everyday law of slavery in the chapter is drawn from Ariela J. Gross, *Double Character: Slavery and Mastery in the Antebellum Southern* Courtroom (Princeton, NJ, 2000). For a comprehensive overview of slavery and the law in the U.S. South, see Thomas D. Morris, *Southern Slavery and the Law, 1619–1860* (Chapel Hill, NC, 1996). Walter Johnson, "Inconsistency Contradiction, and Complete Confusion: The Everyday Life of the Law of Slavery," *Law & Social Inquiry* 22 (1997) reviews this book and gives an excellent critical review of the debate over slavery, liberalism, and capitalism in the U.S. South.

For general interpretations of the relationship of law, capitalism, and slavery, one must start with Eugene D. Genovese, *Roll, Jordan, Roll: The World The Slaveholders Made* (New York, 1976), 25–46. Mark Tushnet, *The American Law of Slavery, 1810–1860: Considerations of Humanity and Interest* (Princeton, NJ, 1981) carries forward many of Genovese's insights in a book-length treatment; Genovese reviews the book in Eugene D. Genovese, "Slavery in the Legal History of the South and the Nation," *Texas Law Review* 59 (1981) 969–98. James Oakes, *Slavery and Freedom: An Interpretation of the Old South* (New York, 1990) gives an alternative view of slaveholders as liberal capitalists and contains an excellent discussion of slavery and liberalism. Perhaps the most extreme version of this interpretation is Robert W. Fogel, *Without Consent or Contract: The Rise and Fall of American Slavery* (New York, 1989), an updated version of Robert W. Fogel and Stanley L. Engerman, *Time on the Cross: The Economics of American Negro Slavery*, 2 vols. (New York, 1989). Perhaps the most persuasive interpretation of slavery and the economy by an economic historian is offered by Gavin Wright in *The Political Economy of The Cotton South: Households, Markets and Wealth in the Nineteenth Century* (New York, 1978) and *Old South, New South: Revolutions in the Southern Economy Since The Civil War* (New York, 1986). Jenny Bourne Wahl, *The Bondsman's Burden: An Economic Analysis of the Common Law of Southern Slavery* (New York, 1998) somewhat mechanistically applies the notion that the common law seeks efficiency to lawsuits regarding slaves. Alan Watson, *Slave Law in the Americas* (Athens, GA, 1989) puts U.S. slavery law in comparative context.

There has not been a great deal of intellectual history on slavery law. Two important pieces are Gregory Alexander, *Commodity & Propriety: Competing Visions of Property in American Legal Thought, 1776–1970* (Chicago, 1997), putting slavery in the context of property theory and law, and William W.

Fisher, III, "Ideology and Imagery in the Law of Slavery," *Chicago-Kent Law Review* 68 (1993), 1051–86, examining the rhetoric of slave cases. Patricia Williams, *The Alchemy of Race and Rights* (New York, 1991) has an insightful exploration of the meaning of property from the slave's perspective. Jon-Christian Suggs, *Whispered Consolations: Law and Narrative in African American Life* (Ann Arbor, MI, 2000) provides insight into slaves' understanding of law in their daily lives.

For general treatments of whether the U.S. South developed a distinctive legal system, see Paul Finkelman, "Exploring Southern Legal History," *North Carolina Law Review* 64 (1985), 77–116, as well as the essays collected in David J. Bodenhamer and James W. Ely, Jr., eds., *Ambivalent Legacy: A Legal History of the South* (Jackson, MS, 1984).

On slavery, family law, and sexuality, see Margaret Burnham, "An Impossible Marriage: Slave Law and Family Law," *Law and Inequality* 5 (1987), 187–225, and A. Leon Higginbotham, Jr. and Barbara K. Kopytoff, "Racial Purity and Interracial Sex in the Law of Colonial and Antebellum Virginia," *Georgetown Law Journal* 77 (1989), 1967–2029. A wonderful study of a single case in which an enslaved rape victim fought back – and stood trial for the murder of her master – is Melton A. McLaurin, *Celia: A Slave* (Athens, GA, 1991). Dylan C. Penningroth, *The Claims of Kinfolk: African American Property and Community in the Nineteenth-Century South* (Chapel Hill, NC, 2003) is a brilliant treatment of the relationship between family and property claims among African Americans before and after slavery, drawing heavily on local court records. Important works on the slave family more generally include Herbert Gutman, *The Black Family in Slavery and Freedom, 1750–1925* (New York, 1976), Brenda Stevenson, *Life in Black and White: Family and Community in the Slave South* (New York, 1996), and Cheryll Ann Cody, "There Was No 'Absalom' on the Ball Plantations: Slave-Naming Practices in the South Carolina Low Country, 1720–1865," *American Historical Review* 92 (1987).

One of the best books on slavery and criminal law is Edward L. Ayers, *Vengeance and Justice: Crime and Punishment in the 19th-Century American South* (New York, 1984). Christopher Waldrep, *Roots of Disorder: Race and Criminal Justice in the American South 1817–1880* (Urbana, IL, 1998) compares legal and extra-legal forms of racial control before and after the Civil War. Sally E. Hadden, *Slave Patrols: Law and Violence in Virginia and the Carolinas* (Cambridge, MA, 2001) is an excellent study of the foremost mechanism of law enforcement in the South.

Early writing on slavery and criminal justice tended to emphasize the procedural protections afforded slaves in criminal trials. See, e.g., Daniel J. Flanigan, "Criminal Procedure in Slave Trials in the Antebellum South," *Journal of Southern History* 40 (1974), 537–64; A.E. Keir Nash, "A More Equitable Past? Southern Supreme Courts and the Protection of the Antebellum Negro," *North Carolina Law Review* 48 (1970), 197–241; A.E. Keir Nash, "Fairness and Formalism in the Trials of Blacks in the State Supreme Courts of the Old South," *Virginia Law Review* 56 (1970), 64–100; A.E. Keir Nash, "Negro Rights, Unionism, and Greatness on the South Carolina Court of Appeals: The Extraordinary Chief Justice John Belton O'Neall," *South Carolina Law Review* 21 (1969), 141–90; and Arthur F. Howington, *What Sayeth the Law: The Treatment of Slaves and Free Blacks in the State and Local Courts of Tennessee* (New York, 1986). For a rather different view, see Judith K. Schafer, "The Long Arm of the Law: Slave Criminals and the Supreme Court in Antebellum Louisiana," *Tulane Law Review* 60 (1986), 1247–68 and Philip J. Schwarz, *Twice Condemned: Slaves and the Criminal Laws of Virginia, 1705–1865* (Baton Rouge, LA, 1988).

Much of the writing regarding the everyday law of slavery has been occupied with the question of whether particular legal rules, such as "caveat emptor" or the "fellow servant rule," played out differently in the South than in the North. This evidence is offered to prove or disprove the thesis that slavery was a paternalist or a capitalist system. Articles in this vein include Robert J. Cottrol, "Liberalism and Paternalism: Ideology, Economic Interest, and the Business Law of Slavery," *American Journal of Legal History* 31 (1987), 359–73; Andrew Fede, "Legal Protection for Slave Buyers in the U.S. South: A Caveat Concerning *Caveat Emptor*," *American Journal of Legal History* 31 (1987), 322–58; and Paul Finkelman, "Slaves as Fellow Servants: Ideology, Law, and Industrialization," *American Journal of Legal History* 31 (1987), 269–305.

Other works have emphasized the question of whether slaves were in fact "persons" or merely "property" under the law: A. Leon Higginbotham, Jr. and Barbara K. Kopytoff, "Property First, Humanity Second: The Recognition of the Slave's Human Nature in Virginia Civil Law," *Ohio State Law Journal* 50 (1989) 511–40; Arthur F. Howington, "'Not in the Condition of a Horse or an Ox,'" *Tennessee Historical Quarterly* 34 (1975), 249–63; and J. Thomas Wren, "A Two-Fold Character: The Slave as Person and Property," *Southern Studies* 24 (1985), 417–31.

Thomas Russell's work demonstrates the central role the state played in the slave market: see "A New Image of the Slave Auction: An Empirical Look at the Role of Law in Slave Sales and a Conceptual Reevaluation of Slave Property," *Cardozo Law Review* 18 (1996), 473–524; "Articles Sell Best Singly: The Disruption of Slave Families at Court Sales," *Utah Law Review* (1996), 1161–1208; and "South Carolina's Largest Slave Auctioneering Firm," *Chicago-Kent Law Review* 68 (1993), 1241–82.

Other important works for the study of the commercial law of slavery include Judith K. Schafer, *Slavery, Civil Law and the Supreme Court of Louisiana* (Baton Rouge, LA, 1994); Walter Johnson, *Soul by Soul: Life Inside the Antebellum Slave Market* (Cambridge, MA 1999); Richard H. Kilbourne, Jr., *Debt, Investment, Slaves: Credit Relations in East Feliciana Parish, Louisiana, 1825–1885* (Tuscaloosa, AL, 1995); and Jonathan D. Martin, *Divided Mastery: Slave Hiring in the American South* (Cambridge, MA, 2004).

Slavery and the Constitution/Abolitionism
On slavery and the issue of comity, see Paul Finkelman, *An Imperfect Union: Slavery, Federalism, and Comity* (Chapel Hill, NC, 1981). Still one of the best sources on anti-slavery and the Constitution is William Wiecek, *The Sources of Anti-Slavery Constitutionalism in America, 1760–1848* (Ithaca, NY, 1977). Harold M. Hyman and William M. Wiecek, *Equal Justice Under Law: Constitutional Development 1835–1875* (New York, 1982) gives a broad overview of the constitutional crisis and its aftermath. See also Mark E. Brandon, *Free in the World: American Slavery and Constitutional Failure* (Princeton, NJ, 1998).

Other important works on abolitionism include James Oliver Horton and Lois E. Horton, *In Hope of Liberty: Culture, Community and Protest Among Northern Free Blacks, 1700–1860* (New York, 1997); Peter P. Hinks, *To Awaken My Afflicted Brethren: David Walker and the Problem of Antebellum Slave Resistance* (University Park, PA, 1997); Ronald G. Walters, *The Antislavery Appeal: American Abolitionism After 1830* (Baltimore, 1976); Julie Roy Jeffrey, *The Great Silent Army of Abolitionism: Ordinary Women in the Antislavery Movement* (Chapel Hill, NC, 1998); Richard S. Newman, *The Transformation of American Abolitionism: Fighting Slavery in the Early Republic* (Chapel Hill, NC, 2002); Demetrius L. Eudell, *The Political Language of Emancipation in the British Caribbean and the U.S. South* (Chapel Hill, 2002); Patrick J. Rael, *Black Identity and Black Protest in the Antebellum North* (Chapel Hill, NC, 2002); David A.J. Richards "Abolitionist Feminism, Moral Slavery, and the Constitution: 'On the Same Platform of Human Rights,'" *Cardozo Law Review* 18 (1996), 767–843; J. Morgan Kousser, "'The Supremacy of Equal Rights': The Struggle Against Racial Discrimination in Antebellum Massachusetts and The Foundations of The Fourteenth Amendment," *Northwestern University Law Review* 82 (1988), 941–1010; James O. Horton & Lois E. Horton, "A Federal Assault: African Americans and The Impact of The Fugitive Slave Law of 1850," *Chicago-Kent Law Review* 68 (1993), 1179–97; David A.J. Richards, "Public Reason and Abolitionist Dissent, *Chicago-Kent Law Review* 69 (1994), 787–842; and Elizabeth B. Clark, "'The Sacred Rights of the Weak': Pain, Sympathy, and the Culture of Individual Rights in Antebellum America," *Journal of American History* (1995), 463–93.

On pro-slavery constitutionalism, see James Oakes, "'The Compromising Expedient': Justifying a Proslavery Constitution," *Cardozo Law Review* 17 (1996), 2023–56; John Patrick Daly, *When Slavery Was Called Freedom: Evangelicalism, Proslavery and the Causes of the Civil War* (Lexington, KY, 2002); and Kermit L. Hall and James W. Ely, Jr., eds., *An Uncertain Tradition: Constitutionalism an the History of the South* (Athens, GA, 1989).

The leading book on the Dred Scott case is still Don E. Fehrenbacher, *Slavery, Law, and Politics: The Dred Scott Case in Historical Perspective* (New York, 1981). See also Earl M. Maltz, "The Unlikely Hero of Dred Scott: Benjamin Robbins Curtis and the Constitutional Law of Slavery," *Cardozo Law Review* 17 (1996),

1995–2016; Lea S. VanderVelde and Sandhya Subramanian, "Mrs. Dred Scott," *Yale Law Journal* 106 (1996), 1047–1120; and the introductory essay to Paul Finkelman, *Dred Scott v. Sandford: A Brief History with Documents* (New York, 1997). On *Prigg v. Pennsylvania*, see Barbara Holden-Smith, "Lords of Lash, Loom, and Law: Justice Story, Slavery, and *Prigg v. Pennsylvania*," *Cornell Law Review* 78 (1993), 1086–1149 and Earl M. Maltz, "Majority, Concurrence, and Dissent: *Prigg v. Pennsylvania* and the Structure of Supreme Court Decisionmaking," *Rutgers Law Journal* 31 (2000), 345–398. Another important fugitive slave case is discussed in Paul Finkelman "Slavery And Legal Ethics: Legal Ethics and Fugitive Slaves: The Anthony Burns Case, Judge Loring, and Abolitionist Attorneys," *Cardozo Law Review* 17 (1996), 1793–1858. The personal liberty laws are discussed in Thomas D. Morris, *Free Men All: The Personal Liberty Laws of the North 1780–1861* (Baltimore, 1974).

CHAPTER 10: THE CIVIL WAR AND RECONSTRUCTION

LAURA F. EDWARDS

This chapter brings together four strands in the historiography of the Civil War and Reconstruction: the legal history of the period, which tends to focus on the institutional development of law and government; scholarship on African American history and Southern history, which has roots in social history; women's history and recent work inspired by feminist theory that views the period through the analytical lens of gender; and scholarship on questions of labor in the nineteenth century, which tend to cluster in either the antebellum or the postwar period, but which does not always deal directly with the Civil War and Reconstruction.

Traditionally, legal and political histories of the Civil War and Reconstruction have tended to focus on federal policy, particularly the implications of the Reconstruction amendments not only for the status of African Americans but also for the trajectory of constitutional law and the powers of the federal government. Because the emphasis is on federal policy, the focus tends to be on dynamics in the national government and abstract debates about racial inequality rather than on domestic conditions within the South, where those policies were directed (at least initially). See, for instance, Bruce Ackerman, *We the People, vol. 2: Transformations* (Cambridge, MA, 1998); Herman Belz, *Abraham Lincoln, Constitutionalism, and Equal Rights in the Civil War* (New York, 1998); Michael Les Benedict, *A Compromise of Principle: Congressional Republicans and Reconstruction, 1863–1869* (New York, 1974); Richard Franklin Bensel, *Yankee Leviathan: The Origins of Central State Authority in America, 1859–1877* (Cambridge, 1990); LaWanda Cox and John H. Cox, *Politics, Principle, and Prejudice, 1865–1866: Dilemma of Reconstruction America* (New York, 1963); Harold Hyman, *A More Perfect Union: The Impact of the Civil War and Reconstruction on the Constitution* (New York, 1973); David E. Kyvig, *Explicit and Authentic Acts: Amending the U.S. Constitution, 1776–1995* (Lawrence, KS, 1996); William E.

Nelson, *The Fourteenth Amendment: From Political Principle to Judicial Doctrine* (Cambridge, MA, 1988); and Phillip S. Paludan, *A Covenant with Death: The Constitution, Law, and Equality in the Civil War Era* (Urbana, IL, 1975). While focusing on the same issues, recent work has rooted legal and political debates in social context, revealing new complexities and contingencies. See, for instance, Michael Vorenburg, *Final Freedom: The Civil War, the Abolition of Slavery, and the Thirteenth Amendment* (New York, 2001). Eric Foner's *Reconstruction: America's Unfinished Revolution* (New York, 1988) combines not only the traditional emphasis of legal and political history with social history but also scholarship on the South and the North.

The work on the Civil War and Reconstruction associated with or inspired by the Freedmen and Southern Society project, based at the University of Maryland, moved the scholarly focus to the South. The volumes in the project deal with federal policies, but consider Southern African Americans' interaction with them. They also integrate questions about the South's transition to capitalist production into a narrative traditionally concerned with the connection between race and civil and political rights. For early pivotal work in the series, see Ira Berlin, Joseph P. Reidy, and Leslie S. Rowland, eds., *Freedom: A Documentary History of Emancipation, 1861–1867, Series 2: The Black Military Experience* (New York, 1982); Ira Berlin, Barbara J. Fields, Thavolia Glymph, Joseph P. Reidy, and Leslie S. Rowland, eds., *Freedom: A Documentary History of Emancipation, 1861–1867, Series 1, vol. 1: The Destruction of Slavery* (New York, 1985); and Ira Berlin, Stephen F. Miller, and Leslie S. Rowland, eds. "Afro-American Families in the Transition from Slavery to Freedom," *Radical History Review* 42 (1988), 89–121. For related scholarship, see Barbara J. Fields, *Slavery and Freedom on the Middle Ground: Maryland during the Nineteenth Century* (New Haven, 1985); Eric Foner, *Nothing But Freedom: Emancipation and Its Legacy* (Baton Rouge, LA, 1983); and Julie Saville, *The Work of Reconstruction: From Slave to Wage Laborer in South Carolina, 1860–1870* (New York, 1994). This scholarship is influenced by comparative approaches to emancipation, which also emphasizes freedpersons' political agency and labor relations. See for instance, Thomas C. Holt, *The Problem of Freedom: Race, Labor, and Politics in Jamaica and Britain* (Baltimore, 1992). This body of work also owes an intellectual debt to W. E. B. DuBois's *Black Reconstruction: An Essay Toward a History of the Part Which Black Folk Played in the Attempt to Reconstruct Democracy in America, 1860–1880* (New York, 1935).

One important implication of this approach has been the recovery and analysis of African Americans' use of law in a variety of forums, including the federal army, the Freedmen's Bureau, and state and local courts. See Nancy D. Bercaw, *Gendered Freedoms: Race, Rights, and the Politics of Household in the Delta, 1861–1875* (Gainesville, FL, 2003); Laura F. Edwards, *Gendered Strife and Confusion: The Political Culture of Reconstruction* (Urbana, IL, 1997); Noralee Frankel, *Freedom's Women: Black Women and Families in Civil War Era Mississippi* (Bloomington, IN, 1999); Dylan Penningroth, *The Claims of Kinfolk: African*

American Property and Community in the Nineteenth-Century South (Chapel Hill, NC, 2003); Diane Miller Sommerville, *Rape and Race in the Nineteenth-Century South* (Chapel Hill, NC, 2004); and Leslie A. Schwalm, *A Hard Fight for We: Women's Transition from Slavery to Freedom in South Carolina* (Urbana, IL, 1997). In its emphasis on African Americans' use of law, such work is related to but distinct from scholarship in Southern legal history, which tends to focus on the institutional development of law. See, for instance, Edward L. Ayers, *Vengeance and Justice: Crime and Punishment in the Nineteenth-Century American South* (New York, 1984); Michael S. Hindus, *Prison and Plantation: Crime, Justice, and Authority in Massachusetts and South Carolina, 1767–1878* (Chapel Hill, NC, 1980); and Christopher Waldrep, *Roots of Disorder: Race and Criminal Justice in the American South, 1817–80* (Urbana, IL, 1998).

Scholarship in Southern history has traditionally emphasized politics and policy, both military and civilian, highlighting the experiences of white Southerners who supported the Confederacy. Influenced by social history, the scholarship on emancipation, and the legacy of C. Vann Woodward's *Origins of the New South, 1877–1913* (Baton Rouge, LA, 1951), recent work has considered class divisions and political conflict among white Southerners both before and after the Civil War. Although not specifically about legal issues, this work suggests vast differences among whites in the region that ultimately shaped law and government not only within the Confederacy but also at the state level after Reconstruction. See, for instance, Daniel W. Crofts, *Reluctant Confederates: Upper South Unionists in the Secession Crisis* (Chapel Hill, NC, 1989); Wayne K. Durrill, *War of Another Kind: A Southern Community in the Great Rebellion* (New York, 1990); Paul D. Escott, *Many Excellent People: Power and Privilege in North Carolina, 1850–1900* (Chapel Hill, NC, 1985); Drew Gilpin Faust, *Mothers of Invention: Women of the Slaveholding South in the American Civil War* (Chapel Hill, NC, 1996); Steven Hahn, *The Roots of Southern Populism: Yeoman Farmers and the Transformation of the Georgia Upcountry, 1850–1890* (New York, 1983); and Armstead Robinston, "Beyond the Realm of Social Consensus: New Meanings of Reconstruction for American History," *Journal of American History* 68 (1981), 276–97. A related body of scholarship has considered the development of sharecropping, tracing the legal and economic development of an institution that defined the region's poverty: Roger L. Ransom and Richard Sutch, *One Kind of Freedom: The Economic Consequences of Emancipation* (Cambridge, 1977); Jonathan Weiner, "AHR Forum: Class Structure and Economic Development in the American South, 1865–1955," *American Historical Review* 84 (1979), 970–1006; and Harold D. Woodman, *New South, New Law: The Legal Foundations of Credit and Labor Relations in the Postbellum Agricultural South* (Baton Rouge, LA, 1995).

The work on gender has emphasized connections among forms of legal inequality that historians once treated separately, highlighting similarities among race, class, and gender and positing new ways of understanding the experiences of men and women of both races in this period. By placing women at the center of the analysis, this body of scholarship also challenges traditional narratives that emphasize the expansion and then retraction of civil and political rights in this period. In particular, see: Peter W. Bardaglio, *Reconstructing the Household: Families, Sex, and the Law in the Nineteenth-Century South* (Chapel Hill, NC, 1995); Bercaw, *Gendered Freedoms*; Nancy Cott, *Public Vows: A History of Marriage and the Nation* (Cambridge, MA, 2000); Edwards, *Gendered Strife and Confusion*; Schwalm, *A Hard Fight for We*; Amy Dru Stanley, *From Bondage to Contract: Wage Labor, Marriage, and the Market in the Age of Slave Emancipation* (New York, 1998); LeeAnn Whites, *The Civil War as a Crisis in Gender: Augusta, Georgia, 1860–1890* (Athens, GA, 1995). The scholarship on Northern white women's activism reveals important – often problematic – connections between efforts to achieve racial and gender equality. See, for instance, Ellen Carol DuBois, *Feminism and Suffrage: The Emergence of an Independent Women's Movement in America, 1848–1869* (Ithaca, NY, 1978); Carol Faulkner, *Women's Radical Reconstruction: The Freedmen's Aid Movement* (Philadelphia, 2004); Nancy A. Hewitt, *Women's Activism and Social Change: Rochester, New York, 1822–1872* (Ithaca, NY, 1984); Julie Roy Jeffrey, *The Great Silent Army of Abolitionism: Ordinary Women in the Anti-Slavery Movement* (Chapel Hill, NC, 1998); and Louise Michele Newman, *White Women's Rights: The Racal Origins of Feminism in the United States* (New York, 1999).

The status of working people and the labor movement has long been associated with the historiography on the Civil War and Reconstruction. See Eric Foner, *Free Soil, Free Labor, Free Men: The Ideology of the Republican Party Before the Civil War* (New York, 1970) and David Montgomery, *Beyond Equality: Labor and the Radical Republicans, 1862–1872* (New York, 1967). Recent work in labor history has highlighted the inequalities inherent within the concept of free labor before and after the Civil War. The emphasis on the limitations of laborers' legal rights also suggests the parallels between the legal status of working-class men and other subordinated groups, namely African Americans and women. See William E. Forbath, "The Ambiguities of Free Labor: Labor and the Law in the Gilded Age," *Wisconsin Law Review* 4 (1985), 767–817; Cindy Hahamovitch, *The Fruits of Their Labor: Atlantic Coast Farmworkers and the Making of Migrant Poverty, 1870–1945* (Chapel Hill, NC, 1997); Alex Lichtenstein, *Twice the Work of Free Labor: The Political Economy of Convict Labor in the New South* (New York, 1996); Gunther Peck, *Reinventing Free Labor: Padrones and Immigrant Workers in the North American West, 1880–1930* (Cambridge, 2000); Robert J. Steinfeld, *The Invention of Free Labor: The Employment Relation in English and American Law and Culture, 1350–1870* (Chapel Hill, NC, 1991); Steinfeld, *Coercion, Contract, and Free Labor in the Nineteenth Century* (Cambridge, 2001); and Christopher L. Tomlins, *Law, Labor, and Ideology in the Early American Republic* (New York, 1993). Other work makes explicit connections between class and gender in the problematic place of wage laborers outside the South. See, for instance, Eileen

Boris, *Home to Work: Motherhood and the Politics of Industrial Homework in the United States* (New York, 1994); Jeanne Boydston, *Home and Work: Housework, Wages, and the Ideology of Labor in the Early Republic* (New York, 1990); and Stanley, *From Bondage to Contract.*

CHAPTER 11: LAW, PERSONHOOD, AND CITIZENSHIP IN THE LONG NINETEENTH CENTURY

BARBARA YOUNG WELKE

In conceptualizing legal individuality in the long nineteenth century, I found myself again and again drawn to the visual image of a tessellation. A tessellation is formed by the repetition of a shape or set of shapes covering a plane without gaps or overlapping. Whether the term or definition is familiar or not, I suspect that every reader has seen one. The most famous may be those of M. C. Escher. Examples from his work can serve for the uninitiated. Escher's *Reptiles* (1943) features a single repeating image of a lizard in different rotations. His *Mosaic II* (1957), is constructed from (or yields) a series of creatures, statues, and objects. (For examples of Escher tessellations and an introduction to tessellation generally, see http://library.thinkquest.org/16661/escher.html) Three features are critical: a figure or figures are repeated, the borders of each figure give shape to adjacent figures, and collectively the figures cover the plane. Hence, no single shape in a tessellation is self-defining; they are interlocked and interdependent. Equally critically to my project, tessellations are often visually confusing; some shapes remain in the background, even as they give definition to others.

This essay offers points of access to pursue in the project of tessellating the borders of belonging as the first step in constructing a literature that has not fully acknowledged itself. Scholars in a range of subfields, including women's, Native American, African American, Asian American, Mexican American, and labor history since at least the 1970s, and, in some important cases well before, have been mapping the component figures that chart the borders of legal individuality. Without that scholarship I could not have written the preceding chapter. But that said, there is no historiography of legal individuality. A variety of factors meant that the concept of border maintenance in the selfish service of one sector of the population was hidden, cast instead as specific gender, race, ethnic. or temporal exclusions. It is only by reading both across time and across scholarship that has painstakingly charted the legal disabilities of those outside the borders of belonging by virtue of race, gender, ethnicity, and citizenship that the borders themselves become visible, can be seen as purposeful, persistent, and shared, and through them that the character of white male privilege across the sweep of the long nineteenth century is clear. With that in mind, the underpinning strategy outlined in this essay might be referred to by the shorthand: border-crossing reading.

Both by virtue of the breadth of the topic and my approach to it, this bibliographic essay is different from those that accompany other chapters in these volumes. Just as other chapters survey more fully particular areas of law that I only touch on, their accompanying bibliographic essays offer extensive readings relating to those topics. It is not my intent to make this essay needlessly duplicative of others. With that in mind, I have included at the end of this essay a list of other bibliographic essays in the three volumes to which I would expect readers might productively turn. In the other direction, I have not limited myself to works of legal history. In recent years, a growing number of scholars who do not see themselves as legal historians or their work as legal history have turned to legal sources. Their work offers critical insights into legal individuality, the expression and experience of law in everyday life, and the multiple, often competing, contradictory worlds that law creates. Moreover, reading works of social, economic, political, and cultural history alongside legal history or in light of legal transformations of the time helps in understanding the mutually constitutive quality of law and society. Finally, I have included key works of legal and political theory relating to law, liberalism, and citizenship that I have found fundamental in thinking about legal individuality.

The essay itself is divided into two parts. Part I features a vertical reading of literature relating to three broad, deeply intertwined topics central in the history of legal individuality in the long nineteenth century: property, race, and citizenship. Part II privileges a horizontal reading of literature addressing four key moments that are traditionally cast as decisive turning points in the long nineteenth century – the Revolutionary era; the Age of Jackson; the Civil War and Reconstruction; and Redemption, Empire, and the Progressive State – as they relate to legal individuality. Because I am reading both horizontally and vertically, there is repetition in works cited. I have limited full citations to the first reference of a work and have listed multiple works on a given point in reverse chronological order.

Part I

Property, race, and citizenship were deeply intertwined in the history of legal individuality in the long nineteenth century. As a result, we could argue over where it seems most appropriate to introduce the literature related to any number of topics. My decision about where to introduce a particular literature reflects my sense of what the issue involved was most fundamentally about. I begin with property because rights to and control of property and nation fundamentally shaped both law relating to race and citizenship. I encourage the reader in thinking about the three categories to read the literature cited here with all three categories – property, race, and citizenship – in mind.

Property. To take the measure of property in the history of legal individuality requires thinking about the nature of property in its fullest sense. Property included property in the self (self-ownership) and property in others, both of which were fundamentally related to more traditional understandings of property as land and things (real and personal property) and the right to inherit, purchase, own, convey, and devise. In its most expansive sense, property related to the extent and boundaries of the nation and, in turn, to who had a right to claim and speak in the name of them as citizens.

The idea of self-ownership was itself new and evolved over the course of the nineteenth century. Good starting points for thinking about self-ownership and its realization and protection in law include Myra C. Glenn, *Campaigns Against Corporal Punishment: Prisoners, Sailors, Women, and Children in Antebellum America* (Albany, 1984); Elizabeth B. Clark, "Self-Ownership and the Political Theory of Elizabeth Cady Stanton," *Connecticut Law Review* 21 (1989). 905–41; Clark, "'The Sacred Rights of the Weak': Pain, Sympathy, and the Culture of Individual Rights in Antebellum America," *Journal of American History* 82 (1995), 463–93; and Amy Dru Stanley, *From Bondage to Contract: Wage Labor, Marriage, and the Market in the Age of Slave Emancipation* (New York, 1998).

Slavery represented the quintessential denial of self-ownership. The literature on slavery is vast. I recommend as starting points work that I have found especially helpful in thinking about legal individuality. On the law of slavery, see Thomas D. Morris, *Southern Slavery and the Law, 1619–1860* (Chapel Hill, NC, 1996). Walter Johnson, *Soul by Soul: Life Inside the Antebellum Slave Market* (Cambridge, MA,1999) focuses on a critical juncture in the transformation of persons to property: the slave market. Ariela J. Gross, *Double Character: Slavery and Mastery in the Antebellum Southern Courtroom* (Princeton, 2000) follows slave market transactions into the courtroom. Both consider the implications of slavery on both sides of the color line. See also in this regard Cheryl I. Harris, "Whiteness as Property," *Harvard Law Review* 106 (1993), 1709–91 and George Lipsitz, *The Possessive Investment in Whiteness: How White People Profit from Identity Politics* (Philadelphia, 1998).

The denial of personhood was at the heart of anti-slavery campaigns. See, in this regard, Jean Fagan Yellin, *Women and Sisters: Anti-Slavery Feminists in American Culture* (New Haven, CT, 1990); Clark "The Sacred Rights of the Weak"; David Brion Davis, *The Problem of Slavery in the Age of Revolution, 1770–1823* (2nd ed., New York, 1999); and Davis, *Inhuman Bondage: The Rise and Fall of Slavery in the New World* (New York, 2006). See also Davis, *In the Image of God: Religion, Moral Values, and Our Heritage of Slavery* (New Haven, CT, 2001). For a recent work that suggests that although property themselves, some slaves managed to acquire property, see Dylan C. Penningroth, *The Claims of Kinfolk: African American Property and Community in the Nineteenth-Century South* (Chapel Hill, NC, 2003).

On the experience of slavery for African Americans, I recommend beginning with *Narrative of the Life of Frederick Douglass, An American Slave, Written by Himself*, ed. David W. Blight (Boston, 1993) and *Harriet A. Jacobs, Incidents in the Life of a Slave Girl, Written by Herself*, ed. Jean Fagan Yellin (Cambridge, MA, 1987). And on the meaning of emancipation and freedom for African Americans, see Ira Berlin et al., eds., *Freedom: A Documentary History of Emancipation*, 4 vols. (New York, 1982–94); Barbara Jeanne Fields, *Slavery and Freedom on the Middle Ground: Maryland During the Nineteenth Century* (New Haven, CT, 1985); and Eric Foner, "The Meaning of Freedom in the Age of Emancipation," *Journal of American History* 81 (1994), 435–60.

Slavery provided the touchstone against which the freedom of all others in the nineteenth century was measured. But, as this chapter highlights, it was by no means the only example of the denial of self-ownership. One of the ways in which law gave form to white men as self-owning individuals and women as not was through marriage and the law of coverture. For treatises on the law of coverture, see William Blackstone, *Commentaries on the Laws of England*, 4 vols. (Chicago, 1979; orig. pub. 1765–69) and Tapping Reeve, *The Law of Baron and Femme, Parent and Child, Guardian and Ward, Master and Servant, and of the Powers of the Courts of Chancery* (1816). For monographs that address men's and women's rights within marriage over the full sweep of the nineteenth century, see Michael Grossberg, *Governing the Hearth: Law and the Family in Nineteenth-Century America* (Chapel Hill, NC, 1985); Nancy F. Cott, *Public Vows: A History of Marriage and the Nation* (Cambridge, MA, 2000); and Hendrik Hartog, *Man & Wife in America: A History* (Cambridge, MA, 2000).

On married women's legal rights to property before property reform in the 1830s, see Marylynn Salmon, *Women and the Law of Property in Early America* (Chapel Hill, NC, 1986). Laurel Thatcher Ulrich, *A Midwife's Tale: The Life of Martha Ballard, Based on Her Diary, 1785–1812* (New York, 1990) and Suzanne Lebsock, *The Free Women of Petersburg: Status and Culture in a Southern Town, 1784–1864* (New York, 1984) offer insight into how legal constraints shaped women's daily lives up to the Civil War. On married women's property reform before and after the Civil War, see Norma Basch, *In the Eyes of the Law: Women, Marriage, and Property in Nineteenth-Century New York* (Ithaca, NY, 1982); Reva B. Siegel, "The Modernization of Marital Status Law: Adjudicating Wives' Rights to Earnings, 1860–1930," *Georgetown Law Journal* 82 (1994), 2127–2211; Siegel, "The First Woman's Rights Claims Concerning Wives' Household Labor, 1850–1880," *Yale Law Journal* 103 (1994), 1073–1217; and Stanley, *From Bondage to Contract*. On comparisons between slavery and marriage, see Elizabeth B. Clark, "Matrimonial Bonds: Slavery and Divorce in Nineteenth-Century America," *Law and History Review* 8 (1990), 25–53 and Stanley, *From Bondage to Contract*. On the impact of coverture on women's pursuit of personal injury claims after the Civil War and into the early twentieth century, see Barbara Y. Welke, *Recasting American Liberty: Gender, Race, Law and the Railroad Revolution, 1865–1920* (New York, 2001).

Even as married women's property reform gave married women greater, if still limited, rights to property, their rights to reproductive independence – and hence property in the self – were narrowed dramatically. On the criminalization of abortion and birth control, see Linda Gordon, *Woman's Body, Woman's Rights: Birth Control in America* (rev. ed. New York, 1990) and Leslie J. Reagan, *When Abortion Was a Crime: Women, Medicine, and Law in the United States, 1867–1973* (Berkeley, 1997).

White men's property right in themselves was tested by the development of wage labor. As the work of labor historians suggests, what came to be called "free labor" might have been called more accurately "not so free labor" or "free labor only by comparison." See in this regard Christopher L. Tomlins, "A Mysterious Power: Industrial Accidents and the Legal Construction of Employment Relations in Massachusetts, 1800–1850," *Law and History Review* 6 (1988), 375–438; Robert J. Steinfeld, *The Invention of Free Labor: The Employment Relation in English and American Law and Culture, 1350–1870* (Chapel Hill, NC, 1991); Tomlins, *Law, Labor, and Ideology in the Early American Republic* (New York, 1993); and Steinfeld, *Coercion, Contract, and Free Labor in the Nineteenth Century* (New York, 2001). Industrialization intensified the importance of the racialized and gendered safeguards of the borders of belonging.

Throughout the long nineteenth century the law presumed that men were providers, that husbands had the right to their wives' labor and persons, and that married working women's primary identities were those of wife and mother. Husbands' rights could trump race as is shown by the work of Todd Stevens, "Tender Ties: Husbands' Rights and Racial Exclusion in Chinese Marriage Cases, 1882–1924," *Law & Social Inquiry* 27 (2002), 271–305. On judicial interpretation of homestead exemption laws, see Alison D. Morantz, "There's No Place Like Home: Homestead Exemption and Judicial Constructions of Family in Nineteenth-Century America," *Law and History Review* 24 (2006), 245–96. On wrongful death laws, see John Fabian Witt, "From Loss of Services to Loss of Support: Wrongful Death, the Origins of Modern Tort Law, and the Making of the Nineteenth Century Family," *Law and Social Inquiry* 25 (2000), 717–55. On husbands' right to their wives' labor and persons and reluctance to acknowledge the same rights in African American families in the South following emancipation, see Chapter 2 in Linda K. Kerber, *No Constitutional Right to Be Ladies: Women and the Obligations of Citizenship* (New York, 1998); and Stanley, *From Bondage to Contract*. The same assumptions shaped workmen's compensation law and policymakers' assumptions about men's and women's work after the turn of the twentieth century. On workmen's compensation, see John Fabian Witt, *The Accidental Republic: Crippled Workingmen, Destitute Widows, and the Remaking of American Law* (Cambridge, 2004). On the "gendered imaginary" regarding work and home and its operation in law, see Alice Kessler-Harris, *In Pursuit of Equity: Women, Men, and the Quest for Economic Citizenship in 20th-Century America* (New York, 2001). On protective labor legislation more particularly, see also Judith Baer, *The Chains of Protection: The Judicial Response to Women's Labor Legislation* (Westport, CT, 1978) and Nancy Woloch, *Muller v. Oregon: A Brief History with Documents* (Boston, 1996).

On efforts to exclude women from professions such as law and medicine and to maintain professions as white men's domain, see Mary Roth Walsh, *"Doctors Wanted, No Women Need Apply": Sexual Barriers in the Medical Profession* (New Haven, CT, 1977); D. Kelly Weisberg, "Barred from the Bar: Women and Legal Education in the United States, 1870–1890," in D. Kelly Weisberg, ed., *Women and the Law: A Social Historical Perspective, vol. II, Property, Family and the Legal Profession* (Cambridge, MA, 1982), 231–258; Michael Grossberg, "Institutionalizing Masculinity: The Law as a Masculine Profession," in Mark C. Carnes and Clyde Griffen, eds., *Meanings for Manhood: Constructions of Masculinity in Victorian America* (Chicago, 1990), 133–51; Neil R. McMillen, *Dark Journey: Black Mississippians in the Age of Jim Crow (Urbana, 1989)*; and Ellen Carol DuBois, "Taking the Law into Our Own Hands: Bradwell, Minor, and Suffrage Militance, in the 1870s," in Ellen Carol DuBois, ed., *Woman Suffrage & Women's Rights* (New York, 1998), 114–38. But also see Eric Foner, *Freedom's Lawmakers: A Directory of Black Officeholders During Reconstruction* (rev. ed., Baton Rouge, LA, 1996), on the extraordinary interlude of Reconstruction.

Emancipation ended the regime of property in persons, but it did not give African Americans or others equal access to the land. For excellent work on post-Reconstruction legal stratagems to ensure the pool of black agricultural laborers in the South, see Eric Foner, "The Politics of Freedom," in Foner, *Nothing But Freedom: Emancipation and Its Legacy* (Baton Rouge, LA, 1983), 39–73 and Evelyn Nakano Glenn, *Unequal Freedom: How Race and Gender Shaped American Citizenship and Labor* (Cambridge, MA, 2002). Glenn is also essential reading for placing actions in the post-Reconstruction South in a national context involving Mexican Americans and Mexicans in the Southwest and West, and Japanese and Chinese in the West and Hawaii. See also Neil Foley, *The White Scourge: Mexicans, Blacks, and Poor Whites in Texas Cotton Culture* (Berkeley, 1998); Linda Gordon, *The Great Arizona Orphan Abduction* (Cambridge, MA, 1999); and Gunther Peck, *Reinventing Free Labor: Padrones and Immigrant Workers in the North American West, 1880–1930*. On convict labor, see Alex Lichtenstein, *Twice the Work of Free Labor: The Political Economy of Convict Labor in the New South* (London, 1996) and David M. Oshinsky, *"Worse Than Slavery:" Parchman Farm and the Ordeal of Jim Crow Justice* (New York, 1996). On the importance of vagrancy laws in enforcing the labor of racialized others – women, as well as men – at the end of the nineteenth century, see Kerber, *No Constitutional Right to be Ladies*; Stanley, *From Bondage to Contract*; and Glenn, *Unequal Freedom*.

On Western expansion and the dispossession of Native Americans of land, see Frederick E. Hoxie, *A Final Promise: The Campaign to Assimilate the Indians, 1880–1920* (Lincoln, 1984); Sidney L. Harring, *Crow Dog's Case: American Indian Sovereignty, Tribal Law, and United States Law in the Nineteenth Century* (New York, 1994); Emily Greenwald, *Reconfiguring the Reservation: The Nez Perces, Jicarilla Apaches, and the Dawes Act* (Albuquerque, 2002); and Jeffrey Ostler, *The Plains Sioux and U.S. Colonialism from Lewis and Clark to Wounded Knee* (New York, 2004). On the dispossession of Mexican (-Americans) of land by and following the Mexican-American war, see María E. Montoya, *Translating Property: The Maxwell Land Grant and the Conflict over Land in the American West, 1840–1900* (Berkeley, 2002) and Gordon, *The Great Arizona Orphan Abduction*.

The work of many scholars highlights the tightening of racial boundaries on land ownership at the end of the nineteenth century in the North and West. On restrictive covenants, see David Delaney, *Race, Place & the Law, 1836–1948* (Austin, 1998). James W. Loewen, *Sundown Towns: A Hidden Dimension of American Racism* (New York, 2005) argues that beginning from 1890 a majority of incorporated places outside the South barred settlement by African Americans. On miscegenation law and land ownership, see Peggy Pascoe, "Race, Gender, and the Privileges of Property: On the Significance of Miscegenation Law in the U.S. West," in Valerie J. Matsumoto and Blake Allmendinger, eds., *Over the Edge: Remapping the American West* (Berkeley, 1999), 215–30. On the adoption of alien land laws in many Western states in the same temporal context, see Mae M. Ngai, *Impossible Subjects: Illegal Aliens and the Making of Modern America* (Princeton, 2004). For the pre-Civil War analogue to limits on settlement by free blacks, see Leon Litwack, *North of Slavery: The Negro in the Free States, 1790–1860* (Chicago, 1961).

What restrictive covenants, miscegenation laws, and alien land laws did for private property at the end of the nineteenth century, Jim Crow did for public space. Important works to consider include C. Vann Woodward, *The Strange Career of Jim Crow* (3rd rev. ed., 1955; New York, 1974); Howard N. Rabinowitz, *Race Relations in the Urban South, 1865–1890* (Urbana, IL, 1980); Charles A. Lofgren, *The Plessy Case: A Legal-Historical Interpretation* (New York, 1987); and Welke, *Recasting American Liberty*.

Throughout the long nineteenth century legal and extra-legal violence was essential in enforcing the borders of belonging. Violence safeguarded white men's claims to property in themselves, others, and land itself and the space of the nation. On the South in particular, see Edward L. Ayers, *Vengeance and Justice: Crime and Punishment in the Nineteenth-Century American South* (New York, 1984). On the development of the law of self-defense, see Richard Maxwell Brown, *No Duty to Retreat: Violence and Values in American History* (New York, 1991). On a husband's right to kill his wife's lover in the heat of passion, see Hendrik Hartog, "Lawyering, Husbands' Rights, and 'the Unwritten Law' in Nineteenth Century America," *Journal of American History* 84 (1997), 67–96. On domestic violence and the law, more generally, see Elizabeth H. Pleck, *Domestic Tyranny: The Making of Social Policy Against Family Violence From Colonial Times to the Present* (New York, 1987) and Linda Gordon, *Heroes of Their Own Lives: The Politics and History of Family Violence* (New York, 1988).

The literature on lynching is vast. Most of it focuses on lynchings by whites of African Americans. For an introduction to this literature, see McMillen, *Dark Journey*; W. Fitzhugh Brundage, *Lynching in the New South, Georgia and Virginia, 1880–1930* (Urbana, IL, 1993); Grace Elizabeth Hale, *Making Whiteness: The Culture of Segregation in the South, 1890–1940* (New York, 1998); and Christopher Waldrep, *The Many Faces of Judge Lynch: Extralegal Violence and Punishment in America* (New York, 2002). For Ida B. Wells telling analyses of the underlying purposes of lynching, see Ida B. Wells-Barnett, *On Lynchings: Southern Horrors, A Red Record, Mob Rule in New Orleans* (Salem, NH, 1993; orig. pub. 1892, 1895, and 1900). On the anti-lynching campaign, see Jacquelyn Dowd Hall, *Revolt Against Chivalry: Jessie Daniel Ames and the Women's Campaign Against Lynching* (rev. ed. New York, 1993). As recent work shows, lynching was a tool of control used against racial minorities generally in enforcing the borders of belonging in the long nineteenth century. See William D. Carrigan and Clive Webb, "The Lynching of Persons of Mexican Origin or Descent in the United States, 1848 to 1928," *Journal of Social History* 37 (2003), 411–38.

Violence as a tool of control protecting and extending white property claims was not, of course, limited to lynching. See, in this regard, Glenda E. Gilmore, *Gender & Jim Crow: Women and the Politics of White Supremacy in North Carolina, 1896–1920* (Chapel Hill, NC, 1996) on the Wilmington massacre; Alfred L. Brophy, *Reconstructing the Dreamland: The Tulsa Riot of 1921: Race, Reparations, and Reconciliation* (New York, 2002). On rape and other violence against women see Diane Miller Sommerville, *Rape & Race in the nineteenth-century South* (Chapel Hill, NC, 2004); Lisa Lindquist Dorr, *White Women, Rape, & the Power of Race in Virginia, 1900–1960* (Chapel Hill, NC, 2004); Laura F. Edwards, *Gendered Strife and Confusion: The Political Culture of Reconstruction* (Urbana, 1997); Hannah Rosen, "'Not That Sort of Women': Race, Gender, and Sexual Violence during the Memphis Riot of 1866," and other essays in Martha Hodes, ed., *Sex, Love, Race: Crossing Boundaries in North American History* (New York, 1999); Jacquelyn Dowd Hall, "'The Mind That Burns in Each Body': Women, Rape, and Racial Violence," *Southern Exposure* 12:6 (1984), 61–71; and Darlene Clark Hine, "Rape and the inner lives of Black women in the Middle West: Preliminary thought on the culture of dissemblance," *Signs* 14:4 (1989), 912–920. On anti-Chinese violence, see John Wunder, "Anti Chinese Violence in the American West, 1850–1910," in John McLaren, Hamar Foster, and Chet Orloff, eds., *Law for the Elephant, Law for the Beaver: Essays in the Legal History of the North American West* (Regina, Saskatchewan, 1992), 212–36; and Victor Jew, "'Chinese Demons": The Violent Articulation of Chinese Otherness and Interracial Sexuality in the U.S. Midwest, 1885–1889," *Journal of Social History* 37 (2003), 389–410. On the role of violence in relations with Native Americans, see Patricia Nelson Limerick, *The Legacy of Conquest: The Unbroken Past of the American West* (New York, 1987) for a broad survey and Jeffrey Ostler, *The Plains Sioux and U.S. Colonialism from Lewis and Clark to Wounded Knee* (New York, 2004) for an extended telling of one example. On violence and empire more generally, especially focused on the end of the nineteenth century, see Paul A. Kramer, *The Blood of Government: Race, Empire, the United States, and the Philippines* (Chapel Hill, NC, 2006); Angel Velasco Shaw and Luis H. Francia, eds., *Vestiges of War: The Philippine-American War and the Aftermath of an Imperial Dream, 1899–1999* (New York, 2002); Lou Perez, *The War of 1898: The United States and Cuba in History and Historiography* (Chapel Hill, NC, 1998); and Sally

Engle Merry, *Colonizing Hawaii: The Cultural Power of Law* (Princeton, 2000). On law and the construction of the boundaries of the nation more generally, see the excellent collection of essays, many of which relate to the long nineteenth century, *Legal Borderlands: Law and the Construction of American Borders*, Mary L. Dudziak and Leti Volpp, eds., *American Quarterly* 57 (2005).

Race. W. E. B. Du Bois did not use the term "tessellation" in *The Souls of Black Folk* (1903), but he might have. It is a good place to begin reading. Throughout the long nineteenth century, giving legal definition to and the policing of race and racial boundaries were fundamental to the borders of belonging. Beyond Du Bois, the reading opportunities are rich. Legal scholars working in the field known as Critical Race Theory have been especially important in making intelligible the operation of racial privilege and racial exclusions in American law. For an introduction to this scholarship, see Neil Gotanda, "A Critique of 'Our Constitution is Color-Blind,'" *Stanford Law Review* 44 (1991), 1–68; Kimberlé Crenshaw, Neil Gotanda, Gary Peller, and Kendall Thomas, eds., *Critical Race Theory: The Key Writings that Formed the Movement* (New York, 1995); Richard Delgado and Jean Stefancic, eds., *Critical Race Theory: The Cutting Edge* (Philadelphia, 2000); Patricia J. Williams, *The Alchemy of Race and Rights* (Cambridge, MA, 1991); Adrien Kathrine Wing, ed., *Critical Race Feminism: A Reader* (New York, 1997); and Angela P. Harris, "Equality Trouble: Sameness and Difference in Twentieth-Century Race Law," *California Law Review* 88 (2000), 1923–2015. Barbara J. Fields, "Ideology and Race in American History" in J. Morgan Kousser and James M. McPherson, eds., *Region, Race, and Reconstruction: Essays in Honor of C. Vann Woodward* (New York, 1982), 143–77 remains a foundational article on race in American history. See also Charles W. Mills, *The Racial Contract* (Ithaca, NY, 1997).

Works outside of legal history that are nonetheless important for understanding the assumptions behind and justifications for race-related legislation in the long nineteenth century, include Winthrop D. Jordan, *White over Black: American Attitudes Toward the Negro, 1550–1812* (Chapel Hill, NC, 1968); John Higham, *Strangers in the Land: Patterns of American Nativism, 1860–1925* (New York, 1969); George M. Frederickson, *The Black Image in the White Mind: The Debate on Afro-American Character and Destiny, 1817–1914* (New York, 1971); Alexander Saxton, *The Indispensable Enemy: Labor and the Anti-Chinese Movement* (Berkeley, 1971); Ronald Takaki, *Iron Cages: Race and Culture in 19th Century America* (New York, 1979); Joel Williamson, *The Crucible of Race: Black-White Relations in the American South Since Emancipation* (New York, 1984); Robert A. Williams, Jr., *The American Indian in Western Legal Thought: The Discourses of Conquest* (New York, 1990); David Gutíerrez, *Walls and Mirrors: Mexican Americans, Mexican Immigrants, and the Politics of Ethnicity* (Berkeley, 1995); Matthew Frye Jacobson, *Barbarian Virtues: The United States Encounters Foreign Peoples at Home and Abroad, 1876–1917* (New York, 2000); and Laura Briggs, *Reproducing Empire: Race, Sex, Science, and U.S. Imperialism in Puerto Rico* (Berkeley, 2003).

Because of slavery, the legal history of race relating to black-white relations dwarfs all others. In addition to the work cited in the preceding section, see Johnson, *Soul by Soul*; Gross, *Double Character*; Litwack, *North of Slavery* and *Been in the Storm So Long*; Ira Berlin, *Slaves Without Masters: The Free Negro in the Antebellum South* (1976; New York, 1992); McMillen, *Dark Journey*; Gilmore, *Gender & Jim Crow*; Steven Hahn, *A Nation Under Our Feet: Black Political Struggles in the Rural South, From Slavery to the Great Migration* (Cambridge, MA, 2003); and Hale, *Making Whiteness*. For collections of race laws in the United States beginning in the late nineteenth century, see Gilbert Thomas Stephenson, *Race Distinctions in American Law* (New York, 1910); Charles S. Mangum, Jr., *The Legal Status of the Negro* (Chapel Hill, NC, 1940); and Pauli Murray, comp. and ed., *States' Laws on Race and Color* (1951; Athens, GA,1997). Stephenson's work, it should be noted, is an elaborate justification of "race distinctions" in law which he contrasts with unjustified "race discrimination." His work is usefully read as an early twentieth-century defense of race legislation; it is also, though, a useful collation of statutes and institutional practices. Both Stephenson and Murray include laws related to racial groups other than African Americans.

As Stephenson's and Murray's collections highlight, race as a foundation for the borders of belonging was not limited to the law discriminating between black and white. It was fundamental to Euro-Indian relations; defined naturalization from the first naturalization law in 1790 through the long nineteenth century; underlay immigration restriction from its beginning in the late nineteenth century; and fundamentally shaped both law and actions taken in the shadow of the law for all racial minorities. On naturalization see Ian Haney Lopez, *White By Law: The Construction of Race* (New York, 1996). On the role of race in immigration restriction and enforcement, see Martha Gardner, *The Qualities of a Citizen: Women, Immigration, and Citizenship, 1870–1965* (Princeton, 2005); Kitty Calavita, "Law, Citizenship, and the Construction of (Some) Immigrant 'Others'", 30 *Law & Social Inquiry* (2005), 401–20; Ngai, *Impossible Subjects*; Erika Lee, *At America's Gates: Chinese Immigration During the Exclusion Era, 1882–1943* (Chapel Hill, NC, 2003); Leti Volpp, "Obnoxious to Their Very Nature': Asian Americans and Constitutional Citizenship," 8 *Asian L. J.* (2001), 71–87; Lucy E. Salyer, *Laws Harsh as Tigers: Chinese Immigrants and the Shaping of Modern Immigration Law* (Chapel Hill, NC, 1995); Richard P. Cole and Gabriel Chin, "Emerging from the Margins of Historical Consciousness: Chinese Immigrants and the History of American Law," *Law and History Review* 17 (1999), 325–64; Bill Ong Hing, *Making and Remaking Asian America Through Immigration Policy, 1850–1990* (Stanford, 1990); and David Langum, *Law and Community on the Mexican California Frontier: Anglo-American Expatriates and the Clash of Legal Traditions, 1821–1846* (Norman, OK, 1987). Also helpful is Erika Lee, "Immigrants and Immigration Law: A State of the Field Assessment," *Journal of American Ethnic History* 18 (1999), 85–114. Only recently have scholars begun to focus on the legal construction of race for Mexican Americans.

See, in this regard, Glenn, *Unequal Freedom*; Gordon, *The Great Arizona Orphan Abduction*; and although much of the author's focus is on later in the twentieth century, George A. Martinez, "The Legal Construction of Race: Mexican-Americans and Whiteness," *Harvard Latino Law Review* 2 (1997): 321–38 and "Forum. Whiteness and Others: Mexican Americans and American Law," *Law and History Review* 21 (2003), 109–213. On the impact of law on relations between blacks and Native Americans, see Tiya Miles, *Ties That Bind: The Story of an Afro-Cherokee Family in Slavery and Freedom* (Berkeley, 2005); and Claudio Saunt, *A New Order of things: Property, Power, and the Transformation of the Creek Indians, 1733–1816* (New York, 1999).

One part of the project of understanding the role of race in American law is marking the normative, here whiteness. A critical starting point for reading is Harris, "Whiteness as Property." See also Gordon, *The Great Arizona Orphan Abduction*. Whereas white privilege in law has been a focus of Critical Race Theorists, work on whiteness has not generally focused on law. One important exception is Lipsitz, *The Possessive Investment in Whiteness*. See also Devon W. Carbado, "Racial Naturalization," *Legal Borderlands*, 633–58. For review essays surveying the field of whiteness studies, see the symposium, "Scholarly Controversy: Whiteness and the Historians' Imagination," *International Labor and Working Class History* 60 (2001), 1–92; Peter Kolchin, "Whiteness Studies: The New History of Race in America," *Journal of American History* 89 (2002), 154–73; and Daniel Wickberg, "Heterosexual White Male: Some Recent Inversions in American Cultural History," *Journal of American History* (2005), 136–57. Works of cultural and political history that chart the construction of whiteness and manliness through the lenses of European immigration, the white working class, nationbuilding, and empire, although explicitly not legal history and only rarely, if at all, even referring to law, nonetheless provide important contextualization for understanding the boundaries of legal individuality. Key are Reginald Horsman, *Race and Manifest Destiny: The Origins of American Racial Anglo-Saxonism* (Cambridge, MA, 1981); Alexander Saxton, *The Rise and Fall of the White Republic: Class Politics and Mass Culture in Nineteenth-Century America* (New York, 1990); David R. Roediger, *The Wages of Whiteness: Race and the Making of the American Working Class* (New York, 1991); Gail Bederman, *Manliness & Civilization: A Cultural History of Gender and Race in the United States, 1880–1917* (Chicago, 1995); and Matthew Frye Jacobson, *Whiteness of a Different Color: European Immigrants and the Alchemy of Race* (Cambridge, MA, 1998).

The privileges that inhered in whiteness created incentives to pass as white; in turn, the legal and administrative structures created to protect the boundaries of whiteness provided a foundation for breeching those boundaries. On passing and racial indeterminacy before as well as after the Civil War see, Ariela Gross, "Litigating Whiteness: Trials of Racial Determination in the Nineteenth-Century South," *Yale L. J.* 108 (1998): 109–88; Ira Berlin, *Slaves without Masters: The Free Negro in the Antebellum South* (New York, 1974); Peggy Pascoe, "Miscegenation Law, Court cases, and Ideologies of 'Race' in Twentieth Century America," *Journal of American History* 83 (1996), 44–69; and Earl Lewis and Heidi Ardizzone, *Love on Trial: An American Scandal in Black and White* (New York, 2001). For a sophisticated consideration of passing applied to illegal Chinese immigrants, see Kitty Calavita, "The Paradoxes of Race, Class, Identity, and 'Passing': Enforcing the Chinese Exclusion Acts, 1882–1910," *Law and Social Inquiry* 25 (2000), 1–40.

There is an extensive literature on the legal regulation of interracial sex and marriage. Peggy Pascoe's work convincingly shows that these laws and the enforcement of them were in significant part about protecting white men's property claims. But miscegenation laws were also about asserting and maintaining racial boundaries or at least the boundary between whites and racial others. See Pascoe, *What Comes Naturally: Miscegenation Law in U.S. History* (unpublished manuscript in author's possession, forthcoming Oxford University Press); Pascoe "Race, Gender, and the Privileges of Property;" Pascoe, "Miscegenation Law, Court Cases, and Ideologies of 'Race' in Twentieth-Century America;" Martha Hodes, *White Women, Black Men: Illicit Sex in the 19th-Century South* (New Haven, CT, 1997); and Joshua D. Rothman, *Notorious in the Neighborhood: Sex and Families Across the Color Line in Virginia, 1787–1861* (Chapel Hill, NC, 2003). A great deal of the work cited here is part of a move toward a more complex understanding of race, and race relations and the law both under slavery and in its aftermath.

Citizenship. It seems obvious to say that U.S. citizenship took shape in the long nineteenth century, but it is a point worth considering. Citizenship was not after all defined in the U.S. Constitution. Only over the course of the nineteenth century did citizenship acquire the weight we ascribe to it today. Since the late 1980s there has been a surge in scholarly interest in the history of citizenship. The sources of this renewed interest are many, but include such factors as the U.S. bicentennial, the end of the Cold War, the impending (and now past) end of a century in which the nation-state became the acknowledged foundation for rights, heightened anxiety over immigration in a postindustrial economy, and a focus on globalization and questions it has raised of what next after the nation-state. The outpouring of excellent work has come from virtually every field. For an introduction to citizenship studies, see Bart van Steenbergen, ed., *The Condition of Citizenship* (Thousand Oaks, CA, 1994); and Gershon Shafir, ed., *The Citizenship Debates: A Reader* (Minneapolis, 1998).

Important historical considerations of citizenship that take in much or all of the long nineteenth century include James H. Kettner, *The Development of American Citizenship, 1608–1870* (Chapel Hill, NC, 1978); Gerald L. Neuman, *Strangers to the Constitution: Immigrants, Borders, and Fundamental Law* (Princeton, 1996); and Rogers M. Smith, *Civic Ideals: Conflicting Visions of Citizenship in U.S. History* (New Haven, CT, 1997). See also Linda Kerber's OAH Presidential

Address, "The Meanings of American Citizenship," *Journal of American History* 94 (1997), 833–54. On the constitution and rights aspiration, see Hendrik Hartog, "The Constitution of Aspiration and 'The Rights That Belong to Us All,'" *Journal of American History* 74 (1987), 1013–34.

Although "citizenship" is, as Linda Kerber notes, "an equalizing term," on closer inspection of the long nineteenth century it was not a guarantee of equal rights to even most of those who could claim its mantle; it served equally as a tool of exclusion and subordination. Up to the Civil War, the citizenship of free African Americans was at best questioned, at worst denied, and mostly irrelevant in providing protection against denials of employment, freedom of movement, or protecting basic civil rights such as jury service or voting. See Kettner, *The Development of American Citizenship* and Smith, *Civic Ideals*. While those held in slavery could not hope to make claims based on citizenship, until the Supreme Court's decision in *Dred Scott*, the question of national citizenship for free blacks was not clear. On the *Dred Scott* case, in addition to Kettner and Smith, see Don E. Fehrenbacher, *The Dred Scott Case, Its Significance in American Law and Politics* (New York, 1978); Paul Finkelman, *Dred Scott v. Sandford: A Brief History with Documents* (Boston, 1997); and Lea VanderVelde and Sandhya Subramanian, "Mrs. Dred Scott," *Yale Law Journal* 106 (1997), 1033.

For women, the equation was different. No one questioned that they were citizens; citizenship simply did not mean for them what it meant for men. Linda K. Kerber's pioneering study, *No Constitutional Right to Be Ladies*, traces the gendered history of obligation in U.S. citizenship from the Revolutionary era through the twentieth century. Critical theoretical considerations that similarly highlight the subordinate character of women's citizenship include Carole Pateman, *The Sexual Contract* (Stanford, 1988) and Nancy Fraser and Linda Gordon, "Civil Citizenship against Social Citizenship?: On the Ideology of Contract-versus-Charity," *The Condition of Citizenship*, 90–107. Whereas men did not risk losing their citizenship through marriage, women did. On this point, in addition to Kerber, *No Constitutional Right to Be Ladies*, see Candace Lewis Bredbenner, *A Nationality of Her Own: Women, Marriage, and the Law of Citizenship* (Berkeley, 1998); Nancy F. Cott, "Marriage and Women's Citizenship in the United States, 1830–1934," *American Historical Review* 103 (1998), 1440–74; Cott, *Public Vows*; Martha Gardner, *The Qualities of a Citizen: Women, Immigration, and Citizenship, 1870–1965* (Princeton, 2005); Nancy Isenberg, *Sex and Citizenship in Antebellum America* (Chapel Hill, NC, 1998); and Leti Volpp, "Divesting Citizenship: On Asian American History and the Loss of Citizenship Through Marriage," *UCLA L. Rev.* 53 (2005), 405–83.

The Civil War transformed the equation, if not ultimately the substance, of citizenship for African Americans, women, and Americans more generally. On the constitutional impact of the Civil War, emancipation, the Civil Rights Act of 1866, and what are collectively referred to the Reconstruction Amendments (Thirteenth, Fourteenth, and Fifteenth Amendments), see Eric Foner,

"Rights and the Constitution in Black Life during the Civil War and Reconstruction," *Journal of American History* 74 (1987), 863–83; Harold M. Hyman and William M. Wiecek, *Equal Justice Under the Law: Constitutional Development 1835–1875* (New York, 1982); Robert J. Kaczorowski, "To Begin the Nation Anew: Congress, Citizenship, and Civil Rights After the Civil War," *American Historical Review* 92 (1987), 45–68; Michael Vorenberg, *Final Freedom: the Civil War, the Abolition of Slavery, and the Thirteenth Amendment* (New York, 2001); and William E. Nelson, *The Fourteenth Amendment: From Political Principle to Judicial Doctrine* (Cambridge, MA, 1988). Bill Novak argues that it is only with the Fourteenth Amendment that citizenship became the "primary constitutional marker of access, status, privilege, and obligation." See William J. Novak, "The Legal Transformation of Citizenship in Nineteenth-Century America," in Meg Jacobs, William J. Novak, and Julian Zelizer, eds., *The Democratic Experiment: New Directions in American Political History* (Princeton, 2003), 85–119.

Yet whatever their promise, the Supreme Court's interpretation of the Thirteenth, Fourteenth, and Fifteenth Amendments in the quarter-century following their adoption rendered their promise largely hollow for African Americans as well as for women. For work discussing specific cases, see the following: on the Slaughterhouse cases, see the recent reinterpretations by Ronold M. Labbé and Jonathan Lurie, *The Slaughterhouse Cases: Regulation, Reconstruction, and the Fourteenth Amendment* (Lawrence, KS, 2003) and Michael A. Ross, *Justice of Shattered Dreams: Samuel Freeman Miller and the Supreme Court During the Civil War Era* (Baton Rouge, LA, 2003); on *Plessy*, see Lofgren, *The Plessy Case*; and Welke, *Recasting American Liberty*. On the Reconstruction Amendments and women's suffrage, see Ellen Carol DuBois, "Outgrowing the Compact of the Fathers: Equal Rights, Woman Suffrage, and the United States Constitution, 1820–1878," and "Taking the Law into Our Own Hands: *Bradwell*, *Minor*, and Suffrage Militance in the 1870s," both reprinted in DuBois, *Woman Suffrage & Women's Rights* (New York, 1998), 81–113, 114–138 and Kerber, *No Constitutional Right to Be Ladies*. On black disfranchisement despite the Fifteenth Amendment, see J. Morgan Kousser, *The Shaping of Southern Politics: Suffrage Restriction and the Establishment of the One-Party South, 1880–1910* (New Haven, CT, 1974) and Michael Perman, *Struggle for Mastery: Disfranchisement in the South, 1888–1908* (Chapel Hill, NC, 2001). Only for Chinese Americans did the birthright citizenship clause of the Fourteenth Amendment assure the limited protection of citizenship and only for those Chinese born in the United States. On the Supreme Court's decision in Wong Kim Ark, see Salyer, *Laws Harsh as Tigers*; and Lee, *At America's Gates*. On the limits of that protection, in addition to the above, see also Lisa Lowe, *Immigrant Acts: On Asian American Cultural Politics* (Durham, NC, 1996); and Ngai, *Impossible Subjects*.

Mexican American, African American, and Native American women who suddenly found themselves citizens through territorial incorporation, emancipation, or allotment learned that U.S. citizenship could mean a loss of rights as they became subject to coverture, the primary determinant of women's legal status. See Wendy Wall, "Gender and the Citizen Indian," in Elizabeth Jameson and Susan Armitage, eds., *Writing the Range: Race, Class, and Culture in the Women's West*, (Norman, OK, 1997); Stanley, *From Bondage to Contract*; Cott, *Public Vows*; Montoya, *Translating Property*; and Katherine Franke, "Becoming a Citizen: Reconstruction Era Regulation of African American Marriages," *Yale Journal of Law and Humanities* 11 (1999), 251–309.

Moreover, beginning in the shadow of Reconstruction, the limits on who had an opportunity to become a citizen tightened, both through interpretation of the naturalization law and through new and increasingly stringent restrictions on immigration beginning with the Page Act (1875) and continuing through the National Origins Act (1924). On naturalization, see Lopez, *White by Law* and John Tehranian, "Performing Whiteness: Naturalization Litigation and the Construction of Racial Identity in America," *Yale Law Journal* 109 (2000), 817–48. On immigration restriction, in addition to Neuman, see Higham, *Strangers in the Land*; Mary Sarah Bilder, "The Struggle Over Immigration: Indentured Servants, Slaves, and Articles of Commerce," *Missouri Law Review* 61 (1996), 743–824; Sucheng Chan, ed., *Entry Denied: Exclusion and the Chinese Community in America, 1882–1943* (Philadelphia, 1994); Salyer, *Laws Harsh as Tigers*; Robert Chang, *Disoriented: Asian Americans, Law, and the Nation State* (New York, 1999); John C. Torpey, *The Invention of the Passport: Surveillance, Citizenship, and the State* (New York, 2000); Lee, *At America's Gates*; and Ngai, *Impossible Subjects*. To place immigration restriction in a longer frame, see also Kunal Parker, "From Poor Law to Immigration Law: Changing Visions of Territorial Community in Antebellum Massachusetts," *Historical Geography* 28 (2000), 61–85 and Forum: "Citizenship as Refusal 'Outing' the Nation of Immigrants" *Law and History Review* 19 (2001), 583–660.

Through the long nineteenth century sovereignty, not U.S. citizenship, was the first goal of most American Indian tribes. On borders and sovereignty, see Vine Deloria, Jr. and David E. Wilkins, *Tribes, Treaties, & Constitutional Tribulations* (Austin, 1999); David E. Wilkins and K. Tsianina Lomawaima, *Uneven Ground: American Indian Sovereignty and Federal Law* (Norman, OK, 2001); and Ostler, *The Plains Sioux and U.S. Colonialism*. Native Americans' relationship to the United States is productively thought of in a long-term context of nation and empire that includes the overseas expansion at the end of the nineteenth century. On empire and citizenship, see José A. Cabranes, *Citizenship and the American Empire* (New Haven, CT, 1979); Smith, *Civic Values*; Merry, *Colonizing Hawaii*; and Ngai, *Impossible Subjects*.

Finally, on the census, belonging, and citizenship, see Melissa Nobles, *Shades of Citizenship: Race and the Census in Modern Politics* (Stanford, 2000); and Naomi Mezey, "Erasure and Recognition: The Census, Race, and the National Imagination," 97 *Northwestern Law Review* (Summer 2003), 1701–68.

Part II

At least since Joan Kelly's pioneering essay, "Did Women Have a Renaissance?," reprinted in Joan Kelly, *Women, History, and Theory: The Essays of Joan Kelly* (Chicago, 1984), we have known to be wary of unquestioning acceptance of the historical turning points we inherit. Kelly's work directly inspired U.S. women's historians to question whether the American Revolution was a revolution for women. Applying Kelly's observation to the question of legal individuality in the long nineteenth century makes work that chronologically bridges acknowledged/accepted turning points especially important. Equally important is juxtaposing topics that share a historical moment, but are generally written by historians working in different subfields. I provide recommendations for both kinds of reading, focusing on four chronological moments: the Revolutionary Era; the Age of Jackson; the Civil War and Reconstruction; and Redemption, Empire, and the Progressive State.

Revolutionary Era. On the Revolutionary era and women's legal status, see Linda K. Kerber, *Women of the Republic: Intellect & Ideology in Revolutionary America* (New York, 1980). Joan R. Gunderson, "Independence, Citizenship and the American Revolution," and Ruth Bloch, "The Gendered Meaning of Virtue in Revolutionary America," both in *Signs: Journal of Women in Culture and Society* 13 (1987), 37–58; Carroll Smith-Rosenberg, "Dis-covering the Subject of the 'Great Constitutional Discussion,' 1786–1789," *Journal of American History* 79 (1992), 841–73; and Kerber, *No Constitutional Right to Be Ladies* (Chapter 1) are especially helpful in exploring the way in which gendered assumptions of women's dependence provided a critical foundation for situating men as independent. Ulrich, *A Midwife's Tale*, although not a work of legal history, captures the continuities in women's legal status and lives across the Revolutionary era.

Nor was the Revolution the revolution that historians once thought it to be for African Americans. Slavery was present at, even fundamental to, the creation of the new nation. See in this regard, Edmund S. Morgan, *American Slavery, American Freedom: The Ordeal of Colonial Virginia* (New York, 1975) with Kathleen M. Brown, *Good Wives, Nasty Wenches, and Anxious Patriarchs: Gender, Race, and Power in Colonial Virginia* (Chapel Hill, NC, 1996). On African Americans and the Revolution itself, see Ira Berlin and Ronald Hoffman, eds., *Slavery and Freedom in the Age of the American Revolution* (Charlottesville, VA, 1983); Gary B. Nash, *The Forgotten Fifth: African Americans in the Age of Revolution* (Cambridge, MA, 2006). Work on the Revolutionary era and after that reevaluates the economic role of slavery in Northern states, highlights the slow pace of emancipation there, and considers the consequences of both factors for African Americans and for whites' conceptions of African Americans as rights-bearing people is essential for seeing the borders of belonging. See, in particular, Ira Berlin, *Many Thousands Gone* (Cambridge, MA, 1998) and Joanne Pope Melish, *Disowning Slavery: Gradual Emancipation and "Race" in New England, 1780–1860* (Ithaca, NY, 1998). On the law of slavery in the South and the impact of the

Revolution, see Morris, *Southern Slavery and the Law*. Robin L. Einhorn, *American Taxation, American Slavery* (Chicago, 2006), traces the origins of limited or anti-government rhetoric to slaveholders and highlights its operation in fundamentally shaping tax policy from the colonial era, through the Revolution and Civil War, with a lasting legacy to the present. On the Civil War as a catalyst in the transformation of global capitalism and the role of the imperial state in extracting labor in its service, see Sven Beckert, "Emancipation and Empire: Reconstructing the Worldwide Web of Cotton Production in the Age of the American Civil War," *American Historical Review* 109 (2004), 1405–38.

On Native Americans, a good beginning point for reading across the Revolutionary era is Richard White, *Middle Ground: Indians, Empires, and Republics in the Great Lakes Region, 1650–1815* (New York, 1997).

The shift to reason as the foundation for consent, the centrality of children to this rethinking, and then the use of children as an example to exclude others, including women and African Americans, on the grounds that they too lacked the capacity to reason required in a government based on reasoned consent is powerfully traced in Holly Brewer, *By Birth or Consent: Children, Law, & the Anglo-American Revolution in Authority* (Chapel Hill, NC, 2005).

Age of Jackson. The "Age of Jackson" is not, as Robin Einhorn puts it so succinctly in *American Taxation, American Slavery*, "what it used to be" (201). The expansion of white male suffrage takes on a less democratic cast when read against Indian removal and the narrowing of suffrage for women and African Americans in the North. On African Americans in the Jacksonian era, see Litwack, *North of Slavery*; Berlin, *Slaves Without Masters*; and Morris, *The Southern Law of Slavery*. On Indian removal, see Garrison, *The Legal Ideology of Removal: The Southern Judiciary and the Sovereignty of Native American Nations* (Athens, GA, 2003) and Jill Norgren, *The Cherokee Cases: The Confrontation of Law and Politics* (New York, 1996). On changes in women's lives and women's growing activism, good starting points for reading include Ellen Carol DuBois, *Feminism and Suffrage: The Emergence of an Independent Women's Movement in America, 1848–1869* (Ithaca, NY, 1978); Nancy Hewitt, *Women's Activism and Social Change: Rochester, New York, 1822–1872* (Ithaca, NY, 1984); and DuBois, *The Elizabeth Cady Stanton ~ Susan B. Anthony Reader: Correspondence, Writings, Speeches* (Boston, 1992). On women's pursuit of child custody and the erosion of male patriarchal privilege, see Michael Grossberg, *A Judgment for Solomon: The D'Hauteville Case and Legal Experience in Antebellum America* (New York, 1996). On women's activism in the abolitionist movement and its role in shaping the first women's movement, see Yellin, *Women and Sisters*. On the history of suffrage, see Alexander Keyssar, *The Right to Vote: The Contested History of Democracy in the United States* (New York, 2000). The threat to mastery though was not just from women and racial others; industrial transformation played a key role in limiting white men's independence even as it was proclaimed by the doctrine of "free labor." Key works on the legal construction of "free labor" are cited in Part I in the section, "Property."

The Civil War and Reconstruction. In reconsidering the Civil War as a turning point, it is important to look beyond the South and slavery to other subject groups, including, among others, women generally and Native Americans. The Civil War does not merit an index entry in Michael Grossberg's path-breaking study of family law, *Governing the Hearth: Law and the Family in Nineteenth-Century America* (Chapel Hill, NC, 1985). Grossberg's carefully crafted heading, "Americans Fashion Racial Restrictions," in a chapter on "Matrimonial Limitations" is broad enough to take in antebellum prohibitions on slave marriage and postbellum anti-miscegenation laws. See also in this regard Cott, *Public Vows*; Peter W. Bardaglio, *Reconstructing the Household: Families, Sex, & the Law in the Nineteenth-Century South* (Chapel Hill, NC, 1995); and Ostler, *The Plains Sioux and U.S. Colonialism*.

Emancipation itself reads differently paired with the Homestead Act and the criminalization of abortion. The literatures here are uneven, from the overwhelming scholarship on the Civil War and emancipation, to the smaller, but sophisticated literature on the history of abortion regulation, to a relative dearth of scholarship on the Homestead Act. As starting points on emancipation and Reconstruction, see Litwack, *Been in the Storm So Long*; Foner, *Reconstruction*; and Hahn, *A Nation Under Our Feet*. On the limits of free labor for freedmen and freedwomen, see especially Stanley, *From Bondage to Contract* and Kerber, *No Constitutional Right to be Ladies*. And on the mixed freedom of marriage for freedmen and freedwomen, see especially Franke, "Becoming a Citizen"; Stanley, *From Bondage to Contract*; and Cott, *Public Vows*. On abortion, see Gordon, *Woman's Body, Woman's Right*; James C. Mohr, *Abortion in America: The Origins and Evolution of National Policy, 1800–1900* (New York, 1978); and Reagan, *When Abortion Was a Crime*. And on the Homestead Act, the brief coverage of the Act provided in Lawrence M. Friedman, *A History of American Law* (2nd ed., New York, 1985).

Redemption, Empire, and the Progressive State. Possibly no historical moment has undergone more dramatic historical reinterpretation than the final quarter of the nineteenth century and the dawning of the twentieth. From a time when respectable historians could and did portray Redemption, Jim Crow, and black disfranchisement as positive developments – routing out corruption (Redemption), restoring the proper balance of things (disfranchisement), and protecting the rights of all (separate but equal), the Southern solution to the race question came to be seen as distinctly undemocratic, a turning away from the promise of the Civil War and Reconstruction. Even in this interpretation though the South remained cut off from the nation; the North's only responsibility was in losing interest. Yet even Woodward's *Strange Career of Jim Crow* argued that the Southern solution to the race question was made possible by a broader rethinking of race in the context of Western expansion and empire. Added to this, more recent work has suggested that the Southern solution to the race question was not backward looking, but in fact was distinctly modern. Yet even here race remains separate – a projection of Du Bois's prediction that "the problem of the twentieth century is the problem of the color line." (Du Bois, *The Souls of Black Folk* (1903; New York, 1994). And, as importantly, the literature of the Progressive era has remained largely separate from literature on the South and on Western expansion. Incorporating race into a broader picture and reading across a periodization that divides at the "Progressive era" to include topics ranging from Redemption, Jim Crow, and black disfranchisement; to allotment and consolidation of white land ownership in the West more generally; to immigration restriction; to the criminalization of birth control and adoption of protective labor legislation; to empire is critical not simply for seeing the terms of legal individuality at the end of the nineteenth century and the beginning of the twentieth but also for seeing how the safeguarding of the borders of belonging fundamentally gave shape to the twentieth-century American state.

On the legal aspects of Redemption and their implications for African American freedom in the South, see Foner, "The Politics of Freedom," in Foner, *Nothing But Freedom: Emancipation and Its Legacy* (Baton Rouge, LA, 1983), 39–73. On Jim Crow, see Woodward, *The Strange Career of Jim Crow* and Welke, *Recasting American Liberty*. On disfranchisement, see Kousser, *The Shaping of Southern Politics*; Gilmore, *Gender and Jim Crow*; and Perman, *Struggle for Mastery*.

On the criminalization of birth control, see Mohr, *Abortion in America*; Gordon, *Woman's Body, Woman's Right*; and Carroll Smith Rosenberg, *Disorderly Conduct: Visions of Gender in Victorian America* (New York, 1985), 217–44. On the development of the two-channel welfare state, see Linda Gordon, ed., *Women, the State, and Welfare* (Madison, WS, 1990); Gordon, *Pitied But Not Entitled: Single Mothers and the History of Welfare* (Cambridge, MA, 1994); Anna R. Igra, *Wives without Husbands: Marriage, Desertion, and Welfare in New York, 1900–1935* (Chapel Hill, NC, 2006); and Igra, "Likely to Become a Public Charge: Deserted Women and the Family Law of the Poor in New York City, 1910–1936," *Journal of Women's History* 11 (2000), 59–81; and Witt, *The Accidental Republic*. On protective labor legislation, see Baer, *Justice in Chains*; William E. Forbath, *Law and the Shaping of the American Labor Movement* (Cambridge, MA, 1989); Woloch, *Muller v. Oregon*; and, most importantly, Kessler-Harris, *In Pursuit of Equity*. Incursions on working-class white men's independence at the end of the nineteenth and early twentieth centuries, as in the Jacksonian era, made the borders of legal individuality relating to race and gender all the more fundamental. See Stanley, *From Bondage to Contract*; Michael Willrich, "Home Slackers: Men, the State, and Welfare in Modern America," *Journal of American History* 87 (2000), 460–89; and Frank Tobias Higbie, *Indispensable Outcasts: Hobo Workers and Community in the American Midwest, 1880–1930* (Champaign, IL, 2003).

On spatial boundaries, belonging, and the nation, see Salyer, *Laws Harsh as Tigers*; Lee, *At America's Gates*; Ngai, *Impossible Subjects*; and Sucheng Chan, "Exclusion of Chinese Women," in Sucheng Chan, ed., *Entry Denied: Exclusion and the Chinese Community in America, 1882–1943* (Philadelphia, 1991) on the

Chinese Exclusion Act and related legislation. On allotment, see N. C. Carter, "Race and Power Politics as Aspects of Federal Guardianship over American Indians: Land-Related Cases, 1887–1924," *American Indian Law Journal* 4 (1976), 197–248; Janet A. McDowell, *The Dispossession of the American Indian, 1887–1934* (Bloomington, IN, 1991); Hoxie, *A Final Promise*; and Emily Greenwald, *Reconfiguring the Reservation*. On the consolidation of white land ownership in the West more generally, see Glenn, *Unequal Freedom*; Gordon, *The Great Arizona Orphan Abduction*; Gunther Peck, *Reinventing Free Labor: Padrones and Immigrant Workers in the North American West, 1880–1930* (New York, 2000); and Montoya, *Translating Property*. On property exclusions based on race, see Glenn, *Unequal Freedom*; Delaney, *Race, Place, and the Law*; and Leowen, *Sundown Towns*.

On legal aspects of empire, see Cabranes, *Citizenship and the American Empire*; Raymond Carr, *Puerto Rico: A Colonial Experiment* (New York, 1984); Juan R. Torruella, *The Supreme Court and Puerto Rico: The Doctrine of Separate and Unequal* (Rio Piedras, P. R., 1988); Smith, *Civic Ideals*; Merry, *Colonizing Hawaii*; Christina Duffy Burnett and Burke Marshall, eds., *Foreign in a Domestic Sense: Puerto Rico, American Expansion, and the Constitution* (Durham, NC, 2001); and Ngai, "From Colonial Subject to Undesirable Alien." David Healy, *Drive to Hegemony: The United States in the Carribbean, 1898–1917* (Madison, WI, 1988) is helpful for providing an understanding of U.S. actions from the Spanish-American War through the Jones Act. See also Kirstin L. Hoganson, *Fighting for American Manhood: How Gender Politics Provoked the Spanish-American and Philippine-American Wars* (New Haven, CT, 1998) for its framing of empire and manhood.

It is also important to think across key "expansions" of citizenship in this period for the more complicated understanding of "inclusion" that reading them collectively presents, including the Jones Act (Puerto Rican citizenship), the Nineteenth Amendment (1920, woman suffrage), and the Indian Citizenship Act (1924). The literature on woman suffrage is very large; starting points include Eleanor Flexnor, *Century of Struggle: The Woman's Rights Movement in the United States*, rev. ed. (Cambridge, MA, 1975); Paula Baker, "The Domestication of Politics: Women and American Political Society, 1789–1920," *American Historical Review* 89 (1984), 620–47; DuBois, *Woman Suffrage & Women's Rights*; and Gilmore, *Gender & Jim Crow*. On the battle over women's jury service that followed suffrage, see Kerber, *No Constitutional Right to Be Ladies* and Gretchen Ritter, "Jury Service and Women's Citizenship Before and After the Nineteenth Amendment," *Law and History Review* 20 (2002), 479–516. On the Indian Citizenship Act and the Jones Act, see Smith, *Civic Ideals* and Kevin Bruyneel, "Challenging American Boundaries: Indigenous People and the 'Gift' of U.S. Citizenship," *Studies in American Political Development* 18 (2004), 130–43. Finally, on key naturalization cases that narrowed the meaning of the word "white" in the act and the tightening of immigration restriction both in the 1920s, see Lopez, *White By Law*; and Ngai, *Impossible Subjects*.

In the introduction to this essay, I explained that, in keeping with the chapter that this essay accompanies, the goals here would be different: more a way of reading than an exhaustive list of sources to which one should turn. I also promised a list of other chapters in the volumes to which readers might productively turn for more exhaustive reading lists on a number of the topics addressed in this essay. I recommend considering from Volume I: Chapter 2, The Law of Native Americans; Chapter 6, Penality and the Colonial Project: Crime, Punishment, and the Regulation of Morals; Chapter 7, Law, Population, Labor; Chapter 8, The Fragmented Laws of Slavery; Chapter 9, The Transformation of Domestic Law; Chapter 13, Law and the Origins of the American Revolution; and Chapter 14, Confederation and Constitution. From Volume II: Chapter 1, Law and the American State, from the Revolution to the Civil War; Chapter 5, Criminal Justice in the United States, 1790–1920: A Government of Laws or Men?; Chapter 6, Citizenship and Immigration Law, 1800–1924: Resolutions of Membership and Territory; Chapter 7, Federal Policy, Western Movement, and Consequences for Indigenous Peoples, 1790–1920; Chapter 8, Marriage and Domestic Relations; Chapter 9, Slavery, Anti-Slavery, and the Coming of the Civil War; Chapter 10, The Civil War and Reconstruction; and Chapter 19. Politics, State-Building, and the Courts, 1870–1920. And from Volume III: Chapter 6, Criminal Justice in the United States; Chapter 11, The Rights Revolution in the United States; Chapter 12, Race and Rights; and Chapter 13, Heterosexuality as a Legal Regime.

CHAPTER 12: LAW IN POPULAR CULTURE, 1790–1920

NAN GOODMAN

There are several legal histories that give popular legal developments their due. Of these Lawrence M. Friedman, *History of American Law* (New York, 1985); Maxwell Bloomfield, *American Lawyers in a Changing Society: 1776–1876* (Cambridge, MA, 1976); and Morton J. Horwitz, *The Transformation of American Law, 1780–1860* (Cambridge, MA, 1977), which delivers a Marxist interpretation, are among the best.

General histories of the Unites States abound, but the one with the best eye for popular history is Howard Zinn, *A People's History of the United States* (New York, 1980). Other historical studies that focus on the contributions of popular culture, but with slightly narrower scopes are Daniel Feller, *The Jacksonian Promise: America, 1815–1840* (Baltimore, 1995) and two ground-breaking studies by Richard Slotkin. *The Fatal Environment: The Myth of the Frontier in The Age of Industrialization, 1800–1890* (New York, 1985), and *Regeneration Through Violence: The Mythology of the American Frontier; 1600–1860* (Middletown, CT, 1973).

The subject of how law interacts with popular culture has been transformed by much recent social theory. The most influential and lucid explanations of this transformation are to be found in essays by Frederic Jameson, "Reification and Utopia in Mass Culture" *Social Text* 1 (1979); Robert Cover, "Nomos and Narrative," in Martha Minow, Michael Ryan, and Austin Sarat, eds., *Narrative, Violence, and the Law: The Essays of Robert Cover* (Ann Arbor, MI, 1992); Hendrik Hartog, "Pigs and Positivism," *Wisconsin Law Review* (1985); J. Rosen, "The Social Police," *The New Yorker* (Oct. 20, 1997); Lawrence, M. Friedman, "Law, Lawyers, and Popular Culture," 98 *Yale Law Journal* 98 (1989), 8. That the disciplinary power of law can be seen in enforcement mechanisms like the prison has also been established by Michel Foucault in his masterful *Discipline and Punish: The Birth of the Prison* (New York, 1979).

A number of the books that contribute to and make use of this theory are Richard K Sherwin, *When Law Goes Pop: The Vanishing Line between Law and Popular Culture* (Chicago, 2000); Steve Redhead, *Unpopular Cultures: The Birth of Law and Popular Culture* (New York, 1995); Eric A. Posner, *Law and Social Norms* (Cambridge, MA, 2000); and Austin Sarat and Thomas R. Kearns, eds., *Law in the Domains of Culture* (Ann Arbor, MI, 1998). Robert C. Ellickson, *Order Without Law: How Neighbors Settle Disputes* (Cambridge, MA, 1991) applies a new understanding of law to specific land use questions in Northern California.

There are countless excellent studies of the literary and artistic manifestations of popular culture and its circulation throughout the nineteenth century as a whole. Studies of particular popular culture events include Richard Wightman Fox and T.J. Jackson Lears, *The Power of Culture: Critical Essays in American History* (Chicago, 1993), whose chapter on the Beecher-Tilton trial is both detailed and entertaining. The best book, encyclopedic in scope, on the actual inventions and technologies of ordinary life through the ages is Sigfried Giedion, *Mechanization Takes Command* (New York, 1948).

Many works on popular culture in the nineteenth century give literary culture more space than any other subculture. The most comprehensive of these is David S. Reynolds, *Beneath the American Renaissance: The Subversive Imagination in the Age of Emerson and Melville* (Cambridge, MA, 1989). Another general study more related to late-century artifacts of popular culture is David E. Shi, *Facing Facts: Realism in American Thought and Culture, 1850–1920* (New York, 1995). Several invaluable studies focus on particular popular literary genres, like Lee Clark Mitchell, *Westerns: Making the Man in Fiction and Film* (Chicago, 1996) and Jane Tompkins, *West of Everything: The Inner Life of Westerns* (New York, 1992). The best study of this kind is Michael Denning, *Mechanic Accents: Dime Novels and Working-Class Culture in America* (New York, 1987); Karen Halttunen, *Murder Most Foul: The Killer and the American Gothic Imagination* (Cambridge, MA, 1998) traces the nineteenth- and twentieth-century fascination with crime in America back to Puritan and eighteenth-century exposes. Similar early links can be found in Nancy Ruttenburg, *Democratic Personality: Popular Voice and the Trial of American Authorship* (Stanford, CA 1998). One of the best books on the connections between minstrelsy and both black and white culture is Eric Lott, *Love & Theft: Blackface Minstrelsy and the American Working Class* (New York, 1995). There are also several good studies of nineteenth-century literary texts that theorize the connection between legal and literary culture: Brook Thomas, *American Literary Realism and the Failed Promise of Contract* (Berkeley, CA, 1997); Wai Chee Dimock, *Resides of Justice: Literature, Law, Philosophy* (Berkeley, CA, 1996); Nan Goodman, *Shifting the Blame: Literature, Law, and the Theory of Accidents* (Princeton, NJ, 1998); Robert A. Ferguson, *Law and Letters in American Culture* (Cambridge, MA, 1984); and James Boyd White, *Heracles's Bow: Essays on the Rhetoric and Poetics of the Law* (Madison, WI, 1985).

Once neglected, the subject of women's popular culture is now perhaps the most thoroughly covered. The best of it includes Jean Fagin Yellin, *Women & Sisters: The Antislavery Feminists in American Culture* (New Haven, CT, 1989); one of the earliest and least tendentious books is Barbara J. Berg, *The Remembered Gate: Origins of American Feminism: The Woman & The City, 1800–1860* (New York, 1978). Lori D. Ginzberg, *Women and the Work of Benevolence: Morality, Politics, and Class in the 19th Century United States* (New Haven, CT, 1990) offers an unusually coherent narrative of middle-class women's work, as does Mary P. Ryan's, *Women in Public: Between Banners and Ballots, 1825–1880* (Baltimore, 1990). A controversial approach to women's sentimental culture is Ann Douglas, *The Feminization of American Culture* (New York, 1977). A book that focuses on only one area of reform and therefore offers an enormous wealth of concentrated detail is Ruth Rosen, *The Lost Sisterhood: Prostitution in America, 1900–1918*. Less overtly interested in reform, but very valuable on the subject of divorce in the nineteenth century is Hendrik Hartog, *Man & Wife in America: A History* (Cambridge, MA, 2000). A brief but extremely useful study that addresses itself to women's social and moral position, with a special interest in the literary manifestations thereof, is Rachel Bowlby, *Just Looking: Consumer Culture in Dreiser, Gissing and Zola* (New York, 1985).

CHAPTER 13: LAW AND RELIGION, 1790–1920

SARAH BARRINGER GORDON

Primary Sources

The single richest collection of primary documents for the entire period is contained in Anson Phelps Stokes, *Church and State in the United States: Historical Development and Contemporary Problems of Religious Freedom Under the Constitution*, 3 vols. (New York, 1950).

Constitutional provisions at both the state and federal level are key to understanding the public law of religion and have been the subject of extensive and often bitter litigation. State constitutions are collected in C.J. Antieau, *Religion Under the State Constitutions* (Brooklyn, NY, 1965) and *Constitutions of the States and the United States* (Albany, 1938). Constitutional conventions where delegates debated the law of religion are also valuable. See, for example, New York, *Reports of the Proceedings and Debates of the Convention of 1821* (New York, 1821). Debates at the federal level surrounding the adoption of the religion clauses are less revealing: see U.S. Congress, *Debates and Proceedings in the Congress of the United States* (Washington, DC, 1834), vol. 1. Their paucity partially explains the intensity of modern debate over the religious commitments (or lack thereof) among the Framers of the Bill of Rights.

State and federal court decisions are also vital to the increasingly sophisticated understanding of government and its relation to religious individuals and institutions among American citizens. State supreme court opinions, especially in the Early Republic, set the standard for the next century and beyond. In New York, Massachusetts, Delaware, and Pennsylvania the jurisprudence of religion delineated boundaries around religious liberty and the privileges of religious institutions and provoked a rebuke from Thomas Jefferson, "Whether Christianity is Part of the Common Law?" in P. L. Ford, ed., *The Writings of Thomas Jefferson* (New York, 1892), 360–67.

Equally important, commentators wrote extensively on whether and how Americans and their governments were religious or respected religious commitments. The work of Associate Justice Joseph Story, including his *Commentaries on the Constitution of the United States*, 3 vols. (Boston, 1833) 3: sections 1865–73; James Kent, *Commentaries on American Law*, 4 vols. (New York, 1832); Christopher G. Tiedemann, *The Unwritten Constitution of the United States* (New York, 1890); Thomas M. Cooley, *Constitutional Limitations* (1868; New York, 1972), and other treatise writers all attempted to provide a uniform and defensible explanation of American law and decision making in the field. In addition, foreign observers of the young nation provided valuable insight into how religion functioned formally and informally in both law and politics. See, e.g., Alexis de Tocqueville, *Democracy in America*, trans. Henry Reeve (1833; London, 1875) and James Viscount Bryce, *The American Commonwealth* (London, 1888).

Religious writing in the field is also extensive and includes the work of apologists, such as Philip Schaff, *America: A Sketch of its Political, Social and Religious Character* (1855; Cambridge, MA, 1961); B. F. Morris, *Christian Life and Character of the Civil Institutions of the United States Developed in the Official and Historical Annals of the United States* (Philadelphia, 1864); and Sanford Cobb, *The Rise of Religious Liberty in America: A History* (New York, 1902).

The private law of religion, including church polity, property, and philanthropic undertakings, is less well treated in the literature, but does include an important and comprehensive treatise by Carl Zollman, *American Civil Church Law* (New York, 1917). See also William H. Roberts, *Laws Relating to Religious Corporations* (Philadelphia, 1896) and Patrick J. Dignan, *A History of the Legal Incorporation of Catholic Church Property in the United States, 1784–1932* (New York, 1935).

The Federal Religion Clauses

The importance and controversy surrounding Supreme Court opinions in this area in recent history have elevated attention paid to the Federal Constitution's treatment of religion. The result is an enormous body of work, much of it focused on whether the Framers intended to remove religion from government entirely or whether they had a more integrated relationship in mind. Some scholars have proposed that the word "religion" means different things in the establishment context than for free exercise claims or that the tensions between a regime of perfect disestablishment and one of perfect toleration mean that the Constitution must have been conceived with perfect neutrality between religion and secular interests in mind: see Lawrence Tribe, *American Constitutional Law* (Mineola, NY, 1978), 826–33 and Philip Kurland, *Religion and the Law of Church and State and the Supreme Court* (Chicago, 1962).

The lack of any precise answer to such vexing questions has produced intense battles among proponents of one or the another perspective on what should be done and how that relates to what the Framers intended. For example, recent studies have probed what a concept such as separation of church and state should be understood to have meant in the late eighteenth century and how the phrase has been manipulated over the past two centuries. See, e.g., the work of Daniel L. Dreisbach, *Thomas Jefferson and the Wall of Separation Between Church and State* (New York, 2002) on Jefferson's letter to the Danbury Baptists and Philip Hamburger's *Separation of Church and State* (Cambridge, MA, 2002), both valuable if often tendentious monographs on separationism and its motivation, as well as Mark DeWolfe Howe, *The Garden and the Wilderness* (Boston, 1965), a readable and thoughtful essay on the long history of separation from the perspective of early believers, such as Roger Williams, Massachusetts Baptists, and the like. See also, for example, Jon Meacham, *American Gospel: God, the Founding Fathers, and the Making of a Nation* (New York, 2006) and Brooke Allen, *Moral Minority: Our Skeptical Founding Fathers* (Chicago, 2006), warring books published recently that take diametrically opposed positions on the Founders' religious commitments, the latest salvos in a war that has raged more or less intensely for fifty years. Such battles have drawn bemused reflections from historians, many of whom argue that scarce records reveal more about the political climate of the late eighteenth century than guidance for contemporary society and its legal troubles. See, e.g., Kenneth R. Bowling, "'A Tub to the Whale': The Founding Fathers and the Adoption of the Bill of Rights," *Journal of the Early Republic* 8 (1988), 223.

On the federal law of religion before 1920, the controversy over Mormon polygamy dominates; see Sarah Barringer Gordon, *The Mormon Question: Polygamy and Constitutional Conflict in Nineteenth Century America* (Chapel Hill, NC, 2002). On the theory that the United States was a "Christian nation," see Linda Przybyszewski, "Judicial Conservatism and Protestant Faith: The Case of Justice David J. Brewer," *Journal of American History* 91 (2004), 471–96.

State Law of Religion

The contest over interpretation of the federal religion clauses has meant that scholarship on the laws of particular states (Virginia excepted) has been far less voluminous, even though state law governed for most of American history. See Merrill D. Peterson and Robert C. Vaughan, *The Virginia Statute for Religious Freedom: Its Evolution and Consequences in American History* (New York, 1988); William G. McLoughlin, *New England Dissent, 1630–1833: The Baptists and the Separation of Church and State*, 2 vols. (Cambridge, MA, 1971); Mark Douglas McGarvie, *One Nation Under Law: America's Early National Struggles to Separate Church and State* (DeKalb, IL, 2004); Sarah Barringer Gordon, "Blasphemy and the Law of Religious Liberty in Nineteenth-Century America," *American Quarterly* 52 (2000); Leonard W. Levy, *Blasphemy in Massachusetts: Freedom of Conscience and the Abner Kneeland Case* (New York, 1973); Michael W. McConnell, "The Origins and Historical Understanding of Free Exercise of Religion," *Harvard Law Review* 103 (1990), 1511–12: R. Laurence Moore, *Religious Outsiders and the Making of Americans* (New York, 1987); and Stuart Banner, "When Christianity Was Part of the Common Law," *Law & History Review* 16 (1998), 27–62.

On the new market in religion in the early nineteenth century and the reformist impulse, see Mary P. Ryan, *Cradle of the Middle Class* (New York, 1981); Charles Sellers, *The Market Revolution* (New York, 1991); R. Laurence Moore, *Selling God: American Religion in the Marketplace of Culture* (New York, 1994); Paul E. Johnson, *A Shopkeeper's Millennium* (New York, 1978); Sean Wilentz and Paul E. Johnson, *The Kingdom of Matthias* (New York, 1994); Louis P. Masur, "Religion and Reform in America, 1776–1860," in John F. Wilson, ed., *Church and State in America* (Wesport, CT, 1986), 225–50; and Elizabeth B. Clark, "The 'Sacred Rights of the Weak': Pain, Sympathy, and the Culture of Individual Rights in Antebellum America," *Journal of American History* 82 (1995), 463–93.

On the state law of religion in education, see, e.g., Samuel W. Brown, *The Secularization of American Education, as Shown by State Legislation, Constitutional Provisions, and Supreme Court Decisions* (New York, 1912); Edward Larson, *The Blaine Amendment in State Constitutions* (Grand Rapids, MI, 1993); Alvin W. Johnson, *The Legal Status of Church-State Relationships in the United States* (Minneapolis,1934); and Michael Grossberg, "Teaching the Republican Child: Three Antebellum Stories about Law, School, and the Construction of American Families," *Utah Law Review* (1997), 429–60. On tax exemptions and Sabbath legislation, see Carl Zollman, *American Civil Church Law*; William Addison Blakely, ed., *American State Papers Bearing on Sunday Legislation* (1911; New York, 1970); and American Civil Liberties Union, *Religious Liberty in the United States Today* (New York, 1939).

On morals legislation and Prohibition, as well as Progressive impulses and the relationship between scientific and religious thought in the late nineteenth and early twentieth centuries, see Louis Menand, *The Metaphysical Club: A Story of Ideas in America* (New York, 2001), which is very wide ranging, but insightful on legal ideas of tolerance and their relationship to religion and science; Edward Larson, *Summer for the Gods: The Scopes Trial and America's Debate over Creation and Evolution* (New York, 1997); Susanna Blumenthal, "The Deviance of the Will: Policing the Bounds of Testamentary Freedom in Nineteenth-Century America," *Harvard Law Review* 119 (2006), 959; and Gaines M. Foster, *Moral Reconstruction: Christian Lobbyists and the Federal Legislation of Morality, 1865–1920* (Chapel Hill, NC, 2002).

CHAPTER 14: LEGAL INNOVATION AND MARKET CAPITALISM, 1790–1920

TONY A. FREYER

A constitutive theory of legal innovation and market relations is suggested by Douglass C. North, *Institutions, Institutional Change, and Economic Performance* (Cambridge, 1990) and Clifford D. Shearing, "A Constitutive Conception of Regulation," in Peter Grabosky and John Braithwaite, eds., *Business Regulation in Australia's Future* (Canberra, 1993). An excellent overview of the changing legal historiography and methodologies measured against the influence of James Willard Hurst – which fits readily into a constitutive theory – is "Engaging Willard Hurst: A Symposium," *Law and History Review* 18 (2000), vii–222. Three surveys of the American law of property, contract, tort, and corporations during the long nineteenth century – which reference the contrasting British legal history – are Lawrence M. Friedman, *A History of American Law* (New York, 1985), which follows a Hurstian argument; Peter Karsten's frankly revisionist cultural and institutional analysis, *Heart Versus Head: Judge-Made Law in Nineteenth-Century America* (Chapel Hill, NC, 1997); and Kermit L. Hall, *The Magic Mirror: Law in American History* (New York, 1989). For an expressly instrumental interpretation of law see Morton J. Horwitz, *The Transformation of American Law, 1780–1860* (Cambridge, MA, 1977) and *The Transformation of American Law, 1870–1960: The Crisis of Legal Orthodoxy* (New York, 1992).

For the theme of law, sectional diversity, the federal polity, and market relations see Harry N. Scheiber, "Federalism and the American Economic Order, 1789–1910," *Law and Society Review* 10 (1975), 57–118 and his "Property Law, Expropriation, and Resource Allocation by Government, 1789–1910," *Journal of Economic History* 33 (1973), 232–51; Tony A. Freyer, *Producers Versus Capitalists: Constitutional Conflict in Antebellum America* (Charlottesville, VA, 1994); Timothy S. Huebner, *The Southern Judicial Tradition, State Judges and Sectional Distinctiveness, 1790–1890* (Athens, GA, 1999); and Lawrence M. Friedman, "The Law Between the States: Some Thoughts on Southern Legal History," Tony A. Freyer, "The Law and The Antebellum Southern Economy: An Interpretation," and Harry N. Scheiber, "Federalism, the Southern Regional Economy, and Public Policy Since 1865," all in James W. Ely, Jr., and David J. Bodenhamer, eds., *Ambivalent Legacy: A Legal History of the South* (Jackson, MS, 1984). For the influence of the federal courts on business within the federal system see Edward A. Purcell, Jr., *Litigation and Inequality: Federal Diversity Jurisdiction in Industrial America, 1870–1958* (New York, 1992) and Tony

A. Freyer, *Forums of Order: The Federal Courts and Business in American History* (Greenwich, CT, 1979).

Useful studies of legal-constitutional institutions and culture, including the U.S. Supreme Court, are Henry J. Bourguignon, *The First Federal Court: The Federal Appellate Prize Court of the American Revolution, 1775–1787* (Philadelphia, 1977); Forrest McDonald, *Novus Ordo Seclorum: The Intellectual Origins of the Constitution* (Lawrence, KS, 1985); Michael Kammen, *A Machine That Would Go of Itself* (New York, 1994); R. Kent Newmyer, *John Marshall and the Heroic Age of the Supreme Court* (Baton Rouge, LA, 2001); Harold M. Hyman and William M. Wiecek, *Equal Justice Under Law: Constitutional Development, 1835–1875* (New York, 1986); Linda Przybyszewski, *The Republic According to John Marshall Harlan* (Chapel Hill, NC, 1999); and Edward A. Purcell, *Brandeis and the Progressive Constitution: Erie, the Judicial Power, and the Politics of the Federal Courts in Twentieth-Century America* (New Haven, 2000). For the bearing of legal-constitutional change and the market on the rise of regulation see William J. Novak, *The People's Welfare, Law and Regulation in Nineteenth-Century America* (Chapel Hill, NC, 1996), Morton Keller, *Affairs of State: Public Life in Late Nineteenth-Century America* (Cambridge, MA, 1977) and his *Regulating a New Economy: Public Policy and Economic Change in America, 1900–1933* (Cambridge, MA, 1990); and Thomas K. McCraw, *Prophets of Regulation: Charles Francis Adams, Louis D. Brandeis, James M. Landis, and Alfred E. Kahn* (Cambridge, MA, 1984). For the ubiquitous *Swift* doctrine, see Tony Freyer, *Harmony & Dissonance: The Swift & Erie Cases in American Federalism* (New York, 1981).

Studies of the substantive law and ideological-institutional context of the public and business corporation are John Lauritz Larson, *Internal Improvement: National Public Works and the Promise of Popular Government in the Early United States* (Chapel Hill, NC, 2001); Herbert Hovenkamp, *Enterprise and American Law, 1836–1937* (Cambridge, MA, 1991); Naomi R. Lamoreaux, *The Great Merger Wave* (Cambridge, 1985); Alfred D. Chandler, Jr., *The Visible Hand: The Managerial Revolution in American Business* (Cambridge, MA, 1977); and James Willard Hurst, *The Legitimacy of the Business Corporation in the Law of the United States, 1780–1970* (Charlottesville, VA, 1970). These studies should be reconsidered in light of Gregory A. Mark, "The Court and the Corporation: Jurisprudence, Localism, and Federalism," *Supreme Court Review* (1993), 403–37 and, regarding corporate governance and the separation of owners and management, Allen D. Boyer, "Activist Shareholders, Corporate Directors, and Institutional Investment: Some Lessons from the Robber Barons," *Washington and Lee Law Review*, 50 (1993), 977–1042; and, most importantly, the massive new empirical findings in Susan Pace Hamill, "From Special Privilege to General Utility: A Continuation of Willard Hurst's Study of Corporations," *American University Law Review* 49 (1999), 81–180.

This chapter's interpretation of several sub-themes draws on the following. For professional legal culture see Samuel Haber, *The Quest for Authority and Honor in the American Professions, 1750–1900* (Chicago, 1991); F. Thornton

Miller, *Juries and Judges Versus the Law, Virginia's Provincial Legal Perspective, 1783–1828* (Charlottesville, VA, 1994); and William G. Thomas, *Lawyering for the Railroad Business: Law and Power in the New South* (Baton Rouge, LA, 1999). On antitrust see Martin J. Sklar, *The Corporate Reconstruction of American Capitalism, 1890–1916: The Market, the Law, and Politics* (Cambridge, 1988) and Tony A. Freyer, *Regulating Big Business: Antitrust in Great Britain and America 1880–1990* (Cambridge, 1990). The noteworthy yet too often forgotten issue of the stock law is considered in J. Crawford King, Jr., "The Closing of the Southern Range: An Exploratory Study," *Journal of Southern History* 48 (1982). For the changing political party and public discourse regarding market capitalism within which legal-constitutional innovation evolved, see Larson, *Internal Improvement*; Keller, *Affairs of State*; Eric Foner, "The Meaning of Freedom in the Age of Emancipation," *Journal of American History* 81 (1994), 435–60; and Walter T. K. Nugent, *From Centennial to World War: American Society, 1876–1917* (Indianapolis, 1977).

The law's contrasting identification of "otherness" is explored in many sources. The conflicted status of free labor itself is considered in Christopher L. Tomlins, *Law, Labor, and Ideology in the Early American Republic* (Cambridge, 1993); Robert J. Steinfeld, *Coercion, Contract, and Free Labor in the Nineteenth Century* (Cambridge, 2001); and Ruth O'Brien, *Workers' Paradox: The Republican Origins of New Deal Labor Policy, 1886–1935* (Chapel Hill, NC, 1998). The arbitrary impact of law and market relations on blacks in the post-Civil War South is examined in Gavin Wright, *Old South, New South: Revolutions in the Southern Economy Since the Civil War* (New York, 1986); Harold D. Woodman, "Post-Civil War Southern Agriculture and Law," *Agricultural History* 53 (1979), 319–37; and a revisionist study, Richard Holcombe Kilbourne Jr., *Debt, Investment, Slaves, Credit Relations in East Feliciana Parish Louisiana, 1825–1885* (Tuscaloosa, AL, 1995). On gender, see Amy Dru Stanley, *From Bondage to Contract Wage: Labor, Marriage, and the Market in the Age of Emancipation* (Cambridge, 1998) and Joan Hoff, *Law Gender & Injustice: A Legal History of U.S. Women* (New York, 1991). An introduction to the unique legal-constitutional and market position of Native Americans is Sydney Harring, *Crow Dog's Case: American Indian Sovereignty, Tribal Law, and United States Law in the Nineteenth Century* (Cambridge, 1994). A good overview of the Chinese in the legal-constitutional order and market is Charles J. McClain, *In Search of Equality: The Chinese Struggle Against Discrimination in Nineteenth-Century America* (Berkeley, 1994).

For the institutional and cultural imperatives of otherness and market capitalism reflected in tort and bankruptcy law see the following. On tort accident claims, see Barbara Young Welke, *Recasting American Liberty: Gender, Race, Law, and the Railroad Revolution, 1865–1920* (Cambridge, 2001) and Nan Goodman, *Shifting the Blame: Literature, Law, and the Theory of Accidents in Nineteenth-Century America* (Princeton, 1998). These works revise an instrumental or moralistic view of tort law: Gary T. Schwartz, "Tort Law and the Economy in

Nineteenth-Century America: A Reinterpretation," *Yale Law Journal*, 90 (1981), 1717–75; Robert J. Kaczorowski, "The Common Law Background of Nineteenth-Century Tort Law," *Ohio State Law Journal*, 51 (1990), 1127–99; and Randolph E. Bergstrom, *Courting Danger: Injury and Law in New York City, 1870–1910* (Ithaca, 1992). This chapter's casting of failed debtors as society's most conspicuous losers is suggested by Peter J. Coleman, *Debtors and Creditors in America: Insolvency, Imprisonment for Debt and Bankruptcy, 1607–1900* (Madison, WI, 1974); Bruce H. Mann, *Republic of Debtors Bankruptcy in the Age of American Independence* (Cambridge, MA, 2002); Edward J. Balleisen, *Navigating Failure Bankruptcy and Commercial Society in Antebellum America* (Chapel Hill, NC, 2001); and David A. Skeel, Jr., *Debt's Dominion: A History of Bankruptcy Law in America* (Princeton, 2001).

The leading work on the law of slavery and free blacks remains Thomas D. Morris, *Southern Slavery and the Law, 1617–1860* (Chapel Hill, NC, 1996); see also Robert W. Fogel, *Without Consent or Contract: The Rise and Fall of American Slavery* (New York, 1989). Joshua D. Rothman's extensive use of legal sources, if not his interpretation, in *Notorious in the Neighborhood: Sex and Families Across the Color Line in Virginia, 1787–1861* (Chapel Hill, NC, 2003) shows that property-holding free blacks usually won in debtor-creditor disputes. Alfred L. Brophy explores the contentious public discourse of law, literature, and religion arising from antebellum market capitalism in "'A revolution which seeks to abolish law must end necessarily in despotism': Louisa McCord and Antebellum Southern Legal Thought," *Cardozo Women's Law Journal* 5 (1998), 33–77 and "'Over and above . . . there broods a portentous shadow, – the shadow of *law*': Harriet Beecher Stowe's Critique of Slave Law in *Uncle Tom's Cabin*," *Journal of Law and Religion*, 12 (1995–96), 457–506. A revisionist account of the potential for justice in the Thirteenth Amendment is Michael Vorenberg, *Final Freedom: The Civil War, the Abolition of Slavery, and the Thirteenth Amendment* (Cambridge, 2001); see also William E. Nelson's *Fourteenth Amendment: From Political Principle to Judicial Doctrine* (Cambridge, MA, 1988).

This chapter locates legal-constitutional innovation and market capitalism within a macroeconomic context drawn primarily from Stanley L. Engerman and Robert E. Gallman, eds., *The Cambridge Economic History of the United States, Vol. II: The Long Nineteenth Century* (Cambridge, 2000), especially Clayne Pope, "Inequality in the Nineteenth Century," 109–42; Stanley L. Engerman, "Slavery and Its Consequences for the South in the Nineteenth Century," 329–66; Stanley, L. Engerman and Kenneth L. Sokoloff, "Technology and Industrialization, 1790–1914," 367–402; Naomi R. Lamoreaux, "Entrepreneurship, Business Organization, and Economic Concentration," 403–34; Richard Sylla, "Experimental Federalism: The Economics of American Government, 1789–1914," 483–541; and Stuart M. Blumin, "The Social Implications of U.S. Economic Development," 813–64. See also Stuart M. Blumin, *The Emergence of the Middle Class Social Experience in the American City, 1760–1900* (Cambridge, 1989).

CHAPTER 15: INNOVATIONS IN LAW AND TECHNOLOGY, 1790–1920

B. ZORINA KHAN

The major arguments in this chapter are based on my reading of more than a thousand appellate decisions at the state and federal levels. Unattributed statistics on the distribution of lawsuits were computed from the population of reported cases. Figures 15.1 to 15.4 reflect numerical counts of lawsuits used to construct samples that illustrate tendencies over time, even if the specific numbers do not represent the entire population of disputes in that category. General historical data were drawn from the U.S. Bureau of the Census, *Historical Statistics of the United States, Colonial Times to 1970* (Washington, DC, 1975). Stanley Lebergott, *The American Economy: Income, Wealth and Want* (Princeton, NJ, 1962) and *Pursuing Happiness: American Consumers in the Twentieth Century* (Princeton, NJ, 1993) provide information of the diffusion of goods and services in the early twentieth century.

Introduction and Conclusion

The introductory epigraph is from *New York Trust Company et al. v. Eisner*, 256 U.S. 345, 349 (1921). Justice Holmes's view of the relationship between history and law was shared by Benjamin Cardozo: "Not logic alone, but logic supplemented by the social sciences becomes the instrument of advance"; see *The Growth of Law* (New Haven, CT, 1924), 73. The epigraph in the conclusion is from Benjamin Cardozo, *The Nature of the Judicial Process* (New Haven, CT, 1921), 66.

Thomas Paine felt that "in America THE LAW IS KING" (capitalized in the original text), *Common Sense* (Philadelphia, 1776), Chapter III, 49. Alexis de Tocqueville argued that American courts wielded enormous political power: "Scarcely any question arises in the United States which does not become, sooner or later, a subject of judicial debate"; see Alexis de Tocqueville, *Democracy in America*, ed. J. P. Mayer, trans. George Lawrence (1835; New York, 1969), vol. I, Chapter 8, 311. For the Jefferson quote, see the inscription at the Jefferson Memorial in Washington, DC, which is taken from his letter to Samuel Kercheval of July 12, 1810. A typical statement that illustrates the view that our times are unique appears in the Office of Technology Assessment, *Intellectual Property Rights in an Age of Electronics and Information* (Washington, DC, 1986). Daniel Boorstin characterized the United States as a republic of technology in *The Republic of Technology: Reflections on Our Future Community* (New York, 1978).

I have benefited from reading the work of Stanley Engerman and Kenneth Sokoloff on the role of institutions in economic history. For a synopsis of their arguments, see Kenneth L. Sokoloff and Stanley L. Engerman, "Institutions, Factor Endowments, and Paths of Development in the New World," *Journal of Economic Perspectives* 14 (2000), 217–32 and "Institutional and Non-Institutional Explanation of Economic Differences," in Claude Menard and Mary Shirley, eds., *Handbook of New Institutional Economics* (New York, 2005).

For a somewhat different and ahistorical perspective, which views the specific choice of appropriate institutions (markets, courts, or the political process) as key to formulating effective social policy, see Neil Komesar, *Imperfect Alternatives: Choosing Institutions in Law, Economics and Public Policy* (Chicago, 1994). I obtained insights into the operation of colonial courts from an extensive dataset of district court cases, which is described in B. Zorina Khan, "'Justice of the Marketplace': Legal Disputes and Economic Activity on the Northeastern Frontier, 1700–1860" (unpublished paper, 2003).

The standard legal histories include Morton J. Horwitz, *The Transformation of American Law, 1780–1860* (Cambridge, MA, 1977) and *The Transformation of American Law, 1870–1960: The Crisis of Legal Orthodoxy* (New York, 1992); Lawrence M. Friedman, *A History of American Law* (New York, 1973); and James Willard Hurst, *Law and the Conditions of Freedom in the Nineteenth-Century United States* (Madison, WI, 1956). See also Kermit L. Hall, *The Magic Mirror: Law in American History* (New York, 1989). Edward L. Glaeser and Andrei Shleifer argue, "During the Progressive Era at the beginning of the 20th century, the United States replaced litigation by regulation as the principal mechanism of social control of business" in "The Rise of the Regulatory State," *NBER Working Paper No. 8650* (2001).

Critics of the subsidy thesis regard the most effective rebuttal to be simply an objective and extensive reading of lawsuits and legal procedures. They highlight the complementary relationship among legislature, the Constitution, and the judiciary. Peter Karsten, *Heart Versus Head: Judge-Made Law in Nineteenth-Century America* (Chapel Hill, NC, 1997) argues that court decisions on contracts, torts, and property law tended to protect workers and were not perceptibly biased toward defendants or capitalist developers. See also Tony A. Freyer, *Producers Versus Capitalists: Constitutional Conflict in Antebellum America* (Charlottesville, VA, 1994). Gary T. Schwartz critically reviewed Horwitz's interpretation of negligence doctrines in "Tort Law and the Economy in Nineteenth-Century America: A Reinterpretation," *Yale Law Journal* 90 (1982), 1717–75 and "The Character of Early American Tort Law," *UCLA Law Review* 36 (1989), 641–718.

Benjamin Cardozo points to the pursuit of social welfare as the ultimate objective of the legal system, "Sooner or later, if the demands of social utility are sufficiently urgent, if the operation of an existing rule is sufficiently productive of hardship or inconvenience, utility will tend to triumph." See Benjamin Cardozo, *The Growth of Law*, 117. Cardozo, *The Nature of the Judicial Process* also highlights the use of analogy in judicial decision making. Cass Sunstein, "On Analogical Reasoning," *Harvard Law Review* 106 (1993), 741, 786, argues that analogical reasoning allows greater long-term flexibility.

Patents

The section on patent and copyright laws primarily draws on B. Zorina Khan, *The Democratization of Invention: Patents and Copyrights in American Economic*

Development (Cambridge, 2005). For accounts of the development of the American patent system see also Bruce Bugbee, *The Genesis of American Patent and Copyright Law* (Washington, DC, 1967); B. Zorina Khan and Kenneth L. Sokoloff, "The Early Development of Intellectual Property Institutions in the United States," *Journal of Economic Perspectives* 15 (2001), 233–46; and B. Zorina Khan, "Property Rights and Patent Litigation in Early Nineteenth-Century America," *Journal of Economic History* 55 (1995), 58–97. B. Zorina Khan, "Married Women's Property Laws and Female Commercial Activity: Evidence from United States Patent Records, 1790–1895," *Journal of Economic History* 56 (1996), 356–88, examines the influence of changes in state laws on patenting activities by women.

For a synopsis of an extensive project that analyzes the market for assignments, see Naomi Lamoreaux and Kenneth L. Sokoloff, "Long-Term Change in the Organization of Inventive Activity," *Science, Technology and the Economy* 93 (1996), 1286–92. See also B. Zorina Khan and Kenneth L. Sokoloff, "Institutions and Democratic Invention in 19th Century America: Evidence from the 'Great Inventors,' 1790–1930," *American Economic Review* (2004), 395–401. The standard reference on the development of international patent harmonization is Edith Penrose, *Economics of the International Patent System* (Baltimore, 1951). B. Zorina Khan and Kenneth L. Sokoloff, "The Innovation of Patent Systems in the Nineteenth Century: A Comparative Perspective (2002) discuss American exceptionalism and highlight the importance of low fees and an examination system in accounting for the nature of American patenting relative to other countries. The liberality of American laws to foreign inventors is addressed in F. A. Seely, "International Protection of Industrial Property," in *Proceedings and Addresses: Celebration of the Beginning of the Second Century of the American Patent System* (Washington, DC, 1892), 205.

Copyright

Stephen Breyer highlights the arguments against widespread copyright protection in "The Uneasy Case for Copyright: A Study of Copyright in Books, Photocopies and Computer Programs," *Harvard Law Review* 84 (1970), 281–351. A useful nineteenth-century source is G. H. Putnam, *The Question of Copyright* (New York, 1896). Legal scholars have recently directed significant attention to copyright issues. Books on the subject include Paul Goldstein's *Copyright's Highway: The Law & Lore of Copyright from Gutenberg to the Celestial Jukebox* (New York, 1994) and Jessica Litman, *Digital Copyright* (Amherst, 2001). Benjamin Kaplan, *An Unhurried View of Copyright* (New York, 1968) outlines the history of U.S. copyright law, whereas Lyman Patterson, *Copyright in Historical Perspective* (Nashville, 1968) is somewhat broader. See also Mark Rose, *Authors and Owners: The Invention of Copyright* (Cambridge, MA, 1993). Aubrey J. Clark examines lobbying for reforms in international copyright laws: see *The Movement for International Copyright in Nineteenth Century America* (Washington, DC,

1960); whereas the perspective of British groups is analyzed in John Feather, *Publishing, Piracy and Politics: An Historical Study of Copyright in Britain* (New York, 1994). The best source on the right to privacy is still Samuel D. Warren and Louis D. Brandeis, "The Right to Privacy," *Harvard Law Review* 4 (1890), 193–220. Good introductions to economic issues in copyright and intellectual property include William M. Landes and Richard A. Posner, "An Economic Analysis of Copyright Law," *Journal of Legal Studies*, 43 (1989), 325–63 and Stanley M. Besen and Leo J. Raskind, "Introduction to the Law and Economics of Intellectual Property," *Journal of Economic Perspectives* 5 (1991), 3–27.

Railroad Transportation

Albert Fishlow surveys the development of transportation in "Internal Transportation in the Nineteenth and Early Twentieth Centuries," in Stanley L. Engerman and Robert E. Gallman, eds., *The Cambridge Economic History of the United States, Vol. II* (Cambridge, 2000), 543–642. The issue of accidents on steamboats is addressed in Richard N. Langlois, David J. Denault, and Samson M. Kimenyi, "Bursting Boilers and the Federal Power Redux: The Evolution of Safety on the Western Rivers," *University of Connecticut Working Paper* (1995). For a different view, see John G. Burke, "Bursting Boilers and the Federal Power," *Technology and Culture* 7 (1966), 1–23. The law of railroads has been discussed in a large number of books and articles, the most scholarly and comprehensive of which is James W. Ely's *Railroads and American Law* (Lawrence, KS, 2001). Ely emphasizes the role of legislators in shaping railroad policies and the contribution of inefficient regulation to the decline of the railroads. Richard C. Cortner, *The Iron Horse and the Constitution* (Westport, CT, 1993) focuses on federal and constitutional issues. Robert Riegel, "Standard Time in the United States," *The American Historical Review* 33 (1927), 84–89, discusses the events leading to the adoption of standard time.

Bankruptcy and tort laws in relation to the railroads have also been well investigated. Bradley Hansen, "The People's Welfare and the Origins of Corporate Reorganization: The Wabash Receivership Reconsidered," *Business History Review* 74 (2000), 377–406, finds no evidence for the view that courts radically transformed creditors' rights in the 1880s. Instead, he proposes that the features of equity receivership in the Wabash decision were consistent with earlier precedents and with the attempt to further public welfare. Peter Tufano points to the link between legally mandated governance mechanisms and financial innovations that allowed distressed firms to obtain funding in "Business Failure, Judicial Intervention, and Financial Innovation: Restructuring U.S. Railroads in the Nineteenth Century," *Business History Review* 71 (1997), 1–40. See also Albro Martin, "Railroads and the Equity Receivership: An Essay on Institutional Change," *Journal of Economic History* 34 (1974), 685–709.

A comprehensive analysis of the railroad and mining industries in terms of workplace safety is provided in Mark Aldrich, *Safety First: Technology, Labor, and Business in the Building of American Work Safety, 1870–1939* (Baltimore, 1997). A key guide to the impact of state legislation to offer insured benefits to workers is Price Fishback and Shawn Kantor, *Prelude to the Welfare State: The Origins of Workers' Compensation* (Chicago, 2000). Fishback and Kantor argue that the state laws were associated with greater certainty for working families. They show that all parties concerned – firms, workers, and insurers – benefited from the introduction of workers' compensation, in part because workers paid for some of the increase in benefits through lower wages. However, in industries where unions predominated, such as the building trades, employees were able to successfully counter the tendency for workers to bear the incidence of the compensation laws. See also Price Fishback and Shawn Kantor, "NonFatal Accident Compensation Under the Negligence Liability System at the Turn of the Century," *Journal of Law, Economics, and Organization* 11 (1995), 406–33; Price Fishback and Seung-Wook Kim, "Institutional Change, Compensating Differentials and Accident Risk in American Railroading, 1892–1945," *Journal of Economic History* 53 (1993), 796–823; and Price Fishback, "Liability Rules and Accident Prevention in the Workplace: Empirical Evidence from the Early Twentieth Century," *Journal of Legal Studies* 16 (1987), 305–28.

Telegraph

My main printed source for lawsuits relating to the telegraph was William Cook, *A Treatise on Telegraph Law* (New York, 1920). Background information on the impact of the telegraph can be obtained from Tom Standage, *The Victorian Internet: The Remarkable Story of the Telegraph and the Nineteenth Century's On-Line Pioneers* (London, 1998). George Rogers Taylor, *The Transportation Revolution: 1815–1860* (New York, 1951) argues that "in an age of revolutionary developments in transportation and communication, perhaps the most drastic change resulted from the magnetic telegraph." See also Alexander J. Field, "The Magnetic Telegraph, Price and Quantity Data, and the New Management of Capital," *Journal of Economic History* 52 (1992), 401–13 and H. H. Goldin, "Governmental Policy and the Domestic Telegraph Industry," *Journal of Economic History* 7 (1947), 53–68. Several law review articles have proposed the application of the common carrier model to the Internet, including James B. Speta, "A Common Carrier Approach to Internet Interconnection," *Federal Communications Law Journal* 54 (2002), 225–79.

Medical Technology and Public Health

Stanley J. Reiser, *Medicine and the Reign of Technology* (Cambridge, 1978) is an excellent general introduction to the history of medical technology. Paul Starr argues that the history of American medicine can be explained by market expansion, and he highlights the links among engineering, sanitation technology and the public health movement in the second half of the nineteenth century in *The Social Transformation of American Medicine* (New York, 1982). A good survey of public health administration and law is James A. Tobey, *Public Health*

Law (New York, 1947). Anita Bernstein, "Engendered by Technologies," *North Carolina Law Review* (2001), 1–113, claims that medical technologies discriminated against women and promoted the interests of professionally trained male doctors. The best work on medical malpractice from an historical perspective is Kenneth Allen de Ville, *Medical Malpractice in Nineteenth-Century America: Origins and Legacy* (New York, 1990). See also James C. Mohr, *Doctors and the Law: Medical Jurisprudence in Nineteenth-Century America* (New York, 1993). Philip R. Reilly, *The Surgical Solution: A History of Involuntary Sterilization in the United States* (Baltimore, 1991) provides an overview of the eugenics movement. Paul A. Lombardo, "Medicine, Eugenics, and the Supreme Court: From Coercive Sterilization to Reproductive Freedom," *Journal of Contemporary Health Law & Policy* 13 (1996), 1, points out that "the most powerful vehicle of the eugenic ideology was the law." For the history of abortion, see Leslie J. Reagan, *When Abortion Was a Crime: Women, Medicine, and Law in the United States 1867–1973* (Berkeley, 1997) and James C. Mohr, *Abortion in America: The Origins and Evolution of National Policy, 1800–1900* (New York, 1979).

Automobiles

The most comprehensive treatise on early automobile law remains Xenophon P. Huddy, *The Law of Automobiles* (Albany, NY, 1906 and subsequent editions). The family agency doctrine is described in the seventh edition of this work, published in 1924. Arthur F. Curtis, who wrote the preface for the 1924 edition, noted, "The ever increasing number of decisions relating to the law of automobiles brings new burden to the lawyer. The question constantly before him is 'How can I keep step with the progress in this, the most actively litigated branch of the law?'" For an overview of the early history of the automobile, see James J. Flink, *America Adopts the Automobile* (Cambridge, MA, 1970) and John Chynoweth Burnham, "The Gasoline Tax and the Automobile Revolution," *Mississippi Valley Historical Review* 48 (1961), 435–59. Contemporary discussion of insurance issues include Robert Riegel, "Automobile Insurance Rates," *Journal of Political Economy* 25 (1917), 561–79 and Morris Pike, "Some Aspects of the Compulsory Automobile Insurance Movement," *Proceedings of the Casualty Actuarial Society* 9 (1922), 23–37.

CHAPTER 16: THE LAWS OF INDUSTRIAL ORGANIZATION, 1870–1920

KAREN ORREN

The best entry into the interpretive twists and turns on *Lochner* jurisprudence is Gary Rowe, "Lochner Revisionism Revisited," *Law & Social Inquiry* 24 (1999), 221. From there, three useful books are Morton J. Horwitz, *The Transformation of American Law, 1870–1960: The Crisis of Legal Orthodoxy* (New York, 1992); Herbert Hovenkamp, *Enterprise and American Law, 1836–1937* (Cambridge, MA, 1991); and Howard Gillman, *The Constitution Besieged: The Rise and Demise of Lochner Era Police Powers Jurisprudence* (Durham, NC, 1993). In the earlier "laissez-faire" vein, see Arnold M. Paul, *Conservative Crisis and the Rule of Law: Attitudes of the Bench and Bar, 1887–1895* (Ithaca, NY, 1960) and Benjamin R. Twiss, *Lawyers and the Constitution: How Laissez Faire Came to the Supreme Court* (Princeton, NJ, 1942).

An article that highlights the distinctive role of labor in the jurisprudence of the period is Charles McCurdy, "The 'Liberty of Contract' Regime in American Law," in Harry Scheiber, ed., *Freedom of Contract and the State* (Stanford, CA, 1998). For precursors of the historical frame of the present chapter, and a general introduction to labor in constitutional jurisprudence, see Karen Orren, *Belated Feudalism: Labor, the Law, and Liberal Development in the United States* (Cambridge, 1991) and "Labor Regulation and Constitutional Theory in the United States and England," *Political Theory* 22 (1994), 98–123. An introduction to formalism of the era, and to the concept of jurisdiction in particular, is Duncan Kennedy, "Toward an Historical Understanding of Legal Consciousness: The Case of Classical Legal Thought in America, 1850–1940," *Research in Law and Sociology* 3 (1980), 24.

Invaluable chapters on the Commerce Clause are found in Charles Fairman, *Reconstruction and Reunion, 1864–88* and Owen M. Fiss, *Troubled Beginnings of the Modern State, 1888–1910*, in the Oliver Holmes Devise History of the United States Supreme Court (New York, 1971–87). On antitrust, see James May, "Antitrust Practice and Procedure in the Formative Era: The Constitutional and Conceptual Reach of State Antitrust Law, 1880–1918," *University of Pennsylvania Law Review* 135 (1987), 495 and "Antitrust in the Formative Era: Political and Economic Theory in Constitutional and Antitrust Analysis, 1880–1918," *Ohio State Law Journal* 50 (1989), 257; and Rudolph J. Peretz, "The 'Rule of Reason' in Antitrust Law: Property Logic in Restraint of Competition," *Hastings Law Journal* 40 (1989), 285.

Good summary treatments of Lochner era collective action cases are Ellen Kelman, "American Labor Law and Legal Formalism: How 'Legal Logic' Shaped and Vitiated the Rights of American Workers," *St. John's Law Review* 58 (1983), 1 and Haggai Hurvitz, "American Labor Law and the Doctrine of Entrepreneurial Property Rights: Boycotts, Courts, and the Juridical Reorientation of 1886–1895," *Industrial Relations Law Journal* 8 (1986), 307. The causal role of state institutions is highlighted in William E. Forbath, "The Shaping of the American Labor Movement," *Harvard Law Review* 102 (1989), 1109; Christopher Tomlins, *The State and the Unions: Labor Relations, Law, and the Organized Labor Movement in America, 1880–1960* (Cambridge, 1985; and Victoria C. Hattam, "Economic Visions and Political Strategies: American Labor and the State, 1865–1896, *Studies in American Political Development* 4 (1990), 82. On the law of industrial accidents, see Lawrence M. Friedman and Jack Ladinsky, "Social Change and the Law of Industrial Accidents," *Columbia Law Review* 67 (1967), 50; Arthur Larson, "The Nature and Origins of Workmen's Compensation," *Cornell Law Quarterly* (1951–52), 206; and John Fabian Witt,

"Toward a New History of American Accident Law: Classical Tort Law and the Cooperative First Party Insurance Movement," *Harvard Law Review* 114 (1998), 690.

Helpful discussions of ultra vires contracts are Edward H. Warren, "Executed Ultra Vires Transactions," *Harvard Law Review* 23 (1910), 495; Charles E. Carpenter, "Should the Doctrine of Ultra Vires Be Discarded," *Yale Law Journal* 33 (1923), 49; and Clyde L. Colson, "The Doctrine of *Ultra Vires* in United States Supreme Court Decisions," *West Virginia Law Quarterly* 179 (1936). An introduction to changing shareholders' rights in the Lochner era is provided by William J. Carney, "Fundamental Corporate Changes, Minority Shareholders, and Business Purposes," *American Bar Foundation* 69 (1980) and Brett W. King, "The Use of Supermajority Voting Rules in Corporate America: Majority Rule, Corporate Legitimacy, and Minority Shareholder Protection," *Delaware Journal of Corporate Law* 21 (1996), 895. For an overview of the business corporation covering these years see J. Willard Hurst, *The Legitimacy of the Business Corporation in the Law of the United States, 1780–1970* (Charlottesville, VA, 1970); Harold Marsh, Jr., "Are Directors Trustees?" *The Business Lawyer* 35 (1966); and William W. Bratton, "The New Economic Theory of the Firm: Critical Perspectives from History," *Stanford Law Review* 41 (1989), 1471.

Thomas R. Lee, "Stare Decisis in Historical Perspective: From the Founding Era to the Rehnquist Court," *Vanderbilt Law Review* 52 (1999), 647 provides an entry point to the subject of legal precedent. On rights jurisprudence see Joseph William Singer, "The Legal Rights Debate in Analytical Jurisprudence from Bentham to Hohfeld," *University of Wisconsin Law Review* 975 (1982). The classic treatment of Lochner era rights as administered in labor law is Walter Wheeler Cook, "Privileges of Labor Unions in the Struggle for Life," *Yale Law Journal* 27 (1918), 779.

CHAPTER 17: THE MILITARY IN AMERICAN LEGAL HISTORY

JONATHAN LURIE

There are numerous works in both American legal history and American military history. Not surprisingly, they tend to emphasize one or the other fields. However, scholarship that bridges the two, such as sources in American military legal history, remain scant, with few exceptions. A more meaningful approach for the interested reader is to seek insights within articles or possibly within books in related fields. If one is willing to look, valuable pieces of scholarship are available. It should be emphasized that the multiple sources listed in notes and bibliographies of the following works are also important.

General sources of American legal and military history, which acknowledge the role of military law and justice to varying extents, include Kermit Hall, *The Oxford Companion to the Supreme Court* (New York, 2005) and *The Oxford Companion to American Law* (New York, 2002); Lawrence M. Friedman, *American*

Law in the 20th Century (New Haven, CT, 2002); John Whiteclay Chambers II, *The Oxford Companion to American Military History* (New York, 1999); and Alan R. Millett and Peter Maslowski, *For the Common Defense: A Military History of the United States of America* (New York, 1984). See also Jonathan Lurie, *Arming Military Justice: The Origins of the U.S. Court of Military Appeals* (Princeton, NJ, 1992) and *Pursuing Military Justice: The History of the United States Court of Appeals for the Armed Forces* (Princeton,1998). Lurie's volumes have been revised and abridged as *Military Justice in* America: *The U.S. Court of Appeals for the Armed Forces, 1775–1980* (Lawrence, KS, 2001).

Pre-Civil War studies include Richard Kohn, *Eagle and Sword: The Federalists and the Creation of the Military Establishment in America, 1783–1802* (New York, 1975). See also Richard Kohn, ed., *The United States Military Under the Constitution of the United States, 1789–1989* (New York, 1991), particularly the essays by Richard Morris (41–60), Richard Kohn (61–94), Harold Hyman (175–92), and Jonathan Lurie (405–30). See also Theodore Crackel, *Mr. Jefferson's Army: Political and Social Reform of the Military Establishment, 1801–1809* (New York, 1987), which can be studied in conjunction with Russell F. Weigley's *The History of the United States Army* (Bloomington, IN, 1984). The famous but now forgotten conflict between a commanding general, Andrew Jackson, and an insistent federal district judge, Dominick Hall, is treated in the Note, "Andrew Jackson and Judge D. A. Hall," *Louisiana Historical Quarterly* 5 (1922), 538–70. The episode of the intended as opposed to actual mutiny on the American ship *Somers* is the subject of an article by Frederick Van de Water, "Panic Rides the High Seas," *American Heritage 12* (1961), 20–23, 97–99 and a book by Harrison Hayford, *The Somers Mutiny Affair* (New York, 1960). James Fenimore Cooper's perceptive insights concerning this incident are discussed in Lurie, *Arming Military Justice*, and James Grossman, *James Fenimore Cooper* (New York, 1949).

For the Civil War era, see the first hundred pages of Philip Paludan's *A Covenant with Death: Law and Equality in the Civil War Era* (Urbana, IL, 1975). This section of Paludan's book focuses on the work of Francis Lieber whose "General Orders 100" was an important precursor to the Uniform Code of Military Justice adopted by Congress in 1863. See also Frank L. Klement, *The Limits of Dissent: Clement L. Vallandigham and the Civil War* (Lexington, KY, 1970) and *Dark Lanterns: Secret Political Societies, Conspiracies, and Treason Trials in the Civil War* (New York, 1984); and Mark E. Neely, Jr. *The Fate of Liberty* (New York, 1991). Neely's study broke new ground in exploring Lincoln's unprecedented suspension of habeas corpus and his involvement – greater than any other president before him – in review of courts-martial. It is an excellent supplement to Harold M. Hyman's, *A More Perfect Union: The Impact of the Civil War and Reconstruction on the Constitution* (Boston, 1975). See also Thomas Turner, *Beware the People Weeping: Public Opinion and the Assassination of Abraham Lincoln* (Baton Rouge, LA,1982); see in particular pages 138–54, in which Turner provides information on contemporary opinion – both public and private – concerning the merits of trial by military commission instead of a civilian court. See also Louis Fisher, *Military Tribunals and Presidential Power: American Revolution to the War on Terrorism* (Lawrence, KS, 2005); Arthur Schlesinger, Jr., *War and the Constitution: Abraham Lincoln and Franklin D. Roosevelt* (Gettysburg, PA, 1988); and John Whiteclay Chambers II, *To Raise an Army: The Draft Comes to Modern America* (New York, 1987).

The tensions between military rule and civilian control during the Civil War are discussed though not emphasized in Charles Fairman's sprawling but still useful volume, *Reconstruction and Reunion, 1864–1888, Part I* (New York, 1971). Fairman has some interesting insights concerning the Civil War in an earlier article, "The Law of Martial Rule and the National Emergency," *Harvard Law Review* 55 (1942), 1253–1302. An early contribution to the debate over the extent to which a court-martial should reflect norms of civilian criminal procedure may be found in Thomas Anderson, "Is a Court-Martial a Criminal Court?" *United Service* 6 (1882), 297–301. The growth of scholarship concerning military law during the late nineteenth century can be seen in Rollin Ives, *A Treatise on Military Law* (New York, 1886), whereas the most comprehensive source for military law prior to the post–World War II era is William Winthrop, *Military Law and Precedents* (Washington, 1920). A sympathetic introduction to Winthrop's work may be seen in George S. Prugh, "Introduction to William Winthrop's *Military Law and Precedents*," *Revue de Droit Penal Militaire et de Droit de la Guerre* [Review of Military Justice and the Law of War] 27 (1988), 437–59.

The debate over the relevance of constitutional protection of civil rights as applied to American citizens who are members of the armed forces is explored by Gordon Henderson in "Courts-Martial and the Bill of Rights: The Original Practice," *Harvard Law Review* 71 (1957), 293–324. Henderson's conclusions were questioned in Frederick Bernays Wiener's exhaustive rebuttal, "Courts-Martial and the Constitution: The Original Understanding," *Harvard Law Review* 72 (1957), 1–49, 266–304. Both Henderson's and Wiener's analyses should be considered in the light of J. D. Droddy, "King Richard to Solorio: The Historical and Constitutional Bases for Court-Martial Jurisdiction in Criminal Cases," *Air Force Law Review* 30 (1989), 91–133. See also Wiener's "American Military Law in the Light of the First Mutiny Act's Tricentennial," *Military Law Review* 126 (1989), 1–88.

The very important controversy between Army Judge Advocate General Enoch Crowder and his one-time close associate, Samuel Ansell, is treated thoroughly in Lurie, *Arming Military Justice*. See also Samuel Ansell, "Some Reforms in our System of Military Justice," *Yale Law Journal* 32 (1922), 146–55; Terry W. Brown, "The Ansell-Crowder Dispute: The Emergence of General Samuel T. Ansell," *Military Law Review* 35 (1967), 1–45; David A. Lockmiller, *Enoch H. Crowder: Soldier, Lawyer, and Statesman* (Columbia, SC, 1955); Herbert

F. Margulies, "The Articles of War, 1920: The History of a Forgotten Reform," *Military Affairs* 43 (1979), 85–89; and William Herbert Page, "Military Law – A Study in Comparative Law," *Harvard Law Review* 32 (1919), 349–73.

The history of the drafting, enactment, and later revisions of the Uniform Code of Military Justice (1950) is explored in Lurie's two volumes cited above. Of course, debate – much of it negative – over the fairness and quality of military justice preceded and followed its adoption. See, for example, Peter Irons, *Justice at War: The Story of the Japanese American Internment Cases* (New York, 1982). Consider also, the treatment of the Nazi saboteurs during World War II; see Louis Fischer, *Nazi Saboteurs on Trial: A Military Tribunal and American Law* (Lawrence, KS, 2003). See also Note "Can Military Trials be Fair? Command Influence over Courts-Martial," *Stanford Law Review* 2 (1950), 547–58 and Bernard Landman, Jr., "One Year of the Uniform Code of Military Justice: A Report of Progress," *Stanford Law Review* 4 (1952), 491–508.

By far the most vigorous debates, both scholarly and public, occurred during the era of the Vietnam War. See Donald W. Hansen, "Judicial Functions of the Commander," *Military Law Review* 41 (1968), 1–54 and "Free Speech in the Military," *New York University School of Law* 53 (1978), 1102–23; Edward F. Sherman, "The Civilianization of Military Law," *Maine Law Review* 22 (1970), 3–103 and "The Military Court and Servicemen's First Amendment Rights," *Hastings Law Journal* 22 (1971), 325–73; Charles Scheisser and Daniel Benson, "A Proposal to Make Courts-Martial Courts: The Removal of Commanders from Military Justice," *Texas Tech Law Review* 7 (1976), 539–600; John S. Cooke, "The United States Court of Military Appeals, 1975–77: Judicializing the Military Justice System," *Military Law Review* 76 (1977), 43–163; Luther West, *They Call it Justice: Command Influence and the Court-Martial System* (New York, 1977); John Douglass, "The Judicialization of Military Courts," *Hastings Law Journal* 22 (1971), 213–35; Daniel Benson, "The United States Court of Military Appeals," *Texas Tech Law Review* 3 (1971), 1–21; Homer F. Moyer, Jr., *Justice and the Military* (1972); and Robert Sherrill, *Military Justice is to Justice as Military Music is to Music* (New York, 1970). Sherrill's book, written by a journalist unfamiliar with the history of the UCMJ, is typical of the popular concern with matters military during the Vietnam War. Of much greater value is Michal Belknap's *The Vietnam War on Trial: The My Lai Massacre and the Court-Martial of Lieutenant Calley* (Lawrence, KS, 2002). The best account of the Slovik tragedy is William Bradford Huie, *The Execution of Private Slovik* (New York, 1970). The reader should remember that, when it took place, the United States was still at war, desertion in time of war has traditionally been punishable by death, and that November 1944 represented a very difficult time for the American war effort. See also Jonathan Lurie, "Military Justice 50 Years After Nuremberg: Some Reflections on Appearance v. Reality," *Military Law Review* 149 (1995), 178–86.

The best treatment of Cold War and post-Cold War military justice is Elizabeth Lutes Hillman, *Defending America: Military Culture and the Cold War*

Court-Martial (Princeton, NJ, 2005). Her more than eighty pages of notes offer the interested reader an impressive amount of contemporary source material. See also Richard H. Kohn, "Posse Comitatus: Using the Military at Home, Yesterday, Today and Tomorrow," *Chicago Journal of International Law* 4 (2003), 165–92 and Diane H. Mazur, "Rehnquist's Vietnam: Constitutional Separatism and the Stealth Advance of Martial Law," *Indiana Law Journal* 77 (2002), 701–85. Mazur argues that, under the leadership of Chief Justice William Rehnquist, the U.S. Supreme Court had supported a doctrine that places the military as "a society apart from civilian society." This policy, if consistently acquiesced in, can only have very serious implications for American civil liberties. Finally, see the anthology edited by Eugene Fidell and Dwight Sullivan, *Evolving Military Justice* (Annapolis, MD, 2002).

CHAPTER 18: THE UNITED STATES AND INTERNATIONAL AFFAIRS, 1789–1919

EILEEN P. SCULLY

General

Relevant and suggestive works are found across several disciplines, including law, international relations, diplomatic history, and colonial studies. At least since the mid-1980s, contending interpretations of Westphalia, sovereignty, nationalism, and territorial boundaries have marked battle lines in the intense polarization of opinion about American activities, economic globalization, and the unstable world order. A useful orientation into these complexities is Charles S. Maier, "Consigning the Twentieth Century to History: Alternative Narratives for the Modern Era," *American Historical Review* 105 (2000), 807–31.

The World of Westphalia

The pivotal shift among scholars to a more historically anchored, though decidedly normative view of the interstate system as a society of nations can be traced back to Hedley Bull, *The Expansion of International Society* (New York, 1985). From there, deconstructionist methodologies yielded a contingent, mutable, and problematic interstate system, well laid out in John G. Ruggie, "Territoriality and Beyond: Problematizing Modernity in International Relations," *International Organization* 47 (1993), 139–74 and J. Samuel Barkin and Bruce Cronin, "The State and the Nation: Changing Norms and the Rules of Sovereignty in International Relations," *International Organization* 48 (1994), 107–30.

Much of the post-1985 literature focusing on Westphalia in particular comes at the past with a purposeful and hopeful eye ahead to supra-national authority and preemptory norms. The "Charter conception" is retrospectively discerned and affirmed in Richard Falk, "The Interplay of Westphalia and Charter Conceptions of International Legal Order," in Richard Falk et al., *International Law: A Contemporary Perspective* (Boulder, 1985), 116–42. The terms and implications of the 1648 Peace of Westphalia are discussed succinctly in David Held,

Democracy and the Global Order: From the Modern State to Cosmopolitan Governance (Stanford, 1995) and Charles W. Kegley, Jr. and Gregory A. Raymond, *Exorcising the Ghost of Westphalia: Building World Order in the New Millennium* (Upper Saddle River, NJ, 2002).

Donald J. Puchala provides an interpretative, factually informative account in "Western Europe," in Robert H. Jackson and Alan James, eds., *States in a Changing World: A Contemporary Analysis* (Oxford, 1993). David P. Fidler, "International Human Rights Law in Practice: The Return of the Standard of Civilization," *Chicago Journal of International Law* 2 (2001), 137–57 discusses "Westphalian mechanics" and the complicated evolution of norms. Gerrit Gong, *The Standard of 'Civilization' in International Society* (Clarendon, 1984) presents an historical, rather than strictly legalistic, analysis and offers particularly strong chapters on China and Japan.

Westphalia as very much the continuation of the earlier international system is found in Stephen D. Krasner, "Westphalia and All That," in Judith Goldstein and Robert O. Keohane, eds., *Ideas and Foreign Policy* (New York, 1993), 235–63. Andreas Osiander, "Sovereignty, International Relations, and the Westphalian Myth," *International Organization* 55 (2001), 251–87 argues that "the accepted IR narrative about Westphalia is a myth," inasmuch as "the Peace of Westphalia . . . confirmed and perfected . . . a system of mutual relations among autonomous political units" that, far from claiming sovereignty, each appreciated the need for consensus and a higher communal good.

David Kennedy, "International Law and the Nineteenth Century: History of an Illusion," *Qinnipiac Law Review* 17 (1997) 99–138 laid the foundations for a close, rather nostalgic study of pre-positivist international law classics. Kennedy's protégé Anthony Anghie has published notable contributions pointing to a pre-imperialist multipolar system of different cultural-religious zones in "Finding the Peripheries: Sovereignty and Colonialism in Nineteenth-Century International Law," *Harvard International Law Journal* 40 (1999), 1–80. Colonialism is presented as the *raison d'etre* of European-centered international law in Anghie, "Colonialism and the Birth of International Institutions: Sovereignty, Economy, and the Mandate System of the League of Nations," *New York University Journal of International Law and Politics* 34 (2002), 513–633. International law as a property regime is explicated in Charles Lipson, *Standing Guard. Protecting Foreign Capital in the Nineteenth and Twentieth Centuries* (Berkeley, 1985).

David J. Bederman, "Intellectual Genealogies," *International Legal Theory* 6 (2000), 10 offers a lively corrective to this view of positivism as "some sort of juggernaut, an angry and vengeful god sacrificing naturalist sources on the altar of State expediency and consent, only to be itself consumed in the general wars it spawned in 1914 and 1939." Contemporary American understandings of positivism are well represented in review essays found in *North American Review* 60 (1845), 301–328 and *The United States Democratic Review* 21 (1847),

23–32, together with Nicholas Onuf, "Henry Wheaton and 'The Golden Age of International Law,'" *International Legal Theory* 6 (2000).

The United States and Westphalia

Historians of U.S. foreign relations have drawn inspiration from postmodern inflections of the "state," "national security," "diplomacy," and so on, but seem ultimately bound to causation, agency, and context. These difficulties and disconnections are explored with particular keenness in Andrew J. Rotter, "Saidism without Said: Orientalism and U.S. Diplomatic History," *American Historical Review* 105 (2000) and Melvyn P. Leffler, "New Approaches, Old Interpretations, and Prospective Reconfigurations," *Diplomatic History* 19 (1995).

The Cambridge History of American Foreign Relations, edited by Warren Cohen (New York, 1993), presents interpretative essays by leading scholars covering the full span of American international affairs, with comprehensive bibliographic references to particular eras and episodes. On the Jeffersonian-Hamiltonian tension, recent works include Doron S. Ben-Atar, *The Origins of Jeffersonian Commercial Policy and Diplomacy* (New York, 1993); Robert Tucker and David Hendrickson, *Empire of Liberty: The Statecraft of Thomas Jefferson* (Oxford 1990); and Peter S. Onuf, *Jefferson's Empire: The Language of American Nationhood* (Charlottesville, VA, 2000). Careful archival work and interdisciplinary perspectives are brought together in James R. Sofka, "The Jeffersonian Idea of National Security: Commerce, the Atlantic Balance of Power, and the Barbary War, 1786–1804," *Diplomatic History* 21 (1997).

Westphalia and the Constitutional Order

Restatement (Third) of the Foreign Relations Law of the United States (New York, 1987) is the authoritative reference work for current practice and its historical antecedents. Beginning in the early 1980s, the controversial use of executive authority and heated public policy clashes over "original intent" sent concerned scholars back to late eighteenth-century primary texts, generating a sizeable body of work on war powers, checks and balances, treaties, judicial deference on "political questions," and the extent to which U.S. government actions abroad must answer to the Constitution. Notable contributions on the role of federal courts in sorting out where the Constitution begins and ends include Thomas M. Franck, *Political Questions/Judicial Answers: Does the Rule of Law Apply to Foreign Affairs?* (Princeton, NJ, 1992) and David Gray Adler, "Court, Constitution, and Foreign Affairs," in David Gray Adler and Larry N. George, eds., *The Constitution and the Conduct of American Foreign Policy* (Lawrence, KS, 1996), 19–56. Detlev F. Vagts, "The United States and Its Treaties: Observance and Breach," *American Journal of International Law* 95 (2001), 313–34 makes a persuasive case that the United States has historically been generally compliant with treaty obligations, provided those duties had been modified through reservations and stipulations to mesh with domestic arrangements.

Among historians, the return to original texts produced, most notably, "The Constitution and American Life: A Special Issue" *Journal of American History* 74 (1987).

The most careful, thoughtful, and measured work on the founding generation and international law is Peter Onuf and Nicholas Onuf, *Federal Union, Modern World: The Law of Nations in an Age of Revolutions, 1776–1814* (Madison, WI, 1993). Douglas J. Sylvester examines late eighteenth-century American understandings of international law in "International Law as Sword or Shield? Early American Foreign Policy and the Law of Nations," *NYU Journal of International Law and Politics* 32 (1999), 1–87. Additional relevant works include Stewart Jay, "The Status of the Law of Nations in Early American Law," *Vanderbilt Law Review* 42 (1989), 819–49; Michael Zuckert, "Natural Rights in the American Revolution: The American Amalgam," in Jeffrey N. Wasserstrom et al., eds., *Human Rights and Revolution* (Lanham, MD, 2000); David Armitage, "The Declaration of Independence and International Law," *William and Mary Quarterly* 59 (2002), 1–32; Daniel Lang, *Foreign Policy in the Early Republic: The Law of Nations and the Balance of Power* (Baton Rouge, LA, 1985); and Stephen Peter Rosen, "Alexander Hamilton and the Domestic Uses of International Law," *Diplomatic History* 5 (1981), 183–202.

Entry points on the place of international law in federal courts include Friedrich Kratochwil, "The Role of Domestic Courts as Agencies of the International Legal Order," in Richard Falk, et al., eds., *International Law: A Contemporary Perspective* (Boulder, 1985), 236–63 and Jack L. Goldsmith, "Federal Courts, Foreign Affairs, and Federalism," *Virginia Law Review* 83 (1997). A particularly important contribution is G. Edward White, "The Transformation of the Constitutional Regime of Foreign Relations," *Virginia Law Review* 85 (1999), which reliably sets out the nineteenth-century "orthodox view" of foreign affairs as a wholly constitutional exercise focused on treaty obligations.

The post-Cold War tendency of several Supreme Court justices to reference decisions of foreign and international courts prompted a return to the distant past; the results are well represented in Curtis A. Bradley and Jack L. Goldsmith, "Federal Courts and the Incorporation of International Law, *Harvard Law Review* 111 (1998); Roger P. Alford, "Agora: The United States Constitution and International Law: Misusing International Sources to Interpret the Constitution," *American Journal of International Law* 98 (2004); and Gerald L. Neuman, "Agora: The United States Constitution and International Law: The Uses of International Law in Constitutional Interpretation," *American Journal of International Law* 98 (2004).

Constitutionalism and Territoriality

Nicholas G. Onuf, "Sovereignty: Outline of a Conceptual History," *Alternatives* 16 (1991), 425–46 presents historically grounded, incisive analysis. Daniel Philpott, "Sovereignty: An Introduction and Brief History," *Journal of*

International Affairs 48 (1995), 353–68 is presented as a corrective to revisionist accounts. Benjamin M. Ziegler, *The International Law of John Marshall* (Chapel Hill, NC, 1939) endures as a foundation reference. James Anaya, *Indigenous Peoples in International Law* (Oxford, 2000) provides a cogent, deeply knowledgeable analytical narrative.

Revisionist readings of the long nineteenth century appear to be converging on a great captivity narrative, in which free-ranging travelers were tethered by passports and stripped of their citizenship on the slightest pretext and women were appended to husbands through derivative nationality. In this nearly unrecognizable global confinement, anthropomorphic Absolute Sovereigns haughtily laid claim to vast territorial realms, emblazoning signs of vassalage on anybody and anything in sight, locking the doors against those deemed unworthy and undesirable. Donna R. Gabaccia, "Is Everywhere Nowhere? Nomads, Nations, and the Immigrant Paradigm of United States History," *Journal of American History* (1999), 1115–34 finds that the few migratory nomads who managed to slip through the cracks wished only to be left to "the mundane task of finding work," but were hegemonically constructed as "Immigrants" and met at every turn by the preemptory demands of States for "passports, heath inspections, taxes, military service, departure, naturalization and loyalty." James A. R. Nafziger, "The General Admission of Aliens Under International Law," *American Journal of International Law* 77 (1983) points to a time before presumptuous sovereigns "complicated the free movement of persons," with "little, in principle, to support the absolute exclusion of aliens" (810).

Accepting that "emigration" and "sovereignty" are constructs, they were nonetheless wrested from more oppressive constructs, a process explored with great care and sophistication in Gordon Wood, *The Creation of the American Republic, 1776 1787* (New York, 1969) and Edmund S. Morgan, *Inventing the People: The Rise of Popular Sovereignty in England and America* (New York, 1988). Eric T. Dean, Jr., "Stephen A. Douglas and Popular Sovereignty," *The Historian* 57 (1995) provides a detailed and perceptive entry point for antebellum debates on sovereignty. Gary Lawson and Guy Seidman, *The Constitution of Empire. Territorial Expansion and American Legal History* (New Haven, CT, 2004) is authoritative on the subject. Mark W. Bailey, "Moral Philosophy, the United States Supreme Court, and the Nation's Character, 1860–1910," *Canadian Journal of Law and Jurisprudence* 10 (1997), 249–71 is especially useful as a starting point backward to prior work. Subject-citizen status is explored in Christina Duffy Burnett and Burke Marshall, eds. *Foreign in a Domestic Sense: Puerto Rico, American Expansion and the Constitution* (Durham, NC 2001) and Kelvin A. Santiago-Valles, *Subject People and Colonial Discourses. Economic Transformation and Social Disorder in Puerto Rico, 1898–1947* (New York, 1994). Drawing on archives across the world, Paul A. Kramer, "Race-Making and Colonial Violence in the U.S. Empire: The Philippine-American War as Race War," *Diplomatic History* 30 (2006) greatly extends the reach of earlier work on the subject. The expansion of ancient consular jurisdiction into modern extraterritoriality is examined through a focus on the U.S. Court for China in Shanghai in Eileen P. Scully, *Bargaining with the State from Afar: American Citizenship in Treaty Port China* (New York, 2001).

The end of the Cold War by 1989 reopened constitutional and governance questions long presumed closed, such as the expulsion of state-level governments from foreign affairs, the boundaries of "international commerce," and the place of international law in the American legal system. On states as potential players in diplomacy, lively, provocative work was made even stronger by internal debate. See "Special Issue: The United States Constitution in its Third Century: Foreign Affairs: Distribution of Constitutional Authority: The Roles of States and Cities in Foreign Relations," *American Journal of International Law* 83 (1989); Peter J. Spiro, "The Role of the States in Foreign Affairs," Part II, *University of Colorado Law Review* 70 (1999); and Curtis A. Bradley "Symposium Overview: A New American Foreign Affairs Law?" *University of Colorado Law Review* 70 (1999).

Volitional Allegiance

American identity as a unique historical proposition is explored in John Murrin, "A Roof Without Walls. The Dilemma of American National Identity," in Richard Beeman et al., eds., *Beyond Confederation: Origins of the Constitution and American National Identity* (Chapel Hill, NC, 1987), 342–44 and Robert Calhoon, "The Reintegration of the Loyalists and the Disaffected," in Jack Greene, ed., *The American Revolution: Its Character and Limits* (New York, 1987).

Three works that are usefully read with and against one another are James H. Kettner, *The Development of American Citizenship in U.S. History 1608–1870* (Chapel Hill, NC, 1978); Rogers Smith, *Civic Ideals: Conflicting Visions of Citizenship in U.S. History* (New Haven, CT, 1997); and Peter H. Schuck, "The Re-Evaluation of American Citizenship," *Georgetown Immigration Law Journal* 12 (1997). Nancy F. Cott, "Marriage and Women's Citizenship in the United States, 1830–1934," *American Historical Review* (1998), 1440–74 remains authoritative for the period covered and is complemented very well by Candice Bredbenner, *A Nationality of Her Own: Women, Marriage, and the Law of Citizenship* (Berkeley, 1998).

A perceptual breakthrough among scholars came with Gerald Neuman's alignment of resident aliens and sojourning nationals in *Strangers to the Constitution. Immigrants, Borders, and Fundamental Law* (Princeton, NJ, 1996). The state-federal tug of war over resident aliens is well covered in T. Alexander Aleinikoff, "Federal Regulation of Aliens and the Constitution," *American Journal of International Law* 83 (1989). An especially rich and appropriately restrained interpretation of emerging travel and identity protocols, proposing the concept of states "embracing" individuals, rather than commodifying or entrapping them, is John Torpey, *The Invention of the Passport: Surveillance,*

Citizenship and the State (Cambridge, 2000). Peter Spiro, "Dual Nationality and the Meaning of Citizenship," *Emory Law Journal* 46 (1997) presents exclusive nationality as an anachronism, making the case for more expansive "external citizenship" that would end penalties against migratory laborers.

A New International "Rule of Law"

Gordon Levin, Jr. *Woodrow Wilson and World Politics: America's Response to War and Revolution* (New York, 1968) is the most widely read work on the subject and is well complemented by Thomas Knock, *To End all Wars: Woodrow Wilson and the Quest for a New World Order* (New York 1992). Tony Smith, *America's Mission: The United States and the Worldwide Struggle for Democracy in the Twentieth Century* (Princeton, NJ, 1994) is unsparing in its critique, but nonetheless is rare in its positive overall appraisal of U.S. democratizing projects abroad.

An *American Journal of International Law Symposium* on The Hague Peace Conference 94 (2000) recovers this important chapter of history. Original material from the League of Nations codification project can be found in supplements to the *American Journal of International Law* in the late 1920s, available on JSTOR. Christopher R. Rossi, *Broken Chain of Being: James Brown Scott and the Origins of Modern International Law* (London, 1998) links early twentieth-century legal internationalism to fifteenth- and sixteenth-century natural law classics, with bibliographic references leading to additional valuable works.

Ethan A. Nadelmann, *Cops Across Borders. The Internationalization of U.S. Criminal Law Enforcement* (University Park, PA, 1993) provides an analytical framework and detailed case studies of the emergence of international regimes to combat drug trafficking, prostitution, and so on. Emily S. Rosenberg, *Financial Missionaries to the World: The Politics and Culture of Dollar Diplomacy, 1900–1930* (Cambridge, MA, 1999) examines the changing portfolio of U.S. "national interests."

CHAPTER 19: POLITICS, STATE-BUILDING, AND THE COURTS, 1870–1920

WILLIAM E. FORBATH

Overviews

There are not many broad, synthetic narratives by American legal and political historians about the processes of social and economic change, state-building, and governmental expansion that unfolded between Reconstruction and World War I. Recently, scholars in other disciplines – political science and historical sociology – have taken the lead in understanding the whole shape and push of these developments. The classic work by a legal historian is J. Willard Hurst, *Growth of American Law* (Boston, 1950). Key syntheses by political historians are Morton Keller, *Affairs of State: Public Life in Late Nineteenth Century America* (Cambridge, 1977) and *Regulating a New Economy: Public Policy and Economic*

Change in America, 1900–1933 (Cambridge, 1990); Barry Karl, *The Uneasy State: The United States from 1915 to 1945* (Chicago, 1983); and Louis Galambos and Joseph Pratt, *The Rise of the Corporate Commonwealth* (New York, 1982). The historical sociologist Theda Skocpol and the political scientists Stephen Skowronek and Karen Orren have produced important new accounts of the emergence of the modern American state, with keen attention to the clash of old and new institutional actors, contending elites and social movements, and the ways they shaped American political development. Stephen Skowronek, *Building a New American State: The Expansion of National Administrative Capacities, 1877–1920* (New York, 1982) pays particular attention to the role of courts. See also Stephen Skowronek and Karen Orren, *The Search for American Political Development* (New York, 2004) and Theda Skocpol, *Protecting Soldiers and Mothers: The Political Origins of Social Policy in the United States* (Cambridge, 1992). A valuable, pioneering essay on the importance of this work for legal history and vice versa is Daniel Ernst, "Law and American Political Development, 1877–1938," *Reviews in American History* 26 (1998), 205–19.

Classical Legal Liberalism

The *locus classicus* on classical legal liberalism is the widely cited but unpublished manuscript by Duncan Kennedy, *The Rise and Fall of Classical Legal Thought* (1975, privately printed in Cambridge, 1998), a portion of which is found in "Towards an Historical Understanding of Legal Consciousness: The Case of Classical Legal Thought in America, 1850–1940," *Research in Law & Society* 3 (1980). Kennedy analyzes the emergence of a systematic and integrated, as well as classically liberal, structure of private law thought in the treatise writing and judicial opinions of the late nineteenth century. Essays by Robert Gordon brilliantly explore the links and tensions between this structure of thought and the professional identity, actions, and aspirations of the emerging corporate bar of that era: see Robert Gordon, "Legal Thought and Legal Practice in the Age of American Enterprise, 1870–1920," in G. Geison, ed., *Professions and Professional Ideologies in America* (Chapel Hill, NC, 1983) and "The Ideal and the Actual in the Law: Fantasies and Practices of New York City Lawyers, 18701910," in Gerald Gawalt, ed., *The New High Priests: Lawyers in PostCivil War America* (Westport, CT, 1984). The most thorough and compelling legal-intellectual history of classical legal liberalism and its critics is Morton Horwitz, *The Transformation of American Law, 1870–1960: The Crisis of Legal Orthodoxy* (New York, 1992).

Parallel to the emergence of a historiography of classical legal liberalism as a coherent and powerful system of thought in the private law domain was a historical reassessment of the genesis and meaning of classical liberal public law or "laissez-faire constitutionalism" in the late nineteenth and early twentieth century. As with private law, the history of the era's public law long remained in the grip of the law's contemporary Progressive critics. Historians echoed the Progressives' own accounts of "laissez-faire" doctrine as the work product of pro-big business, anti-reform-minded jurists, whose ideas sprang from association with the corporate bar. A more deeply historical view of the intellectual origins of laissez-faire constitutionalism in antebellum Jacksonian and abolitionist thought appears in Alan Jones, "Thomas M. Cooley and 'Laissez-Faire Constitutionalism': A Reconsideration," *Journal of American History*, 53 (1967), 751–71; Charles McCurdy, "Justice Field and the Jurisprudence of Government-Business Relations: Some Parameters of Laissez-Faire Constitutionalism, 1863–1897," *Journal of American History*, 61 (1975), 970–1005; William E. Forbath, "Ambiguities of Free Labor: Labor and the Law in the Gilded Age," *Wisconsin Law Review* (1985), 767–817; and Howard Gilman, *The Constitution Besieged: The Rise and Demise of Lochner Era Police Powers Jurisprudence* (Durham, NC, 1993). On the broader elite reform movement that styled itself "Liberalism"and provided the cultural milieu in which classical legal liberalism was forged, see John G. Sproat, *"The Best Men": Liberal Reformers in the Gilded Age* (New York, 1968).

Progressivism and the Legal Progressives

The literature on Progressivism is vast. Key overviews include Robert H. Wiebe, *The Search for Order, 1877–1920* (New York, 1967); Arthur Link and Richard McCormick, *Progressivism* (Arlington Heights, IL, 1983); and Morton Keller, *Regulating a New Society*. A revealing article on the vocabulary of Progressivism is Daniel T. Rodgers, "In Search of Progressivism," *Reviews in American History*, 10 (1982) 113–32. Daniel T. Rodgers, *Atlantic Crossings: Social Politics in a Progressive Age* (Cambridge, 2000) places American Progressivism in a transatlantic context.

On the legal Progressives' critique of laissez-faire and classical legal liberalism, see generally Morton Horwitz, *The Transformation of American Law, 1870–1960*. For the more thoroughgoing critiques of the nation's legal and constitutional system forged by Progressive thinkers outside the legal fraternity, see Eldon J. Eisenach, *The Lost Promise of Progressivism* (Lawrence, KS, 1994) and Dorothy Ross, *The Origins of American Social Science* (New York, 1991). Insightful studies of legal Progressive efforts to rework American law from within include Edward Purcell, *Brandeis and the Progressive Constitution: Erie, the Judicial Power, and the Politics of the Federal Courts in Twentieth-Century America* (New Haven, CT, 2000); Melvyn Urofsky, *Louis D. Brandeis and the Progressive Tradition* (Boston, 1981); Natalie E. H. Hull, *Roscoe Pound and Karl Llewellyn: Searching for an American Jurisprudence* (Chicago, 1997); Natalie E. H. Hull, "Restatement and Reform: A New Perspective on the Origins of the American Law Institute," *Law and History Review*, 8 (1990), 55–96; and G. Edward White, "The American Law Institute and the Triumph of Modernist Jurisprudence," *Law and History Review*, 15 (1997), 1–47. On legal Progressives as mediators between twentieth-century Progressive state-building and nineteenth-century legal and constitutional orders and outlooks, see William E. Forbath, "The Long Life of Liberal America: Law and State-Building in the

U.S. and the U.K.," *Law & History Review* 24 (2006) 179–92. On the U.S. Supreme Court's conflicts and accommodations with – and variations on – Progressivism, see Alexander M. Bickel and Benno C. Schmidt's superb volume of the *Oliver Wendell Holmes Devise History of the Supreme Court, The Judiciary and Responsible Government, 1910–1921* (New York, 1984); see also William E. Forbath, "The White Court (1910–1921): A Progressive Court?" in Christopher Tomlins, ed., *The United States Supreme Court: The Pursuit of Justice* (Boston, 2005).

Judges as State-Builders

A superb treatment of this theme to which I am indebted is Daniel Ernst, "Law and American Political Development, 1877–1938." On late nineteenth-century expansions of federal jurisdiction, federal common law, and federal judicial supervision of state and national administrative and regulatory initiatives, see Tony A. Freyer, *Forums of Order: The Federal Courts and Business in American History* (Greenwich, CT, 1979); Edward Purcell, *Litigation & Inequality: Federal Diversity Jurisdiction in Industrial America, 1870–1958* (New York, 1992); and Edward Purcell, *Brandeis and the Progressive Constitution*. On the expanded use of equity and judge-tried cases, see Stephen N. Subrin, "How Equity Conquered Common Law: The Federal Rules of Civil Procedure in Historical Perspective," *University of Pennsylvania Law Review* 135 (1987), 909–1002. On "government by injunction" and the expansion of judicial regulation of organized labor and industrial conflict, see William E. Forbath, *Law and the Shaping of the American Labor Movement* (Cambridge, 1991). And on the role of courts in restructuring railroads and other large corporations via equity receiverships, see Gerald Berk, *Alternative Tracks: The Constitution of American Industrial Order, 1865–1917* (Baltimore, 1994). The rise of the modern Municipal Court and its Progressive array of "social courts" and social experts and administrators is the subject of Michael Willrich, *City of Courts: Socializing Justice in Progressive Era Chicago* (Cambridge, 2003).

Antitrust, the Railroads and ICC, and the Labor Question

The key work on the first three decades of federal antitrust law and the broader legal and political contests over corporate consolidation is Martin J. Sklar, *The Corporate Reconstruction of American Capitalism, 1890–1916* (Cambridge, 1988). Also valuable are the several essays on the interplay of legal and economic thought in the formation of antitrust law in Herbert Hovenkamp, *Enterprise and American Law, 1836–1937* (Cambridge, 1991). State common law and statutory constraints on corporate expansion, and the economic and political presuppositions of that body of law, are well explored in James May, "Antitrust Practice and Procedure in the Formative Era: The Constitutional and Conceptual Reach of State Antitrust Law, 1880–1918," *University of Pennsylvania Law Review* 135 (1987) 495–593 and "Antitrust in the Formative Era: Political and Economic Theory in Constitutional and Antitrust Analysis, 1880–1918,"

Ohio State Law Journal 50 (1989) 257–395. Morton Horwitz, "*Santa Clara* Revisited: The Development of Corporate Theory," *West Virginia Law Review* 88 (1985), 173–224 is essential for its insights into the influence on law of new economic doctrines about increasing returns to scale and the "inevitability" of the large-scale firm.

On the play of group and corporate interests in the shaping of railroad regulation, much scholarly ink has been spilled. For a recent overview, see James W. Ely, Jr., *Railroads and American Law* (Lawrence, KS, 2001). My own views on the formation of the Interstate Commerce Commission and its vexed relations with the federal judiciary were shaped by Stephen Skowronek, *Building a New American State*, and my understanding of Thomas Cooley's work as the first ICC chair by Gerald Berk, *Alternative Tracks*. For the anti-laissez-faire outlook of Henry Carter Adams, see Henry C. Adams, *Relation of the State to Industrial Action* (Baltimore, 1897). On the court-like and adversarial legalist character of American regulatory agencies in comparative perspective, see Robert Kagan, *Adversarial Legalism: The American Way of Law* (Cambridge, 2003).

The rise of "government by injunction" and the courts' signal role in governing the employment relationship and the boundaries of workers' collective action are explored in William E. Forbath, *Law and the Shaping of the American Labor Movement* (Cambridge, 1991), as are the courts' and legal culture's influence on organized labor's strategies and outlooks. For a comparative perspective, see William E. Forbath, "Courts, Constitutions and Labor Politics in England and America: A Study of the Constitutive Power of Law," *Law and Social Inquiry* 16 (1991), 1–34. On the persistence of old master-servant common law categories and authoritarian values in the common law of industrial America, see also James B. Atleson, *Values and Assumptions in American Labor Law* (Amherst, MA, 1983); Christopher L. Tomlins, *The State and the Unions: Labor Relations, Law, and the Organized Labor Movement in America, 1880–1960* (Cambridge, 1985); and Karen Orren, *Belated Feudalism: Labor, the Law and Liberal Development in the United States* (Cambridge, 1991). Still essential for understanding the emergence of the labor injunction in railroad labor disputes is Gerald G. Eggert, *Railroad Labor Disputes: The Beginnings of Federal Strike Policy* (Ann Arbor, MI, 1967). On unions' efforts in state legislatures and Congress to reform or repeal judge-made law and "government by injunction," and their failure, see Victoria C. Hattam, "Economic Visions and Political Strategies: American Labor and the State, 1865–1896, *Studies in American Political Development* 4 (1990), 82–129; Daniel Ernst, "The Labor Exemption, 1908–1914," *Iowa Law Review* 74 (1989), 1151–73; Julie Greene, *Pure and Simple Politics: The American Federation of Labor and Political Activism, 1881–1917* (Cambridge, 1998); and George I. Lovell, *Legislative Deferrals: Statutory Ambiguity, Judicial Power, and American Democracy* (New York, 2003).

Valuable insights about the reform outlooks and strategies of Progressive lawyers and jurists are found in Tomlins, *State and Unions*; Daniel R. Ernst, "Common Laborers? Industrial Pluralists, Legal Realists and the Law of

Industrial Disputes, 1915–43," *Law and History Review* 11 (1993); and Andrew Wender Cohen, *The Racketeer's Progress: Chicago and the Struggle for the Modern American Economy, 1900–1940* (New York, 2004).

Peculiarities of the American Welfare State

On American responses to the social question and American welfare state formation in comparative and transatlantic perspective, see Daniel Rodgers, *Atlantic Crossings* and Theda Skocpol et al., eds., *Protecting Soldiers and Mothers*; *The Politics of Social Policy in the United States* (Princeton, NJ, 1988) and *States, Social Knowledge, and the Origins of Modern Social Policies* (Princeton, NJ, 1996).

The essential work on the creation of workers' compensation as a critical moment in American welfare state formation is John Fabian Witt, *The Accidental Republic: Crippled Workingmen, Destitute Widows, and the Remaking of American Law* (Cambridge, 2004) to which I am indebted for insights into the rise of actuarial thinking in American law and its clashes with classical liberal legal precepts in cases like *Ives* and in broader contests between public and private forms of insurance. For an innovative comparison of public social insurance with the private aggregating and risk-spreading work of the early twentieth-century plaintiffs' personal injury bar, settling accident cases based on actuarial tables, and "average" values of accidents with private insurance companies, see also Samuel Issacharoff and John Fabian Witt, "The Inevitability of Aggregate Settlement: An Institutional Account of American Tort Law," *Vanderbilt Law Review* 57 (2004), 1571–636.

For broader historical accounts of the United States' extensive reliance on private insurance and private employer-administered health care and pension programs to fashion a publicly subsidized "private welfare state" alongside the country's scantier public welfare state, see Jennifer Klein, *For All These Rights: Business, Labor, and the Shaping of America's Public-Private Welfare State* (Princeton, NJ, 2003) and Jacob S. Hacker, *The Divided Welfare State: The Battle over Public and Private Social Benefits in the United States* (New York, 2002). On the judicialization of the administration of workers' compensation and the rise of the administrative law judge, see Philippe Nonet, *Administrative Justice: Advocacy and Change in a Government Agency* (New York, 1969); see also Robert Kagan, *Adversarial Legalism*.

Race, Nation- and State-Building, and the Illiberal Constitution

The plenary power doctrine encapsulated and formalized in constitutional law the myriad collective decisions to locate much important state-building and expansion of national power outside the pale of liberal norms. The doctrine and choices were bound up with broader conceptions of national sovereignty and racial notions of nationhood animating the law and politics of mass immigration, westward expansion (and "Indian policy"), and imperial adventure. T. Alexander Aleinikoff, *Semblances of Sovereignty: The Constitution, the State, and*

American Citizenship (Cambridge, 2002) superbly chronicles the general development of "sovereignty law" in these contexts, extending his discussion from the formative decades around the turn of the century down to the present. Sarah Cleveland, "Powers Inherent in Sovereignty: Indians, Aliens, Territories, and the Nineteenth Century Origins of Plenary Power over Foreign Affairs," *Texas Law Review* 81 (2002), 1–284 examines the development of the doctrine itself in these same contexts. On the racial dimensions of the era's legal, constitutional, and social scientific discourses about immigration, Indian policy, and the status of America's colonial possessions, I am much indebted to Mark Weiner, *Americans Without Law: Citizenship, Juridical Racialism, and State Modernization* (New York, 2006).

The key legal history of Chinese exclusion is Lucy Salyer, *Law Harsh As Tigers: Chinese Immigrants and the Shaping of Modern Immigration Law* (Chapel Hill, NC, 1995), which recounts the San Francisco Chinese community's campaign of habeas challenges to summary exclusion procedures, Congress's response, and the vast measure of administrative autonomy that Congress gave the federal Immigration Bureau and the Court upheld. For a magisterial history of U.S. immigration policy, with careful attention to the interplay of law, politics, and administrative state-building, see Aristide R. Zolberg, *A Nation by Design: Immigration Policy in the Fashioning of America* (New York, 2006). For a useful legislative history, see Edward P. Hutchinson, *Legislative History of American Immigration Policy 1798–1965* (Philadephia, 1981). Kunal Parker's chapter in Volume II (Chapter 6, Citizenship and Immigration Law, 1800–1924: Resolutions of Membership and Territory) also brims with insight.

On the expansion and "modernization" of the Bureau of Indian Affairs and the "assimilationist era" in federal Indian policy, see Frederick E. Hoxie, *A Final Promise: The Campaign to Assimilate the Indians, 1880–1920* (Lincoln, NE, 1984) and Francis Paul Prucha, *The Great Father: The United States Government and the American Indians*, vol. 2 (Lincoln, NE, 1984). A general history with valuable insights into federal policy is Richard White, *"It's Your Misfortune and None of my Own": A History of the American West* (Norman, OK, 1991). Mark Weiner, *Americans Without Law* illuminates the centrality of law and liberty and the divergent "capacities" of different "races" for liberal self-rule in the racial hierarchies constructed by the new social sciences and the importance of these hierarchies in Supreme Court doctrine about Native Americans and the native subjects of the United States' new colonial possessions. For some of the complexities and open-ended debates of the era's "racial sciences," see George W. Stocking, Jr., *Race, Culture, and Evolution: Essays in the History of Anthropology* (Chicago, 1982) and "The Turn-of-the-Century Concept of Race," *Modernism/Modernity* 1 (1994), 4–16.

The historiography of the United States' late nineteenth-century imperial adventures is vast and knotty. For a learned synthesis, see Walter Lafeber, *The Cambridge History of American Foreign Relations: The American Search for*

Opportunity, 1865–1913, vol. 2 (Cambridge, 1995). On the Spanish-American War in particular, see Joseph Smith, *The Spanish-American War: Conflict in the Caribbean and the Pacific, 1895–1902* (London, 1994), and on the ensuing experiments in colonial rule and administration, see Winfred Lee Thompson, *The Introduction of American Law in the Philippines and Puerto Rico, 1898–1905* (Fayetteville, SC, 1989) and Stuart Creighton Miller, *"Benevolent Assimilation": The American Conquest of the Philippines, 1899–1903* (New Haven, CT, 1982). On Henry Cabot Lodge and American empire, see William C. Widenor, *Henry Cabot Lodge and the Search for an American Foreign Policy* (Berkeley, 1980), and on the "Teutonic origins" thesis that Lodge, Henry Adams, and other leading thinkers embraced to explain Anglo-Americans' distinct role in the history of liberty and distinct "racial capacity" for self-rule compared to the world's other "races," see Reginald Horsman, *Race and Manifest Destiny: The Origins of American Racial Anglo-Saxonism* (Cambridge, 1981); see also Dorothy Ross, *The Origins of American Social Science*. On the anti-imperialists, see Robert L. Beisner, *Twelve Against Empire: The Anti-Imperialists, 1898–1900* (New York, 1968). Finally, for insightful discussions of the *Insular Cases*, see Christina Duffy Burnett, "A Note on the *Insular Cases*," and the other essays gathered in Christina Duffy Burnett and Burke Marshall, eds., *Foreign in a Domestic Sense: Puerto Rico, American Expansion, and the Constitution* (Durham, NC, 2001).

Wartime State-Building, Peacetime Dismantling

For a general history of the wartime expansion of the national government's presence and myriad new functions in economic and social life, see David M. Kennedy, *Over Here: The First World War and American Society* (New York, 1980). On the wartime federal agencies and their management of the economy, see Keller, *Regulating a New Economy*; and Ellis W. Hawley, *The Great War and the Search for a Modern Order: A History of the American People and Their Institutions, 1917–1933* (New York, 1979); Hawley offers a nuanced account of the plans and proposals to make the agencies permanent features of American government, the defeat of those plans, and the subtler institutional changes that endured. Progressives' role in wartime state-building and their efforts to make the war an engine of social reform are also well explored in Karl, *The Uneasy State*. Bickel and Schmidt, *The Judiciary and Responsible Government, 1910–1921* offers a detailed examination of the Supreme Court's response to wartime state-building. On the Court's return to antebellum "normalcy" under Chief Justice Taft, see the thoughtful discussion in Robert Post, "Defending the Lifeworld: Substantive Due Process in the Taft Court Era," *Boston University Law Review* 78 (1998), 1489–1545.

NOTES ON CONTRIBUTORS (IN ORDER OF APPEARANCE)

MARK R. WILSON is Assistant Professor of History at The University of North Carolina, Charlotte

HUGH C. MACGILL is Oliver Ellsworth Research Professor at The University of Connecticut School of Law, Hartford

R. KENT NEWMYER is Professor Emeritus of History at the University of Connecticut, Storrs, and Professor of Law and History at The University of Connecticut School of Law, Hartford

ALFRED S. KONEFSKY is University at Buffalo Distinguished Professor at the University at Buffalo Law School, State University of New York

KERMIT L. HALL was, at the time of his death on 13th August 2006, University President and Professor of History at the University at Albany, State University of New York

ELIZABETH DALE is Associate Professor of History at the University of Florida, Gainesville

KUNAL M. PARKER is Professor of Law at the Cleveland-Marshall College of Law, Cleveland State University

DAVID E. WILKINS is Professor of American Indian Studies at the University of Minnesota, Minneapolis

NORMA BASCH is Professor Emerita of History at Rutgers University, Newark

ARIELA GROSS is Professor of Law and History at the University of Southern California, Los Angeles

LAURA F. EDWARDS is Professor of History at Duke University

BARBARA YOUNG WELKE is Associate Professor of History and Professor of Law at the University of Minnesota, Minneapolis

NAN GOODMAN is Associate Professor of English at the University of Colorado, Boulder

SARAH BARRINGER GORDON is Arlin M. Adams Professor of Constitutional Law and Professor of History at the University of Pennsylvania

TONY A. FREYER is University Research Professor of History and Law at the University of Alabama. Research for his chapter was supported by Dean Kenneth C. Randall, University of Alabama Law School Foundation, and the Edward Brett Randolph Fund

B. ZORINA KHAN is Associate Professor of Economics at Bowdoin College and Research Fellow at the National Bureau of Economic Research

KAREN ORREN is Professor of Political Science at the University of California, Los Angeles

JONATHAN LURIE is Professor of History at Rutgers University, Newark, and Adjunct Professor of Law at Rutgers Law School, Newark

EILEEN P. SCULLY is a Faculty Member in History at Bennington College

WILLIAM E. FORBATH is Angus Wynne, Sr. Professor of Civil Jurisprudence, Lloyd M. Bentsen Chair in Law and Professor of History at the University of Texas, Austin

INDEX